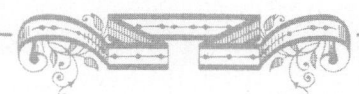

# THE
# BRADMAN
## *Albums*

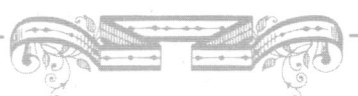

A portrait shot of Don Bradman, 1928.

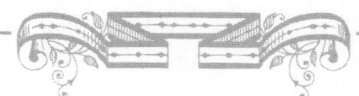

# THE BRADMAN Albums

SELECTIONS FROM
SIR DONALD BRADMAN'S
OFFICIAL COLLECTION

VOLUME 1
1925–1934

WITH AN INTRODUCTION BY
SIR DONALD BRADMAN, A.C.

Macdonald
Queen Anne Press

## PUBLISHER'S NOTE

*In order to retain the authentic style of the original Bradman albums, a minimal amount of new typesetting has been done. Most of the newspaper clippings, and all the letters, telegrams and photographs have been reproduced as they appear in the albums.*

A 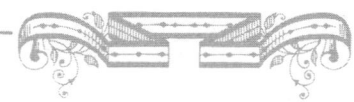 BOOK

© Copyright Introduction, diary extracts and commentaries by Sir Donald Bradman,
Weldons Pty Limited 1987
© Copyright Design Weldons Pty Limited 1987
First published in Great Britain in 1988 by
Queen Anne Press, a division of
Macdonald & Co (Publishers) Ltd
3rd Floor, Greater London House, Hampstead Road, London NW1 7QX

A BPCC plc Company

Produced in Australia by Rigby Publishers
a division of Weldons Pty Limited, Sydney, Australia

Designer   Susan Kinealy

Assembly artist   Catherine Martin

Calligraphy   Margrit Eisermann

Endpapers   Margo Snape

Illustration on slip case   Painting of Donald Bradman by Ivor Hele, *c.* 1946

**British Library Cataloguing-in-Publication Data**

Bradman, Sir Donald
  The Bradman albums
  1. Bradman, Sir Donald
  2. Cricket players — Australia — Biography
  I. Title
  796.35'8'0924 GV915.B7

ISBN 0-356-15411-4

Typeset by Savage Type, Brisbane, Australia.
Printed and bound in Australia by Griffin Press Limited, Adelaide.

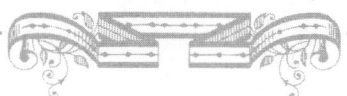

# Contents

## VOLUME 1

*Facing pages listed*

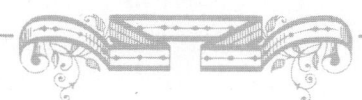

# Introduction

When I was a lad of about thirteen, a small paragraph about me appeared in a Sydney newspaper called *Smith's Weekly*. My father subscribed to the paper because he enjoyed its racy style and its publishing of bizarre items which did not appear in the more conventional press. But it was my mother's eagle eye which spotted the unusual paragraph about the young Bradman, referred to as "crack bat", and an incident which occurred in the school playground involving a cricket ball. She cut it out and pasted it in a small, black-covered exercise book. The world will never know whether she had a premonition of things to come.

That exercise book became the repository of cuttings about my early cricket matches in Bowral and indeed housed reports of events up to about the time of my first Sheffield Shield match.

From then on, as the volume of publicity grew, the keeping of scrap books in a variety of forms became something of a hobby indulged in by my mother, my wife, some relatives, a cricket loving brother-in-law, even in later years my literary agent in London, and, quite incredibly, by cricket lovers who were complete strangers.

As the collection increased in size so did my possession of odd pieces of cricketana, and by the time my active playing career was at an end, I occasionally lent items of interest for exhibitions designed to raise funds for charity or other worthy causes.

Hedley Brideson, who was the chief librarian of the State Library of South Australia, became aware of the existence of such memorabilia. As a devoted cricket lover himself, and with a deep understanding of library matters, he made approaches to me, mainly on the grounds that it would be tragic if such important relics were not preserved for posterity. We were both members of the Adelaide Rotary Club and so met almost every week in a social environment, during which time Hedley never missed a chance to press his claim.

It took a very long time, but finally he persuaded me to place my scrap books in the custody of the library for the purpose of producing from them a series of albums in chronological order, tastefully setting out the main parts of both newspaper articles and photographs.

The work commenced. The library staff attacked their task with diligence and enthusiasm, but it became apparent in the very first week that my collaboration was essential. Unfortunately, much of the material was kept at random, even just thrown into cardboard boxes, and I was the only person capable of identifying various cuttings and naming, for instance, the personnel in photographs — as well as the date and place of origin. In addition to the cuttings, a remarkable statistical book, *Bradman the Great*, by B. J. Wakely was available, from which the season by season figures could be compiled.

The upshot was that almost every week for some years I spent many hours at the library assisting the staff to clarify the source and period of items being used. The finished product of fifty-two magnificently bound leather volumes now permanently housed in the Mortlock library on North Terrace, Adelaide, and available for public scrutiny and for historic purposes is a credit to Brideson's foresight and the excellent work of the staff.

Rigby Publishers conceived the idea of condensing the material into two volumes and of publishing them for sale to the general public, using the library books as the basis. So, with the blessing of the Mortlock library and myself, this project was put in hand.

It covers most of the important happenings in my first class career which began on the Adelaide Oval in December 1927 (happily with a century) and ended on the same ground in March 1949. The latter occasion was a Sheffield Shield match between South Australia and Victoria, and I only agreed to play as a gesture because the match was set aside as a benefit for Arthur Richardson. Regrettably, my final act was to sprain my ankle (due to an uncovered sunken water tap on the field) and limp into the dressing room.

Being neither fit nor in form, my inability to bat in South Australia's second innings was of little consequence, but of course I was sad that my final exit from the playing arena I loved so much was in such a fashion.

Bradman, about 12 years old, takes block in the back yard.

"Bradman's Cottage" where the Bradman family lived in Yeo Yeo *c.* 1909. This was Don Bradman's first home. The restored cottage has been removed to the Temora Rural Museum.

Bowral cricket team *c.* 1924. Bradman's father (George) is the tall man standing third from right in the back row. Bradman's uncle (Geo. Whatman) is seated in the middle of the centre row.

Looking back over what in cricket terms was a long career, I have cause to be thankful for the many wonderful experiences along the road. It would be foolish to say there were not moments of sadness as well. But life has to be lived each day as and when it occurs. Decisions must be taken in the light of circumstances as they exist at the time, not with the reflective hindsight of a historian reviewing the situation years later.

Enthusiasm and youth easily surmount difficulties and they enabled me to regard the traumatic body-line season as a temporary hiccup. But the happenings of 1934 were much more serious. There was the decision to start a completely new career in another state with all the business and social implications for my wife and me, coupled with a near fatal illness which threatened my future cricket career. It was a period of great anxiety and uncertainty.

These problems had largely been resolved and I was secretly contemplating retirement from cricket when the war broke out. Everything had to be subjugated to the national task confronting all men and women and when hostilities ceased, I was so immersed in restructuring my business life and rebuilding my health that sport had a very low priority. I did not contemplate at that time a return to the international arena and would have scoffed at any suggestion that 1948 would prove to be the pinnacle of my cricketing life. But as the fates decreed, Australia's victory at Leeds in 1948, and my part in it, must surpass all other moments of sporting satisfaction.

In retrospect, and surveying the broad canvas, I suppose more than anything else I look back and say I am grateful that as the son of simple country parents, and without the benefit of wealth, power or influence, but with only the talents bestowed upon me by nature, I was able to occupy the highest posts the Australian cricket world had to offer. As a result I was given the opportunity for much of that period to impart my interpretation of the character of this wonderful game which has meant so much to cricket lovers everywhere. In so doing, I am happy in the knowledge that I did not betray the responsibility entrusted to me and I was enabled, I hope, to enhance the best traditions of the sport.

Inevitably the face of cricket changes with the passage of time. The game must adapt to the social era in which people live. Nobody, fifty years ago, could have foreshadowed night cricket, coloured clothing, white balls and so on, but I do not resile from such happenings providing we are able to preserve the underlying character-building edifice upon which the game was founded.

This responsibility must be shouldered with care and foresight by contemporary players and administrators because they are now the custodians of a valued trust for future generations.

Sir Donald Bradman, A.C.
Adelaide, 1987

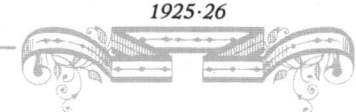

# *1925~6, 1926~7, 1927~8*
# *Seasons*

Leaving school at the age of fourteen I gave up cricket and devoted a whole summer to tennis, largely due to the influence of a favourite uncle.

At the end of the following summer I was persuaded to play cricket again but only batted twice, making 0 and 66.

My serious cricket career began in season 1925–26 and this volume commences at that point.

The following season, after some initial matches with the Bowral team, I was chosen to represent Southern Districts in Country Week, the St. George first grade team and the New South Wales second XI, and I also achieved the cherished ambition of playing on the famous Sydney Cricket Ground.

Finally 1927–28 brought representation for New South Wales in the Sheffield Shield side.

*Don Bradman*

Don Bradman's home at Bowral.
The cricket oval at Bowral, on which some of Don Bradman's early cricket experience was gained, is opposite the young cricketer's home. It has since been renamed the Bradman Oval.

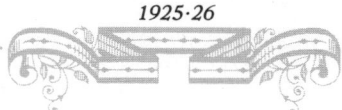

Don Bradman aged 17 years.

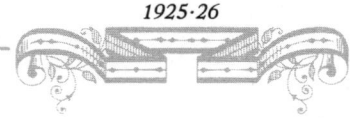

## — SEASON 1925-26 —

| TITLE | GAME | | SCORES | |
|---|---|---|---|---|
| Second Class | Bowral | Berrima | 53 | n.o. |
| | " | Port Kembla | 7 | B. |
| | " | Bundanoon | 34 | n.o. |
| | " | Comb. Moss Vale | 54 | n.o. |
| | " | Sutton Forest | 26 | n.o. |
| | Bowral District | Kenmore | 58 | C. |
| | Bowral | Exeter | 59 | n.o. |
| | " | - | 9 | n.o. |
| | " | Wingello "A" | 234 | B. |
| | " | Moss Vale "A" | 14 | C. |
| | " | Port Kembla | 60 | C. |
| | " | - - | 31 | n.o. |
| | " | Moss Vale "A" | 66 | C. |
| | " | Bowral "B" | 105 | B. |
| | " | - - | 1 | C. |
| | " | - - | 0 | C. |
| | " | - - | 30 | n.o. |
| | " | - - | 30 | n.o. |
| | " | Berrima | 25 | L.B.W. |
| | " | - | 0 | C. |
| | " | Robertson | 2 | C. |
| | " | Bundanoon | 120 | C. |
| | " | Moss Vale | 300 | C. |
| | | Total runs | 1318 | |

### — SUMMARY —

AVERAGES

| | Innings | N.O's. | H.S. | Runs | Average |
|---|---|---|---|---|---|
| Second Class | 23 | 9 | 300 | 1318 | 94·14 |

DON BRADMAN broke Bowral District Record twice scoring 234 and 300.

**BOWRAL v MOSS VALE**, at Moss Vale, 15 May - 12 June 1926.  (Final match in the Berrima District Cricket Competition).

| Bowral | - First Innings | 672 for 9 wickets |
|---|---|---|
| | - Second Innings | - |
| Moss Vale | - First Innings | 134 |
| | - Second Innings | 200 |

Bowral won by an innings and 338 runs.

| DON BRADMAN | - Caught | 300 |
|---|---|---|

The rules provided that the match had to be played to a finish.   It lasted five Saturday afternoons.

---

E.T. No. 2.

COMMONWEALTH OF AUSTRALIA—POSTMASTER-GENERAL'S DEPARTMENT.

## TELEGRAM.

Station from *Burwood*   Words / Check   Remarks   No....................

Time and Date } Lodged  *11 25*  */26*   To *Don Bradman ....*

*This message has been received subject to the Post and Telegraph Act and Regulations.*

*Horsey  Keep your tail up good luck to record breaker*

*Yates*

Time received at this Office.

This telegram was received prior to the third Saturday's play, when Don Bradman's memorable score probably brought him to the notice of the New South Wales State selectors.

# Sports and Games.

## CRICKET.

### FINAL FOR THE TOM MACK CUP.

The final between Bowral A and Moss Vale A for the Tom Mack Cup resulted in a runaway victory for the Bowral team by an innings and 338 runs.

Moss Vale saw the match through like sports and the Bowral captain congratulated them on having made such a good uphill fight on the last day.

The Bowral Cricket Club thus retains the Cup until next year when the district teams fight for it once more. Detailed scores are as follows :

### Bowral.—First Innings.

| | |
|---|---|
| Don. Bradman, c Prigg, b Ryder | 300 |
| O. Prior, b S. Tickner | 52 |
| G. Whatman, b S. Tickner | 227 |
| S. Cupitt, run out | 4 |
| V. Bradman, b Aynsley | 1 |
| E. Waine, b S. Tickner | 36 |
| G. S. Bensley, b S. Tickner | 1 |
| O. Knopp, b S. Tickner | 11 |
| N. Sinden, c Cowley, b Soden | 5 |
| A. Stephens, not out | 7 |
| Sundries | 28 |
| | ___ |
| Nine wkts for | 672 |

Innings declared closed.

Dick Whatman did not bat owing to a broken toe.

### Moss Vale.—First Innings.

| | |
|---|---|
| H. Toose, c D. Bradman, b Prior | 21 |
| R. Tickner, c V. Bradman, b Waine | 16 |
| T. Galbraith, st Whatman, b Waine | 33 |
| R. Cowley, b D. Bradman | 24 |
| E. Prigg, c Sub. b Prior | 0 |
| S. Tickner, b Prior | 17 |
| E. V. Soden, b Prior | 1 |
| G. Aynsley, c Sinden, b Prior | 3 |
| J. Hunt, not out | 0 |
| Sundries | 19 |
| | ___ |
| Total | 134 |

Bowling.—E. Waine, 2 wkts for 16 ; A. Stephens, 0 for 33 ; D. Bradman, 1 for 25 ; O. Prior, 5 for 41.

Fielding.—N. Sinden.

### Moss Vale.—Second Innings.

| | |
|---|---|
| G. Aynsley, st Whatman, b Waine | 0 |
| R. Tickner, b Bensley | 91 |
| E. V. Soden, c Sinden, b Waine | 11 |
| H. Toose, c V. Bradman, b Stephens | 41 |
| S. Tickner, b D. Bradman | 10 |
| T. Galbraith, b D. Bradman | 11 |
| R. Cowley, b Bensley | 9 |
| E. Prigg, not out | 0 |
| J. Hunt, b D. Bradman | 3 |
| Sundries | 24 |
| | ___ |
| Total | 200 |

W. Chipperfield and H. Ryder were absent during the match.

Bowling.—E. Waine, 2 wkts for 49 ; G. Bensley 2 for 31 ; V. Bradman, 0 for 29 ; O. Prior, 0 for 21 ; A. Stephens, 1 for 33 ; D. Bradman, 3 for 14.

Fielding.—O. Prior.

# 1318 RUNS

## AVERAGE OF OVER 100

## BOY OF 17

### DISTRICT RECORD OF 300

BOWRAL, Monday.

That the district record score of 300 by Don Bradman, a lad of 17, in Bowral's final competition match against Moss Vale, was no fluke is shown by the young cricketer's other performances during the season.

In the club's competition matches he played 12 innings (three not out), for 985 runs, an average of 109.4.

In addition to winning the batting average, he was second in bowling, with an average of 8.1 for 35 wickets;

*Don Bradman*

he won the trophy for most catches, 16, and the trophy for best fielding. Including non-competition matches, he played 21 innings, eight not out, for 1318, average 101.3, took 51 wickets at an average of 7.8, and held 26 catches.

His best batting performances were 300 against Moss Vale in the final match for the Mack Cup, 234 against Wingello (premiers 1924-25), 120 against Bundanoon in the semi-final for the cup, and 105 against Bowral R

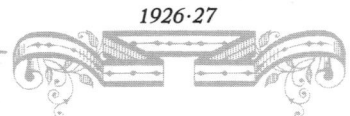

## — SEASON 1926-27 —

| TITLE | GAME | | SCORES | |
|---|---|---|---|---|
| Second Class | Bowral | Robertson | 12 | C. |
| - | | - | 35 | C. |
| - | | Exeter | 170 | n.o. |
| - | | Moss Vale | 22 | B. |
| N.S.W. Possibles | | N.S.W. Probables | 37 | n.o. |
| Southern Districts | | South Coast | 62 | n.o. |
| Bowral | | Mittagong | 13 | B. |
| S.D. Country Week | | Riverina | 43 | C. |
| - - - | | Far North | 24 | B. |
| - - - | | W. Sub. & C.Cumb. Comb. | 41 | B. |
| - - - | | Newcastle | 27 | B. |
| - - - | | West | 25 | C. |
| Combined City | | Combined Country | 98 | C. |
| Moss Vale | | Leichhardt | 103 | n.o. |
| N.S.W. 2nd XI | | Victoria 2nd XI | 43 | B. |
| - - - | | - - - | 8 | B. |
| St. George Colts | | Waverley Colts | 167 | C. |
| Combined City | | Newcastle | 10 | C. |
| Bowral | | Moss Vale | 28 | n.o. |
| - | | - | 320 | n.o. |
| First Grade | St. George | Petersham | 110 | R.O. |
| - | | Waverley | 75 | C. |
| - | | Glebe | 22 | B. |
| - | | Gordon | 11 | B. |
| - | | Randwick | 54 | n.o. |
| - | | Waverley | 1 | C. |
| - | | Western Suburbs | 16 | C. |
| | | Total runs | 1577 | |

## — SUMMARY —

### AVERAGES

| | Innings | N.O's. | H.S. | Runs | Average |
|---|---|---|---|---|---|
| Second Class | 20 | 6 | 320 x | 1288 | 92·00 |
| First Grade | 7 | 1 | 110 | 289 | 48·16 |
| All Matches | 27 | 7 | 320 x | 1577 | 78·85 |

DON BRADMAN broke Bowral District record again - 320 not out - in competition final for "Tom Mack" Cup.

He scored a century on his first appearance in First Grade cricket - 110 - St. George v. Petersham.

Alf Stephens (captain of Bowral cricket team), photographed on the concrete pitch at his home, *Grantham*, at Bowral, where Don Bradman had much of his early practice.

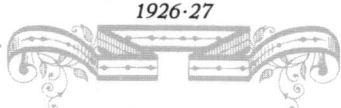
Don Bradman aged 18 years.

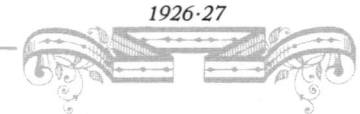

At the commencement of the 1926/27 season, a scheme was devised to try to find promising players, especially bowlers and the New South Wales Cricket Association organised a cricket practice on the Sydney Cricket Ground No. 2 so that the Selectors could witness country talent.

NEW SOUTH WALES  CRICKET ASSOCIATION

Address all Communications
to The Secretary.

Telephone: B3541.

HH/IM

254a GEORGE STREET,

SYDNEY.

5th October, 1926.

D. Bradman, Esq.,
C/o A. Stephens, Esq.,
Boolwey Street,
BOWRAL.

Dear Sir:

The State Selectors have had under consideration your record in cricket in the past season, and in view of such record they particularly desire to see you in action.

For this purpose I would like you to attend practice at the Sydney Cricket Ground on Monday next, 11th instant. Practice commences at 4 p.m. and continues through out the afternoon. Should you be able to attend as requested, please let me know in order that I may inform the Selectors who will be on the watch for you and in order that I may advise you as to the further particulars. My Association is prepared to pay your fare from Bowral and return and should you deem it necessary to remain in Sydney overnight you will be reimbursed to the extent of your accommodation.

I sincerely trust that you will give this matter the consideration its importance warrants and hope that you will realise that this is an opportunity which should not be missed. If you will be able to attend, let me know immediately and state the time you hope to arrive in Sydney. Should you find it impossible to attend on the 11th, please inform me if any other Monday in the near future would be suitable, and I will have arrangements made accordingly.

Yours faithfully,

SECRETARY.

Group photograph taken at Bowral *c.* 1925.
Geo. Bradman (Don's father) is in the back row wearing a hat.
Dick Whatman (Don's uncle) is in the middle row, wearing a cap and with a grey moustache.
Don Bradman is in the second front row wearing a cap.

Bowral Cricket Ground, *c.* 1925. Don Bradman's father is the umpire at square leg. The ground has since been renamed, and is now called Bradman Oval.

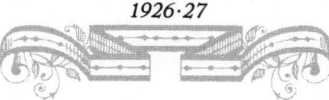

**E.T. No. 2a.**

COMMONWEALTH OF AUSTRALIA.—POSTMASTER-GENERAL'S DEPARTMENT.

# URGENT TELEGRAM.

*This message has been received subject to the Post and Telegraph Act and Regulations.*
*All complaints to be addressed in writing to the Deputy Postmaster-General.*

**NOTE.**—The figures at bottom of message represent the time received at this Office.

No._____
Office Date Stamp

| Station from. | No. of Words. | Check. | Time Lodged. | Date Lodged. | Remarks. |
|---|---|---|---|---|---|

Sydney 41 2 50Pm 9th

D Bradman

Davis and Westbrook

Bowral

You are selected play trial match

Sydney Cricket Ground Wednesday tenth commencing

ten oclock fares will be paid wire stating whether

available

Secretary Cricket Association

2 46h

---

**NOT FOR CUMBERLAND.**

DON BRADMAN, the seventeen-year-old Bowral cricketer, who was invited by the State selectors to visit Sydney and practise at the Cricket Ground, is not going to play with Central Cumberland, as announced. Bradman was willing to play, but the expense of coming to Sydney every weekend is too great. Cumberland is not in a position to contribute in this direction. Surely the New South Wales Cricket Association can do something in the matter. The coaching scheme now in operation, which promises to have good results, is costing nothing at present. Money spent in assisting country cricketers to come to Sydney and show their worth is not wasted. Some provision is made in the scheme for expenses of country players, and it now remains to be seen whether the association is sincere in its desire to produce cricketers. If New South Wales is to "find" players expenses must be incurred, and Bradman should be assisted by the association to play with Cumberland.

## ST. GEO. WANTS BRADMAN

BOWRAL, Saturday.

Negotiations are afoot for Don Bradman, the young Bowral cricketer, to play first grade with St. George this season. St. George have offered to defray Bradman's expenses for weekly visits to Sydney.

---

<u>N.S.W. CRICKET ASSOCIATION</u> - "Probables" v "Possibles", at Sydney Cricket Ground, 10 November 1926.

| | | | |
|---|---|---|---|
| "Possibles" | - First Innings | 237 | |
| | - Second Innings | - | |
| "Probables" | - First Innings | 302 for 9 wickets | |
| | - Second Innings | - | |
| | "Probables" won by 65 runs. | | |

| | | |
|---|---|---|
| <u>DON BRADMAN</u> | - | 37 n.o. |

This was a Trial match to select a State team to play in the Sheffield Shield match against Queensland.

Don Bradman was not chosen.

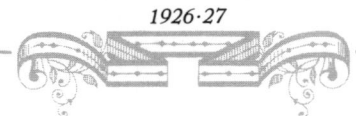

## THE PROBABLES.

BACK ROW    R. Osborne (North Sydney), A. G. Scanes (St. George), A. Jackson (Balmain),
L. Gwynne (Manly), L. Wall (Paddington), N. Campbell (Gordon).
FRONT ROW    G. Morgan (Glebe), H. Hooker (Mosman), A. Kippax (Waverley, captain),
R. McNamee (Randwick), D. Seddon (Petersham).

## THE POSSIBLES.

BACK ROW    J. Fisher (Balmain), S. King (Petersham), J. Foskett (Glebe), D. Mullarkey
(St. George), C. Nicholls (Cumberland), J. Carter (Randwick), A. McGrath (North Sydney),
G. Amos (Marrickville), R. Loder (Northern District).
FRONT ROW    F. Jordan (Glebe), D. Bradman (Bowral), R. E. Gostelow (Paddington),
H. C. Steele (Marrickville, captain), H. Waghorn (St. George), A. Hall (Cumberland).

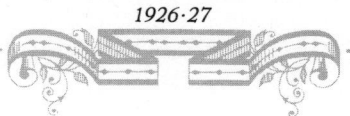

Although Don Bradman was not picked in the State team he was asked to play for the Goulburn District Team against the South Coast in a Trial at Goulburn, after which the "Southern Country Week" side would be chosen.

In this Trial he made top score (62 retired) and took four wickets for 35.

## SOUTHERN COUNTRY WEEK TEAM

BACK ROW    A. Sieler, M. Linder, E. Chapman, A. Bice, K. Murray, H. McGuick, G. Coulter.
FRONT ROW    N. Broderick, H. Webster, L. Sieler (Captain), J. Gray, D. G. Bradman.

## DON. BRADMAN.

### BOWRAL'S MOST FAMOUS CRICKETER.

After achieving a splendid cricket record in his native town, Donald has gone to Sydney, where he plays with St. George. Good judges in the metropolis say Don. will soon take his place in interstate contests. Our photo, by courtesy of the Telegraph Pictorial.

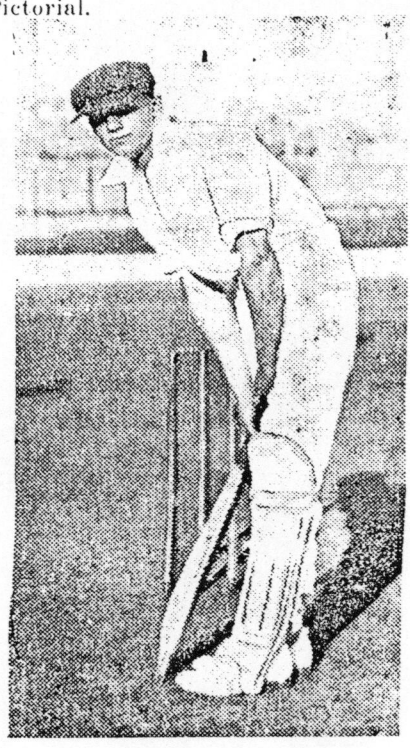

## BRADMAN'S DOUBLE

———

St. George closed their innings at six for 389, against Petersham at Petersham Oval Petersham began badly, and lost three wickets for 23. Lawes partnered Andrews, and the pair added 73 for the fourth wicket, the latter being well caught by Corps off Waghorn when he reached the half century. Andrews had batted patiently for 80 minutes, and gave a hot chance at 29 off King.

Lawes made 63 in two hours' batting, and hit 11 boundaries.

Everett played a lively innings for 44. He was in for 30 minutes, and knocked 32 in boundary hits.

Ellem showed good form for 32 in 40 minutes.

For St. George, Bradman followed up his score of 110 made last week by securing three of the Petersham batsmen for 26 runs.

### ST. GEORGE
#### First Innings

| | | |
|---|---|---|
| JONES, c Graham, b Everett .. .. | 0 |
| LOUDEN, b Everett .. .. .. .. | 14 |
| MULLARKEY, lbw., b Kennett .. | 31 |
| FAIRFAX, c Graham, b Kennett.. | 17 |
| BRADMAN, run out.. .. .. .. .. | 110 |
| MEALEY, c Ellem, b Graham .. .. | 27 |
| TARGETT, not out .. .. .. .. .. | 150 |
| ADAMS, not out .. .. .. .. .. | 4 |
| Sundries .. .. .. .. .. .. .. | 36 |

Six for .. .. .. .. .. .. 389
Innings closed.
Bowling: Everett 2-44, King 0-41, Kennett 2-83, Graham 1-34, Andrews 0-95, McInnes 0-56.
Fall of Wickets: 0, 34, 69, 104, 301, 377.

### PETERSHAM
#### First Innings

| | | |
|---|---|---|
| ROFE, b Waghorn .. .. .. .. .. | 6 |
| GRAHAM, c Mullarkey, b Waghorn | 2 |
| BENJAMIN, c Louden, b Adams .. | 4 |
| ANDREWS, c Corps, b Waghorn .. | 50 |
| McINNES, c Mealey, b Bradman .. | 10 |
| LAWES, c and b Mealey .. .. .. | 63 |
| EVERETT, c Bradman, b King .. | 44 |
| ELLEM, run out .. .. .. .. .. | 32 |
| KENNETT, b Bradman .. .. .. .. | 18 |
| KING, not out .. .. .. .. .. | 1 |
| QUINEY, c Fairfax, b Bradman .. | 11 |
| Sundries .. .. .. .. .. .. | 20 |

Total .. .. .. .. .. .. 261
Bowling: Waghorn 3-59, Adams 1-34, Fairfax 0-29, King 1-66, Mealey 1-20, Bradman 3-26, Louden 0-7.
Fall of Wickets: 3, 6, 23, 96, 111, 178, 198, 244, 247, 261.

#### Second Innings

| | | |
|---|---|---|
| ROFE, lbw., b Mullarkey .. .. .. | 6 |
| GRAHAM, not out .. .. .. .. .. | 29 |
| ANDREWS, c and b Louden .. .. | 7 |
| BENJAMIN, not out .. .. .. .. | 19 |
| Sundry .. .. .. .. .. .. .. | 1 |

Two for .. .. .. .. .. .. 62
Bowling: Mullarkey 1-24, Louden 1-26, Targett 0-11.
Fall of Wickets: 13, 24, 62.
St. George won on the first innings by 128 runs.

---

BOWRAL v MOSS VALE, at Moss Vale.

| Bowral | - First Innings | 480 |
|---|---|---|
| | - Second Innings | |
| Moss Vale | - First Innings | 73 |
| | - Second Innings | |

DON BRADMAN - 320 n.o.

Having started the season in the country and having played for Bowral in the District Competition, Don Bradman was eligible to take part in the season's final match.

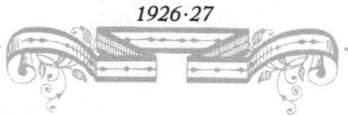
## CRICKET.

### DON BRADMAN SPARKLES.

Bowral cricketers continued their innings against Moss Vale in the final for the Pickard Cup and honor caps at Moss Vale on Saturday last, and look to have the match already won, having a first innings lead of 407. Bowral were just all out at closing time for 480. Cupitt played his best knock of the season and after compiling 60 was bowled by a beautiful ball from Stan. Browne.

After giving a poor exhibition the previous Saturday, Don Bradman excelled himself on this occasion, and the few spectators were given a rare treat. Getting his eye in quickly, Don. commenced to pepper the bowling, and was not long in reaching his century, after which he gave a remarkable exhibition of batting activity. Never before has the Moss Vale bowling received such an unmerciful flogging ; good and bad were treated alike, the balls whizzing to every part of the field, and only those who attempted to stop them know how much ginger was behind them. His experience in Sydney first-class cricket this season has made a marked improvement in Bradman's play, and he gave one of the most exhilerating displays one could wish to see. By making the phenomenal score of 320 not out, in which there were six sixers, he broke the district high score record of 300 made by himself against Moss Vale last season. He had a few lives, but then he was after runs off every ball, and after all, how many such scores are made in any class of cricket without a few chances being given ?

#### Moss Vale.

| | |
|---|---|
| First Innings | 73 |

#### Bowral.—First Innings.

| | |
|---|---|
| D. Bradman, not out | 320 |
| A. Stephens, c Elkin, b Chipperfield | 30 |
| V. Bradman, b R. Tickner | 13 |
| S. Cupitt, b S. Browne | 60 |
| P. Pearson, run out | 7 |
| G. Bensley, b R. Tickner | 0 |
| R. Whatman, b R. Tickner | 0 |
| S. Willis, c and b S. Browne | 15 |
| E. Waine, run out | 6 |
| J. Hill, b R. Tickner | 5 |
| Sundries | 24 |
| | |
| Total | 480 |

One Bowral player was absent.

## DON BRADMAN MAKES HIS DEBUT IN 1926-27

One of the greatest chapters in the history of the club was season 1926-27, which introduced the record-smashing Don Bradman to first grade and ultimately international cricket. It was a season St. George will remember. The first grade side, which finished fifth, had its best season, second grade was seventh and third grade won the competition—the club's first premiership success. The club fielded a team in the Municipal and Shire competition for the first time. It came 15th.

Individual performances in first grade were excellent and large crowds attended Hurstville Oval to see the matches. Century makers were A. Scanes 167 and 108; C. Targett 150 n.o., D. Bradman 110, D. Mullarkey, 104 n.o. In giving a review of the first grade, Mr. R. L. Jones, in the annual report, stated that A. Scane's 108 against Manly was one of the most brilliant innings of the season and this player was a valuable asset to the club. C. Targett's 150 not out against Petersham, one of

R. L. JONES

the strongest bowling sides in the competition, was a splendid effort. In this same match, Don Bradman—the Bowral player, who joined St. George and made his debut in grade cricket—registered an excellent performance is scoring 110. Des Mullarkey also scored a splendid century against University.

In winning the batting average, Scanes, with 547 runs at 49.72, just headed Bradman, who scored 289 runs at 48.16 in six completed innings. Bob Louden, with 405 runs at 33.75, finished second to Scanes in the aggregate. Targett scored 328 runs at 41, Mullarkey 379 at 31.58 and

Stan Mealey 306 at 30.6. Alan Fairfax was next best with 227 at 25.22, followed by Ted Adams 221 at 27.62 and R. L. Jones 198 at 28.28.

E. W. Adams, A. Scanes and H. King, who were called on to bowl for lengthy periods, rendered good bowling performances. Adams captured 17 wickets at 18.05, Scanes 14 at 19.78, Waghorn 14 at 30.64 and H. King 20 at 34.5. Alan Fairfax took eight wickets, Sid Hutchison and Stan Mealey five each.

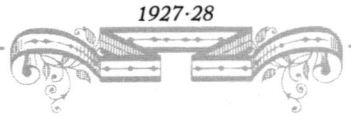

## — SEASON 1927-28 —

| TITLE | GAME | | SCORES | |
|---|---|---|---|---|
| Second Class | St. George Super Grade | Mosman | 2 | C. |
| | St. George - Uni. Comb. | Riverina | 125 | n.o. |
| | New South Wales | Broken Hill | 46 | S. |
| | Bohemians | Parkes | 18 | R.O. |
| | - | Canowindra | 0 | B. |
| | - | Cowra | 7 | B. |
| | - | Grenfell Juniors | 33 | C. |
| | - | Cootamundra | 1 | R.O. |
| | - | Dudauman | 12 | B. |
| | - | Canberra | 7 | B. |
| | Bowral | Combined City | 86 | B. |
| | Parramatta | Combined Grade | 0 | C. |
| First Grade | St. George | Petersham | 4 | B. |
| | - | | 7 | B. |
| | - | Randwick | 7 | C. |
| | - | Paddington | 130 | n.o. |
| | - | University | 2 | C. |
| | - | Marrickville | 40 | n.o. |
| | - | Manly | 47 | C. |
| | - | Randwick | 87 | C. |
| | - | Balmain | 56 | n.o. |
| | | North Sydney | 22 | B. |
| Sheffield Shield | New South Wales | South Australia | 118 | C. |
| " " " | " " | " " | 33 | B. |
| " " " | " " | " " | 2 | C. |
| " " " | " " | " " | 73 | C. |
| " " " | | Victoria | 31 | LBW. |
| " " " | | " | 5 | B. |
| " " " | | " | 7 | S. |
| " " " | | " | 134 | n.o. |
| " " " | | Queensland | 0 | B. |
| " " " | | " | 13 | C. |
| | | Total runs | 1155 | |

## — SUMMARY —

### AVERAGES

| | Innings | NO's. | H.S. | Runs | Average |
|---|---|---|---|---|---|
| First Class | 10 | 1 | 134 x | 416 | 46·22 |
| Sheffield Shield | 10 | 1 | 134 x | 416 | 46·22 |
| First Grade | 10 | 3 | 130 x | 402 | 57·42 |
| Other Second Class | 12 | 1 | 125 | 337 | 30·63 |
| All Second Class | 22 | 4 | 130 x | 739 | 41·05 |
| All Matches | 32 | 5 | 134 x | 1155 | 42·79 |

DON BRADMAN scored a century on his first appearance in Sheffield Shield cricket - 118.

Council Chambers,
Hurstville
9th. December 1927.

D. Bradman, Esq.,
C/- N.S.W. Cricket Association,
254, George Street,
SYDNEY.

Dear Sir,

At the meeting of my Council held
last evening, attention was directed to the
fact that two members of the St. George District
Cricket Club had conferred upon them the very
great honor of being selected to represent this
State against Victoria and South Australia in the
forthcoming "Sheffield Shield" Cricket matches,
and as one of those selected, I was directed to
convey to you the hearty congratulations of the
Council, and the hope that when the occasion
arises, you will indeed prove a very worthy
representative, and thus justify the confidence
reposed in you by the selectors.

Yours faithfully,

Town Clerk.

## NEW SOUTH WALES CRICKET ASSOCIATION
### Southern Tour — December 1927

BACK ROW  N. Phillips, F. Jordan, A. Scanes, S. Everett, T. J. E. Andrews, D. G. Bradman,
A. Jackson, W. A. Oldfield.
FRONT ROW  G. Morgan, A. F. Kippax (Captain), Dr. F. V. McAdam (Manager), R. McNamee,
A. Mailey.

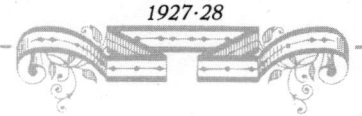

# New South Wales v South Australia

NEW SOUTH WALES v SOUTH AUSTRALIA, at Adelaide, 16, 17, 19 and 20 December 1927.

| New South Wales | - First Innings | 519 |
| | - Second Innings | 150 |
| South Australia | - First Innings | 481 |
| | - Second Innings | 189 for 9 wickets |
| | New South Wales lost by 1 wicket. | |

| DON BRADMAN | - c. N.L. Williams b. J.D. Scott | 118 |
| | b. C.V. Grimmett | 33 |

The Selectors had intended to make DON BRADMAN twelfth man in this match but A.A. Jackson developed a boil on his knee and had to be omitted.     This meant that Bradman was included in the eleven.

He faced a stern test in his first first-class match, for the opposing bowlers included C.V. Grimmett, then perhaps the best bowler in Australia; moreover, he was suffering from an injured hand.

He went in just before tea on the first day, and promptly hit two fours off Grimmett in his first over.    He reached 50 in sixty-seven minutes, and was 65 not out at the close of play after one and three-quarter hours' batting.    The next morning he reached his century, after two hours forty-one minutes, and was last out, just before lunch, after a stay of three hours eight minutes; he hit eight fours.    He was the twentieth Australian batsman to make a century on his début in first-class cricket.

In the second innings, Bradman went in before lunch on the last day, he batted for sixty-four minutes and made 33 runs, before being bowled off his pads soon after lunch.

## BRADMAN'S BRILLIANT DEBUT

Kippax continued his plucky innings, with Bradman at the other end also piling up the runs, but just before the luncheon interval the N.S.W. captain was caught by Alexander after having made a brilliant 143.    When Mailey went, clean bowled, Bradman faced Scott and was caught by Williams. He had played a magnificent innings for 118, a great debut in Sheffield Shield cricket.

### NEW SOUTH WALES
#### First Innings

| | |
|---|---|
| N. E. Phillips, b Whitfield | 112 |
| G. Morgan, b Scott | 11 |
| T. J. E. Andrews, c Williams, b Grimmett | 58 |
| A. Kippax, c Alexander, b Williams | 143 |
| A. Scanes, c Williams, b Schneider | 44 |
| W. A. Oldfield, c Hack, b Grimmett | 12 |
| D. Bradman, c Williams, b Scott | 118 |
| F. Jordan, lbw, b Scott | 1 |
| S. C. Everett, st Hack, b Grimmett | 5 |
| A. Mailey, b Scott | 0 |
| R. McNamee, not out | 1 |
| Sundries | 14 |
| Total | 519 |

#### BOWLING

| | O. | M. | R. | W. |
|---|---|---|---|---|
| Scott | 19.6 | 1 | 99 | 4 |
| Whitfield | 17 | 3 | 43 | 1 |
| Grimmett | 31 | 1 | 160 | 3 |
| Williams | 11 | — | 70 | 1 |
| Lee | 17 | 1 | 76 | — |
| Schneider | 6 | — | 39 | 1 |
| Alexander | 3 | — | 14 | — |
| Johnson | 1 | — | 4 | — |

Scott 6 no-balls. Whitfield 1 wide, 2 byes, 5 leg-byes, 1 wide, 6 no-balls.
Fall of wickets — 15, 137, 224, 250, 298, 306, 400, 511, 514, 519.

#### Second Innings

| | |
|---|---|
| N. E. Phillips, lbw, b Grimmett | 11 |
| A Scanes, c Whitfield, b Grimmett | 26 |
| T. J. Andrews, b Scott | 20 |
| A. Kippax, c and b Grimmett | 0 |
| G. Morgan, b Grimmett | 34 |
| D. Bradman, b Grimmett | 33 |
| S. C. Everett, c Harris, b Scott | 8 |
| F. Jordan, lbw, b Grimmett | 0 |
| W. A. Oldfield, c Richardson, b Grimmett | 4 |
| A. A. Mailey, c Schneider, b Grimmett | 5 |
| R. McNamee, not out | 1 |
| Sundries | 8 |
| Total | 150 |

#### BOWLING

| | O. | M. | R. | W. |
|---|---|---|---|---|
| Grimmett | 21.7 | 5 | 57 | 8 |
| Scott | 17 | 3 | 46 | 2 |
| Whitfield | 7 | 1 | 25 | 0 |
| Williams | 2 | 0 | 13 | 0 |

Scott, 5 no-balls and 1 wide, 1 bye, 1 leg-bye.

### SOUTH AUSTRALIA
#### First Innings

| | |
|---|---|
| K. J. Schneider, c and b Mailey | 108 |
| G. W. Harris, c and b Andrews | 77 |
| V. Y. Richardson, b Jordan | 80 |
| W. C. Alexander, st Oldfield, b Mailey | 42 |
| E. A. Johnson, st Oldfield, b Andrews | 0 |
| H. E. P. Whitfield, b Jordan | 15 |
| A. Hack, c Morgan, b Everett | 45 |
| P. K. Lee, st Oldfield, b Mailey | 28 |
| C. V. Grimmett, not out | 43 |
| J. D. Scott, c Phillips, b Everett | 0 |
| N. L. Williams, b Everett | 21 |
| Sundries | 22 |
| Total | 481 |

#### BOWLING

| | O. | M. | R. | W. |
|---|---|---|---|---|
| Everett | 26.7 | 4 | 92 | 3 |
| McNamee | 22 | 11 | 34 | 0 |
| Jordan | 21 | 1 | 65 | 2 |
| Mailey | 50 | 9 | 143 | 3 |
| Andrews | 18 | 0 | 86 | 2 |
| Phillips | 7 | 0 | 22 | 0 |
| Morgan | 3 | 0 | 17 | 0 |

8 byes, 12 leg-byes, 2 no-balls.

#### Second Innings

| | |
|---|---|
| K. J. Schneider, lbw, b McNamee | 11 |
| G. W. Harris, b McNamee | 18 |
| V. Y. Richardson, b McNamee | 0 |
| W. C. Alexander, b Andrews | 49 |
| E. A. Johnson, b Mailey | 0 |
| H. E. P. Whitfield, run out | 17 |
| A. Hack, b McNamee | 6 |
| P. K. Lee, not out | 27 |
| C. V. Grimmett, c Oldfield, b McNamee | 32 |
| J. D. Scott, c Phillips, b Mailey | 14 |
| N. L. Williams, not out | 0 |
| Sundries | 15 |
| Total | 189 |

#### BOWLING

| | O. | M. | R. | W. |
|---|---|---|---|---|
| Everett | 3 | 0 | 16 | 0 |
| McNamee | 29.2 | 12 | 53 | 5 |
| Jordan | 4 | 0 | 13 | 0 |
| Mailey | 28 | 2 | 79 | 2 |
| Andrews | 6 | 1 | 13 | 1 |

4 byes, 11 leg-byes.
Fall of wickets — 27, 27, 34, 112, 116, 117, 131, 158.

## LIKE A VETERAN

### BRADMAN'S DEBUT

THAT AUSTRALIA has unearthed another "topnotcher" is the opinion expressed by old interstate and international cricketers who watched Don Bradman compile a century in his innings in Sheffield Shield cricket.

Though only nineteen years old he played like a veteran, devoid of nerves, cracking Grimmett twice for four at the very outset of his innings and completing his hundred by sweeping Lee to the leg boundary.

Bradman is a natural batsman. He uses his feet well and though he hit hard and made strokes all round the wicket not for a moment did he take the slightest risk.

**DON BRADMAN, ST. GEORGE COLT.**

Made a century in his first match in the Sheffield Shield. A product of Bowral he is short, quick on his feet drives crisply, fields smartly, and has a fine temperament for big cricket.

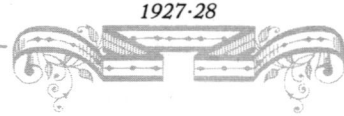

**TELEGRAM.**

This message has been received subject to the Post and Telegraph Act and Regulations.

Seb. C112, 7/1926   NOTE—The figures at bottom of message represent the time received at this Office.

| Station from. | Words. | Amount. | Time Lodged. | Date Lodged. | Remarks. |
|---|---|---|---|---|---|

REP

X 186 SYDNEY 17 126 AR 24 TH    01198

D BRADMAN HOTEL WINDSOR

QUEEN ST MELBOURNE

GOOD LUCK DON HOPE FINGER BETTER MUM

WRITING LOVE

MAY

E.T. No. 2

**COMMONWEALTH OF AUSTRALIA.—POSTMASTER-GENERAL'S DEPARTMENT.**

## RECEIVED TELEGRAM.

| Station From. | Words. | Charge. | Time and Date Lodged. | No. |
|---|---|---|---|---|
| SA 2 | BOWRAL | 18 9 | AM 19TH | |

Remarks.

To DON BRADMAN
CARE ALLEN KIPPAX
ADELAIDE CRICKET GROUND

MY HEARTIEST CONGRATULATIONS ON YOUR GREAT INNINGS EVERYBODY BOWRAL DELIGHTED FROM UNCLE

Sched. C 107—6/1926

Time received at this Office.

## RECEIVED TELEGRAM

| Station From. | Words. | Charge. | Time and Date Lodged. | No. |
|---|---|---|---|---|
| Bowral NSW | 16 | | 10-10 a 20th | |

Remarks.

To Don Bradman
Sheffield Cricket Team
Adelaide

Hearty congratulations from all your bowral friends and Well wishes

Time received at this Office.

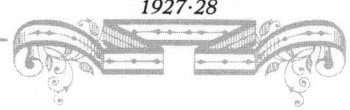

*Extract from Bowral newspaper*

### THANKS FROM DON.

From Don himself we have the following characteristic note :—

Whilst playing cricket in Adelaide on the present tour I received the following telegram from Bowral :— "Hearty congratulations from all your Bowral friends and well wishers."

There was no signature but it would appear to have been sent from the local residents, and as I cannot thank anyone in particular I would like you to convey my sincerest thanks and appreciation to those people who have sent me messages of congratulation.

The whole trip has been wonderful and the experience which one gains on such a trip is a great benefit for all future occasions.

Beyond that it is very gratifying to know that one's efforts are also appreciated by the people of Bowral and wherever I go I will always cherish very happy memories of the town where I learnt my cricket.

Once again, may I thank one and all for the great kindness shown to me, and while I am in the game I will do my best to live up to the standards expected, both on and off the field.

Yours very sincerely,
D. G. BRADMAN.

Charles Bannerman, the first man to make a century in Test cricket (165 not out for Australia at Melbourne in the 1876–77 season), gives Don Bradman some advice.

Arthur Mailey selected a team and called it "The Bohemians".
A special blazer was created and the players toured country centres in New South Wales.

## ARTHUR MAILEY'S *BOHEMIANS*

BACK ROW   F. Merchant, C. Nicholls, E. L. Waddy, J. Ellis, J. C. Bancks, C. Wright, T. J. E. Andrews, C. Spencer.
FRONT ROW   N. Cameron, A. Mailey, D. G. Bradman.

*Taken at Dudauman, N.S.W., 1928*

# Bowral Honors Her Cricket Hero.

## PRESENTATION OF GOLD WATCH AND CHAIN TO DON BRADMAN.

### INTERSTATE PLAYERS LAUD THE BOWRAL BOY.

There was an exceptionally large attendance at the Reception and Dance given in Bowral on Friday night in honor of Don. Bradman and the visiting St. George players. Such a tribute of respect and admiration has rarely been paid to a resident in these districts and Don might have been pardoned had he shown some little sign of swelled head. But his greetings of old friends and his reply to the speeches made in his praise was marked by a modesty of demeanor that explains the rapid progress he has made in the affections of his new associates in the game. For the most notable feature of the speeches of the visitors, from Richardson downwards, was the evident pleasure they had in praising their new associate. As Mr. Westbrook said, Don Bradman had endeared himself to the public not only by his masterly cricket but by his character, which was the same in private life as on the cricket field.

Mayor Stephens has every reason to feel satisfied with the success of his first official effort to promote sport and sociability in Bowral. Everyone was in the happiest mood and the reception was one of the most successful functions ever held in the town—a success which was repeated on Loseby Park the following day.

After dancing had been indulged in for some time to the strains of Mr. Beavan's orchestra, Mr. Mailey and other visiting and local cricketers were invited to take seats on the platform. The Mayor then introduced local players to the visitors, after which he proceeded with the presentation. He said there was no need to tell them that they had met primarily to do honor to Don Bradman. They had also to extend to Mr. Mailey and the visitors from St. George a very hearty welcome. Mr. Kippax was being married that night and some of their expected visitors were at the wedding, but they would be along on Saturday. When he (the Mayor) first got the idea of opening the turf wicket in Loseby Park, he asked Don Bradman to bring along a team. Don was too modest to do that, but he interested Mr. Jones in the project and on Saturday, Bowral would have a red letter day in cricket. The occasion was a fitting one to show Don that his services to N.S.W. cricket and to Bowral were appreciated in the town in which he had first won his laurels. It was no mean achievement for a country boy to go to Sydney and in his first season win second place in the Sheffield Shield averages and second place in first grade averages in Sydney. The great wish of his Bowral admirers was to see him in an Australian team. (Applause).

Mr. P. A. Westbrook said he was a little nervous in the presence of Mr. Mailey who not only played good cricket but made good humorous pictures. He did not think they should wait till a man was dead before they told him how they admired his good qualities. Rather would be endorse the sentiment of the legend which greeted the return of a wanderer to his own land, " We love you and we tell you so." Whether it was keeping books, playing tennis, driving a car or wielding a bat, the smartest man of his age known to the speaker was Don Bradman. To keep up his wicket when others had fallen disastrously was the supreme test of a cricketer and that their young guest had done. He was undoubtedly one of the greatest cricketers in the State. They were proud of the illustrious deeds performed by the incomparable boy from Bowral. (Applause).

Mr. Mailey did not claim to be a wonderful judge of cricket, but one of the best innings he had ever seen was Don Bradman's knock at Adelaide. He was undoubtedly a coming international. Not only was Don a fine cricketer, but he was a good sportsman. They were lucky to have produced so fine a chap as Don.

The Mayor presented Bradman with a handsome gold watch and chain saying that he would live long to wear them and go far in the cricket world.

Mr. Bradman, who was received with " For He's a Jolly Good Fellow," was evidently overcome by the extreme cordiality of his reception. He said that after the glowing remarks of the chairman he found difficulty in putting his feelings into words. In the first place there were several people he had to thank for whatever success he had made. Mr. Stephens had got him the chance to have a knock in Sydney. Mr. Jones and Mr. Cush had given him his next chance for if he hadn't got into St. George he could not have gone further. Then, when that was achieved, Mr. Westbrook had given him time off, for without that it would have been impossible for him to retain his place in his Club. Cricket was a wonderful character builder and he had met some of the finest of men amongst his cricket associates. He thanked them all from the bottom of his heart and hoped he would never do anything to make them regret they had given him their present.

An excellent supper was served by the ladies.

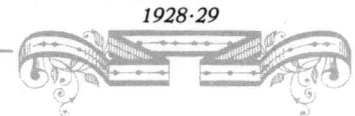

# 1928 -29 Season

The pinnacle of ambition for every Australian cricketer is to be selected in a side to tour England.

Selection for a Test team within Australia is really a higher honour because you are one of the best eleven, whereas it is possible for a tourist not to play in even one Test.

A lucky break which brought me a century in each innings against Queensland ensured a place in the first Test team in 1928-29 but scores of 18 and 1 were not sufficient for me to hold my position and I was dropped for the second Test.

Chosen again for the third, in which I made 79 and 112, I clinched a regular place and was never again omitted from an Australian team.

*Don Bradman*

## — SEASON 1928-29 —

| TITLE | GAME | | SCORES | |
|---|---|---|---|---|
| Second Class | District | Bexley Waratahs | 3 | L.B.W. |
| | Kippax's XI | Lismore | 0 | C. |
| | - - | Taree | 19 | B. |
| | - - | Wauchope | 71 | C. |
| | Gladesville | S.M. Herald | 149 | C. |
| | Exhibition | Newcastle | 5 | B. |
| | New South Wales C.A. XI | | 34 | S. |
| | - - - - | Tamworth | 20 | B. |
| | | | 128 | n. o. |
| | - - - - | Singleton | 117 | C. |
| | - - - - | Maitland | 0 | L.B.W. |
| | Oldfield's XI | Menangle | 6 | C. |
| | St. George Team | Richmond Aerodrome | 52 | C. |
| | - - | Kippax's XI | 61 | n. o. |
| First Grade | St. George | Gordon | 107 | B. |
| | - | Manly | 34 | C. |
| | - | North Sydney | 46 | C. |
| | - | Petersham | 74 | C. |
| First Class | The Rest | Australia | 14 | C. |
| | - - - | | 5 | B. |
| | An Australian XI | England | 58 | n. o. |
| | - - - | | 18 | L.B.W. |
| | New South Wales | | 87 | B. |
| | - - - | | 132 | n. o. |
| | - - - | | 15 | C. |
| Sheffield Shield | - - - | Queensland | 131 | C. |
| | - - - | | 133 | n. o. |
| | - - - | South Australia | 5 | C. |
| | - - - | - - | 2 | B. |
| | - - - | - - | 35 | C. |
| | - - - | - - | 175 | C. |
| | - - - | Victoria | 1 | B. |
| | - - - | - | 71 | n. o. |
| | - - - | | 340 | n. o. |

| TITLE | GAME | | SCORES | |
|---|---|---|---|---|
| Test | Australia | England | 18 | L.B.W. |
| | - | - | 1 | C. |
| | - | - | 79 | B. |
| | - | - | 112 | C. |
| | - | - | 40 | C. |
| | - | - | 58 | R.O. |
| | - | - | 123 | C. |
| | - | - | 37 | n. o. |
| | | Total runs | 2616 | |

## — SUMMARY —

AVERAGES.

| | Innings | N.O's. | H.S. | Runs | Average |
|---|---|---|---|---|---|
| Test | 8 | 1 | 123 | 468 | 66·85 |
| Sheffield Shield | 9 | 3 | 340x | 893 | 148·83 |
| Other First Class | 7 | 2 | 132 | 329 | 65·80 |
| All First Class | 24 | 6 | 340x | 1690 | 93·88 |
| First Grade | 4 | 0 | 107 | 261 | 65·25 |
| Other Second Class | 14 | 2 | 149 | 665 | 55·41 |
| All Second Class | 18 | 2 | 149 | 926 | 57·87 |
| All Matches | 42 | 8 | 340x | 2616 | 76·94 |

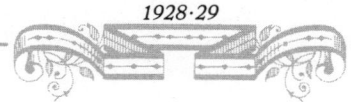

DON BRADMAN's aggregate of 1690 was a record for an Australian season.

He scored seven centuries in first-class matches in one season - sharing this Australian record with W.R. Hammond.

Bradman was second for Australia in the Test Match batting averages.

His aggregate of 468 was the highest on record for any Test series by a batsman under the age of twenty-one.

He was the youngest player in the world to score a century in a Test Match.

His aggregate of 893 runs and his average of 148·83 for Sheffield Shield Matches were records for New South Wales, and his average of 140·87 in all matches for New South Wales was the highest on record.

Of those who have played over twenty innings, his average of 78·00 was then a record for batsmen under the age of twenty-one.

His aggregate of 2106 was then a record for a batsman of under twenty-one for runs scored in Australia.

Bradman made nine centuries in first-class cricket before he was twenty-one; two centuries were made in Test Matches between England and Australia.

He won the St. George Club batting average.

Don Bradman aged 20 years.

# DON BRADMAN–WONDER CRICKETER OF 1928

## Eight Years Ago "Smith's Weekly" Picked the Hero of To-day

## MARKED HIM AT THE AGE OF 12 FOR PRESENT HONORS

### BY J. MATHERS.

ABOUT eight years ago, a sub-editor of "Smith's Weekly," with a humorous flair for writing head-lines, unsuspectingly predicted the greatness of an obscure little lad who was subsequently to write his name in the highest company of International cricket.

The little chap was playing in the school yard when he hit a ball that balanced on the top of a post, then ran along the edge of a paling fence, and performed a few more tricks before it ultimately came to rest on the ground.

The incident was published exclusively in "Smith's" in a par which referred to him as "A crack bat." Don Bradman was the lad.

To-day he is THE crack bat.

"I've still got that cutting from 'Smith's,'" proudly admitted Bradman the other evening during the course of a chat over the dinner table.

"And, although many nice things have been written about me, that first paragraph still takes the bun."

### BOUNDING BALL

SAW a curious thing at a junior cricket match at Bowral (N.S.W.) recently. Don Bradman (crack bat) sent a ball over the boundary fence. It struck half a brick, rebounded on to a fence post, poised there for an appreciable time and ran along the top of the palings the whole length of a panel of fencing before descending outside the boundary.—"John."

Reprinted from "Smith's Weekly" of eight years ago, by courtesy of Smith's Newspapers Ltd.

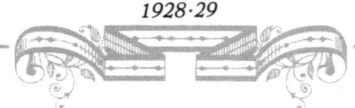

# New South Wales v Queensland

NEW SOUTH WALES v QUEENSLAND, at Brisbane (Exhibition Ground), 27, 29, 30, 31 October and 1 November 1928.

| New South Wales | - First Innings | 248 |
| | - Second Innings | 401 for 4 wickets |
| Queensland | - First Innings | 324 |
| | - Second Innings | 322 |

New South Wales won by 6 wickets.

| DON BRADMAN | - c. L.P. O'Connor b. H.M. Thurlow | 131 |
| | not out | 133 |

DON BRADMAN made a century in each innings of this match, the first of the four occasions on which he did so. He completed his century in two hours forty-four minutes and he batted altogether for three hours thirty-two minutes, and hit fourteen fours.

Bradman went in soon after lunch on the fourth day at 121 for 1, and had reached 88 not out by the close of play. Next morning he took thirty-four minutes to complete his second century of the match, after batting three hours thirty-one minutes.

A hundred in each innings had been scored on only ten previous occasions in Sheffield Shield Matches.

THE WINNING HIT.—Bradman and Love running between the wickets after Bradman had made the winning hit in the Sheffield Shield match, giving victory to New South Wales.

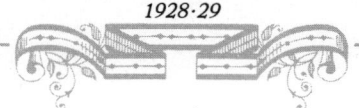

# BRADMAN'S DOUBLE.
## CENTURY IN EACH INNINGS.
## NEW SOUTH WALES WINS.

(By R. Hartigan.)

## Two Surprises

UNTIL yesterday the youthful D. Bradman, of New South Wales was merely an "outside" possibility in a test match sense. His double century in Brisbane brings him well into the calculations of unofficial selectors. Whether it will have the same effect on the official four remains to be seen.

Tradition dies hard. And test cricket is full of traditions. Selectors, both here and in England, are cautious innovators.

They may find a feat like young Bradman's disturbing. It was really the kind of thing that should have been done by an acknowledged "eligible." With the Englishman, Larwood, making test batsmen look cheap in Melbourne, the riddle of the Australian Eleven becomes no easier, while the need for the best solution is more apparent. There is glorious uncertainty in many places—not only on the pitch.

Everybody is anxiously awaiting the personnel of the first Test team. May be there will be some surprises.

\* \* \* \*

Will Vic. Richardson or Billy Woodfull captain the team?

\* \* \* \*

Bradman and Jackson will be hard to leave out.

### QUEENSLAND.—First Innings.

| | |
|---|---|
| L. O'Connor, c. Love, b. Hooker | 72 |
| R. K. Oxenham, c. Nicholls, b. M'Namee | 1 |
| F. J. Gough, b. Hooker | 67 |
| W. Rowe, c. Nicholls, b. Morgan | 15 |
| F. C. Thompson, l.b.w., b. Hooker | 29 |
| O. Nothling, b. Morgan | 18 |
| Knowles, c. Love, b. Morgan | 2 |
| R. Higgins, c. Morgan, b. Hooker | 58 |
| P. M. Hornibrook, c. Love, b. Hooker | 0 |
| E. Bensted, not out | 36 |
| H. M. Thurlow, b. Hooker | 1 |
| Sundries | 25 |
| **Total** | **324** |

Byes, 11, leg-byes, 10, no balls 4.

Wickets fell at 21, 150, 155, 176, 230, 254, 258, 320, 320, 324.

#### BOWLING.

| | O. | M. | R. | W. |
|---|---|---|---|---|
| Nicholls | 17 | 1 | 64 | 0 |
| Hooker | 24.3 | 6 | 46 | 6 |
| M'Namee | 29 | 7 | 85 | 1 |
| Carter | 11 | 0 | 47 | 0 |
| Morgan | 11 | 1 | 36 | 3 |
| Campbell | 5 | 0 | 21 | 0 |

### NEW SOUTH WALES.—First Innings.

| | |
|---|---|
| R. Loder, b. Thurlow | 1 |
| A. Jackson, c. Hornibrook, b. Nothling | 50 |
| D. Bradman, l.b.w., b. Thurlow | 131 |
| A. Kippax, b. Thurlow | 47 |
| G. Morgan, l.b.w., Thurlow | 4 |
| S. Love, c. O'Connor, b. Thurlow | 5 |
| C. Nicholls, b. Thurlow | 2 |
| H. Hooker, b. Oxenham | 0 |
| J. Carter, l.b.w., Oxenham | 0 |
| R. M'Namee, not out | 0 |
| N. Campbell, b. Oxenham | 0 |
| Sundries | 8 |
| **Total** | **248** |

Leg byes 4, no balls 4.

Wickets fell at: 7, 120, 213, 227, 246, 247, 248, 248, 248, 248.

#### BOWLING.

| | O. | M. | R. | W. |
|---|---|---|---|---|
| Hornibrook | 12 | 2 | 52 | 0 |
| Thurlow | 15 | 3 | 59 | 6 |
| Oxenham | 18.2 | 3 | 56 | 3 |
| Nothling | 8 | 1 | 22 | 1 |
| Rowe | 5 | 0 | 15 | 0 |
| Bensted | 6 | 0 | 30 | 0 |
| Thompson | 1 | 0 | 6 | 0 |

### Second Innings.

| | |
|---|---|
| A. Jackson, c. Nothling, b. Rowe | 71 |
| R. Loder, run out | 49 |
| D. Bradman, not out | 133 |
| A. Kippax, c. Hornibrook, b. Rowe | 96 |
| G. Morgan, b. Thurlow | 6 |
| H. Love, not out | 31 |
| Sundries | 15 |
| **Total for four wickets** | **401** |

Wickets fell at 121, 121, 306, 322.

Byes 11, leg byes 3, no-ball 1.

#### BOWLING.

| | O. | M. | R. | W. |
|---|---|---|---|---|
| Hornibrook | 20.4 | 3 | 62 | 0 |
| Thurlow | 21 | 2 | 94 | 1 |
| Oxenham | 29 | 3 | 77 | 0 |
| Nothling | 13 | 0 | 52 | 0 |
| Bensted | 9 | 0 | 35 | 0 |
| Rowe | 11 | 3 | 45 | 2 |
| Thompson | 8 | 3 | 21 | 0 |

New South Wales won by six wickets and three runs.

Umpires, Messrs. J. A. Scott and J. P. Orr. Official scorers, Messrs. J. G. Bell (acting for New, South Wales) and W. R. Grice.

### QUEENSLAND—Second Innings.

| | |
|---|---|
| E. Bensted, b M'Namee | 0 |
| L. O'Connor, b Hooker | 2 |
| P. Hornibrook, c Nicholls, b Hooker | 16 |
| R. K. Oxenham, b Morgan | 7 |
| F. J. Gough, c and b Carter | 39 |
| F. C. Thompson, not out | 158 |
| E. Knowles, b Campbell | 30 |
| W. Rowe, b Nicholls | 22 |
| O. Nothling, c Nicholls, b Hooker | 3 |
| R. Higgins, b M'Namee | 33 |
| E. Thurlow, c Morgan, b Hooker | 1 |
| Sundries | 11 |
| **Total** | **322** |

Fall of wickets: 1, 10, 19, 43, 82, 157, 206, 215, 295.

#### BOWLING.

| | O. | M. | R. | W. |
|---|---|---|---|---|
| Nicholls | 9 | 2 | 50 | 1 |
| M'Namee | 27 | 5 | 93 | 2 |
| Hooker | 31.6 | 5 | 72 | 4 |
| Morgan | 9 | 2 | 28 | 1 |
| Campbell | 6 | 0 | 37 | 1 |
| Carter | 7 | 1 | 31 | 1 |

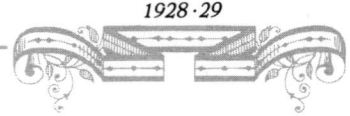

The time received at this office is shown at the foot of the form.
The first line of this telegram contains the following particulars in the order named.

S. 16. C.39. 1928

| Station from. | Words. | Time and Date Lodged. | No. |

W 219   SYDNEY   20   3-50 PM   1 ST

D BRADMAN   £46
CARLTON HOTEL
BRISBANE

CONGRATULATIONS YOU LITTLE CORKER TELL ALAN AND ARCHIE
CAN COME IN FRONT DOOR
HERB GELDARD

---

The time received at this office is shown at the foot of the form.
The first line of this Telegram contains the following particulars in the order named.

Sch. C220/1

| Station from. | Words. | Time and Date Lodged. |

ADELAIDE   15   5-2 P   1 ST

DON BRADMAN
HOTEL CARLTON BRISBANE

CONGRATULATIONS SELF ALSO ALAN KIPPAX KEEP DOING IT
VIC RICHARDSON

---

| STATION FROM. | WORDS. | TIME AND DATE LODGED. | No. | C et No. |
|---|---|---|---|---|
| Bowral | 16. | 2 5p 30th | | By |

Remarks.

This message has been received subject to the Post and Telegraph Act
and Regulations.
The time received at this Office is shown at the foot of the Form.
Sch. C/37/1928.—C.9 85.—B 2028.

To   Don Bradman
Cricket Ground
Bne

Congratulations from us all
here on your wonderful
fighting innings
Stephens

A New South Wales blazer worn by Don Bradman, together with a pair of his boots, his pads, and a ball used in his first match with a New South Wales Sheffield Shield Team at Broken Hill, 1927.

## ENGLAND v. AUSTRALIA
## Second Test Match
*Sydney, 14–20 December 1928*

BACK ROW    W. M. Woodfull, W. H. Ponsford, H. Ironmonger, D. J. Blackie, O. E. Nothling, H. L. Hendry.
FRONT ROW    V. Y. Richardson, C. V. Grimmett, J. S. Ryder (Captain), D. G. Bradman, W. A. Oldfield, A. F. Kippax.

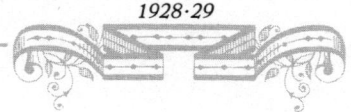
The first line of this Telegram contains the following particulars in the order named.

| STATION FROM. | WORDS. | TIME AND DATE LODGED. | No. | C'ct No. ........... |
|---|---|---|---|---|

Goulburn NSW. 13 — 9 50 a 30 — A By ...........

Remarks.

This message has been received subject to the Post and Telegraph Act and Regulations.
The time received at this Office is shown at the foot of the Form.
Sch 12-7/1928.—C.9085.—B.2.'28.

To Don Bradman
cricket ground

Bris

Throat hoarse from cheering.
Congratulations Archie too

Claude

---

# *Of Test Class*

## *Bradman's Great Promise*

DON. G. BRADMAN, the 20-year-old New South Wales batsman, who performed with remarkable consistency in both innings against Queensland, looks like developing into the cricketer of the season. His Brisbane performances with the bat, allied to the fact that he is a wonderful deep fieldsman, must bring him strongly into the picture for selection in Australia's team to meet England at the Exhibition Ground on November 30.

Bradman is a remarkable youth. When he made his first appearance in a Sheffield Shield match at Adelaide last season he staggered the cricket world by scoring 118 and 33. He failed in the second game against Queensland, and did only fairly in the first Victorian match, but in the return game against South Australia he scored 73, and added fresh glory to his name in the return Victorian match by scoring 134 not out. These fine performances were supplemented by many stirring deeds in Sydney club cricket, from which he emerged with the fine average of 57.42 per innings.

Bradman's promise does not rely solely on his ability to get runs; rather is it the manner in which he scores them that emphasises his potentialities as a test-match player of the near future. Both his great innings in Brisbane bore the hall-mark of true batsmanship. He not only scored his runs freely, but showed a remarkable timing eye and a knowledge of positional placing that one could hardly find bettered even in the play of a seasoned campaigner. Bradman's on and leg shots were delightful to watch for power and crispness. His partiality for these strokes is not restricted to one type of bowler, and every Queenslander was given a taste of his punishing powers at points from fine leg right round to the on drive.

It is many years since the Brisbane public saw so strong a batsman in on-side of the wicket play. However, Bradman's versatility was not confined to these picturesque shots, as he made many choice back cuts, and at times kept both point and covers alert. He is a great cricket find, and New South Wales is congratulated upon introducing such a brilliant batsman.

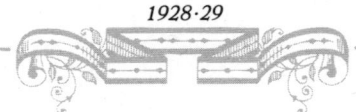

# New South Wales v M.C.C.

NEW SOUTH WALES v M.C.C. TEAM, at Sydney, 9, 10, 12 and 13 November 1928.

New South Wales - First Innings     349
                - Second Innings    364 for 3 wickets

M.C.C. Team     - First Innings     734 for 7 wickets dec.
                - Second Innings   -

                Drawn.

DON BRADMAN   - b. A.P. Freeman       87
               not out              132

This was DON BRADMAN's first match against an International team, and his century in the second innings would be easily his best performance up to this time.   In the first innings, Bradman went in at 38 for 3.  He was 6 not out overnight and reached 50 next morning in eighty-five minutes, batting for two hours eleven minutes and hitting eight fours. His second innings was even better, going in soon after lunch on the last day at 115 for 3, he reached 50 in sixty-five minutes, and 100 in two hours eight minutes; he and Alan Kippax put on 249 undefeated for the fourth wicket, in two hours thirty-six minutes.   Bradman hit fourteen fours, mostly hard drives, in a brilliant innings.

*Kelleway and Bradman adjourning for the lunch interval to-day.*

# DON BRADMAN
# HITS UP A BRILLIANT 87
## DEFIES ENGLISH TEST BOWLERS

## THE SCORES

Scores:—

### ENGLAND.—First Innings.

| | |
|---|---|
| H. Sutcliffe, b Kelleway | 67 |
| D. R. Jardine, b Hooker | 140 |
| E. Tyldesley, c Oldfield, b Kelleway | 1 |
| W. R. Hammond, run out | 225 |
| E. Hendren, c Campbell, b Bradman | 167 |
| M. Leyland, not out | 47 |
| L. Ames, b Morgan | 25 |
| A. P. F. Chapman, c Gregory, b Morgan | 16 |
| M. W. Tate, not out | 21 |
| Sundries (byes 12, leg byes 5, wides 2, no-balls 6) | 25 |

Seven wickets (closed) for .. 734
Fall of wickets: 1-148, 2-158, 3-263, 4-596, 5-622, 6-675.

### BOWLING

| | O. | M. | R. | W. |
|---|---|---|---|---|
| Gregory | 29 | 2 | 130 | 0 |
| Kelleway | 37 | 6 | 140 | 2 |
| Nicholls | 12 | 0 | 68 | 0 |
| Hooker | 34 | 3 | 150 | 1 |
| Campbell | 14 | 0 | 119 | 0 |
| Morgan | 14 | 1 | 47 | 2 |
| Bradman | 5 | 0 | 55 | 1 |

Kelleway and Morgan each bowled 3 no-balls, Morgan and Nicholls each one wide.

### ENGLAND

First innings—7 for 734
Innings declared closed.

### NEW SOUTH WALES
#### First Innings

| | |
|---|---|
| MORGAN, b Hammond | 1 |
| JACKSON, b Tate | 4 |
| ANDREWS, c Chapman, b Tate | 14 |
| A. KIPPAX, lbw, b Hammond | 64 |
| D. BRADMAN, b Freeman | 87 |
| C. E. KELLEWAY, not out | 93 |
| J. M. GREGORY, st. Ames, b Tate | 7 |
| W. A. OLDFIELD, c Ames, b Freeman | 33 |
| C. NICHOLLS, c Jardine, b Freeman | 26 |
| H. HOOKER, c Hammond, b Freeman | 14 |
| N. CAMPBELL, c Chapman, b Freeman | 0 |
| Sundries | 6 |
| **Total** | **349** |

Fall of Wickets: 1-5, 2-7, 3-38, 4-128, 5-196, 6-266, 7-268, 8-328, 9-347, 10-349.

#### BOWLING

| | O. | M. | R. | W. |
|---|---|---|---|---|
| Tate | 28 | 3 | 98 | 3 |
| Hammond | 17 | 3 | 64 | 2 |
| Freeman | 37.2 | 3 | 136 | 5 |
| Larwood | 4 | 1 | 10 | 0 |
| Leyland | 12 | 1 | 35 | 0 |

### Second Innings

| | |
|---|---|
| JACKSON, run out | 40 |
| MORGAN, c Ames, b Larwood | 18 |
| ANDREWS, b Tate | 19 |
| KIPPAX, not out | 136 |
| BRADMAN, not out | 132 |
| Sundries | 19 |
| **Three wickets for** | **364** |

Fall: 42, 72, 115.

#### BOWLING

| | O. | M. | R. | W. |
|---|---|---|---|---|
| Tate | 15 | 2 | 36 | 1 |
| Hammond | 15 | 0 | 73 | 0 |
| Freeman | 25 | 3 | 81 | 0 |
| Leyland | 12 | 1 | 61 | 0 |
| Larwood | 16 | 5 | 23 | 1 |
| Jardine | 3 | 0 | 22 | 0 |
| Hendren | 5 | 0 | 18 | 0 |
| Sutcliffe | 4 | 1 | 21 | 0 |

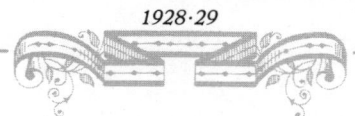
# TWO CENTURIES.

## Bradman and Kippax.

Thanks to Kippax and Bradman, New South Wales averted an innings defeat by England at the Sydney Cricket Ground yesterday. Each exceeded a century in a partnership originated when the outlook was far from bright. At stumps, New South Wales, with seven wickets in hand, was still 21 runs short of England's first innings total. The match was drawn. The three previous games of the visitors resulted similarly

Kippax and Bradman wore down and finally took complete control of England's best bowlers, who did not gain a wicket during the afternoon. They came together after Morgan had been beaten by Larwood's pace, Andrews had mistimed Tate, and Jackson's hesitancy had cost him his wicket. Another wicket at that stage would have put the hope of victory into the hearts of the Englishmen. The score then was 115. Larwood had not been overworked, and Freeman was experimenting with supreme confidence. But they, and then Tate, Hammond, and Leyland were mastered, and might have been routed but for the fact that during the last half hour of the game, Chapman used his batsmen in their stead.

It was not until Kippax had attained his century and Bradman was within a few runs of his, that Jardine, Hendren, and Sutcliffe were given the ball. Then there was no chance of the game being other than drawn.

*Showing a section of the huge crowd on the hill, and the scoring board at one stage of the game,*

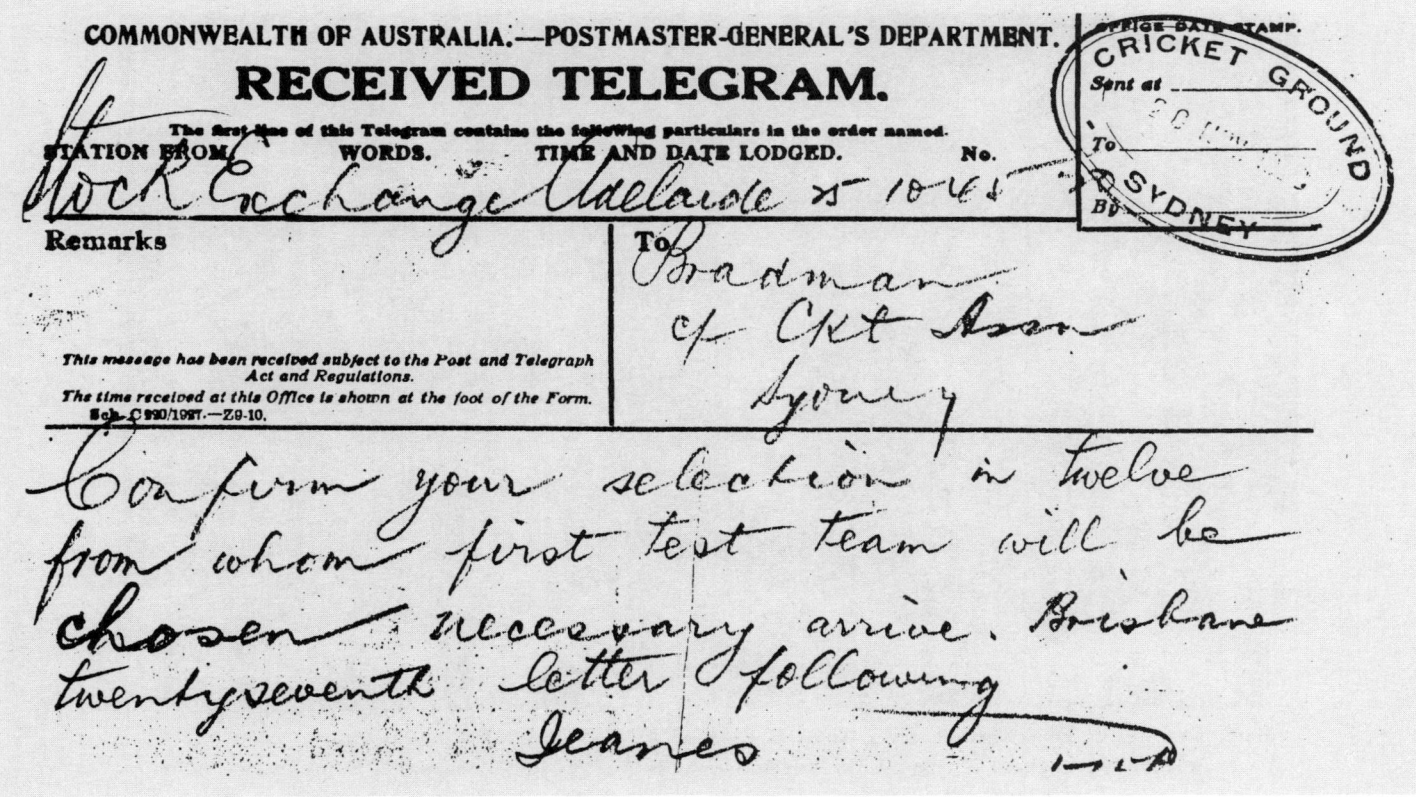

Telegram notifying Don Bradman of his selection in a Test team for the first time.

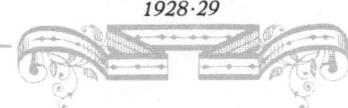

# Australia v England
## First Test Match

AUSTRALIA v ENGLAND, First Test Match, at Brisbane
(Exhibition Ground), 30 November, 1,3,4 and 5 December 1928.

| Australia | - First Innings | 122 |
| | - Second Innings | 66 |

| England | - First Innings | 521 |
| | - Second Innings | 342 for 8 wickets dec. |

Australia lost by 675 runs.

| DON BRADMAN | - lbw. b. M.W. Tate | 18 |
| | c. A.P.F. Chapman b. J.C. White | 1 |

DON BRADMAN's introduction to Test Match cricket was an unhappy experience. In the first innings, he went in on the third morning at 71 for 5, and batted for thirty-three minutes, hitting four fours, before falling at 101 for 6; his 18 was, in fact, the third highest score. He was very disappointed at being given out lbw., because he had tried to place the ball behind the square-leg umpire, thinking it would miss the leg stump.

In the second innings Bradman only faced two balls, being caught off the second one. It was the first time in his life he had seen a wet wicket of this nature, and of course he had never played on one.

## THE M.C.C. TOURING TEAM
### 1928–29

BACK ROW    G. W. Duckworth, L. E. G. Ames, C. P. Mead, M. W. Tate, E. Hendren, G. Geary.
CENTRE ROW    M. Leyland, S. Staples, W. R. Hammond, Mr. F. C. Toone (Manager), H. Sutcliffe, H. Larwood, A. P. Freeman.
FRONT ROW    E. Tyldesley, J. C. White, A. P. F. Chapman (Captain), D. R. Jardine, J. B. Hobbs.

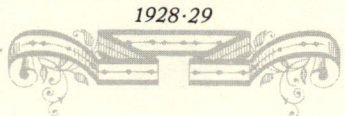

Bradman proudly wears his first Australian XI blazer.

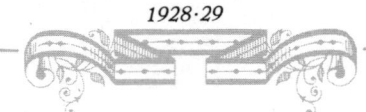

# BRADMAN MAKES TEST DEBUT

*Don Bradman, making his first stroke in Test cricket in the match at Brisbane. He made 18 in the first innings and 1 in the second.*

**BRADMAN OUT** leg-before-wicket to Tate, after he had scored 18 in great style in the first Test at Brisbane.

## THE SCORES

### ENGLAND—First Innings.

| | |
|---|---|
| J. B. HOBBS, run out .. .. .. .. | 49 |
| H. SUTCLIFFE, c Ponsford, b Gregory .. .. .. .. .. .. | 38 |
| C. P. MEAD, lbw, b Grimmett .. | 8 |
| W. R. HAMMOND, c Woodfull, b Gregory .. .. .. .. .. .. | 44 |
| E. R. JARDINE, c Woodfull, b Ironmonger .. .. .. .. .. .. | 35 |
| E. HENDREN, c Ponsford, b Ironmonger .. .. .. .. .. .. | 169 |
| A. P. F. Chapman, c Kelleway, b Gregory .. .. .. .. .. .. | 50 |
| M. W. TATE, c Ryder, b Grimmett | 26 |
| H. LARWOOD, lbw, b Hendry .. | 70 |
| J. C. WHITE, lbw, b Grimmett .. | 14 |
| G. DUCKWORTH, not out .. .. | 5 |
| Leg-byes 10, no-balls 3 .. .. .. | 13 |
| Total .. .. .. .. .. .. | 521 |

Fall: 1-85, 2-95, 3-103, 4-161, 5-217, 6-291, 7-319, 8-443, 9-495, 10-521.

### BOWLING.

| | O. | M. | R. | W. |
|---|---|---|---|---|
| Gregory .. .. | 41 | 2 | 142 | 3 |
| Grimmett .. | 40 | 2 | 167 | 3 |
| Kelleway .. | 34 | 9 | 77 | 0 |
| Ironmonger . | 44.3 | 18 | 79 | 2 |
| Ryder .. .. | 6 | 2 | 23 | 0 |
| Hendry .. .. | 10 | 1 | 20 | 1 |

Kelleway bowled three no-balls.

### ENGLAND—Second Innings.

| | |
|---|---|
| J. H. HOBBS, lbw, b Grimmett .. | 11 |
| H. SUTCLIFFE, c sub. (Oxenham), b Ironmonger .. .. .. .. .. | 32 |
| C. P. MEAD, lbw, b Grimmett .. .. | 72 |
| W. R. HAMMOND, c sub. (Thompson), b Ironmonger .. .. .. | 28 |
| J. R. JARDINE, not out .. .. .. | 65 |
| E. HENDREN, c Ponsford, b Grimmett .. .. .. .. .. .. | 45 |
| A. P. F. CHAPMAN, c Oldfield, b Grimmett .. .. .. .. .. | 27 |
| M. W. TATE, c Bradman, b Grimmett .. .. .. .. .. .. .. | 20 |
| H. LARWOOD, c Ponsford, b Grimmett .. .. .. .. .. .. | 37 |
| Leg-byes 3, no-balls 2 .. .. | 5 |
| Eight wickets (closed) for | 342 |

Fall: 25, 69, 127, 165, 228, 263, 285, 342.

| | o. | m. | r. | w. |
|---|---|---|---|---|
| Ironmonger | 50 | 20 | 85 | 2 |
| Grimmett | 44.1 | 8 | 131 | 6 |
| Hendry .. .. | 27 | 6 | 79 | 0 |
| Ryder .. .. | 14 | 3 | 42 | 0 |

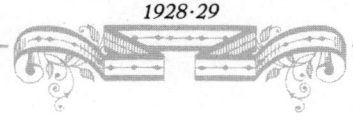

## AUSTRALIA—First Innings.

| | | |
|---|---|---:|
| W. M. WOODFULL, c Chapman, b Larwood | | 0 |
| W. H. PONSFORD, b Larwood | | 2 |
| A. KIPPAX, c and b Tate | | 16 |
| H. L. S. HENDRY, lbw, b Larwood | | 30 |
| C. E. KELLEWAY, b Larwood | | 8 |
| J. RYDER, c Jardine, b Larwood | | 33 |
| D. G. BRADMAN, lbw, b Tate | | 18 |
| W. A. OLDFIELD, lbw, b Tate | | 2 |
| C. V. GRIMMETT, not out | | 7 |
| H. IRONMONGER, b Larwood | | 4 |
| J. M. GREGORY, absent | | 0 |
| Bye, 1, leg-bye 1 | | 2 |
| Total | | 122 |

Fall: 1-0, 2-7, 3-24, 4-40, 5-71, 6-101, 7-105, 8-116, 9-122, 10-122.

### BOWLING.

| | O. | M. | R. | W. |
|---|---:|---:|---:|---:|
| Larwood | 14.4 | 4 | 32 | 6 |
| Tate | 21 | 6 | 50 | 3 |
| Hammond | 15 | 5 | 38 | 0 |

## ENGLAND

| | |
|---|---:|
| First Innings | 521 |
| Second Innings Eight wickets for | 342 |

Innings declared closed.

## AUSTRALIA

| | |
|---|---:|
| First Innings | 122 |

### Second Innings.

| | | |
|---|---|---:|
| W. H. PONSFORD, c Duckworth, b Larwood | | 6 |
| W. M. WOODFULL, not out | | 30 |
| A. KIPPAX, c and b Larwood | | 15 |
| H. L. HENDRY, c Larwood, b White | | 6 |
| J. RYDER, c Larwood, b Tate | | 1 |
| D. BRADMAN, c Chapman, b White | | 1 |
| W. A. OLDFIELD, c Larwood, b Tate | | 5 |
| C. V. GRIMMETT, c Chapman, b White | | 1 |
| H. IRONMONGER, c Chapman, b White | | 0 |
| C. E. KELLEWAY, absent | | 0 |
| J. M. GREGORY, absent | | 0 |
| Sundry | | 1 |
| Total | | 66 |

Fall of Wickets: 1-6, 2-33, 3-46, 4-47, 5-49 6-62, 7-66, 8-66.

### BOWLING

| | O. | M. | R. | W. |
|---|---:|---:|---:|---:|
| Larwood | 7 | 0 | 30 | 2 |
| Tate | 11 | 3 | 26 | 2 |
| White | 6.3 | 2 | 7 | 4 |
| Hammond | 1 | 0 | 2 | 0 |

## Fender and the Bridge

Mr. Fender, passing through to Brisbane, said he had not seen Bradman. What he wanted was a close-up view of the harbor bridge:—

"Oh! have you seen our Bradman."
 And the pressman winked an eye.
He was talking to a sad-man
 Who was passing Sydney by.
"I have seen your lovely harbor,
 And I want to see your bridge;
May have converse with a barber,
 And inspect a mountain ridge.
"But I haven't seen your Bradman."
 And Friend Fender rattled on,
"Do not think I am a madman—
 It's a bridge I gaze upon."
And his eye turned to the far wood
 While the pressmen murmured,
 "Well,
Our Bradman's seen your Larwood—
 That's another tale to tell!"

# Bradman Brilliantly Dismisses Hobbs

The Australian fielding had been much better than expected on Friday, but on Saturday it fell off a lot, a few of the men moving very slowly under the stress of the long outing. Bradman continued the star fieldsman, his speed saving lots of boundaries, and his swift throwing keeping the batsmen from risking what should have been easy runs. Grimmett, Woodfull and Kippax were the best of the other fieldsmen, with Oldfield also first-rate and tireless.

The position had swung a bit against England. Though not scoring fast, Hammond and Jardine were shaping all right against good bowling. The best features of the cricket at this time, however, were the bowling of Gregory and the brilliancy in the field of Bradman, whose quickness over the ground and brilliant returns had the batsmen forgoing runs they might have trotted to other fieldsmen.

The first three men fell l.b.w. at Elder's end, all three missing the ball in trying to force it to the on side, with Hendren close up at silly short leg. Bradman and Ryder batted best, the colt particularly well.

DON BRADMAN, whose dismissal of Hobbs made him the hero of the day.

One other little thing I would like to refer to is Bradman's fielding in the country. He excelled himself. He knew that there was a great responsibility on his shoulders. He knew that probably everybody was watching his efforts to retrieve a lost position that Australians held many years ago as great outfielders. That being so, he did not fail. He chased the ball round the boundary, picked it up either with one hand or both, and returned like a pistol shot to bowler or wicketkeeper. He should have no regrets for his showing during the day's play.

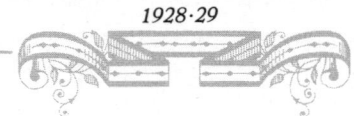
IS the youthful New South Wales cricket star, Don Bradman, to be sacrificed because, like many other players, he failed with the bat in the first Test match at Brisbane?

Bradman saved many runs in the field at Brisbane, and he is too great a colt to be dropped like hot coal after his first experience in Test cricket. He should be given the chance to make good in the match commencing at the Sydney Cricket Ground to-morrow.

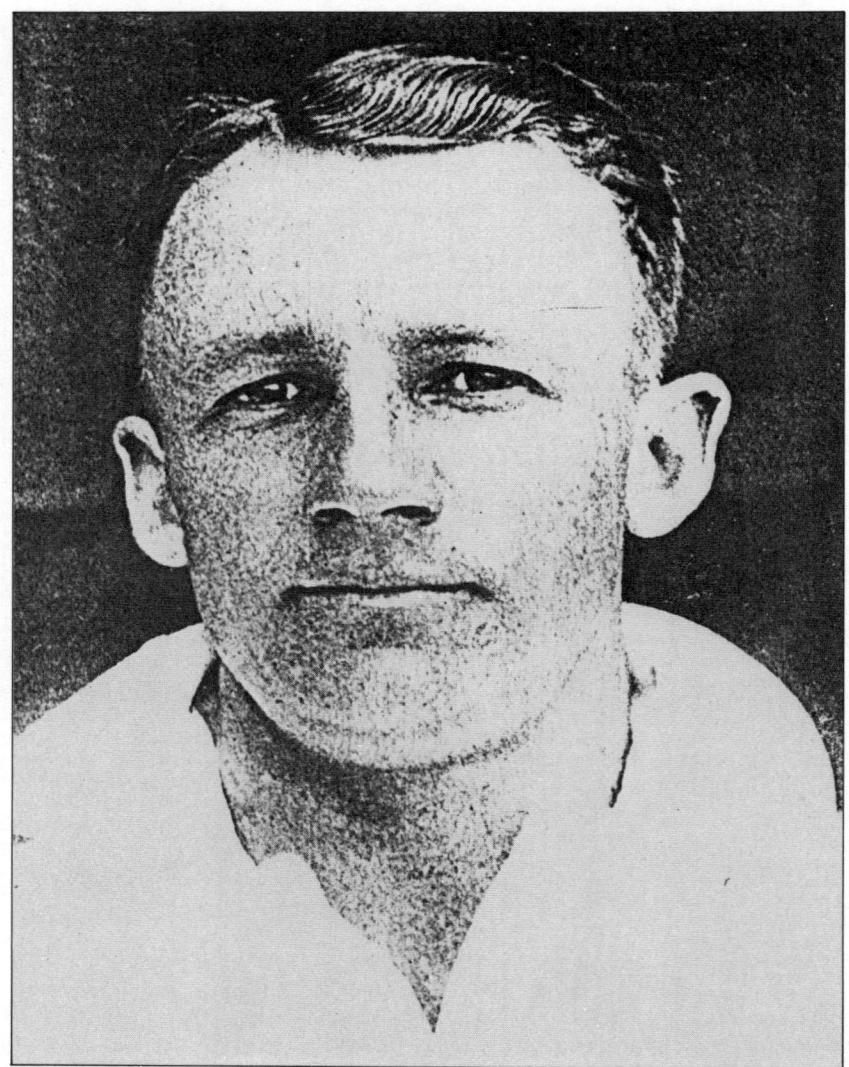

Don Bradman in Brisbane while participating in his first Test Match.

AUSTRALIA v ENGLAND (Second Test Match), at Sydney, 14, 15, 17, 18, 19, 20 December 1928.

DON BRADMAN was one of the twelve chosen for the Australian team for the Second Test Match, but on the morning of the match he was excluded from the eleven and made twelfth man. However, Ponsford broke a bone in his finger when batting in Australia's first innings, and Bradman therefore had to field all through the England innings of 636, including 251 from Hammond. Australia lost in the end by 8 wickets.

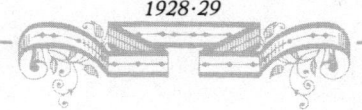

# *Australia v England*
## *Third Test Match*

AUSTRALIA v ENGLAND, Third Test Match, at Melbourne, 29 and 31 December 1928, 1,2,3,4 and 5 January 1929.

| Australia | | | |
|---|---|---|---|
| | - First Innings | 397 | |
| | - Second Innings | 351 | |
| England | | | |
| | - First Innings | 417 | |
| | - Second Innings | 332 for 7 wickets | |

Australia lost by 3 wickets and England won the rubber and retained the Ashes.

| DON BRADMAN | - b. W.R. Hammond | 79 |
|---|---|---|
| | c. G. Duckworth b. G. Geary | 112 |

In the first innings DON BRADMAN went in late on the first day. He was 26 not out overnight, and reached 50 on the second morning after a further hour. At lunch, he was 60 not out, and he batted altogether for three hours fourteen minutes to reach 79; he hit nine fours, and scored his runs at the rate of 24 an hour, off 223 balls.

His second innings was even better, and he reached his first century in Test Match cricket. Going in on the fifth day, he was 9 not out at lunch, he took two hours twenty-three minutes to reach 50 and was 60 at tea. Thereafter, he brightened up considerably; he began to use his feet to jump out to drive, with the result that his second 50 took only eighty-three minutes, the century taking three hours forty-six minutes altogether. He was finally caught at the wicket, after batting for four hours seven minutes, and hitting seven fours.

Up till that time, he was the youngest player ever to make a century in a Test Match; he was then twenty years 129 days. No Australian batsman had up till then scored a Test Match century with so little first-class experience behind him as only eleven matches.

# HOW YOUNGSTERS BATTLED
# FOR THEIR COUNTRY

### BRADMAN AND a'BECKETT, AGED 41 BETWEEN THEM, SHOW ENGLAND GREAT CRICKET

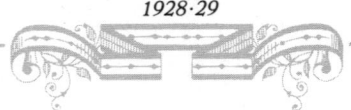
# TEST SCORE BOARD

## AUSTRALIA

### First Innings

| | |
|---|---:|
| Richardson, c Duckworth, b Larwood .. .. .. .. .. | 3 |
| Woodfull, c Jardine, b Tate .. | 7 |
| Hendry, c Jardine, b Larwood | 23 |
| Kippax, c Jardine, b Larwood | 100 |
| Ryder, c Hendren, b Tate .. | 112 |
| Oldfield, b Geary .. .. .. .. | 3 |
| Bradman, b Hammond .. .. | 79 |
| a'Beckett, c Duckworth, b White .. .. .. .. .. .. | 41 |
| Grimmett, c Duckworth, b Geary .. .. .. .. .. .. | 5 |
| Oxenham, b Geary .. .. .. | 15 |
| Blackie, not out .. .. .. .. | 2 |
| Extras .. .. .. .. .. .. | 7 |
| **Total** .. .. | **397** |

Fall of Wickets:—5, 15, 57, 218, 282, 287, 373, 383, 394, 397.

### BOWLING

| | O. | M. | R. | W. |
|---|---:|---:|---:|---:|
| Larwood .. .. | 37 | 3 | 127 | 3 |
| Tate .. .. .. .. | 46 | 17 | 87 | 2 |
| Geary .. .. .. | 31.5 | 4 | 83 | 3 |
| White .. .. .. | 57 | 30 | 64 | 1 |
| Hammond .. . | 8 | 4 | 19 | 1 |
| Jardine .. .. .. | 1 | 0 | 10 | 0 |

Extras: Four byes, three leg byes.

### Second Innings

| | |
|---|---:|
| Woodfull, c Duckworth, b Tate | 107 |
| Richardson, b Larwood .. .. | 5 |
| Hendry, st Duckworth, b White | 12 |
| Kippax, b Tate .. .. .. .. .. | 41 |
| Ryder, b Geary .. .. .. .. | 5 |
| Bradman, c Duckworth, b Geary | 112 |
| Oldfield, b White .. .. .. .. | 7 |
| a'Beckett, b White .. .. .. .. | 6 |
| Oxenham, b White .. .. .. .. | 39 |
| Grimmett, not out .. .. .. .. | 4 |
| Blackie, b White .. .. .. .. | 0 |
| Extras .. .. .. .. .. .. | 13 |
| **Total** .. .. | **351** |

Fall of Wickets:—7, 60, 138, 143, 201, 226, 252, 345.

### BOWLING

| | O. | M. | R. | W. |
|---|---:|---:|---:|---:|
| Larwood .. .. . | 16 | 3 | 37 | 1 |
| Tate .. .. .. | 47 | 15 | 70 | 2 |
| White .. .. .. | 56.5 | 20 | 107 | 5 |
| Geary .. .. .. | 30 | 4 | 94 | 2 |
| Hammond .. . | 16 | 6 | 30 | 0 |

Extras: Six byes, seven leg byes.

YOUTH COMES INTO ITS OWN.—Bradman, of New South Wales, and a'Beckett, of Victoria, coming on after lunch to resume the thrilling partnership in the third Test, which effectively vindicated the claims of youth to help shape Australia's Test destinies.

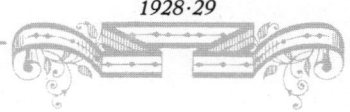

## ENGLAND

### First Innings

| | |
|---|---:|
| Hobbs, c Oldfield, b a'Beckett | 20 |
| Sutcliffe, b Blackie .. .. .. | 58 |
| Hammond, c a'Beckett, b Blackie .. .. .. .. .. .. | 200 |
| Chapman, b Blackie .. .. .. | 24 |
| Hendren, c a'Beckett, b Hendry | 19 |
| Larwood, c and b Blackie .. . | 0 |
| Jardine, c and b Blackie .. .. | 62 |
| Geary, lbw, b Grimmett .. .. | 1 |
| Duckworth, b Blackie .. .. | 3 |
| Tate, c Kippax, b Grimmett .. | 21 |
| White, not out .. .. .. .. .. | 8 |
| Extras .. .. .. .. .. .. | 1 |
| | ———— |
| Total .. .. 417 | |

Fall of Wickets:—28, 161, 201, 238, 364, 364, 381, 385, 391, 417.

## BOWLING

| | O. | M. | R. | W. |
|---|---:|---:|---:|---:|
| a'Beckett .. .. .. | 37 | 7 | 92 | 1 |
| Hendry .. .. .. | 20 | 8 | 35 | 1 |
| Grimmett .. .. | 55 | 14 | 114 | 2 |
| Oxenham .. .. | 35 | 11 | 67 | 0 |
| Blackie .. .. .. | 44 | 13 | 94 | 6 |
| Ryder .. .. . | 4 | 0 | 14 | 0 |

Extra: One bye.

### Second Innings

| | |
|---|---:|
| Hobbs, lbw, b Blackie .. .. | 49 |
| Jardine, b Grimmett .. .. .. | 33 |
| Hammond, run out .. .. .. | 32 |
| Sutcliffe, lbw, b Grimmett .. | 135 |
| Hendren, b Oxenham .. .. .. | 45 |
| Chapman, c Woodfull, b Ryder | 5 |
| Tate, run out .. .. .. .. .. | 0 |
| Duckworth, not out .. .. .. | 0 |
| Geary, not out .. .. .. .. | 4 |
| Extras .. .. .. .. .. | 29 |
| | ———— |
| Total (for 7 wickets) .. 332 | |

Fall of Wickets.—105, 199, 257, 318, 326, 328, 328.

Bowling.—Grimmett, 2 for 96; Oxenham, 1 for 44; Blackie, 1 for 75; Ryder, 1 for 16; a'Beckett, none for 39; Hendry, none for 33.

England won by three wickets.

### Bradman's Century.

When, however, Bradman, pulling White for 4, all run, reached his 100 after being 225 minutes at the wickets, the demonstration was remarkable. The crowd rose to its feet and cheered itself hoarse. Cheer after cheer rang round the ground, and it was some moments before play could be resumed. The Englishmen welcomed the respite, the whole eleven reclining on the ground, leaving the field clear for the boy who had done such a wonderful performance and the partner who had made it possible for such a feat.

# Bradman Leaps to Fame

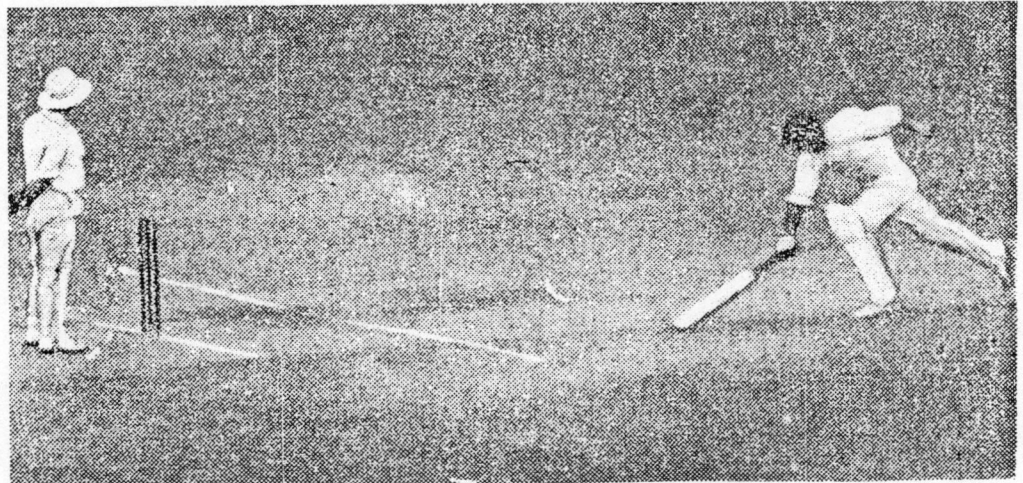

HIS FIRST CENTURY—and his second Test, a feat of which any cricketer might be proud—Bradman, the N.S.W. colt, regaining his crease after running for four, which brought his score up to the century.

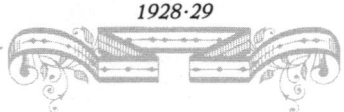

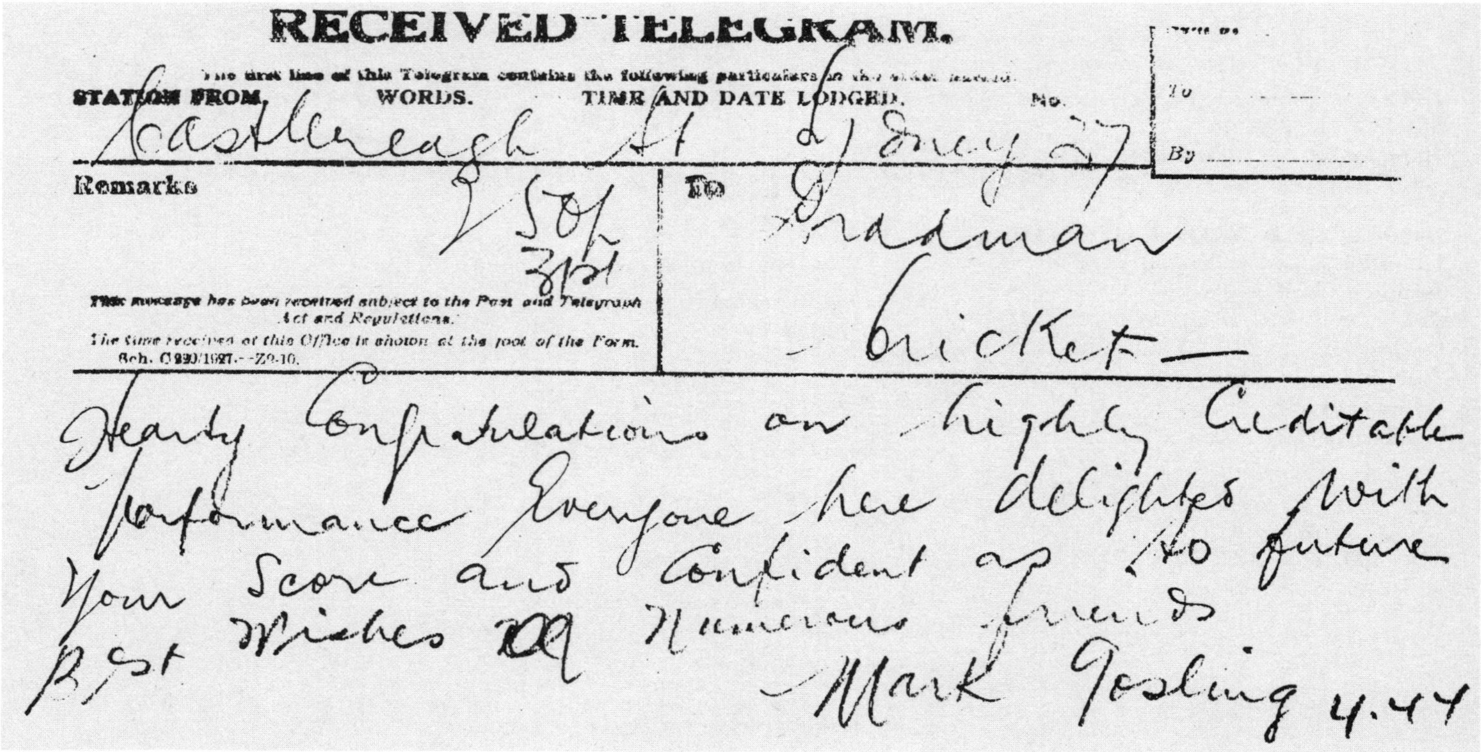

## RECEIVED TELEGRAM.

The first line of this Telegram contains the following particulars in the order named.

STATION FROM.    WORDS.    TIME AND DATE LODGED.    No.    To

Castlereagh St Sydney 27

Remarks    To    Bradman

cricket

This message has been received subject to the Post and Telegraph Act and Regulations.
The time received at this Office is shown at the foot of the Form.
Sch. O 990/1927.—Z9-10.

Hearty Congratulations on highly creditable performance Everyone here delighted with your score and confident of No future Best wishes XX Numerous friends
Mark Gosling 4.44

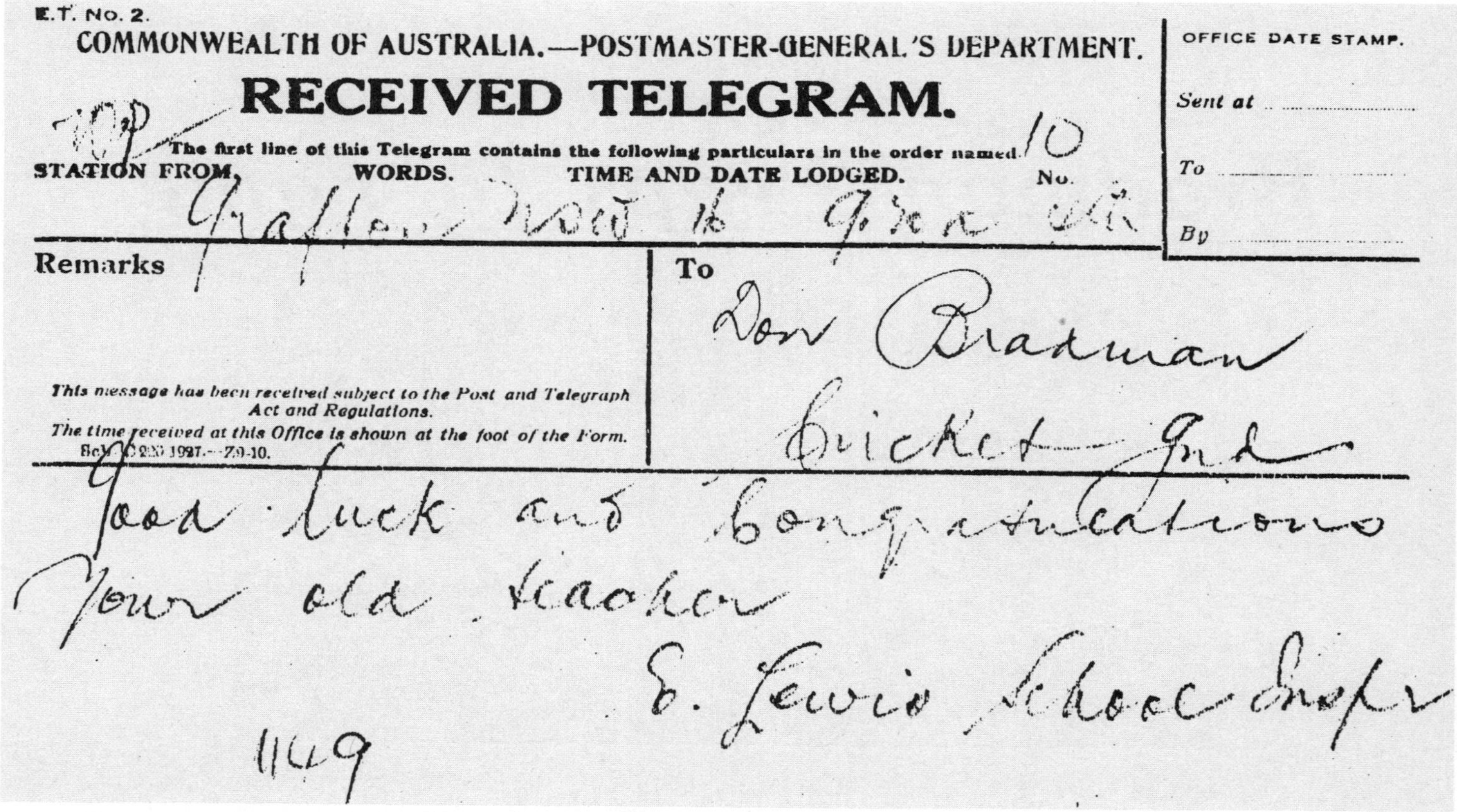

---

E.T. No. 2.

COMMONWEALTH OF AUSTRALIA.—POSTMASTER-GENERAL'S DEPARTMENT.

OFFICE DATE STAMP.

## RECEIVED TELEGRAM.

The first line of this Telegram contains the following particulars in the order named.

STATION FROM.    WORDS.    TIME AND DATE LODGED.    No.

Grafton NSW 16    10

Sent at
To
By

Remarks    To    Don Bradman

cricket Gnd

This message has been received subject to the Post and Telegraph Act and Regulations.
The time received at this Office is shown at the foot of the Form.
Sch. O 990/1927.—Z9-10.

Good luck and Congratulations
your old teacher
E. Lewis School Inspr

1149

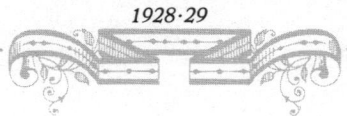

E.T. No. 2.

No.

COMMONWEALTH OF AUSTRALIA.—POSTMASTER-GENERAL'S DEPARTMENT.

Office Date Station

# TELEGRAM.

*This message has been received subject to the Post and Telegraph Act and Regulations.*
*All complaints to be addressed in writing to the Deputy Postmaster-General.*

C.77.    **NOTE.**—The figures at bottom of message represent the time received at this Office.

| Station from. | No. of Words. | Check. | Time Lodged. | Date Lodged. | Remarks. |
|---|---|---|---|---|---|

W 18. ROZELLE NSW 12 11-30 AM 4 TH

D BRADMAN     0   C2S

HOTEL WINDSOR MELBOURNE

HEARTY CONGRATULATIONS ON YOUR WONDERFUL CENTURY

CUSH

FL1226f

---

*This message has been received subject to the Post and Telegraph Act and Regulations.*
*All complaints to be addressed in writing to the Deputy Postmaster-General.*

C.77.    **NOTE.**—The figures at bottom of message represent the time received at this Office.

-4.JAN.1929

| Station from. | No. of Words. | Check. | Time Lodged. | Date Lodged. | Remarks. |
|---|---|---|---|---|---|

S 47 SYDNEY 16 5.G PM 4-TH

0 1081

DON BRADMAN

AUSTRALIAN ELEVEN

MELBOURNE

EVERYBODY WANTS TO LIVE BOWRAL BRADMANS TOWN

CONGRATULATIONS DON

MORRIS YATES

# New South Wales v Victoria

## NEW SOUTH WALES SHEFFIELD SHIELD TEAM
*January 1929*

BACK ROW    A. E. Marks, N. L. Morris, B. A. Cooper, C. O. Nicholls, Mr. F. M. Cush (Manager), A. G. Fairfax, D. C. Seddon, D. G. Bradman.
FRONT ROW    W. C. Andrews, A. A. Jackson, A. F. Kippax (Captain), T. J. E. Andrews, W. A. Oldfield.

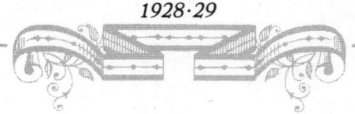

NEW SOUTH WALES v VICTORIA, at Sydney, 24, 25, 26, 28 and 29 January 1929.

New South Wales - First Innings    713 for 6 wickets dec.
                 - Second Innings    -

Victoria         - First Innings    265
                 - Second Innings   510 for 7 wickets

                   Drawn.


DON BRADMAN      - not out           340

Just prior to the commencement of this match, DON BRADMAN had arranged to have his name put on the William Sykes cricket bat.    To celebrate this arrangement the manufacturers gave Bradman a new bat and without any oiling or preparation, he took it to the wicket, made this score with it, and never used it again, because the manufacturers took it back and used it for display purposes.

This was the match in which Bradman first displayed his potentialities as a record-breaker. Going in shortly before lunch on the first day at 76 for 1, he reached 50 in eighty-five minutes, and 100 in three hours nine minutes, being 129 not out at the close of play after three hours fifty-one minutes.    The next morning when he was 133, he completed 1,000 runs for the season, for the first time in his career,  and it was the earliest (January 25) until then, by a New South Wales batsman.    At 20 years 151 days, he was the youngest batsman ever to reach 1,000 runs in an Australian season.    By lunchtime he had reached 196, this score taking five hours fifty-seven minutes, and the next 50 came in only thirty-four minutes.    The 300, which he reached just before tea, took seven hours thirty-three minutes, and when New South Wales declared, he had been at the wicket for eight hours eight minutes, and had hit thirty-eight fours.    At eight hours eight minutes, this was in point of time the longest innings he had played, and it was the longest ever played for New South Wales in a Sheffield Shield Match. 340 was then the highest score by a New South Wales player in any Sheffield Shield Match, and the highest score made on the Sydney Cricket Ground.    It was the highest score ever made by a batsman under twenty-one, and he was the youngest Australian to play an innings of 300 and over.    Bradman was also then the youngest batsman to make a treble-century as well as a hundred in each innings, both before reaching the age of twenty-one, and he was the youngest batsman to make a double-century for New South Wales in a Sheffield Shield Match.

# Don Bradman— -Young Breaker of Cricket Records

## 340 NOT OUT

### BRADMAN'S GREAT SCORE

### N.S.W. DECLARES

## COLT'S 1207 IN FIRST CLASS MATCHES

Don Bradman, by his play in the Sheffield Shield match—N.S.W. v. Victoria—has won the right to have his name inscribed with those of Australia's mightiest batsmen

## FAULTLESS BRADMAN

### IMPROVED STROKE PLAY

### HIS GREAT INNINGS

#### (By M. A. Noble)

Bradman gave a fine exhibition of stroke play and some square cuts had plenty of power behind them. One would feel more at ease if he stood up straighter and got more on top of the ball.  His onside play was faultless, and he did not repeat his former error of making the leg-glance too fine

It was a great physical feat, as well as a great innings.

Early last season before I had seen him make a run, H. H. Massie, the old international and great hitter of the eighties, after watching his batting said: "Bradman is going to be a fine batsman.  He isn't afraid to hit the ball." How true his prophecy was is quite evident now.

Fingleton played his part in keeping an end intact while Bradman swatted the bowling.

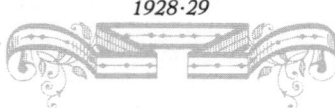

# ANOTHER CENTURY BY DON BRADMAN.

D. G. Bradman scoring his 100th run, a glance off Ironmonger, in yesterday's big innings in the Sheffield Shield match against Victoria.

D. G. Bradman, who is 129 not out, is shown back-cutting Ironmonger.  J. L. Ellis is the Victorian wicket-keeper.

Miniature autographed cricket bats and cricket ball trophies displayed in the Mortlock Library Collection.

LEFT     Sykes bat used by Don Bradman in scoring 340 not out for New South Wales v. Victoria, 1929, at that time the highest score ever made at the Sydney Cricket Ground.

RIGHT     Warsop bat used by Don Bradman in scoring his first Test century, 112 v. England, Melbourne 1929. The Don Bradman autograph bat, made by Wm Sykes Ltd, was produced at a later date.

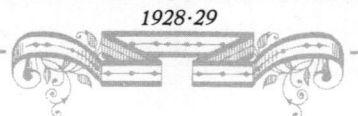

Don Bradman wearing the honour cap and badge presented to him by
Mr. J. J. Giltinan to commemorate his 340 not out against Victoria. Mr. Giltinan, in
association with Victor Trumper, was one of the men responsible for the
establishment of Rugby League football in New South Wales.

## RECEIVED TELEGRAM.

| Station From | Words. | Charge. | Time and Date Lodged. | No. |
|---|---|---|---|---|

SYDNEY 19 12 3PM 30TH

Remarks.

To DON BRADMAN ESQ 296
SOUTH AUSTRALIAN CRICKET ASSN
ADELAIDE

This message has been received subject to the Post and Telegraph
Act and Regulations

CONGRATULATIONS ON BREAKING MY UNCLES RECORD GOOD LUCK WRITING
GILBERT MURDOCH

Time received at this Office.

The previous highest score made on the Sydney Cricket Ground was 321 by William Lloyd Murdoch.

# Australia v England
# Fourth Test Match

AUSTRALIA v ENGLAND, Fourth Test Match, at Adelaide, 1,2,4,5,6,7 and 8 February 1929.

| Australia | - First Innings | 369 |
|---|---|---|
| | - Second Innings | 336 |
| England | - First Innings | 334 |
| | - Second Innings | 383 |

Australia lost by 12 runs.

| DON BRADMAN | - c. H. Larwood  b. M.W. Tate | 40 |
|---|---|---|
| | run out | 58 |

DON BRADMAN's first innings began early on the third day, with the score 145 for 4; 34 not out at lunch, he was dismissed soon afterwards, being caught in the slips.     In making 40, he carried his season's aggregate to 1247, thus passing the previous record by an Australian for a season's aggregate in Australia.

His second innings was much sounder, and all but won the match for Australia.     He batted for sixty-eight minutes for 16 not out overnight, and completed his 50 next morning after another forty-three minutes.     His 58 was made in two hours eighteen minutes (25 runs an hour), and included four fours.

# ENGLAND'S TEST VICTORY.

## THE SCORES.

The scores:—

### ENGLAND.—First Innings.

| | | |
|---|---|---|
| J. B. Hobbs, c Ryder, b Hendry | .. | 74 |
| H. Sutcliffe, stp Oldfield, b Grimmett | | 64 |
| W. R. Hammond, not out | | 119 |
| D. R. Jardine, lbw, b Grimmett | .. | 1 |
| E. Hendren, b Blackie | | 13 |
| A. P. F. Chapman, c a'Beckett, b Ryder | | 39 |
| G. Duckworth, c Ryder, b Grimmett | | 5 |
| H. Larwood, b Hendry | | 3 |
| G. Geary, run out | | 3 |
| M. W. Tate, b Grimmett | | 2 |
| J. C. White, c Ryder, b Grimmett | | 0 |
| Sundries | | 11 |
| **Total** | | **334** |

Fall of wickets: One for 143, two for 143, three for 149, four for 179, five for 246, six for 263, seven for 270, eight for 308, nine for 312, ten for 334.

### BOWLING.

| | O. | M. | R. | W. |
|---|---|---|---|---|
| a'Beckett | 21 | 7 | 44 | 0 |
| Hendry | 31 | 14 | 49 | 2 |
| Blackie | 29 | 7 | 57 | 1 |
| Grimmett | 52.1 | 12 | 102 | 5 |
| Oxenham | 35 | 14 | 51 | 0 |
| Ryder | 5 | 1 | 20 | 1 |

## THE SCORES.

### ENGLAND.—First Innings, 334.
### Second Innings.

| | | |
|---|---|---|
| J. B. Hobbs, c Oldfield, b Hendry | . | 1 |
| H. Sutcliffe, c Oldfield, b a'Beckett | | 17 |
| W. R. Hammond, c and b Ryder | .... | 177 |
| D. R. Jardine, c Woodfull, b Oxenham | | 98 |
| E. Hendren, c Bradman, b Blackie | . | 11 |
| A. P. F. Chapman, c Woodfull, b Blackie | | 0 |
| H. Larwood, lbw, b Oxenham | .... | 5 |
| G. Geary, c and b Grimmett | | 6 |
| M. W. Tate, lbw, b Oxenham | | 47 |
| J. C. White, not out | | 4 |
| G. Duckworth, lbw, b Oxenham | .... | 1 |
| Byes 6, leg-byes 10 | | 16 |
| **Total** | | **383** |

Fall of wickets: One for 1, two for 21, three for 283, four for 296, five for 297, six for 302, seven for 327, eight for 337, nine for 381, ten for 383.

### BOWLING.

| | O. | M. | R. | W. |
|---|---|---|---|---|
| a'Beckett | 27 | 9 | 41 | 1 |
| Hendry | 28 | 11 | 56 | 1 |
| Grimmett | 52 | 15 | 117 | 1 |
| Oxenham | 47.4 | 21 | 67 | 4 |
| Blackie | 39 | 11 | 70 | 2 |
| Ryder | 5 | 1 | 13 | 1 |
| Kippax | 2 | 0 | 3 | 0 |

### AUSTRALIA.—First Innings.

| | | |
|---|---|---|
| W. M. Woodfull, st Duckworth, b Tate | | 1 |
| A. Jackson, lbw, b White | | 164 |
| H. L. Hendry, c Duckworth, b Larwood | | 2 |
| A. F. Kippax, b White | | 3 |
| J. Ryder, lbw, b White | | 63 |
| D. G. Bradman, c Larwood, b Tate | | 40 |
| E. L. a'Beckett, b White | | 36 |
| R. K. Oxenham, c Chapman, b White | | 15 |

| | | |
|---|---|---|
| W. A. Oldfield, b Tate | ............. | 32 |
| C. V. Grimmett, b Tate | .......... | 4 |
| D. J. Blackie, not out | ............. | 3 |
| Leg-byes 5, wide 1 | ............. | 6 |
| **Total** | | **369** |

Fall of wickets: One for one, two for six, three for 19, four for 145, five for 227, six for 287, seven for 323, eight for 336, nine for 365.

### BOWLING.

| | O. | M. | R. | W. |
|---|---|---|---|---|
| White | 60 | 16 | 130 | 5 |
| Tate | 42 | 10 | 77 | 4 |
| Larwood | 37 | 6 | 92 | 1 |
| Geary | 12 | 3 | 32 | 0 |
| Hammond | 9 | 1 | 32 | 0 |

Tate bowled one wide.

## THE SCORES.

### ENGLAND.—First Innings, 334.
### Second Innings, 383.
### AUSTRALIA.—First Innings, 369.
### Second Innings.

| | | |
|---|---|---|
| W. M. Woodfull, c Geary, b White | .. | 30 |
| A. Jackson, c Duckworth, b Geary | .. | 36 |
| H. L. Hendry, c Tate, b White | .. | 5 |
| A. Kippax, c Hendren, b White | .. | 51 |
| J. Ryder, c and b White | .......... | 87 |
| D. G. Bradman, run out | ............ | 58 |
| E. L. a'Beckett, c Hammond, b White | | 21 |
| R. K. Oxenham, c Chapman, b White | | 12 |
| W. A. Oldfield not out | ............ | 15 |
| C. V. Grimmett, c Tate, b White | .... | 9 |
| D. Blackie, c Larwood, b White | .... | 0 |
| Sundries—Byes 9, leg-byes 3 | ... | 12 |
| **Total** | | **336** |

### BOWLING.

| | O. | M. | R. | W. |
|---|---|---|---|---|
| Larwood | 20 | 4 | 60 | 0 |
| Tate | 37 | 9 | 75 | 0 |
| White | 64.5 | 21 | 126 | 8 |
| Geary | 16 | 2 | 42 | 1 |
| Hammond | 14 | 3 | 21 | 0 |

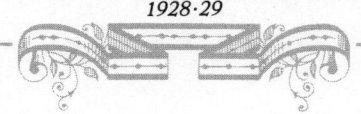

# Final Day a Real Epic in Cricket

## Great & Determined Batting Foiled by White's Rare Bowling

### *Bradman Plays Glorious Hand The Run Out a Tragedy*

### THE BRADMAN PART.

Both a'Beckett and Oxenham displayed great gameness in their fighting spirit in endeavoring to hold the fort whilst Bradman, who was batting at his best, endeavored to make victory certain for Australia. With Bradman in, Australia looked to be in a winning position, as the young Welshman was particularly aggressive, coupled with absolute soundness, and made his strokes perfectly. His drives were clean and hard, and rarely failed to reach the fence. The crowd was worked up to a very high pitch of excitement at the magnificence of his batting, and during the time he was striking so quiet were the people that one could have almost heard a pin drop.

### THE CROWD GRIPPED.

Then Bradman would play a scoring stroke, and the pent-up feelings of the crowd would be let loose in one mighty roar immediately followed by the deadly silence, as the people once more lapsed into that tenseness as they watched the young batsman setting about his task with that grim determination characteristic of him.

### "NO PEN CAN DESCRIBE IT."

It was great, wonderful, and no pen could possibly explain the brilliancy of the game. The great, determined batting on the one hand, and the formidable attack of White, on the other. The bowling of Tate and Hammond from one end, sending them along outside the off stump, just to keep down the runs, leaving the ultimate result of the issue to White, at the other end.

## Bradman Kisses the Ball

D. G. Bradman, who missed Tate in the deep field in the first innings of the Englishmen, made no mistake when fielding in a similar position today, he caught Hendren.

As soon as the new South Welshman had the ball safely clasped in his hands he raised it to his lips and kissed it.

His action created much laughter among the women onlookers.

### BRADMAN'S RUN OUT.

The running-out of Bradman was the turning point in to-day's play. At the time he was batting with supreme assurance. The occasion might have been the second innings of a club match when a draw was inevitable for all the effect it had on his self-control. He had, in conjunction with Oxenham, made 50 runs for the seventh wicket, and with Oldfield brought Australia to within 29 runs of victory when the incident occurred. There was not a run's value in Oldfield's stroke, which was travelling fairly easily in the direction of Hobbs. Oldfield's call, however, was confident. Bradman had the option of saying "No" or of staying in his crease. In the former event Oldfield might have got back. In the latter event Oldfield would have been run out. It was a most difficult situation for the 20-year-old batsman. He chose wrongly, as the event proved, for he had no hope of gaining his ground in face of Hobbs's accuracy and Duckworth's sheer certainty.

Before that Bradman's innings was one of the most attractive of the match. Of his batting skill there was no doubt. That was proved against all the bowlers, and especially when he turned Hammond, who had placed his fielding strength on the off. Thereafter the Australians had their backs to the wall. They fought gamely against constant pressure, but from Bradman's dominance the batting descended to patchiness, with occasional lucky strokes. Oxenham, next to Bradman, was the best of to-day's batsmen. He was undaunted by the occasion, and showed possession of match temperament. It was but a forlorn hope which Oldfield and Grimmett led when 23 runs were required after lunch. Everyone was imbued with the belief that a wicket meant the loss of the match. And so it proved, for Blackie subsequently was tempted to destruction.

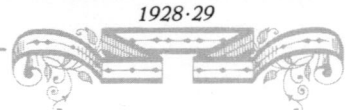

Clarrie Grimmett, Pat Davis, Don Bradman, John Davis.
*Adelaide, February 1929*

R. V. Thomas (former holder with Pat O'Hara Wood of World's Doubles Tennis Championship at Wimbledon) with
Don Bradman.
*Adelaide, February 1929*

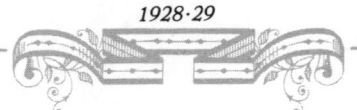

# *Australia v England*
# *Fifth Test Match*

AUSTRALIA v ENGLAND, Fifth Test Match, at Melbourne, 8, 9, 11, 12, 13, 14, 15 and 16 March 1929.

| Australia | - First Innings | 491 |
| | - Second Innings | 287 for 5 wickets |
| England | - First Innings | 519 |
| | - Second Innings | 257 |

Australia won by 5 wickets.

| DON BRADMAN | - c. M.W. Tate b. G. Geary | 123 |
| | not out | 37 |

In the first innings DON BRADMAN went in to bat directly after lunch on the fourth day, at 203 for 3, and played a splendid innings.   He reached 50 in seventy-one minutes, and was 62 not out at the tea interval, completing his century in two hours fifty-two minutes, and being 109 not out, after three hours one minute.   Next morning, he continued his fifth-wicket partnership with A.G. Fairfax until they had added 183, in three hours thirty-three minutes;  this stand was then a record for Australia's fifth wicket in any Test Match. Bradman was then caught at short-leg after batting for three hours thirty-seven minutes; he hit eight fours and when he had made 5 he passed the aggregate record for an Australian season - 1534.

Australia had reached 204 for 5 when Bradman went in on the eighth morning, taking one hour and twelve minutes to score 37 runs.

# THE TEST SCORE BOARD

## ENGLAND
### First Innings

| | | |
|---|---|---:|
| Hobbs, lbw., b Ryder | | 142 |
| Jardine, c Oldfield, b Wall | | 19 |
| Hammond, c Fairfax, b Wall | | 38 |
| Tyldesley, c Hornibrook, b Ryder | | 31 |
| Duckworth, c Fairfax, b Hornibrook | | 12 |
| Hendren, c Hornibrook, b Fairfax | | 95 |
| Leyland, c Fairfax, b Oxenham | 137 |
| Larwood, b Wall | | 4 |
| Geary, b Hornibrook | | 4 |
| Tate, c a'Beckett (sub), b Hornibrook | | 15 |
| White, not out | | 9 |
| Extras (4 byes, 6 leg byes, 1 wide, 2 no balls) | | 13 |
| Total | | 519 |

Fall of Wickets: 64, 146, 235, 240, 260, 401, 409, 428, 470, 519.

### BOWLING

| | O. | M. | R. | W. |
|---|---:|---:|---:|---:|
| Wall | 49 | 8 | 123 | 3 |
| Hornibrook | 48 | 8 | 142 | 3 |
| Oxenham | 45.1 | 15 | 86 | 1 |
| Grimmett | 25 | 11 | 40 | 0 |
| Fairfax | 27 | 4 | 84 | 1 |
| Ryder | 18 | 5 | 29 | 2 |
| Kippax | 3 | 1 | 2 | 0 |

Fairfax, one no ball; Wall, one no ball, one wide.

### Second Innings

| | | |
|---|---|---:|
| Hobbs, c Fairfax, b Grimmett | | 65 |
| Jardine, c Oldfield, b Wall | | 0 |
| Larwood, b Wall | | 11 |
| Hammond, c Ryder, b Fairfax | | 16 |
| Tyldesley, c Oldfield, b Wall | | 21 |
| Hendren, b Grimmett | | 1 |
| Leyland, not out | | 53 |
| Tate, c Fairfax, b Hornibrook | | 54 |
| Geary, b Wall | | 3 |
| White, c Oxenham, b Wall | | 4 |
| Duckworth, lbw., b Oxenham | | 9 |
| Extras (byes 19, leg-byes 1) | | 20 |
| Total | | 257 |

Fall of Wickets: 1, 19, 75, 119, 123, 131, 212, 217, 231, 257.

### BOWLING

| | O. | M. | R. | W. |
|---|---:|---:|---:|---:|
| Wall | 26 | 5 | 66 | 5 |
| Hornibrook | 19 | 5 | 51 | 1 |
| Fairfax | 7 | 0 | 20 | 1 |
| Grimmett | 24 | 7 | 66 | 2 |
| Oxenham | 24.3 | 1 | 34 | 1 |

## AUSTRALIA
### First Innings

| | | |
|---|---|---:|
| Woodfull, c Geary, b Larwood | | 102 |
| Jackson, run out | | 30 |
| Kippax, c Duckworth, b White | | 38 |
| Ryder, c Tate, b Hammond | | 30 |
| Bradman, c Tate, b Geary | | 123 |
| Fairfax, lbw., b Geary | | 65 |
| Oxenham, c Duckworth, b Geary | | 7 |
| Oldfield, c and b Geary | | 6 |
| Grimmett, not out | | 38 |
| Wall, c Duckworth, b Geary | | 9 |
| Hornibrook, lbw., b White | | 26 |
| Extras (byes 6, leg-byes 9, wides 2) | | 17 |
| Total | | 491 |

Fall of Wickets: 54, 142, 203, 203, 386, 399, 409, 420, 432, 491.

### BOWLING

| | O. | M. | R. | W. |
|---|---:|---:|---:|---:|
| Larwood | 34 | 7 | 83 | 1 |
| Tate | 62 | 26 | 108 | 0 |
| Geary | 81 | 36 | 105 | 5 |
| White | 75 | 22 | 136 | 2 |
| Hammond | 16 | 3 | 31 | 1 |
| Leyland | 3 | 0 | 11 | 0 |

Geary bowled two wides.

### Second Innings

| | | |
|---|---|---:|
| Hornibrook, b Hammond | | 18 |
| Oldfield, b Hammond | | 48 |
| Woodfull, b Hammond | | 35 |
| Jackson, b Geary | | 46 |
| Kippax, run out | | 28 |
| Ryder, not out | | 57 |
| Bradman, not out | | 37 |
| Extras | | 18 |
| Five wickets for | | 287 |

Australia won by five wickets.
Fall of wickets: 51, 80, 129, 158, 204.

Bowling (lunch): Larwood, no wicket for 66; Tate, none for 60; White, none for 24; Geary, one for 31; Hammond, three for 53.

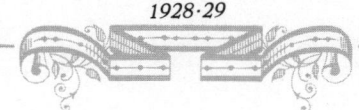

# ST. GEORGE-

# -BOTH OF THEM-

# ATTACK ENGLISH DRAGON!

## *Miracle Was Needed in Test*

## *and St. George Provided It*

### TWO YOUNGSTERS BUILD UP
### AUSTRALIA'S SCORE

**Bradman-Fairfax Live on After Fifth
Wicket Record Coalition**

#### DOUBLE LUNCHEON DISASTER REPAIRED

(By Our Special Representative.)

MELBOURNE, Tuesday.
—When it was considered that only a miracle could save Australia from a debacle in to-day's Test duel, Bradman and Fairfax—both from St. George Club, Sydney—came forward and produced the required miracle.

Bradman.

Woodfull.

They not only broke the Australian Test fifth wicket record, but also definitely defeated the English bowling, and put their side in a hopeful position after the doubly disastrous crash of Woodfull and Ryder when only 203 runs were on the board.

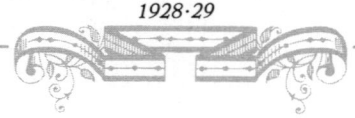

# A CONSISTENT SCORER.

D. G. Bradman, who made 109 not out in the test match at the Melbourne Cricket Ground yesterday.

## WICKET TRUE

—

### BUT MAY PLAY TRICKS

—

### DRIZZLING RAIN

—

**BY C. G. MACARTNEY.**

MELBOURNE, Wednesday.

DESPITE the fairly heavy rain which fell early to-day, the wicket played truly, and showed no signs of being badly affected. At the same time, it may play some tricks before the dampness entirely disappears.

A wicket of this nature should never get really bad, owing to the absence of sun. The ball may probably turn, but slowly. Bradman continued his aggressive methods, again using his feet nicely to White, but eventually fell to a rather weak stroke off Geary. He had played a grand innings full of fight and attack, and one that will long be remembered on the Melbourne ground.

His partnership with Fairfax had vastly improved the situation for Australia, and he had used tactics far too infrequently in evidence nowadays.

Fairfax pursued his solid defensive methods, presenting a broad blade to everything. Geary got through his defence with a straight and faster ball, and his highly-creditable initial Test innings closed. Marked mainly by soundness, his display was of immense assistance to Australia when needed.

### Greasy Wicket

It was lucky that the rain, which came in the night, was only sufficient to make the surface of the wicket greasy, and quite good for batting purposes. Commencing carefully this morning and discovering the true condition of the wicket, Bradman opened out on the bowlers, making fine strokes One splendid powerful on-drive was stopped by Tate's left hand at forward shortleg. The next ball was mistimed and Tate took an easy catch.

The great value of Bradman's innings cannot be fully estimated. He showed pluck, resource, stamina, and fighting qualities above the ordinary He made the runs at the proper time, when they were badly needed. He has thoroughly proved his temperament and ability.

---

Station from.    Words.    Time and Date Lodged.    No.

66 SYDNEY 16 10 22 AM

0  256

DON BRADMAN

WINDSOR HOTEL MELBOURNE

CONGRATS JUST AS WELL YOU PLAY CRICKET BETTER THAN FIVE HUNDRED

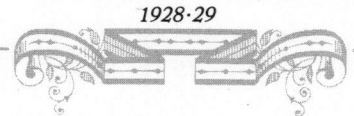

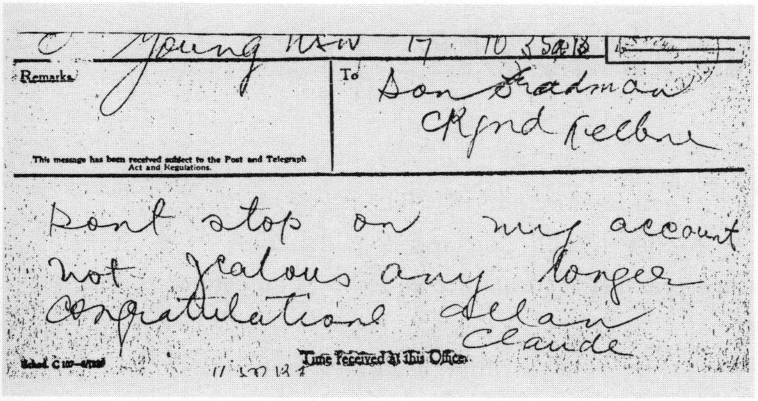

C Young NSW 17 10 ...

Remarks | To Don Bradman C/Rynd Melbne

This message has been received subject to the Post and Telegraph Act and Regulations.

Dont stop on my account not jealous any longer congratulations Alan Claude

Time Received at this Office.

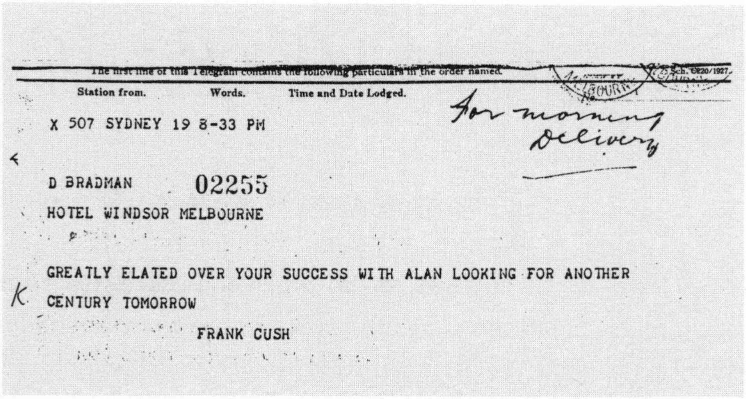

---

The first line of this Telegram contains the following particulars in the order named.

Station from. | Words. | Time and Date Lodged.

X 507 SYDNEY 19 8-33 PM

For morning delivery

D BRADMAN 02255
HOTEL WINDSOR MELBOURNE

GREATLY ELATED OVER YOUR SUCCESS WITH ALAN LOOKING FOR ANOTHER
CENTURY TOMORROW

FRANK CUSH

A glorious study of W. R. Hammond making a cover drive during his great tour of Australia, 1928–29.

# 1929-30 Season

The world's record score in first class cricket which I achieved in 1930 came by chance, not by design, but undeniably it gave me intense satisfaction and confidence.

It was not so much the score itself but rather that I had made the runs by aggressive stroke play in quicker time than anybody else.

Then selection for England, which is the goal of every Australian cricketer, made me feel proud that I had lived up to the hopes and ambitions of my parents and friends.

*Don Bradman*

## — SEASON 1929-30 —

| TITLE | GAME | | SCORES | |
|---|---|---|---|---|
| Second Class | Mick Simmons | Horderns | 32 | C. |
| | Combined Grade | Lane Cove | 3 | B. |
| | Kippax's XI | Taree | 7 | B. |
| | " | Wauchope | 37 | C. |
| | New South Wales C.A. | Moree | 13 | n.o. |
| | " | " | 96 | C. |
| | Mick Simmons | Wyong | 53 | B. |
| | New South Wales C.A. | Orange | 5 | B. |
| | " " " | Dubbo | 88 | L.B.W. |
| | " " " | Parkes | 76 | B. |
| | " " " | Far West | 50 | C. |
| | " " " | Bathurst | 83 | B. |
| | Sun | Theatricals | 39 | R.O. |
| | New South Wales C.A. | G.P.S. | 62 | n.o. |
| | "Restmore" | Tidmarsh's XI | 141 | C. |
| | Tidmarsh's XI | Narooma | 107 | n.o. |
| | " | Bega | 127 | n.o. |
| | Gladesville | S.M. Herald | 228 | n.o. |
| | Combined Grade | Riverina | 126 | n.o. |
| | Australia | Colombo | 40 | C. |
| | New South Wales | Newcastle | 111 | C. |
| First Grade | St. George | Glebe | 180 | n.o. |
| | " | Balmain | 18 | C. |
| | " | North Sydney | 8 | C. |
| | " | " | 37 | C. |
| | " | Cumberland | 54 | n.o. |
| | " | Randwick | 187 | C. |
| | " | Mosman | 65 | C. |
| First Class | New South Wales | M.C.C. | 157 | B. |
| | Australia | The Rest | 124 | C. |
| | " | " | 225 | L.B.W. |
| | " | Western Australia | 27 | C. |
| | " | Tasmania | 20 | L.B.W. |
| | " | " | 139 | C. |
| Sheffield Shield | New South Wales | Queensland | 48 | R.O. |
| | " " " | " | 66 | C. |

| TITLE | GAME | | SCORES | |
|---|---|---|---|---|
| Sheffield Shield | New South Wales | Queensland | 3 | C. |
| | " " " | " | 452 | n.o. |
| | " " " | South Australia | 2 | r.o. |
| | " " " | " | 84 | L.B.W. |
| | " " " | " | 47 | C. |
| | " " " | Victoria | 89 | B. |
| | " " " | " | 26 | n.o. |
| | " " " | " | 77 | C. |
| | | Total runs | 3659 | |

## — SUMMARY —

**AVERAGES**

| | Innings | N.O.'s. | H.S. | Runs | Average |
|---|---|---|---|---|---|
| Sheffield Shield | 10 | 2 | 452x | 894 | 111·75 |
| Other First Class | 6 | 0 | 225 | 692 | 115·33 |
| All First Class | 16 | 2 | 452x | 1586 | 113·28 |
| First Grade | 7 | 2 | 187 | 549 | 109·80 |
| Other Second Class | 21 | 6 | 228x | 1524 | 101·60 |
| All Second Class | 28 | 8 | 228x | 2073 | 103·65 |
| All Matches | 44 | 10 | 452x | 3659 | 107·61 |

DON BRADMAN's aggregate of 894 in Sheffield Shield Matches passed by one run the record for New South Wales which he had established the previous season.

His average in all first-class matches of 113·28 was also the highest, up till then, by a New South Wales batsman in a season.

He won the New South Wales Sheffield Shield batting average.

He won the St. George Club batting average.

He broke the St. George Club record twice - 180 n.o. and 187.

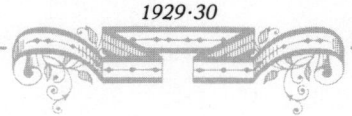

# New South Wales v M.C.C.

NEW SOUTH WALES v M.C.C. TEAM, at Sydney, 22, 23, 25 and 26 November 1929.

| New South Wales | - First Innings | 629 for 8 wickets dec. |
| | - Second Innings | 305 for 3 wickets |
| M.C.C. Team | - First Innings | 469 |
| | - Second Innings | 204 for 2 wickets |

Drawn.

DON BRADMAN  - b. T.S. Worthington          157

DON BRADMAN started this innings on a perfect wicket.    Going in at 26 for 1 on the first morning, he reached 50 in three-quarters of an hour, and was 71 not out at lunch; his century was achieved in one hour forty-three minutes, and when he was bowled by the last ball before tea, he had batted for two hours fifty-five minutes.    He hit sixteen fours, and features of his innings were his masterly placing and his power off the back foot.

# RUN A MINUTE
## COLTS' BRILLIANT DISLPAY

D. G. Bradman bowled by S. Worthington with the last ball before the tea interval.  Bradman made 157 in an entertaining innings.

## NEW SOUTH WALES—First Innings.

| | |
|---|---|
| A. FAIRFAX, lbw, b Allom .. .. .. | 14 |
| A. JACKSON, c Benson, b Allom .. | 49 |
| D. BRADMAN, b Worthington .. .. .. | 157 |
| A. KIPPAX, c Dawson, b Bowley .. .. | 38 |
| A. MARKS, c and b Bowley .. .. .. | 33 |
| A. ALLSOPP, c Turnbull, b Allom .. .. | 117 |
| S. McCABE, b Worthington .. .. .. .. | 90 |
| C. ANDREWS, not out .. .. .. .. .. | 11 |
| W. A. OLDFIELD, c Duleepsinhji, b Worthington .. .. .. .. .. .. .. | 3 |
| H. HOOKER, not out .. .. .. .. .. | 6 |
| Byes 20, leg-byes 13, no-balls 3 .. .. | 36 |
| Eight wickets (closed) for .. .. | 629 |

Fall: 26, 143, 292, 372, 417, 602, 613, 618.

| | | | | | | | | | |
|---|---|---|---|---|---|---|---|---|---|
| Barratt | 30 | 1 | 130 | 0 | Bowley | 13.3 | 0 | 80 | 2 |
| Allom | 27 | 1 | 127 | 3 | Woolley | 16 | 0 | 77 | 0 |
| Worthington | 21 | 1 | 151 | 3 | Duleepsinhji | 4 | 0 | 28 | 0 |

Worthington 2 no-balls, Woolley 1.

## N.S.W.—Second Innings.

| | |
|---|---|
| A. FAIRFAX, lbw, b Worthington .. .. | 19 |
| A. JACKSON, not out .. .. .. .. .. | 164 |
| C. ANDREWS, c and b Woolley .. .. .. | 17 |
| A. MARKS, lbw, b Woolley .. .. .. | 26 |
| A. ALLSOPP, not out .. .. .. .. .. | 63 |
| Byes 8, leg-bye 1, no-balls 3 .. .. .. | 12 |
| Three wickets (closed) for .. .. | 305 |

| | | | | | | | | | |
|---|---|---|---|---|---|---|---|---|---|
| Allom | 19 | 0 | 92 | 0 | Duleepsinhji | 4 | 0 | 24 | |
| Worthington | 13 | 1 | 63 | 1 | Dawson | 3 | 0 | 30 | 0 |
| Woolley | 12 | 0 | 84 | 2 | | | | | |

Allom bowled 2 no-balls, Worthington 1 no-ball.

## M.C.C.—First Innings.

| | |
|---|---|
| E. W. DAWSON, c Hooker, b Fairfax .. | 3 |
| A. H. H. GILLIGAN, lbw, b Hooker .. | 45 |
| K. S. DULEEPSINHJI, b Dupain .. .. | 34 |
| F. E. WOOLLEY, b Fairfax .. .. .. .. | 219 |
| M. J. TURNBULL, c and b Bradman .. | 100 |
| S. WORTHINGTON, c and b Hooker .. | 7 |
| G. B. LEGGE, c Andrews, b Dupain .. | 42 |
| E. T. BENSON, b Fairfax .. .. .. .. | 0 |
| F. BARRATT, not out .. .. .. .. .. | 12 |
| M. J. C. ALLOM, b Fairfax .. .. .. .. | 2 |
| E. H. BOWLEY, absent .. .. .. .. .. | 0 |
| Leg-byes 3, wides 2 .. .. .. .. .. | 5 |
| Total .. .. .. .. .. .. .. | 469 |

Fall: 11, 82, 96, 361, 386, 446, 446, 454, 469.

| | | | | | | | | | |
|---|---|---|---|---|---|---|---|---|---|
| Dupain | 25 | 2 | 117 | 2 | McCabe | 12 | 1 | 56 | 0 |
| Fairfax | 27.3 | 2 | 102 | 4 | Bradman | 12 | 0 | 83 | 1 |
| Hooker | 23 | 0 | 102 | 2 | Marks | 1 | 0 | 4 | 0 |

Fairfax and Dupain each a wide.

## Second Innings.

| | |
|---|---|
| A. H. GILLIGAN, b Hooker .. .. .. | 15 |
| E. W. DAWSON, not out .. .. .. .. | 19 |
| K. S. DULEEPSINHJI, not out .. .. .. | 36 |
| Sundries .. .. .. .. .. .. .. | 4 |
| One wicket for .. .. .. .. .. | 74 |

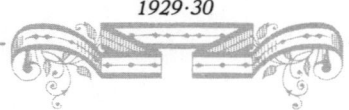

# W. M. Woodfull's XI
## v
## J. S. Ryder's XI
## (Test Trial Match)

W.M. WOODFULL's XI v J.S. RYDER's XI (Test Trial Match), at Sydney, 6, 7, 9, 10 and 11 December 1929.

| | | |
|---|---|---|
| W.M. Woodfull's XI | - First Innings | 309 |
| | - Second Innings | 541 |
| J.S. Ryder's XI | - First Innings | 663 |
| | - Second Innings | 191 for 9 wickets |
| | Woodfull's XI lost by 1 wicket. | |

| | | |
|---|---|---|
| DON BRADMAN | - c. A.A. Jackson b. R.K.Oxenham | 124 |
| | lbw. b. C.V. Grimmett | 225 |

Starting his innings late on the second day, at 85 for 2, DON BRADMAN reached 50 in fifty-eight minutes and was 54 not out overnight. Next morning his century came up in two minutes over two hours altogether and he was caught in the slips after batting for two hours forty-six minutes; he hit sixteen fours.

In the second innings he was 205 not out at the close of the third day's play. He reached 50 in eighty minutes, 100 in two hours eighteen minutes, and 200 in three hours thirty-four minutes; going from 150 to 200 in only twenty-six minutes. He made 275 runs altogether during the day, in five hours twenty-five minutes. The next morning after thirty-three minutes' play, he was out lbw., for 225; his whole innings took only four hours twelve minutes, and he hit a five and twenty-eight fours. Up to that time, Bradman was the first Australian ever to make two hundreds in the same match twice in Australia. This was also his third century in successive innings.

**BRADMAN'S QUAINT POSE** after missing an attempt to glance Alexander. Don carried his score from 54 to 124 and was 205 not out in the second innings.

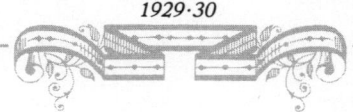

# BRADMAN BATS ALL DAY

## RUN-SCORING MACHINE

---

## BOWRAL COLT MAKES AUST. CRICKET HISTORY

---

## FOLLOWS FIRST INNINGS CENTURY WITH 205 NOT OUT

---

## WOODFULL XI's HARD FIGHT

### (By GEORGE THATCHER.)

HATS off to Don. Bradman, greatest Australian run-getter since the war! Bradman made Australian cricket history at the Sydney Cricket Ground yesterday, in the third day's play of the Australian XI. trial game. The Bowral youth batted five and a half hours, scored 273 runs during the day, and followed his first innings' score of 124 with a brilliantly compiled 205 not out. Bradman is the only Australian to reach his double century on the one day, and the first cricketer to score a century in his first innings and 200 in the second in a first-class match at the Sydney Cricket Ground. Woodfull's XI. were dismissed for 309 in the first innings, the last six wickets falling for 40 runs. In the follow-on, 341 runs have been added for two wickets.

SEVERAL months ago an erudite critic broadcast the opinion that Don Bradman would be a comparative failure on English wickets.

No reasons were advanced, but the expert was of opinion that Bradman had many faults, was lacking in stroke play, and would be in trouble to bowlers who were able to "do a bit." Let us hope that the critic was at the S.C.G. yesterday.

### Convincing Display

Bradman has scored many runs on the S.C.G. in his brief career, but never as convincingly as yesterday. He batted all day—5½ hours—scored 273 runs, turned his Saturday's score into 124, and followed with 205 not out.

A quarter of an hour to go Bradman wanted 32 for his double century. An over from Marks gave him 15. Second last over before time he hit Grimmett for 15, and then attempted to "suicide."

The catch went astray, and Bradman resumes to-day. If he so desires he might easily reach the 300.

Bradman is not a stylist, but he is the most effective batsman in Australia.

Ponsford has scored more runs in a day, but not against bowlers of the quality of Grimmett, Oxenham and Whitfield.

Don's performance is a happy augury for a great time in England. He should make many more records in the next few seasons.

---

RYDER'S ELEVEN—First Innings.

| | |
|---|---|
| A. JACKSON, c Kippax, b Hornibrook | 182 |
| W. H. PONSFORD, c Rigg, b Blackie | 131 |
| J. RYDER, c Rigg, b Hornibrook | 6 |
| S. McCABE, c Kippax, z Burrows | 35 |
| A. MARKS, c Kippax, b Blackie | 83 |
| W. HORROCKS, lbw. b Blackie | 25 |
| A. E. P. WHITFIELD, c Bradman, b Hornibrook | 68 |
| R. K. OXENHAM, not out | 84 |
| C. WALKER, c Wall, b Bradman | 12 |
| C. V. GRIMMETT, c Blackie, b Wall | 13 |
| H. ALEXANDER, c Allsopp, b Wall | 6 |
| Byes 8, leg-byes 8, no-ball 1, wide 1 | 18 |
| Total | 663 |

Fall: 278, 347, 364, 424, 472, 482, 594, 621.

| | | | | | | | |
|---|---|---|---|---|---|---|---|
| Wall | 27.7 | 0 | 131 | 2 | Blackie | 29 0 163 3 |
| Hornibrook | 22 | 4 | 102 | 3 | Bradman | 11 0 56 1 |
| | | | | | Burrows | 14 1 77 1 |
| Fairfax | 27 | 0 | 116 | 0 | | |

Wall 1 no-ball, Burrows 1 wide.

Second Innings.

| | |
|---|---|
| S. J. McCABE, c Fairfax, b Blackie | 46 |
| A. MARKS, run out | 14 |
| W. HORROCKS, c Burrows, b Blackie | 5 |
| H. WHITFIELD, l.b.w., b Blackie | 19 |
| C. WALKER, run out | 9 |
| R. K. OXENHAM, c and b Hornibrook | 4 |
| A. JACKSON, c Ellis, b Hornibrook | 15 |
| H. ALEXANDER, b Hornibrook | 8 |
| W. PONSFORD, not out | 8 |
| J. RYDER, not out | 9 |
| Byes 8, leg byes 6 | 14 |
| Eight for | 152 |

55, 65, 76, 97, 104, 115, 131, 138.

| | | | | | | |
|---|---|---|---|---|---|---|
| Wall | 5 | 0 | 20 | 0 | Hornibrook | 16 3 50 3 |
| Fairfax | 2 | 0 | 19 | 0 | Blackie | 15 2 49 3 |

W. M. WOODFULL'S ELEVEN—First Innings

| | |
|---|---|
| W. M. WOODFULL, st Walker, b Oxenham | 36 |
| A. FAIRFAX, c and b Alexander | 25 |
| A. F. KIPPAX, st Walker, b Grimmett | 17 |
| A. ALLSOPP, b Oxenham | 4 |
| D. G. BRADMAN, c Jackson, b Oxenham | 124 |
| K. RIGG, b Whitfield | 73 |
| A. O. BURROWS, b Oxenham | 7 |
| J. ELLIS, lbw, b Oxenham | 4 |
| D. BLACKIE, c McCabe, b Grimmett | 0 |
| P. M. HORNIBROOK, st Walker, b Grimmett | 2 |
| T. WALL, not out | 0 |
| Byes 4, l.b. 9, w 3, n.b. 1 | 17 |
| Total | 309 |

Fall: 50, 85, 93, 98, 269, 286, 298, 299, 301, 309.

| | | | | | | |
|---|---|---|---|---|---|---|
| Alexander | 11 | 1 | 71 | 1 | Grimmett | 15 2 68 3 |
| Whitfield | 12 | 2 | 46 | 1 | Marks | 3 0 26 0 |
| Oxenham | 14.6 | 3 | 42 | 5 | McCabe | 2 0 39 0 |

Alexander 3 wides, 1 no-ball.

Second Innings.

| | |
|---|---|
| W. M. WOODFULL, c and b Grimmett | 43 |
| A. FAIRFAX, st Walker, b Grimmett | 26 |
| D. BRADMAN, lbw, b Grimmett | 225 |
| A. KIPPAX, c Walker, b Oxenham | 170 |
| A. ALLSOPP, c McCabe, b Grimmet | 5 |
| K. RIGG, c Ponsford, b McCabe | 5 |
| A. O. BURROWS, c and b Grimmett | 0 |
| J. ELLIS, b Oxenham | 24 |
| D. BLACKIE, b Grimmett | 11 |
| P. HORNIBROOK, c Alexander, b Grimmett | 1 |
| T. WALL, not out | 2 |
| Byes 14, leg-byes 7, wides 3, n.b 1 | 25 |
| Total | 541 |

Fall of wickets: 94, 160, 378, 394, 417, 418, 495, 524, 530, 541.

| | | | | | | |
|---|---|---|---|---|---|---|
| Alexander | 11 | 0 | 73 | 0 | Grimmett | 33 3 173 7 |
| Whitfield | 14 | 0 | 71 | 0 | McCabe | 7 1 42 1 |
| Oxenham | 30.5 | 7 | 97 | 2 | Marks | 6 0 45 0 |
| Ryder | 5 | 0 | 15 | 0 | | |

Alexander 1 wide, 1 no-ball, Whitfield 2 Wides.

The game will be concluded to-day.

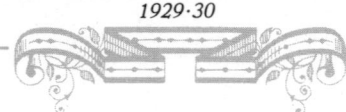

Bradman, l.b.w. for 225, returns to the pavilion at Sydney Cricket Ground.

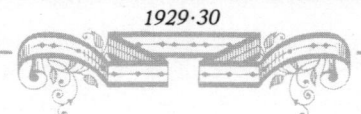

# New South Wales v Queensland

NEW SOUTH WALES v QUEENSLAND, at Sydney, 3, 4, 6 and 7 January 1930.

New South Wales - First Innings    235
                - Second Innings    761 for 8 wickets dec.

Queensland      - First Innings    227
                - Second Innings    84

New South Wales won by 685 runs.

DON BRADMAN    - c. H. Leeson   b. A. Hurwood    3
                  not out                    452

DON BRADMAN opened the first innings, but was caught at the wicket after seven minutes, scoring only 3 runs.

Going in at 22 for 1 soon after lunch on the second day, he completed 50 in fifty-one minutes, 100 in an hour and forty-four minutes, and 200 in three hours five minutes, to be 205 not out at the close of play ten minutes later.    He completed 1,000 runs for the season when 176 (4 January), the earliest date, until then, a New South Wales batsman had ever reached this aggregate; and he took only eleven innings.    On the third day, he carried on to pass W.H. Ponsford's two-year-old record score of 437, till then the highest score ever made in first-class cricket.    He reached 300 in four hours forty-eight minutes, and was 310 not out at lunch.    After six hours seventeen minutes he reached 400, and twenty-nine minutes later broke the record; he hit forty-nine fours.    His 452 was the highest score ever made in a first-class match.    Bradman became the only New South Wales batsman twice to make a score of over 300.    His match aggregate of 455 was also the highest on record.    At 21 years 132 days, he was the youngest player ever to make 400. Bradman's partnership with A.F. Kippax for the third wicket was a record for matches between New South Wales and Queensland, and in any match against Queensland.    His time for reaching 400 (six hours seventeen minutes) was the fastest on record (Ponsford scored 400 in seven hours seventeen minutes), and his time for reaching 300 (four hours forty-eight minutes) was the fastest for New South Wales.    His forty-nine fours were the highest number of boundaries ever hit in an innings in a Sheffield Shield Match, and his 196 were the most runs scored in boundaries.

## NEW SOUTH WALES XI AGAINST QUEENSLAND

BACK ROW    Wendell Bill, D. Bradman, A. Fairfax, S. C. Everett, H. Davidson, S. J. McCabe.
FRONT ROW    A. Marks, S. Burt, A. F. Kippax (Captain), H. Chilvers, and C. Andrews. A. Allsopp is absent.

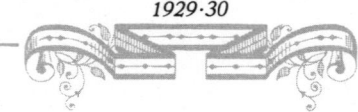

# Bradman Tops 1000 in Successive Seasons

## Dashing, Record-Smashing, Bradman Makes 205 Not Out.

## GREAT BAT MAKES A THOUSAND

### PARTNERSHIP OF 272 WITH KIPPAX

### N.S.W's BIG LEAD

#### (By J. MATHERS.)

RECORD BREAKER

DON BRADMAN reached his 1000 runs for the season in his innings of 205 not out against Queensland on Saturday. He performed the same feat last season.

WHAT a dramatic setting late yesterday afternoon at the Sydney Cricket Ground for any dashing batsman!

A huge crowd that made the old green hill look black. Grandstands around the ground packed with hero-worshippers. The atmosphere heavy with tobacco smoke. The band playing popular strains from the "Gondoliers." The sun slowly casting its long shadows across the beautifully trimmed lawn. Cheers of appreciation that acted as sweet music to the ears of the batsman.

What an incentive to make runs and to make them dashingly like Don Bradman did yesterday afternoon!

#### BRADMAN 1000 RUNS

Every run he made was applauded. Every ten he scored was noted. Every fifty was cheered. His century passed, and the crowd began to settle down for records. Quickly he put the 150 mark behind his sparkling effort. Then with 176 opposite his name on the scoring board the crowd thunderously applauded him.

To make sure that everybody in the crowd was aware of the applause, the man in the scoring room painted up the information: "Bradman, 1000 runs this season." The applause broke out afresh, and Bradman took his cap off his head in appreciation. Bradman 1000 runs this season. Bradman 1000 runs last season.

A ceramic plaque of the English wicket-keeper, George Duckworth.

Miniature bat made of Tasmanian fiddleback blackwood presented to Don Bradman in March 1930 by the Prince of Wales Theatre, Hobart, Tasmania, to recognise his world's record score of 452 not out. The wording on the gold map of Tasmania reads:
March 1930
Presented by the Prince of Wales Theatre
to Don Bradman,
holder of the world's record score of 452 not out.

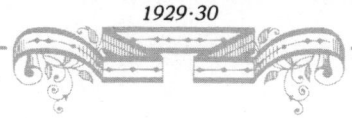
## NEW SOUTH WALES
### First Innings.

| | |
|---|---:|
| Andrews, st Leeson, b Hurwood | 56 |
| Bradman, c Leeson, b Hurwood | 3 |
| Marks, c Hurwood, b Thurlow | 40 |
| Kippax, lbw, b Thurlow | 15 |
| McCabe, c Leeson, b Thurlow | 15 |
| Allsopp, c and b Hurwood | 9 |
| Fairfax, b Brew | 20 |
| Everett, c Bensted, b Brew | 41 |
| Davidson, lbw, b Hurwood | 14 |
| Burt, b Thurlow | 10 |
| Chilvers, not out | 6 |
| Extras | 6 |
| Total | 235 |

Fall of wickets.—3, 1, 106, 133, 144, 144, 192, 211, 227.

### BOWLING

| | O. | R. | M. | W. |
|---|---:|---:|---:|---:|
| Thurlow | 18.1 | 83 | 1 | 4 |
| Hurwood | 22 | 57 | 6 | 4 |
| Bensted | 6 | 39 | — | — |
| Brew | 8 | 50 | — | 2 |

### Second Innings

| | |
|---|---:|
| C. Andrews, c Levy, b Hurwood | 16 |
| Fairfax, st Leeson, b Hurwood | 10 |
| Bradman, not out | 452 |
| Kippax, b Rowe | 115 |
| McCabe, c Leeson, b Hurwood | 60 |
| Marks, c Bensted, b Hurwood | 5 |
| Allsopp, b Hurwood | 66 |
| Everett, c Goodwin, b Hurwood | 4 |
| Davidson, c and b Goodwin | 22 |
| Extras | 11 |
| Eight wickets for | 761 |

(Innings declared closed).

Fall of wickets.—22, 33, 305, 461, 469, 645, 669, 760.

### BOWLING

| | O. | M. | R. | W. |
|---|---:|---:|---:|---:|
| Thurlow | 55 | 0 | 147 | 0 |
| Hurwood | 34 | 1 | 179 | 6 |
| Bensted | 13 | 0 | 70 | 0 |
| Brew | 6 | 0 | 61 | 0 |
| Rowe | 19 | 0 | 143 | 1 |
| Thompson | 15 | 0 | 90 | 0 |
| Gough | 4 | 0 | 40 | 0 |
| Levy | 2 | 0 | 20 | 0 |
| Goodwin | 0.1 | 0 | 0 | 1 |

## QUEENSLAND
### First Innings

| | |
|---|---:|
| Levy, c Everett, b Fairfax | 6 |
| O'Connor, c Andrews, b Fairfax | 21 |
| Thompson, lbw, b Chilvers | 1 |
| Rowe, b McCabe | 11 |
| Gough, c Marks, b McCabe | 14 |
| Bensted, c Davidson, b McCabe | 51 |
| Hurwood, b Chilvers | 4 |
| Goodwin, c Marks, b Fairfax | 67 |
| Brew, b McCabe | 20 |
| Leeson, c Davidson, b McCabe | 14 |
| Thurlow, not out | 3 |
| Extras | 15 |
| Total | 227 |

Fall of wickets.—18, 40, 42, 63, 100, 126, 157, 185, 214, 227.

### BOWLING

| | O. | M. | R. | W. |
|---|---:|---:|---:|---:|
| Fairfax | 15 | 1 | 53 | 3 |
| McCabe | 13.1 | 5 | 36 | 5 |
| Chilvers | 20 | 5 | 52 | 2 |
| Burt | 8 | 1 | 25 | 0 |
| Everett | 10 | 1 | 46 | 0 |

Fairfax, two no-balls; Chilvers, one no-ball.

### Second Innings.

| | |
|---|---:|
| Levy, b Everett | 0 |
| O'Connor, b McCabe | 17 |
| Bensted, b Everett | 3 |
| Goodwin, run out | 4 |
| Thompson, lbw, b Everett | 0 |
| Rowe, c Bradman, b Chilvers | 1 |
| Gough, b Allsopp, b Chilvers | 20 |
| Brew, c Davidson, b Everett | 26 |
| Hurwood, b Everett | 6 |
| Leeson, not out | 2 |
| Thurlow, b Everett | 0 |
| Extras | 5 |
| Total | 84 |

Fall of Wickets.—0, 3, 19, 19, 23, 42, 51, 75, 84, 84.

### BOWLING

| | O. | M. | R. | W. |
|---|---:|---:|---:|---:|
| Everett | 8.5 | 1 | 23 | 6 |
| Fairfax | 7 | 3 | 12 | 0 |
| Chilvers | 8 | 0 | 22 | 2 |
| McCabe | 5 | 3 | 15 | 1 |
| Burt | 2 | 0 | 7 | 0 |

Chilvers, 1 no-ball, 1 wide; Everett, 1 no-ball.

Bradman caught Leeson bowled Hurwood.

Remarks

This message has been received subject to the Post and Telegraph Act and Regulations.
The time received at this Office is shown at the foot of the Form.
Seh. C425—10/1929.

"Announcer"
27. C
Cricket Ground

**THE INFORMATION ON THE BACK OF THIS FORM WILL INTEREST YOU**

Congrats to Don hope he beats Ponsfords record from The Girl admirers

# Don Bradman Gives Amazing Display to Break Ponsford's World Record

## PAST 437

◆

### COLT'S GREAT OVATION

---

### TERRIFIC HITTING

#### McCABE AND ALLSOPP HELP TO PILE UP HUGE SCORE

Cricket records toppled before the flashing bat of Don Bradman to-day. One after the other they fell, the crowd often wondering what they were going to cheer next.

It did not disturb the St. George colt. He kept piling up the runs in great style, repeatedly burning the grass with a terrific drive to the boundary. When he ran past the 400 mark the crowd gave him a great round of applause, in which even an umpire joined.

Still he went, until he wanted eight to break Ponsford's world record of 437. That did not even affect him. He hit two fours and was 438, the crowd going wild with delight. Even the Queenslanders crowded around him and gave him three cheers. By that time the N.S.W. score had reached 750.

Bradman starting to run after back-cutting Hurwood.

**NEW SOUTH WALES v QUEENSLAND**
Sydney Cricket Ground, January 1930. Bradman pulls
Thurlow to the square leg boundary to make a
world's record. The highest score ever made in one
innings in a first class match. 452 not out.

# DON BRADMAN MAKES CRICKET HISTORY

**ON TIP TOES OF EXCITEMENT** in the members' stand as Bradman drew closer to Ponsford's record high score of 437. When the St. George wonder passed that score the oldest member took off his hat and cheered.

**HERO OF THE LADIES, TOO**!—There were extraordinary scenes of enthusiasm at the Cricket Ground when Bradman walked in at the close of the New South Wales innings, with 452 not out to his name.

# A GREAT SCORE AND A GREAT RECORD

*Don Bradman at the wickets immediately after he made the stroke that broke the world's batting record.*

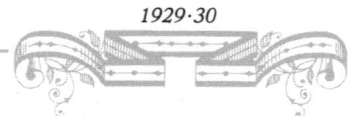

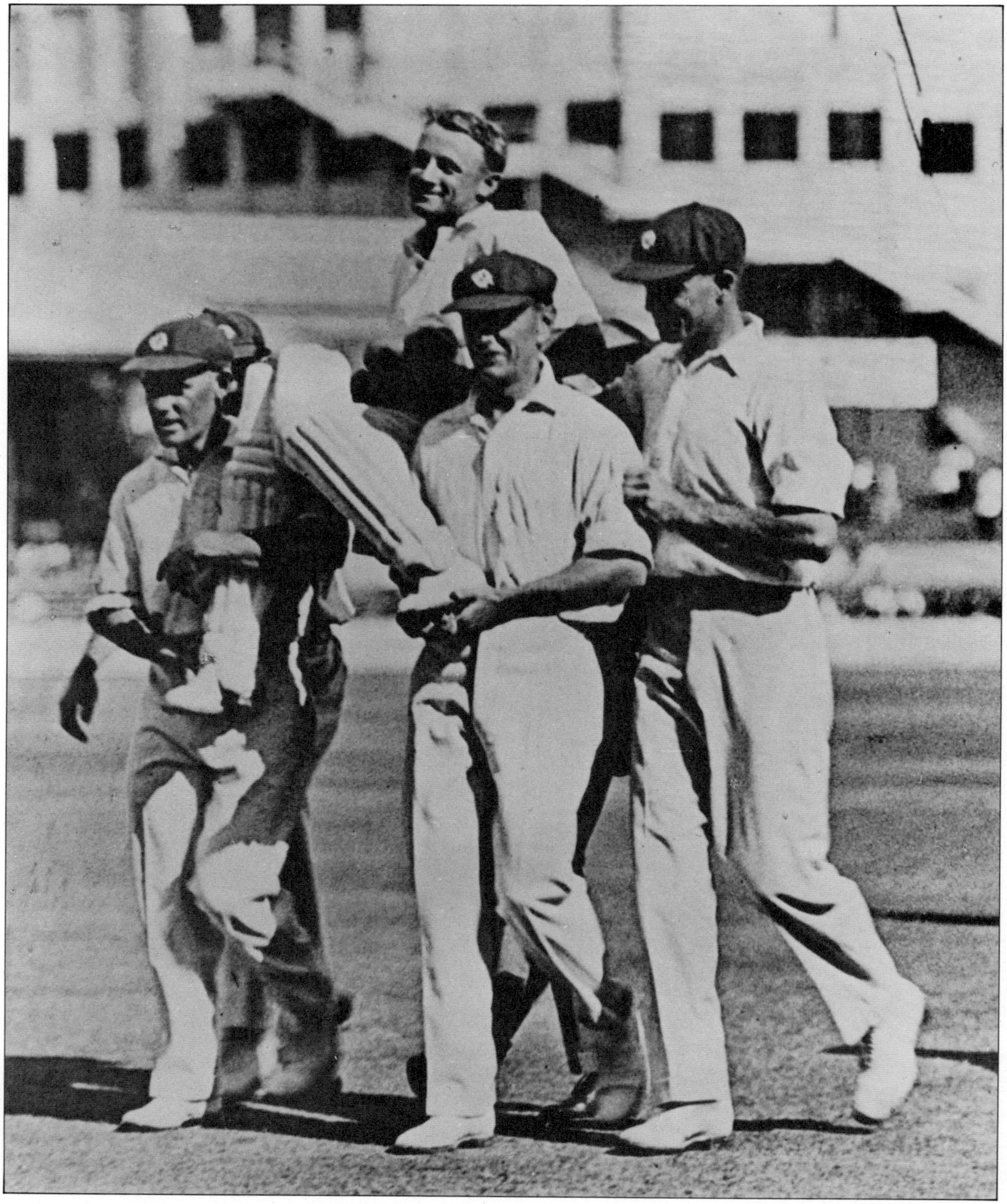

Bradman being carried off the field by Queensland players after making the world's record score of 452 not out.

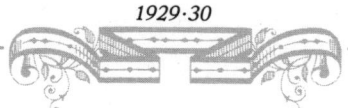

BOWLER WKTS. RUNS
GOODWIN 1
LEVY 20
O CONNOR
COUCH 40
ROWE 1 143
THOMPSON 90
BREW 61
BENSTEAD 70
HURWOOD 6 179
THURLOW 147
N.S.W. 1ST INS 235
QUEENSLD 1ST INGS 227
BATSMEN
BRADMAN 452
DAVIDSON 22
8 FOR 761
BATSMEN OUT F OF W
ANDREWS 16 22
FAIRFAX 10 33
KIPPAX 115 305
McCABE 60 461
MARKS 5 469
ALLSOPP 66 649
EVERETT 4 669
SUNDRIES 11

Scoreboard at Sydney Cricket Ground recording Bradman's world's record score.

T.G. No. 42A. USE THE TELEPHONE TO SEND YOUR TELEGRAMS.
COMMONWEALTH OF AUSTRALIA.—POSTMASTER-GENERAL'S DEPARTMENT.

RECEIVED TELEGRAM
URGENT RATE

The first line of this Telegram contains the following particulars in the order named.

| STATION FROM. | WORDS. | TIME AND DATE LODGED. | No. |
| --- | --- | --- | --- |
| Melbourne | 15 | 3.52 | |

OFFICE DATE STAMP: CRICKET GROUND 6 JAN 1930 SYDNEY

Sent at / No. / By

Remarks

This message has been received subject to the Post and Telegraph Act and Regulations.
The time received at this Office is shown at the foot of the Form.
Sch. C425—6/1929.

To Don Bradman
C.G.

THE INFORMATION ON THE BACK OF THIS FORM WILL INTEREST YOU

Congratulations great feat player
your ability deserves the
honor. Ponsford

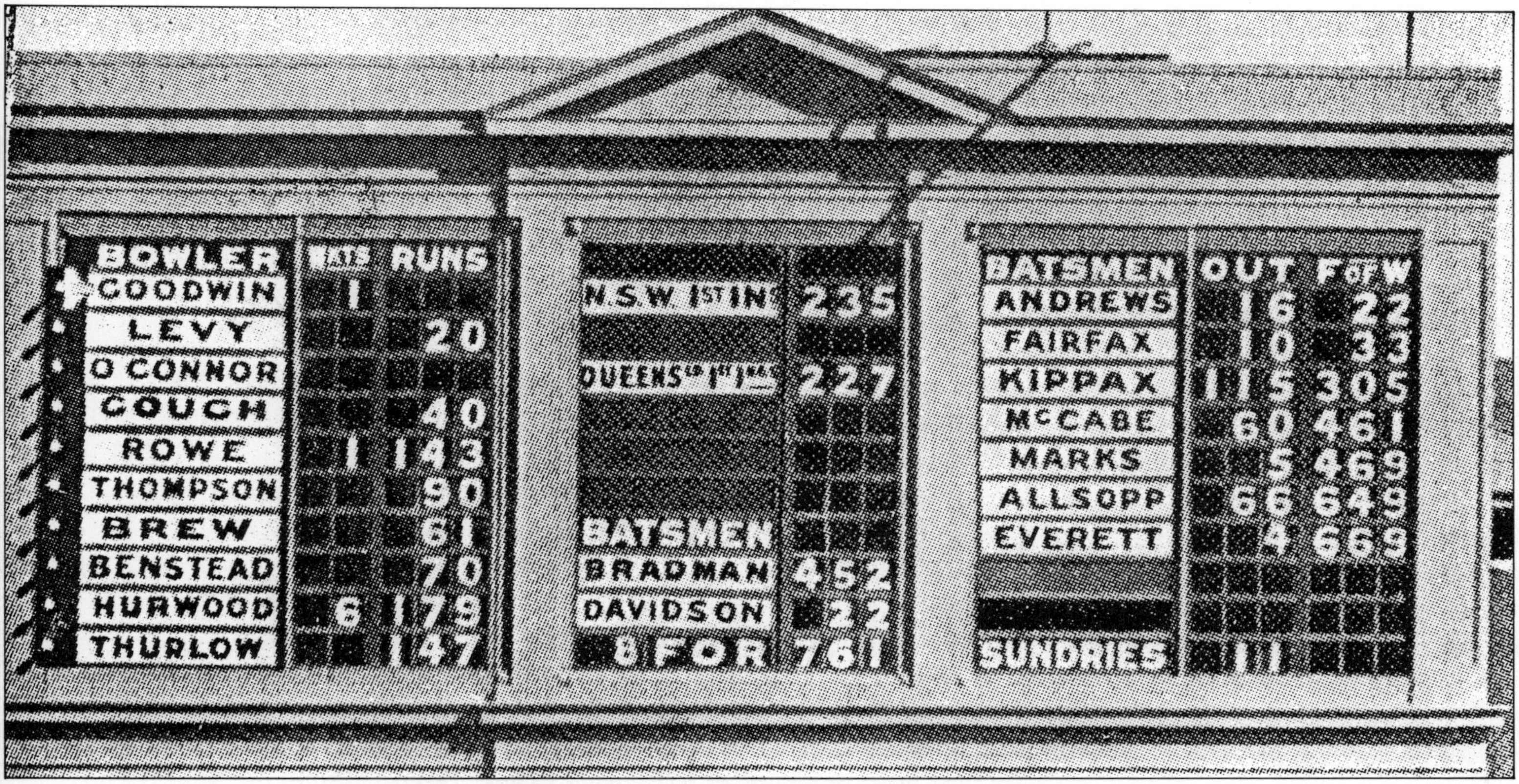

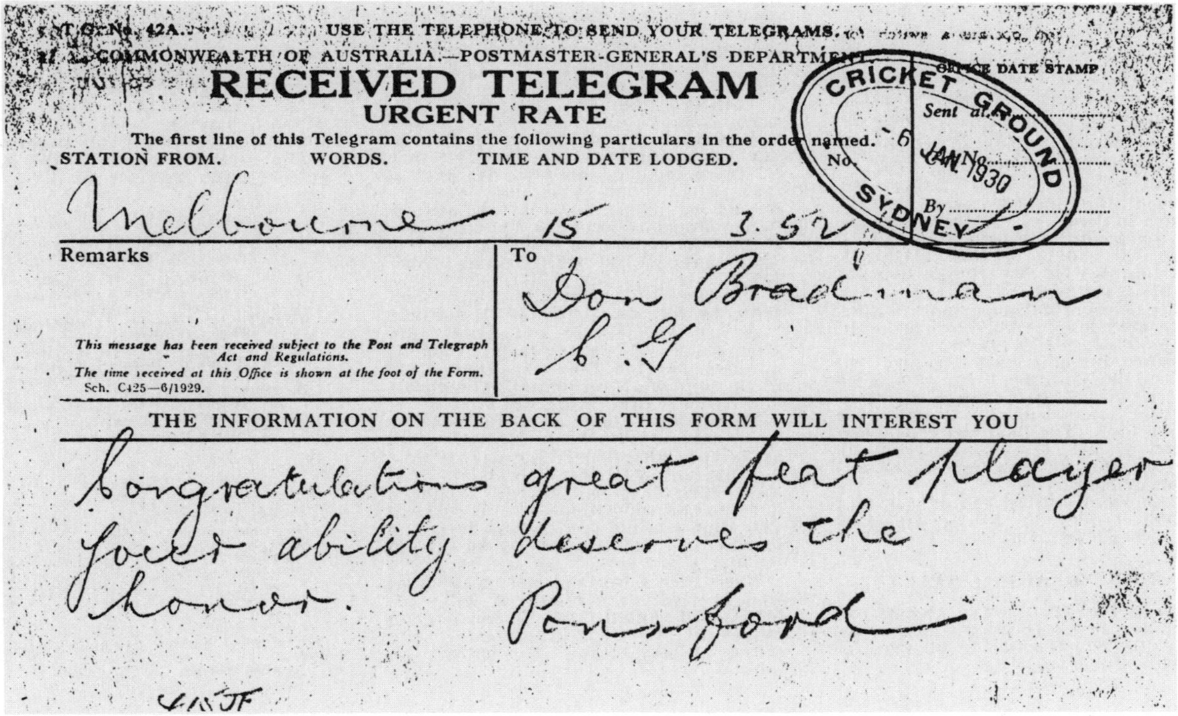

Before Don Bradman made his 452 not out, Ponsford held the World's Record Score, 437 made against Queensland in Melbourne in December 1927.

# Ponsford's
# World's Big Cricket Record
# OUT AT 437

## HISTORIC INNINGS

## VICTORIA 793

**MELBOURNE, Saturday.**

W. H. Ponsford made history to-day by scoring 437 against Queensland.

He beat his own record of 429, made against Tasmania.

Congratulations showered on the brilliant Victorian from all sides as record after record was broken.

VICTORIA had made 400 for the loss of two wickets when the match was resumed against Queensland to-day.

Ponsford, who was 23 not out, had Ryder for his partner. Early Ponsford might have been out, as he reached forward to Gill, and missed; O'Connor, the Queensland 'keeper, did not take the ball cleanly, and a good chance was missed of stumping the record breaker.

After batting 91 minutes Ryder, in trying to drive Nothling, mistimed, and he was caught by Rowe. He batted 91 minutes for 70. His partnership with Ponsford realised 143.

Scaife, the promising young junior, did not stay long, being bowled by the ex-New South Wales player, Amos.

Ponsford brought 300 against his name in 397 minutes. He was plied with leg theory after lunch by Benstead and Thompson, but it had little effect on him. The field was repeatedly changed by the Queensland captain, O'Connor, and the scoring became exceptionally slow.

Hartkopf only stayed 28 minutes, and was then bowled by Amos, who had taken two wickets for 98.

### RECORD BREAKING STARTS

When he had been at the wickets for 500 minutes, Ponsford reached 353, thus beating his own record for Victoria in Sheffield Shield matches.

Clem Hill's record of 365 against New South Wales in 1900 was the next to go. The feat was greeted by a burst of cheering. All the Queenslanders joined in the congratulations to Ponsford. The Victorian total was 660 when Ponsford's score was 366.

Ponsford had been bating 553 minutes when he reached 400. He had two scores left to beat—Maclaren's 424 for Lancashire against Somerset over 30 years ago, and his own, 429 against Tasmania. Thompson and Amos resumed leg theory bowling to Ponsford. When Ponsford was 419 the score had passed Victoria's second highest in these games—724 against South Australia.

A stolen run after the wicket had been thrown down from the field, made Ponsford 420. Play was again very slow, Ponsford making only 11 in 25 minutes. At 742 Ellis was snapped up in the slips by Nothling, off Thompson, and seven wickets were down.

There was some applause when Thompson, after consultation with O'Connor, abandoned his leg theory, but his first ball was a wide on that side. The next ball Ponsford banged hard to the leg boundary, and reached 430, thus beating his own record, and leaving no more records to be broken by him.

There was a renewal of the applause that greeted his breaking of Hill's record, and again the Queenslanders joined in the congratulations. The crowd at once began to leave the ground.

Ponsford was batting 621 minutes for his 437, and hit 43 fours.

After that Victorian wickets fell rapidly. Morton joined Blackie, but was caught before he could score. Ironmonger was the next man, and scored a single when Blackie, who had to face Amos, was bowled just on 6 o'clock, without having improved his score since the departure of Ponsford.

The attendance was 10,977, and the gate receipts £481 10s 6d.

Scores:—

**VICTORIA**

**First Innings**

| | | |
|---|---|---:|
| W. M. WOODFULL, run out | | 31 |
| W. H. PONSFORD, c and b Amos | | 437 |
| H. L. HENDRY, b Gough | | 129 |
| J. RYDER, c Rowe, b Nothling | | 70 |
| J. SCAIFE, b Amos | | 18 |
| A. E. V. HARTKOPF, b Amos | | 15 |
| C. SINDREY, c Bensted, b Rowe | | 27 |
| J. ELLIS, c Nothling, b Thompson | | 15 |
| D. BLACKIE, b Amos | | 35 |
| F. M. MORTON, c O'Connor, b Amos | | 0 |
| H. IRONMONGER, not out | | 1 |
| Sundries | | 15 |
| **Total** | | **793** |

Bowling:

| | O. | M. | R. | W. |
|---|---:|---:|---:|---:|
| Amos | 29 | 0 | 148 | 5 |
| Hurwood | 28 | 3 | 133 | 0 |
| Gill | 19 | 0 | 91 | 0 |
| Nothling | 26 | 6 | 101 | 1 |
| Bensted | 20 | 0 | 95 | 0 |
| Rowe | 13 | 1 | 65 | 1 |
| Thompson | 22 | 2 | 74 | 1 |
| Gough | 10 | 1 | 56 | 1 |
| Lister | 2 | 0 | 15 | 0 |

Thompson bowled five wides and Bensted one.

Stumps drawn.

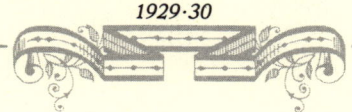

306 STOCK EX ADELAIDE 17 3-36 PM

ADMAN 1-1239

ICKET GROUND SYDNEY

EARTY CONGRATULATIONS FROM SOUTH AUSTRALIAN CRICKET ASSOCIATION
ND SELF YOUR WONDERFUL ACHIEVEMENT

EANES

arks

message has been received subject to the Post and Telegraph Act and Regulations.
time received at this Office is shown at the foot of the Form.
C435—10/1929.

To Don Bradman
C/- The announcer
S.G.

4-1P45

THE INFORMATION ON THE BACK OF THIS FORM WILL INTEREST YOU

Accept my congratulations on your magnificent innings
Jack Munro

To Don Bradman
C.G.

message has been received subject to the Post and Telegraph Act and Regulations.

Heartiest Congrats & best wishes to Don Bradman hope you continue good work against England next year
Donald Geddes Mayor Parkes

575 JT Time received at this Office.

...ALTH OF AUSTRALIA—POSTMASTER-GENERAL...

URGENT TELEGRAM.

Words Check Remarks No.

CRICKET GROUND -6 JAN 1930 SYDNEY

To Don Bradman

received subject to the Post and Telegraph Act and Regulations.

difficult

Received at this Office.

...HONE TO SEND YOUR TELEGRAMS.

...OSTMASTER-GENERAL'S DEPARTMENT

TELEGRAM

...T RATE

...the following particulars in the order named. TIME AND DATE LODGED. No.

CRICKET GROUND Sent at 6 JAN 1930 C'ct No. SYDNEY

16 3-50

To Don Bradman
Sy Ckt Ground

THE INFORMATION ON THE BACK OF THIS FORM WILL INTEREST YOU

you masterful ... records.
Alick and Staff
Cootamundra

...Post and ... is shown at the foot of the Form.

... received at this Office is shown ... 8/1929.

D. G. Bradman
C/- Mick Simmons Ltd
Haymarket. 1399a

THE INFORMATION ON THE BACK OF THIS FORM WILL INTEREST YOU

Hearty Congratulations best of luck
Jean and Nancy
Annandale

1.52 pm WE

# AUSTRALIAN ELEVEN.

## OFFICIAL ANNOUNCEMENT CONFIRMS FORECAST.

### WOODFULL APPOINTED AS CAPTAIN.

#### Ryder's Omission Severely Criticised.

(BY OUR SPECIAL REPRESENTATIVE.)

At 3.15 o'clock yesterday afternoon Mr. R. A. Oxlade, chairman of the Board of Control, announced the names of the 17th Australian Eleven to tour England. They were identical with those forecast in the "Herald" yesterday.

More than an hour later another announcement was made to the effect that W. M. Woodfull has been appointed captain, and V. Y. Richardson vice-captain, and Woodfull, Richardson, and Kippax will comprise the selection committee on tour.

It was not until nearly 6 o'clock that the decision to refuse the selectors' request to be allowed to choose a 16th player was known.

Comment on the omission of Ryder was general. Apart from that the selection has given satisfaction. It is regarded as representative of Australian cricket to-day.

Twelve of the team have had previous test match experience, but Woodfull, Ponsford, Oldfield and Grimmett are the only members who have previously visited England.

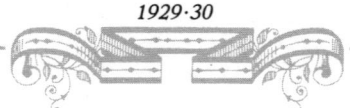

HOW AUSTRALIA SIGNS ITSELF

### THE TEAM.

W. M. Woodfull (Vic.), capt.
V. Y. Richardson (S.A.), vice-capt.
E. L. a'Beckett (Vic.)
D. G. Bradman (N.S.W.).
A. Fairfax (N.S.W.).
C. V. Grimmett (S.A.).
P. M. Hornibrook (Q.).
A. Hurwood (Q.).
A. Jackson (N.S.W.).
A. F. Kippax (N.S.W.).
S. J. McCabe (N.S.W.).
W. A. Oldfield (N.S.W.).
W. H. Ponsford (Vic.).
C. M. Walker (S.A.).
T. M. Wall (S.A.).

CURRENT FOR THE YEAR 1930.

**NEW SOUTH WALES**

*ORTA RECENS* *QUAM* *PURA NITES*

# The Bearer of this Credential,

MR. DONALD GEORGE BRADMAN
(a member of the Australian Cricket Team),

*a respected resident of this State, is*

*proceeding on a visit to* Great Britain

and the Continent of Europe.

*Any courtesy that may be*
*afforded to him will be valued on*
*his part and will be appreciated*
*by this Government.*

*J R Savin*

*Prime Minister*
*of the State of New South Wales*
*in the Commonwealth of Australia.*

*Signature of Bearer :–*

Premier's Office.

Sydney, 31st January, 19 30.

---

Australian Board of Control for International Cricket

**AUSTRALIAN XI ENGLISH TOUR, 1930.**

W. L. KELLY MANAGER
T. HOWARD TREASURER

V.C.A. Buildings
cr Flinders St & Collins Place
MELBOURNE
January 31 st. 1930

Dear Sir/  Please accept my heartiest congratulations on your
selection as a Member of the 17 th. Australian Team for England.

I am enclosing herewith some information regarding your
Passport, Taxation Department requirements, Luggage Etc, which
requires your immediate personal attention, also particulars of
the arrangements made for the trip to Tasmania & Western Australia.

With kind regards

Yours truly

*W. L. Kelly*

To/ D.G.Bradman Esq.

Don Bradman in 1930 wearing his first touring blazer.

AUSTRALIAN BOARD OF CONTROL FOR INTERNATIONAL CRICKET
AUSTRALIAN Xl ENGLISH TOUR 1930
SOME INFORMATION FOR PLAYERS.                31-1-1930.

### PASSPORT, LUGGAGE ETC.

Every member of the Team must have a passport to leave Australia.
Please obtain an "Application for Passport" from the Customs Dep't,
read all the instructions on theback of the form very carefully and
make the necessary arrangements to have a passport issued to you.

NOTE. 1.   The cost of Photos. and Passport are a charge against the
           receipts of the tour and will be refunded to you.
      2.   No Passport will be issued by the Customs Department until
           a Certificate from the Taxation Department has been obtained
           by you certifying that your Income Tax return has been made
           and the tax (if any) paid.
      3.   Every Player must have his Passport "vised" by the Customs
           Department for travelling overland through Switzerland,
           Italy and France.

                         -------

With regard to luggage, have your kit bags, trunks and suit cases
painted distinctly with bands, one inch wide, of the Australian
colours. (Green and Gold).        All heavy trunks must be put
on board the "Orford" at your HOME PORT.

### BLAZER, CAP, TIE ETC.

Please leave your order for these articles at once with
"Hardings Mercery" , Number 1a, Hunter Street, Sydney.
This is very necessary if you are to get delivery before sailing.
Also arrange with William Hollins and Coy. of 227 Flinders Lane,
Melbourne and 50 York Street, Sydney, to be measured for sets of
"Yiyella" trousers, shirts and pyjamas :- (The gift of the Viyella Co.)
These goods will be delivered to the team on arrival in England.

                         --------

### TASMANIAN AND WEST AUSTRALIAN TRIP?.

Arrangements have been made with the Manager of the Hotel
Alexander, Spencer Street, Melbourne, to provide accomodation
forplayers from Queensland, New South Wales, South Australia
on arrival on Friday morning March 7th.
Lunch will be served at the Hotel Alexander.
The team will leave Melbourne at 3 p.m. the same day for
Launceston per the "S. S. Nirana".
Suit Cases and Kit Bags of Players from New South Wales,
South Australia and Queensland required on this trip, will be
picked up at Spencer Street Station on arrival and placed on
the "Nairana".
Victorians will deliver their own luggage to the boat.

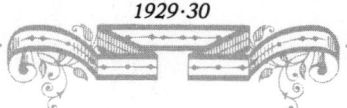

# The Man and His Record

This young man, not yet 22 years of age, with but three years' experience in big cricket, has startled the cricket world by making the highest score in first class cricket.

His record is truly astounding.

**1926-1927:**

Country cricket: 320 n.o., 300, 234 — the three highest scores made in the Bowral district.

**1927-1928:**

Sheffield Shield cricket: 118, 33, 31, 5, 0, 13, 2, 73, 7, 134 n.o. Total, 416 runs. Average 46.2, second highest for the N.S.W. team.

**1928-1929:**

Sheffield Shield cricket: 131, 133 n.o., 1, 71 n.o., 5, 2, 35, 175, 340 n.o. Test cricket: 18, 1, 79, 112, 40, 58, 123, 37 n.o. Other first class fixtures: Trial match, 14, 5; v. England, 87, 132 n.o., 58 n.o., 18, 15. Total, 1,690 runs in the season, a record for first class cricket in Australia. Average, 93.9 runs, first in Shield averages.

**1929-1930:**

Sheffield Shield cricket: 48, 66, 2, 84, 89, 26 n.o., 3, 452 n.o., 47, 77. Other first class fixtures: v. M.C.C., 157; Test Trial, 124, 225. Total, 1,400 runs. Average, 127.2 runs. First in Shield averages.

**RECORDS HELD IN FIRST CLASS CRICKET.**

452 n.o., highest score in first class cricket in the world.

1,690 runs, highest number of runs scored in one season in Australia.

7 centuries in one season in Australia, held jointly with Hammond, M.C.C.

Over 1,000 runs in successive seasons, held jointly with W. Ponsford, Vic.

Youngest player in the world to score over 400 runs in a first class match.

2 separate innings of over 100 in one day, shared with Ranjitsinghi.

A century in each innings in a match, twice.

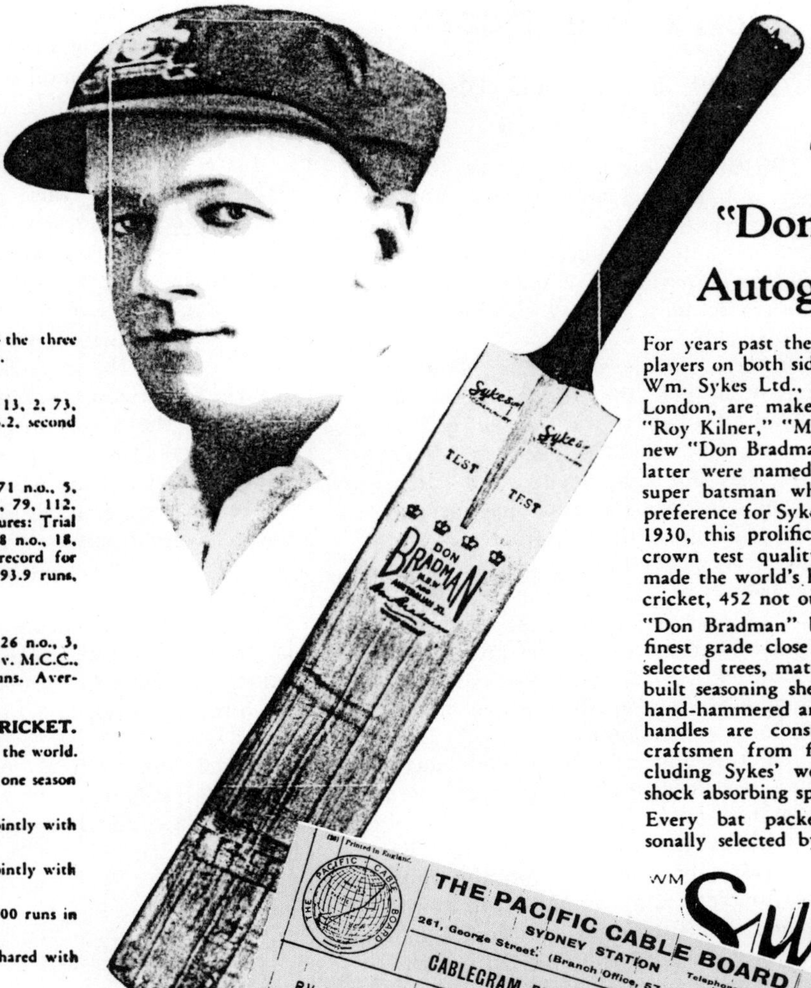

# The "Don Bradman" Autograph Bats

For years past the majority of test match players on both sides have used Sykes' bats. Wm. Sykes Ltd., of Horbury, Yorks and London, are makers of the world-famous "Roy Kilner," "Maurice Leyland" and the new "Don Bradman" autograph bats. The latter were named in honor of Australia's super batsman who, in 1928, showed his preference for Sykes-made bats. In January, 1930, this prolific run-getter, using a 4-crown test quality "Don Bradman" bat, made the world's highest score in first class cricket, 452 not out.

"Don Bradman" bats are made from the finest grade close bark willow, cut from selected trees, matured in our scientifically built seasoning sheds. Each blade expertly hand-hammered and face-compressed. The handles are constructed by experienced craftsmen from finest Sarawak cane, including Sykes' well-known treble rubber shock absorbing spring.

Every bat packed for export is personally selected by one of our principals.

WM Sykes LTD
BRITAINS SPORTS SPECIALISTS
London

Printed in England.

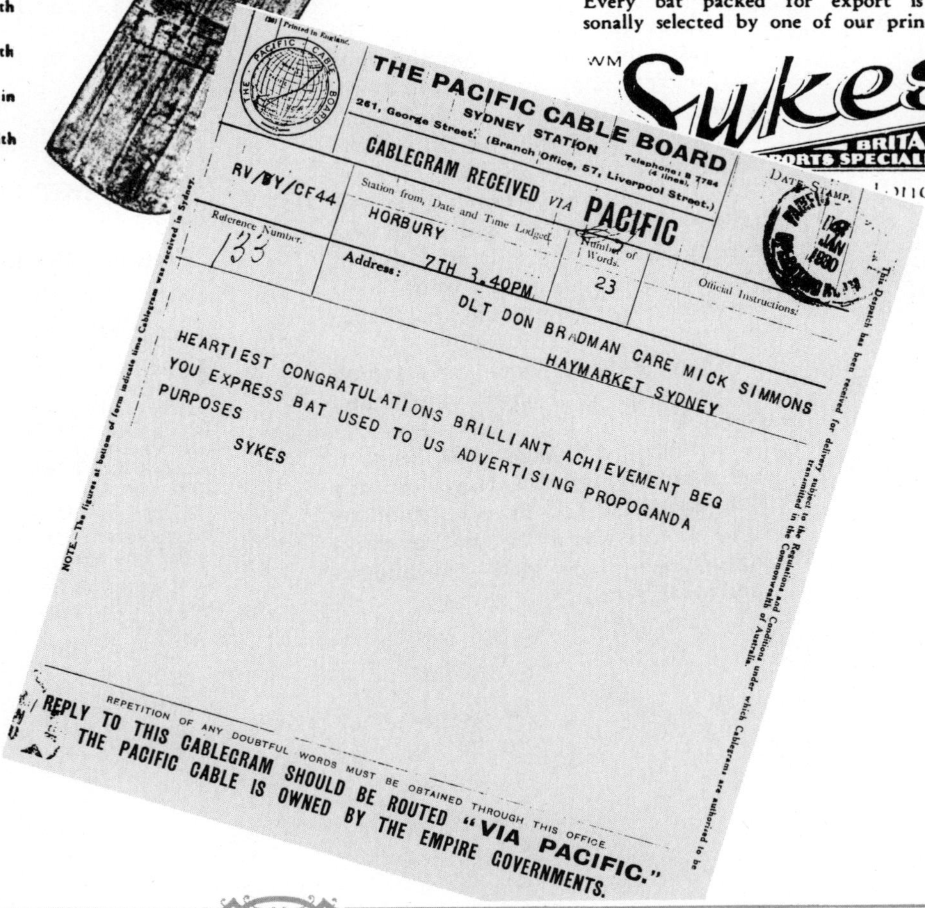

THE PACIFIC CABLE BOARD
SYDNEY STATION
261, George Street. (Branch Office, 57, Liverpool Street.) Telephone: B 7784 (4 lines).

CABLEGRAM RECEIVED VIA PACIFIC

RV/BY/CF44

Station from, Date and Time Lodged. HORBURY 7TH 3.40PM

Reference Number. 133

Number of Words. 23

Date Stamp. JAN 1930

Official Instructions:

Address: DLT DON BRADMAN CARE MICK SIMMONS HAYMARKET SYDNEY

HEARTIEST CONGRATULATIONS BRILLIANT ACHIEVEMENT BEG YOU EXPRESS BAT USED TO US ADVERTISING PROPOGANDA PURPOSES

SYKES

NOTE—The figures at bottom of form indicate time Cablegram was received in Sydney.

This Despatch has been received for delivery subject to the Regulations and Conditions under which Cablegrams are authorised to be transmitted in the Commonwealth of Australia.

REPETITION OF ANY DOUBTFUL WORDS MUST BE OBTAINED THROUGH THIS OFFICE.

REPLY TO THIS CABLEGRAM SHOULD BE ROUTED "VIA PACIFIC."
THE PACIFIC CABLE IS OWNED BY THE EMPIRE GOVERNMENTS.

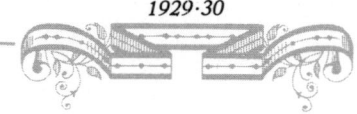

# Don's Big Score

## HOW IT FEELS TO BREAK A RECORD.

Writing of his record score of 452 not out in the Queensland match, Don says:—

I do not set much store on the making of records. I make it a rule always to play for my side, and not for myself.

I have never placed my own interest before the interests of my team. If I broke a record I have been glad, but only because I have felt that my side needed the runs.

On one occasion and one occasion only, however, I definitely and deliberately set out to establish a record.

The highest individual score in first-class cricket was the one record I wanted to hold, and the opportunity came my way in the return match against Queensland.

At the end of the second day's play (Saturday) I was some 200 odd runs not out.

I spent the evening quietly with some friends, and then on the Sunday, on reflecting on the state of the game, it occurred to me that I had just a chance of topping Billy Ponsford's record score of 437.

The conditions were all in my favor. The state of the game was exactly right, and I felt sure that if I could only do my part I would have the necessary support at the other end.

When Monday came, everything worked out as I had hoped and planned.

The mood to make runs was on me, and, topping the third century and then the fourth, the moment came when I was at last within striking distance of my goal—the highest individual score.

My score was 434, so that four more runs were wanted when I faced Thurlow, Queensland's fast bowler, against whom earlier in the season Woodfull had had his hand broken.

Here I had a curious intuition. While Thurlow was preparing to bowl, I seemed to sense that the ball would be a short-pitched one on the leg stump, and I could almost feel myself getting ready to make my shot before the ball was delivered.

Sure enough, it pitched exactly where I had anticipated, and, hooking it to the square-leg boundary, I established the only record upon which I had set my heart.

Many people have asked me to describe my feelings when I realised that I had accomplished this performance.

The best description I can offer is that I felt as a man who had achieved a specific task which he had set himself to do, and having done it was satisfied.

I was not excited, and I cannot say that I suffered any reaction. My feeling was one of complete satisfaction.

## "FOR MUM," SAYS DON

### Famous Cricket Colt Leaves Trophy at Home

*"There's a spot in me heart
That no colleen may own."*

HANDED a handsome rose bowl in recognition of his world's record score of 452 not out against Queensland, Don Bradman, at last night's dinner to the N.S.W. members of the Australian Eleven, explained why he had selected such a present.

"There is someone who will treasure this bowl more than I do," he said.

"I refer to my mother. The rose bowl is for her."

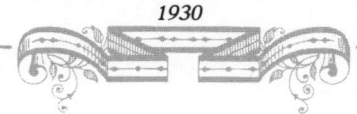

# *1930*
# *Australian Tour of England*

The days between selection for an English tour and departure are usually nostalgic and 1930 was no exception. I attended many farewells, as did two of my young team mates, Alan Fairfax and Archie Jackson, shown photographed with me, and all our hopes were high.

Sadly they did not achieve their goals. Both had mediocre tours of England. I was a pall-bearer at Archie's funeral less than three years later whilst Alan suffered much ill health and died at the very young age of 48.

A tour to England in those days was a marvellous experience. This one embraced visits to Hobart, Launceston and Perth (where matches were played) before leaving Australia.

The shipboard life, with stops at Colombo, Aden, Suez and Port Said, was exciting. The Suez Canal gave no hint of the tragedy which lay ahead.

Rome was a highlight. Even now I think St. Peter's Cathedral the most wonderful structure I have seen, with the Milan Cathedral also marvellous.

Switzerland was incredibly beautiful and in its own way so was Paris, though to an unsophisticated lad like me, somewhat overpowering.

What an education for a young country lad and how wonderful that cricket could make it possible.

*Don Bradman*

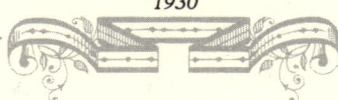

Don Bradman, Alan Fairfax, Archie Jackson.

# Australian Cricketers' Tour, 1930—The Selected Team

D. G. BRADMAN,
N.S.W. — Batsman.

A. JACKSON,
N.S.W. — Batsman.

A. F. KIPPAX,
N.S.W. — Batsman.

W. H. PONSFORD,
Victoria — Batsman.

W. A. OLDFIELD,
N.S.W. — 1st Wicket-keeper.

C. W. WALKER,
S.A. — 2nd Wicket-keeper.

A. FAIRFAX,
N.S.W. — All-rounder.

A. HURWOOD,
Queensland — Bowler.

S. McCABE,
N.S.W.—All-rounder.

P. M. HORNIBROOK,
Queensland — Bowler.

E. L. a'BECKETT,
Victoria — All-rounder.

V. RICHARDSON,
S.A.—Batsman (Vice-Capt.).

W. M. WOODFULL,
Victoria — Batsman (Captain).

T. M. WALL,
South Australia — Fast Bowler.

C. V. GRIMMETT,
South Australia — Slow Bowler.

**TEST MATCHES—OPENING DATES.**
June 13 (Nottingham); June 27 (Lord's);
July 11 (Leeds); July 25 (Manchester);
August 16 (The Oval).

*Programme:*

April 30, May 1 and 2, v. Worcestershire, at Worcester.
May 3, 5, and 6, v. Leicestershire, at Leicester.
May 7, 8, and 9, v. Essex, at Leyton.
May 10, 12, and 13, v. Yorkshire, at Sheffield.
May 14, 15, and 16, v. Lancashire, at Liverpool.
May 17, 19, and 20, v. M.C.C., at Lord's.
May 21, 22, and 23, v. Derbyshire, at Chesterfield.
May 24, 26, and 27, v. Surrey, at The Oval.
May 28, 29, and 30, v. Oxford University, at Oxford.
May 31, June 2 and 3, v. Hampshire, at Southampton.
June 4, 5, and 6, v. Middlesex, at Lord's.
June 7, 9, and 10, v. Cambridge University, at Cambridge.
June 13, 14, 16, and 17, FIRST TEST, at Nottingham.
June 18, 19, and 20, v. Surrey, at The Oval.
June 21, 23, and 24, v. Lancashire, at Manchester.
June 27, 28, 30, and July 1, SECOND TEST, at Lord's.

July 2, 3, and 4, v. Yorkshire, at Bradford.
July 5, 7, and 8, v. Notts, at Nottingham.
July 11, 12, 14, and 15, THIRD TEST, at Leeds.
July 16 and 17, v. Scotland, at Glasgow.
July 18, 19, and 21, v. Scotland, at Edinburgh.
July 22 and 23, v. Durham, at Sunderland.
July 25, 26, 28, and 29, FOURTH TEST, at Manchester.
July 30 and 31, v. Somerset, at Taunton.
August 2, 4, and 5, v. Glamorgan, at Swansea.
August 6, 7, and 8, v. Warwickshire, at Birmingham.
August 9, 11, and 12, v. Northamptonshire, at Northampton.
August 16, etc., FIFTH TEST, at The Oval.
August 23, 25, and 26, v. Gloucestershire, at Bristol.
August 27, 28, and 29, v. Kent, at Canterbury.
August 30, September 1 and 2, v. Sussex, at Brighton.
September 3, 4, and 5, v. South of England XI., at Folkestone.
September 6 and 8, v. Club Cricket Conference.
September 10, 11, and 12, v. an English XI., at Scarborough.

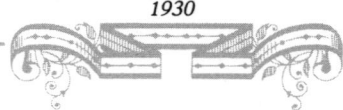

# PROUDEST MOMENT IN DON.'S LIFE.

## BERRIMA DISTRICT HONORS GREATEST CRICKETER OF HIS TIM STIRRING SCENE OF UNPARALELLED ENTHUSIASM

### "A GREAT CRICKETER AND A PERFECT GENTLEMAN."

There was every reason why Tuesday night was to Don Bradman, as he said, the proudest moment of his life. To but few of the world's teeming millions is given such an experience as was Don's on Tuesday.

In the bosom of his family and surrounded by the friends of his youth, he received from the people of the Berrima District an ovation that is without precedent. The Empire Theatre was crowded with youth and beauty, and venerable age had also come to honor the most amazing cricketer of his time.

And through it all the hero of the hour bore himself so modestly that a stranger might well have doubted if he were the centre of all this great commotion.

To his old friends Don was just the same quiet, happy youth with whom they had played and worked with no presentiment that in a few short years their mate would be a world's hero. Youngsters who model themselves upon Australia's most eminent cricketer will not suffer from swelled head nor boast of deeds that made them famous. It says something for the great game that it produces men of the character of Bradman.

Don arrived at the theatre with his father and mother and stood outside for a few moment whilst the Bowral Band played "Advance Australia Fair." He was greeted with hearty cheers.

Inside the theatre dancing was something of a task so crowded was the floor. But who cared? They were there to acclaim Don the best in the world, and nothing else mattered much.

When the time came for the presentation, Mr. Alf. Stephens, President of the Cricket Association took the chair. He was supported by Mr. Reg. Tickner, Secretary of the Association, and the Mayors of Bowral and Moss Vale.

Apologies read included one from Mr. F. Cush, who said Bradman was one of the finest characters who had ever graced the cricket field. He would worthily uphold the prestige and honor of Australia.

Mr. Stephens then asked the Mayor of Bowral (Ald. Sheaffe) to welcome Mr. Bradman on behalf of the citizens.

Ald. Sheaffe said it was his pleasant duty as Mayor to represent the town in extending a welcome to Don and to wish him success on the other side. They were not saying good-bye, for Don would soon be back and he hoped he would bring with him a considerable quantity of the Ashes. Don possessed a temperament that would enable him to do well anywhere. "It's not cricket" was applied when something fell below the moral standard, and in Don they had a man who had taken the best lessons of cricket to heart. They all wished him the best of luck on the trip and a happy return to Australia.

Mr. P. A. Westbrook said their motto that night might well be "We are proud of you, Don, and we tell you so." Maybe Sydney and St. George might claim this distinguished cricketer, as theirs, but he was especially a product of the Berrima District. As they watched the progress of Don in the Old Land they would feel that he had been one of them. In his early formative life in Bowral in education and in school games he had acquired that mental alertness and that sterling character which distinguished him on the cricket field and off it. There were many good cricketers in Australia, but they had there that night the foremost cricketer of his time . (Prolonged applause.) Donald had done more than conquer the mysteries of cricket, he had made a conquest of himself. His wonderful success had not turned his head, and he came back to them the same bonny boy, quite unspoiled, and recognising his old mates just the same as when he went away. When at a city presentation he referred to his mother, he had revealed the true hall mark of his heart. He was the great cricketer and the perfect gentleman. Turning to Don he said, "The eyes of the world are on you, Don, but no one will take more interest in your career than those in this district who know you best."

"For He's a Jolly Good Fellow," sang the crowd.

Then Mr. Stephens read Don's cricket record.

' And he's not done yet," interjected Tom Cummins to renewed cheering.

"He is the youngest batsman in the world to have done such things," continued Mr. Stephens. "We are very proud of him in Bowral and in the district, and glad to find him the same unassuming lad as ever."

Mr. Stephens handed Don a pair of silver entree dishes and a wallet well-filled with notes.

### DON MAKES A SPEECH.

When Don rose to reply there was another outburst and "For He's a Jolly Good Fellow" was sung.

"This is the proudest evening of my life," he commenced, "to be able to return to Bowral to say good-bye to the friends I made when a boy and to see those who helped me a bit along the road. First my parents taught me to be a cricketer off the

## OUR DON.
A Portrait Study by Kelvey Luke.

field as well as on. It was not 'did you win,' but 'did you play the game' that made the man.

"Next came Mr. Westbrook. After leaving school I spent five years with Mr. Westbrook before going to Sydney. Everything lay in his hands, but at great inconvenience he let me go to Sydney. It was due to him that I got my chance in big cricket. Then the games played in the district helped me in many ways. When we play at Lords—the mecca of cricket—Alf. Stephens will be there and it will be like old times to have so true a friend over there. I hope to be able to say goodbye to all my old friends, but if I miss any I hope they will take the will for the deed. I thank you for this opportunity of saying goodbye, and hope when I come back that I shall still be able to regard you one and all as my friends."

And then again "For He's a Jolly Good Fellow."

Mr. Stephens then announced that Mr. Kelvey Luke had presented a fine portrait study of Don to the High School. He was sure it would be appreciated there, for Don had been dux of the school as well as playing cricket there.

## A SURPRISE FOR ALF.

Mr. A. A. South here caused a diversion by producing a large parcel and asking Mr. Stephens to accept a present from the Cricket Association on the eve of his departure for England. In business, in sport, in public life, Mr. Stephens always played the game. He must have made great sacrifices to serve the public as alderman and Mayor. Their present was a token of the esteem in which their President was held by his fellow cricketers throughout the district. They wished him God speed and a safe return. Mr. South then presented Mr. Stephens with a handsome office set.

Mr. Stephens said they had taken him by surprise and he was very grateful to the Association for giving him so valuable a present. The Association was a happy body and its members all tried to play cricket on the field and off. He took occasion to thank Mrs. Woolard and her helpers for the supper, Mr. Arthur Meeks for the decorations, and everybody who had helped to make the function such a great success. It was a great tribute to Don and he was worthy of it.

Dancing was resumed and supper partaken of. This last item proved somewhat of an undertaking, as some five or six sittings were necessary to provide for all. The ladies fully earned the thanks given them for their work.

Don left Bowral on Thursday to join his comrades at Moss Vale, en route to Lords.

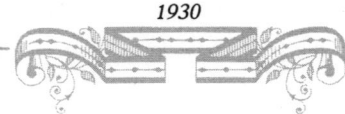

## THURSDAY, 6 MARCH

*Harry Grose and Billy Tidmarsh helped me pack cabin trunk, 2 suitcases, cricket bag and attache case.*
*Good-bye to Ellimatta. Trunk to Billy's for him to put on board "Orford". Lunch in town with Harry. Completed Power of Attorney with Solicitor.*
*Sister May and I set out for Bowral at 3.30.*
*Dinner at home. Mother, Father, Vic, May and I went to Moss Vale to catch train at 9.30 p.m.*
*Large crowd on the station. Flashlight photographs.*
*Band was playing. Train pulled out at 10.12 p.m.*
*Lee Hunt, Billy Williams and others said au revoir on Goulburn Station at 11.25 p.m.*
*Pulled out soon afterwards, then to bed.*

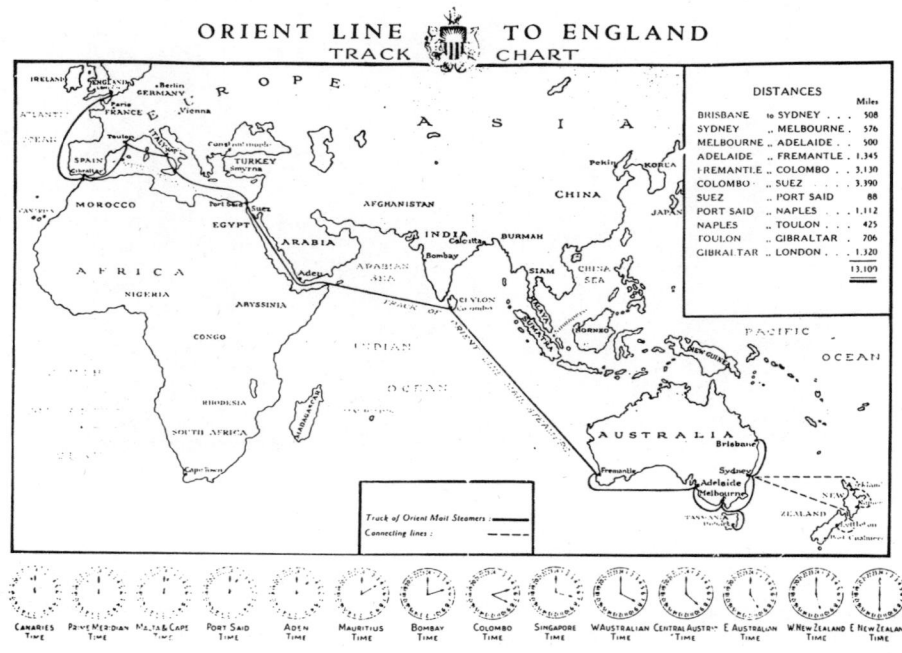

## MATCHES PLAYED EN ROUTE TO ENGLAND

| TITLE | | GAME | | SCORES | |
|---|---|---|---|---|---|
| Second Class | Australia | Colombo | 40 | C. | |
| First Class | " | Tasmania | 20 | L.B.W. | |
| | " | " | 139 | C. | |
| | " | Western Australia | 27 | C. | |
| | | Total runs | 226 | | |

The Australian Team commenced their 1930 English tour with a visit to Tasmania and played two games against the State at Launceston and Hobart.

They travelled from Melbourne to Launceston in the S.S."Nairana" on 7th March, and returned to Melbourne on the 17th March in the R.M.S. "Orford" which they rejoined in Perth after an overland journey.

The Team arrived in Perth by train on 21st March and sailed for England in the R.M.S."Orford" on 24th March.

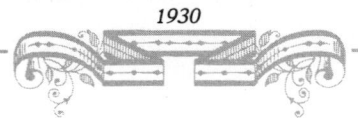

TUESDAY, 25 MARCH

*Played the various deck games.*
*Played piano. Swam and in general enjoyed the boat life.*
*Beautiful day. Nice calm sea.*
*Dance at night.*

WEDNESDAY, 26 MARCH

*Draw for the deck games out and everyone crowding around the notice board.*
*I played in the various games as drawn with the following results:*
*Quoit Tennis — Men's Doubles. With R. Whitehouse beat J. Harrison and R. H. Walters 6–3.*
*Ball Tennis — Men's Singles. Beat Nat Seamens 6–0. Mr. Tatchell senr. 6–4.*
*Deck Quoits — Singles. Beat Dr. Brown 21–7.*
*Quoit Tennis — Mixed Doubles. With Mrs. Whitehead beat Father Clancy and Miss Whitehead 6–2.*
*Deck Quoits — Men's Doubles. With J. Armstrong beat A. Jenner and S. Goldman 21–9.*
*Swim in between times. Carnival night. The boys all dressed up and had a fine night.*

SUNDAY, 30 MARCH

*Usual routine on board.*
*Concert in the lounge at night.*
*Wonderful sunset in the evening.*

MONDAY, 31 MARCH

*Game of tennis and swim before breakfast.*
*Beat Mr. Gay 6–1 in ball tennis singles then beat Kippax 6–0 in semi-final.*
*Final played at 3 o'clock before a large gallery and I beat Alec Hurwood 6–1, 7–5.*

TUESDAY, 1 APRIL

*Swim before breakfast.*
*Day of finals. Jackson won peg quoits. a'Beckett won bucket quoits. Fairfax and partner won doubles of quoit tennis. Oldfield and Fisher won doubles of deck quoits.*
*Oldfield beaten in final of deck quoits singles by Fisher Cooper after magnificent game 21–20 in deciding game. A wrong decision by the umpire and we prematurely chaired Bertie, later having to do the same to Cooper.*
*Very heavy rainstorm at night.*

## COOLEST SPOT ON THE SHIP.

Australian cricketers en route to England enjoyed the Orford's swimming pool. Bradman and McCabe are in the water.

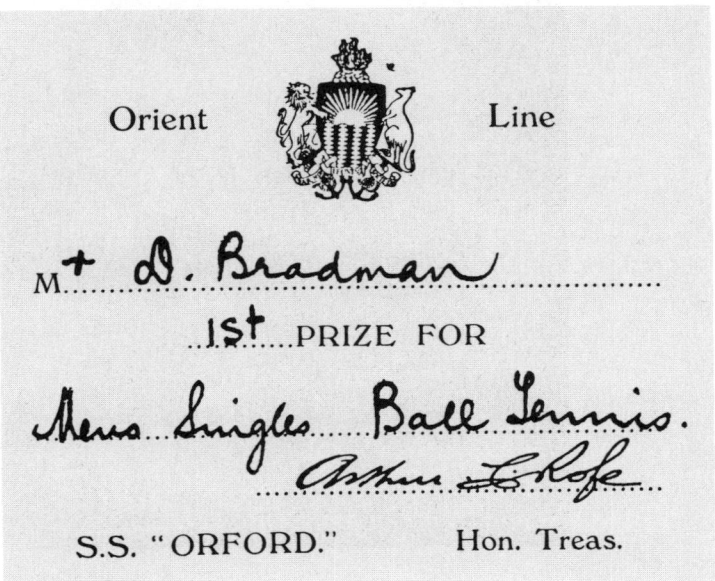

Orient      Line

Mʳ D. Bradman ...........

...1st... PRIZE FOR

Mens Singles Ball Tennis.

Arthur L. Rofe

S.S. "ORFORD."        Hon. Treas.

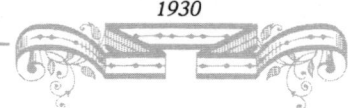

## WEDNESDAY, 2 APRIL

In port at Colombo. Cricket officials came on board and met us. Ashore 9 a.m. in launch. To Millers for a topee each.
By cars to Mt. Lavinia, Galle Face Hotel. Rickshaws, cars honk honk, oxen, policemen, bungalows, squirrel, native quarters, people.
Buddhist temple, shoes off. Orchids and perfumes.
Round promenade, racecourse etc. Fernandez Studios.
Cricket ground. Black and white native dress. Game 11 to 6.
Lost toss. Batted. Made 40. Ponsford batted finely for 62.
Australia 240. Colombo 1 for 50. Rained during adjournment.
Dinner 8.30 p.m. at Galle Face Hotel. The Governor presided. Concluded at 10 p.m. Caught launch 10.30.
Boarded the "Orford" which pulled out at 11 p.m.
Marvellous day. Buildings, foliage, natives etc., an eye opener. Standard of cricket quite high.
100 cents 1 rupee = 1/6. 10d per day good pay.
Lawns, gardens, and coconut palms a fine sight.

## WEDNESDAY, 9 APRIL

Deck games, swimming etc.
Ponsford and McCabe beat my partner and I 6–4 in the quarter-finals of the men's ball tennis and they ultimately won.
Miss Staley and I beat Smith and Mrs. Poulton 6–3 in semifinal of mixed doubles ball tennis.
Passed more ships and land during day.
Calcutta Sweep was closed and auctioned at night realising over £200. Captain's No. 353.
Passed German ship about 11 p.m.

## AUSTRALIA'S TEST TEAM.

ADEN, April 9.
The cricketers to-night showed themselves sticklers for etiquette. Despite an announcement that evening dress would be optional, owing to the intense heat in the Red Sea, only one dined in informal clothing. The players are all fit. Some are losing weight, owing to strenuous exercise in continuous heat. Bradman is half a stone lighter. Grimmett is practising a new googly.

## THURSDAY, 10 APRIL

Cooler weather, strong headwind and a heavy sea.
Miss Staley and I beat Miss Harrison and Alec Hurwood 9–7, 2–6, 6–3 in the final of the mixed doubles ball tennis.
It was a wonderful struggle and we all enjoyed it. Wringing wet at the finish.
Dancing in the evening.

## FRIDAY, 11 APRIL

Quiet restful day.
Saw a wonderful school of dolphins.
Must have been 50 of them quite close to the ship. Very large ones and they sprang out of the water and swam away at an amazing speed.
Gymkhana in the afternoon on deck.
Passed interesting islands during the day.
Presentation of prizes in the evening, had selected a silver butter dish and a travelling clock with my chits.

Mosque, Cinnamon Gardens, Colombo.

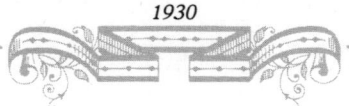

The Pyramids.

## SUCCESSFUL IN SHIP'S SPORTS.
### (By Radio from R.M.S. Orford.)
April 11.

The Australian cricketers figured prominently in the ship's sports, A'Beckett, Bradman, Fairfax, Hurwood, Jackson, McCabe, Ponsford, and Oldfield to-night receiving between them 14 prizes.

---

### SATURDAY, 12 APRIL

*Up at 5.30. Lying in Suez Harbour. Town visible. Bad smell. Doctor's examination 6.30. Ashore in launch at 8.30. Left at 8.50 per special silver train. Lunch on board 10.30. Arrived Cairo 12.50. Irrigation fields fed from waters of Nile. Small irregular patches of clover, lucerne, cotton etc. Water wheels, oxen, donkeys, camels. Small native settlements with mud huts. Wonderful oasis in desert. Terrific babble at Cairo. Per Cook's cars to museum. Saw Tutankhamen's relics etc. To Citadel Mosque. Alabaster throughout, gorgeous chandeliers, windows, view of city. Through amazing dirty hovels in narrow streets among myriads of people to Bazaar. To pyramids and Sphinx. Camels from Mena House to top and back. Afternoon tea Mena House. Shepherd's Hotel for dinner. Magnificent scene at rear. Gardens all lit up with Chinese electric lanterns. Uniformed military band played wonderful music. Dance band played in the ballroom for dancing. Wonderful hotel. Native employees. Bright costumes. Meals peculiar. Wore topees all day. Bright hot sunshine in day but cold night.*

# AUSTRALIA'S TEST TEAM ON THE VOYAGE

*HAVE THEY GONE FOR THE ASHES?—Our crick-eters, with the unmistak-able Australian air of casual amusement, are seen wandering around the ruins of Pompeii.*

**WEDNESDAY, 16 APRIL**

*Breakfast 7.30. Doctor's examination, passport etc. Under Dibbs (Pickford's man) per Fiat to Pompeii, at 10 a.m. Saw small museum. Via gates to city. Inspected it all.*
*Mt. Vesuvius in background 5 miles away. Left at 12.20.*
*Lunch at Hotel Suisse. By cars to Solfatara. Back to Hotel Royale for afternoon tea. Driving around saw the King's Palace, Royal and Fascist police and interesting sights.*
*Left by train at 5.50 for Rome. Wonderful greenery and intense cultivation. Rich soil. Every available inch cultivated. Fruit trees, beans and grape-vines together.*
*Intermittent rain. Sky overcast. Heavy thunderstorms.*
*Arrived Rome 9.20. To Hotel Grand. Great place.*
*First impressions of Rome are of greatness.*

View from the top of St. Peter's, Rome.

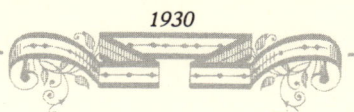

House of the Vettii, Pompeii.

The Church of Trinita Dei Monti, Rome.

Public Bakehouse and Mills, Pompeii.

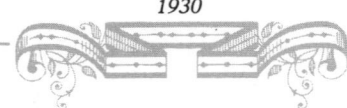

## SUNDAY, 20 APRIL

*Breakfast 8.45. Dull. Mountains obscured by the clouds.*
*10.30 by ferry boat Lucerne to Vitznan over lake — an hour's run. Tram to Rigi-Kulm, another hour's run up the mountain side.*
*The rails merely guide the funicular train — cogs in a rail in the centre do the driving.*
*Snow plow in front. Amazing sight going up through the clouds. Fir trees laden with snow in singles, patches and forest. Gullies, cliffs, snow-drifts. Beautiful Hotel at Rigi. 7,000 feet high.*
*After dinner a snowfight, Australian XI v The Press.*
*Great fun. Then the clouds lifted. Glorious sunny day, blue sky, occasional floating cloud.*
*No pen could describe the grandeur of the scene.*
*Lakes below — enchanting shades of green on the flat with snow capped mountains dotted with fir trees as a background for everything.*
*Coming down was simply too beautiful for words.*
*Back to Hotel via ferry. Maybe it is the finest scenery in the world here in Switzerland.*
*Walking round after dinner saw statue of sleeping lion, carved out of solid rock.*
*Watches, opera glasses and woodwork here.*

## MONDAY, 21 APRIL

*Up at 6 a.m. Caught train 7.25 a.m.*
*Temperature 40°. Fresh and wonderful air. Snow clad mountains guard the town on all sides.*
*Pretty journey to the Border at Basle 9 a.m.*
*Here we had to pass the French Customs Officials.*
*Fine trip through Troyes and rural country. Train breakdown held us up an hour.*
*Paris 5.50 p.m. Elysées Palace Hotel, 12 Rue de Mariguau.*
*Six of us occupied the Prince's Royal Suite.*
*Went to Folies Bergère in the evening, probably the finest vaudeville programme in the world.*

## TUESDAY, 22 APRIL

*Per Char-a-banc on a tour round Paris.*
*Cathedral of Notre Dame. Started in 12th century and took 300 years to build. Similar in style to Milan. Outstanding features are 20 statues of Kings along Church front above entrance door and the beautiful circular coloured windows.*
*To Arc de Triomphe under which is the grave of the unknown soldier. Placed a wreath thereon.*
*With Jack Craig up to top of Eiffel Tower.*
*Fine view of the city. Seine River and the Bois.*
*To Luna Park. Paramount Theatre and dance in Latin Quarter at night. Strange customs.*
*Shows open all night.*

## WEDNESDAY, 23 APRIL

*Bus to Gare-du-Nord. Left station 12.15 for Calais.*
*Arrived Calais 3.30. Passed Customs. Changed money.*
*Arrived Dover 5 p.m. Official welcome by the Mayor and Lord Harris. Train to London. Arrived at Victoria Station 7.35 p.m. Met by huge crowd including Hobbs and Chapman.*
*Driven in fleet of Austin cars to Midland Grand Hotel. St. Pancras.*
*Dinner. Then chat with H. O. Sykes, Mr. Weaver, Mr. and Mrs. Dunning.*
*Sykes gave members of our team a bat, pair of pads, and pair of batting gloves each.*
*Myself 6 bats, 2 pair gloves and a pair of pads.*

The Lucerne Lion, known as the sleeping lion of Lucerne.

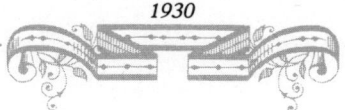

The first tour of England is a great thrill for any young player. The restful boat journey over, new places to visit, the experience of playing on famous grounds, a host of things which at one time were only dreams.

On arrival in London the weather felt like mid-winter but did not dampen the warm welcome and the start of some life long friendships.

The ensuing months were filled with interesting and exciting events. We became the first cricketers to speak to Australia on the wireless telephone — then in its infancy and since outmoded by more modern technology.

Dinners were held in some of London's historic buildings such as the Guildhall and the Merchant Taylors Hall. The opportunity was provided to visit other renowned places whilst there were occasional but very pleasant days for relaxation on scenic golf courses.

Matches were not confined to England. The beauty of Scotland entranced us and we were fascinated by the lovely city of Edinburgh.

All these things were to be savoured to the full knowing they would be followed in due course by the peaceful boat journey home where one could relax and appreciate that the effort for Australia had been worth while.

Many times I reflected on the pleasure it would give me to relate my experiences to family and friends, especially to a loving and self-effacing mother without whom nothing would have been possible.

*Don Bradman*

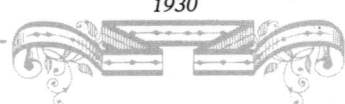

The team on its arrival at Victoria Station, London.

LEFT TO RIGHT   S. J. McCabe, A. Fairfax (behind), D. G. Bradman, P. Hornibrook, T. W. Wall, C. W. Walker, A. F. Kippax, A. P. F. Chapman, A. Hurwood, A. Jackson, T. Howard, Field Marshal Viscount Lord Plumer, W. M. Woodfull, Lord Decies, Mr. W. L. Kelly.

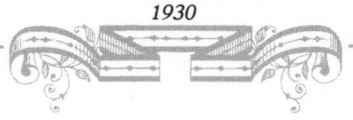

## — SEASON 1930 —

| TITLE | GAME | | SCORES | |
|---|---|---|---|---|
| Second Class | Australia | Scotland | 140 | B. |
| | - | C.C. Conference | 70 | C. |
| First Class | - | Worcestershire | 236 | C. |
| | - | Leicestershire | 185 | n.o. |
| | - | Yorkshire | 78 | C. |
| | - | Lancashire | 9 | B. |
| | - | - | 48 | n.o. |
| | - | M.C.C. | 66 | B. |
| | - | - | 4 | L.B.W. |
| | - | Derbyshire | 44 | C. |
| | - | Surrey | 252 | n.o. |
| | - | Oxford | 32 | B. |
| | - | Hampshire | 191 | C. |
| | - | Middlesex | 35 | B. |
| | - | - | 18 | L.B.W. |
| | - | Cambridge | 32 | C. |
| | - | Surrey | 5 | C. |
| | - | Lancashire | 38 | C. |
| | - | - | 23 | n.o. |
| | - | Yorkshire | 1 | L.B.W. |
| | - | Somerset | 117 | C. |
| | - | Glamorgan | 58 | B. |
| | - | - | 19 | n.o. |
| | - | Northampton | 22 | B. |
| | - | - | 35 | C. |
| | - | Gloucestershire | 42 | C. |
| | - | - | 14 | B. |
| | - | Kent | 18 | L.B.W. |
| | - | - | 205 | n.o. |
| | - | The South of England | 63 | L.B.W. |
| | - | Leveson-Gower's XI | 96 | B. |
| Test | - | England | 8 | B. |
| | - | - | 131 | B. |
| | - | - | 254 | C. |
| | - | - | 1 | C. |
| | - | - | 334 | C. |

| TITLE | GAME | | SCORES | |
|---|---|---|---|---|
| Test | Australia | England | 14 | C. |
| | - | - | 232 | C. |
| | | Total runs | 3170 | |

## — SUMMARY —

### AVERAGES

| | Innings | N.O's. | H.S. | Runs | Average |
|---|---|---|---|---|---|
| Test — | 7 | 0 | 334 | 974 | 139·14 |
| Other First Class | 29 | 6 | 252 x | 1986 | 68·48 |
| All First Class | 36 | 6 | 334 | 2960 | 98·66 |
| Second Class | 2 | 0 | 140 | 210 | 105·00 |
| All Matches | 38 | 6 | 334 | 3170 | 99·09 |

### THURSDAY, 24 APRIL

Dull and drizzly. Stan McCabe in bed ill.

To Stuart Surridges. 2 "Perfect" bats, pair of pads.

Official welcome at Australia House by the High Commissioner (Sir Granville Ryrie), Percy Chapman, "Plum" Warner, Mr. Fenton.

Luncheon at the Savoy Hotel. Welcome by the Duke of Gloucester, Field Marshal Lord Plumer, Lord Decies, Lord Harris and others.

Thence to Lord's for our first practice. Soft slow wickets.

Muggy weather. Sweater, 2 shirts and 2 pairs trousers from Jaeger's. Photo. for them.

4 pairs trousers, 3 pairs pyjamas, 1 dozen pairs socks and 4 shirts from Viyella's. Beautiful presents.

Guests of H. O. Sykes at National Liberal Club for dinner and the evening.

The Australians, some of whom were experiencing English conditions for the first time, practising at Lord's shortly after arrival.

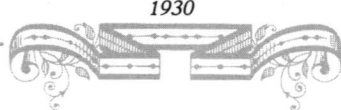

The Long Room, Lord's.

The Ill-fated Sparrow.

Where's the sparrer, Miss? Every schoolboy in England seems to know that in the museum at Lord's he may see, preserved in a glass case, a humble London sparrow who, by the manner of his death, bowled out by Jahangir Khan at Lord's in 1936, achieved immortal fame.

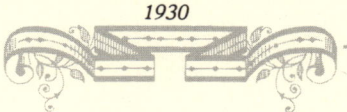

Bradman practising at Lord's prior to the commencement of the first match.
The initial stage of a cover drive.

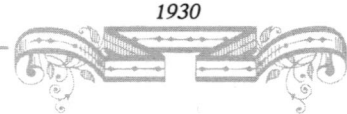

SATURDAY, 26 APRIL

*Practice at Lord's in the morning.*
*Metropolitan Railway to Wembley. Guests of the council for dinner. Welcomed by Sir Charles Clegg.*
*To seats after dinner. Massed bands played, community singing. Sir Philip Snowden. The King and the Duke of York sitting near us.*
*Crowd of nearly 100,000 stood bare-headed and sang God Save the King, accompanied by the bands, then cheered and waved programmes. Great spectacle.*
*Grandstands all around close to playing area. King was introduced to the players and then took his seat in the box 5 yards from us. Huddersfield Town v Arsenal was the big Soccer Cup Final Tie. I left at half time. Train to Kings Cross. Train to Leeds.*
*Arrived Leeds 10.15 p.m. Met by Sykes and home with them.*

WEDNESDAY, 30 APRIL

*To Worcester ground. On the river bank this ground was 10 feet under water a while back.*
*Now beautiful, bright sunny day — cold wind. Wicket slow, easy, fielding ground excellent. Cathedral in background — pretty surroundings. Worcester 131. Grimmett and Fairfax best bowlers.*
*Aust. 1 for 199. Woodfull 95 n.o. Self 75 n.o. Jackson 24. I felt well after getting a start and my new bat was excellent.*
*At night we attended a dinner in the Guildhall given us by the Lord Mayor.*
*Fine speech by "Plum" Warner.*

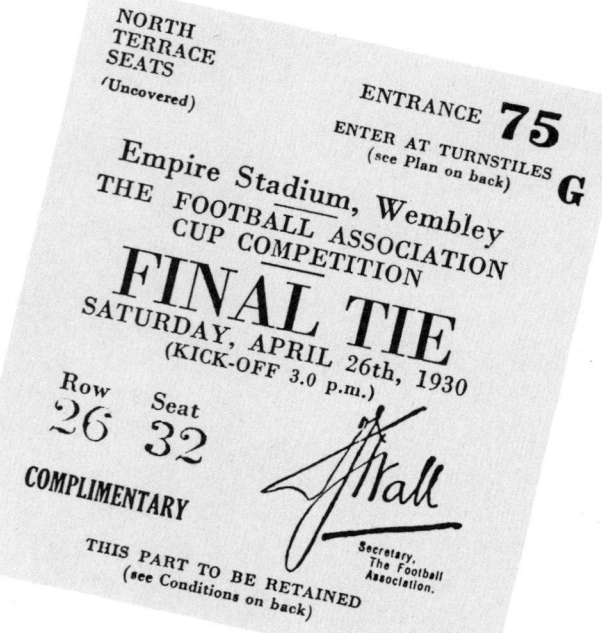

NORTH TERRACE SEATS
(Uncovered)

ENTRANCE 75
ENTER AT TURNSTILES
(see Plan on back)

G

Empire Stadium, Wembley
THE FOOTBALL ASSOCIATION
CUP COMPETITION
FINAL TIE
SATURDAY, APRIL 26th, 1930
(KICK-OFF 3.0 p.m.)

Row 26   Seat 32

COMPLIMENTARY

Secretary,
The Football
Association.

THIS PART TO BE RETAINED
(see Conditions on back)

LONDON. PICCADILLY. CIRCUS.

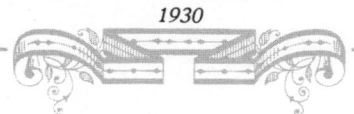

# Australians v Worcestershire

AUSTRALIANS v WORCESTERSHIRE, at Worcester,
30 April, 1 and 2 May 1930.

| Australians | - First Innings | 492 for 8 wickets dec. |
| | - Second Innings | - |
| Worcestershire | - First Innings | 131 |
| | - Second Innings | 196 |

Australians won by an innings and 165 runs.

DON BRADMAN - c. C.F Walters  b. G.W. Brooke    236

Making the most successful début on English wickets of any batsman in history, DON BRADMAN soon showed form as convincing as anything he had done in Australia.    He went in after tea on the first day at 67 for 1, and scored fast enough to reach 50 in an hour, and at the close of play, after one and a half hours' batting, he was 75 not out.    The next morning, he reached his century in a further half-hour, and was 173 by lunch-time, having added 98 in the two hours before lunch.    He completed 200 in four hours ten minutes, and at 236 was well caught at short-leg off a skier.    He was in for four hours thirty-six minutes, and hit twenty-eight fours. Despite the strangeness of the wicket, he displayed his whole range of strokes, his off-driving and cutting being particularly attractive.

Bradman's 236 was the highest score ever made by a batsman on his first appearance on English wickets, and it was the highest score made by a visiting batsman in his first innings of a tour of England.

At 21 years 247 days, Bradman was then the youngest player from overseas to score a double-century in England, and was then the only Australian to make a century in his first matches both in Australia and England.

Woodfull leads his team on to the Worcester ground.

C. V. Grimmett, A. G. Fairfax, W. M. Woodfull, A. A. Jackson, D. G. Bradman, V. Y. Richardson, W. A. Oldfield,
T. W. Wall, S. J. McCabe, P. M. Hornibrook.

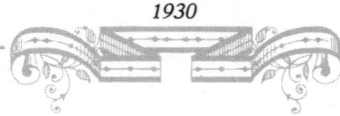

## WORCESTERSHIRE.

| 1st Innings. | | 2nd Innings. | |
|---|---|---|---|
| M. F. S. Jewell, c Fairfax, b Grimmett | 7 | hit wkt., b Hornibrook | 10 |
| Wright, lbw, b Grimmett | 28 | run out | 18 |
| Nichol, run out | 8 | c Hornibrook, b Grimmett | 1 |
| Gibbons, not out | 31 | b Hornibrook | 22 |
| Fox (V.), lbw, b Grimmett | 0 | c Oldfield, b Grimmett | 28 |
| C. F. Walters, st Oldfield, b Grimmett | 21 | c and b Grimmett | 44 |
| Root, st Oldfield, b Fairfax | 9 | b Grimmett | 48 |
| Brooke, b Fairfax | 2 | b Grimmett | 0 |
| Styler, run out | 13 | lbw, b Hornibrook | 1 |
| H. A. Gilbert, b Fairfax | 0 | absent ill | 0 |
| Jackson, lbw, b Fairfax | 0 | not out | 4 |
| Extras | 12 | Extras | 20 |
| Total | 131 | Total | 196 |

## AUSTRALIANS.

| | |
|---|---|
| W. M. Woodfull, b Brooke | 133 |
| A. Jackson, c Walters, b Brooke | 24 |
| D. G. Bradman, c Walters, b Brooke | 236 |
| S. McCabe, c Root, b Brooke | 15 |
| V. Y. Richardson, run out | 24 |
| A. Fairfax, c Root, b Jackson | 0 |
| E. L. a'Beckett, c Gilbert, b Root | 24 |
| W. A. Oldfield, c Jackson, b Root | 4 |
| C. V. Grimmett, not out | 15 |
| T. Wall, not out | 9 |
| Extras | 8 |
| Total (8 wkts. dec.) | 492 |

P. M. Hornibrook did not bat.

## BOWLING.

### WORCESTERSHIRE.—First Innings.

| | O. | M. | R. | W. | | O. | M. | R. | W. |
|---|---|---|---|---|---|---|---|---|---|
| Wall | 8 | 1 | 21 | 0 | Hornibrook | 7 | 1 | 22 | 0 |
| a'Beckett | 6 | 4 | 2 | 0 | Fairfax | 12.3 | 2 | 36 | 4 |
| Grimmett | 24 | 12 | 38 | 4 | | | | | |

### Second Innings.

| | O. | M. | R. | W. | | O. | M. | R. | W. |
|---|---|---|---|---|---|---|---|---|---|
| Wall | 11 | 5 | 22 | 0 | Hornibrook | 17 | 5 | 30 | 3 |
| Fairfax | 21 | 8 | 45 | 0 | a'Beckett | 11 | 3 | 25 | 0 |
| Grimmett | 28.3 | 13 | 46 | 5 | McCabe | 3 | 1 | 8 | 0 |

### AUSTRALIANS.—First Innings.

| | O. | M. | R. | W. | | O. | M. | R. | W. |
|---|---|---|---|---|---|---|---|---|---|
| Root | 43 | 9 | 112 | 2 | Brooke | 36 | 1 | 148 | 4 |
| Jackson | 25 | 1 | 105 | 1 | Wright | 18 | 1 | 68 | 0 |
| Gilbert | 4 | 0 | 30 | 0 | Gibbons | 2 | 0 | 21 | 0 |

Umpires.—Hardstaff and Oates.

Worcester batted first but were soon out to the bowling of Grimmett and Fairfax and their total of 131 was quickly surpassed by the big partnership between Bradman and Woodfull.

The Australian team are in the field with Grimmett bowling.

A shot down the gully eludes Major Jewell at slip.

Bradman and Woodfull going out to resume their innings after the adjournment.

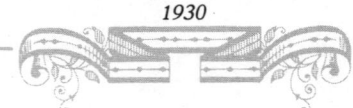

# Record Breaker Bradman Adds Another To His List

## GREAT 236

### CHEERED WILDLY BY CROWD

### VICTORY IN SIGHT

("Sun" Special)

WORCESTER, Thursday.
Don Bradman made cricket history to-day in the match against Worcester. This young record-breaker in his first innings in England astonished the critics by the manner in which he flogged the bowling to every point of the field, and in 280 minutes he rattled up a brilliant 236, the highest score by an Australian against Worcester.

It was a wonderful display, and the crowd cheered and cheered him on his way to the pavilion.

**WORCESTER, Thursday.**
In his first match in England, Don Bradman has covered himself with glory.
Woodfull gained the honor of the first century of the tour, while Bradman played a magnificent innings in compiling 236.

WORCESTER GROUND, Thursday.
Don Bradman, in his first match of the tour, has given England a sample of his brilliant batsmanship.

**Playing against Root, the bowler who last tour played havoc with the Australian Eleven batsmen, the Bowral colt top-scored with 236, after Woodfull had thrown his wicket away for 133. His effort amazed the spectators, and staggered the critics.**

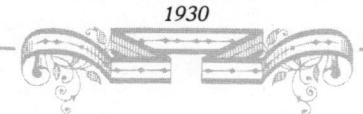

"I'm glad to see it. He's a champion. There's no doubt about that. Bradman has my heartiest congratulations." said Mr. H. H. Massie, the famous hard-hitting batsman of old, when he heard that Don Bradman had eclipsed his own feat of 1882.

THE whole world in sport is singing the praises of Don Bradman, not alone for having broken the long-standing record established by Hugh Hamon Massie, the most brilliant Australian batsman of his time, but for the brilliancy with which he made the runs and delighted the crowds.

**DON BRADMAN AT 21 YEARS**

### THE 1930 FEAT

DON BRADMAN, at the age of 21, eclipsed the 1882 record, making 236 in 4 hours 40 minutes against Worcestershire at Worcester on April 30 and May 1, 1930, hitting twenty-eight 4's and seven 3's.

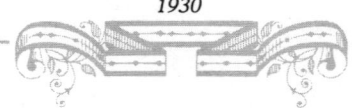

# Australians v Leicestershire

**AUSTRALIANS v LEICESTERSHIRE**, at Leicester, 3 and 5 May 1930.

| | | |
|---|---|---|
| Australians | - First Innings | 365 for 5 wickets |
| | - Second Innings | - |
| Leicestershire | - First Innings | 148 |
| | - Second Innings | - |
| | Drawn. | |
| **DON BRADMAN** | - not out | 185 |

DON BRADMAN went in at the end of the first day at 18 for 1, and after forty minutes' batting was only 9 not out at the close of play. The next morning he batted for two and a quarter hours before reaching 50. After lunch he reached his century, and when rain stopped play at 5.30 p.m., he had batted for five hours seventeen minutes for 185 not out, including sixteen fours.

Bradman thus equalled the performance of W.M. Woodfull in 1926, who made a double-century and a century in his first two innings in England.

### LEICESTERSHIRE.

| | |
|---|---|
| Shipman, c Wall, b Grimmett | 63 |
| Berry, c Ponsford, b Grimmett | 50 |
| Armstrong, st Walker, b Grimmett | 3 |
| Bradshaw, lbw, b Grimmett | 0 |
| Riley, c and b Grimmett | 0 |
| A. T. Sharp, st Walker, b Grimmett | 5 |
| Astill, c McCabe, b Wall | 7 |
| Geary, lbw, b Wall | 6 |
| J. A. de Lisle, not out | 2 |
| Sidwell, st Walker, b Grimmett | 6 |
| Snary, b Wall | 0 |
| Extras | 6 |
| | |
| Total | 148 |

### AUSTRALIANS.

| | |
|---|---|
| W. H. Ponsford, lbw, b Geary | 25 |
| A. Jackson, b Geary | 4 |
| D. G. Bradman, not out | 185 |
| A. F. Kippax, c Sidwell, b Snary | 22 |
| S. McCabe, b Geary | 2 |
| V. Y. Richardson, c Armstrong, b Geary | 100 |
| A. Fairfax, not out | 21 |
| Extras | 6 |
| | |
| Total (for 5 wkts.) | 365 |

C. V. Grimmett, C. W. Walker, A. Hurwood, and T. Wall did not bat.

### BOWLING.

#### LEICESTERSHIRE.—First Innings.

| | O. | M. | R. | W. | | O. | M. | R. | W. |
|---|---|---|---|---|---|---|---|---|---|
| Wall | 16.5 | 1 | 37 | 3 | Grimmett | 25 | 8 | 46 | 7 |
| Hurwood | 12 | 5 | 18 | 0 | McCabe | 4 | 2 | 3 | 0 |
| Fairfax | 16 | 4 | 38 | 0 | | | | | |

In the unfinished innings the Leicester bowling figures were:

| | O. | M. | R. | W. | | O. | M. | R. | W. |
|---|---|---|---|---|---|---|---|---|---|
| Shipman | 22 | 2 | 59 | 0 | Astill | 30 | 2 | 99 | 0 |
| Snary | 29 | 6 | 89 | 1 | Armstrong | 9 | 2 | 27 | 0 |
| Geary | 35 | 9 | 85 | 4 | | | | | |

Umpires.—Bestwick and Buswell.

# Unparalleled Performance by Remarkable Bradman

Bradman, after reaching his 100, commenced to hit out at a terrific pace, a square cut off Geary going to the fence. The third hundred took 55 minutes only and Bradman was now monopolising the scoring. Scenting another double century he went on steadily, declining to "have a fling." Fairfax batted for an hour for a dull 15. Storm clouds were threatening at the tea adjournment and heavy rain fell later, causing 20 minutes' delay. Play was resumed in a cold wind. Bradman went after the runs, pasting the bowlers whom the slippery ball handicapped. Rain drove the players from the field at 5.25 p.m. There was no further play for the day, when the score was five for 365, Bradman being 185 and Kippax 21.

This morning, owing to heavy rain, it was decided to abandon the game. Bradman was thus cheated of his second successive double century. His 185 had taken 320 minutes, and included 16 fours.

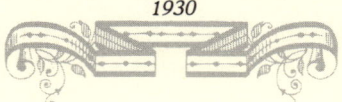

Bradman punishes a loose ball from Astill.
Richardson is backing up.

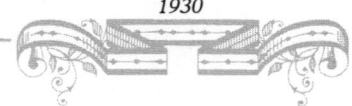

# Australians v Surrey

AUSTRALIANS v SURREY, at the Oval, 24 May 1930.

| Australians | - First Innings | 379 for 5 wickets |
| | - Second Innings | - |
| Surrey | - Did not bat | |
| | Drawn. | |

DON BRADMAN - not out      252

Rain restricted play to the first day of this match.    The light was bad and DON BRADMAN played a superb innings on a soft but easy wicket.    In the hour before lunch he made 28, and after lunch completed 50 in one and a half hours, 100 in two hours twenty-five minutes, and his second century took only another eighty minutes.    When rain stopped play he had scored 252 in four hours fifty minutes, including twenty-nine fours.    He had stands of 116 for the second wicket with W.M. Woodfull, 113 for the third wicket with V.Y. Richardson, and 129 unfinished for the sixth wicket with A.G. Fairfax.

This was the highest score for an Australian or any other Touring team v. Surrey, and it was also the highest score for an Australian or any other Touring team at the Oval.

Played at the Oval, May 24, 26 and 27. Drawn. Score:—

### AUSTRALIANS.

| | |
|---|---|
| W. M. Woodfull, c Shepherd, b Fender | 50 |
| A. Jackson, c Brooks, b Allom | 9 |
| D. G. Bradman, not out | 252 |
| V. Y. Richardson, c Stroud, b Allom | 32 |
| W. H. Ponsford, lbw, b Fender | 1 |
| S. McCabe, c Fender, b Allom | 2 |
| A. Fairfax, not out | 28 |
| Extras | 5 |
| **Total (5 wkts.)** | **379** |

W. A. Oldfield, P. M. Hornibrook, T. Wall, and C. V. Grimmett did not bat.

SURREY.—P. G. H. Fender, M. J. C. Allom, D. R. Jardine, E. G. Stroud, Hobbs, Sandham, Ducat, Shepherd, Gregory, Brooks, and Lock.

### BOWLING.

| | O. | M. | R. | W. | | O. | M. | R. | W. |
|---|---|---|---|---|---|---|---|---|---|
| Allom | 34 | 8 | 74 | 3 | Fender | 21 | 1 | 75 | 2 |
| Lock | 22 | 5 | 73 | 0 | Shepherd | 20 | 5 | 46 | 0 |
| Stroud | 16 | 1 | 66 | 0 | Gregory | 10.4 | 1 | 40 | 0 |

Umpires.—King and Buswell.

BRADMAN'S MASTERY AT SURREY.

This was the match in which the youthful batsman scored 252 not out and earned the highest praise from the English critics for his mastery of the bowling and his delightful freedom of action.

# SUPER BOY

## BRADMAN IN EXCELSIS

### REPLY TO FENDER

*(Special to "The Sun" by Arthur Mailey)*

*Don Bradman signalised his first appearance at Kennington Oval by playing a glorious innings for 252 not out, against Surrey, in a score of 379 for 5 wickets.*

*A feature of the play which distinguished Bradman's great knock was that six other batsmen, five of whom were got out, scored only 122 runs between them, a tribute to the quality of the bowling.*

The Bowral boy, after a rather cautious start, took complete control of the bowling. Although Fender, who

*One of Bradman's many strokes.*

in his book on the M.C.C. tour last year disparaged Don's batting, carefully placed the field to block his hits, the batsman forced openings in all directions. He scored 200 in 225 minutes, his 252 in 290 minutes, gave only one chance—a sharp one when he was 207—and made 156 of his runs in fours. Woodfull batted solidly, and at the end of the day Fairfax was painfully slow.

Bradman needs only 78 to complete his 1000 runs before the end of May, a feat achieved only by four men.

Bradman played magnificent cricket, but tired towards the end of the afternoon. He flogged the bowling to a standstill. Fairfax was painfully slow, and should have helped Brad-man when he was fatigued. He scored only four while Bradman was adding 54 during one period of their partnership. At 6 o'clock he seemed determined to play till stumps were drawn at 6.30, instead of forcing the pace. Bradman, despite his tiredness, courageously endeavored to score quickly, as a big first innings score gives the side a greater chance of victory.

As the batsmen returned to the pavilion the crowd surged on to the ground and mobbed Bradman. Policemen had difficulty in forcing a passage for the young Australian, who was given a great ovation.

### WHAT FENDER SAID

*Bradman was one of the most curious mixtures of good and bad batting I have ever seen. He made shots of the truly magnificent type, but never being able to avoid the really bad ones or the badly made ones . . . If practice, experience and hard work enable him to eradicate faults . . . he may well become a very great player . . . He will always be in the category of the brilliant and unsound ones . . . He does not inspire one with any confidence that he desires to take the only course that will lead him to a fulfilment of that promise*

*He does not correct mistakes or look as if he were trying to do so.*

---

TELEPHONES:—HOP 3707 & 6868

PHILIP & GEORGE GEEN,
Surveyors,
Auctioneers & Estate Agents.

PHILIP GEEN, F.A.I.
GEORGE GEEN, F.A.I.
CHARLES GEEN.
WALTER GEEN, M.A.F.S.I.

YORK HOUSE,
199, WESTMINSTER BRIDGE RD.

LONDON, S.E.I.
(CLOSE TO THE COUNTY HALL)

26/5/30

Dear Mr Bradman —

I have seen W. G. Grace Arthur Shrewsbury, R. Abel & all the big guns, but never have I had the pleasure before of watching such a wonderful innings as yours of Saturday. I beg to thank you & wish you a glorious career.

Yours faithfully
Chas Geen

## THE GUARDS

### TRAMS AND PALACES

*(Special to "The Sun" by Arthur Mailey.)*

LIVERPOOL, Thursday.
While the Australian team was waiting in a sitting room at the North Western Hotel to talk to Australia, Kippax said to Fairfax: "What are you going to say to your mother, Alan?"

Fairfax replied," I'll tell her that I have seen the changing of the guard at Buckingham Palace."

Kippax rejoined: "What on earth is the use of telling her about that? She can see the changing of the guards at the Waverley tram depot any day."

Bradman, who was playing the piano, collapsed over the keyboard.

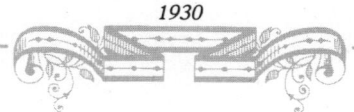

*Monday, 26 May*

*Awakened early. Phone call from Australia came through. I spoke to Mum, Dad, May, Mr. and Mrs. Cush, Mr. and Mrs. Jones. Uncanny feeling. Voices clear but very suggestive of power and distance. The radio phone has only been open for three weeks.*
*Rain. No play today.*
*Into Imperial Advertising Co. Received camera, film, safety razor, pocket knife, wristlet watch.*
*To the Coliseum Theatre in the afternoon with Stan. Round London afterwards.*
*Surrey County C.C. dinner in Skinner's Hall at night. H. D. Levenson-Gower, "Plum" Warner, Lord Chelmsford and others spoke. Beautiful old hall built in 1300 odd.*

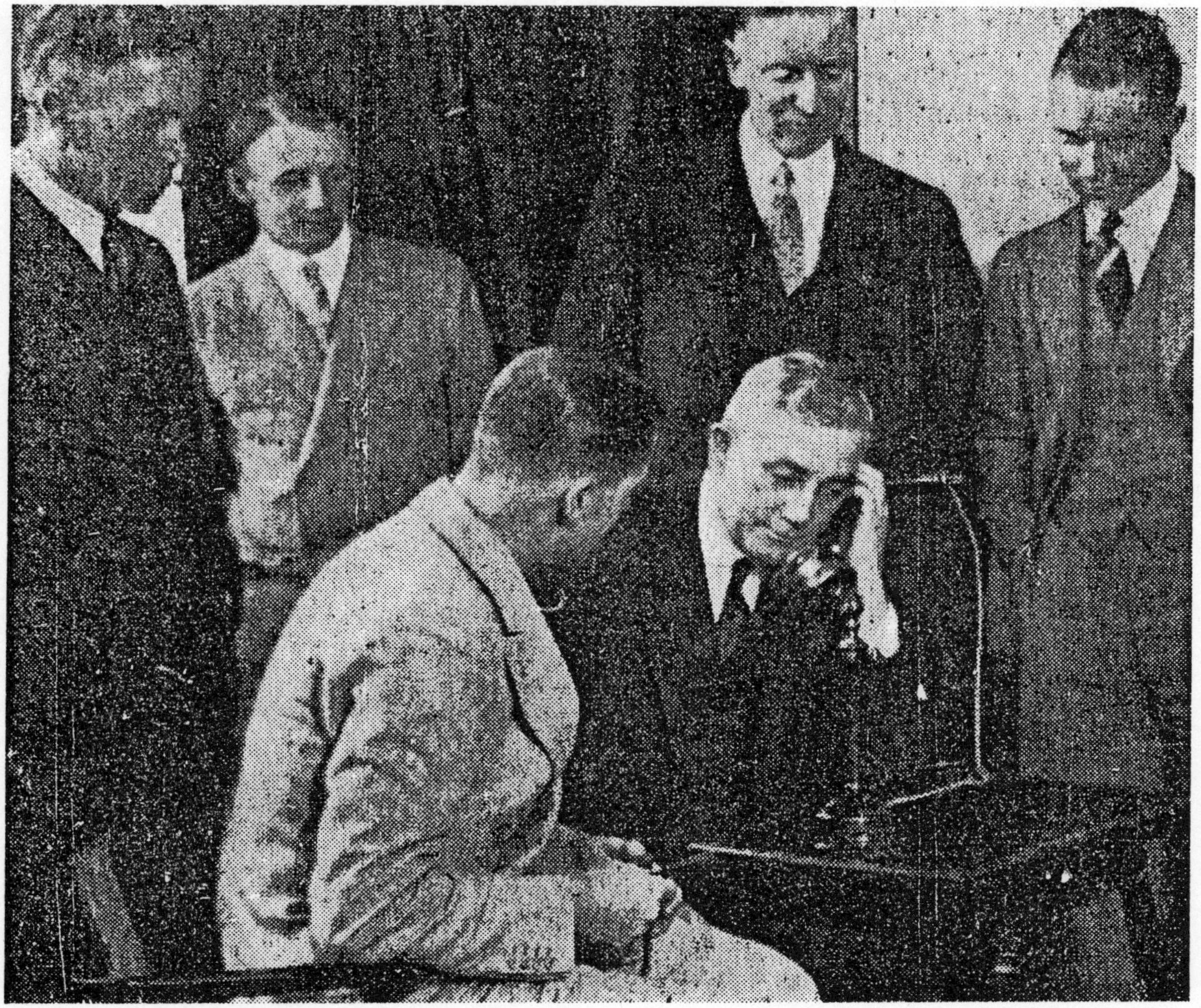

AUSTRALIAN CRICKETERS ENDEAVOURING TO SPEAK TO THEIR RELATIVES AT home by telephone from Liverpool this morning. Left to right (standing): Mr. Mailey, D. G. Bradman, Mr. Kelly and S. McCabe. Seated: A. F. Kippax and Mr. Howard (speaking).

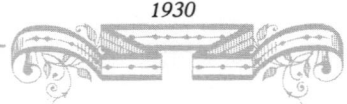

# 'PHONING THE TEST CRICKETERS

**TEST CRICKETERS' RELATIVES AND FRIENDS** spoke to them in England by 'phone yesterday, from the offices of Mr. L. A. W. Pearce, St. James Building. L. to R.: Mrs. Oldfield, Betty Howard, on arm of Mrs. Tom Howard's chair, Mrs. Cush, Mrs. Jones, Mrs. Kippax (seated), Mrs. Pearce, Mr. F. M. Cush (almost obscured by Miss Oldfield), Miss Bradman, Mrs. Bradman (seated), M. A. Noble, Mrs. Jackson, almost hiding E. A. Dwyer, Mrs. Fairfax, Mr. Bradman, R. L. Jones, and, in front, L. A. W. Pearce.

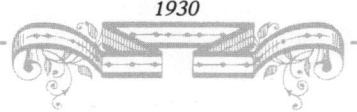

# Australians v Hampshire

AUSTRALIANS v HAMPSHIRE, at Southampton, 31 May and 2 June 1930.

| Australians | - First Innings | 334 |
| | - Second Innings | - |
| Hampshire | - First Innings | 151 |
| | - Second Innings | 175 |

Australians won by an innings and 8 runs.

DON BRADMAN - c. C.P. Mead b. G.S. Boyes 191

DON BRADMAN went in first at 3.30 p.m., and was 28 by tea-time. Rain held up the game, and when play resumed he reached 47, thus completing 1,000 runs before the end of May, and becoming the only Touring batsman ever to complete his 1,000 runs before the end of May. Next morning, he completed his 50, and thereafter continued in his most brilliant form. He reached 100 in a further hour, and was 156 at lunch. When he was out, he had scored 191 in four hours, including a six and twenty-six fours.

Played at Southampton, May 31, June 2 and 3, Australians winning by an innings and 8 runs. Score:—

## HAMPSHIRE.

| 1st Innings. | | 2nd Innings. | |
|---|---|---|---|
| Brown, run out | 56 | c Hornibrook, b Grimmett | 47 |
| A. L. Hosie, c Wall, b Grimmett | 12 | c and b Grimmett | 24 |
| W. G. Lowndes, c Woodfull, b Hornibrook | 5 | c Bradman, b Hornibrook | 1 |
| Mead, c McCabe, b Grimmett | 0 | c Fairfax, b Hornibrook | 0 |
| Newman, c Fairfax, b Grimmett | 10 | b Grimmett | 18 |
| Kennedy, b Grimmett | 5 | c Hornibrook, b Grimmett | 8 |
| Captain T. O. Jameson, c Oldfield, b Grimmett | 27 | b Hornibrook | 19 |
| Lord Tennyson, c Jackson, b Wall | 15 | b Grimmett | 24 |
| Creese, lbw, b Grimmett | 9 | c Bradman, b Grimmett | 10 |
| Boyes, not out | 4 | st Oldfield, b Grimmett | 15 |
| Herman, c Hornibrook, b Grimmett | 3 | not out | 0 |
| Extras | 5 | Extras | 9 |
| Total | 151 | Total | 175 |

## AUSTRALIANS.

| | |
|---|---|
| D. G. Bradman, c Mead, b Boyes | 191 |
| A. Jackson, c Boyes, b Herman | 0 |
| W. H. Ponsford, b Newman | 29 |
| A. F. Kippax, c Kennedy, b Boyes | 20 |
| W. M. Woodfull, st Brown, b Boyes | 4 |
| S. McCabe, b Lowndes | 65 |
| A. Fairfax, c Hosie, b Boyes | 14 |
| W. A. Oldfield, lbw, b Kennedy | 1 |
| C. V. Grimmett, c Brown, b Boyes | 1 |
| T. Wall, lbw, b Boyes | 0 |
| P. M. Hornibrook, not out | 0 |
| Extras | 9 |
| Total | 334 |

## BOWLING.

### HAMPSHIRE.—First Innings.

| | O. | M. | R. | W. | | O. | M. | R. | W. |
|---|---|---|---|---|---|---|---|---|---|
| Wall | 9 | 1 | 36 | 1 | Hornibrook | 18 | 2 | 49 | 1 |
| Fairfax | 7 | 1 | 22 | 0 | Grimmett | 20.4 | 4 | 39 | 7 |

### Second Innings.

| | O. | M. | R. | W. | | O. | M. | R. | W. |
|---|---|---|---|---|---|---|---|---|---|
| Wall | 12 | 1 | 39 | 0 | Grimmett | 29.3 | 5 | 56 | 7 |
| Fairfax | 4 | 0 | 20 | 0 | Hornibrook | 22 | 4 | 51 | 3 |

### AUSTRALIANS.—First Innings.

| | O. | M. | R. | W. | | O. | M. | R. | W. |
|---|---|---|---|---|---|---|---|---|---|
| Kennedy | 30 | 5 | 89 | 1 | Boyes | 26 | 4 | 90 | 6 |
| Herman | 9 | 1 | 47 | 1 | Creese | 2 | 0 | 13 | 0 |
| Newman | 18 | 3 | 80 | 1 | Lowndes | 3 | 0 | 6 | 1 |

Umpires.—Chester and Parry.

The County Ground, Southampton, headquarters of Hampshire.

### SATURDAY, 31 MAY

*Taxi to Southampton ground. Light bad. Rain about. Lord Tennyson, just back from America, Captain of Hampshire, won toss and batted.*

*Big opening partnership until I ran Brown out. Then they collapsed for 152. Clarrie 7 for 39.*

*Woodfull, to give the chance of making 1,000 runs in May, sent me in to open with Archie.*

*Wicket not easy, light bad, bowling good and Archie out for a duck. It was the hardest fight for runs I ever had. 28 n.o. at tea.*

*Rain — 15 minutes late going out. Ponsford clean bowled. I wanted 7 and rain started. Newman sportingly tossed up 2 slows. Two fours made me 47, 1,001 runs at average of 143 and a record.*

*Immediately left the field and play ceased for the day.*

*Dramatic game. Dramatic event.*

*To the Empire Theatre in the evening.*

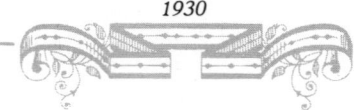

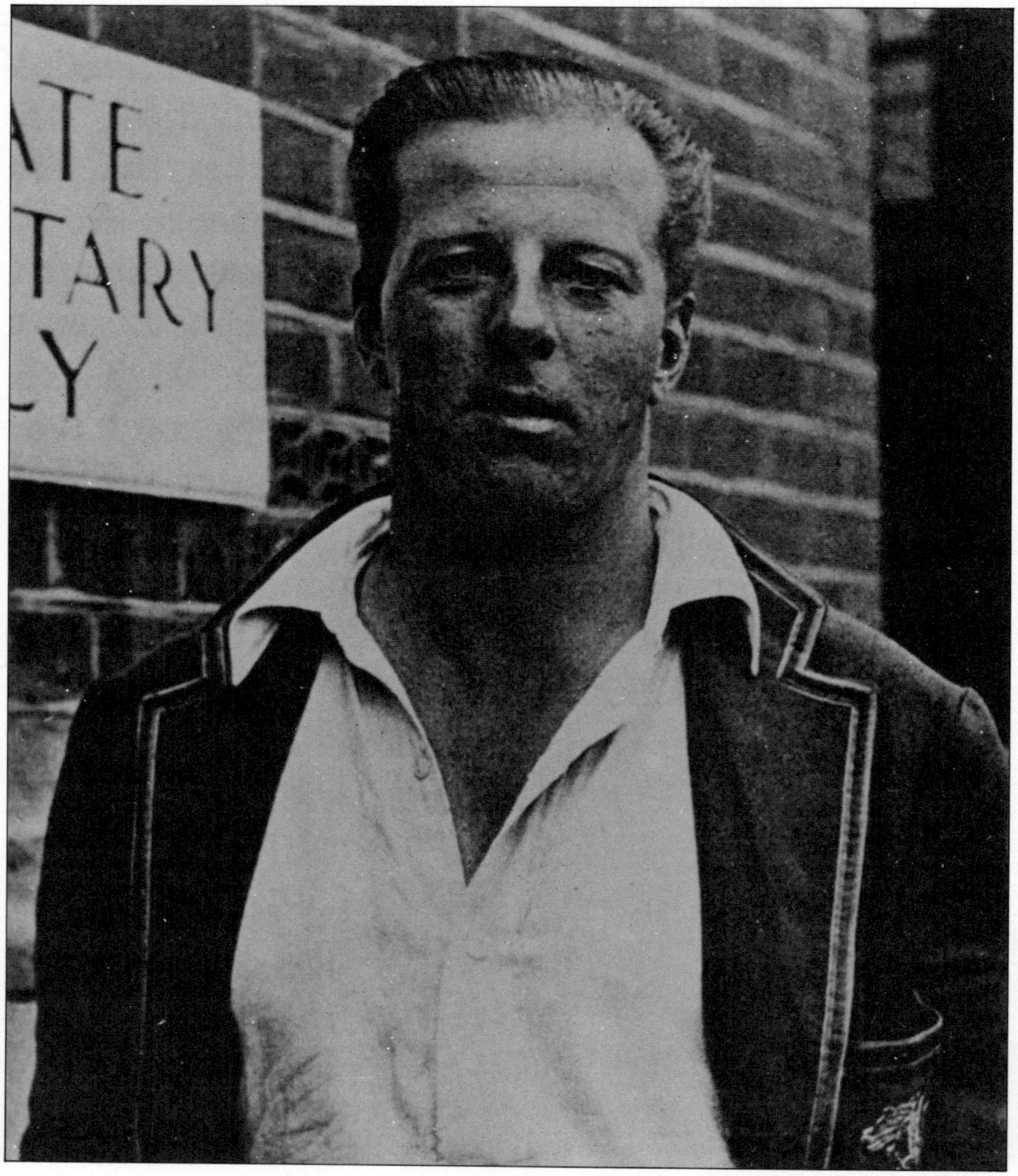

Lord Tennyson, Captain of Hampshire.

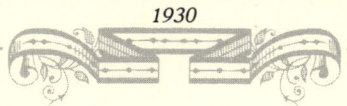

Bradman and Ponsford open Australia's innings in the historic match in which
Bradman completed his 1,000 runs before the end of May.

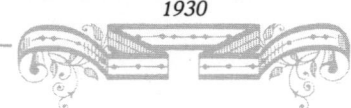
# Bradman Just Reaches His Goal

## RACE AGAINST RAIN FOR 1000 RUNS

## Dramatic Achievement v. Hampshire

### GRIMMETT REAPS ANOTHER HARVEST

The main interest in the first day's play between Australia and Hampshire at Southampton on Saturday centred on Bradman's bid for his 1000 runs by the end of May. The Sydney record-breaker just reached his goal to the accompaniment of a cloudburst, the feeling of the big crowd being so tense that there was hardly a murmur as Bradman crept towards his objective.

Factors which made the feat possible were Grimmett's deadly bowling—he took 7 wickets for 39—and a splendid throw-in by Bradman himself, which dismissed Brown, Hampshire's top scorer, when he was well set.

# DON BRADMAN JOINS THE "IMMORTALS."

**(BY CLARENCE MOODY)**

TO thousands who regard Victor Trumper as one of the most illustrous of cricket immortals, it may seem like sacrilege to mention a present-day player in the same breath, yet already Don Bradman is being compared with him, not only by Australians, but by English authorities.. Likewise, with Charlie Macartney, whose dazzling batting so often recalled Trumper.

We all trust that the time is a long way off when the cricket world will have to express its final verdict of Bradman. He has had only three seasons in Australia in first-class company, and experience of the vagaries of an English season may be expected to further mould his style, so that it is really absurd to compare him now with finished artists.

The lad from Bowral has, however, made wonderful scores, which place him in the highest class of world run-getters. His first month in England has been the most sensational an Australian batsman ever had, and to compare his figures with those for the first season of any of his predecessors would make the latter look puny. Even a comparison with the second seasons in England of Trumper and Macartney for the first 10 matches is overwhelmingly in favor of Bradman. Thus:—

Victor Trumper, 1902 (an exceptionally wet season).—v. London County 9-64, Notts 47, Surrey 101, Essex 9, Leicestershire 20-14, Oxford 121, M.C.C. 105-86, England 18-14, Yorkshire 38-7, Lancashire 70. Total, 723 runs, for 15 innings, average 48.2.

C. G. Macartney, 1912.—v. Notts 84-4, Northants 127, Essex 208, Surrey 123-5, M.C.C. 74-20, Oxford 21, South Africa (Test) 21, Warwickshire 90-27, Middlesex (Australia did not bat), Cambridge 21—804 for 12 innings, average 67.

D. G. Bradman.—v. Worcester 236. Leicestershire 18 n.o., Essex (did not play), Yorkshire 78, Lancashire 9-48 n.o., M.C.C. 66-4, Derbyshire 44, Surrey 252 n.o., Oxford 32, Hampshire 191—1145 runs for 11 innings, 3 n.o., average 143.12.

#### FIGURES NOT EVERYTHING

Those figures extol Bradman as a super rungetter, even if we take into account that the 1902 and 1912 opponents were of higher grade than those of 1930, but there are reasons quite apart from mere figures why Trumper and Macartney were ranked among the elect, why they argue in England whether Victor was a greater batsman than W. G. Grace or Ranji.

A batsman may compile huge scores so frequently that he becomes a match-winning factor, but the sign manual of true greatness is ability to so punish superior bowling that the bowler loses command of length, and becomes easy meat for the less gifted batsmen.

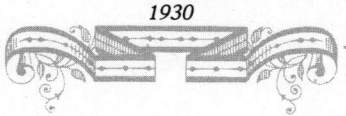

June 1. 1930.

LAXMAN 6505.

15, TEDWORTH SQUARE,
CHELSEA.

Dear Bradman.

A line to Congratulate you most sincerely on your very great batting which has brought you 1,000 runs before the end of May — a wonderful feat, & more wonderful than ever in your case because you have accomplished it in fewer innings than Grace, or Hayward or Hallows. I hope you will go on & prosper, for your batting, & I may add your fielding, have given the greatest possible delight to everyone.

Once more my best wishes & Congratulations.

Yours sincerely,

P. F. Warner.

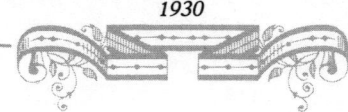

TELEGRAMS,
LORD'S GROUND LONDON.
TELEPHONE Nº:
PADDINGTON 0144 (PAVILION.)
PADDINGTON 5884 (PAVILION.)
PADDINGTON 3131 (TENNIS COURT.)
PADDINGTON 4675 (HOTEL.)

June. 3ʳᵈ 1930

## Lord's Cricket Ground,
### London, N.W. 8.

My dear Bradman. May I add
my congratulations to the very
many you have. and will
receive. on your notable
and magnificent performance
of your '1000.' Runs.
You have. well deserved.
this record which will
place you. amongst. the.
greatest. of cricketers. for.
all. times

Jf McCrae

H.D. Stevenson Evans

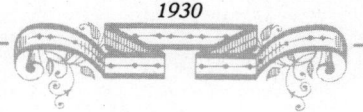

# Australia v England
## First Test Match

**A**lthough I scored a century in the first Test at Nottingham, Australia lost the game. We reversed the position in the second Test at Lord's where my innings of 254 was, in my opinion, the most technically perfect of my career.

The game was memorable because in it, Ranji's nephew Duleepsinhji scored a "never to be forgotten" 173.

I had the pleasure of chasing every run and catching him out.

*Don Bradman*

---

AUSTRALIA v ENGLAND, First Test Match, at Nottingham, 13, 14, 16 and 17 June 1930.

| Australia | - First Innings | 144 |
|---|---|---|
| | - Second Innings | 335 |
| England | - First Innings | 270 |
| | - Second Innings | 302 |
| | Australia lost by 93 runs. | |

| DON BRADMAN | - b. M.W. Tate | 8 |
|---|---|---|
| | b. R.W.V. Robins | 131 |

In the first innings DON BRADMAN went in at 6 for 2. The pitch was very nasty after heavy rain overnight and Bradman was bowled a quarter of an hour later for 8.

His second innings was much better. Going in at 12 for 1 at the end of the third day, Bradman batted for thirty-five minutes and was 31 not out at the close of play. The next day he almost succeeded in winning the match for Australia. He reached his century after batting for three hours thirty-five minutes, and was out at 131 after batting for four hours twenty minutes; he hit ten fours.

He was the first Australian to score a century in a Test Match at Nottingham.

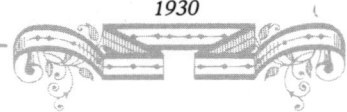

## ENGLAND

| First Innings | | Second Innings | |
|---|---|---|---|
| J. B. HOBBS, c Richardson, b McCabe | 78 | st Oldfield, b Grimmett | 74 |
| H. SUTCLIFFE, c Hornibrook, b Fairfax | 29 | retired hurt | 58 |
| W. R. HAMMOND, lbw, b Grimmett | 8 | lbw, b Grimmett | 4 |
| F. E. WOOLLEY, st Oldfield, b Grimmett | 0 | b Wall | 5 |
| E. P. HENDREN, b Grimmett | 5 | c Richardson, b Wall | 72 |
| A. P. F. CHAPMAN, c Ponsford, b Hornibrook | 52 | b Wall | 29 |
| H. LARWOOD, b Grimmett | 18 | b Grimmett | 7 |
| R. W. V. ROBINS, not out | 50 | b McCabe | 4 |
| M. W. TATE, b Grimmett | 13 | c Kippax, b Grimmett | 24 |
| R. TYLDESLEY, c Fairfax, b Wall | 1 | b Grimmett | 5 |
| W. DUCKWORTH, lbw, b Fairfax | 4 | not out | 14 |
| Byes 4, leg-byes 7, no-ball 1 | 12 | Byes 5, leg-byes 1 | 6 |
| Total | 270 | | 302 |

Fall: 53, 63, 63, 71, 153, 188, 218 241, 242, 270.

125, 137, 147, 211, 250, 260, 283, 302, 302.

### BOWLING

| | O. | M. | R. | W. | O. | M. | R. | W. |
|---|---|---|---|---|---|---|---|---|
| Wall | 17 | 4 | 47 | 1 | 26 | 4 | 67 | 3 |
| Fairfax | 21.4 | 5 | 51 | 2 | 15 | 4 | 58 | 0 |
| Grimmett | 32 | 6 | 107 | 5 | 30 | 4 | 91 | 5 |
| Hornibrook | 12 | 3 | 30 | 1 | 11 | 4 | 35 | 0 |
| McCabe | 7 | 3 | 23 | 1 | 14 | 3 | 42 | 1 |

Fairfax a no-ball.

## AUSTRALIA

| First Innings | | Second Innings | |
|---|---|---|---|
| W. M. WOODFULL, c Chapman, b Tate | 2 | c Chapman, b Larwood | 4 |
| W. H. PONSFORD, b Tate | 3 | b Tate | 39 |
| A. FAIRFAX, c Hobbs, b Robins | 14 | c Robins, b Tate | 14 |
| D. G. BRADMAN, b Tate | 8 | b Robins | 131 |
| A. F. KIPPAX, not out | 64 | c Hammond, b Robins | 23 |
| S. J. McCABE, c Hammond, b Robins | 4 | c Cropley (sub.), b Tate | 49 |
| V. Y. RICHARDSON, b Tyldesley | 37 | lbw, b Tyldesley | 29 |
| W. A. OLDFIELD, c Duckworth, b Robins | 4 | c Hammond, b Tyldesley | 11 |
| C. V. GRIMMETT, st Duckworth, b Robins | 0 | c Hammond, b Tyldesley | 0 |
| P. M. HORNIBROOK, lbw, b Larwood | 0 | st Duckworth, b Robins | 5 |
| T. WALL, b Tyldesley | 0 | not out | 8 |
| Byes 4, leg-byes 4 | 8 | | 22 |
| Total | 144 | | 335 |

Fall: 4, 6, 16, 57, 61, 105, 134 140, 144, 144.

12, 93, 152, 229, 296, 316, 316, 322, 324, 335.

### BOWLING

| | O. | M. | R. | W. | O. | M. | R. | W. |
|---|---|---|---|---|---|---|---|---|
| Larwood | 15 | 8 | 12 | 1 | 5 | 1 | 9 | 1 |
| Tate | 19 | 8 | 20 | 3 | – | – | – | 3 |
| Tyldesley | 21 | 8 | 53 | 2 | – | – | – | 3 |
| Robins | 17 | 4 | 51 | 4 | – | – | – | 3 |

After winning the toss, England batted first and were all out for 270 in 4¼ hours.

Woodfull and Ponsford opened Australia's innings.   In less than an hour, Woodfull, Ponsford and Bradman were out for 16.

Tate bowled Ponsford for 3 and Bradman for 8.

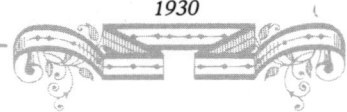

Trent Bridge Ground.

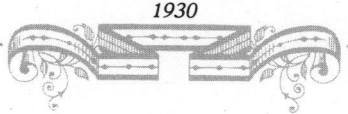
In the first innings, after Ponsford, Woodfull and Bradman were out for only 16, Kippax gave a great display of masterly cricket under very difficult conditions, making 64 not out.

A. F. Kippax.

Maurice Tate.

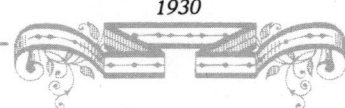

England led on the first innings by 126 runs and, scoring 302 in the second, left Australia 429 to get for victory.

She managed only 335.

# AUSTRALIA BEATEN.

## By Margin of 93 Runs.

## BRADMAN MAKES RECORD SCORE.

## *KELLEWAY "DIPS LID" TO BRADMAN*

### ⚡ By C. E. KELLEWAY. ⚡

DAME Fortune changed her face and this time it was England who suffered instead of Australia.

Sutcliffe was unable to continue his innings and as if that was not bad enough Larwood was unable to bowl owing to illness. The absence of the Notts express bowler might easily place England in a serious position if the wicket remains good.

Larwood provides the shock tactics for Chapman, who rarely bowls him for long periods Tate provides the marathon efforts, while every effort is made to move the batsmen from the other end, using every wile Chapman can think of.

However, Australia began to lose possession of the game when Ponsford left before establishing the position. Kippax, too, was dismissed before getting into his stride, the English bowlers fighting like demons to overcome the bad luck brought about by the absence of their leading bowler.

Even on this last day the match is providing thrills in plenty for the onlookers, whose enthusiasm was dampened by the bad news that greeted them as Chapman led his depleted team on the field.

S. J. McCabe

Optimism pervaded the Australians' dressing room at Nottingham before play commenced.

When Ponsford and Bradman arrived they told Kippax not to change his clothes.

But, unfortunately, Kippax was needed sooner than members of the team had hoped.

The experience of Copley, a second eleven Notts professional who found himself thrust unexpectedly from obscurity into a test game, is a unique one, and a milestone in his cricket career. Some are born to greatness, others, like Copley, have it thrust upon them.

It is not hard to imagine how tense the feelings of the crowd were as the fall of each wicket was eagerly prayed for, while all sorts of plans flashed through their minds, only to be squashed before they gained utterance.

McCabe and Bradman carried on regardless of the tense feelings of the onlookers, and, despite the many bowling changes and deft moves of the various fieldsmen.

### IT'S UP TO DON.

Don carried the responsibility thrust upon his young shoulders like a veteran used to many campaigns.

A fighting spirit is admired by all, and the only solace afforded England was that given by the thought of the long road to hoe before Australia could win

Before now I have used the expression "opportunist," when referring to McCabe. It was expressive of the way he forced his way first into the team to tour England, and when there to earn his place in this match.

Now he appears in a fresh light, and this time opportunity has given him the chance to demonstrate that he possesses the real fighting spirit tradition has given to all the greatest of Australian cricketers whether as batsmen, bowlers, or fieldsmen.

The virile young manhood of Australia has justified itself again, this time on the cricket field, and, whatever the ultimate result of the Tests, everyone must admire their entry into the most severe test of their lives when they severely twitched the lion's tail.

### ATTENTION MR. LYON!

Well, Mr. Lyon, how do you relish the reply courteous to your scathing and uncalled for criticism? How did the boy walk out yesterday?

Bradman once again gave the "lie direct" to his detractor, giving a display ranking among those great efforts that make Australian teams feared more when desperately striving for victory, than when merely pushing along in festive spirit.

By this display Don has entered the select few who have made a century in their first Test match in England.

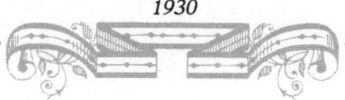

Bradman bowled by Robins for 131.

# Brilliant Don Bradman First Test Match

## BRADMAN HELD THE FORT

### Disturbances in the Homes

MANY previously happy homes were nearly wrecked in the early hours by: (1) enthusiastic husbands who kept unenthusiastic wives awake, cheering as they listened-in to the cricket scores; (2) unenthusiastic husbands similarly disturbed by enthusiastic wives; unenthusiastic parents dragged out of bed to make little Willie switch off the radio.

One man of my acquaintance shouted to his wife, some time about 1 a.m.: "If you don't stop that durn radio I'll sue for divorce and name your hero, Bradman, as the primary cause of cruelty and neglect!"

### Indomitable Don

Don Bradman, whose score of 131 was the highest of the match.

## ASHES UNSAFE

### Bradman's "Iron Nerves"

(Published in the "Daily Mail")

LONDON, Tuesday.

"None can say, after Nottingham, that the Ashes are safe," says the "Daily Mail," in a leading article. "It should be remembered that the Australians, in an uphill battle, made a record score in the fourth innings of a Test in England. The youthful Bradman showed nerves of iron and the poise of a veteran. Cricketers will be proud of England's success and still prouder to think that it was accomplished against foemen such as these."

THURSDAY, 19 JUNE

By tube to the Oval. Wicket wet and Clarrie took 4 for 2 off 7 overs. Self 5. Woodfull a good century.

To the Royal Albert Hall at night to see Harold Williams in "Hiawatha". Over 900 performers on the stage. Magnificent spectacle, fine music.

Beautiful hall. Like the old Roman Coliseum in shape. Tiers of boxes which are let annually. We had the Royal Suite.

Met Harold, Dr. Sargent, orchestral conductor, and Indian Chief at interval.

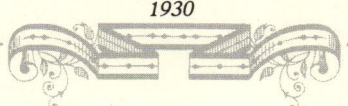
"Hiawatha."

Harold Williams

Royal Albert Ho

19 June 19

Harold Williams shakes hands with Bradman.

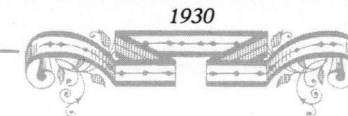

*WEDNESDAY, 25 JUNE*

*Up early and went by bus to "H. M. Voice" factory at Hayes. Shown all over. Best organised and equipped place I've yet seen.*
*Cup of tea and few words from Manager who gave our Captain a portable gramophone.*
*Next to Grosvenor House, Park Lane, where the Dowager Countess of Darnley gave us a dinner.*
*Her husband was the late Hon. Ivo. Bligh.*
*Very distinguished gathering including — Stanley Bruce, Madame Melba, many Lords etc.*
*I sat alongside Colonel Bishop V.C., said to be the greatest aviator in the World War.*
*Dinner finished at 3 p.m. Thence to West Kent golf course — played in the rain.*
*Kahane and McGloin gave us a very enjoyable party and dance evening at their home.*

# OUR LIONS IN LONDON ALL
## THE RAGE

### Luncheon to Team — "Ashes" on the Table — Cricket Menu—Notable People at Famous Gathering

Although it is many moons since Margaret Baxter lived in Sydney, she is still keenly interested in the doings of Australians, and, of course, is following the movements of our Test cricketers with the greatest enthusiasm.

*Writing by a recent mail, she tells of the luncheon given in honor of the team, at which the Dowager Countess of Darnley and the committee of the International Sportsmen's Club were "hosts."*

THE special thrill was the "Ashes," contained in a rather impressive-looking urn, mounted on a small pedestal, that stood before the Countess of Darnley's place at the table.

Everybody told you "Who was who"—in many cases merely mistaken identity, except Woodfull and Bradman, whose photographs are so prominent in the English papers that everyone in England must recognise them.

### The Menu

THE menu which, of course, was bristling with "cricket," read:—

*Melon Freppe Woodfull.*
*Truite Saumonee a la Chapman.*
*Supreme de Volataille a la Test.*
*Pomme Noisette de Lord's*
*Salad Australian.*
*Aspereges International aux deus.*

*Peche et Fraise Melba.*
*Delicatesses Dame Darnley.*
*Cafe Wallaby.*

### At the Party

MANY whose names are of great interest to Australia were among those present.

Dame Nellie Melba chatted animatedly to everyone. Lord Richard Neville, Mr. and Mrs. Stanley Bruce, Mrs. Lindsay, who is very interested in Melbourne. You will remember that she is a daughter of the late Sir William and Lady Clarke.

Mrs. Lindsay's daughter sat next to Don Bradman, and was the centre of attraction. Lord and Lady Stradbroke were there, too.

The speeches, which were short, were flavored with cricket terms, and the gathering was a jolly one.

Archie Jackson with some of the hostesses.

Jim Bancks (of Ginger Meggs fame) second from left, Arthur Mailey in plus fours,
Kippax with umbrella, and Bradman.

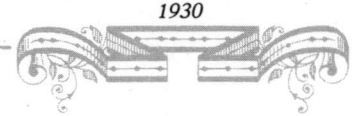
THURSDAY, 26 JUNE

With Clarrie to Paddington Recreation Ground re moving
pictures. To the House of Commons and House of Lords.
Shown over. Had dinner there with the Minister of War,
Attorney General, Trevor Wignall and Oldfield.
Driven to Wimbledon. During the afternoon I saw Andrews
and Kingsley v Hughes and Lee; Hillyard, Von Kehrling,
Tilden, Perry, Aussem, Heeley, Hopman, Willard, Crawford,
Moon, Allison, Van Ryn, Cochet, Brugnon, Miss Ryan and
Helen Wills.
Tilden and Helen Wills played magnificently.
Centre court a wonderful sight. 14,000 people.
No. 1 also good. Others no accommodation.
Met Willard of Australian Davis Cup team there.
St. Pancras for dinner.
Into His Majesty's Theatre. Saw "Bitter Sweet"; fine light
operatic show.

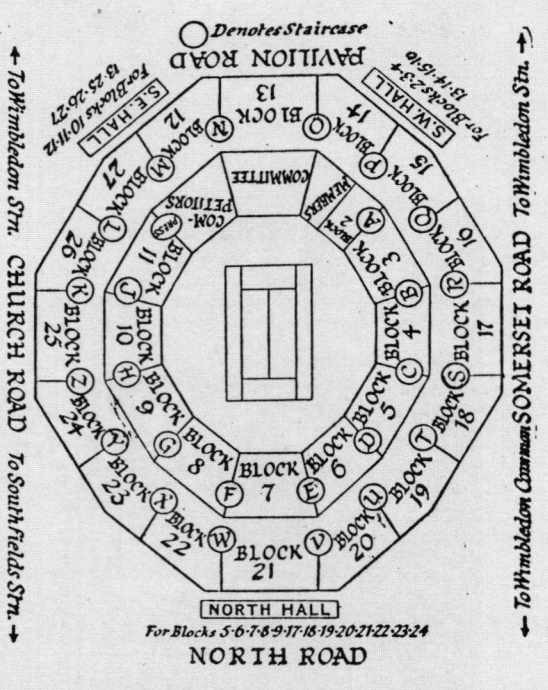

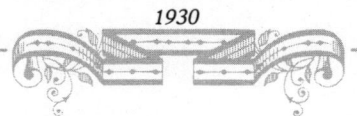

# Australia v England
# Second Test Match

AUSTRALIA v ENGLAND, Second Test Match, at Lord's, 27, 28, 30 June, 1 July 1930.

| | | |
|---|---|---|
| Australia | - First Innings | 729 for 6 wickets dec. |
| | - Second Innings | 72 for 3 wickets |
| England | - First Innings | 425 |
| | - Second Innings | 375 |

Australia won by 7 wickets.

| | | |
|---|---|---|
| DON BRADMAN | - c. A.P.F. Chapman b. J.C. White | 254 |
| | c. A.P.F. Chapman b. M.W. Tate | 1 |

DON BRADMAN considers his first innings of 254 to be the most perfect he ever played. He went in on the second day, and took forty-five minutes to reach 50. He was 54 at the tea adjournment, and went on to complete his century in one and three-quarter hours. At the close, Bradman was 155 not out, after batting for only two and three-quarter hours. On Monday morning, he was 231 at lunch and was caught at extra-cover after a superb innings which lasted five hours twenty minutes; he hit twenty-five fours.

On the fourth day, Bradman went in at 16 for 1, survived only 2 balls, before he was caught in the gully, with the score 17 for 2.

Bradman's score of 254 was the highest score ever made at Lord's, and the highest score ever made in a Test Match in England. He was the youngest batsman also to score a double-century in a Test Match for Australia. Having made 385 in two consecutive innings, he created a record for Australia.

Played at Lord's, June 28, 30, July 1 and 2, Australia winning by seven wickets. Score:—

### ENGLAND.—First Innings.

| | |
|---|---|
| Hobbs, c Oldfield, b Fairfax | 1 |
| Woolley (F. E.), c Wall, b Fairfax | 41 |
| Hammond, b Grimmett | 38 |
| K. S. Duleepsinhji, c Bradman, b Grimmett | 173 |
| Hendren, c McCabe, b Fairfax | 48 |
| A. P. F. Chapman, c Oldfield, b Wall | 11 |
| G. O. Allen, b Fairfax | 3 |
| Tate, c McCabe, b Wall | 54 |
| R. W. V. Robins, c Oldfield, b Hornibrook | 5 |
| J. C. White, not out | 23 |
| Duckworth, c Oldfield, b Wall | 18 |
| Byes, 2; l.-b., 7; n.b., 1 | 10 |
| **Total** | **425** |

### Second Innings.

| | |
|---|---|
| Hobbs, b Grimmett | 19 |
| Woolley (F. E.), hit wkt., b Grimmett | 28 |
| Hammond, c Fairfax, b Grimmett | 32 |
| K. S. Duleepsinhji, c Oldfield, b Hornibrook | 48 |
| Hendren, c Richardson, b Grimmett | 9 |
| A. P. F. Chapman, c Oldfield, b Fairfax | 121 |
| G. O. Allen, lbw, b Grimmett | 57 |
| Tate, c Ponsford, b Grimmett | 10 |
| R. W. V. Robins, not out | 11 |
| J. C. White, run out | 10 |
| Duckworth, lbw, b Fairfax | 0 |
| Byes, 16; l.-b., 13; w., 1 | 30 |
| **Total** | **375** |

### AUSTRALIA.—First Innings.

| | |
|---|---|
| W. M. Woodfull, st Duckworth, b Robins | 155 |
| W. H. Ponsford, c Hammond, b White | 81 |
| D. G. Bradman, c Chapman, b White | 254 |
| A. F. Kippax, b White | 83 |
| S. McCabe, c Woolley, b Hammond | 44 |
| V. Y. Richardson, c Hobbs, b Tate | 30 |
| W. A. Oldfield, not out | 43 |
| A. Fairfax, not out | 20 |
| Byes, 6; l.-b., 8; w., 5 | 19 |
| **Total (6 wkts. dec.)** | **729** |

C. V. Grimmett, P. M. Hornibrook, and T. Wall did not bat.

### Second Innings.

| | |
|---|---|
| W. M. Woodfull, not out | 26 |
| W. H. Ponsford, b Robins | 14 |
| D. G. Bradman, c Chapman, b Tate | 1 |
| A. F. Kippax, c Duckworth, b Robins | 3 |
| S. McCabe, not out | 25 |
| Byes, 1; l.-b., 2 | 3 |
| **Total (3 wkts.)** | **72** |

### BOWLING.

#### ENGLAND.—First Innings.

| | O. | M. | R. | W. | | O. | M. | R. | W. |
|---|---|---|---|---|---|---|---|---|---|
| Wall | 29.4 | 2 | 118 | 3 | Hornibrook | 26 | 6 | 62 | 1 |
| Fairfax | 31 | 6 | 101 | 4 | McCabe | 9 | 1 | 29 | 0 |
| Grimmett | 33 | 4 | 105 | 2 | | | | | |

#### Second Innings.

| | O. | M. | R. | W. | | O. | M. | R. | W. |
|---|---|---|---|---|---|---|---|---|---|
| Wall | 25 | 2 | 80 | 0 | Hornibrook | 22 | 6 | 49 | 1 |
| Fairfax | 12.4 | 2 | 37 | 2 | Bradman | 1 | 0 | 1 | 0 |
| Grimmett | 53 | 13 | 167 | 3 | McCabe | 3 | 1 | 11 | 0 |

#### AUSTRALIA.—First Innings.

| | O. | M. | R. | W. | | O. | M. | R. | W. |
|---|---|---|---|---|---|---|---|---|---|
| Allen | 34 | 7 | 115 | 0 | Robins | 42 | 1 | 172 | 1 |
| Tate | 64 | 16 | 148 | 1 | Hammond | 35 | 8 | 82 | 1 |
| White | 51 | 7 | 158 | 3 | Woolley | 6 | 0 | 35 | 0 |

#### Second Innings.

| | O. | M. | R. | W. | | O. | M. | R. | W. |
|---|---|---|---|---|---|---|---|---|---|
| Tate | 13 | 6 | 21 | 1 | Robins | 9 | 1 | 34 | 2 |
| Hammond | 4.2 | 1 | 6 | 0 | White | 2 | 0 | 8 | 0 |

### FALL OF THE WICKETS.

#### ENGLAND.—First Innings.

| 1 | 2 | 3 | 4 | 5 | 6 | 7 | 8 | 9 | 10 |
|---|---|---|---|---|---|---|---|---|---|
| 13 | 53 | 105 | 209 | 236 | 239 | 337 | 363 | 387 | 425 |

#### AUSTRALIA.—First Innings.

| 1 | 2 | 3 | 4 | 5 | 6 |
|---|---|---|---|---|---|
| 162 | 393 | 585 | 588 | 643 | 672 |

#### ENGLAND.—Second Innings.

| 1 | 2 | 3 | 4 | 5 | 6 | 7 | 8 | 9 | 10 |
|---|---|---|---|---|---|---|---|---|---|
| 45 | 58 | 129 | 141 | 147 | 272 | 329 | 354 | 372 | 375 |

#### AUSTRALIA.—Second Innings.

| 1 | 2 | 3 |
|---|---|---|
| 16 | 17 | 22 |

Umpires.—Chester and Oates.

K. S. Duleepsinhji.

Duleepsinhji back cuts a ball out of reach of Hornibrook whilst Oldfield looks on.

# TWO IDOLS

## BRADMAN --- DULEEP.

### FLAXEN HAIR

**(From Our Special Representative)**

**LONDON, Saturday.**

THERE are two idols in this Test match—Don Bradman and K. S. Duleepsinhji, and, following on the latter's great display yesterday, everyone is eagerly awaiting the youthful Australian's appearance at the wickets to-day.

The English crowd has taken to Bradman as a gallery of flappers take to a cinema idol, and nothing appealed so much to their imagination as this youth with uncovered flaxen hair, tearing around the boundary yesterday, fielding ball after ball magnificently.

Time and again the ground literally shook with applause as he flashed along, dipped and, picking the ball up one-handed, returned it to the wicketkeeper unerringly.

It was glorious seeing that brilliant youth dashing everywhere, and the one hope to-day was that he would get going at the batting crease. A big score from Bradman would be as popular as "Duleep.'s."

His Majesty the King shaking hands with the Australian players.

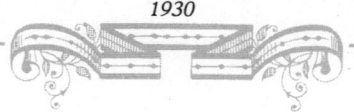

On the second day England were all out for 425 runs.
After Woodfull and Ponsford had worn down the English bowling in an opening stand of 162,
Bradman went in at 3.30 p.m.

Ponsford scores past Chapman in the gully off a ball from Tate.

Bradman cuts one too wide for Chapman to reach.
Duckworth (wicket-keeper) and Allen watch the ball go.

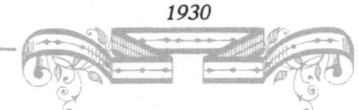

# HOW DON BRADMAN GAVE AUSTRALIA HER CHANCE

### Brilliant Hitting at the Right Time Turns the Tide Against England—Bowlers Fail

BOY BRADMAN at the wicket yesterday, when he added to Australia's impressive position by scoring 155 not out. His run-a-minute scoring was applauded by the great crowd.

### BRADMAN'S BRILLIANCE

To do justice to D. Bradman's batting it is necessary to use the language of superlatives and compare it with the acting of Miss Marie Tempest. Both are so exquisitely right in the general design and in the polished execution of every detail. Bradman on Saturday was as audacious as Macartney in the second innings of the Lord's Test Match of 1926. His cutting was as safe and brilliant as that of Duleepsinhji on the previous day. He played the ball on the leg side as deftly as Hendren had, and Woolley for all his advantage in height was not so very much the more powerful off-driver. Bradman's innings began, so to speak, in the middle, for he had no need to play himself in. He was still in the middle of it when stumps were drawn, for he had not begun to lift the ball off the ground as they do who propose to get on or get out when it makes no difference which of their alternative objects they achieve. He has, in fact, played the first part of an extremely steady innings, treating each ball sent down to him strictly on its merits as he discerns them. And yet he has scored 155 runs in 2½ hours.

If one were to begin particularizing his strokes there would be no end to this account, but one of them must be specially noted. Hammond was put on at the Pavilion end to bowl defensively, and was doing his job quite well. Naturally he had a defensive field, with only one man in the slips. He sent down a fast, good-length ball which broke back viciously at the top of the off and middle stumps. Bradman met it with an orthodox-looking back stroke which had the effect of a late cut. The ball flew, and clearly was meant to fly, wide of the solitary slip and fine enough to beat the deep third-man. White, who was so successful in slowing down the scoring in Australia, could do nothing with him. He *chasséed* out to the pitch of the good-length balls, and altered the direction of them as well as their length to suit his purpose, so that he could drive them where the fieldsmen were not. The crowd twice paid him unusual but well-deserved compliments. They gave Tate one of the loudest rounds of applause heard during the afternoon when he succeeded in bowling a maiden over to him. And once when he shaped to cut at a dangerous ball from that bowler some 2,000 people appealed for the expected catch at the wicket, and were badly scored off when he checked his stroke.

Poster praising Bradman's performance during the third Test match against England at Leeds, 1930. His 334 was the highest score made in any Test match anywhere, up to that time.

Daily
At Dawn

# The Natal Mercury

Saturday
July 12, 1930

# BRADMAN VERSUS ENGLAND

PUBLISHED BY THE CENTRAL NEWS AGENCY, LIMITED.

Don Bradman's score of 334 in the third Test against England at Leeds in 1930 made headlines in Natal, South Africa.

After being 155 not out on Saturday, Bradman commenced on Monday morning and passed Duleepsinhji's score of 177 runs to complete his 200 after batting for 4 hours 5 minutes.

An unsuccessful attempt to catch Kippax    Inset : Bradman acknowledges cheers on the completion of his 200th run.

Bradman and Kippax added 192 runs for the third wicket in 2 hours 38 minutes.

Bradman was caught out at 2.50 p.m. on Monday, after scoring 254 runs.

The Lord's score board at the conclusion of Australia's record-breaking innings.

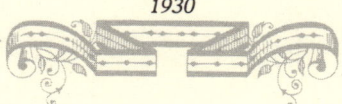

After the wonderful Australian victory, this enormous crowd gathered beneath the team's dressing-room window, calling for the players to appear on the landing.

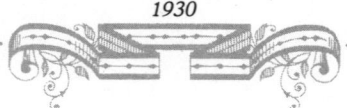

# RARE MIRACLE
## OF THE GAME

---

## BRADMAN, CRICKET PHENOMENON

---

## WIN OFF OWN BAT

---

"GUARDIAN" SERVICE

LONDON, Sunday.

"IN Bradman, Australia has a cricket phenomenon, one of the rare miracles of the game —a player who can almost beat a side off his own bat," states the "Sunday Times" in a warm tribute.

"The Observer" states that his huge innings was almost faultless.

His technique and dominance made every bowler assume the role of an indispensable means to the batsman's purpose, without any other purpose.

**"When Bradman was gone, the light seemed to go out of the game,"** adds the paper.

Maclaren, in the "Evening Standard," states that Bradman has been compared with Macartney, but that his methods are different.

### NEVER INDISCREET

"It was sometimes possible to get Macartney out by inciting him early to play a characteristic stroke, which nobody else would attempt, but Bradman never allows himself any liberty," adds Maclaren.

A ND Bradman, the youth who has the whole of England spellbound.

He just pounded that English bowling into helplessness.

His dazzling effort thoroughly demoralised the English atack, and quickly changed the Australian position from an uphill fight to a bold, threatening challenge.

He plays so many grand innings, each of which seems more brilliant than the last, that it is difficult to pronounce which is his really greatest feat.

**But yesterday's exhibition nust go down in history as a cricketing classic.**

## GULLIVER'S TOUR AMONG THE LILLIPUTIANS.
### (WITH MR. PUNCH'S COMPLIMENTS TO MR. BRADMAN.)

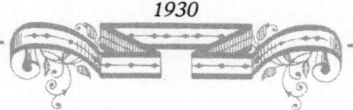

# Australia v England
## Third Test Match

In a long career there are many outstanding memories but I suppose the opening day of the third Test at Leeds must rank as the greatest in my cricketing life.

To break the world's record Test score was exciting. To do so against Australia's oldest and strongest rival was satisfying.

More than anything else, however, was the knowledge that I had scored the runs at such a fast rate and therefore provided entertainment for the spectators.

Details are set out in the following pages and provide a historic account of events.

It is worth mentioning that immediately following this record score I was completely beaten by a young and relatively unknown "googly" bowler, Ian Peebles, in the Manchester Test.

The wheels of fortune remorselessly turn.

*Don Bradman*

---

AUSTRALIA v ENGLAND, Third Test Match, at Leeds, 11, 12, 14 and 15 July 1930.

| Australia | - First Innings | 566 |
| | - Second Innings | - |
| England | - First Innings | 391 |
| | - Second Innings | 95 for 3 wickets |
| | Drawn. | |

DON BRADMAN — c. G. Duckworth b. M.W. Tate 334

In making 334 in this Test Match, DON BRADMAN virtually re-wrote the record book. His total of 309 at the end of the first day consisted of 105 before lunch, 115 between lunch and tea, and 89 between tea and stumps, a performance without parallel in Test history.

He went in on the first morning and completed 50 in forty-nine minutes and after ninety-nine minutes he reached his century, thus joining V.T. Trumper (1902) and C.G. Macartney (1926) in scoring a century before lunch on the first day of a Test Match. Bradman went from 150 to 200 in forty minutes, and reached 200 after batting for only three hours thirty-four minutes. By the tea interval, his score was 220. He carried on in the same wonderful form, and after batting five hours fourteen minutes, he broke R.E. Foster's record of 287 (Foster had batted for six hours fifty-nine minutes). He ended the day with 309 not out, and off the last ball of the day, he reached his 2,000 runs for the season. Next morning, Bradman added another 25 runs before being caught at the wicket. He was in for six hours twenty-three minutes and hit forty-six fours.

Rain prevented the chance of an Australian victory, but England had to follow on, and in the second innings J.B. Hobbs was run out by a magnificent piece of fielding by Bradman.

Bradman, at twenty-one years 318 days, was the youngest batsman in history to reach an aggregate of 2,000 runs in an English season, and he was the youngest ever to reach 1,000 runs in Test cricket, in his seventh Test and his thirteenth innings. His match aggregate of 334 was then the highest for any Test Match between England and Australia.

His 334, was the highest score made in any Test Match anywhere, and it was also the highest score ever made in a first-class match on the Leeds ground. This was also the most runs scored in succession in Test Matches by any batsman before being dismissed. Bradman's time for reaching

100 (ninety-nine minutes) was the fastest on record by an Australian in a Test Match in England; his time for reaching 200 (three hours thirty-four minutes) was the fastest in any Test Match, and his time for reaching 300 (five hours thirty-six minutes) was the best by an Australian in a Test in England.    His total of 309 runs in a single day's play was the most made in one day in any Test Match anywhere, and his partnership of 229 for the third wicket with A.F. Kippax broke the record for that wicket against England.

Bradman became the first player to make two double-centuries in Tests in England and against England, and the first Australian to make more than one Test Match double-century;  this was his fourth double-century in first-class matches in England, more than any other Australian batsman had achieved before.    Up to this time he had made 589 runs in three successive Test innings . (254, 1, 334), a Test Match record, he had also made 720 in four successive Test innings (131, 254, 1, 334), then a record for all Tests.    His 728 in five successive Test innings (8, 131, 254, 1, 334) was an Australian record.    It was also the fourth successive Test in which he had made a century.    In helping to increase the total by 506 while he was in, he broke the record for Test Matches between England and Australia, and by out-scoring the next highest scorer by 257 broke another Test Match record.

Bradman's forty-six fours were a record number of boundaries for all Test Matches.

![England takes the field.]

England takes the field.

H. Larwood, H. Sutcliffe, G. Geary, W. R. Hammond, K. S. Duleepsinhji, R. Tyldesley, M. W. Tate (partly hidden), G. Duckworth, J. B. Hobbs, A. P. F. Chapman, M. Leyland.

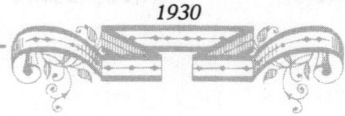

Played at Leeds, July 11, 12, 14, and 15. Drawn. Score:—

## AUSTRALIA.

| | |
|---|---|
| W. M. Woodfull, b Hammond | 50 |
| A. Jackson, c Larwood, b Tate | 1 |
| D. G. Bradman, c Duckworth, b Tate | 334 |
| A. F. Kippax, c Chapman, b Tate | 77 |
| S. McCabe, b Larwood | 30 |
| V. Y. Richardson, c Larwood, b Tate | 1 |
| E. L. a'Beckett, c Chapman, b Geary | 29 |
| W. A. Oldfield, c Hobbs, b Tate | 2 |
| C. V. Grimmett, c Duckworth, b Tyldesley | 24 |
| T. Wall, b Tyldesley | 3 |
| P. M. Hornibrook, not out | 1 |
| Byes, 5; l.-b., 8; w., 1 | 14 |
| **Total** | **566** |

## ENGLAND.—First Innings.

| | |
|---|---|
| Hobbs, c a'Beckett, b Grimmett | 29 |
| Sutcliffe, c Hornibrook, b Grimmett | 32 |
| Hammond, c Oldfield, b McCabe | 113 |
| K. S. Duleepsinhji, b Hornibrook | 35 |
| Leyland, c Kippax, b Wall | 44 |
| Geary (G.), run out | 0 |
| Duckworth, c Oldfield, b a'Beckett | 33 |
| A. P. F. Chapman, b Grimmett | 45 |
| Tate, c Jackson, b Grimmett | 22 |
| Larwood, not out | 10 |
| Tyldesley R., c Hornibrook, b Grimmett | 6 |
| Byes, 9; l.-b., 10; n.-b., 3 | 22 |
| **Total** | **391** |

### Second Innings.

| | |
|---|---|
| Hobbs, run out | 13 |
| Sutcliffe, not out | 28 |
| Hammond, c Oldfield, b Grimmett | 35 |
| K. S. Duleepsinhji, c Grimmett, b Hornibrook | 10 |
| Leyland, not out | 1 |
| Leg-byes | 8 |
| **Total 3 wkts.** | **95** |

## BOWLING.
### AUSTRALIA.—First Innings.

| | O. | M. | R. | W. | | O. | M. | R. | W. |
|---|---|---|---|---|---|---|---|---|---|
| Larwood | 33 | 3 | 139 | 1 | Tyldesley | 33 | 5 | 104 | 2 |
| Tate | 39 | 9 | 124 | 5 | Hammond | 17 | 3 | 46 | 1 |
| Geary | 35 | 10 | 95 | 1 | Leyland | 11 | 0 | 44 | 0 |

### ENGLAND.—First Innings.

| | O. | M. | R. | W. | | O. | M. | R. | W. |
|---|---|---|---|---|---|---|---|---|---|
| Wall | 40 | 12 | 70 | 1 | Hornibrook | 41 | 7 | 94 | 1 |
| a'Beckett | 28 | 8 | 47 | 1 | McCabe | 10 | 4 | 23 | 1 |
| Grimmett | 56.2 | 16 | 135 | 5 | | | | | |

### Second Innings.

| | O. | M. | R. | W. | | O. | M. | R. | W. |
|---|---|---|---|---|---|---|---|---|---|
| Wall | 10 | 3 | 20 | 0 | Hornibrook | 11.5 | 5 | 14 | 1 |
| a'Beckett | 11 | 4 | 19 | 0 | McCabe | 2 | 1 | 1 | 0 |
| Grimmett | 17 | 3 | 33 | 1 | | | | | |

Umpires.—Bestwick and Oates.

## FALL OF THE WICKETS.
### AUSTRALIA.—First Innings.

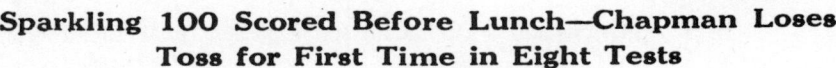

| 1 | 2 | 3 | 4 | 5 | 6 | 7 | 8 | 9 | 10 |
|---|---|---|---|---|---|---|---|---|---|
| 2 | 194 | 423 | 486 | 491 | 508 | 519 | 544 | 565 | 566 |

### ENGLAND.—First Innings.

| 1 | 2 | 3 | 4 | 5 | 6 | 7 | 8 | 9 | 10 |
|---|---|---|---|---|---|---|---|---|---|
| 53 | 64 | 123 | 206 | 206 | 289 | 319 | 370 | 375 | 391 |

### ENGLAND.—Second Innings.

| 1 | 2 | 3 |
|---|---|---|
| 24 | 74 | 94 |

# BRADMAN V. ENGLAND:

### Eclipses Record Test Score of 287
### Made by R. E. Foster in 1903

## WEAK ENGLISH BOWLING FLOGGED

W. G. GRACE.

### Sparkling 100 Scored Before Lunch—Chapman Loses Toss for First Time in Eight Tests

England's bowlers battered and exhausted; Don Bradman, aged twenty-one, the world's wonder batsman, triumphant and 309 not out after smashing still more records.

Such was the close of the first day of the Leeds Test match yesterday. "It was Bradman's day," says Mr. C. G. Macartney, the famous Australian cricketer, whose exclusive description of the match appears on page 6. Comments by Mr. P. J. Moss, the "Daily Mirror" Sports Editor, are on page 18.

By an amazing display of hurricane hitting Bradman beat the previous highest Test score of 287 made by R. E. Foster for England at Sydney in 1903, and his own personal record of 254 made in the match at Lord's. He nearly doubled the highest score (170) made by Dr. W. G. Grace, the "father" of cricket, against the Australians in 1886.

R. E FOSTER

He is the only player to obtain a century in four successive Tests, and has equalled the feat of Trumper and Macartney in scoring a Test century before lunch. He has not yet made two separate centuries in a Test match. Bardsley did in 1909.

Bradman going out to bat at Leeds.

V. T. Trumper.

A glorious and world famous action photograph of Victor Trumper — probably one of the best known and most widely distributed photographs in existence.
In 1902 Trumper became the first man to score a century before lunch on the opening day of a Test match, a feat subsequently emulated by Macartney (1926) and Bradman (1930).

Bradman at the completion of a full-blooded drive.

C. G. Macartney in action during his innings at Headingley in 1926
when he made a century before lunch.

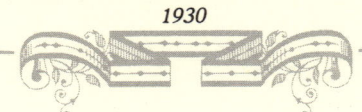

# ALL EYES ON BRADMAN AT HEADINGLEY.

All intent upon the performance of Bradman during yesterday's play in the Test match.

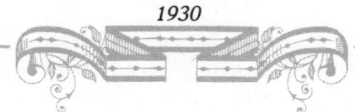

## DON BRADMAN'S SMILE.

Don Bradman, the greatest favourite who has ever come from Australia, acknowledging the wild cheering of the crowd at Headingley, Leeds, yesterday, when he broke the record for the highest score in a Test match. This boy of twenty-one slaughtered our bowling, made 309, and won all hearts.

Bradman acknowledges plaudits from the crowd during his world's record Test innings.

# DON REMEMBERS THE GIRL
## HE LEFT BEHIND!

---

## Pal of His Childhood Days
## Now Lives in Sydney

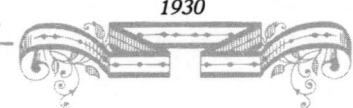

DON BRADMAN.

---

## WAS THAT JOKE NEAR THE TRUTH?

*Perhaps the wag who wired Don Bradman that "his girl wanted him back" was nearer the truth than he realised, for a girl working in the city blushingly acknowledges Don as a childhood friend.*

Daughter of an old Bowral family, she came to Sydney in the days before Don began shattering cricket records.

BUT when Don first gave city crowds a glimpse of his ability he sought out the girl, and the friendship was resumed. And even now Don keeps in touch.

The young lady's 21st birthday did not escape the young champion's memory. Shortly before it he cabled asking if he might send a present!

So this girl, who is on the friendliest terms with the much sought after cricket hero, may perhaps be excused the enjoyment of her friends' envy.

## DON, YOUR GIRL WANTS YOU HOME!

(From Our Special Representative with the Team.)

LEEDS, Monday.

Compliments are pouring in to Bradman. Chapman's mild "Confound him!" at the century before lunch on Friday developed into a "Blast him!" over the week-end.

A telegram which delighted Don, received anonymously from London, read: "Your house is on fire. Your girl wants you back—so go home."

## How to Beat Don

Someone sent Don Bradman a wire saying: "Your house is burning, your girl wants you back—hurry home!"

Absurd! This is not the way to distract a chap of Don's phlegmatic nature. It is only waste of ninepence and a dozen words to appeal to the imagination of a cricketer—they live only in a moment and on the wicket. For the guidance of the English, whom Peter loves as brothers and pities as lame dogs to be helped over stiles, a little advice is proffered. There is no charge. Don can be got rid of very easily by taking the fire to him. The English back-stop or silly point should be armed with matches, with which he could set fire to Don's hair, pants, pads, or shirt at critical moments during the game. Or a Mills bomb could be rung-in occasionally in place of the ball. If these failed to put the boy off his game, what about digging an elephant trap overnight in the middle of the wicket—a big hole 20 feet square with sharp stakes in the bottom? This, if lightly covered with grass, would engulf all the Australian players in pairs and relieve England of the necessity of batting at all!

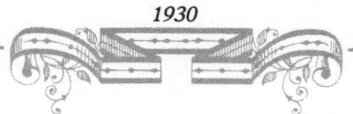

Jessie Menzies — the girl from Bowral.

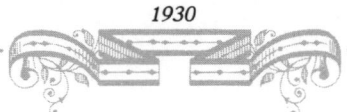

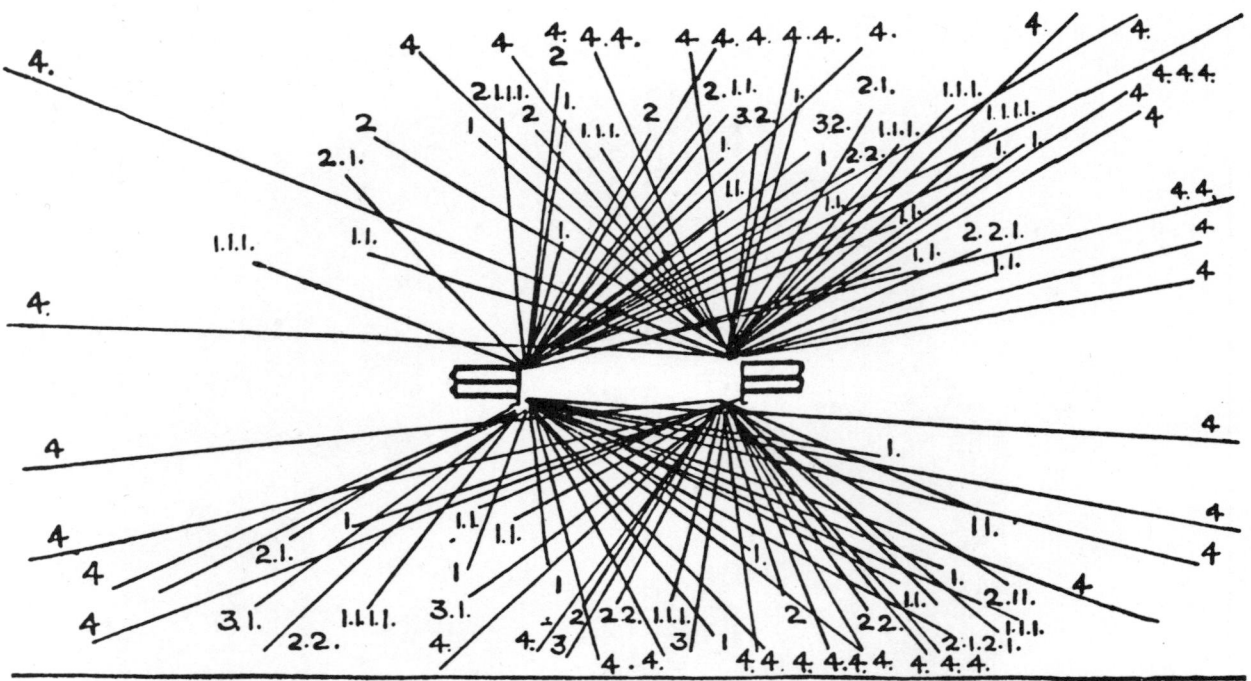

**HOW BRADMAN MADE HIS 334 RECORD.**

The end of a record innings. Bradman caught by Duckworth off Tate, who is seen appealing.

A beautiful action photograph of Tate.

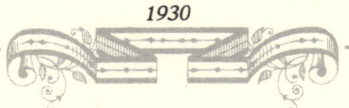

The crowd according Bradman an ovation when coming in after making the world's record Test score of 334.

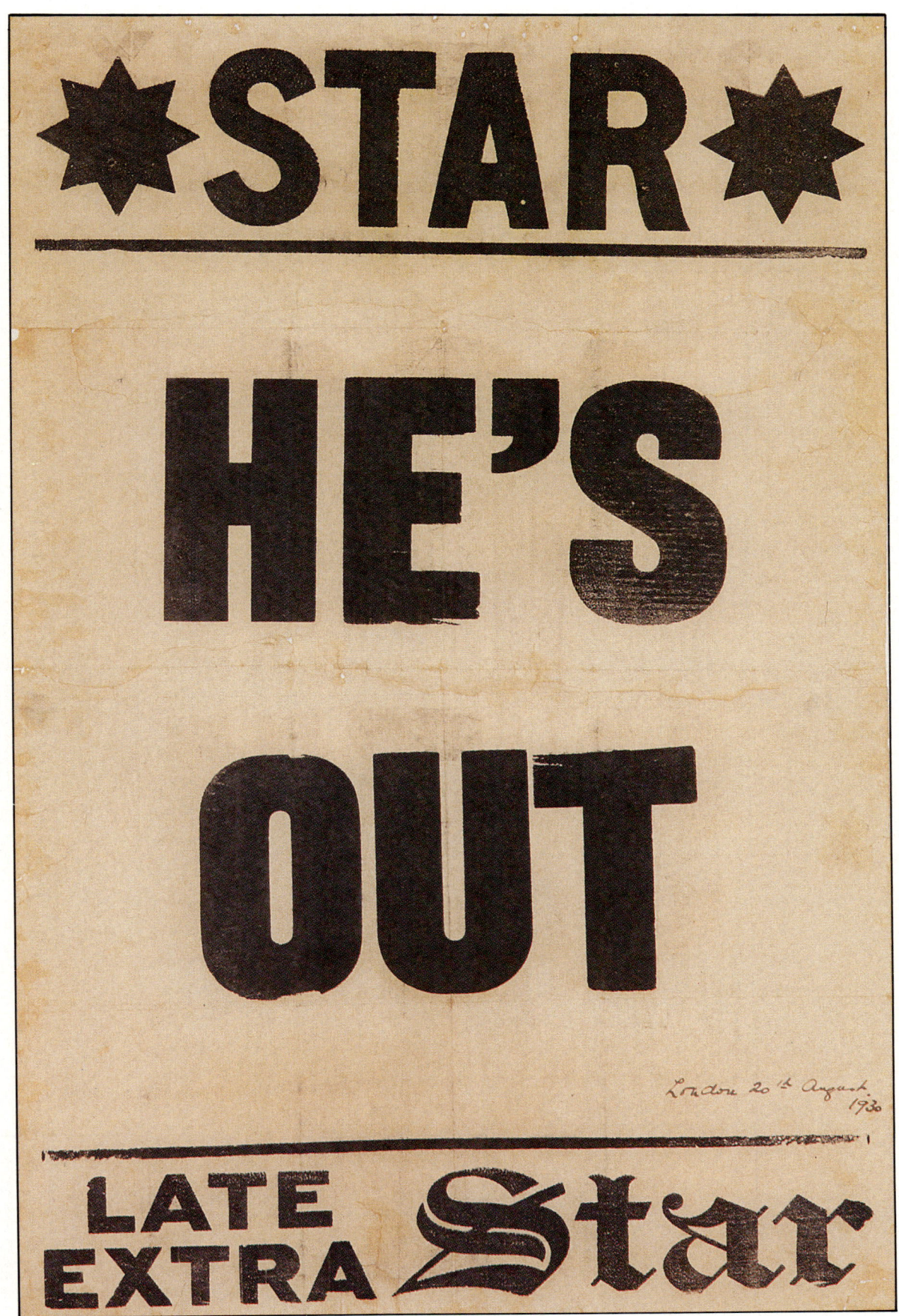

Poster announcing the end of Don Bradman's remarkable innings in the final Test match against England in 1930, when he scored 232.

# — CRICKET —
## 1930 — AUSTRALIAN TEAM IN ENGLAND
### Shewing Individual Scores, Averages & results in all Matches

— Note —

Scores against Scotland & London Clubs are not included in the Averages and Aggregates, which refer to First Class Matches only.

| Match | Result | D.G. BRADMAN | A.F. KIPPAX | W.M. WOODFUL | W.H. PONSFORD | A. JACKSON | S. McCABE | V. RICHARDSON | A. FAIRFAX | E. a'BECKETT | W. OLDFIELD | P. HORNIBROOK | C. GRIMMETT | A. HURWOOD | T. WALL | C. WALKER |
|---|---|---|---|---|---|---|---|---|---|---|---|---|---|---|---|---|
| Worcester | Won - Innings & 165 runs | 236 | — | — | 133 | — | 24 | 15 | 24 | 0 | 24 | 4 | — | 15* | — | 9* |
| Leicester | Drawn | 185* | 22 | — | 25 | — | 2 | 100 | 21* | 4 | — | — | — | — | 9* | — |
| Essex | Won - by 207 runs | — | 57 / 42 | 54 / 4 | 39 / 26 | 7 / 27 | 5 / 6 | — | 12 / 53* | 0 / 30 | 16* / 14* | 7 | 0 | — | — | — |
| Yorkshire | Drawn | 78 | 3 | 121 | 6 | — | 16 | 45 | — | 14 | — | 6 | 23* | — | — | 3 |
| Lancashire | Drawn | 9 / 48* | 40* / 6* | 21 | 40 / 19 | 39 / 0 | 18 | — | 3 | — | 0 | 0 | 0 | — | 4 | — |
| M.C.C. | Drawn | 66 | 24 / 18 | 52 / 7 | 82* / 15 | 64 / 5 | 34 | — | 26 | — | 6 / 11 | 4 | 15 | 5 | 2 | 0 / 10* |
| Derbyshire | Won - by 10 wickets | 44 | 25 | — | 131 | 63 / 18* | 5 | 10 | 20 | 14 | — | 2* | — | 15 | 0 | — |
| Surrey | Drawn | 252* | — | 50 | — | 9 | 2 | 32 | 28* | — | — | — | — | — | — | — |
| Oxford Uni. | Won - Innings & 158 runs | 32 | 56* | 220 | — | — | 91 | — | — | DNB | DNB | DNB | — | DNB | DNB | DNB |
| Hampshire | Won - Innings & 8 runs | 191 | 20 | 4 | 29 | 0 | 65 | 14 | — | 0* | — | — | — | 0 | — | — |
| Middlesex | Won - by 5 wickets | 35 / 18 | 102 / 13* | 10 / 5 | 14 / 26 | 31 / 17* | — | 34 | 11 | 4 | 21 | — | — | — | — | 5* |
| Cambridge Uni. | Won - Innings & 134 runs | 32 | 32 | 216 | 7 | 25 | 96 | 34 | — | 28 | — | 6 | 8* | 9* | — | DNB |
| ENGLAND | Lost - by 93 runs | 8 / 131 | 64* / 23 | 2 / 4 | 3 / 39 | — | 49 / 4 | 29 / 14 | 14 / 4 | 4 / 1 | — | — | 0 / 0 | 0 / 8* | — | — |
| Surrey | Drawn | 5 | 36 | 27 | 42 | 37* | 36 | — | 67* | — | — | — | — | DNB | DNB | — |
| Lancashire | Drawn | 38 / 23* | 120 | 27 | 52 | 34 / 36* | 13 / 12 | 63 | 34* | 20 | — | 9 | 0 | — | — |
| ENGLAND | Won - by 7 wickets | 254 | 83 / 3 | 155 / 26* | 81 / 14 | — | 44 / 25* | 30 / 20* | 43* | DNB | DNB | DNB | DNB | DNB | — |
| Yorkshire | Won - by 10 wickets | — | 3 | 46 | 143 | 40 | 30* / 6* | 10 | 4 | — | 6* | — |
| Notts. | Drawn | — | 89* / 93 | 79 / 58 | 79 / 22 | 6 | 69 / 55 | 3 | 38 / 5* | 5* | — | 6 | 0 | 6 | — | 5 |
| ENGLAND | Drawn | 334 | 77 | 50 | — | 1* | 30 | 29 | 2 | 24 | 1* | — | — | 3 | — | — |
| Scotland | Drawn | Scotland scored 3-129 (Wrath) then abandoned (rain) |  |  |  |  |  |  |  |  |  |  |  |  |  |  |
| Scotland (W) | Drawn | 140 | 65 | 6 | — | 52* | — | 43 | 8 | — | — | 3 | — | 2* | 0 | — |
| Durham | No Play | No Play (Wet Play owing to rain) |  |  |  |  |  |  |  |  |  |  |  |  |  |  |
| ENGLAND | Drawn | 14 | 51 | 54 | 83 | — | 4 | 2 | 49 | 3 | 50 | — | — | 1* | — | — |
| Somerset | Won - Innings & 158 runs | 117 | 30 | 8 | 118 | — | 27 | — | 24 | 4* | 16 | 16 | — | 10 | 0 | 0 |
| Glamorgan | Drawn | 58 / 19* | — | 39 / 11 | 53 / 35* | 53 | 3 | 8 | 18* | 8 | — | 2 | 0 | — | 0 | — |
| Warwickshire | Drawn | Warwickshire scored 3-102 (Match abandoned - rain) |  |  |  |  |  |  |  |  |  |  |  |  |  |  |
| Northants | Drawn | 22 / 35 | 20 / 10 | 116 | 9 | 52 | — | 7 | 13 | 22 | 16* / 2 | 2 | 12 | 3 | — | 0* |
| ENGLAND | Won - Innings & 39 runs | 232 | 28 | 54 | 110 | 73 | 54 | 53* | 34 | — | 6 | 7 | 6 | — | 0 | 0* |
| Gloucester | Drawn (a tie) | 42 / 14 | 14 | 51 | 8 / 25 | 0 / 34 | 12 | 2 | 9 / 4 | 7* | 4 | 12 / 7* | 0 / 14 | 0 | 7 | — |
| Kent | Drawn | 18 / 205* | 16 | 50* / 21 | 45 | 21 / 11 | 16 / 6 | 4 | 4 | — | — | 0 | 45 | 12* | — | — |
| Sussex | Drawn | 102 / 158 | 10 / 38 | 15 / 12 | 24 / 15 | 2 / 16 | 13 | 6 | 7 | — | 2* / 59* | 38 | 5 | 61 | 12* | — |
| Sth England | Drawn | 63 | 0 | 34 | 76 | 14 | 53 | 10 | 43 | — | — | — | — | 40* | — | — |
| London Clubs | Won - Innings & 41 runs | 70 | 63 | 69 | 0 | 25 | 14 | — | — | — | — | — | 0 | 0 | — | 7* |
| English XI | Drawn | 96 | 59 | 24 | 24 | 8* | 8 | — | 0 | — | DNB | — | 3 | — | 6 | — |
| **AGGREGATE** |  | 2960 | 1447 | 1434 | 1425 | 1097 | 1012 | 832 | 540 | 397 | 225 | 232 | 237 | 190 | 105 | 43 |
| **AVERAGE** |  | 98.66 | 57.88 | 57.36 | 49.13 | 34.28 | 32.64 | 26.83 | 25.71 | 24.81 | 18.75 | 12.88 | 11.85 | 10.55 | 8.07 | 4.77 |

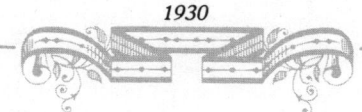

# ADMIRER'S £1,000 FOR BRADMAN

## 'TEST' WIZARD IN REAL LIFE DRAMA

### CROWD OF 33,000 ON VERGE OF HYSTERIA.

"Boy" Bradman, Australia's record-smashing batsman, who scored 334, was the centre of a dramatic incident during the match yesterday.

A telegram was taken out on to the ground and handed to Bradman. It was from Mr. Arthur Whitelow, a wealthy Australian who lives in London, asking him to accept £1,000 "as a mark of admiration for his wonderful performance."

Bradman, quietly pocketing the telegram, took his place in the field. Later he replied: "I cannot express in words my deep appreciation of your wonderful offer. I hope to thank you personally at an early date."

## IN PUBLIC EYE

Mr. Arthur E. Whitelaw,
Australian, in London, gave £1000 to
Don Bradman.

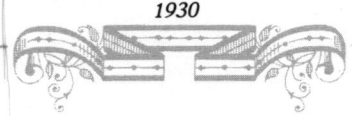
MELBOURNE, Sunday.
Mr. Arthur Ernest Whitelow was born in Auburn, Victoria, and after being associated with his father and brothers in a wallpaper business in Flinders-street successfully established a proprietary soap throughout the world. He went to England 14 years ago, and has paid many visits to Australia since, the last occasion being in 1928. When living in Melbourne he was captain of the Commercial Travellers' Association interstate cricket team. Mr. Whitelow has written a book on bridge that is well-known in England.

82, PORTLAND PLACE,
W.
13th July 1930

Dear Don

Pardon the liberty. I am glad to learn that you have accepted the £1000 which I offered. May I suggest that I deposit the money in one of the Australian banks such as Bank of Australasia for your credit. They would send you a form for signature and you could operate on your account almost immediately. You are fortunate in saving a further £60 odd owing to Exchange, should you transfer the money to Sydney. I was greatly impressed by your remarkable feats with the bat and being an Australian (Melbourne) I was happy to pay tribute to your phenomenal performances. I trust you will favour me with a visit to Australia House (5th floor) and if you can find it convenient to call about 12.30 p.m. any day we could go along to the Moorgate for a chop but I don't quite know how you are going to have the day off. However if this does not fit in perhaps you could have dinner with us at this flat one evening when you are in London and bring a pal. Fix your own date.

On hearing from you which bank you wish the £1000 paid into I shall do the needful with profound pleasure. Kind regards

Yours sincerely
A.E. Whitelow

P.S. perhaps you will prefer me to pay £100 into a current a/c and the other £900 into fixed deposit a/c (withdrawable at say 14 days notice) as in the way your money would be earning interest also but please yourself!

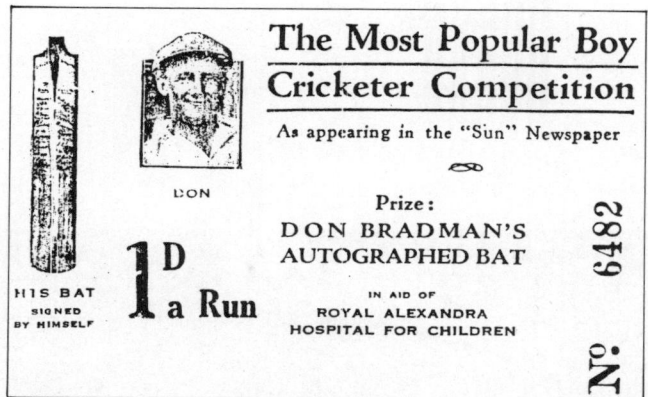

*SUNDAY, 20 JULY*

Train from Buchanan Street Station at 10.30 to Gleneagles, arriving there at noon. The finest hotel I've ever been in. Beautifully appointed with French Restaurant, ballroom, private and public dining rooms, post office, bank, swimming pool and everything.

There are the King's and Queen's golf courses of 18 holes each.

Nine hard tennis courts, croquet lawns, bowling green, flower and vegetable gardens, aerodrome, own fish in pond and the whole of the gardens wonderfully laid out in lawns, gardens, drives etc.

Tariff very high — 30/- per day minimum.

Bedroom, bath and sitting room suite £6/15/- per day with no meals.

All owned and run by L. M. S. Railway whose guests we were for the day.

Played 18 holes on the King's Course after lunch. Got wet in rain.

Afternoon tea at five and thence by car to Glasgow.

On the way back we went partly round Loch Lomond and saw lovely Loch Catherine.

Saw a rail plane testing ground.

Sick at night. Straight to bed.

## Famous Autographs

"Runs" will be scored by the contenders for Don's famous bat, autographed by every member of the Australian and English first Test Match teams in 1928.

Before Don went over the water to worry Percy Chapman and break the proud spirit of the giant Larwood, he had an idea that he would like to do something for the kiddies at the Royal Alexandra, so he gave the bat. Now an appeal is made to all the Great Public Schools of New South Wales, to all the colleges, to all young cricketers and cricket enthusiasts, to send in nominations to Mr. Moss, the secretary of the Royal Alexandra Hospital, at the offices in Kembla Building.

"Runs" will take the form of 1d tickets. All the money received from the sale of tickets (or special donations that may be made for the purpose) will go to endow in perpetuity a cot to be known as the "Don Bradman Cot."

The age limit for competitors is 21 years, and "The Sun" will publish progress reports, also the names and photographs of entrants, until August 31, when the competition closes.

Gleneagles Hotel and Golf Courses.

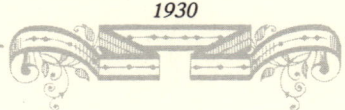

SUNDAY, 27 JULY

*After lunch to Sir Edwin Stockton's home.*
*Played golf with Mrs. Stanley Bruce. Played Clarrie tennis.*
*Met Ranjitsinhji there.*
*Back to hotel for dinner.*

BACK ROW   The Hon. S. M. Bruce, Mr. W. Kelly (Manager of the team), Lt. Col. H. H. Shri Sir Ranjitsinhji Vibhaji (Ranji), Woodfull,
Ponsford, Mr. W. Ferguson (Scorer), Jackson, Hurwood, a'Beckett.
FRONT ROW   Grimmett, Oldfield, Bradman, Lady Stockton, Sir Edwin Stockton, Mrs. S. M. Bruce, Walker, Wall.

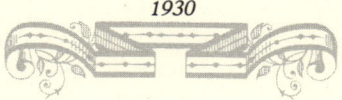

"Ranji" and "Duleep".

Mr. Tobey Peel, Arthur Mailey and others at bowls.

Sir Edwin takes a movie of Oldfield, Ponsford and Hurwood.

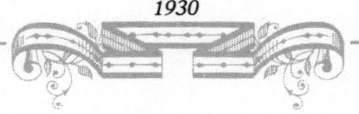

# Australia v England
## Fourth Test Match

AUSTRALIA v ENGLAND, Fourth Test Match, at Manchester, 25, 26 and 28 July 1930.

Australia — First Innings 345
— Second Innings -

England — First Innings 251 for 8 wickets
— Second Innings -

Drawn.

DON BRADMAN — c. K.S. Duleepsinhji b. I.A.R. Peebles 14

DON BRADMAN went in on the first afternoon at 106 for 1 on a turning pitch and survived uneasily for half an hour, being dismissed with the score 138 for 2. He found great difficulty in detecting Peebles' 'wrong-un' owing to the poor light.

Australia won the toss and batted, but the turf was so soft that play was delayed for half an hour.

Ponsford and Woodfull put on 106 for the first wicket; later Bradman was all at sea against Peebles.

## Bradman, c Duleepsinhji, b Peebles ..................... 14

THUS passed, for one innings at least, the greatest danger to England's chance of a victory in the fourth Test match, which began at Manchester to-day.

### AUSTRALIA.—First Innings.

| | |
|---|---|
| W. M. Woodfull, c Duckworth, b Tate | 54 |
| W. H. Ponsford, b Hammond | 83 |
| D. G. Bradman, c Duleepsinhji, b Peebles | 14 |
| A. F. Kippax, c Chapman, b Nichols | 51 |
| S. McCabe, lbw, b Peebles | 4 |
| V. Y. Richardson, b Hammond | 1 |
| A. Fairfax, lbw, b Goddard | 49 |
| W. A. Oldfield, b Nichols | 2 |
| C. V. Grimmett, c Sutcliffe, b Peebles | 50 |
| P. M. Hornibrook, c Duleepsinhji, b Goddard | 3 |
| T. Wall, not out | 1 |
| Byes, 23; l.-b., 3; n.-b., 7 | 33 |
| Total | 345 |

### ENGLAND.—First Innings.

| | |
|---|---|
| Hobbs, c Oldfield, b Wall | 31 |
| Sutcliffe, c Bradman, b Wall | 74 |
| Hammond, b Wall | 1 |
| K. S. Duleepsinhji, c Hornibrook, b McCabe | 54 |
| Leyland, b McCabe | 35 |
| A. P. F. Chapman, c Grimmett, b Hornibrook | 1 |
| Tate, c Ponsford, b McCabe | 15 |
| Nichols, not out | 7 |
| I. A. R. Peebles, c Richardson, b McCabe | 6 |
| Duckworth, not out | 0 |
| Byes, 13; l.-b., 12 | 25 |
| Total (8 wkts.) | 251 |

Goddard did not bat.

### BOWLING ANALYSIS.
#### AUSTRALIA.—First Innings.

| | O. | M. | R. | W. |
|---|---|---|---|---|
| Nichols | 21 | 5 | 33 | 2 |
| Tate | 30 | 11 | 39 | 1 |
| Goddard | 32.1 | 14 | 49 | 2 |
| Peebles | 55 | 9 | 150 | 3 |
| Leyland | 8 | 2 | 17 | 0 |
| Hammond | 21 | 6 | 24 | 2 |

#### ENGLAND.—First Innings.

| | O. | M. | R. | W. |
|---|---|---|---|---|
| Wall | 33 | 9 | 70 | 3 |
| Fairfax | 13 | 5 | 15 | 0 |
| Grimmett | 19 | 2 | 59 | 0 |
| Hornibrook | 26 | 9 | 41 | 1 |
| McCabe | 17 | 3 | 41 | 4 |

### FALL OF THE WICKETS.
#### AUSTRALIA.—First Innings.

| 1 | 2 | 3 | 4 | 5 | 6 | 7 | 8 | 9 | 10 |
|---|---|---|---|---|---|---|---|---|---|
| 106 | 138 | 184 | 189 | 190 | 239 | 243 | 330 | 338 | 345 |

#### ENGLAND.—First Innings.

| 1 | 2 | 3 | 4 | 5 | 6 | 7 | 8 |
|---|---|---|---|---|---|---|---|
| 108 | 115 | 119 | 192 | 199 | 222 | 237 | 247 |

Umpires.—Chester and Hardstaff.

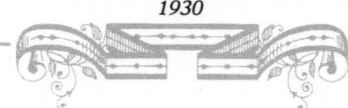

# But Hobbs and Sutcliffe Make Great Chase After Total of 345

### Fairfax and Grimmett—the Bowler— Knock the Men Who Had Got Our Best Batsmen Out

### Wall Gets Rid of Famous Openers; England, Five for 221

("Pictorial" Special Service.)

HOBBS, England's stalwart opening batsman, was one of our first obstacles.

GRIMMETT, upon whom Australia's hopes are once more centred.

MANCHESTER, Saturday.

When, after a good start, disaster loomed for Australia in the fourth Test, with the cheap dismissal by Peebles of Bradman, and the quick fall of our other hopes, the "tail" came to light. Fairfax and Grimmett made a great stand, and the total score was 345.

Faced with a formidable task, England's famous opening pair, Hobbs and Sutcliffe, made a great stand, taking the partnership to 108 before Wall got them both. At stumps England had lost five wickets for 221.

## BRADMAN'S AMAZING CATCH

Bradman brought off a catch to get Sutcliffe out which will live long in the memory of all those who witnessed it. Sutcliffe had brought his score to 74 by masterly strokes when he lifted a ball from Wall on the leg side to within a yard from the boundary line.

Bradman had a glaring sun in his eyes; there was a danger of his being tripped up by the feet of people who squatted about, but, having riveted his unerring eye on to the ball he calmly waited for it and held it as he fell back among the crowd.

From where I was there seemed a doubt whether Bradman had made the catch within the playing area. He himself signalled that he was on the right side of the boundary line, and on Hardstaffe being appealed to he decided that the catch was a legitimate one, and Sutcliffe had to go.

## Elusive Don

The most elusive player in the team is probably Don Bradman. Sometimes he is missing for hours. Seldom is he seen after dinner in the lounge or during the Australian innings excepting when he is out on the field.

Last night we arrived from Manchester, and stayed at the historic Castle Hotel at Taunton.

Somebody suddenly discovered that Don was missing. Mr. Kelly rushed around the hotel: page-boys darted here and there calling his name; somebody suggested he had been kidnapped; others said he had missed the connection at Bristol.

When the search was at its highest the soft sound of music was heard issuing from the music-room, and there was Don quietly playing a little tune he had heard at a show a night or two previously.

This team does not like blatant publicity, which, after all, is an asset to people who are in the public eye. I have often seen the players disappear through the stage door of a theatre because curious people were waiting at the front of the theatre to see them leave.

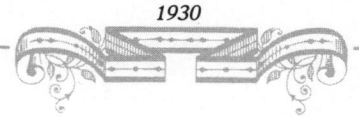

# Another
# Of Don's Good Deeds

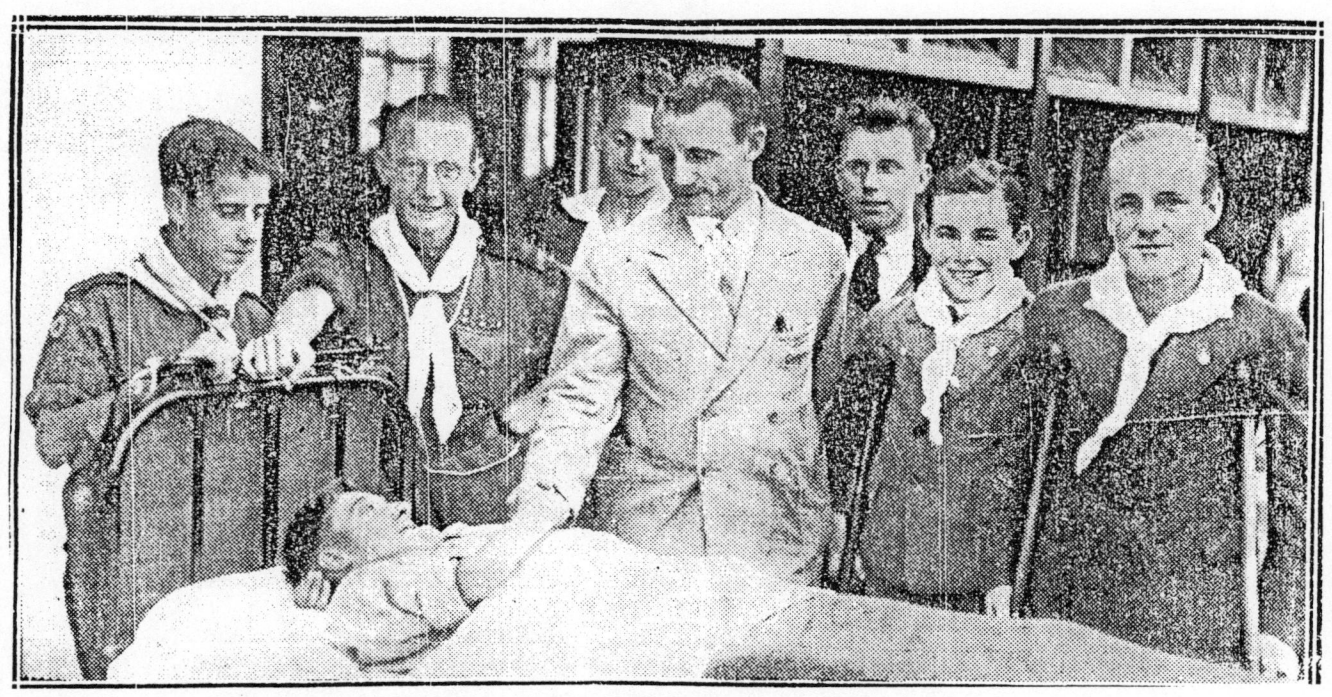

Don Bradman dressed immaculately in grey flannels
greeting a Boy Scout patient at a Northampton hospital, which was visited by the Australian cricketers
last month.

## *BRADMAN TALKIE*

("*Sun*" *Special*)

*LONDON, Monday.*

London's first
British Movietone
News theatre in
Shaftesbury - av-
enue features an
interview with
Bradman, who il-
lustrates his
strokes and de-
scribes them in a
clear, hard voice.

*Don Bradman*

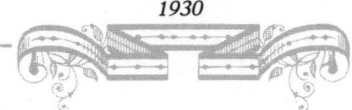

# Australia v England
## Fifth Test Match

A week before my 22nd birthday the final Test was played at the Oval and Australia won by a wide margin.

It was the culmination of a hard series in which our young team, under the inspiring leadership of Bill Woodfull, moulded into a fine combination.

We were given little chance at the outset by the critics but the Australian players improved far more rapidly than had been anticipated.

My own double century in the fifth Test was made under somewhat difficult batting conditions and in some ways was the most valuable one of the series. In later years Larwood claimed it gave rise to the birth of body-line, a theory which I dispute; but that is another story.

The whole tour was a wonderful experience and certainly laid the foundation for the balance of my career.

*Don Bradman*

---

AUSTRALIA v ENGLAND, Fifth Test Match, at the Oval, 16, 18, 19, 20 and 22 August 1930.

| | | |
|---|---|---|
| Australia | - First Innings | 695 |
| | - Second Innings | - |
| England | - First Innings | 405 |
| | - Second Innings | 251 |

Australia won by an innings and 39 runs, and won the rubber and the Ashes.

DON BRADMAN - c. G. Duckworth b. H. Larwood 232

Rain and bad light held up play on the second day, and after sixty minutes at the wicket, DON BRADMAN was 27 not out overnight. He batted the whole of the third day, which was again interfered with by rain, and after four hours twenty-eight minutes, he was 130 not out. The wicket was difficult on the fourth morning and Bradman reached 200 - his third double-century of the series - in six hours twenty-three minutes. He and A.A. Jackson put on 243 for the fourth wicket in four and three-quarter hours before Jackson was out. At lunch he was 228 and twenty minutes afterwards he was caught at the wicket.

Bradman had played an innings of immense value to Australia, who were 570 for 5, or 165 ahead, when he was out and his relentless determination to make a big score in the interests of his side was never more apparent.

He finished with an aggregate of 974 in seven innings, a record for any player in any Test series. His 232 was at that time the highest in any Test Match at the Oval. Bradman's and Jackson's partnership of 243 for the fourth wicket broke the record for Test Matches between England and Australia.

His last five Test innings this season thus totalled 835 (254, 1, 334, 14, 232), which was a Test Match record.

For the Fifth Test Match, Australia made one change to their team; Richardson was dropped for Jackson.

In the English side, Wyatt, Whysall and Larwood took the places of Chapman, Goddard and Nichols. Wyatt replaced Chapman as Captain.

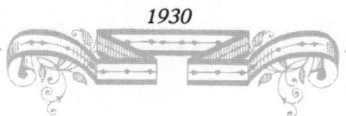

Don Bradman and wicket-keeper Charlie Walker.

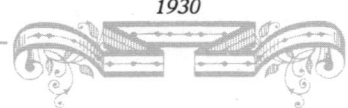

England won the toss and batted for the whole of the first day and scored 316 for 5 wickets.

## SCORES.

### ENGLAND.—First Innings.

| | |
|---|---|
| J. B. Hobbs, c Kippax, b Wall | 47 |
| H. Sutcliffe, c Oldfield, b Fairfax | 161 |
| W. W. Whysall, lbw, b Wall ..,.. | 13 |
| K. S. Duleepsinhji, c Fairfax, b Grimmett | 50 |
| W. R. Hammond, b McCabe .... | 13 |
| M. Leyland, b Grimmett ........ | 3 |
| R. E. S. Wyatt, c Oldfield, b Fairfax | 64 |
| M. W. Tate, st Oldfield, b Grimmett | 10 |
| H. Larwood, lbw, b Grimmett ..... | 19 |
| G. Duckworth, b Fairfax ........ | 3 |
| I. A. R. Peebles, not out ......... | 3 |
| 17 leg byes, 2 no-balls ........ | 19 |
| Total | 405 |

Fall of wickets: 68, 97, 162, 190, 197, 367, 379, 379, 391, 405.

#### BOWLING.

| | O. | M. | R. | W. |
|---|---|---|---|---|
| Wall | 37 | 6 | 96 | 2 |
| Fairfax | 31 | 9 | 52 | 3 |
| Grimmett | 66.2 | 18 | 135 | 4 |
| McCabe | 22 | 4 | 49 | 1 |
| Hornibrook | 15 | 1 | 54 | 0 |

Wall and McCabe each bowled a no-ball.

### Second Innings.

| | |
|---|---|
| J. B. Hobbs, b Fairfax .......... | 9 |
| H. Sutcliffe, c Fairfax, b Hornibrook .......................... | 54 |
| W. W. Whysall, c Hornibrook, b Grimmett ..................... | 10 |
| K. S. Duleepsinhji, c Kippax, b Hornibrook .................... | 46 |
| W. R. Hammond, c Fairfax, b Hornibrook ..................... | 60 |
| M. Leyland, b Hornibrook ...... | 20 |
| R. E. S. Wyatt, b Hornibrook ...... | 21 |
| M. W. Tate, run out .............. | 0 |
| H. Larwood, c McCabe, b Hornibrook | 5 |
| G. Duckworth, b Hornibrook ...... | 15 |
| I. A. R. Peebles, not out ......... | 0 |
| Sundries ..................... | 21 |
| Total | 251 |

Fall of wickets: 17, 37, 118, 135, 189, 207, 208, 220, 248, 251.

Bowling: Wall, none for 25; Fairfax, one for 21; Grimmett, one for 90; Hornibrook, seven for 92; McCabe, none for 2.

### AUSTRALIA.—First Innings.

| | |
|---|---|
| W. M. Woodfull, c Duckworth, b Peebles ..................... | 54 |
| W. H. Ponsford, b Peebles ........ | 110 |
| D. G. Bradman, c Duckworth, b Larwood ..................... | 232 |
| A. F. Kippax, c Wyatt, b Peebles .. | 28 |
| A. Jackson, c Sutcliffe, b Wyatt.. | 73 |
| S. J. McCabe, c Duckworth, b Hammond ..................... | 54 |
| A. Fairfax, not out ............ | 53 |
| W. A. Oldfield, c Larwood, b Peebles | 34 |
| C. V. Grimmett, lbw, b Peebles .. | 6 |
| T. M. Wall, lbw, b Peebles ........ | 0 |
| P. M. Hornibrook, c Duckworth, b Tate .................... | 7 |
| Byes 22, leg-byes 18, no-balls 4 | 44 |
| Total | 695 |

Fall of wickets: 159, 190, 263, 506, 570, 594, 670, 684, 684, 695.

#### BOWLING.

| | O. | M. | R. | W. |
|---|---|---|---|---|
| Larwood | 48 | 6 | 132 | 1 |
| Tate | 65.1 | 12 | 153 | 1 |
| Peebles | 71 | 8 | 204 | 6 |
| Wyatt | 14 | 1 | 58 | 1 |
| Hammond | 42 | 12 | 70 | 1 |
| Leyland | 16 | 7 | 34 | 0 |

Tim Wall bowling. Parry (umpire) and Hobbs look on.

Sutcliffe playing to Grimmett. Hornibrook and Oldfield keenly watch events.

A general view of the match in progress. Hundreds of people viewed the game from the windows of the houses opposite, many having paid large sums of money for these window seats.

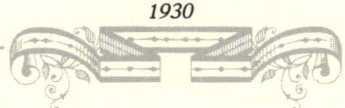

Just before the tea interval, England were in a bad way, because the fifth man was dismissed when the total was only 197.
Then Wyatt went in and played well.

Wyatt, England's new Test Captain, playing the first ball he received from Grimmett.

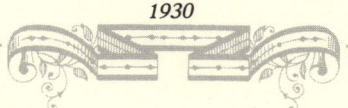

Thus ended a good day for England. The Australians stuck to their work well, but it may be questioned if, Wall excepted, the bowling had been as good as it was in other Tests. The fielding was first class until the last hour when it became a bit ragged, though Bradman remained a champion, his returns being wonderful.

Sutcliffe and Wyatt are mobbed by the crowd before they can get off the playing arena at the conclusion of the first day's play. Together they had added 119 runs, Sutcliffe being 138 not out.

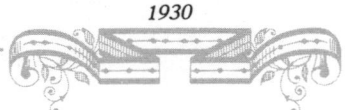

Sutcliffe snicks a ball from Wall which flies harmlessly through slips between Hornibrook and McCabe, although the latter makes a great effort. Oldfield and Sutcliffe anxiously watch its flight.

Sutcliffe c. Oldfield b. Fairfax. Hornibrook and McCabe appeal but Oldfield is certain.

A group of interested spectators at the Oval.
Don Bradman gave his autograph to the boy in the foreground who sent him this photograph in appreciation.

W. A. Oldfield — Australia's great wicket-keeper.

Ponsford pulls one from Peebles to leg.

Play was resumed at 5.15. The rain was insufficient to affect the pitch or make the ball slippery, except for a short period.

Bradman cut the first ball from Peebles' uncompleted over for a single. Tate came on at the other end. The light was still indifferent. Bradman turned Tate's first ball for two, but he seemed to be baffled by the two succeeding deliveries.

Since Peebles dismissed Bradman at Manchester there have been mild controversies whether the record-breaker would be master on this occasion. Consequently, the spectators watched the duel with great interest, but appeals against the light were upheld at 5.25, and the battle was deferred.

Play was resumed at 5.30.

Bradman and Woodfull scored steadily against Peebles and Tate, the latter cover-driving for four, which Wyatt mainly chased. Bradman was getting ones and twos by neat taps behind the wicket. Twice he penetrated Peebles' leg-traps, and once he jumped out and slammed the slow bowler for two. Apparently he decided to have a good look at the bowling before attempting punishment.

Bradman handled Tate with his customary skill, glancing neatly. He also gained three by lifting Peebles over the leg traps' heads.

Bradman's innings began at 5.15 p.m. on the second day, after Ponsford was out for 110. Woodfull and Ponsford had taken the score to 159 for 1 wicket.

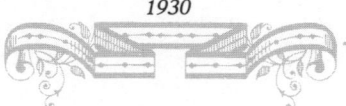
Bradman and Kippax resumed their innings on the third day (Tuesday).

Wyatt brings off a wonderful one-handed catch to dismiss Kippax. Hammond, Kippax, Duckworth, Wyatt, Larwood.

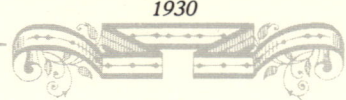

Bradman pulls a ball from Peebles to leg.

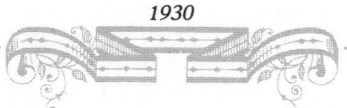

Jackson and Bradman going out to bat during the third day's play. They were not separated until 1 o'clock on Wednesday.

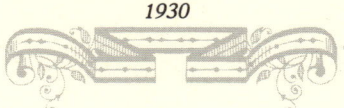

Bradman acknowledges the cheers of the crowd on completing his first century. Hobbs is applauding also.

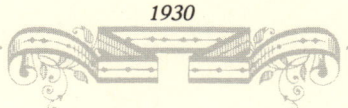

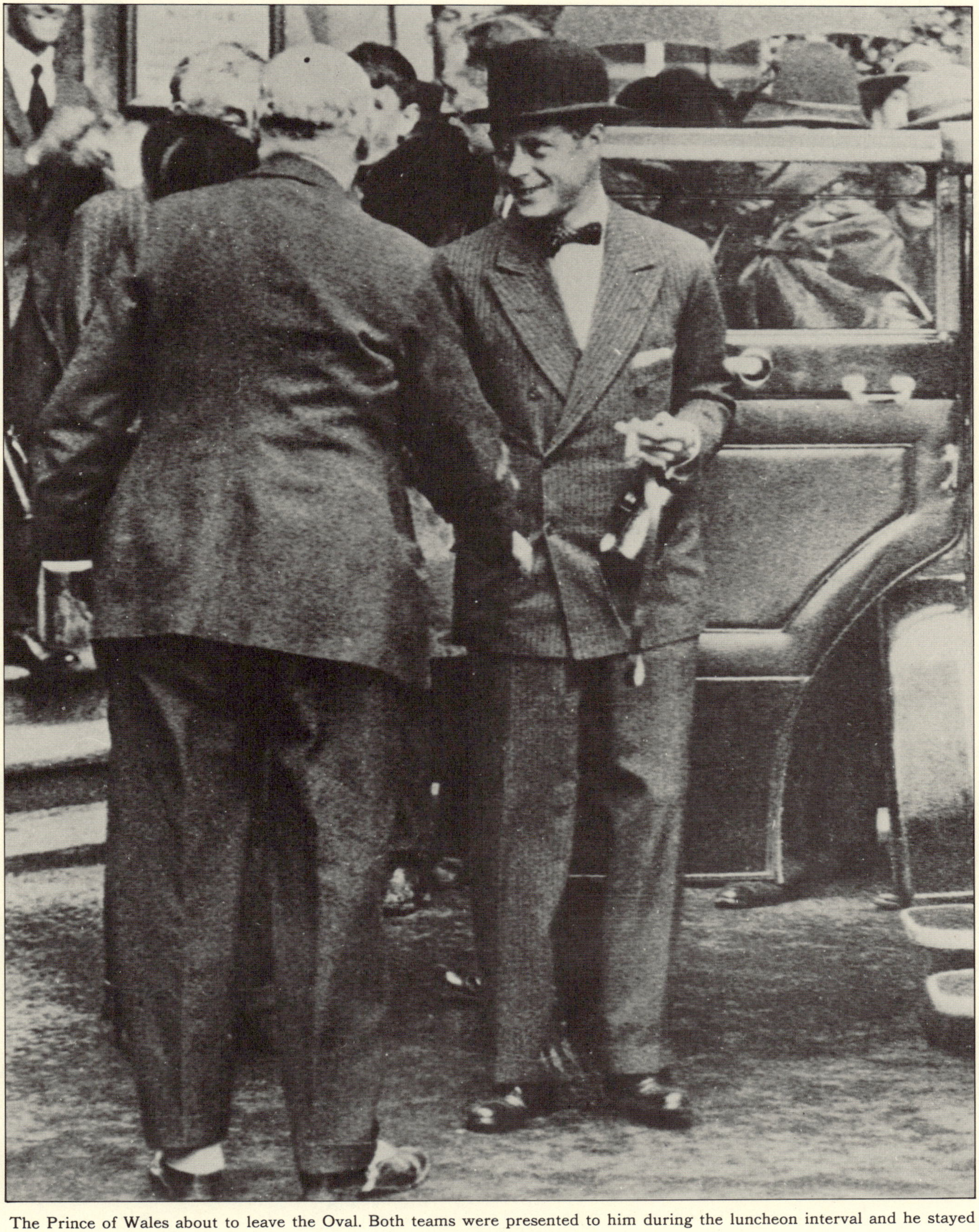

The Prince of Wales about to leave the Oval. Both teams were presented to him during the luncheon interval and he stayed to watch the game.

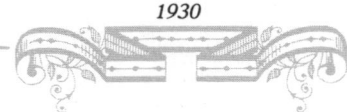

The score was 371 for 3 wickets at lunch.      Rain prevented play until 3 p.m. but after 50 minutes, further rain caused a postponement with the score at 402.
The umpires ordered play to resume at 25 minutes past 6.
In those 5 minutes 1 run was added.

Play was suspended owing to bad light and the wicket area roped off as usual.
The crowd are very interested to see what the pitch looked like.

Bradman makes the shot which puts Australia's total level with that of England in the first innings.
Hammond is preparing to chase the ball.

# LARWOOD IN ROLE OF "KILLER"

## BRADMAN WINCED WITH PAIN

## JACKSON, TOO, WAS STRUCK HARD

# ANXIOUS MOMENTS

LONDON, Wednesday.

This Bradman is lion-hearted, physically and figuratively.

He made a double century despite the whirlwind rib-breaking shock tactics of Larwood.

DON was doubled up with pain when a terrifically fast ball struck him in the chest. Shortly afterwards another Larwood ball crashed on to his fingers.

It would be hard to realise the pain he was suffering as he flogged the bowling. When Jackson shook him by the hand after his double century Don winced in agony.

*Larwood*

It was real cricket courage. Larwood was in his most dangerous mood, reminiscent of his Australian visit. Balls bumped from the pitch at high speed, and it seemed as if Bradman and Jackson would be seriously injured.

Jackson threw up his head in pain when a Larwood ball struck his chest. He afterwards seemed to be sick, frequently leaning on his bat.

Later, a ball from Hammond cracked him on the elbow.

They were anxious moments for Australia as the balls hurtled towards the batsmen's heads.

Umpire Parry attends to an injury to Bradman caused by a "bumper" from Larwood who looks on.

# Another Masterly Century For Bradman

Before lunch at The Oval was a glorious period for Australia to-day, and provided the most courageous batting I have ever seen. Despite the most difficult wicket, Bradman and Jackson gave the English public an exhibition of versatility, pluck, and determination rarely seen on a cricket field. The dangerous wicket helped the bowlers, who made the ball fly, Larwood being particularly vicious. Frequently the lads, after being hit, writhed in pain, but, bruised and battered from head to toe, they carried on. The eyes of the Australian women were moistened by tears, as though Jackson and Bradman were their own sons. Certainly it was a wonderful display of courage to withstand such a terrific onslaught.

Jackson's fighting innings justified the selectors' wisdom, while words cannot be found for Bradman's wonderful versatility on all types of wickets. He has silenced his critics for ever.

Bradman acknowledges the cheers of the crowd on completing his 200 runs.

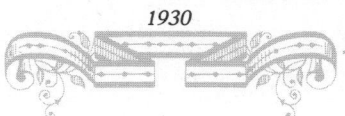

Bradman, seated next to the driver in this car, is seen waving to Alf Stephens (former Mayor of Bowral and Captain of Bowral Cricket Club) whose face can be seen past the nose of the grey horse.

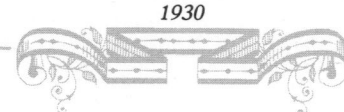

As Hobbs was about to commence his last Test innings for England the Australian players, led by Woodfull, formed a circle around him and gave three cheers.
Hobbs acknowledges this recognition of his great career.

*WEDNESDAY, 20 AUGUST*

*Continued game. Difficult, dangerous wicket.*
*Archie and I made a stand. I was given out caught by*
*Duckworth off Larwood for 232 but did not hit the ball.*
*I scored 98 before lunch and broke all previous records for*
*a series of Tests.*
*Others all batted well.*
*Three cheers for Hobbs when he came out.*
*To the Alhambra Theatre at night to see "All Quiet on the*
*Western Front".*

A splendid photograph of Hobbs showing his beautifully relaxed stance.

# FIFTH TEST.

## Australia's Great Victory.

### INNINGS AND 39 RUNS.

The closing scene of the match showing crowds of spectators rushing towards the players as they leave the field.

# OUR MIRACLE

## BRADMAN WON THE ASHES

### AVERAGE OF 139

### WORTH TWO OF ANY OTHER

#### (By Clarence Moody)

Australia has regained the Ashes and established a pronounced ascendancy in the eternal struggle with 50 wins against 47. While it is a triumph for youth under the guidance of a splendid captain, the presence in the team of a world-beating batsman is primarily responsible for our happy position.

ENGLAND has been taught a lesson and seems determined to profit by it for the next series of Tests to be played in Australia in 1932-33.

Comparatively few Australians, and probably no Englishman, expected such a glorious result before the 1930 series of matches was begun. An English writer has said this week that it was a miracle that a team which in May was regarded as being only of county strength, should have won the Ashes.

Don Bradman is the miracle, confirming in the most striking fashion my contention, based on a long experience of Tests, that the country which possesses a super-champion batsman will invariably win a rubber.

D. G. Bradman    C. V. Grimmett

If Australia, possessing Bradman with Grimmett the best bowler or either side, could not win the rubber she never would.

### ORIGIN OF "THE ASHES"

After Australia had beaten England in England for the first time in 1882 *The Sporting Times* printed a mock obituary notice lamenting the death of English cricket and adding that "the body will be cremated and the ashes taken to Australia."

When, in the following winter, the Hon. Ivo Bligh (later Lord Darnley) took a team to Australia and reversed the result, certain ladies burned a stump, sealed the ashes in an urn and presented it to him. In his will Lord Darnley bequeathed the urn to M.C.C. It is to be seen now in the Imperial Cricket Memorial Gallery at Lord's.

Thus "the ashes" are not mythical. They do not, however, change hands, but are kept permanently at the Headquarters of Cricket.

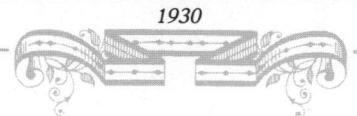

# Australians
# v
# Mr. H. D. G. Leveson-Gower's XI

AUSTRALIANS v MR. H.D.G. LEVESON-GOWER's XI, at Scarborough, 10, 11 and 12 September 1930.

Australians     - First Innings     238
                - Second Innings   -

Mr. Leveson-Gower's  - First Innings     218 for 9 wickets dec.
       XI          - Second Innings   247

               Drawn.

DON BRADMAN   - b. C.W.L. Parker          96

Wilfred Rhodes.

DON BRADMAN started his innings on the second day at 30 for 1, and had reached 73 in an hour and forty-eight minutes before bad light stopped play. Next morning, the wicket was again rather difficult, but he carried his score to 96 before being bowled off his pads in trying to hook a ball which kept very low. This was an historic occasion because it was the last time that Wilfred Rhodes played in a first class match, and it is interesting to record that subsequently Rhodes said he considered Bradman to be the greatest batsman of all time.

Scarborough Cricket Ground.

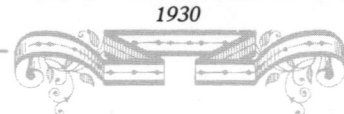

# THE AVERAGES.

### Interesting Statistics.

#### (By "Veteran.")

The Australian Test team which has just concluded its English tour will go down to cricket history as one of the most successful that has ever visited the old land. Out of 34 matches played, only one was lost, and it cannot be said that any of the drawn games were unfavourable to the visitors, although one exciting tie was played.

During the tour the Australians scored 12,335 runs for the loss of 348 wickets, or an average of 35.4 runs per wicket, while their English opponents made 10,562 runs for 470 wickets, an average of 22.4, thus giving a substantial balance in the Australians' favour. The last three Australian teams which have visited England have fared as follow:—

| Year. | Won. | Lost. | Drawn. | Tie. |
|---|---|---|---|---|
| 1921 .. .. .. .. .. | 22 | 2 | 14 | 0 |
| 1926 .. .. .. .. .. | 14 | 1 | 22 | 0 |
| 1930 .. .. .. .. .. | 12 | 1 | 20 | 1 |

Following are the averages and other statistics for the tour:—

### Batting.

| | Inns. | N.O. | Runs. | H.S. | Aver. |
|---|---|---|---|---|---|
| Bradman .. .. | 38 | 6 | 3,170 | 334 | 99 |
| Woodfull .. .. | 28 | 1 | 1,568 | 216 | 58 |
| Kippax .. .. .. | 34 | 7 | 1,510 | 158 | 55.9 |
| Ponsford .. .. | 35 | 4 | 1,429 | 220* | 46 |
| Jackson .. .. .. | 36 | 4 | 1,149 | 118 | 35.8 |
| McCabe .. .. .. | 35 | 2 | 1,013 | 96 | 30.6 |
| Richardson .. .. | 32 | 1 | 832 | 116 | 27.1 |
| Fairfax .. .. .. | 28 | 6 | 565 | 63 | 25.6 |
| a'Beckett .. .. | 25 | 5 | 454 | 67* | 22.7 |
| Oldfield .. .. | 17 | 4 | 225 | 43* | 17.8 |
| Hornibrook .. .. | 28 | 8 | 241 | 59* | 12 |
| Grimmett .. .. | 23 | 3 | 237 | 50 | 11.8 |
| Hurwood .. .. | 21 | 1 | 193 | 61 | 9.6 |
| Wall .. .. .. | 20 | 7 | 107 | 40* | 8.2 |
| Walker .. .. .. | 16 | 6 | 50 | 10* | 5 |

### Century List.

| | | |
|---|---|---|
| Bradman .. .. .. .. | Worcester | 236 |
| Bradman .. .. .. .. | Leicestershire | 185* |
| Bradman .. .. .. .. | Surrey | 252* |
| Bradman .. .. .. .. | Hampshire | 191 |
| Bradman .. .. .. .. | England 1st Test | 131 |
| Bradman .. .. .. .. | England 2nd Test | 254 |
| Bradman .. .. .. .. | England 3rd Test | 334 |
| Bradman .. .. .. .. | West of Scotland | 140 |
| Bradman .. .. .. .. | Somerset | 117 |
| Bradman .. .. .. .. | England 5th Test | 232 |
| Bradman .. .. .. .. | Kent | 205* |
| Woodfull .. .. .. .. | Worcestershire | 138 |
| Woodfull .. .. .. .. | Yorkshire | 121 |
| Woodfull .. .. .. .. | Cambridge Uni. | 216 |
| Woodfull .. .. .. .. | Surrey | 141 |
| Woodfull .. .. .. .. | England 2nd Test | 155 |
| Woodfull .. .. .. .. | Northampton | 116 |
| Ponsford .. .. .. .. | Derbyshire | 133 |
| Ponsford .. .. .. .. | Oxford Uni. | 220* |
| Ponsford .. .. .. .. | Yorkshire | 143 |
| Ponsford .. .. .. .. | England 5th Test | 110 |
| Kippax .. .. .. .. | Middlesex | 102 |
| Kippax .. .. .. .. | Lancashire | 120 |
| Kippax .. .. .. .. | Sussex | 158 |
| Kippax .. .. .. .. | Sussex | 102* |
| Richardson .. .. .. | Leicestershire | 100 |
| Richardson .. .. .. | Northampton | 116 |
| Jackson .. .. .. .. | Somerset | 118 |

* Signifies not out.

## AUSTRALIAN CRICKET TEAM IN ENGLAND
### 1902

BACK ROW   (reading from left to right) W. P. Howell, H. Trumble, J. V. Saunders, W. W. Armstrong, A. J. Hopkins.

MIDDLE ROW   (reading from left to right) V. Trumper, J. J. Kelly, R. A. Duff, J. Darling, M. A. Noble, C. Hill.

FRONT ROW   (reading from left to right) S. E. Gregory, H. Carter.

## Averages of the Australians in England, 1902.

### BATTING.

| | Innings. | Not out. | Highest Score. | Total Runs. | Average. |
|---|---|---|---|---|---|
| V. Trumper............ | 53 | 0 | 128 | 2570 | 48.47 |
| M. A. Noble............ | 48 | 5 | 284 | 1416 | 32.93 |
| C. Hill................ | 52 | 1 | 136 | 1614 | 31.64 |
| R. A. Duff............ | 58 | 5 | 183 | 1507 | 28.43 |
| W. W. Armstrong...... | 51 | 10 | 172* | 1087 | 26.51 |
| A. J. Hopkins........ | 54 | 8 | 105* | 1202 | 26.13 |
| J. Darling.......... | 51 | 5 | 128 | 1113 | 24.19 |
| S. E. Gregory........ | 52 | 6 | 86 | 980 | 21.71 |
| H. Trumble.......... | 30 | 6 | 68 | 426 | 17.75 |
| J. J. Kelly.......... | 34 | 8 | 75 | 398 | 14.72 |
| E. Jones.......... | 21 | 1 | 40 | 254 | 12.70 |
| H. Carter............ | 20 | 5 | 31 | 121 | 8.06 |
| W. P. Howell........ | 24 | 6 | 14 | 95 | 5.27 |
| J. V. Saunders........ | 34 | 9 | 9* | 84 | 3.36 |

### The Century List.

| | |
|---|---|
| V. Trumper.. .. | 11 = 128, 127, 125, 121, 120, 119, 113, 109, 105, 104, 104. |
| C. Hill .. | 4 = 136, 123, 119, 104. |
| M. A. Noble .. | 3 = 284, 113, 100. |
| R. A. Duff .. | 2 = 183, 182. |
| J. Darling .. | 2 = 128, 116. |
| W. W. Armstrong .. | 1 = 172*. |
| A. J. Hopkins .. | 1 = 105*. |

* Not out.

### BOWLING.

| | Runs. | Wickets. | Average. |
|---|---|---|---|
| H. Trumble ................ | 1988 | 140 | 14.20 |
| J. V. Saunders.............. | 2173 | 127 | 17.11 |
| W. W. Armstrong .......... | 1410 | 81 | 17.40 |
| A. J. Hopkins ............ | 669 | 38 | 17.60 |
| W. P. Howell ............ | 1215 | 68 | 17.86 |
| M. A. Noble ............ | 1947 | 98 | 19.85 |
| E. Jones.... ............ | 1456 | 71 | 20.50 |
| V. Trumper .............. | 415 | 20 | 20.75 |

# STRAIGHT HOME

## WITH DON'S BAT

"I am taking it straight home to have a big swipe with it," said George Lethbridge, of Mowbray House School yesterday, when he received the Don Bradman bat presented to him for heading the scores in the big competition in aid of the Royal Alexandra Hospital for Children.

The presentation was made at the hospital yesterday by the Lord Mayor (Alderman Marks).

"The amount of money raised was wonderful," said Alderman Marks, referring to the £733 which was collected by the competition. He paid a tribute to "The Sun," through whose efforts that amount was raised by penny votes

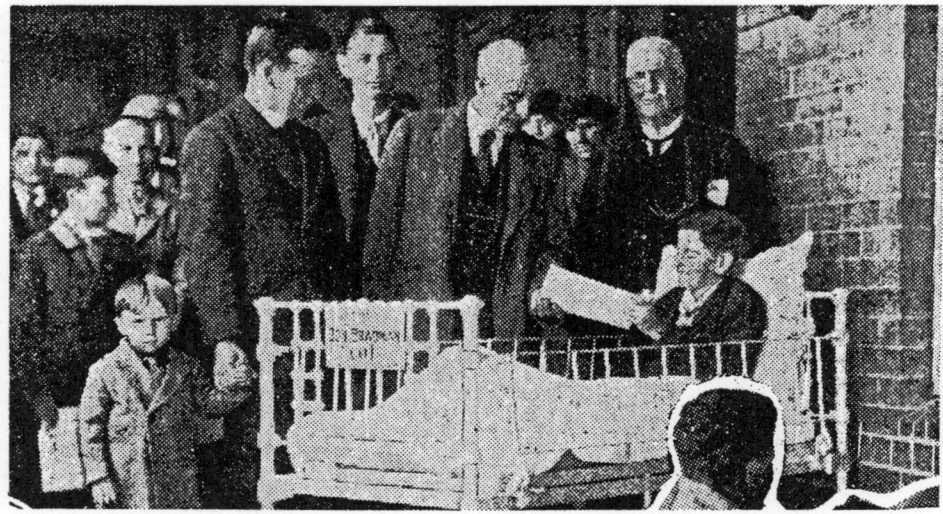

PROUD, Clifford Seaton, who was presented with the Don Bradman bat at Royal Alexandra Hospital by the Lord Mayor. Sir Charles Clubbe and Rev. A. Morris Yates (organiser) behind Ald. Marks.

## Bon Voyage to Don Bradman

AU REVOIR, FLEET STREET.—No Australian cricketer has received so many plaudits from the London press as Don Bradman. Here's a picture of Don after having been tendered a send-off luncheon in Fleet-street by "Truth's" London manager, Mr. Claude Watt (on the left).

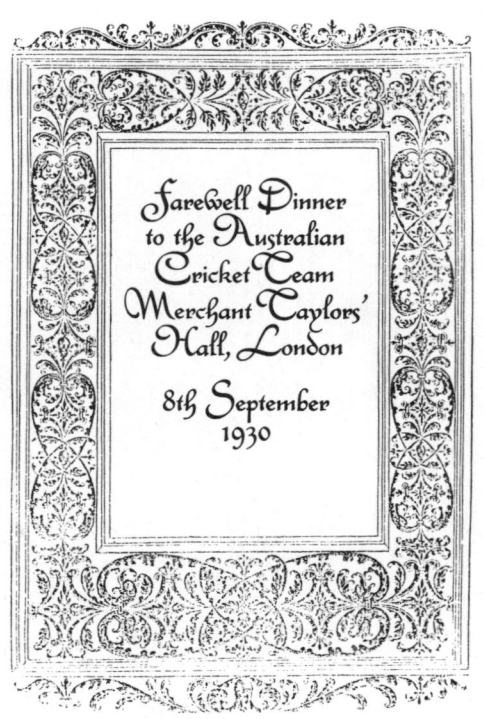

Farewell Dinner
to the Australian
Cricket Team
Merchant Taylors'
Hall, London

8th September
1930

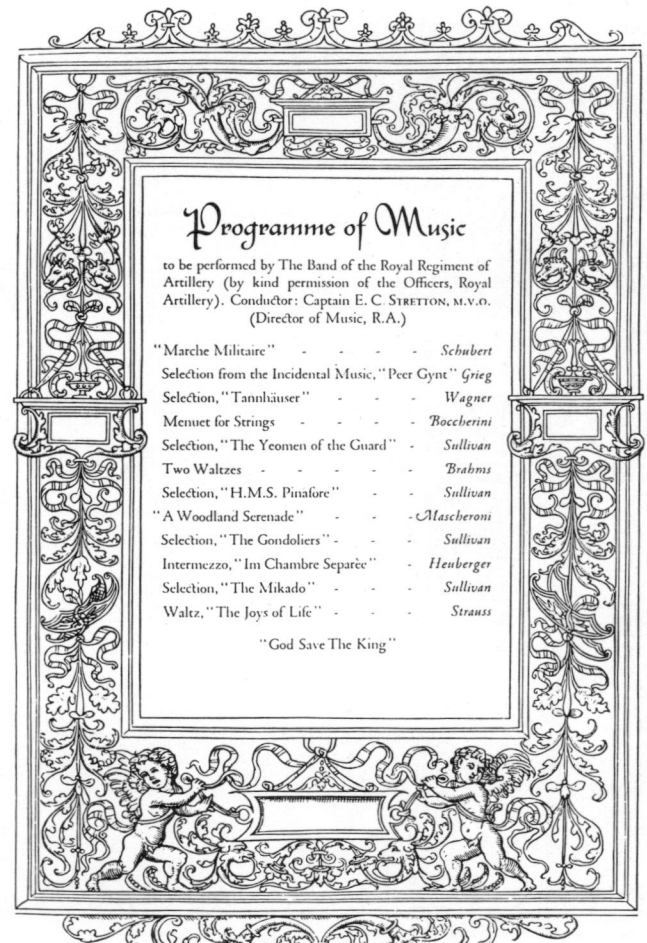

## Programme of Music

to be performed by The Band of the Royal Regiment of Artillery (by kind permission of the Officers, Royal Artillery). Conductor: Captain E. C. STRETTON, M.V.O. (Director of Music, R.A.)

"Marche Militaire" - - - *Schubert*
Selection from the Incidental Music, "Peer Gynt" *Grieg*
Selection, "Tannhäuser" - - - *Wagner*
Menuet for Strings - - - *Boccherini*
Selection, "The Yeomen of the Guard" - *Sullivan*
Two Waltzes - - - - *Brahms*
Selection, "H.M.S. Pinafore" - - *Sullivan*
"A Woodland Serenade" - - *Mascheroni*
Selection, "The Gondoliers" - - *Sullivan*
Intermezzo, "Im Chambre Separée" - *Heuberger*
Selection, "The Mikado" - - *Sullivan*
Waltz, "The Joys of Life" - - - *Strauss*

"God Save The King"

## Toasts

### His Majesty The King

National Anthem

First verse sung by Mr. Kennerley Rumford
Second verse sung by Dame Clara Butt
First verse repeated by entire assembly

### Our Australian Guests

*Proposed by* Sir James Barrie
*Responses by* Mr. W. M. Woodfull & Mr. W. L. Kelly

SONGS - "The Lost Chord" - *Sullivan*
"Land of Hope and Glory" - *Elgar*

Land of Hope and Glory, Mother of the Free,
How shall we extol thee, who are born of thee?
Wider still and wider shall thy bounds be set;
God, who made thee mighty, make thee mightier yet.
—A. C. BENSON
Dame Clara Butt

### Cricket

*Proposed by* The Lord Harris
*Response by* H.H. The Maharaja Jamsaheb of
Nawanagar

### The Chairman

*Proposed by* The Viscount Ullswater

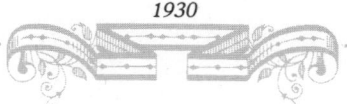

Don Bradman autographing bats at Sykes' factory, Horbury.

## TWO AUSTRALIAN CHAMPIONS.

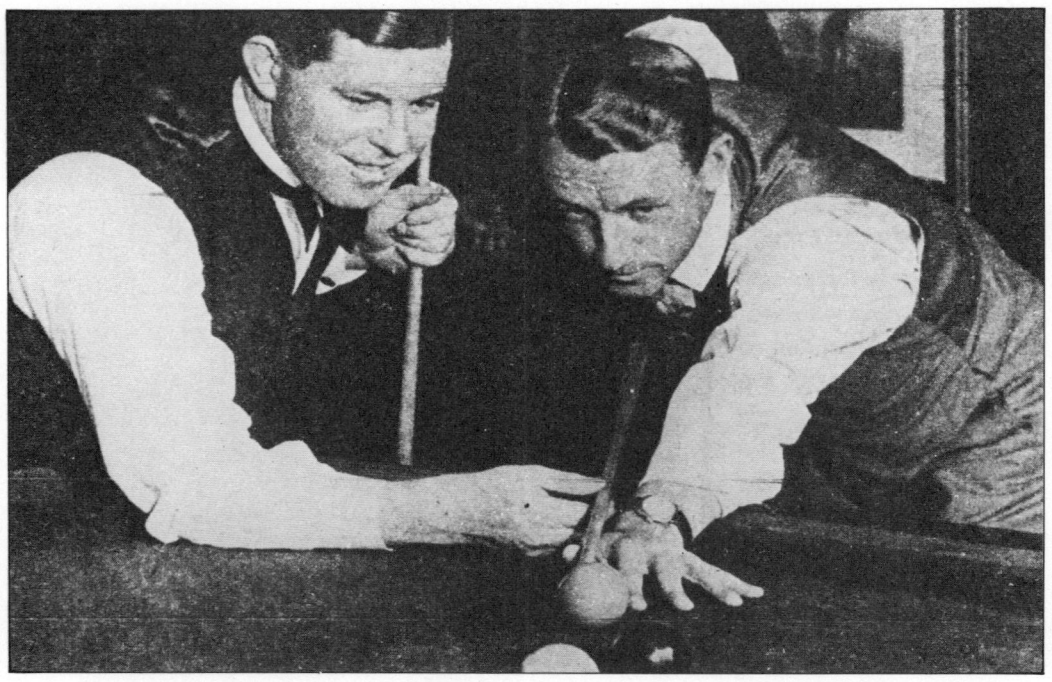

Walter Lindrum (left), world's billiards champion, coaching Don Bradman in London.

# BRADMAN MAKES A NEW RECORD.

**DON BRADMAN** is almost as facile with "the ivories" as he is with the willow. Latest picture, by air mail, shows him making a record at Columbia's London studio, with Harold Williams, Australian artist.

SATURDAY, 20 SEPTEMBER

*Doing jobs in London. S. T. Garland Advertising Coy, Rolex and others.*
*To Elstree Studios after lunch with Whitelaws. Mr. Grossman showed us around. Met Wee Georgie Wood, Seymour Hicks, Joyce Kennedy, Margot Grahame, Edmund Greon and other actors and actresses also Monty Banks, the producer.*
*To Bushy Hotel for afternoon tea.*
*Geoff and I then went to the New Morris Hall "Tedmore Club". Gave them a bat and they presented me with a wallet.*
*To Whitelaws for dinner and afterwards to see "The Three Musketeers" at Theatre Royal, Drury Lane.*
*Afterwards to the "Kit Kat" Club.*

Bradman presents a cricket bat to the "Tedmore Club" at the New Morris Hall. Geoff Whitelaw is on the extreme right.

Elstree Studios.

LEFT TO RIGHT   Mr. Arthur Whitelaw, Geoff Whitelaw, Seymour Hicks, Don Bradman, Margot Grahame and one of the Western Brothers.

# CHAMPION IS REAPING HANDSOME FORTUNE DURING MARVELLOUS TOUR IN ENGLAND

## Manager Kelly Cannot Chain Young Napoleon

### DON WRITES FOR PAPERS, MAKES MOVIE-TONES, AND IS PHOTOGRAPHED TO BOOST WIRELESS SETS

*WHEN Don Bradman comes back to Australia the Cricket Board of Control will yammer and squeal. There'll be a great clucking among the cricket-governing hens!*

*This superb young cricketer, showing as much initiative and acumen in business as he does at the batting crease, has snapped like a lot of pack-thread the tangle of prohibitions and restrictions woven by the Board of Control to debar Australian players from making any money from their cricketing fame.*

*Like Alexander with his sword, Don with his bat, has slashed through all those restraining knots. Being in his own class as a batsman, he is also a law unto himself.*

*Manager Kelly has not ventured to suppress Don's business activity, excepting in part. The young wonder batsman, in his first triumphant tour in England, is reported by "Smith's" London office to have probably accumulated enough capital to set himself up in business when he returns to Australia.*

*Good luck to him! "Smith's" welcomes Bradman's bold defiance of the Board of Control, a fussy body which tries to treat Australia's cricketing champions as a team of underpaid gladiators. Why shouldn't Bradman be allowed to protect his future?*

Don Bradman, Mr. Kelly and Geoffrey Tebbutt.
(Taken during the 1930 Australian tour of England.)

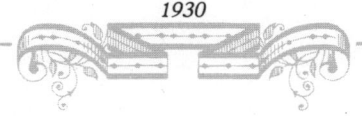

# Will Don Bradman Be Bossed By The Board of Control?

FROM "Smith's" London office yesterday came the story of the prowess of Don Alexander Napoleon Bradman, the cricketer who hit the fussy Controllers to leg, with as much coolness and determination as he showed in smiting the English bowlers.

"Pompous rules and regulations of the Board of Control have been cut, slashed, and smitten into scraps," says our London office by special radio. "The Red Tape is scattered in little pieces.

"By means of his unprecedented batting, Don Bradman has placed himself on a pinnacle where he is not only supreme among cricketers, but may be as independent in his attitude towards the Controllers, as Dr. W. G. Grace made himself in England in a past generation."

(Dr. W. G., as a "lilywhite" amateur, made his cricket more profitable than that of any professional in England; but because of W.G.'s unapproachable records, none of the Gentlemen of England ever ventured to question the Doctor's amateur status.)

Radio from "Smith's" London office goes on to tell us:

"Don has done things during this tour which no lesser player would have dared to attempt. The Board of Control has been simply left gasping.

"Early in the tour, it will be remembered, the Manager and the Board of Control were perturbed by the Australian team's acceptance of £100 a man, for boosting a special line of cigarettes. According to cables received in England, a number of Australian newspapers uttered mugwump protests against this 'exploitation' of cricket fame. Opinion in England did not seem to be at all perturbed by the incident.

"Again, the Management and Board were at great pains to prevent the Australian players from signing autograph books for schoolboys.

"But Don Bradman went ahead with as full serenity as he displayed when he was scoring 334 and 232 in Test matches.

"About a month ago he startled Manager Kelly and the cricketing world at large by writing a series of newspaper articles for the London 'Star.' This action was open and defiant.

"All England knows the history of the campaign undertaken by the Australian Board of Control against cricketing player-writers. It meant the removal of Arthur Mailey from Test cricket, even though Mailey by profession is a journalist.

"So far as I can gather from reliable information, Manager Kelly was greatly surprised when he learned of Bradman's series of articles. But Kelly took no action. Thus the manager condoned an obvious breach of the ironbound rule against player-writers, which had been laid down so firmly by the Board of Control.

"But this was only the beginning of Don's Napoleonic pursuit of his own destiny.

"Since then, Bradman has made a movie-tone demonstrating his strokes.

"He has signed his autograph on hundreds of cricket bats.

"I am informed that he even agreed to sign a contract to appear in one of the London halls during the fifth Test.

"But this last boldness was too much for the distressed Manager Kelly, who nipped the scheme in the bud.

"Latest demonstration of Don's independence is to be seen in London shop windows, which display his photograph in large sizes, advertising a wireless set of well-known brand."

That Bradman received a gift of £1000 from the ex-Australian merchant Arthur Whitelaw has been widely published. "Smith's" man in London does not know whether the champion consulted the manager before accepting this princely douceur.

"Don has had a valued adviser," continues "Smith's" radio message from London. "His mentor is an ex-Victorian cricketer, who has been Don's close associate ever since the tour opened.

"England, on the whole, seems rather pleased that Bradman may be able to establish himself in business in Australia, as a result of his phenomenal brilliance on this tour. He is a national (or Imperial) hero to the English cricketing public as well as to Australians."

The foregoing news from England will be read with deepest interest by Australians; and "Smith's" ventures the opinion that outside the more fussy members of the Board of Control, few Australians will harshly criticise the triumphant young cricketer.

When a young champion devotes himself to a game, he sacrifices his commercial prospects during critical years of his life.

One of Australia's most successful business men, Sir Mark Sheldon, said recently to a "Smith's" writer:—

"In the life of a young man there comes a time when he must decide between business and sport. He may look forward to progress in his business career, or he may make himself a champion on the tennis court or the cricket field. But he cannot do both."

So it is with Bradman. If he is to devote himself to Australian cricket, as a champion batsman with perhaps twenty years of international duty before him on the playing field, he is surely entitled to consolidate his present chances, even in terms of money.

Off the field Bradman is employed by Mick Simmons Ltd.; a valuable asset to that firm. Naturally Mick Simmons Ltd. do not tell what salary he is paid. When "Smith's" asked Simmons' manager yesterday whether Don would come back to Australia to join the rest of us in suffering a wage-cut, Simmons Ltd. laughed quite pleasantly and told the inquirer to go to the devil.

But if the Board of Control had everything its own way, that is the experience it would expect Australia's greatest batsman of all time to undergo obediently and cheerfully.

It will be interesting to see whether the Australian Board of Control will fall into the blunder of attempting any punitive action against Australia's greatest batsman.

# THE CRICKETERS

## SAIL FOR HOME.

### Bradman Still Fancy Free.

LONDON, Sept. 27.

The representative of the Australian Press Association with the Australian cricketers says:—Compared with the Orford, on which the Australians journeyed to England, the Oronsay, which Ponsford, Bradman, Wall, Fairfax, Hornibrook, and Walker joined, was an empty ship. Many friends farewelled them at St. Pancras Station, but as few visitors were allowed to come to the dismal docks, the players saw the last of England in the quietest fashion.

Hornibrook was disappointed because his wife and baby, who were bound to Colombo to meet him, were unable to stand the sea journey, and left the steamer at Melbourne. Among the trophies which Hornibrook is taking home are a fox mask and brush, secured during a cubbing meet near Leicester, where he was the guest of Sir Arthur Hazlerigg. Bradman seemed depressed at leaving the scenes of his many triumphs, but the others were in high spirits, and looking forward to the next tour.

The servants of the Midland Hotel, the team's London headquarters, have many mementoes of the Australians' stay. The valet who attended the team is bursting with pride at gifts of an old blazer and some car gloves.

The team's baggage includes golf clubs, because, with few exceptions, they have become converts to golf during the tour. Hornibrook took a fishing rod aboard, and Ponsford carried a phonograph, which had aided in keeping up the team's spirits since they left.

Macartney and Mrs. Macartney are aboard, and the scorer (Mr. Ferguson) will travel overland on Monday, joining the Oronsay at Toulon. Oldfield, Hurwood, Jackson, a'Beckett and the manager (Mr. Kelly) leave London on Wednesday, also embarking at Toulon.

No announcement has been made by the team, but it is understood that the financial result of the tour is an improvement on the 1926 tour.

## AT ST. PANCRAS.

A shrill chorus of cooees by the women hockey players gave a real Australian flavour to the crowded send-off at St. Pancras Station. As usual Bradman held an unceasing reception, and assured many inquirers that he was not leaving a sweetheart behind in England. Ponsford said that the time could not pass quickly enough for him to be home. Wall looked very fit after his minor scalp operation. Fairfax was phlegmatic, and viewed everything as a matter of course. Bradman told an interviewer, "It isn't good-bye, it is only au revoir. I hope to be back in 1934, if my cricket is still good enough." Ponsford cryptically remarked, "I may not be paying another visit to England."

There was great enthusiasm as the train left. Bradman was still hanging out of the window as the train disappeared.

The secretary of the M.C.C. (Mr. W. Findlay) was present on behalf of the club.

The Drawing Room, R.M.S. *Oronsay.*

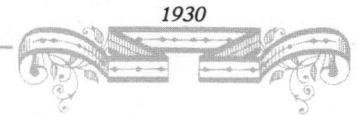

SATURDAY, 18 OCTOBER

*In Colombo Harbour on awakening.*
*Ashore early. Foenander presented me with silver model of*
*Buddhist Temple on behalf of the natives of Colombo.*
*Enthusiasts on the wharf in hundreds.*
*To Dia's rubber plantation where we were shown all over*
*the Estate, how the tapping was done, the rubber made etc.,*
*and they gave us a sheet of rubber each.*
*To his own home where he has birds, animals, deer etc.*
*Thence to rest home for tea and to Mt. Lavinia for dinner.*
*After that to the museum and a look over the zoo. Keeper*
*offered me monkeys.*
*Dinner at Foenander's home. Evening on boat.*
*Pulled out at 12.*

S. P. Foenander holds Woodfull's son in his arms as Bradman is presented with a silver model of
the Buddhist Temple.

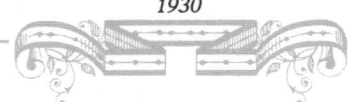
# HOME, DON

## BY AIR AND CAR
### CONDUCTED TOUR

A giant American motor corporation—General Motors—is to reintroduce Don Bradman to his fellow-Australians.

It will receive him and his fellow-players at Perth on October 28.

The whole Australian team, whose cohesion has been its strongest point, is to be broken at Adelaide on November 1. From that moment it will become a comet with a long tail—Bradman being the head, and the rest of the team the tail. In Adelaide, in Melbourne and in Sydney Bradman is to be the guest of General Motors.

## To See Home Folks

From Adelaide General Motors will bring him to Melbourne in a National Airways three-engine passenger 'plane, where receptions arranged by General Motors will be held. On Tuesday, November 4, Bradman will be taken in the same 'plane from Melbourne to Goulburn, and thence in a General Motors car to his home in Bowral. On the following day he is to be driven to Sydney at the head of a party of General Motors cars, which will contain officials of General Motors and his parents.

There will be an official welcome at the Town Hall, followed by a luncheon given by General Motors, and in the evening he will be entertained at the home of a well-known General Motors official. Finally, he will be presented with a General Motors car.

Bradman being welcomed at Theatre Royal, Perth.

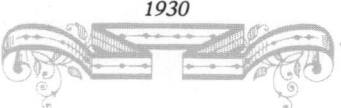

Don Bradman on the Transcontinental train.

Arriving at Parafield aerodrome en route to Melbourne.

# DON BRADMAN

## Arrives by 'Plane at Melbourne.

### WELCOMED BY BIG CROWD.

### CRICKETERS ABSENT.

MELBOURNE, Sunday.

The arrival to-day of Don Bradman, a day ahead of the rest of the Australian Eleven, drew a crowd of 10,000 to Essendon Aerodrome.

Bradman was expected to arrive from Adelaide by 'plane at 3.30 this afternoon, but it was not until 5.30 that the 'plane reached Essendon. The crowd by this time had considerably diminished, but the welcome by hundreds of people who rushed the 'plane almost before it had stopped was none the less hearty.

It was noticeable that not one cricketer of note or a cricket official could be seen in the crowd. It was the reception of a popular sporting hero by a crowd of sightseers, in which curiosity and hero-worship were the principal features.

When Bradman landed he was immediately lost in the crowd, and only the forcible attentions of a strong body of police enabled him to reach a lorry draped with the Australian flag that was to serve as a platform.

The captain of the 1921 Australian Eleven, Mr. W. W. Armstrong, welcomed Bradman. He said that it was a welcome to the first of the team which had won the ashes. The credit of victory belonged to all the members of the team, but Bradman was the first to reach Melbourne, and was thus first to be welcomed.

Bradman, who was smiling as usual, said he was overwhelmed at the reception, and that, although there had been many welcomes, this was the best of them all. He apologised for having been late, and said that the 'plane was late leaving Adelaide, and was then delayed by head winds. Bradman added that he hoped to be returning to England as a member of the Australian Eleven in 1934.

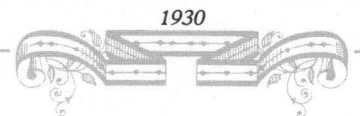

Leaving Essendon aerodrome. Bradman is on the right of Pilot Shortridge with the
"Southern Cloud" behind.

"Wizard" Smith, Don Bradman and his brother Vic setting off by car from Goulburn aerodrome.

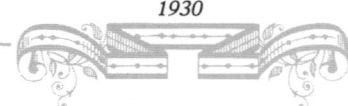

# GLIMPSES OF "DON" —

**HIS MOTHER.**—Proudest moment of all for Don was when his mother clasped him in her arms, and smilingly he kissed her.

*HOME!—Don seems well content. His happy smile is indicative of his appreciation of home, the cheers of the townspeople, a new car, and—a charming sister.*

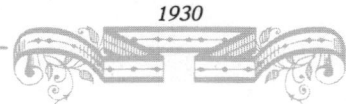

Bradman greeted by his father (on his left) and his brother Vic.

A proud mother gratefully accepts a bunch of red roses.

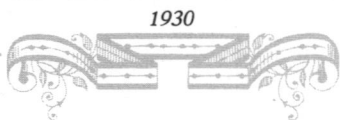

**DON BRADMAN,** world's most famous batsman, addressing his friends when he reached Bowral last night.

Silver model of Buddhist Temple presented to Don Bradman in 1930 by cricket lovers in Colombo.

A cinema advertising poster in Sydney, *c.* 1931.

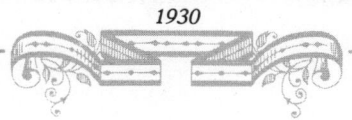

### WEDNESDAY, 5 NOVEMBER

*Left Bowral 9.45. Raced to Sydney with Wizard Smith. Did 82 m.p.h. at one stage of the trip.*
*Changed into my Chev at Liverpool. Drove into Sydney and reached Mick Simmons' at noon.*
*Public and staff gave me a magnificent welcome.*
*Received by all and sundry.*
*General Motors gave me a lunch at the Royal Automobile Club.*
*Lord Mayor, Chief Secretary and others there.*
*Evening at Holt's home in Woollahra.*
*Later to the Sydney Town Hall.*
*A musical programme was broadcasted and General Motors asked the Chief Secretary Mark Gosling to hand me the keys of my special Don Bradman Model Chevrolet motor car.*
*He made a speech. I replied. I also gave keys of G. M. Charity car to the Lord Mayor.*
*All broadcasted.*
*Finished at 10 p.m.*

En route from Bowral to Sydney, Bradman and "Wizard" Smith changed into the little red Chevrolet which General Motors later presented to Bradman. Bradman's sister May looks on.

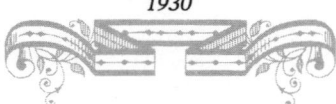

Arriving at Mick Simmons Ltd., Sydney.

## No Jealousies

Referring to Don Bradman, Jackson said that there were no personal jealousies in the team and Bradman was just as popular as the rest among his team-mates despite his great success. However in between matches or after the day's play, they did not see much of the young champion, who had made many friends outside. Not one member of the team raised any objection to Bradman leaving the team at Adelaide.

**SLIPPED HOME** and dodged the welcoming crowds.—Cricketer Archie Jackson, happy with his proud mother and sister.

## THE SILENCE OF DON BRADMAN

### Serious, and With Nothing to Say

Eight months or so ago Don Bradman went away a smiling boy. Now he has come back thinner, maturer, and much more serious.

HE stoutly refuses to say a word to the public through the newspapers.

After his reception at Bowral yesterday Bradman was asked by the "Pictorial" for some impressions of the tour. He declined to give them.

He declined to discuss English crowds, his own success, or his future, Woodfull, or the rest of the team.

When it was suggested that it was unusual for a prominent Australian to return from abroad and decline to talk, Bradman replied, "It is not unusual with me; I have not given anything to a newspeper since I landed!"

Obviously, Bradman has his mind made up in a certain direction.

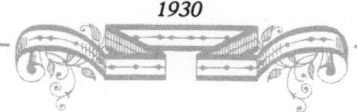

# DON BRADMAN
## WELCOME
### LOSEBY PARK, BOWRAL
## SATURDAY, DEC. 6

Electric Light. Monster Sports & Carnival

Vic Bradman (Don's brother) cleaning his Ford whilst father relaxes on the running board.

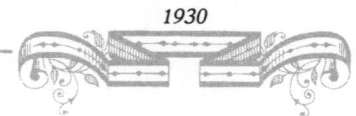

During the 1930 tour of England I wrote my life story. It was published as *Don Bradman's Book*, and a London newspaper ran serialised articles from it. They are set out on the following pages.

Because of space limitations, certain of the less relevant material has been excluded and some editing has been done to preserve continuity and the general tenor of the text.

Only matters which occurred prior to the English tour were published before the tour ended. By this stipulation I believed I was acting within the framework of my contract with the Australian Board of Control, but in due course the Board fined me £50 for a "technical" breach.

My conscience remains clear that I acted entirely within the spirit and meaning of the contract.

*Don Bradman*

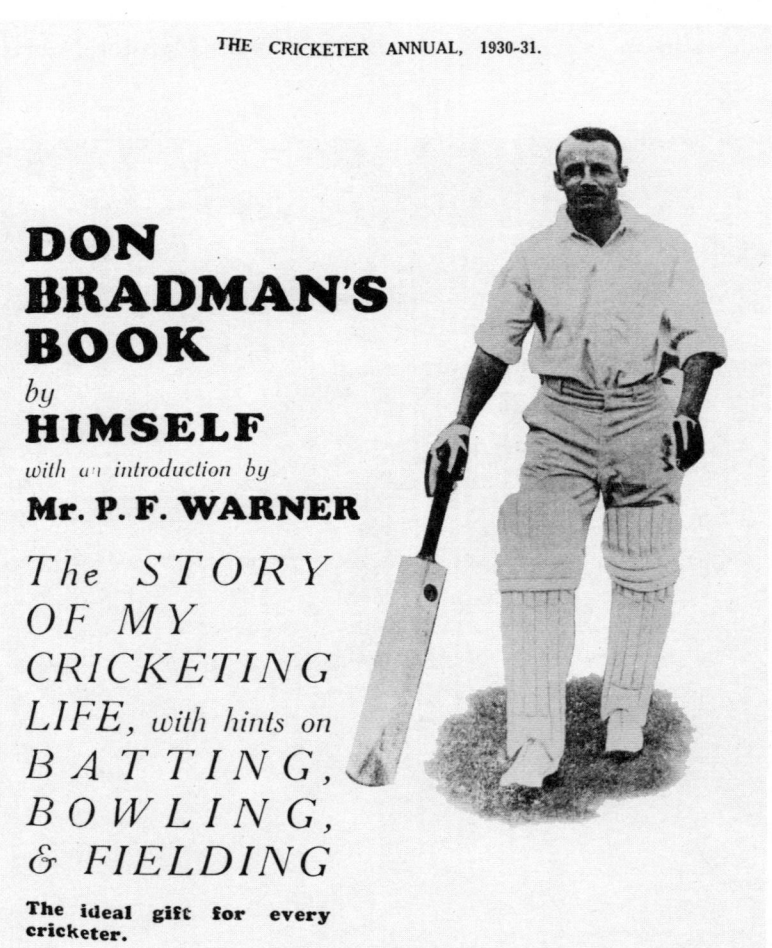

THE CRICKETER ANNUAL, 1930-31.

**DON BRADMAN'S BOOK**
*by*
**HIMSELF**
*with an introduction by*
**Mr. P. F. WARNER**

The *STORY OF MY CRICKETING LIFE, with hints on* BATTING, BOWLING, *&* FIELDING

**The ideal gift for every cricketer.**

*(Just Published)*
*16 pages of illustrations 12/6 net.*

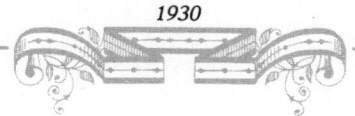

# INTRODUCTION

MR. BRADMAN has paid me a high compliment in asking me to write an introduction to his book, for it is ten years since I played first-class cricket, and he, at the age of 22, is, to-day, the world's greatest batsman. It may be that Mr. Bradman discovered in a "Has Been" a love of and delight in the game of games as great as his own, but whatever the reason, it is a gesture from youth to age which I am human enough to appreciate sincerely.

Before giving my impressions of Mr. Bradman's cricket, I should like to say that his book is charmingly written. Modest and generous to a degree, he admits that he was always learning something new. There is no finality in anything, certainly not in cricket — and Mr. Bradman, genius as he is, is always ready to improve. Over and over again one reads: "I learnt much from this innings," or words to that effect, and if ever there was a generous tribute to an opponent, it is his appreciation of the bowling of I. A. R. Peebles in the Test Match at Old Trafford.

The whole book breathes the right spirit, and there are many human touches, as, for instance, his description of his last day at his home, at Bowral, the pride of his people at his selection, and his happiness in their pride — he evidently possesses that filial piety which the Romans used to commend so highly — and his first sight of England and the lovely country between Dover and London, through "the garden of England" — though the men of Worcestershire say that they do not argue this point, for they *know* that that title belongs to them.

Of his many wonderful innings Mr. Bradman writes very briefly, and with most becoming reserve, and his enjoyment of every moment of the tour is manifest.

There are three chapters on batting, bowling, and fielding, and he admits that he enjoys fielding as much as batting. In his chapter on batting he writes: "I once read that W. G. said that in playing back to a ball never put your legs in front of the wicket." Mr. Bradman ventures to disagree with this, but W. G., in contradistinction to Mr. Bradman, did not always write his own books, and whoever wrote that sentence was inaccurate, for in point of fact W. G. nearly always had his legs in front of the stumps when playing back on a sticky wicket, and they were not small legs either!

As for Mr. Bradman's own performances in England, they were unique in the annals of cricket. In all matches he scored 3,170 runs, with an average of 99.06. He made eleven three-figure innings — six of these over 200 — and in the Test Matches his scores were 8, 131, 254, 334 (a world's record), 14, and 232 — 974 runs, with an average of 139.14! These great innings followed on two seasons' unbroken success in Australia, and it is no exaggeration to say that not even W. G. — at Mr. Bradman's age — had attained so world-wide a reputation.

What were the secrets of his triumphal march through England? First — immense natural skill. Secondly — an idealism which urged him to learn everything he possibly could, and to profit by the lessons learnt. Thirdly — tremendous concentration of mind; and fourthly, like C. B. Fry before him, great physical strength. Fifthly — extreme fitness; and, lastly, a cool, calm temperament. As to the actual technique of his play, he was blessed with a wonderful eye, steel-like wrists, and small and beautifully neat feet, which a Genée or a Pavlova might have envied, and which made him quite exceptionally quick in moving back or forward to the ball, every stroke fully developed, except, possibly, the straight drive, and, above all, an amazingly strong defence — which, as he says in his chapter on batting, is the keynote of all successful batsmanship in first-class cricket. His hooking of anything the least short was masterful to a degree; he missed nothing on his pads; and he off-drove beautifully; but, above all, the cut, both late and square, was his chief glory. I have seldom seen finer or *safer* cutting — for he was always right on top of the ball.

Again, he watched the ball very closely, and played all his strokes with his nose exactly over the ball — the "smell her, sir, smell her," of the renowned Yorkshireman, Tom Emmett — and his extreme quickness of foot enabled him almost to dictate the length to the bowler — at least, so it appeared in the Test Matches at Lord's and at Headingley. Another noticeable feature of his batting was his placing of the ball, and the absolute certainty with which he hit a full pitch for 4. He seldom played forward, though he was often yards down the pitch to a slow bowler, and he scarcely ever lifted a ball off the ground. His drives clung to the turf, and how clean and powerful they were, and I cannot agree that his eschewing the high drive was a weakness in his play, though so highly do I rate Mr. Bradman's cricket that I am sure he could play any stroke on which he cared to concentrate.

So much for his batting — but he was also a long field of the very highest class, quick to start, a fast runner, and the possessor of a return as swift as an arrow from a bow, and full pitch into the wicket-keeper's hands. Australia have had many fine deep fields, but never a finer — judging him on his form here — and those who were at the Test Match at Headingley will never forget the manner in which he threw down Hobbs's wicket, at Oldfield's end, from deep mid-off. Never have I seen anyone move forward faster to a ball, pick it up more quickly, or throw it in harder.

What is his future? Is he destined to break his own records? Will he one day play an innings of 600 or 700, and put the aggregates of Grace and Hobbs, and their number of centuries, in the shade? Remember, he is only twenty-two, and, given good health, he should have, at least, twenty more years of cricket before him. He seems certain to "plague" and, at the same time, delight England's bowlers for many future seasons — indeed, boys yet unborn are destined to suffer at his hands. Personally, I believe him to be possessed not only of the skill, but of the ambition, the physique, and the temperament, to accomplish these feats. A batsman, as a general rule, does not attain to his best until he is thirty-four or thirty-five, and by the time Mr. Bradman reaches that age he will have had immense experience to build on to his natural skill. Have I praised him too highly? I don't think so, if one remembers his youth, and the fact that it was his first visit to England, and our varying wickets.

Do people realize his astonishing figures? Take the Test Matches. In these the Australians scored 2,743 runs from the bat, of which Bradman contributed no less than 974. Again, he invariably made a huge proportion of the runs scored while he was in — namely, 131 out of 255 at Trent Bridge; 254 out of 423 at Lord's; 334 out of 506 at Headingley; and 232 out of 411 at the Oval. One may also add that *v.* Worcestershire, at Worcester, he scored 236 out of 413; *v.* Surrey, at the Oval, 252 out of 363; and *v.* Kent, at Canterbury, 205 out of 302.

Mr. Bradman looked every inch a cricketer. He was scrupulously neat and smart in his turn-out, and he played the game with rare zest and enjoyment. Short in height, though long in the leg, and with very broad shoulders, he is, from a cricket point of view, finely and compactly built, and one was particularly struck by the fit of his cricket boots on his small feet; and I think that he should present his boots to the Australian nation, to be placed in the pavilion at Sydney, there to be kept in a glass-case for future generations to gaze on, and to inspire them to something like his own nimbleness of foot!

Above all, Mr. Bradman possesses both character and brains, and I feel sure that so well-balanced a personality will remember to "keep a straight bat and a modest mind." Certainly he showed no signs in England that that fair and well-shaped head of his was in danger of requiring a larger-sized cricket cap. On the contrary, he took his long succession of triumphs with a becoming modesty which is reflected in this interesting book of his.

*P. F. Warner*

LONDON,
*November, 1930.*

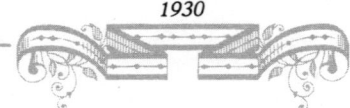

# BRADMAN BEGAN CRICKET
## CAREER AS CHILD

# Games With Golf Ball and Stump

## AUSTRALIA'S STAR BATSMAN
## MADE FIRST CENTURY WHEN 12

> *This is the first instalment of Don Bradman's life story by himself. It relates how he practised cricket shots with a golf ball and a small stump as a child, and how he made his first century when 12.*

I WAS born at Cootamundra, New South Wales, on August 27, 1908, and when two years of age was taken with the rest of the family—I have three sisters, Islet, Lily and May, and one brother, Victor—to Bowral, where my father set up as a carpenter. I was christened Donald George.

Bowral is a beautiful residential town about 80 miles from Sydney, with a winter population of some 3000, which in the summer months reaches larger proportions. The nearest likeness to Bowral in England, is perhaps Bolton Abbey, in Yorkshire.

It was when I went to the town's Intermediate High School that I got my first insight into cricket and games generally. My headmaster, Mr A. J. Lee, was quite a good cricketer, and was ever ready to play with us. He did not, however, act as coach as coaches are understood. We were left almost entirely to our own devices; and, besides, the school did not boast of facilities to be found in England.

I was never coached; I was never told how to hold a bat. I was my own teacher, and the first bat I ever used was the limb of a gum tree. No boy lived near enough to my home to join me in a game, and as often as not I was left to play alone.

My earliest cricket, and much of it that I played when not at school, took this form. Armed with a small stump, which I used as a bat, and throwing a golf ball at the brick part of an old tank a few yards away, I would try to hit the ball on the rebound. I was never satisfied unless I could hit it, say, three times out of four. The small bat made this no easy matter, as the ball came back at great speed, and, of course, at widely differing angles. I found I had to be pretty quick on my feet, and keep my wits about me, and in this way I developed, unconsciously, perhaps, sense of distance and pace.

By the same methods that served as my education as a batsman, I taught myself how to field, how to throw and how to catch—not that I am regarded as an extra safe catch even now, for the records have it that I missed something like five catches in the last series of Test matches in Australia!

I would take a golf ball into the paddock, and, standing a short distance from a fence, throw the ball so as to hit a given spot on the rounded rail.

Because of the shape of the rail, I knew that if I did not land the ball in one particular place, it would shoot off at a tangent, and I would have to set out in search of it. By constant practice, I found I could hit a certain spot on the rail that would make the ball come straight back to me. I was pleased with the accuracy of aim I acquired in this way.

### Bats Lopped from Gum Trees

I HAVE often been asked whether the frequency with which I hit the stumps when fielding, has been more by accident than design. There is, of course, an element of luck in hitting the stumps from a distance, or from an awkward angle, but if I were forced to a definite statement, I would say that the games I played as a small boy gave to me any accuracy of aim I may possess.

The lonely hours I spent with the tennis ball, and the golf ball, had no object in view other than passing the time, and I enjoyed playing about by myself. I did not know then that I was training my hand and eye to work together. I loved to be out of doors, and I had to amuse myself, and that is how I came to use the expedients of the old brick wall and the rail of the fence.

From five, until I was 10 years of age, I was in the primary school, and our ground, which was the common playground, was separated from that of the High School, but we had the privilege of standing at the gateway that shut our pitch from that of the seniors; and it was a privilege that I embraced as often as possible. And the day soon came when I was allowed to go into the ground of the higher school to see what I could do against the bowling of the bigger boys.

Our cricket, as I have said, was done in the school-yard, the bell post, that shot up in the centre of the yard, serving as the wicket, which, by the way, was indicated by chalk marks. We made our own bats, which, having been lopped from some gum tree, were more the shape of a baseball bat. The conformation of them demanded straight driving. The ball was compo., the pitch dirt; and pads were absolutely unknown. The boy who got hold of the ball was the bowler, and he batted when he got the other fellow out.

Cricket, even under such primitive conditions, was a joy to me and I was always happy when I played the game whether by myself, or with a crowd of boys.

My days at school were completely happy days. Besides winning some distinction at cricket, I played for the school football XV., and in events for boys of my age, I won the 100 yards, 220 yards, and the quarter and half-mile championships.

I also represented the school at tennis.

### Early Successes
### With Bowral Team

WHAT may be said to be the first match of note in which I took part was for a school team against one some eight miles from my home. I was still in the primary or junior school; but our side boasted several players of the high or senior school.

I would not then be more than 11 years of age. The match was played on what is known as Glebe Park at Bowral—a very fine recreation ground. We, however, did not wage war on the recognised or regular cricket pitch—the football ground was reckoned good enough for us. The wicket was plain dirt.

Our captain won the toss and went in to bat. From the other side, a left-handed bowler got a wicket first ball; with his second he spread-eagled the stumps of the second batsman, and I arrived in my first cricket match to stand between him and the hat trick.

How and why the first ball sent down to me did not hit my stumps, I shall never be able to tell. But having survived it, I remained to carry out my bat for 55.

As I had now reached the high school I was selected to play against Mittagong School —deadly rivals, whose battle-ground was three miles away.

The game was fought on a real cricket pitch—that is, one of concrete covered with matting, on which our rivals had won some renown through the medium of a fast bowler. It was in this match that I scored my first century—115 not out, out of a total of 156. I was then 12 years of age. We won the match and I was, I considered, pardonably proud.

The next day when we lined up in the playground at school the headmaster called out: "I understand that there is a certain boy among you who scored a century yesterday against Mittagong. Well, that is no reason or excuse why you should have left a bat behind."

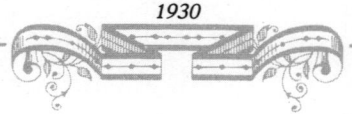

The bat was recovered and all was well. Meantime, Mittagong were thirsting for revenge, and a return match came about as a matter of course. My share in it was 72, or thereabouts, not out.

I was having something approaching organised cricket when I was 12 years old, in the sense that one afternoon each week, from 2 o'clock to 4.30, I was one of picked schoolboys to engage in what were known as scratch matches. One side would go in, and if they were not all out by 3.30, they were forced to declare, so that, as far as possible, each boy should have batting practice.

One of my greatest joys at this time was to be allowed to act as scorer for the Bowral Town team. They played competition games against clubs with grounds within a radius of about 25 miles. My uncle was captain of the Bowral team.

There was an occasion when Bowral had a match with Moss Vale, at which one of the Bowral players did not turn up, and I, who had set out to score, filled the breach.

No words of mine can adequately express my feelings—a speck of a boy, rigged out in short trousers, playing for the redoubtable Bowral and against their near and avowed rivals, Moss Vale! It was almost too much. However, going in at the fall of the eighth wicket, wielding a man's full-sized bat, I scored 37 not out.

That was my first appearance in senior cricket and I was 13 years of age. The following Saturday, when the match was continued, I was sent in first, and scored 29 not out. Then back to the position of scorer. But I did not mind; I was glad to be inside the fence.

### Happy Boy With First Real Bat

IT was about this time that I came into possession of a real bat. And I was now the happiest boy ever. It was given to me by a Mr. Cupitt, a member of the Bowral Town team. It was man's size; but that did not matter. It was a bat with a splice, and not one chopped out of

the limb of a gum tree. That bat meant almost everything in the world to me.

With a saw my father cut three inches off the bottom, and rounded it off at the foot, and I went into the paddock with my prized possession. I played shots at imaginary balls till the light failed. I was happy.

When 13 years of age I set out on the greatest adventure of my young and crowded life. For then it was that I beheld the Sydney ground and saw for the first time first-class cricket. My father had taken me to Sydney from Bowral, my home, some 80 miles away. I was quite a little fellow in knickerbockers, but I remember how the enormous crowd and the magnificence of the ground fired and captured my fancy.

It was amazing and unforgettable. I thought then, and still think, it is the finest ground in the whole world.

The Fifth Test match between England and Australia was in progress, and although I was quite a boy then, I have still vivid memories of seeing first Macartney, in all his glory, making 170; then a magnificent innings by Woolley; and I can recall still a brilliant catch made by "Johnny" Taylor.

During one of the intervals my father took me by the hand and we walked round the ground to take a peep at the pavilion, and perhaps rub shoulders with the players. I vividly remember my feelings at that moment. I turned to my father:

"I shall never be satisfied until I play on this ground," I said.

He smiled with affectionate tolerance. As it turned out, my next visit to the Sydney Cricket Ground was when I stepped on it as a player—nor did I see another first-class match until then.

At the end of the second day's play, business called my father back to Bowral. I was naturally disappointed that I could not remain until the end, but I had seen enough to rouse my ambition to become a great cricketer.

**DON BRADMAN**

# A RECORD 300 IN COUNTRY MATCH
## SIX WEEKS' SATURDAY FINAL PLAYED OUT

# Invitation to Sydney for First Try-out on Turf

AFTER leaving school I entered the service of Mr Percy Westbrook, the head of a real estate business in Bowral. At this time I was very fond of tennis, and I decided to give up cricket and devote myself entirely to the other game, and for one whole summer I played no cricket at all. Perhaps the explanation is that the facilities for tennis were generous and the readier, for my Uncle Dick had a court, and I was always free to play on it.

Still, with cricket so surely in my blood, I was bound to come back to it sooner or later. Toward the end of the following summer I joined the Bowral Town Club, but my return to cricket was to me a painful experience. The very first time I turned out (in a match played on Glebe Park), I made a duck, caught and bowled, and I feel that I must at the time have wished that I had stuck to tennis.

I only took part in two more matches that season—one the semi-final of a competition against Wingello. I had the great good fortune to make the top score for my side—66—but Bowral were beaten. That was the finish of my cricket for the season, but I had had enough to force me to a definite decision to make cricket my real, if not my only, game, though I still coquetted with tennis.

Although from the day I could do little more than toddle I played bat and ball of sorts, I would mark my beginning as a serious cricketer as from the season 1925–26. I was then 17 years of age, and I was enrolled as a regular member of the Bowral Town Club.

The games took place on Saturday afternoons. I have little or no data to guide me, but I well remember that the first score of note in my first big and pretentious season was a competition

game against Wingello, who, in the previous term, had defeated Bowral in the semi-final and had gone on to win in the last round of all against Moss Vale.

In the Wingello team there was a very fine bowler named O'Reilly, and though I had not played against him I knew that he was a better bowler than I had hitherto encountered. Whether that knowledge brought me inspiration I cannot tell, but it is a curious circumstance that throughout my career I have invariably won greatest distinction when opposed to avowedly dangerous and accomplished bowlers.

When I went in to bat against O'Reilly, I took this view, a view I shall hold to the end of my cricketing days—it is I and the bowler for it.

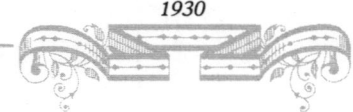

## Carried Out His Bat For 234

BECAUSE O'Reilly played ducks and drakes in the previous season in the final of the tournament, it did not follow that he would do so against Bowral. At all events, I had no qualms when I faced him, and I treated his bowling according to my idea of what it was worth. I stayed at the wicket for two hours and three-quarters, and carried out my bat for 234; in the last 50 runs I hit four sixes and six fours.

I have given much prominence to the name of O'Reilly. I have done so because the following year he was picked to represent New South Wales in the Sheffield Shield team. He was a medium-paced bowler, could make the ball turn both ways, but never achieved any outstanding success on turf wickets. However, he often proved much of a demon on concrete, as he was indeed on the resumption of the game a week later: I did not add to my score, being bowled first ball by O'Reilly.

But I had need to be abundantly satisfied. I had knocked up three centuries for the local team before we set out to play in the final against Moss Vale, against whom I had played as a lad in short trousers.

The rules of the competition decreed that the match should be played to a finish, to the end of the following season if necessary! The days devoted to it were Saturdays, the playing hours from 2 o'clock in the afternoon until 6 in the evening.

The rivalry between the two clubs was intense. Partisanship was white hot. My uncle, George Whatman, was captain of Bowral, and like a good uncle he won the toss. He did me the honor of sending me in first. My partner was a left-hander. The end of the afternoon had almost come before we were separated: then the partnership was broken by the dismissal of the senior member. At the close of play I was 80 not out.

Back to Bowral we went, to return to Moss Vale on the following Saturday. And when stumps were pulled at the end of that second day I was 279 not out, and my uncle, still in possession, had knocked up 100 or thereabouts. And only one wicket down!

Came the third Saturday when, after taking my score to exactly 300, I was caught on the boundary. At the close of that afternoon Bowral's score was 600 for six wickets, my uncle being not out 220. On the fourth Saturday my uncle was bowled without making another run. The match was not over until the sixth Saturday, and then we beat Moss Vale by an innings.

## Tried Out on Sydney Ground

NOT unnaturally, the match created a stir. Folk in Sydney got to hear about it and a well-known cartoonist revelled in it. He first pictured "Young Don" running up and down the wicket like a little rabbit, then as a full-grown man, next stage as a fellow old and rheumaticky and bent, with a beard touching the ground, and as a grand finale two of us on the top of the heavens asking Saint Peter where the Moss Vale cricket pitch was, so that we might finish the match.

That match is talked about to this day in terms of amazement and incredulity. It will go down into history as a match that took six weeks to decide—as a world's record, and a record for the district, in that I scored more runs than any other batsman had ever done in a single innings.

While still playing for the local team at Bowral I began to have visions of winning a place in First Grade cricket. The time came when I was all eager expectation for the picking of what was known as the Southern Country Week team, a side composed of the proved best players of a district which embraced a wide area—hundreds of square miles, including Bowral.

Before the Country Week team was selected, however, I received a wire from the secretary of the New South Wales Association, asking me to come to Sydney to have a turn at the nets, and the receipt of this "command" created a lot of excitement in my home. My father accompanied me to Sydney. We made the journey almost in silence, but, needless to say, we were eloquent in thought.

It is a trait in my make-up which it is quite impossible to explain, that I am almost a total stranger to that species of nervousness common to most people whenever involved in an unusual happening. I did not quake or fear when I approached the Sydney ground. I was neither conscious of my boyishness nor the exacting test I was about to undergo. The feeling I had was only one of great joy, and a relish for adventure.

When I was called to Sydney, it was felt that I would be sorely, if not fatally, handicapped because I was a total stranger to turf wickets. Further—that my "style" in vastly different conditions would be all against me. The trial took place under the eyes of various New South Wales experts; but they were unknown to me, and I went on with my batting in my own way.

I faced the bowling, and did my best to hit it. Whether I made any impression or not I had no idea. When my "knock" was over I simply packed up and went back to Bowral, and as far as possible tried to convince myself that I had done well.

Sydney Cricket Ground where Bradman had his first try-out on a turf wicket.

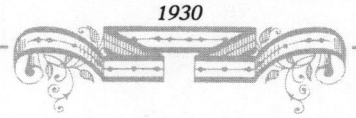

# ENTRY TO FIRST GRADE CRICKET
## A CENTURY FOR ST. GEORGE

# Selected to Play in Shield Match in Adelaide

AS luck would have it, it was not very long before I received a second call from Sydney, this time to play in a trial match organised by the New South Wales Cricket Association, with the idea of helping in the selection of sides to compete for the Sheffield Shield.

I had my first innings on the Sydney Ground, and scored 37 not out. The result was that although I was not chosen to go to Queensland, as I hoped, the New South Wales Cricket Association asked the selectors of the Southern Country Week side to pick me for a trial at Goulburn, which is some 50 miles from Bowral. That was done, and I scored 62 not out, and took four wickets, a performance which led to my being in the Country Week team.

My selection to play in the Country Cricket Week team placed me in a rather curious dilemma. I had also been asked to play in the Country Tennis team, and as both these events meant a week in Sydney I went to Mr Westbrook, my employer, to arrange for leave.

Mr Westbrook, to whom I owe a deep debt of gratitude, had never placed any obstacle in the way of my getting away from work, but on this occasion he made this stipulation.

"Don," he said, "you can only have one week in Sydney. You can have the tennis week or the cricket week, but you cannot have both."

I thought the matter over. The cricket week came before the tennis week. That may or may not have decided me, but ultimately I decided to take the cricket week. And that was the end of the battle between cricket and tennis.

The Country Cricket Week duly came round. All the chosen players collected in Sydney, and some eight teams met to do battle. The play lasted from Monday to Friday, with a different match each day. My record for that week was not too good—my highest score for the five matches being 46, and my lowest 21.

I was now beginning to wonder and speculate how my cricketing future would shape itself, when Mr R. L. Jones asked me whether I would play regularly in Sydney for the St. George Club, which meant opening the door to first grade cricket.

Mr Jones, by the way, is one of the gentlemen who assisted in the selection of the 1930 Australian team, and represents New South Wales on their selection committee.

## Playing First Grade For St. George

AS the result of negotiations, arrangements were made for me to play every Saturday for St. George in the Sydney First Grade competition. My first Grade match for St. George was against Petersham on the Saturday of "Country Week," and in this game I was run out after making 110. That was my first century on a turf wicket. On the following Monday I was selected to represent a combined country team side against a combined First Grade team of Sydney, captained by Charlie Macartney.

My luck held. I scored 98. Macartney, I remember, made a glorious century, and one of the other players on our side was Charlie Andrews, who later became a member of the New South Wales Shield team.

After much cogitation, and not a little trepidation, I decided that it would be in my best interests if I lived in Sydney. I found the weekly journey to and from Bowral—a two and a half hours' run—a matter of some inconvenience.

The thought of leaving home and all its happy associations hurt. My work was completely pleasant; I could have desired no more generous or considerate master; but whatever the cost I was determined to make the plunge. I delayed making it, however, for some time, especially as Mr Westbrook, far from offering any objection to my being away from business every Saturday—his busiest and most important day of the week—encouraged me. So I remained at Bowral and I came to be selected to represent New South Wales against Victoria in a second XI match on the Sydney ground.

In my first innings I made 42, which was the top score. In the second I stepped back to play the ball and hit it good and hard, and, of course, started to run. I had run a single and was coming back for the second run when I noticed the square-leg umpire with his hand up, by way of signalling that I was out. I pulled up to learn that in making the shot I had touched the stumps and removed the bails, and of course I had to go.

Having played for Bowral in the district competitions, I was eligible to take part in the final match of the season. Their opponents were Moss Vale, against whom, in the previous season, I had scored 300. There was much of the "needle" in the match. The nearer the neighbor, the keener the rivalry: it is the same the world over.

## 320 For Bowral in Country Final

MOSS VALE were in high feather when they won the toss, but they were all out after batting some two hours and a half. At six o'clock that night—the match started at half-past two—I was 58 not out. We resumed, according to regulations, on the following Saturday afternoon. Bowral scored 480, of which I made 320 not out. Whether, as a result of my huge score, I do not know, but a rule was passed that no First Grade player, which by that time I had become, was free to play in such competitions; he was ever afterward barred.

There was much said about this particular performance: at least, it attracted notice, and from what afterwards transpired, I feel that it established me permanently as a first-class player.

It now dawned on me more than ever, that, having to travel to and from Bowral, my opportunity for practice on turf was impossibly small. There was only concrete to play on round and about my home, and besides, I felt it to be of first importance that I should have as much practice as possible against first-class bowlers, and under the best conditions.

Before I went to live in Sydney I was selected to represent New South Wales in a Sheffield Shield match at Adelaide, and I left my native State for the first time in my life.

The journey to Adelaide, to my young mind, was like travelling to the other end of the earth, and it had the effect of intensifying a desire that had developed and which I confess I encouraged, to see the world.

I was fully conscious of the great honor that had come my way in the space of two short years. The previous summer was my first in Grade cricket, and now I was to play for my State against South Australia. I was then entering my 19th year.

My selection to play in this match fired me with a real desire to give of my very best. I realised that it might be only a short step from interstate cricket to a place in the Australian side against England, and as I was already dreaming of one day getting to England, I was now more than ever determined to make good.

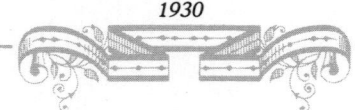

# GRIMMETT GREATEST BOWLER
## IN WORLD, SAYS BRADMAN

# First Melbourne Appearance

## BEST LESSONS TAUGHT BY BATTING FAILURES

MY trip with the New South Wales Shield team from Sydney to Adelaide was one that I shall never forget. For the first and only time in cricket history the team was sent via Broken Hill, where we stayed a short while and played a match.

It was the first time I had ever spent a night in a train, and, not being accustomed to it, of course had very little sleep. The weather was very hot—being practically mid-summer in one of the hottest parts of Australia—and I tried to keep myself cool with the aid of an electric fan (the direct result of which was to give me a cold in the eye) and I felt anything but well when we reached Broken Hill the next morning.

On the same journey, Archie Jackson developed a boil on his knee, so that instead of our enjoying a trip down one of the silver mines with the rest of the team, our manager (Dr. McAdam) politely made Archie and me go to bed in preparation for the match next day.

The match was duly played, and what an experience! There was not a blade of grass on that oval from one end to the other; the soil was a deep red with, in some parts, dust a couple of inches deep, a concrete wicket, and—I have never seen this anywhere else—the bowler had to run up on a concrete approach.

Considering that the ground had not received any rainfall to speak of for about two years, these conditions were not to be wondered at. Anyway, some of us played in sand shoes. I played in my ordinary walking shoes—anything but cricket boots with sprigs in, for they were useless. We couldn't allow our fast bowler to bowl for fear of injury, and the locals put up a very good showing, with the result that we eventually had to fight hard to win.

At the conclusion of the game I somehow managed to get the ball, and still have it as a souvenir of the first match I ever played with a New South Wales Sheffield Shield side.

Then came my real chance under the very best of conditions at Adelaide. In the South Australian side was Clarrie Grimmett, and I felt that if I could do well against such a redoubtable bowler I was well on the way to my goal. N. E. Phillips and Tommy Andrews took the edge off the bowling, and when I went in Alan Kippax was playing brilliantly.

### Scores 118 in Adelaide Match

ALAN, I remember, was far from well that day and had to retire twice, owing to indisposition caused by the excessive heat, but together we put on 111 for the sixth wicket, and eventually I was out after scoring 118, having felt that I had made a creditable debut.

In spite of our huge total of 519, we eventually lost the match by one wicket in one of the most exciting finishes ever played. Their last man was in and four runs were required. The ball was bowled, shot along the ground, beat the batsman and went so close to the wicket that the wicket-keeper failed to stop it, and they ran four byes while the fieldsman chased it.

This excitable finish and wonderful victory was largely brought about by the magnificent bowling of Clarrie Grimmett in our second innings. He was practically unplayable, taking eight wickets for 57. I was one of his victims after having scored 33 (our top scorer made 34), but felt when the match was over that I had gained a considerable amount of cricket knowledge of which I had known nothing before.

Clarrie Grimmett and I are excellent friends, and there is no player with whom I would feel more at home in asking advice. In fact, it is characteristic of the make-up of most top-flight cricketers that they are always ready and willing to give a word in season to the young player, provided he is keen and anxious to learn.

Unfortunately, players are very often misunderstood, and the impression gained is that they have no desire to assist others. It is entirely wrong, and in my experience no elder player has ever declined to give me advice when I asked for it.

One evening during this South Australian game, I felt honoured when Clarrie asked me along to his home. We spent a very pleasant evening together, and Clarrie's tales of his previous trip to England interested me very much indeed.

It is an education to watch Grimmett spinning a small soft rubber ball on a table. He just simply makes a fool of one, and it is impossible to tell where or how it is going to break.

At that time I thought Clarrie Grimmett the best bowler I had then met. Today I unhesitatingly say that Grimmett is the best bowler I have ever met, and in my opinion the greatest bowler in the world. With it all he is a most modest, unassuming fellow, and an extremely likeable personality.

### Watching Two "Billys" in Melbourne

AND so, leaving Adelaide with pleasant memories, we journeyed on to Melbourne, to make the acquaintance of the two "Billys"—"Billy" Ponsford and "Billy" Woodfull, the latter afterward destined to be my skipper in our English tour.

It was my first appearance on the Melbourne ground, and with a modest 31 and 5 against Victoria I considered myself a failure. Although a little disappointed with my non-success, I was pleased to see two magnificent scores by both the men I was anxious to see in action, notwithstanding the fact that I helped to chase the runs.

This gave me an opportunity of watching their methods, and so increased my cricket education. To my mind, watching the class player is one of the happiest and most effective means of learning the art of cricket.

Coming back home, my first appearance for New South Wales on the Sydney Cricket Ground was against Queensland. It seemed like the realisation of an ambition walking out to bat, but very soon that dream was altered, and I was taught what I still consider to be the best lesson I have ever learnt in cricket.

The previous batsman had got out off the last ball of an over, and when I went in Alan Kippax was taking strike to slow bowler Gough.

The first ball Kippax gently pushed to mid-on, and we ran one. It all appeared so simple to me that before the next ball had been bowled, I made up my mind to do the same thing.

Sure enough I tried, but instead of the ball coming slowly and turning as I anticipated, it went straight through and fast, taking with it my middle stump. Motto: Never make up your mind what to do with a ball before it is bowled, and also gauge the pace of the wicket before you attempt a risky shot.

It seemed a long way back to the pavilion, but I consider that getting a "duck" that day has saved me getting many since.

In this game Alan Kippax played the game of his life. Those who saw the late Victor Trumper tell me that Alan is more like him than any other batsman we have. Would that I could have seen an innings by this great Australian master.

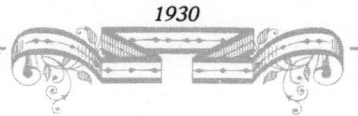

# TEST SELECTION BECOMES A REALITY
## THE TRAGIC BRISBANE STORY

SEASON 1928/9 opened very unpromisingly for me. Selected to play in a trial match at Melbourne—Rest of Australia v Australia—I did nothing at all, scoring 14 and 5 in my two innings. The following week the scoring of two separate hundreds in the one match against Queensland, one of whose bowlers was Hornibrook, seemed to put me on the crest of the wave, for when I returned to Sydney I was selected to represent New South Wales against England on the Sydney Cricket Ground.

I have reason to remember my debut in that game. Three of our best men were out for a mere 20-odd runs, the time was 10 minutes to six with a fading light, when my turn came to bat. I could not have asked for anything better, and had my captain asked me to wait until next day and sent someone else in that night, I would have been disappointed, for it seemed just the incentive I required to do well.

Anyway, I managed to stay there until six o'clock, finally taking my score to 87 next day, and making 132 not out in the second innings. In the first innings of this game Freeman bowled me with a prodigious leg break.

To play for New South Wales against England was the fulfilment of one of my minor ambitions, and I had been looking forward to this match, being especially anxious to make acquaintance with the famous Jack Hobbs. The great Surrey batsman stood down in this match so that the pleasure of seeing him at the crease was deferred.

Naturally I was particularly glad that I had done something in this game, for the whole cricketing world of Australia was by now buzzing with excitement over the selection of the Australian team to play at Brisbane in the first Test Match.

Following the New South Wales game, I was selected to play for an Australian XI against England, and in this game my scores were 58 not out and 18, and then came the day when the team was to be finally selected and announced.

Frankly I was hopeful of being selected to play, and yet as the time drew near for the announcement of the side I felt some misgivings, and was not too confident. After dinner in the evening, I waited in my lodgings to hear the team broadcast. At the hour at which it should have been made known, it was given out that it would be put over later. The next announcement was that the selectors were still deliberating, and I decided to wait up no longer, but go off to bed.

"I have a chance", I assured myself, "but on the other hand I might be passed over; but whatever I say or do or think will not get me a place"—that is how I reckoned.

So I told my landlady "I shall find out whether I am in the team or not in the morning when the newspapers arrive", and with that went off to my room.

I had not been under the blankets 10 minutes when the announcer's voice came from the loud speaker in the next room. The names were broadcast in alphabetical order, and Bradman was the first name to be called.

I cannot say that I suffered any reaction. I was not conscious of excitement, but felt perfectly satisfied that I had accomplished a task which I had definitely set about trying to do. To me it acted as a sleeping draught—in fact I slept so soundly that I was late for work next morning (but forgiven), and that is how I came to realise I had achieved my ambition in Australian cricket of getting into the Australian Eleven and being entitled to receive and wear a green and gold blazer with the coat of arms on the pocket.

Then came the great day when I took the field at Brisbane under the captaincy of Jack Ryder. It was in this Test that many things of great importance occurred, and history was made. Off the last ball but one before lunch on the first day, Sutcliffe was out to a magnificent catch by Ponsford, and then after lunch I had the good fortune to be associated with Oldfield in the running out of Jack Hobbs.

But England's other batsmen carried on. Patsy Hendren played a most magnificent innings of 169, definitely giving the lie to that oft-repeated statement that "he had not the Test match temperament". I hope whoever said that of Patsy was there that day.

Then we saw Larwood, not reputed to be a batsman, making 70 runs in excellent style, until at last they were all out for 521.

Still we were not downhearted as we watched Woodfull and Ponsford go to the wickets.

But Larwood ran riot. Woodfull, in his first Test match in Australia, was out to a marvellous catch (which Chapman alone of all fieldsmen could have taken) for 0. Ponsford was clean bowled and we were all out for 122.

Our skipper gallantly tried to stem the tide, making top score for the side, 33. My own contribution to our total was a mere 18. England batting a second time scored 342 for eight wickets, when Chapman applied the closure.

The task set us in normal circumstances would have been an impossible one, but even the Gods seemed to be against us, for the weather broke, to develop a wicket that poked fun at the batsmen and rejoiced the heart of the bowler.

Jack White revelled in it—he captured 4 of our wickets for 7 runs. I can still picture Maurice Tate—he couldn't get hold of the ball to go and bowl quickly enough.

I would not deny England the least credit for the mightiness of her victory, but Chapman and his followers, I am sure, will grant that Dame Fortune frowned on Australia this time.

To me and my countrymen this Test in Brisbane will ever remain a painful memory. It was some grounding for a lad of 20 to play in a side defeated by the greatest number of runs in Test history.

But the tragic part of the game was that not only did England win by the most runs in Test history—675—but the game marked the finish of the careers of Jack Gregory and Charlie Kelleway.

Jack Gregory suffered a recurrence of an old knee trouble, and broke down so badly that he did not take part in the latter stages of the game. Charlie Kelleway developed ptomaine poisoning, which necessitated his staying in bed for some days, and affected his health for weeks afterwards.

A perfect specimen of physical manhood walked into the English dressing-room, his knee heavily bandaged, and, with tears in his eyes, remarked "Boys, I have played my last game against you".

The person who felt it most keenly was Jack Gregory himself.

A great—a noble—cricketer was Gregory. Undoubtedly one of the greatest of all Australia's fast bowlers, the greatest slip-fieldsman I ever saw, and, when in the mood a magnificent hitter. What his breakdown meant to Australia need not be stressed—he was a tower of strength: Memory of him and his prodigious deeds will never fade. It is impossible to exaggerate the loss both to Australia and the game.

Then picture Charlie Kelleway lying in bed in his room at the hotel, listening in on a little portable wireless set to his team mates being defeated, powerless to lift a finger to help them in a battle he would have given anything to be in.

This too marked the finish of Kelleway's Test match career.

Thus I participated in what proved to be the last game these two great all-round cricketers ever played for Australia, and I regretted very deeply that such was the case.

However the first Test was over and we came back to Sydney for the second. Twelve men were selected to represent Australia, and 15 minutes before the match began our captain advised me in our dressing room that I was 12th man. I was very disappointed, for it was the first time in my life I had reached the standard of a team and then been dropped out of the actual playing eleven, but I was determined to get back in that side.

Another regrettable incident happened in this match. After scoring but 5 runs in his first innings, Ponsford had a small bone broken in his left hand by a ball from Larwood, and took no further part in cricket that season.

This necessitated my fielding throughout the whole of the English innings, and gave me a wonderful opportunity to watch closely that masterful innings played by Wally Hammond in scoring 251. It seemed that nothing would ever get him out, and we were a very surprised team of cricketers when he eventually did make that vital mistake.

I watched his marvellously powerful off drives, the soundness of his defence, and his methods, all of which appeared to be typical of himself and nobody else.

The second Test, like the first, was lost, and it was now a case of do or die. Our selectors, in their desperation, and encouraged by popular clamour, decided that they might as well be killed for a sheep as a lamb. They embarked on a gamble. They called up Oxenham, a'Beckett and myself, each largely untried.

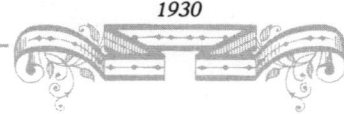

# ENGLAND'S GREAT OPENING PAIR
## MAGNIFICENT DEFENCE ON STICKY WICKET IN MELBOURNE

THIS third Test I shall never forget. Here was cricket in one of its most capricious moods; first the advantage was with one country, then with the other, and the match went to the seventh day before the issue was settled. We won the toss, and we praised the Gods. It is notorious that all shrewd judges have always looked suspiciously at the Melbourne wicket on the first day—it must always be taken more or less on trust up to lunch time.

This day I saw what was then the greatest opening attack in the world, Tate and Larwood, putting everything they knew into their bowling, the result of which was that Australia were soon three wickets down for 57 runs.

I have never seen at any time faster bowling than that of Larwood on this day. The ball seemed literally to fly through the air, and come off the pitch at a terrific speed. What great knocks for Australia Alan Kippax and Jack Ryder played in this game.

Ryder we all knew for a wonderful fighter, but Kippax was accused of lacking the Test Match temperament, and in addition faced the possibility of being dropped from the next match, as he had not done well in the two previous games.

How he replied to his critics is well known, and his brilliant century goes down as one of the greatest innings played in that series.

Profiting from my previous experiences, I managed to come through this match, having attained another goal, that of scoring a century in a Test match, also getting 79 in the second innings, thereby, I hoped, making my place secure in the remaining games.

Once again I witnessed the spectacle of Wally Hammond making a double century in a Test match, and once again I closely watched his batting. Then came a magnificent display by Hobbs and Sutcliffe on a Melbourne "sticky dog", reputed to be the worst wicket in the world when really bad.

One of the greatest thrills I got out of cricket was on this day at Melbourne, when Hobbs and Sutcliffe showed what great batsmen could do on a sticky wicket.

My youth had denied me the opportunity of seeing much of this famous, history-making pair, but exaggeration of the magnitude of the feat they accomplished is impossible. England, on a wicket that we felt had been ruined by rain—at least one cruelly against the batsman of whatever standing—were set to get 332 runs to win. Only those with actual experience of the Melbourne ground after rain, followed by sunshine, can have any conception of its atrociousness.

With reason, Australia took victory for granted. "If England makes a century on such a dog of a wicket, they will have done wonders." That was popular prediction. It was any odds on Australia.

Hobbs and Sutcliffe performed what all those who saw the match regarded as a miracle. No cricketers ever showed such determination.

It was a revelation to me. I had never imagined that even these two giants could bat on such a wicket. I expected to see them get out with every ball that was sent down, but try as we might, we could not shift them.

They were struck from top to toe; but by sheer grit they stayed together until they had brought 105 runs on the board and opened the way to a victory that seemed impossible of attainment.

Hobbs was out LBW to Blackke for 49, but the worth of his innings must not be appraised by the mere number of runs that came from his bat. Those 49 runs represented a greater accomplishment than many a century, and were little less wonderful than the 135 scored by Sutcliffe who, curiously enough, like Hobbs, was out leg before.

Their batting on a sticky wicket had been an education to me, and I stored up in my mind for future use the example set by these two great batsmen on this particular day.

It was in this game that Jack Hobbs gave an instance of his wonderful knowledge of the game. In the late afternoon he was seen to signal with his bat to the pavilion, and at the end of the next over Hendren ran out with a couple of bats. Jack tried them both, but eventually resumed batting with his own bat.

We learned afterwards that Hobbs had sent a message to Chapman that in the event of a wicket falling before close of play Jardine should be sent in instead of Hammond, so that the latter could be reserved for the following day, when the wicket might be more to his liking.

There was nothing wrong whatever in Hobbs' action in sending a message to his captain, and I mention the incident only to show how an observant player can help his side.

Hobbs lost his wicket shortly afterwards, and with Jardine holding the fort until the close of play, England pulled the game around the following day, and won a memorable and meritorious victory.

It fell to my lot to chase George Geary's winning hit to the boundary, and the ball, with a gold shield on it, was afterwards presented to me by the Victorian Cricket Association as a memento of my first Test century.

After this historic Test at Melbourne I went on to Adelaide to play for New South Wales against South Australia in a Sheffield Shield match.

Owing to the fact that Victor Richardson had not proved a success as an opening batsman in the second and third Test matches, Australian critics were now calling loudly for a new man to open the Australian innings.

Some of them suggested that I should take his place, and I believe this was primarily the reason why, in our next Shield match, I was sent in to open the innings for New South Wales.

It did not matter to me what position I was in, for I was always prepared to do whatever my captain desired, but nevertheless I always had a slight preference for being opening batsman.

However, as events turned out, my scores in this were two and five, and fate seemed to decree that my regular position in future was to be a first wicket down batsman, and that is the position in which I am generally sent in to bat today. It is not from choice that I go in first wicket down, and I really cannot say that I have a penchant for any particular position now, but as previously stated, my destiny just seemed to work itself out.

Rather an amusing little incident occurred immediately I returned to Sydney after this game. A friend of mine in conversation informed me that he had just had a talk with a man in reference to myself. (This man, of course, did not know me at all.)

"No wonder Don Bradman failed in Adelaide", this man had remarked, "success in the Test Match in Melbourne evidently turned his head, and he was scarcely sober all the time he was in Adelaide. How could he make runs in that condition?"

Could a better illustration of the fickleness of the public be required?

Throughout my life I have been a strict teetotaller, and I can honestly say that I have never had a drink in my life. Yet because I failed, a person unknown to me had to find some excuse for my failure.

Had I been a success in Adelaide the remark would never have been passed.

Luckily my friend knew the correct circumstances, and did not hesitate to tell this fellow what he thought of his statement.

# A SYDNEY RECORD SCORE
## MORE TESTS IN AUSTRALIA

BEFORE the fourth Test I played for New South Wales against Victoria on the Sydney Cricket Ground. It was a notable game for me in that I scored 340 not out in less than 8 hours. This was the highest individual score that had been made on the Sydney Cricket Ground up to that time and the highest by a New South Wales player against Victoria.

Naturally such an innings lifted my confidence, as did the many congratulatory messages I received. The one I prized most came from the brother of the famous W. L. Murdoch, who, up to then, had held the record for the Sydney Cricket Ground.

Following this Shield game I set out for the fourth Test in Adelaide in company with Archie Jackson who was to make his first appearance in international cricket and was destined to be the youngest batsman to score a century in his first Test. Archie and I stayed at an Adelaide hotel but for some reason the rest of the team were quartered at Glenelg, which is on the beach some miles outside the city.

The match produced a succession of thrills and a hair raising finish. It will ever be remembered for the wonderful performance of Hammond who scored 119 not out and 177, and for the truly magnificent display given by Archie Jackson. Without hesitation I class this innings of his as one of the finest I have ever seen.

We were left with 349 runs to get to win in the fourth innings. The fortunes of the game swung this way and that, but the moment came when we were in a winning position. We were within 29 runs of victory with three wickets to fall, and with Oldfield as my partner I saw every prospect of getting the necessary runs.

Then came tragedy. Oldfield hit a ball from White to Hobbs at cover-point, and we tried for a run, but Hobbs was too smart for me, and I was run out.

## Felt He Had Let Down Side

NEEDLESS to say, I was bitterly disappointed, as I felt that I had let down my side—and those 29 runs were still wanted with but Grimmett and Blackie to go in. I made for the shower bath, but when I found that Blackie, the last man, was about to face the bowling and 12 runs had to be got for victory, I stole out of the bathroom, and, robed in a towel, I peered through the window on to the ground.

The agony of it all! If Blackie would only hold his end up so that Oldfield might knock off the runs! If—! And then Blackie hit out at White with all his might. Larwood, running full tilt, near the square-leg boundary, got to the ball and held it. And so England won by 12 runs.

Blackie was crestfallen, but even so he held to his sense of humour. When asked, "What were you thinking when Jack White pitched that ball up to you?"

"I said to myself," answered Blackie, "how the boys will cheer when they see me hit him for six."

Before the fifth and final Test match, I played on the Sydney ground against the English team. As luck would have it, the weather ruined the game. But it afforded me an opportunity of making acquaintance with a wicket affected by rain.

My only other experience of playing on such a wicket was in my first Test, at Brisbane. I was tremendously anxious to do well. The number of runs I got was small, but even so I learned much in the way of realising the kind of stroke-making demanded by a wicket that was far from being hard and plumb—the kind of wicket which, I was assured, was more or less common in England. So I decided that my education was the more complete.

The last Test at Melbourne was a grim fight from start to finish. We were a very young side. Alan Fairfax, a St. George club mate of mine, was making his first appearance in a Test match, as were also Hornibrook and Wall. Although England had already won the Ashes, we were mightily keen and anxious to win the last of the series.

In this match, Fairfax and I had the distinction of setting up a record fifth wicket partnership for Australia. We were especially proud and glad, for we were not only members of the same club, but the only club to have two representatives in our country's team.

We lost the toss and we had the misfortune to be denied the services of Grimmett on the second day, Clarrie being unable to bowl because of an injured knee.

## Australia's Win in Fifth Test

ENGLAND'S first innings in this memorable fifth Test at Melbourne was notable for another Hobbs century. This was his 12th century against Australia, and his fifth on the Melbourne ground. His batting was superb, and it was not until the end of the day's play that he got his leg in front of one from Jack Ryder.

Leyland, who had come into the team in place of Chapman, who was ill with an attack of influenza, made his first Test appearance, and after surviving a difficult chance when he was 13, went on to swell the number of players who have scored a century in a first Test match. His off-side play and his drives were particularly good, and his knock coming late in the innings, helped England to reach the respectable total of 519.

The opinion of the experts was that since we would have to take fourth innings, the odds were emphatically against Australia. Much, therefore, depended on how we fared in our first innings.

Woodfull set us a good example by staying at the crease three hours and a half. Archie Jackson was unfortunate in being run out when set, but ultimately we got to within 20 odd runs of England's total. In our innings Geary must have accomplished something like a record by sending down 81 overs.

Tim Wall did some fine work with the ball in England's second innings, and when they were out for the moderate total of 257, we saw there was a definite chance of victory. Our score rose steadily until an Australian victory was in sight, and it was a real pleasure to me to be at the wicket with my captain, Jack Ryder, when the winning runs were made.

When I realised that we were bound to win, my one desire was to see Ryder make the winning hit, for he had been a wonderful fellow in the previous matches, and my wish that he should get the winning hit was shared by everybody.

The runs which gave Australia her one victory in the series, however, were byes.

Before these came, Ryder had hit a ball toward the boundary and Maurice Tate was so sure that it was a four that he grabbed a couple of stumps so as to add to his score of souvenirs. Tate just roared when he saw that the ball had not reached the boundary, and to the accompaniment of much good-humoured banter restored the stumps.

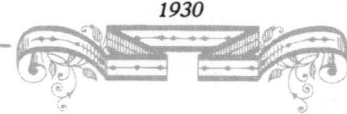

# FONDNESS FOR MUSIC

## A WORLD'S RECORD SCORE AGAINST QUEENSLAND

THERE were jubilant scenes on the Melbourne Cricket Ground at the end of the fifth Test, Jack Ryder being carried off shoulder high and losing his bat and his cap in the process.

We didn't have much time for celebrations because Fairfax, Jackson, Kippax and I had to catch the train back to Sydney. The vast crowd and the excitement made it impossible for us to get a taxi. In the end the four of us boarded a horse drawn cab. One of us sat on the dickey with the driver, two squeezed inside the vehicle with our luggage, and the fourth stood on the back step holding on like grim death. What a way for victorious players to leave the ground.

After a brief stay in Sydney I next went on a country tour with a N.S.W. Association side, visiting several fine centres. At Singleton our first four batsmen made centuries and the fifth a duck, whereupon the innings was closed—a rather unusual happening. At Maitland I was given out LBW for 0 to a ball which I'm sure would have missed the leg stump by a foot. But obeying the umpire without showing dissent was part of my training. [It was later in life that I read the probably apocryphal story of Dr. W. G. Grace who, in similar circumstances, is alleged to have said to the umpire—"listen my man the people came here to see me bat not to watch you umpire".]

So 1928/9 had been a long and eventful season. My 1690 runs in first class cricket was the highest aggregate yet compiled in Australia in one season and had paved the way for my future career.

During the fourth Test at Adelaide I had been offered and had accepted a three year appointment with Mick Simmons Ltd, a large sports goods establishment in Sydney and this, coming just as the first signs of a depression were emerging, was of considerable importance and comfort.

I was glad to get some respite from cricket at the season end and to relax at two of my hobbies, a little golf and some piano playing.

Season 1929/30 came round in due course. Just prior to the opening of the cricket year, I celebrated my 21st birthday, and this season, as it turned out, was an auspicious one for me. The season however opened quietly enough as far as I was concerned. The first inter-state game was against Queensland at Brisbane, and in spite of some good bowling by Hornibrook and Oxenham, we won a close game by 23 runs. My scores were 48 and 66. On our side that day were Arthur Mailey and Dr. R. H. Bettington.

After this match we returned to Sydney to play the M.C.C. side captained by A. H. H. Gilligan, which was on its way to New Zealand. In this game no fewer than four New South Wales players made centuries. In the first innings Alan Kippax scored 108, Allsopp 117, and I got 157. In the second innings Archie Jackson scored 168 not out.

This match was noteworthy to me inasmuch as it was the first occasion on which I saw Duleepsinhji bat. His reputation had already reached Australia, and naturally we were all anxious to see him. He only made 34, but even during his short stay at the wickets, I, like everybody else, was much impressed by the gracefulness of his strokes.

In the same match I saw Frank Woolley at what must have been his very best. He played a delightful innings of 219. I had seen him once before when he played in the fifth Test match at Sydney in 1921. Then, of course, I was a very small boy, but I have a distinct recollection of one or two strokes he then made—glorious shots they were. I never dreamed when I first saw him at Sydney that I would ever play against him on the same ground.

My next game was also at Sydney and this was a game to which a great deal of importance was attached. With the idea of helping them in their task of team building, our selectors arranged a trial match between teams captained by Jack Ryder and Billy Woodfull. As might be supposed, the greatest interest was taken in the trial, for here was the material on which the selectors would work.

Jack Ryder had on his side, in addition to himself, Archie Jackson, Ponsford, Grimmett, McCabe, Oxenham, C. Walker, A. Marks, W. Horrocks, H. Whitfield and H. H. Alexander. Woodfull's XI, in the order of going in, were Woodfull, Fairfax, Kippax, Bradman, A. Allsopp, K. Rigg, A. G. Burrows, J. E. Ellis, Don Blackie, Hornibrook and Wall.

The game lasted five days, and altogether 1704 runs were scored for 39 wickets, Ryder's side ultimately winning, after an exciting finish, by one wicket.

Archie Jackson played a magnificent innings of 182, which, though not of the same worth as his century in his first Test at Adelaide, nevertheless denoted the cricket genius. We also saw Ponsford back to form, to prove that he was none the worse from the effects of the broken hand which he had suffered the previous season when batting against Larwood.

Our team, that is Woodfull's, finished up 350 runs behind on the first innings, mainly because of the destructive bowling of Oxenham, who varied his pace and flighted the ball in a way that was wonderful. He was in his most deadly mood.

In our second innings Kippax made a very fine 170, and I had the good fortune to score a century in the first innings, and when we followed on in the afternoon I went in first and made a double century.

My next interstate match was for New South Wales against South Australia at Adelaide. We not only lost by five wickets, but had the misfortune to have our slow bowler, Campbell, injured. After sending down nine overs in the first innings, he had his finger smashed so badly

that he could not bowl. Being the only other slow bowler on our side, I was called on to bowl—perhaps that is why we did not do very well.

Stan McCabe played two delightful innings, and Allsopp also acquitted himself with every credit on this, his first appearance at Adelaide.

In our second innings Grimmett bowled with tremendous effect. Some of the balls he sent down to me were the most difficult I had ever been called on to play. I was absolutely tied up, and made to look like a schoolboy. I never had such a bad time, but somehow I remained to make 84, and then Grimmett, as he should have done long before, got me out l.b.w.

### Chilvers Reminiscent of Grimmett

FROM Adelaide we journeyed to Melbourne, to play a drawn game with Victoria. In this match my scores were 89 and 26 not out. Here Jack Ryder's luck was dead out. He was out for a duck in the first innings, and only scored a single in the second, and it is fair to assume that his misfortune at Melbourne had its effect on his chance of going to England.

Campbell, who had played at Adelaide, was still nursing his damaged finger, and a young player named H. Chilvers was brought from Sydney to take Campbell's place at Melbourne.

Chilvers in many respects reminds one of Grimmett, and in this, his first important game, he created a very favourable impression. Indeed, he came very near being selected to tour England. In Chilvers, I believe New South Wales has a slow bowler of unusual promise.

Stan McCabe who, at Adelaide, had scored 69 and 79, obtained 70 in his first innings, and 50 not out in his second at Melbourne. He was a model of consistency. This match at Melbourne was also notable for the very excellent wicket-keeping of Davidson, of the Waverley Club, and he, like Chilvers, was considered to be well in the running for selection.

This finished the New South Wales "away" matches for the season, and I say frankly that I was not sorry. It is not possible for those unfamiliar with the conditions under which we play in Australia to understand the strain imposed on players who take part in interstate matches. Already I had travelled from Sydney to Brisbane, from Brisbane back to Sydney, from Sydney to Adelaide, from Adelaide to Melbourne, and then back to Sydney. The long train journeys are a severe test of physical endurance.

For instance, the journey from Sydney to Adelaide means 32 hours in the train; from Sydney to Brisbane, 27 hours; and from Sydney to Melbourne, 16 hours. Many of these trips are done in terrific heat, which leaves one limp and almost good for nothing, and the day's rest we enjoy on the completion of the journey is as necessary as it is welcome.

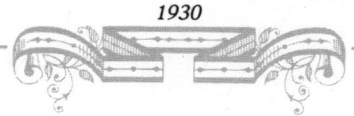

## Individual Score Record Broken

AFTER leaving Melbourne on the last day of 1929, we were due to play our return game with Queensland on the Sydney ground on January 3. I give these details, because this match was associated with what I regard as one of the outstanding events of my career.

I do not set much store on the making of records, and throughout my whole career, I have made it a rule, and have never departed from it, always to play for my side, and not for myself. I have never placed my own interest before the interests of my team, and if I made a new record I have been glad, but mainly because I have felt that my side needed the runs.

On this occasion, however, I definitely and deliberately set out to establish a record. The highest individual score in first-class cricket was one record I wanted to hold, and the opportunity came my way in this match.

New South Wales batted first, and both sides completed an innings for comparatively small scores. At the end of the second day's play (Saturday), I was some 200 odd runs not out. I spent the evening quietly with some friends, and then on the Sunday, on reflecting on the state of the game, it occurred to me that I had just a possibility of topping Billy Ponsford's record score of 437.

The conditions were splendidly in my favor. The state of the game was exactly right, and I felt sure that if I could only do my part I would have the necessary support at the other end. When Monday came, everything worked out as I had hoped and planned.

The mood to make runs was on me, and topping the third century, and then the fourth, the moment came when I was at last within striking distance of my goal—the highest individual score.

My score was 434, so that four more runs were wanted when I faced Thurlow, Queensland's fast bowler, against whom earlier in the season Woodfull had his hand broken.

Here I had a curious premonition. While Thurlow was preparing to bowl, I seemed to sense that the ball would be a short-pitched one on the leg stump, and I could almost feel myself getting ready to make my shot before the ball was delivered.

True enough, it pitched exactly where I had anticipated, and hooking it to the square leg boundary I established the only record on which I had set my heart, subsequently going to 452 not out.

Many people have asked me to describe my feelings when I realised that I had accomplished this performance. The best description I can offer is that I felt as a man having set himself a specific task, had achieved it, and having done so, was satisfied. I was not excited, and I cannot say that I suffered any reaction. My feeling was one of complete satisfaction.

# SHOOTING RABBITS WHEN CHOSEN FOR ENGLAND
## YOUTH OF TEAM STAGGERS SOME
## AUSTRALIAN CRITICS

MANY times I have been asked if I were physically tired after making the record score of 452. I can honestly say I was not. It has to be remembered that I made my runs on two separate days with a Sunday intervening.

I had actually scored slightly over 200 runs on each of the two days, and as a strain on my physical powers this innings does not compare with the 124 and 225 I scored in one day in the first and second innings of the trial game a month before.

I was not only fortunate in the way my innings was split up, but I was also fortunate that the state of the game so helped me that first Alan Kippax, then McCabe, and later Allsopp were able to stay with me for lengthy periods, while I was going along to the record. Shortly afterward our innings was declared closed, with my individual total at 452 not out.

Physically I was so comfortable that I felt I could have gone on indefinitely, providing of course that I did not make that vital mistake which all batsmen are liable to make. But, after all, games are meant to be won. I was playing for New South Wales and not for Don Bradman and I did not complain when our captain applied the closure.

And here I am glad to be able to tell you that the first telegram of congratulation I received was from Billy Ponsford whose record I had broken.

This is another instance of the splendid good feeling and spirit of goodwill which is ever an outstanding feature of the wonderful game of cricket.

There was an amusing incident following the making of my record. A traveller employed by the same firm as myself became so excited that he jumped the fence, ran across the ground and attempted to lift me onto his shoulder.

I was too much of a handful for him however, and he fell with me on his chest.

Before I left for England, at a farewell and presentation by my firm, this traveller gave me

a miniature Don Bradman bat of pure gold in the form of a tie-pin; it is one of my most treasured possessions.

So many messages of congratulation reached me from all over Australia that I was glad of the opportunity of broadcasting my thanks to the Australian public through the medium of 2BL Sydney.

Curiously enough, the 452 I made against Queensland was my only three figure score in interstate cricket in this season.

I did not play so much Grade cricket in 1929/30, owing to the claims of New South Wales, but on two occasions when I turned out for them, I broke the St. George club record twice by scoring first 180 not out, and then 187 in a later game.

These Grade games, by the way, are played on two Saturday afternoons, and are usually very exciting affairs. Runs have to be made quickly if they are to be of any use to the side, and for that reason they appeal to me.

It is no uncommon experience in these Grade games to find oneself opposed to players who were in the New South Wales side with you just previously. For instance Archie Jackson plays for Balmain, Alan Kippax is a Waverley player, while McCabe plays for Mosman.

Before the end of the season there came the selection of the Australian team for England. Having permitted myself to think that I had a chance of being chosen to make the trip to England, I was at the same time prepared for disappointment.

It is part of my mental make-up not to take anything for granted. The view I took was that if our selectors decided I was good enough, I would be picked as a matter of course.

With but a little exaggeration, everybody in Australia constituted himself a selector. The picking of the side developed into an epidemic; teams were built and teams were scrapped after long established fashion.

Every potential Australian player was dis-

sected, myself among the number. A number of critics openly expressed the opinion that I would not be a success under English conditions; that my style was next to impossible, that it smacked of the bush, and so on.

"This country lad" it was written, "with his cross bat, will be no good on English wickets." Such criticism neither stung nor hurt me, but it did make me determined that if selected I would do my best to confound my critics.

I was not unused to this criticism, and I recall that Maurice Tate took me aside when saying good-bye at Melbourne. "Don," he said, "learn to play a straighter bat before you come to England, or you will never get any runs."

I am ready to admit in the freest, frankest manner that I make no pretensions as to style, but having discovered and proved that I could make runs in Australia by my own methods, I felt that they would be effective in England. If they were not, then, I said, "I'll alter them to suit the conditions there".

While the various experts were discovering faults in my method of batting and fearing my failure if I were sent to England, I was spending a few quiet days at my home in Bowral. Even at little restful Bowral, however, the selection of the team was the subject of common talk. My father, mother, sisters and brother were perhaps more than mildly excited; and as the day approached for the broadcasting of the names they were all anxiety.

I can honestly say that I was the least agitated, but to ensure something like peace of mind, I kept to myself, as far as possible aloof from the many family councils and inquests that were held.

On the afternoon that the names of the Australian team were to be officially announced, my brother Victor and myself decided to go for a trip into the country.

At the moment the team was made known we were shooting rabbits.

It was not until we were on our way back

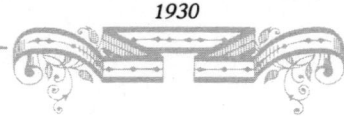

home that we learned from friends that I had been picked. It seemed too good to be true, and it took me some time to realise that I was really going Home, to begin an adventure on which every Australian cricketer, whatever his station, sets his heart.

I had no relations known to me in England; but it did not matter—my ambition was to be fulfilled.

When the names of the 1930 Australian touring side were given to the world, the experts gasped with astonishment. There was some plain writing and plain speaking; the worst possible fate was bound to be ours; we were too young and inexperienced—in fact we were lambs going to the slaughter.

We were told that youth and enthusiasm were fine qualities, no doubt, and that was about all that could be said for us. The likelihood that we would bring back the Ashes was regarded more in a spirit of hope than faith.

I can understand the attitude of those who were against the dropping of Jack Ryder, Australia's leader in the previous series of Tests, but this was a matter entirely for the selectors; I was equally pleased to be going to England under Woodfull's leadership. They are excellent fellows both.

Here are the names of the 15 players who were selected: W. M. Woodfull (Victoria), Capt.; V. Y. Richardson (South Australia), Vice-captain; W. H. Ponsford (Victoria); A. F. Kippax (New South Wales); A. Jackson (New South Wales); W. A. Oldfield (New South Wales); S. J. McCabe (New South Wales); A. Fairfax (New South Wales); D. G. Bradman (New South Wales); C. V. Grimmett (South Australia); T. Wall (South Australia); P. M. Hornibrook (Queensland); A. Hurwood (Queensland); E. L. a'Beckett (Victoria); C. W. Walker (South Australia).

Mr. W. L. Kelly was manager; Mr. T. H. Howard (Treasurer); and Mr. W. Ferguson scorer and baggage man; while later Arthur James, of Tasmania, was appointed masseur.

Woodfull, Ponsford, Oldfield and Grimmett were in England with the 1926 team, but the rest of us were making the English trip for the first time.

The days before my actual departure to join the team were happy and busy ones.

There were farewells here and farewells there; with preparations and presentations it was one long round of excitement, and I was not sorry when at last my bags were packed and on the way to the station.

# TEST TEAM REACHES LONDON
## BRADMAN ENJOYS SHIP LIFE

# Renewing Acquaintance with English Cricketers

FOR myself, the great adventure actually began on Thursday, March 6, 1930, when I set out from Sydney for Bowral, so that I might have my last meal in New South Wales at home. Those few hours with my folk are of my sweetest memories—the pride of my parents, the joy I know they felt, their hopes and prayers.

Time raced, and away I went to Moss Vale, some six miles from Bowral, to join the other members of the New South Wales party, en route for Melbourne.

My parents, sisters and brother accompanied me to Moss Vale, where they were reinforced by a large circle of friends who turned out to say "goodbye".

The parting over, the journey to Melbourne began.

Arrived in Melbourne, the N.S.W. portion of the Test team picked up the South Australian and Victorian contingents, and on the afternoon of the next day, after being entertained by the Commercial Traveller's Club, we boarded the Nairana for Launceston.

There was no dinner for me that night; I was dreadfully seasick, which was a new and painful experience. I was grateful when morning came to find that I was still living. And not only so, but to begin a delightful trip up the Tamar River to Launceston. I was mightily glad to get ashore, though I had been privileged to feast on a panorama of gorgeous scenery.

We reached Launceston at 9 o'clock in the morning, and began a match with Tasmania before lunch. The ground here was as pretty as any I have seen, its setting rich in restfulness and most picturesque. We won the match easily.

In it, Stan McCabe made his first century in first class cricket.

A trip to the Great Lake followed. Some of the boys went a-fishing, but I am afraid their haul was more remarkable for leanness than opulence; the fish in fact, were shy to bite that day. The Tasmanian Cricket Association having entertained us at a farewell supper, we proceeded by cars to Hobart.

Unhappily there was no play on the first day owing to rain, so that the game in which Billy Ponsford and I made centuries was left drawn.

While in Hobart, the Prince of Wales Theatre very kindly presented me with a half-size cricket bat made of beautiful Tasmanian blackwood. After the manner of a careful souvenir collector, I immediately sent it home.

We were the guests of the Theatre to supper, and on the following morning were entertained by the Governor, Sir James O'Grady, at Government House.

The match having perforce been given up as a draw, we boarded the Orford and started for Melbourne. Once again I was reduced to a state of worse than limpness; I was frightfully seasick all the way.

Arriving at Melbourne, we were officially received in the Town Hall by the Lord Mayor, and later the Victorian Cricket Association gave us a farewell dinner at the Hotel Alexander. From Melbourne we went by train to Perth, a long and tiring journey occupying 5 days and 6 nights on the train.

Following more entertainment and an uneventful match against West Australia we rejoined the Orford at Fremantle for the final stage of our great adventure.

Having on my journey to and from Tasmania proved an impossible sailor, I was not a little apprehensive as to what would happen before I reached Europe. The gods be praised. The sea was beautifully calm all the way, and I did not miss a meal from the time we left Fremantle until we disembarked at Naples.

Life aboard the ship appealed to me immensely, and I revelled in the various games. We were as one big happy family; and in the different sports we were fortunate to win a fair share of the prizes.

On the morning of April 2 we woke to find ourselves at Colombo. Breakfast over, we went ashore at once to buy a topee each. And decked out in that most necessary head-dress, we had a beautiful drive to Mount Lavinia; later to visit a Buddhist Temple. We were profoundly impressed by all the sights we saw.

The cricket enclosure was a pleasant surprise; it was an excellent ground, and a big crowd turned out to paint a picture of many colours. The people were most enthusiastic, and they had infinitely more than a nodding acquaintance with the game.

Back defensive shot.

Start of drive.

Early position for a back leg glance.

Bradman demonstrating the late cut.

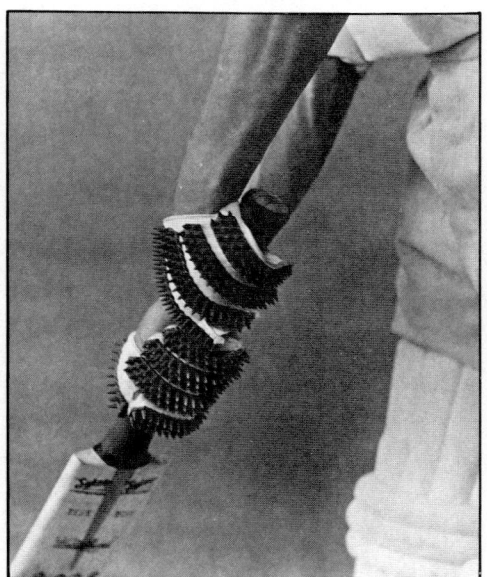

Bradman's grip.

Bradman demonstrates the forward leg glance.

Bradman demonstrating a square cut off the front foot.

Bradman making a hook shot. Position after contact.

Bradman making a forward defensive shot. Note how the right hand has been lowered to the bottom of the handle.

SUNDAY, SEPTEMBER 6, 1931

# BRADMAN IS GOING TO ENGLAND!

"TRUTH" PRINT, KIPPAX STREET, SYDNEY.

There was much public speculation surrounding an offer made by the Accrington Club for Don Bradman to play in the Lancashire League.

## Had First Ride on Camel

UNFORTUNATELY, there was rain, but there was not the slightest disposition to grumble. Folk just sat in silence to wait for a resumption of the game. The standard of play was appreciably higher than I had expected. The weather was hot and trying, and as might be supposed we felt it more than a trifle strange and awkward playing in topees.

We batted first, and Ponsford was top scorer. The local bowlers were quite good, especially one, Ed. Kelaart, who did not a little destruction. Rain prevented the local side batting for more than a short time, and when the match had to be given up they had lost one wicket.

We were given a dinner at the Galle Face Hotel, at which the Governor presided. Rejoining the Orford, we resumed the usual ship life until Saturday, April 12, when we landed at Suez and berthed in the harbor. After breakfast, we went ashore and caught the train for Cairo. There we visited the museum where repose relics of Tutankhamen; the Citadel Mosque, and did the rounds of the bazaar. Our next trip was to the Pyramids. And I had my first ride on a camel. Never again!

We took tea at Mena House and then back to Shepheard's Hotel, to be regaled there by a wonderful band, and to loll in the beautiful gardens. We were away very early the following morning for Port Said. The railway runs parallel for some distance with the canal, and looking from the train windows it was a weird experience to see ships' funnels sticking out of what seemed to be the desert. Aboard the Orford again, we landed two days later at Naples.

Our arrival at Naples broke new and wonderful ground for me; it marked the beginning of a glorious round of sight-seeing. First, we visited Pompeii; thence to Solfatara, where we walked in the crater of this now extinct volcano; afterward to Rome to see St. Peter's, St. Paul's, the Vatican City, the Vatican Museum, and to gaze in awe and admiration at the Victor Emmanuel Memorial. We placed a wreath on the Unknown Warrior's grave, looked into the Forum, saw the grave of John Keats, went to the Catacombs, the Colosseum, and we were received by Sir Roland Graham, the British Ambassador in Italy.

From Rome we proceeded to Milan where we visited La Scala theatre and the Cathedral, gazed at that famous painting of the Last Supper, and then on through entrancing scenery, through the St. Gothard tunnel, to Switzerland, where some of the boys saw snow for the first time in their lives. We stayed a night at Lucerne, and on the following morning took a ferry to Vitznau on to Rigi-Kulm, where in gorgeous sunshine we had a regular snowball fight. Great fun!

And then to Paris where, of course, we did most of the sights, visiting Notre Dame, Arc de Triomphe, where we placed a wreath on the Unknown Warrior's grave.

I was fortunate to meet in Paris an Australian boy and with him I drove around the magic city later to view it from the top of the Eiffel Tower. Wonderful panorama!

## Soul-Stirring Journey to London

OUR trip across the Channel was perfect, scarcely a ripple, and we arrived at Dover in high feather, the happiest party ever to be given an official reception, and welcomed by Lord Harris. The feeling that at last we had come Home was indescribable. To see the white cliffs of Dover for the first time, to be among folk who claimed us as their very own captured us entirely.

Only those who recall their first journey from Dover to London can appreciate how soul-stirring it is, how immensely different from any other journey. The green, its richness, the colour of the country-side, the perfect peace of it all—never have I beheld nor yet have I been so moved by the picture that was painted.

We were enthusiastically and most cordially welcomed on our arrival in London, and how happy we were to renew acquaintance with Jack Hobbs and Percy Chapman, who were among the vast crowd at the station to greet us. We made the Midland Hotel, St. Pancras, our headquarters. Crowded indeed were all the days which were to follow.

First, a reception at Australia House, where we were received by Sir Granville Ryrie, the High Commissioner of Australia; a luncheon given by the members of the Sportsman's Club, at which were many distinguished people—the Duke of Gloucester, Lord Harris, Lord Decies, Field-Marshal Lord Plumer, and many other celebrities.

As soon as possible we made for Lord's. How we all itched to get there! I found Lord's different from what it had been represented to me. It is a magnificent ground. We had a little practice on turf that was very soft, a new and strange experience to me.

We were about early next morning, and our first duty was to place a wreath on the Cenotaph, and then attend the Anzac memorial service at St. Clement Dane's Church.

We were entertained at lunch by the Lord Mayor of London, and in the afternoon were present at an Anzac reunion at Australia House, where I had the pleasure of meeting Sir George Fuller, the Agent-General of New South Wales, whose home town is also mine, Bowral.

Our programme did not permit of our going to Lord's next day, but we managed to squeeze in a little practice on the Saturday, when from Lord's we went to Wembley as the guests of the Football Association, to see the cup final between Arsenal and Huddersfield Town.

Of Association football I have but little knowledge—different from Archie Jackson, who, I understand, is a distant relation of Alex Jackson, the most famous player of the Huddersfield club. But if the game was largely strange to me, I enjoyed it immensely. It was the sight which I gazed on that appealed to me most. Few short of 100,000 people were present, and when the King arrived they stood to attention as one man and sang the National Anthem with a spontaneity and enthusiasm that thrilled me as I have never been thrilled before.

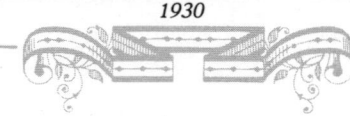

# WHEN GRIMMETT TOOK ALL
## 10 YORKSHIRE WICKETS

# Bradman's Story of English Tour

## SWEATERS NEEDED IN BITTERLY COLD WEATHER

ON the Monday following the Test team's arrival in England, we had a fair amount of practice at Lord's, and then came our first match with Worcester. Naturally, we looked forward to it with every keenness. We were much concerned, however, about Stan McCabe and Alan Kippax, who were feeling far from their normal selves. We were all charmed with the Worcester ground; its situation is delightful, and we saw it lit up by brilliant sunshine. But, oh, the weather was cold! One's thickest sweater was not enough, for even then the wind seemed to cut into our very bones.

Grimmett and Fairfax, though they had had no serious practice for a couple of months, bowled remarkably well, Grimmett especially so, taking five for 46 and four for 38, so that Worcester were got out cheaply, and we won the match by an innings.

This was my first experience of an English wicket, and, of course was the first time I had batted against Root, who I remembered had gone through the previous Australian side. I am sure he was not at his best on this occasion, and besides the wicket was too easy to give him much assistance. I scored 236, and Billy Woodfull made 133. This innings on the pretty Worcester ground put me on good terms with myself, inasmuch as it gave me that confidence I felt I needed.

Although we knew that Worcester were not a strong side, our victory over them acted as a tonic, for be it remembered that many of us were playing under conditions wholly foreign to us. Altogether, our stay at Worcester was a happy and interesting one. The Mayor received us officially at the historic Guildhall, and, speaking for myself, I fell in love with the old city.

From Worcester we travelled to Leicester, breaking our journey en route at Birmingham. Here we had some curious cricket. Leicester batted first and scored 130 without losing a wicket. Then Grimmett and Wall bowled with such effect that the side were all out for 148. We made a sorry start to our innings, and were pardonably apprehensive when Archie Jackson was out to the first ball sent to him by George Geary, and Ponsford was soon out leg before, also to that great bowler.

### Geary Bowls With Little Luck

THE conditions were anything but encouraging to us. However, after the dismissal of Jackson and Ponsford the tide began to run in our favour. I would like to say that Geary bowled at his very best in this match and had little luck. I considered that his bowling was better than it had been in Australia. Vic. Richardson hit two glorious sixes in a great century, and profiting by the excellent batting practice I had at Worcester, I managed to score 185 before bad light and rain stopped play. I found the wicket much more difficult than those I had been accustomed to and most of the time the ball had to be watched carefully right on to the bat—it couldn't be trusted to come along straight and true as it does on the good old Sydney ground. I learned a good deal at Leicester.

There was no play at all on the third and last day of the match, and after a dreary day in the pavilion we packed up and returned to London for our next match with Essex at Leyton. This game marked our first appearance on a London ground. I was a spectator on this occasion. The match with Essex was notable for the excellence of the bowling of Hornibrook, who at one stage took six wickets in the Essex first innings for 11 runs, and we won by 207. The weather conditions were extremely unpleasant, the wind being bitterly cold and piercing—not at all cricket weather.

From Leyton we went north, to Sheffield, to play Yorkshire at Bramall Lane. As might be supposed, we were prepared for a hard fight. The ground was far from wealthy in the matter of grass, many bare patches reminding us that the football season—Sheffield United play at Bramall Lane—was but recently over. It was in this match that Clarrie Grimmett performed the great feat of taking all 10 wickets—and 10 Yorkshire wickets at that!

His figures were:—

| Overs | M. | Runs | Wickets |
|---|---|---|---|
| 22.3 | 8 | 37 | 10 |

Clarrie was not a bowler at Bramall Lane that day; he was a wizard. He seemed to do as he pleased, and as he captured wicket after wicket I am sure that every one of us inwardly prayed that he might accomplish the next to impossible. And when he bowled Bowes, the young fast bowler, neck and crop, and brought the innings to an end, our admiration of Clarrie knew no bounds.

Grimmett, by the way, is the third Australian bowler to take all 10 wickets in a match in England. In his first game in England Bill Howell accomplished the feat against Surrey at the Oval. That was in 1889. In 1921, Arthur Mailey got Gloucester out.

What made this performance of Grimmett more remarkable was that he did not go on until Yorkshire had scored 46. He began by bowling Holmes, then he got Oldroyd out leg before, and having disposed of Sutcliffe, who threatened to stay indefinitely, he had every batsman who followed in his pocket. Grimmett took the last seven wickets in 65 minutes for 16 runs.

### Hearty Yorkshire Roar For Grimmett

HOW the crowd rose to him! I can hear and feel the heartiness, the sincerity of that deep-chested Yorkshire roar now. Congratulations showered on Clarrie from everybody and everywhere. I have never seen such masterful, such mystifying bowling, and I doubt whether I ever shall.

The bowler is often denied the praise due to him; it is the bowler, just as surely as the batsman, who makes victory possible. We were all mightily pleased that after Grimmett had struck his best form, and it was only fitting that the ball with which he worked such havoc should afterward be mounted and presented to him.

We much regretted that the weather ruined the match. On the Sunday I played golf with A. T. Barber, the young Yorkshire captain, at a place some 50 miles from the city, a place that, compared to Sheffield itself, was Arcadia.

Woodfull here made his second century of the tour; I scored 78, on the slowest wicket I had so far encountered, and in the making of it I made my first acquaintance with the bowling of Wilfred Rhodes, who was playing Test cricket before I was born.

There was none of the old man about him; his action was a thing of grace. Rhodes is a wonderful veteran!

From Sheffield we journeyed to Liverpool to play Lancashire on the picturesque ground at Aigburth, surely one of the most beautiful grounds in England. And it was at Aigburth that we had our first experience of an English summer day. How we relished it! And how welcome after frowning, forbidding Sheffield!

Altogether, our visit to Aigburth was a very pleasant one. The match at one period was in such a position that the County conjured up visions of victory. Lancashire, for whom their captain, Eckersley, played what was considered to be about his best innings, scored 176.

We went in to bat late in the day, and had a very bad hour or so, losing five wickets for 63. This was my first meeting with the old Australian, Ted McDonald, and I am ready to bear testimony to his greatness as a bowler. It was not a very happy meeting for me, as "Mac" (as he is commonly called) knocked my middle stump out of the ground in the second over. Although he has been a fast bowler now for many years, I would say he is still to be numbered among the world's best.

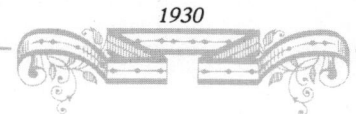
# BRADMAN DETERMINED TO
## PROVE CRITIC WRONG

## Makes 252 Not Out Against Surrey

FOLLOWING Lancashire we had an interesting tussle with M.C.C. at Lord's. To my surprise we found that the ground slopes from side to side and therefore the pitch is not entirely level. I made 66 useful runs and then pulled one onto my stumps "down the hill" (as they say).

There is a wonderful atmosphere surrounding Lord's and I fell in love with the place straight away. Which was more than I could say about Chesterfield where we played Derbyshire. Not because I didn't like the place, but purely because of the bitter cold. I sat in the dressing room waiting for my turn to bat, wearing all my cricket gear, a sweater, a blazer, and an overcoat before a glowing fire. Worse than that was being struck twice in succession when at the wicket by lively deliveries from Stan Worthington, both of which hit me on the bare thigh in exactly the same place. Boy did they hurt.

In our game with Surrey at the Oval, which followed our visit to Chesterfield, there was a curious contre-temps. When the umpires went into the field they discovered that the larger stumps used in County matches had been pitched. There was a hue and cry for the old stumps but these could not be procured for fully a quarter of an hour, and then fresh holes had to be made so that they might be used.

I look on my visit to the Oval as one of the red letter days of my life, for I had long known the Oval by reputation as the happy hunting ground of Jack Hobbs, and as the scene of many memorable games between England and Australia. And here of course, under the shadow of the towering gasometer, was to be played the fifth and last Test match of our tour.

I cannot say I was filled with joy at the sight of the gasometer, but I remember that I could not help thinking what the good people of Bowral would think if it were dumped in their midst one quiet night.

I hope for pardon when I say I had a particularly personal reason for looking forward to my first match against Surrey. Fender, the Surrey captain, besides being a great captain of a great county, is also a leading critic; and if I have not misunderstood him, he did not think too highly of my batting or my fielding during the last series of Tests in Australia.

I am not at all susceptible to criticism, but I need not make any secret of the fact that I was filled with a quiet determination to do well at the Oval.

I am not gloating over the fact that on this day I made 252 not out, but I did feel that if this innings had not put me on my feet as far as Fender was concerned, I at least had learned a good deal about an English wicket. I was to find out later that I had much more to learn about English wickets.

All this time, of course, we were trying to get into trim for the Test matches. A short but pleasant match at Oxford gave me a chance to see the finals of the inter-collegiate eights—a great spectacle.

Seeing the highways and byways of rural England is one of the charms of a cricketing tour such as ours. I would not like to say offhand just which particular stretch of country pleased me most, but I know I thoroughly enjoyed our motor drive to Southampton by way of the New Forest for our game with Hampshire.

Bradman pulls one from Lock to the leg boundary.

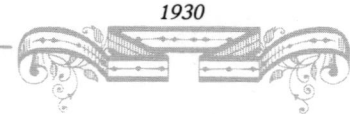

# THOUSAND RUNS IN MAY

## TRIBUTE TO HAMPSHIRE CAPTAIN

THE first day of our match with Hampshire was May 31, and I was naturally wondering if I would have an opportunity of reaching the 1000 mark. As luck would have it, Lord Tennyson won the toss, and when Brown started the Hampshire batting in great style, I felt that by failing at Oxford I had allowed the golden opportunity to slip.

Brown was hitting with such gusto that he seemed likely to stay indefinitely, but the fates were on my side, for when Brown had got 56 I ran him out. The ball was driven to me between mid-off and extra cover, and immediately the stroke was made I ran to meet the ball. I stopped the ball with my foot, one of the things I always advocate not doing if one can help it, and over-ran it.

Brown, when he saw that I had not got hold of the ball, decided that the stroke was worth a couple, and started out for his second run. I turned and grabbed the ball, and although I was practically broadside on to the wickets, I took the chance of throwing him out, and somehow managed to knock the middle stump out of the ground. It was the biggest fluke that ever happened—a 100 to one chance had come off.

With Brown disposed of, Grimmett simply skittled out the rest of the Hampshire batsmen; he took seven wickets for 56. In his usual kind and considerate way, Woodfull, as keen on my getting 1000 runs as I was myself, sent me in with Archie Jackson to open the innings.

I had more than a fright when Jackson was out in the first over for a duck, for I must confess I was more anxious than I had ever been. I felt the occasion and the special circumstances very much indeed—in fact, I was never more disturbed in my mind about getting runs.

Here was something I had to do to-day, or perhaps never at all. I had the fear that the feat was impossible. There was the quick fall of Jackson, but, worse, the weather. It had broken, and, when I had made 28, rain stopped play. The hands of the pavilion clock were simply rushing round to 6.30, and there we were looking at the rain coming down in torrents. The weather had baulked me.

Just when I had given up hope, the rain ceased, and out we went to resume play. I made runs as quickly as I could, but when I was seven short of the coveted figure there was more rain. I could not have complained if umpires and players had rushed pell-mell to the pavilion. That excellent sportsman, Lord Tennyson, who was captain of Hampshire, decided on one more over. I saw him approach the bowler and, although I have no exact knowledge of what he said, I think I could make a good guess. At all events, I had first one full toss to leg and then a "long hop," both of which I sent to the boundary, and then we bolted for shelter.

### English Wickets Dry
### Out Quickly

I WAS thankful when it was all over, and glad to be the first Australian to make a thousand runs before the end of May. I consider I was only able to accomplish this feat owing to the great bowling of Clarrie Grimmett, and the wonderful sportsmanship of the captains, Woodfull and Lord Tennyson, and the bowler at the time, Jack Newman.

Apart from the congratulations of Woodfull and all my colleagues, I had delightful messages from Hammond and Hallows, who, along with the late W. G. Grace and Tom Hayward, are the only Englishmen who have scored 1000 runs in May.

Following what to me will always be remembered as one of the most memorable days of my cricketing life, we were entertained by Lord Forster, a former Governor-General of Australia, and in his earlier years a great cricketer.

Saturday's rain had reduced the pitch to the most difficult that I had so far played on in England. To me, after all the rain had fallen, it was remarkable that the pitch had so far recovered that play was at all possible early on Monday. But wickets in England seem to dry out with incredible quickness, and while in the process of drying are easy most times. Wickets in Australia under similar conditions would become sticky. I was especially glad to have the experience of a rain-affected pitch at Southampton.

I was successful beyond all my expectations, and went on to score 191, with McCabe (65) next highest scorer. Grimmett maintained his superb bowling in the Hampshire second innings by again capturing seven wickets. In the end we won rather easily by an innings and eight runs.

From Southampton we travelled to London for our match with Middlesex at Lord's, and at the same time availed ourselves of an opportunity to visit the royal military tournament at Olympia—a magnificent spectacle, different from anything I had ever seen.

The next two games were against Middlesex and Cambridge University. On the Sunday we were the guests of Viscount Downe at luncheon, and on the same day we had the great joy of going to Sandringham, where we had the honour of being received by the King and Queen. To all of us the occasion was a momentous one.

The King and Queen made us feel entirely at home. The absence of anything in the nature of formality put us at our ease immediately. The King showed the liveliest interest in our tour. It was all a red-letter day. We were free to roam the grounds, and his Majesty saw to it that we made every use of our cameras. And the boys got some great pictures, which they will ever treasure.

The gardens were gorgeous, the museum teemed with interest; we made a tour of the stables, and visited the very beautiful church where their Majesties worship when they are in residence at Sandringham. The day was all too short.

We had now come to the eve of the first Test match. Interest in it was tremendous; to us it meant a vast deal, more than mere words can tell. We were keyed up to the highest pitch, but I can truthfully say that, young side though we were, and largely untried, we looked forward to it with every confidence.

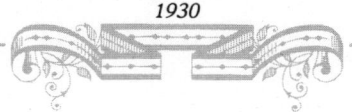

# BRADMAN DESCRIBES LOSS OF
## FIRST TEST IN ENGLAND

## Thought He Could Swing Game Round

AND now the stage was set for the first Test match at Trent Bridge, Nottingham, the first of our five games with England. The second was to be played at Lord's, the third at Leeds, the fourth at Manchester, and the fifth and last at the Oval, Kennington.

About this time it was very interesting to read what the English newspaper critics thought of us and our chances at Nottingham. I don't think I am giving away any secrets when I say that we were no little amused by the daily dissection we had to undergo in the press.

Some writers could see no hope for us at all. According to them, we were good enough for the counties, but when it came to the Tests we would be overwhelmed. We had no bowlers, and our batsmen were not good enough. And so on.

One or two critics whom we, of course, regarded as more discerning than their fellows, saw real possibilities in our ability both to make runs and take wickets. To them we were an improving side, and with the material we had, if we went on improving, we would be more and more dangerous opponents as the season wore on.

That was exactly our point of view. When we landed in England, we had one intention and one intention only. We were out to win the Ashes, and all our games and all our schemes, if I may use the word, had this one end in view. We worked together as a team for this one purpose; we discussed our opponents and analysed them in private, just as we were discussed and analysed in print, and you may be sure we added to our knowledge as we went along in readiness for the day.

I do not mean to suggest that we did not take our other games seriously. We took every game seriously, but our main consideration was to get our bowlers and batsmen used to the changed conditions under which we were playing. We tried all we knew to adapt ourselves to the different paced wickets, and every day and every game saw us becoming more and more used to the English pitches.

For myself I found that the ball had to be watched very carefully, especially at the start of an innings. Still, I was very pleased with the way I had been able to adapt myself to English conditions, and frankly I, for one, was quietly confident that there was a prospect of an Australian victory at Nottingham.

All followers of cricket are well aware that we lost this first Test at Nottingham, but I will always contend that we came very near to winning. When England's second innings closed on the Monday evening, we were left with 429 runs to get to win, and although this seemed a rather formidable total to face in the fourth innings of a match, I was optimistic about our chances.

Before close of play on Monday, we had lost Woodfull's valuable wicket, and the position on the Tuesday morning was that we had all day to bat and 369 runs to get to win—roughly, a run a minute. I felt confident that we could get them.

Ponsford and myself were not out overnight, but early in the day's play Billy was unlucky to get a real beauty from Tate—it was one of the finest balls I have ever seen Maurice bowl.

I kept one eye on the scoreboard and the other on the clock, and despite the loss of these two wickets, a win for Australia was still on the cards. If I could only keep the score moving along steadily until tea-time we could just pull off a great victory.

It may seem a boastful thing to say, but I really thought I could swing the game round. At lunch time we were in a comfortable position. The score was 198 for three—Woodfull, Ponsford and Kippax—my score being 88 and McCabe 33.

Shortly after lunch McCabe was caught by Copley, of the Notts ground staff, who was acting as substitute for Sutcliffe. It was a splendid catch, taken low down at mid-on. Up to this time we had been moving along in good style, and I was sorry to see McCabe go.

We now wanted 200 to win, with 195 minutes to play. I took stock of the position while waiting for Vic Richardson to come in, and decided that a win was still possible. I told myself that if I could only keep my wicket intact the rate of scoring could be speeded up in the last hour, when the bowlers were tired.

Alas for all my schemes and hopes! With another 38 runs knocked off, Robins pitched up an ordinary looking ball on the off. Judging that it would pass my stumps, I covered my wickets with my pads as I thought, and held my bat away from the ball. I must have been completely deceived, for the ball, which, as I have said, I made no attempt to play, hit my off stump.

### Felt He Had
### Thrown Away Game

I BLAME myself yet for this shocking lapse on my part. I really felt that I had thrown away the game, and the fact that I had scored 131 did not give me much satisfaction in the circumstances. When walking off the field that day I was more disappointed than if I had made a duck, for I felt I had let Australia down.

At the tea interval our defeat was inevitable. Richardson, in a fine effort to pull the game round, had missed one from Tyldesley, and when Fairfax was caught on the leg boundary by Robins, the end was in sight. Tim Wall hit a glorious six to leg—the only six of the

match—but this defiant gesture could not save us, and with exactly an hour left for play we were beaten by 93 runs.

The weather played us a scurvy trick; the rain that delayed the game on the second day being all against us; but the fact that Sutcliffe could not continue his innings owing to an injury, and that England on the last day were deprived of the services of Larwood, ill with gastritis, may be said to have levelled up matters as far as the bad luck was concerned.

There were many outstanding features in this very interesting game. Jack Hobbs batted magnificently in both innings; his defensive play was the best I have ever seen, and now and then he flashed out a shot of real genius. The fielding of Chapman was positively uncanny, and I don't know any other player who could have taken the catch that sent back Woodfull in the first innings.

Tate bowled long and well in our second innings; surely no other bowler could have sent them down with so much heart and vim. He did good work for England in this Test match, but his best patch was at the beginning of our first innings on the Saturday afternoon.

It was a disastrous start for us, reminiscent of that day at Brisbane when Larwood bundled out our opening batsmen. Ponsford was bowled round his legs, Woodfull was caught by Chapman, and I played on—all inside eight overs. At this stage Tate had taken three wickets for seven runs, and I fancy we never really recovered from this shock. Alan Kippax played a heroic innings of 64 not out. It was one of his very best.

When we came to review the match, taking everything into account, we thought we had no reason to be despondent. We had lost, it is true, but then again there was a time on the final afternoon when a win for Australia was a reasonable expectation.

We had done much better than was expected of us in some quarters, and we could now look forward to the second Test with some confidence. We certainly left Nottingham with the feeling that next time it might be our turn.

By taking five wickets in each innings, Clarrie Grimmett had established a moral superiority that was bound to tell in our favor in the long run. All the same, as the golfers have it, we were now one down and four to go.

During our stay at Nottingham we were invited to Welbeck Abbey by the Duke of Portland, where we met Mr Stanley Bruce, a former Prime Minister of Australia, and Mrs Bruce. Our visit to Welbeck Abbey was vastly interesting, and in signing the visitors' book we dipped our pens into ink wells made out of hoofs of Carbine, the history-making Australian racehorse.

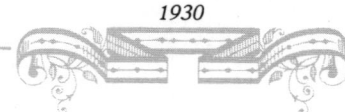

# BRADMAN'S STORY OF SECOND
## TEST IN ENGLAND

## Great Catch Dismisses Him at 254

### CHAPMAN'S GALLANT INNINGS WITH THREE MIGHTY SIXES

OUR next two inconclusive matches were against Surrey and Lancashire—both ruined by the weather.

Returning to London for the second Test at Lord's, we were the guests of the Dowager Countess of Darnley, whose husband as the Honorable Ivo Bligh will ever be remembered in international cricket. The countess, to our great interest, told us the original story of the "ashes". We afterwards took lunch at the House of Commons, and were shown over the Houses of Parliament. I had one of the greatest days of my life—I went to Wimbledon, where I saw all the great tennis players in the world.

We were now experiencing something like real cricket weather, and with a warm sun overhead and a hard, fast wicket for the second Test match, we were on good terms with ourselves at Lord's. If only Woodfull were lucky enough to win the toss!

England made three changes in the side that won at Nottingham—Sutcliffe and Larwood were still unfit, and Tyldesley (r.) was dropped. The newcomers were Duleepsinhji, G. O. Allen, and J. C. White. We played exactly the same eleven as at Nottingham.

Much to our disappointment, England again won the toss, and, of course, had first use of one of the best wickets I have played on in England. The English batting was surprisingly uneven. After getting rid of Hobbs, thanks to a smart catch behind the wickets, we were on our toes for the rest of the day, and only a really splendid innings by Duleepsinhji saved the English total from mediocrity.

Duleep made a memorable debut. He tackled Grimmett in a way that few batsmen dare. That he should deliberately throw away his wicket before the close of play on Friday—for that was his evident intention—is something I cannot profess to understand. England's total was not far off 400, it is true, but that is not a safe score in a four-day match.

When England left off with a total of 425 runs, there were many who thought that this figure was good enough to win the match, and I understood that one expert was doubtful if we would save the follow-on.

Cricket is a funny game, and anything may happen, of course. In a Test match played at Sydney, long before I was born, England made only 45 runs in the first innings and won the match by 13 runs; and in another Test match —also at Sydney long years ago—Australia's first innings' total was 586 runs, yet Australia lost by 10 runs.

I will not say that we faced this England total of 425 light-heartedly, but we were hopeful of making a decent reply, if we could only count on the weather. It is all in our favor that we are accustomed to huge totals in Australia, and an aggregate of 400 or 500 does not necessarily send our hearts into our boots.

### King Brought Luck to England

THE Australian reply to the English total at Lord's will surely rank as one of the best performances of any Australian touring side. Woodfull and Ponsford gave us a magnificent send-off. They took the sting out of the bowling, and undoubtedly paved the way for what was to follow.

During the afternoon, the King visited the ground, and play was stopped while the English and Australian players were presented to His Majesty. Immediately on the resumption of play, Ponsford lost his wicket by giving a simple catch in the slips to Hammond off White. And it was facetiously said that the best bowler in England was the King.

When I joined Woodfull, our score was 162 for one wicket, and I was glad to find that the pace of the pitch was exactly to my liking. This was my first Test at Lord's, and I was naturally very anxious to do well.

Woodfull was playing so finely, meeting every ball plumb in the centre of his bat, that I could afford to go for the bowling. We stayed together until Woodfull was stumped in practically the last over of the day, and by scoring 231, we had made a new second-wicket Test record for Lord's. At the close of play my score exactly equalled Woodfull's 155, and our total was 393 for two wickets.

We were now in an exceptionally strong position, and with ordinary luck we were bound to leave off with a big enough lead to make the English side fight hard to save the game.

Kippax, McCabe, Richardson, Oldfield and Fairfax all made runs, and at 729 for six wickets, Woodfull applied the closure.

At one time during my innings on the Monday, I had hopes of beating R. E. Foster's record Test score of 287. This record was put up at Sydney, and as a Sydney player, I felt it was only fitting that I should take the record back to Sydney. I was trying very hard, and I believe I would have succeeded but for an unbelievable catch by Chapman—at mid-off.

During my long innings I had been very careful not to lift a single ball, but on this occasion I slashed a loose ball from White well wide of the English captain, as I thought. I have seen Chapman make several amazing catches, but to this day I cannot think how he got his hand to that ball.

Anyway, it ended my innings at 254, and I walked back to the pavilion telling myself that it never paid to be rash with a fieldsman like Chapman in the vicinity.

As it proved, our huge total was not quite a winning one. England batted so stubbornly —Chapman playing a gallant innings of 121, in which he hit three mighty sixes off Grimmett—that we had to go in again to make 72 runs to win.

Our friends had a mild shock before we got them. First, Ponsford was bowled by Robins; then Chapman made another remarkable catch which sent me back to the pavilion; next Kippax was caught behind the wicket—and all three of us were out with the score at 22.

### Woodfull as Steady as a Rock

ALL this time, however, Woodfull was as steady as a rock and he and McCabe knocked off the runs—and the Test match score was now all square.

There can be no two opinions of the Lord's game. We won on our merits, and we felt that we could face the remaining games with high hopes of further success. Our batting had pulled us through in this match, but Fairfax, in the first innings, and Grimmett, in the second, had bowled nobly and well. Tim Wall had also bowled courageously.

In this Test match at Lord's I achieved another record (for me). I bowled one over for one run; it was one of the best overs I ever sent down, but Billy Woodfull did not think so, for he took me off straight away.

We went on to Bradford to play Yorkshire the following day. I think some of us were suffering from the reaction of the Test match, and it was a blessing for us that Ponsford was in his usual good form. Our score-sheet made curious reading: Woodfull 3, Ponsford 143, Bradman 1, McCabe 40, Jackson 46, Richardson 3. Once again, Grimmett was too much for the Yorkshire batsmen, and our score of 302 enabled us to win by 10 wickets.

Grimmett, Fairfax and I stood down for the next match against Notts, who achieved the distinction of making the highest score—433 —registered against us during the tour.

To my intense delight I was free to see the finals of the lawn tennis championships at Wimbledon, at which the King and Queen were present. And my pleasure was all the greater for seeing the mixed doubles won by my countryman, Jack Crawford, and Miss Ryan.

Having taken a trip up the Thames as far as Richmond, and had a look around London, I set out for Leeds for the third Test, by car, which was something of an adventure, though a pleasant one.

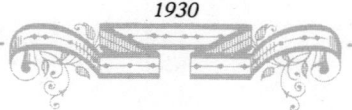

# BRADMAN BREAKS RECORD
## WITH 334 IN THIRD TEST
## Admirer Presents Him With £1000

LEEDS was decidedly in the grip of the Test match fever when we arrived there to play the third of the series. This great Yorkshire city was simply buzzing with excitement; the hotels were full, the streets were crowded with visitors, and every train was pouring more and more people into the town. The wonder was how they were all to get accommodation at Headingley.

Both teams put up at the same hotel, and as one could not move without rubbing shoulders with this or that cricketing celebrity, it was very difficult to keep one's mind off the coming struggle.

England brought in Sutcliffe, Larwood, R. Tyldesley, Geary and Leyland in place of J. C. White, G. O. Allen, R. M. V. Robins, Woolley and Hendren. We had Ponsford and Fairfax on the sick list, and Archie Jackson and a'Beckett came into the team.

We had a stroke of good fortune when Woodfull won the toss, but made a tragic beginning, Archie Jackson turning the fifth ball of Tate's opening over into the hands of Larwood at short leg.

When I went out to start my innings, I had not handled a bat for nine days, and I was perhaps fortunate to find the pitch playing nice and easy. I am afraid it is impossible for me to describe my innings in any detail. I can only say that from the first I was perfectly at home, and was lucky to get more than my share of the bowling.

At lunch time I had reached my first century out of a total of 136, but lost Woodfull at 194.

With the assistance of Kippax, I reached 220 at the tea interval, and it was then that I gave a thought to the record I had missed at Lord's.

It was about six o'clock, I think, that I topped R. E. Foster's 287, and I am afraid it is impossible to convey by mere words the pleasure I felt in achieving this distinction, nor will I attempt to do so; but here I wish to say how deeply touched I was by the whole-hearted applause of the great Yorkshire crowd.

The fact that a formidable total was being run up against their country was altogether forgotten, and I am sure there will always be a warm place in my heart for Leeds. Kippax left before close of play, and when stumps were drawn the score stood at 458 for three. I just managed to top the third century and was left not out with 309.

I believe I've been credited with the intention of going on to score 500! Nothing so ambitious crossed my mind. I consider I was very lucky to strike my best form on an ideal batsman's wicket, and if I thought about it at all it was that the morrow could look after itself.

As it turned out, the wicket was much faster on the Saturday, and on this wicket Larwood and Tate were a different pair of bowlers altogether. This was obvious when Larwood bowled McCabe with a ball that looked to me absolutely unplayable. Tate found an early victim in Richardson, and then came my turn. I snicked a ball from Tate, when 334, and Duckworth did the rest.

## 577 Thought Good Enough to Win

IF I had any feelings about my innings, it was one of gratitude that I had been instrumental in putting my country in a strong position, and I may hint that we felt that our total of 577 was good enough to win.

Just before I left the dressing-room on the Saturday morning to continue my innings, a telegram was handed to me. This was the message:—

"Your house is on fire, and your girl wants you."

Needless to say, the telegram was unsigned.

Later in the day, while we were fielding, a telegram was handed to Woodfull. This wire was to the effect that an Australian admirer wanted to give me £1000, in recognition of my score. My first thought was that my old friend the practical joker was at work again, but Billy Woodfull assured me that it was all right. Still, I could hardly believe it.

I returned to my place on the leg boundary like one in a dream. Those of you who have been kind enough to read my narrative so far will understand what this handsome gift meant to me. The donor was Mr A. E. Whitelaw, of Australia House; and, it was one of my first duties on returning to London to thank Mr Whitelaw for his wonderful present.

Much to our disappointment the game ended in a draw, and while anything may happen at cricket, I think it will be admitted that England was in a critical position when stumps were drawn for good on Tuesday evening.

The game to my mind turned decidedly in our favour when a'Beckett dived at a ball played gently to mid-on by Hobbs. There was some little discussion as to whether this was a legitimate catch; I was in an excellent position to see, and thought the catch a perfectly good one.

Hammond played a real man's innings, and although he was more restrained than is his wont, he did a great day's work for his side. We were glad to see Duleepsinhji sent back just when he looked like repeating his Lord's performance. He was unlucky to get a ball from Hornibrook that first swerved and then broke beautifully from leg to hit the wickets.

England lost five good wickets for 212 before the close of play, so that we were in a very strong position. We hoped to drive home our advantage on Monday, but heavy rain on Sunday night and Monday morning left us kicking our heels in the pavilion.

Woodfull was prepared to start play shortly after two, but the English captain would not agree, and it was not until half-past five that we resumed the game.

## Duel Between Duckworth and Grimmett

THERE was only something like 50 minutes' play altogether, and the spectators who had waited patiently all day saw an interesting duel between Duckworth and Grimmett.

Duckworth has no pretensions to being a first-class bat, but he showed real grit in the way he stood up to both Wall and Grimmett. His 33 runs were a valuable contribution, and meant more than the mere figures represent. He was batting on Saturday evening and on Monday, and we did not get rid of him until noon on Tuesday, by which time he had seen the score taken from 206 to 289.

The delay on Monday had lessened enormously our chances of a win, but the unexpected stand made by Hammond and Duckworth made our task an almost hopeless one. It was something, however, to have made England follow on.

We sent back Hobbs, Hammond, and Duleepsinhji before an appeal for bad light was sustained, and the match abandoned as a draw. As England were still 80 runs behind our first innings total, I need not stress the fact that we were in a winning position.

The demonstration that followed the appeal for bad light when Hobbs and Sutcliffe were batting was unfortunate, but the umpires are the best judges in a matter of this kind, and their decision, while disappointing to us, must be regarded as the right one.

Naturally the advantage we had set up at Leeds was highly gratifying to us, for many of our friends at the start of the season did not conceal their belief that we were in for a bad time during the Tests. It had taken some of our players a long time to find their form—in fact Archie Jackson and Hurwood could do nothing right, and to have to take the field at Leeds without both Ponsford and Fairfax was a knock-down blow in itself.

However, we had done better than was expected at Nottingham; we had done better still at Lord's, and we were in a winning position at Leeds. There now remained Old Trafford, and, failing a decision there, the fifth Test at the Oval to be played to a finish.

As a rule, I am blessed with a cheerful outlook, but somehow I could not bring myself to take a rosy view of our prospects at Manchester. I don't know why I should have had any misgivings regarding the fourth Test. I felt certain in my own mind that if we could only draw at Old Trafford we would win at the Oval, and my state of mind was probably affected by the fear that there might not be a fight to a finish after all. Anyhow, I kept my thoughts to myself, and hoped for the best.

Between the third and fourth Tests, our programme took us to Scotland—first to Edinburgh and then to Glasgow. I had been looking forward to seeing Scotland, and it was a big disappointment that the rain curtailed play both in the east and west.

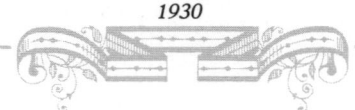

# BRADMAN HAD MOST UNHAPPY
## TIME WITH PEEBLES

# Unable to Detect Spin of Ball

## RAIN CAUSES ABANDONMENT OF OLD TRAFFORD TEST

BILLY PONSFORD and Alan Fairfax both having been reported fit, we took it as a happy augury that for the Test at Old Trafford we would turn out the same side as won at Lord's. I was sorry that Archie Jackson had to stand down, but all he said was: "What does it matter if we win?"

England brought in three new bowlers for this match, Larwood gave way to Nichols, the Essex fast bowler; Geary was replaced by Goddard, of Gloucester; and I. A. R. Peebles, of Oxford and Middlesex, took the place of R. Tyldesley. Those three, with Tate and Hammond, made up what was perhaps the strongest bowling combination we had to face in the whole series of Tests.

This game gave every promise of producing a grim struggle. It was full of tense moments while it lasted, and there were many thrills; but after two full days' play the rain put an end to all possibility of a definite result.

I shall indulge in no speculation as to what might have happened. All the same we were very well pleased that the match had ended in a draw, and that, as we had hoped, the last Test at the Oval would decide the destination of the Ashes.

As to the game itself, I need deal very briefly with the two days' play. Woodfull was not very keen about winning the toss, but having won it he decided to bat, and he and Ponsford gave us a good start on a damp wicket with a slow outfield, the score being 106 before Woodfull left to a catch behind the wicket.

When I got to the crease I found Peebles bowling extraordinarily well; and, as confession is said to be good for the soul, I may as well admit that for the first time in my life I was unable to detect a bowler's leg break from his "bosey". I watched Peebles as closely as I knew how, but it was no use. Neither by watching his hand nor the ball could I detect it, and definitely, this day, his bowling was too good for me. I had a most unhappy time! First I was almost clean bowled, then Hammond might have caught me in the slips, but these bits of good fortune did not help me much, for I was soon out, caught by Duleepsinhji in the slips off Peebles.

Afterwards, in discussing the bowling with Woodfull, Ponsford, and Kippax, I found that they also had difficulty in detecting the "bosey" sent down by Peebles. I am still puzzled to know why I couldn't, but it was some consolation to hear them say this.

### Fourth Test
### Had To Be Abandoned

PONSFORD was bowled by a real beauty from Hammond, but Kippax had a piece of bad luck in losing his wicket, a ball from Nichols that looked like hitting him on the face bouncing off the shoulder of his bat into the hands of Chapman. Then Hammond produced another good one to bowl Richardson, and with five wickets down for 190, we were not doing too well.

It was freely whispered that we could not possibly get 250, but a fine stand by Fairfax and Grimmett helped us to reach 345. Grimmett's 50 was a heroic effort, and his defence in playing the excellent bowling was an object lesson, while now and again he flashed out the strokes of a master batsman.

England's reply to our total was 251 for eight wickets, but we were perhaps fortunate to get three wickets at very little cost on the Monday evening. At the close of play on Saturday, England's total was 221 for five. Sutcliffe had batted with fine confidence, but Hobbs was not himself at all; and after we had got rid of the opening pair, only Duleep and Leyland looked like making runs. However, it was not until half-past five on Monday that a resumption was possible, and then Stan McCabe did some fine bowling in this last hour's play. He made the ball come off the pitch at a surprising pace, and by capturing the wickets of Leyland, Tate and Peebles for 14 runs, he put us in a good position. But that was the end as it proved, for when we reached the ground on Tuesday morning the pitch was water-logged, and the match was there and then abandoned.

With only one Test to go to determine the rubber we used the matches against Somerset, Glamorgan, and Warwickshire as practice, but they proved of little value because of bad weather and we relied on the nets at the Oval for our final preparation.

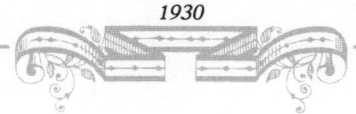

# BRADMAN TELLS STORY OF
## ASHES-WINNING TEST

## Oldfield Great Behind Wickets

### PONSFORD PLAYS BEST INNINGS OF HIS CAREER

CAME Saturday, August 16, the first day of the all-important Test. The interest in this game was extraordinary; the fact that it was the rubber match, and that it was to be played to a finish, made it like the last act of a thrilling drama.

We were confident, but the sensational dropping of Percy Chapman put our team into great spirits. We were simply amazed at the omission of Chapman. Here was a born leader, an inspiration to his side, a man who had captained England in the previous four games, a player who up to this time had the most successful Test season of his career, and one who had, in addition to saving scores of runs, taken several phenomenal catches. And he was dropped on the eve of the decisive game of the series!

As a left-hand batsman Chapman was a distinct foil to Grimmett, the bowler we mainly relied upon, and, to my mind, he was the most likely batsman in England to knock Clarrie off his length.

The moral effect on the English players must have been considerable. The fact that Chapman was not to play was wonderful news to us, and we could have wished for no better tonic.

England's new captain was R. E. S. Wyatt, of Warwickshire, a man with a great reputation as an all-round cricketer, but lacking, I believe, Chapman's magnetic personality. The other England changes were Whysall and Larwood in place of Nichols and Goddard. Ames, of Kent; Hendren and Parker, the Gloucestershire left-hand bowler, were present, but omitted from the eleven finally selected to play.

We made one change. Even though Vic. Richardson had made a century in the previous match, our selectors preferred Jackson in this played-to-a-finish game, believing that his inclusion would strengthen our batting.

After a period of uncertain weather "the day" dawned bright and clear, and the playing conditions were ideal in every respect. As the winning or losing of the toss might mean the winning or losing of the game, we awaited this part of the proceedings with more than ordinary interest.

We were kept in no suspense. The coin had barely reached the ground when a mighty cheer told us that Wyatt had won the first round.

### Sutcliffe Plays Wonderful Innings

SENSATION came early, for despite the cleverness of Hobbs and Sutcliffe in running between the wickets, two runouts might easily have occurred. Once Kippax missed a golden opportunity, while a great effort on the part of Grimmett just missed the stumps.

Hobbs and Sutcliffe were quite at home with the bowling, and looked like staying indefinitely when just before lunch Hobbs pulled a short-pitched ball from Wall right into the hands of Alan Kippax.

Clarrie Grimmett had Whysall in trouble immediately, and very nearly secured his wicket first over, but it was left to Wall to get him also—l.b.w. to a yorker.

Duleep batted beautifully, and reached his 50 in no time; then he made a very bad shot in trying to lift Grimmett into the outfield, and was caught behind the bowler.

Hammond also started in great style, but was unlucky in that he pulled a ball on to his wicket; and with Leyland bowled before he got started, our position at the tea interval was grand. It was not so grand, however, at 6.30.

Wyatt came in to an amazing ovation, and it is not to be wondered that he made a shaky start. He soon settled down to play solid, determined cricket, and he batted with such effect that he was still there at the close of play. Meanwhile Sutcliffe was holding one end safe, and he, too, was still unconquered at the end of the day.

His was a wonderful innings. I cannot remember that he gave a single chance, his only blemish being an uppish snick through the slips off Wall when in the eighties.

There was much thinking in our camp that weekend, and when Monday came—nice and clear again—we set about our task cheerfully. Before going on the field Fairfax jokingly told us that the last time he wore the particular pair of trousers he had on he took four wickets. It was a prophetic remark!

Early on the Monday morning our hearts sank when Hornibrook dropped a "sitter" off Wyatt in the slips, Wall again being the sufferer. But then Fairfax got to work, and aided splendidly by Oldfield, England were all out before lunch.

Too much praise cannot be given to Sutcliffe and Wyatt for their record partnership stand. Then, too, all our bowlers, except Hornibrook, who did not seem to be able to strike his form, stuck to their task manfully, and, I thought, bowled very well.

Behind the stumps, Oldfield gave the greatest exhibition of wicket-keeping it has been my privilege to witness. He was perfection, and one cannot say more than that. His catching of Wyatt on the leg-side was the high-watermark of a great display.

### Ponsford Breaks Larwood Hoodoo

WE opened as usual with our famous Victorian pair. Woodfull had the burdens of a captain on his shoulders, and Ponsford had not only to contend with Larwood, the man who seemed to have a hoodoo on him, but he had also in mind the fact that he had never been able to get runs at the Oval.

Is it any wonder then that we watched very anxiously those first few overs, and I can tell you it was heartening to us to see how Ponsford disposed of the Larwood hoodoo and the Oval bogey.

Ponsford, to my mind, played the greatest innings of his career, and at the other end "Steadfast" (our nickname for Woodfull) held the fort in the inimitable Woodfull manner.

All through his innings Ponsford played with remarkable confidence, and I have never seen him so satisfied with his own performance as he was on this day. His only mistake was a hard chance to Duckworth, off Tate, when in the forties.

Woodfull was lucky to escape in a similar manner when he was six. Unfortunately for Duckworth he received hard chances at very critical times, and just failed to hold them.

At the tea adjournment Ponsford was very ill, and he knew he couldn't carry on much longer, so that when his wicket fell shortly afterward we were not surprised.

Taking all the circumstances into consideration, his was, indeed, a magnificent performance.

Then came my own turn, but, on going out to bat, rain caused a stoppage before I had reached the crease. Going out again later I had scored three when an appeal against the light by our skipper was upheld, and once more we adjourned to the pavilion.

A third time we went out, only to see Woodfull caught behind the wickets off Peebles. Though he did not score many runs, Woodfull had played a very fine innings for his side.

Kippax and I played out time, and with our score standing at 215 for two against England's total of 405 the game was in a fairly even position.

Tuesday was fine once more and conditions were ideal for batting, but it was not long before we lost Kippax, out to a beautiful one-handed catch by Wyatt at short leg off Peebles.

Archie Jackson, out of form and not too confident, was also facing an ordeal. As soon as he came in, he hit a ball to Hobbs, called, and we ran.

I can well believe that our supporters didn't dare to look as Hobbs threw the ball at the wicket. The ball—thrown underhand—missed the stumps by a hair's-breadth with Archie two

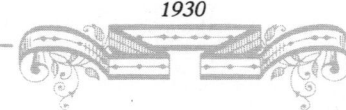

yards from the crease—and we ran one from the overthrow.

After this escape, we gradually settled down, and slowly but surely gained the upper hand, though I was fortunate in being missed by Duckworth off Hammond when in the eighties. George, to date, had had a bad match.

At lunch Jackson and I were still together, but during the interval there was a heavy shower of rain. While waiting for it to stop we had the honor of meeting the Prince of Wales, and he jovially chatted with us while waiting for the weather to clear.

We resumed after three o'clock, but batting was not so easy a matter now, and Archie received one or two painful knocks. Down came the rain and once again we adjourned.

Following a disagreement by the captains, the umpires inspected the wicket and came to the amazing decision that play should start at 6.25—five minutes before stumps were drawn.

## McCabe Lays on the Wood

WE had to go out, of course, and, incidentally, we were subjected to a good deal of barracking from a section of the crowd because we refused to take risks to score. Only 13 balls were sent down, but it was more important to us that we should keep our wickets than make runs during these two very critical overs.

Think what a wicket falling at that stage of the game would have meant to Australia. However, we survived, and next morning continued the game on a somewhat difficult and slightly damp drying wicket. Larwood made the ball fly, and we had a very trying time against good bowling during the period before lunch.

At length Archie was out to a simple catch in the covers after having got over by far the hardest part of the wicket. Apart from the nearly run-out, he gave but one chance, a very hard one on the leg side to Duckworth, and played a most praiseworthy innings in every way. Certainly he was slow, but his policy was justified. We had put on 243 for the fourth wicket under difficult conditions, and in doing so had created a new Test match record.

McCabe started to lay the wood on quickly, and soon livened things up. He gave a most difficult chance to Hammond in the slips, but his innings was beautiful and daring.

Shortly after lunch I was given out, caught by Duckworth off Larwood. Though still trying hard, I felt our position was by now fairly secure.

Fairfax and Oldfield carried on, each in turn playing the best innings I have seen from either of them in Test cricket. Larwood made an excellent catch to dismiss Oldfield, while Alan played a "not out".

Peebles took the bowling honours, and he deserved them, for he was always troublesome and doing something with the ball. The other English bowlers all did heroic work, and their figures are no indication whatever of their fine efforts.

After such a long spell in the field, Hobbs and Sutcliffe had an unenviable experience in having to open England's second innings with less than an hour left for play. It was Jack's Test farewell, and as we rallied round and gave him three hearty cheers when he reached the crease I felt genuinely sorry that this was to be the finish of a wonderful Test career.

Hobbs started well and was most unfortunate in pulling a short-pitched ball onto his stumps. I really think this marked the beginning of the end for England. Duleep, Hammond and Sutcliffe all batted well in a plucky effort to pull the game around, but to no avail.

With the last man in I dropped Hammond in the outfield thereby losing my chance to get a cherished souvenir, but shortly afterwards Alan Fairfax made no such mistake and pocketed the ball.

I thought Australia deserved to win "The Ashes". We were slightly the better side in all departments, especially fielding.

To be on the winning side was a proud moment for me, especially under such a great leader as Woodfull, whose birthday fell on the concluding day. A wonderful present.

Bradman leg glances Hammond to the boundary. Duckworth anxiously looks on.

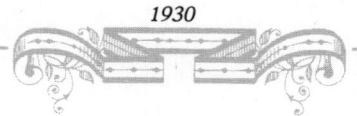

# CONCLUDING MATCHES ON TOUR

## PRAISE FOR OFFICIALS AND UMPIRES

AFTER the last Test match we still had to play some county games and a couple of so-called Festival matches, but after the excitement at the Oval they became of minor significance.

I do not wish to use this as an excuse but I'm sure the feeling of anti-climax contributed to the extraordinary happenings against Gloucestershire.

A see-saw game found the scores dead level with our last two batsmen at the wickets. Without a run being scored, 18 more balls were bowled before Hornibrook was given out LBW and for the first time ever a county had played a tie with the Australians. In a more light hearted manner we breezed through a match against Kent, the festival match at Folkestone and finally the fixture at Scarborough.

Before that a delightful farewell dinner was tendered to us by Sir Kynaston Studd, President of M.C.C., at which the legendary and whimsical Sir James Barrie entertained us with a humorous speech. I became "Mr. Badman"—a "dark and gloomy figure".

Almost a dwarf in stature, Barrie adored cricket.

When stumps were drawn at Scarborough our tour was over and sadly we had seen Wilfred Rhodes play his last first class match. I never saw this great Yorkshireman in his prime but his record is sufficient to show what a wonderful cricketer he had been. Even in this his last game he put up an excellent bowling performance against us. It had been an honour and a privilege to be his opponent.

I have already remarked on what was thought of our chances when we left Australia. We were regarded as a team of boys, inexperienced, and setting out to learn. The English Press did not forget to remind us of our youth on our arrival, and I can recall a humorous cartoon centring round a baby's bottle.

Perhaps this criticism was all to the good, for it showed at least that too much was not expected of us. I can say this, however: we had confidence in ourselves, in our team-mates, and above all, we had complete faith in our captain.

Woodfull was the rudder of our ship. His performances on the cricket field are well known—always at his best when things were going against us—but his value to us off the field is known only to those who had the good fortune to come in contact with him. It was this looking up to our leader that so materially helped to make these boys a team.

Personally, I have never played under anyone for whom I had more respect or in whom I placed more implicit trust; and all the time I felt I just could not let him down, but must give of the utmost that was in me, and I am sure every member of our little band felt the same way.

Every match saw us learning, getting more accustomed to these new conditions, and becoming a team, until at last, at the Oval, we achieved what every one of us was striving for, victory in the deciding Test match.

I think everyone will agree with me when I say that credit for our success should go, not to any individuals, but to the whole 15 players. It was the way we stuck to one another, smiled, and were happy in all circumstances, that was largely responsible for the success of the team.

Then, too, the other members of our party must not be forgotten. Mr Kelly's iron hand was severely criticised at times but it was very often a God-send to us. The fact that our dressing room was for us, and not the general public, was a very great comfort on many occasions, while the autograph hunters did not give us so much trouble as they would have done otherwise.

## Unfortunate in Striking
## Wet Summer

THEN there was Tom (Mr Howard) who guarded the finances, always doing his job without any noise or fuss, and always trying to help the young chaps along.

Arthur James, of Tasmania, our masseur, was always smiling and efficient. He didn't mind doing anything for the boys, even if it wasn't exactly his job.

And last, but not least, comes our scorer, "Bill" Ferguson, commonly called "Ferg", "Fergie" or "Brickdust". He has often been spoken of as indispensable. He was the nearest to it on this tour of anyone I know. Never missed scoring a run, kept amazing detailed records of every match, looked after our bags like a detective, acted the part of manager or treasurer if either official happened to be away, and was laundry superintendent as well.

He just seemed to do everything, and all the time not a murmur of complaint and 100 per cent efficiency. When Bill Ferguson retires he will be a remarkable man who can hope to fill his place.

At the start of the tour we struck very cold weather and, coming on top of an Australian summer, we found the change rather trying. I have known a player go on the field with two undershirts, a heavy flannel shirt, and two sweaters, and still be shivering.

We were unfortunate in striking a wet summer, but this only seemed to make the fine days we had all the more delightful. Toward the close when playing in the south of England, we had a short experience of a few really hot days. A decided advantage of the cooler weather was that one did not tend to tire out so quickly.

The wickets, too, were so varied that we rarely saw two alike. This was a wonderful experience for our young players, and I doubt if there is any type of wicket that was not encountered at least once on the tour. Fast wickets, slow wickets, wickets where the ball turned both slowly and quickly, two-paced wickets, every conceivable kind were met with on some occasion. To me they seemed to play more easily when slightly damp than when perfectly dry, and whereas in Australia we always dread rain on the pitch it was often very welcome here.

The county grounds are mostly very pretty and well kept. Sometimes the dressing rooms were not of the best, and facilities for the players, such as sight-boards, etc., were not what we had been accustomed to, but, even so, any shortcoming in the matter of the screens seems to make the game more of a sport. The bowlers were grateful for a little more assistance.

## Word of Praise for
## English Umpires

PRACTICALLY every County fielded a strong side, and even against the weakest team we could not afford to take them cheaply. The players' general knowledge of the game and its tactics seems to be better in England than in Australia.

The professional cricketer, who has to earn his living at the game, must necessarily know it from A to Z, and in England one notices how much more a bowler bowls to his field, and in various ways combats a batsman. I am not sure that these things make for brighter cricket, but we were enabled to learn a lot by watching these players.

Then, too, I would like to add a word of praise for the English umpires. They undoubtedly are the best in the world. Match after match they gave us entire satisfaction in that most difficult position, and only when we met a bad umpire (which was very rarely) did we fully appreciate the efficiency of the rest.

Then the wonderful hospitality shown us by the English public must not, and cannot, be forgotten. This was the first occasion I had been outside Australia, but at all times was I made to feel at home by those with whom I came in contact.

Every one of us regretted we could not accept the many invitations that were extended to us by various people to stay at their homes, but, nevertheless, these invitations were greatly appreciated. The warmth of our welcome everywhere was simply wonderful and made us feel at home in this dear old land.

Altogether I cannot imagine any happier experience than to tour England as an Australian cricketer. To travel the length and breadth of the country, to visit old-fashioned towns and busy cities, to look on scenery much more beautiful than anything I had ever imagined, was an unending delight.

It was my great desire to go to England, and now that this desire has been fulfilled, I can truthfully say I enjoyed every minute of the trip. So much so that I am already looking forward to the day when the next Australian side will set out for England, and hoping with all my heart that I shall be one of the party.

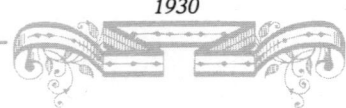

## Bradman's Methods.

THE "BOY" WONDER of cricket, Don Bradman, may become the Pepys of the game.

Only a few of his most intimate friends are aware that he keeps a diary and makes very full entries in it every day.

One of Bradman's closest friends whilst he was in England for the Test matches tells me that he has been allowed to glance at a few pages of the famous cricketer's diary.

He said : "Every night, no matter how tired he felt, Bradman kept his diary up to date. It is a wonderful book. He has entered in it his impressions of English cricket and players, the towns he visited, and the various personalities he met.

"I was amazed at the neatness of the penmanship and the diversity of idea. Very few things seem to escape Bradman's notice. He is a very keen observer, and expresses himself so clearly and quickly that I feel sure, if the diary could be published just as it is, it would be a world's ' best-seller.'

"He makes entries about his hobbies, too. These include piano-playing—perhaps you did not know that he is a fine pianist—golf and tennis. Bradman told me that at one time he seriously considered taking up tennis and dropping cricket. That, of course, was before he became world-famous.

"But you can take it from me—Bradman's diary is a most interesting book, for it is instructive as well as being a reflection of places, games and people as they appear to him."

"Star", London, 1.11.30.

### Don Bradman's Book.

I hear that Don Bradman's book will be out towards the end of next month with an introduction by P. F. Warner. It is founded mainly on the diary, which, as I mentioned recently, he kept assiduously from the beginning to the end of the Australians' tour, and it will also have a record of his batting hits.

"Eastern Daily Press," Norwich, 30.10.30.

Bradman's cricketing book has been published. Mr. P. F. Warner contributing an introduction.

"Morning Herald", Sydney, 21.11.30.

## WONDER BATSMAN.

### BRADMAN CONFESSES PEEBLES WAS HIS "BOGEY MAN."

That I. A. R. Peebles was his " bogey man " is the frank confession of Australia's wonder batsman, made in " Don Bradman's Book" (Hutchinson, 12s 6d), published to-day, and that not only he but other members of the team were completely baffled by Peebles at times.

Writing of the fourth Test match at Old Trafford, played last July, Bradman says: " When I got to the crease I found Peebles bowling extraordinarily well, and . . . I may as well admit that for the first time in my life I was unable to detect a bowler's leg break from his ' bosey.' I watched Peebles as closely as I knew how, but it was no use. Neither by watching his hand nor the ball could I detect it, and definitely this day his bowling was too good for me. I had a most unhappy time!" In a preface to the book, Mr P. F. Warner pays a glowing tribute to the author, and predicts for him an even greater future.

"Edinburgh Evening News", 21.11.30.

## BRADMAN'S BOOK.
### Fond of Fielding.

### Mr. P. F. Warner's Prophecy.

LONDON, Nov. 19.

"I love fielding, and would just as soon field as bat at any time," writes Bradman in Don Bradman's book, "The Story of My Cricketing Life, with Hints on Batting, Bowling, and Fielding," published by Hutchinson's. Bradman dedicates the book "To my dearest mother and father."

Mr. P. F. Warner, who has written the introduction, refers to Bradman's feet as "small and beautifully neat, which Pavlova might have envied." He does not agree that Bradman's eschewing the high drive is a weakness in play. Bradman could play any stroke on which he cared to concentrate. He predicts that Bradman will play between 600 and 700 innings, and that he will put the aggregates and the centuries of Grace and Hobbs in the shade.

"Argus", Melbourne, 21.11.30.

Your cricketing customers should be told of " Don Bradman's Book " (Hutchinson, 12s. 6d.). " Plum " Warner, in his introduction to the book, draws attention to the many valuable hints on batting, bowling and fielding that Don passes on to his readers. This is a handsomely-produced volume with many full-page illustrations.

"The Week", Brisbane, 28.11.30.

" Don Bradman's Book," in which the author tells the story of his cricketing life from his schooldays to the end of the recent Australian tour, will be published by Messrs. Hutchinson immediately.

"Times Literary Supplement", London, 20.11.30.

## SPORT AND TRAVEL.

Don Bradman's Book. By Don Bradman, with an Introduction by P. F. Warner. London: Hutchinson and Co., Ltd. Price, 12s. 6d.

The game of cricket has given many outstanding personalities to the world of sport, but perhaps none has been so prominent as Don Bradman, Australia's wonder batsman. Fully entitled to be described as the world's greatest bat, not only because to his credit lies the highest individual score ever made in first-class cricket, but also because of his consistently great batting, his book—in which he gives the romantic and interesting story of his cricketing life, together with hints on batting, bowling and fielding— will be welcomed by all sportsmen, and all the more because of the fact that his big achievements in Test cricket in England during the summer are still fresh in the public mind. The book is modestly, as well as charmingly, written, and his appreciation of the play of other cricketers is not the least attractive feature. Don Bradman's hints on how to play cricket will be a valuable guide to all cricketers, young and old, but the most interesting part of his delightful book is that which deals with his earliest successes on his old school playground at Bowral. "I was never coached," writes Bradman. "I was my own teacher, and the first bat I ever used was the limb of a gum tree. . . . Armed with a small stump which I used as a bat, and throwing a golf ball at the brick part of an old tank a few yards away, I would try to hit the ball on the rebound. I was never satisfied until I could hit it, say, three times out of four. The small bat made this no easy matter, as the ball came back at great speed, and of course at widely differing angles." No wonder Bradman developed an "eye" for a ball and a sense of distance and pace! When one remembers his record-breaking achievements on the cricket field, it is difficult to realise that Don Bradman is only 22 years old.

"Cork Examiner", 3.12.30.

## BRADMAN AS AUTHOR

### Will Put Grace in Shade

LONDON, November 19.

"I love fielding, and would just as soon field as bat any time," writes Don Bradman, in "Don Bradman's Book: the Story of My Cricketing Life " with hints on batting, bowling, and fielding. The book has been published by Hutchinson's. Bradman dedicates the book to "my dearest mother and father."

Mr. P. F. Warner, in an introduction, refers to Bradman's feet as "small and beautifully neat, which Pavlova might have envied." He denies that Bradman's eschewing of the high drive is his weakness in play. Bradman, he thinks, could play any stroke on which he cared to concentrate. He predicts that Bradman will play 600 or 700 innings, and put the aggregates and centuries of Grace and Hobbs in the shade.

"Chronicle", Adelaide, 27.11.30.

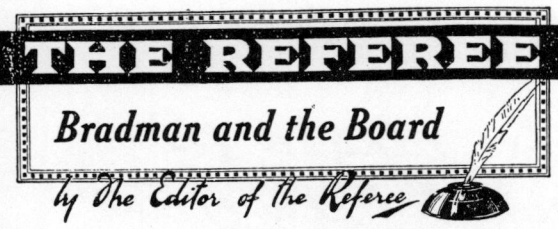

## Bradman and the Board

*by The Editor of the Referee*

BY unanimous decision the Cricket Board of Control determined that Don Bradman did commit a breach of the agreement the players made with it on becoming members of the Australian team. He is censured and fined £50. The clause under which this charge, on the report of the manager, is sustained, contains the following:—

"NEITHER the manager, treasurer, nor any player shall accept employment as a newspaper correspondent or do any work for or in connection with any newspaper or any broadcasting, and no member of the team other than the manager shall directly or indirectly, in any capacity whatever, communicate with the Press nor give any information concerning matters connected with the tour to the Press or to any other servant or agent thereof."

THE Board interprets this literally, that is, that it applies to any writing on any subject whatever no matter how far from cricket it may be. For instance, if Bradman had written a treatise on How Bees Make Honey from Bowral Blossoms, he would have been open to censure and penalty.

THE book written by Bradman in England dealt with his life. The rights were sold to publishers who in their turn disposed of the serial rights to newspapers in which it was published. This book included comments on the tour in England, but none of this part of it appeared in the serial press until the tour had concluded.

BRADMAN himself apparently took the view that C. V. Grimmett had also written a book and had it published, and that if for it official sanction was not necessary, his own book would come under the same category. Grimmett's book appeared as a serial. Did the Board sanction that?

ON the legal ruling of the Board now it appears, however, that any writing of any kind published in the newspapers breached the agreement. It may be assumed then that Grimmett's life as published in the newspapers was a technical breach in the same way as Bradman's. What has the Board to say about this? If a censure was insufficient to meet the case of Bradman's technical breach—and in the public mind that is what it amounts to—why has he been singled out?

IT is clear that the Board must either remit the penalty of £50 imposed on Bradman or make further inquiries into the activities of other members, who apparently have not been reported by the manager.

THE Board owes this to the public which keeps the game, and the Board alive. It owes it to itself to show that it is no hole and corner affair and that when its judicial functions are called into action they are exercised with the rigid impartiality of a court of justice.

THE breach of which Bradman is adjudged guilty is purely technical, otherwise the entire £150 should have been impounded. In the circumstances censure by the Board is ample to convey to Bradman himself and other players of the future, that the agreement must be understood by them and the authority of the Board rigidly observed. The Board cannot allow the matter to rest as it now stands.

# DON BRADMAN STATES HIS CASE

## "My Honest Belief Is That I had Not Acted Contrary To The Agreement"

## HE ABIDES BY THE BOARD'S RULING

Don Bradman has handed to "The Referee" the following statement explaining the position in relation to the Board and the agreement. He points out that, while he abides by the decision of the Board, he cannot see eye to eye with it in determining that he has committed a breach of the spirit of the agreement:—

"FOR some months past a great deal has been said and written as to whether I had committed a breach of contract with the Australian Board of Control, or not.

"At its meeting, the Board considered I had broken the contract—passed a vote of censure, and decided to withhold, not the £150 they were entitled to, but one-third of that amount, viz., £50.

"Up to the date of the meeting I refrained from making any public statement in regard to the matter because I did not consider such an action would be fair to the Board, and until they gave their decision no comment was necessary from me.

"Now the matter is over, I feel I should meet the requests of newspapers and cricket enthusiasts, to tell them just what happened. And as it is quite obvious that the general public are not fully aware of the circumstances surrounding the case, I feel that they should be informed also. Consequently I have decided to state the facts as they actually occurred.

"During our tour of England a firm of literary agents approached me with an offer to write for them my life story, or autobiography, combined with hints on the various phases of cricket. After due consideration I agreed, and forthwith commenced to write. My arrangements with the literary agents provided for the sale to them of the British serial rights of the book.

"Shortly afterwards this firm negotiated with, and sold to the 'Star,' a London evening newspaper, these serial rights. The literary agents advised me of what they had done.

"I stipulated that nothing whatever relating to the tour in progress must be published in any shape or form prior to my return to Australia. This stipulation was strictly adhered to, and at no time did one word appear concerning the tour. This latter portion of the book was published in the 'Star' after I returned to Australia.

"At no time did I communicate in any way with any person connected with this newspaper. I did not receive any payment from the 'Star' newspaper, nor did I receive any additional payment from the literary agents because of the book being published in the 'Star.'

"In other words, it was a direct sale from the agents to the newspaper of the serial rights of the book, and I was not concerned in the matter beyond, as previously stated, stipulating the publications must cease at the point where the story reached the selection of the Australian team for England.

"Had I thought for one moment I was violating my contract with the Board I would not have written that book. At the time I did not think I was committing a breach. I am still of the same opinion. May I add here that I was courteously received by the Board, and appreciated their action in asking me to attend their meeting, thereby giving me an opportunity of stating my case.

"It was with a great deal of regret that I learned their decision, because of my firm and honest belief that I had not acted contrary to the agreement, for no sum of money, no matter how large, would compensate me if my honor or character would be affected in the slightest degree.

"However, I must abide by the Board's ruling. Naturally, I am extremely disappointed. Nevertheless, I am prepared to accept their decision in the proper spirit, and trust, that in writing this statement, I have succeeded in making the position fully understood."

Mr L. Bradman

63 Queen Vic Building
Sydney
Jan 3/30

Dear Sir

As one who has played the good old game for over 50 years I hereby extend to you my sympathy, and also express my contempt for the miserable attempt on the part of the N.S.W. Board of control to besmirch your reputation. Believe me the cricket loving public hold you in high esteem, and many to whom I have spoken have expressed themselves in terms of disgust at the unwarranted and injudicious action of the board. However don't let this scandalous treatment daunt your courage or in any way affect your career. Play the game as you have always done for the love of it. No doubt the action taken against you was a result of envy and jealousy which if looked at from a right angle is rather complimentary, for envy and jealousy are really admissions of inferiority. With kind regards and best wishes

I am yours faithfully

W. H. Hartley.

The *Don Bradman* Special CRICKET BOOT

| Material | Size |
|---|---|

# Here's
## *the famous*
# Don
# Bradman

You may be sure the Wonder Batsman wears the best Cricket Boots obtainable anywhere. He's seen and tried many brands and from them all chooses McKeown's.

*and here are his favorite*

# Boots

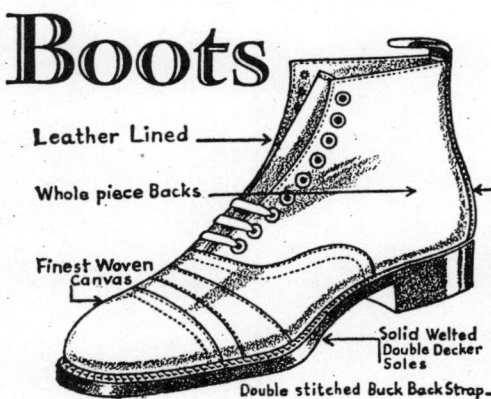

Leather Lined

Whole piece Backs

Finest Woven Canvas

Solid Welted Double Decker Soles

Double stitched Buck Back Strap

**Now you can get exactly the same make and quality Boots as Don Bradman Wears—at DAVID JONES'**

They've whole piece backs in selected fine woven canvas, solid leather double decker soles specially constructed to withstand spiking; white buck back-strap double stitched; and are leather lined throughout—each boot bearing a facsimile signature of Don Bradman himself. Special displays this week at both Stores.

| Sizes and Half-sizes, | **22/6** | Youths' sizes, 1-4, | **21/-** |
|---|---|---|---|

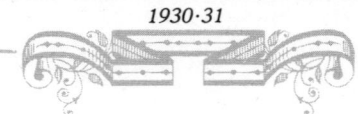

# 1930 - 31 Season

fter a season in England I found it took some time to accustom myself again to Australian pitches. However there was the incentive of my first encounter with the West Indies, who made their inaugural Test tour of Australia, and their mercurial cricket gave a foretaste of the years ahead.

*Don Bradman*

## — SEASON 1930-31 —

| TITLE | GAME | | SCORES | |
|-------|------|--|--------|--|
| Second Class | New South Wales C.A. | G.P.S. | 106 | C. |
| | Gladesville | Victorian Teachers | 202 | C. |
| | - | S.M. Herald | 89 | C. |
| | Kippax's XI | Eacham Association | 34 | C. |
| | - - | Cairns | 90 | C. |
| | - - | - | 103 | C. |
| | - - | Innisfail | 25 | C. |
| | - - | Townsville | 13 | C. |
| | - - | North Queensland | 113 | C. |
| | - - * | Ayr | 107 | C. |
| | - - | Bowen | 12 | C. |
| | - - | Mackay | 148 | n.o. |
| First Grade | St. George | Northern Districts | 49 | C. |
| | " | - | 50 | n.o. |
| | " | Marrickville | 116 | n.o. |
| First Class | Australia | The Rest | 73 | B. |
| | - | - - | 29 | C. |
| | New South Wales | West Indies | 73 | C. |
| | " " | - - | 22 | C. |
| | " " " | - - | 10 | B. |
| | " " " | - - | 73 | L.B.W. |
| Sheffield Shield | " " " | South Australia | 61 | C. |
| | " " " | - " | 121 | C. |
| | " " " | - " | 258 | B. |
| | " " " | Victoria | 2 | C. |
| | " " " | - | 33 | C. |
| | " " " | - | 220 | C. |
| Test | Australia | West Indies | 4 | C. |
| | " | - - | 25 | C. |
| | " | - - | 223 | C. |
| | " | - - | 152 | C. |
| | " | - - | 43 | C. |
| | " | - - | 0 | B. |
| | | Total runs | 2679 | |

## — SUMMARY —

AVERAGES

| | Innings | N.O's. | H.S. | Runs | Average |
|--|---------|--------|------|------|---------|
| Test | 6 | 0 | 223 | 447 | 74·50 |
| Sheffield Shield | 6 | 0 | 258 | 695 | 115·83 |
| Other First Class | 6 | 0 | 73 | 280 | 46·66 |
| All First Class | 18 | 0 | 258 | 1422 | 79·00 |
| First Grade | 3 | 2 | 116 x | 215 | 215·00 |
| Other Second Class | 12 | 1 | 202 | 1042 | 94·72 |
| All Second Class | 15 | 3 | 202 | 1257 | 104·75 |
| All Matches | 33 | 3 | 258 | 2679 | 89·30 |

# New South Wales v South Australia

NEW SOUTH WALES v SOUTH AUSTRALIA, at Sydney, 7, 8, 10 and 11 November 1930.

New South Wales - First Innings    228
                - Second Innings  396

South Australia  - First Innings    124
                - Second Innings  287

              New South Wales won by 213 runs.

DON BRADMAN   - c. D.E. Pritchard b. C.S. Deverson     61
                 c. M.G. Waite b. C.S. Deverson    121

Going in at 8 for 1 on the first morning, DON BRADMAN took ninety-six minutes to reach 50, just before lunch. Soon after the interval, he was caught at first slip, having batted for an hour and forty-eight minutes; he hit seven fours. The score was 126 for 5 when he was out, and he had carried his aggregate in four consecutive innings for New South Wales to 637, the most on record.

His second innings was much better; he went in at 7 for 1, just after lunch on the second day, reached 50 in seventy-two minutes, and was 87 at tea-time. His century came soon afterwards, in two hours five minutes. He was out at 228 for 3, being caught at cover off a hard drive. He batted for only two hours twenty-two minutes, and hit thirteen fours, his cover-driving being particularly powerful.

In five consecutive innings for New South Wales, he had thus made 758 runs, a record for that State.

Bradman cuts one from Carlton to Pritchard at slip.

### BRADMAN'S GRIP

The wind was as keen and cold after luncheon. In the pavilion, upstairs and the windows. The bowling continued downstairs, many sought shelter behind spirited and met further success. Bradman at 61 edged a good length fast one from Deverson low and Pritchard at deep first slip held it very nicely. Bradman at first played defensively to get practice, but after passing 40 he unwound some of his characteristic strokes on the cut. He batted an hour and three-quarters, and hit seven fours. It was not, however, a real Bradman innings in timing and placing, though it spoke eloquently of his judgment and self-control that in the circumstances he could play so solidly and get the runs two months after his last grip of the bat. 5-61-126.

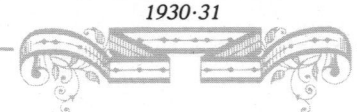

# Australia v West Indies
## First Test Match

AUSTRALIA v WEST INDIES, First Test Match, at Adelaide, 12, 13, 15 and 16 December 1930.

| | | |
|---|---|---|
| Australia | - First Innings | 376 |
| | - Second Innings | 172 for no wicket |
| West Indies | - First Innings | 296 |
| | - Second Innings | 249 |

Australia won by 10 wickets.

DON BRADMAN — c. G. C. Grant b. H. C. Griffith    4

DON BRADMAN went in at 55 for 1 after lunch on the second day, and was caught at third slip, with the score 64 for 3; he was in for a quarter of an hour.

In the West Indies' second innings, Bradman obtained his first wicket in a Test Match, dismissing I. Barrow lbw., in the last over of the third day.

# AUSTRALIA v. WEST INDIES

At Adelaide, December 12, 13, 15, 1930. G. C. Grant won the toss from W. M. Woodfull and batted.

## WEST INDIES—First Innings.

| | |
|---|---|
| C. A. ROACH, st Oldfield, b Hurwood | 56 |
| L. S. BIRKETT, c and b Grimmett | 27 |
| G. HEADLEY, c Wall, b Grimmett | 0 |
| F. R. MARTIN, b Grimmett | 39 |
| L. N. CONSTANTINE, c Wall, b Grimmett | 1 |
| E. L. BARTLETT, lbw b Grimmett | 84 |
| J. C. GRANT, not out | 53 |
| I. BARROW, c Bradman, b Grimmett | 12 |
| G. FRANCIS, lbw, b Hurwood | 5 |
| O. C. SCOTT, c Fairfax, b Grimmett | 3 |
| H. C. GRIFFITH, b Hurwood | 1 |
| Byes 6, leg-byes 8, no-balls 1 | 15 |
| **Total** | **296** |

Fall: 58, 58, 118, 123, 131, 245, 269, 293, 295, 296.

| | | | | |
|---|---|---|---|---|
| Wall | 16 | 0 | 64 | 0 |
| Fairfax | 11 | 1 | 36 | 0 |
| Grimmett | 48 | 19 | 87 | 7 |
| Hurwood | 36.1 | 14 | 55 | 3 |
| McCabe | 12 | 3 | 32 | 0 |
| Bradman | 1 | 0 | 7 | 0 |

## Second Innings

| | |
|---|---|
| C. A. ROACH, b Hurwood | 9 |
| G. HEADLEY, st Oldfield, b Grimmett | 11 |
| L. N. CONSTANTINE, b Grimmett | 14 |
| L. S. BIRKETT, st Oldfield, b Grimmett | 64 |
| F. R. MARTIN, run out | 3 |
| G. C. GRANT, not out | 71 |
| E. L. BARTLETT, c Grimmett, b Hurwood | 11 |
| I. C. BARROW, lbw, b Bradman | 27 |
| O. C. SCOTT, c Kippax, b Hurwood | 8 |
| G. R. FRANCIS, b Hurwood | 3 |
| H. GRIFFITH, st Oldfield, b Grimmett | 10 |
| Sundries | 18 |
| **Total** | **249** |

Wall 0-20, Hurwood 4-86, Grimmett 4-96, McCabe 0-15, Bradman 1-8, Fairfax 0-6.

## AUSTRALIA.—First Innings.

| | |
|---|---|
| W. H. PONSFORD, c Birkett, b Francis | 24 |
| A. JACKSON, c Barrow, b Francis | 31 |
| D. G. BRADMAN, c Grant, b Griffith | 4 |
| A. F. KIPPAX, c Barrow, b Griffith | 146 |
| S. J. McCABE, c and b Constantine | 90 |
| W. M. WOODFULL, run out | 6 |
| A. FAIRFAX, not out | 41 |
| W. A. OLDFIELD, c Francis, b Scott | 15 |
| C. V. GRIMMETT, c Barrow, b Scott | 0 |
| A. HURWOOD, c Martin, b Scott | 0 |
| T. WALL, lbw, b Scott | 0 |
| B. 2, l.b. 10, n.b. 7 | 19 |
| **Total** | **376** |

Fall: 56, 59, 64, 246, 269, 341, 374, 374, 74, 375.

| | | | | |
|---|---|---|---|---|
| Francis | 18 | 7 | 43 | 2 |
| Constantine | 22 | 0 | 89 | 1 |
| Griffiths | 28 | 4 | 69 | 2 |
| Scott | 20.5 | 2 | 83 | 4 |
| Martin | 29 | 3 | 73 | 0 |

Francis 2 n.b., Griffiths 5 n.b.

## SECOND INNINGS

| | |
|---|---|
| W. H. Ponsford, not out | 85 |
| A. Jackson, not out | 65 |
| Sundries | 9 |
| **No wickets for** | **159** |

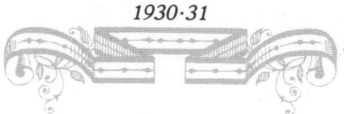

# WEST INDIES CRICKET TEAM
*Australian Tour 1930–31*

BACK ROW   G. Headley, C. A. Roach, E. A. C. Hunte, F. I. de Caires, O. C. Scott, O. S. Wight, I. Barrow, E. L. St. Hill.

CENTRE ROW   H. C. Griffith, N. N. Constantine, Mr. J. E. Seheult (Assistant Manager), G. C. Grant (Captain), Mr. R. H. Mallett (Manager), L. S. Birkett (Vice-Captain), F. R. Martin, E. L. Bartlett, G. Francis.

FRONT ROW   J. E. D. Sealey.

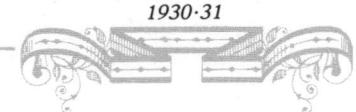

# New South Wales v South Australia

NEW SOUTH WALES v SOUTH AUSTRALIA, at Adelaide, 18, 19, 20 and 22 December 1930.

| New South Wales | - First Innings | 610 |
| | - Second Innings | - |
| South Australia | - First Innings | 166 |
| | - Second Innings | 310 |

New South Wales won by an innings and 134 runs.

DON BRADMAN - b. V. Y. Richardson 258

Going in on the first morning at 24 for 1, DON BRADMAN assisted A.A. Jackson in a brilliant partnership which added 334 for the second wicket in three hours forty-three minutes. This partnership of 334 was a record for the second wicket in a Sheffield Shield Match. After lunch, Bradman reached 50 in seventy-nine minutes, and 100 in two hours eight minutes; he later hit so hard that he went from 150 to 200 in thirty-eight minutes, completing 200 in three hours fifty-four minutes; he was bowled, at 448 for 3, just before the close of play. He had been at the wicket for four hours forty-nine minutes and had hit thirty-seven fours. This was the tenth double-century of Bradman's career, more than any other Australian has ever made.

In South Australia's second innings he took 3 wickets for 54.

## N.S.W. BEATS SOUTH AUSTRALIA

### An Innings to Spare: S.A. Batsmen Break Down

At Adelaide, December 18, 19, 20, and 22, 1930. A. F. Kippax won the toss from V. Y. Richardson, and batted. First day, three for 455, Jackson and Bradman put on 334 for the second wicket. Bradman batted 4 hours 49 minutes for 258, and hit 37 fours. Jackson made 166 in 3 hours 49 minutes, and hit 15 fours. The second wicket stand is a record for Sheffield Shield cricket. N.S. Wales won by an innings and 134 runs.

Scores:—

**N.S.W.—First Innings**

| | | |
|---|---|---|
| A. JACKSON, c Richardson, b Waite | | 166 |
| J. FINGLETON, st Walker, b Grimmett | | 6 |
| D. G. BRADMAN, b Richardson | | 258 |
| A. F. KIPPAX, b Grimmett | | 42 |
| S. J. McCABE, lbw, b Carlton | | 7 |
| A. FAIRFAX, b Grimmett | | 38 |
| W. BILL, lbw, b Grimmett | | 0 |
| H. S. LOVE, lbw, b Grimmett | | 4 |
| H. HOOKER, b Carlton | | 45 |
| H. CHILVERS, run out | | 23 |
| W. HUNT, not out | | 15 |
| Byes 4, leg byes 2 | | 6 |
| Total | | 610 |

Fall: 24, 358, 448, 465, 500, 500, 506, 549, 589, 610.

| | | | | |
|---|---|---|---|---|
| Wall | 23 | 0 | 89 | 0 |
| Carlton | 20.2 | 0 | 99 | 2 |
| Lee | 38 | 4 | 144 | 0 |
| Grimmett | 48 | 5 | 180 | 5 |
| Waite | 7 | 0 | 54 | 1 |
| Richardson | 8 | 0 | 38 | 1 |

**SOUTH AUSTRALIA—First Innings**

| | | |
|---|---|---|
| G. W. HARRIS, b Hunt | | 11 |
| H. C. NITSCHKE, c Hooker, b Chilvers | | 69 |
| D. E. PRITCHARD, b Chilvers | | 18 |
| V. Y. RICHARDSON, c McCabe, b Chilvers | | 25 |
| A. HACK, lbw, b Hunt | | 4 |
| P. K. LEE, not out | | 13 |
| N. G. WAITE, b Hunt | | 0 |
| T. A. CARLTON, c Love, b Chilvers | | 2 |
| C. V. GRIMMETT, c and b Chilvers | | 0 |
| T. M. WALL, lbw, b Hunt | | 14 |
| C. V. WALKER, b Hunt | | 0 |
| Byes 6, leg-byes 4 | | 10 |
| Total | | 166 |

Fall: 39, 70, 128, 133, 133, 134, 141, 141, 166, 166.

| | | | | |
|---|---|---|---|---|
| Fairfax | 6 | 1 | 23 | 0 |
| Hunt | 17.7 | 4 | 36 | 5 |
| Hooker | 13 | 2 | 29 | 0 |
| Chilvers | 21 | 3 | 68 | 5 |

**Second Innings.**

| | | |
|---|---|---|
| G. W. HARRIS, c Kippax, b Bradman | | 25 |
| H. C. NITSCHKE, c Fingleton, b Hunt | | 102 |
| A. HACK, b Hunt | | 25 |
| V. Y. RICHARDSON, b Hunt | | 17 |
| D. E. PRITCHARD, b Hunt | | 1 |
| P. K. LEE, b Bradman | | 25 |
| N. G. WAITE, lbw, b Chilvers | | 0 |
| C. V. GRIMMETT, b Chilvers | | 26 |
| T. CARLTON, st Love, b Bradman | | 15 |
| T. M. WALL, not out | | 45 |
| C. V. WALKER, b Hooker | | 16 |
| B 11, lb 2 | | 13 |
| Total | | 310 |

Fall: 47, 103, 159, 167, 192, 193, 209, 235, 267, 310.

| | | | | |
|---|---|---|---|---|
| Hooker | 9.6 | 0 | 20 | 1 |
| Fairfax | 2 | 0 | 7 | 0 |
| Hunt | 38 | 8 | 105 | 4 |
| Chilvers | 32 | 8 | 81 | 2 |
| Bradman | 12 | 2 | 54 | 3 |
| McCabe | 8 | 2 | 20 | 0 |
| Kippax | 4 | 2 | 10 | 0 |

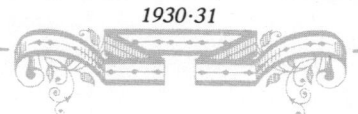

## NEW SOUTH WALES SHEFFIELD SHIELD CRICKET TEAM
### Southern Tour 1930

BACK ROW   S. J. McCabe, H. S. Love, H. Hooker, G. Stewart, O. W. Bill, J. Fingleton, W. Hunt.

FRONT ROW   D. G. Bradman, A. A. Jackson, A. F. Kippax (Captain), Mr. F. Buckle (Manager), H. C. Chilvers, A. G. Fairfax.

Bradman, if lacking the grace of his partner, was, as usual, all out for runs. He put terrific force into his shots, in making 258 in 4 hours 49 minutes, 37 of which rattled the pickets. He treated the bowling with scant respect, and off one over from Carlton scored 17 and off one from Waite 18. Pulls and on-drives gave him a great number of his runs, although all parts of the field suffered during his onslaught. An indication of how Bradman dominated the scoring, after Jackson's dismissal, is shown by the third-wicket partnership with Kippax, which yielded 90, of which he made 77. His last hundred runs were made in 78 minutes. At the end of the day the score was 455 for three wickets, Kippax 20 and McCabe 1 being not out.

### Tenth Two Hundred Innings

BRADMAN'S ability to compile big scores rivals that of Walter Lindrum at billiards. One cannot foresee what feat in fast and prodigious scoring he will not next achieve. He makes 300 in a day in a Test. He makes a century before luncheon in a Test. He makes his thousand before the end of May. He makes a world's record of 452 in far less time than many others have taken to make much less than half the runs. And now he has made 200 in an innings a tenth time, though his first of these was played less than two years ago. W. G. Grace's record includes thirteen innings exceeding 200, the first played in 1866 and the last thirty years later. If Don Bradman be still a power in cricket thirty years hence, how many innings over 200 will he have made? He has ten at present.

### Has No Limitations

ONE unparalleled element in Don Bradman's cricket is that in his perspective there is neither limitation to achievement nor adherence to any rule of thumb idea. For instance if he had opened the second innings for New South Wales against Queensland in Sydney, he would not have reduced the game to a barndoor affair with time. While the sun shone and the wicket was perfect he would have tried to win the match before the day closed. What a colossal difference between that outlook on a game and the one disclosed by the tactics of those who did bat that day.

It was seen on Friday last when Bradman, who did not go in first and was out before stumps were drawn, scored 252 against South Australia. In the speed of his rungetting, without degenerating into slogging or mere big-hitting, he scores very fast, through the great power of his shots, and their placing and the use he makes of his feet in getting to the ball.

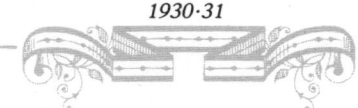

# Australia v West Indies
## Second Test Match

AUSTRALIA v WEST INDIES, Second Test Match, at Sydney, 1, 3 and 5 January 1931.

| | | | |
|---|---|---|---|
| Australia | - First Innings | 369 | |
| | - Second Innings | - | |
| West Indies | - First Innings | 107 | |
| | - Second Innings | 90 | |

Australia won by an innings and 172 runs.

DON BRADMAN — c. I. Barrow b. G.N. Francis     25

DON BRADMAN went in at 12 for 1, early on the first day, but was caught at the wicket off a rising ball after forty minutes.

He thus brought his Test Match aggregate since 14 June 1930 to 1,003, in 201 days - until then the quickest 1,000 runs ever scored in Test Matches.

## SECOND TEST.

### West Indies' Forlorn Showing.

### AUSTRALIA WINS.

### Innings and 172 Runs.

Twenty-four minutes sufficed to end the West Indies' innings this morning, and Australia won by an innings and 172 runs.

SCORES.

AUSTRALIA.—First Innings, 369.
WEST INDIES.—First Innings, 107.

Second Innings.

| | |
|---|---|
| C. A. Roach, c Kippax, b McCabe | 25 |
| L. S. Birkett, c McCabe, b Hurwood | 8 |
| G. Headley, c Jackson, b Hurwood | 2 |
| F. R. Martin, c McCabe. b Hurwood | 0 |
| L. N. Constantine. b Hurwood | 8 |
| I. Barrow, c McCabe, b Ironmonger | 10 |
| G. Francis, c Oldfield, b Ironmonger | 0 |
| G. C. Grant, not out | 15 |
| O. C. Scott, c Woodfull, b Ironmonger | 17 |
| H. C. Griffith, lbw, b Grimmett | 0 |
| E. L. Bartlett, absent | 0 |
|     Bye 1, leg-byes 2, wide 1, no-ball 1 | 5 |
|     Total | 90 |

Fall of wickets: 26, 32, 32, 42, 53, 67, 67, 90, 90.

BOWLING.

| | O. | M. | R. | W. |
|---|---|---|---|---|
| Fairfax | 5 | 1 | 21 | 0 |
| Hurwood | 11 | 2 | 22 | 4 |
| McCabe | 7 | 0 | 20 | 1 |
| Ironmonger | 4 | 1 | 13 | 3 |
| Grimmett | 3.3 | 1 | 9 | 1 |

Hurwood bowled a wide and Ironmonger a no-ball.

Australia won by an innings and 172 runs.

Scores:—

### AUSTRALIA.—First Innings.

| | |
|---|---|
| W. H. Ponsford, b Scott | 183 |
| A. Jackson, c Francis, b Griffith | 8 |
| D. G. Bradman, c Barrow, b Francis | 25 |
| A. F. Kippax, c Bartlett, b Griffith | 10 |
| S. J. McCabe, lbw, b Scott | 31 |
| W. M. Woodfull, c Barrow, b Constantine | 58 |
| A. Fairfax, c Constantine, b Francis | 15 |
| W. A. Oldfield, run out | 0 |
| C. V. Grimmett, b Scott | 12 |
| A. Hurwood, c Martin, b Scott | 5 |
| H. Ironmonger, not out | 3 |
|     Byes 6, leg-byes 5, wides 5, no-balls 3 | 19 |
|     Total | 369 |

Fall of wickets: 12, 52, 69, 140, 323, 341, 344, 361, 364, 369.

BOWLING.

| | O. | M. | R. | W. |
|---|---|---|---|---|
| Francis | 27 | 3 | 70 | 2 |
| Constantine | 18 | 2 | 56 | 1 |
| Griffith | 28 | 4 | 57 | 2 |
| Martin | 18 | 1 | 60 | 0 |
| Scott | 15.4 | 0 | 66 | 4 |
| Birkett | 10 | 1 | 41 | 0 |

Birkett bowled 2 and Griffith 3 wides, Francis 1 and Griffiths 2 no-balls.

### WEST INDIES.—First Innings.

| | |
|---|---|
| C. A. Roach, run out | 7 |
| L. S. Birkett, c Hurwood, b Fairfax | 3 |
| G. Headley, b Fairfax | 14 |
| F. R. Martin, lbw, b Grimmett | 10 |
| G. C. Grant, c Hurwood, b Ironmonger | 6 |
| L. N. Constantine, c Bradman, b Grimmett | 12 |
| I. Barrow, c Jackson, b Fairfax | 17 |
| G. Francis, b Grimmett | 8 |
| O. C. Scott, not out | 15 |
| H. Griffith, c Kippax, b Grimmett | 8 |
| E. L. Bartlett, absent, hurt | 0 |
|     Byes 6, no-ball 1 | 7 |
|     Total | 107 |

Fall of wickets: 3, 26, 36, 36, 57, 63, 80, 88, 107.

BOWLING.

| | O. | M. | R. | W. |
|---|---|---|---|---|
| Fairfax | 13 | 4 | 19 | 3 |
| Hurwood | 5 | 1 | 7 | 0 |
| Grimmett | 19.1 | 3 | 54 | 4 |
| Ironmonger | 13 | 3 | 20 | 1 |

Fairfax bowled a no-ball.

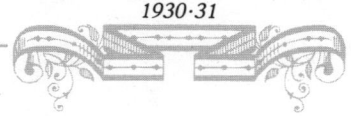

# SECOND TEST.

## TO-DAY'S PLAY.

### Australia Makes 369.

#### WEST INDIES' COLLAPSE.

The second test match between Australia and the West Indies was resumed in beautiful weather this morning. The outfield was faster than on the first day, and the pitch harder, but inclined to kick from the part which had not been under cover.

This was evident when from Constantine's third ball Woodfull was caught at the wicket without addition to the score.

Fairfax, next in, made 15 while Ponsford was scoring 2. He detected Constantine's slower ball, and forced one of them to the on for four after a succession of hard-earned singles. Constantine had three overs before Francis relieved him, but fielding at backward point, close in, was responsible for a great catch low down to dismiss Fairfax.

Oldfield had a brief stay. Called for a short run by Ponsford, he had his stumps thrown down by Headley from cover. Three wickets had fallen for 21.

Grimmett was generously cheered. When 2 he was missed at third slip by Grant off Francis, and from an overthrow as Grimmett was standing out of his crease 350 appeared in 335 minutes. He was not comfort..e, and made several miss-hits.

Scott came on at 356. Ponsford determined to punish him, but in the slow bowler's second over he ran down the pitch, swung, but just touched the ball, which bowled him. Eight for 361. Ponsford had been in 348 minutes for 183, including 11 fours. In the same over Scott clean bowled Grimmett.

The innings ended when Martin caught Hurwood at mid-off for 369, made in 358 minutes. Six wickets had fallen for 46 in a little over an hour.

With less than a quarter of an hour before lunch, Roach and Birkett began the West Indies innings against Fairfax and Hurwood. In Fairfax's second over Birkett was nicely caught by Hurwood at second slip for 3. Lunch was taken.

Headley was Roach's partner after lunch, and the batsmen played Fairfax and Hurwood with extreme caution, most of the runs coming from glances and turns. At 17 Grimmett displaced Hurwood. Similar defensive tactics were adopted.

Fairfax got the second wicket when Headley, in attempting a cover drive, dragged a ball well outside the off-stump hard on. He was 14 and the score 26.

At 31 Ironmonger was brought on and Grimmett changed ends. Martin had placed Grimmett grandly through the covers from the southern end and repeated the stroke from the other end. While Roach was stolid, Martin looked for runs and rapidly reached double figures. Then he went lbw to Grimmett, the third wicket falling at 36.

Grant came in. Grimmett had a fairly deep field but a silly point and silly leg. Ironmonger had two short slips and a very close third man. The visitors' next disaster was when Roach was run out. He responded to a short call by Grant and lost the verdict; although his bat appeared to have slid over the crease in time. As Bartlett could not bat, the West Indies were in a desperate position with virtually five out for 36.

For Constantine, next in, Grimmett had a deep inner ring and an outer ring of three on the fence. Twice Constantine swept the slow bowler round. Bradman was in time to prevent the first reaching the boundary. While Grant was playing like a rock, occasionally scoring with a back-cut, Constantine was choosing the ball to hit. Ironmonger kept runs down. When Constantine was 11 Ironmonger missed an exceptionally hot return to his left hand.

Constantine continued to swing at Grimmett, and eventually was caught by Bradman nearly square on the fence for 12. Five for 57. The field closed in again for Barrow.

Grant was the next victim. He gave Hurwood an easy catch at first slip off Ironmonger, after being in 33 minutes for 6. Six for 63.

Barrow and Francis adhered to defensive methods. Neither used his feet facing Grimmett. At 80 Fairfax displaced Ironmonger, who had bowled 12 overs, costing 16 runs. In the last over before tea Francis, stepping back to pull Grimmett, was bowled, the score at the interval being 80 for seven wickets.

Scott joined Barrow after the interval. His first scoring stroke was a four from an off-drive off Grimmett. He went down the pitch as none of his predecessors had done. Then he lost Barrow, well caught at the second attempt by Jackson, off Fairfax. He had been in 37 minutes for 17. Scott continued to be enterprising. With Griffith in, both ran down the pitch to Grimmett. They brought up 100 in 127 minutes, the first 50 having taken 70.

The innings ended when Griffith was caught by Kippax fairly deep on the on, off Grimmett. Not a batsman on the West Indies side had reached 20. The innings of 107 had lasted 133 minutes.

#### WEST INDIES BAT AGAIN.

Facing a deficit of 262, the West Indies opened their second innings with Roach and Birkett against the bowling of Fairfax and Hurwood at five minutes to 5.

The batsmen were more adventurous than in the first innings and 16 runs came from the first five overs.

Excellent bowling by Hurwood, who at one stage had taken three wickets for nine, and good slip catching by McCabe and Jackson, accounted for another bad start. Then Roach was splendidly caught by Kippax low down at square leg off McCabe for 25. The fourth wicket fell at 42.

The attendance was 18,025, and the gate takings £1370/6/9.

## BRADMAN'S SONG.

### "Every Day is a Rainbow Day for Me."

Mr. Don Bradman, the famous cricketer, was present at the Grand Opera House last night to hear his song "Every Day is a Rainbow Day for Me," which is introduced in the pantomime "Beauty and the Beast." The song, composed by Mr. Bradman to words by Mr. Jack Lumsdaine, was sung by Miss Elsie Hosking, and proved pleasantly melodious and sentimental, with a refrain in which saxophones and brasses vigorously supported the vocal theme, ere it was taken up smartly by a well-trained ballet.

After the song there was great applause for the composer as he walked on to the stage, accompanied by Mr. George Marlow. Mr. Bradman said he had enjoyed very much the experience of hearing for the first time this composition sung in public. "I hope," he added, amid renewed applause, "that we shall be able to apply the title of this song to our experiences in Australia in the year now opening, and that every day will be a rainbow day for us." On his own behalf and that of Mr. Lumsdaine, he presented a box of chocolates to Miss Hosking, and complimented her and the orchestra and ballet upon the performance. "It is a very great pleasure and a very great honour to sing this song," said Miss Hosking, in reply. There was warm applause also for the members of the West Indies team, who were present.

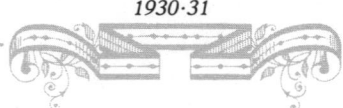

# Australia v West Indies
## Third Test Match

AUSTRALIA v WEST INDIES, Third Test Match,
at Brisbane (Exhibition Ground), 16, 17, 19 and 20 January 1931.

| Australia | - First Innings | 558 |
|---|---|---|
| | - Second Innings | - |
| West Indies | - First Innings | 193 |
| | - Second Innings | 148 |

Australia won by an innings and 217 runs, and won the rubber.

DON BRADMAN    - c. G.C. Grant b. L.N. Constantine    223

Going in at 1 for 1, early on the first day, DON BRADMAN batted brilliantly and faultlessly; he completed 50 in eighty minutes, and his second-wicket stand with W.H. Ponsford added 229 in two hours forty-two minutes.    At tea, he was 129; afterwards, he reached 200 in four hours eleven minutes, and at the close of play, after batting for four hours fifty minutes, he was 223 not out, having passed V.T. Trumper's 214, previously the highest score by an Australian batsman in a home Test Match. He and A.F. Kippax added 193 for the third wicket in two minutes less than two hours.

By scoring 223 runs in a day, he made the most runs ever scored in one day's play in a Test Match in Australia.  This was the second time that he had scored more than 200 in a day's play in a Test Match; up till then, no one else had done so more than once.

On a drying wicket next morning, Bradman stayed for only seven minutes, and did not add to his score, being caught off a skier at square-leg.  Batting for four hours fifty-seven minutes, he hit twenty-four fours. His 223 was a record for an Australian in a Test Match in Australia.  It was also the highest score against a West Indian team on tour in Australia, and the highest in a Test Match on the Exhibition Ground, Brisbane.

His partnership of 229 with Ponsford was up till then the highest for the second wicket in any Test Match in Australia, and his partnership of 193 with Kippax equalled the highest for the third wicket for Australia in a Test Match in Australia.

## THIRD TEST MATCH

### AUSTRALIA.—First Innings.

| | | |
|---|---|---:|
| A. JACKSON, lbw, b Francis | | 0 |
| W. H. PONSFORD, c Birkett, b Francis | | 109 |
| D. G. BRADMAN, c Grant, b Constantine | | 223 |
| A. F. KIPPAX, b Birkett | | 84 |
| S. J. McCABE, c Constantine, b Griffith | | 8 |
| W. M. WOODFULL, c Barrow, b Griffith | | 17 |
| A. FAIRFAX, c Sealy, b Scott | | 9 |
| R. K. OXENHAM, lbw, b Griffiths | | 48 |
| W. A. OLDFIELD, not out | | 38 |
| C. V. GRIMMETT, c Constantine, b Francis | | 4 |
| H. IRONMONGER, c Roach, b Griffith | | 2 |
| B 2, lb 7, nb 7 | | 16 |
| Total | | 558 |

Fall: 1, 230, 423, 434, 441, 462, 468, 543, 551, 558.

| | O | M | R | W |
|---|---|---|---|---|
| Francis | 23 | 4 | 76 | 3 |
| Constantine | 26 | 2 | 74 | 1 |
| Griffith | 33 | 4 | 133 | 4 |
| Scott | 24 | 0 | 125 | 1 |
| Martin | 27 | 3 | 85 | 0 |
| Sealy | 3 | 0 | 32 | 0 |
| Birkett | 7 | 0 | 16 | 1 |
| Grant | 1 | 0 | 1 | 0 |

Francis, 4nb; Griffith, 2 nb; Sealy, 1 nb.

### WEST INDIES.—First innings.

| | |
|---|---:|
| C. A. ROACH, lbw, b Oxenham | 4 |
| F. R. MARTIN, lbw, b Grimmett | 21 |
| J. E. D. SEALEY, c McCabe b Ironmonger | 3 |
| G. C. GRANT, c McCabe, b Grimmett | 8 |
| L. N. CONSTANTINE, c Fairfax, b Ironmonger | 9 |
| L. S. BIRKETT, lbw, b Oxenham | 8 |
| G. HEADLEY, not out | 102 |
| I. BARROW, st Oldfield, b Grimmett | 19 |
| G. R. FRANCIS, b Oxenham | 8 |
| O. C. SCOTT, b Oxenham | 0 |
| H. C. GRIFFITH, c McCabe, b Grimmett | 8 |
| Sundries | 3 |
| Total | 193 |

Fall: 5, 23, 41, 60, 94, 116, 159, 180, 182, 193.

| | O | M | R | W |
|---|---|---|---|---|
| Fairfax | 7 | 2 | 13 | 0 |
| Oxenham | 30 | 15 | 39 | 4 |
| Ironmonger | 26 | 15 | 43 | 2 |
| Grimmett | 41.3 | 3 | 93 | 4 |

### Second Innings

| | |
|---|---:|
| C. A. ROACH, b McCabe | 1 |
| F. R. MARTIN, lbw, b Oxenham | 11 |
| G. HEADLEY, c Oldfield, b Ironmonger | 28 |
| L. N. CONSTANTINE, lbw, b Oxenham | 7 |
| G. C. GRANT, run out | 10 |
| L. S. BIRKETT, b Grimmett | 13 |
| I. BARROW, st Oldfield, b Grimmett | 17 |
| J. E. D. SEALEY, not out | 2 |
| O. C. SCOTT, lbw, b Grimmett | 15 |
| G. R. FRANCIS, not out | 2 |
| J. E. D. SEALY, not out | 16 |
| G. R. FRANCIS, c Oldfield, b Grimmett | 7 |
| H. GRIFFITH, c Bradman, b Grimmett | 12 |
| Sundries | 11 |
| Total | 148 |

Fall: 13, 29, 47, 58, 72, 82, 94, 113, 128, 148

| | O | M | R | W |
|---|---|---|---|---|
| Fairfax | 6 | 2 | 6 | 0 |
| McCabe | 7 | 1 | 16 | 1 |
| Oxenham | 18 | 5 | 37 | 2 |
| Ironmonger | 15 | 8 | 29 | 1 |
| Grimmett | 14.3 | 3 | 49 | 5 |

The excellent attendance was attributed, to a certain extent, to a desire on the part of the public to see Bradman, Ponsford, Kippax, M'Cabe, and other heroes of the recent English tour in action, and the big crowd had no cause for complaint. The only blemish of Bradman's double century was the early chance. Thereafter he pounded the bowling to all parts of the ground. Ponsford also was seen at the top of his form, and it was a great treat to witness two of the world's best batsmen mercilessly punish bowling that was never ragged, and was invariably of a good length. Before they were separated they had carried the total to 230, and that the rate of scoring was fast can be gauged from the fact that the 200 appeared in 138 minutes.

## RAPID SCORING.

The troubles of the West Indian bowlers were continued with the appearance of Kippax, who, commencing slowly, also aided Bradman to pile up a big total. The rate of scoring during the afternoon was as follows:—

50 runs in 41 minutes.
100 runs in 69 minutes.
150 runs in 110 minutes.
200 runs in 138 minutes.
250 runs in 183 minutes.
300 runs in 221 minutes.
350 runs in 241 minutes.
400 runs in 267 minutes.
428 runs in 294 minutes.

The century-makers have a spell. Bradman quenches his thirst while Ponsford takes a well-earned rest.

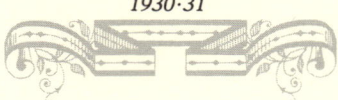

George Headley completing one of his famous hook shots.
His score of 102 not out was the first century ever scored by a West Indian in a Test match against Australia.

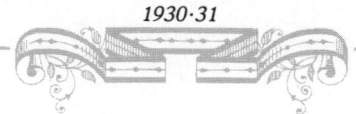

No team can give a "life" to that record-breaking batsman, Don Bradman, without paying dearly. The West Indies, in the third Test, at the Exhibition yesterday, had the mortification of seeing the Bowral boy missed in the slips when four, and after Archie Jackson had been disposed of without scoring. But before the day had ended they had grown tired of gnashing their teeth in disappointment and despair of "what might have been." Bradman profited by his error, made no more mistakes, and gave the fieldsmen one of the most gruelling afternoons of leather-hunting they have ever had the misfortune to suffer.

## More Popular Than Ever.

The few critics who have declared that Bradman's popularity was on the wane must have received a surprise when the great crowd which attended the Test match at the Exhibition Ground yesterday rose en masse and cheered themselves hoarse while the wonder batsman walked to the wickets. The trivial dispute with the Board of Control, which resulted in their fining Bradman £50, did not make the public forget what Don had done for Australian cricket. This warm-hearted, unspoiled boy is everything that a sportsman should be. His glad smile when the runs are literally flying from his bat, his characteristic hand waves when congratulations are heaped upon him, and his modesty when he has been the deciding factor which meant victory, all endear him to the hearts of the public. It was typical of him yesterday, when Ponsford beat him to the century, that he led the thunderous applause, hurried down the pitch, and congratulated the Victorian champion. Ponsford returned the compliment two minutes later, and again the crowd appropriately appreciated true sportsmanship.

## Bradman's Brilliant Brisbane Innings

BRISBANE fans had a treat on Friday. At the close of the day's cricket Don Bradman was 223 not out made in 290 minutes. There were 24 boundaries, and he reached the 200 in 251 minutes.

After tea Bradman laid the wood on with a vengeance, straight driving and pulling with terrific force against brilliant fielding.

## Another Record Broken.

By making 223 not out Bradman has broken the record for the highest individual score made by an Australian in a Test match played in Australia. S. E. Gregory, against England at Sydney in 1894, knocked up 201, and this record stood until Victor Trumper, in the Test match against the South Africans at Adelaide in 1910-11 season, exceeded it by compiling 214. J. S. Ryder, playing for Australia at Adelaide in 1924-25, registered 201 not out, and thus equalled Gregory's record for an Australian against England in Australia. R. E. Foster (England) batting against Australia on the Sydney Cricket Ground during the 1903-4 season made 287. Bradman will be hot-foot after Foster's figures to-day.

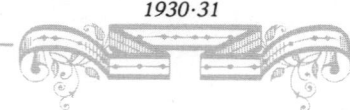

# New South Wales v Victoria

NEW SOUTH WALES v VICTORIA, at Sydney, 24, 26, 27 and 28 January 1931.

| New South Wales | - First Innings | 196 |
| | - Second Innings | 417 for 9 wickets dec. |
| Victoria | - First Innings | 318 |
| | - Second Innings | 202 for 6 wickets |
| | Drawn. | |

| DON BRADMAN | - c. B.A. Barnett b. H.H. Alexander | 33 |
| | c. K.E. Rigg b. H. Ironmonger | 220 |

DON BRADMAN went in at 14 for 1, early on the first morning, and hit up 33 in forty-seven minutes, before being brilliantly caught at the wicket on the leg side.

New South Wales opened their second innings early on the third day. Bradman reached 50 in eighty-seven minutes, and 100 in two hours fifty-four minutes shortly before tea; at 76 he completed his 1,000 runs for the season, being again the first batsman to do so. Afterwards he continued to bat soundly, and completed 200 in four hours forty-two minutes, six minutes before the close of play, being 208 not out overnight. Next morning, he stayed for another twenty minutes, until, at 415 for 7, he gave a catch to cover, after batting for five hours eight minutes; he hit thirteen fours. He and O.W. Bill added 234 for the fifth wicket in two hours ten minutes - this was the highest for that wicket against Victoria. In being the first (or only) batsman for the third time to reach 1,000 runs in an Australian season, he surpassed the performances of C.Hill and W.H. Ponsford.

## Great Was the Glee

WHEN Barnett caught Bradman on the leg-side, the Victorians in the field jumped as one man in their chorussed shout of "How's that?" Men in the field are always delighted to see him depart as soon as possible. As a well-known cricketer remarked on Saturday, "Your best chance to get rid of Bradman is before he settles down. If he gets his eye in, it is odds on his making a century, and you never can tell how far he will go on after that." He has, nevertheless, made only two centuries against Victoria, 340 and 134, both not out, and both in Sydney. His Melbourne centuries have been compiled in Test matches.

# N.S.W. v. VICTORIA
## First Innings Win For Victoria

Sydney Cricket Ground, January 24, 26, 27, 28. Won on first innings by Victoria by 122 runs. With four wickets in hand, Victoria required 91 runs to win outright. Gross gate was £1424/4/-.

**NEW SOUTH WALES—First Innings 196**

Second Innings

| | | |
|---|---|---|
| D. G. BRADMAN, c Rigg, b Ironmonger | | 220 |
| S. J. McCABE, b Alexander | | 20 |
| A. F. KIPPAX, c and b Blackie | | 26 |
| A. MARKS, b Ironmonger | | 9 |
| A. G. FAIRFAX, c O'Brien, b Blackie | | 12 |
| W. BILL, b Blackie | | 100 |
| W. HUNT, c Rigg, b Blackie | | 16 |
| J. FINGLETON, st Barnett, b Blackie | | 4 |
| W. OLDFIELD, c Darling, b Ironmonger | | 1 |
| H. HOOKER, not out | | 0 |
| Sundries | | 9 |
| Nine wickets (closed) for | | 417 |

Fall: 26, 103, 126, 157, 391, 412, 415, 417, 417.

| | | | | |
|---|---|---|---|---|
| Alexander | 18 | 1 | 89 | 1 |
| Ironmonger | 22.4 | 0 | 91 | 3 |
| a'Beckett | 13 | 0 | 58 | 0 |
| Ryder | 4 | 0 | 39 | 0 |
| Blackie | 23 | 2 | 101 | 5 |
| Hendry | 3 | 0 | 20 | 0 |
| Darling | 2 | 0 | 10 | 0 |

Darling and Ironmonger each 1 w.

**VICTORIA—First Innings 318**

Second Innings

| | | |
|---|---|---|
| H. L. HENDRY, c Oldfield, b Hunt | | 1 |
| L. P. O'BRIEN, c Hunt, b McCabe | | 11 |
| J. RYDER, lbw, b Hunt | | 36 |
| K. RIGG, c Hunt, b Chilvers | | 98 |
| H. OAKLEY, c Oldfield, b Hunt | | 29 |
| L. DARLING, c Kippax, b Chilvers | | 0 |
| B. BARNETT, not out | | 11 |
| B 2, lb 1, w 2, nb 5 | | 10 |
| Six wickets for | | 202 |

Fall: 14, 35, 92, 148, 149, 202.

| | | | | |
|---|---|---|---|---|
| Fairfax | 9 | 4 | 14 | 0 |
| Hunt | 23 | 9 | 38 | 3 |
| McCabe | 10 | 2 | 25 | 1 |
| Chilvers | 30.4 | 7 | 66 | 2 |
| Hooker | 13 | 4 | 26 | 0 |
| Bradman | 8 | 1 | 16 | 0 |
| Marks | 3 | 1 | 4 | 0 |
| Fingleton | 1 | 0 | 3 | 0 |

Fairfax, 2 w and 3 nb; Hooker, 2 nb.
Umpires: W. G. French and H. Armstrong.

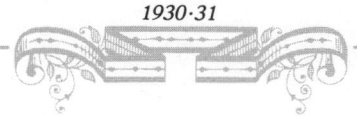

# DON: AS PRINCE CHARMING

## SURPRISE CALL ON OLD LADY

## MRS. CAMPBELL, 85, IS HAPPY NOW

## THRILL OF A TALK WITH HER IDOL

## "WONDERFUL BOY"

**By J. MATHERS**

Only a stodgy pen would describe Don Bradman as a Knight of the Willow, but he has nevertheless proved, by a kindly action, that chivalry is not dead.

TO a dear old lady of Dulwich Hill, Mrs. Lydia Campbell, he is Prince Charming.

Mrs. Campbell is 85, and rarely leaves her home, so that she had no opportunity of seeing her young hero on the field.

Love of cricket came to Mrs. Campbell years ago. when her husband excelled at the game. He was a teacher at Dapto for 35 years.

"I was so devoted to my husband's success in cricket," Mrs. Campbell explained, "that when I first read about Don Bradman I wanted to meet him to shake him by the hand."

### COULD IT COME TRUE?

It seemed a wild dream, but sometimes dreams come true. Relatives took a hand.

A young fellow called at Mick Simmons' shop and told Don about Mrs. Campbell. It was pointed out that he would be in the neighborhood at a church function; could he call? Don said he would if he could, and he'd try.

Mrs. Campbell knew nothing about it.

### DRESSED IN "SUNDAY BEST"

After tea on the evening of the function, one of her grand-daughters suggested that she should put on her "Sunday best," for she thought it was possible that Don Bradman would call.

*Mrs. Lydia Campbell, of Dulwich Hill, has longed to see Don Bradman. How he made a surprise call on her is told in the story.*

"It seemed too good to be true," admitted Mrs. Campbell.

At eight o'clock there was a knock at the door, and the inquiry, "Does Mrs. Campbell live here?"

"Well, tell her that Don Bradman would like to see her."

And Australia's cricket giant walked into the sitting room. The Prince Charming leaned against the piano, and gratified the heart of the old lady with a short but happy conversation.

### KNEW ALL ABOUT HIM

Mrs. Campbell showed him newspaper cuttings of every comment and criticism about himself. from the time he entered big cricket. She has kept as complete a record of Bradman as any cricket historian could desire. To-day she is happy, because her greatest wish has been gratified.

"I've seen him," she said yesterday, "and I think he is just as wonderful as a boy as he is a cricketer, and I would like to tell his mother that."

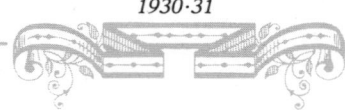

## BRADMAN'S SONG RECORDED.

A gramophone record of Don Bradman's musical composition. "Every Day is a Rainbow Day for Me," has been made by the Columbia Company at Homebush. The composer autographed the wax record.

Recording by Columbia of Don Bradman's song "Every Day is a Rainbow Day for Me".

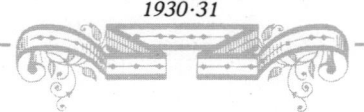

# Australia v West Indies
# Fourth Test Match

AUSTRALIA v WEST INDIES, Fourth Test Match, at Melbourne, 13 and 14 February 1931.

| | | |
|---|---|---|
| Australia | - First Innings | 328 for 8 wickets dec. |
| | - Second Innings | - |
| West Indies | - First Innings | 99 |
| | - Second Innings | 107 |

Australia won by an innings and 122 runs.

DON BRADMAN   - c. C.A. Roach  b. F.R. Martin      152

The wicket on the first day of the first innings was perfect. Going in after tea at 50 for 1, DON BRADMAN reached 50 in forty-five minutes, his fastest in a Test Match, and when stumps were drawn he had batted only seventy-eight minutes to be 92 not out. After overnight rain, the wicket was sticky next morning, and before he had added to his score Bradman was missed at silly point off F.R. Martin. After that, he mastered the conditions, and continued to bat brilliantly, reaching 100 in one hundred and two minutes; and when he was caught in the deep at 286 for 5, he had made 152 in two hours thirty-four minutes, including two fives and thirteen fours; the last 60 of them came in seventy-six minutes on the second morning on a wicket all against good batsmanship.

At 59 runs an hour, this was his fastest Test Match century.

## TO-DAY'S PLAY.

### MELBOURNE, Saturday.

Heavy rain during the night on a wicket that was covered only at the creases made conditions unfavourable for the batsmen when the fourth test was resumed on the Melbourne Cricket Ground to-day. The ball rose awkwardly, and in Martin's first over Headley missed Bradman at silly point. Francis had opened the bowling, and was also causing trouble, Bradman being struck on the foot and the body with successive deliveries. Woodfull, scoring off each bowler, brought the score to 200 in 133 minutes. In Francis' third over Woodfull was run out, Bradman not responding to his call for an easy run. Woodfull had made 83 in 142 minutes, with seven fours. Bradman hit Francis past point for four, and off-drove Martin for three, to reach 100 in 102 minutes. Neither bowler was taking advantage of the favourable conditions, and Constantine replaced Francis at 220, Jackson pulling him for four. Constantine also remained for three overs only, and Birkett took his place. Bradman pulled his first ball for four. Martin's length was erratic, and Bradman pulled him for five, all run, Constantine just ambling after the ball. The score reached 250 in 182 minutes. Constantine came back again instead of Birkett, and Jackson skied a fast bumping ball to Birkett in the slips. He had batted for 44 minutes.

An extraordinary incident occurred when McCabe and Bradman became tangled up in a run, and, with both men at the same end, Constantine easily removed the bails at the other end. Bradman immediately raced off, and the umpire tried vainly to bring him back, at the same time pointing to McCabe. Bradman was cheered when he returned with Fairfax. He reached 150 in 147 minutes in the same over by swinging Constantine to the fine leg boundary. One run later Bradman was plendidly caught at long off by Roach, who had to run some distance. Batting for only 154 minutes, Bradman made 152, and hit 15 fours and two fives. Fairfax and Kippax were both in difficulties, Fairfax twice just steering the ball over the heads of the fieldsmen.

At lunch Fairfax was seven and Kippax 5, and the score five for 297.

Against inaccurate bowling and on a wicket that was not as treacherous as before, the scoring quickened after lunch. Kippax pulled Constantine to the leg boundary twice in one over, and Fairfax pulled Martin in the same direction. At 24 Kippax played over a ball from Martin, and was bowled for 24, made in 32 minutes, and including three fours. Oxenham was out without scoring, Constantine taking a spectacular catch at silly-leg. Oldfield hit the next ball just over the bowler's head. Fairfax endeavoured to pull Martin, and was nicely caught at deep mid-on. The innings was then declared closed, with the score eight for 328, made in 249 minutes. Martin bowled unchanged to-day, his figures being 21.2 overs, 54 runs, three maidens, and three wickets.

After a delay of 20 minutes, during which first the light and then the heavy roller was used, the West Indies second innings was opened by Roach and Constantine at 12 minutes past 3 o'clock. The bowlers were Fairfax and Ironmonger. In Fairfax's second over Roach was out lbw. Headley had made 1 when he was struck a severe blow with a ball from Ironmonger. He took some time to recover, and should have been stumped. In the same over Constantine swung at a rising ball from Fairfax, and was easily caught at silly leg. Fairfax was making the ball rise awkwardly at times. In Ironmonger's next over Fairfax took a clever right hand catch close in at third slip, and dismissed Headley. At tea the score was three for 43.

Australia won by an innings and 122 runs.

Scores:—

### WEST INDIES.—First Innings, 99.
### Second Innings.

| | |
|---|---|
| C. A. Roach, lbw, b Fairfax | 7 |
| L. N. Constantine, c Kippax, b Fairfax | 10 |
| G. Headley, c Fairfax, b Ironmonger | 11 |
| L. S. Birkett, c Jackson, b Ironmonger | 13 |
| C. G. Grant, c McCabe, b Ironmonger | 3 |
| F. R. Martin, c Oldfield, b Fairfax | 10 |
| E. L. Bartlett, b Fairfax | 6 |
| I. Barrow, c Oxenham, b Ironmonger | 13 |
| O. C. Scott, not out | 20 |
| H. O. Griffith, b Grimmett | 4 |
| A. Francis, c Jackson, b Grimmett | 0 |
| Sundries | 10 |
| | |
| Total | 107 |

### AUSTRALIA.—First Innings.

| | |
|---|---|
| W. H. Ponsford, st Barrow, b Constantine | 24 |
| W. M. Woodfull, run out | 83 |
| D. G. Bradman, st Roach, b Martin | 152 |
| A. Jackson, c Birkett, b Constantine | 15 |
| S. McCabe, run out | 2 |
| A. Fairfax, c Birkett, b Martin | 16 |
| A. Kippax, b Martin | 24 |
| H. Oxenham, c Constantine, b Griffith | 0 |
| W. Oldfield, not out | 1 |
| Sundries | 11 |
| | |
| Eight wickets for | 328 |

Innings declared closed.

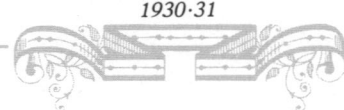

# Australia v West Indies
# Fifth Test Match

AUSTRALIA v WEST INDIES, Fifth Test Match, at Sydney, 27, 28 February, 2 and 4 March 1931.

| | | |
|---|---|---|
| Australia | - First Innings | 224 |
| | - Second Innings | 220 |
| West Indies | - First Innings | 350 for 6 wickets dec. |
| | - Second Innings | 124 for 5 wickets dec. |

Australia lost by 30 runs.

| | | |
|---|---|---|
| DON BRADMAN | - c. G.N. Francis b. F.R. Martin | 43 |
| | b. H.C. Griffith | 0 |

DON BRADMAN went in soon after tea on the second day, at 7 for 1, when the pitch was at its most spiteful, and played a brilliant innings, displaying sure judgement of which ball to hit and which to leave alone. He made 43 in fifty-one minutes (50 runs an hour) before being well caught in the slips.

On the fourth morning, he went in at 49 for 1, when the wicket was rather easier than in the first innings, but still unpleasant after more rain and sun; and, pinned down by H.C. Griffith, he swung wildly across a straight good-length ball and was bowled for his first 'duck' in a Test Match; he was third out at 53, after staying for ten minutes.

## Still They Gazed

WHEN Don's "duck" was recorded against the West Indies the colored tourists nearly threw a seven. The "rattle in the timberyard" was the most beautiful music they had heard during the tour.

But "The Hill" was stunned, and this is how the fans looked when "Truth's" artist found them long after "stumps."

Don has a lot on his mind these days, however, and a "duck" is a poultry affair in his young life. It certainly pleased the West Indies more than it hurt him.

## Don in Another Role

THOUGH Don Bradman's mother is naturally delighted with his achievements as a cricketer, and in perfect agreement with the general public's acclamation thereof—it's a way mothers have—a happening of his schoolboy days must give her even a warmer glow of satisfaction.

It was an oppressively sultry day, and in the languid atmosphere of the school many impatient glances were cast at the clock. "Who's for a swim?" was heard in stealthy whispers throughout the room as closing bell time drew near, the noise going unheeded by a sympathetic master. Directly school was dismissed there was a rush for Oxley's waterhole, the swimming pool favored by Bowral schoolboys.

·Don Bradman

Half-way across the paddock the first batch saw a woman waving her arms and running towards them, and Don, making a dash and sizing up the situation, as he ran, dived fully clothed and booted into the water and rescued her little girl who had slipped and fallen in. This quick perception has stuck to him, to his advantage in his career as a cricketer.

When Prince George recently visited the Sykes factory at Horbury, where the Don Bradman bats are made, Mrs. Sykes, wife of the managing director, asked him to sign an autograph album. The Prince complied with the request and so became associated with some folk well known in Bowral. The only other signatures in the book are those of Don Bradman and Mr. and Mrs. Alf. Stephens, who visited the factory last year.

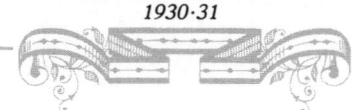

# The Accrington Story

In August 1931 Australia was in the midst of a bad depression.

My contract with Mick Simmons Ltd. was due to expire early in 1932. I had no wish to continue a business career so closely allied to sport and was contemplating my whole future when Learie Constantine inquired through my friend Claude Spencer whether I would be interested in playing cricket in the Lancashire League.

Whilst the prospect did not really attract me I felt bound to ascertain what was involved and whether it might prove attractive in the short term.

The following pages detail the negotiations and tell of the culmination whereby I signed a tri-partite two year agreement to remain in Sydney.

It is of interest and importance because this decision determined that I would never leave my home country nor become a professional cricketer.

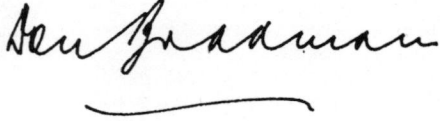

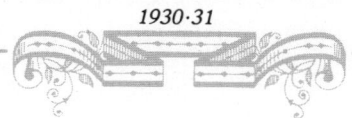

# RUMOR BOWLS AT BRADMAN

## TALK OF LEAVING AUSTRALIA

## NEGOTIATIONS SAID TO BE IN TRAIN

## HARD TO HOLD HERE

### (By A. G. MOYES)

**Has the persistent rumor that Australia may lose Don Bradman any foundation?**

ALTHOUGH there is at the moment nothing official, it is said that negotiations are even now proceeding which may deprive us of the run-getting machine.

When Bradman was smashing records in England it was freely stated that more than one county would welcome him with open arms.

It will also be recalled that on his return to Australia friction developed and finally he was haled before the Board of Control, censured, and fined for what was at the most a technical breach of his agreement.

Certain of Bradman's friends have for months held the opinion privately that he would return to England and recently the rumors have gained ground.

#### SIX MONTHS TO RUN

Bradman is now with Mick Simmon's, Ltd., and it is said that his contract has six months to run.

Being young and ambitious, he will naturally seek the best market and it will be an extremely difficult task to keep him in this country.

One would regret intensely to see other countries getting the benefit of skill which is Australian in birth and development, even though a cricketer is as much entitled to reward for skill as the singer or the actor.

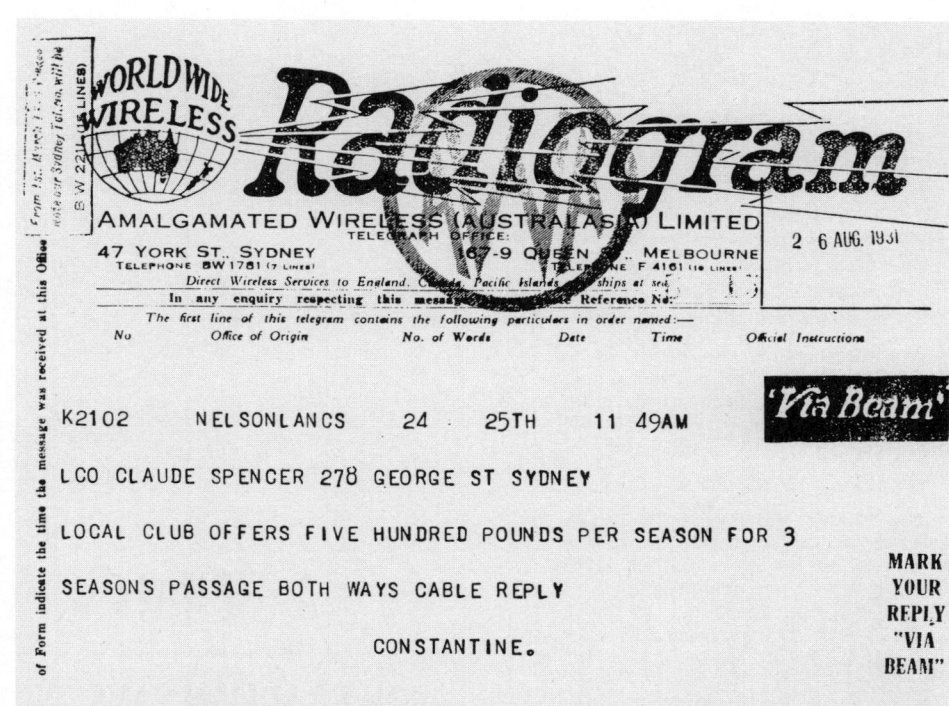

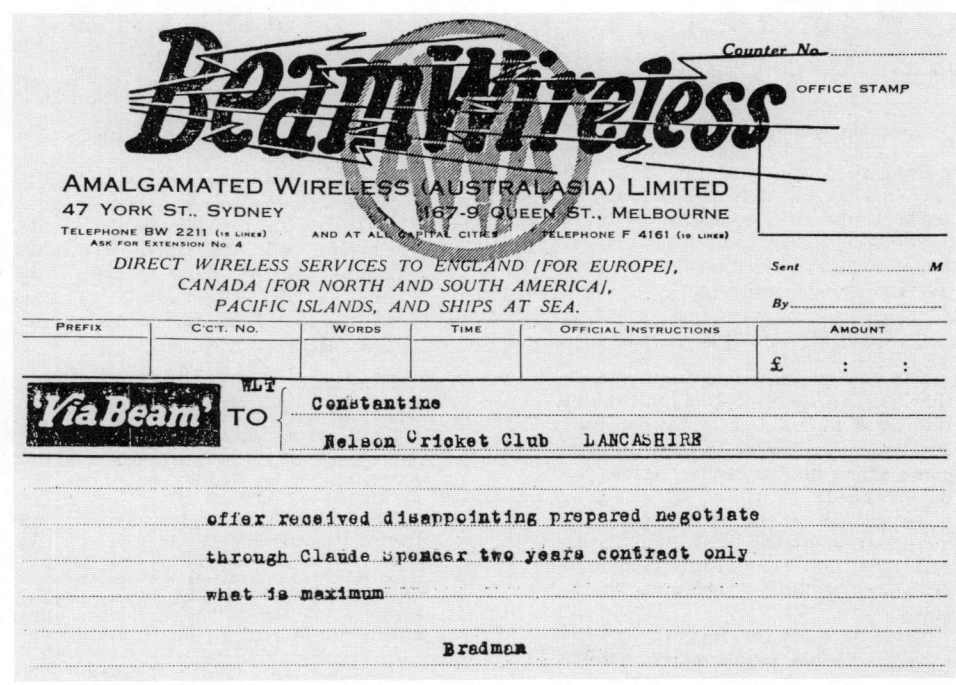

# Shall We Lose Bradman?

## SECRET!

## "Tempting Offer"

### FOR LEAGUE

("Sun" Special)

*LONDON, Monday.*

The "Evening News" declares that the Accrington Cricket Club (Lancashire League) is negotiating through third parties to engage Don Bradman, and that the offer made to the famous Australian is a record in League cricket.

The discussions, the paper adds, are so secret that even Bradman is not aware of the name of the club on behalf of which the offer is being made.

**(Published in the "Daily Mail")**

The "Daily Mail" says: Bradman recently wrote to a friend, who is interested in the Nelson Club, stating that he was willing to come to England. As Nelson is committed to Constantine, the West Indian all-rounder, for three years, it could not, under the Lancashire rules, engage a second professional, so the hint was passed on to another club. This was reported to be Accrington, which made Bradman a tempting offer.

*Don Bradman*

The Accrington Club secretary refused to say more than: "We have not signed on Bradman."

### 'County Backs Club'

The "News-Chronicle" understands that the Lancashire County Club is interested in the Accrington proposal. Bradman is reported to be willing to come, "provided suitable terms can be arranged."

He would spend two years, as qualification period, with Accrington, and then join the county, which is probably backing Accrington financially.

There is a strong feeling that the county officials ought to go outside county-born players in order to brighten county cricket.

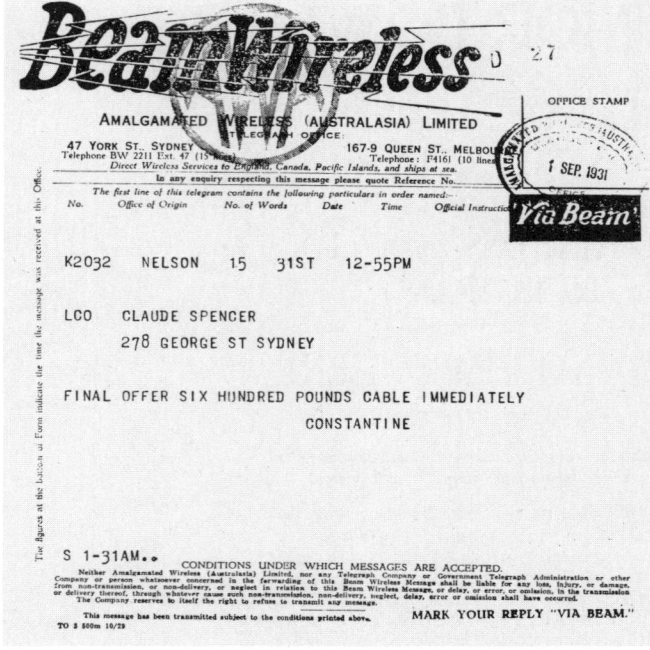

# A SPHINX

## DON BRADMAN SAYS "NO"

### ENGLISH OFFER

### ASKED MANY QUESTIONS

(By Claude Corbett)

**Don Bradman would drive a King's Counsel insane!**

**With that inscrutable smile playing all the time, Bradman could not be drawn into discussing the offer made to him to play League cricket in Lancashire.**

Bradman refused to answer all questions except one:

"Will you deny that you have received an offer to play for a Lancashire League club?"

"No!" was the reply.

Bradman likes being asked questions by pressmen which he does not want to answer. He admitted it. Also, he naively remarked, "It is wonderful what you fellows know." This with the immovable smile so characteristic of him.

### Smile Still There

Bradman, when informed that the offer made to him by Accrington was said to be the largest ever made a man to play professional cricket in the Lancashire League, desired to know what amounts had been paid.

The information was not available, but the smile did not fade.

"Do they play only on Saturday afternoons in Lancashire?"

"Are there any obligations other than to play cricket?"

"Do they want their professionals to coach?"

Don had a lot of questions to ask, but no information to give—except that he would not deny he had received an offer.

In any case, whether he accepts the offer or not, Bradman will not be lost to Australian cricket this season. He will be available to play against the South Africans, and is hopeful of getting a lot of runs.

### Interesting Story to Tell

An interesting point arises. Should Bradman go to England and return to Sydney each summer, would he be selected for New South Wales and Australia against the Sheffield Shield States and England? Coaching and playing in Adelaide made no difference to Patsy Hendren as far as England was concerned. There shouldn't be any trouble in that direction for Bradman.

Don has an interesting story to tell, one that would receive world-wide publicity—provided he clinches negotiations.

But when he will tell it is another thing.

All that he will say at present is "No!" when asked will he deny that he has received an offer from England.

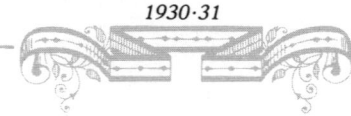

THE
Wagga Daily Advertiser

This is true liberty, when freeborn men
Having to advise the public, may speak free.
—Milton.

SATURDAY, SEPTEMBER 5, 1931

## BRADMAN AND HIS CRITICS

The controversy at present centring on Bradman seems to arise from the fact that Bradman is a business man, as well as a cricketer. This is a logical attitude on the part of Bradman since big cricket, like all other commercialised sport, is a business, despite the warm protestations of "lily-white" amateurs that it is not. Bradman did not frame the conditions which govern the sport; what he has done was to give a decided fillip to the gate receipts at any match in which he played, and surely he cannot be blamed for getting the best terms for himself while his ability and popularity are at the zenith. Cricket is Bradman's business, as well as his recreation. Being an astute young man, as well as the cricketing genius of the century, he sees the position clearly. How many of our great cricketers, such as Victor Trumper, have gone into retirement with only a testimonial match as a reward for years of brilliant play which helped to swell the exchequers of the clubs and associations? There are many positions open to the cricketer at the height of his success, but when his powers are spent it is another story. In effect, Bradman might say: "I have not created the present position in regard to the payment of players. I have every right to commercialise my cricketing genius in the best market. If the best market is in England and I must go abroad, then I shall be one of many Australians who took the same course to their undoubted advantage."

The Accrington Cricket Club has offered Bradman excellent terms and security of employment to play for it. Many hands have been held up in pious horror at this action. Followers of the game, particularly those who sit in the pavilion, are shocked to the very core of their being at what an English newspaper describes as "throwing gold into the balance." This is sheer humbug, for similar conditions exist at our very door. How many footballers are walking about country towns, having been "imported" from Sydney and elsewhere? In a modified form the same thing applies to cricket in the cities of Australia, while in England the trade in, and barter of, professional players is a flourishing industry. Those who are questioning Bradman's good taste are not in the main altogether sincere. Had he been a mediocre player his departure would scarcely have stirred a ripple of comment. He would have slipped quietly away like many another Australian to fresh fields and pastures new. This impinges on another matter of good taste. By virtue of his truly wonderful performances on the cricket field Bradman lives in the spotlight of publicity. Considering that he is a very young man the publicity and criticism evoked by his every action cannot but have a detrimental effect upon a sensitive nature. Bradman shares with other prominent people of the world the pinpricks of comment of many of lesser calibre. In this connection the following cabled comment from the "News-Chronicle" is worthy of quotation: "Accrington's acquisition of Bradman is a doubtful gain to English cricket. It introduces an alien atmosphere of barter and purchase. Lancashire already abounds in the uninspiring and 'efficient' type of batting, in which Bradman is unrivalled. Moreover, his relatively poor performances recently argue the awful possibility that his astounding records here may have been more fortunate than was originally supposed." It might appear from the foregoing that Bradman committed a grave error, in the judgment of the writer, in being born an Australian. For years England has been praying for an English cricketer of the "uninspiring" type of Bradman. The Accrington club is willing, nay anxious, to secure Bradman, despite his "relatively poor performances recently." If Australia is to retain the "ashes" we cannot afford to lose Bradman, who is willing to devote himself entirely to cricket. That being the case, shorn of all hyperbole, the cricket authorities must make some effort to keep Bradman in the land of his birth.

**Beam Wireless** D 273

AMALGAMATED WIRELESS (AUSTRALASIA) LIMITED
TELEGRAPH OFFICE:

47 YORK ST., SYDNEY
Telephone BW 2211 Ext. 47 (15 lines)

167-9 QUEEN ST., MELBOURNE
Telephone: F4161 (10 lines)

*Direct Wireless Services to England, Canada, Pacific Islands, and ships at sea.*

**In any enquiry respecting this message please quote Reference No.**

OFFICE STAMP
6 SEP 1931
AMALGAMATED WIRELESS (AUST.) CENTRAL

*The first line of this telegram contains the following particulars in order named:—*

| No. | Office of Origin | No. of Words | Date | Time | Official Instructions |
|---|---|---|---|---|---|
| W2242 | ACCRINGTON | 105 | | 1030AM.... | |

'Via Beam'

RP10/50 WLT BRADMAN SYDNEY.

CONFIRMING TELEPHONE CONVERSATION, ARRIVE ENGLAND APRIL EIGHTEENTH. DUTIES FINISH SEPTEMBER THIRD. PLAY THIRTY MATCHES BETWEEN THESE DATES, TWENTY OF WHICH ON SATURDAYS. DURATION MATCH FIVE HOURS. ATTEND GROUND FOR PRACTICE EACH TUESDAY WEDNESDAY THURSDAY EVENING, NO GROUNDWORK. WE OFFER FEE L 600. ESTIMATE L 150 TALENTS AND COLLECTIONS. EVERY CONFIDENCE L 150 EXHIBITION MATCHES. CONTRACT TWO YEARS, WE PAY PASSAGE BOTH WAYS. BOARD RESIDENCE COST YOU L 2 WEEKLY. WE UNDERSTAND SUNDAY CHRONICLE OFFER YOU L 150 FOR CRICKET ARTICLES. PROSPECTS OF OTHER BUSINESS ARRANGEMENTS. DECISION EXPECTED AND DESIRED IN SEVEN DAYS IF POSSIBLE, CONDITIONS SIMILAR TO CONSTANTINE.

The figures at the bottom of Form indicate the time the message was received at this Office.

CONDITIONS UNDER WHICH MESSAGES ARE ACCEPTED.

Neither Amalgamated Wireless (Australasia) Limited, nor any Telegraph Company or Government Telegraph Administration or other Company or person whatsoever concerned in the forwarding of this Beam Wireless Message shall be liable for any loss, injury, or damage, from non-transmission, or non-delivery, or neglect in relation to this Beam Wireless Message, or delay, or error, or omission, in the transmission or delivery thereof, through whatever cause such non-transmission, non-delivery, neglect, delay, error or omission shall have occurred.
The Company reserves to itself the right to refuse to transmit any message.

This message has been transmitted subject to the conditions printed above.

**MARK YOUR REPLY "VIA BEAM."**

TO 3 500m 10/29

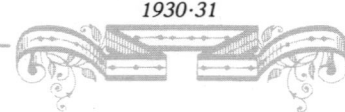
# THE VALUE OF DON BRADMAN

BEYOND all the denials, it appears to be established that the Australian cricket team is likely to lose Mr. Don Bradman, its most fertile run-getter.

Following a policy which began a few years ago, an English cricket club has made Mr. Bradman an offer which, with a view to establishing his future, he will possibly accept.

No doubt his acceptance would bring a certain criticism upon him by people who believe that he should stick to Australia and help to win Test Matches for her.

In a world in which talent is marketed like wheat or cotton or rubber, Mr. Bradman merely follows the usual procedure. He did not make the world, and it would be grossly unfair to blame him for following its usages. Australia's singers and artists and other professional folk go abroad, and, finding, as a rule, that they can do better abroad than in their own country, remain away. Few of us, if offered a sum which appeared as large to us as the very handsome wages offered must appear to Mr. Bradman, would refuse to go to London or anywhere else for it. In this case the admonition may well be quoted: "Let him that is without sin among ye cast the first stone."

At the same time it is most regrettable that the world is so constituted that talent should thus be marketed. So far, cricket has been a sport singularly free from the commercialism which bids for players. Far better for cricket should it remain so.

No doubt it is an excellent thing for a club to have a champion cricketer in its team, but the old system of breeding and training champions was a far more satisfactory way than buying them. It gave a genuine local pride which cannot be marketed nor valued— "the praise no man can buy."

That it will rebound to the general detriment of the game is certain. What pride can there be in England that a team of hired Australian professionals win a match against Australia?

At least the Australian artist abroad keeps his nationality. Melba was always the Australian prima donna, George Lambert signed his pictures frequently "G. W. Lambert, of Australia." The professional cricketer, after the statutory period of residence, becomes an English cricketer, and it becomes his painful duty to slog the bowling of his old team-mates or take the wickets which before it was his duty and pride to keep up. It is not a pleasant position for any man who has pride in the country of his birth.

Moreover, it tends to reduce Test cricket to a farce. If Great Britain is able to buy our most promising cricketers as they appear, and the habit grows, what Australian will be interested enough to go out to the Cricket Ground to see a team, largely composed of former Australian cricketers, wallop a team from which all the brightest talent has been bought by the enemy?

Bradman, playing for Australia on an Australian wicket, was a magnet to tens of thousands of enthusiastic spectators.

However, it is not much use to protest. If English clubs propose to strengthen their sides by purchase, there is no more to be said, and no young man can afford to reject a good offer from a mere reason of sentiment. It looks as if in future Australia may be the breeding ground of England's cricketers.

OUR DON.
Speculation is rife in the world of cricket as to whether Don will accept a tempting offer to leave Australia

# What Has Australia Done For Bradman ?

## FINED HIM FOR EATING THE FRUIT

### OF HIS OWN GENIUS

## Emotional Outbursts About His Doing What Most Great Australians Have Done

## DIDN'T GET HIS SKILL BY ACT OF PARLIAMENT

WHY all this outcry about Don Bradman? One would think the young cricketing genius had violated one of the commandments simply because he has enough business ability to consider his own future.

He has been offered a lucrative position in the English cricket world. Why shouldn't he accept it? There is no excuse for the pitiful wails which are resounding throughout Australia. Bradman is a free agent. A marvellous gift has been bestowed on him. It is sheer stupidity to imagine that it is his duty to remain in the land of his birth if his gift is more valuable elsewhere.

TELEPHONES—
F 5244
F 4272
F 2463

COMMONWEALTH OF AUSTRALIA
HOUSE OF REPRESENTATIVES

FEDERAL MEMBERS' ROOMS.

TEMPLE COURT.

422-428 COLLINS STREET.

MELBOURNE. C. 1.

7th September, 1931.

Mr. Don Bradman.

My dear Friend,

I resent deeply the criticism that you have been subjected to. I resent it strongly the contemptible fining of you after your return with your glorious record. I know in the past that snobs and cads on the Selecting Committee insulted our best cricketers, and sent home a second-rate team under McAllister. I know also that many international cricketers who helped to win glory for Australia suffered want in their old age, and some of them even had to pay admission to see cricket played. Under these circumstances and using all the wisdom I have garnered in seventy seven years, I strongly advise you to accept the position that has been offered you, and when you have saved enough to ensure your middle and old-age from want, then act as you please.

As to the critics in England, they are all on a par with the snobs who made certain cricketers, even though they had helped them to win matches, go in a certain door that the Gentlemen cricketers never entered. That is enough for the English critics.

You are welcome to use this letter in any way, and only illness prevented my taking public action to answer your critics.

Wishing you a long and happy life, surrounded by health and happiness,

Yours fraternally and affectionately,

W. Maloney

## BRADMAN'S TURN TO BE ANNOYED.

### "TIME TO COMMENT WHEN, AND IF, I SIGN."

Don Bradman, the famous Australian Test cricketer, is extremely annoyed at comments appearing in British newspapers on the offer made by the Accrington Cricket Club.

British newspapers are "pulling him to pieces without cause," declares Bradman, who says it would be time for them to comment if and when he signed the contract with the Accrington Club.

He points out (says the British United Press) that he has not yet signed the contract.

It is reported that a firm in Sydney has made a counter-offer to Bradman, who, however, declares that he knows nothing of any such offer.

A prominent Sydney sportsman has offered Bradman £50 if he will stay in Australia (says Reuter) so that he will be available to play against England at the end of next year.

It is expected that others will follow the Sydney sportsman in their endeavour to keep the Test match record scorer in his own country.

Accrington, which is a member of the Lancashire Cricket League, is stated to have offered Bradman £25 a week to play for the club. Bradman, who had an average score of 139 during the last Test tour, is bound by an undertaking not to play in England for two years after the conclusion of the last Test tour.

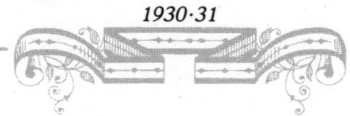

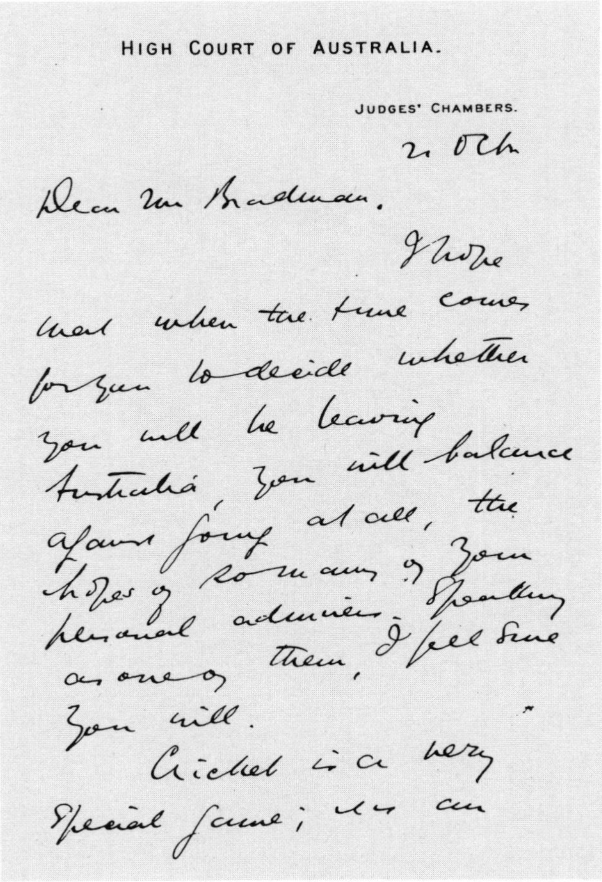

**HIGH COURT OF AUSTRALIA.**

JUDGES' CHAMBERS.

21 Oct.

Dear Mr Bradman,

I hope that when the time comes for you to decide whether you will be leaving Australia, you will balance against going at all, the hopes of so many of your personal admirers. Speaking as one of them, I feel sure you will.

Cricket is a very special game; it is an institution with a literature & tradition & history — quite its own. In all of that you have already a place apart and I promise to be the most historic place of all. E.g. Macdonnell promised to fill a greater place in it than he did, largely when he became he less came to be identified with Australia.

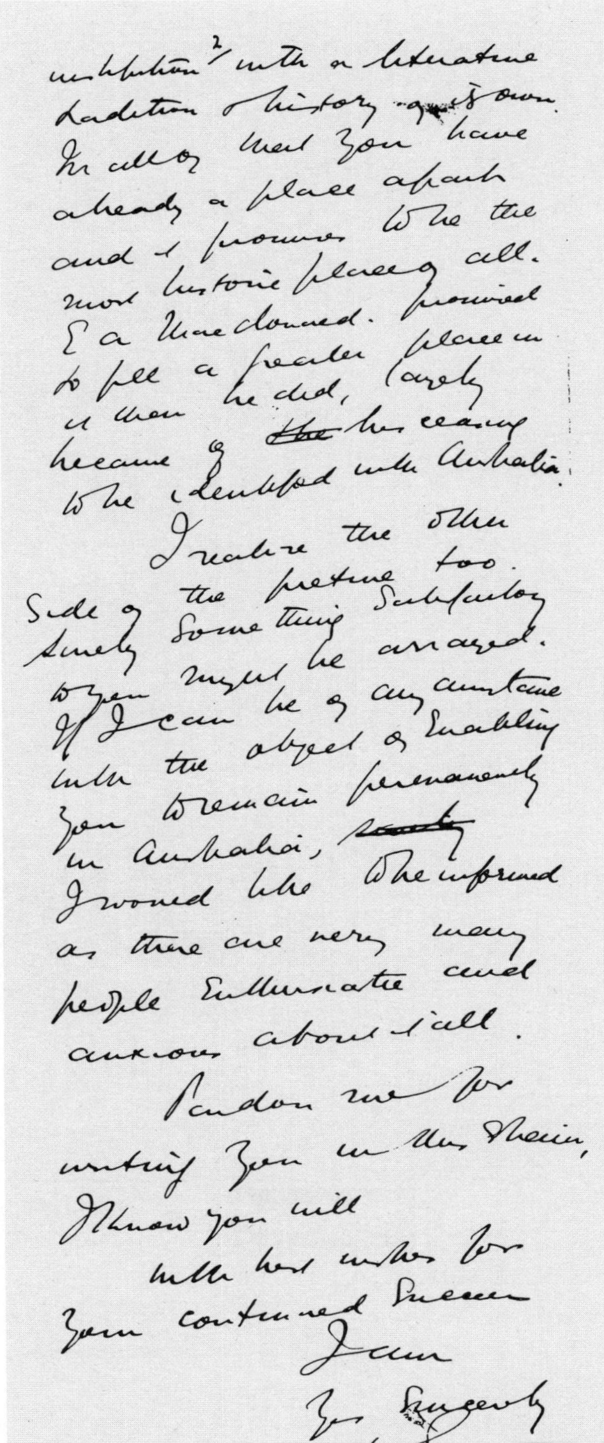

I realize the other side of the picture too. Surely something satisfactory to you might be arranged. If I can be of any assistance with the object of enabling you to remain permanently in Australia, I would like to be informed as there are very many people enthusiastic and anxious about it all.

Pardon me for writing you in this strain, I know you will.

With best wishes for your continued success

I am

Yours Sincerely

H Starke

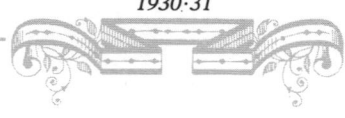

Victoria

Don Bradman

Dear little boy, take the advice of an old woman, Hit while the iron is hot; Australia soon forgets England never, You were not too well treated on your return with the greatest record in Cricket, Go & marry an heiress, with your face & record you can.

Good Luck.

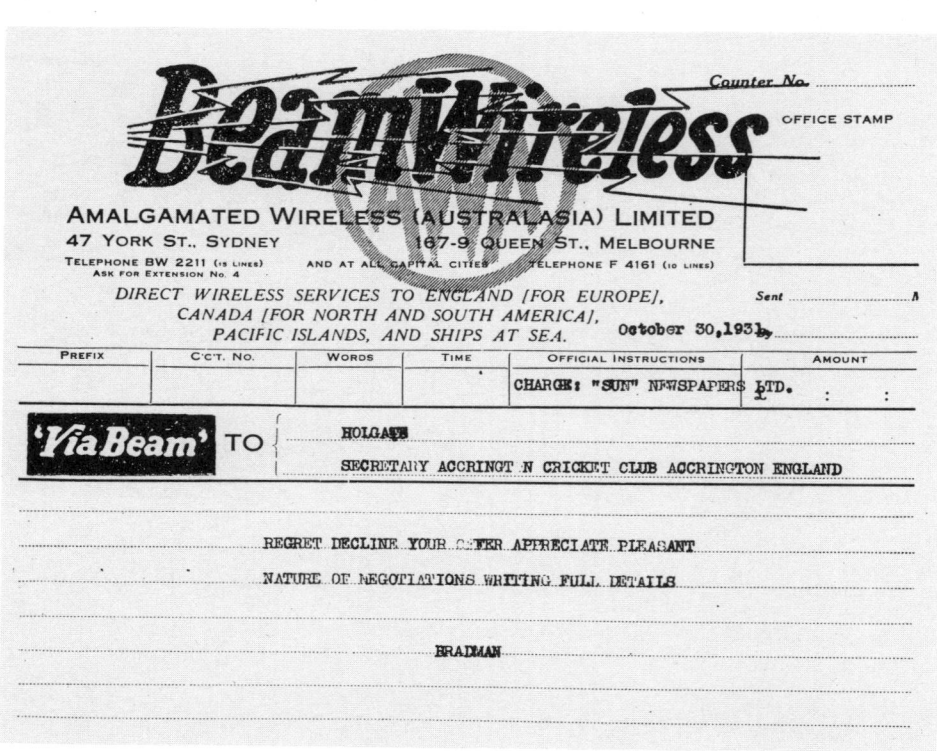

When "The Daily Telegraph" first published the story that there was something in the wind. it caused a sensation.

Cables to and from England ran hot. Bradman was cross-examined in a manner that would have done credit to an eminent K.C.

*"But this is home," smiles Don.*

"Will he go?" was asked throughout Australia—for Don is an Australian figure.

Again, we tell you that he will not go!

On Monday, Bradman saw the Accrington contracts for the first time, and then came the conflict between home ties and an attractive and well-paid life as a professional cricketer.

It was a tough problem, and one that could not be decided in a moment.

## Signing of Contract

Then came a bomb (to Bradman) in the shape of a local offer, that settled the argument.

This afternoon was a memorable one in our cricket history, for it marks the signing of the contract that will keep Bradman in Sydney.

The parties to the contract are:—

**Associated Newspapers Ltd.,**
**Messrs. F. J. Palmer and Son, Ltd.,**

**2UE Broadcasting Station.**

It will take effect on February 2 next year, when Don's present engagement with Mick Simmons. Ltd., will expire.

The great batsman will write constructive cricket articles for Associated Newspapers. His wonderful cricket brain is well known to those who follow the game, and he wields the pen with the same facility as he does the bat.

This feature should appeal to all readers, who appreciate expert comment from one who knows so intimately the game and its players.

It was obvious that no single firm could hope to compete with the magnificent offer from England, but the three, working in conjunction, have been able to go far enough to hold the champion.

**It is only fair to Bradman to emphasise the fact that Bradman is losing financially by remaining in Australia, but, as he said to-day, "This is home."**

"I am delighted," said Don, with a happy smile, "that I am staying here. I did not want to go away or to lose touch with Australian cricket. Now I am happy."

So are we all.

## Amazing Career

Bradman's cricket career has been one series of extraordinary achievements. It is only five years since he was brought from Bowral for a trial, and in that short space of time he has won a place among the immortals of the game

His records are so numerous and so well known to everyone that it would be waste of time to repeat them. His world's record of 452 not out is the high-water mark, but his batting in the last series of Tests in England, including, as it did, a Test record and two other scores of over 200, will probably never be equalled.

Possessing exceptional stamina, and with eye, wrist and feet working in perfect unison, he has created a new standard.

In five short years he has shattered records by the dozen, and has written with his bat new pages in the "Book of Cricket."

Had he gone to Accrington he would have been lost to international cricket. The game would have lost one of its brightest jewels.

Now he will shed his lustre over the Sheffield Shield and Test Match field instead of wasting his brilliance in the comparative obscurity of League cricket.

## The "Triple Alliance"

Upon completion of the arrangements this afternoon, the mutual congratulations included the following statement of Mr. J. T. Smith (general manager of F. J. Palmer and Son):—

"I am very delighted that the scheme has matured, and that our firm, in association with Station 2UE and Associated Newspapers, has been the means of retaining this great cricketer to serve the Australian game. It would have been a great pity if this country had lost him. This, thanks to our triple alliance, has been averted."

Mr. C. V. Stevenson, speaking for Station 2UE, said:—

"Naturally I am very pleased as the result of our negotiations, through the agency of Reuters, to be associated with Messrs. Palmer and Son and Associated Newspapers in securing the services of Don Bradman for Australia, and I am sure that the radio public throughout Australia, will appreciate the outcome of the efforts that have been made by all concerned."

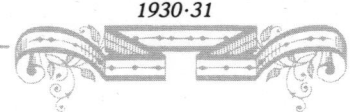

HIGH COURT OF AUSTRALIA.

JUDGES' CHAMBERS.

2/11/31

Dear Mr Bradman

I was
delighted to see your decision
in the press, and to receive
your letter in reply. Every
cricket lover in the world
will be delighted. I wish
you a continuance of your
phenomenal success.

Believe me
Yrs Sincerely
W Evatt.

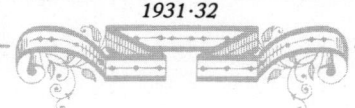

# *1931-32 Season*

The 1931–32 season was notable for my first and only appearance against South Africa in Test matches.

Aided by some good fortune I finished with a Test average of 201.5 for the season but this in no sense reflected the skill and quality of the South African bowlers who suffered cruel misfortune from missed catches.

There was also the unique second class match at Blackheath in which I made 100 in 3 overs.

*Don Bradman*

## BRADMAN ON THE PROGRAMME

### PROGRAMME

| | | | | | |
|---|---|---|---|---|---|
| 1 | " Bohemian Girl " Overture | | ... | ... | Balfe |
| 2 | Quis Est Homo ... | ... | ... | ... | Rossini |
| 3 | Rendez-vous ... | ... | ~~ | ... | Aletter |
| 4 | Humoresque ... | ... | ... | ... | Dvorak |
| 5 | " Gloria " ... | ... | ... | ... | Mercadante |
| 6 | Excerpt " La Mascotte ... | ... | ... | Audran |
| 7 | Mazur ... | ... | ... | ... | Nemerowsky |

GOD SAVE THE KING.

### For Sunday Recitals—See Papers

**Strict silence is requested during the performance of each item.**

CHILDREN IN ARMS NOT ADMITTED.

W. G. LAYTON.
Town Clerk

*It seems that the name of Bradman is on everyone's lips. It was even on the organ recital programme at the Town Hall on Sunday evening. Read down the initial letters of the names of the composers, and you will realise that in Sydney there is at least one musician-cricketer, the man who arranged this programme.*

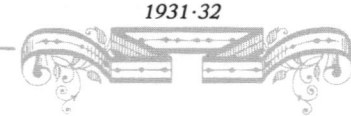

# PROUDEST BOY IN SYDNEY

## DON BRADMAN WAS THE REMEDY

WHO is the proudest boy in Sydney to-day? Albert Bridges, a nine-year-old patient in Sydney Hospital, will take a lot of beating.

Because Don Bradman heard that Albert had wished to meet him, he paid an unobtrusive visit to the boy and gave him an autographed photograph.

Albert, who lives at Newtown, was born with a deformed foot and, though he could not join in the games of his mates, he took a keen interest in sport.

This month he had the foot amputated and now he is looking forward to the day when, with an artificial limb, he will be able to play cricket.

A few days ago his aunt wrote to Don Bradman, telling him he was her nephew's idol, and how he wanted to meet him.

The boy got a shock yesterday when a nurse said, "A gentleman wants to see you. His name is Bradman."

Don Bradman is as great a fellow as he is a cricketer, the boy told his envious ward mates after his visitor had gone.

One hospital rule was broken last night. A peg that usually supports a temperature chart propped up the picture of a young man with a cricket bat. It bore the autograph—"Don Bradman."

# THE 4 OURS

# OUR HARBOUR
# OUR BRIDGE
# OUR "SMITHY"
# OUR "DON"

## DON BRADMAN.

### Former Master's Praise.

Recent criticism of Don Bradman drew a spirited defence yesterday from Inspector Ewing, of the Education Department, who was the cricketer's headmaster when he was a schoolboy in Bowral.

Addressing the visiting Victorian and Western Australian schoolgirls, Mr. Ewing said: "I taught Don as a little boy, and hope that all the people I taught have the same spirit. To statements that Don suffers from swelled head, I give an unqualified denial.

"I saw him before he went to England and when he came back," Mr. Ewing proceeded. "I saw him quite recently, and he has been a visitor at my home. He is the same Don Bradman I knew as a boy. Don is a fine lad, and I am very pleased indeed at his success."

WHEN Phar Lap was giving an exhibition gallop at Randwick on Saturday I recalled the suggestion of a correspondent before the latest Melbourne Cup. He declared that the greatest draw card would be for Don Bradman to be Phar Lap's jockey, as both were "stayers." Bradman, the correspondent added, was country-bred, and knew all about horses.

# HIS £50

## Return It to Don

### GRIMMETT'S CASE

#### (By Arthur Mailey)

Clarrie Grimmett, that quiet, peaceful, law-abiding slow-bowler of South Australia, must surely be spending some restless nights.

He is alleged to have written a book and allowed it to be published in newspapers while on tour with the 1930 Australian XI.

Don Bradman committed the same crime, and the Board of Control stopped £50 from his allowance.

Under the agreement with the players, the board reserves the right to punish those whose behavior whilst on tour is considered to be unsatisfactory, and the publication of newspaper articles is a breach of the agreement.

#### Not Stampeded

The fact that it is nearly 12 months since the team returned is sufficient proof that the board is not being stampeded into giving a hasty decision regarding the peaceful Clarrie Grimmett's case.

The board, with a wealth of legal men at its command, is anxious to do the right thing and act consistently. If the peaceful Clarrie is guilty of the same offence as Don, he will probably be fined £50.

I cannot imagine the little South Australian roaring with laughter at the thought of this; but there must be a better way out of the embarrassing position than this.

Both these cricketers are first offenders, and might be treated as such.

One has almost 20 years' honest cricket behind him, and the other probably 20 years' interesting cricket ahead of him. It would be a graceful and generous gesture if the board refunded Bradman £50, and allowed Grimmett's case to drop altogether.

If this is not done, and Grimmett is found guilty, we might have the unpleasant action of Grimmett's first two Test Match allowances being garnisheed.

# New South Wales
## v
## South Africa

SOUTH AFRICAN TEAM
*1931–32*

BACK ROW   A. J. Bell, C. L. Vincent, K. F. Viljoen, E. L. Dalton, S. S. L. Steyne, S. H. Curnow, L. S. Brown.
CENTRE ROW   J. A. J. Christy, H. W. Taylor, Mr. Tandy (Manager), H. B. Cameron, Q. McMillan, N. A. Quinn.
FRONT ROW   X. Balaskas, E. A. Van der Merwe, B. Mitchell.

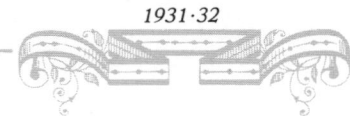
NEW SOUTH WALES v SOUTH AFRICANS, at Sydney, 13, 14, 16 and 17 November 1931.

| | | | |
|---|---|---|---|
| New South Wales | - First Innings | 168 | |
| | - Second Innings | 430 for 3 wickets | |
| South Africans | - First Innings | 425 | |
| | - Second Innings | 190 for 3 wickets dec. | |
| | Drawn. | | |

| | | |
|---|---|---|
| DON BRADMAN | - c. and b. Q. McMillan | 30 |
| | - c. A.J. Bell b. D.P.B. Morkel | 135 |

DON BRADMAN's first innings was not one of his best. Going in just before lunch on the second day, he batted for eighty-seven minutes, before giving an easy return catch. He helped to raise the score from 1 for 1 to 98 for 3.

Declaring at the end of the third day, the South Africans gave New South Wales a day (five hours) to make 448 to win. Going in just after lunch, at 81 for 1, Bradman batted in his most brilliant form; he reached 50 in only thirty-seven minutes, and 100 in one hundred minutes; just before tea he was caught at backward point. He had batted for two hours eight minutes and was out at 297 for 2, having put on 216 for the second wicket with J.H. Fingleton; he hit fifteen fours.

## — SEASON 1931-32 —

| TITLE | GAME | | SCORES | |
|---|---|---|---|---|
| Second Class | St. George | Epping | 80 | n.o. |
| | Rydalmere | Balmain | 8 | c. |
| | Own Team | Wyong Colts | 13 | c. |
| | " " | " " | 74 | B. |
| | Kippax's XI | Lithgow | 52 | B. |
| | - | Parkes | 124 | c. |
| | - | Forbes | 137 | c. |
| | - | Grenfell | 7 | c. |
| | - | Young | 111 | c. |
| | - | Murrumburrah | 63 | c. |
| | - | Wagga | 130 | n.o. |
| | - | Tumut | 0 | c. |
| | - | Gundagai | 88 | B. |
| | - | Yass | 85 | n.o. |
| | Own Team | Bathurst | 21 | c. |
| | Scot's College | School XI | 130 | c. |
| | Rothwell's Team | Newcastle | 66 | c. |
| | Bradman's Girls XI | McCabe's Girls XI | 18 | c. |
| | Kippax's XI | Paddington | 66 | c. |
| | Bradman's Team | Kippax's Team | 45 | B. |
| | Blackheath | Lithgow | 256 | c. |
| | Gladesville | Mosman Juniors | 8 | c. |
| | Mailey's Team | Callan Park | 143 | B. |
| | N.S.W.C.A. | Fairfax Juniors | 52 | B. |
| | Celebrities | Theatricals | 84 | n.o. |
| | Kippax's Team | St. Stanislaus | 4 | c. |
| First Grade | St. George | Northern Districts | 17 | n.o. |
| | - | Manly | 46 | r.o. |
| | - | Randwick | 246 | c. |
| | - | C Cumberland | 30 | c. |
| | - | University | 50 | L.B.W. |
| | - | | 67 | c. |
| | - | Paddington | 128 | c. |
| | - | Gordon | 201 | S. |
| First Class | New South Wales | South Africa | 30 | c. |
| | - - - | - - - | 135 | c. |
| | - - | | 219 | c. |
| Sheffield Shield | - - - | Queensland | 0 | c. |
| | - - - | Victoria | 23 | c. |
| | - - | | 167 | B. |
| | - - | South Australia | 23 | B. |
| | - - | - - | 0 | B. |
| Test | Australia | South Africa | 226 | L.B.W. |
| | - - | - - | 112 | c. |
| | - - | - - | 2 | c. |
| | - - | - - | 167 | L.B.W. |
| | - - | - - | 299 | n.o. |
| | | Total runs | 4053 | |

## — SUMMARY —

| AVERAGES | Innings | N.O's. | H.S. | Runs | Average |
|---|---|---|---|---|---|
| Test | 5 | 1 | 299x | 806 | 201·5 |
| Sheffield Shield | 5 | 0 | 167 | 213 | 42·6 |
| Other First Class | 3 | 0 | 219 | 384 | 128· |
| All First Class | 13 | 1 | 299x | 1403 | 116·9 |
| First Grade | 8 | 1 | 246 | 785 | 112·1 |
| Other Second Class | 26 | 4 | 256 | 1865 | 84·7 |
| All Second Class | 34 | 5 | 256 | 2650 | 91·3 |
| All Matches | 47 | 6 | 299x | 4053 | 98·8 |

Bell, Cameron, Bradman. Bradman swings Quinn for four.

## BRADMAN'S INNINGS ENDS.

DON BRADMAN'S first 100 against South Africa were made in 100 minutes and the 135 in 2hr 8min. One has seen him score still faster in big cricket. In this innings Bradman was not continuously forcing the pace, though it might have seemed to the South Africans that he was, it being their first experience of him. He had two stoppages, both for the purpose of having sticking plaster or adhesive tape put on to his blistered hand. The second application seemed to make his grip of the bat handle less satisfactory than it had been. H. B. Cameron after a while placed his field cleverly for Bradman and cut off a few of his intended fours.

\* \* \*

TO watch Bradman was a very interesting lesson in the art of batting for any observant young cricketer present. Vincent's length bowling to Fingleton and Bell looked perfect, but the same bowling to Bradman looked easy to manipulate for runs. He either played right back and whipped the ball wide of mid-on, or straight past the bowler by sheer power of wrists combined with delicate placing, or he late cut it. He moved into it and drove lustily despite the off field being cleverly placed to stop the drives.

\* \* \*

BRADMAN'S method of dealing with McMillan's slows was also educative to young batsmen. To a ball tossed a wee bit into the air, he jumped in and clipped it on the full, at the same time placing it to beat mid-on or square leg. At times mid-on would be moved a bit square to cut off the ball, then Bradman would hit it past the stumps. Mid-on would move in a bit, and then the ball would flash yards wider on the outside. It was the art of Trumper in placing the ball. The difference between Bradman and Fingleton in making the length of the ball suit the bat and then in placing it, was very striking.

A. J. Bell fell over to take a difficult low down catch yesterday off Morkel, when Bradman, who made 135, was racing for runs.

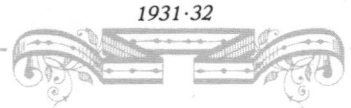

# Australia v South Africa
## First Test Match

AUSTRALIA v SOUTH AFRICA, First Test Match, at Brisbane, 27 and 28 November, 2 and 3 December 1931.

| Australia | - First Innings | 450 |
| | - Second Innings | - |
| South Africa | - First Innings | 170 |
| | - Second Innings | 117 |

Australia won by an innings and 163 runs.

DON BRADMAN    - l.b.w. b. C.L. Vincent    226

Going in at 32 for 1 on the first morning, on a very fast wicket, DON BRADMAN made a dreadful start. At 3 he was almost caught at square-leg, and at 10 and 15 he was missed in the slips. After that he found the pace of the pitch. He was 30 not out at lunch and reached 50 in sixty-two minutes, then took a further hour and twenty-two minutes to reach three figures. He was 108 at tea, and reached 200, just before the close of play, in four hours thirteen minutes, being 200 not out overnight. His hooking and his forcing shots to the on were particularly devastating. When he was 111 he reached an aggregate of 2,000 runs in all Test Matches.

Hitting out next morning he soon passed V.T. Trumper's 214 made in 1910-11, which had been the highest score by an Australian batsman in a home Test Match. However at 226 he was out l.b.w. to C.L. Vincent. His innings lasted four hours thirty-seven minutes and included twenty-two fours. This was his ninth century in all Test Matches, and he was the only batsman who had scored a double-century in his first Test Match v. South Africa.

This was the first Test Match to be played on the Brisbane Cricket Ground.

## SCORES.

**AUSTRALIA.—First Innings .. .. 450**

**SOUTH AFRICA—First Innings.**

| | |
|---|---|
| F. H. Curnow, b. Ironmonger .. .. | 11 |
| J. A. J. Christy, b. Wall .. .. .. | 24 |
| B. Mitchell, run out .. .. .. .. | 58 |
| H. B. Cameron, st. Oldfield, b. Grimmett .. .. .. .. .. | 4 |
| H. W. Taylor, b. Wall .. .. .. .. | 41 |
| E. L. Dalton, c. and b. Ironmonger | 11 |
| Q. M'Millan, c. Oxenham, b. Ironmonger .. .. .. .. .. .. .. | 0 |
| D. P. B. Morkel, c. M'Cabe, b. Ironmonger .. .. .. .. .. .. | 3 |
| C. L. Vincent, c. Nitschke, b. Grimmett .. .. .. .. .. | 10 |
| N. A. Quinn, c. Rigg, b. Ironmonger | 1 |
| A. T. Bell, not out .. .. .. .. .. | 1 |
| Sundries .. .. .. .. .. .. .. | 6 |
| **Total .. .. .. .. .. .. .. 170** | |

Fall of wickets: 25, 44, 49, 129, 140, 140, 152, 157, 168.

### BOWLING.

| | O. | M. | R. | W. |
|---|---|---|---|---|
| Wall .. .. .. .. | 28 | 14 | 39 | 2 |
| M'Cabe .. .. .. | 11 | 4 | 16 | 0 |
| Grimmett .. .. | 41.1 | 21 | 49 | 2 |
| Ironmonger .. .. | 47 | 29 | 42 | 5 |
| Oxenham .. .. | 11 | 5 | 18 | 0 |

**Second Innings.**

| | |
|---|---|
| F. H. Curnow, b. Grimmett .. .. | 8 |
| J. A. J. Christy, c. M'Cabe, b. Ironmonger .. .. .. .. .. .. .. | 15 |
| B. Mitchell, b. Wall .. .. .. .. | 0 |
| H. B. Cameron, b. Ironmonger .. | 21 |
| H. W. Taylor, c. Oxenham, b. Ironmonger .. .. .. .. .. .. .. | 47 |
| E. L. Dalton, b. Wall .. .. .. .. | 6 |
| D. P. B. Morkel, b. Wall .. .. .. | 5 |
| Q. M'Millan, c. Nitschke, b. Wall | 0 |
| C. L. Vincent, c. Rigg, b. Wall .. | 1 |
| N. A. Quinn, c. M'Cabe, b. Ironmonger .. .. .. .. .. .. .. | 0 |
| A. T. Bell, not out .. .. .. .. .. | 0 |
| Sundries (6 byes, 5 leg-byes, 3 no-balls) .. .. .. .. .. .. | 14 |
| **Total .. .. .. .. .. .. 117** | |

Fall of wickets: 16, 19, 34, 78, 97, 111, 111, 117, 117.

### BOWLING.

| | O. | M. | R. | W. |
|---|---|---|---|---|
| Wall .. .. .. .. | 15.1 | 7 | 14 | 5 |
| Ironmonger .. .. | 30 | 16 | 44 | 4 |
| Grimmett .. .. | 15 | 3 | 45 | 1 |

Ironmonger bowled two no-balls and Wall one.

## SCORES.

**AUSTRALIA.—First Innings.**

| | |
|---|---|
| W. H. Ponsford, c. Mitchell, b. Bell .. .. .. .. .. .. .. .. | 19 |
| W. M. Woodfull, l.b.w., b. Vincent .. .. .. .. .. .. .. .. | 76 |
| D. G. Bradman, l.b.w., b. Vincent .. .. .. .. .. .. .. .. | 226 |
| A. F. Kippax, c. Cameron, b. Vincent .. .. .. .. .. .. .. | 1 |
| S. J. M'Cabe, c. Vincent, b. Morkel .. .. .. .. .. .. .. | 27 |
| H. C. Nitschke, c. Cameron, b. Bell .. .. .. .. .. .. .. .. | 6 |
| R. K. Oxenham, b. Bell .. .. .. | 1 |
| C. V. Grimmett, b. Bell .. .. | 14 |
| W. A. Oldfield, not out .. .. .. | 56 |
| T. Wall, l.b.w., b. Quinn .. .. | 14 |
| H. Ironmonger, b. Quinn .. .. | 2 |
| Sundries .. .. .. .. .. .. .. | 8 |
| **Total .. .. .. .. .. .. .. 450** | |

Fall of wickets: 32, 195, 211, 292, 316, 320, 380, 407, 446.

### BOWLING.

| | O. | M. | R. | W. |
|---|---|---|---|---|
| Bell .. .. .. .. | 42 | 5 | 120 | 4 |
| Morkel .. .. .. | 13 | 1 | 57 | 1 |
| Quinn .. .. .. | 38.3 | 6 | 113 | 2 |
| Vincent .. .. .. | 34 | 0 | 100 | 3 |
| M'Millan .. .. .. | 10 | 0 | 52 | 0 |

Byes 5, leg-bye 1. Morkel bowled a wide, and Quinn a no-ball.

A costly mistake. Bradman, when only 10 runs were showing to his credit, snicked one through slips, the ball being missed by first and second slip, who both attempted the catch.

Don Bradman made 200 not out to-day. He was dropped by Vincent and Mitchell when he was 10 and 15!

# Bradman Requires Only 15 Runs to Break Trumper's Record

## MIGHTY BRADMAN.

### A GLORIOUS INNINGS.

### NEW RECORDS IN SIGHT.

### By CAPTAIN E. W. BALLANTINE.

In any kind of cricket, 341 in five hours would be a good day's work, and at the moment there are only six wickets disposed of to place Australia in a happy frame of mind. Whatever the weather may be, those runs are on the board, and there are four wickets in hand. But the South Africans have themselves to blame for this position of affairs. Out of the 341 runs, Don. Bradman has made 200, a greater proportion than we in England experienced, when during those five Tests in 1930, out of 2743 runs off the bat, he had to be content with only 974, and that is but little over a third! Yesterday's cricket found the young glutton for runs near two-thirds of the runs scored. Is there any limit to the scoring powers of this human machine? We were formerly concerned about "Billy" Ponsford and his 400,'s, 300's, and 200's, and ordinary centuries, but Don. Bradman seems likely to eclipse all the surprises that we had then.

### AFTER ANOTHER RECORD.

Although living so many miles away from Bradman, I have taken a great interest in his performances in first-class cricket, and I find that he has contributed as many as nine Test innings of three figures in four seasons, and this Test season is but a day old. I saw his two such innings in 1928-29, and I saw his four in England in 1930, but I had to be content to read about his two more three-figure scores against the West Indies, while I was following the English team through South Africa. Not content with overtaking the individual score in Test matches between England and Australia, of the late "Tip" Foster of 287, made at Sydney in 1903-4—a record which had stood for 27 years, when Don. Bradman made 334 at Leeds—he is now attacking another record, that held by the late Victor Trumper, of 214 not out, made against the South Africans in the Test match at Adelaide in 1910-11. South Africa had already paid for Bradman's disposal by Eddie Gilbert for a "duck," and now South Africa are going through it with themselves contributory.

### CLEVER ANTICIPATION.

Bradman and M'Cabe were ideal batsmen to take advantage of a tired attack. Both are enterprising, and possess a multitude of strokes, fearless, and powerful. The former did most of the scoring while M'Cabe was getting a sight of the ball. M'Cabe's timing, however, was uncertain, and his stroke-making inaccurate. There was an unusual lack of confidence, which was expressed in the snick to second slip, which Vincent, moving to the right forward, took low down. It was a clever piece of anticipation. With Nitschke as partner, Bradman quickly increased the score with strokes all round the wicket. He made three delightful strokes off half-volleys on the off stump, which were forced wide of mid-on, with plenty of power. Since passing the forties the Australian champion played with great skill, and completely dominated the play. His wonderful footwork and powerful back play were responsible for the bowlers' inability to keep him quiet as he quickly approached the two hundred. Nitschke was splendidly caught by Cameron on the leg side. There was an element of bad luck in his dismissal, though it was excellent cricket. Oxenham was bowled by the same bowler. He played forward and outside an inswinger. On the fast-rising wicket Bradman was able to exploit his magnificent late cut fearlessly and with great power. This is one of the prettiest and most dangerous strokes in cricket. Bradman is its master.

### THE DOUBLE CENTURY.

Too much credit cannot be given to the Africans for their plucky, accurate, and resourceful bowling, and their unflagging efforts in the field. In fact, their outcricket is of a much higher calibre than was at first supposed. Bradman's race for the double century against the clock had the crowd on its toes. It was an interesting duel of tactics between a versatile batsman, well set, and good-length left-hand bowling and a well-placed field. Bradman won, and the crowd went home delighted with a great day's cricket.

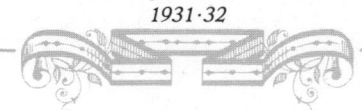

# BRADMAN BREAKS MORE TEST MATCH RECORDS

## TO-DAY'S TEST AT BRISBANE

### World's Champion Scores
### 226 vs. S. Africa

### TEST AVERAGE 100

### Australia 450 : South Africa
### 42 for 1 at Tea

Special to the "Ceylon Observer—Copyright

BRISBANE, Saturday

BRADMAN established a new record to-day in the first Test at Brisbane, for the highest individual score against South Africa, beating the previous record of 214 made by Victor Trumper at Adelaide in 1910.

Bradman's Test average is now 100.

At the lunch interval to-day Australia were 446 for 9.

Australia's innings terminated for 450, Oldfield being unbeaten at 56.

South Africa lost Curnow at 25 and at the tea interval had scored 42 for 1.

## GROUND TOO SMALL.

### CROWD BREAKS BOUNDS.

The tremendous crowd at the Test on Saturday proved far too big for the ground after lunch. The spectators seated around the pickets in the outer were pushed against the fence by the thousands behind, and in desperation they began knocking out the palings of the fence with empty bottles and their bare fists. In a twinkling small gaps appeared on both sides of the ground. Emboldened by their success, more palings were knocked off, and the appearance of a groundsman only created a target for orange peels and other rubbish. Armed with a hammer, he endeavoured to repair some of the damage, but the crowd spirited away the loose palings. As soon as he turned his back there was an orgy of destruction, quelled only by the belated appearance of a policeman.

# New South Wales v South Africa

<u>NEW SOUTH WALES v SOUTH AFRICANS</u>, at Sydney, 7 and 8 December 1931.

| | | |
|---|---|---|
| New South Wales | - First Innings | 500 |
| | - Second Innings | - |
| South Africans | - First Innings | 185 for 1 wicket |
| | - Second Innings | - |
| | Drawn. | |
| <u>DON BRADMAN</u> | - c. S.H. Curnow  b. Q. McMillan | 219 |

DON BRADMAN was again in brilliant form and gave no chance in making his second successive double-century against the Tourists. He made 50 in sixty-six minutes, 100 in two hours seven minutes, 200 in three hours thirty-four minutes, and altogether batted for six minutes under four hours for his 219, the highest score for New South Wales v. the South Africans. The score was 348 for 7 when he was out; he hit fifteen fours.

**NEW SOUTH WALES.—First Innings**

| | |
|---|---|
| J. H. FINGLETON, lbw, b Morkel.... | 2 |
| O. W. BILL, c Morkel, b Bell ... ... | 10 |
| D. G. BRADMAN, c Curnow, b Mc-Millan | 219 |
| S. J. McCABE, c Christy, b Bell .... | 28 |
| A. MARKS, c Cameron, b Bell ...... | 6 |
| C. SOLOMON, st Cameron, b McMillan ... .... .... .... .... ... .... | 11 |
| W. A. OLDFIELD, c Mitchell, b McMillan ... .... .... ... .... ... | 29 |
| W. HUNT, c Curnow, b McMillan... | 45 |
| S. HIRD, c Cameron, b McMillan.... | 101 |
| G. AMOS, st Cameron, b McMillan.... | 24 |
| H. THEAK, not out .... .... .... ... | 10 |
| Byes 13, l.b. 2 .... .... .... .... | 15 |
| | |
| Total  .... .... .... .... .... ... | 500 |

Fall: 8, 14, 102, 116, 159, 258, 348, 436, 485, 500.

| | | | | | | | | |
|---|---|---|---|---|---|---|---|---|
| Bell | 26 | 2 | 107 | 3 | Quinn | 20 | 1 | 105 0 |
| Morkel | 8 | 0 | 33 | 1 | McMil'n | 23.4 | 0 | 189 6 |
| Vincent | 11 | 0 | 51 | 0 | | | | |

**SOUTH AFRICA—First Innings**

| | |
|---|---|
| J. A. CHRISTY, c Hunt, b Theak .... | 27 |
| S. CURNOW, not out .... ... ... ... | 81 |
| D. MORKEL, not out .... .... ... | 70 |
| Sundries .... .... .... .... ... .... | 7 |
| | |
| One wicket for  .. .... .... .... | 185 |

Bowling: Amos 0-31, Theak 1-54, McCabe 0-27, Hunt 0-29, Hird 0-30, Bradman 0-7.

D. G. Bradman, who made 219 in the first innings for N.S.W. at the Cricket Ground yesterday, steps out to off-drive the slow bowler, Q. McMillan.

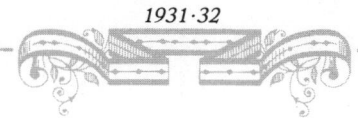

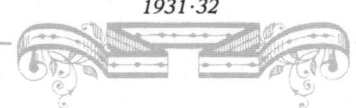

# Australia v South Africa
## Second Test Match

AUSTRALIA v SOUTH AFRICA, Second Test Match, at Sydney, 18, 19 and 21 December 1931.

| | | |
|---|---|---|
| Australia | - First Innings | 469 |
| | - Second Innings | - |
| South Africa | - First Innings | 153 |
| | - Second Innings | 161 |

Australia won by an innings and 155 runs.

DON BRADMAN - c. K.J. Viljoen  b. D.P.B. Morkel    112

DON BRADMAN went in just before lunch on the second day and continued in magnificent form.    At lunch he was 11 not out;  he reached 50 in eighty-five minutes, was 90 not out at the tea interval and reached 100 in two hours twenty-seven minutes, being finally caught in the deep.    He batted for two hours thirty-five minutes and hit ten fours.

Up till then Bradman was the only batsman to score four or more centuries in successive innings off a Touring team's bowling.

## AUSTRALIA LOSES TOSS AND WINS SECOND TEST

*Sydney Cricket Ground, December 18, 19, 21, 1931.  H. B. Cameron won the toss from W. M. Woodfull.  Australia won by an innings and 155 runs.*

### SOUTH AFRICA—First Innings

| | |
|---|---|
| J. A. J. CHRISTY, c Nitschke, b Grimmett | 14 |
| B. MITCHELL, b McCabe | 1 |
| D. P. B. MORKEL, st Oldfield, b Grimmett | 20 |
| H. B. CAMERON, b Wall | 11 |
| H. W. TAYLOR, c Lee, b Grimmett | 7 |
| K. C. VILJOEN, b Ironmonger | 37 |
| E. L. DALTON, b Grimmett | 21 |
| C. L. VINCENT, not out | 31 |
| L. S. BROWN, b McCabe | 2 |
| N. A. QUINN, lbw., b McCabe | 5 |
| A. J. BELL, b McCabe | 0 |
| Leg-byes 3, wide 1 | 4 |
| **Total** | **153** |

Fall: 6, 31, 36, 54, 62, 91, 136, 143, 153, 153.

Wall .. .. 18  3 46 1  Ironm'ger 12  1 38 1
McCabe .. 12  5 13 4  Lee .. .. 7  1 24 0
Grimmett 24 12 28 4
Wall 1 wide.

### SECOND INNINGS

| | |
|---|---|
| J. A. J. CHRISTY, c Woodfull, b Ironmonger | 41 |
| B. MITCHELL, c Oldfield, b Wall | 24 |
| D. P B. MORKEL, lbw., by Grimmett | 17 |
| H. B. CAMERON, b Wall | 0 |
| H. TAYLOR, c Grimmett, b Ironmonger | 6 |
| K. VILJOEN, b Grimmett | 0 |
| E. L. DALTON, c Bradman, b Ironmonger | 14 |
| C. L. VINCENT, c Ponsford, b Grimmett | 35 |
| L. S. BROWN, c Wall, b Lee | 8 |
| N. A. QUINN, st Oldfield, b Grimmett | 1 |
| A. P. BELL, not out | 1 |
| Byes 5. leg-byes 8, no-ball 1 | 14 |
| **Total** | **161** |

Fall: 70, 80, 89, 100, 100, 100, 122, 144, 160, and 161.
Grimmett 20.3 9 44 4  Iron'ger   19 10 22 3
Wall .. 18  5 31 2  Lee .. .. 13  4 25 1
McCabe .. 3  0 25 0
Umpires: G. Hele and G. Borwick.

### AUSTRALIA.—First Innings

| | |
|---|---|
| W. H. PONSFORD, b Quinn | 5 |
| W. M. WOODFULL, c Mitchell, b Vincent | 58 |
| K. E. RIGG, b Bell | 127 |
| D. G. BRADMAN, c Viljoen, b Morkel | 112 |
| S. J. McCABE, c Christy, b Vincent | 79 |
| H. C. NITSCHKE, b Bell | 47 |
| K. LEE, c Cameron, b Brown | 0 |
| W. A. OLDFIELD, c Cameron, b Bell | 8 |
| C. V. GRIMMETT, not out | 9 |
| T. WALL, c Morkel, b Bell | 6 |
| H. IRONMONGER, c Cameron, b Bell | 0 |
| Byes 5, leg-byes 12, wide 1 | 18 |
| **Total** | **469** |

Fall: 6, 143, 254, 317, 432, 433, 444, 457, 467, 469.
Bell .. 46.5  6  110 5  Vincent 34  5 75 2
Morkel 12  2  33 1  Brown 29  3 100 1
Quinn 42 10  95 1  Mitchell 1  0  8 0
Brown, a wide.

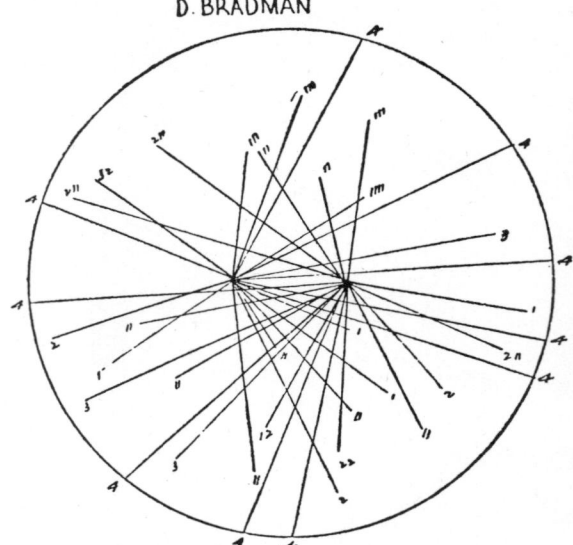

## D. BRADMAN

*The diagram shows that 76 runs were made by Bradman to the on-side, and only 36 on the off-side.  Behind the wicket on the off-side he made only six runs, and three of these were practically square.  ·His ten boundary hits consisted of two past mid-off, two past mid-on or the bowler, five between square leg and extra long on, and one to fine leg on the glance.  Only 24 runs were made by him behind the wicket.  If there is a moral in his stroke-placing it is that he favors in-front-of-the-wicket strokes on both sides, with a good preference to on-side shots.*

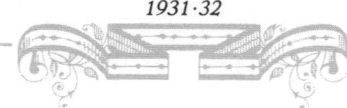

# Australia v South Africa
# Third Test Match

AUSTRALIA v SOUTH AFRICA, Third Test Match, at Melbourne, 31 December 1931, 1, 2, 4, 5 and 6 January 1932.

| Australia | - First Innings | 198 |
| | - Second Innings | 554 |
| South Africa | - First Innings | 358 |
| | - Second Innings | 225 |

Australia won by 169 runs, and won the rubber.

| DON BRADMAN | - c. H.B. Cameron b. N.A. Quinn | 2 |
| | - l.b.w. b. C.L. Vincent | 167 |

Going in at 11 for 1 on the first morning, on a perfect wicket, DON BRADMAN took ten minutes to open his score, and after another four minutes was caught at the wicket, at 16 for 2.

In the second innings, Bradman went in just after tea, at 54 for 1, and promptly attacked and mastered the bowling, driving and pulling in his most brilliant form. He reached 50 in sixty-four minutes, and when stumps were drawn thirty-four minutes later, he was 97 not out. He drove the first ball of the next day for 3, to complete his third century of the series. He was out at 328 for 2, just before lunch; he hit eighteen fours.

His partnership of 274 with W.M. Woodfull for the second wicket was the highest second-wicket stand in all Test cricket.

## THIRD TEST MATCH
At Melbourne C.G., December 31, January 1, 2, 4, 5, 1932.

### AUSTRALIA—First Innings
| | | |
|---|---|---|
| W. M. WOODFULL, c Cameron, b Bell | | 7 |
| W. H. PONSFORD, b Bell | | 7 |
| D. G. BRADMAN, c Cameron, b Quinn | | 2 |
| A. F. KIPPAX, c Bell, b Quinn | | 52 |
| S. J. McCABE, c Morkel, b Bell | | 22 |
| K. E. RIGG, c Mitchell, b Bell | | 68 |
| E. L. a'BECKETT, c Mitchell, b Quinn | | 6 |
| W. A. OLDFIELD, c Vincent, b Quinn | | 0 |
| C. V. GRIMMETT, c Morkel, b Bell | | 9 |
| T. M. WALL, not out | | 6 |
| H. IRONMONGER, run out | | 12 |
| B. 1, l.b. 4, w. 1, n.b. 1 | | 7 |
| **Total** | | **198** |

Fall: 11, 16, 25, 71, 135, 143, 143, 173, 179, 198.

| | | | | | | | | | |
|---|---|---|---|---|---|---|---|---|---|
| Bell | 26.1 | 9 | 69 | 5 | Vincent | 12 | 0 | 32 | 0 |
| Quinn | 31 | 13 | 42 | 4 | McMillan | 2 | 0 | 22 | 0 |
| Morkel | 3 | 0 | 12 | 0 | Christy | 3 | 0 | 14 | 0 |

Morkel 1 wide and Bell 1 n.b.

### Second Innings
| | | |
|---|---|---|
| W. M. WOODFULL, c Mitchell, b McMillan | | 161 |
| W. H. PONSFORD, c Mitchell, b Bell | | 34 |
| D. G. BRADMAN, lbw, b Vincent | | 167 |
| A. F. KIPPAX, c Curnow, b McMillan | | 67 |
| S. J. McCABE, c Mitchell, b McMillan | | 71 |
| K. E. RIGG, c Mitchell, b Vincent | | 1 |
| E. L. a'BECKETT, b Vincent | | 4 |
| W. A. OLDFIELD, lbw, b McMillan | | 0 |
| C. V. GRIMMETT, not out | | 16 |
| T. WALL, b Vincent | | 12 |
| H. IRONMONGER, b Quinn | | 0 |
| Byes 17, leg-byes 3, no-ball 1 | | 21 |
| **Total** | | **554** |

Fall: 54, 328, 408, 519, 521, 521, 524, 530, 550, 554.

| | | | | | | | | | |
|---|---|---|---|---|---|---|---|---|---|
| Quinn | 36.4 | 6 | 113 | 1 | McMillan | 33 | 3 | 150 | 3 |
| Bell | 36 | 6 | 101 | 1 | Morkel | 4 | 0 | 15 | 0 |
| Vincent | 55 | 17 | 154 | 4 | | | | | |

Bell 1 no-ball.

### SOUTH AFRICA—First Innings
| | | |
|---|---|---|
| B. MITCHELL, c McCabe, b Wall | | 17 |
| S. H. CURNOW, b Grimmett | | 47 |
| J. A. J. CHRISTY, c McCabe, b Ironmonger | | 16 |
| H. W. TYLOR, lbw, b Grimmett | | 11 |
| D. P. B. MORKEL, lbw, b Ironmonger | | 33 |
| H. B. CAMERON, st Oldfield, b Ironmonger | | 39 |
| K. VILJOEN, c Wall, b McCabe | | 111 |
| C. L. VINCENT, c Oldfield, b Wall | | 16 |
| Q. McMILLAN, c Oldfield, b Wall | | 29 |
| N. A. QUINN, b McCabe | | 11 |
| A. J. BELL, not out | | 10 |
| Byes 3, leg-byes 13, no-balls 2 | | 18 |
| **Total** | | **358** |

Fall: 39, 79, 89, 108, 163, 183, 225, 329, 333, 358.

| | | | | | | | | | |
|---|---|---|---|---|---|---|---|---|---|
| Wall | 37 | 5 | 98 | 3 | a'Beck't | 18 | 5 | 29 | 0 |
| Iron'ger | 49 | 26 | 72 | 3 | McCabe | 21.3 | 4 | 41 | 2 |
| Grim'ett | 62 | 23 | 100 | 2 | | | | | |

AUSTRALIA.—First Innings, 198.
Second Innings, 554.

SOUTH AFRICA.—First Innings, 358.
### Second Innings.
| | | |
|---|---|---|
| S. H. Curnow, b Grimmett | | 9 |
| B. Mitchell, c and b Grimmett | | 46 |
| J. A. J. Christy, c Oldfield, b Ironmonger | | 63 |
| H. W. Taylor, b Grimmett | | 38 |
| D. P. B. Morkel, b Ironmonger | | 4 |
| H. B. Cameron, lbw, b Ironmonger | | 13 |
| K. C. Viljoen, b Ironmonger | | 2 |
| C. L. Vincent, c Ponsford, b Grimmett | | 34 |
| Q. McMillan, c Wall, b Grimmett | | 1 |
| N. A. Quinn, not out | | 0 |
| A. J. Bell, b Grimmett | | 0 |
| Byes 8, leg-byes 6, no-ball 1 | | 15 |
| **Total** | | **225** |

Fall of wickets: 18, 120, 133, 138, 178, 186, 188, 208, 225, 225.

BATTALIONS OF CARS were marshalled in the park outside the M.C.G. during the Test cricket match on Saturday—an eloquent testimony to the popularity of the game.

H. B. Cameron, South Africa's Captain who brilliantly caught Bradman for 2 off N. A. Quinn in the first innings.

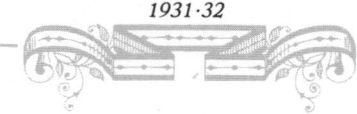

# BEST KNOCK OF CAREER

## AFRICANS Amazed AT DON'S Great MASTERY

BRADMAN, THE MAGICIAN

## WOODFULL Drove HARD AND Played SUPERBLY

## Visitors Want Quick Wickets

### (From Our Special Representative)

**MELBOURNE, Sunday.—Unless the South Africans can get a couple of quick wickets to-morrow, their Test chances are well-nigh hopeless.**

**Bradman on Saturday played one of the greatest knocks of his career, and Woodfull was as solid as a rock.**

IF Bradman and Woodfull bat in the same form as on Saturday afternoon runs will be common.

They played superbly, Bradman being particularly brilliant and, in fact, played what is generally conceded to be the greatest cricket of his career.

When he went to the wickets after Ponsford's dismissal it was evident that he was in his most dashing mood. He pranced about the pitch at the bowler's end, eager to get into action, and before long he was there with his flashing bat, driving and pulling with extraordinary power, until he had the crowd marvelling at the extraordinary manner in which he treated length bowling.

Any bowler in the world would have been easy for Bradman on that wicket, and as one of the Australians remarked after the game, "Thank goodness he is on our side."

### Worth Seeing

The South Africans could talk of nothing else. They were amazed at the skill of the champion, and even though he may have ruined their chance of winning the Test, they are delighted at having seen Bradman in such a remarkable innings.

It is something they are never likely to forget, and will give them food for discussion whenever a brilliant innings is played.

In common with others, I had believed that Bradman had reached his peak, but now I am convinced he is still improving.

Woodfull played one of his best knocks, and although he had only two fours in his score, he drove with great power, and exploited the covers more than ever before. The boundaries are long in Melbourne, and on any other ground Woodfull would have had many more runs to his credit.

He and Bradman will make a fresh start to-morrow, with the Australian score 46 ahead of that of South Africa, with the loss of one wicket.

That position, from an Australian point of view, is really good, for the wicket is still in perfect condition, and there is not the slightest indication of rain.

But South Africa needs another quick wicket to make a win possible, for even then, with Kippax, Rigg and McCabe all in century-making form, they have some formidable obstacles to overcome.

The "ups and downs" of this match have been extraordinary, and every player is enjoying the game thoroughly.

There is promise of many more thrills before the Test ends, and there is plenty to attract another big crowd to-morrow.

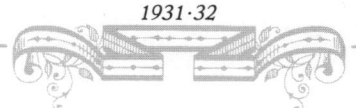

# EXCITED CROWD

## BRADMAN WAS MAGNET

**(From Arthur Mailey)**

MELBOURNE, Monday.

Bradman, magnet to draw the crowd to any game in which he plays, was said to be responsible for the excited clamoring of the huge gathering of enthusiasts outside the Melbourne Cricket Ground to-day. Test veterans said they had never seen its like.

Melbourne people had heard about Bradman, but the champion had not given of his best in previous games here, and to-day they poured in to see this amazing fellow they had read so much about. It became apparent when Bradman walked to the wickets on Saturday that he was still mentally winking under his first innings failure.

Thanks to Ponsford, who was, because of his recent failures in a similar frame of mind, and Woodfull, Bradman found the stage set to his liking. The Victorian opening pair had knocked the newness off the ball, the wicket was one of the easiest ever seen on the M.C.G., and the score stood at 54 for one wicket. Then the storm broke on the Africanders. In less than 100 minutes, 150 odd runs had been scored and this morning the Australians went to the wickets with the deficit knocked off.

Bradman with an admirer, "Curly" Jones.

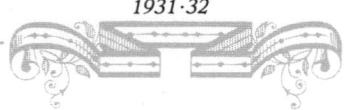

# New South Wales v Victoria

NEW SOUTH WALES v VICTORIA, at Sydney, 22, 23, 25 and 26 January 1932.

| New South Wales | - First Innings | 348 |
| | - Second Innings | 389 for 4 wickets dec. |
| Victoria | - First Innings | 204 |
| | - Second Innings | 294 |

New South Wales won by 239 runs.

| DON BRADMAN | - c. S.A. Smith b. H. Ironmonger | 23 |
| | - b. L.E. Nagel | 167 |

In the first innings, DON BRADMAN went in at 72 for 1, just before lunch on the first day; he batted for forty-nine minutes, before being caught at short-leg at 119 for 3.

In the second innings, going in at 28 for 1, early on the third morning, he took thirty-seven minutes to reach double figures, and one and a half hours to get to 50. After lunch, he reached his century in two hours forty-six minutes. Soon after tea, his leg stump was up-rooted when he was going for another big hit; he batted for three hours forty-four minutes and hit twenty-two fours. He completed 1,000 runs for the season when 86, in his tenth innings.

BRADMAN, shaping like some irresponsible youth, had made 6 and Fingleton 40 and it was 1 for 80 at luncheon. Don did not look to be stopping there. He was making risky shots without the usual care, and not timing these. Once, in trying to pull McCormick he hit the ball into his pads and another with the end of the bat into the pitch. Fingleton was cramped against the faster bowlers and leg-theorists, but relished Ironmonger whom he drove with glee between mid-off and cover for three fours. The bowlers had their tactics and stuck to them, and the fielding was very fine, that of Oakley on the off and Smith brilliant at on.

BRADMAN and Fingleton re-appeared wearing broad-brimmed white hats; some of the Victorians did so too. But a'Beckett bowled bare-headed, though young as he is he has no thick growth on the roof to keep off fierce rays of the sun. The hats brought luck to the bowlers.

* * *

FIRST ball after luncheon was delivered by Nagel from the pavilion end. It was a trifle off the wicket and Fingleton trying the cut was snapped up by a'Beckett at first slip. Batting an hour and three-quarters for 40 the Waverley man shaped best against Ironmonger off whom he forced every run possible. But he failed to apply the power to any rare ones that were pitched up from a'Beckett or the men of pace.

* * *

THOUGH shaping better since luncheon Bradman was a relaxed irresponsible Don for a change. Just as one sensed that he was emerging from the light-and-airy role into that of the champion he stepped back to one from Ironmonger a little short of good length. This footwork made the ball shorter and then a sharp, wristy, perfectly-timed pull with the ball travelling about three feet from the ground looked a boundary. It was in front of the umpire. But Smith was there and he snapped up the catch with the confident air of a man who knows how to time the hottest shots.

### N.S.W.—First Innings.

| | | |
|---|---|---:|
| J. H. FINGLETON, c a'Beckett, b Nagel | | 40 |
| W. BILL, c Barnett, b McCormick | | 27 |
| D. G. BRADMAN, c Smith, b Ironmonger | | 23 |
| S. J. McCABE, b Barnett, b Ironmonger | | 106 |
| R. NUTT, c Darling, b a'Beckett | | 15 |
| S. HIRD, b Barnett, b McCormick | | 23 |
| A. F. KIPPAX, c and b Darling | | 36 |
| W. A. OLDFIELD, c Oakley, b Darling | | 2 |
| W. HUNT, c Darling, b Ironmonger | | 0 |
| W. J. O'REILLY, not out | | 26 |
| H. THEAK, run out | | 17 |
| B. 16, l.b. 11, w. 5, n.b. 1 | | 33 |
| **Total** | | **348** |

Fall: 72, 80, 119, 174, 238, 274, 291, 296, 302, 348.

McCormick 15.2 4 42 2, I'monger 20 2 94 3, Smith 5 0 33 0, a'Beckett 15 3 44 1, Darling 9 0 39 2, Nagel 14 1 63 1

McCormick and Darling each 2 w., and Nagel 1. Nagel 1 n.b.

### VICTORIA.—First Innings.

| | | |
|---|---|---:|
| J. THOMAS, lbw, b McCabe | | 19 |
| L. DARLING, lbw, b McCabe | | 5 |
| L. P. O'BRIEN, c Oldfield, b Theak | | 38 |
| J. RYDER, b McCabe | | 20 |
| H. OAKLEY, b O'Reilly | | 48 |
| E. L. a'BECKETT, b O'Reilly | | 3 |
| L. BARNETT, b O'Reilly | | 4 |
| L. NAGEL, lbw, b McCabe | | 30 |
| S. SMITH, c Bradman, b Hird | | 16 |
| E. L. McCORMICK, c McCabe, b Hird | | 8 |
| H. IRONMONGER, not out | | 3 |
| B. 6, l.b. 3, n.b. 1 | | 10 |
| **Total** | | **204** |

Fall: 28, 37, 82, 88, 103, 113, 170, 172, 200, 204.

Theak 13 1 39 2, Hunt 10 3 15 0, McCabe 18 4 57 3, Hird 6.6 0 25 2, O'Reilly 21 6 52 3, Bradman 1 0 6 0

### NEW SOUTH WALES.—First Innings

| | | |
|---|---|---:|
| O. W. BILL, lbw, b McCormick | | 15 |
| J. FINGLETON, lbw, b Smith | | 40 |
| D. G. BRADMAN, b Nagel | | 167 |
| A. F. KIPPAX, c Barnett, b McCormick | | 44 |
| S. J. McCABE, not out | | 103 |
| R. NUTT, not out | | 8 |
| B. 3, l.b. 3, w. 2, n.b. 2 | | 12 |
| **Four wickets (closed) for** | | **389** |

Fall: 28, 106, 216, 303.

McC'm'k 13 0 54 2, Smith 14 1 100 1, a'Beckett 13.3 0 68 0, Darling 3 0 34 0, I'monger 17 4 52 0, Ryder 4 0 12 0, Nagel 12 1 57 1

### VICTORIA.—Second Innings

| | | |
|---|---|---:|
| J. THOMAS, st Oldfield, b Hunt | | 70 |
| L. P. O'BRIEN, c Kippax, b Hunt | | 34 |
| L. DARLING, lbw. b Hird | | 23 |
| J. RYDER, run out | | 13 |
| H. OAKLEY, not out | | 93 |
| E. L. a'BECKETT, c Fingleton, b Theak | | 14 |
| L. BARNETT, c and b Theak | | 3 |
| L. NAGEL, b Hird | | 10 |
| J. SMITH, c Nutt, b O'Reilly | | 7 |
| E. L. McCORMICK, c Hird, b McCabe | | 16 |
| H. IRONMONGER, c McCabe, b Bradman | | 1 |
| Sundries | | 10 |
| **Total** | | **294** |

BOWLING: Theak 2-64, McCabe 1-18, O'Reilly 1-73, Hunt 2-67, Hird 2-58, Bradman 1-4.

N.S.W. won outright.

Fall of wickets: 93, 114, 131, 149, 202, 218, 235, 248, 294.

Poster announcing Don Bradman's decision in 1931 not to play in the Lancashire League, but to remain in Australia.

Brockton Point Cricket Ground, Vancouver, Canada, 1975.

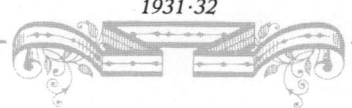

# Australia v South Africa
## Fourth Test Match

AUSTRALIA v SOUTH AFRICA, Fourth Test Match, at Adelaide, 29, 30 January, 1 and 2 February 1932.

| Australia | - First Innings | 513 |
| | - Second Innings | 73 for no wicket |
| South Africa | - First Innings | 308 |
| | - Second Innings | 274 |

Australia won by 10 wickets.

| DON BRADMAN | - n.o. | 299 |
| | - (did not bat). | |

DON BRADMAN continued his overpowering mastery over the South African bowlers with another magnificent innings. Going in at 9 for 1, ten minutes before lunch on the second day, he scored 2 before the interval. Afterwards, he reached 50 in sixty-two minutes; 84 not out at tea, completing his fourth century of the series in two hours thirteen minutes. After being in for only three hours twenty-four minutes he was 170 not out at the close of play. When he had scored 109, he completed 1,000 runs for the season (including six centuries) off the South African bowling alone. Next morning he took eighty minutes to make the 30 he needed for his double-century off the Tourists' bowling. At the end of the innings Bradman was 299 not out. He batted for six hours thirty-six minutes and hit twenty-three fours. His 299 was the highest score ever made in any Test Match in Australia. This was the ninth double-century he had scored in Australia and his stand of 78 with W.J. O'Reilly was the highest ninth-wicket partnership in any Test Match v. South Africa. His last two Test innings thus totalled 466, a record.

---

### AUSTRALIA v SOUTH AFRICA
Fourth Test match at Adelaide, January 29, 30, February 1 and 2, 1932.

**SOUTH AFRICA—First Innings**

| | |
|---|---|
| S. H. CURNOW, c Ponsford, b Grimmett | 20 |
| B. MITCHELL, c and b McCabe | 75 |
| J. A. J. CHRISTY, b O'Reilly | 7 |
| H. W. TAYLOR, c Rigg, b Grimmett | 78 |
| H. B. CAMERON, lbw. b Grimmett | 52 |
| D. P. B. MORKEL, c and b Grimmett | 0 |
| K. S. VILJOEN, c and b Grimmett | 0 |
| C. L. VINCENT, not out | 48 |
| Q. McMILLAN, b Grimmett | 19 |
| N. A. QUINN, c Ponsford, b Grimmett | 1 |
| A. J. BELL, lbw, b O'Reilly | 2 |
| Sundries | 6 |
| **Total** | **308** |

Fall: 27, 45, 165, 202, 204, 204, 243, 286, 300, 308.

| | | | | | |
|---|---|---|---|---|---|
| Thurlow | 27 | 6 | 53 | 0 | Hunt 10 1 25 0 |
| McCabe | 17.6 | 6 | 34 | 1 | Grim'ett 47 11 116 7 |
| O'Reilly | 39.4 | 10 | 74 | 2 | |

O'Reilly 4 no-balls.

**AUSTRALIA—First Innings**

| | |
|---|---|
| W. M. WOODFULL, c Morkel, b Bell | 82 |
| W. H. PONSFORD, b Quinn | 5 |
| D. G. BRADMAN, not out | 299 |
| A. F. KIPPAX, run out | 0 |
| S. J. McCABE, c Vincent, b Bell | 2 |
| K. E. RIGG, c Taylor, b Bell | 35 |
| W. A. OLDFIELD, lbw, b Vincent | 23 |
| C. V. GRIMMETT, b Bell | 21 |
| W. HUNT, c Vincent, b Quinn | 0 |
| W. J. O'REILLY, b Bell | 23 |
| H. M. THURLOW, run out | 0 |
| Sundries | 23 |
| **Total** | **513** |

| | | | | | |
|---|---|---|---|---|---|
| Bell | 40 | 2 | 142 | 5 | McMillan 9 0 53 0 |
| Quinn | 37 | 5 | 114 | 2 | Morkel 18 1 71 0 |
| Vincent | 34 | 5 | 110 | 1 | |

Umpires: G. Hele and G. Borwick.

**Second Innings**

| | |
|---|---|
| B. MITCHELL, c O'Reilly, b Grimmett | 95 |
| S. H. CURNOW, b McCabe | 3 |
| J. A. J. CHRISTY, b Grimmett | 51 |
| H. W. TAYLOR, b O'Reilly | 84 |
| H. B. CAMERON, b O'Reilly | 4 |
| C. L. VINCENT, b Grimmett | 5 |
| K. VILJOEN, b Grimmett | 1 |
| D. P. MORKEL, b Grimmett | 15 |
| Q. McMILLAN, c Hunt, b Grimmett | 3 |
| N. A. QUINN, b Grimmett | 1 |
| A. J. BELL, not out | 0 |
| Sundries | 12 |
| **Total** | **274** |

Fall: 22, 103, 224, 232, 240, 246, 262, 268, 274, 274.

| | | | | | |
|---|---|---|---|---|---|
| Thurlow | 12 | 1 | 33 | 0 | Grimmett 49 17 83 7 |
| McCabe | 14 | 1 | 51 | 1 | Hunt 6 1 14 0 |
| O'Reilly | 42 | 13 | 81 | 2 | |

**AUSTRALIA.—First Innings, 513**

**Second Innings**

| | |
|---|---|
| W. M. WOODFULL, not out | 37 |
| W. H. PONSFORD, not out | 27 |
| Sundries | 9 |
| No wickets for | 73 |

| | | | | | |
|---|---|---|---|---|---|
| Quinn | 3 | 0 | 5 | 0 | McMillan 7 0 23 0 |
| Morkel | 2 | 0 | 5 | 0 | Vincent 7 0 31 0 |

Umpires: G. Hele and G. Borwick.

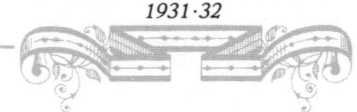

# BRADMAN'S NEW RECORDS AGAINST AFRICA

## Eclipses All Scores With 299, and Australia Leads by 205

**Adelaide Oval enthusiasts found the weather holding up splendidly on Monday when 15,000 saw Don Bradman hold the fort throughout the innings and carry his bat out for 299. As in the case of Kippax when Bradman was 199, so Thurlow, when Bradman was 299, was run out trying to make the desired single.**

**Bradman has the crowds and cricketers beaten. They know he is a prodigy. But every big innings he plays astonishes them afresh. He is invincibly the Lindrum of cricket. On the first three days 55,400 people paid £3890.**

WITH the exception of Woodfull, Bradman in this match has had his fellow batsmen eclipsed. This continued on Monday when he resumed with Rigg against the reinvigorated South African bowlers.

Rigg's 35 was painstaking, but there was nothing attractive about it. He made several good drives past mid-on, but lost his wicket at 327 to a very poor stroke, being caught by Taylor at cover in attempting to cut a half-pitched ball from Bell, who was nevertheless bowling splendidly and without luck.

[In what may be termed his first Test series Rigg has batted quite admirably, to make 127, 68, 1, and 35. He may be expected to let his rungetting strokes and power flow a little more buoyantly in future now that he has had his Test match salting.—"Not Out."]

Oldfield made several fine drags off Vincent and Quinn in compiling 23, but lost his wicket l.b.w. to Vincent in attempting to force him to the on-side.

Bradman received a tremendous ovation from a crowd of about fifteen thousand on reaching his double century, which occupied 4 hours 44 minutes.

His last fifty took an hour and 35 minutes. His batting before lunch was in sharp contrast to that of Saturday. He did not appear to time the ball well, and it was only during the latter portion of his second hundred that he was making the strokes with his customary magnificent execution. He was badly missed at fine slip by Mitchell off Bell when 185, and for a brief period the African bowler was on top of both Bradman and Oldfield. He should have secured the 'keeper's wicket as well as Bradman's; it was really a hard piece of luck for the visitors, who were sticking to their work with great vim.

Honors were fairly even before noon the bowlers having as much to say as the batsmen, with the luck of the game in the batsmen's favor. At lunch time the Australians had reached 389 for 5 wickets.

Bradman continued in a happier mood after lunch. He now made his runs in his best form and there was tremendous excitement on the ground as the champion approached the 300 mark with Grimmett playing well for 21, O'Reilly batting ably for 23, and Thurlow assisting. However, it was not to be as in a similar case to that of Kippax, a runout closed the innings, Thurlow being the victim, when the record-breaker was without one of the coveted goal.

Bradman batted for 6 hours 36 minutes for his 299, and hit 23 boundaries. The whole innings lasted 6 hours 53 minutes.

[Bradman's 299 is this third double century against the South Africans, the others being 226 in the first Test and 219 in the return match with New South Wales. He has not only made a century in each of the four Tests but one in every match against the South Africans. His aggregate of 806 is the greatest on record in a South African series. He has, moreover, equalled the phenomenal effort by W. R. Hammond for the last English team against Australia when the Gloucestershire man made 251, 200, 32, 119 not out, and 177 in successive innings in the second, third, and fourth Tests. The memory of these innings no doubt inspires the prophecies of P. F. Warner and A. E. R. Gilligan that England will defeat Australia next season.—"Not out."]

The South Africans deserved a lot of priase for the vim they put into their work in the field, patricularly as the luck was favoring the batsmen. Bell bowled magnificently to-day and if he had had the least bit of luck would have secured the wickets of Bradman and Oldfield. The fast bowler mixed his pace splendidly and occasionally got in a very fast rising ball. Quinn also bowled well and for several overs worried Bradman considerably, keeping him entirely on the defensive.

[A. P. Bell came out of the ordeal with honors of the ball. His 5 for 142, with chances missed, and handicapped by a sore heel, coming in the wake of 3 for 120, 5 for 140, 5 for 69, and 1 for 101, attest his gameness. Bell has bowled grandly. If any English bowler of pace next season be as good the Tests will provide stirring fighting cricket.—"Not Out."]

The fielding all-round was sound, though it lacked the all-round speed of the Australians. Cameron made his bowling changes well, but a lot of runs were given away by the offside field being far too deep, particularly when slow bowler McMillan was operating, singles being made comfortably.

South Africa lost Curnow early in the second innings, being bowled by McCabe. The batting effort of Christy and Mitchell looked like giving the visitors a rough fighting chance, though when he was well set Grimmett bowled Christy for 51. It was 2 for 124 at the end. Mitchell 54 not out and Taylor 11 not out.

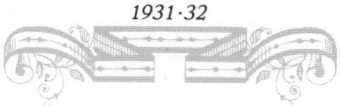
On the Sunday of the fourth Test, Don Bradman relaxed with friends at tennis.
Davis Cup player Don Turnbull is on the right.

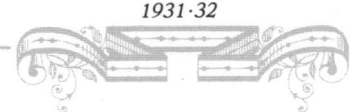

# Australia v South Africa
## Fifth Test Match

AUSTRALIA v SOUTH AFRICA, Fifth Test Match, at Melbourne, 12 and 15 February 1932.

DON BRADMAN strained a ligament in his ankle as a result of a fall in the dressing-room just before the Australians took the field, and apart from fielding on the second day during the South Africans' second innings, took no part in the match.

**THE THRILL** of his young lifetime. A handshake with Don Bradman! The famous batsman appeared to enjoy the daring of this young "fan" who approached him while he watched the fifth Test from the pavilion.

## FIFTH TEST MATCH

(Melbourne, February 12, 13 (no play) 14, 1932. H. B. Cameron won toss from W. M. Woodfull. Australia won by an innings and 72, thus winning all five Tests.

### SOUTH AFRICA.—First Innings

| | |
|---|---|
| B. MITCHELL, c Rigg, b McCabe | 2 |
| S. H. CURNOW, c Oldfield, b Nash | 3 |
| J. A. J. CHRISTY, c Grimmett, b Nash | 4 |
| H. W. TAYLOR, c Kippax, b Nash | 0 |
| K. G. VILJOEN, c sub, (Darling), b Ironmonger | 1 |
| H. B. CAMERON, c McCabe, b Nash | 11 |
| D. P. B. MORKEL, c Nash, b Ironmonger | 1 |
| C. L. VINCENT, c Nash, b Ironmonger | 1 |
| Q. McMILLAN, st Oldfield, b Ironmonger | 0 |
| N. A. QUINN, not out | 5 |
| A. J. BELL, st Oldfield, b Ironmonger | 0 |
| Sundries | 8 |
| **Total** | **36** |

Fall: 7, 16. 16, 17, 19, 25, 31, 31, 33, 36.

Nash .. .. 12 6 18 4 McCabe .. 4 1 4 1
Iron'ger 7.2 5 6 5

### Second Innings

| | |
|---|---|
| J. A. J. CHRISTY, c and b Nash | 0 |
| S. H. CURNOW, c Fingleton, b Ironmonger | 16 |
| A. J. BELL, c McCabe, b O'Reilly | 6 |
| B. MITCHELL, c Oldfield, b Ironmonger | 4 |
| H. B. CAMERON, c McCabe, b O'Reilly | 0 |
| D. P. B. MORKEL, c Rigg, b Ironmonger | 0 |
| H. W. TAYLOR, c Bradman, b Ironmonger | 2 |
| K. VILJOEN, c Oldfield, b O'Reilly | 0 |
| C. L. VINCENT, not out | 8 |
| Q. McMILLAN, c Oldfield, b Ironmonger | 0 |
| N. A. QUINN, c Fingleton, b Ironmonger | 5 |
| Byes 3, leg-byes 1 | 4 |
| **Total** | **45** |

Fall: 0, 12, 25, 30, 30, 30, 32, 32, 33, 45.

Nash .. .. 7 4 4 1 Iron'ger 15.3 7 18 6
O'Reilly 9 5 19 3

### AUSTRALIA.—First Innings

| | |
|---|---|
| W. M. WOODFULL, b Bell | 0 |
| J. FINGLETON, c Vincent, b Bell | 40 |
| K. E. RIGG, c Vincent, b Quinn | 22 |
| A. F. KIPPAX, c Curnow, b McMillan | 42 |
| S. J. McCABE, c Cameron, b Bell | 0 |
| L. NASH, b Quinn | 13 |
| W. A. OLDFIELD, c Curnow, b McMillan | 11 |
| C. V. GRIMMETT, c Cameron, b Quinn | 9 |
| W. J. O'REILLY, c Curnow, b McMillan | 13 |
| H. IRONMONGER, not out | 0 |
| D. G. BRADMAN, absent | 0 |
| Sundries | 3 |
| **Total** | **153** |

Fall: 0, 51, 75, 75, 112, 125, 131, 148, 153, 153.

Bell .. .. 16 0 52 3 Quinn .. .. 19.3 4 29 3
Vincent 11 2 40 0 McMillan 8 0 29 3
Umpires: G. Hele and G. Borwick.

## Don Meets His Huge Audience

Don Bradman last night was introduced by 2UE to the large army of admirers who will listen to his broadcasts from this station. From left to right: Mr. J. T. Smith, general-manager of F. J. Palmer and Son, Ltd., Mr. C. V. Stevenson, managing-director of 2UE, Don Bradman, and Uncle Lionel, manager of 2UE.

# BOWLING to BRADMAN

## A Task that Proved Too Much for the Springboks

### By

### A. J. BELL

A. J. Bell, the Springbok fast bowler, had a great many opportunities of studying the great Australian batsman, Bradman. He bowled to Bradman in seven matches, often for an entire day, without once getting his wicket. "Most people in South Africa," he says "seem to be under the impression that Bradman is a great forward player. This is quite erroneous. He is the finest back player any of us have ever seen."

*A. J. Bell—an action study.*

OU never hear the name Bradman in Australia. He is simply, Our Don.

There were thousands of cricketing enthusiasts at the quayside, all of whom greeted us with the usual formula: "Wait till Our Don gets you." In Sydney we were received by the New South Wales Cricket Association and there we met many old friends of South African cricketers, including Jack Gregory, Sam Ryder, Bert Oldfield, Charlie McCartney, and dozens of others. Of course we were most anxious to get a glimpse of Don Bradman.

Imagine our surprise on seeing a tiny fellow in a neat grey suit, and then finding him to be the redoubtable Don Bradman.

Enough has been written about him to fill a book. But off the field he has a remarkable personality, more especially when one considers that four years ago he was a nonentity in the small township of Bowral and now is easily the most magnetic figure in the world of cricket. He is a good conversationalist, obviously out to learn all that he can, and he gives one the impression of being an astute business man. You feel when you talk to him that he is probing you. His eyes are never still. You feel that he will not be satisfied until he knows all about your bowling and your batting. You can see that he makes a close study of cricket and has unusual powers of concentration.

He does not talk about himself to any marked degree. He takes all his amazing performances as a matter of course. He tells you quite candidly that he is determined to better his previous records

Our first encounter with Don was on the Sydney Oval when we played New South Wales for the first time. Neville Quinn had been left out of this game in order to be a surprise packet for the first Test Morkel and I had a few overs at Don, and he did not impress us as anything out of the ordinary. Quentin McMillan and Cyril Vincent then took over the bowling. For about 80 minutes Don put up a very scratchy display, finally ending his innings at ?? caught and bowled by McMillan.

NATURALLY we were all somewhat elated and felt that we more or less had the measure of him. On the last day of the match we declared, leaving New South Wales 450 to get to win. We disposed of Wendill Bill, and Bradman came in. McMillan promptly was given the ball. But this was not the same Bradman. McMillan's first ball was a good length, fast spinner. Don ran about five yards up the pitch and cracked it like a bullet past mid-on to the pickets (the

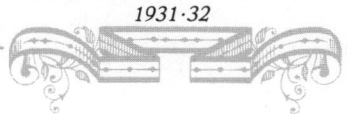

boundary). After this we were entertained to one of the most magnificent exhibitions of footwork any of us had ever seen.

Don never allowed McMillan to pitch the ball anywhere near a decent length, but hit it on the full-toss all the time. This rather changed our views about the little wizard. However, we put our faith in Neville Quinn. He bowled over the wickets in Australia, making the ball do a little either way.

Arriving at Brisbane we soon realised that Don had shown them the way of dealing with McMillan. The story of the first Test match is simply this— Bradman was dropped twice before he had scored 20, and on both occasions off Neville Quinn. In Brisbane Don broke Trumper's record against the 1910 Springboks, giving a magnificent display of forceful hitting.

Most people in South Africa seem to be under the impression that Bradman is a great forward player. This is quite erroneous. He is the finest forcing back player any of us have ever seen. To slow bowling he uses his feet marvellously, placing the ball when and where he likes. Against fast and medium bowling he does not score at quite the same phenomenal rate, but employs entirely different tactics.

One pitches a good length on his leg stump and the ball gathers another coat of paint off the pickets of the fine leg boundary, and one's bowling average increases by another four. If you bowl the ball just short of a length on the off pin he takes great pains over his shot and is content to push it down the gully for a single, or just out of reach of the unfortunate fielder.

We tried for four and a half months to get him caught in the slips by bowling short just outside the off stump. His wonderful placing and command over the ball made life absolutely untenable for gully and point.

WHEN batting Bradman always seems, to the weary bowler at any rate, to assume a sort of cynical grin, which rather reminds one of the Sphinx. We tried to shift that grin; but I think Neville Quinn was the only one of us successful, and that was in the third Test at Melbourne when Cameron caught him for two.

His command of shots is nothing short of marvellous. He seems to know just what kind of ball you are going to bowl and where you are going to bowl it. He makes up his mind in a flash and does not hit the ball to the fielder as a great many do, but places it just out of reach and grins cheerfully.

To bowl to him is heart-breaking. He takes risks but never seems to pay the cost which his temerity deserves. His hook shot is incredible. He steps right back on to the wicket (one does not see much wicket when he is batting) and cracks the ball plumb in the middle of the bat about 99 times out of 100. When he does mistime the ball, and that is very infrequently, the ball does not shoot up into the air and fall into the avaricious wicket-keeper's hands, but drops harmlessly on the ground. This is due to the fact that with every shot he plays he intends the ball to hit the ground just a couple of yards from his feet. In all his shots he seems to turn the wrist over so that on the completion of the stroke the face of his bat is towards the ground.

The remarkable thing about the little wizard is that while fast and medium bowling is fresh he contents himself by never attempting to score in front of the wicket, but glides the ball down the leg side, or hits it like a bullet between point and third man. This last shot of his is, I think, his favourite.

If I ever play against Don Bradman again I think the best thing to do will be to bowl the fast full toss straight for the top of the off-stump. That seems to be the only ball he is content to pat back to the bowler. On second thoughts, however, he probably would work out a counter-offensive and land it up against the pickets in his usual manner!

BRADMAN'S running between the wickets was an eye-opener. I have seen him make nearly 200 runs in one day and at the end of the day seem to the weary bowlers to run faster than when he began at 12 o'clock. He runs for everything. He hits the ball just short of cover-point and runs a quick single. Cover-point comes in and he then places it just out of reach of his left hand. He does this to every fielder in the team.

Consequently, when Don comes in nobody knows where to stand, and they pray fervently either that he'll go out, or that six o'clock will hurry up.

Another remarkable thing about Bradman is that he never seems to perspire. Our bowlers used to get through three or four shirts a day, but Don comes out in an immaculate silk shirt at noon and at six o'clock it is still an immaculate silk shirt.

At Adelaide the temperature was 108 in the shade. Don was in the course of making 299. We were all just about exhausted, but Don—he was as fresh as a new pin. The only sign of his 180 runs was a tiny little damp spot in the middle of his back.

Apart from Don's actual play in the field he is looked upon as a national hero in Australia. He is easily the greatest drawing-card in the cricket world of to-day; probably the greatest of all time. We had an instance of this in the third Test at Melbourne. Don was 97 not out on the previous night.

*"When he is batting Bradman always seems to assume a sort of cynical grin which reminds one of the Sphinx."*

## ALEXANDER BELL

*South African Lion Heart.*

We started the next day at noon. Old players and officials of the Melbourne cricket ground told us that they had never seen such a queue at the members' gate. At the commencement of play there were 32,000 people.

Needless to say Don dispatched the first ball for three, making his 100. If I remember he got 160 odd and lost his wicket just prior to the luncheon adjournment. On the re-opening of play at 1.45 the crowd numbered about 20,000, which goes to prove that 12,000 at least only came to the ground to see Don get his century.

AS regards his fielding I saw both Andrews and Pellew in the Australian side that played in South Africa in 1919 and they were considered to be among the world's best. I think it only fair to say that Bradman outshines any outfield in the world.

His running is phenomenal. If he sees a ball travelling towards the boundary he suddenly starts off after what seems to be a certain four, and to everybody's amazement he stops it with his foot just on the boundary.

He then throws it back in much the same way as "Tupps" Owen-Smith. One of Don's idiosyncrasies is that no matter whether the batsmen are still running or are stationary in their crease he still pelts the ball straight at the wicket. If throwing square to the wicket he hits it from the boundary once in three times.

Our running between the wickets was very bad and to some degree I think Don Bradman was responsible. One never knew how quickly he was capable of disarranging the wickets from a boundary throw.

His ground fielding was exceptionally good; but the Australians who toured England in 1930 aver that he is not a very safe catch. Whether this is so we really never had a chance of observing. As in his batting his judgment of the pace of the ball in the field is wonderful.

HE is the perfect example for the budding cricketer. He neither smokes nor drinks. He keeps reasonably early hours and looks after himself very carefully. He does a course of physical training, and combines it with wrestling. As regards the bogy of golf he seems rather to explode that theory. He is very fond of the game, plays off about eight and wins various competitions. So much for golf affecting the strokes of a batsman!

He plays the piano remarkably well, and plays most tunes he is asked either from ear or music. His only downfall against the South Africans was at a charity meeting when Eric Dalton beat him in a ping-pong match.

To sum up Don is rather a difficult job. He has done enough to make 20 average men swollen-headed. And yet that is the last thing one could accuse him of. He has a queer way of talking about himself. To all appearances he is batting well, and yet he will tell you quite candidly that he never bats well on the day following a big score. We could never detect a flaw in his batting.

HE is one of the most magnetic personalities I have ever met in the course of my cricket career. He speaks with a strong Australian accent. Quite definitely he is an Australian. He is proud of it and Australia is proud of him. Whether he has reached the zenith of his powers cannot be said. But I think Alan Kippax hit the nail on the head when he said to me: "If Don played for the West Indies they would be the leading cricketing country. If he played for New Zealand they would be the leading cricketing country. If he played for England they would be the leading cricketing country. If he played for South Africa they would be the leading cricketing country."

And at that I leave it.

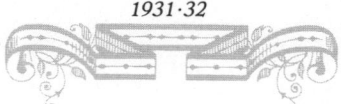

Coaching the youngsters, 1932.

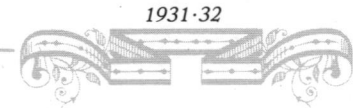

# OUR DON BRADMAN

## The Up-to-the-Minute Song Hit

### A SNAPPY FOX TROT SONG

Written in appreciation of the Match Winning and Record Breaking
Efforts of

*AUSTRALIA'S BATTING PHENOMENON*

Our Don And I ask you is he
Our Don Now I ask you is he

an-y good Our Don
an-y good Our Don

Brad-man As a bats-man he can sure lay on the wood
Brad-man As a bats-man he is cer-tain-ly "Plum Pud"

# *1932*
# *Tour of Canada and the U.S.A.*

This unique tour, organised by Arthur Mailey, was primarily a goodwill visit.

The composite Australian side was captained by Vic Richardson and frequently played against 15 or 18 men under a variety of conditions.

First class cricket is not played in America though the records tell of an era in the early part of the 20th century when cricket was strong in Philadelphia. The Canadian bowler Bart King was, according to his performances in England in 1908, up to world class.

I believe our mission to revive and create interest was successful, though I gravely doubt whether cricket will ever become a major sport in that part of the world.

We were fortunate to participate in a tour largely free of the stresses and strains of a Test tour.

The Brockton Point ground must surely be the prettiest in the world.

There were the thrills of seeing Niagara Falls, New York and other famous places, and of meeting the legendary Babe Ruth at a baseball match. We visited the heart of the American automobile industry, Detroit, then on to the so-called gangster city Chicago (where we found beautiful gardens — but no gangsters), and back across Canada through the great prairie lands.

Then came a brief sojourn in the Canadian Rockies which contain scenery of incredible beauty but scarcely enough flat country for a cricket ground.

After a farewell look at Vancouver we journeyed south to San Francisco and Los Angeles and played our final matches in Hollywood, where the British contingent, led by that doyen of actors, Charles Aubrey Smith, an ex-English cricketer of renown who was later knighted for his services to the film industry, were resolutely keeping the cricket flag flying.

It was a fitting place to end a remarkable tour which may never be repeated.

*Don Bradman*

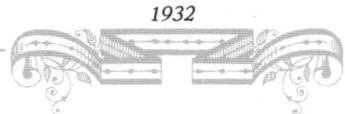

LEFT TO RIGHT    Vic Bradman, Don Bradman, Jessie Menzies, Jean Menzies, Lily Menzies, Roy Menzies.

Mrs. Don Bradman.

## FAMOUS CRICKETER'S HONEYMOON TOUR

Don Bradman and his wife, formerly Miss Jessie Menzies, photographed on board the *Niagara* at Auckland. Don Bradman is a member of Mailey's Australian cricket team which is to tour Canada.

Don and Jessie Bradman.

Mrs. Marshall, Don Bradman, Misses Aldwood, Mrs. Don Bradman and Dave Marshall on board *Niagara*.

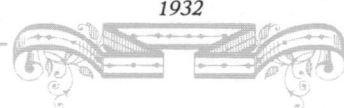

## – SEASON 1932 –

| TITLE | GAME | | SCORES | |
|---|---|---|---|---|
| Second Class | Mailey's Team | Cowichan | 60 | C. |
| ,, | ,, | Victoria B.C. | 94 | C. |
| ,, | ,, | Vancouver | 110 | n.o. |
| ,, | ,, | ,, | 42 | C. |
| ,, | ,, | ,, | 180 | C. |
| ,, | ,, | Toronto | 27 | n.o. |
| ,, | ,, | ,, | 11 | B. |
| ,, | ,, | ,, | 40 | C. |
| ,, | ,, | ,, | 52 | C. |
| ,, | ,, | Guelph | 260 | C. |
| ,, | ,, | Ridley College | 10 | n.o. |
| ,, | ,, | ,, | 109 | C. |
| ,, | ,, | Montreal | 95 | S. |
| ,, | ,, | ,, | 200 | n.o. |
| ,, | ,, | ,, | 92 | B. |
| ,, | ,, | Ottawa | 105 | C. |
| ,, | ,, | ,, | 114 | B. |
| ,, | ,, | New York | 45 | C. |
| ,, | ,, | ,, | 117 | C. |
| ,, | ,, | ,, | 0 | C. |
| ,, | ,, | ,, | 8 | C. |
| ,, | ,, | ,, | 35 | C. |
| ,, | ,, | ,, | 57 | C. |
| ,, | ,, | Detroit | 26 | B. |
| ,, | ,, | Windsor | 24 | C. |
| ,, | ,, | Chicago | 4 | B. |
| ,, | ,, | ,, | 10 | C. |
| ,, | ,, | ,, | 13 | C. |
| ,, | ,, | ,, | 41 | C. |
| ,, | ,, | Winnipeg | 2 | C. |
| ,, | ,, | ,, | 14 | C. |
| ,, | ,, | Regina | 116 | n.o. |
| ,, | ,, | Moose Jaw | 110 | C. |
| ,, | ,, | ,, | 100 | n.o. |

| TITLE | GAME | | SCORES | |
|---|---|---|---|---|
| Second Class | Mailey's Team | Yorkton | 115 | C. |
| ,, | ,, | Saskatoon | 88 | B. |
| ,, | ,, | Edmonton | 34 | C. |
| ,, | ,, | ,, | 159 | n.o. |
| ,, | ,, | Calgary | 39 | n.o. |
| ,, | ,, | ,, | 69 | n.o. |
| ,, | ,, | Vancouver | 103 | n.o. |
| ,, | ,, | ,, | 125 | n.o. |
| ,, | ,, | Victoria B.C. | 88 | C. |
| ,, | ,, | ,, | 171 | B. |
| ,, | ,, | San Francisco | 123 | B. |
| ,, | ,, | ,, | 29 | C. |
| ,, | ,, | Santa Barbara | 121 | L.B.W. |
| ,, | ,, | Hollywood | 42 | C. |
| ,, | ,, | ,, | 52 | n.o. |
| ,, | ,, | ,, | 18 | n.o. |
| ,, | ,, | ,, | 83 | n.o. |
| | | Total runs | 3782 | |

\* The 260 made at Guelph was then the highest score ever made in Canada.

## – SUMMARY –

AVERAGES

| | Innings | N.O's. | H.S. | Runs | Average |
|---|---|---|---|---|---|
| Second Class | 51 | 14 | 260 | 3782 | 102·1 |
| All Matches | 51 | 14 | 260 | 3782 | 102·1 |

Victoria, capital city of British Columbia.

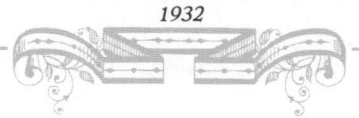

MAILEY'S TEAM v COWICHAN, at Duncan, Vancouver Island, on 17 June 1932.

| | | |
|---|---|---|
| Mailey's Team | - First Innings | 503 for 8 wickets |
| | - Second Innings | - |
| Cowichan | - First Innings | 184 |
| | - Second Innings | - |

DON BRADMAN    - c. and b. Baiss        60

Wicket - matting on grass.

The road to Duncan.

# Australian Cricket Team Opens Tour With Display That Amazes Big Crowd

## MAILEY'S TEAM

### Wins First Match in Canada.

VANCOUVER, June 17.
In the first match of their tour, played at Duncan, the Australian cricket team defeated a representative team of the Cowichan Club. They gave the greatest exhibition of batting in the cricket history of Vancouver Island. The Australians made 503 for seven wickets, and declared. Their opponents made 184. Cowichan batted eighteen and fielded eleven.

### Cowichan's Innings

| | |
|---|---|
| H. A. Rhodes, c Carter, b Mailey | 1 |
| R. Walton, b Mailey | 22 |
| F. H. Allwood, c McCabe, b Mailey | 0 |
| J. H. Ryall, c McCabe, b Mailey | 7 |
| C. T. Mayo, c Carter, b Fleetwood-Smith | 35 |
| L. A. S. Cole, b Mailey | 16 |
| A. E. S. Liggatt, c McCabe, b Fleetwood-Smith | 8 |
| E. C. Ball, lbw, b Fleetwood-Smith | 7 |
| W. U. Mowbray, b Fleetwood-Smith | 39 |
| A. E. Green, by Mailey | 0 |
| A. Gillespie, c Rofe, b Mailey | 2 |
| W. Unsworth, c Rofe, b Fleetwood-Smith | 4 |
| G. G. Baiss, c Kippax, b Fleetwood-Smith | 35 |
| F. C. Williams-Freeman, b Mailey | 0 |
| J. Hine, b Mailey | 0 |
| A. G. H. Tisdall, b Mailey | 3 |
| G. A. Jobling, b Mailey | 0 |
| A. Leighton, b Mailey | 1 |
| Extras | 4 |
| **Total** | **184** |

### Australia's Innings

| | |
|---|---|
| V. Richardson, c Leggatt, b Cole | 76 |
| R. Nutt, c Leggatt, b Cole | 31 |
| D. Bradman, c and b Baiss | 60 |
| A. F. Kippax, b Baiss | 59 |
| S. McCabe, c Green, b Rhodes | 150 |
| K. Tolhurst, c Ryall, b Rhodes | 22 |
| E. Rofe, c Ryall, b Rhodes | 21 |
| P. Carney | 2 |
| H. Carter, not out | 23 |
| A. A. Mailey, not out | 51 |
| Extras | 8 |
| **Total (for 8 wkts)** | **503** |

L. Fleetwood-Smith did not bat.

### Bowling Analysis

| Cowichan Innings: | O. | R. | W. |
|---|---|---|---|
| S. McCabe | 4 | 5 | 0 |
| A. A. Mailey | 19 | 64 | 11 |
| L. Fleetwood-Smith | 15 | 111 | 6 |
| Australian Innings: | O. | R. | W. |
| E. C. Ball | 11 | 70 | 1 |
| A. Leighton | 8 | 98 | 0 |
| L. A. S. Cole | 7 | 99 | 3 |
| H. A. Rhodes | 8 | 88 | 3 |
| G. G. Baiss | 8 | 77 | 1 |
| W. Mowbray | 2 | 27 | 0 |
| C. T. Mayo | 2 | 35 | 0 |

Don and Jessie Bradman on their wedding day, 30 April 1932.

Jessie Bradman (née Menzies) on her wedding day, 30 April 1932.

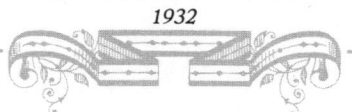

Don Bradman, Parks Commissioner, Jessie Bradman, Dick Nutt, Bill Ives in Stanley Park, Vancouver.

*. . . Stayed at Vancouver Hotel.*
*Before lunch we went to the ground, Brockton Point, and I*
*doubt if there is a prettier ground in the world. On the sides*
*are the most beautiful trees imaginable; Vancouver Harbour*
*is on two sides of the ground, further away.*
*From one portion of the Harbour the seaplane to Victoria*
*takes off and along the other portion the beautiful big ferries*
*steam up and down.*

MAILEY'S TEAM v MAINLAND ALL-STARS, at Brockton Point ground, Vancouver, on 21 June 1932.

| | | |
|---|---|---|
| Mailey's Team | - First Innings | 287 for 6 wickets dec. |
| | - Second Innings | - |
| Mainland | - First Innings | 64 |
| | - Second Innings | - |

| | | |
|---|---|---|
| DON BRADMAN | - retired | 110 |

Wicket - matting on grass.

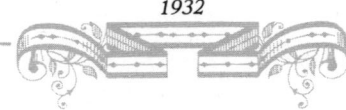

# Don Bradman Proves Master With Cricket Bat on Local Crease

**World's Greatest Player Scores 110, Not Out, Against Home Squad**

**Australians Give Finished Exhibition in Winning Game 267 to 64**

### By BILLY FINLAY

Don Bradman, Australia's Babe Ruth of cricket, did his stuff with bat and ball for the edification of Vancouver fandom at the Brockton Point crease yesterday afternoon.

The master batsman of cricket, in scoring 110 runs before retiring undefeated at the wicket, gave a magnificent display of hitting. He showed in many ways that he is a cricket genius and his performance was a treat to watch.

Bradman was the man who the enthusiasts wanted to see. His name was on everybody's lips. He is a medium sized youth with a stern countenance, and how he can whale a cricket ball.

It was interesting to listen to the various remarks, such as:

"Isn't he just grand?"

"I don't know where he gets all that driving power."

"He must have a wonderful pair of wrists and his timing must be perfect."

"Just look how he stands. His footwork is about perfect and he seems to be always in position to hit any kind of a ball."

### BRADMAN A GENIUS

No matter what the Vancouver bowlers did, Bradman was their master all the way. Time and again the field was changed but the Aussie ace would look around and find an opening for a good clean hit or a out that would roll far from a fielder.

Bradman gave a finished exhibition of the art of handling a cricket bat. He only gave one chance and that was late after he had started to open up, when he sent a high catch to Pinkham in the long field and the fielder muffed the catch.

The Australian All-Stars in giving their first exhibition of a three-game series with Mainland players, looked just like Connie Mack's Athletics, the St. Louis Cards or the New York Yankees would in playing a select side of city league baseball boys.

### LOCALS BADLY OUTCLASSED

The visitors simply overwhelmed the local stars with class. They scored 287 runs for six wickets on a wet pitch and with only an hour left to play went out and retired the home squad for the small number of 64 runs.

It was a wet day for cricket. Morning play was stopped owing to rain and it was 2:15 in the afternoon before the captains and officials finally decided to start hostilities in a drizzly rain, which lasted most of the afternoon. There must be something wrong with the cricket colony of this big city. The attendance was disappointing for such a notable affair. Probably they are waiting for the sunshine.

## AUSTRALIA INNINGS

| | |
|---|---|
| Richardson, c Bullen, b Dobbie | 3 |
| Nutt, c Peel, b Bullen | 25 |
| Bradman, retired | 110 |
| Kippax, c Pinkham, b Bullen | 74 |
| McCabe, b Bullen | 58 |
| Tolhurst, not out | 14 |
| Mailey, c Dobbie, b Gillespie | 0 |
| Extras | 3 |
| | |
| Total for 6 wickets (declared) | 287 |

Carney, Carter, Fleetwood-Smith and Rofe did not bat.

### Bowling Analysis

| | O. | M. | R. | W. |
|---|---|---|---|---|
| Rivers | 11 | 0 | 63 | 0 |
| Dobbie | 8 | 0 | 64 | 1 |
| Scott | 3 | 0 | 14 | 0 |
| Ivamy | 9 | 0 | 50 | 0 |
| Bullen | 7 | 0 | 27 | 3 |
| Gillespie | 5.5 | 0 | *3 | 1 |
| Reed | 1 | 0 | 13 | 0 |

## MAINLAND ALL-STARS INNINGS

| | |
|---|---|
| Reed, stpd. Carter, b Mailey | 4 |
| Scott, c McCabe, b Mailey | 1 |
| Carey, c Tolhurst, b Fleetwood-Smith | 17 |
| Pinkham, b Mailey | 0 |
| Rivers, c Bradman, b Mailey | 9 |
| Bullen, c Mailey, b Fleetwood-Smith | 8 |
| Dobbie, b Mailey | 0 |
| Ivamy, c Carney, b Mailey | 0 |
| Johnston, b Mailey | 10 |
| Gillespie, stpd. Carter, b Fleetwood-Smith | 7 |
| Peel, not out | 6 |
| Extras | 2 |
| | |
| Total | 64 |

### Bowling Analysis

| | O. | M. | R. | W. |
|---|---|---|---|---|
| McCabe | 4 | 0 | 16 | 0 |
| Mailey | 7.1 | 2 | 24 | 7 |
| Fleetwood-Smith | 4 | 0 | 22 | 3 |

Umpires—Redgrove and St. John Davey.

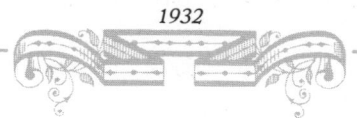

*. . . Then commenced our journey through the Canadian
Rockies, some of the most magnificent scenery in the world.
Gorgeous fir trees everywhere, running snow rivers,
waterfalls and always on top of everything the towering
Rockies which are always covered with snow.
I was rather disappointed in the sleeping berths which are
the Pullman type.*

Phil Carney and Ed Rofe alongside a C.P.R. monster.

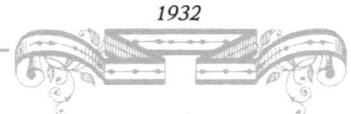

View of Yonge Street, Toronto.

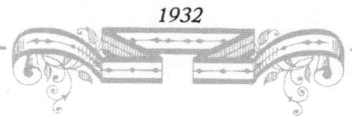

MAILEY'S TEAM v WESTERN ONTARIO, at Guelph, on 4 July 1932.

| Mailey's Team | - First Innings | 479 for 7 wickets |
| | - Second Innings | - |
| Western Ontario | - First Innings | 88 |
| | - Second Innings | - |

DON BRADMAN    - c. and b. Kelly    260

Wicket - matting on grass.

Ontario Reformatory, Guelph.

# Aussies' Win Featured by Don Bradman

Guelph. Ont., July 5.—Don Bradman, world's premier batter, knocked up 260 runs, a new Canadian record, as the touring Australian cricket team defeated a Western Ontario team yesterday by a one-sided margin. Batting first, the Western Ontario side of 18 men found the Aussies' bowling puzzling and were all out with a total of 88 runs. The visitors amassed 479 runs for seven wickets and then declared.

Bradman demonstrated his ability to pile up a score when he assailed the bowling and drove with abandon all over the field. He was eventually caught by Kelly.

McCabe added the impressive total of 119 to the Antipodeans' score before he was bowled by Jones. Richardson was not out with 40 runs to his credit when the innings closed.

Jones, bowled by Fleetwood-Smith after amassing 23 runs, made the best showing of the Western Ontario side. He also was the most effective bowler against the Aussies, with four wickets for 77 runs. A. Youngman, with 18, and Cronin with 18, were the only others able to solve the tourists' bowling with any success.

McCabe was deadly, taking 11 wickets for a mere 33 runs, while Fleetwood-Smith was almost as effective, with five wickets for 25 runs.

**—Western Ontario.—**

| | |
|---|---:|
| Inglis, b. McCabe | 10 |
| Kelly, l.b.w., McCabe | 2 |
| Jones, b. Fleetwood-Smith | 23 |
| Stanley, l.b.w., McCabe | 5 |
| Metcalfe, b. McCabe | 0 |
| McLeod, b. Ives | 0 |
| McIntyre, b. McCabe | 0 |
| Downing, b. McCabe | 0 |
| Cronin, b. McCabe | 12 |
| Youngman, b. McCabe | 18 |
| McCartney, b. Fleetwood-Smith | 4 |
| Arnold, stpd. Nutt, b. Fleetwood Smith | 3 |
| Simpson, b. Fleetwood-Smith | 1 |
| Illingworth, not out | 1 |
| Tuckett, b. McCabe | 0 |
| Howlett, b. McCabe | 2 |
| Stephens, b. McCabe | 1 |
| Jude, b. Fleetwood-Smith | 1 |
| Extras | 5 |
| Total | 88 |

**—Australians.—**

| | |
|---|---:|
| Richardson, not out | 40 |
| Kippax, l.b.w., Kelly | 19 |
| Bradman, c. and b. Kelly | 260 |
| McCabe, b. Jones | 119 |
| Fleetwood-Smith, b. Jones | 0 |
| Nutt, b. Downing | 1 |
| Tolhurst, c. and b. Jones | 31 |
| Ives, b. Jones | 4 |
| Extras | 5 |
| Total (for seven wickets) | 479 |

**—Bowling Analysis.—**

McCabe, 11 wickets for 33 runs; Ives, one wicket for 25 runs; Fleetwood-Smith, five wickets for 25 runs.

Downing, one wicket for 44 runs; Jones, four wickets for 77 runs; Kelly, two wickets for 74 runs.

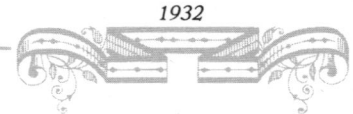

*. . . After the game we were driven to Niagara Falls to a banquet as the guests of the Parks Commission.*
*The Niagara River joins lakes Erie and Ontario and the big Horseshoe Falls are in Canada.*
*Across the River is America and they have a small Niagara Falls, not nearly so big or beautiful. Both falls are illuminated at night by coloured search-lights and to see either falls, Americans must cross over into Canada.*
*Very wonderful spectacle. Can't see bottom for spray or stand at top on street.*

The Boulevard, Queen Victoria Park, Niagara Falls.

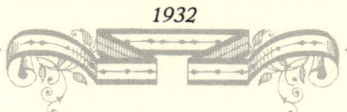

Don and Jessie Bradman outside Waterman's Pen Shop, Montreal.

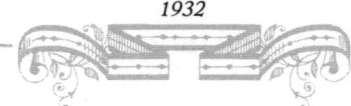

# Bradman's 200, Not Out, Features Second Day Of Aussies' Visit

## AUSTRALIAN CRICKETERS.

### Bradman's Double Century.

MONTREAL, July 8.

Don Bradman on Friday showed cricket enthusiasts why he is regarded as one of the best batsmen the game has produced, when, against the best local bowling, he scored 200 not out in the second of a series of three one-day matches between the Australians and an all-Montreal team. Montreal, batting 15, was dismissed for 77. The tourists scored 331 for three.

MAILEY'S TEAM v MONTREAL, at Molson Stadium, on 8 July 1932.

| | | |
|---|---|---|
| Mailey's Team | - First Innings | 331 for 3 wickets |
| | - Second Innings | - |
| Montreal | - First Innings | 77 |
| | - Second Innings | - |

DON BRADMAN - n.o.        200

### MONTREAL

| | |
|---|---|
| A. T. Bates, b. Mailey | 1 |
| F. T. Broadbelt, lbw McCabe | 4 |
| H. A. Lartigue, st Carter, b Mailey | 19 |
| H. Proctor, lbw Mailey | 19 |
| J. Robinson, b Fleetwood-Smith | 2 |
| L. G. Spooner, b Mailey | 10 |
| G. J. C. Potter, c and b Fleetwood-Smith | 4 |
| L. Clarke, b Fleetwood-Smith | 1 |
| T. G. Douglass, b Fleetwood-Smith | 0 |
| H. S. C. Leach, not out | 11 |
| A. J. Burgess, b Fleetwood-Smith | 0 |
| R. A. Wyatt-Jones, c Bradman, b Fleetwood-Smith | 4 |
| H. Smith, c and b Mailey | 1 |
| C. Bond, b Fleetwood-Smith | 0 |
| R. S. Thorpe, b Fleetwood-Smith | 0 |
| Leg bye | 1 |
| Total | 77 |

### BOWLING ANALYSIS

| | O. | M. | R. | W. |
|---|---|---|---|---|
| McCabe | 6 | 0 | 17 | 1 |
| Mailey | 14 | 0 | 45 | 5 |
| Fleetwood-Smith | 9 | 3 | 14 | 8 |

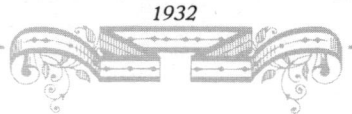

## MAILEY'S TEAM.

### Arrival in New York.

NEW YORK, July 13.

The Australian cricketers were greeted on arrival in New York by several hundreds of Australian and British people, including members of the West Indian team, which they will play to-morrow. The visitors were loudly cheered.

Mr. Arthur Mailey informed the representative of the Australian Press Association that the team had had a splendid trip and thus far had been slightly successful and pleased with the results. "We have had top gates everywhere," he said. "We heard a great deal about the depression but saw none of it."

Don Bradman said that he was somewhat troubled by the heat, but was in excellent condition, as also were his team mates. He was enjoying the trip very much.

MAILEY'S TEAM v NEW YORK WEST INDIANS,

at Innisfail Park, on 15 July 1932.

| Mailey's Team | - First Innings | 276 for 7 wickets |
|---|---|---|
| | - Second Innings | - |
| N.Y. West Indians | - First Innings | 222 |
| | - Second Innings | - |

| DON BRADMAN | - c. Brown b. Richardson | 117 |
|---|---|---|

### West Indians

| | |
|---|---|
| B. Clarke, st. Carter, b. Fleetwood-Smith | 19 |
| H. Richardson, c. V. Richardson, b. Mailey | 13 |
| A. Mayers, st. Carter, b. Mailey | 41 |
| R. Alder, b. Fleetwood-Smith | 9 |
| J. K. Ragbir, b. Fleetwood-Smith | 0 |
| V. Ollivierre, b. Fleetwood-Smith | 14 |
| A. Dash, c. Richardson, b. Fleewood-Smith | 65 |
| R. Griffith, b. Fleetwood-Smith | 0 |
| A. Walcott, l. b. w. Fleetwood-Smith | 19 |
| S. Trottman, b. McCabe | 13 |
| C. Brown, not out | 24 |
| Extras | 5 |
| Total | 222 |

Runs at fall of each wicket—24, 54, 66, 66, 95, 104, 104, 179, 184, 222.

### Australians

| | |
|---|---|
| V. Richardson, l. b. w. Clarke | 22 |
| R. N. Nutt, l. b. w. Trottman | 21 |
| Don Bradman, c. Brown, b. Richardson | 117 |
| S. J. McCabe, c. Clarke, b. Richardson | 82 |
| E. L. Tolhurst, c. Ragbir, b. Ollivierre | 10 |
| W. Ives, b. Ollivierre | 17 |
| E. Rolfe, l. b. w. Clarke | 3 |
| P. Carney, not out | 0 |
| Extras | 4 |
| Total (seven wickets) | 276 |

Runs at fall of each wicket—27, 60, 228, 252, 269, 271, 276.

H. Carter, A. Mailey and L. O'B. Fleetwood-Smith did not bat.

### BOWLING ANALYSIS

#### West Indians

| Bowlers | O. | M. | R. | W. |
|---|---|---|---|---|
| McCabe | 50 | 1 | 20 | 1 |
| Ives | 12 | 0 | 11 | 0 |
| Fleetwood-Smith | 108 | 2 | 106 | 7 |
| Mailey | 78 | 1 | 80 | 2 |

#### Australians

| Bowlers | O. | M. | R. | W. |
|---|---|---|---|---|
| Mayers | 32 | 0 | 23 | 0 |
| Clarke | 72 | 2 | 84 | 2 |
| Trottman | 42 | 0 | 63 | 1 |
| Griffith | 18 | 0 | 36 | 0 |
| Alder | 24 | 0 | 24 | 0 |
| H. Richardson | 24 | 0 | 37 | 2 |
| Ollivierre | 24 | 1 | | 2 |

# Bradman's 117 Gives Victory To Australia

### Antipodean Cricket Team Beats West Indians by 54 Runs, 3 Wickets to Spare

Don Bradman, leading batsman of the Australian cricketers, delivered the century for which New York devotees of England's national pastime had been waiting in the second match against a picked eleven of the West Indian cricketers, of New York, at Innisfail Park before 2,000 onlookers yesterday afternoon. This achievement by the man who made a score of 334 in one of the last test matches in England, helped the team from "down under" to notch a decisive victory by fifty-four runs, with three wickets to spare.

## AUSTRALIANS IN NEW YORK.

NEW YORK, July 16.

After dismissing the West Indian team on Friday for 222 runs, the Australians passed that total with the loss of two wickets and then played out time.

Don Bradman at Innisfail Park.

# Don Meets Babe

By Daniel in the New York World Telegram

Babe Ruth today was bound to a promise. When the Australian cricket team visits this part of the country again next May the Bam will try his hand at the old English game and bat against the visitors from Down Under. He made that arrangement with Don Bradman, the Ruth of the cricketeers and star of the Aussies, at the Stadium yesterday.

Bradman and his teammates, sitting with the crippled Babe in mezzanine boxes, watched the Yankees beat the White Sox again, 7 to 2, sweeping the series of five games.

"I'll try this cricket business," chuckled Ruth. "Maybe it's my game. Now, why don't you put on a Yankee uniform and see what you can do against our kind of pitching?" he suggested to Bradman. "Maybe baseball is your game." But Bradman begged off. He had to be on his way to Detroit.

The Babe was surprised by Bradman's lack of size and weight. The greatest batsman cricket yet has boasted is no bigger than Joey Sewell. Don weighs 145 pounds, is 24 years of age, and, according to the cricket experts, is a Willie Keeler rather than a Ruth—a scientist rather than a powerhouse. Bradman hits them "where they ain't, and has been known to score more than 1,600 runs in a little more than fourteen days of cricket.

"From what they were telling me I thought you were a husky guy," remarked Ruth. "But us little fellows can hit 'em harder than the big ones!" roared the Bam, and at once the proper spirit of camaraderie was established.

## DON KNOWS

They watched the game closely, Johnny Allen pitching for the Yankees, Pete Daglia for the White Sox. In the second inning, with one out, Arndt Jorgens grounded to Red Kress.

"Now watch this closely," suggested Guide Ruth, who was intent on teaching all the finer points to Bradman.

"Jove a double play!" ejaculated Don. "Hey, what's this?" snorted the Babe. "I was told to point out the tricks of the game and you holler 'double play.' You don't need any teaching. Seen much of this game?"

Little Bradman smiled. "Oh, yes; we have lots of baseball in Australia and I have taken a keen interest in it. I'd like to play baseball myself."

"Well, what strikes you most forcibly? What's the big difference between baseball and cricket?" Ruth asked. "The catches of the outfielders? The work of the infielders? Those things always impress the English."

Little Mr. Bradman smiled again. "No there is nothing extraordinary about the catches or the inner fielding. You professionals do nothing else. You work up to the leagues and then you must be exceptional or they chuck you out." Mr. Ruth chuckled. "I'll say!" he snorted.

"In addition, baseball players are equipped with heavy gloves," Don continued. "It isn't the actual playing of the game that impresses me. It's the quick decision, the businesslike way in which the test is conducted.

"In two hours or so the match is finished. Each batter comes up four or five times. Each afternoon's play stands on its own."

## COULD LEARN FROM BASEBALL

"Yes, cricket could learn a lot from baseball," Bradman went on. "Our matches are prolonged for days and days. Only four or five batsmen may come up in an afternoon's play. There is more snap and dash to baseball."

There was little conversation through the game. The Babe s resplendent in brown sports co white striped trousers, buckski shoes and a white cap—the true n bob.

In the fifth inning the Austr lians were aroused. Frankie Cr setti drove a home run, with two bases, to left centre. As Bob See and Elias Funk chased after t ball Crosetti went scamperi around the bags. On he came, a there was a play at the plate. T Aussies were on their feet. But n Bradman.

"A beauty in the right spot," w Don's comment. "That was off googlie ball," remarked Fleetwoo Smith, star bowler of the visitor who is quite a googlie-ball throw himself. A googlie, m'lads, is pitch with twist and spin to it— short, a curve.

The game ultimately got a laug out of Bradman. In the sevent inning the boys got up to stretc "What's all this about?" ask Don.

"Just an old American custo that takes the place of tea!" roar the Babe—and then 'Arry Steven of Derbyshire, sent up his bo with tiffin—ginger ale y'know.

Don Bradman and Babe Ruth watching baseball in New York.

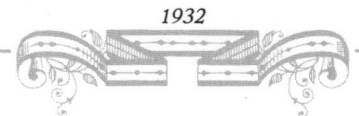

# BRADMAN HELD UP

---

## Mailey's Team At Chicago

---

## POLICE ESCORT

### FROM ARTHUR MAILEY

CHICAGO, Sunday.

A thrilling welcome awaited Mailey's team at Chicago. The Mayor's representative, who is well-known as "Greeter" Gaw, received the team, with a police escort, which, with screeching sirens, travelled at a terrific pace through the held-up traffic.

Bradman's straw hat blew skywards among the skyscrapers, necessitating the return of the police patrol, who recovered the hat from a souvenir-hunter on the sidewalk.

This reception was in contrast with that at Detroit, where the team experienced some difficulty with the immigration officials after crossing from Detroit, U.S.A., to Windsor, where they played a match. The team was dressed in flannels. They crossed the river to Canada, but were unable to return without passports.

Carter, luckily, had his. He returned to the hotel and rummaged through the players' baggage, recovering the passports and enabling them to return to Detroit after the match.

The team will play for four days at Chicago, then going to Winnipeg, travelling westward.

Grant Park, Chicago.

In the background is Stevens Hotel, the world's largest, with 5,000 bedrooms.

Chicago.

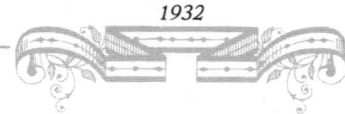

MAILEY'S TEAM  v  ILLINOIS CRICKET ASSOCIATION, at Grant Park, on 25 July 1932.

Mailey's Team    - First Innings      185 for 9 wickets
                 - Second Innings     -

Illinois         - First Innings      103
                 - Second Innings     -


DON BRADMAN      - b. Watt                         13


# CHICAGO GUARDS MAILEY'S XI. WITH GUNS

**(From ARTHUR MAILEY)**
**CHICAGO, Tuesday.**

IF there were any intending kidnappers at Grant Park, Mailey's team did not see them.

A police escort, with belts bristling with cartridges, and uncovered guns, cleared spectators from the playing field—adding a typically Chicagoan touch to the match.

✢ The ground is a reclaimed area between Michigan Avenue and Lake Michigan, in a beautiful setting with skyscrapers in the background, casting shadows over the playing arena.

The wicket, however, was distinctly dangerous, causing Australian batsmen much concern.

✢ Bradman was the subject of much scrutiny from the representatives of all nations, and hid himself in a tent until entering the field, when the police escort cleared the way.

Bradman and others sacrificed their wickets in each innings owing to the dangerous pitch, realising that an appearance for Australia against England next season was more important.

Fleetwood-Smith is greatly improved, and has taken almost 150 wickets in a month

✢ The Australians won the match—against Illinois Cricket Association—easily, compiling 186 runs for nine wickets (declared), while Illinois totalled 103 for 17 wickets. Bradman was bowled by Watt for 13, and Nutt hit up 86 retired.

The team is being royally entertained everywhere, especially in Chicago, where the people are determined to impress the visitors that the city's reputation for crime is not deserved.

The team will leave for Winnipeg—where the second Test will be played—to-morrow.

| | | | | | |
|---|---|---|---|---|---|
| Harburg. | c Mailey b McCabe. | 10. | | | |
| Williams. | c Nutt b Ives. | 5. | | | |
| Clarke. | c Richardson b McCabe. | 1. | McCabe. | 3/17. | |
| Joyce. | c Bradman b Smith. | 10. | Ives. | 1/13. | |
| Knights. | Bowled Kippax. | 8. | Smith. | 9/26. | |
| Wilkins. | Run Out. | 0. | Kippax. | 3/25. | |
| Watt. | Bowled McCabe. | 0. | | | |
| Sims. | c Bradman b Smith. | 1. | | | |
| Crompton. | Bowled Smith. | 5. | | | |
| Anderson. | c Richardson b Smith. | 0. | | | |
| Catling. | Bowled Kippax. | 2. | | | |
| Tindall. | c Ives b Smith. | 23. | | | |
| Butcher. | Bowled Smith. | 4. | | | |
| Graly. | Bowled Smith. | 7. | | | |
| Davidson. | St. Richardson b Smith. | 0. | | | |
| Smith. | Not Out. | 5. | | | |
| Gawthorp. | c Ives b Smith. | 0. | | | |
| Ryan. | c & b Kippax. | 0. | | | |
| Sundries. | | 22. | | | |
| | | 103. | | | |

| | | | | | |
|---|---|---|---|---|---|
| Richardson. | c & b Wilkins. | 0. | | | |
| Nutt. | St. Sims b Smith. | 86. | Watt. | 1/11. | |
| Bradman. | Bowled Watt. | 13. | Wilkins. | 2/29. | |
| Kippax. | c Watt b Wilkins. | 1. | Knight. | 1/35. | |
| McCabe. | c Anderson b Knight. | 10. | Smith. | 2/38. | |
| Tolhurst. | L.B.W. Smith. | 16. | Butcher. | 1/16. | |
| Ives. | Bowled Butcher. | 7. | Anderson. | 2/21. | |
| Kofe. | c Wilkins b Anderson. | 8. | Graly. | 0/20. | |
| Mailey. | c Gawthorp b Anderson. | 14. | Tindall. | 0/4. | |
| Carney. | Not Out. | 17. | | | |
| Smith. | Not Out. | 2. | | | |
| Sundries. | | 11. | | | |
| | 9 for | 185. | | | |

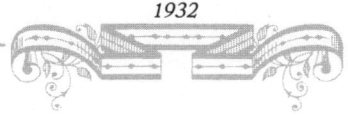

MAILEY'S TEAM v REGINA, at Saskatchewan Co-op. grounds, on 1 August 1932.

| | | |
|---|---|---|
| Mailey's Team | - First Innings | 240 for 5 wickets |
| | - Second Innings | - |
| Regina | - First Innings | 123 |
| | - Second Innings | - |

| | | |
|---|---|---|
| DON BRADMAN | - n.o. | 116 |

Wicket - matting on composition.

Mr. H. S. Carter, Keith Tolhurst, Don Bradman, Jessie Bradman and Leslie Fleetwood-Smith in Regina.

# Bradman Carries Bat Over Century Mark; Locals Show Up Well

### Over 2,000 Reginans Witness Exhibition by Famous Antipodeans

Australia's touring cricketers, led by the educated bat of Don Bradman, world-famous run-getter, and the deceptive bowling of Arthur Mailey, veteran manager of the team, proved too strong for 17 selected Regina players in an exhibition match played at Saskatchewan Co-op. grounds, Monday afternoon, winning by five wickets and 117 runs. The Regina team scored a total of 123 runs in one and a half hour's batting, to which the visitors replied with a total of 240 runs for the loss of five wickets, Bradman scoring 116 not out.

The local players gave an excellent account of themselves in all departments of the game. Their fielding was unmarred by mistakes and earned them the praise of the famous visitors, while their batting, though expectedly weaker than that of their opponents, at least proved more productive than the combined bats of the All-Canadian side which had faced the Australians at Winnipeg the previous Saturday. The local bowling, too, was sound and of good length — so good, indeed, that few of the famous batsmen opposing it but treated it with circumspection and respect.

### Have Complete Command

While the visitors had complete command of the situation while at the wicket, they earned their runs by skilful placement shots rather than by the mighty boundary hits the majority of the spectators were inclined to expect. In the slogging line, major honors were virtually "stolen" from the mighty Bradman and the stylish Kippax, by two of Regina's younger element, the most dashing innings of the afternoon being that of young Maurice Grant, who, last man in for the locals, carried his bat for 17 runs, composed of two sixes, a four, and a single. Don Leighton showed equally scant respect for the great reputations of such bowlers as Arthur Mailey, famous dispenser of "googlies," Ives and Fleetwood-Smith. He also slashed out a driving six, added two fours, and garnered a total of 14 in a short but merry knock.

Exceptionally smart fielding by Woodhams and Keymer, particularly, cut short prolific Australian stands, while the team conspired to display a snappiness on the ball which cut off many runs, being added thereto by the "dead" nature of the outfield.

### Mailey Disastrous

Arthur Mailey, veteran trickster with the ball, had a disastrous effect on promising Regina rallies, his deliveries accounting for 10 wickets taken at the small cost of six runs apiece. Aided by the stellar stumping of Captain Vic Richardson, the Australian wicketkeeper, Mailey continually "teased" the locals into leaving their crease by his deceptive cross breaks and varying length. Ives' medium to fast deliveries at the other end made an excellent foil for the veteran, and few, if any, of the locals were left in comfort when at bat.

In amassing his 116 not out, Bradman played a careful, precise innings, using as his chief scoring medium a short placement shot to which invariably went where the local fielders were not. Not until he had reached the coveted "century" did the world's most famous cricketer and holder of many batting records open his shoulders and show his mettle.

The visitors were tendered a banquet after the game by the local cricket organization, and Tuesday they oppose a selected side at Moose Jaw. Thence they go to Yorkton to stage an exhibition there.

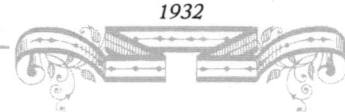

MAILEY'S TEAM v MOOSE JAW, at Moose Jaw, on 2 August 1932.

| Mailey's Team | - First Innings | 302 for 5 wickets |
| | - Second Innings | - |
| Moose Jaw | - First Innings | 102 |
| | - Second Innings | - |

DON BRADMAN - c. Wright b. Kenyon 110

Wicket - matting on composition.

# AUSSIES WIN AT MOOSE JAW

## Men From 'Down Under' Score 302 Runs for Five Wickets Against 102

MOOSE JAW, Sask., Aug. 2.— Scoring 302 runs for five wickets the touring Australian cricket team defeated a selected side of Moose Jaw cricketers who could only muster 102 amongst the 17 local players.

Don Bradman, star batsman of the Cornstalks, scored a brilliant 110 before going out to a magnificent catch by Jim Wright who took the ball almost on the ground after diving full length for it. Charles Kenyon was the bowler and Bradman had hit out at a slow full toss. Kippax carried his bat for a stylishly played 76 runs, not out, while Richardson, captain of the Aussies, was run out from the last hit of the match, having scored 30.

### Moose Jaw Bowlers

For the locals, Joe Buckley took two wickets for 42 runs, while C. Kenyon who got Bradman's wicket was the only other bowler to take a wicket, two batsmen being run out. Kenyon's lone wicket cost 30 runs. Fourteen bowlers were used by Moose Jaw, Hadley Jones having 23 runs knocked off him without success, W. Page giving away 23 runs, R. Buckley 19, J. Wright 16, N. Buckley seven, J. Cole, 13, W. Stedmond 16, G. Richards 32, W. Stedmond 16, G. Richards 32, W. S. Thain 22, W. McLeod nine, J. Hampson 23 and A. Ingleby 16 runs, all without taking a wicket. Extras accounted for 10 of the Australians' runs.

#### Moose Jaw

| | |
|---|---|
| J. Wright b. McCabe | 1 |
| O'Hara c. Nutt b. Ives | 7 |
| W. Page b. McCabe | 0 |
| H. Jones b. McCabe | 0 |
| W. McLeod b. McCabe | 19 |
| J. Cole c. Carney b. McCabe | 0 |
| J. Buckley b. Ives | 0 |
| W. Stedmond b. McCabe | 2 |
| R. Howland c. Rofe b. Fleetwood-Smith. | 15 |
| R. Buckley b. Mailey | 0 |
| W. Thain stpd. Richardson b. Mailey .. | 0 |
| C. Kenyon b. Fleetwood-Smith | 9 |
| N. Buckley b. McCabe | 28 |
| Whitridge b. Mailey | 3 |
| Langdon b. Mailey | 2 |
| Hampson c. Kippax b. McCabe | 0 |
| Ingelby, not out | 1 |
| Extras | 13 |
| | |
| Total (for 17 wickets) | 102 |

#### Bowling Analysis

| | Overs | Mdn. Overs | Runs | Wkts. |
|---|---|---|---|---|
| McCabe | 7.4 | 1 | 27 | 7 |
| Ives | 5 | 1 | 15 | 2 |
| Mailey | 8 | 0 | 44 | 6 |
| Fleetwood-Smith. | 6 | 3 | 5 | 2 |

#### Australia

| | |
|---|---|
| Carney, run out | 8 |
| Rofe stmpd. Howland, b. J. Buckley.. | 11 |
| Bradman c. Wright b. Kenyon | 110 |
| McCabe c. Cole b. J. Buckley | 57 |
| Kippax, not out | 76 |
| Richardson, run out | 30 |
| Extras | 10 |
| | |
| Total (for five wickets) | 302 |

#### Bowling Analysis

| | Overs | Mdn. Overs | Runs | Wkts. |
|---|---|---|---|---|
| J. Buckley | 10 | 1 | 42 | 2 |
| H. Jones | 10 | 2 | 23 | 0 |
| W. Page | 2 | 0 | 23 | 0 |
| R. Buckley | 2 | 0 | 19 | 0 |
| J. Wright | 3 | 0 | 16 | 0 |
| N. Buckley | 2 | 0 | 7 | 0 |
| A. Ingelby | 2 | 0 | 16 | 0 |
| J. Cole | 2 | 0 | 13 | 0 |
| W. Stedmond | 3 | 0 | 16 | 0 |
| G. Richards | 2 | 0 | 32 | 0 |
| W. Thain | 3 | 0 | 22 | 0 |
| W. McLeod | 1 | 0 | 9 | 0 |
| C. Kenyon | 4 | 0 | 30 | 1 |
| J. Hampson | 4 | 0 | 23 | 0 |

Transportation, milling and packing centre, Moose Jaw.

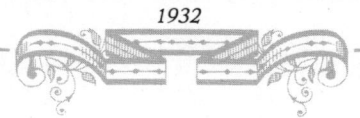

MAILEY'S TEAM v SASKATOON, at Saskatoon, on 6 August 1932.

| Mailey's Team | - First Innings | 418 for 7 wickets |
| | - Second Innings | - |
| Saskatoon | - First Innings | 101 |
| | - Second Innings | - |

DON BRADMAN    - b. Wrightson          88

Wicket - matting on ant bed.

## MAILEY'S TEAM.

### VANCOUVER, Aug. 8.

The Australian cricketers, in a match at Saskatoon, scored 418 for the loss of seven wickets. Saskatoon made 101.

## Spins Ball

**L. O. FLEETWOOD-SMITH**
A great bowler; this player bowls left hand and spins the ball in a most confusing manner. He is the only left-handed "googley" bowler in first class cricket and he's a great skittler of stumps.

| | | | | |
|---|---|---|---|---|
| Parr. | Bowled McCabe. | 7. | | |
| Goulding. | c & b Ives. | 1. | | |
| Wade. | Bowled McCabe. | 0. | | |
| Street. | c McCabe b Ives. | 5. | | |
| Wilson. | Bowled Ives. | 5. | McCabe. | 8/30. |
| Christian. | Bowled Ives. | 0. | Ives. | 4/14. |
| Chater. | c & b McCabe. | 8. | Mailey. | 5/30. |
| Nelson. | Bowled McCabe. | 3. | Smith. | 2/21. |
| Roney. | Bowled McCabe. | 3. | | |
| Bennett. | Bowled McCabe. | 2. | | |
| Marriott. | c Smith b Mailey. | 1. | | |
| Millns. | Bowled Smith. | 2. | | |
| Walls. | St. Richardson b Mailey. | 7. | | |
| Fraser. | c Richardson b Mailey. | 9. | | |
| Wrightson. | Bowled Mailey. | 0. | | |
| Mercer. | Bowled Smith. | 10. | | |
| Saunders. | Not Out. | 2. | | |
| Strutton. | c Carney b McCabe. | 6. | | |
| Cooper. | c McCabe b Mailey. | 16. | | |
| Sundries. | | 6. | | |
| | | 101. | | |

| | | | | |
|---|---|---|---|---|
| Tolhurst. | L.B.W. Millns. | 41. | Wilson. | 2/55. |
| Ives. | St. Saunders b Wilson. | 6. | Street. | 0/7. |
| Bradman. | Bowled Wrightson. | 88. | Christian. | 1/72. |
| McCabe. | c Wade b Wilson. | 121. | Millns. | 1/36. |
| Kippax. | c Millns b Christian. | 82. | Roney. | 0/63. |
| Nutt. | Not Out. | 61. | Wrightson. | 1/39. |
| Rofe. | L.B.W. Chater. | 2. | Walls. | 0/54. |
| Mailey. | c Millns b Chater. | 4. | Gibbons. | 0/29. |
| Carney. | Not Out. | 1. | Wade. | 0/37. |
| Sundries. | | 12. | Chater. | 2/12. |
| | | 7 fcr 418. | | |

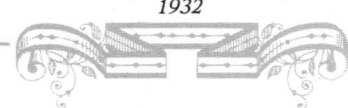
MAILEY'S TEAM v EDMONTON, at South Side Athletic Park, on 9 August 1932.

| | | | |
|---|---|---|---|
| Mailey's Team | - First Innings | 323 for 3 wickets | |
| | - Second Innings | - | |
| Edmonton | - First Innings | 59 | |
| | - Second Innings | - | |

DON BRADMAN - n.o.                    159

## MAILEY'S TEAM.

## Bradman in Good Form.

EDMONTON, Aug. 9.
Compiling 50 runs in the first 15 minutes D. G. Bradman led the touring Australians in a convincing victory over a selected Edmonton team of 18. Bradman flogged the bowling unmercifully, scoring 159 not out. S. J. McCabe scored a fine 121 before he was caught by Weaver off Ebdon. The Edmonton players were unable to cope with the Australian bowling, and were all out for 59.

| | | | | |
|---|---|---|---|---|
| Fleetwood Smith. | c Gallimore b Hesketh. | 0. | Hesketh. | 1/72. |
| Carney. | St. Field b Merritt. | 27. | Hodgson. | 0/31. |
| Bradman. | Not Out. | 159. | Weaver. | 0/24. |
| McCabe. | c Weaver b Ebdon. | 121. | Rimmell. | 0/55. |
| Kippax. | Not Out. | 12. | Comley. | 0/44. |
| Sundries. | | 4. | Merritt. | 1/11. |
| | | | Dieroff. | 0/55. |
| | 3 for | 323. | Ebdon. | 1/17. |
| | | | Edwards. | 0/8. |
| | | | Avison. | 0/6. |
| | | | | |
| Dieroff. | c & b Mailey. | 5. | | |
| Weaver. | c Bradman b Weaver. | 4. | | |
| Comley. | Bowled Ives. | 5. | | |
| Merritt. | c Kippax b Ives. | 3. | | |
| Hesketh. | Bowled Ives. | 1. | | |
| Avison. | c Tolhurst b Mailey. | 2. | | |
| Rimmell. | Bowled Ives. | 3. | | |
| Hodgson. | St Nutt b Mailey. | 1. | | |
| Jones. | Bowled Mailey. | 14. | | |
| Gallimore. | c Bradman b Ives. | 0. | | |
| Ebdon. | c Ives b Mailey. | 0. | Ives. | 11/22. |
| Pugh. | Bowled Ives. | 0. | Mailey. | 6/29. |
| Thomas. | Bowled Ives. | 0. | | |
| Cox. | c Mailey b Ives. | 6. | | |
| Field. | c Nutt b Ives. | 0. | | |
| Stewart. | Not Out. | 3. | | |
| Parker. | Bowled Ives. | 4. | | |
| Edwards. | c McCabe b Ives. | 0. | | |
| Sundries. | | 8. | | |
| | | 59. | | |

Don and Jessie Bradman at Edmonton.

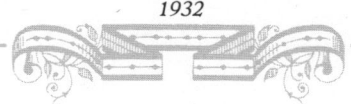

The Gallery at Banff.

"Million dollar" plunge at Banff.

Lake Louise — Pearl of the Rockies.

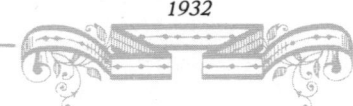

# BRADMAN PASSES 3,000 -RUN MARK FOR TOUR

## *Famous Australian Batsman Hits Out Another Century*

### Scores 125, Not Out, Against Vancouver Colts, to Pass 3,000 Mark for Tour—Aussies Win Final Match on Mainland by 128 Runs and Four Wickets—To Play Here Today

DON BRADMAN

VANCOUVER, Aug. 15.—The touring Australian cricket team added another victory to their long list of triumphs when they defeated Vancouver Colts, batting nineteen men and captained by Arthur Mailey of the Australians, by 128 runs and four wickets. The match was featured by Don Bradman's score of 125 not out, bringing the total runs made by this famous Aussie batsman on the present tour to more than three thousand.

The Australians gave a brilliant exhibition of batting, scoring their runs in two hours and ten minutes. After losing Carter with 2 on the score board, Kippax and Bradman carried the count to 52 before Kippax was caught by Strickland for 31. Carney, Rofe, Ives and Fleetwood-Smith were soon disposed of, but Richardson assisted Bradman to carry the score to 175 before Richardson was caught on the boundary by Carey for 35. He had three 6's and two 4's.

### SCORES QUICKLY

Tolhurst and Bradman then hit the bowling to all corners of the field, and when stumps were drawn the peerless Bradman had hit up 125, not out, and Tolhurst had scored 56, not out. Bradman batted two hours and five minutes and hit two 6's and seventeen 4's, while Tolhurst, during his stay of thirty minutes, hit three 6's and six 4's. When Bradman had made 70 he had scored 3,000 runs for the tour.

The Colts, under the direction of the famous Mailey, played well. Hendy carried his bat for 39, Ward hit up 18, and Lester, Stuart-Smith and Johnstone each made 12. Mailey scored 25. Bradman had the best bowling analysis for the Australians, taking six wickets for 25 runs. McCabe took nine for 60.

MAILEY'S TEAM v BRITISH COLUMBIA COLTS, at Brockton Point, on 15 August 1932.

| | | | |
|---|---|---|---|
| Mailey's Team | - First Innings | 286 for 7 wickets | |
| | - Second Innings | - | |
| British Columbia | - First Innings | 157 | |
| | - Second Innings | - | |

| | | |
|---|---|---|
| DON BRADMAN | - n.o. | 125 |

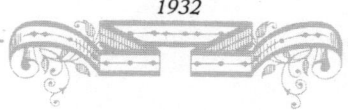

MAILEY'S TEAM v NORTHERN CALIFORNIA ALL-STARS, at Kezar Stadium,
on 20 August 1932.

| | | |
|---|---|---|
| Mailey's Team | - First Innings | 268 for 2 wickets dec. |
| | - Second Innings | - |
| Nthn. California | - First Innings | 20 |
| | - Second Innings | 33 |

| | | |
|---|---|---|
| DON BRADMAN | - b. Trenholm | 122 |

Wicket - matting on grass.

# Bradman's Bat Baffles Bowlers
## ✦ ✦ ✦ ✦ ✦ ✦ ✦ ✦ ✦
## Down Under' Cricketeers on Top

### By FRANK PERCY
#### Former Captain St. Francis Xavier College, Liverpool

Dapper Don Bradman, the Babe Ruth of Australian cricket, had only to unlimber his shoulders four times at Kezar Stadium to convince devotees of the game, as well as amaze first-timers at watching the pastime, that he came by his cognomen meritoriously. The four mighty heaves—all in succession—landed the ball high in the grandstand and aided a victory by the Australian tourists of an inning and 215 runs over an all-star aggregation selected from the best of the Northern California players.

To the local mind, untutored in such a score reckoning, this means that locals batted first, made 20 for the full dismissal of the side, and batted a second time around making 33. Between these two innings, Australia went to bat, but scored 268 with the loss of only tow wickets, which means for only two outs, where ten have to be made.

Bradman lived up to all that has been said about him. He played a magnificent all-around-the-wicket game—never gave a really easy chance at being caught out—and cut them through the slips, to leg, and deep on—cutting, slicing and when he felt in the mood, slugging that ball to every quarter of the stadium. He wore out four California bowlers—pitchers to the local cogniscenti—and when his wicket finally fell it was when he took a careless cut at a slow rising ball.

### TOLHURST ALSO STARS IN RUN GETTING

His partner in the lucrative run getting stand was E. Tolhurst, who gathered 117 runs to Bradman's 122. All pitches seemed alike to this pair, and an idea of their punishment of the bowling can be gathered from the fact that they made 168 runs in 34 minutes. Bradman's innings included five sixes (four in succession) and eight fours. Tolhurst gathered one six and thirteen fours.

Watching these cracks from down under makes people wonder when the rest of the team gets to bat, but it may be a different story today, when the pick of the California bowlers face them, being held in reserve for today's match.

For the locals Percival and Ochinal and Trenholm did yeoman work, but they were up against a combination of classic batting, lightning fielding and every kind of bowling. From the crack of the bat these Australians were on their toes and slips, cover point and midposition

players—contemporary to our infielders in baseball—were like ferrets on that ball. One slip was all that a California matsman had to make—one unguarded tap with the bat, and the ball glanced into an eagle-eyed fielder's hand.

### LOUD SPEAKER HELPS CROWD APPRECIATE GAME

The crowd liked the match and showed a rare aptitude toward learning it. A loud speaker, handled to a Queen's taste by Bob Davie, explained every point of the pastime, and made it easy for fans—at least let them know when applause was in order. There were two kinds of action, the parade of the California players to the crease-home plate to the uninitiated, and back to the bench, and the parade of bowlers to face Bradman and Tolhurst.

Ochinal made a splendid running shoestring catch to dismiss Mailey, first Anzac batter up, and it was Trenholm who clean bowled Bradman, but even a Bradman can weary of placing the most wicked looking pitches into the stands. Percival was the fly—the only fly—in Bradman's ointment. He played slips (something akin to shortstop) to the Aussie slugger and few runs went through his position.

As for the visiting bowlers, when a man gets 15 wickets for 26 runs, and his mate takes five for twelve runs, they must have something on the ball. McCabe had a medium to lightning paced delivery, while his fellow conspirators, Maley and Fleetwood Smth, used a "googly" akn to that deceptive knuckle ball. "Sep" Carter, 54-year-old wicket keeper for the visitors, as hawk-eyed a man as ever squatted behind the wickets—catcher to the baseball fan—won the crowd by his matchless work. His handling of those lightning deliveries and his masterly knowledge of where a ball was going to break stamps him as one of the greatest in the game today.

# Australians Humble Local Cricket Team

### CALIFORNIANS WILL HAVE 18 MEN ON TAP TODAY

The teams play again today at Kezar, and the Californians will have eighteen men in the lineup, a much reinforced side. They will have a change in the bowling selection, and more confidence, yhich is what they needed today facing such a remarkable outfit of machine-like opponents. The score:

#### NORTHERN CALIFORNIA ALL-STARS
##### First Inning

| | |
|---|---|
| Ochenal, c. Mailey, b. McCabe | 0 |
| Tull, b. McCabe | 0 |
| Clark, b. Mailey | 1 |
| Braga, c. Bradman, b. Mailey | 2 |
| Broome, c. Tolhurst, b. McCabe | 0 |
| Blackman, c. Tolhurst, b. Mailey | 0 |
| Percival, c. McCabe, b. Mailey | 10 |
| Stott, b. McCabe | 0 |
| Price, c. and b. McCabe | 3 |
| Butcher, run out | 0 |
| Trenholm, c. Fleetwood-Smith b. McCabe | 0 |
| Housen, b. Mailey | 1 |
| Nahaplet, c. Richardson, b. Mailey | 0 |
| Johnson, not out | 0 |
| Stott, run out | 0 |
| Extras | 3 |
| Total | 20 |

##### Bowling Analysis
McCabe, 7 wickets for 5 runs; Mailey, 5 wickets for 12 runs.

##### Second Inning

| | |
|---|---|
| Tull, c. Bradman, b. McCabe | 1 |
| Ochinal, c. Fleetwood-Smith, b. McCabe | 0 |
| Clark, b. Fleetwood-Smith | 0 |
| Braga, run out | 0 |
| Broome, c. Bradman, b. Fleetwood-Smith | 1 |
| Blackman, c. Mailey, b. McCabe | 4 |
| Percival, b. Fleetwood-Smith | 2 |
| Stott, b. Fleetwood-Smith | 8 |
| Price, b. McCabe | 2 |
| Butcher, b. McCabe | 6 |
| Trenholm, b. Fleetwood-Smith | 8 |
| Housen, b. McCabe | 1 |
| Nahaplet, c. Carney, b. McCabe | 5 |
| Johnson, c. Fleetwood-Smith, b. McCabe | 0 |
| Stone, not out | 0 |
| Extras | 2 |
| Total | 33 |

##### Bowling Analysis

| | |
|---|---|
| McCabe. | 8/21. |
| Smith. | 5/12. |

##### AUSTRALIA

| | |
|---|---|
| Mailey, c. Ochinal, b. Trenholm | 10 |
| Tolhurst, not out | 117 |
| Bradman, b. Trenholm | 122 |
| Extras | 19 |
| (Innings declared closed) | |
| Total, 268 for two wickets. | |

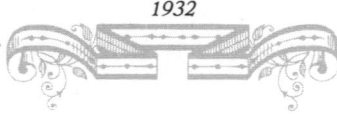

Kezar Stadium.

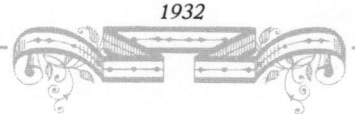

The famous Carpinteria grapevine.
"Under the shade of the old vine, in the primitive days of '50, was held the first election in Santa Barbara County."

MAILEY'S TEAM v MONTECITO, at the Peabody Stadium, on 24 August 1932.

| Mailey's Team | - First Innings | 387 for 6 wickets |
| | - Second Innings | - |
| Montecito | - First Innings | 58 |
| | - Second Innings | - |
| DON BRADMAN | - | 121 |

Wicket - matting on grass.

# BRADMAN AGAIN

## CENTURY IN CALIFORNIA

### ("Sun" Special)

SANTA BARBARA, CAL., Thursday.
The Australian touring cricketers yesterday defeated the Montecito Cricket Club at the Peabody Stadium very easily.

The local team, batting 18, were all out for 58. McCabe took 8 wickets for 30, Ives 4 for 10, and Fleetwood-Smith 5 for 12. The Australians lost six wickets for 387, Bradman hitting 121, Kippax 54, Nutt 58, Tolhurst 52, and Ives 46 not out.

The lineups and scores:
Australians—Capt. Victor Y. Richardson 18, Allen F. Kippax 54, Donald G. Bradman 121, S. J. McCabe 15, R. N. Nutt 58, E. K. Tolhurst 52, W. Ives 46 not out, P. Carney 18 not out, extras 5.

Montecito—D. Roberts 2, H. Yeoman 0, H. Maynard 11, R. Crow 2, M. Hall 9, F. Mills 3, J. Turnbull 0, A. Clayton 5, C. Boulton 1, Capt. W. A. Creasy 8, J. Flint 1, P. Aitken 0, E. Wilson 1, J. Washington 3, W. Wright 3, W. Minniken 1, R. Creasy 0, J. Tye 0, extras 9.

The Australians are on their way home after winning not only every match played on the American continent, but also a tilt with the famed "Ashes" team of England, one of the oldest and most famed cricket combinations. They will leave for Hollywood this morning, where they will play the film capital's crack team before sailing for Australia.

Ives.      4/11.
Smith.     5/10.
McCabe.    8/29.

Hollywood actors take time off from filming *Fu Man Chu* to have a photograph taken with the Australian players.

TOP   Boris Karloff.   FIRST ROW   A. Mailey, an actor, V. Richardson, the Director.
CENTRE   H. Carter.   SECOND ROW   E. Rofe, R. Nutt, W. Ives, S. McCabe.
THIRD ROW   P. Carney, L. Fleetwood-Smith, Myrna Loy, K. Tolhurst, A. Kippax, D. Bradman.
FRONT ROW   Desmond Roberts, an actor, Charles Aubrey Smith.

A. Mailey, Boris Karloff, Leslie Howard, Mrs. Howard, Desmond Roberts, V. Richardson.

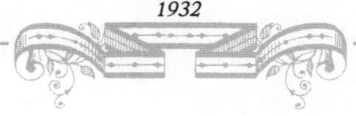
MAILEY'S TEAM v HOLLYWOOD, at University Campus grounds, on 26 August 1932.

| Mailey's Team | - First Innings | 144 for 2 wickets |
| | - Second Innings | - |
| Hollywood | - First Innings | 114 |
| | - Second Innings | - |

DON BRADMAN - n.o.    52

## AUSTRALIAN CRICKETERS.

LOS ANGELES, Aug. 27.
The Australian cricket team (144 for two wickets) defeated Hollywood cricket club (114 for 18 wickets). Scorers: V. Y. Richardson, 42; S. J. McCabe, 26; D. G. Bradman, 52 not out; A. F. Kippax, 24 not out. Hollywood batted first and darkness stopped the game, with Bradman and Kippax going strongly.

| | | | | |
|---|---|---|---|---|
| Roberts. | St. Carter b Smith. | 13. | | |
| Greaves. | c Carney b McCabe. | 2. | | |
| Maynard. | Bowled McCabe. | 0. | | |
| Whitley. | Bowled Ives. | 20. | | |
| Hoyle. | Bowled Smith. | 3. | | |
| Thomas. | c Kippax b Ives. | 0. | | |
| Hall. | Bowled Smith. | 6. | | |
| Karloff. | Bowled Ives. | 12. | | |
| Wright. | c Richardson b Ives. | 0. | | |
| Harper. | Bowled Ives. | 0. | | |
| Smith. | c Richardson b Smith. | 24. | | |
| Kinnell. | Bowled Smith. | 1. | McCabe. | 2/7. |
| Harper. | Bowled Smith. | 5. | Ives. | 6/59. |
| Du Domaine. | Bowled Smith. | 6. | Smith. | 9/31. |
| Finlayson. | Bowled Ives. | 0. | | |
| Moore. | Bowled Smith. | 4. | | |
| Brown. | c Ives b Smith. | 0. | | |
| Cross. | Not Out. | 1. | | |
| Sundries. | | 17. | | |
| | | **114.** | | |

| | | | | |
|---|---|---|---|---|
| Richardson. | c Thomas b Harper. | 42. | Roberts. | 0/32. |
| McCabe. | c Wright b Harper. | 26. | Du Domaine. | 0/37. |
| Bradman. | Not Out. | 52. | Wright. | 0/6. |
| Kippax. | Not Out. | 23. | Harper. | 2/57. |
| Sundry. | | 1. | Whitley. | 0/11. |
| | 2 for **144.** | | | |

## TAMED BY A GOOGLY!

## An "Emperor" Meets His Master

"Sunday Sun" Special

LOS ANGELES, Saturday.

A FEARSOME figure in the mask of Foo Man Chew, the huge Boris Karloff stood on the set in the Metro-Goldwyn-Mayer studio thundering out his commands in the voice of a powerful Oriental emperor.

Then came the fade out. The scene shifted to Hollywood's cricket field, and it was the same Boris, considered the best batsman in the movie colony's team, who a little later floundered about in a most undignified manner against the slows of Fleetwood-Smith.

The Australians spent the morning visiting the exclusive Metro studio, which resembles a great self-contained cosmopolitan colony.

They saw various pictures being made by Maureen O'Sullivan, Jean Harlow, Mary Astor, Clark Gable, the three Barrymores, Walter Huston, Mitchell Lewis, Marie Dressler, Myrna Loy, David Torrance, and Boris Karloff.

### Australians Watch

The match, which followed was viewed by a crowd of movie people, mostly English, with a smattering of Australians, including "Snowy" Baker.

The Australians won, 144 for two wickets to 114 for 18.

Scorers were:—Richardson (42), McCabe (26), Bradman (52, not out), Kippax (24, not out). Darkness stopped the game, with Bradman and Kippax going strong.

The final match will be played on Sunday, when Aubrey Smith will captain the locals.

Charles Aubrey Smith shows his style at the crease.

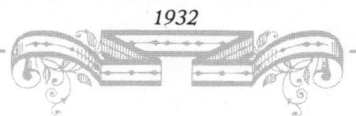
MAILEY'S TEAM v HOLLYWOOD, at University Campus grounds, on 28 August 1932.

| Mailey's Team | - First Innings | 182 for 2 wickets |
| | - Second Innings | - |
| Hollywood | - First Innings | 164 |
| | - Second Innings | - |

DON BRADMAN   - n.o.                              83

## MAILEY'S TEAM.

## Tour Ends at Hollywood.

HOLLYWOOD, Aug. 27.
The Australian cricketers ended their tour on Sunday by defeating Hollywood Cricket Club by 182 for two wickets to 164 for 20 wickets. The Australians sail on Wednesday from San Francisco.

The home team occupied two and a half hours at the creases. The Australians made their runs in an hour and a quarter, when darkness stopped play.

McCabe made 48, Richardson 47, Bradman 83 not out, and Tolhurst 3 not out.

Fleetwood-Smith took seven wickets for 39, McCabe three for 37, Mailey eight for 50, and Ives one for 20. Playing with Hollywood were H. B. Warner, Desmond Roberts, Claude King, and Murray Kinnell, of the motion picture colony. Roberts, who was a former English player, scored 66. Motion pictures were taken.

Leaving San Francisco for home.

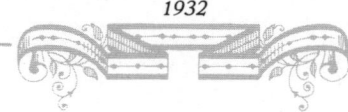

```
Matches Played.                             51.
   "    won outright.                        4.
   "     "   on first innings.              40.
   "    lost on first innings.               1.
   "    drawn.                               6.
```

```
Stumpings.          H. Carter.            31.
                    V.Y.Richardson.        9.
                    R.Nutt.                7.
```

```
Catches.            McCabe.               55.
                    Richardson.           34.
                    Fleetwood-Smith.      31.
                    Bradman.              27.
                    Mailey.               27.
                    Ives.                 26.
                    Kippax.               23.
                    Tolhurst.             22.
                    Nutt.                 22.
                    Carney.               17.
                    H.Carter.             11.
                    Rofe.                 11.
                    W.Carter.              2.
```

## BATTING FIGURES.

| Name. | Inns. | N.O's. | Runs. | H.S. | Average. |
|---|---|---|---|---|---|
| Bradman. | 51 | 14 | 3779 | 260 | 102.1 |
| McCabe. | 47 | 4 | 2361 | 157 | 54.9 |
| Kippax. | 43 | 9 | 1853 | 132 | 54.5 |
| Nutt. | 41 | 11 | 1402 | 109 | 46.7 |
| Tolhurst. | 42 | 12 | 1285 | 117x | 42.8 |
| Bramble. | 1 | 0 | 36 | 36 | 36 |
| Richardson. | 44 | 3 | 1380 | 147 | 33.6 |
| Ives. | 29 | 12 | 444 | 46x | 26.1 |
| H.Carter. | 10 | 5 | 100 | 27x | 20 |
| Carney. | 21 | 8 | 201 | 27 | 15.4 |
| Rofe. | 26 | 6 | 280 | 40 | 14 |
| Vaughan. | 1 | 0 | 14 | 14 | 14 |
| Mailey. | 20 | 2 | 236 | 51x | 13.1 |
| Fleetwood-Smith. | 11 | 3 | 39 | 23 | 4.8 |
| W.Carter. | 2 | 1 | 1 | 1 | 1 |

## BOWLING FIGURES.

| Name. | Wickets. | Runs. | Average. |
|---|---|---|---|
| McCabe. | 189 | 1139 | 6 |
| Ives. | 92 | 678 | 7.3 |
| Fleetwood-Smith. | 238 | 1788 | 7.5 |
| Mailey. | 203 | 1755 | 8.6 |
| Bradman. | 24 | 240 | 10 |
| Kippax. | 20 | 225 | 11.2 |
| Richardson. | 5 | 103 | 20.6 |
| Carney. | 2 | 89 | 44.5 |
| Rofe. | 0 | 15 | - |
| Tolhurst. | 0 | 19 | - |
| Nutt. | 0 | 29 | - |

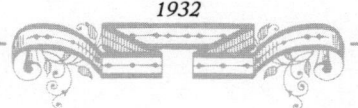

OWN BOWLING FIGURES.

| OPPONENTS. | WICKETS. | RUNS. |
|---|---|---|
| Victoria. | 7 | 43 |
| Vancouver. | 2 | 12 |
| Toronto. | 2 | 49 |
| New York. | 2 | 27 |
| Chicago. | 0 | 4o |
| Calgary. | 3 | 13 |
| Vancouver. | 6 | 25 |
| San Francisco. | 1 | 9 |
| Hollywood. | 1 | 16 |

24 wickets.   24o runs.   10 average.

Number of catches taken.     27.

Number of centuries scored         18
including double centuries.          2

OWN BATTING FIGURES.

| OPPONENTS. | HOW OUT. | RUNS. | OPPONENTS. | HOW OUT. | RUNS. |
|---|---|---|---|---|---|
| Cowichan. | Caught. | 60. | Windsor. | Caught. | 24. |
| Victoria. | " | 94. | Chicago. | Bowled. | 4. |
| Vancouver. | Not Out. | 110. | " | Caught. | 10. |
| " | Caught. | 42. | " | " | 13. |
| " | " | 180. | " | " | 41. |
| Toronto. | Not Out. | 27. | " | " | 2. |
| " | Bowled. | 11. | Winnipeg. | " | 14. |
| " | Caught. | 40. | Regina. | Not Out. | 116. |
| " | " | 52. | Moose Jaw. | Caught. | 110. |
| Guelph. | " | 260. | " | Not Out. | 100. |
| Ridley College. | Not Out. | 10. | Yorkton. | Caught. | 115. |
| " | Caught. | 109. | Saskatoon. | Bowled. | 88. |
| Montreal. | Stumped. | 95. | Edmonton. | Caught. | 34. |
| " | Not Out. | 200. | " | Not Out. | 159. |
| " | Bowled. | 92. | Calgary. | " | 39. |
| Ottawa. | Caught. | 105. | " | " | 69. |
| " | Bowled. | 114. | Vancouver. | " | 103. |
| New York. | Caught. | 45. | " | " | 125. |
| " | " | 117. | Victoria. | Caught. | 88. |
| " | " | 0. | " | Bowled. | 171. |
| " | " | 8. | San Francisco. | " | 123. |
| " | " | 35. | " | Caught. | 29. |
| " | " | 57. | Santa Barbara. | L.B.W. | 121. |
| Detroit. | Bowled. | 26. | Hollywood. | Caught. | 42. |
| | | | " | Not Out. | 52. |
| | | | " | " | 18 |
| | | | Hollywood. | Not Out. | 83. |

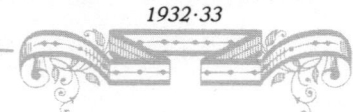

# 1932 -33 Season

As long as cricket is played it is doubtful whether there will ever be a more turbulent season than 1932/33.

The name "body-line" was coined to describe the type of bowling used by England. Fast leg-theory was an inadequate description, for reasons which become evident in articles dealing with the matches.

Umpires evidently regarded the tactics as "legal" under the laws, but other aspects of this form of attack were considered so detrimental to the interests of cricket that ultimately legislation was introduced to prevent a repetition of such events.

It was often stated that "body-line" was invented for my special benefit; in other words to curb my ability to make runs. Whether that was true or not I am quite certain that no batsman could ever succeed in consistently making big scores against such tactics. Worse still, nobody would continue to face the hazards associated with "body-line".

It is on record that when the great W. R. Hammond had to bat against a modified version of it from the West Indians, Martindale and Constantine, he indicated that either this form of bowling ceased or he would retire.

At the commencement of the season, ill health, combined with an argument with the Australian Board of Control over my writing activities, further militated against my ability to concentrate and altogether it was a most unhappy season.

In retrospect perhaps I can take satisfaction in saying that my own part in events may have been largely responsible for outlawing tactics so foreign to cricket.

*Don Bradman*

## — SEASON 1932-33 —

| TITLE | GAME | | SCORES | |
|---|---|---|---|---|
| Second Class | Zingari | St. Paul's University | 15 | r.o. |
| | No. 3 Trial Team | No.1 Trial Team | 145 | C. |
| | Press | Navy | 53 | n.o. |
| | Palmers | Mick Simmons | 84 | n.o. |
| | Coaching Team | N. Sydney Juniors | 148 | C. |
| | New South Wales | Ex-Internationals | 98 | C. |
| | St. George | Bowral District | 154 | C. |
| | " | " " | 71 | S. |
| | " | " " | 159 | B. |
| First Grade | " | Gordon | 108 | n.o. |
| | " | Mosman | 105 | n.o. |
| | " | Manly | 112 | C. |
| | " | Balmain | 134 | C. |
| | " | Waverley | 53 | C. |
| First Class | Combined W.A. | England | 3 | C. |
| | " | " | 10 | C. |
| | An Australian XI. | " | 36 | L.B.W. |
| | " | " | 13 | B. |

| TITLE | GAME | | SCORES | |
|---|---|---|---|---|
| | New South Wales | - | 18 | L.B.W. |
| | - - - | - | 23 | B. |
| | - - - | - | 1 | B. |
| | - - - | - | 71 | C. |
| Sheffield Shield | - - - | Victoria | 238 | C. |
| | - - - | - | 52 | n.o. |
| | - - - | - | 157 | C. |
| | - - - | South Australia | 56 | C. |
| | - - - | - | 97 | B. |
| Test | Australia | England | 0 | B. |
| | - | - | 103 | n.o. |
| | - | - | 8 | C. |
| | - | - | 66 | C. |
| | - | - | 76 | B. |
| | - | - | 24 | C. |
| | - | - | 48 | B. |
| | - | - | 71 | B. |
| | Total runs | | 2610 | |

## — SUMMARY —

### AVERAGES

| | Innings | N.O's. | H.S. | Runs | Average |
|---|---|---|---|---|---|
| Test | 8 | 1 | 103x | 396 | 56·5 |
| Sheffield Shield | 5 | 1 | 238 | 600 | 150· |
| Other First Class | 8 | 0 | 71 | 175 | 21·8 |
| All First Class | 21 | 2 | 238 | 1171 | 61·6 |
| First Grade | 5 | 2 | 134 | 512 | 170·6 |
| Other Second Class | 9 | 2 | 159 | 927 | 132·4 |
| All Second Class | 14 | 4 | 159 | 1439 | 143·9 |
| All Matches | 35 | 6 | 238 | 2610 | 90· |

# WILL HE PLAY?

## CONTROL BOARD RE-AFFIRMS WRITING BAN

### CRICKET DRAMA WORTHY OF TEST FINALE

## GAME, NOT MAN

### BOARD WOULD CONSIDER HIS APPLICATION

A cricket drama worthy of the vital moments of a Test finale was staged in Sydney yesterday.

While the steamer Monowai was steaming into Sydney Harbor with Don Bradman aboard, returning from the tour of America and Canada, the Board of Control was re-affirming its embargo on player-writers.

The sensation caused by the board's announcement was followed by a still greater sensation with Bradman's declaration that if the board had said its last word he would not be available for Test cricket against the Englishmen.

"I have signed a contract to write articles," stated Bradman, "and I must keep it. I cannot let cricket interfere with my work."

It is, of course, unthinkable that Bradman will not play for Australia, and doubtless a satisfactory way out of the impasse will be found. Associated Newspapers Ltd. will not stand unreasonably in the way of Bradman playing Test cricket.

# New South Wales v Victoria

NEW SOUTH WALES v VICTORIA, at Sydney, 4, 5, 7 and 8 November 1932.

| | | |
|---|---|---|
| New South Wales | - First Innings | 475 |
| | - Second Innings | 82 for 1 wicket |
| Victoria | - First Innings | 404 |
| | - Second Innings | 150 |
| | New South Wales won by 9 wickets. | |

| | | |
|---|---|---|
| DON BRADMAN | - c. L.P. O'Brien b. L.O'B. Fleetwood-Smith | 238 |
| | - not out | 52 |

Going in at 16 for 1 just after lunch on the second day, DON BRADMAN took only half an hour to complete 50, and only seventy-three minutes to reach his century. His 200 took two hours fifty-two minutes, and just before the close of play, he was fourth out with the score at 355. He had batted for only three hours twenty minutes and hit thirty-two fours. His time for reaching 200 in this match, was the fastest ever achieved in a Sheffield Shield match.

His second innings started at 19 for 1, soon after the start of the fourth day's play, and lasted only forty-one minutes, his eighth boundary was the winning hit.

## SHIELD SCORES

### VICTORIA—First Innings

| | |
|---|---|
| W. M. WOODFULL, run out | 74 |
| W. H. PONSFORD, c Kippax, b Hird | 200 |
| L. O'BRIEN, st Oldfield, b Hird | 15 |
| K. E. RIGG, lbw, b O'Reilly | 0 |
| L. DARLING, c Fingleton, b O'Reilly | 0 |
| J. THOMAS, b Hird | 5 |
| B. A. BARNETT, lbw, b Bradman | 36 |
| D. J. BLACKIE, c Oldfield, b O'Reilly | 20 |
| L. O. FLEETWOOD-SMITH, b O'Reilly | 38 |
| H. ALEXANDER, c Hird, b O'Reilly | 1 |
| H. IRONMONGER, not out | 3 |
| Sundries | 12 |
| Total | 404 |

Fall of Wickets: 138, 185, 188, 188, 205, 304, 354, 378, 383, 401.

### BOWLING:

| | O. | M. | R. | W. |
|---|---|---|---|---|
| Theak | 18 | 1 | 64 | 0 |
| McCabe | 8 | 0 | 44 | 0 |
| Hill | 27 | 5 | 48 | 0 |
| O'Reilly | 44.4 | 17 | 81 | 5 |
| Hird | 23 | 0 | 115 | 3 |
| Cummins | 7 | 0 | 32 | 0 |
| Bradman | 3 | 0 | 8 | 1 |

### VICTORIA.—First Innings .. .. .. 404
### Second Innings

| | |
|---|---|
| W. M. WOODFULL, st Oldfield, b Hird | 83 |
| L. O'BRIEN, c Theak, b McCabe | 13 |
| K. E. RIGG, run out | 10 |
| L. DARLING, b Hird | 2 |
| J. THOMAS, not out | 24 |
| B. J. BARNETT, c Bradman, b Hird | 0 |
| D. J. BLACKIE, st Oldfield, b Hird | 1 |
| L. O. FLEETWOOD-SMITH, c Bill, b Hird | 5 |
| H. ALEXANDER, c Theak, b Hird | 6 |
| H. IRONMONGER, run out | 0 |
| W. H. PONSFORD, abs., injured | 0 |
| Sundries (leg-byes 4, wide 1, no-ball 1) | 6 |
| Total | 150 |

### BOWLING

| | O. | M. | R. | W. |
|---|---|---|---|---|
| Theak | 5 | 0 | 24 | 0 |
| Hill | 10 | 1 | 15 | 0 |
| O'Reilly | 20 | 8 | 26 | 0 |
| Hird | 17.4 | 1 | 56 | 6 |
| McCabe | 3 | 0 | 13 | 1 |

Hird bowled a wide and McCabe a no-ball.

### NEW SOUTH WALES.—First Innings

| | |
|---|---|
| W. BILL, b Fleetwood-Smith | 19 |
| J. H. FINGLETON, l.b.w., b Alexander | 6 |
| D. G. BRADMAN, c O'Brien, b Fleetwood-Smith | 238 |
| A. F. KIPPAX, c Barnett, b Alexander | 52 |
| S. J. McCABE, c Fleetwood-Smith, b Alexander | 56 |
| H. THEAK, b Alexander | 39 |
| S. HIRD, c Barnett, b Alexander | 6 |
| F. CUMMINS, b Alexander | 13 |
| W. O'REILLY, b Alexander | 0 |
| W. A. OLDFIELD, not out | 22 |
| C. HILL, b Ironmonger | 10 |
| Sundries (byes 8, leg-byes 6) | 14 |
| Total | 475 |

### BOWLING

| | O. | M. | R. | W. |
|---|---|---|---|---|
| Alexander | 22 | 1 | 95 | 7 |
| Darling | 7 | 0 | 40 | 0 |
| Fleetwood-Smith | 19 | 0 | 145 | 2 |
| Ironmonger | 26.1 | 2 | 96 | 1 |
| Blackie | 19 | 1 | 85 | 0 |

### N.S.W.—Second Innings

| | |
|---|---|
| J. H. FINGLETON, not out | 20 |
| O. W. BILL, b Alexander | 8 |
| D. G. BRADMAN, not out | 52 |
| Sundries | 2 |
| One wicket for | 82 |

Fall of Wicket: 1-19.

### BOWLING

| | O. | M. | R. | W. |
|---|---|---|---|---|
| Alexander | 3 | 0 | 23 | 1 |
| Darling | 1 | 0 | 7 | 0 |
| Fleetwood-Smith | 5 | 0 | 27 | 0 |
| Ironmonger | 5 | 2 | 17 | 0 |
| Blackie | 1.2 | 0 | 6 | 0 |

Sundries: One bye, one leg-bye.

New South Wales won by nine wickets.

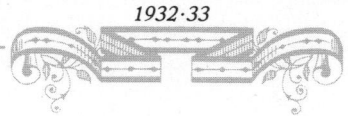

# Bradman's Entrancing 235 in 3½ Hours

## Trumper Never Batted More Amazingly: Fleetwood-Smith Bowls With Tenacity, Grit and Sting

BRADMAN went in when one wicket was down for 16 at 5 minutes past 2, and, at once began to unfold amazing forcing strokes off the middle stump to the on-side. These were impressively diversified with perfectly-placed humming off-strokes on the drive and the cut. Fleetwood-Smith, the new bowler, came at him. As though both men felt the challenge, the contest between them, under conditions made for the batsman, was one of the most fascinating I have ever witnessed.

HERE was a colt making his first appearance against the best living batsman, and that batsman in the mood to attack with eerie skill and tremendous vigor.

THE colt came at him and under a heavy pounding kept them well up and made the ball spin and turn back. Through perfect footwork and the most wonderful placing of the ball, and with stinging power and consummate wrist action, Bradman punished him. And he never wilted for an instant. An ordinary visitor to the ground not knowing much about cricket, might have thought Fleetwood-Smith a neophyte with the ball, with the scoreboard providing evidence in support. But I reckon he bowled grandly against the batting wonder of the times.

AS the battle went along and captain Woodfull kept the colt hard at it, the impression created on one's mind was, that while Bradman is greater than ever, another new Australian bowler of very high class had been found, one possessing what an old cricketing friend terms "guts."

THE first day in this game was worthy of rank with the best whenever New South Wales and Victoria have been at one another. The second day was still greater, perhaps unsurpassed in the entire series seen in Sydney, because while the batting was glorious, the bowlers never at any stage lost their zest, the bowling its precision, and the fielding its speed and certainty. It was cricket in excelsis and a wonderful preliminary skirmish for the Test. There were 24,656 people, with the gate £1198. Rarely has a Saturday crowd had such a feast of the finest things in cricket while basking in such beautiful sunshine, a thorough contrast in weather to Friday.

### BRADMAN THE AMAZING

BRADMAN, in at 2.5 p.m., met the first ball with such precise timing, wristiness and power as he turned it to the on that one instantly thought of Trumper. From that moment he took charge as Victor used to do. Those present at this time will, one believes, agree that nothing finer in batting has ever been seen on the famous ground. Trumper, Ranji, Macartney, MacLaren, Mackay, Hobbs, Foster—not one in his great moments bent this, and Trumper alone perhaps equalled it.

### A FIERCE DUEL

FLEETWOOD-SMITH relieved Darling, and after a few balls turning from the off, Bradman started on him. He drove one straight to the fence by that crisp, wristy back-stroke of which he is a master. Then stepping in he drove another with consummate placing between the mid-offs. It went to the fence. One dropped a bit shorter and with a venomous hook it travelled to the pickets at square leg. Then came the last ball of the over. It pitched near, good-length just outside the line of Bradman's legs. He shaped as though expecting the ball to break away from him to leg, but it turned the other way and his bat meeting it sent it uppishly towards mid-on. Fleetwood-Smith, who is a very fine fieldsman, moved across, but the ball touched and passed between his hands to pitch short of Ironmonger, and then run on to the boundary. It was a miss by the bowler, a mistimed shot by the batsman. That made Bradman 41. He then reached 51 in half an hour out of 62 scored since he had gone in.

### SCORES 65 IN 35 MINUTES

WITH the fighting aggressiveness of a bull terrier Bradman used his feet with uncanny precision in making the ball suit him and again attacked the left-hander. First he whipped one on the pull for four, the pace giving the field no chance of intercepting it. Then another past extra mid-off flashed to the fence, two for one past cover and another straight past the bowler to the sight board. His 65 were made in 35 minutes, with the crowd incessantly applauding.

THE score was 93, when Wendell Bill, pushing at a well-pitched off-break from Fleetwood-Smith, found it whip back sharply and, grazing the top of his glove hit the off stump. His 19 were carefully made.

KIPPAX had the pleasure of witnessing the duel from the other end for a while. The first hour produced 126 with Bradman, who had gone in first wicket down, now 90, and Fleetwood-Smith 1 for 81. Here a break in play occurred for close on ten minutes owing to a mishap to Ponsford. Blackie came on to bowl from the southern end. Bradman whipped the first ball to forward square leg. Close to the fence after a sharp run in trying to save the four with his foot, Ponsford trod on the ball and then ran on along the fence to finally lean against it in pain. Another fieldsman returned the ball. Ponsford had strained his foot beneath the instep, and four of his mates carried him from the sight board side across the field to the dressing room, where Mr. Langridge attended him. He did not appear again and Oakley fielded in his place.

### HIS CENTURY IN 70 MINUTES

THIS mishap broke up the orgy of run-getting for a time. The score was 145 with Bradman 95 and Kippax 22 when it happened. The 150 were made in an hour and 25 minutes. At 154 Bradman was cheered, when, by scoring three off Ironmonger, the board signalled his century. But "one short" brought it back to 99. He got another single next over and his hundred was completed in an hour and ten minutes with 13 boundaries. This against very fine bowling and brilliant fielding was superlative batting. Things simmered down now until

tea when it was 192 for two wickets, Bradman 124 and Kippax 40. Five bowlers had been tried.

### THE HOOK THAT SKIED IT

BEFORE another run was scored Kippax pulled a short one from Fleetwood-Smith to deep long leg a trifle square, but Thomas, out near the fence, missed it. The batsman explained subsequently that he had lost sight of the fieldsman through the spectators making a background of white out there. When he had scored 50 Kippax tried to hook a short-pitched one from Alexander, but mistiming, it flew straight up and wicket-keeper Barnett held it. His 50 were made in an hour and a quarter by attractive batting, though the placing was not nearly so clever as that of Bradman. The third wicket stand had added 128, and Bradman was now 141.

STEADY batting by Bradman and McCabe with Blackie keeping a fine length, swinging a trifle from the leg and bowling nothing loose and Ironmonger pegging away at the other end saw runs come yet more slowly than before. Bradman reached 150 at a quarter to 5 with the total 236. He was getting to the ball more than McCabe who was playing very steadily. Bradman scored well by placing his drives to get between a very deep mid-off (O'Brien) and the extra mid-off, some bringing fours and others ones or twos.

### FLEETWOOD GETS HIM

AT 277 Bradman was 180 and he reached the 200 at 304. He had tired, but here he commenced to vigorously attack again. He jumped into Fleetwood-Smith and skied one wide of very deep mid-off. Next ball he did the same and it went uppishly wide of extra mid-off. The following ball went high beyond the ordinary mid-off position and O'Brien, stationed deep out there, ran back and took a splendid catch, jumping with the two hands over his head. It was ten minutes to six when this happened and Bradman had scored 235 with the total 855. He batted 3½ hours and as he came in from the fields amidst cheers everyone said, "He's a wonder." Bradman is just that.

### YOU CANNOT PLACE HIM

AN uncanny eye. Wrists as flexible as steel. Unparalleled in placing the ball, unless Trumper was his equal, and one is inclined to think he was not. And perhaps unequalled by any other batsman in his judgment of the length. This quality he possesses to an extraordinary degree. Bradman has developed into a greater batsman than ever, with his on-side battery absolutely bewildering to bowlers and captains in placing the field. Those of us able to look back through the years know what great cricketers owe to their game. But Bradman is one of the cricketers to whom the game likewise owes something.

## THE ENGLISH TEAM

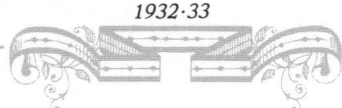

LEFT TO RIGHT, BACK ROW    E. Paynter, L. E. G. Ames, H. Verity, W. E. Bowes, F. R. Brown, T. B. Mitchell, H. Larwood.
FRONT ROW    The Nawab of Pataudi, R. E. S. Wyatt, D. R. Jardine (Captain), H. Sutcliffe, M. Leyland.
INSET    W. Voce, M. W. Tate, G. Duckworth, W. R. Hammond, P. F. Warner, G. O. Allen.

(E. Sampey, photograph)

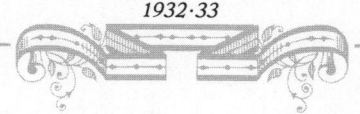

# Australia v England
# First Test Match

AUSTRALIA v ENGLAND, First Test Match, at Sydney, 2, 3, 5, 6 and 7 December 1932.

DON BRADMAN was unable to play in the First Test Match early in December owing to ill health, and in his absence Australia lost by 10 wickets.

Bradman had signed a contract with a newspaper to report the Test Matches, which had brought him into dispute with the Australian Board of Control, and he had for some weeks been the centre of a heated controversy on the subject.    The 'player-writer' controversy was eventually solved by the newspaper in question releasing Bradman from his contract, and he played no cricket for nearly a month while he attempted to recover his health.

## FIRST TEST MATCH

Played at Sydney Cricket Ground, December 2, 3, 5, 6, and 7, 1932.  Woodfull won the toss from Jardine.  England won by 10 wickets and one run.  Gross attendance, 158,125, and gate £14,863.

### AUSTRALIA.—First Innings

| | | |
|---|---|---|
| W. M. WOODFULL, c Ames, b Voce | | 7 |
| W. H. PONSFORD, b Larwood | .... | 32 |
| J. H. FINGLETON, c Allen, b Larwood | | 26 |
| A. F. KIPPAX, lbw, b Larwood | | 8 |
| S. J. McCABE, not out | ...... | 187 |
| V. Y. RICHARDSON, c Hammond, b Voce | | 49 |
| W. A. OLDFIELD, c Ames, b Larwood | | 4 |
| C. V. GRIMMETT, c Ames, b Voce | | 19 |
| L. NAGEL, b Larwood | .... .... | 0 |
| W. J. O'REILLY, b Voce | .... .... | 4 |
| T. W. WALL, c Allen, b Hammond | | 4 |
| B 12, lb 4, nb 4 | .... .... | 20 |
| **Total** | | **360** |

FALL: 22, 65, 82, 87, 216, 231, 299, 300, 305, 360.

Larwood  31 5 96 5  Ham'nd  14.2 0 34 1
Voce .. .. 29 4 110 4  Verity .. 13  4 35 0
Allen .. .. 15 1 65 0
Voce 3 n-b, Larwood, 1 n-b.

### AUSTRALIA.—Second Innings

| | | |
|---|---|---|
| W. M. WOODFULL, b Larwood | .... | 0 |
| W. H. PONSFORD, b Voce | .... | 2 |
| J. H. FINGLETON, c Voce, b Larwood | | 40 |
| S. J. McCABE, lbw, b Hammond | | 32 |
| V. Y. RICHARDSON, c Voce, b Hammond | | 0 |
| A. F. KIPPAX, b Larwood | .... .... | 19 |
| W. A. OLDFIELD, c Leyland, b Larwood | | 1 |
| C. V. GRIMMETT, c Allen, b Larwood | | 5 |

| | | |
|---|---|---|
| L. NAGEL, not out | ... .... ... .... | 21 |
| T. W. WALL, c Ames, b Allen | .... | 20 |
| W. J. O'REILLY, b Voce | .... .... | 7 |
| B 2, l-b 12, n-b 2, w 1 | .... .... .... | 17 |
| **Total** | | **164** |

FALL: 2, 10, 61, 61, 100, 104, 105, 113, 151, 164.

Larwood  18  4 28 5   Hammond 15 6 37 2
Voce .. .. 17.3 5 54 2   Verity .. 4 1 15 0
Allen .. .. 9  5 13 1
Allen 1 no-ball and a wide, Voce a no-ball.

### ENGLAND—First Innings

| | | |
|---|---|---|
| H. SUTCLIFFE, lbw, b Wall | .... | 194 |
| R. E. S. WYATT, lbw, b Grimmett | .... | 38 |
| W. R. HAMMOND, c Grimmett, b Nagel | | 112 |
| NAWAB OF PATAUDI, b Nagel | .... | 102 |
| M. LEYLAND, c Oldfie'd, b Wall | .... | 0 |
| D. R. JARDINE, c Oldfie'd, b McCabe | | 27 |
| H. VERITY, lbw, b Wall | .... .... | 2 |
| G. O. ALLEN, c and b O'Reilly | .... | 19 |
| L. AMES, c McCabe, b O'Reilly | .... | 0 |
| H. LARWOOD, lbw, b O'Reilly | .... | 0 |
| W. VOCE, not out | .... .... .... | 0 |
| B 7, l-b 17, n-b 6 | .... .... | 30 |
| **Total** | | **524** |

FALL: 112, 300, 423, 423, 470, 479, 518, 522, 522, 524.

Wall  .. 38  0 104 3   McCabe  15  2 42 1
Nagel  .. 43.4 9 110 2   Kippax  3  1  3 0
O'Reilly  67 32 117 3   Grimmett 64 21 118 1
Wall and O'Reilly 3 no-balls.

### ENGLAND.—Second Innings

| | | |
|---|---|---|
| H. S. SUTCLIFFE, not out | ... .... | 1 |
| R. E. S. WYATT, not out | ... .... | 0 |
| No wickets for | .... .... ... ... .... | 1 |

BOWLING: McCabe 0-1.
UMPIRES: G. Hele (S.A.), and G. Borwick (N.S.W.).

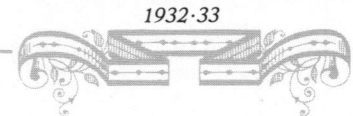

# New South Wales v Victoria

NEW SOUTH WALES v VICTORIA, at Melbourne, 26 and 27 December 1932.

New South Wales   - First Innings        388
                     - Second Innings     8 for no wicket

Victoria             - First Innings        258
                     - Second Innings     -

                     Drawn.

DON BRADMAN      - c. E.H. Bromley b. H. Ironmonger    157
                    - (did not bat)

New South Wales were sent in to bat after the first two days had been washed out by rain.     After the lunch interval DON BRADMAN took his place and soon settled down.     His first 50 was compiled in one and a half hours, and after tea he reached his century in two hours thirty-seven minutes.     He then lashed out making his last 50 in half an hour before being well caught at long-on, at 338 for 4. He batted altogether for three hours nineteen minutes and hit sixteen fours.

When he was 130, he completed 10,000 runs in all first-class cricket, in his 126th innings; he was at twenty-four years 121 days the youngest batsman ever to reach 10,000 runs.

Scores:—

### NEW SOUTH WALES.—First Innings.

| | |
|---|---|
| J. H. Fingleton, lbw, b Nagel | 85 |
| W. Brown, not out | 35 |
| D. G. Bradman, c Bromley, b Ironmonger | 157 |
| S. J. McCabe, lbw, b Alexander | 48 |
| A. F. Kippax, c King, b Ironmonger | 17 |
| S. Hird, c Barnett, b Ironmonger | 3 |
| F. Cummins, c Bromley, b Ironmonger | 15 |
| H. S. Love, lbw, b Alexander | 1 |
| W. J. O'Reilly, c and b Alexander | 2 |
| W. Howell, b Alexander | 5 |
| G. Stewart, c Darling, b Ironmonger | 7 |
| Byes 6, leg-byes 7 | 13 |
| Total | 388 |

Fall of wickets: 145, 248, 308, 338, 340, 341, 345, 369, 369, 388.

#### BOWLING.

| | O. | M. | R. | W. |
|---|---|---|---|---|
| Alexander | 26 | 3 | 107 | 4 |
| Nagel | 24 | 1 | 90 | 1 |
| Ironmonger | 30.2 | 6 | 87 | 5 |
| Fleetwood-Smith | 14 | 0 | 73 | 0 |
| Darling | 4 | 0 | 18 | 0 |

#### SECOND INNINGS.

| | |
|---|---|
| W. Howell, not out | 7 |
| G. Stewart, not out | 1 |
| No wicket for | 8 |

#### BOWLING.

| | O. | M. | R. | W. |
|---|---|---|---|---|
| Bromley | 1 | 0 | 8 | 0 |

### VICTORIA.—First Innings.

| | |
|---|---|
| W. H. Ponsford, b Howell | 12 |
| W. M. Woodfull, c Love, b O'Reilly | 19 |
| L. Darling, b O'Reilly | 4 |
| L. O'Brien, c McCabe, b O'Reilly | 53 |
| S. King, run out | 30 |
| E. Bromley, c Stewart, b McCabe | 84 |
| B. Barnett, b O'Reilly | 39 |
| L. Nagel, not out | 5 |
| L. Fleetwood-Smith, c O'Reilly, b Howell | 1 |
| H. Alexander, b Howell | 0 |
| H. Ironmonger, b Howell | 0 |
| Bye 1, leg-byes 8, wide 1, no-ball 1 | 11 |
| Total | 258 |

Fall of wickets: 32, 32, 36, 84, 174, 235, 255, 258, 258, 258.

#### BOWLING.

| | O. | M. | R. | W. |
|---|---|---|---|---|
| Stewart | 13 | 0 | 61 | 0 |
| McCabe | 7 | 0 | 34 | 1 |
| Howell | 25 | 6 | 69 | 4 |
| O'Reilly | 24 | 9 | 52 | 4 |
| Hird | 5 | 0 | 23 | 0 |
| Bradman | 2 | 0 | 8 | 0 |

Stewart a wide, O'Reilly a no-ball.

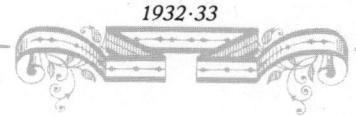

# BRADMAN'S 157

## IN SHIELD MATCH.

### Glimpses of Old Form.

### N.S.W. SEVEN FOR 348.

MELBOURNE, Monday.

Don. Bradman, whose form for the second test match has been the subject of so much speculation, to-day made 157 in 199 minutes in the Sheffield Shield match between New South Wales and Victoria, on the Melbourne Cricket Ground.

His batting until he reached his century lacked the audacity for which he is famous, but his last 50 were made in less than 30 minutes.

Fingleton made a solid 85, and McCabe, who was quieter than usual, made 48 in 81 minutes.

In the concluding stages of the day's play there was a surprising change in the aspect of the game. Just before Bradman was caught the board showed 338 for three wickets; at the end of the day the total was 348 for seven wickets.

Except towards the end of the day there were no fireworks. The test men apparently were grateful for the opportunity of getting good match practice.

The match had been delayed for two days by rain; to-day was delightfully sunny, and a cool breeze blew all day. The rain had kept the outfield slow, but the wicket, although slow, appeared to be in good order. Evidently in the expectation that the wicket and ground would be faster on the next day, Woodfull, much to the general surprise of the crowd, on winning the toss sent New South Wales in to bat. But his confidence in his bowlers was misplaced.

Bradman was evidently determined to recover his form; he took few risks. It was a batsman's innings, and gave his supporters confidence in his ability to display his best form in the test match on Friday. The way in which he batted after making his century delighted the crowd. He received a remarkable ovation as he came in.

Fingleton, who opened the innings, batted very well. He was the essence of solidity. His defence was sound, and his judgment excellent, and he scored all round the wicket, with a partiality for leg glances, at which he received plenty of practice. He batted 163 minutes and hit two fours. He and Brown had to pare down the bowling, and only 30 runs were made in the first hour.

In the last over before lunch Brown was struck on the body by a ball from Alexander. He was obviously in pain, and did not resume after lunch, but he will be fit to bat to-morrow. Brown, although worried occasionally by Ironmonger, was solid and showed good judgment.

McCabe did not worry much about runs or the rate of scoring.

## IRONMONGER BEST.

The bowlers had a difficult task on a dead wicket. Ironmonger was the most impressive. He maintained his accuracy to a marked degree, turned the ball from leg a little, although slowly, and was watched with care. Twice Fingleton mishit streakily through the slips, and Brown also had escapes. At one period after lunch Ironmonger and Nagel had the batsmen very subdued, but could not take wickets. Nagel generally was ineffective, his length being defective, and his direction was not good.

Fleetwood-Smith bowled some good balls, but they were too few to make him effective. He generally over-pitched them, and quick-footed batsmen like Bradman and McCabe scored heavily.

The fielding generally was not impressive, although Bromley, the former Western Australian player, gained applause for his agility in the long field and smart throwing. He cleverly caught Bradman, running in some distance.

The attendance was 21,187, and the takings were £1011.

# DON'S PROTEST

## In Strong Terms

### MAN'S LIVING

### BOARD MEDDLES

MELBOURNE, Friday.

On learning that the Board of Control had re-affirmed the player-writer rule, Bradman, adhering to his previous policy, advised Associated Newspapers Ltd. that it was his wish to honor his contract with them—which of course, meant he could not play cricket. Associated Newspapers, however, requested Bradman to take the field with the Australian team, stating their intention of sacrificing his services to them to enable him to play.

#### BOARD'S ACTION

Bradman this morning made the following statement:—

"Through the generosity of Associated Newspapers Ltd., who requested me to play for Australia instead of occupying a seat in the Press-box, I have been enabled to play in the second Test; and to the great cricket loving public of Australia may I express my extreme pleasure at being able to represent my country once more?

"Even though the Board of Control continues to prevent me from earning an honorable and permanent living from the occupation of journalism, it allows other Australian XI. players to broadcast their comments freely, despite the fact that broadcasting, to them, is only a temporary occupation.

"While the difference between journalism and radio work is so small as to make any distinction appear ridiculous, the board had all the facts before them at this meeting, and their legislation means they are able to dictate to players the means whereby they shall earn their living. If any player wishes to make a living in a channel which is unacceptable to the board, he is not going to be allowed to play for his country.

#### A PROTEST

"Only through the generosity of my employers am I enabled to play to-day. While doing so, I must emphatically protest against the Board of Control being allowed to interfere with the permanent occupation of any player. To my mind, the board was never meant to have the power of directing the business activities of the players. It is certainly no encouragement for anyone to remain in Australia when such restrictions are brought in."

#### BOARD CRITICISED

MELBOURNE, Friday.

In a leading article, "The Sun-News Pictorial" says: "It must be generally admitted that Bradman is one of the greatest batsmen the world has ever seen. Perhaps he is the greatest. Undoubtedly he is a match-winner. But, because he is earning his living as a cricket writer, and broadcasts his views on cricket, he has come into conflict with a small body of non-playing cricketers who happen to control the game in Australia.

"If Bradman decides that he must go on earning his living by writing on cricket, this little body of autocrats declares that he cannot go on playing Test cricket, however much the public want him to do so. In other words, it is prepared to defy public opinion and sacrifice Bradman, to have its own way. . . ."

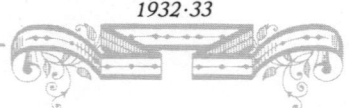

# Australia v England
# Second Test Match

AUSTRALIA v ENGLAND, Second Test Match, at Melbourne, 30, 31 December 1932, 2 and 3 January 1933.

| Australia | - First Innings | 228 |
|---|---|---|
|  | - Second Innings | 191 |
| England | - First Innings | 169 |
|  | - Second Innings | 139 |

Australia won by 111 runs.

| DON BRADMAN | - b. W.E. Bowes | 0 |
|---|---|---|
|  | - - not out | 103 |

In the first innings DON BRADMAN went in with the score at 67 for 2, and was bowled first ball; he attempted to hook a ball outside the off-stump which was not nearly short enough to hook, and a wild swing dragged the ball down on to his leg stump.

In his second innings he went in at 12.54 p.m. on the third morning with the score 27 for 2, with the result of the match depending almost entirely upon him, and he succeeded to such an extent that he virtually won the match off his own bat.    At lunch he was 25, reached 50 in ninety-three minutes, and had raised his score to 77 by tea-time.    Completing his century in two minutes over three hours Bradman's 103 not out lasted three hours five minutes, and he hit seven fours off 146 balls.    His defence was magnificent, and his courage in standing up to the 'body-line' bowling was equally admirable.

This was his seventh century v. England in Tests.

# THE TEST MATCH SCORES

### AUSTRALIA—First Innings

| | |
|---|---|
| W. M. Woodfull, b Allen | 10 |
| J. H. Fingleton, b Allen | 83 |
| L. P. O'Brien, run out | 10 |
| D. G. Bradman, b Bowes | 0 |
| S. J. McCabe, c Jardine, b Voce | 32 |
| V. Y. Richardson, c Hammond, b Voce | 34 |
| W. A. Oldfield, not out | 27 |
| C. V. Grimmett, c Sutcliffe, b Voce | 2 |
| T. W. Wall, run out | 1 |
| W. J. O'Reilly, b Larwood | 15 |
| H. Ironmonger, b Larwood | 4 |
| Byes 5, leg-byes 1, wides 2, no-balls 2 | 10 |
| **Total** | **228** |

Fall of wickets: 29, 67, 67, 131, 156, 188, 191, 200, 222, 228.

#### BOWLING

| | O. | M. | R. | W. |
|---|---|---|---|---|
| Larwood | 20.3 | 2 | 52 | 2 |
| Voce | 20 | 3 | 54 | 3 |
| Allen | 17 | 3 | 41 | 2 |
| Hammond | 10 | 3 | 21 | 0 |
| Bowes | 19 | 2 | 50 | 1 |

Allen bowled two wides. Larwood bowled two no-balls.

### ENGLAND—First Innings

| | |
|---|---|
| H. Sutcliffe, c Richardson, b Wall | 52 |
| R. E. S. Wyatt, l.b.w., b O'Reilly | 13 |
| W. R. Hammond, b Wall | 8 |
| Nawab of Pataudi, b O'Reilly | 15 |
| M. Leyland, b O'Reilly | 22 |
| D. R. Jardine, c Oldfield, b Wall | 1 |
| L. E. G. Ames, b Wall | 4 |
| G. O. Allen, c Richardson, b O'Reilly | 30 |
| H. Larwood, b O'Reilly | 9 |
| W. Voce, c McCabe, b Grimmett | 6 |
| W. E. Bowes, not out | 4 |
| Bye 1, leg-byes 2, no-balls 2 | 5 |
| **Total** | **169** |

Fall of wickets: 30, 43, 83, 98, 104, 110, 122, 138, 161, 169.

#### BOWLING

| | O. | M. | R. | W. |
|---|---|---|---|---|
| Wall | 21 | 4 | 52 | 4 |
| O'Reilly | 34.3 | 17 | 63 | 5 |
| Grimmett | 16 | 4 | 21 | 1 |
| Ironmonger | 14 | 4 | 28 | 0 |

Wall bowled two no-balls.

### AUSTRALIA—Second Innings

| | |
|---|---|
| W. M. Woodfull, c Allen, b Larwood | 26 |
| J. H. Fingleton, c Ames, b Allen | 1 |
| L. P. O'Brien, b Larwood | 11 |
| D. G. Bradman, not out | 103 |
| S. J. McCabe, b Allen | 0 |
| V. Y. Richardson, l.b.w., b Hammond | 32 |
| W. A. Oldfield, b Voce | 6 |
| C. V. Grimmett, b Voce | 0 |
| T. W. Wall, l.b.w., b Hammond | 3 |
| W. J. O'Reilly, c Ames, b Hammond | 0 |
| H. Ironmonger, run out | 0 |
| Byes 3, leg-bye 1, wides 4, no-ball 1 | 9 |
| **Total** | **191** |

Fall of wickets: 1, 27, 78, 81, 135, 150, 150, 184, 186, 191.

#### BOWLING

| | O. | M. | R. | W. |
|---|---|---|---|---|
| Larwood | 15 | 2 | 50 | 2 |
| Allen | 12 | 1 | 44 | 2 |
| Bowes | 4 | 0 | 20 | 0 |
| Voce | 15 | 2 | 47 | 2 |
| Hammond | 10.5 | 2 | 21 | 3 |

Allen bowled four wides and Voce bowled a no-ball.

### ENGLAND—Second Innings

| | |
|---|---|
| H. S. Sutcliffe, b O'Reilly | 33 |
| M. Leyland, b Wall | 19 |
| Nawab of Pataudi, c Fingleton, b Ironmonger | 5 |
| W. R. Hammond, c O'Brien, b O'Reilly | 23 |
| D. R. Jardine, c McCabe, b Ironmonger | 0 |
| L. E. G. Ames, c Fingleton, b O'Reilly | 2 |
| R. E. S. Wyatt, l.b.w., b O'Reilly | 28 |
| G. O. Allen, stpd. Oldfield, b Ironmonger | 23 |
| H. Larwood, c Wall, b Ironmonger | 3 |
| W. Voce, b O'Reilly | 0 |
| W. E. Bowes, not out | 0 |
| Sundries | 3 |
| **Total** | **139** |

Bowling: O'Reilly, 5 for 58; Ironmonger, 4 for 26; Wall, 1 for 20.

Australia won by 111 runs.

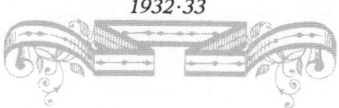

Bradman bowled Bowes for 0.

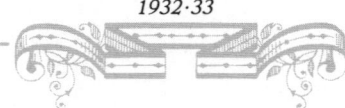

# BRADMAN'S CENTURY

## Cheered by Englishmen.

## BRILLIANT INNINGS.

### Crowd's Great Demonstration.

### DOGGED FIGHT FOR THE TEST.

#### Many Australian Batsmen Fail.

##### WORLD'S RECORD ATTENDANCE OF 68,188.

(FROM OUR SPECIAL REPRESENTATIVE.)

MELBOURNE, Monday.

England requires to reach a total of 251 in the second innings to win the second test match with Australia at the Melbourne Cricket Ground. Batting for three-quarters of an hour this afternoon, Sutcliffe and Leyland made 43 of the runs, and all wickets are intact.

Australia again surprisingly failed with the bat, scoring only 191 in the second innings. The team was saved from utter collapse by Don Bradman, who played a magnificent fighting innings. He passed his century with the last man in amid the greatest enthusiasm, and was 103 not out when the innings ended.

The Englishmen performed splendidly on a wicket which did not assist the fast bowlers. Hammond made an excellent effort, taking three wickets for 21 runs, and Larwood, Allen, and Voce all contributed to the good work.

Bradman showed that the wicket was easy enough, but it should prove of more assistance to Australia's spin bowlers than it was to the men of pace.

A world's record crowd of 68,188 was thrilled by a day's play full of incident.

### BRADMAN'S TRIUMPH.

There were amazing scenes and a wonderful demonstration when Bradman reached his century with the last man, Ironmonger, his partner. It seemed as if every man, woman, and child in the huge crowd was shouting and cheering. The ovation was sustained for minutes.

Bradman made a glorious return to the list of great scorers. At last he was the master batsman again, and in his eighth innings against Jardine's team he made a great century when every run was needed. The record-breaker has made faster hundreds, but never one that was more appreciated.

The crowd was dismayed and delighted in turn as the fortunes of this great test varied.

Australia's grip on the game was loosened, but Bradman remained to attack the English bowlers. He overcame the leg theory, and played a confident and brilliant innings.

#### FAST BOWLERS.

After Richardson had held a beautiful catch to give O'Reilly his fifth wicket and to finish the English innings with the score only 169, Australia had a lead of 59 runs, with England to have last use of the wicket. The failure of the bowlers to dismiss Sutcliffe or Leyland was upsetting, but it remains to be seen just how much the winning of the toss will mean to Australia to-morrow.

To-day the wicket was easy enough, notwithstanding the fact that the English fast bowlers had a good measure of success. The ball did not lift high from the pitch, and without a spin bowler in the team England appeared likely to be seriously handicapped.

Once again several of the Australian batsmen played with a painful lack of confidence and enterprise. The side should have done much better with weather and wicket conditions so favourable, but only Woodfull, Richardson, and Wall gave Bradman real support. Wall made only three runs, but pluckily defended his wicket, and gave Bradman the strike during a stay of over half an hour. Fingleton, the hero of the first innings, scored only one, and McCabe failed to make a run. Fingleton was the first to be dismissed. He opened the innings with Woodfull at 22 minutes past 12, and in the second over touched an out-swinger from Allen, and was caught behind the wicket. O'Brien made only 11, but was apparently quite confident till Larwood beat him with a splendid length ball, which took the off stump.

England's shock bowlers had performed splendidly to get two wickets with only 27 runs on the board. The hopes of the crowd changed to doubts concerning the ability of the batsmen to overcome the fierce attack, but encouraging applause swelled to roars of enthusiasm as Bradman and Woodfull, once more a great test pair, engaged in a steady, sound partnership for the third wicket. Woodful held on gallantly, as he did in the first innings. He batted in his old dogged fashion for 85 minutes, and his 26 runs were worth infinitely more than they showed on paper.

Woodfull fell to Larwood's leg trap, and when he played a defensive shot, popping the ball into the hands of Allen at forward short leg, it appeared as if he thought the ball would rise more quickly than it did.

McCabe's failure to score before a ball from Allen, which he attempted to drive, hit the off stump, caused Australian hearts to sink once again, and then Richardson came with a graceful if not aggressive innings in a stand with Bradman. These were the last of the recognised batsmen in the team, and four were down for 81 when they became associated.

### RICHARDSON AND VOCE.

Richardson played Voce easily, swinging him to the leg boundary, and caused the left-hander to change his field from the leg to the off side. With Bradman he appeared likely to stay for a productive partnership, but when he had made 32 he succumbed to a delivery from Hammond, which found him with his leg in front of the wicket, and he was out leg before wicket.

As in the second innings of the first test at Sydney, when he also got rid of Richardson, Hammond rallied to England's aid with a bowling effort which meant much to his side. Hammond operated from the grandstand end, and kept an accurate length, varying his pace cleverly. He got more out of the slow pitch than any of the other bowlers, and even Bradman was not prepared to take liberties with Hammond. It was Voce bowling a steady length and swinging the ball at times who beat Oldfield and Grimmett, but Hammond came again and dismissed Wall and O'Reilly.

Wall had won the admiration of the spectators by his defence and his alertness in working the strike for Bradman, who refused singles in order to keep his partner away from the bowling. Eventually Wall went low to Hammond, and O'Reilly playing carefully and leaving the scoring to Bradman, was caught behind the wicket.

When Wall departed Bradman had reached 96, and when O'Reilly left he was still two runs short of a century. The crowd was intensely excited, being as eager to see Bradman attain the three-figure mark as to see him score runs for the side.

#### HIS CENTURY.

Ironmonger had two balls from Hammond to play, and he survived them, although the first went close to his wicket. Bradman, waiting for the loose ball, and aiming at keeping the strike, played five balls from Voce, and lifted the last of the over to near the on boundary, running three. Thus he made his score 101 after batting for just over three hours, and the Englishmen joined in the applause which greeted the champion. Bradman still had to fight for his side, but at 5 o'clock, after he had scored two more runs, he called for a run after driving the ball, and Ironmonger, slow to get going, was run out. Bradman's placing was skilfully executed, and this was one of the outstanding features of his innings. His on-driving of Larwood and straight-driving of Allen were made with delightful ease. He also indulged in an occasional late cut, one beautiful shot off Hammond resulting in a boundary. He hit seven fours, and now that he has shown he is in something like his old form he will have confidence for further big matches ahead.

Bradman scored his first 50 in 93 minutes, and the remaining runs were added in 89 minutes. His innings was absolutely chanceless. For a time Larwood's leg field had worried him, but later he was definitely on top of the bowling, being restrained only against the accurate attack of Hammond and Voce.

Bradman has established another record, for he has now made seven centuries in tests with England, and no other Australian batsman has achieved that honour. Trumper and Woodfull are each credited with six centuries. Bradman commenced his test career only four years ago, and three of his centuries have been scored at Melbourne.

The only Englishmen who have made more than six centuries against Australia are Hobbs with 12 and Sutcliffe with eight.

### THE BOWLERS.

Jardine handled his bowlers well, and both he and Woodfull have enhanced their reputations for leadership by the manner in which they have controlled their attacks and placed their fields in this match. Jardine gave Bowes a chance before the shine was off the ball, but Bowes sent down four ineffective overs, and was not afterwards used.

Larwood bowled better than in the first innings, although he was not able to make the ball fly. After two overs from the grandstand end he changed to the other wicket to get full advantage from the light cross breeze, and it was from that end that he secured the wickets of O'Brien and Woodfull. It appeared that Jardine was anxious to change him after the first over, and that he bowled Allen to enable Voce to operate from the other end, but when Allen dismissed Fingleton in his first over he was kept going. Allen's direction became rather erratic, and one ball went to the boundary for four wides, but he did his share by beating McCabe, as well as Fingleton.

Voce, with his easy action, looked as if he could bowl all day if required. He maintained an accurate attack after Richardson had dealt with a few loose deliveries. Both Voce and Larwood employed off and leg side slips. Hammond's good work has already been commented upon, and his success proved most welcome to Jardine, who must have been more than satisfied to have dismissed Australia on such a wicket for 191 runs.

### SUTCLIFFE AND LEYLAND.

The English captain decided that Leyland and not Wyatt should be Sutcliffe's opening partner for the second innings. The pair commenced at 5.15 p.m. to the bowling of Wall and O'Reilly, but after three overs by the fast bowler, Woodfull brought on Ironmonger to complete a spin attack, and near the end gave Grimmett a turn from O'Reilly's end.

Ironmonger bowled three successive maidens after Sutcliffe had hit his first ball to the leg boundary, and O'Reilly had some accurate overs; but the spin bowlers were not able to dissolve the opening partnership. They will get a further chance to-morrow, when the wicket may help them to turn the ball.

Sutcliffe batted much better than in the first innings, although O'Reilly's faster ball once beat him all the way. He was eager to hit anything loose, and there were four fours included among his 33 runs. Leyland has made only 10 runs. He showed good defence, but he gained four for a slashing straight hit off Grimmett. The play closed brightly, Sutcliffe hitting Grimmett's last delivery to the fence.

### AMAZING CROWD.

The attendance was the largest that has ever attended a cricket match. The figures were officially announced as 68,188, the takings being £5790. The previous attendance record was established last Friday, when the figures were 63,994, the takings being £5577. The record takings, £6207/18/, were received at Sydney in 1928-9.

It is interesting to note that the crowd to-day closely approached the record football attendance at the Melbourne ground, which was made this year, when 69,724 persons were present.

Some of the outer gates were closed long before play commenced to-day—as early as 6.15 a.m. a tram carried some 30 enthusiasts to the ground, and two hours later there were long queues of people awaiting admission.

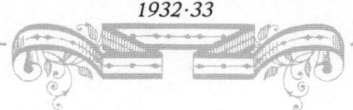

# Australia v England
## Third Test Match

AUSTRALIA v ENGLAND, Third Test Match, at Adelaide, 13, 14, 16, 17, 18 and 19 January 1933.

| | | |
|---|---|---|
| Australia | - First Innings | 222 |
| | - Second Innings | 193 |
| England | - First Innings | 341 |
| | - Second Innings | 412 |

Australia lost by 338 runs.

| | | |
|---|---|---|
| DON BRADMAN | - c. G.O. Allen b. H. Larwood | 8 |
| | - c. and b. H. Verity | 66 |

This was certainly the most unpleasant Test Match played, the 'body-line' attack rousing the crowd to furious barracking, and moving the Australian Board of Control to protest to the M.C.C.

Going in at 1 for 1 on the second afternoon, DON BRADMAN failed again in his first innings, staying for eighteen minutes and 17 balls before giving a simple catch to short square-leg in defending his head from a fast rising ball, at 18 for 2.

In the end, Australia were set to make 532 to win on a worn wicket. Bradman came in at 12 for 2 on the fifth evening, and played a brilliant if rather hectic innings. Some of his strokes were amazing, as he sometimes retreated to square-leg to try to hit H. Larwood's and W. Voce's leg-theory to the unprotected off side. He hit up 50 in sixty-four minutes, and then, having hit ten fours, drove H. Verity over the on boundary for 6 (the first he ever hit in Australia, and his first in a Test Match) before being caught and bowled next ball. He made 66 in seventy-three minutes.

Bradman also had the distinction of bowling W.R. Hammond for 85 with a full-pitch, just before the close of the fourth day.

## THIRD TEST MATCH

Played at Adelaide January 13, 14, 16, 17, 18, and 19. Jardine won the toss from Woodfull. England won by 338 runs. Attendance 172,346, and gate £16,241.

**ENGLAND.—First Innings**

| | |
|---|---|
| H. SUTCLIFFE, c Wall, b O'Reilly | 9 |
| D. R. JARDINE, b Wall | 3 |
| W. R. HAMMOND, c Oldfield, b Wall | 2 |
| L. E. G. AMES, b Ironmonger | 3 |
| M. LEYLAND, b O'Reilly | 83 |
| R. E. S. WYATT, c Richardson, b Grimmett | 78 |
| E. PAYNTER, c Fingleton, b Wall | 77 |
| G. O. ALLEN, lbw, b Grimmett | 15 |
| H. VERITY, c Richardson, b Wall | 45 |
| W. VOCE, b Wall | 8 |
| H. LARWOOD, not out | 3 |
| B 1, l-b 7, n-b 7 | 15 |
| **Total** | **341** |

FALL: 4, 16, 16, 30, 186, 196, 228, 324, 336, 341.

| | | | | | | |
|---|---|---|---|---|---|---|
| Wall | 34.1 | 10 | 72 | 5 | | |
| O'Reilly | 50 | 19 | 82 | 2 | | |
| Iron'ger | 20 | 6 | 59 | 1 | | |
| Grimmett | 28 | 6 | 94 | 2 | | |
| McCabe | 14 | 3 | 28 | 0 | | |

Wall bowled 3 n-b, and O'Reilly 4.

**ENGLAND.—Second Innings**

| | |
|---|---|
| H. SUTCLIFFE, c O'Brien (sub), b Wall | 7 |
| D. R. JARDINE, lbw, b Ironmonger | 56 |
| R. E. S. WYATT, c Wall, b O'Reilly | 49 |
| G. O. ALLEN, lbw, b Grimmett | 15 |
| W. R. HAMMOND, b Bradman | 85 |
| M. LEYLAND, c Wall, b Iron'ger | 42 |
| L. E. G. AMES, b O'Reilly | 69 |
| H. VERITY, lbw, b O'Reilly | 40 |
| H. LARWOOD, c Bradman, b Ironmonger | 8 |
| E. PAYNTER, not out | 1 |
| W. VOCE, b O'Reilly | 8 |
| B 17, l-b 11, n-b 4 | 32 |
| **Total** | **412** |

FALL: 7, 91, 123, 154, 245, 296, 394, 395, 403, 412.

| | | | | | | |
|---|---|---|---|---|---|---|
| Wall | 29 | 6 | 75 | 1 | | |
| O'Reilly | 50.3 | 21 | 79 | 4 | | |
| Iron'ger | 57 | 21 | 87 | 3 | | |
| Grimmett | 35 | 9 | 74 | 1 | | |
| McCabe | 16 | 0 | 42 | 0 | | |
| Bradman | 4 | 0 | 23 | 1 | | |

Wall 2 n-b, O'Reilly 1, and McCabe 1.

**AUSTRALIA.—First Innings**

| | |
|---|---|
| J. H. FINGLETON, c Ames, b Allen | 0 |
| W. M. WOODFULL, b Allen | 22 |
| D. G. BRADMAN, c Allen, b Larwood | 8 |
| S. J. McCABE, c Jardine, b Larwood | 8 |
| W. H. PONSFORD, b Voce | 85 |
| V. Y. RICHARDSON, b Allen | 28 |
| W. A. OLDFIELD, retired hurt | 41 |
| C. V. GRIMMETT, c Voce, b Allen | 10 |
| T. W. WALL, b Hammond | 6 |
| W. J. O'REILLY, b Larwood | 0 |
| H. IRONMONGER, not out | 0 |
| B 2, l-b 11, n-b 1 | 14 |
| **Total** | **222** |

FALL: 1, 18, 34, 51, 131, 194, 212, 218, 222, 222.

| | | | | | | |
|---|---|---|---|---|---|---|
| Larwood | 25 | 6 | 55 | 3 | | |
| Allen | 23 | 4 | 71 | 4 | | |
| Ham'nd | 17.4 | 4 | 30 | 1 | | |
| Voce | 14 | 5 | 21 | 1 | | |
| Verity | 16 | 7 | 31 | 0 | | |

Voce bowled a no-ball.

**AUSTRALIA.—Second Innings**

| | |
|---|---|
| W. M. WOODFULL, not out | 73 |
| J. H. FINGLETON, b Larwood | 0 |
| W. H. PONSFORD, c Jardine, b Larwood | 3 |
| D. G. BRADMAN, c and b Verity | 66 |
| S. J. McCABE, c Leyland, b Allen | 7 |
| V. Y. RICHARDSON, c Allen, b Larwood | 21 |
| C. V. GRIMMETT, b Allen | 6 |
| T. W. WALL, b Allen | 0 |
| W. J. O'REILLY, b Larwood | 5 |
| H. IRONMONGER, b Allen | 0 |
| W. A. OLDFIELD (absent) | — |
| B 4, l-b 2, n-b 5, w 1 | 12 |
| **Total** | **193** |

FALL: 3, 12, 100, 116, 171, 183, 183, 192, 193.

| | | | | | | |
|---|---|---|---|---|---|---|
| Larwood | 19 | 3 | 71 | 4 | | |
| Allen | 17.2 | 5 | 50 | 4 | | |
| Ham'nd | 9 | 3 | 27 | 0 | | |
| Voce | 4 | 1 | 7 | 0 | | |
| Verity | 20 | 12 | 26 | 1 | | |

Allen 2 n-b and a wide, Larwood 2 n-b, and Verity 1.

UMPIRES: G. Hele (S.A.) and G. Borwick (N.S.W.).

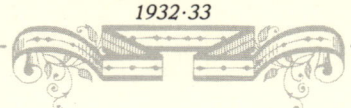

W. M. Woodfull struck over the heart by a ball from H. Larwood.

# TENSE SCENES AT TEST.

## Oldfield Struck by Ball.

## CROWD HOOTS LARWOOD.

## Australia 119 Behind on First Innings.

## PONSFORD'S GREAT STAND FOR 85.

(FROM OUR SPECIAL REPRESENTATIVE)

ADELAIDE, Monday.

There was an ugly scene at Adelaide Oval this afternoon when the Australian wicketkeeper, W. A. Oldfield, who was batting in the third test match, was struck on the head by a ball from the English fast bowler, H. Larwood.

Oldfield staggered a few yards from the wicket and then fell to the ground. After assistance he was able to walk to the dressing-room, but later he was in a groggy state. He is now in the care of a doctor, who is a personal friend, and is reported to be "very comfortable."

The crowd demonstrated against the English players, especially Larwood, who was hooted continuously while he ran to the wicket during the next couple of overs. At one stage it appeared as if there might be serious developments, but the agitated crowd settled down to watch the Englishmen batting in their second innings.

Australia was dismissed for 222 runs. Ponsford continued a splendid stand, reaching 85, and Oldfield had batted pluckily for 41 before he was forced to retire.

England, with a first innings lead of 119 runs, lost Sutcliffe cheaply in the second innings, but Jardine and Wyatt had taken the score to 85 when stumps were drawn.

W. A. Oldfield.

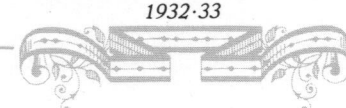

Larwood bowling.

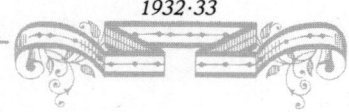

## ANGRY CROWD.

Never before has there been a test match with which so many unpleasant happenings, both on and off the field, have been associated The severe knock sustained by Woodfull when struck by a ball from Larwood on Saturday, and the published reports of Woodfull's subsequent emphatic protest to the English manager, Mr. Warner, against the tactics of the visiting team, had increased the antipathy of sections of the crowd towards the visiting team. They gave vent to bitter feeling by jeering at the captain (Jardine) almost every time he fielded the ball, and on one occasion, when he raced after a ball which reached the fence, many of those near the spot hooted and shouted abusive remarks to the English captain.

The injury to Oldfield, coming at a time when the Australian wicketkeeper was making as plucky a stand as ever he made in a test match caused the crowd to demonstrate in a manner which suggested that there might be serious developments. Police officers were alert to prevent any trouble, and, fortunately, the crowd subsided somewhat, although Larwood and Jardine continued to be subjected to hooting and cat-calls.

When Woodfull was hit on Saturday Larwood was operating to an off field. To-day Jardine had started him with leg theory, and later the fast bowler changed his field frequently. Just before Oldfield was injured Larwood had returned to the leg theory attack having several fieldsmen close in on the leg side and only one man in slips.

Oldfield was being applauded for a pretty glance to the boundary but soon afterwards he failed to connect when he attempted to swing the ball to leg and was struck on the right side of the head. Oldfield dropped his bat and staggered a few yards from the wicket and then fell to his knees.

A roar of mingled excitement and annoyance broke from the crowd. The fieldsmen and the batsman at the other end—Wall—rushed to Oldfield's aid and Allen ran to the dressing-room to secure a jug of water and a towel. He was followed on to the field by Woodfull who was cheered by the crowd Oldfield seemed to have recovered quickly, and walked back to the grandstand without assistance, but soon after reaching the dressing-room he was in great pain. His head had not been cut, but there was a bad bruise and Dr C. E. Dolling an Australian selector who attended Oldfield, stated that he was suffering from slight concussion.

Oldfield, after a long rest, was taken in an ambulance to the home of Dr. K. N. Steele a friend with whom he has been staying at Glenelg. To-night Dr Steele stated that Oldfield was "very comfortable," although he had suffered a bad knock. There was a swelling above the right temple which was spreading to above the eye, and the player was still affected slightly by the shock.

### LARWOOD HOOTED.

When the play was resumed many of the spectators, including some in the grandstand were in an excited state and they hooted Larwood roundly. Each time he ran to the bowling crease Larwood was hooted and jeered at, but after a few overs the demonstration became less pronounced, although a few continued to hoot the bowler to the end of the innings.

When Jardine appeared with Sutcliffe to open England's second innings there were further hoots, to which some of the crowd responded with cheers, but after Sutcliffe's early dismissal the barrackers became tired and in the concluding stages the play was watched in comparative silence.

Members of the English team, questioned concerning the Oldfield incident, stated that the ball was pitched on the stumps, but Oldfield, who crouched to swing the ball to leg, missed it and was struck. Some appeared to think that the ball had come through a trifle slower from the pitch than some previous deliveries.

### PONSFORD'S INNINGS.

Ponsford and Richardson had resumed the home innings to-day with four wickets down for 109 and at 131 Richardson played a ball from Allen on to his wicket. Ponsford continued his splendid innings and reached top score for the match—85. He gave a difficult chance to Hammond off Allen on Saturday when three and another to Verity off Voce to-day when 75, but his form after a shaky start against Allen on Saturday was most impressive, and Ponsford, who had been dropped for the second test, should now be assured of retaining his place. Apart from his splendid courage the feature of his innings was magnificent stroke play, his driving, cutting, and pulling being perfectly executed. He took a few knocks from Larwood, twice being struck in the back during one over, when he turned to protect his wicket.

Oldfield, had engaged with Ponsford in a sixth-wicket stand of 63 runs. He was missed on the leg side by Ames off Hammond when 26, but otherwise his form was excellent. He made many neat shots and a square drive to the fence off Larwood aroused enthusiasm. Oldfield was struck when the score was 218, Grimmett having been dismissed previously. O'Reilly and Wall were quickly bowled, and the innings realised 222 runs.

### VOCE BOWLS.

An x-ray examination had disclosed that Voce, who had experienced a recurrence of ankle trouble, had not broken a bone. Fears of the English managers that the big left-hander might not be able to bowl again in the test were allayed, and to-day Voce took the field with the ankle well bandaged. He was not called upon to bowl until close to the luncheon adjournment. Voce bowled steadily, and after lunch was successful in gaining Ponsford's wicket, the batsman missing a ball on the leg side and being bowled.

The wicket was slow and easy, and gave the bowlers no assistance. Larwood bowled at a good speed, and the persistent Allen was accurate. Allen broke a troublesome partnership when he got Richardson.

England, with a first innings lead of 119 runs, commenced the second innings at ten minutes to four, Jardine again opening with Sutcliffe. Only seven runs had been scored, all of them by Sutcliffe, when that batsman swung on to a rising ball from Wall, and was beautifully caught by the substitute fieldsman O'Brien at deep fine leg. Richardson was the wicketkeeper in the absence of Oldfield.

There should have been another early wicket for Wyatt, who had been moved higher in the batting order, was missed in the slips by O'Reilly off Wall when only nine, and later he gave a chance behind the wicket to Richardson off Ironmonger. Thanks to Wyatt's enterprise, particularly against Grimmett, 50 runs were scored in 56 minutes, but later the spin bowlers quietened the batsmen, Jardine being particularly restrained. The English captain batted 24 minutes before scoring a run, and he had occupied the creases for over two hours, being 24 not out.

With nine wickets to fall England, with the substantial first innings lead, is now 204 runs to the good. The wicket to-day was splendid, but may show some signs of wear when the Australians bat in the last innings.

### PAYNTER'S MISHAP.

The English left-handed batsman E. Paynter injured his right ankle when fielding this afternoon. He failed to save a four when Grimmett hit a ball to fine leg, and when near the fence, slipped and jarred his ankle. Paynter did not rise for a few moments, and he was assisted from the playing area by Jardine and Hammond.

Later Paynter returned to the field, the 12th man, Brown, having filled his place.

### THE ATTENDANCE.

The attendance to-day was 32,527, and the takings were £3008.

For the three days the aggregates are: Attendance, 122,790; takings, £12,440. The takings already exceed those for the six days of the test at Adelaide four seasons ago, when the amount was £12,404, the aggregate attendance being 138,895.

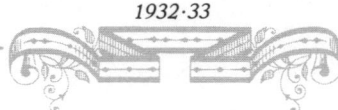

"Plum" Warner, Manager M.C.C. Team, was loyal to the Captain
D. R. Jardine on tour, but privately was opposed to "body-line" tactics.

Larwood bowling to Bradman.

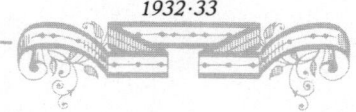

# MAMMOTH TASK.

## AUSTRALIA 411 RUNS BEHIND.

## Four Wickets down for 120.

### BRADMAN BRILLIANTLY SCORES 66.

### Ponsford, Fingleton, and McCabe Fail.

**ADELAIDE, Wednesday.**

### ENGLISH INNINGS.

Light rain during the early morning had not harmed the wicket, which played remarkably well for the fifth day of the match. The pitch was slightly worn in places, but although the spin bowlers were able to turn the ball, the batsmen were not seriously inconvenienced, and Wall was not able to extract from the pitch the same life produced later by Larwood and Allen.

Ames and Verity began the day's play, and were still together at the luncheon adjournment, having added 89 runs to the overnight score of 296 for six wickets. Ames, who made his first good test score, might have been stumped off Grimmett when 28, and Verity when 25 snicked a ball from Wall, which the wicketkeeper (Richardson) failed to hold. Ames later batted with confidence, and made good strokes, especially on the drive. His 69 runs occupied 164 minutes, and he was bowled by O'Reilly when the score was 394. With only a leg-bye added Verity, who had made 40 of a partnership of 98 in 110 minutes, was dismissed lbw. by the same bowler. As in the first innings, Verity batted stubbornly, revealing an occasional neat stroke, and his double success with the bat caused veterans to recall the fact that the left-handed bowler who preceded him in the famous Yorkshire team, Wilfred Rhodes, rose from last to first position in the English batting list.

### THE SPIN BOWLERS.

The spin bowlers did most of the work, while the Englishmen batted to-day. O'Reilly came to light with a splendid finishing effort, and Ironmonger, who during the innings sent down 57 overs, was particularly accurate. Grimmett was unfortunate to have Ames missed, but his bowling is not worrying the English batsmen as it did in former years. Bradman, who had taken Hammond's wicket yesterday, had a couple of overs, but was punished by Ames.

Jardine did not take any risks, but sent in Paynter as the tenth batsman. Paynter, who had Leyland to run for him, limped badly with his injured ankle, and winced with pain when he made a stroke. He did not field to-day, the 12th man, Brown, taking his place, and it was the Nawab of Pataudi who brought out the drinks.

The Australian fielding slumped somewhat during the Ames-Verity partnership, and O'Brien misfielded when a run-out might have occurred. Later Bradman made a great effort to catch Voce, running many yards, but was unable to hold the ball with his outstretched right hand.

### LARWOOD'S CHANGE.

On a dead wicket, Larwood commenced bowling in devastating fashion when Australia batted in the second innings at 19 minutes past three. His first over was a maiden to Fingleton, and in his second over he bowled Fingleton with the third ball, Woodfull having scored the only single off the English fast bowler. His third over was another maiden, and the first ball of his fourth over was cut by Ponsford to Jardine at short gully.

Larwood had commenced with an off-field, having four men in slips, with Allen in his customary position of silly square leg. He bowled five overs before he left the field to have damaged spikes fixed, and when he commenced the fourth and fifth overs with an off-field still placed, the crowd, although disappointed with Australia's disastrous start, generously applauded the bowler.

Some saw significance in the placing of the field. Did it mean that the leg theory was to be scrapped, they asked, or was Larwood influenced by his early success in persevering with his off-field?

The answer came in Larwood's seventh over. Commencing his second turn with the ball he bowled his sixth over to an off-field, but evidently decided that a change was necessary when both Woodfull and Bradman hit him round to leg for singles, and at the end of the over, he motioned to Jardine that he desired the field to be altered. The English captain assented, and there was only one man in slips.

The change was the signal for a storm of hooting and derisive shouts, and there was a demonstration as Larwood ran to the bowling crease. The noise was punctuated with cheers when Bradman or Woodfull executed a good stroke off Larwood, but there were shouts of annoyance when Woodfull had to duck to avoid a ball and Bradman crouched to meet a bumping one

which he hit to leg for a single. Voce previously had bowled with his customary leg field, but the left-hander was harmless, being unable to make the ball fly on the lifeless wicket.

### BRADMAN'S EXHIBITION

Until the leg-theory began, the crowd had been treated to a fine exhibition of stroke play, Bradman being superb. He attacked all bowlers, treating Hammond with scant respect, and punishing Verity, who had bowled maidens to Woodfull. Anything short or overpitched from Allen was dealt with, and Bradman glanced and drove Larwood in a manner that roused the crowd to enthusiasm. His stroke execution was perfect, and the usually stolid Woodfull seemed inspired by his display, and himself made some excellent drives and neat cuts and hits to leg.

Naturally the leg-theory attack cramped Woodfull's style, but it seemed as if Bradman then decided on a "do or die" effort, and he became even more aggressive. In Larwood's first over with the changed field, Bradman swung fiercely at balls on the leg side, but failed to connect. After reaching 50 in 64 minutes, he punished Verity, scoring 11 runs, including two fine fours for pulls off one over. Facing the left-hander again, he thrilled the crowd with a magnificent hit for six, the ball sailing over the on-boundary and into the crowd seated in front of the main grandstand. The ball struck a woman on the right forearm, but she was only slightly injured, and was able to walk from the ground after attention by the ambulance.

Bradman had made 66 of the 88 runs registered while he was at the wickets with Woodfull, when he drove the next ball hard back to the bowler, and Verity held the catch.

### McCABE GOES.

His dismissal marked the end of any faint hope of winning that Australia might have possessed, and soon after he had gone, Woodfull also lost McCabe. The hero of the first test at Sydney recorded a double failure, having made only seven when he swung a short ball from Allen high to fine leg, where Leyland held the catch. The shot was a beautiful one, but apparently McCabe had forgotten the presence of Leyland.

Fingleton had the unenviable experience of failing to score in either innings. He felt for a ball on the leg stump, but missed it, and was bowled. Ponsford had swished at a few balls on the off-side in Larwood's third over before being caught in his fourth over.

Woodfull is 36 not out, having played an exceptionally fine innings. Although slow, for he has batted for 131 minutes, he made several excellent strokes. Richardson had not scored when an appeal against the dull light at half-past five was upheld, and shortly afterwards stumps were drawn.

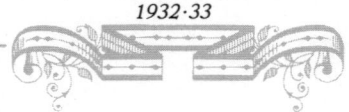

# A CRISIS IN CRICKET.

## Summing Up the Situation.

### (BY DR. ERIC P. BARBOUR.)

Since 1912, when the memorable dispute occurred between leading players and the Board of Control, Australian cricket has pursued the even tenor of its way undisturbed by storms of any magnitude. During the past week we have reached the climax of a storm that has been brewing all through the season. That climax has been precipitated, not, as some are inclined to think, by Oldfield's injury, and not, as others have unworthily suggested, by Australia's defeat in the third test. It has been brought to a head by two very serious protests, one by Woodfull, captain of the Australian eleven, the other by the Australian Board of Control. Newspaper criticism has only been provocative of argument, and, as might be expected, has allowed the main issue to be obscured in a maze of repartee and biting rejoinder. But the action of the Australian captain and the controlling body immediately lifts the question out of the realms of a newspaper dispute into those of a pressing international crisis in the world of cricket. Woodfull is known throughout Australia and England as a sportsman of the first water; no Australian captain has ever been more highly respected, either by his own men or by his opponents. Matters must indeed be serious when he expresses himself as forcibly as he is reported to have done in Adelaide. The Board of Control is composed of men who have given many years, in some cases a lifetime, to the service of cricket. They are elected in the most democratic manner possible; they are placed in the position by the vote of the delegates of the various associations, who in turn are elected to the association by the vote of the members of the constituent clubs. It would not be possible to devise a system of election that would make the board more truly representative of Australian cricket.

We may not agree with all that it does in matters of policy, any more than we agree with all the actions of a Ministry which we have helped to put into office; but we must admit that the Board of Control is composed of men who are regarded as sportsmen in the best sense of the word, and to whom the welfare of the game of cricket is a more serious consideration than the winning or losing of a rubber. They have seen fit to cable to the M.C.C., the controlling body of English cricket, two very grave statements, firstly, that in their opinion the policy of body bowling pursued by Jardine's team is unsportsmanlike; secondly, that it has caused intensely bitter feeling among the players, and unless stopped at once, is likely to upset friendly relations existing between Australia and England, meaning, of course, cricket relations.

## OPPOSITION IN ENGLAND.

It may now fairly be said that an overwhelming majority of Australian cricketers and enthusiasts has expressed its condemnation of the tactics. Even in England, notwithstanding a perfectly natural tendency among some to back up their own side, there is a large and steadily growing body of famous men who are against them. Such players as A. C. Maclaren, the Jam Sahib Ranjitsinhji, Sir Stanley (F. S.) Jackson, Arthur Gilligan, Rev. J. H. Parsons, and even Frank R. Foster, the greatest leg-theory bowler of all time, have expressed their disapproval.

By a majority verdict, it stands condemned at the bar of public opinion. The question now is, what are we going to do about it? There are many who, like the writer, would have felt more comfortable if the board had not sent any formal protest. We all cling tightly to our own estimate of ourselves as sportsmen, and tend to resent any action that might lead other people to think that we are "squealers," or bad sportsmen. But I have heard this unlovely word used so loosely in Australia that I have ceased to have much respect for it. I have heard it used at the Stadium when a boxer has had the temerity to object to being hit low. The gentlemen on the back benches who use the word so freely would probably run for miles, if they were asked to enter the ring and pull on a glove. In fact, as far as the sporting world is concerned, no man can point out any abuse of the proprieties, or even any illegality, on the other side, without the certainty of someone calling him a "squealer."

## BOARD'S BROAD VIEW.

The Board of Control is taking a broader and bigger view. Personal considerations and amour propre do not weigh so heavily with them as the proud position of the great game of cricket, and the Imperial relations connected with it.

Some people have suggested that matters should be allowed to go on as they are until the close of the season, when a conference of the representatives of the two countries should be held to discuss the matter. At first sight this would appear to be the best solution; but what is going to happen in the interval? As a matter of fact, anything is likely to happen. If a man of the mild nature of Woodfull cannot restrain himself at the present juncture, what may happen among the more hot-headed members of the side, whose patience is daily and weekly being worn out by a continuance of tactics that make it impossible for them to play decent cricket, and subject them to constant physical pain and discomfort?

It is common property that serious disagreements have already occurred between the members of the English team themselves on this question; is the board to wait until a personal clash takes place between members of opposing teams? I am not suggesting that anything of the kind is contemplated, nor would it be applauded, but human nature can only stand a certain amount of goading, and the Board of Control, which should be in a position to know, evidently thinks that the players have reached the limit of their patience. And, in any case, why should our batsmen, great cricketers and great fellows, be called upon to endure a further battering extending over many weeks, just in order that armchair critics in Sydney and Melbourne may be able to sit back and complacently congratulate themselves on being good sportsmen?

Let us be fair. We hear of a lot of heroics from a few non-cricketers and a very few ex-cricketers, who say "Why don't they stand up and take it?" I do not believe that the majority of these critics would face the music for five minutes. I do not believe that there is in Australia, or in the world, for that matter, a fairer sportsman than W. M. Woodfull, or a gamer player. I also believe that if the English batsmen had been subjected to their own attack, the tactics would have been stopped long before the third test. Hobbs refused to take it even for one match from Bowes, and Bowes is a joke in comparison to Larwood.

## RETALIATION NOT RIGHT.

Another alternative that has been suggested is retaliation. Strong as is the temptation to put this into operation, no argument can make it right. Even the proverb, "Set a thief to catch a thief," is not as morally true as "Two blacks do not make a white." It would be a different matter if public opinion decided that the tactics were fair, but in that case it would be imitation, and not retaliation.

The ideal solution of the matter would have been for Mr. Jardine to realise, even at this late hour, that his tactics are outside the pale of good sportsmanship, and voluntarily to withdraw them. It seems, however, that he has gone so far with them that there is no likelihood of a withdrawal from the position he has taken up, unless instructed by the M.C.C.

For all that we know, the tactics that Jardine is now using may have been dictated by that body, or by its selectors.

It could not have been an easy matter for the Board of Control to compose the cable that has been sent to the M.C.C., nor could it have been an easy matter to send it. We may take it as certain that the board would not have taken so drastic a step unless it had very definite facts before it for its justification.

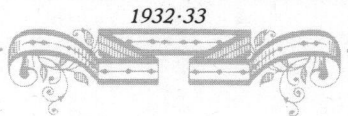

11 Lower Bayview Street,
McMahon's Point.
SYDNEY. 30th.Jany.1933.

The Secretary,
M.C.C.
Lords Cricket Ground.
LONDON.

Dear Sir,

Only after considerable thought have I dared to write
this letter to the controlling body in cricket. In doing so
however, I have but one thought in my mind which is"the betterment
of our glorious game of cricket".

I have taken the liberty of presuming my letter will be read to the
members of the M.C.C. Should my presumption be correct then it
is quite possible that, after hearing the contents, the members
will think it preposterous of me to have the temerity to even
dream of making a suggestion to them. Should they take this view
no harm will be done. On the other hand if they are prepared to
listen to my suggestion I would feel very honoured.

At the present moment a rather unfortunate state of affairs exists.
The Australian Board of Control and the M.C.C. are somewhat at
variance over the tactics employed by theEnglish bowlers on their
present tour of Australia. On such a subject I wish to make no
comment except this. For some years past there has been a
growing feeling amongst those in control of affairs that the task
of bowlers, year after year, has become more difficult. As
evidence of their belief in this fact the M.C.C. recently passed
leglisation increasing the size of the stumps and altering the
L.B.W. rule, thereby making the bowler's task slightly easier.
Surely then, with the present controversy at its height, there
could not be a more opportune moment than the present, for passing
further leglisation which would materially assist all bowlers for
all time and also, if my reasoning is correct, would make cricket
better and brighter with scarcely any arguments against it.

My suggestion is one which may have been made before. On that
occasion however the necessity of any further addition to the rules
was probably not so apparent. Being purely a batsman myself,
this new rule would affect me just the same as it would affect
every other batsman. I wish to stress this fact. My suggestion,
if ever carried, would not be to my advantage in any way whatsoever.

In addition to the existing rule covering a Leg-before-wicket
decision why not add the following:-

2.

"If with part of his person the striker stops the ball which in
the opinion of the umpire at the bowler's wicket shall have been
pitched on the off side of the wicket as to the striker and would
have hit the wicket, the striker is out "Leg Before Wicket".

Pardon me for further presumption but I would like to add my
reasons for believing in the success of this experiment.

Batsmen's leg-guards have been considerably improved to withstand
knocks from the ball. This was done to protect the batsman's legs,
not to allow him to protect his wicket with those pads. To-day
we find batsmen so proficient in the art of using their feet, that a
bowler, pitching the ball off the wicket, has no chance whatever of
hitting the stumps. The new rule as suggested, would force the
batsmen to play at the ball. Allowing the ball to pass outside
the off stump merely by covering the wicket with the pads, would
be a thing of the past.

In addition to the wickets bowlers would obtain by L.B.W. decisions
under the new rule, slip catches and such like would become much
more frequent because of the batsman being forced to play at the
ball. To-day a man bowling off breaks has an extremely difficult
task obtaining wickets so that new bowlers coming on, are inclined
to turn to a more successful type which is leg break bowling.
Under the new rule an off break bowler would probably be more
successful than a leg break bowler and yet no advantages whatsoever
would be taken away from the leg breakbowler. In fact the leg
break bowler would gain considerably too.
With a right hand leg breakbowler operating to a left hand batsman
the new rule would definitely assist the bowler. No batsman would
suffer any more disadvantage than another and there is no type of
bowling which would not receive assistance.

Unquestionably teams would make less runs. To my mind it would be
in the best interests of the game if this was so. And yet none of
the skill in handling a bat is taken away from the batsman.

The decision which the umpire would be called upon to make, should
not be any more difficult than the present decisions, especially the
L.B.W. decision after the ball has snicked the bat. As always the
player would accept the umpire's decision without quibble.

I cannot see anything against the suggestion. Apparently many
arguments may be used in favour of it.

As previously stated my love of and devotion to cricket where men
should use a bat and a ball, causes me to offer this humble
suggestion at a time when the predominance of bat over ball has
become the subject of so much comment.

Compared with the members of your Club I am but an inexperienced
youth but in a short space of time I have learned to love our grand
game and if I have taken up your time with an impracticable idea I
apologise.

Yours Sincerely,

In retrospect it is interesting to observe that Bradman received no acknowledgement of his
private letter to M.C.C. advocating an extension of the l.b.w. rule to the off side but that
years later M.C.C. changed the law, substantially incorporating Bradman's suggestion.

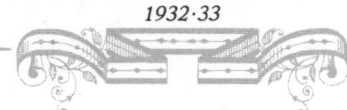

# Australia v England
## Fourth Test Match

AUSTRALIA v ENGLAND, Fourth Test Match, at Brisbane, 10, 11, 13, 14, 15 and 16 February 1933.

| | | |
|---|---|---|
| Australia | - First Innings | 340 |
| | - Second Innings | 175 |
| England | - First Innings | 356 |
| | - Second Innings | 162 for 4 wickets |

Australia lost by 6 wickets, and England won the rubber and regained the Ashes.

| | | |
|---|---|---|
| DON BRADMAN | - b. H. Larwood | 76 |
| | - c. T.B. Mitchell  b. H. Larwood | 24 |

The score was 133 for 1 on the first day when DON BRADMAN went to the wicket at 3.25 p.m. in great heat.    He made a subdued and uncertain start, being 14 at tea-time, but gradually settled down, again using his unorthodox square-cut on the retreat against the 'body-line' bowling.    He scored 50 in eighty-eight minutes, and was 71 not out overnight after two hours sixteen minutes' batting.    When he was 48, he completed his 1,000 runs for the season.    Next day, Bradman batted for only another twenty minutes before H. Larwood hit his leg stump in his third over, as he again drew away and tried to cut.    He was out at 264 for 4, after batting for two hours thirty-six minutes;  he hit eleven fours.
On the fourth evening, Bradman went in at 46 for 1 and though he cut Larwood for 10 in an over, he had batted for only thirty-two minutes when, drawing away again, he lobbed an easy catch to square-cover at 79 for 2.

Arriving at Brisbane railway station.

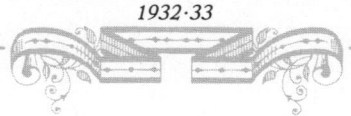

## FOURTH TEST MATCH

Played at the Brisbane Cricket Ground, February 10, 11, 13, 14, 15 and 16. Woodfull won the toss from Jardine. England won by six wickets, thus winning the "Ashes." Attendance, 93,143, gate £10,935.

### AUSTRALIA.—First Innings

| | | |
|---|---|---|
| W. M. WOODFULL, b Mitchell | | 67 |
| V. Y. RICHARDSON, st Ames, b Hammond | | 83 |
| D. G. BRADMAN, b Larwood | | 76 |
| S. J. McCABE, c Jardine, b Allen | | 20 |
| W. H. PONSFORD, b Larwood | | 19 |
| L. S. DARLING, c Ames, b Allen | | 17 |
| E. H. BROMLEY, c Verity, b Larwood | | 26 |
| H. S. LOVE, lbw, b Mitchell | | 5 |
| T. W. WALL, not out | | 6 |
| W. J. O'REILLY, c Hammond, b Larwood | | 6 |
| H. IRONMONGER, st Ames, b Hammond | | 8 |
| B 5, l-b 1, n-b 1 | | 7 |
| Total | | 340 |

FALL: 133, 200, 233, 264, 267, 292, 315, 317, 329, 340.

| | | | | | | | | |
|---|---|---|---|---|---|---|---|---|
| Larwood | 31 | 7 | 101 | 4 | Mitchell | 16 | 5 | 49 | 2 |
| Allen | 24 | 4 | 83 | 2 | Verity | 27 | 12 | 39 | 0 |
| Hammond | 23 | 5 | 61 | 2 | | | | | |

Larwood a no-ball.

### AUSTRALIA.—Second Innings

| | | |
|---|---|---|
| W. M. WOODFULL, c Hammond, b Mitchell | | 19 |
| V. Y. RICHARDSON, c Jardine, b Verity | | 32 |
| D. G. BRADMAN, c Mitchell, b Larwood | | 24 |
| W. H. PONSFORD, c Larwood, b Allen | | 0 |
| S. J. McCABE, b Verity | | 22 |
| L. S. DARLING, run out | | 39 |
| E. H. BROMLEY, c Hammond, b Allen | | 7 |
| H. S. LOVE, lbw, b Larwood | | 3 |
| T. W. WALL, c Jardine, b Allen | | 2 |
| W. J. O'REILLY, b Larwood | | 4 |
| H. IRONMONGER, not out | | 0 |
| B 13, l-b 9, n-b 1 | | 23 |
| Total | | 175 |

FALL: 46, 79, 81, 91, 136, 163, 169, 169, 171, 175.

| | | | | | | | | |
|---|---|---|---|---|---|---|---|---|
| Larwood | 17.3 | 3 | 49 | 3 | Verity | 19 | 6 | 30 | 2 |
| Allen | 17 | 3 | 44 | 3 | Mitchell | 5 | 0 | 11 | 1 |
| Hammond | 10 | 4 | 18 | 0 | | | | | |

Larwood 1 no-ball.

### ENGLAND.—First Innings

| | | |
|---|---|---|
| D. R. JARDINE, c Love, b O'Reilly | | 46 |
| H. SUTCLIFFE, lbw O'Reilly | | 86 |
| W. R. HAMMOND, b McCabe | | 20 |
| R. E. S. WYATT, c Love, b Ironmonger | | 12 |
| M. LEYLAND, c Bradman, b O'Reilly | | 12 |
| L. E. G. AMES, c Darling, b Ironmonger | | 17 |
| G. O. ALLEN, c Love, b Wall | | 13 |
| E. PAYNTER, c Richardson, b Ironmonger | | 83 |
| H. LARWOOD, b McCabe | | 23 |
| H. VERITY, not out | | 23 |
| T. B. MITCHELL, lbw, b O'Reilly | | 0 |
| B6, l-b 12, n-b 3 | | 21 |
| Total | | 356 |

FALL: 114, 157, 165, 188, 198, 216, 223, 264, 356, 356.

| | | | | | | | | |
|---|---|---|---|---|---|---|---|---|
| Wall | 33 | 6 | 66 | 1 | Bromley | 10 | 4 | 19 | 0 |
| O'Reilly | 67.4 | 26 | 120 | 4 | Bradman | 7 | 1 | 17 | 0 |
| Ironm'ger | 42 | 19 | 69 | 3 | Darling | 2 | 0 | 4 | 0 |
| McCabe | 23 | 7 | 40 | 2 | | | | | |

Watt 2 no-balls and O'Reilly 1.

### ENGLAND.—Second Innings

| | | |
|---|---|---|
| D. R. JARDINE, lbw, b Ironmonger | | 24 |
| H. SUTCLIFFE, c Darling, b Wall | | 2 |
| M. LEYLAND, c McCabe, b O'Reilly | | 86 |
| W. R. HAMMOND, c Bromley, b Ironmonger | | 14 |
| L. AMES, not out | | 14 |
| E. PAYNTER, not out | | 14 |
| B 2, l-b 4, n-b 2 | | 8 |
| Four wickets for | | 162 |

FALL: 5, 78, 118, 138.

| | | | | | | | | |
|---|---|---|---|---|---|---|---|---|
| Wall | 7 | 1 | 17 | 1 | Ironm'ger | 35 | 13 | 47 | 2 |
| O'Reilly | 30 | 11 | 65 | 1 | McCabe | 7.4 | 2 | 25 | 0 |

McCabe 2 no-balls.

UMPIRES: B. Hele (S.A.), G. Borwick (N.S.W.).

# AUSTRALIA'S GOOD DAY.

## Three Wickets for 251.

## ENGLISH BOWLING MASTERED.

### Fine First-Wicket Partnership.

### WOODFULL, RICHARDSON, BRADMAN SCORE WELL.

### Larwood Uses Leg Theory Unsuccessfully.

FROM OUR SPECIAL REPRESENTATIVE WITH THE TEAMS.

BRISBANE, Friday.

Batting first on an easy wicket at the Brisbane Cricket Ground to-day, Australia scored 251 runs with the loss of three wickets in the fourth Test match with England.

This is the greatest number of runs that has been scored on the first day of any Test match this season. It was the first occasion on which the Australian batsmen had mastered the English bowling.

Woodfull and Richardson gave the side a wonderful start, scoring 133 runs for the opening wicket, and Bradman, after an uncertain beginning, hammered home the advantage.

Woodfull scored 67 and Richardson 83. McCabe went for 20, but Bradman has made 71 not out.

An outstanding feature was that Larwood failed to take a wicket. His attack varied from off to leg theory. The crowd was delighted when, during the partnership of Woodfull and Richardson, the fast bowler's field was moved back to the off. There was some hooting on occasions, but the demonstrations were mild.

The visiting players had a gruelling time in the field, as the weather was oppressive, but they stuck to their task well.

To-night, the weather was still warm and sultry. The forecast for to-morrow is as follows:— "Fine and hot by day with light to moderate northerly wind, but some probability of a thunderstorm towards evening. A cool southerly change during the night."

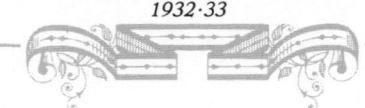

# ENGLAND WINS ASHES.

## Fourth Test Victory.

## MARGIN OF SIX WICKETS.

## Paynter Scores Six with Winning Hit

## JARDINE'S CAPTAINCY A BIG FACTOR.

## Mr. Warner Praises O'Reilly.

(FROM OUR SPECIAL REPRESENTATIVE WITH THE TEAM.)

BRISBANE, Thursday.

England won the fourth test match against Australia at Brisbane by six wickets, and so regained the "ashes," lost at the Oval in 1930.

England's winning score was 162 for four wickets, two wickets falling for 55 runs to-day. Hammond was caught off Ironmonger for 14. and Leyland was caught off O'Reilly, when he had carried his overnight score of 66 to 86.

The winning hit was appropriately made by Paynter, to whom England owes much for her victory, when he lifted a slow full toss sent down by McCabe for six.

The joint manager of the English team, Mr. P. F. Warner, after the match, praised the bowling of O'Reilly and Ironmonger, and referred to O'Reilly as "a really great bowler."

The Englishmen have definitely proved their superiority over Australia during the series, and the captaincy of Jardine has been a match-winning factor.

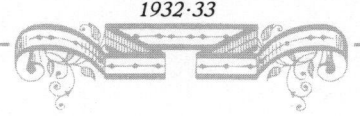

# WARNER AND JARDINE.

## STATEMENTS TO PRESS.

In a statement to the Press, Mr. Warner said: "We are naturally proud and delighted at recovering the ashes, but the Australians true to tradition, fought hard, and the bowling of O'Reilly and Ironmonger was of a very high order. Our bowling invariably has been extremely good, and the fielding, inspired by Jardine, who made many fine catches, has been splendid. The secret of our success has been loyal co-operation of the whole team, both on and off the field. In the words of Lord Roberts, 'The men have been splendid.'"

The captain, D. R. Jardine, in a statement, said: "For the last two months I have been receiving a regular host of letters from Australians of goodwill from all over this Dominion. I would like to take this opportunity of thanking them and assuring them that the letters have been greatly appreciated by the M.C.C. team and myself. The number of these letters alone has prevented me from answering them personally. It is, however, just these correspondents who appreciate silence instead of comment or criticism on matters of controversy from visitors and guests. They would, I think, echo the hope that the game of cricket is all that matters, and the best and only thing to do is to get on with it, for there is little if anything wrong with it. Personally, I have been thrice lucky in the side which it has been my proud privilege to lead. No captain, I feel sure, has received or could ask for greater help, sympathy, and utter loyalty than has fallen to my lot. We are proud of our fortune and success against our valiant and determined opponents under Mr. Woodfull, and condole with them on their sad loss through the death of Mr. Archie Jackson."

## MATCH REVIEWED.

Had Love stumped Verity or had Ponsford caught that batsman early on Tuesday, the ninth wicket stand of England's first innings would have been considerably shortened, and there were other "ifs" about the match, but Australia secured an advantage when Woodfull won the toss and Woodfull and Richardson gave the side a magnificent start with 133 runs for the first wicket.

While some of the English batsmen have not performed up to their best form, the visitors' batting generally has been more reliable than that of Australia. The bowling of Larwood, well supported by that of Allen and others, has been strikingly successful, and the fielding in the Brisbane test has been superior to that of the home team.

In this test, the Englishmen revealed better teamwork than in any previous match of the tour. Jardine set a high standard in the field, and the placing of his men and the handling of his bowlers caused his reputation to be enhanced. Jardine has carried out his job in his own way, and although his slow batting was not to the liking of the spectators, it was purposeful, and laid the foundation for England's scores.

### THE LEG THEORY.

The leg-theory will always be associated with Jardine's name. In this match it has not caused much excitement, because of the easy nature of the wicket.

Incidentally the members of the committee appointed by the Board of Control to report upon the question of leg-theory bowling—Messrs. Hartigan, Noble, Woodfull, and Richardson—have all been associated with the Brisbane match, and no doubt they have had a preliminary discussion. All four have previously expressed opposition to the tactics.

### BRADMAN'S LAPSES.

At two or three stages in this match Australia appeared to be in a most promising position, but on each occasion the Englishmen caused the home team's grip to loosen.

The batting of Bradman against Larwood's shock attack caused intense disappointment. Woodfull made solid stands, and other players registered good performances, but the match-winning effort expected of Bradman did not materialise.

Bradman scored 71 not out on the first day, but he lost a glorious opportunity to overcome the menace of Larwood, when on the second day he again faced that bowler, who had to operate on a lifeless wicket. Bradman, adopting risky methods and leaving his wicket exposed, failed to add many runs, and in the second innings he again fell to Larwood after a brief display of brisk batting.

England from the outset pinned faith to the shock attack, unsettling Bradman, but at Brisbane that attack was less menacing than at Sydney and Adelaide, because of the nature of the pitch. Bradman has failed to dominate the batting as he did in England in 1930, and it remains to be seen whether he will punish Larwood's bowling in the fifth test.

### O'REILLY'S SUCCESS.

One of the happiest features from the Australian point of view has been the development of O'Reilly, who was a test "discovery" when the South Africans were here last season. In the four matches played O'Reilly has taken 24 wickets, and only Larwood, with 28, has exceeded that tally. O'Reilly, besides proving himself a high-class spin bowler, has revealed splendid determination and stamina. If he improves his batting against fast bowling he will be even more valuable to Australia.

### THE ATTENDANCES.

A crowd of 1591 witnessed the last day's play, the gate takings being £66/6/6. For the match the aggregates were:—Attendance, 93,143; takings, £9735/8/.

The question of whether a test match should be played at Brisbane, when the next English team tours is one likely to be keenly discussed, and it is probable that if the opinion of the leaders of the present team is sought it will be found that they are against Brisbane having a test, in February at any rate. Players of both teams have found a week of hot and muggy weather extremely trying, and one member of the home team, who is not a bowler, states that he has lost 12lb in weight since the play commenced.

The accommodation at the Brisbane Cricket Ground, while much improved since the South Africans were here, is not yet sufficiently good to meet requirements, and so far as the financial aspect is concerned it cannot be denied that thousands of pounds more would have been taken at Melbourne or Sydney with the match fluctuating in such an interesting manner.

The good of Queensland cricket must be taken into consideration and there is evidence of a growing appreciation of the finer points of the game by the Brisbane public. Why the Board of Control should have fixed the Brisbane test for February and why the team should have to revisit Adelaide and Melbourne for matches against the States after the fifth test at Sydney are questions which have caused much comment among the touring players. They will have to return from Adelaide to Sydney to embark for New Zealand.

### THREE TESTS TO ONE.

England has now won three tests to Australia's one. The fifth and concluding match of the series will be commenced at the Sydney Cricket Ground next Thursday. For a time this morning, it seemed that play might not be resumed to-day, as steady light rain had set in during the morning, but the weather cleared temporarily, and there had not been sufficient rain at Woolloongabba to damage the wicket. Light rain was falling when the match ended at 20 minutes past one, and an hour later there were heavy showers.

Until McCabe was put on for the last over and served up a full toss for Paynter to hit when only four runs were required to give England victory, the Australians gave nothing away, O'Reilly and Ironmonger maintaining a steady attack.

Hammond found that he could not get Ironmonger through the field with his drives, and eventually he had a hit, and mistimed the ball, which was taken by Bromley at cover. Hammond had made the same mistake in several other innings on this tour, and his inability to keep the ball on the grass with his off and cover drives, has provided one of the main reasons for his failure to score as heavily as in 1928-9.

### LEYLAND'S EFFORT.

Leyland, who had batted in a restrained manner when partnered by Jardine in a second wicket stand on Wednesday, carried on slowly. He used his pads to stop awkward balls from the spin bowlers, who gained some little assistance from a pitch which had lasted surprisingly well in a match extending to six days. After he had lifted Ironmonger for two fours, Leyland had a chance to reach the century, but the left-hander did not get beyond 86, equalling Sutcliffe's top-score for the match.

Leyland fell to the vimful O'Reilly, feeling forward for a good ball, which he edged to McCabe at slip. Leyland's innings was unusually slow for him, but he had played the part allotted him by Jardine, and, even though he had batted for nearly four hours, he had hit nine boundaries.

### MR. WARNER'S FEARS.

O'Reilly and Ironmonger continued to bowl with accurate length and direction, O'Reilly showing more dash than on the previous day, and Mr. Warner afterwards stated that he had left the ground for a few minutes following Leyland's dismissal, so fearful was he that the two bowlers might bring about a collapse. He was reassured by the wireless broadcast, and returned to the ground in time to see the finish. Ames and Paynter soon settled the issue, the former lifting O'Reilly for six, and Paynter making 14 runs in three scoring strokes—two fours and a six.

It was fitting that Paynter should make the winning hit, for the fighting stand of that left-handed batsman when he had not fully recovered from illness was one of the outstanding features of the match.

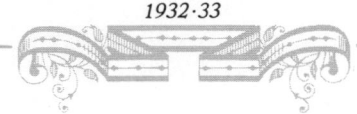

# Australia v England
# Fifth Test Match

AUSTRALIA v ENGLAND, Fifth Test Match, at Sydney, 23, 24, 25, 27 and 28 February 1933.

| Australia | - First Innings | 435 |
| | - Second Innings | 182 |
| England | - First Innings | 454 |
| | - Second Innings | 168 for 2 wickets |

Australia lost by 8 wickets.

| DON BRADMAN | - b. H. Larwood | 48 |
| | - b. H. Verity | 71 |

DON BRADMAN went in very early on the first morning, with the score 0 for 1, and again played a brilliant if rather reckless innings against the fast leg-theory, this time he was bowled, just before the lunch interval.    He batted for seventy-one minutes and the score was only 64 for 3 when he left. When his score was 28, he reached his 3,000 runs in all Test Matches.

The score was again 0 for 1 when Bradman batted on the fourth morning, being 22 not out at lunch, and he was again in daring form, some of his cutting of the 'leg-theory' being most spectacular.    He reached 50 in seventy-six minutes, and appeared almost to have mastered H. Larwood, but was deceived by H. Verity who yorked him with his faster ball as he jumped in to drive.    He hit nine fours. During his innings, Bradman was hit by Larwood, receiving a painful blow on the arm as he drew away to cut a rising ball.

This was Bradman's first Test Match v. England at Sydney, and it was the eighth successive Test in which he exceeded 50 in one innings or the other.

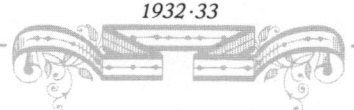
# FIFTH TEST MATCH

Played at Sydney Cricket Ground, February 23, 24, 25, 27 and 28. England won by eight wickets and five runs. Woodfull won the toss from Jardine. Attendance 136,790, and gate £11,997.

## AUSTRALIA.—First Innings

| | |
|---|---|
| V. Y. RICHARDSON, c Jardine, b Larwood | 0 |
| W. M. WOODFULL, b Larwood | 14 |
| D. G. BRADMAN, b Larwood | 48 |
| L. P. O'BRIEN, c Larwood, b Voce | 61 |
| S. J. McCABE, c Hammond, b Verity | 73 |
| L. S. DARLING, b Verity | 85 |
| W. A. OLDFIELD, run out | 52 |
| P. K. LEE, c Jardine, b Verity | 42 |
| W. J. O'REILLY, b Allen | 19 |
| H. ALEXANDER, not out | 17 |
| H. IRONMONGER, b Larwood | 1 |
| B 13, l-b 9, w 1 | 23 |
| **Total** | **435** |

FALL: 0, 59, 64, 163, 244, 328, 385, 414, 430, 435.

| | | | | | | | |
|---|---|---|---|---|---|---|---|
| Larwood | 32.2 | 10 | 98 | 4 | Ham'nd | 8 0 32 0 |
| Voce | 24 | 4 | 80 | 1 | Verity | 17 3 62 3 |
| Allen | 25 | 1 | 128 | 1 | Wyatt | 2 0 12 0 |

Voce bowled a wide.

## AUSTRALIA.—Second Innings

| | |
|---|---|
| V. Y. RICHARDSON, c Allen, b Larwood | 0 |
| W. M. WOODFULL, b Allen | 67 |
| D. G. BRADMAN, b Verity | 71 |
| L. P. O'BRIEN, c Verity, b Voce | 5 |
| S. J. McCABE, c Jardine, b Voce | 4 |
| L. S. DARLING, c Wyatt, b Verity | 7 |
| W. A. OLDFIELD, c Wyatt, b Verity | 5 |
| P. K. LEE, b Allen | 15 |
| W. J. O'REILLY, b Verity | 1 |
| H. ALEXANDER, lbw, b Verity | 0 |
| H. IRONMONGER, not out | 0 |
| B 4, n-b 3 | 7 |
| **Total** | **182** |

FALL: 0, 115, 135, 139, 148, 161, 177, 178, 178, 182.

| | | | | | | | |
|---|---|---|---|---|---|---|---|
| Larwood | 11 | 0 | 44 | 1 | Voce | 10 0 34 2 |
| Allen | 11.4 | 2 | 54 | 2 | Verity | 19 9 33 5 |
| Ham'nd | 3 | 0 | 10 | 0 | | |

Allen 3 no-balls.

## ENGLAND.—First Innings

| | |
|---|---|
| H. SUTCLIFFE, c Richardson, b O'Reilly | 56 |
| D. R. JARDINE, c Oldfield, b O'Reilly | 18 |
| W. R. HAMMOND, lbw, b Lee | 101 |
| H. LARWOOD, c Ironmonger, b Lee | 98 |
| M. LEYLAND, run out | 42 |
| R. E. S. WYATT, c Ironmonger, b O'Reilly | 51 |
| L. E. G. AMES, run out | 4 |
| E. PAYNTER, b Lee | 9 |
| G. O. ALLEN, c Bradman, b Lee | 48 |
| H. VERITY, c Oldfield, b Alexander | 4 |
| W. VOCE, not out | 7 |
| B 7, l-b 7, n-b 2 | 16 |
| **Total** | **454** |

FALL: 31, 153, 245, 310, 330, 349, 374, 418, 434, 454.

| | | | | | | | |
|---|---|---|---|---|---|---|---|
| Alexan'r | 35 | 1 | 129 | 1 | Lee | 40.2 11 111 4 |
| McCabe | 12 | 1 | 27 | 0 | Darling | 7 5 30 |
| O'Reilly | 45 | 7 | 100 | 3 | Bradman | 1 0 40 |
| Ironm'ger | 31 | 13 | 64 | 0 | | |

O'Reilly bowled 2 no-balls.

## ENGLAND.—Second Innings

| | |
|---|---|
| R. E. S. WYATT, not out | 61 |
| D. R. JARDINE, c Richardson, b Ironmonger | 24 |
| M. LEYLAND, b Ironmonger | 0 |
| W. R. HAMMOND, not out | 75 |
| B 6, l-b 1, n-b 1 | 8 |
| **Two wickets for** | **168** |

FALL: 43, 43.

| | | | | | | | |
|---|---|---|---|---|---|---|---|
| Alexander | 11 | 2 | 25 | 0 | Lee | 12.2 3 52 0 |
| Alexand'r | 11 | 2 | 25 | 0 | McCabe | 5 2 10 0 |
| O'Reilly | 15 | 5 | 32 | 0 | Darling | 2 0 70 |
| Ironm'ger | 26 | 12 | 34 | 2 | | |

O'Reilly 1 no-ball.

UMPIRES: G. Hele (S.A.), and G. Borwick (N.S.W.).

The crowd removed pickets from the fence.

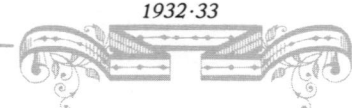

# AUSTRALIA'S RECOVERY.

## Five Wickets for 296.

## RUNS SCORED AT FAST RATE.

## Larwood Gets Three Quick Wickets.

## YOUNG LEFT-HANDERS SHOW SKILL.

## McCabe Tops the Score with 73.

Batting first in the fifth test match with England, at the Sydney Cricket Ground yesterday, Australia scored 296 runs for the loss of five wickets. It was the fastest scoring on the first day of a test this season.

The batsmen made an excellent recovery. The first three wickets fell for 64 runs, of which Bradman scored 48. He was bowled by Larwood, who, in his previous over, dismissed Woodfull. Richardson was caught in Larwood's first over, before a run had been scored.

O'Brien and McCabe put on 99 runs for the fourth wicket. McCabe and Darling added 81 for the fifth wicket. Darling and Oldfield were engaged in an unfinished sixth wicket stand, which produced 52 runs.

McCabe, who was more restrained than usual, scored 73. The left-handers, O'Brien and Darling, gave early chances, but later batted attractively. O'Brien was missed three times off Larwood, and Darling gave chances off Hammond and Allen.

Larwood, who bowled 21 overs, captured the first three wickets with only 14 runs against him, and later was unlucky not to secure O'Brien's wicket. Allen, who played after a trial at the nets, failed to take a wicket, and 89 runs were scored from his bowling.

The forecast for to-day is:—Mostly fine and warm, with squally westerly to south-westerly winds, but a cool change becoming more pronounced at night.

D. G. Bradman (48) attempts to glance a ball from Larwood which takes his leg stump.

# CROWD HOOTS JARDINE

## At Cricket Ground.

## CAPTAIN COMPLAINS ABOUT ALEXANDER.

## England Requires 153 to Win.

## AUSTRALIA DISMISSED FOR 182.

## Woodfull and Bradman Lack Support.

### VERITY'S SUCCESS ON WEARING WICKET.

There was a demonstration by sections of the big crowd witnessing the play in the fifth test match at the Sydney Cricket Ground yesterday afternoon, when the English captain, D. R. Jardine, complained to Umpire Borwick about fast bowler H. Alexander running on the wicket.

The crowd jeered and counted out Jardine, and the "barracking" broke out afresh when he patted spots on the wicket.

Alexander in his third over changed to bowling round the wicket, and Jardine made a further complaint. In his fourth over a ball struck Jardine a severe blow on the left side, and many of the spectators cheered and applauded, although the visiting captain was obviously in pain.

England requires a second innings total of 164 to win the match, and has made 11 of the runs. Australia yesterday collapsed on a wicket which gave assistance to some of the bowlers, especially Verity. This left-hander bowled accurately, and finished with five wickets for 33 runs.

Bradman batted aggressively for 71, and Woodfull played a dogged innings for 67; but Lee (15) was the only other batsman to reach double figures.

Larwood secured Richardson's wicket before a run had been scored; but his figures were one for 44 when he left the field at half-past three. He was suffering from bruised feet, and did not return to the field.

England had finished the first innings with a lead of 19 runs, Bradman having made a magnificent catch to dismiss Allen, who had scored 48.

The crowd numbered 43,324, being more than 10,000 greater than Saturday's attendance.

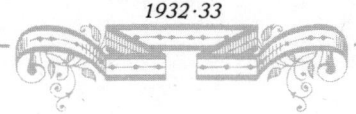

# BRADMAN BECOMES HUMAN

### By Cricketer

A great struggle has been nipped in the bud by much cricket that no Australian of old would have recognised as that of his breed. We can "smell" a psychological collapse in the downfall of Australia at Sydney yesterday, after their score had stood at 100 for one wicket. This time Larwood was more or less tamed by the genius of Bradman. But the opportunity was missed entirely; on a hard wicket Verity was able to take five wickets for 33, one of the most extraordinary performances ever achieved on a dry Australian pitch in a Test match by a slow left-handed bowler. Throughout these Test matches Verity has been hard to hit; he has kept the runs down and has consistently made the batsmen think. Yet five wickets for 33 would be an exceptional performance even on a "sticky" wicket at Bradford against representative players.

When the first Test match began at Sydney last November I suggested that there were not more than five players at Woodfull's call who would be certain to hold their places in a strong English county side for batting alone. This view was challenged by several correspondents, who, I fancy, overrated the skill of Ponsford, McCabe, Richardson, and Kippax. To-day we can see that Australia possesses only two really great batsmen—Woodfull and Bradman.

### Batting Without Tenacity

The batting yesterday lacked the proper Australian tenacity. Richardson tried to pull the second ball Larwood sent to him; McCabe cut a ball, before he was "set," into the hands of Jardine. O'Brien did not play himself in; he, too, was out trying to cut. ("It isn't a business stroke," said Wilfred Rhodes long ago.) Darling also got out through trying a swinging hit to leg. Even Woodfull scored at a pl... ....... quick pace—for him. What of the current notion that we are "playing the Australians at their own game" whenever our batsmen make 350 runs in ten hours? The Australian batsman has always been quick and severe at the sight of a bad ball; yesterday, though, they seem to have lost their traditional knack of mingling offence proportionately with defence. The low scores of the Australians in this rubber have been the consequence of poor all-round batting and of admirable all-round bowling. Though Larwood has provided the spearhead of Jardine's attack, the other bowlers have never lost a chance; somebody or other has usually jumped to his cue. Not for many years has an England eleven shown a more consistent all-round ability than that of Jardine's team. But we have received flattery from an Australian "tail" of unprecedented length.

### Bradman's Genius

The innings of Bradman tells vividly of genius. He declined to be enchained by the leg-trap. Like a great player, he sought to solve the problem by creative batsmanship; he moved aside on quick feet and cut the fast "bumpers" in dazzling style. Years ago we admired the swift-witted way in which J. T. Tyldesley countered Armstrong's *slow* leg theory. At Nottingham in 1905 Armstrong attempted to save Australia from defeat by pitching his slow stuff wide to leg with the field set appropriately. MacLaren watched ball after ball go by, declining the risk of hitting a catch to leg. Tyldesley walked backwards a few steps and cut the leg balls to the off-side, where no fieldsmen were placed. Every cricketer applauded Tyldesley's resource, and rightly so. But if it was genius to tackle slow leg theory in this warlike way, what must we say of Bradman's brilliant swordsmanship to the off-side against leg bowling faster than any seen on fast Australian turf for years?

Bradman, I believe, put more genius into his cricket yesterday than into any of his mechanical double centuries of 1930. None the less, he is a psychological enigma. For the typical Bradman—the automatic scoring machine of a year or two ago—never gave the bowler a chance, never hit the ball into the air, never exposed a single flaw in his mechanism. He scored fast, but he scored with a heart-breaking canniness. To-day he is playing with the brilliance of a Tyldesley or a Macartney—and with Tyldesley's and Macartney's adorable fearlessness and hint of mortal fallibility. And such is the modern conception of cricket that Bradman is now being reprimanded even by his friends for his sudden evolution into a human and sporting batsman. He has found a cricketer's heart; he is no longer a robot. The game is enriched by the new-born Bradman; he may lose his average of 200.17 an innings; but he takes his place in the immortal company of cricketers who have gripped the imagination and used their bats like lances of chivalry. I have not often this winter wished to see the Test matches; usually the play has been all against my idea of lovely and generous sport. But I would gladly have walked a long way to see Bradman yesterday.

### An Escape from Bondage

He has at last escaped from bondage to his own technique; he is now able to go beyond it, to send his spirit on bold adventures into the unknown. An artist should be free to transcend his skill, to take brave chancy flights a little higher than he knows his wings will take him. If Larwood has wakened up the spirit of Bradman, and transformed him from a worker by the book of arithmetic into a romantic lover of hazards, then Larwood has not only won the rubber for England but also has given to cricket another Trumper—who never could support an average of a hundred! Even in his new and more fallible shape Bradman has scored runs heavily enough. Here is his performances this winter: 0, 103 not out, 8, 66, 76, 24, 48, and 71.

Bradman's complete record in Test cricket against England, South Africa, and the West Indies is almost beyond belief: 18, 1, 79, 112, 40, 58, 123, 37 not out, 8, 131, 254, 1, 334, 14, 232, 4, 25, 223, 152, 43, 0, 226, 112, 2, 167, 299 not out—and then the innings he has played this season. Of course, no human being could "keep up" the monotonous consistency of Bradman's scores of 1929-32. The great point of it all is that Bradman, who once was scarcely human, is now definitely human, and therefore greater than ever. We have admired him in the past; now we shall begin to watch him with something warmer than admiration.

"Cricketer" was the pseudonym for Neville Cardus

# ENGLISH BOMBSHELL-

## F. R. FOSTER TELLS

## England Is Shamed By The Victory

**(RADIO FROM "SMITH'S" LONDON OFFICE. COPYRIGHT.)**

"**JARDINE IS WELCOME TO THE ASHES, AT THE PRICE ENGLAND PAID FOR THEM.**"

*Thus Frank R. Foster, the famous English bowler, opened his statement in London to "Smith's Weekly." And he went on:—*

"Say this from me to the captain of the English Eleven in Australia:—

"**DOUGLAS JARDINE, I AM ASHAMED OF ENGLAND'S WIN. I WILL FACE YOU ON YOUR RETURN WITH THESE WORDS ON MY LIPS.**

"You allowed Woodfull to beat you in every sense of the word Cricket.

"Woodfull won the Second Test by clean methods. We won our four matches by other methods.

"I take my hat right off to Woodfull, for resisting the temptation to retaliate in body-line bowling. **Cricket history has no finer example of sportsmanship.**

"My name has been used in the body-line controversy, in connection with Warner's tour of 1911–1912. I indignantly repudiate the suggestion that I ever used body-line bowling.

"I may have struck men by accident. What fast bowler hasn't? But I never deliberately sent the ball at a batsman's head or body. I aimed always for good length balls. Batsmen like Hobbs or Macartney were never struck by me, because they knew how to use their feet.

## Allen Should Lead England

"Being a left-handed bowler, I never once in my whole cricket career bowled over the wicket. A left-arm bowler, bowling over the wicket, immediately becomes a body-liner, for he cannot possibly see the three stumps.

"**Body-line bowling is quite different from the leg-theory, which I understand and which I bowled.**

"I am sorry that Nottingham, through Larwood and Voce, figures so conspicuously in the cloud surrounding England's victory.

"**ALLEN HAS PROVED HIMSELF A PERFECT GENTLEMAN, AND ON HIS ABILITY AND SPORTSMANSHIP HE SHOULD BE ENGLAND'S CAPTAIN.**

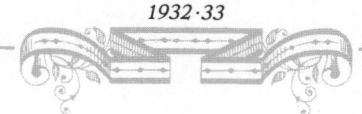

# -AT DOUGLAS JARDINE

## "UNWORTHY USES"

### Great Bowler Indignant Against Jardine

# TACTICS OF CAPTAIN

"Allen displayed strength of character in resisting Jardine's 'body-line' influence.

"I greatly regret Larwood's actions. As the finest fast bowler that England has seen for thirty years, he is too good to resort to any kind of leg theory.

"Unless the Marylebone Cricket Club does uphold the protest from the Australian Board of Control, the game will be ruined in the coming season. Even schoolboy fast bowlers, encountering difficult wickets and expert batsmen, will bowl bumpers deliberately at the man instead of the wicket.

"Body-line bowling must be abolished. The only solution is to give the umpire power to no-ball.

**"AND IT MUST BE DONE BEFORE THE 1934 SEASON, AS JARDINE MAY STILL BE CAPTAIN WHEN THE AUSTRALIANS VISIT US."**

Foster then concluded his statement to "Smith's Weekly" with a comment on Warner's presence in the visiting party, and a revelation regarding the body-line plan. Both were highly significant. Regarding Warner, he said:—

"In the whole history of cricket, there have never previously been two managers sent to Australia with an English Eleven.

'WARNER WAS SENT TO KEEP THE PEACE. THE CABLE SENT BY THE AUSTRALIAN BOARD OF CONTROL IS EVIDENCE THAT HE FAILED IN HIS OBJECT'."

Foster's final statement concerning Jardine contains the honest indignation of a sportsman who has felt himself misused:—

"BEFORE JARDINE LEFT ENGLAND, HE CAME FREQUENTLY TO MY FLAT IN THE ST. JAMES, AND SECURED FROM ME MY LEG-THEORY FIELD PLACINGS.

'I had no hint that these would be used for body-line bowling.

'I WOULD LIKE ALL MY OLD FRIENDS IN AUSTRALIAN CRICKET TO KNOW THAT I AM SORRY THAT MY EXPERIENCE AND MY ADVICE WERE PUT TO SUCH UNWORTHY USES."

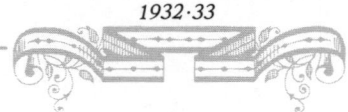

# THE BOWLING CONTROVERSY.

## TEXT OF THE CABLES.

———————————

During the tour of the M.C.C. team in Australia in 1932-33, exception was taken in that country to the methods adopted by certain of the visiting bowlers, and long correspondence by cable between the M.C.C. and the Australian Board of Control followed. Below will be found, in chronological order, the text of these cables, together with—in proper sequence—a short report of meetings bearing upon the subject.

### From Australian Board of Control to M.C.C., Jan. 18, 1933.

" Body-line bowling has assumed such proportions as to menace the best interests of the game, making protection of the body by the batsmen the main consideration.

" This is causing intensely bitter feeling between the players as well as injury. In our opinion it is unsportsmanlike.

" Unless stopped at once it is likely to upset the friendly relations existing between Australia and England."

### From M.C.C. to Australian Board of Control, Jan. 23, 1933.

" We, Marylebone Cricket Club, deplore your cable. We deprecate your opinion that there has been unsportsmanlike play. We have fullest confidence in captain, team and managers and are convinced that they would do nothing to infringe either the Laws of Cricket or the spirit of the game. We have no evidence that our confidence has been misplaced. Much as we regret accidents to Woodfull and Oldfield, we understand that in neither case was the bowler to blame. If the Australian Board of Control wish to propose a new Law or Rule, it shall receive our careful consideration in due course.

" We hope the situation is not now as serious as your cable would seem to indicate, but if it is such as to jeopardize the good relations between English and Australian cricketers and you consider it desirable to cancel remainder of programme we would consent, but with great reluctance."

### From Australian Board of Control to M.C.C., Jan. 30, 1933.

" We, Australian Board of Control, appreciate your difficulty in dealing with the matter raised in our cable without having seen the actual play. We unanimously regard body-line bowling, as adopted in some of the games in the present tour, as being opposed to the spirit of cricket, and unnecessarily dangerous to the players.

" We are deeply concerned that the ideals of the game shall be protected and have, therefore, appointed a committee to report on the action necessary to eliminate such bowling from Australian cricket as from beginning of the 1933-34 season.

"We will forward a copy of the Committee's recommendations for your consideration, and it is hoped co-operation as to its application to all cricket. We do not consider it necessary to cancel remainder of programme."

The committee appointed consisted of Messrs. R. J. Hartigan (Queensland) representing the Board of Control; W. M. Woodfull, V. Y. Richardson and M. A. Noble.

### From M.C.C. to Australian Board of Control, Feb. 2, 1933.

"We, the Committee of the Marylebone Cricket Club note with pleasure that you do not consider it necessary to cancel the remainder of programme, and that you are postponing the whole issue involved until after the present tour is completed. May we accept this as a clear indication that the good sportsmanship of our team is not in question?

"We are sure you will appreciate how impossible it would be to play any Test Match in the spirit we all desire unless both sides were satisfied there was no reflection upon their sportsmanship.

"When your recommendation reaches us it shall receive our most careful consideration and will be submitted to the Imperial Cricket Conference."

### From Australian Board of Control to M.C.C., Feb. 8, 1933.

"We do not regard the sportsmanship of your team as being in question.

"Our position was fully considered at the recent meeting in Sydney and is as indicated in our cable of January 30.

"It is the particular class of bowling referred to therein which we consider is not in the best interests of cricket, and in this view we understand we are supported by many eminent English cricketers.

"We join heartily with you in hoping that the remaining Tests will be played with the traditional good feeling."

The Australian Board of Control, meeting on April 21, 1933, considered a proposal submitted to them by the special sub-committee set up to consider the question of "body-line" bowling and cabled M.C.C. asking that body to give the proposal their consideration. The cable read as follows: "Australian Board adopted following addition to Laws of Cricket in Australia, namely:—

"Any ball delivered which, in the opinion of the umpire at the bowler's end is bowled at the batsman with the intent to intimidate or injure him shall be considered unfair and 'No-ball' shall be called. The bowler shall be notified of the reason. If the offence be repeated by the same bowler in the same innings he shall be immediately instructed by the umpire to cease bowling and the over shall be regarded as completed. Such bowler shall not again be permitted to bowl during the course of the innings then in progress."

"Law 48a shall not apply to this Law. Foregoing submitted for your consideration and it is hoped co-operation by application to all cricket."

### From M.C.C. to Australian Board of Control, June 12, 1933.

"The M.C.C. Committee have received and carefully considered the cable of the Australian Board of Control of April 28th last. They have also received and considered the reports of the Captain and Managers of the cricket team which visited Australia 1932-1933.

"With regard to the cable of the Australian Board of Control of April 28th last, the Committee presume that the class of bowling to which the proposed new law would apply is that referred to as 'body-line' bowling in the Australian Board of Control's cable of January 18th. The Committee consider that the term 'body-line' bowling is misleading and improper. It has led to much inaccuracy of thought by confusing the short bumping ball, whether directed on the off, middle or leg stump, with what is known as 'leg-theory.'

*The Board meeting referred to as April 21, was in fact held on April 28.

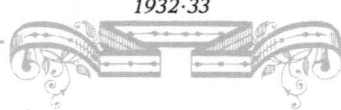

"The term ' body-line ' would appear to imply a direct attack by the bowler on the batsman. The Committee consider that such an implication applied to any English bowling in Australia is improper and incorrect. Such action on the part of any bowler would be an offence against the spirit of the game and would be immediately condemned. The practice of bowling on the leg stump with a field placed on the leg side necessary for such bowling is legitimate, an l has been in force for many years. It has generally been referred to as ' leg-theory.' The present habit of batsmen who move in front of their wicket with the object of gliding straight balls to leg tends to give the impression that the bowler is bowling at the batsman, especially in the case of a fast bowler when the batsman mistimes the ball and is hit.

"The new Law recommended by the Australian Board of Control does not appear to the Committee to be practicable. Firstly, it would place an impossible task on the umpire, and secondly, it would place in the hands of the umpire a power over the game which would be more than dangerous, and which any umpire might well fear to exercise.

"The Committee have had no reason to give special attention to ' leg-theory' as practised by fast bowlers. They will, however, watch carefully during the present season for anything which might be regarded as unfair or prejudicial to the best interests of the game. They propose to invite opinions and suggestions from County Clubs and Captains at the end of the season, with a view to enabling them to express an opinion on this matter at a Special Meeting of the Imperial Cricket Conference.

"With regard to the reports of the Captain and Managers, the Committee, while deeply appreciative of the private and public hospitality shewn to the English Team, are much concerned with regard to barracking, which is referred to in all the reports, and against which there is unanimous deprecation. Barracking has, unfortunately, always been indulged in by spectators in Australia to a degree quite unknown in this Country. During the late tour, however, it would appear to have exceeded all previous experience, and on occasions to have become thoroughly objectionable. There appears to have been little or no effort on the part of those responsible for the administration of the game in Australia to interfere, or to control this exhibition. This was naturally regarded by members of the team as a serious lack of consideration for them. The Committee are of opinion that cricket played under such conditions is robbed of much of its value as a game, and that unless barracking is stopped, or is greatly moderated in Australia, it is difficult to see how the continuance of representative matches can serve the best interest of the game.

"The Committee regret that these matters have to be dealt with by correspondence and not by personal conference. If at any time duly accredited representatives of Australian Cricket could meet the Committee in conference, such conference would be welcomed by M.C.C."

### *From Australian Board of Control to M.C.C., Sept. 22, 1933.*

" We note that you consider that a form of bowling which amounted to a direct attack by the bowler on the batsman would be against the spirit of the game. We agree with you that Leg-theory Bowling as it has been generally practised for many years is not open to objection. On these matters there does not appear to be any real difference between our respective views.

"We feel that while the type of bowling to which exception was taken in Australia, strictly was not in conflict with the Laws of Cricket, yet its continued practice would not be in the best interests of the game. May we assume that you concur in this point of view and that the teams may thus take the field in 1934 with that knowledge ?

"We are giving consideration to the question of barracking and you may rely upon our using our best endeavours to have it controlled in future tours.

"We are most anxious that the cordial relations which have so long existed between English and Australian cricket shall continue."

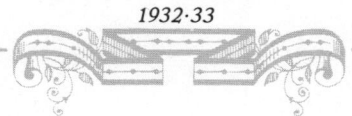

### From M.C.C. to Australian Board of Control, Oct. 9, 1933.

" The M.C.C. Committee appreciate the friendly tone of your cable and they heartily reciprocate your desire for the continuance of cordial relations.

"In their view the difference between us seems to be rather on the question of fact than on any point of interpretation of the Laws of Cricket or of the spirit of the game. They agree and have always agreed that a form of bowling which is obviously a direct attack by the bowler upon the batsman would be an offence against the spirit of the game.

"Your team can certainly take the field with the knowledge and with the full assurance that cricket will be played here in the same spirit as in the past and with the single desire to promote the best interests of the game in both countries.

"The Committee much appreciate your promise to take the question of barracking into consideration with a view to ensuring that it shall be kept within reasonable bounds.

"Your team can rely on a warm welcome from M.C.C., and every effort will be made to make their visit enjoyable."

### From Australian Board of Control to M.C.C., Nov. 16, 1933.

" We appreciate the terms of your cablegram of October 9 and assume that such cable is intended to give the assurance asked for in our cablegram of September 22.

" It is on this understanding that we are sending a team in 1934."

---

A joint meeting of the Advisory County Cricket Committee and the Board of Control of Test Matches at Home, at which the county captains were present, was held at Lord's on Thursday, November 23, 1933, to consider the replies received from the counties to the M.C.C.'s circular letter in regard to fast leg-theory bowling.

A decision was reached that no alteration of the Law was desirable. It was agreed that any form of bowling which is obviously a direct attack by the bowler upon the batsman would be an offence against the spirit of the game.

It was decided to leave the matter to the captains in complete confidence that they would not permit or countenance bowling of such type.

---

### From M.C.C. to Australian Board of Control, Dec. 12, 1933.

" Reference your cable of November 16th, you must please accept our cable of October 9th, which speaks for itself, as final.

" We cannot go beyond the assurance therein given. We shall welcome Australian cricketers who come to play cricket with us next year. If, however, your Board of Control decide that such games should be deferred, we shall regret their decision.

" Please let us know your Board's final decision as soon as possible and in any event before the end of the year."

### From Australian Board of Control to M.C.C., Dec. 14, 1933.

" With further reference to your cable of October 9 and your confirmatory cable of December 12 in reply to ours of November 16, we, too, now regard the position finalised. Our team will leave Australia on March 9."

### From M.C.C. to Australian Board of Control, Dec. 14, 1933.

" Thank you for your cable. We are very glad to know we may look forward to welcoming the Australians next summer. We shall do all in our power to make their visit enjoyable."

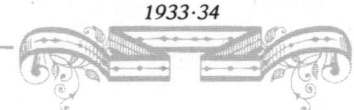

# 1933-34 Season

The 1933/34 season was the end of an era.

Born and bred in New South Wales, and not being of a nomadic disposition, I would have preferred to end my cricket days in that State. But economic considerations dominated my decision to obtain employment which would free me from dependence on sport as a livelihood.

In due course, I grew to love my adopted State, but in 1934 I felt rather like a boy leaving home.

Prior to the summer of 1933/34 I made a study of the laws of cricket and passed an umpire's exam, not with the idea of ever becoming an umpire, but merely to educate myself.

In general my form throughout the season was good and at the end I was gratified and honoured to be appointed Vice-Captain of the team to tour England.

Unfortunately, there were already warnings that my health needed watching. Even though passed by the Board doctors in Sydney, I went, at my own expense, to an Adelaide specialist and confided in him my doubts as to whether I could stand up to the English tour. He ordered complete rest until reaching England.

This undoubtedly helped, but in retrospect my spasmodic lapses on tour reflected an underlying malady which suddenly erupted and nearly ended my life, as well as my career.

But that is a matter for the end of 1934.

*Don Bradman*

## — SEASON 1933-34 —

| TITLE | GAME | | SCORES | |
|---|---|---|---|---|
| Second Class | North Sydney | Marrickville | 24 | S. |
| | Sun-Palmers | M.S. Radio Club | 83 | C. |
| - | - | - | 71 | C. |
| - | - | - | 63 | C. |
| - | - | - | 28 | S. |
| | N.S.W.C.A. | Mudgee | 87 | B. |
| - | | Dubbo | 100 | C. |
| - | | Cowra | 49 | B. |
| - | | Holbrook | 58 | B. |
| - | | Albury | 109 | C. |
| - | | - | 51 | B. |
| - | | Leeton | 48 | B. |
| - | | Orange | 6 | B. |
| | Bradman's Team | N. Sydney School | 37 | C. |
| | Bankstown | C. Cumberland | 30 | S. |
| | Bradman's Team | Oldfield's XI | 144 | B. |
| | N.S.W. | Newcastle | 183 | C. |
| First Grade | North Sydney | Waverley | 19 | C. |
| | - | W. Suburbs | 127 | S. |
| | - - | Petersham | 62 | C. |
| First Class | Richardson's XI | Woodfull's XI | 55 | C. |
| | Blackie Ironmonger | Testimonial | 101 | C. |
| | N.S.W. | Rest of Australia | 22 | C. |
| | Collins-Kelleway-Andrews | Testimonial | 92 | B. |

| TITLE | GAME | | SCORES | |
|---|---|---|---|---|
| Sheffield Shield | N.S.W. | Queensland | 200 | C. |
| | - | - | 253 | B. |
| | - | South Australia | 1 | B. |
| | - | - - | 76 | C. |
| | - | Victoria | 187 | n. o. |
| | - · | - | 77 | n. o. |
| | - · | - | 128 | C. |
| | | Total runs | 2571 | |

## — SUMMARY —

AVERAGES -

| | Innings | N.O's | H.S. | Runs | Average |
|---|---|---|---|---|---|
| Sheffield Shield | 7 | 2 | 253 | 922 | 184·4 |
| Other First Class | 4 | - | 101 | 270 | 67·5 |
| All First Class | 11 | 2 | 253 | 1192 | 132·4 |
| First Grade | 3 | - | 127 | 208 | 69·3 |
| Other Second Class | 17 | - | 183 | 1171 | 68·8 |
| All Second Class | 20 | - | 183 | 1379 | 68·9 |
| All Matches | 31 | 2 | 253 | 2571 | 88·6 |

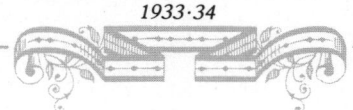

# DON IS NOW QUALIFIED TO UMPIRE

## PASSED HARD TEST LAST NIGHT

### (By A. G. Moyes)

"Now, Don, you are the injured striker and play the ball. In the excitement you and your substitute both run, and the wicket at the batting end is put down before your colleague has made good his ground. What would be the decision on appeal?"

This and similar questions (incidentally the injured striker would be out) were fired at Don Bradman last night at the N.S.W.C.A. rooms, when he sat for the N.S.W. Cricket Umpires examination, and passed it with honors.

The Board of Examiners comprised umpires Fred. Lyons, Alf Jones, George Borwick, W. French, Jack Gairns, and secretary Harry Armstrong, and they put Don through his paces. There were no trick questions. Everything asked affected a situation which might arise.

### Some Questions

There was the old catch as to which umpire adjudicated in the case of hit wicket. It is the job of the man at square leg. There was the lazy fieldsman who leaned against the fence while he fielded the ball. This is allowable.

Also the speedy one, who, after fielding the ball, had to save himself by putting a hand on the fence, giving away a four, and the chap who leaned back over the fence to take the catch, which would, of course, be out.

Then came the stationary ball and the batsmen who decided to run while it lay on the ground midway between the wicket, the fieldsman who picked it up, threw at the wicket and missed, the ball reaching the fence. "How many runs" was the question, and the answer was given promptly. No runs can be scored unless the batsman hits the ball.

Of course, the l.b.w. law came into play and also that relating to the no-ball.

It was a most interesting and instructive evening. There sitting round a table were the examiners and the world's greatest batsman. Between them was a board, with the pitch properly marked out, stumps erected, and with colored counters for batsmen, bowlers and fieldsmen.

And if a man can pass the test he need have no doubt as to his knowledge of the rules.

### Another Record

Mr. H. Armstrong, hon. secretary of the New South Wales Cricket Umpires' Association, said after the meeting:—"Don Bradman has certainly set up another record in passing an examination on the laws of cricket before the board of examiners of the New South Wales Cricket Umpires' Association. I offer Don my hearty congratulations. I certainly shows how keen he is on his game.

"He felt (when he spoke to me some few weeks ago) that it was not sufficient that one should be efficient in the actual playing of cricket only, but that he should be efficient in his knowledge of the laws under which he plays. I wish other leading players would follow Don and study the laws governing the game they play.

"I have seen wickets lost simply through the ignorance of the players.

"The board of examiners of my association would be very pleased at any time to deliver lectures to any club or any cricket association in New South Wales. Several country centres have already been visited lectures given, and afterwards umpires' associations formed.

"It should be the aim of every country cricket association to have affiliated to it an umpires' association. This would do a wonderful lot of good for cricket in the country.

"I hope all payers and associations will avail themselves of the opportunity to increase their knowledge of the laws of cricket."

N.S.W. CRICKET UMPIRES ASS'N

H. ARMSTRONG HON. SEC
A. C. JONES HON. TREAS

254a George Street,
Sydney

August 2nd 19·33

Mr D.G. Bradman

Mc Mahons Point

North Sydney

Dear Sir

It gives me very great pleasure on behalf of the Examination Board of the above Association, to inform you that you did on the 1st inst, pass the Examination on the Laws of Cricket. You have passed the Examination with great credit. The Board wishes to congratulate you on the example you have set, and hope that other prominent players will follow in your footsteps.

Yours faithfully,

Henry J. Armstrong
Hon Secretary

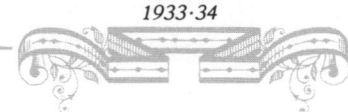

# New South Wales v Queensland

NEW SOUTH WALES v QUEENSLAND, at Brisbane,
3, 4, 6 and 7 November 1933.

| New South Wales | - First Innings | 494 for 4 wickets dec. |
| | - Second Innings | - |
| Queensland | - First Innings | 183 |
| | - Second Innings | 140 |

New South Wales won by an innings and 171 runs.

DON BRADMAN - c. C.W. Andrews b. R.M. Levy    200

DON BRADMAN started the season in dazzling form. He went in on the second morning with the score 101 for 1, and took only thirty-four minutes to reach 50 and an hour and thirty-two minutes to complete his century. He was caught on the boundary just after reaching 200 after batting for three hours four minutes. He went from 150 to 200 in only twenty-four minutes, and on one occasion took 23 runs in an over off E.R.H. Wyeth's bowling. He hit twenty-six fours and he and W.A. Brown added 294 for the second wicket, the score being 426 for 3 when Bradman was out.

His partnership of 294 with Brown was a second-wicket record for matches between New South Wales and Queensland.

# BRADMAN'S WISARDRY

## Sparkling Double Century by Genius

## Brown's Graceful Orthodoxy

## Queenslanders Gruelling Day

By "THIRD MAN."

*WHO could say, after drinking in the delights of the glorious batting feast that Bradman and Brown provided on Saturday afternoon, that cricket had lost its charm; that bodyline had killed the game; or that the dyed-in-the-wool enthusiast would in future find all his cricket thrills in watching the exhibitions of unadulterated "slogging" that a few people, who misinterpreting entirely the psychology of the cricket public, essayed to introduce in Brisbane recently.*

DON BRADMAN.

*Those who attended the Cricket Ground on Saturday went away with memories of a master innings by a master batsman. For sheer audacity it excelled anything that we have seen in Sheffield cricket for many a long day; for brilliant of execution it must have equalled the brightest efforts of any previous genius of the willow; for effective run-getting it could have been surpassed by nothing that ever any batsman ever devised. Twenty-six fours in a total of 200 was the result of uncanny placement, and of making openings where, if one relied on orthodox stroking, none really existed!*

The crowd at the Cricket Ground was not as large as had been expected, possibly on account of the big race meeting. But the 5,000 odd who did attend will for ever be the envy of those who failed to witness what will go down in the history of Queensland cricket as one of the finest exhibitions of the game that it has been our good fortune to see.

At one end there was Brown playing all the orthodox shots in cricket with consummate grace and ease, his dainty flicking of the ball away to leg, his forceful square cut, and a vigorous off-drive drawing the plaudits of the crowd again and again.

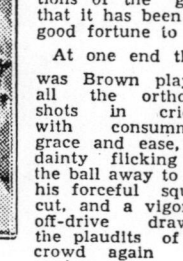

A. KIPPAX

### TRIUMPH OF UNORTHODOXY.

AT the other end was Bradman. And if his partner shone in orthodoxy, then the little champion positively sparkled in unorthodoxy. Balls that according to all the tenets of cricket should have been handled with a meticulous straight bat, were rudely dispatched boundary-wards with a blade that artistically flashed across the line of flight without recording the suggestion that the user thereof was indulging in the "cross-bat," so despised by his rare orthodox confreres of the willow. Never was the mastery of Bradman more exemplified than in that single off-theory over of Thompson's when every ball was cracked to the unprotected leg, while the covers presented the appearance of an overstacked paddock of flannel-clad fieldsmen.

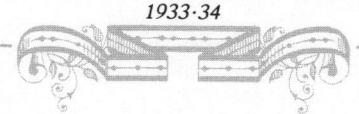

# New South Wales v Victoria

NEW SOUTH WALES v VICTORIA, at Melbourne, 22, 23, 26 and 27 December 1933.

| New South Wales | - First Innings | 355 |
| | - Second Innings | 144 for 1 wicket |
| Victoria | - First Innings | 382 |
| | - Second Innings | 200 |
| | Drawn. | |

| DON BRADMAN | - n.o. | 187 |
| | - n.o. | 77 |

DON BRADMAN's batting dominated this match to an extraordinary degree. His first innings commenced just after tea on the second day and a strained back at first compelled him to take things easily. However, he was 68 not out overnight after ninety-three minutes' batting.

Next morning, he continued to play Victoria almost single-handed. He showed great skill in keeping the bowling; but despite all his efforts his side was 27 runs behind on the first innings. His century had been completed in 178 minutes and altogether he batted for four hours fifty-four minutes, hitting thirteen fours.

Bradman opened the second innings with A.F. Kippax on the fourth evening, when New South Wales had an hour and forty-three minutes to make 228 to win.

## NEW SOUTH WALES.—First Innings.

| | |
|---|---|
| J. H. Fingleton, lbw, b Ebeling | 76 |
| W. A. Brown, lbw, b Fleetwood-Smith | 23 |
| D. G. Bradman, not out | 187 |
| A. F. Kippax, b Fleetwood-Smith | 23 |
| A. McGilvray, b Fleetwood-Smith | 11 |
| R. Rowe, c Barnett, b Fleetwood-Smith | 5 |
| W. A. Oldfield, c Darling, b Fleetwood-Smith | 2 |
| H. Chilvers, b Ironmonger | 5 |
| W. J. O'Reilly, lbw, b Fleetwood-Smith | 6 |
| F. Mair, c Barnett, b Ironmonger | 3 |
| W. Howell, b Fleetwood-Smith | 2 |
| Sundries (byes 8, leg-byes 2, no-balls 2) | 12 |
| Total | 355 |

Fall of wickets: 88, 130, 199, 231, 251, 259, 280, 299, 316, 355.

### BOWLING.

| | O. | M. | R. | W. |
|---|---|---|---|---|
| Ebeling | 29 | 7 | 53 | 1 |
| Nagel | 20 | 3 | 70 | 0 |
| Ironmonger | 30 | 10 | 51 | 2 |
| Fleetwood-Smith | 32 | 3 | 138 | 7 |
| Bromley | 7 | 0 | 31 | 0 |

Scores:—

## VICTORIA.—First Innings.

| | |
|---|---|
| W. M. Woodfull, c and b Howell | 60 |
| W. H. Ponsford, c Fingleton, b O'Reilly | 30 |
| L. P. O'Brien, run out | 86 |
| K. E. Rigg, c Oldfield, b Chilvers | 20 |
| L. S. Darling, c O'Reilly, b Howell | 91 |
| E. H. Bromley, c O'Reilly, b Howell | 13 |
| B. Barnett, c and b Howell | 20 |
| L. E. Nagel, not out | 17 |
| H. I. Ebeling, c Oldfield, b O'Reilly | 32 |
| L. Fleetwood-Smith, c Chilvers, b O'Reilly | 2 |
| H. Ironmonger, c McGilvray, b Howell | 1 |
| (Byes 2, leg-byes 2, wides 2, no balls 4) | 10 |
| Total | 382 |

Fall of wickets: 45, 134, 170, 260, 292, 325, 328, 371, 375, 382.

### BOWLING.

| | O. | M. | R. | W. |
|---|---|---|---|---|
| McGilvray | 21 | 2 | 65 | 0 |
| Howell | 38.5 | 11 | 97 | 5 |
| O'Reilly | 43 | 9 | 92 | 3 |
| Chilvers | 33 | 7 | 85 | 1 |
| Mair | 6 | 0 | 33 | 0 |

Mair bowled two wides and a no-ball; Howell bowled three no-balls.

## NEW SOUTH WALES.—First Innings, 355.
### Second Innings.

| | |
|---|---|
| A. F. Kippax, c Barnett, b Ebeling | 28 |
| D. G. Bradman, not out | 77 |
| R. Rowe, not out | 39 |
| One wicket for | 144 |

Fall of wicket: 54.

### BOWLING.

| | O. | M. | R. | W. |
|---|---|---|---|---|
| Ebeling | 10 | 0 | 56 | 1 |
| Nagel | 3 | 0 | 28 | 0 |
| Ironmonger | 9 | 0 | 26 | 0 |
| Bromley | 3 | 0 | 26 | 0 |
| Darling | 2 | 0 | 8 | 0 |

Victoria won on the first innings by 27 runs.

Scores:—

## VICTORIA.—First Innings, 382.
### Second Innings.

| | |
|---|---|
| W. M. Woodfull, lbw, b O'Reilly | 15 |
| W. H. Ponsford, b O'Reilly | 40 |
| L. P. O'Brien, c Rowe, b O'Reilly | 29 |
| K. Rigg, c Howell, b O'Reilly | 19 |
| L. S. Darling, c Oldfield, b O'Reilly | 53 |
| E. H. Bromley, lbw, b O'Reilly | 0 |
| B. A. Barnett, b McGilvray | 13 |
| L. Nagel, b O'Reilly | 10 |
| H. I. Ebeling, b O'Reilly | 15 |
| L. O. B. Fleetwood-Smith, not out | 1 |
| H. Ironmonger, b O'Reilly | 0 |
| Sundries, byes 3, no-balls 2 | 5 |
| Total | 200 |

Fall of wickets: 24, 70, 94, 144, 144, 161, 178, 195, 200, 200.

### BOWLING.

| | O. | M. | R. | W. |
|---|---|---|---|---|
| McGilvray | 23 | 5 | 51 | 1 |
| Howell | 33 | 15 | 54 | 0 |
| O'Reilly | 35 | 14 | 50 | 9 |
| Chilvers | 24 | 11 | 38 | 0 |
| Kippax | 2 | 1 | 2 | 0 |

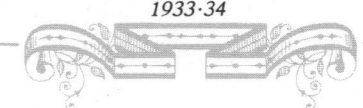

# O'REILLY'S

## Great Bowling.

## NINE FOR 50.

## State's Bid for Victory.

MELBOURNE, Wednesday.

W. J. O'Reilly performed a remarkable bowling feat in the concluding day's play of the Sheffield Shield match between New South Wales and Victoria, at the Melbourne Cricket Ground. O'Reilly, who sent down 35 overs, took nine Victorian wickets for 50 runs.

His effort was unavailing. Victoria won the match on the first innings.

O'Reilly's wonderful effort resulted in Victoria being dismissed in the second innings for 200 runs. New South Wales made an effort to knock up the 228 runs required for an outright win; but at the end of play the score was 144 for one wicket.

O'Reilly was accorded a magnificent ovation when he ran from the ground to the pavilion, after his bowling feat. In an attempt to make the win sure after a lead had been established on the first innings. Victorian batsmen fell victims to his magnificent bowling. The only batsman who troubled him was L. S. Darling, who had most to do with keeping his figures from assuming record proportions. Those who feared that O'Reilly's power to strike had diminished were treated to a display of strong, hostile bowling.

A bright spot in the day was the attempt by Bradman and Kippax to force an outright victory.

The official figures for to-day were:— Attendance, 8553; receipts, £293/4/8. For the match the figures were: Attendance, 51,214; receipts, £2019/19/3.

### PONSFORD GOES.

With a lead of 27 runs on the first innings and one wicket down for 64, Victoria seemed assured of victory on the first innings when the match was resumed in perfect weather.

Ponsford and O'Brien continued the batting, but their combination was soon broken up when O'Reilly bowled Ponsford with the third ball of his over. Ponsford did not add a run to his overnight score of 40. Rigg added 19 runs, and was then caught by Howell in the slips off O'Reilly. With two more wickets down for an extra 30 runs, Victoria's position was less bright. Darling joined O'Brien, and the century was passed.

O'Brien made only seven runs in an hour's play, and then made seven in a few minutes off Chilvers' over. Darling, after getting his bearings, began to play with sparkle. While O'Brien had taken 165 minutes to reach 26, Darling scored 27 in 38 minutes. O'Brien and Darling remained together till lunch, when the score was three for 144.

### SPLENDID BOWLING.

After lunch O'Reilly caused a sensation. Howell bowled a maiden, and then O'Reilly took over at the other end. On the fourth ball O'Brien was caught by Rowe, fielding at mid-off, who ran round behind the bowler for the catch. Four were down for 144. Then Bromley came in to face O'Reilly, and was trapped lbw on the sixth ball, and another wicket was down for 144. Two wickets had gone for none, and O'Reilly had taken five for 34. Barnett joined Darling, and finished the over. Howell bowled out his over for one run. Then O'Reilly resumed. Darling was nearly caught at silly point by Fingleton, but

he cut the next ball to the fence for four. Darling reached 50 in Howell's next over. In O'Reilly's next over an lbw appeal against Darling was disallowed, but he was out the next ball, being caught behind by Oldfield. Six wickets were down for 161, all taken by O'Reilly for 40. Since lunch O'Reilly had taken three wickets for six runs.

Nagel joined Barnett, and they faced out three successive maidens from Howell and O'Reilly. Chilvers took the bowling, and Barnett turned the first for a four to square-leg. McGilvray bowled the next for two runs, and in his next over clean bowled Barnett for 13. Seven wickets were down for 178. Ebeling went in to partner Nagel. O'Reilly was given the ball again, and bowled a maiden. In O'Reilly's next over he bowled Ebeling for 15 on the last ball. Fleetwood-Smith came in five minutes before tea, as Victoria reached 200 after 339 minutes' play. Nagel was clean bowled by O'Reilly in the next over. Ironmonger went in, and O'Reilly bowled him with the next ball. Victoria was all out for 200, and O'Reilly had taken nine wickets for 50.

### BRADMAN AND KIPPAX.

After tea New South Wales had apparently decided to go for the runs, 228 being needed. Bradman and Kippax opened to the bowling of Ebeling and Nagel, and they commenced in a merry style, stealing every opportunity for a single. In 20 minutes they had made 34 runs.

Fifty runs were reached in half an hour, and then Kippax was caught behind by Barnett off Ebeling. He had played defiantly for 34 minutes, making 28, including three fours. Rowe went in, and the score mounted rapidly to 100, made in 68 minutes. Bradman reached his 50 on the next ball. With half an hour's play remaining 125 were needed to win—an impossible task—and New South Wales could only reduce the deficit. At stumps Bradman and Rowe were still in, and the score was one for 144.

**DON BRADMAN STARRED AGAIN** when the Sheffield Shield game at last began yesterday. This was one of the many vigorous drives he made during his innings of 77.

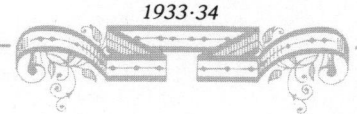

# New South Wales v Queensland

NEW SOUTH WALES v QUEENSLAND, at Sydney, 30 December 1933, 1, 2 and 3 January 1934.

| | | |
|---|---|---|
| New South Wales | - First Innings | 614 for 6 wickets dec. |
| | - Second Innings | - |
| Queensland | - First Innings | 372 |
| | - Second Innings | 158 |

New South Wales won by an innings and 84 runs.

DON BRADMAN — b. F. M. Brew      253

DON BRADMAN was again in devastating form against Queensland. He went in at 94 for 1, just before tea on the second day, and at 118 for 2 was joined by A.F. Kippax in a long partnership. At the close of play he was 122 not out, after an hour and forty-six minutes. Next morning he added a further 131 runs before lunch in ninety-eight minutes; he completed 200 in three hours five minutes, and then went from 200 to 250 in sixteen minutes. Kippax was out at 481 for 1, the pair having added 363 runs for the third wicket in two hours fifty-two minutes. Bradman threw his wicket away just before lunch, having batted for three hours twenty-four minutes; he hit four sixes and twenty-nine fours. When he was 189 he completed his 1,000 runs for the sixth successive season. The 2nd of January was the earliest that a New South Wales batsman had reached 1,000 for the season.

His partnership of 363 with Kippax was the highest for the third wicket by any Australians anywhere. Added to his scores of 187ˣ and 77ˣ in his previous match, this score of 253 raised the number of runs he had made in successive innings to 517.

131 runs was the most that anyone had ever scored before lunch in Australia.

## NEW SOUTH WALES.

| | |
|---|---|
| J. H. Fingleton, c Bensted, b Brew | 42 |
| W. A. Brown, c Levy, b Oxenham | 50 |
| D. G. Bradman, b Brew | 253 |
| A. F. Kippax (Capt.), c Yeates, b Oxenham | 125 |
| R. Rowe, c Leeson, b Oxenham | 7 |
| A. G. Chipperfield, c Leeson, b Andrews | 84 |
| A. D. McGilvray, not out | 34 |
| C. J. Hill, not out | 2 |
| B. 8, L.B. 2, W. 5, N.B. 2 | 17 |

Six wickets (closed) for ......... 614

H. C. Chilvers, F. Easton and W. Howell did not bat.
Fall: 94, 118, 481, 487, 507, 610.

### NEW SOUTH WALES—BOWLING.

| | O. | M. | R. | W. | O. | M. | R. | W. |
|---|---|---|---|---|---|---|---|---|
| McGilvray | 14 | 3 | 36 | — | 8 | 1 | 18 | 1 |
| Hill | 30.4 | 12 | 51 | 3 | 13 | 8 | 13 | 1 |
| Chilvers | 48 | 17 | 95 | 2 | 22.3 | 5 | 62 | 6 |
| Howell | 43 | 16 | 79 | 1 | 15 | 3 | 35 | 1 |
| Chipperfield | 25 | 3 | 88 | 2 | 5 | 1 | 19 | — |
| Kippax | 5 | — | 16 | — | | | | |
| Bradman | 1 | — | 2 | — | | | | |

Chilvers, 1 wide       McGilvray, 2 wides.

## QUEENSLAND.

| | | | |
|---|---|---|---|
| G. G. Cook, lbw, b Chilvers | 24 | —c Chipperfield, b Chilvers | 2 |
| F. M. Brew, run out | 14 | —c Bradman, b Howell | 23 |
| C. W. Andrews, c Bradman, b Chipperfield | 38 | —lbw, b Hill | 8 |
| F. C. Thompson, st Easton, b Chipperfield | 92 | —st Easton, b Chilvers | 10 |
| R. M. Levy (Capt.), b Chilvers | 45 | —c and b Chilvers | 16 |
| E. C. Bensted, c Easton, b Howell | 0 | —st Easton, b Chilvers | 29 |
| T. Allen, run out | 86 | —c Chipperfield, b McGilvray | 0 |
| R. K. Oxenham, st Easton, b Hill | 51 | —st Easton, b Chilvers | 24 |
| A. H. Tait, not out | 3 | —c Easton, b Chilvers | 35 |
| H. Leeson, c Chipperfield, b Hill | 14 | —not out | 0 |
| H. S. Gamble, c Easton, b Hill | 0 | —run out | 0 |
| L.B. 4, W. 1 | 5 | B. 8, L.B. 1, W. 2 | 11 |

Total ......... 372      Total ......... 158

Fall: 24, 43, 109, 183, 192, 238, 353, 356, 372.

Fall: 1, 14, 39, 49, 90, 95, 97, 153, 158.

### QUEENSLAND—BOWLING.

| | O. | M. | R. | W. |
|---|---|---|---|---|
| Gamble | 6 | — | 17 | — |
| Bensted | 19 | 2 | 97 | — |
| Brew | 25 | 1 | 176 | 2 |
| Oxenham | 42 | 9 | 116 | 3 |
| Tait | 10 | 1 | 77 | — |
| Cook | 4 | — | 32 | — |
| Andrews | 3 | — | 19 | 1 |
| Levy | 5 | — | 63 | — |

Bensted, 1 wide.
Cook, 4 wides.
Tait, 1 no-ball.
Umpires: G. Borwick and H. Armstrong.

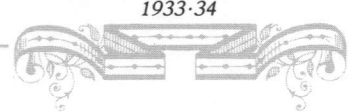

# BRILLIANT BATTING.

## Bradman and Kippax in Record Partnership.

### 363 RUNS IN 172 MINUTES.

### Four Sixes in Bradman's Innings of 253.

Kippax and Bradman, batting brilliantly against Queensland at the Sydney Cricket Ground yesterday, established an Australian record for a third wicket partnership. They added 363 runs to the New South Wales score in 172 minutes. Two hundred runs were scored in 105 minutes before lunch yesterday, this being one of the most extraordinary periods of play in the history of the famous ground.

Bradman, who made 253 runs in 204 minutes yesterday, hit four sixes off the bowling of the Queensland captain, Levy. Kippax scored 125 in 172 minutes.

The home team's innings closed with six wickets down for 614. Chipperfield contributed 84 runs. Queensland, requiring 242 runs to avert an innings defeat, had lost four wickets for 70 runs at the close of play.

The amazing Don Bradman in hitting humour.

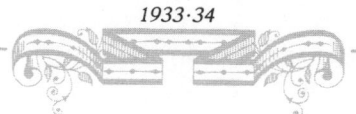

# New South Wales v Victoria

NEW SOUTH WALES v VICTORIA, at Sydney, 26, 27, 29 and 30 January 1934

| New South Wales | - First Innings | 672 for 8 wickets dec. |
| | - Second Innings | - |
| Victoria | - First Innings | 407 |
| | - Second Innings | 274 for 5 wickets |
| | Drawn. | |

DON BRADMAN - c. L.S. Darling b. L.O'B. Fleetwood-Smith    128

DON BRADMAN, though not in the best of health, hit out with great vigour when he went in on the first day. Despite his early self-effacement he reached 50 in fifty-seven minutes, completed 100 in eighty-seven minutes, and batted altogether for only an hour and thirty-six minutes.    He finished up by hitting L.O'B. Fleetwood-Smith for three sixes in an over before being caught in the deep.    He hit four sixes and seventeen fours.    His rate of scoring averaged 80 an hour and after his slow start his last 118 runs were actually scored in fifty-eight minutes.

In four successive innings for New South Wales he thus scored 645 runs (187$^x$, 77$^x$, 253, 128), a record for that State.

BACK ROW   W. A. Brown, A. G. Chipperfield, C. J. Hill, H. J. Theak, W. J. O'Reilly, O. W. Bill, W. A. Oldfield.
FRONT ROW   R. Rowe, D. G. Bradman, A. F. Kippax (Captain), J. H. Fingleton, H. C. Chilvers.

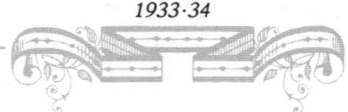

# Hail Bradman

## OVER 91 IN ALL BIG GAMES

### (By A. G. Moyes)

THE story of Bradman has often been told and yet not all of it, for the future is before us and perhaps not for another twenty years will we fully realise his influence on the game which he plays so well and to which he is such an ornament.

As I watched him make his glorious 253 against Queensland my mind slipped back seven years—it seems less than that—to the day when he came to Sydney for a trial.

The wire that Harold Heydon despatched on that occasion is a precious possession now, pasted away in one of the scrap books that tell of trials and triumphs, of success and failure—chiefly the former—the story on paper of the greatest run-getter that the game has ever seen.

And Don is more than a run-getter. Behind the powerful wrists is a cricket brain that makes one wonder. As Kingsford-Smith thrills the world with the majesty of his skill and organisation, so does Bradman compel our admiration with his exceptional ability, resource and daring.

He is not the purposeful plodder, but rather the gay cavalier of cricket, his bat a banner waving in the air as he ventures forth to run a course with the unhappy bowler.

### He Goes Fast

Examine his scores and you will find that he does not loiter. He carries the war into the enemy territory, for behind his batsmanship is the same ideal as burned so brightly in Trumper and Macartney.

Not until 1927-8 season did he play for the State, and his first innings, a century in Adelaide, was merely a forecast of things to come. In the next season came his first Test and then a setback when he was dropped, but on being reinstated he proved with his bat that the selectors were wrong.

And so it has gone on, in sickness and in health, one long triumph, with here and there the dull patches of failure sewn loosely on the garment of success.

A good thing, these failures, for they teach us that Don is human, whereas we, in our enthusiasm, place him on a pedestal and blame him, rather than ourselves, if he at times becomes unsettled.

One wonders how one of his age

has stood it all. At times the bitter criticism from those who should know better, must have been galling. From England have come cabled comments, cheap and childish at times, based always on wrong premises and grossly unfair, and in our own land, too, have we always been reasonable?

We know that we have not, and yet our champion, young as he is, has come through it all quite unspoilt and wishing only to be left alone to live peacefully as a private citizen.

### Look At Them

His records in big cricket are so well known as not to need repetition. His figures are given below and are so staggering that they need no comment.

Suffice it to say that Bradman has drawn level with Ponsford and Trumper on the century list, with Woodfull 44, Clem Hill 45, Armstrong 46, Macartney 52 and Bardsley 56 alone ahead of him.

He has only to continue in the game to leave them all far behind.

In conclusion, it is time that we made use of his brains. He should be vice-captain of our team for England, and he will come back ready to lead Australia in the years to come.

### SEASON BY SEASON

| Season. | I. | N.O. | R. | H.S. | Avge. |
|---|---|---|---|---|---|
| 1927-8 .. | 10 | 1 | 416 | 134x | 46.22 |
| 1928-9 .. | 24 | 6 | 1690 | 340x | 93.88 |
| 1929-30 . | 16 | 2 | 1586 | 452x | 113.28 |
| 1930 .. | 36 | 6 | 2960 | 334 | 98.66 |
| (In England) | | | | | |
| 1930-1 .. | 18 | — | 1422 | 258 | 79.00 |
| 1931-2 .. | 13 | 1 | 1403 | 299x | 116.91 |
| 1932-3 .. | 21 | 2 | 1171 | 238 | 61.63 |
| 1933-4 .. | 10 | 2 | 1064 | 253 | 133.00 |
| Totals | 148 | 20 | 11,712 | 452x | 91.5 |

### AN ANALYSIS

| | I. | N.O. | R. | H.S. | Avge. |
|---|---|---|---|---|---|
| New South Wales v. Victoria .. .. | 20 | 7 | 1937 | 340x | 148.21 |
| New South Wales v. South Australia | 20 | — | 1269 | 258 | 63.45 |
| New South Wales v. Queensland .. | 11 | 2 | 1299 | 452x | 144.33 |
| Australian XI. matches .. .. | 13 | — | 926 | 225 | 71.23 |
| English teams .. .. .. .. .. | 30 | 4 | 1506 | 157 | 57.53 |
| South Africa .. .. .. .. .. | 8 | 1 | 1190 | 299x | 170.00 |
| West Indies .. .. .. .. .. | 10 | — | 625 | 223 | 62.50 |
| In England .. .. .. .. .. | 36 | 6 | 2960 | 334 | 98.66 |
| Totals .. .. .. .. .. | 148 | 20 | 11,712 | 452x | 91.5 |

### TEST MATCHES

| | I. | N.O. | R. | H.S. | Avge. |
|---|---|---|---|---|---|
| Australia v. England .. .. .. .. | 23 | 2 | 1838 | 334 | 87.52 |
| Australia v. West Indies .. .. .. | 6 | — | 447 | 223 | 74.50 |
| Australia v. South Africa .. .. .. | 5 | 1 | 806 | 299x | 201.59 |
| Totals .. .. .. .. .. | 34 | 3 | 3091 | 334 | 99.7 |

### CENTURY LIST
#### For Australia

| | | | | | | | |
|---|---|---|---|---|---|---|---|
| v. England (Tests) .. .. .. .. | 334 | 254 | 232 | 131 | 123 | 112 | 103x |
| v. West Indies (Tests) .. .. .. | 233 | 152 | | | | | |
| v. South Africa (Tests) .. .. | 299x | 226 | 167 | 112 | | | |
| In England (other than Tests) .. | 252x | 236 | 205 | 191 | 185x | 117 | |

#### For N.S.W.

| | | | | | | | |
|---|---|---|---|---|---|---|---|
| v. England .. .. .. .. .. | 157 | 132x | | | | | |
| v. South Africa .. .. .. .. | 219 | 135 | | | | | |
| v. Victoria .. .. .. .. .. | 340x | 238 | 220 | 187x | 167 | 158 | 134x |
| v. South Australia .. .. .. .. | 258 | 175 | 121 | 118 | | | |
| v. Queensland .. .. .. .. | 452x | 253 | 200 | 133x | 131 | | |
| Australian XI. and Benefit Games .. | 225 | 139 | 124 | 101 | | | |

x Not Out.

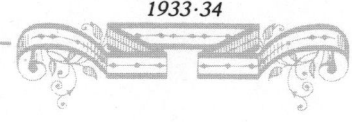

# New South Wales Cricket Association

CABLE & TELEGRAPHIC ADDRESS: "STUMPS"
ADDRESS ALL COMMUNICATIONS TO THE SECRETARY
TELEPHONES: B3541, B5556
WL.HH

254A GEORGE STREET, SYDNEY

Twentieth
February
1934

Mr. D.G. Bradman,
C/o Mr. J. Menzies,
MITTAGONG

Dear Sir,

Your letter of the 14th inst.
notifying the Association of your intention
to live in Adelaide was read to the Association at its meeting last evening.

I have been directed to inform
you that the decision was noted with regret.
The Association, however, decided to place on
record its appreciation of the wonderful services rendered by you to cricket in this State,
and instructed me to convey to you its best
wishes for your success in your new sphere of
life.

I have very much pleasure in
conveying this resolution to you, and I would
like to add my own personal expressions of
appreciation and good wishes to the foregoing.

Yours sincerely,

SECRETARY

# CRICKETERS FOR ENGLAND.

## Selection Widely Approved.

### CHIPPERFIELD A SURPRISE.

#### Bradman Appointed Team's Vice-captain.

The Board of Control announced yesterday that the Australian selectors—Dr. C. E. Dolling, and Messrs. E. A. Dwyer and W. M. Woodfull—had chosen the following 16 cricketers for the tour of England:—

| | |
|---|---|
| B. A. Barnett (Vic.). | C. V. Grimmett (Sth. Aus.). |
| D. G. Bradman (N.S.W.). | A. F. Kippax (N.S.W.). |
| E. H. Bromley (Vic.). | S. J. McCabe (N.S.W.). |
| W. A. Brown (N.S.W.). | W. A. Oldfield (N.S.W.). |
| A. G. Chipperfield (N.S.W.). | W. J. O'Reilly (N.S.W.). |
| L. S. Darling (Vic.). | W. H. Ponsford (Vic.). |
| H. I. Ebeling (Vic.). | T. W. Wall (South Australia). |
| L. Fleetwood-Smith (Vic.) | W. M. Woodfull (Vic.). |

The Board of Control appointed Woodfull captain, and Bradman vice-captain. Woodfull, Bradman, and Kippax will comprise the selection committee on tour.

One of the outstanding features of the selection was the inclusion of Chipperfield. This came as a surprise to the general public, although many keen judges had advocated his selection.

Interviews with cricket officials and players indicated almost unanimous approval of the selectors' work, although regret was expressed by many that it had been found necessary to omit Richardson and Fingleton.

# SOME PEEPS INTO THE PAST

## *Those Who Shared In The Making Of A Champion*

### By A. G. Moyes

HOW many people thought when Associated Newspapers, 2UE and Palmer's combined together and retained Bradman for Australia, that he would two years later be appointed vice captain of the Australian XI? It was a most gratifying result and it happened exactly two years from the day on which Bradman's contract commenced.

# Bradman For S.A. In Three Weeks

## IN BROKER'S FIRM

### Champion Tells

### BUSINESS FUTURE

#### (By A. G. Moyes)

DON BRADMAN will take up his residence in Adelaide in about three weeks and thus will make the move for qualification before he leaves for England with the Australian side.

Mr. Harry Hodgetts made that statement to me over the 'phone from Adelaide to-day.

Mr. Hodgetts was in great glee.

"I am very fond of Don," he said, "and am looking forward to having him as a member of my share-broking firm," he said.

"He wanted a career outside cricket, so that he could play the game as a recreation, and I will see that he gets it

#### For Australia

"He will be able to play cricket when and where he likes, and the big thing is that there is no possibility of Australia losing him.

"We will look after him, and of course it will be a big thing for our cricket.'

"Don will live in Kensington Gardens and will play with Kensington, the club with which I am associated," added Mr Hodgetts.

The fact that Don will reside in Adelaide before leaving for England means that he will be qualified for South Australia as from the start of next season. There is a three months' qualification, and, had he waited until he returned from abroad, he would have missed half the season.

#### Bradman's Statement

Bradman confirmed Mr. Hodgetts's statement over the 'phone to-day.

"You can make the statement officially from me," he said, "that I have accepted the position with Mr. Hodgetts's firm, and that I will go to Adelaide before the team sails for England."

Bradman also intimated that he would not be available for the match between N.S.W. and Western Australia on Friday week.

Thus the champion, who has meant so much to New South Wales cricket

*Mr. H. W. Hodgetts*

during the past six or seven years, has definitely severed his connection with it.

#### Another Viewpoint

There cannot be any two opinions about the loss which our cricket will sustain. Bradman has been the backbone of the side, and, as a draw card, has probably never been equalled in the history of the game.

It has been an education to the younger generation to bat with him, and Billy Brown is one who makes no secret of the lessons that he learned from Bradman.

There is, however, another point of view, and it may be that, with the overshadowing influence withdrawn, our other players may develop their powers to a greater degree.

## NOT ILL

### BUT NEEDS A REST

### DOCTOR'S ADVICE

### TO DON BRADMAN

ADELAIDE, Tuesday.

BRADMAN will not play with the Australian team until he arrives in England, it was announced to-day. He did not go by train to Perth with the rest of the team, but will catch the Orford on Thursday.

It is stated that Bradman's doctor told him it would be in the best interests not to play until he arrived in England. He needed a rest, and the sea trip would probably make him completely fit.

Reports that Bradman is ill are emphatically contradicted. He has had a little too much cricket and needs a rest.

There was a rush to find the cricketers' carriage when the express reached Adelaide and officials of the S.A. Cricket Association and local players greeted the team.

#### "Team of Gentlemen"

Outside the platform gate Woodfull and his men had to force their way through crowds of admirers to get to the official breakfast.

Members of the team brought confirmation of the news that Badcock would be coming to Adelaide to play for South Australia.

About 50 cricketers and others attended the breakfast.

The South Australia C.A. president (Mr. Scrymgour) said he was sure the team would uphold the honor of cricket according to the highest traditions.

"When the team leaves for England, England's authorities will say this is a team of gentlemen and sportsmen," he declared.

The secretary of the Australian Board of Control (Mr. Jeanes) will travel to Colombo with the team.

# Don is Here

DON BRADMAN and his wife arrived unexpectedly in the Melbourne express today to take up residence in South Australia before Don's departure to England.. A picture of the couple in the garden of Mr. H. W. Hodgetts' home at Kensington Park.

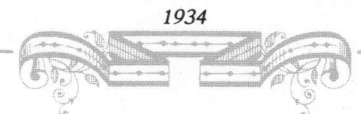

# 1934
# Australian Tour of England

I began the 1934 tour under a cloud. My health had been causing anxiety and the doctor ordered complete rest with no cricket on the forward journey.

Fortunately, I was able to get through the tour and play my full part though on many occasions I felt well below par.

After the last match and just prior to the scheduled sailing date, my incipient appendicitis flared up. An urgent operation was followed by some days of anxiety and my wife came over to join me.

After a few weeks in hospital there followed a period of convalescence and sight-seeing in England, Scotland and the Continent.

We returned to Australia in January 1935.

*Don Bradman*

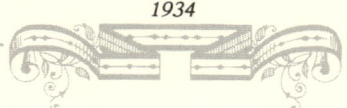

The Australian cricket team and the Davis Cup tennis players on board *S.S. Orford*.

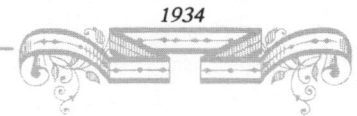

# BRADMAN ON HIS HEALTH

## "DIFFERENT MAN" AFTER RESTFUL VOYAGE

WHILE Don Bradman and eight other members of the Australian cricket team, completing the journey to England by sea, yesterday visited Gibraltar, where Bradman told Tom Clarke, our Special Correspondent, that he is as fit as ever, the first member of the team to reach this country, W. A. Oldfield, arrived in London last night after travelling across France.

### From TOM CLARKE,
### Our Special Correspondent with the Australian Team

ON BOARD THE ORIENT LINER
ORFORD, Sunday.

**"After this long rest, I am a different man."**

That is what Don Bradman told me this afternoon in the course of an informal chat about the reports in regard to his health.

I had gone ashore with him when the Orford called at Gibraltar, and I asked him if he had seen the recent stories and pictures purporting to reveal his unfitness.

He replied: "I have heard of them, but I have paid no attention to them. But these innuendoes are recabled to Australia, and I think it unfair to my wife that she should be falsely alarmed by stories that I am ill."

I said: "Well, Don, no one seeing you now would credit such stories."

He replied: "I am feeling as fit as ever."

### Wonderful Rest

He went on to explain that 18 months ago he was certainly "under the weather" and badly wanted a holiday, but got no chance during the busy season till this sea voyage, which had been a wonderful rest.

**He was not surprised that we thought he looked seedy at Colombo.**

"Of course I am a bad sailor," he said, "and if we get bad weather in the Bay of Biscay I may look like nothing on earth at Southampton. But once ashore, and it will be all 'dinkum.'"

### Putting on Weight

Meantime Bradman has put on weight, and as far as the ship's games are an index, his alert eyes are as marvellously quick as ever, and his agility with his wrists and feet is that of a really fit man.

I cannot assume medical prescience, as appears to be the case of some people who are determined to exhibit Bradman as a sick man. But if he is not now—as he said during our talk—as fit as all the rest of the team, then I am a Dutchman.

His problem, like that of all his colleagues, is more psychological than physical, and that is inevitable in the circumstances of these vitally interesting and important Tests.

All the members of the group on board the Orford, now that England is within what may be described without offence as "barracking" distance and they are feeling the effects of cooler weather, are showing greater activity in limb-loosening exercises.

In the last two days Woodfull, Ponsford, and Grimmett, together with Bradman, have been especially active with the ball at tennis.

# CRICKETERS

## Arrive in England.

### WELCOME AT SOUTHAMPTON.

LONDON, April 25.

The special correspondent of the Australian Press Association at Southampton says:—The sun broke through the clouds as the Orford approached the wharf. Most of the Australian test cricketers lined the decks, waving to friends on shore. The main welcome naturally awaits the team in London in the afternoon, but Sir Henry Bencraft, a former member of the committee of the M.C.C., boarded the ship to greet the players on behalf of the M.C.C., in company with the Mayor of Southampton. There were some "Coo-ees" from Australians in the crowd as the ship berthed, which met with a similar response from the passengers.

W. M. Woodfull was not seen on the deck, but O'Reilly and other newcomers leaned happily over the rails to get their first glimpse of England.

Players and passengers crowded in the ship's lounge to hear Sir Henry Bencraft briefly and cheerfully welcome the team. He referred to the pleasing coincidence that cricketers and tennis players, both in search of trophies held by England, were arriving by the same ship.

Woodfull, responding, paid a tribute to the warmth of the welcome and the efforts made to make the cricketers feel at home, even though they had not yet set foot in England.

While the gangway was being lowered, D. G. Bradman entertained the team in the music-room at the piano, playing popular tunes, to which the cricketers sang. W. J. O'Reilly has greatly benefited from the voyage. He has practically recovered from his wrist injury, and has increased his weight by 11lb. Bradman and H. J. Ebeling suffered from the heavy weather in the Bay of Biscay, but quickly revived in the smooth waters of the Channel. Bradman has gained weight in the past few days, and is now looking quite fit for the first match.

Paradoxically, the world's greatest batsman arrived without a bat, Bradman having decided to obtain a fresh stock here.

The team are great phonograph enthusiasts. No sooner had they boarded the train for London than they produced an instrument and a large supply of cheerful records to while away the time occupied by the Customs examination.

### "COMING TO PLAY CRICKET."

In a leading article, commenting on the arrival of "certain giants from the other side of the world," "The Times" suggests that "there is no need for alarm, because they are merely coming to play cricket, and will be heartily welcome."

"Anyone who continues trying to make bad blood," the article states, "deserves to be tied to a roller and bowled at for an hour by Wall and Larwood."

The "Daily Telegraph" asks if it would be treason to suggest that the Englishmen should not bother themselves too much over "the ashes," and expresses the opinion that the games between the visitors and the county teams will be more important for the future of cricket.

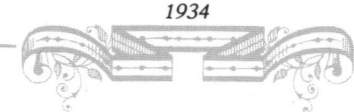

# LONDON'S WELCOME TO THE AUSTRALIANS

## BRADMAN ON LARWOOD

### *"Not Worrying About Him"*

### WOODFULL'S HOPE

### Win the Ashes and Retire

**L**ONDON accorded a great welcome to the Australian Test cricketers yesterday.

Immediately after their arrival at Waterloo from Southampton, W. M. Woodfull, the captain, and Don Bradman, vice-captain, drove with other members of the party to Whitehall to lay a wreath on the Cenotaph, and were greeted by great crowds with ringing cheers and shrill "cooees."

A *Daily Mail* "close-up" of Don Bradman's smiling response to the enthusiastic reception at Waterloo. He looks fit enough!

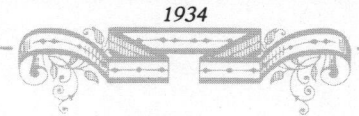

My second tour of England began in traditional style at Worcester. It was a crucial opening because my health had been worrying me for weeks and as an act of deliberate policy it was agreed that I should play to try and dispel doubts as to my fitness.

By a great effort I was able to do the job, but in retrospect I am sure it took considerable toll of my reserves of strength and was partly the cause of my later failures.

There followed very shortly my first "duck" on English soil, at Cambridge, then another against Hampshire.

Illogically, I went on to make a century in seventy-five minutes against Middlesex at Lord's, which, now that my career is over, I rate as probably the best innings I ever played against an English county.

Some days I felt quite well; others languid and off colour.

The pattern continued to unfold in this manner.

*Don Bradman*

## — SEASON 1934 —

| TITLE | GAME | | SCORES | |
|---|---|---|---|---|
| Second Class | Australia | The Army | 79 | C. |
| | " | North of Scotland | 7 | C. |
| | " | " | 2 | B. |
| First Class | " | Worcestershire | 206 | B. |
| | " | Leicestershire | 65 | B. |
| | " | Cambridge University | 0 | B. |
| | " | M.C.C. | 5 | C. |
| | " | Oxford University | 37 | L.B.W. |
| | " | Hampshire | 0 | C. |
| | " | Middlesex | 160 | C. |
| | " | Surrey | 77 | C. |
| | " | Northamptonshire | 65 | C. |
| | " | - | 25 | B. |
| | " | Somerset | 17 | C. |
| | " | Surrey | 27 | C. |
| | " | - | 61 | n.o. |
| | " | Derbyshire | 71 | C. |
| | " | " | 6 | n.o. |
| | " | Yorkshire | 140 | B. |
| | " | Sussex | 19 | B. |
| | " | South of England | 149 | n.o. |
| | " | Levenson-Gower's XI | 132 | S. |
| Test | " | England | 29 | C. |
| | " | " | 25 | C. |
| | " | " | 36 | C. |
| | " | " | 13 | C. |
| | " | " | 30 | C. |
| | " | " | 304 | B. |
| | " | " | 244 | C. |
| | " | " | 77 | B. |
| | | Total runs | 2108 | |

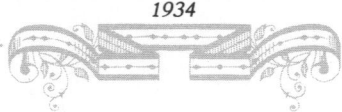

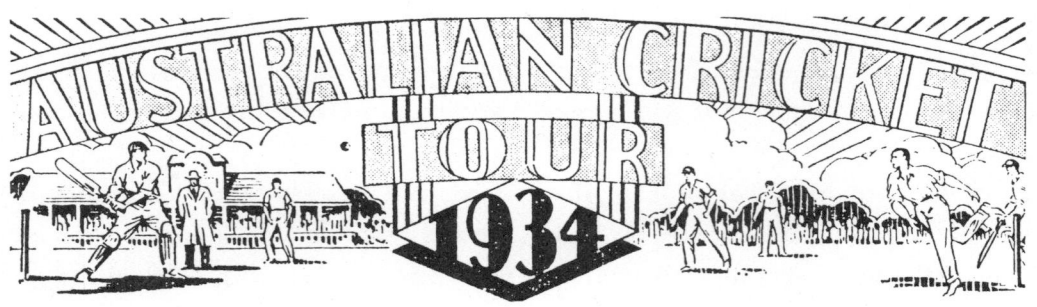

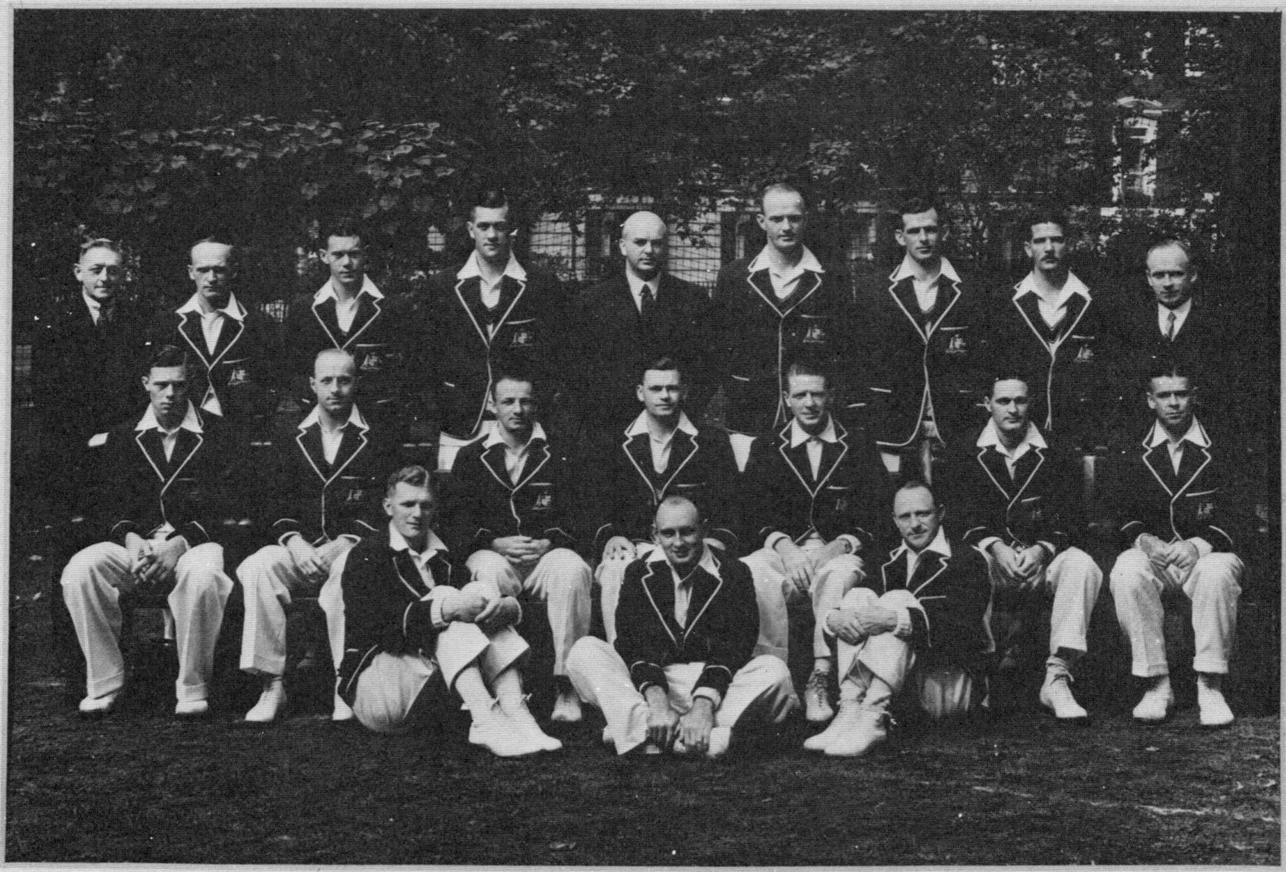

Official Photograph by SASHA

7 Suffolk Street, Pall Mall, S.W.1.

The 18th Australian Cricket Team
1934

BACK ROW W. Ferguson (Scorer and baggage manager), C. V. Grimmett, W. A. Brown, H. Ebeling, H. Bushby (Manager), W. J. O'Reilly, T. W. Wall, L. O'B. Fleetwood-Smith, W. C. Bull (Treasurer).

CENTRE ROW E. H. Bromley, A. G. Chipperfield, D. G. Bradman (Vice-Captain), W. M. Woodfull (Captain), A. F. Kippax, L. S. Darling, W. H. Ponsford.

SEATED B. A. Barnett, S. J. McCabe, W. A. Oldfield.

# *Australians v Worcestershire*

| Australians | - First Innings | 504 |
|---|---|---|
| | - Second Innings | - |
| Worcestershire | - First Innings | 112 |
| | - Second Innings | 95 |

Australians won by an innings and 297 runs.

DON BRADMAN  - b. R. Howorth  206

As in 1930, DON BRADMAN started the Tour with a double-century at Worcester. He went in at 29 for 1, before tea on the first day, and after tea batted with great confidence, reaching 50 in sixty-two minutes, and 100 in a minute less than one and three-quarter hours. He was 112 not out at the close after being in for one hundred and twelve minutes, and his stand with W.M. Woodfull (48) for the second wicket was worth 114 before the latter was out.

Next day, he carried on in brilliant form, completing 200 in three hours twenty-eight minutes, and two minutes later, with the score 359 for 6, he deliberately gave his wicket away. He hit twenty-seven fours. His cutting and hooking were as powerful as ever, and it was noticeable that he was more willing than in 1930 to hit the ball into the air.

No one else, English or Australian, had ever made 200 and over in his first innings of two English seasons; this was Bradman's third century in successive innings and his last five innings thus realized 851 (187$^x$, 77$^x$, 253, 128, 206).

### WORCESTERSHIRE.

| | | | | |
|---|---|---|---|---|
| Mr. C. F. Walters lbw, b Grimmett | 32 | — | c Ebeling b Wall | 5 |
| H. H. Gibbons b Ebeling | 0 | — | c Bromley b O'Reilly | 1 |
| Nawab of Pataudi run out | 14 | — | lbw, b Grimmett | 27 |
| M. Nichol lbw, b Grimmett | 6 | — | c Ponsford b O'Reilly | 1 |
| S. H. Martin c and b O'Reilly | 0 | — | c Bromley b O'Reilly | 20 |
| C. H. Bull st Oldfield b Grimmett | 13 | — | b O'Reilly | 1 |
| Mr. B. W. Quaife c Oldfield b Wall | 20 | — | not out | 13 |
| R. Howorth b Wall | 16 | — | st Oldfield b Grimmett | 14 |
| G. W. Brook b Grimmett | 3 | — | c Ebeling b Grimmett | 2 |
| P. F. Jackson lbw, b Grimmett | 0 | — | b Grimmett | 4 |
| R. T. D. Perks not out | 0 | — | c and b Grimmett | 3 |
| B 2, l-b 6 | 8 | | L-b | 4 |
| | 112 | | | 95 |

### AUSTRALIANS.

| | | | | |
|---|---|---|---|---|
| W. M. Woodfull c Perks b Martin | 48 | C. V. Grimmett c Brook b Howorth | 7 |
| W. H. Ponsford c Nichol b Jackson | 13 | H. I. Ebeling b Perks | 13 |
| D. G. Bradman b Howorth | 206 | T. W. Wall lbw, b Brook | 24 |
| A. F. Kippax b Jackson | 0 | W. J. O'Reilly not out | 25 |
| S. J. McCabe c Brook b Perks | 20 | B 26, l-b 5, n-b 5 | 36 |
| E. H. Bromley c Brook b Howorth | 45 | | |
| W. A. Oldfield c Martin b Howorth | 67 | | 504 |

### AUSTRALIANS BOWLING.

| | Overs | Mdns. | Runs | Wkts. | Overs | Mdns. | Runs | Wkts. |
|---|---|---|---|---|---|---|---|---|
| Wall | 12.3 | 8 | 6 | 2 | 8 | 3 | 9 | 1 |
| Ebeling | 4 | 1 | 10 | 1 | 6 | 1 | 15 | 0 |
| Grimmett | 24 | 7 | 53 | 5 | 15.3 | 7 | 27 | 5 |
| O'Reilly | 16 | 6 | 35 | 1 | 13 | 6 | 25 | 4 |
| Bromley | | | | | 4 | 0 | 15 | 0 |

### WORCESTERSHIRE BOWLING.

| | Overs | Mdns. | Runs | Wkts. |
|---|---|---|---|---|
| Perks | 26 | 2 | 83 | 2 |
| Jackson | 30 | 4 | 95 | 2 |
| Martin | 14 | 4 | 41 | 1 |
| Brook | 22 | 2 | 114 | 1 |
| Howorth | 23 | 0 | 135 | 4 |

Umpires: T. Oates and A. Dolphin.

ON THE FREE LIST. Spectators at Worcester getting an elevated view of the Australians during their opening match. Milton discoursed freely on "the fruit of that forbidden tree". But on the whole, he did it less heatedly than Worcester's Chancellor of the Exchequer probably did on this occasion.

# COUNTY IS SENT OUT FOR 112

## SLOW MAN GETS 5 VICTIMS | A CENTURY FOR BRADMAN

### From ARTHUR MAILEY

**WORCESTER, Wednesday.**

AUSTRALIA made a sensational start in the Test tour, when to-day they rattled through Worcester. An hour after lunch the county had been dismissed for 112.

The county team could not stand up to the Australian bowlers, Grimmett especially being deadly. He took five wickets for 53.

*The dismal showing greatly disappointed a large crowd that thronged the picturesque Worcester ground, which was bathed in brilliant sunshine. The wicket was true and fast.*

Although Ponsford and Kippax went cheaply, the Australians had scored 199 for the loss of three wickets at stumps, Bradman having passed his century.

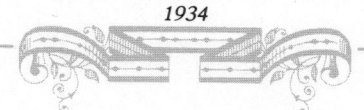

# Bradman Creates Another New Record

## ONLY BATSMAN TO OPEN WITH CENTURY IN TWO ENGLISH TOURS

### Has Now Made 46 Centuries In First-Class Cricket

By J. C. DAVIS ("Not Out.")

DON BRADMAN, the irrepressible, has started the tour in England by adding to his lengthy list of batting records. By making 112 not out on the first day he has scored a century in his first innings on two successive tours. No other Australian ever managed to do that in the past, during which seventeen teams visited England. Very few made even one such century.

In the corresponding match in 1930 (also against Worcestershire) Bradman made 236. That great innings, which electrified England, supplanted the 206 by H. H. Massie against Oxford University in 1882, as the highest by any Australian on his first appearance in England.

THE making of records may be anathema to some few sportsmen, but to Bradman at the wickets it seems inevitable. His skill is so transcending that his brilliant career has been studded with record-breaking achievements. There may not be many more for him to break, unless he keeps on surpassing his own records, which he is now doing.

This vein of run-getting so quickly struck by Bradman was not needed to convince Australians that his health was all right, and that his unparalleled ability to make runs against any kind of bowling had not diminished. It may have been necessary, however, to convince some in England that Bradman is still Bradman, perhaps a-little-better-still Bradman.

That as many as 100 journalists, and half as many photographers, assembled at the Worcester ground, indicates that no tour of the past ever had such intense public glare focussed upon it. If the Australians run into their top form early, as a team, this glare will continue, and the campaign, in that angle, will surpass any other international campaign in any kind of sport.

Bradman has now made 46 centuries in first-class cricket. The highest number by an Australian stands to the credit of Warren Bardsley, viz., 56. The present champion should have no difficulty in eclipsing this figure. He may go close to doing it on the current tour, if he remain free from mishap.

In the bowling of the Australians at Worcester on Wednesday were two very interesting and satisfactory features. One is the accuracy with which Wall bowled. For a fast bowler to send down 12½ overs for 6 runs, and two wickets, on a pitch that seems to have been on the slow side compared with those on which he bowls in Australia, is quite exceptional—in a fast bowler, phenomenal.

Wall, however, has shown that he has become a better bowler, apart from pure speed, than he was on his first tour. Out here, on many occasions since, he has bowled at periods like a real champion. Being supported by another man of pace, in Ebeling, he will be kept fresher on this tour.

The other satisfactory feature is that Grimmett has struck length and form at the start. He, too, will have better support than he had four years ago. This should allow of W. M. Woodfull keeping him as fresh as possible for the Test matches. It is more necessary to spell him from incessant match play now than it was in the past, though on English wickets it is easier for him to turn the ball, and that makes his work lighter.

A full blooded pull makes the close-in leg fieldsman superfluous.

Watching the Australians at Worcester in picturesque surroundings.

dman's autograph is still worth the bother of collecting it. Yester-
he carried his innings to 206 before being cleaned bowled by
arth.

Small Autograph-Hunter. "HAVE YOU GOT BRADMAN?"
Smaller Autograph-Hunter. "NO, BUT I'VE GOT THE SIGNATURE OF A CHAP THAT HAS."

# *Australians v Cambridge University*

AUSTRALIANS v CAMBRIDGE UNIVERSITY, at Cambridge, 9, 10 and 11 May 1934.

| | | |
|---|---|---|
| Australians | - First Innings | 481 for 5 wickets dec. |
| | - Second Innings | - |
| Cambridge Univ. | - First Innings | 158 |
| | - Second Innings | 160 |

Australians won by an innings and 163 runs.

DON BRADMAN - b. J.G.W. Davies          0

DON BRADMAN's first 'duck' in England had little effect on the course of the game. J.G.W. Davies, a slow off-spinner, bowled a ball which appeared to drift across from the leg, but did not turn back as Bradman expected, and hit his off-stump. He had gone in at 42 for 1 on the first morning, and was out to the fourth ball he received at 46 for 2; he was in for four minutes.

## C. B. FRY Says

### Don's Duck

At this point, your Don succeeded in being clean bowled for nothing by Davies—an epoch!

And St. John's College will undoubtedly celebrate to-night.

But I wanted to see Don again. I'm both astonished and annoyed.

It has been explained to me that Don "packed up for the off break," but the ball slipped straight on—it happens to some of us (note the "us")—from around the wicket right-hand.

[*N.B.—I didn't ask Bradman. Didn't dare. Hadn't the heart. Am a bit of a "fan."*]

How English sailors in Melbourne recorded Don Bradman's failure at Cambridge.

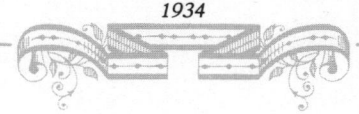

# Australians v Middlesex

AUSTRALIANS v MIDDLESEX, at Lord's, 26 and 28 May 1934.

| Australians | - First Innings | 345 |
| | - Second Innings | 29 for no wicket |
| Middlesex | - First Innings | 258 |
| | - Second Innings | 114 |

Australians won by 10 wickets.

DON BRADMAN — c. J. Hulme b. I.AR. Peebles 160
— did not bat

Having made only 42 runs in his last four innings, DON BRADMAN hit his way back to his most brilliant form. Going in at 5.13 p.m. on the first day at 0 for 1, he reached 50 in forty-nine minutes, and at 6.30, off the last ball of the day, he scored a single to make his score 100 not out, including nineteen fours, in a total of 135 for 2.

Next day he stayed for another forty-seven minutes before being brilliantly caught by J. Hulme on the boundary. In a stay of only two hours four minutes, he hit a six, a five and twenty-seven fours.

## MIDDLESEX.

| | | | |
|---|---|---|---|
| W. F. Price c and b O'Reilly | 23 | — c Ebeling b Wall | 9 |
| G. E. Hart b Ebeling | 1 | — b O'Reilly | 23 |
| J. Hulme b Ebeling | 0 | — b Ebeling | 0 |
| E. Hendren b Wall | 115 | — c and b Grimmett | 35 |
| Mr. R. W. V. Robins lbw, b Grimmett | 65 | — c Kippax b O'Reilly | 12 |
| Mr. G. C. Newman st Barnett b Grimmett | 0 | — b Grimmett | 2 |
| Mr. G. O. Allen lbw, b O'Reilly | 4 | — lbw, b Grimmett | 0 |
| Mr. H. J. Enthoven lbw, b Grimmett | 15 | — c Woodfull b O'Reilly | 19 |
| J. Smith b Wall | 13 | — b Grimmett | 0 |
| Mr. P. F. Judge lbw, b Wall | 0 | — not out | 1 |
| Mr. I. A. R. Peebles not out | 0 | — c Chipperfield b Grimmett | 8 |
| B 10, l-b 10, w 1, n-b 1 | 22 | B 3, l-b 2 | 5 |
| | **258** | | **114** |

## AUSTRALIANS.

| | | | |
|---|---|---|---|
| W. M. Woodfull lbw, b Smith | 0 | | |
| W. H. Ponsford lbw, b Smith | 0 | | |
| D. G. Bradman c Hulme b Peebles | 160 | | |
| L. S. Darling c Price b Smith | 37 | — not out | 9 |
| A. F. Kippax lbw, b Robins | 56 | | |
| A. G. Chipperfield c and b Enthoven | 35 | | |
| B. A. Barnett b Smith | 40 | — not out | 14 |
| C. V. Grimmett c Price b Enthoven | 8 | | |
| H. I. Ebeling st Price b Enthoven | 0 | | |
| T. W. Wall b Enthoven | 0 | | |
| W. J. O'Reilly not out | 7 | | |
| B 1, l-b 1 | 2 | B 4, l-b 1, w 1 | 6 |
| | **345** | **(No wkt.)** | **29** |

### AUSTRALIANS BOWLING.

| | Overs | Mdns. | Runs | Wkts. | Overs | Mdns. | Runs | Wkts. |
|---|---|---|---|---|---|---|---|---|
| Wall | 16 | 3 | 41 | 3 | 7 | 0 | 27 | 1 |
| Ebeling | 18 | 5 | 37 | 2 | 9 | 1 | 21 | 1 |
| O'Reilly | 18 | 4 | 56 | 2 | 15 | 5 | 34 | 3 |
| Grimmett | 19.2 | 2 | 80 | 3 | 12.4 | 5 | 27 | 5 |
| Darling | 4 | 0 | 22 | 0 | | | | |

### MIDDLESEX BOWLING.

| | Overs | Mdns. | Runs | Wkts. |
|---|---|---|---|---|
| Smith | 20.2 | 2 | 99 | 4 |
| Judge | 6 | 0 | 41 | 0 |
| Enthoven | 16 | 2 | 59 | 4 |
| Robins | 12 | 1 | 61 | 1 |
| Peebles | 16 | 0 | 83 | 1 |
| Hulme | 2 | 0 | 8 | 0 |
| Allen | 1.4 | 0 | 15 | 0 |

Umpires : A. Skelding and W. A. Buswell.

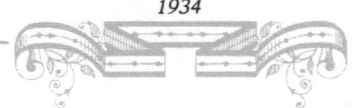

# DAZZLING DISPLAY BY DON BRADMAN

At 118 O'Reilly relieved Wall, who had again kept a good length and had bowled accurately.

When Hendren lifted Grimmett straight for four he reached 50 in 95 minutes, but the next ball beat him badly. Ebeling's right arm was again strained, and it was causing him to throw the ball with his left arm, while he frequently misfielded.

Both batsmen seemed to be on top of the bowling, Hendren's forceful on-side play contrasting to Robins's fine off-side strokes, while now and again each rattled the fence with straight drives.

At 140 Ebeling, despite his arm trouble, relieved Grimmett. Apparently he found it easier to bowl than throw.

## Robins Out

Robins, by glancing O'Reilly for four, ran to 50 in 75 minutes. He on-drove the next ball for three, but when facing Ebeling he was unable to pierce Bradman at cover. At 58 he snicked a ball hard and low, but Wall at third slip failed to hold a difficult chance, although he dived for the ball.

Darling and Grimmett came on at 173, and in the latter's first over Robins in trying to swing a ball to leg, missed and was out l.b.w.

**It was the first appeal that O'Reilly had made all day.**

Newman was the next man in.

Robins batted for 165 minutes, hitting nine fours in his 65. Over 20,000 people cheered Hendren when he cover-drove and cut Darling to the boundary, **but next over Newman,** whom Grimmett had guessing all the time, finally guessed wrong. Barnett had an easy stumping.

With Allen in the 200 appeared in 170 minutes. Allen was completely at sea to Grimmett and O'Reilly, but Hendren continued to upset the field by waiting for Grimmett's break, and then guiding the ball to leg for a single.

**Barnett once anticipated the move, and dived in front of the wicket, but just failed to reach the ball.** Hendren then cut Grimmett for four, reaching 100 in 160 minutes.

Allen, obviously not comfortable, put his leg in front of one from O'Reilly, and at 233 Wall came back with the new ball, and in his second over swung one back and clean bowled Hendren, who hit 11 fours.

**Smith, the next batsman, is a tall man, a fast bowler, and a big hitter, and recently hit nine sixes in one innings. To-day he square cut the first ball he received for**

four, and broke his bat. He got a new one, drove the next for two, then snicked Wall for four, and was then bowled.

Neither Judge nor Enthoven gave over much trouble, and shortly after tea the innings finished for 258.

The post-lunch session proved conclusively that the only way to play slow bowling is to use the feet. **During the past 10 years the fast-footed Englishmen have repeatedly failed before Grimmett, but he was unable to bowl accurately to-day because Hendren and Robins jumped yards down the wicket to kill the break.**

He and O'Reilly bowled as well as they were allowed, and that is the reason why the partnership was so prolific.

Ebeling after lunch was ineffective owing to his injured arm, but Chipperfield was not used.

With Hendren in such a mood it was a wonder that Woodfull did not try some new theory, concentrating on keeping him away from the bowling so that the bowlers could have a go at the other batsmen. However he kept on his orthodox road waiting like Micawber for something to turn up.

## Early Disaster

Australia made a disastrous start. Woodfull took strike, and Smith's second ball hit his pad and went to fine leg. He started to run and the umpire lifted his hand, giving him out l.b.w. Thus Bradman was once again practically an opening batsman, and the crowd gave him a cheer of encouragement. He blocked the first few balls and then nicely late-cut one for a single.

A sigh of relief was followed by a round of applause when Bradman, after missing Judge's first ball drove the second unmistakably for four, followed in the same over by a straight drive for four.

However, in the next over from Smith Ponsford was out l.b.w. to the second ball. This was the sixth leg-before victim out of the 12 wickets that had fallen. Smith did not seem as fast as Wall, but swung rather disconcertingly.

**Darling joined Bradman, who was soon off again on his merry way. He drove and then pulled Judge for fours and then straight-drove Smith for three, scoring 23 out of 24 in 15 minutes.**

Apparently his recent failures had not affected his nerve, for he was attacking the bowling whole-heartedly. Darling, on the other hand, was there for 15 minutes before he pulled Smith for three and broke his duck.

Darling then cover-drove Judge for four and pulled Smith to the boundary, Bradman in the meantime having got fours for an on-

drive off Judge and a late cut off Smith. In 30 minutes 47 appeared, Bradman being 33 and Darling 13.

Darling was dropped at this stage by wicket-keeper Price, who juggled the ball and dropped a difficult chance.

## First Fifty

Fifty runs came in 35 minutes, and Enthoven relieved Judge. Smith kept going, swinging well, and at times keeping low.

Then, at 61, Robins, who has been called Bradman's "hoodoo," came on, and the champion turned the first for a single.

After Darling had scored a lucky three for a snick, Bradman straight-drove Robins for four, but pushed the next uppishly towards square leg.

**Smith bowled a maiden, and then Bradman pulled, off-drove and cover-drove Robins for fours, reaching 57 in 45 minutes, including nine fours.**

Smith then dropped one short, and as it flew, Bradman stooped and smashed it to the leg boundary as though he was making an overhead shot at tennis. This was his 11th four. Then, in the next over, he cover-drove and straight-drove Robins to the boundary.

**Peebles was now brought on in place of Smith, and two to Darling brought up 101 in an hour. Then Bradman, who was laying back his ears and hitting everything in a way that he had not done previously on the tour, late-cut Peebles for his 14th four.**

Enthoven came back into the firing line, and Bradman square cut the first ball for four, and followed it by hooking Peebles for fours three times in one over.

## Crowd Went Mad

When the last over of the day arrived Bradman was 95. He had a chance to run a single, but Darling sent him back, calling out, "No, stay there. Keep it up, Don." Bradman promptly cover-drove Peebles for his 19th four, and then, with a single, reached the century off the last ball of the day.

He had batted for only 75 minutes and had made his last 25 in 15 minutes.

The police escorted him to the pavilion as the cheering crowd surged on to the field.

Australia's runs, thanks to him, were made in 80 minutes, Darling being there for 70 minutes.

# BRADMAN SMITES MIDDLESEX

## By William Pollock

AN innings that thousands of us who love cricket are going to enshrine in our memories was played as the sun went down over Lord's on Saturday.

For more than forty years I have watched great batsmen—W. G., Ranji, Trumper, Frank Woolley, Macartney, Jessop, Hammond, Hobbs—and am grateful for many precious hours from them, but never have I seen a masterpiece of batting more glorious than Don Bradman's 100.

It was supreme, it was epic.

Le Don came in when the Middlesex J. Smith (ex Wiltshire) had got both Woodfull and Ponsford out for noughts with his village blacksmithy fast stuff, and for a ball or two he was not quite sure of himself.

But the bit of luck that all batsmen need at the start was with him, and within five minutes the bowling was his toy.

### All the Shots

His timing was marvellous, the power he got into his strokes extraordinary. Through the covers, straight past the bowlers, round to leg, down through the slips, the ball raced from his almost magic bat. All the shots were his, the whole field his kingdom.

Smith's quickies, Walter Robins's slows, Ian Peebles' length ones, including an occasional googly, were just so much meat and drink to him.

> The ball no question made of ayes or noes,
> but right or left, as struck the player went.

Le Don seemed to be inspired; he danced down the pitch and hit, he flung out his left leg and drove, he lay back and pulled.

### Torrent of Runs

I do not believe that any bowling in the world could have stopped the torrent of his run-making during this wonderful hour and a quarter. It was an honour to bowl and field during such an innings.

It is no more than the frame of the picture to say that he put the ball to the boundary nineteen times, and that he got the one run he wanted for his hundred off the last ball of the evening.

Le Don has played the great innings of the season. If there is anything better to come from him or any one else, may I be there to see and share. The really great things of cricket are treasure.

How rich was Saturday at Lord's, packed by another Test-match-size crowd, made good by Patsy Hondren and Robins before Bradman set his seal upon it.

A powerful drive to the boundary off H. J. Enthoven.

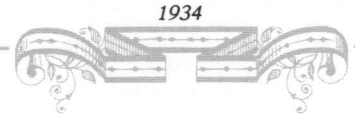

# Australia v England
# First Test Match

AUSTRALIA v ENGLAND, First Test Match, at Nottingham, 8, 9, 11 and 12 June 1934.

| Australia | - First Innings | 374 |
| | - Second Innings | 273 for 8 wickets dec. |
| England | - First Innings | 268 |
| | - Second Innings | 141 |

Australia won by 238 runs.

| DON BRADMAN | - c. W.R. Hammond b. G. Geary | 29 |
| | - c. L.E.G. Ames b. K. Farnes | 25 |

DON BRADMAN contributed less than usual to a convincing Australian victory. In the first innings, he went in six minutes before lunch on the first day, at 88 for 1, and hit 11 runs by lunch-time; after the interval, he continued to force the pace rather hectically, hitting six fours in twenty-nine minutes before being caught at slip. Spectacular as his innings was, it was a surprise on the first day of a Test Match; he was out at 125 for 3.

His second innings was equally spectacular, and included some brilliant strokes as well as some rather eccentric ones; he went in at 32 for 2 on the third afternoon, at a time when Australia, 106 runs ahead on the first innings, needed runs quickly before declaring, and made 21 in thirty-one minutes before the tea interval. He batted rather more soberly for sixteen minutes thereafter, before being caught at the wicket at 69 for 3.

NOTTINGHAM

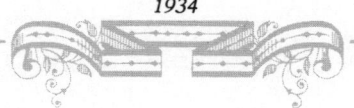

## AUSTRALIA.

| | | | | |
|---|---|---|---|---|
| W. M. Woodfull c Verity b Farnes..... | 26 | — | b Farnes.................. | 2 |
| W. H. Ponsford c Ames b Farnes...... | 53 | — | b Hammond.............. | 5 |
| W. A. Brown lbw, b Geary............ | 22 | — | c Ames b Verity.......... | 73 |
| D. G. Bradman c Hammond b Geary... | 29 | — | c Ames b Farnes.......... | 25 |
| S. J. McCabe c Leyland b Farnes..... | 65 | — | c Hammond b Farnes...... | 88 |
| L. S. Darling b Verity.............. | 4 | — | c Hammond b Farnes...... | 14 |
| A. G. Chipperfield c Ames b Farnes.... | 99 | — | c Hammond b Farnes...... | 4 |
| W. A. Oldfield c Hammond b Mitchell.. | 20 | — | not out.................. | 10 |
| C. V. Grimmett b Geary.............. | 39 | — | not out.................. | 3 |
| W. J. O'Reilly b Farnes............. | 7 | — | c Verity b Geary.......... | 18 |
| T. W. Wall not out................. | 0 | | | |
| B 4, l-b 5, n-b 1.............. | 10 | | B 22, l-b 9.............. | 31 |
| | **374** | | **(Eight wkts., dec.)** | **273** |

## ENGLAND.

| | | | | |
|---|---|---|---|---|
| Mr. C. F. Walters lbw, b Grimmett..... | 17 | — | b O'Reilly................ | 46 |
| H. Sutcliffe c Chipperfield b Grimmett.. | 62 | — | c Chipperfield b O'Reilly... | 24 |
| W. R. Hammond c McCabe b O'Reilly.. | 25 | — | st Oldfield b Grimmett.... | 16 |
| Nawab of Pataudi c McCabe b Wall.... | 12 | — | c Ponsford b Grimmett.... | 10 |
| M. Leyland c and b Grimmett......... | 6 | — | c Oldfield b O'Reilly....... | 18 |
| E. Hendren b O'Reilly.............. | 79 | — | c Chipperfield b O'Reilly... | 3 |
| L. E. G. Ames c Wall b O'Reilly....... | 7 | — | b O'Reilly................ | 12 |
| G. Geary st Oldfield b Grimmett....... | 53 | — | c Chipperfield b Grimmett.. | 0 |
| H. Verity b O'Reilly................ | 0 | — | not out.................. | 0 |
| Mr. K. Farnes b Grimmett............ | 1 | — | c Oldfield b O'Reilly....... | 0 |
| T. B. Mitchell not out............... | 1 | — | lbw, b O'Reilly............ | 4 |
| B .......................... | 5 | | B 4, l-b 3, n-b 1........ | 8 |
| | **268** | | | **141** |

## ENGLAND BOWLING.

| | Overs | Mdns. | Runs | Wkts. | Overs | Mdns. | Runs | Wkts. |
|---|---|---|---|---|---|---|---|---|
| Farnes ......... | 40.2 | 10 | 102 | 5 | 25 | 3 | 77 | 5 |
| Geary ......... | 43 | 8 | 101 | 3 | 23 | 5 | 46 | 1 |
| Hammond ..... | 13 | 4 | 29 | 0 | 12 | 5 | 25 | 1 |
| Verity......... | 34 | 9 | 65 | 1 | 17 | 8 | 48 | 1 |
| Mitchell ....... | 21 | 4 | 62 | 1 | 13 | 2 | 46 | 0 |
| Leyland ........ | 1 | 0 | 5 | 0 | | | | |

## AUSTRALIA BOWLING.

| | | | | | | | | |
|---|---|---|---|---|---|---|---|---|
| Wall .......... | 33 | 7 | 82 | 1 | 13 | 2 | 27 | 0 |
| McCabe ........ | 7 | 2 | 7 | 0 | 2 | 0 | 7 | 0 |
| Grimmett....... | 58.3 | 24 | 81 | 5 | 47 | 28 | 39 | 3 |
| O'Reilly ....... | 37 | 16 | 75 | 4 | 41.4 | 24 | 54 | 7 |
| Chipperfield .... | 3 | 0 | 18 | 0 | 4 | 1 | 6 | 0 |

## FALL OF THE WICKETS.

### AUSTRALIA—First Innings.

| 1 | 2 | 3 | 4 | 5 | 6 | 7 | 8 | 9 | 10 |
|---|---|---|---|---|---|---|---|---|---|
| 77 | 88 | 125 | 146 | 153 | 234 | 281 | 355 | 374 | 374 |

### AUSTRALIA—Second Innings.

| 1 | 2 | 3 | 4 | 5 | 6 | 7 | 8 |
|---|---|---|---|---|---|---|---|
| 2 | 32 | 69 | 181 | 219 | 231 | 244 | 267 |

### ENGLAND—First Innings.

| 1 | 2 | 3 | 4 | 5 | 6 | 7 | 8 | 9 | 10 |
|---|---|---|---|---|---|---|---|---|---|
| 45 | 102 | 106 | 114 | 145 | 165 | 266 | 266 | 266 | 268 |

### ENGLAND—Second Innings.

| 1 | 2 | 3 | 4 | 5 | 6 | 7 | 8 | 9 | 10 |
|---|---|---|---|---|---|---|---|---|---|
| 51 | 83 | 91 | 103 | 110 | 134 | 135 | 137 | 137 | 141 |

Umpires: A. Dolphin and F. Chester.

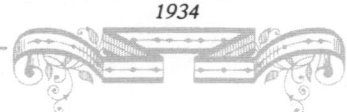

C. F. Walters, the English Captain, spins the coin but W. M. Woodfull called correctly
and decided to bat.

Bradman going out to bat.

Don Bradman disconsolately walks from the wicket after his controversial dismissal, caught W. R. Hammond at first slip.

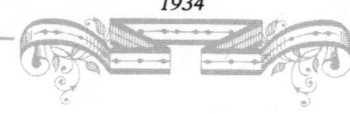

## FRIDAY'S PLAY.

LONDON, June 8.

The special representative of the Australian Press Association at Nottingham says:—The weather was threatening after lunch. Farnes bowled with the dark mass of the members' pavilion behind his arm, as there is only one sight screen on the ground. Bradman drove a no-ball straight to the fence. Rain commenced in Geary's first over and stopped play at 2.25 p.m., the score being 107.

Play was resumed at 2.40 p.m., the ends of the wicket having been protected. Bradman cover-drove and cut Geary for two successive boundaries, and then again played a ball from Farnes into his pads. Brown was playing confidently, particularly against Farnes, but was overshadowed by Bradman's attacking mood.

Bradman was then out in a peculiar manner. He attempted to drive Geary, whom he had just previously straight driven to the fence, and played the ball on to his pads. The ball flew straight up and was caught by Hammond in the slips. Bradman had batted for half an hour, his 29 runs including six fours.

Bradman momentarily hesitated before his departure. It was a patchy innings, his timing being inconsistent, but he always forced the pace. The stoppage caused by rain following lunch deprived him of the opportunity of settling down. McCabe and Brown faced a less satisfactory test position, with three down for 125. Brown played neatly off his legs, but Farnes several times beat his defence. Brown's scoring was almost exclusively by leg glances. McCabe opened cautiously.

Geary, at 146, took his second wicket with a fast straight ball. Brown, attempting an on-drive, walked right in front, and was out lbw. He had batted 85 minutes, and gave a sound, careful display. There were no boundaries among his 22 runs.

### DARLING BOWLED.

Ames attempted to stump Darling from Geary's next ball. Darling began shakily with a fluky four from Verity, raising 150 in 185 minutes. Geary bowled unchanged for more than an hour after lunch. He kept a splendid length, but it was Verity who placed Australia in an awkward position by bowling Darling, who was completely beaten, the ball coming quickly from the pitch. Five were down for 153.

While McCabe plodded watchfully, Chipperfield made an uncomfortable test entry. Ames made a splendid attempt to stump him from a leg-side ball from Geary. Then Chipperfield nicely turned Verity to the square leg fence. Geary was taken off at 4 o'clock and was warmly applauded.

Australia was now struggling for runs against accurate length bowling. McCabe took an hour to score 18, the circumstances justifying caution. Chipperfield, however, seemed intent on playing his natural game.

McCabe, who prettily cover-drove Verity to the boundary, was now showing more aggression. He and Chipperfield were Australia's last batting hopes. Farnes and Mitchell returned to the attack at 186, and McCabe hooked two successive rising balls from Farnes to the boundary, providing the first relief to the grimness since Bradman had left. Then pulling Mitchell hard he raised 200 in 235 minutes. Leyland bowled the last over before tea, McCabe cover-driving him for four, and so reaching 50 in 95 minutes. The score was 206 for five wickets, Chipperfield being 16.

There was a disappointing attendance of not more than 15,000. Rain began during the adjournment and delayed the resumption of play.

Play was resumed at 5.40 p.m. after a delay of 55 minutes. The rain had been only slight, and was not a serious handicap to the bowlers, but the light was poor. Geary and Farnes resumed, the latter taking the new ball in the middle of an over. Then an appeal against the light was upheld.

After a delay stumps were drawn at 6.15 p.m. The score was 207, McCabe being 50 (five fours) and Chipperfield 17. The innings had occupied 250 minutes.

## A TEST COMPLEX.

Apart from Bradman and the unfulfilled intentions of Darling, there was overmuch timidity about the Australian batting. Seeing them in action in county matches, one might have prayed that Nottingham would not produce a test complex, but that was largely what happened.

The selectors, in choosing Brown, doubtless regarded him as an insurance policy on the gamble of winning the toss, but when Woodfull brought him in with the object of solidifying the batting, on Ponsford's departure, it seemed questionable tactics.

It so happened that Bradman had to face an awkward five minutes before lunch, and then the rain interrupted the game immediately after lunch, which meant that Bradman had to start three times, an upsetting thing for a batsman of his methods and in his present mood.

Woodfull was unhappy against Farnes's bowling, and Ponsford must be given great credit for his splendid foundation innings.

Undoubtedly winning the toss on such a wicket, and with an attack which, at any rate, was no better than Australia made it look, should have produced more and easier run-getting, but those anticipating a huge score reckoned without history, for only two centuries, those of Maclaren and Bradman, have been scored in Anglo-Australian tests on the Nottingham ground.

There is, moreover, an ever-present handicap. The batsman who faces the pavilion has to focus the ball against the tightly-packed, darkly-attired members, and Farnes, naturally, using this end, did great service for England, dismissing Woodfull and Ponsford.

It was merciful that the light was bad enough to justify upholding the appeal, for the bowler had just commenced to use a new ball in the favourable circumstance of his own freshness combined with the fact that the batsmen were unsettled by the adjournment, and hampered by the difficult background.

## FARNES'S TEST DEBUT.

Farnes made a highly creditable first test appearance. He bowled a better length, and with more intelligence than at Chelmsford, and also checked himself of the no-ball habit, which usually costs a good many runs. He is a deceptive bowler. He does not take a long run; he moves relatively slowly to the wicket, and then, with a good long swing, thumps the ball down from the top of his height, considerably faster than might have been expected from his action. Though never short of a legitimate length, he bumped the ball sufficiently to worry the batsmen.

Geary showed a shrewd appreciation of his ability to keep the batsmen on the defensive, without allowing his methods to become sufficiently stereotyped for them to play themselves in. All England's bowlers kept a good length, principally because the batsmen had insufficient confidence to knock them off it. Hammond bowled really well, but Walters clearly does not intend to diffuse the energies of his champion batsman on bowling. Verity, apart from shattering Darling's wicket, merely served to confirm the impression that the Australians are competent to deal with spin bowling.

Walters seems to be a knowledgable captain. He rang plenty of changes on the unsettled batsmen. Only one catch was missed, but the Australians' fielding ought to be at least as good as their opponents'. Verity was England's best fieldsman. Hammond, in the slips, had curiously little to do, and, apart from Walters at cover-point, the groundwork was undistinguished.

## "NO MASTER TOUCHES."

The special representative of the Australian Press Association at Nottingham, commenting on the first day's play, states:—

The Nottingham game, which generally lacked the true test atmosphere, reached a disappointing state of suspension in murky gloom, with only five minutes' play after tea.

Prophets who anticipated that each side was so strong in batting that there would be a glut of runs found it hard to believe that half the Australian side was out for 153. England undoubtedly had the better of the day, but there were no master touches about either the bowling or the fielding. The batting, apart from Ponsford's and the later stages of McCabe's innings, also lacked distinction. There were moments, indeed, when it seemed as if Bradman's genius was going to lift the day to test level, and consequently it was a real disappointment when he was dismissed, especially in such an unusual fashion. Some versions of his dismissal state that the ball flew off Ames's gloves before Hammond caught it. There was apparently some doubt among the fieldsmen as to whether it was a catch, but Geary shouted "Catch it."

Bradman earlier had several narrow escapes, but, batting in daredevil style as he was, it would have been pleasant to see him stay in a little longer. Darling similarly refused to be overawed on the occasion of his first test appearance in England, and he went through all the motions of attacking the bowling, failing, however, properly to connect with a single ball. His dismissal occasioned no surprise, but considerable dismay among Australian onlookers.

Mr. H. H. Elliott with his wife and family. (See story below).

# BRADMAN AND AN UNEMPLOYED NOTTS. MINER.

## KINDLY ACTION AT TEST MATCH.

## RADFORD HOME BRIGHTENED.

ONE of the best Test Match stories concerns Don Bradman and an unemployed Notts. miner who was outside the ground on Saturday disconsolate and distressed.

With scarcely a copper to bless himself with the man had little hope of seeing the match at all.

Don Bradman appeared on the scene. He saw the man looking through the gate wistfully, hopelessly, dejected.

### Took Him In.

"Would you like to come in ?" asked the Australian batsman.

In less time than it takes to write these lines Bradman and the miner were on the ground, the former paying for the man's admission and finding him a place in the stand, at the same time giving him a few shillings with which to knock along.

### Colleagues' Help.

When it was discovered that the miner, Mr. Herbert H. Elliott, of Radford, has a wife and eight children, a subscription list was opened, Don Bradman heading the list with a generous donation.

Other cricketers gladly added their names and ere long the fund ran into several pounds.

Elliott's story is that Bradman gave him the surprise of his life when he asked him if he would like to see the match.

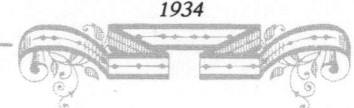
# England All Out—268

## EARLY DISASTER FOR OUR MEN

| BUT BROWN; McCABE GOT RUNS | RACING TO PUT ON A BIG LEAD |
|---|---|

FROM OUR SPECIAL REPRESENTATIVE

**NOTTINGHAM, Monday.**

*ALL THE Australians were relieved when Pataudi went. He is shown here at the nets.*

LEADING England by 106 in the first innings, Australia met early disaster in the first Test to-day, when Woodfull was out for two and Ponsford lost his wicket for five, with the score at 32.

England was saved from utter rout by a partnership of 101 by Hendren and Geary. Both batsmen, however, lost their wickets in quick succession, and the home team was all out for 268.

After the opening bats went, Bradman and Brown attacked the bowling, Bradman playing almost recklessly until he went at 69. Brown was 37 and McCabe 74 (3 for 159) at stumps.

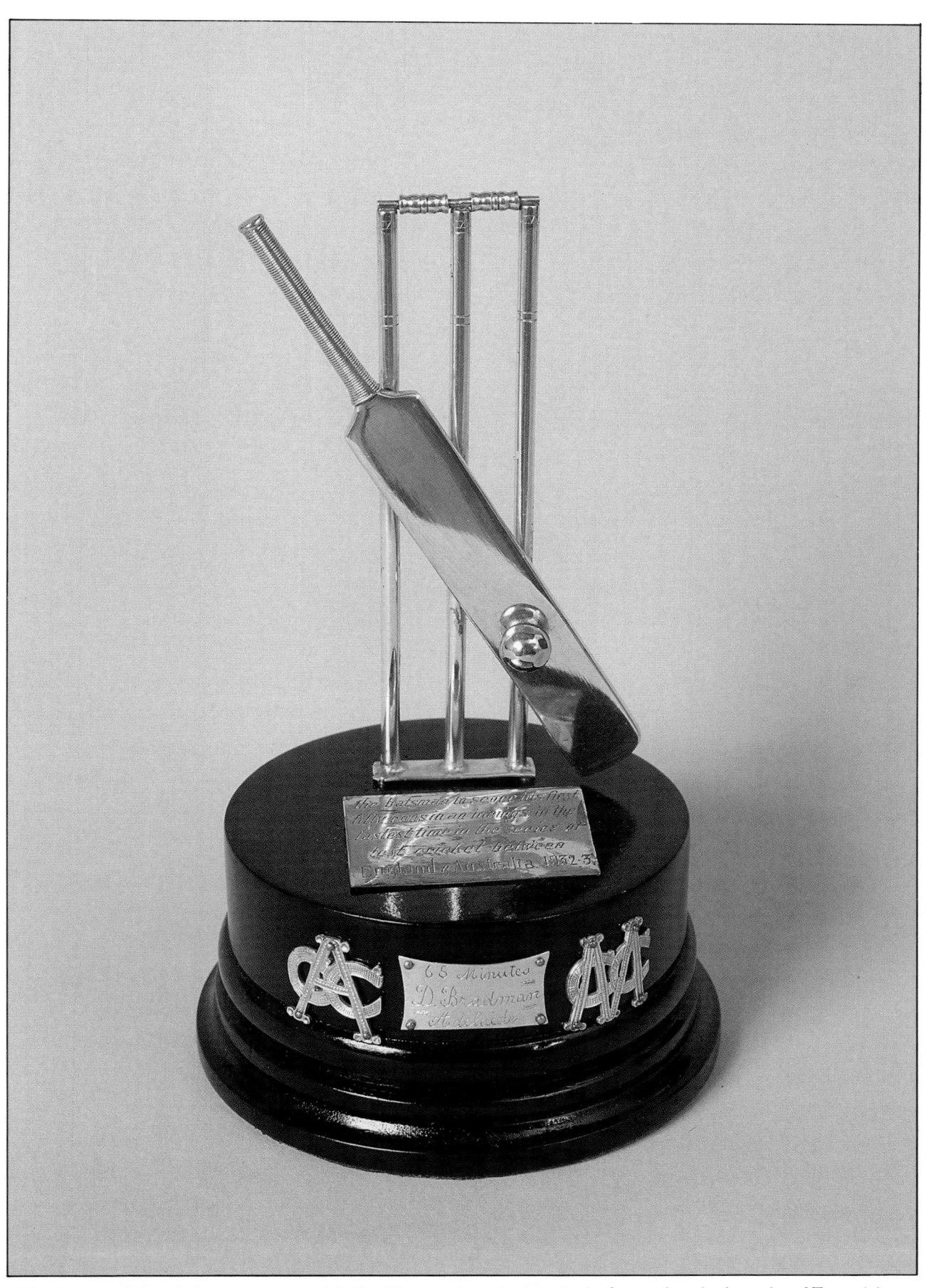

Trophy awarded to the batsman to score his first fifty runs in an innings, in the fastest time, in the series of Test cricket between England and Australia 1932–33. Presented to Don Bradman for scoring his first fifty runs in sixty-five minutes in the third Test at Adelaide.

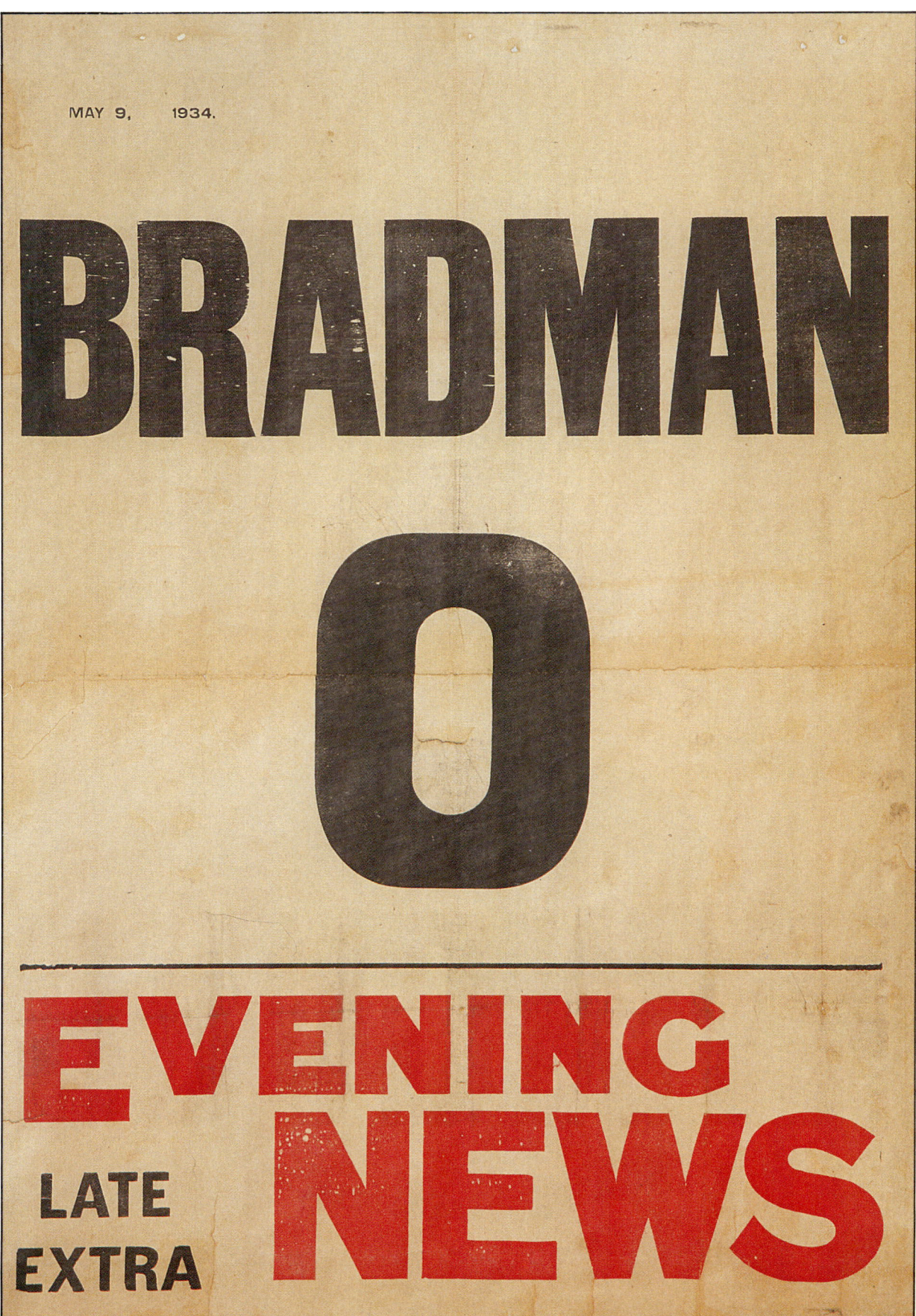

Don Bradman's first duck in England during the 1934 tour was the cause of this poster. The match was against Cambridge University when he was bowled by J. G. W. Davies, later to become a Director of the Bank of England and President of the Marylebone Cricket Club.

# AUSTRALIA'S FIRST TEST WIN

## FIRST TEST CONFOUNDS PROPHETS

### Chipperfield's Courage In Serious Crisis

## WHY DID BRADMAN FAIL?

### Some Critics Say He Is "Sacrificing Accuracy For Showmanship"

(From "The Referee's" Special Representative at Nottingham)

NOTTINGHAM, Tuesday night.

THE first Test has confounded all the prophets. They had predicted immense scores on a wicket apparently perfect for rungetting. But never before has the glorious uncertainty of cricket been better exemplified. The weather, the pitch, and the ground all conspired to make a batsmen's paradise, yet nearly all of the acclaimed giants failed, though the opening batsmen in the first innings looked set for big scores against bowling apparently innocuous, but which improved immensely with the fall of a few cheap wickets.

Don Bradman had little to spare as L. E. G. Ames breaks the wicket in this run-out attempt.

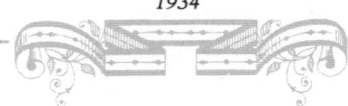

# Australia v England
## Second Test Match

AUSTRALIA v ENGLAND, Second Test Match, at Lord's,
22, 23 and 25 June 1934.

| Australia | - First Innings | 284 |
|---|---|---|
| | - Second Innings | 118 |
| England | - First Innings | 440 |
| | - Second Innings | - |

Australia lost by an innings and 38 runs.

| DON BRADMAN | - c. and b. H. Verity | 36 |
|---|---|---|
| | - c. L.E.G. Ames  b. H. Verity | 13 |

For two days this match was played on a perfect wicket, but rain over the week-end made the conditions ideal for H. Verity.

DON BRADMAN's first innings was played on the second evening, and was another brilliant if rather slapdash affair. In at 68 for 1, he hit seven fours with superb strokes in forty-six minutes, before giving a soft return catch off a defensive stroke to a ball which kicked slightly; he was out at 141 for 2.

After the week-end rain, Australia failed by 7 runs to avert the follow on, and that failure virtually cost them the match.

When Bradman went in for his second innings at 43 for 2, he batted soundly enough for twenty-eight minutes after which he became restless at being chained down by Verity (who was bowling without a deep field), tried to drive him, and only succeeded in giving a catch to the wicket-keeper. He was out at 4.15 p.m. with the score 57 for 3.

A typical London crowd respond to the sunny weather.

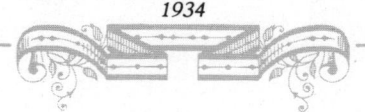

## ENGLAND.

| | |
|---|---|
| Mr. C. F. Walters c Bromley b O'Reilly | 82 |
| H. Sutcliffe lbw, b Chipperfield | 20 |
| W. R. Hammond c and b Chipperfield | 2 |
| E. Hendren c McCabe b Wall | 13 |
| Mr. R. E. S. Wyatt c Oldfield b Chipperfield | 33 |
| M. Leyland b Wall | 109 |
| L. E. G. Ames c Oldfield b McCabe | 120 |
| G. Geary c Chipperfield b Wall | 9 |
| H. Verity st Oldfield b Grimmett | 29 |
| Mr. K. Farnes b Wall | 1 |
| W. E. Bowes not out | 10 |
| L-b | 12 |
| | **440** |

## AUSTRALIA.

| | | | |
|---|---|---|---|
| W. M. Woodfull b Bowes | 22 | — c Hammond b Verity | 43 |
| W. A. Brown c Ames b Bowes | 105 | — c Walters b Bowes | 2 |
| D. G. Bradman c and b Verity | 36 | — c Ames b Verity | 13 |
| S. J. McCabe c Hammond b Verity | 34 | — c Hendren b Verity | 19 |
| L. S. Darling c Sutcliffe b Verity | 0 | — b Hammond | 10 |
| A. G. Chipperfield not out | 37 | — c Geary b Verity | 14 |
| E. H. Bromley c Geary b Verity | 4 | — c and b Verity | 1 |
| W. A. Oldfield c Sutcliffe b Verity | 23 | — lbw, b Verity | 0 |
| C. V. Grimmett b Bowes | 9 | — c Hammond b Verity | 0 |
| W. J. O'Reilly b Verity | 4 | — not out | 8 |
| T. W. Wall lbw, b Verity | 0 | — c Hendren b Verity | 1 |
| B 1, l-b 9 | 10 | B 6, n-b 1 | 7 |
| | **284** | | **118** |

### AUSTRALIA BOWLING.

| | Overs | Mdns. | Runs | Wkts. | Overs | Mdns. | Runs | Wkts. |
|---|---|---|---|---|---|---|---|---|
| Wall | 49 | 7 | 108 | 4 | | | | |
| McCabe | 18 | 3 | 38 | 1 | | | | |
| Grimmett | 53.3 | 13 | 102 | 1 | | | | |
| O'Reilly | 38 | 15 | 70 | 1 | | | | |
| Chipperfield | 34 | 10 | 91 | 3 | | | | |
| Darling | 6 | 2 | 19 | 0 | | | | |

### ENGLAND BOWLING.

| | Overs | Mdns. | Runs | Wkts. | Overs | Mdns. | Runs | Wkts. |
|---|---|---|---|---|---|---|---|---|
| Farnes | 12 | 3 | 43 | 0 | 4 | 2 | 6 | 0 |
| Bowes | 31 | 5 | 98 | 3 | 14 | 4 | 24 | 1 |
| Geary | 22 | 4 | 56 | 0 | | | | |
| Verity | 36 | 15 | 61 | 7 | 22.3 | 8 | 43 | 8 |
| Hammond | 4 | 1 | 6 | 0 | 13 | 0 | 38 | 1 |
| Leyland | 4 | 1 | 10 | 0 | | | | |

### FALL OF THE WICKETS.

#### ENGLAND—First Innings.

| 1 | 2 | 3 | 4 | 5 | 6 | 7 | 8 | 9 | 10 |
|---|---|---|---|---|---|---|---|---|---|
| 70 | 78 | 99 | 130 | 182 | 311 | 359 | 409 | 410 | 440 |

#### AUSTRALIA—First Innings.

| 1 | 2 | 3 | 4 | 5 | 6 | 7 | 8 | 9 | 10 |
|---|---|---|---|---|---|---|---|---|---|
| 68 | 141 | 203 | 204 | 205 | 218 | 258 | 273 | 284 | 284 |

#### AUSTRALIA—Second Innings.

| 1 | 2 | 3 | 4 | 5 | 6 | 7 | 8 | 9 | 10 |
|---|---|---|---|---|---|---|---|---|---|
| 10 | 43 | 57 | 94 | 94 | 95 | 95 | 95 | 112 | 118 |

Umpires: F. Chester and J. Hardstaff.

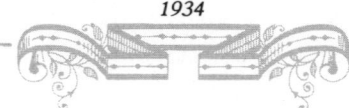

# BROWN MAKES A DASHING CENTURY

## BRADMAN PLAYS WITH GREAT BRILLIANCE | McCABE AGAIN IS SHOWING FIRST-CLASS FORM

## OUR TEAM GETS 192 FOR TWO

From Our Special Representative

LONDON, Saturday.

BATTING until shortly before three o'clock to-day, England compiled 440 in its first innings of the Test. Both Leyland and Ames reached three figures. The Australians made a good start in reply and unless the weather breaks the match seems certain to be drawn.

Ames played a splendid knock for England and thoroughly deserved his century. He was missed behind the wicket by Oldfield off Wall, when at 96, and it would have been strange if he had met with the fate similar to that which befell Chipperfield in the first Test.

When their turn came the Australians made a great start, Woodfull and Brown getting 68 together and then Brown and Bradman giving the bowlers a torrid time until Verity caught and bowled Bradman. McCabe also started in a manner which indicated that he was in tremendous form.

"NO BRIDGE TO-NIGHT, I'M AFRAID. HE'S AT WORK ON A SYSTEM FOR GETTING DON BRADMAN OUT."

Don Bradman watches a cover drive off H. Verity go through to the boundary.

King George shakes hands with Don Bradman and comments on his hand muscles.

An attempted drive into the outfield is mis-hit and H. Sutcliffe, L. E. G. Ames and W. R. Hammond vie to see who shall take the catch.

It was L. E. G. Ames who finally took the catch though the smile on W. R. Hammond's face registers his satisfaction.

*Verity, hero of the second Test.*

# 15 WICKETS

## BRADMAN PUZZLE

## Lost Patience ?

## BOWES WAS EASY

(From Arthur Mailey)
LONDON, Monday.

Although the wicket was damaged by rain, full marks must be given to Hedley Verity, for to-day he beat Australia. Verity bowled magnificently, his typical Yorkshire cricket mentality tantalising the Australians beyond words. He even rendered the great Bradman immobile.

Verity bowled practically all day and finished with the remarkable figures of 15 for 104, equalling Rhodes's record. His greatest and most successful spell was after tea in the second innings, when he took six wickets for 15 runs.

England's convincing win—it was her first success at Lord's since 1896—created tremendous excitement, but I cannot help thinking that had conditions been equal and had the rain not come, England would have been unable to force a win, for none of the bowlers, except Verity, was impressive.

There were two shining examples in Australia's two innings. First we had Chipperfield courageously trying to save a follow-on, and then Woodfull desperately trying to save the innings defeat. It was a colorful day's cricket, and we learned many things.

# Australia v England
# Third Test Match

AUSTRALIA v ENGLAND, Third Test Match, at Manchester, 6, 7, 9 and 10 July 1934.

| Australia | - First Innings | 491 |
| | - Second Innings | 66 for 1 wicket |
| England | - First Innings | 627 for 9 wickets dec. |
| | - Second Innings | 123 for no wicket dec. |
| | Drawn. | |

| DON BRADMAN | - c. L.E.G. Ames b. W.R. Hammond | 30 |
| | - did not bat | |

DON BRADMAN was really not well enough to bat, but he went in at 320 for 4 on the third afternoon; he survived until after tea, when he was 25, and batted altogether for sixty-six minutes and 51 balls. When 26, he gave W.R. Hammond a sharp return chance; he was caught, soon afterwards, at the wicket in trying to cut a rather wide ball.

### ENGLAND.

| | | | |
|---|---|---|---|
| Mr. C. F. Walters c Darling b O'Reilly .. | 52 | — not out.................... | 50 |
| H. Sutcliffe c Chipperfield b O'Reilly ... | 63 | — not out.................... | 69 |
| Mr. R. E. S. Wyatt b O'Reilly ......... | 0 | | |
| W. R. Hammond b O'Reilly............ | 4 | | |
| E. Hendren c and b O'Reilly.........| 132 | | |
| M. Leyland c sub b O'Reilly.........| 153 | | |
| L. E. G. Ames c Ponsford b Grimmett.. | 72 | | |
| J. L. Hopwood b O'Reilly............. | 2 | | |
| Mr. G. O. Allen b McCabe............. | 61 | | |
| H. Verity not out.................. | 60 | | |
| E. W. Clark not out................. | 2 | | |
| B 6, l-b 18, w 2.............. | 26 | B 2, l-b 1, w 1.......... | 4 |
| (Nine wkts., dec.) | 627 | (No wkt.) | 123 |

### AUSTRALIA.

| | | | |
|---|---|---|---|
| W. A. Brown c Walters b Clark.......| 72 | — c Hammond b Allen....... | 0 |
| W. H. Ponsford c Hendren b Hammond | 12 | — not out.................. | 30 |
| S. J. McCabe c Verity b Hammond.....| 137 | — not out.................. | 33 |
| W. M. Woodfull run out............. | 73 | | |
| L. S. Darling b Verity............. | 37 | | |
| D. G. Bradman c Ames b Hammond... | 30 | | |
| W. A. Oldfield c Wyatt b Verity....... | 13 | | |
| A. G. Chipperfield c Walters b Verity... | 26 | | |
| C. V. Grimmett b Verity............. | 0 | | |
| W. J. O'Reilly not out............. | 30 | | |
| T. W. Wall run out................. | 18 | | |
| B 20, l-b 13, w 4, n-b 6......... | 43 | B 1, l-b 2.............. | 3 |
| | 491 | (One wkt.) | 66 |

### AUSTRALIA BOWLING.

| | Overs | Mdns. | Runs | Wkts. | Overs | Mdns. | Runs | Wkts. |
|---|---|---|---|---|---|---|---|---|
| Wall .......... | 36 | 3 | 131 | 0 | 9 | 0 | 31 | 0 |
| McCabe ........ | 32 | 3 | 98 | 1 | 13 | 4 | 35 | 0 |
| Grimmett....... | 57 | 20 | 122 | 1 | 17 | 5 | 28 | 0 |
| O'Reilly ....... | 59 | 9 | 189 | 7 | 13 | 4 | 25 | 0 |
| Chipperfield .... | 7 | 0 | 29 | 0 | | | | |
| Darling........ | 10 | 0 | 32 | 0 | | | | |

### ENGLAND BOWLING.

| | Overs | Mdns. | Runs | Wkts. | Overs | Mdns. | Runs | Wkts. |
|---|---|---|---|---|---|---|---|---|
| Clark .......... | 40 | 9 | 100 | 1 | 4 | 1 | 16 | 0 |
| Allen........... | 31 | 3 | 113 | 0 | 6 | 0 | 23 | 1 |
| Hammond ...... | 28.3 | 6 | 111 | 3 | 2 | 1 | 2 | 0 |
| Verity......... | 53 | 24 | 78 | 4 | 5 | 4 | 2 | 0 |
| Hopwood ...... | 38 | 20 | 46 | 0 | 9 | 5 | 16 | 0 |
| Hendren ...... | | | | | 1 | 0 | 4 | 0 |

### FALL OF THE WICKETS.

**ENGLAND—First Innings.**

| 1 | 2 | 3 | 4 | 5 | 6 | 7 | 8 | 9 |
|---|---|---|---|---|---|---|---|---|
| 68 | 68 | 72 | 149 | 340 | 482 | 492 | 510 | 605 |

**AUSTRALIA—First Innings.**

| 1 | 2 | 3 | 4 | 5 | 6 | 7 | 8 | 9 | 10 |
|---|---|---|---|---|---|---|---|---|---|
| 34 | 230 | 242 | 320 | 378 | 409 | 411 | 419 | 454 | 491 |

**AUSTRALIA—Second Innings.**

| 1 |
|---|
| 1 |

Umpires : J. Hardstaff and F. Walden.

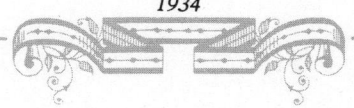

# AUSTRALIANS ILL IN TEST

### ◆

## *BRADMAN GOES HOME TO BED*

## AN EPIC

### O'REILLY'S OVER
---
### CLEVEREST BALL
---
## WATERING OF PITCH

("Sun" Special)

LONDON, Friday.

NEVILLE CARDUS, writing in the "Manchester Guardian," describes O'Reilly's over as one of the most famous in Test history. Walters, he says, was caught off O'Reilly's cleverest ball, that slow off break which he holds back.

He continues: "O'Reilly's next was pitched up well on the leg stump and knocked back Wyatt's middle stump. It was a noble ball. Hammond played back a hideous cross bat off the wrong foot and was defeated by a foot.

"It was one of the most 'transforming' overs, and a brother to the deathless over Jackson bowled in 1905 dismissing three Australians."

### THE KING'S HOPE

The King sent a telegram yesterday to Mr. Harold Bushby, manager of the Australian team, expressing his sympathy with the Australians in their bad luck in having so many players stricken by illness.

The message expressed the hope that the sick players would quickly recover and be able to take part in the Test match to-day.

### "WIMBLEDON THROAT."
---
### CRICKETERS' MISFORTUNE.
---

The special representative of the Australian Press Association at Manchester says:—

"Wimbledon throat" is the best description of the painful malady which caught several of the Australians at a critical moment in the test. Bradman and Chipperfield left the ground before tea on Friday, and went to bed at their hotel. Bradman was slightly better at night; but he, Chipperfield, and Kippax stayed at the hotel on Saturday.

Kippax is the worst sufferer of the three. Woodfull and Brown went to bed immediately they returned from the match on Friday, hoping that the rest would prevent the development of the malady, of which each had slight symptoms. It is generally believed that the visits to Wimbledon were responsible for the illness, which is somewhat similar to that from which Crawford suffered, namely, a combination of biliousness, headache, high temperature, and general weakness, with some symptoms of influenza.

Bradman and Chipperfield were both well on Thursday night. They complained of sickness soon after the start of the match. It is characteristic of the "Wimbledon throat" that the condition suddenly changes. The heat-wave aggravated the ailment, which in infectious, and is leading to fears that it may spread through the team. Dr. Pope, whose services as honorary physician were never more valuable than on the present tour, is busy attending the sufferers.

## INVALIDS

### ◆

## Our Sick List
---
### THE LATEST

(From Arthur Mailey)

MANCHESTER, Midnight.

OF the three invalids most seriously affected by "Wimbledon throat" the probable order of recovery now is Chipperfield, Bradman and Kippax.

Bradman shows signs of recovering in time to bat to-morrow, his temperature having subsided.

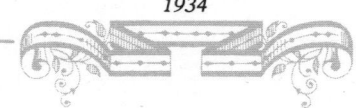

# BRADMAN SHOULD NOT HAVE BATTED

## "A WRAITH OF THE GREATNESS WE ONCE KNEW"

When Bradman slowly strolled to the wicket exactly at 3.35 it was unfortunately all too obvious that he is an ill man. His cheeks are very drawn, and never before have I seen him look so thin.

The smile that for so long has been planted on his face was completely absent, but I think it requires to be stressed that the comparative absence of cheering—I honestly expected a hurricane of applause for a plucky fellow who is fighting the fates as well as his own poor health—was due to the fact that few of the spectators recognised him as he walked to the pitch.

This was not the old dashing Bradman of 1930, nor yet the Bradman of impulsive recklessness of recent days.

He made one or two typical shots, but the one and only time when he showed us the real wonder-worker of the past was when he knocked a ball down hard and then cut it to the off before it could shoot on to his wicket.

This demonstrated that, despite the pains and aches and the nostalgia and the disappointments, he still has the eye, the brain, and the quickness to act in an emergency.

It may seem sloppy and sentimental to say so—and I have nothing to thank Bradman for—but I felt that I was pulling for him as he vainly strove to overcome insuperable obstacles. His was but the wraith of the greatness we once knew.

The man is sick, and I would tear off an arm rather than say one hurtful word about him, but yesterday he reminded me of one who had thrown off his shroud to tilt at taunting cricketing windmills.

### MEDICAL TESTS ?

This will probably be denied—the Australian management are better at denying assertions that afterwards come true than they are at adopting the more sensible course of taking newspaper men into their confidence—but Bradman would have been better served if he had been urged not to bat yesterday.

Courage we can all admire, but surely there are moments when even courage should be discouraged. It has again been repeated to me that sometime this week Bradman will return to London for medical tests and examinations.

That there is something very much the matter with him is palpable, and the sooner the tension on the lad is reduced the better it will be for all concerned.

# THIRD TEST ENDS IN A DRAW

## ENGLAND DECLARES AGAIN | TAME FINISH TO MATCH

(FROM OUR SPECIAL REPRESENTATIVE)

*OLD TRAFFORD GROUND, Tuesday*

THE Third Test match ended to-day in a tame draw, play ceasing at six o'clock—half an hour early—because of the impossibility of a decisive finish.

Australia, in their first innings, averted a follow-on, the tail wagging to such an extent that the last three batsmen scored 13 more runs than were really necessary.

*The hero of the day, from an Australian point of view, was O'Reilly, who scored 30 not out. This meant that England had to bat again, and saved Australia the necessity of playing a defensive second innings.*

England's second innings was closed when 123 had been scored without loss, leaving Australia two hours in which to get 260 runs. The match finished in picnic spirit, Hendren bowling the last over.

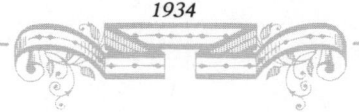

# Don Bradman Is Annoyed

(From "Truth's" Special Rep. with the Australian team.)

(B.U.P. Service.)

MANCHESTER, Saturday.

IT is reported that Bradman is anxious for his wife to join him before the tour is over.

He strenuously opposed the Board of Control's regulation, which prevents the wives of Test match cricketers travelling with the team or being in England at the same time as the team.

**Don Bradman.**

Bradman has urged that his wife be allowed to come to Europe on the same conditions as the wife of his skipper, W. M. Woodfull.

His claim, it is considered, is strengthened because during his present illness he needs special nursing and care.

The Test "widows" listening to broadcasts in 2BL Studios, Sydney.

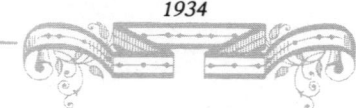

# Australians v Yorkshire

AUSTRALIANS v YORKSHIRE, at Sheffield, 14, 16 and 17 July 1934.

| Australians | - First Innings | 348 |
| | - Second Innings | 28 for 1 wicket |
| Yorkshire | - First Innings | 340 |
| | - Second Innings | 157 |
| | Drawn. | |

DON BRADMAN went in at 2.28 p.m. on the second day at 16 for 1, and started soundly, taking seventy-four minutes to reach 50; then hit out and completed his century in a further twenty-six minutes. He added another 40 in twenty minutes, and then virtually threw his wicket away, going for another big hit, just before tea. He made 140, out of 205 for 2, in exactly two hours, his last 90 coming in forty-six minutes. Bradman's innings included two sixes and twenty-two fours.

DON BRADMAN - b. M. Leyland 140
- did not bat

## YORKSHIRE.

| | | | | | |
|---|---|---|---|---|---|
| H. Sutcliffe run out | 19 | — | absent hurt | 0 |
| A. Mitchell b Grimmett | 36 | — | b Wall | 4 |
| W. Barber st Barnett b Grimmett | 37 | — | b Ebeling | 0 |
| M. Leyland c Barnett b Ebeling | 43 | — | b Wall | 1 |
| C. Turner b Ebeling | 10 | — | b Fleetwood-Smith | 20 |
| Mr. A. B. Sellers b Wall | 104 | — | b Wall | 13 |
| H. Verity c McCabe b Bromley | 9 | — | c McCabe b Darling | 20 |
| T. F. Smailes b Grimmett | 30 | — | lbw, b Fleetwood-Smith | 18 |
| A. Wood c Brown b Grimmett | 4 | — | c and b Fleetwood-Smith | 59 |
| G. G. Macaulay not out | 40 | — | not out | 6 |
| W. E. Bowes b Wall | 0 | — | b Darling | 4 |
| B 2, l-b 6 | 8 | | B 1, l-b 11 | 12 |
| | **340** | | | **157** |

## AUSTRALIANS.

| | | | | |
|---|---|---|---|---|
| W. M. Woodfull c Sellers b Smailes | 54 | | | |
| W. A. Brown c Macaulay b Bowes | 14 | — | lbw, b Macaulay | 12 |
| D. G. Bradman b Leyland | 140 | | | |
| S. J. McCabe b Bowes | 21 | — | not out | 14 |
| L. S. Darling c sub, b Bowes | 45 | | | |
| E. H. Bromley lbw, b Macaulay | 16 | | | |
| B. A. Barnett b Bowes | 7 | | | |
| C. V. Grimmett b Bowes | 8 | | | |
| H. I. Ebeling b Bowes | 27 | | | |
| T. W. Wall b Bowes | 1 | | | |
| L. O'B. Fleetwood-Smith not out | 1 | | | |
| B 10, l-b 3, n-b 1 | 14 | | W | 2 |
| | **348** | | (One Wkt.) | **28** |

## AUSTRALIANS BOWLING.

| | Overs | Mdns. | Runs | Wkts. | Overs | Mdns. | Runs | Wkts. |
|---|---|---|---|---|---|---|---|---|
| Wall | 20.4 | 4 | 48 | 2 | 13 | 4 | 36 | 3 |
| Ebeling | 36 | 12 | 78 | 2 | 12 | 5 | 19 | 1 |
| Bromley | 15 | 2 | 44 | 1 | | | | |
| Grimmett | 40 | 14 | 113 | 4 | 14 | 4 | 30 | 0 |
| Fleetwood-Smith | 28 | 7 | 49 | 0 | 23 | 8 | 39 | 3 |
| McCabe | | | | | 3 | 0 | 17 | 0 |
| Darling | | | | | 1.3 | 1 | 4 | 2 |

## YORKSHIRE BOWLING.

| | Overs | Mdns. | Runs | Wkts. | Overs | Mdns. | Runs | Wkts. |
|---|---|---|---|---|---|---|---|---|
| Bowes | 29.2 | 4 | 100 | 7 | 3 | 1 | 6 | 0 |
| Smailes | 21 | 2 | 68 | 1 | 2 | 1 | 5 | 0 |
| Macaulay | 19 | 5 | 41 | 1 | 5 | 1 | 13 | 1 |
| Turner | 9 | 0 | 53 | 0 | 4 | 3 | 2 | 0 |
| Verity | 6 | 0 | 33 | 0 | | | | |
| Leyland | 4 | 0 | 39 | 1 | | | | |

Umpires: L. C. Braund and C. N. Woolley.

# SPECTACULAR DON

## 140 In 115 Minutes

## 22 FOURS, TWO SIXES

### (From Arthur Mailey)

SHEFFIELD, Monday.

*FIRST 50 in 75 minutes; second 50 in 23 minutes; last 40 in 17 minutes—140 in 115 minutes.*

*THAT is how Don Bradman battered his way to that pinnacle which he attained in 1930, obviously far more spectacularly than on his first tour. He hit 22 fours and two sixes.*

As far as Australia was concerned. Bradman's performance to-day was a satisfying rehearsal for the fourth Test, as the Bramall Lane wicket is similar in character to Leeds.

Also, Don Bradman faced Bowes and Verity, two potential Leeds bowlers.

Against that was the Australians' ineffectiveness against Sellers, who, until this match, had not been a prolific scorer, and Macaulay, whose partnership with Sellers added nearly 100 runs.

*Don Bradman*

Sellers played Wall and Ebeling fairly comfortably, but was all at sea to Fleetwood Smith's wrong - 'un, which, luckily for Sellers, was of a very defective length.

Grimmett appeared lethargic, unlike his previous visit to Sheffield, when he bagged 10 wickets.

The Australians fielded extremely well, and might have kept the Yorkshire score comparatively low, but I do not think Woodfull placed the field to the best advantage.

There were numerous periods of quiet play, which warranted silly-point, and silly mid-on fieldsmen, but I cannot remember one being placed.

Perhaps the bowlers were as much to blame as Woodfull. Sellers played attractively up till the time when he practically sacrificed his innings.

The Australian innings had such a Bradman vein running through it that his success seemed to infuse confidence and life into the batting.

Brown and Woodfull opened for Australia, and the former was batting brightly when he snicked one straight to Macaulay at first slip. Bradman started by glancing Smailes for a single, and then a few overs later pulled Bowes for a glorious four.

### A Close Shave

When eight, Bradman snicked Bowes hard and low to near Leyland, at second slip, but the fieldsman just failed to reach the ball. Turner relieved Bowes at 60, and in his first over Bradman got four for an on-drive, two for a late cut, four for a straight drive, and a single for a glance.

Bradman reached his 50 in 75 minutes, Woodfull having added 22 in the same period. Next over Bradman made four brilliant cover-drives off Verity, but splendid fielding only allowed two to reach the boundary.

A couple of overs later Bradman chopped Verity for four, bringing up 102 in 95 minutes, and then lifted Macaulay straight for six. Only splendid Yorkshire fielding was saving a riot of runs.

At 125, Turner relieved Macaulay, and Bradman hit him for three fours in one over, passing 1000 runs for this tour.

Going great guns, Bradman reached 100 in 98 minutes, his last 50 comprising four singles, 10 fours, and one six. The 150 appeared in 110 minutes, and five runs later Leyland relieved Turner. Bradman got 10 off his first over.

### How He Got His Runs

Woodfull was going along nicely and on drove Smailes for four, and then saw Bradman lift Leyland for six, on-drive him for four, glance him for two, and square-cut him for four, bringing up 200 in 130 minutes, the second hundred taking 35 minutes.

Bowes was the only bowler to keep Bradman comparatively quiet, but in trying a big hit, Don was bowled by Leyland. He had batted just under two hours, and hit 22 fours and two sixes.

Bradman's first 50 included five fours, his score thereafter comprising 17 fours, two sixes, two twos, and six singles.

Bradman's complete strokes, in the order made were:—First 50: 1 1 1 4 1 1 1 2 4 3 1 4 1 3 1 1 4 2 4 1 1 1 1 1 1 1 1 1 1; second 50: 4 4 4 1 6 4 4 4 4 4 4 1 1 1; last 40: 4 4 2 1 6 4 4 1 2 4 4 4.

McCabe, after a shaky start, was settling down to forceful cricket when a ball kept low and skittled his middle stump.

### Bradman's Best

(Published in "The Times")
LONDON, Monday.

The cricket correspondent of "The Times" praises Bradman for one of the greatest exhibitions of his career.

He employed every conceivable stroke, and it became impossible to set a field for him,' he said. After passing 50, Bradman massacred the bowling.

(Published in the "Daily Mail")

Bradman's display was one of the most magnificent and spectacular innings ever played at Sheffield, says the cricket writer of the "Daily Mail." "His invincible wizardry menaces England's Test hopes."

Dick Moulton, the groundsman at Headingley, where the fourth Test will be played, says that last week's rain freshened up the pitch, and the wicket will be good for a lot of runs. Unquestionably it will last for four days, unless there is bad weather.

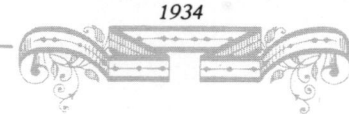

# Australia v England
## Fourth Test Match

With three Tests gone and the scores level, the Leeds match assumed great importance in the fight for "The Ashes".

After failing in the others I was very anxious to make amends. Headingley must be my happy hunting ground because for the second time there I made over 300 in one innings in a Test match.

Critics in some cases rated it a better innings than the one in 1930 though my own assessment would not be so and certainly the scoring rate was slower.

Regrettably it availed Australia nothing because a heavy downpour caused the match to be abandoned as a draw.

Before then I had suffered a bad leg injury in the field and only recovered in time to play in one more game before the final Test.

*Don Bradman*

AUSTRALIA v ENGLAND, Fourth Test Match, at Leeds, 20, 21, 23 and 24 July 1934.

| | | |
|---|---|---|
| Australia | - First Innings | 584 |
| | - Second Innings | - |
| England | - First Innings | 200 |
| | - Second Innings | 229 for 6 wickets |
| | Drawn. | |
| DON BRADMAN | - b. W.E. Bowes | 304 |

At the start of the second day's play, W.E. Bowes still had two balls to bowl of his uncompleted over and DON BRADMAN hit them both off the back foot past the bowler for 4 each.

Bradman continued cautiously after his forceful start, and took ninety-one minutes to reach 50; he completed his century at 2.58 p.m., in three hours eight minutes. His 200 took five hours five minutes. In the last thirty-five minutes, Bradman batted rather light-heartedly and hit two sixes (his first in a Test Match in England), and at the close was 271 not out, made in six hours twenty minutes. This was the fourth time that he had made 200 or more in a Test Match in a day's play. He had a further fifty minutes' batting on the third morning, and for the second time reached 300 in a Test Match at Leeds. Five minutes after completing his 300, Bowes removed his leg stump; he had hit two sixes and forty-three fours in an innings lasting seven hours ten minutes. He scored with equal skill all round the wicket.

Bradman is the only batsman to make two treble-centuries in Test Matches.

Bradman's and W.H. Ponsford's 388 was the highest for the fourth wicket for Australia in any Test Match; it was also a record for the fourth wicket for an Australian or any other Touring team in England. With two sixes and forty-three fours, Bradman scored 184 runs in boundaries.

Later that day, Bradman injured his leg while fielding and had to retire, being unable to play any more cricket for nearly a month.

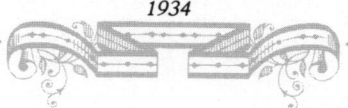

## ENGLAND.

| | | | | |
|---|---|---|---|---|
| Mr. C. F. Walters c and b Chipperfield.. | 44 | — b O'Reilly | 45 |
| W. W. Keeton c Oldfield b O'Reilly.... | 25 | — b Grimmett | 12 |
| W. R. Hammond b Wall | 37 | — run out | 20 |
| E. Hendren b Chipperfield | 29 | — lbw, b O'Reilly | 42 |
| Mr. R. E. S. Wyatt st Oldfield b Grimmett | 19 | — b Grimmett | 44 |
| M. Leyland lbw, b O'Reilly | 16 | — not out | 49 |
| L. E. G. Ames c Oldfield b Grimmett | 9 | — c Brown b Grimmett | 8 |
| J. L. Hopwood lbw, b O'Reilly | 8 | — not out | 2 |
| H. Verity not out | 2 | | |
| T. B. Mitchell st Oldfield b Grimmett | 9 | | |
| W. E. Bowes c Ponsford b Grimmett | 0 | | |
| L-b | 2 | B 1, l-b 6 | 7 |
| | **200** | (Six wkts.) | **229** |

## AUSTRALIA.

| | |
|---|---|
| W. A. Brown b Bowes | 15 |
| W. H. Ponsford hit wkt, b Verity | 181 |
| W. A. Oldfield c Ames b Bowes | 0 |
| W. M. Woodfull b Bowes | 0 |
| D. G. Bradman b Bowes | 304 |
| S. J. McCabe b Bowes | 27 |
| L. S. Darling b Bowes | 12 |
| A. G. Chipperfield c Wyatt b Verity | 1 |
| C. V. Grimmett run out | 15 |
| W. J. O'Reilly not out | 11 |
| T. W. Wall lbw, b Verity | 1 |
| B 8, l-b 9 | 17 |
| | **584** |

### AUSTRALIA BOWLING.

| | Overs | Mdns. | Runs | Wkts. | Overs | Mdns. | Runs | Wkts. |
|---|---|---|---|---|---|---|---|---|
| Wall | 18 | 1 | 57 | 1 | 14 | 5 | 36 | 0 |
| McCabe | 4 | 2 | 3 | 0 | 5 | 4 | 5 | 0 |
| Grimmett | 30.4 | 11 | 57 | 4 | 56.5 | 24 | 72 | 3 |
| O'Reilly | 35 | 16 | 46 | 3 | 51 | 25 | 88 | 2 |
| Chipperfield | 18 | 6 | 35 | 2 | 9 | 2 | 21 | 0 |

### ENGLAND BOWLING.

| | Overs | Mdns. | Runs | Wkts. |
|---|---|---|---|---|
| Bowes | 50 | 13 | 142 | 6 |
| Hammond | 29 | 5 | 82 | 0 |
| Mitchell | 23 | 1 | 117 | 0 |
| Verity | 46.5 | 15 | 113 | 3 |
| Hopwood | 30 | 7 | 93 | 0 |
| Leyland | 5 | 0 | 20 | 0 |

### FALL OF THE WICKETS.

#### ENGLAND—First Innings.

| 1 | 2 | 3 | 4 | 5 | 6 | 7 | 8 | 9 | 10 |
|---|---|---|---|---|---|---|---|---|---|
| 43 | 85 | 135 | 135 | 168 | 170 | 189 | 189 | 200 | 200 |

#### AUSTRALIA—First Innings.

| 1 | 2 | 3 | 4 | 5 | 6 | 7 | 8 | 9 | 10 |
|---|---|---|---|---|---|---|---|---|---|
| 37 | 39 | 39 | 427 | 517 | 550 | 551 | 557 | 574 | 584 |

#### ENGLAND—Second Innings.

| 1 | 2 | 3 | 4 | 5 | 6 |
|---|---|---|---|---|---|
| 28 | 70 | 87 | 152 | 190 | 213 |

Umpires: J. Hardstaff and A. Dolphin.

# ENGLAND SKITTLED FOR 200 RUNS

## But Australia Loses Three For 39 At Stumps: Bowes Deadly

**SENSATIONS IN THE FOURTH TEST**

*GRIMMETT (four wickets) and Oldfield, the peerless 'keeper.*

**BOWLERS HAVE A FIELD DAY**

(From Our Special Representative)

LEEDS, Friday.

AUSTRALIA made a fine start in the fourth Test to-day. England, winning the toss, decided to bat on a perfect wicket, but soon after tea were all out for 200 runs.

Oldfield was magnificent. He dismissed four batsmen—two catches, and two stumpings—and did not allow a bye. The only sundries were two leg byes. Grimmett was more successful than in previous Tests, finishing with four wickets for 57 runs. O'Reilly (three), Chipperfield (two), and Wall took the remaining wickets.

Australia's opening brought sensations. Brown and Ponsford were scoring freely when the former was caught off Bowes. Oldfield, sent in to play out time, was out for a duck, and disaster came when Woodfull, too, went without scoring. Bowes had taken three quick wickets, and stumps were drawn with the score at 39.

England was without the services of Sutcliffe, who had torn a leg muscle, and Walters opened with Keeton, of Notts, who was playing in his first Test. The pair put on 43 before Keeton's wicket fell, but thereafter the bowlers were always on top. Walters (44) was top score of the innings.

JULY 21, 1934.

# BRADMAN BATS AND BATS AND BATS

## EVENING NEWS

**CLOSE OF PLAY**

This poster refers to Don Bradman's score of 304 during the fourth Test at Leeds in 1934.

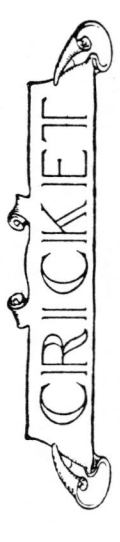

# CRICKET

## 1934 - Australian Team in England

### Showing Individual Scores, Averages & results in all Matches

Compiled and Drawn by E. H. NOBLE

\* Not First Class Matches. Scores in these Matches are not included in the Aggregate or Average.

| Player | Aggregate | Average |
|---|---|---|
| D. G. BRADMAN | 2020 | 84·16 |
| W. A. PONSFORD | 1784 | 77·56 |
| S. J. McCABE | 2078 | 69·26 |
| W. M. WOODFULL | 1268 | 52·83 |
| A. F. KIPPAX | 961 | 50·57 |
| A. G. CHIPPERFIELD | 899 | 40·86 |
| W. A. BROWN | 1308 | 38·47 |
| L. S. DARLING | 1022 | 34·06 |
| B. A. BARNETT | 470 | 33·57 |
| W. J. O'REILLY | 237 | 26·33 |
| W. A. OLDFIELD | 295 | 22·69 |
| E. A. BROMLEY | 312 | 16·42 |
| C. V. GRIMMETT | 255 | 15·00 |
| A. EBELING | 265 | 14·72 |
| T. W. WALL | 84 | 9·33 |
| L. FLEETW-SMIT/H | 24 | 3·42 |

# PONSFORD AND BRADMAN

## DON AGAIN BECOMES THE SCORING MACHINE

### *Verity the Only Bowler to Keep him Quiet*

### BOWES BUMPERS BUMPED OFF

Don Bradman and W. H. Ponsford resume Australia's innings on Saturday.

OH, dear! What a sight. Take that score-board away. I can't bear to look at it. Poor old England is in sackcloth and ashes, and Australia are definitely, decisively and completely cocks of the walk. Oh, dear!

\* \* \*

Mr. Bradman and Mr. Ponsford went to the wickets in the morning, and they liked it so much that they stayed there all day. Nearly all day anyway. Mr. Ponsford thought he'd like some sleep so round about six o'clock he got out after knocking up 181. Mr. Bradman—well, he's still there, and likely to stay there until the start of the next Test.

\* \* \*

Just dry your eyes and have a look at the score—494 for 4. It's a nasty smack in the eye for us, isn't it? At the same time, you must admit that it's a " darn " fine piece of cricket, especially following that sensational business on Friday night, when the tourists lost three wickets in about a quarter of an hour.

\* \* \*

THE partnership of Ponsford and Bradman is surely the most dramatic and the most opportune that has ever happened in big cricket. From the verge of a collapse they took Australia to a position which may mean a very comfortable victory.

\* \* \*

They each got a century, Bradman getting his eighth against England and Ponsford his fourth, and their stand, 388 for the fourth wicket, broke the record of 323 by Hobbs and Rhodes at Melbourne in 1912, which is the highest partnership for any wicket in these Tests.

\* \* \*

Needless to say, Don held the centre of the stage. We saw the real Bradman, the scoring machine, for the first time this year, at least in Test matches.

\* \* \*

BRADMAN was magnificent. Even that word does not do justice to his fine innings. Right from the start he put out of his mind the sorry fate of Australia's early batsmen and clouted each of the two remaining balls of Bowes's devastating over of Friday for 4's.

\* \* \*

Even so, the tall be-spectacled Yorkshireman, together with his county colleague, Verity, remained the heroes of the English wreck.

\* \* \*

As he entered the ground, Bowes was slapped on the shoulders and cheered to the echo by a huge crowd which laid in wait for him, and he had to sprint hard for the pavilion.

\* \* \*

OUT on the field Bowes gave an early shock to Bradman when Don took a wild swipe at a ball which he missed and, unfortunately for England, just missed the stumps. Now if—oh, but what's the good.

\* \* \*

Verity was a pastmaster at the art of keeping the batsmen quiet. At one point he bowled seven maidens in a row. Not even Bradman, who was cracking everybody else all over the place, could steal a run out of Verity.

\* \* \*

BRADMAN had to execute some pretty nifty footwork when facing Bowes, for several times he had to dodge and duck bumpers. Between the overs, Don, saucy-like, walked down the pitch and patted the turf a yard or so from the opposite crease.

\* \* \*

Of course, this brought forth howls of derision. Bowes just smiled and sent down some more. But when Bowes struck Bradman on the head and then on the hip Don just smiled, too—and tried to clout a few more fours.

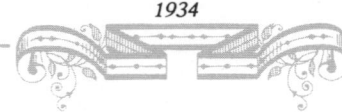

# TRIBUTE TO BRADMAN

## "Best Scoring Batsman I Have Seen"

## ALL THE SHOTS

### Headingley Wicket Still First-Rate

*By* WILFRED RHODES

HEADINGLEY, Saturday

THE scoring machine—that is Bradman—got to work again to-day and our bowlers had to pay tribute, as we all knew they would have to do, as soon as Bradman decided that the time had come for him to move seriously along the run-getting road.

He never hurried—never dashed, as cricketers say—yet at the end of a day on which he was at the wicket for five minutes less than six and a half hours he had 271 runs to his name. He scored over a hundred runs in the last hundred minutes, and just as there was no indication of quick-scoring in his general outlook, so, when he left the field, there was no suggestion that he was tired after the strain of standing at the wicket for so long.

Frankly, I do not know which is the most remarkable feature about this very remarkable young man, who is, all the way round, the best scoring batsman I have seen.

He has all the shots; he can apparently use them at will: he has wonderful strength in his wrists and forearms, and his timing is so perfect that one knows the quickest of eyesight is allied with lightning footwork and an astonishing judgment of the length of a ball; and, with all this, he has the confidence he has a right to have in his power, and a determination that enables him to do almost as he pleases.

I have heard a story that when he was playing his record Australia v. England Test innings at Headingley on the last tour—a record that he may easily beat on Monday morning—he was asked at lunch-time how he felt. His reply was characteristic: "Good for the day."

And I am prepared to believe that when he got up this morning he (knowing the beautiful condition of the Headingley wicket) said to himself: "Well, I think that, seeing we are at Headingley again, I'll get a few runs for Australia, and, incidentally, have a go at topping the 334 innings I played there four years ago."

All to-day he batted like a man determined to fulfil a promise to himself, and he has served Australia as well as a batsman can serve his country. Do not overlook the fact that when Bradman and Ponsford went to the wicket this morning there was the threat of Bowes, the man who took three wickets in 10 balls last night, hanging over their heads.

What happened? Bowes had two balls left in the over in which he took the wickets of Oldfield and Woodfull, and Bradman had to face Bowes. Now Bowes had to loosen himself, and each of the balls was understandably a trifle short. Bradman played two beautiful back shots to get two 4's, and ever afterwards he was the commanding figure of the day.

It maybe that his innings was not an innings for the spectators. They probably looked, after all they have heard of the other Bradman of whom we have seen so much this season, for some fast and furious hitting of the type we saw at Sheffield on Monday. They got the furious hitting, but it was served to them in doses.

Whenever a loose ball was sent along Bradman was there to hit it safely with a wickedly vicious bat—I don't think I have seen a man so vicious with a loose ball as Bradman can be—and all the time he missed very few scoring chances, without ever noticeably seeking to rush the score along. The Bradman we saw to-day was a sound Bradman taking, in the correct way, the right toll of steady bowling on a wicket good enough to delight the heart of any batsman.

He was, so far as I could see, only beaten once, and then, when his score was 56, he played over what appeared to be a half-volley from Mitchell. It was a difficult stumping chance, for Ames would be blinded by the batsman and he would have to guess a little in going for the ball, but nevertheless it was just a chance.

For the remainder of the day, if one excepts the first period in which Bowes desperately tried to bounce the ball, Bradman's bat simply met the ball and dealt with it on its merits. As I saw Bradman's score mount steadily with Ponsford's and Australia's, I had a feeling of sympathy for our bowlers, for I have always said, since I first saw this young man from Australia, that he is the hardest man to keep quiet I have ever bowled to.

### Perfect Timing

He has so many shots—every one of them —he is so sharp at judging the length of a ball, and, what is more, he can place the ball with such astonishing accuracy. When you watch Bradman seriously at work you see hitting as crisp as anything you ever will see, you see forcing back shots played with a dead straight bat, and you see leg hits that are leg hits, made with timing that is the acme of perfection.

Watch Bradman's leg-glide. Not only does he glide the ball to place it, but he jabs hard to help that ball along, and there the steel that is in his wrists and forearms makes itself felt.

It was Bradman all the way to-day, and yet Ponsford, a very fine batsman indeed, took his score from 22 to 181. One cannot give Ponsford too much credit for his brilliant innings, for the fine quality of his shots, and for the readiness of his scoring. His square cutting and his shot placing was good to watch all the time, and he was unlucky to get out as he did, but he was even more unlucky in playing his innings on a day on which Bradman was rejoicing.

Ordinarily, Ponsford's innings would stand head and shoulders above any other innings in a Test match; to-day it just happened that he was overshadowed, as anyone else would have been, by Bradman.

And Ponsford's period of some uncertainty was Bradman's—when Bowes bumped a few balls. With a bit of luck then Bowes might have had both wickets. Bradman, hooking a short one, hit the ball hard to Hopwood's right hand—it would have been an exceedingly good catch had it been made—and Ponsford was very nearly caught by Mitchell at cover. Indeed, some of us will always think that he would have been caught had Mitchell moved quicker to the ball.

### Bowes Tries Hard

Really, you know, on this wicket which was a bit better than it was yesterday (and then it was just about good enough for anything) our only hope to-day was for two quick wickets, either at the start or when the new ball came along at 200.

And when the new ball came along what did we see? Bowes tried his hardest and best with it from the pavilion end, as did Hammond from the top end, and then while the ball was still comparatively new there was the extraordinary spectacle of Bowes bowling to Bradman with a field in which he had one slip—a slip so wide, in fact, that he was almost in the gully.

Here was an indication of the effort that was made to block Bradman's shots, and it was somewhat curious to-day to note that Bradman, who can cut so well, used that stroke only very occasionally.

But it is no easy task trying to block the shots of men like Bradman and Ponsford when they are going well. They made it appear, indeed, that there were constant gaps in our field, so excellent was their placing.

Bradman and Ponsford to-day with their stand of 388 set up a record partnership in England v. Australia Tests. I am happy, with my old colleague Jack Hobbs, to congratulate them on their excellent performance. As I watched them move steadily from the 300 mark towards the 400 mark—Ponsford, I say again, was unfortunate to get out as he did when the pair had put on 388—my memory went back to that match at Melbourne on the 1911-12 tour when Hobbs and I scored 323 for England's first wicket.

I know how tired I was when stumps were drawn that Saturday evening at Melbourne, and I can say this—when Bradman ran off the field to-night he did not look half as tired as I felt that day all those years ago.

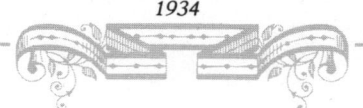

# WICKETS FALL IN CHASE FOR RUNS

## RAIN NOW ONLY HOPE OF DRAW | BRADMAN GETS THREE HUNDRED

(FROM OUR SPECIAL REPRESENTATIVE)

LEEDS, Monday.

WICKETS fell quickly in the fourth Test match this morning, Bradman carried his score to 304 before being bowled by Bowes, but the remaining Australian batsmen, trying to force the pace, were all out for a total of 584.

England, needing 384 to reach Australia's total, went to the wickets shortly before lunch, but at the adjournment had lost Keeton's wicket for only 28 runs. The wicket fell to Grimmett, who completely deceived the batsman with a ball that broke round his legs.

*When the players resumed after lunch, black clouds were gathering, and the possibility of rain interfering with Australia's great chance of a win appeared imminent.*

England lost two more wickets shortly after lunch, and when, early after the tea adjournment, Wyatt was bowled by Grimmett, the home side's position was desperate.

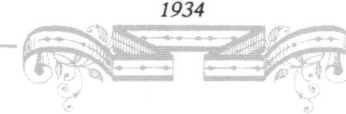

# ON DEFENCE

## ENGLISH BATSMEN

### PLAY DESCRIBED

## O'REILLY'S APPEALS

(From Our Special Representative)

LONDON, Tuesday.

PURELY defensive tactics were adopted by the Englishmen to-day, but in the short period of Test play both Hendren and Ames were dismissed.

Although there was heavy overnight rain the wicket ends had been covered and the start was delayed only eight minutes. The ground appeared damp, but dust swept off the wicket ends after the covers were removed. The sky was overcast and rain threatened. Roughly 5000 were present when Grimmett and O'Reilly opened with maidens to Leyland and Hendren.

Grimmett and O'Reilly each bowled another maiden before fairly heavy rain interrupted play.

Play was resumed after 20 minutes. A couple of runs came from Grimmett and then, in O'Reilly's first over Hendren missed one which came straight through and he was out leg-before. He had batted 215 minutes, and hit five fours.

The Australians crowded in at silly point and silly mid-on, and the batsmen did not attempt to get runs, although Leyland did pull O'Reilly high for four. A few overs later a single brought up 200 in 285 minutes, after which Ames glanced O'Reilly for four.

## In Difficulties

Leyland was in difficulties to a couple of balls from Grimmett, but in the same over he on-drove the slow bowler for four. Ames continued to block carefully until Grimmett tossed up a higher one. Ames tried to swing it and it went hard to square-leg, Brown taking a nice catch.

Leyland relieved a forlorn struggle by straight driving Grimmett for four, but Hopwood seemed hopelessly at sea to O'Reilly, surviving a couple of leg-before appeals which must have been near things.

**O'Reilly's four appeals amused the crowd, although it is many weeks since O'Reilly appealed for anything but the closest of chances.**

Hopwood opened the score by turning O'Reilly for a single just as huge black clouds came over the ground. Leyland in the same over got four for a hard off-drive. Hopwood survived a maiden from Grimmett, at least three balls beating him.

O'Reilly sent down a maiden, and then Hopwood survived another over. Leyland and Hopwood each got a single from O'Reilly as a huge clap of thunder broke.

## Was It a Catch?

In Grimmett's next over Hopwood cocked up a ball and Wall at silly mid-on dived, and the Australians not only unanimously appealed but clapped what seemed a brilliant catch. Oldfield was particularly confident, but the umpire disallowed the appeal.

Then came a terrific downpour. The actual torrential portion of which lasted only three minutes and a half, but the wicket ends, even under the covers, were like mud pies. Subsequent rain would not have prevented an early resumption, as at 2.15 the sun was shining. A. E. R. Gilligan said the only comparable downpour he had seen was in South Africa.

The ground had many big puddles and the asphalt between the pavilion and the ground where the players walk was a big lake. During rain, it was impossible to see across the ground.

## Story Of Inspections

This is what happened after the rain. At 2.45 Woodfull and Wyatt inspected the wicket. The covers were removed revealing that one end of the wicket was still waterlogged.

**At 4 p.m. the captains made a lengthy inspection. The squeegee roller was applied around the pitch.**

Woodfull and Wyatt had another look at 4.30, but decided on a further inspection at 5 p.m.

At that hour the captains disagreed and the umpires examined the wicket. They decided to have another look at 6 p.m. The light was brilliant and no further rain appeared likely. The wicket, however, was still wet.

At 6 p.m. the umpires decided that the match would be abandoned.

The end of Australia's hopes of victory.

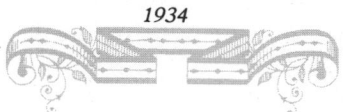

# BRADMAN FIT FOR LAST TEST

## HOLIDAY WITH HIS DOCTOR

*Special " Daily Mail " News*

DON Bradman will play in the fifth and last Test match, which starts at the Oval on August 18.

There have been many conflicting statements about his health, not only concerning the muscle injury that compelled him to retire during the Leeds Test match but also in a general way.

**Actually, neither Bradman nor anyone connected with the Australian team has the slightest doubt about his playing.**

Last week his temperature went up a shade one evening, and there was a fear, which was soon dispelled, that he might have caught a mild attack of influenza.

Since Bradman moved from the Park-lane nursing home of Sir Douglas Shields, where he was receiving treatment for his strained muscle, to the house of his doctor at Farnham Common, near Windsor, he has been very well. His stay there is something of a holiday.

A whole party of visitors went to Farnham yesterday. Bradman is no longer a patient in the strict sense of the word, and in all probability he will remain at Farnham Common until August 14, the day on which the whole of the Australian team returns to its London headquarters.

Sir Douglas Shields' home.

Sir Douglas Shields.

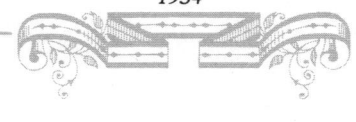

# Australia v England
## Fifth Test Match

After a tour of fluctuating fortunes the fate of "The Ashes" rested on the fifth and final Test.

The toss favoured Australia and, following the Leeds pattern, W. H. Ponsford and I were again associated in a long partnership which made the game safe for Australia.

England suffered cruelly from misfortune. A back injury put Ames out of action. Bowes also was incapacitated for a while. In the midst of these troubles, the gamble of the Selectors in bringing back the 47-year-old Frank Woolley failed. Worse still, he was asked in the emergency to keep wickets, an unfair burden to inflict upon him because at that age and with his physique, there could not have been a more illogical choice.

I can picture now the final stroke of this erstwhile magnificent player falling a hapless victim to the wiles of O'Reilly.

Australia won the rubber and there is no doubt was the better side. It was a fitting end to the captaincy of Woodfull that he should lead Australia to victory in his last Test.

Though we didn't know it at the time, this also proved to be Ponsford's last Test, for he retired at the end of the season.

My own enjoyment of the tour concluded with two festival innings, one at Folkestone and one at Scarborough. The latter innings of 132 in 90 minutes made before lunch on the first day ranks with the Middlesex match as the best stroke play of my career, but did not rate so high in importance because of its picnic nature.

Thus ended an era for never again did I play for Australia without being Captain.

*Don Bradman*

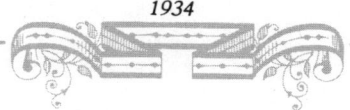

AUSTRALIA v ENGLAND, Fifth Test Match, at the Oval, 18, 20, 21 and 22 August 1934.

| Australia | - First Innings | 701 |
|---|---|---|
| | - Second Innings | 327 |
| England | - First Innings | 321 |
| | - Second Innings | 145 |

Australia won by 562 runs,
and won the rubber and the Ashes.

| DON BRADMAN | - c. L.E.G. Ames b. W.E. Bowes | 244 |
|---|---|---|
| | - b. W.E. Bowes | 77 |

DON BRADMAN's first first-class game for nearly a month found him in the same superb form as at Leeds, and he played another great innings.

Bradman came in at 21 for 1, at 12 noon on the first day, and began quietly, being only 43 at lunch. Afterwards, having reached 50 in ninety-six minutes, he began to score more rapidly, and his century came up in two hours fifty minutes. At tea, he was 150 and in the evening he increased the pressure; his 200 (at 5.50) took four hours forty-three minutes. Finally he was out at 6.23 p.m. after five hours sixteen minutes at the wicket, when he tried to hook a very high bumper and only snicked it to the wicket-keeper. Bradman's innings included a six and thirty-two fours; he made his runs off 272 balls, and blended sound defence and concentration with a brilliant exhibition of stroke-play all round the wicket. W.H. Ponsford also batted well, and contributed 194 to the partnership of 451; this partnership was a world record for the second wicket and it was also a record for any wicket for any Test Match.

This was the second time in first-class cricket that Bradman had made two double-centuries in successive innings but the first time he did so in Test Matches. He also equalled Hammond's feat in twice making 200 or over in consecutive Test Matches. His total of 548 (304, 244) in two successive innings was a Test record for Australia. For the fifth time he made 200 or over in a day's play in a Test Match.

Australia batted again after tea on the third day. Bradman went in at 13 for 1, and again scored easily; he had been in for only twenty-three minutes when, with his score 9, he hooked a short ball from E. Clarke for a huge six. Completing 50 in seventy-eight minutes, he was 76 not out at the close of play, after an hour and fifty-two minutes' batting.

Next morning, after he had added 1 run off H.Verity, he attempted to hook W.E. Bowes second ball, it did not rise as much as he expected and he was bowled. He made 77, including a six and six fours, off 100 balls, in an hour and fifty-six minutes.

His 765 in his last four first-class innings (140, 304, 244, 77) was a record for any Overseas batsman in England.

### AUSTRALIA.

| | | | | |
|---|---|---|---|---|
| W. A. Brown b Clark | 10 | — | c Allen b Clark | 1 |
| W. H. Ponsford hit wkt, b Allen | 266 | — | c Hammond b Clark | 22 |
| D. G. Bradman c Ames b Bowes | 244 | — | b Bowes | 77 |
| S. J. McCabe b Allen | 10 | — | c Walters b Clark | 70 |
| W. M. Woodfull b Bowes | 49 | — | b Bowes | 13 |
| A. F. Kippax lbw, b Bowes | 28 | — | c Walters b Clark | 8 |
| A. G. Chipperfield b Bowes | 3 | — | c Woolley b Clark | 16 |
| W. A. Oldfield not out | 42 | — | c Hammond b Bowes | 0 |
| C. V. Grimmett c Ames b Allen | 7 | — | c Hammond b Bowes | 14 |
| H. I. Ebeling b Allen | 2 | — | c Allen b Bowes | 41 |
| W. J. O'Reilly b Clark | 7 | — | not out | 15 |
| B 4, l-b 14, w 2, n-b 13 | 33 | | B 37, l-b 8, w 1, n-b 4 | 50 |
| | **701** | | | **327** |

### ENGLAND.

| | | | | |
|---|---|---|---|---|
| Mr. C. F. Walters c Kippax b O'Reilly | 64 | — | b McCabe | 1 |
| H. Sutcliffe c Oldfield b Grimmett | 38 | — | c McCabe b Grimmett | 28 |
| F. E. Woolley c McCabe b O'Reilly | 4 | — | c Ponsford b McCabe | 0 |
| W. R. Hammond c Oldfield b Ebeling | 15 | — | c and b O'Reilly | 43 |
| Mr. R. E. S. Wyatt b Grimmett | 17 | — | c Ponsford b Grimmett | 22 |
| M. Leyland b Grimmett | 110 | — | c Brown b Grimmett | 17 |
| L. E. G. Ames retired hurt | 33 | — | absent ill | 0 |
| Mr. G. O. Allen b Ebeling | 19 | — | st Oldfield b Grimmett | 26 |
| H. Verity b Ebeling | 11 | — | c McCabe b Grimmett | 1 |
| E. W. Clark not out | 2 | — | not out | 2 |
| W. E. Bowes absent ill | 0 | — | c Bradman b O'Reilly | 2 |
| B 4, l-b 3, n-b 1 | 8 | | L-b 1, n-b 2 | 3 |
| | **321** | | | **145** |

### FALL OF THE WICKETS.

AUSTRALIA—First Innings.

| 1 | 2 | 3 | 4 | 5 | 6 | 7 | 8 | 9 | 10 |
|---|---|---|---|---|---|---|---|---|---|
| 21 | 472 | 488 | 574 | 626 | 631 | 638 | 676 | 682 | 701 |

AUSTRALIA—Second Innings.

| 1 | 2 | 3 | 4 | 5 | 6 | 7 | 8 | 9 | 10 |
|---|---|---|---|---|---|---|---|---|---|
| 13 | 42 | 192 | 213 | 224 | 236 | 236 | 256 | 272 | 327 |

ENGLAND—First Innings.

| 1 | 2 | 3 | 4 | 5 | 6 | 7 | 8 |
|---|---|---|---|---|---|---|---|
| 104 | 108 | 111 | 136 | 142 | 263 | 311 | 321 |

ENGLAND—Second Innings.

| 1 | 2 | 3 | 4 | 5 | 6 | 7 | 8 | 9 |
|---|---|---|---|---|---|---|---|---|
| 1 | 3 | 67 | 89 | 109 | 122 | 138 | 141 | 145 |

Umpires : F. Chester and F. Walden.

### ENGLAND BOWLING.

| | Overs | Mdns. | Runs | Wkts. | Overs | Mdns. | Runs | Wkts. |
|---|---|---|---|---|---|---|---|---|
| Bowes | 38 | 2 | 164 | 4 | 11.3 | 3 | 55 | 5 |
| Allen | 34 | 5 | 170 | 4 | 16 | 2 | 63 | 0 |
| Clark | 37.2 | 4 | 110 | 2 | 20 | 1 | 98 | 5 |
| Hammond | 12 | 0 | 53 | 0 | 7 | 1 | 18 | 0 |
| Verity | 43 | 7 | 123 | 0 | 14 | 8 | 43 | 0 |
| Wyatt | 4 | 0 | 28 | 0 | | | | |
| Leyland | 3 | 0 | 20 | 0 | | | | |

### AUSTRALIA BOWLING.

| | Overs | Mdns. | Runs | Wkts. | Overs | Mdns. | Runs | Wkts. |
|---|---|---|---|---|---|---|---|---|
| Ebeling | 21 | 4 | 74 | 3 | 10 | 5 | 15 | 0 |
| McCabe | 6 | 1 | 21 | 0 | 5 | 3 | 5 | 2 |
| Grimmett | 49.3 | 13 | 103 | 3 | 26.3 | 10 | 64 | 5 |
| O'Reilly | 37 | 10 | 93 | 2 | 22 | 9 | 58 | 2 |
| Chipperfield | 4 | 0 | 22 | 0 | | | | |

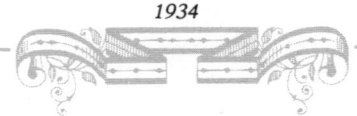

## THE FIRST DAY

The Fifth Test Match between England and Australia opened at the Oval on Saturday morning, August 18. Australia won the toss, and at the close of play her score was 475 for 2 wickets. The feature of the first day was the partnership between Bradman and Ponsford, which began after Brown had been bowled by Clark, and lasted until 6.25, when Bradman, having made 244, was bowled by Bowes.

# AUSTRALIA'S GREAT START.

# Two Wickets Down for 475.

## RECORD-BREAKING PARTNERSHIP.

## Bradman, 244; Ponsford, 205 Not Out.

LONDON, Aug. 18.

The opening day's play in the final test match at The Oval to-day produced the heaviest day's scoring in the history of the tests. When stumps were drawn, Australia had scored 475 runs, with only two wickets down.

Ponsford and Bradman, in an amazing second wicket stand, following the early dismissal of Brown, created a new record for a second wicket partnership, beating the 235 registered by Macartney and Woodfull at Leeds in 1926. They continued in devastating fashion, raising 300, and going on to pass their own record of 388 for any test partnership, recorded for the fourth wicket at Leeds last month. They had added 451 runs in 310 minutes when Bradman was dismissed, having set a brisk rate of scoring from the start.

Missed chances told heavily against England, as, although Bradman's great innings had been absolutely chanceless up to the time of his dismissal, Ponsford was missed off difficult chances at 57 and 68, and gave further chances at 115 and 116.

Bradman scored his ninth century in tests against England, and Ponsford his fifth. Bradman was brilliant throughout his long stay, and among his 244 runs were a six and 32 fours. Ponsford batted for 345 minutes and hit 19 boundaries. Ponsford was several times hit by fast deliveries; but he and Bradman took control of the speed attack, and in the closing stages of their extraordinary partnership they were scoring with ease.

Woodfull's luck in winning the toss meant much to his side, as the batsmen were favoured with a perfect wicket.

Ebeling and Kippax were included in the Australian team, Wall being unfit, and Darling being made 12th man. The England eleven included the veteran Woolley, who, fielding in slips, failed to hold two chances from Ponsford. Hendren was unable to play.

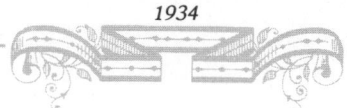

Don Bradman c. L. E. G. Ames b. W. E. Bowes 244, turns to go to the pavilion.

Don Bradman gets in as L. E. G. Ames takes the ball.

# Ponsford Gets 266 And Is Top Scorer

## WALTERS HITS OUT FOR ENGLAND

| LONG CHASE FOR RUNS | MORE MISSED CHANCES |

(FROM OUR SPECIAL REPRESENTATIVE)

### LONDON, Monday.

AUSTRALIA totalled 701 in the first innings of the fifth Test, Ponsford reaching 266 before he hit his wicket—a repetition of his fourth Test dismissal.

*Woodfull 49, Oldfield 42 not out, and Kippax 28 were the only other Australian batsmen to get among the runs.*

England started merrily, due to the cavalier treatment of Ebeling by Walters, who was so severe on the Australian that 23 runs came off his first five overs. Then Woodfull took Ebeling off.

Sutcliffe, too, made some clinking boundary shots, and there was early evidence that England would chase the Australian total, forcing the pace.

The opening pair were unconquered at stumps, 90 being on the board.

# Now Has A Lead Of Over 560 Runs

## ENGLAND'S BAD LUCK IN FIFTH TEST

### BOWES AND AMES ARE ILL | EBELING GETS THE AVERAGE

*EBELING, whose first victim in Test cricket was Hammond.*

From OUR SPECIAL REPRESENTATIVE

**LONDON, Tuesday.**

DUE to the excellent bowling and fielding of the Australian side, and England's misfortunes, the side was all out before tea to-day for 321 runs. Ames, while batting, tore a muscle in his back, and was unable to complete his innings. Bowes is suffering from a fistula, and was unable either to bat or bowl.

*Australia was 380 ahead on the innings, but Woodfull adopting safety-first tactics, decided to bat again. Woolley is keeping wickets for England, and in addition to Gregory, the twelfth man, McMurray, a member of the ground staff, is fielding.*

Ebeling got the bowling average for Australia, taking three wickets for 74, Grimmett took three, and O'Reilly two. In Australia's second innings, Brown was out early for one. The first wicket falling at 13.

*The wicket is still good. Groundsman Martin says that its surface is as good as ever, and he is well satisfied with the way it is standing up. "I do not think that anyone can grumble about its condition," he said.*

Don Bradman b. W. E. Bowes 77.

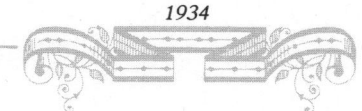

# Australia's Victory By 562 Runs: Grimmett's Five Wkts.

## SWIFT END TO A GAME OF THRILLS

(From Our Special Representative)

LONDON, Wednesday.

*A*USTRALIA HAS WON BACK THE ASHES!

Batting on to-day, the tourists carried their second innings score to 327 runs, and England, needing 708 to win, was dismissed for 145. Australia thus won by 562 runs.

Bowes was England's hero of the day. After undergoing a minor operation in the morning, he insisted on leaving hospital to play for his side, and took five wickets—including those of Bradman and Woodfull—for 55 runs.

Operating on a wicket that was beginning to crumble, Grimmett bowled excellently, finishing with an average of five wickets for 64 runs.

Crowds rushed the field, but the players got the stumps and bails. Ten minutes later only vagrant newspapers blowing across the ground were left to tell the tale of the fight for the Ashes.

The end of the fifth Test at the Oval.

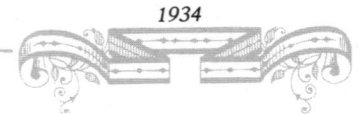

# Australians v An England XI

AUSTRALIANS v AN ENGLAND XI, at Folkestone, 3 and 4 September 1934.

| Australians | - First Innings | 365 for 4 wickets |
|---|---|---|
| | - Second Innings | - |
| An England XI | - First Innings | 279 |
| | - Second Innings | - |
| | Drawn. | |

DON BRADMAN - not out     149

DON BRADMAN went in after lunch on the second day and batted in his most attractive style. He completed 50 in forty-eight minutes, 100 in eighty-seven minutes, and then proceeded from 104 to 134 by hitting A.P. Freeman for 30 in one over (4, 6, 6, 4, 6, 4). His innings lasted only an hour and forty-four minutes (an average of 85 an hour) and included four sixes and seventeen fours. 30 runs was the most ever scored by an Australian off one over. Despite the limited amount of first-class cricket he had played, he was at twenty-six years eight days, the youngest batsman in the history of the game to reach his fiftieth century; moreover he completed fifty centuries in the shortest time from the start of a first-class career. He took only six years 262 days from the date of his debut.

### AN ENGLAND XI.

| | |
|---|---|
| Mr. C. F. Walters b Fleetwood-Smith | 22 |
| J. B. Hobbs c McCabe b Fleetwood-Smith | 38 |
| F. E. Woolley b Wall | 66 |
| W. R. Hammond st Oldfield b Fleetwood-Smith | 54 |
| L. E. G. Ames lbw, b Fleetwood-Smith | 13 |
| Mr. B. H. Valentine c Oldfield b O'Reilly | 5 |
| Lord Tennyson c Fleetwood-Smith b O'Reilly | 1 |
| M. Jahangir Khan c Oldfield b O'Reilly | 6 |
| Mr. M. J. C. Allom not out | 47 |
| Mr. A. P. F. Chapman b O'Reilly | 5 |
| A. P. Freeman b Fleetwood-Smith | 4 |
| B 9, l-b 9 | 18 |
| | 279 |

### AUSTRALIANS.

| | |
|---|---|
| W. H. Ponsford b Freeman | 45 |
| W. A. Brown c Ames b Woolley | 73 |
| S. J. McCabe lbw, b Freeman | 10 |
| A. F. Kippax c Ames b Hammond | 21 |
| D. G. Bradman not out | 149 |
| W. M. Woodfull not out | 62 |
| B 2, l-b 1, w 2 | 5 |
| (Four wkts.) | 365 |

W. A. Oldfield
C. V. Grimmett
T. W. Wall        } did not bat.
W. J. O'Reilly
L. O'B. Fleetwood-Smith

### AUSTRALIANS BOWLING.

| | Overs | Mdns. | Runs | Wkts. |
|---|---|---|---|---|
| Wall | 13 | 3 | 58 | 1 |
| McCabe | 3 | 0 | 10 | 0 |
| Grimmett | 1 | 0 | 1 | 0 |
| O'Reilly | 27 | 10 | 55 | 4 |
| Fleetwood-Smith | 37.5 | 4 | 137 | 5 |

### AN ENGLAND XI. BOWLING.

| | | | | |
|---|---|---|---|---|
| Jahangir Khan | 16 | 1 | 52 | 0 |
| Allom | 20 | 1 | 81 | 0 |
| Hammond | 15 | 0 | 71 | 1 |
| Woolley | 8 | 0 | 28 | 1 |
| Freeman | 31 | 5 | 128 | 2 |

Umpires: F. Chester and A. E. Street.

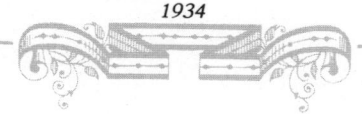

# FOLKESTONE MATCH.

## AUSTRALIA'S RAPID SCORING.

## Bradman Unbeaten after Dashing Century.

LONDON, Sept. 4.

After dismissing the England Eleven for 279, the Australian cricketers scored rapidly in the match at Folkestone to-day. The match was drawn, Australia compiling 365 runs, with the loss of four wickets.

Bradman, who was missed when one, gave a dashing display for 149 not out in 105 minutes, he and Woodfull adding 180 runs in 80 minutes. From one over by Freeman, Bradman scored 30 runs, and altogether he hit four sixes and 17 fours. Woodfull scored 62 not out, and Brown made 73.

Bowling on a wicket giving them some assistance, Fleetwood-Smith and O'Reilly troubled the England Eleven batsmen, with the exception of Allom (Surrey). Fleetwood-Smith finishing with five wickets and O'Reilly with four. Allom scored 47, not out, in 40 minutes, and hit three sixes off Fleetwood-Smith.

### ALLOM'S BIG HITS.

The special representative of the Australian Press Association at Folkestone says:—

When the third and last day of the match was commenced the England Eleven had three wickets down for 186, Hammond being 43 not out and Ames nine not out.

Assisted by a heavy morning and a sea mist, the bowlers proved dangerous immediately on the resumption, the ball often rising awkwardly. Ames hooked O'Reilly for four, but went leg-before-wicket in Fleetwood-Smith's second over. That bowler also troubled Hammond, and after 200 had been raised in 180 minutes Hammond reached forward and was smartly stumped. Fleetwood-Smith had thus claimed Hammond's wicket at each of their two meetings on the tour. Hammond gave a delightful display for 54 in 75 minutes and hit ten fours.

The batsmen were now hopelessly at sea. Valentine was caught behind in O'Reilly's next over, and Lord Tennyson played one shocking stroke before he was caught at long-leg, giving O'Reilly two wickets in three overs. Allom hit mightily, one six off Fleetwood-Smith appropriately landing on top of the tent of the "Brotherhood of Cheerful Sparrows," one of those picturesque organisations which flourish on Kentish grounds.

It was now truly festival cricket. In another over from Fleetwood-Smith Allom pulled him for six, and then on-drove him clean out of the ground. It was one of the greatest hits of the season. Allom's 47 not out in 40 minutes included three sixes and six fours. Nobody else looked like staying, and the team was out for 279. The innings occupied 235 minutes.

O'Reilly was in excellent form, his figures for to-day being 13 overs, 7 maidens, 25 runs, 4 wickets. Chapman, who strained a leg, had Jahangir Khan to run for him.

Opening the Australian innings at 12.40 p.m., Ponsford and Brown batted nicely against the bowling of Allom, Jahangir Khan, Freeman, and Hammond. The English eleven presented a rather unusual appearance in the field, Woolley and Freeman being in the slips, Hammond at third man, and Tennyson in the outfield. Allom and Jahangir Khan each obtained pace from the pitch, but the batting never lacked assurance. At lunch the score was 55, Ponsford being 31 and Brown 22.

### PONSFORD BOWLED.

All went well after lunch, the scoring being steady, but unexciting, until Ponsford hit right across Freeman's leg-break and the middle stump was knocked back. The score was 81, Ponsford having made 45.

The crowd saw highly skilled and graceful play by Brown and Kippax. Freeman bowled splendidly, keeping an immaculate length and occasionally making the ball turn a long way. Soon after Brown had reached 50 in 110 minutes, Kippax was smartly caught at the wicket by Ames, off Hammond.

Lord Tennyson, captaining England in the absence of Chapman, after lunch brought on Woolley, who soon dismissed Brown. The batsman had been at the wickets for 140 minutes, in a chanceless and pretty display. His score was 73.

Bradman, meanwhile, was in a lively mood, placing cleverly, and Woodfull, who came in at 185, began with rare vigour. The 200 appeared in 150 minutes.

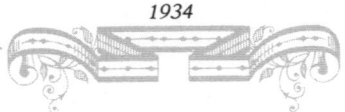

# Australians
## v
# Mr. H.D.G. Leveson-Gower's XI

AUSTRALIANS v MR. H.D.G. LEVESON-GOWER'S XI, at Scarborough, 8, 10 and 11 September 1934.

| Australians | - First Innings | 489 |
|---|---|---|
| | - Second Innings | - |
| Leveson-Gower's | - First Innings | 223 |
| | - Second Innings | 218 |

Australians won by an innings and 48 runs.

DON BRADMAN - st. G. Duckworth b. H. Verity    132

Against an attack consisting of M.S. Nichols, K. Farnes, W.E. Bowes, L.F. Townsend and H. Verity, DON BRADMAN played another brilliant innings.    He went in early on the first day at 14 for 1, made 50 in forty minutes, and reached 100 before lunch in eighty-two minutes.    He then added 32 in eight minutes, going from 96 to 127 in five minutes, including 19 in an over off Verity.    He batted altogether for only one and a half hours, hitting a six and twenty-four fours (102 in boundaries, or seventy-seven per cent).

# AMAZING DON BRADMAN
# IN GLORIOUS WIND-UP TO TOUR
## In 90 Minutes He Scored 132 Runs
## 24 FOURS AND A SIX
## IN TALLY
### Star Fast Bowlers Battered
### After Two Early
### Escapes

**From Our Special Representative**

SCARBOROUGH, Saturday.

GOING to the wickets to-day after Brown was out for three, and facing an attack which included three fast bowlers—Farnes, Bowes, and Nichols—England's star left-hander in Verity, and a high-class slow bowler in Townsend, Don Bradman gave one of the most amazing displays of his extraordinary career, scoring 132—24 fours and one six—in 90 minutes.

Bradman's remarkable score was made prior to the luncheon adjournment in the match here to-day against Mr. H. D. Leveson Gower's XI., and was a fitting climax to the tour for this great batsman, who was the first of the Australians to complete his 2000 runs.

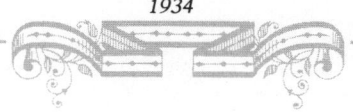

A couple of months ago people were asking what was the matter with Bradman. That marvellous player has answered the question himself, and has shown that he is far greater than ever before.

No one in these days refers to him as a machine. There is in his batting all the old certainty, but interwoven with it is a masterly degree of genius that places him on a pedestal above any batsman, either past or present.

In his last eight innings his total is 1144, and as he was once not out, it gives him an average of 163.4, a complete and satisfactory answer to "what is wrong with Bradman?"

Woodfull led the visitors, who omitted Bromley, Wall, Grimmett and Kippax, Barnett being the 12th man.

The weather was delightfully fine and the wicket in excellent order, so that Woodfull, on winning the toss, did not hesitate to take first use of it.

**Brown and Ponsford opened, but disaster came rather early, as Farnes, who was so successful in his only Test appearance, bowled Brown for three.**

### Rapid Scoring

Apparently Bradman had made up his mind that it was a festival fixture and that the people were entitled to see some spectacular cricket.

When he appeared the onlookers gave him the usual ovation and settled down to enjoy themselves. Don, however, started rather luckily. He was fortunate in snicking Farnes past the leg stump, and then, in the next over, he was almost caught in the slips off Bowes.

The two fast bowlers were making the ball fly high, but were using an off-side field, with only three men on the on-side.

Nichols came on in place of Bowes, and Bradman hooked him and cover-drove him for boundaries in his first over.

The first 50 appeared in 40 minutes, Bradman scoring about three times as fast as Ponsford.

## THE SCORES

### AUSTRALIA v LEVESON-GOWER'S XI.

#### AUSTRALIA—First Innings

| | |
|---|---|
| W. H. PONSFORD, c and b Nichols | 92 |
| W. A. BROWN, b Farnes | 3 |
| D. G. BRADMAN, st Duckworth, b Verity | 132 |
| S. J. McCABE, not out | 69 |
| W. M. WOODFULL, l.b.w., b Verity | 9 |
| L. S. DARLING, b Bowes | 19 |
| A. G. CHIPPERFIELD, not out | 1 |
| Sundries | 12 |
| **Five wickets for** | **337** |

### Quick Changes

Bradman continued to go for the runs and in 40 minutes he ran to 50. Wyatt then made another change in the bowling, Townsend relieving Nichols, but Don greeted the new man by banging him for a couple of fours, bringing up 100 in 70 minutes.

Ponsford seemed to be inspired by Bradman's onslaught and hooked Bowes for a couple of hard fours in one over.

**Townsend did not stay on very long, Verity taking his place. It made no difference to Bradman. In the slow man's first over he hooked him twice for fours and viciously square-cut another to the boundary. Next over he picked Bowes beautifully off his toes sending the ball to the fence, and followed it with a cover-drive for three.**

Nichols relieved Bowes at 140 and Bradman welcomed him as he did the others—a couple of fours—bringing up 150 in 90 minutes.

### 100 in 80 Minutes

It was too much for Wyatt; he brought Farnes on again. It had a quietening effect on Bradman—he only got one four off the over. Next over, amidst tumultous applause, Bradman lifted Verity for four, to reach 100 in 80 minutes. He had hit 18 fours, and celebrated his success by lifting the next ball for six, cover-drove the next for four, and then, just to wind up the over, straight-drove the last like a bullet to the boundary.

Farnes then experienced Bradman's hitting power, for three times Bradman cracked him to the boundary. He followed this by hitting Verity for a four and a single, and then Ponsford, who had been moving along fairly rapidly, reached 50 in 110 minutes.

### 96 in Fours

Then Bradman's innings came to an end. He jumped out, made a big effort to crack Verity for six, missed, and was stumped. He had only been at the wickets 90 minutes and in his amazing 132 was one six and 24 fours.

The scoring slowed down, to what appeared to be a funereal rate after Bradman's departure. In the last over before lunch the 200 appeared in 120 minutes, the players leaving the field at 2 p.m. It was arranged that there would be no tea adjournment and that stumps would be drawn at 6 p.m.

After lunch there were about 14,000 present. Farnes and Nichols took up the attack, and Ponsford square-cut the latter for four. A couple of overs later the Victorian again got two boundaries off Nichols. McCabe was content with occasional singles. Sometimes he was badly beaten and, when six, gave Verity, at square-leg, a fairly easy chance off Farnes, but the Englishman moved too late.

McCabe, by late-cutting Farnes for a couple of fours, brought up 250 in 145 minutes, but next over Ponsford, when eight short of his century, was caught and bowled by Nichols. He had batted 150 minutes and had hit ten fours.

McCabe twice hooked Farnes for four. When 29 McCabe cut Nichols through slips, Wyatt just touching the ball. McCabe then got a four and a three off Farnes, whom Bowes relieved at 284.

Woodfull played a maiden and then McCabe on-drove Nichols for four and late-cut him for a single, becoming the second Australian to reach 2000 runs on the tour.

# OPERATION

## DON BRADMAN

### APPENDIX

## "SOME ANXIETY"

("Sun" Special)

LONDON, Monday.

AN operation for acute appendicitis was performed upon Don Bradman to-day at the hospital of the noted Australian surgeon, Sir Douglas Shields, by his brother, Dr. Clive Shields.

It was stated, after the conclusion of the operation, that Don's condition was as satisfactory as could be expected, though it will not be free from anxiety for a few days, owing to the severity of the attack.

At 10 p.m., a further statement was issued: "Bradman's condition is satisfactory, though still anxious."

At 11.30 it was stated that Bradman's condition was unchanged, and at midnight that he was slightly better, though there was still some anxiety.

The attack began suddenly on Saturday, and became more acute on Sunday.

Bradman will be unable to accompany the remainder of the team when it leaves for Australia next Saturday. The date of his departure cannot be fixed at present.

*"Don"*

### Sudden Illness

(From Arthur Mailey)

Had Bradman not strained a muscle in the Leeds Test, Australia might not have won the Ashes.

His appendicitis symptoms probably would have been obvious weeks ago had they not been camouflaged by the muscular strain, and Don would have shared the operating room with Bromley before the fifth Test.

Bradman was very cheery and apparently in the best of health until

Mrs. Bradman's dash to London.—See Page 11.

the week-end when he became seedy, but did not take it seriously.

This morning, Sir Douglas Shields, at Don's request, examined him and decided that appendicitis was imminent but not necessarily at a critical stage. Nevertheless, an ambulance took him to hospital after lunch and he was operated on at 4 p.m.

# IN RUSH

## London Ticket Mrs. BRADMAN

MRS. DON BRADMAN found to-day that events could move with more rapidity than ever she imagined.

A cable from the surgeon informed her of Don's operation (see story on Page 1), and asked that she make all haste to London. In her anxiety she sought the aid of "The Sun," and in less than two hours she had her steamer ticket, all formalities having been completed.

To catch the Maloja, leaving Perth next Monday, it was at first thought she would need to leave Sydney to-day.

As it was necessary that she motor to her parents' home at Mittagong to secure clothing for the voyage there were but few minutes to spare.

Appeals to the passport office officials and the overseas branch of the Taxation Department met with the most sympathetic response, and, while she was in "The Sun" studio, being photographed for her passport, the initial steps were being made with the preparation of the necessary documents.

Sir Charles Kingsford-Smith, meanwhile apprised of the position, investigated at once the possibility of finding room for Mrs. Bradman in his Centenary air race 'plane on its forthcoming flight to London, but found to his regret that the necessary space could not be made available.

### Eager to Assist

Papers were signed, photographs were printed, and the official forms completed. Rushed to the passport office, the pictures found immediate attention at the hands of officials eager to assist Mrs. Bradman in her anxiety, while at the taxation office the necessary papers were completed with all speed.

It was then discovered that Mrs. Bradman could delay her departure from Sydney until to-morrow and still catch the Maloja, and at Thos. Cook and Sons the bookings were speedily adjusted.

To the bank and back to Cook's was the work of minutes, and a few minutes after noon, less than two hours after Mrs. Bradman had reached "The Sun" office, her taxation clearance had been obtained, her passport and her tickets were in her handbag, and London lay ahead.

Mrs. Bradman later asked "The Sun" to thank all concerned for their courtesy and consideration.

# MEN AND WOMEN OFFER BLOOD

## PROGRESS MUST BE SLOW | NATION IS WATCHING HIS FIGHT

(SPECIAL BEAM SERVICE)

**LONDON, Thursday.**

BRADMAN'S physician, Sir Douglas Shields, told the special representative of "The Telegraph" at 2 p.m. to-day (11 p.m. Sydney time) that the great cricketer's condition had slightly improved.

*At 4.30 p.m. (1.30 a.m. Sydney) this improvement was maintained, and his temperature had fallen.*

His progress, said Sir Douglas, must necessarily be slow for the next day or two, but in the circumstances it was satisfactory.

The whole nation is watching the progress of Bradman in his fight against the complications that followed his operation for appendicitis.

## KING'S PERSONAL INTEREST

Sir Douglas Shields told "The Telegraph" that between 20 and 30 people had called or telephoned the hospital yesterday and to-day offering their blood.

### Royal Sympathy

They included a member of the House of Commons, a prominent footballer, women, newspaper-men, ex-officers who had served with the Australians during the war, Diggers, and others in all walks of life.

**Both friends of Bradman and people of whom he had never heard, hope that the transfusion will be unnecessary, but, in any case, it would be done through the normal hospital services, said Sir Douglas.**

Following the inquiry by the King and Queen before the launching of

H.M. THE KING, who has asked for regular bulletins.

LORD HAILSHAM, who called to see Bradman yesterday

the new Cunarder, the King asked that regular bulletins be sent to Balmoral.

Sir Douglas added that Bradman was delighted to hear his wife had telephoned, but he was not well enough to send a reply.

He appreciates the New South Wales Government's cable offering the use of its services.

"A Lancashire sportsman friend of mine," said Sir Douglas, "also offered to pay Mrs. Bradman's passage.

"The telephone is ringing day and night. A constant stream of callers, and innumerable flowers are arriving."

The inquirers included Lord Hailsham, Sir Herbert Austin, Mr. J. H Thomas (Dominions Secretary), Mr. S. M. Bruce, and Lady Darnley, who sent flowers.

## ANXIOUS MOTHER

### RAY OF THANKFULNESS THAT HELPS HER

BOWRAL, Thursday.—"I am very anxious about Don, particularly as he is so far away," Mrs. Bradman, senior, said to-day.

"The only thing that is helping me to bear up is thankfulness that he became ill before he boarded the boat for Australia, and the knowledge that he is being given the best possible attention," she added.

"On Monday I received a letter from Don, in which he said that it wouldn't be long before he was home.'

# "Don Bradman Has Started To Turn Corner"

## His Physician Gives Best News So Far

## PULSE STRONGER

## Has His Best Night Since The Operation

## IMPROVEMENT LASTS

Mrs. Don Bradman, photographed at Spencer-street station, Melbourne on her way to England.

("Sun" Special)

LONDON, Friday.

SIR DOUGLAS SHIELDS, who is attending Don Bradman, stated late last night that his patient had "started to turn the corner." The latest bulletin issued at 3 o'clock this morning said that Don was having a better night; that his improvement was maintained; and that he was much less restless than on any other night since his operation.

A bulletin issued at 4.30 p.m. yesterday said that Don's temperature had fallen and that the slow rate of improvement was being maintained.

At 8 p.m. it was announced that he was "much the same," but that his pulse was stronger.

Don's progress, said Sir Douglas, must necessarily be slow for the next day or two, but, in the circumstances, it was satisfactory.

Sir Douglas Shields added that between 20 and 30 people had called or telephoned the hospital offering their blood.

They included a member of the House of Commons, a prominent footballer, women, newspaper-men, ex-officers who had served with the

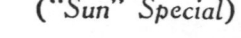

### King's Interest

(Published in the "Daily Mail")

LONDON, Thursday Night.

THE KING has intimated that he wants to know everything about Don Bradman's progress.

Australians during the war, Diggers, and others in all walks of life—both friends of Bradman and people of whom he had never heard.

The famous physician hopes that the transfusion will be unnecessary; but, in any case, it would be done through the normal hospital services.

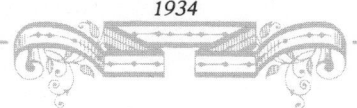

"A Lancashire sportsman friend of mine," said Sir Douglas, "also offered to pay Mrs. Bradman's passage.

"The telephone is ringing day and night. A constant stream of callers and innumerable flowers are arriving."

"That's wonderful news," said Mr. Bradman, sen., when "The Sun" telephoned Sir Douglas Shield's statement to him at Bowral this morning.

"His mother has been terribly worried, and this is the best tidings she has received for years. We will cable Don immediately—I suppose a message addressed care of Sir Douglas Shields would find him?"

"The Sun" suggested that "Don Bradman, London," would be the only address the Post Office would require.

# SHE SMILED

## Good News of Don

## "SUN'S" WIRE

ADELAIDE, Friday.

Holding a telegram from "The Sun," Sydney, relaying the good news about Bradman's improvement in health, which she received at 8 a.m. on the Melbourne express to-day, Mrs. Bradman was smiling happily as she arrived in Adelaide.

She left an hour later in the East-West express, on the last stage of her dash to catch the Maloja for England.

As soon as she reached the platform she showed the telegram to the secretary of the Board of Control (Mr. Jeanes) and Mr. H. W. Hodgetts, her husband's friend and business associate.

"I hope to bring Don back by December," she said, as she boarded the express, still carrying the telegram in her hand.

As the train gathered speed, an elderly woman, a stranger to Mrs. Bradman, ran up to her with a bunch of yellow flowers, and said, "Good luck to you, my dear."

The Australian Test team, minus Don Bradman, leaves for home.

## "OH, DON!"

### Bradmans Re-united

**(Published in the "Daily Mail")**

LONDON, Sunday.

Don. Bradman and his wife were happily reunited at the Lord Warden Hotel at Dover, after Mrs. Bradman had crossed the Channel in a gale, writes Tom Clarke.

Don. motored to the Lord Warden from London, and waited in a reserved room until the manager led his wife to the door, through which she rushed with a cry, "Oh, Don!"

A happy "four-in-hand" tea party followed.

Mrs. Bradman chatted vivaciously about her journey, and later they escaped secretly through the kitchen and drove off in a big car to a secret destination in the country.

JOYFUL REUNION.— An exclusive "Daily Mail" photograph of Mrs. Don Bradman with her husband at Dover. This was the happy ending to her 13,000-miles journey from Australia, whence she was called five weeks ago.

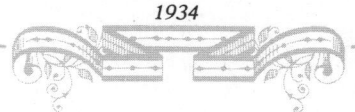

Don and Jessie Bradman spent a few happy days at Perth, Scotland, with Mr. and Mrs. A. K. Bell. A. K. was the head of the firm renowned for the whisky bearing his name.

Don and Jessie Bradman photographed at Victoria Station, London, on their departure for Australia.

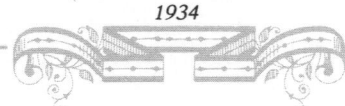

Don and Jessie on arrival at Adelaide from England.

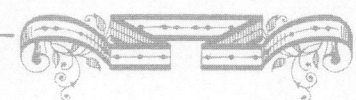

# THE
# BRADMAN
## *Albums*

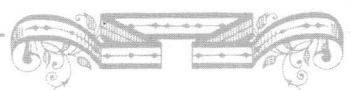

Don Bradman *c.* 1938

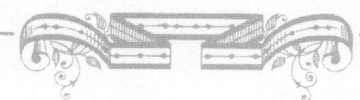

# THE
# BRADMAN
## *Albums*

SELECTIONS FROM
SIR DONALD BRADMAN'S
OFFICIAL COLLECTION

### VOLUME 2
1935–1949

WITH AN INTRODUCTION BY
SIR DONALD BRADMAN, A.C.

Macdonald
Queen Anne Press

A *Queen Anne Press* BOOK

© Copyright Introduction, diary extracts and commentaries by Sir Donald Bradman,
Weldons Pty Limited 1987
© Copyright Design Weldons Pty Limited 1987
First published in Great Britain in 1988 by
Queen Anne Press, a division of
Macdonald & Co (Publishers) Ltd
3rd Floor, Greater London House, Hampstead Road, London NW1 7QX

A BPCC plc Company

Produced in Australia by Rigby Publishers
a division of Weldons Pty Limited, Sydney, Australia

Designer   Susan Kinealy

Assembly artist   Catherine Martin

Calligraphy   Margrit Eisermann

Endpapers   Margo Snape

Illustration on slip case   Painting of Donald Bradman by Ivor Hele, *c.* 1946

**British Library Cataloguing-in-Publication Data**

Bradman, Sir Donald
 The Bradman albums
 1. Bradman, Sir Donald
 2. Cricket players — Australia — Biography
 I. Title
 796.35'8'0924 GV915.B7

ISBN 0-356-15411-4

Typeset by Savage Type, Brisbane, Australia.
Printed and bound in Australia by Griffin Press Limited, Adelaide.

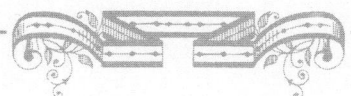

# Contents

## VOLUME 2

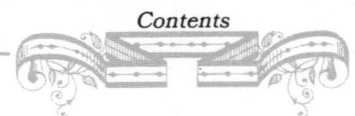

## *Plates*

*Facing pages listed*

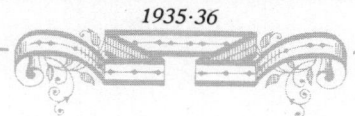

# *1935-36 Season*

**F**ollowing the disastrous end to the 1934 tour of England, my medical adviser said I should not undertake the strenuous tour to South Africa with the Australian team in 1935.

Accepting this advice, I was able to regain health and cricket form in the quieter atmosphere of Sheffield Shield games.

I was also enabled to settle down in my adopted State and pick up the threads of stock and share broking, an occupation which was completely new to me. I badly wanted to follow a business career having no connection with sport and this appeared to be the opportunity I sought.

By the end of the season I felt reasonably sure that the move to South Australia had permanently determined my future activities.

*Don Bradman*

## — SEASON 1935-36 —

| TITLE | GAMES | | SCORES | |
|---|---|---|---|---|
| Second Class | Kensington I | Kensington II | 27 | n.o. |
| | South Australia | Newcastle | 46 | C. |
| | S.A.C.A. | Berri and District | 155 | C. |
| | - | Renmark and District | 81 | St. |
| | Kensington | Clare and District | 5 | C. |
| | " | Clare | 112 | B. |
| | " | Martindale and District | 106 | C. |
| First Grade | " | Adelaide | 60 | C. |
| | " | Colts | 29 | L.B.W. |
| | " | Glenelg | 18 | C. |
| | " | " | 17 | C. |
| | " | East Torrens | 62 | C. |
| | " | Port Adelaide | 101 | L.B.W. |
| | " | " | 0 | B. |
| | " | " | 63 | C. |
| | " | " | 194 | C. |
| | " | Prospect | 69 | B. |
| | " | University | 80 | C. |
| | " | Sturt | 118 | C. |
| First Class | South Australia | M.C.C. | 15 | L.B.W. |
| | " | " | 50 | L.B.W. |
| | " | Tasmania | 369 | C. |
| Sheffield Shield | " | New South Wales | 117 | C. |
| | " | " " | 0 | C. |
| | " | Queensland | 233 | C. |
| | " | " | 31 | C. |
| | " | Victoria | 357 | C. |
| | " | " | 1 | C. |
| | | Total runs | 2516 | |

## — SUMMARY —

AVERAGES -

| | Innings | N O's | H S | Runs | Average |
|---|---|---|---|---|---|
| Sheffield Shield | 6 | 0 | 357 | 739 | 123·1 |
| Other First Class | 3 | 0 | 369 | 434 | 144·6 |
| All First Class | 9 | 0 | 369 | 1173 | 130·3 |
| Other Second Class | 7 | 1 | 155 | 532 | 88·6 |
| First Grade | 12 | 0 | 194 | 811 | 67·5 |
| All Second Class | 19 | 1 | 194 | 1343 | 74·6 |
| All Matches | 28 | 1 | 369 | 2516 | 93·1 |

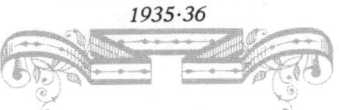

Don and Jessie Bradman photographed in Park Road, Kensington Park outside Harry Hodgett's home.

# BRADMAN OUT

### HEALTH IS REASON

### TO SOUTH AFRICA

### NEXT TOURING SIDE

ADELAIDE, Friday.

DON BRADMAN will not go to South Africa.

His announcement to-day, a little over 24 hours before the selection of the team, that he was unavailable for the tour, will be received with regret by all cricket enthusiasts.

It was anticipated that Bradman would have recovered sufficiently from his illness, and few doubts of his fitness were raised. To-day Bradman said that he had had a very bad time with his health in the last couple of years, and had received definite advice that he was to follow a set programme to make a complete recovery.

This advice could not be ignored, and because of it he would not undertake a strenuous tour. He expressed great regret that he was not going, but said that the rest would ensure his fitness for the next series against the Englishmen.

This recalls a statement made by a well-known English critic, who, commenting on Bradman's health, said that there was a chance of his not going to South Africa. "Perhaps he will rest and await the tour by the next English side," he said. "What a dreadful prospect for England!"

Bradman said that the announcement that he was not to make the tour did not mean that he was not going to play cricket next season. He would play in the Sheffield Shield matches.

## IS WISE

### Will Not Retire

(By A. G. Moyes)

This afternoon I received a wire from Don Bradman informing me that he was officially notifying the Board, most regretfully, that he could not make the trip.

Since Don returned from England, he has been taking things very quietly at Mittagong and has just returned to Adelaide to start his new career with Harry Hodgett, one of the Board members.

When in Sydney he told me that it was extremely unlikely that he would go.

From every point of view, the decision is probably wise.

Don made perfectly clear that this does not indicate any intention of retiring from cricket. He told me that he wanted at least one more trip to England. His unavailability means, of course, that the Board will have to find a captain.

At first glance it would appear that either Oldfield, who led New South Wales, or Ebeling, who captained Victoria, would be chosen; but Victor Richardson, who is a selector, may come into the scheme of things.

## South Australian Cricket Association

INCORPORATED

TELEGRAMS AND CABLES:
"OVAL" ADELAIDE
TELEPHONES
OFFICE: CENT IIII (2 LINES)
OVAL: CENT. 771
SECRETARY:
W. H. JEANES

MANUFACTURES BUILDING
14 PIRIE STREET.
ADELAIDE

19th September, 1935.

Mr. D.G. Bradman,
C/o Messrs. H.W. Hodgetts & Co.,
Cowra Chambers,
Grenfell Street,
ADELAIDE.

Dear Sir,

I have pleasure in advising that at the meeting of the Cricket Committee held last evening, you were appointed with Mr. H.N. Bridgman and Dr. C. E. Dolling to the Interstate Selection Committee for the ensuing season.

The Committee will be gratified if you will accept this appointment.

Yours faithfully,

Secretary.

WHJ/JF.

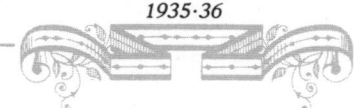

# CRICKET CLUBS PREPARE
## FOR OPENING OF SEASON

### Bradman Leads South Australian Team For First Time

## DISTRICT MATCHES BEGIN NEXT SATURDAY

#### By LONG-ON

In preparation for the first series of cricket matches for the 1935-36 season, which will begin next Saturday, district clubs conducted match practice last Saturday.

D. G. Bradman, for the first time, played in and led a South Australian club team when he captained a Kensington team against an eleven also chosen from the club.

In nearly all the matches the batsmen played under a time limit, so that as many as possible should have an opportunity for practice.

The wickets were generally good and the bowlers did not receive the assistance they have often had from damp pitches in pre-season games. Interesting features of the practices were West Torrens's indication of all-round form against a Prince Alfred College team, Young and Ridings showing good form with the bat, and Fails and Sincock taking wickets cheaply. Batting promise was shown by Whittard, a young Port Pirie batsman playing with Prospect; the fact that every man who batted for Kensington A (Bradman's side) retired voluntarily, and the fine bowling by McKay and Wright in the same match; an unfinished score by Stokes, of St. Peter's College, who top-scored in the match between the college and East Torrens; good bowling by R. and L. B. Power, for Glenelg; V. Y. Richardson's bright batting, and Rossiter's slow bowling at Unley.

Owing to the fact that a suitable ground was not available, Colts did not practice.

# "GREATEST EVER"

### Wilfred Rhodes Pays Fine Tribute To Bradman

## "REAL CRICKET"

From Our Special Representative.— By Air Mail

**LONDON, June 8.**

THE greatest batsman ever seen in the world of cricket. That is how Wilfred Rhodes, writing in the London "Sunday Chronicle," describes Don Bradman.

Bradman is an example of Test match temperament par excellence, he says. His confidence is supreme. No matter how well you bowl at him he seems to be able to place the ball just where he likes.

He makes the bowling suit his batting—which is real cricket and the right spirit of cricket.

"He follows in the footsteps of that other great Australian," Rhodes continues, "Victor Trumper, who once told me that his idea was to hit the first ball he got for four. Bradman isn't afraid of trying that game either."

He goes on to recall Bradman's opening, with two fours, from the first two balls bowled him by Bowes in the Leeds Test last year. "That's what you call confidence."

Lots of people, particularly Australians, he says, do not agree with him that Bradman is the greatest batsman ever.

#### Trumper Compared

"Most 'Aussies' stand firm for Trumper, with his lovely dashing style," he goes on. "They say that Bradman has never had to face such bowlers as the giants of the old days.

"It is certainly interesting to surmise what would have happened had Bradman been up against Foster with his fast left-handers; Barnes, with the new ball, and Douglas as first change.

"But I still think that Bradman would have been head and shoulders above Trumper.

"It would have been a great sight to see Bradman matching his eye and his skill against Sid Barnes's clever bowling—the greatest batsman and the greatest bowler."

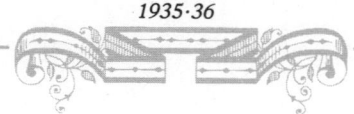

# South Australia v M.C.C.

SOUTH AUSTRALIA v M.C.C. TEAM, at Adelaide, 8, 9, 11 and 12 November 1935.

| | | |
|---|---|---|
| South Australia | - First Innings | 322 |
| | - Second Innings | 187 |
| M.C.C. Team | - First Innings | 371 |
| | - Second Innings | 174 |
| | South Australia lost by 36 runs. | |

| | | |
|---|---|---|
| DON BRADMAN | - lbw. b. J.M. Sims | 15 |
| (Captain) | - lbw. b. J.H. Parks | 50 |

In his first match for South Australia, DON BRADMAN batted like a man who had had no first-class practice for over a year.

In the first innings, going in after lunch on the second day at 64 for 1, he was obviously quite out of touch, but was gradually beginning to time the ball properly once more, when he was lbw. to a top-spinner at 90 for 2; he batted for twenty-three minutes.

South Australia were set to make 224 to win on the last day.

Bradman went in at 29 for 1, after lunch, and, after being completely beaten by his first ball from J.M. Sims, made a painstaking effort to get these runs and to recover his form and confidence. At tea-time, South Australia still wanted 120, in one and three-quarter hours, with six wickets in hand, including that of Bradman, 35 not out; he completed his 50 after an hour and forty-four minutes, but was lbw. next over. His 50, in one and three-quarter hours, was the top score.

BACK ROW   F. A. Ward, E. J. R. Moyle, H. M. Thompson, R. G. Williams, R. A. Parker, A. G. Shepherd.
FRONT ROW   F. H. Collins, C. W. Walker, D. G. Bradman, C. L. Badcock, A. J. Ryan, M. G. Waite.

# England V. South Australia Cricket Begins Today

## Bright Cricket Likely In Adelaide Oval Match

### By LONG ON

D. G. Bradman (S.A. Captain)

E. R. T. Holmes (M.C.C. Captain)

AT NOON today South Australia will begin a four day match against the M.C.C. team of English cricketers. The game should attract a large attendance for from all reports and observation the visiting players are likely to provide the type of cricket which delights the crowd. If they do, it should be a welcome and refreshing change after the dour struggles into which Test cricket seems to have developed.

The Englishmen are not a Test team— judged on Australia-England standards, at least (for they are to play Test matches in New Zealand)—and they are the first to admit it, but they point out that the spare parts which comprise the side may mould themselves into at least the basis of a very formidable Test team by the time the present tour is finished.

Breezy, delightful personalities at the wicket and away from it, their popularity with Australian crowds is assured, and all that remains for them to do is to produce some of the cricket ability their performances in England show them to possess.

MUCH has already been written about the English team, and there is no doubt that with sound opening batsmen such as Parks and Barber—Parks scored 1,633 runs at an average of 33.32, and Barber 2,147 at 42.09 (highest score 255) in the last English season—the side should have more good starts than failures. With that pair to wear down the opening attack and other fine batsmen such as Holmes (only 75 runs short of 2,000 last season), Smith (2,175), Hardstaff, Mitchell-Innes, and Langridge, to follow opposing bowlers will have much food for deep thought.

The bowlers are not perhaps as convincing, although Sims and Langridge each took more than 100 wickets in the last English season, and Read only three fewer than that total. These three bowlers are the mainstays of the side, Sims with his slows, Langridge's left-arm deliveries, and Read with his pace. They are supported by Baxter, who finished second to G. O. Allen in the English bowling averages. He took 42 wickets at an average cost of 13.09 Langridge took his 102 wickets at 19.67, and Sims's 131 cost 20.87 each. Read's figures were 97 wickets at an average cost of 22.16.

Holmes (55 at an average of 31.90) is also a change bowler, and Mitchell-Innes and Lyttelton also occasionally take the ball.

#### Fast Bowler In Action

Adelaide cricket-lovers will almost certainly see Read in action, for he did not play against Western Australia, and the bowling of this man, who, it is declared, is only a little slower than Larwood, will probably be one of the attractive features of the match. He possesses an energetic rather than a smooth, effortless run up to the wicket, but his whole action and delivery shout keenness and enthusiasm.

South Australia should be able to give the Englishmen a harder fight than did Western Australia in the drawn game in Perth, although the Western Australians fared unexpectedly well.

South Australia has a strong batting side. Assuming that one of the batsmen is made twelfth man, it will still have men with century-making possibilities in first-class cricket down to No. 6, and several of those who will follow are capable of making respectable scores, notably Williams, Collins, and Walker.

Badcock and Ryan, who have experience together with the Adelaide Club, although they are now separated in district cricket, will open the innings, and Bradman, Parker, and Moyle will follow probably in that order These five constitute a very powerful batting section and, even against the Englishmen, should be good for many runs.

The bowling, too, is not so well on examination, as might appear first glance. Of course, there is Grimmett, and the experience of L and Wall will also be missed, but Williams and Thompson have the appearance of a very capable opening pair with Collins to carry on the work with the ball before it gets too many "whiskers." Ward, Waite and Ryan will take over the attack from this stage.

Play will begin at noon today.

Following are the opposing teams in probable batting order:—

| M.C.C. TEAM | SOUTH AUSTRALIA |
|---|---|
| J. Parks | C. L. Badcock |
| W. Barber | A. J. Ryan |
| J. Hardstaff | D. G. Bradman (captain) |
| D. Smith | |
| N. S. Mitchell-Innes | R. A. Parker |
| | E. J. R. Moyle |
| C. J. Lyttelton | M. G. Waite |
| James Langridge | R. G. Williams |
| J. Sims | F. H. Collins |
| A. G. Powell | C. W. Walker |
| A. D. Baxter | H. M. Thompson |
| H. D. Read | F. Ward |
| S. C. Griffith | A. G. Shepherd |
| E. R. T. Holmes (captain) | |

# SATISFACTORY DAY FOR
## SOUTH AUSTRALIA

### Five Wickets In Hand And Only 171 Behind M.C.C. Total

### HAT-TRICK TO M. G. WAITE

#### By LONG ON

Although Bradman failed to score heavily, South Australia had reason to be satisfied with the play in the cricket match against the M.C.C. team at the Adelaide Oval on Saturday. With five wickets in hand it is 171 runs behind the Englishmen's total.

Yesterday's steady rain should have little effect on the wicket, which is wholly covered while not in use, but, unless the weather is fine today, it may have some effect in slowing up the outfield. England's innings was closed before lunch on Saturday, chiefly as the result of another burst of brilliant bowling by Waite, who achieved the rare distinction of performing the hat-trick in a first-class match. There is no available record of a similar feat being performed by a South Australian at the Adelaide Oval. The last hat-trick by a member of the South Australian team in a first-class match was by Grimmett against Queensland in Brisbane in February, 1929.

Waite took the wickets of Lyttelton and Baxter with the seventh and last deliveries of one over and clean bowled Read, the last man in, with the first ball of his next over.

GOOD FORM was shown by E. J. R. Moyle (South Australia) after tea in the match against the M.C.C. team at the Adelaide Oval on Saturday. He is shown pulling a ball from Sims to leg.

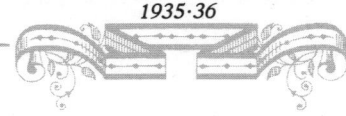
Apart from Lyttelton's powerful hitting—he scored 25 runs in 25 minutes—there was little of note in the M.C.C. batting on Saturday. Ward bowled well for South Australia and deserved better figures than four for 127, his analysis being completely overshadowed by Waite's five for 42.

South Australia opened, a little unexpectedly, with Parker as Badcock's partner, but the decision was justified by results, for the pair gave the side a good start of 64 runs. Bradman, who went in at the fall of the first wicket, was settling down into something like his old-time form, after a not very convincing start, when he was out to an over-spinner. Badcock played a sound, typical innings; Moyle, after tea, was most dashing, and Waite and Williams have already added nearly 40 runs for the sixth wicket.

Parker's innings, however, was one of the most pleasing features of the South Australian innings. He attacked the bowling with surprising confidence and played many fine shots.

### English Bowling

Of the English bowlers Sims stood out. Once he struck a length he seemed always likely to get wickets, and although he finished with only two for 85, he bowled much better than those figures indicate. He possesses the ability to make the ball whip off the pitch and also follows it in occasionally in an endeavor to take possible caught-and-bowled opportunities. Langridge, like most left-arm bowlers, drops the ball on the proverbial three-pence, and, as his figures show—10 overs for 8 runs and two wickets—none of the batsmen felt inclined to take liberties.

Read possesses an extraordinarily energetic run up to the wicket, but although he was undoubtedly fast, he apparently troubled none of the South Australians. Baxter was well above medium pace and kept an excellent length. Human was the outstanding fieldsman.

### Wickets Fall Quickly

Williams and Collins resumed bowling to Langridge (11) and Sims (1) with the score at five for 314. Williams bowled only one over from the southern end and then transferred to the opposite creases, Ward taking up the attack with him. The Adelaide slow bowler was inclined to overpitch his deliveries and Langridge off-drove one full toss to the fence. Sims, who was a batsman of ability before he neglected that branch of the game in order to develop his bowling, gave Langridge sound support. In fact, Langridge was the first to go, being bowled by Ward.

Lyttelton, son of Lord Cobham (president of the M.C.C.), filled the vacancy and before long gave an indication of his hitting ability by on-driving Ward for four. In the next over he repeated the stroke and the score passed 350 in 342 minutes, the last 50 having taken 57 minutes.

Waite's figures suffered when he was brought on to relieve Ward. One ball was pulled high and hard to the square leg fence by Lyttelton, and the next was powerfully off-driven for another four.

A misunderstanding left both batsmen in the middle of the pitch, and Sims made the sacrifice to enable the vice-captain to go on, but he did not continue long, for one run later he was caught at the wicket. Waite bowled Baxter first ball, and Read, the last man came in.

### Waite's Hat Trick

Baxter was dismissed with the last ball of Waite's over, but as both batsmen weathered Collins's over, Waite still had a chance to get the hat trick. Whipping in his fast ball Waite clean bowled Read with the first ball of his next over, thus achieving his objective and finishing off the innings.

The batting times of Sims and Lyttelton provided a striking contrast Sims scored 12 runs in 62 minutes, and Lyttelton 25 in 25 minutes—more than twice as many runs in less than half the time.

### Baxter's Leg Field

South Australia began its innings with Badcock and Parker, and they faced an over each from Baxter and Read without scoring before the luncheon adjournment was taken. Baxter bowled with a pronounced leg field. He had a fine leg, short fine leg, extra short fine leg, a foreward square leg (short) and mid-on in close. In addition he had one slip, deep and very fine, the wicketkeeper (Powell) standing between and almost within reach of slip and short fine leg.

South Australia's first runs were scored off the first ball after lunch, Badcock getting Baxter away in front of slips for two. Parker hit the first four of the innings, pulling a ball from Parks, who bowled an over to permit Baxter and Read to change ends, to the square-led fence.

Read seemed to have few real terrors for the opening pair, for Badcock on-drove him to a deserted deep field for four (all run), and then beautifully late cut him to the fence.

Parker was venturesome. He took the risk of pulling a ball pitched on the wicket by Baxter high to square-leg, rather close to Human, who was running from fine leg. The ball pitched a few yards short of the fence, and rolled up to it. Badcock, still relishing Read's deliveries, slammed a short-pitched ball to the fence behind square-leg. In half an hour after lunch 44 runs were scored—a bright opening.

Sims, the slow bowler, took Baxter's end, and did not strike a length until the end of his over, but, though he was hit hard, fine fielding by Human at square-leg, saved two or three potential boundary shots. South Australia's first 50 was reached in 43 minutes.

### Parker Dismissed

Parker reached 30 as the result of confident batting, but he spent one or two awkward moments against Sims in one over from the slow bowler, and was brilliantly caught and bowled one-handed off the seventh ball. He had batted 62 minutes and hit two fours. With Badcock, he had given the side a good start of 64 runs.

Bradman's entry was the signal for a great outburst of enthusiasm from the crowd, and hand-clapping from the Englishmen. Some minutes elapsed before Bradman opened his score—a single a few yards from the bat towards square-leg—but there was no doubt about a cover-drive to the fence and a straight drive for three, both off Baxter's fast-medium deliveries. Badcock, when 39, was nearly snapped up by Sims off the latter's bowling. The ball struck the ground only inches in front of Sims's hand, as he dived for the catch.

### Bradman Out L.b.w.

Just when Bradman looked like making runs—he had just hooked a beautiful four off the slow bowler—he was out leg-before. He had scored 15 of the 26 runs added for the second wicket.

Moyle was not at ease against Sims's bowling, and it was only by a hairsbreadth that he missed being caught and bowled by Read. He was 18 minutes at the wickets before he opened his score with two for a pushed drive.

The total reached 101 in 106 minutes (the last 50 in 63 minutes), and a minute later Badcock was caught behind the wicket off Read. He hit three fours.

At the tea adjournment the score was three for 101, Moyle being 5 and Ryan the next man in. On the resumption, Moyle batted with much greater confidence, pulling a ball from Sims to the square-leg fence and cutting the same bowler for four more in his next over. The next ball he straight drove for three, and reached the twenties. Ryan was beginning stolidly, leaving the aggression to Moyle, who played the role of chief attacker well. He drove a ball from Sims straight to the sight screen, and was in the thirties in good time.

### Good Length Bowling

With the score at 137 Langridge bowled for the first time, one run being scored off his first over, and none off his second. The scoring rate was practically motionless for some time. Runs scored by Ryan were ironically cheered by a section of the crowd. While Moyle took the score past 150 in as many minutes, the last 50 having taken 44 minutes.

Ryan patiently played ball after ball from Langridge, and then essayed a pull, but Hardstaff, at square leg, leapt into the air and held a one-handed catch. Ryan's 13 runs had occupied 50 minutes.

Waite lost no time in setting about his work, smartly on-driving Parks for four and turning him neatly to leg for two, but he lost Moyle when Langridge accepted a simple chance off his own bowling. The left-arm bowler had taken two wickets for four runs off five overs. Moyle's innings, unimpressive before tea, had been most entertaining since the adjournment. His 39 runs had occupied 77 minutes, and he hit three fours. Waite reached 20 with a late cut for two off Sims, and Williams emulated the shot, but sent the ball to the boundary.

With five minutes to play the score was 197. Three more runs and Lyttelton would be entitled to call for the new ball and would be able to use his fast bowlers. Two or three exciting short singles brought the score to 200 in 213 minutes, the last 50 having taken 53 minutes. The new ball was not used, although Read bowled the last over, and Waite and Williams were still together at stumps.

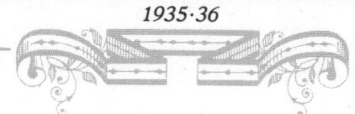

# South Australia v New South Wales

<u>SOUTH AUSTRALIA v NEW SOUTH WALES</u>, at Adelaide, 18, 19, 20 and 21 December 1935.

South Australia    - First Innings      575
                       - Second Innings    -

New South Wales   - First Innings      351
                       - Second Innings   219

        South Australia won by an innings and 5 runs.

<u>DON BRADMAN</u>    - c. and b. R.H. Robinson      117
   (Captain)

On his first appearance in a Sheffield Shield match, DON BRADMAN had made a century for New South Wales v. South Australia, and now, on his first appearance in a Shield match for South Australia, he made another.    He went in after lunch on the first day, at 139 for 1, and, although rather sedate, he showed that he was now much nearer his normal form and fitness.    He completed 50 in an hour and seven minutes, and 100 in two hours eleven minutes.    He was out at 349 for 3 after a chanceless innings of two hours thirty-eight minutes which included seven fours.    His late-cutting was perhaps the best feature of an innings in which he was content to take runs as they came rather than dominate the bowlers.    This was his first century for a side of which he was Captain.

## SHEFFIELD SHIELD COMPETITION
### 1935/36

BACK ROW    F. H. Collins, F. A. Ward, T. W. Wall, R. G. Williams, T. R. O'Connell, E. J. R. Moyle, A. F. Richter.
CENTRE ROW    R. A. Parker, C. W. Walker, D. G. Bradman (Captain), A. J. Ryan, M. G. Waite.
FRONT ROW:    R. A. Hamence, C. L. Badcock.

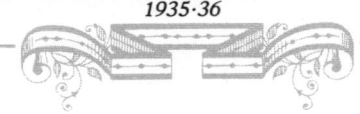

# BRADMAN INSPIRES S.A. TEAM

### By CLEM HILL, the famous Test Cricketer

**South Australia has a wonderful chance of winning the Sheffield Shield this season. Our State has the players, most of them young, and likely to improve. My judgment is based on the matches this season against the Marylebone and New South Wales' teams.**

WHAT is the reason for such optimism? First, there is the influence of Don Bradman. That influence on the young South Australian side has been most pronounced. With his wonderful cricket brain he has imparted a tremendous amount of confidence to the players. Keen and enthusiastic in everything he does, Bradman carries his men with him. His enthusiasm is contagious. His personality is such that the younger players, in whom he has taken an unusually deep interest, regard him as a great leader, and the consequence is that there is never any slackening.

In all my experience I have never seen a South Australian team to be so much on their toes as was the case in the match ended today. Evidently the players were told by Bradman to be on the watch and on the move all the time. It was not only the fact that Bradman was in the side as a batsman; it was also his activity in the field which counted in the players', determination to win.

### RUNNING BETWEEN WICKETS

The South Australian batsmen learnt something, too. The first thing we saw was the improvement in running between the wickets. When Bradman went in Badcock and Parker were content with an easy one when by running fast two could have been scored. They attempted few short singles.

The advent of Bradman altered all that. He had Badcock on his toes, and in half an hour the former Tasmanian had learnt a lesson on how to make runs. In that half hour Badcock had developed from a slow runner between the wickets into a really fast man.

# CLEM HILL ON BRADMAN

Another thing Bradman has done is to stop the silly shots we used to see young players trying. They tried to put the ball around the corner for singles. Such shots were impossible, but the boys tried them.

While he has strengthened the batting, he has tightened up the fielding. Every player has been on his toes, and every one looks the part.

So much for the influence of Bradman on the team.

Another reason for my optimism in expecting South Australia to do well in the Shield matches is the fact that our State has the batsmen. Parker and Moyle are very promising young men, especially Parker. He will go a long way, because he has the strokes and he has confidence in his own ability. He uses his feet well, and his wrist work is excellent.

### CRUDENESS DISAPPEARING

When he first started last year, Moyle was rather crude, but his experience in first-class cricket has improved him out of all knowledge. The crudeness is gradually disappearing, and he is adding polish to his batting. This boy is not afraid to use his feet to a slow bowler, and when he does use his feet, it is not to play the ball, but to hit it. Some of his shots off the Sydney slow bowlers passed mid-off like a shot out of a gun.

And there is Badcock. If the opportunity offers he is likely to be one of the opening batsmen for Australia. He is the man to fill the position. His defence is sound, he has the right temperament, and he can produce strokes all round the wicket. He has improved, and is still improving.

Wall bowled very well. He has had little play in the last two years, and this match will top him up, and soon he will not be far off Tim Wall at his best. South Australia missed Grimmett, but Ward and Waite, who are carrying on in his absence, bowled well without giving runs away with rubbish.

### AN IMPROVED BATSMAN

We have Walker, the wicketkeeper. There is no need for me to say anything about his ability. His 'keeping is as good as ever, and his batting has improved. O'Connell, a left-hander, shaped most confidently at his first appearance in first-class cricket. He was cool, and with a straight bat gave promise of better things. The six he hit off Howell between mid-off and square-leg was a real Nitschke shot. O'Connell shows great promise as a fast medium bowler.

With all these young players developing, I think I am justified in forecasting that South Australia will play a prominent part in the destiny of the Shield this year.

I must not omit reference to Robinson. I was very impressed with this Newcastle boy's batting. A number of his shots were reminiscent of Alan Kippax, and I would not be surprised to learn that he had studied that great Sydney batsman. There is nothing surer than that Robinson will represent Australia.

Don Bradman's South Australian Cricket Association blazer, *c. 1936*.

Adelaide Oval, from the River end, 1986.

# South Australia v Queensland

SOUTH AUSTRALIA v QUEENSLAND, at Adelaide,
24, 26, 27 and 28 December 1935.

| South Australia | - First Innings | 642 for 8 wickets dec. |
| | - Second Innings | - |
| Queensland | - First Innings | 127 |
| | - Second Innings | 289 |

South Australia won by an innings and 226 runs.

DON BRADMAN — c. D. Tallon  b. R.M. Levy          233
  (Captain)

DON BRADMAN returned to his most brilliant form in making his third successive double-century against Queensland.

He went in at 32 for 1, before lunch on the first day, and reached 50 in sixty-five minutes; he ran to his century in one and three-quarter hours, and, going from 150 to 200 in fourteen minutes, completed 200 in two hours forty-eight minutes.    Being 200 at tea-time, he was finally caught at the wicket after batting for three hours eleven minutes; he hit a six and twenty-eight fours, and was out at 374 for 3.

This was the highest score ever made in matches between South Australia and Queensland, and in making double-centuries in three successive innings off the bowling of one State, Bradman achieved something which no one else had ever done.

Don Bradman and C. L. Badcock going out to bat in Adelaide.

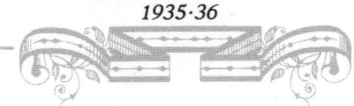

# South Australia v Victoria

SOUTH AUSTRALIA v VICTORIA, at Melbourne,
1, 2, 3 and 4 January 1936.

| South Australia | - First Innings | 569 |
| | - Second Innings | - |
| Victoria | - First Innings | 313 |
| | - Second Innings | 250 for 5 wickets |
| | Drawn. | |

| DON BRADMAN | - c. S. Quin  b. E.H. Bromley | 357 |
| (Captain) | | |

DON BRADMAN went to the wicket early on the first day, at 8 for 1, and when 17 completed 5,000 runs in Sheffield Shield matches;  this was his fifty-fifth innings in Shield matches.

His 50 was completed before lunch in seventy minutes, and his century took only two hours thirty-two minutes.     Going rather faster thereafter, he reached 200 in four hours twenty-seven minutes, and at the close of play was 229 not out, after batting for five hours ten minutes.     Next morning he batted very brilliantly;  after reaching 300 in two minutes under six and a half hours, he hit out ferociously, and completed his century before lunch in ninety-seven minutes,  being 338 at lunchtime;  then, after batting for a minute over seven hours,  he threw his wicket away, being caught near square-leg by the wicket-keeper off a skier.     The score was 510 for 8 when he was out.     His innings included forty fours.

This was the fifth treble-century of his career;  also the fifty-fourth century of his career.

The forty fours and 160 runs he scored in boundaries in this innings were records for South Australia.

This was the highest score ever made in Sheffield Shield cricket against Victoria.

## Score Book

### SOUTH AUSTRALIA—First Innings

| | Runs. | Min. | 4's. |
|---|---|---|---|
| R. A. Parker, c Rigg, b Welch .. .. .. .. .. | 63 | 187 | 6 |
| A. J. Ryan, run out .. | 7 | 15 | 0 |
| D. G. Bradman, c Quin, b Bromley .. .. .. .. .. | 357 | 424 | 40 |
| E. J. Moyle, c Quin, b Welch .. .. .. .. .. .. | 9 | 22 | 1 |
| M. G. Waite, b Gregory | 24 | 50 | 0 |
| A. Richter, c Smith, b Welch .. .. .. .. .. .. | 7 | 35 | 1 |
| T. O'Connell, c Quin, b Plant .. .. .. .. .. .. | 22 | 89 | 3 |
| C. W. Walker, lbw, b Welch .. .. .. .. .. .. | 8 | 27 | 0 |
| F. H. Collins, not out .. | 37 | 70 | 3 |
| F. Ward, stpd. Quin, b Welch .. .. .. .. .. .. | 29 | 45 | 5 |
| T. W. Wall, lbw, b Smith | 0 | 3 | 0 |
| Byes 4, no-balls 2 .. .. | 6 | | |
| | — | — | — |
| Total .. .. .. .. | 569 | 492 | 59 |

Fall: 8, 186, 211, 276, 323, 421, 471, 510, 564, 569.

#### BOWLING

| | Overs. | Mdns. | Runs. | Wkts. |
|---|---|---|---|---|
| Ebeling .. .. .. .. | 4 | 1 | 9 | 0 |
| V. Nagel .. .. .. | 25 | 5 | 85 | 0 |
| Plant .. .. .. .. | 27 | 2 | 86 | 1 |
| Smith .. .. .. .. | 14.1 | 2 | 56 | 1 |
| Welch .. .. .. .. | 25 | 1 | 155 | 5 |
| Gregory .. .. .. | 19 | 1 | 101 | 1 |
| Bromley .. .. .. | 14 | 2 | 71 | 1 |

Nagel bowled two no-balls.

### VICTORIA—First Innings

| | Runs. | Min. | 4's. |
|---|---|---|---|
| K. Rigg, lbw, b Wall .. | 0 | 1 | 0 |
| S. Quin, b Ryan .. .. .. | 52 | 89 | 6 |
| I. Lee, c and b Waite .. | 50 | 148 | 2 |
| V. Nagel, stpd. Walker, b Ward .. .. .. .. .. | 0 | 11 | 0 |
| E. Bromley, c Waite, b Ryan .. .. .. .. .. .. | 1 | 2 | 0 |
| J. Scaife, b Wall .. .. .. | 48 | 146 | 3 |
| J. Plant, c Ryan, b Waite | 42 | 90 | 5 |
| R. Gregory, lbw, b Ward | 80 | 193 | 8 |
| S. Smith, c Walker, b Wall .. .. .. .. .. .. | 22 | 42 | 1 |
| C. Welch, c Ryan, b Wall | 1 | 33 | 0 |
| H. Ebeling, not out .. .. | 1 | 20 | 0 |
| Extras .. .. .. .. .. | 16 | | |
| | — | — | — |
| Total .. .. .. .. .. | 313 | 398 | 25 |

Fall: 0, 83, 123, 125, 126, 180, 263, 306, 310.

#### BOWLING

| | Overs. | Mdns. | Runs. | Wkts. |
|---|---|---|---|---|
| Wall .. .. .. .. | 25.2 | 4 | 77 | 4 |
| O'Connell .. .. | 11 | 1 | 33 | 0 |
| Collins .. .. .. | 13 | 2 | 24 | 0 |
| Waite .. .. .. | 14 | 3 | 45 | 2 |
| Ryan .. .. .. | 18 | 8 | 26 | 2 |
| Ward .. .. .. | 25 | 6 | 77 | 2 |
| Richter .. .. .. | 3 | 0 | 15 | 0 |

Extras, 16 (3 byes, 13 leg-byes).

### VICTORIA—Second Innings

| | Runs. | Min. | 4's. |
|---|---|---|---|
| Rigg, c Ryan, b O'Connell | 124 | 230 | 7 |
| S. Quin, c Bradman, b O'Connell .. .. .. .. .. | 47 | 128 | 0 |
| Lee. run out .. .. .. .. | 13 | 42 | 0 |
| J. Scaife, c Wall, b O'Connell .. .. .. .. .. | 25 | 38 | 2 |
| Bromley, c Walker, b Wall .. .. .. .. .. .. | 2 | 31 | 0 |
| Gregory, not out.. .. .. | 18 | | |
| Plant, not out .. .. .. | 16 | | |
| Extras .. .. .. .. .. | 4 | | |
| | — | | |
| Five wickets for.. .. | 250 | | |

Fall: 111, 159, 206, 213, 219.

Bowling. — Wall 1/15, O'Connell 3/42, Collins 0/66, Ryan 0/6, Richter 0/58, Ward 0/29, Waite 0/30, Bradman 0/0.

(Stumps)

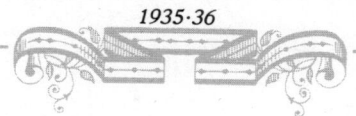

# THE OLD
## And The New
# BRADMAN

### By E. H. M. BAILLIE

*Successive scores of 117, 233, and 357—is any further evidence needed to show that Don Bradman is himself again? Well, what would you say?*

*Personally, I want no more evidence than was provided at the Melbourne Cricket Ground on Wednesday and Thursday of last week. Even admitting that Victoria this season is without some of her crack bowlers, everyone who saw it must admit that Bradman played masterly cricket, of the kind that only he can play.*

SOME may contend that for a man who has scourged the Test bowlers of three countries as he has done in recent years, his feat of last week against a weakened Victorian attack was nothing out of the ordinary. They may also say that with our Test bowlers away it is only to be expected that a batsman of his extraordinary ability would make tremendous scores as a matter of course.

That, however, would not be doing Bradman justice, for several reasons. In the first place, the bowling was quite good. Secondly the severity of his operation at the end of the recent tour of England must have sapped even his remarkable vitality very greatly. This is clearly indicated by the long period of convalescence that was forced upon him, and which led to doubts being raised as to whether he would again be the batting phenomenon of old. Those doubts seem to have been definitely settled by his recent performances.

Next, we must consider the fact that Bradman, in beginning his connection with South Australian cricket, has assumed the leadership of a side that contains many weak links, and requires a lot of building up. When he was playing for New South Wales he was supported by other champion batsmen who could make up for any unexpected failure on his part. Good as some of the South Australian batsmen are, it cannot be claimed that they equal in scoring ability those who have been in the New South Wales team with Bradman in recent years.

## Faces Big Task

Bradman is faced with a Herculean task this season in endeavoring to take South Australia to the top of the tree, and he has done his part in an extraordinary way so far. Not only has he batted in masterly style, but he has, by his enthusiastic leadership, infused a new keenness into the players under him, and has succeeded in developing almost unexpected talent in some of them.

One thing this innings did was to reveal him in a light that was somewhat new to the ordinary cricket follower.

Hitherto Bradman has been looked upon as a cricket cavalier who was always tilting adventurously at windmills. He was the real "killer" of bowlers; a batsman whose flashing blade sent a bright light over every cricket field that he trod, and left a trail of wrecked bowling reputations as it passed. Not for him was the passive role; he must be at the bowler's throat all the time with a grip that was never, or seldom, relaxed.

Not that he could not play the staider game if it became necessary; he occasionally showed that he could do that also, but even in his most passive moods he usually scored much faster than most other batsmen could do. That, however, was not a role that suited his temperament.

Last week, however, we saw a different Bradman. If one had been told that this batting tornado could have kept the brakes on for more than five hours, with hardly a loosening of the tight grip, it would have been a hard thing to believe. Yet that is what we saw on the Melbourne ground last Wednesday. His bat certainly did flash occasionally, but it was very occasionally. For more than five hours he played what for him was a stonewalling game —yet he scored his runs at more than 40 an hour.

It was a new Bradman — a Bradman on whom had been cast a tremendous responsibility, which he shouldered like the champion he is. And what a masterly display of batting he gave! Never in difficulty, meeting every ball with the full face of the bat, never lifting it off the ground except to hit it designedly to a safe spot, he never flattered the bowlers with the faintest suggestion that they would ever get him out.

Then, next day, having placed his side in an impregnable position, he relaxed, and we saw something of the old carefree Bradman in a spell of batting that gave him 128 runs in 114 minutes. It was a wonderful display of clever, brainy batting in every respect, and one of the most remarkable innings of his extraordinary career.

No, there is nothing the matter with Bradman. He is still the champion, with no one to dispute his right to the title. Bradman did not show himself in this game an ostentatious captain, but his hand was on the pulse of the game all the time. There was none of the fussy moving about of fieldsmen that we see so often, none of the constant waving of arms. The fieldsmen seemed to know just what he wanted, and a quiet signal served its purpose. In the handling of his bowlers he struck one as having performed a good job. Altogether it was a great match for Bradman — it would have been even greater had he been able to pull off the outright win for his side.

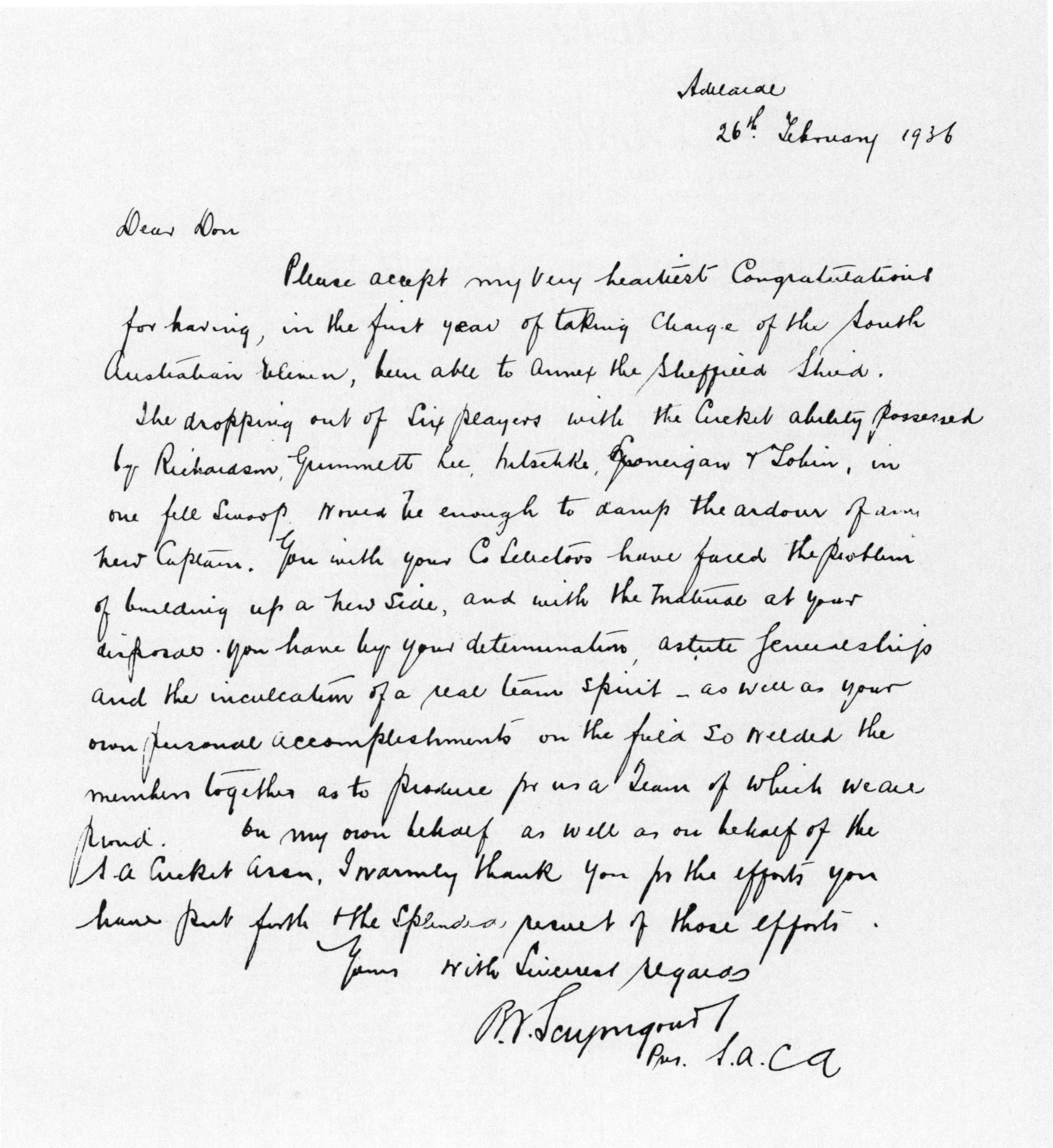

Adelaide
26th February 1936

Dear Don

Please accept my very heartiest Congratulations for having, in the first year of taking Charge of the South Australian Eleven, been able to annex the Sheffield Shield.

The dropping out of Six players with the Cricket ability possessed by Richardson, Grimmett Lee, Nitschke, Gronignan & Tobin, in one fell Swoop, would be enough to damp the ardour of any new Captain. You with your Co Selectors have faced the problem of building up a new Side, and with the Material at your disposal. You have by your determination, astute Generalship and the inculcation of a real team Spirit _ as well as your own personal accomplishments on the field So Welded the members together as to produce for us a Team of which we are Proud. On my own behalf as well as on behalf of the S.a Cricket Assn, I warmly thank you for the efforts you have put forth & the Splendid result of those efforts.

Yours with Sincerest regards

R.V. Scrymgour
Pres. S.a.C.a

---

Letter to Don Bradman from W. B. V. Scrymgour, President of the South Australian Cricket Association.

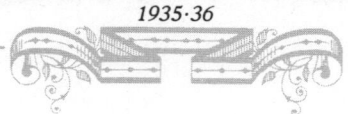

# South Australia v Tasmania

## DON AGAIN AMONG RECORDS

**ADELAIDE, Monday.—Don Bradman sent more cricket records crashing to-day.**

CARRYING his Saturday's score of 127 not out to 369 against Tasmania, he eclipsed Clem Hill's previous highest score for South Australia of 365 not out, made against New South Wales way back in the 1900-1 season at Adelaide.

Bradman's 369 also became the highest score made on the Adelaide Oval.

It was the second time he had topped 300 in an innings this season, a feat equalled only by W. H. Ponsford in the 1927-8 season, and W. G. Grace in 1876.

Bradman has now made six scores in first-class cricket over 300, a feat without parallel. To-day's effort was his 24th double century, and he now needs only one more century to equal the record of Warren Bardsley, who has made 56 hundreds in first-class cricket—the highest number by an Australian.

The champion also brought his aggregate for first-class games this season to 1173, at an average of 130 runs per innings.

### Record Total

Bradman's 369 took only 253 minutes, and included four sixes and 48 fours. He hit 16 off one over from Combes, and at one stage collected 50 runs in 21 minutes.

Hamence, who scored 121, figured in a prolific partnership with Bradman. The former was dismissed when only eight runs were needed to set a new record for a third wicket partnership on Australian grounds. Bradman and Kippax at present hold the record with 363 for N.S.W. against Queensland in 1933-34.

The South Australian total reached 688, a record for the State. The previous best by S.A. was 642 for eight wickets v. Queensland earlier in the season, and 614 for eight wickets v. W.A. at Adelaide in 1929-30.

Scores:—

TASMANIA—First Innings .. .. .. .. 158

**SOUTH AUSTRALIA—First Innings.**

| | |
|---|---|
| BADCOCK, b Thomas .. .. .. .. | 13 |
| WALKER, c Thomas, b Walsh .. .. .. | 11 |
| BRADMAN, c and b Townley .. .. .. | 369 |
| HAMENCE, c and b Townley .. .. .. | 121 |
| LEAK, b Townley .. .. .. .. .. | 19 |
| STAMFORD, run out .. .. .. .. .. | 0 |
| O'CONNELL, c A. Combes, b Thomas .. | 53 |
| WAITE, c Gardiner, b A. Combes .. .. | 43 |
| WARD, c Gardiner, b James .. .. .. | 6 |
| COTTON, b A. Combes .. .. .. .. | 5 |
| SHEPHERDSON, not out .. .. .. .. | 28 |
| Sundries .. .. .. .. .. | 20 |
| | |
| Total .. .. .. .. .. .. .. | 688 |

**BOWLING**

| | O. | M. | R. | W. |
|---|---|---|---|---|
| Walsh .. .. .. .. .. .. | 16 | 0 | 75 | 1 |
| Thomas .. .. .. .. .. .. | 16 | 1 | 91 | 2 |
| Combes .. .. .. .. .. .. | 20.2 | 2 | 116 | 2 |
| James .. .. .. .. .. .. | 15 | 2 | 92 | 1 |
| Townley .. .. .. .. .. | 20 | 2 | 169 | 3 |
| Jeffrey .. .. .. .. .. | 6 | 0 | 54 | 0 |
| Pearsall .. .. .. .. .. | 11 | 0 | 71 | 0 |

**TASMANIA—Second Innings**

| | |
|---|---|
| THOMAS, not out .. .. .. .. .. | 9 |
| M. COMBES, not out .. .. .. .. .. | 10 |
| Sundries .. .. .. .. .. | 10 |
| | |
| No wickets for .. .. .. .. .. | 29 |

Bowling.—Cotton 0-7, Shepherdson 0-9, O'Connell 0-3.

---

| South Australia | - First Innings | 688 |
|---|---|---|
| | - Second Innings | - |
| Tasmania | - First Innings | 158 |
| | - Second Innings | 181 |

South Australia won by an innings and 349 runs.

| DON BRADMAN | - c. and b. R. Townley | 369 |
|---|---|---|
| (Captain) | | |

DON BRADMAN gave another overwhelming performance. He started at 23 for 1, and had ninety-five minutes' batting on the first evening, being 127 not out at the close of play; he had made 50 in forty minutes (his first 40 taking only a quarter of an hour) and 100 in seventy minutes. Next morning he hit with such ferocity that he added 242 runs in two hours thirty-eight minutes, 135 of them before lunch; he completed 200 in two hours fifty-three minutes, and 300 in three hours thirty-three minutes. Eventually, at 552 for 6 he gave a deliberate catch to the bowler. He was batting for only four hours thirteen minutes, and hit four sixes and forty-six fours.

His 369 was the highest score ever made for South Australia and the highest ever made on the Adelaide ground.

This was the sixth treble-century of his career, four of them made in Australia and two in England.

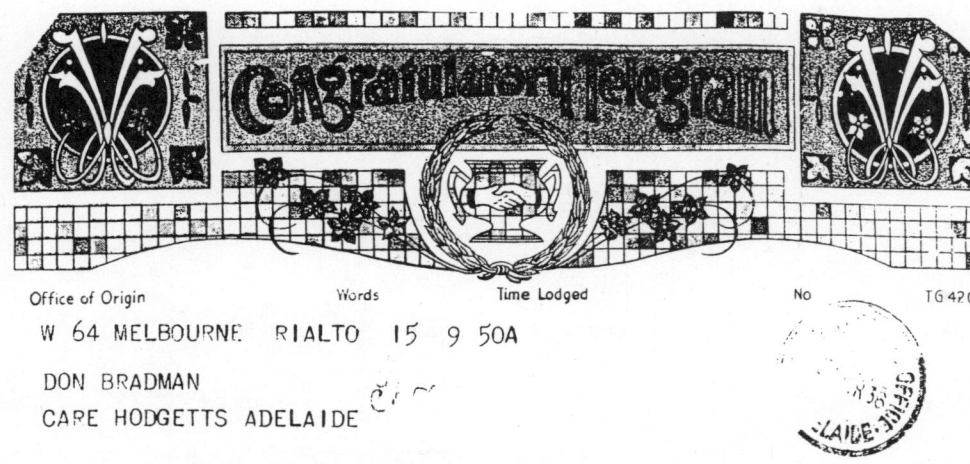

| Office of Origin | Words | Time Lodged | No | TG 426 |
|---|---|---|---|---|

W 64 MELBOURNE RIALTO 15 9 50A

DON BRADMAN

CARE HODGETTS ADELAIDE

CONGRATULATIONS YOU LITTLE DEVIL BREAKING MY RECORD

CLEM HILL MENZIES

9 40A BC

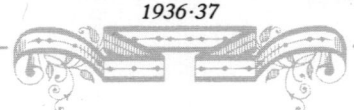

# 1936 - 37 Season

A momentous season opened with my appointment as an Australian Test Selector. Then came a testimonial match for W. Bardsley and J. M. Gregory in which I captained the Rest of Australia against Vic Richardson's all conquering heroes, just returned from South Africa. It was my first tilt against O'Reilly in a first class match.

Great rejoicing at the birth of a son turned to sorrow when the child died after some 36 hours.

But life had to go on. Captaincy of An Australian XI against M.C.C. was followed by my appointment as Captain of Australia against England, a position which I held until retirement in 1948.

My opening gambit ended disastrously when England beat Australia handsomely at Brisbane.

*Don Bradman*

## — SEASON 1936-37 —

| TITLE | GAMES | | SCORES | |
|---|---|---|---|---|
| Second Class | Kensington | Glenelg | 143 | B. |
| | " | Adelaide | 127 | C. |
| | " | " | 2 | n.o. |
| | South Australia | Newcastle | 78 | S. |
| First Class | Bradman's XI | Richardson's XI | 212— | C. |
| | " | " | 13 | C. |
| | An Australian XI | England | 63 | B. |
| | South Australia | - | 38 | C. |
| Sheffield Shield | " | Victoria | 192 | C. |
| | " | " | 31 | C. |
| | " | " | 8 | C. |
| | " | Queensland | 123 | S. |
| | " | New South Wales | 24 | L.B.W. |
| | " | " " | 38 | n.o. |
| Test | Australia | England | 38 | C. |
| | " | " | 0 | C. |
| | " | " | 0 | C. |
| | " | " | 82 | B. |
| | " | " | 13 | C. |
| | " | " | 270 | C. |
| | " | " | 26 | B. |
| | " | " | 212 | C. |
| | " | " | 169 | B. |
| | | Total runs | 1902 | |

## — SUMMARY —

AVERAGES -

| | Innings | N.O's. | H.S. | Runs | Average |
|---|---|---|---|---|---|
| Test | 9 | 0 | 270 | 810 | 90·0 |
| Sheffield Shield | 6 | 1 | 192 | 416 | 83·2 |
| Other First Class | 4 | 0 | 212 | 326 | 81·5 |
| All First Class | 19 | 1 | 270 | 1552 | 86·2 |
| First Grade | 3 | 1 | 143 | 272 | 136·0 |
| Other Second Class | 1 | 0 | 78 | 78 | 78·0 |
| All Second Class | 4 | 1 | 143 | 350 | 116·7 |
| All Matches | 23 | 2 | 270 | 1902 | 90·6 |

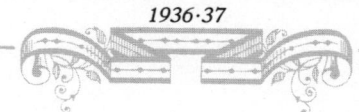

# Rest of Australia v Australia
## (W. Bardsley & J. M. Gregory Testimonial)

THE REST OF AUSTRALIA v AUSTRALIA

(W. Bardsley and J.M. Gregory Testimonial), at Sydney, 9, 10, 12 and 13 October 1936.

| | | |
|---|---|---|
| Rest of Australia | - First Innings | 385 |
| | - Second Innings | 161 for 4 wickets |
| Australia | - First Innings | 363 |
| | - Second Innings | 180 |

Rest of Australia won by 6 wickets.

| | | |
|---|---|---|
| DON BRADMAN | - c. W.J. O'Reilly b. C.V. Grimmett | 212 |
| (Captain) | c. J.H. Fingleton b. C.V. Grimmett | 13 |

This was the first time that DON BRADMAN had faced W.J. O'Reilly in a first-class match, and he mastered him and the others in a brilliant innings.    He went in ten minutes before lunch on the second day, with the score 51 for 4 and O'Reilly bowling at his best; however, he soon settled down, though at first his shots suffered from early-season mistiming.    He got to 50 in fifty-six minutes, and at tea was 94; his century was registered in two hours ten minutes, and then hit out so vigorously that his second century took only sixty-one minutes.    When 200, he was missed in the deep off O'Reilly, and soon afterwards he was caught at long-on, with the score 378 for 7.

He batted for three hours twenty-two minutes, and hit two sixes and twenty-six fours.

This was the fourth time in Australia that he made two double-centuries in successive innings.

His team were set 159 to win in the last innings, and when he went in late on the third day, the score was 63 for 1; this time, however, he failed, being caught at cover when mistiming an off-drive, at 76 for 2. He made his 13 in thirteen minutes.

## D. G. BRADMAN'S TEAM

BACK ROW    K. Gulliver, F. Ward, T. W. Leather, E. S. White, A. D. McGilvray, D. Tallon, H. I. Ebeling.
FRONT ROW    R. Robinson, L. P. O'Brien, D. G. Bradman, C. L. Badcock, R. Morrisby.

## TESTIMONIAL CRICKET

### Australians Beaten By Six Wickets

**D. G. BRADMAN'S XI—First Innings**

| | |
|---|---|
| L. P. O'BRIEN, lbw, b McCormick | 85 |
| C. L. BADCOCK, c Fingleton, b O'Reilly | 18 |
| R. ROBINSON, b O'Reilly | 2 |
| R. O. MORRISBY, b O'Reilly | 4 |
| D. TALLON, b Sievers | 3 |
| D. G. BRADMAN, c O'Reilly, b Grimmett | 212 |
| A. D. McGILVRAY, st Oldfield, b Grimmett | 42 |
| E. S. WHITE, b O'Reilly | 3 |
| F. WARD, not out | 5 |
| H. I. EBELING, lbw, b Grimmett | 0 |
| T. W. LEATHER, st Oldfield, b Grimmett | 0 |
| B, 4, l.b, 2, n.b, 5 | 11 |
| **Total** | **385** |

Fall: 38, 44, 48, 51, 200, 377, 378, 382, 385, 385.

| | | | | | | |
|---|---|---|---|---|---|---|
| McCorm'k | 13 | 0 | 50 | 4 | Grim'ett 30.7 2 116 4 |
| Sievers | 13 | 1 | 49 | 1 | McCabe 4 1 21 0 |
| O'Reilly | 22 | 0 | 96 | 4 | Chip'field 1 0 12 0 |

**Second Innings**

| | |
|---|---|
| L. P. O'BRIEN, lbw, b O'Reilly | 18 |
| C. L. BADCOCK, c Darling, b Grimmett | 43 |
| D. G. BRADMAN, c Fingleton, b Grimmett | 13 |
| R. ROBINSON, c Fingleton, b Grimmett | 57 |
| R. MORRISBY, not out | 18 |
| D. TALLON, not out | 1 |
| Sundries | 11 |
| **Four wickets for** | **161** |

| | | | | |
|---|---|---|---|---|
| Grimmett | 16 | 2 | 82 | 3 | Sievers 3 0 11 0 |
| O'Reilly | 13.6 | 4 | 27 | 1 | McCormick 6 0 30 0 |

Umpires: C. Borwick and A. Christie.

**V. Y. RICHARDSON'S XI—First Innings**

| | |
|---|---|
| J. H. FINGLETON, c Tallon, b Ebeling | 4 |
| W. A. BROWN, b Ward | 111 |
| S. J. McCABE, c O'Brien, b Ebeling | 76 |
| L. S. DARLING, c and b Ward | 3 |
| A. G. CHIPPERFIELD, lbw, b Ward | 3 |
| V. Y. RICHARDSON, c McGilvray, b Leather | 26 |
| M. SIEVERS, c Tallon, b Ward | 0 |
| W. A. OLDFIELD, c Bradman, b Ward | 78 |
| C. V. GRIMMETT, b Ward | 11 |
| W. J. O'REILLY, lbw, b Ward | 7 |
| E. L. McCORMICK, not out | 30 |
| Byes, 7; No Balls, 4 | 11 |
| **Total** | **363** |

Fall: 9, 178, 181, 191, 210, 214, 240, 282, 294, 363.

| | | | | | |
|---|---|---|---|---|---|
| Leather | 16 | 0 | 84 | 1 | Ward 32.3 5 127 7 |
| Ebeling | 21 | 3 | 44 | 2 | McGilvray 7 1 29 0 |
| White | 19 | 3 | 68 | 0 | |

**Second Innings**

| | |
|---|---|
| J. H. FINGLETON, b Leather | 10 |
| W. A. BROWN, l.b.w., b Ebeling | 17 |
| S. J. McCABE, c McGilvray, b Ward | 28 |
| L. S. DARLING, c White, b Ward | 35 |
| A. G. CHIPPERFIELD, l.b.w., b Ward | 10 |
| V. Y. RICHARDSON, c Tallon, b Ebeling | 0 |
| M. SIEVERS, not out | 43 |
| W. A. OLDFIELD, run out | 16 |
| C. V. GRIMMETT, b White | 0 |
| W. J. O'REILLY, l.b.w., b Ward | 1 |
| E. L. McCORMICK, b Ward | 13 |
| B 2, l b 4, n.b. 1 | 7 |
| **Total** | **180** |

Fall: 19, 31, 66, 82, 95, 105, 153, 153, 154, 180.

| | | | | |
|---|---|---|---|---|
| Leather | 7 | 1 | 12 | 1 | White 14 3 26 1 |
| Ebeling | 12 | 4 | 35 | 2 | Ward 16.6 1 100 5 |

---

## BRADMAN-O'REILLY DUEL

# Champion
# Watches The Ball Go By

A dramatic incident in the long looked for duel between Don Bradman and Bill O'Reilly, at the Sydney Cricket Ground yesterday. O'Reilly has beaten Bradman with this one.

# BRADMAN IN FORM.

## 212 Runs in 202 Minutes.

## O'BRIEN AND McGILVRAY BAT WELL.

## The Rest Passes Australia's Total.

Don Bradman, by skilful and daring batting at the Sydney Cricket Ground on Saturday, mercilessly punished the pick of Australia's bowlers to score 212, in 202 minutes, during the second day's play of the Bardsley-Gregory testimonial match.

Once he passed his century, Bradman treated the good-length deliveries of O'Reilly, Grimmett, and McCormick as if they were sent down by school-boys, hitting 26 fours and two sixes.

Bradman came in to bat for the Rest of Australia after four wickets had fallen for 51 runs, but did not sacrifice his wicket until the opposition's total of 363 had been passed.

The disappointment of the day was the failure of the younger players—Badcock, Robinson, Morrisby, and Tallon—who were all dismissed as the result of weak strokes, although Badcock shaped confidently.

The attendance was 19,858, and the gate takings £1240.

## BRADMAN EQUALS BARDSLEY'S RECORD.

Although it was Bradman's first innings in a match this season, it did not stop him from adding another record to his lengthy list. He brought his total to 56 centuries, which equals that of Warren Bardsley, one of the beneficiaries of the testimonial.

An analysis of his scoring rate showed that he made 50 in 56 minutes, 100 in 130, 150 in 168, and 200 in 191 minutes. With McGilvray, he added 177 runs in 78 minutes, McGilvray scoring only 42 of them.

O'Brien gave a grand display. After a confident beginning, he reached 19 shortly after the first wicket fell, but, with the bowling definitely on top, he remained on this figure for half an hour. Then, with Bradman as a partner, he livened up, and combined perfect timing with accurate placements. Once he passed his half century, he attacked the bowling with more vigour than even his more experienced associate. His form should solve the problem of an early left-handed batsman for the tests.

### AUSTRALIA'S INNINGS ENDS.

After nine minutes of bright batting, Australia's innings terminated at 363. Oldfield and McCormick attacked the bowling from the outset, but when Oldfield reached 78, he drove Ward uppishly to Bradman at mid-on, and an easy chance was accepted. Oldfield batted for 112 minutes, hitting six fours, and, apart from a few lucky snicks, early in the innings, he batted with as much judgment as any of his team. McCormick was not out, 30, compiled in 36 minutes. He, too, was confident and astounded the critics with his fine display of stroke-making. Ward finished with seven wickets for 127, off 32.3 overs.

Badcock and O'Brien opened for The Rest, and McCormick, who commenced the attack, bowled with great pace and lifted awkwardly from the pitch several times. Badcock was prone to chase McCormick's off deliveries, and in that bowler's fourth over, he flicked a rising ball finely and Oldfield moved smartly, but could not reach the ball. In his effort he affected Chipperfield's vision at first slip, and the catch was not accepted.

O'Reilly replaced McCormick, with the score at 30, and employed a leg trap, but Badcock placed his first delivery cleverly between the fieldsmen for two, and in the same over lofted him to deep mid-on. Richardson brought Grimmett on from the southern end at 38, and he sent down a maiden to O'Brien. O'Reilly's leg trap met with success in the next over, when Fingleton snapped up a catch at silly-leg from Badcock. The young South Australian scored 18 in pleasing style, but was too venturesome on the leg side.

Robinson arrived, and tapped O'Reilly into the covers for a smartly run single. O'Brien was very sedate. He did not take any risks, and was content to allow runs to come in singles and twos. With the score at 40, he used his feet to Grimmett and cover-drove him to the boundary for the first four of the innings.

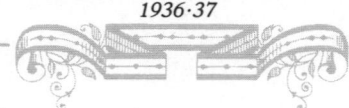

# South Australia v Victoria

SOUTH AUSTRALIA v VICTORIA, at Melbourne, 13, 14, 16 and 17 November 1936.

| South Australia | - First Innings | 386 |
| | - Second Innings | - |
| Victoria | - First Innings | 401 |
| | - Second Innings | 403 for 7 wickets |
| | Drawn. | |

DON BRADMAN, after winning the toss and putting Victoria in did not field on the first day, owing to an attack of gastro-enteritis, and he had had nothing to eat, and was far from well, when he went in on the second afternoon; nevertheless, he played another good innings, against bowlers who included E.L. McCormick, H.I. Ebeling, M.W. Sievers, J. Frederick and R.G. Gregory.

In at 27 for 2, Bradman made 50 in sixty-six minutes, and reached 103 in two hours fourteen minutes. In the next forty-six minutes, he added another 89, the last 42 of them in sixteen minutes. He was missed when 128 off Frederick and caught at deep long-on, just before the close of play. He batted for exactly three hours and hit thirty-two fours.

| DON BRADMAN | - c. L.P. O'Brien b. R.G. Gregory | 192 |
| (Captain) | | |

## THE SCORES

**VICTORIA v. SOUTH AUSTRALIA**
Melbourne C.G., November 13, 14, 16, 17, 1936. Victoria won by 15 runs on the first innings.

### VICTORIA—First Innings.

| | |
|---|---|
| L. P. O'BRIEN, run out | 30 |
| L. S. DARLING, st Walker, b Ward | 39 |
| K. E. RIGG, lbw, b Ward | 97 |
| I. S. LEE, c Badcock, b Waite | 38 |
| R. G. GREGORY, c Richardson, b Cotton | 85 |
| M. SIEVERS, c Waite, b Ward | 54 |
| B. A. BARNETT, c Cotton, b Ward | 20 |
| H. J. PLANT, lbw, b Ward | 20 |
| J. FREDERICKS, c Walker, b Ward | 3 |
| H. I. EBELING, st Walker, b Grimmett | 0 |
| E. L. McCORMICK, not out | 2 |
| Sundries | 13 |
| **Total** | **401** |

Fall: 72, 153, 185, 237, 345, 364, 391, 396, 399, 401.

| | | | | | | |
|---|---|---|---|---|---|---|
| Cotton | 21 | 0 | 82 | 1 | G'mett 37.1 6 112 1 |
| Waite | 13 | 2 | 37 | 1 | Ward 32 3 107 6 |
| Ryan | 22 | 3 | 50 | 0 | |

Cotton 2 wides and 1 no-ball. Waite 1 wide.

### Second Innings

| | |
|---|---|
| K. E. RIGG, c and b Waite | 105 |
| L. P. O'BRIEN, c Waite, b Cotton | 5 |
| L. S. DARLING, lbw, b Cotton | 102 |
| I. S. LEE, c and b Waite | 93 |
| R. S. GREGORY, c and b Waite | 12 |
| M. W. SIEVERS, lbw, b Grimmett | 9 |
| B. A. BARNETT, c Badcock, b Waite | 55 |
| H. J. PLANT, not out | 8 |
| J. FREDERICKS, not out | 5 |
| Sundries | 9 |
| **Seven wickets for** | **403** |

Fall: 24, 210, 224, 253, 266, 381, 394.

| | | | | | | |
|---|---|---|---|---|---|---|
| Cotton | 16 | 0 | 83 | 2 | Ryan 21 4 50 0 |
| Waite | 23 | 1 | 65 | 4 | Ward 24 2 111 0 |
| Grimmett | 30 | 9 | 85 | 1 | |

Cotton 1 wide.

### SOUTH AUSTRALIA—First Innings.

| | |
|---|---|
| C. L. BADCOCK, lbw, b McCormick | 2 |
| R. A. PARKER, st Barnett, b Sievers | 33 |
| A. J. RYAN, lbw, b McCormick | 9 |
| D. G. BRADMAN, c O'Brien, b Gregory | 192 |
| V. Y. RICHARDSON, lbw, b Sievers | 38 |
| R. A. HAMENCE, b Fredericks | 37 |
| C. W. WALKER, b Ebeling | 34 |
| M. J. WAITE, c and b Ebeling | 11 |
| C. V. GRIMMETT, c Barnett, b Ebeling | 8 |
| F. WARD, not out | 3 |
| H. J. COTTON, lbw, b Ebeling | 0 |
| Sundries | 19 |
| **Total** | **386** |

Fall: 3, 27, 104, 187, 295, 336, 372, 377, 386, 386.

| | | | | | |
|---|---|---|---|---|---|
| McCor'k | 15 | 1 | 85 | 2 | Gregory .10 3 27 1 |
| Ebeling | 22.2 | 5 | 74 | 4 | Plant ... 15 6 50 0 |
| Sievers | 13 | 3 | 36 | 2 | Darling . 2 0 5 0 |
| Fred'cks | 15 | 2 | 90 | 1 | |

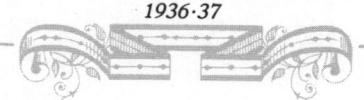

# BRADMAN, A BATTING TORNADO

### By E. H. M. Baillie

*DON BRADMAN has given many amazing batting displays, but few more amazing than that with which he thrilled a crowd of 21,000 people at the Melbourne ground on Saturday in the match between Victoria and South Australia.*

*A sick man on Friday, he was not in his best condition on Saturday, yet he gave a display of which no other batsman would be capable. Reaching his century in 134 minutes, he went on to 192, in another 46 minutes and made the bowling look completely futile. He made his last 42 runs in 16 minutes, and was caught on the fence apparently in trying to hit slow bowler Gregory out of the ground. It was a perfect tornado of batting.*

SOUTH AUSTRALIA'S innings began after lunch on Saturday, after Victoria had scored 401, and at stumps five wickets were down for 295. Of this number Bradman made 192 in one of the most remarkable displays of batting he has ever given. His last three-quarters of an hour was just a burst of frenzied hitting, in which the Victorian bowlers were made to look like schoolboys.

The display was all the more remarkable because of the disabilities under which he batted. An attack of gastro-enteritis kept him off the field on Friday. On Saturday he was looking pale and had not fully regained his appetite, hence he was not feeling at his best. He began shakily against McCormick's fast bowling, but once he settled down no one would have imagined that he had been a sick man.

#### McCORMICK TROUBLES HIM

He went in second wicket down, instead of in his usual first wicket place, the start having been a poor one with only 27 runs on the board, the batsmen out being Badcock and Ryan. McCormick, giving one of the best bowling displays we have ever seen from him, had obtained both wickets, and he unleashed a particularly hostile burst of inspired bowling against the champion. He had Bradman in trouble right away, and the batsman was fortunate to escape an early dismissal for some of his strokes were anything but safe, especially a couple of snicks behind the wicket.

McCormick, however, had had a long spell at the creases for a fast bowler, and he had to have a rest. Bradman was more at home to the other bowlers, although Ebeling sometimes troubled him, but gradually he settled down to better cricket. Flashing shots to all parts of the field came from his bat, and he reached 50 in 66 minutes. Parker, his partner, was playing a steady game, and leaving most of the scoring to his captain. Bradman went rapidly to the nineties, then he had an extraordinarily slow period, taking a long time to reach the century.

Meantime Parker, after a useful hand for 33, and Richardson, who had batted confidently for 38, had been dismissed and when Hammence joined Bradman at eight minutes past five the champion was 98. A single made him 99, and then a flashing four gave him 103, made in 134 minutes. Thus his second 50 had taken 58 minutes, although from 50 to 90 he had scored very fast.

It was 5.13 when he made this four, and he was out at 5.57 for 192, having added no fewer than 89 runs in 46 minutes. By this time McCormick had lost some of his early hostility, and in the later turns that he had at the crease did not trouble Bradman nearly so much. The slower paced bowlers gave him no trouble whatever, and he did just as he liked with them.

With terrific cover and straight drives and powerful pulls he reached 150 in another 32 minutes, but it was the last portion of his innings that was really hectic.

Frederick, the slow bowler, who had tied up the Englishmen, had 28 hit from two overs — 27 of them by Bradman. At 10 minutes to 6 Bradman faced Plant, hit his first three balls each for four, and got 19 off the over.

Then he faced Gregory, and evidently made up his mind that he could hit him out of the ground. The ball went sailing out to Lee, stationed near the sight screen at the railway end. Lee, almost on the fence, got his hands to it, but dropped it. The next ball was swung to long-on, where O'Brien, also on the fence, took the catch. His last 42 were made in 14 minutes, and he was at the wickets 180 minutes for his 192, out of 268 made while he was batting. There were 32 fours in his total, or 128 from boundary hits. When 128 he gave Gregory a difficult chance at deep mid-off from Frederick's bowling, the fieldsman just getting his hands to the ball as it flew over his head and went to the boundary.

The crowd of 21,000, of course, thoroughly enjoyed Bradman's batting, and he had it in a state of great excitement. As he walked back to the pavilion they applauded tumultuously for one of the most remarkable batting displays ever seen on the ground. Bradman obviously was very tired, and he limped slightly as he returned to the pavilion. The pity was that he got out when he did, for his side was far from being in a safe position, being still 106 runs behind the Victorian total.

Bradman, of course, overshadowed all the other batsmen, but Richardson and Parker deserve a word for the way they helped him. Richardson, batting in something like his old style, made his 38 in 59 minutes, with four fours, while Parker stayed 104 minutes in making his 33.

#### VICTORIA LEADS

Play on Monday was frequently interrupted by showers, and it saw the remaining South Australian batsmen battle bravely against a weakened Victorian attack to reach the Victorian total of 401. Sievers was absent through indisposition, and McCormick, after bowling a couple of overs, had to retire with a strained leg. In the circumstances the batsmen were justified in batting carefully, and scoring was very slow. They failed by only 15 runs to gain a first innings lead, but were by no means disgraced.

Hamence, the colt, showed stubborn defence and some style in making 37 in 115 minutes, while Walker, who is by no means deficient in batting ability, batted a minute less for 34, and Waite stayed 69 minutes to make 11. Waite's dismissal was the result of a brilliant c and b effort by Ebeling, the bowler throwing himself at the ball and falling over as he took the catch. The total of 386 runs was made in 374 minutes.

Ebeling took the bowling honors with four for 74, all obtained on Monday, when he had to bear the burden of the attack, at a cost of 18 runs. He had all his usual steadiness and nip, and even troubled Bradman on Saturday. McCormick and Sievers each obtained two wickets and both bowled excellently, McCormick particularly so.

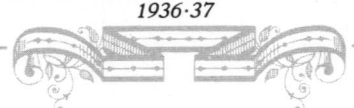
# M.C.C. TEAM
# AUSTRALIAN TOUR
*1936-37*

BACK ROW    C. J. Barnett, A. Fagg, W. Copson, L. B. Fishlock, Captain Howard (Manager).

SECOND ROW    T. H. Wade (emergency wicket-keeper), H. Verity, K. Farnes, T. S. Worthington, W. Voce, J. Hardstaff, J. M. Sims, W. Ferguson (official scorer).

FRONT ROW    L. E. G. Ames, W. R. Hammond, R. W. V. Robins, G. O. Allen (Captain), R. E. S. Wyatt, M. Leyland, G. Duckworth.

# D. R. Jardine on the Test Team

## "Captaincy May Curb Bradman's Bat"

MR. JARDINE wrote thus: "Almost certainly the Australian team which toured South Africa will supply eight or nine of those who will be picked at least for the first Test match.

"V. Richardson, now quite a veteran after captaining South Australia for several years, led the team in South Africa, and from all accounts gave satisfaction. In his absence, Bradman, who has migrated to Adelaide, took over the captaincy of his new State's team.

**"Since Bradman, alone among the active cricketers in Australia, has been invited by the Australian Board of Control to serve on the selection committee, there can be little doubt that he is intended to don Richardson's mantle and lead the Australian XI.**

"Either player would have given a good account of himself as leader, for both know the game thoroughly. English partisans may be excused the hope that the cares of captaincy may put some curb on Bradman's prolific bat. It is at least reasonable to assume that his new role cannot increase his scoring ability.

"There is no dearth of young and promising players to take the places vacated by Woodfull and Ponsford, among others. The best, in all probability, has not been seen of Fingleton, Badcock, and Nitschke, none of whom has ever toured England.

### It Was a Puzzle

"Members of the last two M.C.C. teams in Australia found it hard to understand why Nitschke was never given a trial in a Test match—on record, he must be the most dangerous left-handed batsman in Australia.

"Fingleton has been known as a solid opening batsman and brilliant field for some time, and he will fit into Woodfull's place adequately. Badcock, however, is a comparative newcomer, who has done some remarkable things to bowling that is not in the top class.

"It will be interesting to see if he can repeat his feats in international cricket. Should he do so, he will be ranked almost in Bradman's class.

"One combination at any rate the England XI are unlikely to encounter—a combination which won the rubber for Australia in 1934—Grimmett and O'Reilly. The latter is almost certain to play in every match of the series, but unless the wickets in Australia have been radically and systematically altered again, Grimmett will not find a place in the regular Australian team.

"Wonderful bowler as he has proved

DISCUSSING the possible first Test team of Australia a few weeks ago, D. R. Jardine, in the London "Evening Standard," raised an interesting question—the likely influence on his batting of D. G. Bradman undertaking the captaincy.

Others have discussed this matter out here, but, as a rule, in academic manner.

However, Australian captains are not often handicapped in batting by their responsibilities as leaders. W. W. Armstrong, M. A. Noble, H. L. Collins, W. M. Woodfull, J. Darling, G. H. S. Trott, and W. L. Murdoch were not.

*D. R. Jardine, who thinks the captaincy may affect Don Bradman's batting.*

himself in England, Grimmett in Australia four years ago was but a shadow of himself, and lost his place after the second Test match. After four more years he is unlikely to improve on this—unless there is a famine in Australia of bowlers of youth and class."

\* \* \*

D. R. Jardine's views of H. C. Nitschke will find many a resonant echo of acquiescence in Australia. The South Australian left-hander, by the way, did play against South Africa, and showed rather good form.

But in his reference to the wickets of Australia, Jardine's phrase, "radically and systematically altered once again," does not lie so great a cricketer and so sound a judge! It is incorrect.

### Climatic Influences

We are not getting a succession of the hot summers of years ago. If the wickets anywhere in this country have changed or do change, it is due to climatic influences. In anything like normal weather the wickets of the leading grounds are unsurpassed in the world and, invariably, they are fast.

This season, in Sydney the weather has been at times nippy when the wind is from the south. In two

English matches it was hardly necessary to take refreshments on to the field. Four years ago at the M.C.C. matches there were the half-hourly invasions of the field by the twelfth man carrying a tray.

If some Australian cricketer were to make the remark of Mr. Jardine in relation to the wicket at Lord's or the Oval, what would the English sportsmen think about it?

\* \* \*

Test captains are invariably criticised according to the degree of their success. Some remarkably able captains—A. C. MacLaren for instance—lost, not through inefficiency in leadership, but because the forces they had to handle were not good enough for the task.

One believes that Don Bradman will handle his side ably, and that his doing so will not militate much against his own batting. But will he dissect the strokes and diagnose the methods of the stars of the English team, W. R. Hammond and M. Leyland, and of the others, after the manner of G. H. S. Trott and M. A. Noble, and other great Australian Test leaders, and then arrange the field accordingly, in conjunction with the bowlers?

### Don Bradman's Touch

In the Australian Eleven match Bradman handled his bowling with good judgment, for it was no very deadly array on paper. The field-placing to Leyland's batting was open to discussion and, perhaps, to mild constructive criticism. It was good, and yet possibly it might have been a little better. However, Leyland is a shrewd, keen-witted batsman as well as a very able one. Don Bradman's manipulation of the bowling and field placing to the batting of Hammond and Leyland will be an interesting feature of the test matches, to those who can recall great captains of both countries in the last thirty years or so. One has confidence in his rising to the occasion.

In one of his books J. B. Hobbs wrote:

"I think, perhaps, Noble was the finest skipper I have ever seen; he used to study everyman's shots, and then shut them up. The Australians are far better at saving runs than we; they bottle up your good shots, put men on the boundaries to save the fours, and bowl to keep you quiet. This, I suppose, because in Australia, matches are played out, and they have plenty of time, while we are bound to play to win."

The ablest captains, English and Australian, in bottling your shots invariably left a shot unbottled and angled for the batsman to go for it off the wrong ball. In that little art Trott and Noble were masters.

# Sievers Included For Wet Wicket?

## TEST TEAM IS POWERFUL

### Looks Stronger Than Best English Combination

#### By ARTHUR MAILEY

IF the selectors have chosen M. Sievers, the only surprise in the Australian team for the first Test, beginning in Brisbane on Friday week, because he might be of assistance on a sticky wicket, the idea is a good one.

However, if all players are fit and good weather is indicated when the Test begins, the tall Victorian will probably be 12th man.

The captain and vice-captain will be announced in Adelaide by the Board of Control secretary (Mr. Jeanes). Bradman and McCabe seem certain to fill the positions, respectively.

The twelve from whom the team will be chosen are:—

D. G. Bradman (S.A.).
C. L. Badcock (S.A.).
W. A. Brown (Qld.).
A. G. Chipperfield (N.S.W.).
J. H. Fingleton (N.S.W.).
S. J. McCabe (N.S.W.).
E. L. McCormick (Vic.).
W. A. Oldfield (N.S.W.).
W. J. O'Reilly (N.S.W.).
R. H. Robinson (N.S.W.).
M. S. Sievers (Vic.).
F. A. Ward (S.A.).

In my opinion it is the best possible team, although a good left-hand bowler would improve the side. But assuming that the selectors considered none was at hand, they have done the next best thing.

In any case if there happens to be a sticky wicket in Brisbane, O'Reilly has the necessary accuracy and pace to make good use of it.

For sentimental reasons, I am sorry that Grimmett has been passed over. I never like to see any old player scrapped, but Grimmett has not performed up to expectations this season, nor has he done nearly as well as younger candidates.

The selectors' job is to pick the best players, and, much as I regret Grimmett's omission, it would be a burlesque if they were influenced in their deliberations by sentiment.

On paper the team looks stronger than any team England can put in the field, but, like Allen, the English captain, I think England will put up a better fight than was anticipated a couple of weeks ago.

The recent successes of Verity, Ames, and Leyland have converted what appeared to be an ordinary team into an efficient combination.

### Badcock The "Baby"

The average age of the team is nearly 28 years.

The baby of the side is the 22-year-old Tasmanian, C. L. ("Jack") Badcock, who beats Ray Robinson for that distinction by three weeks.

The veteran of the 12 is W. A. Oldfield, 39 years of age.

The ages of the players are: W. A. Oldfield 39, A. G. Chipperfield 31, W. J. O'Reilly 30, E. L. McCormick 30, J. H. Fingleton 28, D. G. Bradman 28, F. Ward 28, S. J. McCabe 26, M. S. Sievers 24, W. A. Brown 24, R. H. Robinson 22, and C. L. Badcock 22.

## Victorian Opinions

MELBOURNE, Wednesday.

**Dr. R. L. Morton** (chairman of the Executive, Victorian Cricket Association): "It seems an extraordinary thing that no left-hand bowler was included in case of a wet wicket. Test wickets are not covered once play begins.

"Everyone said a good left-hand bowler could not be found, but E. S. White, of New South Wales, has been seen here, and would have been very useful."

**Arthur Liddicut** (former international): "I am pleased at the inclusion of Sievers. The Tests will be played on uncovered wickets and should it rain he will be a distinct menace. There would be no more destructive bowler in the side. The whole selection fulfils the prophecy made ten years ago that the day of fast bowlers was coming to an end because of the gradual loss of pace of Australian wickets."

**Alex Hurwood** (former Test bowler): "Chiefly because he is a left-hand batsman Darling should have been included. He is right in form and the side could do with a left-hander. Otherwise a good team."

**Edgar Mayne** (former international): "I think O'Brien should have been included. A left-hander with Test match temperament and a fine fieldsman, he would have been valuable. I cannot follow the selectors in their choice of Sievers."

**Percy Wallace** (former Victorian fast bowler): "Evidently Sievers has been put in to keep an end going. He is the right type of stock bowler. His deliveries come from a height very solidly on to the pitch. He seems a good selection and should do well."

## S.A. Views

**Clem Hill** (former Test player): "I am pleased Badcock has been chosen. There is no sounder or better defensive batsman in Australia, and if Brown shows no improvement in form for the State on Friday, I will not be surprised if Badcock opened up in the Test. I am surprised Grimmett was dropped for Ward. Evidently age was the deciding factor. Chipperfield, Ward, and Grimmett could not all be included. Sievers probably impressed Bradman in the game between Victoria and South Australia

"If McCormick plays, he and McCabe will probably open the attack, but I would sooner see O'Reilly open than McCabe, as O'Reilly will be more hostile than McCabe with the new ball. I thought Darling would have been chosen in Robinson's place, but evidently the selectors did not want a left-hander."

**Vic. Richardson** (former international): "Sievers is the greatest surprise, but may be played to strengthen the batting tail. Bradman, McCabe, and O'Reilly picked themselves, and nobody could quibble at any of the other selections."

# Australia v England
## First Test Match

AUSTRALIA v ENGLAND, First Test Match, at Brisbane,
4, 5, 7, 8 and 9 December 1936.

| | | |
|---|---|---|
| Australia | - First Innings | 234 |
| | - Second Innings | 58 |
| England | - First Innings | 358 |
| | - Second Innings | 256 |
| | Australia lost by 322 runs. | |

| | | |
|---|---|---|
| DON BRADMAN | - c. T.S. Worthington b. W. Voce | 38 |
| (Captain) | - c. A.E. Fagg b. G.O. Allen | 0 |

DON BRADMAN's first innings started on the second afternoon at 13 for 1, with two boundaries off G.O. Allen in his first over, and he continued to play brilliantly if rather streakily until tea-time, when he was 37 not out. He stayed for ten minutes after the interval, but was caught in the gully when trying to drive a going-away ball off his back foot; the score was then 89 for 2. He batted for seventy-one minutes and played 56 balls. Australia were set to make 381 to win the match, a task which would probably have been too heavy in any event; but rain before the fifth day's play made the result a certainty for England, and W. Voce and Allen exploited a vicious wicket to run through the opposition. Bradman going in soon after the start at 7 for 3, played one ball from Allen, and was caught at third slip from his second; it pitched on a length, lifted sharply, and hit the shoulder of his bat before he could withdraw it.

Bradman's first experience of captaincy in a Test Match was thus a melancholy one.

G. O. Allen smilingly examines Bradman's coin before the
toss to see if it has two heads.

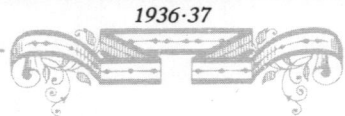

## FULL SCORES.

### ENGLAND.—First Innings.

| | |
|---|---|
| T. S. Worthington, c Oldfield, b McCormick | 0 |
| C. J. Barnett, c Oldfield, b O'Reilly | 69 |
| A. Fagg, c Oldfield, b McCormick | 4 |
| W. R. Hammond, c Robinson, b McCormick | 0 |
| M. Leyland, b Ward | 126 |
| L. E. G. Ames, c Chipperfield, b Ward | 24 |
| J. Hardstaff, c McCabe, b O'Reilly | 43 |
| R. W. V. Robins, c sub. (Brown), b O'Reilly | 38 |
| G. O. Allen, c McCabe, b O'Reilly | 35 |
| H. Verity, c Sievers, b O'Reilly | 7 |
| W. Voce, not out | 4 |
| Sundries (bye 1, leg-byes 3, no-balls 4) | 8 |
| **Total** | **358** |

Fall of wickets: 0, 20, 20, 119, 162, 252, 311, 311, 343, 358.

### BOWLING.

| | O. | M. | R. | W. |
|---|---|---|---|---|
| McCormick | 8 | 1 | 26 | 3 |
| Sievers | 16 | 5 | 42 | 0 |
| O'Reilly | 40.6 | 13 | 102 | 5 |
| Ward | 36 | 2 | 138 | 2 |
| Chipperfield | 11 | 3 | 32 | 0 |
| McCabe | 2 | 0 | 10 | 0 |

Sievers bowled two no-balls, McCormick one, and O'Reilly one.

### Second Innings.

| | |
|---|---|
| T. S. Worthington, st Oldfield, b McCabe | 8 |
| C. J. Barnett, c Badcock, b Ward | 26 |
| A. Fagg, st Oldfield, b Ward | 27 |
| W. R. Hammond, hit wicket, b Ward | 25 |
| M. Leyland, c Bradman, b Ward | 33 |
| L. E. G. Ames, b Sievers | 9 |
| G. O. Allen, c Fingleton, b Sievers | 68 |
| J. Hardstaff, st Oldfield, b Ward | 20 |
| R. W. V. Robins, c Chipperfield, b Ward | 0 |
| H. Verity, lbw, b Sievers | 19 |
| W. Voce, not out | 2 |
| Sundries (byes 14, leg-byes 4, no-ball 1) | 19 |
| **Total** | **256** |

Fall of wickets: 17, 50, 82, 105, 122, 144, 205, 205, 247, 256.

### BOWLING.

| | O. | M. | R. | W. |
|---|---|---|---|---|
| Sievers | 19.6 | 9 | 29 | 3 |
| McCabe | 6 | 1 | 14 | 1 |
| O'Reilly | 35 | 15 | 59 | 0 |
| Ward | 46 | 16 | 102 | 6 |
| Chipperfield | 10 | 2 | 33 | 0 |

McCabe, a no-ball.

### AUSTRALIA.—First Innings.

| | |
|---|---|
| J. H. Fingleton, b Verity | 100 |
| C. L. Badcock, b Allen | 8 |
| D. G. Bradman, c Worthington, b Voce | 38 |
| S. J. McCabe, c Barnett, b Voce | 51 |
| R. H. Robinson, c Hammond, b Voce | 2 |
| A. G. Chipperfield, c Ames, b Voce | 7 |
| M. W. Sievers, b Allen | 8 |
| W. A. Oldfield, c Ames, b Voce | 6 |
| W. J. O'Reilly, c Leyland, b Voce | 3 |
| F. A. Ward, c Hardstaff, b Allen | 0 |
| E. L. McCormick, not out | 1 |
| Byes 4, leg-byes 1, no-balls 5 | 10 |
| **Total** | **234** |

Fall of wickets: 13, 89, 166, 176, 202, 220, 229, 231, 231, 234.

### BOWLING

| | O. | M. | R. | W. |
|---|---|---|---|---|
| Allen | 16 | 2 | 71 | 3 |
| Voce | 20.6 | 5 | 41 | 6 |
| Hammond | 4 | 0 | 12 | 0 |
| Verity | 28 | 11 | 52 | 1 |
| Robins | 17 | 0 | 48 | 0 |

Voce bowled five no-balls.

### Second Innings.

| | |
|---|---|
| J. H. Fingleton, b Voce | 0 |
| C. L. Badcock, c Fagg, b Allen | 0 |
| M. W. Sievers, c Voce, b Allen | 5 |
| W. A. Oldfield, b Voce | 10 |
| D. G. Bradman, c Fagg, b Allen | 0 |
| S. McCabe, c Leyland, b Allen | 7 |
| R. H. Robinson, c Hammond, b Voce | 3 |
| A. G. Chipperfield, not out | 26 |
| W. J. O'Reilly, b Allen | 0 |
| F. A. Ward, b Voce | 1 |
| E. L. McCormick, absent | 0 |
| No-balls | 6 |
| **Total** | **58** |

Fall of wickets: 0, 3, 7, 7, 16, 20, 35, 41, 58.

### BOWLING.

| | O. | M. | R. | W. |
|---|---|---|---|---|
| Voce | 6.3 | 0 | 16 | 4 |
| Allen | 6 | 0 | 36 | 5 |

Voce bowled five no-balls and Allen one.

# FIRST BALL SHOCK FOR ENGLAND

# Worthington Dazed When Wicket Went

(From Neville Cardus)

BRISBANE, Friday.

THE beginning of the Test was catastrophe, and pandemonium was unleashed.

McCormick's first ball, which he bowled like a hurricane, pitched short and rose high at Worthington's left shoulder.

Worthington hooked impulsively, his stroke skied it, and Olded, after starting late, ran forward, all frenzy and voracity, and held the catch. Poor Worthington stood dazed a moment, then departed, head down.

In the same over McCormick struck Fagg amidships and the agony was abated while Fagg retired to dry dock for repairs. McCormick's next ball rose near Fagg's cranium, and we could see for ourselves that McCormick's two short-legs were not merely decorative but accessory, at least for a while until the ball lost its newness.

But one of McCormick's short-legs was moved to the slips, and the rising angle of his attack became generally more in accordance with the modern batsman's view of respectable fast bowling. In quick sequence Barnett cut McCormick for four, edged him dangerously for four, cut him again with a great hammerswing from the shoulder.

The struggle could be felt intensely, for all nerves were taut; a grand bone of contention was being gnawed by the various dogs. But Barnett was cool and brave, and though Leyland could not do as he wished the English temperature eased a little.

In fact, a massive off-drive for six by Barnett from Ward let a momentary breeze blow; he hit the next ball for four arrogantly in the manner of a man in a beleagured city attempting a sortie.

## A Morning's Work

Barnett was mainly admirable. But the batting still needed certainty of touch; I felt that both Leyland and Barnett were often obliged to play strokes which the bowlers wanted them to make, and which they themselves would raher have evaded.

Still, no further disaster occurred before half-past one when the cricketers came in to lunch after a scalding morning's work. I thought it was a good wicket for good bowlers and good batsmen.

Brisbane Cricket Ground, 1985.

Ceramic mug struck to commemorate the 150th anniversary of the Marylebone Cricket Club.

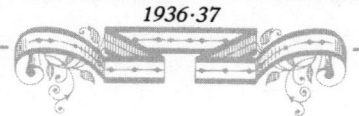

# CARDUS MARVELS AT DON'S TYPICAL START

### (From Neville Cardus)

BRISBANE, Saturday.

THERE was a congested crowd when at high noon the Test umpires attended to the stumps and fixed them like students of trigonometry.

The pitch looked like a Roman pavement discovered by antiquarians or a grave or an historic barrow containing the honorable bones of departed and disillusioned bowlers.

The day's first ball, from Ward, was cut for four by Robins. He cut it when it was about to bounce for the second, but by no means the last time.

Then in O'Reilly's opening over three boundaries occurred, an exquisite leg glance and a dangerous pull by Hardstaff, and a glorious leg glance by Robins.

The attack was hereabout rather disreputable and Hardstaff twice drove Ward to the off in his happiest Trent Bridge vein.

I emphasise this excellent form of Hardstaff, because his poor cricket latterly has upset the English batting balance and put an abnormal responsibility on Hammond and Barnett, whose natural talents for free stroke play have been cramped and confined by defensive responsibilities.

More than ever I am persuaded that England will score plenty of runs in the Test Matches, though not always perhaps will we find O'Reilly so out of mood as he has been generally in this engagement, the picture of lumbering, bald-headed and rather unhopeful endeavor.

### Call Grimmett?

Robins was as good as Hardstaff, nimble of feet, cutting late with a terrier alacrity, and putting beauty of rhythm in his cover drive.

In half-an-hour Robins and Hardstaff scored 40, and struck a note of happy easeful challenge, which was new to an English innings this tour. It may be necessary for Australia to recall Grimmett.

Hardstaff was caught from an effort to sweep O'Reilly to leg: Even the gesture of the stroke told us that Hardstaff is escaping from the complicated interstices of self-doubt.

Robins fell to a catch on the offside soon after Hardstaff departed, a bad shot under the ball, but again I liked the offensive gesture.

O'Reilly's tail stood up visibly. Yesterday it was as low to the ground as that of a dog which has been severely reprimanded.

### McCormick Missed

Allen and Verity proceeded obstinately. Verity was very studious as he attended to O'Reilly's changes of pace, solving them like a sixth form mathematician, sometimes counting on his fingers surreptitiously.

Allen tried to drive, but could not quite time his strokes: still he stayed in, and aided Verity, who would not get out. Once again I felt some weakness of penetration in the Australian forces.

Just before lunch, Oldfield had to leave the field, owing to a hit in the face, but he returned, as, of course, he would return to any cricket match if he had his way, even if he needed a bath chair.

On the perfect wicket. McCormick was sadly missed.

Allen struck a full toss from O'Reilly for four: the Australians were allowing the game to drift the other way now.

### Superb Catch

The ground was packed after lunch and one man sat in an adjacent roof and watched the play for nothing.

There were many ladies content to stand in positions of discomfort, risking pretty clothes and disfiguring pretty faces by wearing the hideous smoked glasses which I am sorry to find are fashionable in Australia.

A woman of looks should be prepared to suffer sun blindness rather than go about with the windows of the soul hidden from our masculine view.

Verity, at length, decided to hit O'Reilly to leg, and was caught square: Something had to be done, I suppose, for the game was becoming static.

With Voce in last, Allen ran out and smote O'Reilly for four, and a straight six and died fighting, caught superbly at mid-on by McCabe from another "damn the consequences" gesture.

It took Australia almost an hour to capture England's last two wickets, which fell to O'Reilly, and so lent a gentle touch of varnish to the great bowler's analysis.

So concluded the drama's first act, and during the interval part of the crowd had another opportunity to inspect the Press box. It is a pity we are not a handsomer lot, but I hope we look intellectual enough.

### Frenzied Opening

In the most frenzied atmosphere I can remember in Test cricket, Australia's innings began. The roars were colossal when Badcock at once drove Allen straight for three and pulled him for four.

And when suddenly Badcock played on by pulling his stroke askew in a back defensive effort the sky was split by the noise. It was gladiatorial: I expected the lions and the Christians.

Bradman was heralded with trumpets and trombones of acclamation as he walked to the wicket, and the whole of the multitude's orchestra crashed out as he cut Allen for four and pulled him gigantically for four.

Then Voce missed the edge of Bradman's bat by a hair's breadth, and hysteria let out its shriek: It was a lucky escape. But heavens, what a game this cricket is in Australia. What a battleground is made of a cricket field: How I shall greet the green peacefulness next year of Worcester and Horsham. I love the grandeur of Test Matches here, the strain and the power, but I am a man of peace, and this is war.

### Bradman Machine

Allen rested after a few overs, in which he seemed not only willing but anxious to break his back for the cause. Hammond relieved him and the tension eased, though Fingleton once of twice rekindled panic by a hesitant slip stroke. Bradman missed one or two, but I felt the wonderful engine of his technique at work: the dynamo was throbbing all right, in spite of a fortunate slice through the slips off Allen when he was 21.

Bradman often begins against fast bowling as though some deep periodic law of fallibility works in him, making him one of the human family.

His genius has its own logic and authority. Apparently he is free to play off any foot, and transform into greatness and grandeur what in other players would be errors fatal and unlovely. There is the gamin about him somehow.

Fingleton defended stoutly, a worthy anonymous helpmate to the darling and paragon of the crowd.

### Bradman On Leash

Though Allen bowled with heroic intent, he was expensive, and Verity came on, secret and self-contained as an oyster. His bowling looked amiable on the flawless wicket, but it contained an inward obliquity. The words of his mouth were smother than butter, but war was in his heart.

He lured Bradman into second thoughts, and at once he insulted the great man by placing a silly point. Then Verity skilfully put him on a leash.

Meanwhile the afternoon became cool and cloudy. Perhaps Verity will yet have his desire.

# Test Is
# Forgotten
# In Crisis

FROM OUR SPECIAL REPRESENTATIVE

LONDON, Saturday.

The first Test is given little space in the newspapers. The "Daily Mirror" devotes 14 pages to the King and Mrs. Simpson and gives inches to the cricket match.

The Test story is half-way down the sporting page and has a single-column heading.

"The Times" says that those who suggested free scoring by some of the English batsmen following the Queensland match must have been disappointed by the first innings.

Thanks, however, to a brave stand by Leyland and Barnett, England made a grand recovery, but still is in an unenviable position.

The "Daily Herald" praises Allen for a real captain's innings.

The "Manchester Guardian" calls it England's chastening hour, and deplores the irresolute batting.

"Sporting Life" says it might have been worse—a lot worse indeed. There was a danger early in the game that the Australian bowlers would go through the side.

A pull to leg over Ames's head to the fence.

# CREDIT TO ALLEN

## Attack Well Handled

(From W. M. Woodfull)

BRISBANE, Monday.

ENGLAND was on top to-day and it looked a rattling good combination.

Allen handled his bowling to perfection.

Patience and confidence were features of Fingleton's century—a Herculean effort.

McCabe started with characteristic freedom and vigor. Fingleton bided his time.

Allen used Robins early, an excellent move, for it provided variety, while, in addition, the spin and flight might upset a batsman.

Then came a shortish one from Voce, certainly the right ball to pull, and none can pull better than McCabe, but he lofted it, to give an easy catch three-quarters of the way out—Voce, two maidens and one wicket. McCabe could just as easily have kept it along the carpet.

A perpetual buzz followed our next disaster, for Robinson, before he had an opportunity to settle down, played forward to a good length delivery from Voce, tickled it, and Hammond nonchalantly took the catch low down. Voce, two for 2, off 19 deliveries.

Sending a catch to Hammond is as safe as testing your petrol supply with a lighted match.

Robinson could hardly be blamed for his dismissal. He played the obvious stroke, but was a shade inside the ball.

### England On Top

A couple from Robins, whose length had improved, stood up sharply, with the result that Verity joined him at the bowling crease.

It might be that Allen was influenced by the proximity of the total to 200, so Voce sought temporary harborage in the field. His speed had been impressive and his direction irreproachable.

Fingleton showed great self control under this most powerful nerve tension. He had just passed his previous highest Test score against England.

Chipperfield made an indefinite stroke at a good length ball from Voce and was caught at the wicket. Chipperfield must back up better. He loses valuable singles.

### Sorry Morning

It had been a sorry morning for Australia, and I could not help thinking that two of the wickets lost should have been saved.

In making a shot off a ball such as Chipperfield got, the right foot should be carried back and across the wicket. He endeavored to play it without moving his feet.

Allen was in a quandary over the new ball. He apparently knows Sievers's weakness against the slows.

Verity looked to be bowling too fast early to-day, but later he slowed up, with much better effect.

Imperturbable patience was the feature of Fingleton's century. His innings was invaluable. There was no seasonal gust and dwindle about his knock, but a steady flow of confident strokes.

This evenness of temperament is a big factor in his success, and none can compute just how far that goes towards making an international batsman. It was a Herculean effort. He scored all round the wicket, but favored the square cut.

### A Great Captain

Bradman impressed me in very marked degree with his genius for captaincy and field placing. Two English wickets fell as a direct result of his very clever leadership and O'Reilly's skilful bowling. Both Hardstaff's and Verity's dismissals were most intelligent and well-planned moves.

I believe that when Bradman has had the necessary experience of two or three more Test matches as skipper he will prove himself to be one of the brainiest captains Australia has had for several seasons.

Will his own batting suffer through the cares of leadership? My own opinion is that it definitely will not, because he has always that wonderful gift of confidence when he arrives at the crease.

His interlude on Saturday provided the most exhilarating part of the Test match. Some of his strokes were positively cheeky, but still remained brilliant in a combination of amazing footwork and superb timing. But his style has altered since he made his double and treble centuries in England six years ago. Then he was probably the most correct cricketer Australia had ever sent to our shores. He never lifted a ball off the ground and took no risks at all. Now he is ever seeking runs with uncanny strokes which are the delight of lovers of both orthodox and unorthodox cricket.

Bertie Oldfield's wicket-keeping deserves special mention. He kept as well as he has ever done in his long and splendid career.

I should say O'Reilly is a 50 per cent. better bowler with Bertie behind the stumps.

Australia's fielding was a class above that of the Englishmen. There was more snap about their work and greater anticipation by the fieldsmen. The returns of Fingleton and Badcock in particular were outstanding.

### Opening Batsman

Allen has still one problem to solve to finding an opening batsman with Barnett. Worthington is not a No. 1. I would prefer him to go in No. 6. I should have preferred a Barnett-Fagg partnership, especially after their success in the Queensland match. Wyatt's loss is considerable and I fear he will not appear until the fourth Test.

Fingleton's century was a masterpiece, and the immense value of his innings can best be described by saying that he saved Australia in exactly the same way that Leyland had done for England.

Voce can congratulate himself on a great bowling performance. I have rarely seen him so accurate or deadly.

Verity kept an ideal length and tied down every batsman. Robins also found his English bowling form, and Allen must be delighted at the totally unexpected change of fortune, his bowlers having all struck form at the psychological moment.

Bradman has my entire sympathy in the loss of McCormick, as this leaves Australia without a bowler of pace. Some will say that this is the luck of the game, but the luck was not helpful to Australia.

Badcock must have warm praise for the excellent catch which dismissed Barnett. He had the sun right in his eyes, but made as neat a catch as could be possible at a somewhat critical stage for Australia.

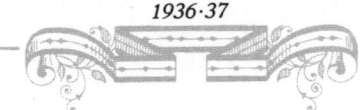

# AUSTRALIA FACES DIFFICULT PROBLEM.

BRISBANE, Tuesday.

Australia, faced with the task of making 381 runs in the fourth innings to win the first test match against England, suffered a crushing blow in the last 10 minutes of play this afternoon when Fingleton, after unsuccessfully appealing against the light, played the first ball from Voce on to his wicket.

Six appeals against the light were made before stumps were drawn at 5.55 p.m. in the middle of the second over, the score being three.

England's second innings to-day was marked by dramatic fluctuations of fortune and by batting which was mostly dour and defensive. The innings realised 256 runs. The captain, G. O. Allen, by a fighting innings for 68, swung the game England's way after the team's overnight grip of the match had been loosened.

Honours of the day were shared with Allen by the Australian slow bowler, F. Ward, who kept an end going for most of the innings, and captured five wickets, making his tally for the innings six wickets for 102 runs. Sievers took three wickets.

Bradman was not greatly troubled by his injured left ankle and he held a remarkable catch to dismiss Leyland off Ward.

At midnight, light, steady rain was falling, but nothing definite about the state of the wicket will be known until late on Wednesday morning.

## SIX APPEALS

### AGAINST BAD LIGHT.

BRISBANE, Tuesday.

In the closing stages of the English innings, the light became dull with heavy clouds. Allen naturally did not think of appealing against the light, as he was well set and the bowlers were tired. When Fingleton and Badcock walked out at 5.45 p.m. to open Australia's innings, it was anticipated that they would appeal against the light, and Fingleton did this after having the sightboard shifted and before a ball was bowled. Umpires Borwick and Scott conferred briefly and refused the appeal. Fingleton then played defensively at the first ball from Voce, and touched it into his stumps.

It was a dramatic moment for the crowd, and the shack was greater because Fingleton saved Australia with a great century in the first innings. He walked slowly from the wicket, and his disappointment was obvious.

Sievers, who was sent to join Badcock, also appealed unsuccessfully before he played a ball, and he made two more appeals, the umpires conferring on each occasion. Sievers, after blocking one ball out of his wicket, played Voce towards Allen at short leg and ran. It seemed that he would run his partner out, but Allen made a wide return to the wicketkeeper, Ames, who, after scrambling for the ball, missed with a throw at the stumps as Badcock got home.

Badcock then appealed against the light, making the fifth appeal in the over. This time the umpires did not bother to confer, but merely exchanged glances, and then signalled that play should continue.

The sixth appeal came after four balls in Allen's over, when Badcock spoke to the umpires, who conferred again, and then announced that stumps would be drawn. It was 5.55 p.m., and the light was hardly worse than it had been when previous appeals were disallowed.

The weather to-night was steamy and unsettled. Some light rain fell at 9 o'clock, and half an hour later there was a sharp shower. Up to a late hour there had been no more rain, but it was a period of considerable anxiety for members of both teams. The rain which fell would have a beneficial effect on the wicket, as it would tend to bind it, and perhaps it would make a good wicket out of one that might have proved troublesome. If further heavy rain falls there will be the possibility of a "sticky" wicket, on which England's left-handed bowler Verity would be deadly.

The State Meteorologist says that conditions are more uncertain than they have been of late, but he believes that to-morrow should be mostly fine, with the likelihood of some thunder. A little rain would probably improve the wicket. A heavy storm might result in a "sticky" wicket. To-day, there was one small patch outside the leg stump of the right-handed batsman at the pavilion end, and this helped Ward to turn the ball. Experts believe that the spin bowlers are bound to receive some assistance from the pitch to-morrow.

To win the match, Australia will have to make history, as no team has scored 381 runs in the fourth innings of a test and won. The greatest score in the fourth inning was 411 by England in 1924-25, but the team was beaten.

### ENGLISH GRIP LOOSENED.

The Englishmen's tight hold on the match was loosened when Fagg, Hammond, and Ames all fell before lunch in a period when only 49 runs were scored. Bradman had his men on their toes during that tense hour and a half. The pendulum swung Australia's way again when Leyland was brilliantly caught by Bradman. Allen played a courageous innings in which his control and defence surprised those who regarded him simply as a forcing batsman. Allen's 68 was his highest score against Australia. He batted for three and a quarter hours.

Ward, the hero of Australia's bowlers to-day, impressed with his stamina, control, and pluck. He varied his deliveries in a manner that made the batsmen cautious. He was aided by Bradman's shrewd placing of the field.

### OLDFIELD'S RECORD.

Oldfield, by two stumpings, broke the record of the English wicketkeeper A. Lilley, who dismissed 84 batsmen in tests between England and Australia.

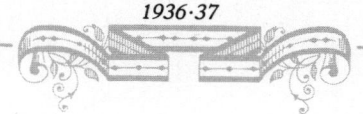

# ALLEN'S MATCH.

## Devastating Bowling.

## ENGLAND'S TEST WIN.

## Australian Debacle.

(BY DENZIL BATCHELOR.)

BRISBANE, Wednesday.

For four days the test match was fought out closely and desperately, with neither side ever holding an unassailable advantage. To-day in one hour of nightmare cricket, unforgettably and fantastically melodramatic, England won by 322 runs.

Never has the game staged a more incalculable denouement. Never have conquering cricketers, given not a shadow of a chance on current form, proved more emphatically that so long as cricket is played, the age of miracles can never be regarded as past.

This was the team that represented the country which had proved incapable of holding its own against South Africa and the West Indies. This was the team which fought in vain to stave off decisive defeat from New South Wales and narrowly escaped loss by an innings in its match in Sydney against an Australian Eleven. This was the team which for the first two days of the Queensland match fought a losing battle against the weakest Australian cricket State. To-day this team routed the massed strength of Australia.

The last phantom hope for Australia was dissipated by the second ball Allen bowled this morning. The ball, sliced as delicately as by a razor, spun from Badcock's bat to Fagg's hand, widespread as a hipbath. The victory of Wotan in the Melbourne Cup was a foregone conclusion compared with the dismissal of both Australia's opening batsmen without a run between them.

### BRADMAN, NOUGHT.

But that was but a mild surprise compared with what was to come. After the third wicket had fallen—Voce heeling over to hold Sievers's incautious flick at a flier from Allen—an electric tension settled on the crowd as Bradman made his way to the wicket.

Already an atmosphere of disaster loomed menacingly over the field. A panic clap of relief greeted the fact that Bradman survived his first ball. It was the only chance the crowd had of clapping Bradman's batsmanship to-day. His second ball kicked from the pitch. The batsman drew away from it as he made his stroke. A moment later the English team was clustering round Fagg to shake the giant-killing hand that had caught the most incalculable batsman in the world.

Badcock, Fingleton, and Bradman back in the pavilion without a run among them! From that moment Australia batted as if this was the one unforgettable fact in history. It was not the wicket that gave the victory to the bowlers. Verity, the great left-hander, Robins, Leyland, and Hammond were not needed. The two fast bowlers, irresistible as juggernauts, prolonged their onslaught to the gates of victory.

### CHIPPERFIELD FIGHTS BRAVELY.

Allen, bowling against the wind, seemed to be able to get a slight kick out of the wicket—that was more than could be extracted from the best of Australian batsmen. Chipperfield alone swung a rustic and speculative bat to good purpose, and remained unbeaten, except morally, with nearly half the runs scored by the side to his credit. In Australia's darkest hour he was still able to drive a victorious fast bowler into and past an unguarded deep-field.

Magnificent as Allen's figures were, they might have been better if his slips had charitably not given Chipperfield and Ward further "lives," but if the batsmen had had as many lives as cats, there was no gainsaying the English captain in his hour of triumph.

### VOCE'S FINE BOWLING.

With two heroic innings to his credit, and this magnificent bowling feat, this should be spoken of far down the echoing corridors of time as Allen's match—if Voce had not been playing in it. The left-hander bowled nobly to-day. He shattered Oldfield's wicket with a bombshell of a yorker. One remembers the old saying that no one ever bowled W. G. Grace a yorker—he always made a full pitch of it. To anyone less than a W.G., a lightning yorker on the wicket is an uncomfortable ball, and Oldfield did not look less of a batsman than anyone in the side for having succumbed to one.

Robinson's wicket also fell to Voce. The young batsman, for whom such a great future is predicted, swung a wild hooking shot at a "kicker," and was ignobly and comfortably caught at first slip.

The end came with the bowling of Ward, his nose injured through hooking one of Allen's faster balls with that part of him in preference to his bat. Voce's final lightning bolt blasted Ward's wicket a few minutes after one o'clock—in nice time for lunch, if anyone still had an appetite for such funeral-baked meats.

England's win after a first hour of apparently irrevocable disaster, recalls the victory at Adelaide during the last tour, and the utter and final subjugation of the Australian batsmen to-day was an even more devastating coup de grace than Chapman's team inflicted in the first test match on the Brisbane ground eight years ago. Whether Australia was less than Australia in this match, or whether the real England has been seen for the first time remains to be proved in four unpredictable test matches to come.

Allen and his men have covered themselves with glory in winning what was perhaps the most surprising test match in history.

# SELECTORS NOT STAMPEDED BY BIG DEFEAT

## Sievers Likely 12th Man If McCormick Is Fit

### From ARTHUR MAILEY

**BRISBANE, Wednesday.**

**T**HE Australian cricket selectors tonight chose the same 12 players for the second Test against England, beginning on Friday, December 18, as met defeat by 322 runs in Brisbane today.

| | | | |
|---|---|---|---|
| Bradman | Badcock | Brown | Fingleton |
| Chipperfield | McCabe | McCormick | Oldfield |
| O'Reilly | Robinson | Sievers | Ward |

**I congratulate the selectors. In the face of defeat they have refused to be stampeded.**

A week ago the selectors thought, most critics thought, and probably most Australians thought, that the team was the best Australia could field, and nothing has happened in the meantime to dissipate that idea.

We cannot consign the players with whom we were experimenting to the scrapheap and retain those on whom we depended and were equally unsuccessful.

**Badcock and Robinson are two promising cricketers, and it would be a tragedy if they were dropped, and I think that when the five Tests are over, we will find that O'Reilly has been our best bowler.**

Ward bowled extremely well, and looked about twice as good as O'Reilly, but it was not O'Reilly's true form.

### Brown's Place

Brown will automatically come into the side as an opening batsman, with Badcock batting lower down, and Sievers probably twelfth man.

Sievers got a few wickets in the second innings, but they were of tired batsmen. He never seemed to have the batsmen in trouble, and one of his victims, Allen, sacrificed his wicket.

**It is quite possible that McCormick will not be fit to play, in which case, Sievers would go into the side, and a good Sydney fieldsman played as twelfth man.**

### No Other Bowler

There is no bowler in Australia capable of taking McCormick's place, except R. Halcombe, of Western Australia, but as his delivery is regarded as doubtful, it might prove embarrassing to the whole team if he were chosen.

It is no use putting a bowler in the team simply because he is labelled "fast". He must be a wicket-getter. It would be far better for Sievers and McCabe to open the bowling, then allow O'Reilly and Ward, and to a lesser degree Chipperfield, get the Englishmen out.

There doesn't seem to be anybody else in Australia likely to do better, although Grimmett can be labelled a wicket-getter, but his inclusion would mean a weakening of the batting, which we can ill-afford to weaken. On Saturday and again today, our genuine batsmen finished at the sixth wicket.

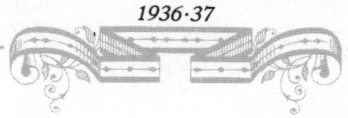

ustralia's defeat in Brisbane, after being hot favourites, was followed by a veritable hiding in Sydney where rain sealed Australia's fate after England had made a grand start.

But the weather God reversed his favours at Melbourne where Australia benefited.

The resultant battle of tactics was fascinating. At one stage I ordered my bowlers not to take wickets. But G. O. Allen saw through the move and closed. He was too late. There wasn't time to ravage our batsmen before stumps. Fine weather from then on and we were home.

An earlier declaration would have sealed Australia's fate in the match and for the series.

How easy to be wise in retrospect.

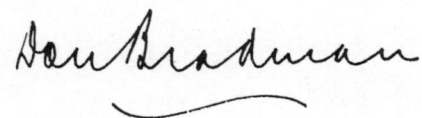

# ENGLISH CRITICS CAUTIOUS

### INDEPENDENT CABLE SERVICE

### LONDON, Thursday.

THE general feeling in England is one of cautious optimism regarding the prospects of the second Test match.

Everybody is eagerly discussing the possibilities of this most criticised English Test team repeating the Brisbane victory.

The Daily Express is non-committal, but states that O'Brien's inclusion should greatly strengthen Australia's batting. "Australia should also be heartened at McCormick's return to fitness."

The Daily Herald: "The game may be as sensational and as dramatic as the first Test."

News Chronicle: "Brown's absence is to be regretted. He is the Hobbs of Australia. Even without Brown, Australia may have less anxiety with the new opening pair than England has with hers."

## Importance Of Toss

The Daily Mail: "Victory may depend on the winning of the toss."

The Times: "England was the better side in Brisbane, and will continue to be from the standpoint of general equipment so long as Australia relies so overwhelmingly on Bradman.

"If he fails, Australia crashes. It has a woefully long tail."

Morning Post: "England's chances must be rated high. If the wicket is normal, England's attack and defence are not inferior to Australia's—always excepting the possibility of a great long innings from Bradman, than whom not even Hammond can more completely demoralise bowling."

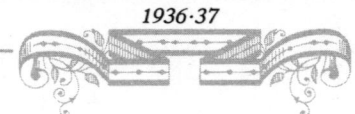

# Australia v England
# Second Test Match

AUSTRALIA v ENGLAND, Second Test Match, at Sydney, 18, 19, 21 and 22 December 1936.

| Australia | - First Innings | 80 |
| | - Second Innings | 324 |
| England | - First Innings | 426 for 6 wickets dec. |
| | - Second Innings | - |

Australia lost by an innings and 22 runs.

| DON BRADMAN | - c. G.O. Allen b. W. Voce | 0 |
| (Captain) | - b. H. Verity | 82 |

After England had batted for the first two days, overnight rain presented Australia with their second sticky wicket in succession, and DON BRADMAN made his second successive 'duck'; on this occasion he went in at 1 for 1, early on the third morning, and played an indeterminate stroke to a good-length ball, to be easily caught at short-leg, first ball.

Forced to follow on after lunch, 346 behind, Australia and Bradman did much better in the second innings, on a rapidly-improving wicket; he went in at 38 for 1, and was 12 not out at the tea interval.

On reaching 27, he passed C. Hill's aggregate of 2660, the previous record for an Australian in Tests between England and Australia, this being his thirty-fourth innings, against Hill's seventy-six. He completed 50 in an hour and fifty-two minutes, and was 57 not out at 6 p.m., after five minutes' further play.

Next morning he continued his careful progress. He lost J.H. Fingleton after 124 had been added for the second wicket in a minute over two and a half hours, and soon afterwards was himself bowled by H. Verity. He lifted his head in attempting to hook a slow long hop. He batted for two hours fifty-two minutes and 139 balls for his 82, and hit six fours.

## THE SCORES.

### ENGLAND.—First Innings.

| | |
|---|---|
| A. Fagg, c Sievers, b McCormick .... | 11 |
| C. J. Barnett, b Ward ........... | 57 |
| W. R. Hammond, not out ......... | 231 |
| M. Leyland, lbw, b McCabe .... | 42 |
| L. E. G. Ames, c sub. (Robinson), b Ward ........... | 29 |
| G. O. Allen, lbw, b O'Reilly ...... | 9 |
| J. Hardstaff, b McCormick ........ | 26 |
| H. Verity, not out ................ | 0 |
| Byes 8, leg-byes 8, wide 1, no-balls 4 | 21 |

Six wickets for ............. 426
(Innings declared closed.)
Fall of wickets: 27, 118, 247, 351, 368, 424.

### BOWLING.

| | O. | M. | R. | W. |
|---|---|---|---|---|
| McCormick ...... | 20 | 1 | 79 | 2 |
| Sievers .......... | 16.2 | 4 | 30 | 0 |
| Ward ........... | 42 | 8 | 132 | 2 |
| O'Reilly ........ | 41 | 17 | 86 | 1 |
| Chipperfield .... | .13 | 2 | 47 | 0 |
| McCabe .......... | 9 | 1 | 31 | 1 |

McCormick bowled a wide and four no-balls.

### AUSTRALIA.—First Innings.

| | |
|---|---|
| J. H. Fingleton, c Verity, b Voce.... | 12 |
| L. P. O'Brien, c Sims, b Voce ..... | 0 |
| D. G. Bradman, c Allen, b Voce .. | 0 |
| S. J. McCabe, c Sims, b Voce .... | 0 |
| A. G. Chipperfield, c Sims, b Allen .. | 13 |
| M. W. Sievers, c Voce, b Verity .. | 4 |
| W. A. Oldfield, b Verity .......... | 1 |
| W. J. O'Reilly, not out .......... | 37 |
| E. L. McCormick, b Allen ........ | 10 |
| F. A. Ward, b Allen ............. | 0 |
| C. L. Badcock, absent ........... | 0 |
| Bye 1, leg-bye 1, no-ball 1 ...... | 3 |

Total ..................... 80
Fall of wickets: 1, 1, 1, 16, 28, 30, 31, 80, 80.

### BOWLING.

| | O. | M. | R. | W. |
|---|---|---|---|---|
| Voce ............. | 8 | 1 | 10 | 4 |
| Allen ............. | 8.7 | 1 | 19 | 3 |
| Verity ............ | 3 | 0 | 17 | 2 |
| Hammond ......... | 4 | 0 | 6 | 0 |
| Sims ............. | 2 | 0 | 20 | 0 |
| Robins ........... | 1 | 0 | 5 | 0 |

Allen bowled a no-ball.

### Second Innings.

| | |
|---|---|
| L. P. O'Brien, c Allen, b Hammond | 17 |
| J. H. Fingleton, b Sims .......... | 73 |
| D. G. Bradman, b Verity ........ | 82 |
| S. J. McCabe, lbw, b Voce ........ | 93 |
| A. G. Chipperfield, b Voce ...... | 21 |
| C. L. Badcock, lbw, b Allen ...... | 2 |
| M. W. Sievers, run out .......... | 24 |
| W. A. Oldfield, c Ames, b Voce ... | 1 |
| W. J. O'Reilly, b Hammond ...... | 3 |
| E. L. McCormick, lbw, b Hammond | 0 |
| F. A. Ward, not out ............. | 1 |
| Leg-byes 3, no-balls 4 ........ | 7 |

Total .................. 324

### BOWLING.

| | O. | M. | R. | W. |
|---|---|---|---|---|
| Voce ............ | 19 | 4 | 66 | 3 |
| Allen ............ | 19 | 4 | 61 | 1 |
| Hammond ...... | 15.7 | 3 | 29 | 3 |
| Sims ........... | 17 | 0 | 80 | 1 |
| Verity .......... | 19 | 7 | 55 | 1 |
| Robins ......... | 7 | 0 | 26 | 0 |

Allen bowled three no-balls, and Voce bowled one no-ball.

# ENGLAND IN FAVOURABLE POSITION.

## SECOND TEST MATCH.

## Three Wickets for 279 Runs.

### HAMMOND'S CHANCELESS CENTURY.

### Badcock Attacked by Illness.

England, with 279 runs scored and only three wickets down, was in a favourable position at the end of the first day's play in the second test match against Australia at the Sydney Cricket Ground yesterday.

Fagg was dismissed by McCormick for 11, but Barnett, who gave a difficult chance off Ward when 26, stayed with Hammond until the score reached 118. Hammond and Leyland were then associated in a third wicket partnership of 129 runs.

From England's point of view, the most unsatisfactory feature was that the slowest period came just when the batsmen might have been expected to hurry the score along. That was after tea, when Leyland was extremely stoggy. Leyland was dismissed by McCabe under the new lbw rule for 42, but at the drawing of stumps Hammond was 147 not out.

It was Hammond's eighth century in tests against Australia and his fourth in tests in Sydney. He requires only 15 more runs to complete an aggregate of 2000 runs against Australia.

The Australians, disappointed early when Bradman lost the toss, suffered a setback when Badcock, who was suffering from gastric trouble and had a high temperature, had to be taken back to his hotel after lunch. It is doubtful whether he will be able to play to-day should his services be required.

# HUGE TASK FOR AUSTRALIA IN THE SECOND TEST

## By A. G. Moyes

ENGLAND 6 for 426 after 489 minutes batting.

Walter Hammond not out 231 after batting for 460 minutes, with 27 fours.

Thus two days have gone and England's first innings is not completed. Next Friday is Christmas Day and the second Test is to start on January 1. Players please note!

Yesterday, as on Friday, three wickets fell and 147 runs were added, which after all was slow work. Then came rain and there was no more play after 4.31 p.m., although the umpires did not let us go until an hour later.

What will be the effect of the rain, and will there be any more? If we have seen the last of it then the wicket should be as good as when the game started and that will help Australia. We will wait and see hoping that the weather will be with us.

Yesterday Badcock was again unable to play. He was in bed at his hotel listening instead of chasing the ball. It is hoped that he will be able to bat to-morrow, but what if Bradman had won the toss? We would have batted ten men probably.

England started off again at noon on a War of Attrition and it looked as though she would get through the pre-lunch session without loss.

The came the first thrill of the day — for Australia, when Ames hit a loose one— a very loose one—to cover and young Ray Robinson hugged the ball as though it had come out of his Christmas stocking.

Then lunch and Allen came in, but he had a look around and then missed one from Bill O'Reilly. Five for 368 was better and O'Reilly looked much happier.

Hardstaff was next to join Hammond, and the fieldsmen gathered round him in rather an embarrassing manner. I have no doubt Hardstaff likes them personally, but distance lends enchantment, especially when first you go to the wickets.

He stayed there for 73 minutes and provided his share of the limited excitement of the day because when he was 11 he hit Bill O'Reilly to square leg, and Ray Robinson dropped it. Poor Ray, He had done so well.

The excitement, however, had not died down when attention was directed to the stumps. McCabe it was who caught the eye as he showed the umpire a broken wicket, the result of the batsman's foot coming into contact with it. The appeal was negatived.

It was Joe's lucky day, but such things are always on the cards as when a stroke is made there is always the urge to follow the ball with the eye.

Over! Ward bowls to Hammond, who jumps in to drive. Ward grabs with both hands, but drops the ball. Hammond misses! His wicket would have been a real help at that stage.

Then came tea with 5 out for 418, with only 67 runs added between the two adjournments less 15 minutes for loss of time on account of rain.

The players come out again and after Ward had bowled an over, McCormick swings into action again with a new ball. He measures out his normal run whereas earlier he had reduced it by the length of the wicket almost, and Hardstaff turns the first to leg for two.

The second curved past the bat and a stump went flying through space while Hardstaff walked out and the board showed 6 for 424.

It was Verity who came next. He played one, touched the next and it slithered out of Oldfield's gloves. Another miss—but the ball was wet and the gloves could not grip it.

Still it looked promising as McCormick was a real force again, but then came rain in plenty, an appeal from Bradman and the end of play for the day.

It was then about 4.30, and an hour later, after the captains had disagreed, the umpires decided to let the debate hold over until to-morrow at twelve.

And thousands of people were no doubt glad to get home and change into dry clothes.

# PSYCHOLOGICAL COLLAPSE

## Bradman & Fingleton Help To Turn The Tide

(By GEORGE THATCHER.)

## O'REILLY'S "SIXES"

WHILE excuses could have been made for the Brisbane debacle, there was absolutely no reason why the Australians batted with such futility in the pre-lunch period at the Sydney Cricket Ground yesterday. Australia went for 80, and at one time it looked as if the record low score would not be exceeded. Now, with nine wickets in hand in its second knock, Australia should save an innings defeat.

THE wicket in the early period had been affected by rain, but, apart from a little "lift," it was completely without viciousness, and it is rather amazing that once again the English fast bowlers created an Australian rout on a pitch that should have helped the "spinners."

Bill Voce started the rabble. He had O'Brien caught with the last ball of his first over, and Bradman went the first ball of his next. Two balls later McCabe was out, and, with three wickets down for one, Australia's position was hopeless. The first three batsmen were dismissed as a result of bad cricket rather than marvellous bowling.

### Weak Shots

O'Brien tried to glance a ball that swung across his wicket, and was caught in the slips. Bradman played forward to a shortish ball from Voce that came slowly off the pitch, and, to the consternation of the crowd, he provided Allen at short leg with a "sitter."

McCabe's ball pitched outside the off stump, came through a little higher than usual. There was absolutely no excuse for the shot. Chipperfield chanced his arm, scored several fours and then gave Sims an easy catch off a half-volley. Oldfield was bowled with a full-toss. So, when McCormick and O'Reilly were associated, seven had fallen for 31 in 70 minutes. Neither O'Reilly nor McCormick has any pretensions to batting quality. Still, they played the right game. O'Reilly wielded a very hefty blade, and McCormick kept out quite a number of good deliveries. O'Reilly's three sixes changed the demeanor of a crowd that had been disappointed at the failure of the stars.

While Voce bowled accurately, his figures and those of Allen were very flattering. I feel that a little more courage on the part of the early Australians would have kept out England for the loss of two or three wickets until luncheon. Australia always with that mental hazard of a wet wicket in its mind surrendered without a fight.

Fingleton, after a dour innings, fell to the only really difficult ball of the period.

A famous English journalist put it to me this way: "I came 13,000 miles to see England win the Ashes. I want to see them win on their merits, but I hate victory when the other side capitulates." Those were harsh words, but, in my opinion, they were quite justified.

It would serve no good purpose in making repeated excuses for our batting failure. Australians must learn to bat on wickets on which the ball "pops" and occasionally "lifts" with a little viciousness.

It looks very much as if we have developed a crop of "cream-puff" batsmen.

### Bad Start

We started badly in the second innings, and lost O'Brien to a shocking shot. Then Fingleton and Bradman gradually wore down the English attack. Fingleton played superbly. He took lots of the new "pill," and did not make a mistake. Fingleton isn't a stylist, and even in club cricket those who did not know him would not pick him for the champion he is. A steady eye, firm defence, and courage—lots of the latter—are his main assets. While he went steadily on his way, Bradman played without distinction. Never have I seen him quite so subdued. Occasionally he made a good shot, but more often than not his timing was at fault, and Verity and Robins shaved his stumps with balls that turned at fair pace.

Allen should have had him caught on the on-side by Robins when he was 24. That chance was sharp, but not over difficult. Bradman, instead of placing the ball, smashed it in baseball style. The position of the game did not warrant such recklessness.

Now, with nine wickets in hand, Australia has a chance to rehabilitate itself. I am not for one moment suggesting that we can win. Bradman's form is too bad for that. In the first half-hour this morning he will have to survive another leg-stump battery by Allen and Voce. Should he overcome that period, England can look out for trouble.

The wicket during the second innings to-day wasn't a batsman's paradise, although it was probably more helpful to the bowlers than will be the case to-day. Hammond was the only bowler who got any life out of the wicket after lunch. I was rather amazed that Allen did not use him more. Verity had a great chance, but he was too fast.

Certainly he beat Bradman very badly on one occasion, but he would have had more success with slow "spinners," bowling to the off field in the fashion made famous by Wilfred Rhodes.

Voce appeared tired after his early morning effort, and I still think that Australia will score heavily in the Tests if our openers can make a moderate stand.

There is just a chance that Jack Badcock will bat to-day. He will be a big help, and if McCabe can carry on the good work after Bradman and Fingleton go, England may be set 150 runs. Then the elements, which, in the present series, have been very much against Australia, may come to our aid.

England's out-cricket yesterday has probably convinced Allen that a third fast bowler will be necessary in the Melbourne Test. His "spinners," Sims, and Robins, are altogether too expensive on a wicket that should have helped them. They may be more costly to-day. A second defeat looks like being Australia's portion, but it is hoped that we will go down fighting, and that the capitulation of the first innings will not be repeated to-day.

O'Brien's failure to overcome Voce will probably mean he will be dropped from the Melbourne Test. Fleetwood-Smith's success yesterday in Melbourne makes him a certainty.

Chipperfield will have to score runs to hold his place.

The Australian selectors should watch to-day's cricket with a good deal of interest.

And in the next few days a decision should be made concerning the availability of Billy Brown.

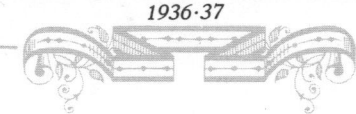

# INCIDENTS IN THE TEST TO-DAY

Bradman playing a ball from Hammond at the Sydney Cricket Ground to-day. In the background is a section of "The Hill."'

Bradman, bowled by Verity at the Sydney Cricket Ground to-day. The fieldsman facing him is Hammond.

# Weak Australian Attack Main Factor In The Defeat

## BATTING COLLAPSED WITH DISMISSAL OF McCABE

### By ARTHUR MAILEY

**E**NGLAND won the second Test match yesterday by dismissing Australia for 323, thus scoring by an innings and 22 runs.

The Australians lost because they depended too much on two men—Bradman and O'Reilly.

I feel tempted to make some excuses for the weather and its effect on the wicket when the Australians were about to bat, but I cannot find any excuse other than the feebleness of the Australian attack for England's score of 426 for the loss of six wickets.

Hammond, with all his dourness and caution, was master of the Australian bowlers, and if the wicket had been perfect on Monday morning, and Allen had decided to continue batting, it is possible that Hammond would have monopolised the strike and batted for another day at least.

### Perfect Wicket

This closure meant that Hammond sacrificed the opportunity of creating a world's record Test score, but Hammond realised that his services to England were more important.

Australia yesterday batted on a wicket which seemed as perfect as one might expect on the first day, yet after a good start the tail fell away, and could not amass more runs than the meanest batsmen that ever played cricket.

Thus I feel that England beat Australia on merit alone.

Australia did not possess a batsman who could bowl like Hammond, nor did it possess a bowler who could bowl to the field as did Verity, Voce, Hammond, and Allen.

Had the wicket been sticky throughout the game England would probably have won by a greater relative margin, because not only can Englishmen bat on sticky wickets, but they are equally competent in bowling on them.

McCabe played a glorious innings yesterday, and deserves full marks. When he left the bottom fell out of Australia's chances.

Fingleton played another fine innings, and might have turned a possible defeat into victory had the position been such that he could have carried less responsibility.

Bradman, that amazing fellow who makes extraordinary strokes, was more or less moody.

He is seldom governed by the condition of the game. In the face of defeat he makes the most amazing strokes, and gets away with them. Yesterday he made a vicious pull shot and lost his wicket.

I have seen him make a similar stroke, and the ball flew like a bullet to the boundary. The stroke, which brought about his downfall yesterday, did not go to the boundary. It seemed to cannon off his pads on to his wicket.

McCabe was graceful and artistic, and seldom wasted energy on futile flourishings of the bat.

Despite, however, these individual displays of cricket, England seemed the better-balanced team.

Badcock, who appeared at the ground in the afternoon, then came in. Siever's name had gone up on the board, but the crowd soon recognised it was Badcock, and gave the young player a grand reception.

Naturally subdued, he nevertheless showed an impregnable defence until "Gubby" Allen turned one back from the off and the ball, keeping low, rapped Badcock on the pads, and he was, out under the new l.b.w. rule.

### McCabe In Control

With Sievers as partner, McCabe took control of the situation and manoeuvred for the strike. The tall Victorian held his wicket up well.

It looked as if England might be given some runs to chase, but that useful change bowler, the tea interval, came to the rescue.

McCabe and Sievers restarted confidently enough, but the former then stepped in front of a straight one from Voce and attempted to glide it to leg. An appeal for l.b.w. was upheld, but McCabe stood his ground, as if expecting a favorable verdict.

Members of the English team freely admitted later that McCabe had hit the ball. It was bad luck for McCabe and Australia.

The sixth wicket had fallen at 318, but the whole side was out at 324, so that, while the main batsmen of the team gave rise to hopes for better things to come, the "tail" appears as big as ever.

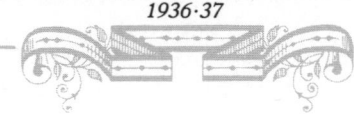

# BRADMAN NOT FULLY SUPPORTED BY TEAM

## POSITION DISTURBS CRICKET OFFICIALS

### Serious Handicap To Captaincy

IT is known that the Australian cricket selectors and the Board of Control are disturbed by a suggestion that the Test team is not pulling together, and that Bradman has not had the support generally given to an Australian captain.

The discussions have not yet reached an official stage.

Some members of the team have not been giving Bradman the co-operation that a captain is entitled to expect.

There is definitely, and has been for some time, an important section of the team that has not seen eye to eye with Bradman, either on or off the field.

## Little Team
### Work On Field

In the circumstances Bradman's captaincy has been seriously handicapped.

There is no doubt that the present Australian team, quite apart from the ill-luck in weather, and the unexpected failures) of leading batsmen, has looked less like a team, when fielding, than any of its predecessors since the war.

There is no question of any present member of the team displacing Bradman as captain.

In cricket circles it has been suggested that Victor Richardson should be called back to heal a breach that does not go deeply, and to co-ordinate the team into the combination it showed in South Africa.

### Reluctance To
#### Make Change

But Australian selectors, unlike English, are loath to change captains during a season.

It is unlikely, therefore, that Richardson, or anybody else, will be called upon.

Meantime, strenuous efforts are being made behind the scenes to gain for Bradman the support that an Australian captain must have from his men.

In view of this position the method of control of Tests becomes interesting.

The Board of Control appoints the selectors for the season; the selectors choose the team for each match; the board then approves of each team, and appoints its captain.

## Alterations
### Must Be Made

#### By ARTHUR MAILEY

It is quite obvious that the Australian selectors will be compelled to make severe alterations in the Australian team.

I do not favor drastic changes, but something must be done to improve the batting of the team, especially the tail end.

Unfortunately, all-rounders are scarce at the moment, and we must depend on specialists in batting and bowling.

Fleetwood-Smith must come in.

His selection is not altogether a war-time measure.

He would have been chosen probably had we won the first two Tests.

### Would Be A
#### Dangerous Bowler

He is quite a different bowler from O'Reilly, Ward, or Grimmett.

Being a left-hander, he would be a dangerous bowler under the new l.b.w. rule, because he spins viciously back from the off.

Whether Ward or O'Reilly is dropped is a problem for the selectors, but I would favor the omission of Sievers as a bowler and O'Brien as a batsman, and in their places Fleetwood-Smith and Brown, if available.

And if the selectors feel that O'Reilly, Fleetwood-Smith, McCormick, Chipperfield, and McCabe are sufficient to launch a satisfactory attack, I would omit Ward and select Allen, from Queensland, or Gregory of Victoria.

Allen scored a century against Fleetwood-Smith over the weekend, and a century against England at Ipswich.

Finally, I would not favor the inclusion of a left-hand opening batsman against Voce, despite the fact that O'Brien played a plucky knock in the second innings.

Voce's out-swinger to a left-hander is a masterpiece of work.

# BRADMAN DENIES LACK OF TEAM LOYALTY

---

## MATES WENT OUT OF WAY TO HELP

---

## SEEKS SYMPATHETIC UNDERSTANDING

---

## ALL TRIED VERY HARD

"THE statements that there has not been complete harmony amongst the members of the Australian Eleven are, in my opinion, completely without foundation."

That is Don Bradman's reply to assertions that have aroused wide interest and concern among cricket followers.

"My team mates have, in many cases, gone out of their way to help me and make my job as captain easier," he said to-day.

"They have all tried very hard and the non-success of the team cannot be attributed to any lack of effort on their part," he declared.

"It is unfortunate that a rumor such as this should be spread at a time when the Australian Eleven has suffered two successive defeats; probably it is an attempt to find a reason for the defeats.

"More good would accrue if the Englishmen were given due credit for well-deserved victories, and if the Australian team were accorded more sympathetic understanding from those people who really know nothing about the inner workings.

"I have never yet played in an Australian Eleven which was not 100 per cent. loyal to its captain, and I know that I never will."

---

## CLEARS UP ALL RUMORS

### (By A. G. Moyes)

Cricketers generally will be glad to know that Bradman does not consider that there is any truth in rumors that he was not enjoying the whole-hearted support of members of his team.

His views, coming on top of the statement given to "The Sun" yesterday by S. J. McCabe, should remove all wrong impressions.

That there have been rumors is undoubted, and they have been gathering in volume.

### Brought Into Open

Thus, when reference was made to them, it was imperative that the subject be fully ventilated and cleared up at once.

Then, if we lose the Ashes, there can be no suggestion that it was the result of any outside or inside influence, but purely a matter of cricket skill under the conditions in which the games were played. That is as it should be.

That should now finish the rumors which have persisted for weeks. In the long run it may prove a real blessing that they were brought out into the open and scotched.

# *Australia v England*
## *Third Test Match*

AUSTRALIA v ENGLAND, Third Test Match, at Melbourne, 1, 2, 4, 5, 6 and 7 January 1937.

| | | |
|---|---|---|
| Australia | - First Innings | 200 for 9 wickets dec. |
| | - Second Innings | 564 |
| England | - First Innings | 76 for 9 wickets dec. |
| | - Second Innings | 323 |

Australia won by 365 runs.

| | | |
|---|---|---|
| DON BRADMAN | - c. R.W.V. Robins b. H. Verity | 13 |
| (Captain) | - c. G.O. Allen b. H. Verity | 270 |

On this occasion the luck of the toss and the weather decisively favoured Australia.    DON BRADMAN's first innings began at 7 for 1 early on the first day, and lasted only twenty-eight minutes and 22 balls before he put up an easy catch to square-leg, to make the score 33 for 2.    His first five Test innings this season had thus produced only 133 runs, which, by a coincidence, was exactly the same as he had made in his first five Test innings in 1934.

After England had been dismissed on another 'glue-pot' wicket on the second day, the wicket had virtually recovered when Bradman went in at 2.50 p.m. on the third day, and he at once began to show his old mastery.    Rain interrupted play on three occasions, without making the wicket more difficult; in fact, Bradman took advantage of the fact that the bowlers had trouble in gripping the slippery ball.    Bradman had completed 50 in eighty-five minutes, and after an hour and forty minutes was 56 not out.    He reached 4,000 runs in all Test cricket when he was 18.

He then proceeded to bat the whole of the fourth day.    He was 164 not out at the tea interval, completed 200 at 5.15, after five hours fifty-four minutes, and was 206 when J.H. Fingleton was dismissed at 443 for 6; he and Bradman had added 346 for the sixth wicket, in six hours four minutes.    In the last half-hour, Bradman increased the pace of his scoring and at the close, after six hours thirty-nine minutes, was 248 not out - his first double-century v. England in a Test Match in Australia.    During the day, he scored 192 runs thus breaking the record for an Australian in a Test Match against England in Australia, previously held by C. Hill, who made 182 in one day in 1897-8.

His stand of 346 with Fingleton was the highest for the sixth wicket in any first-class match in Australia.

Suffering from a chill on the fifth morning, Bradman batted rather listlessly for a further fifty-nine minutes, and his first aggressive stroke skied the ball wide of mid-on, where G.O. Allen took a good catch.    His 270, in seven hours thirty-eight minutes, included twenty-two fours, and he was out to his 375th ball at 549 for 9.

His time of seven hours thirty-eight minutes was the longest he had ever batted in a Test Match and the longest innings ever played by an Australian in a Test Match in Australia.

His 270 was the highest score in the second innings of any Test Match and was also the highest 'Captain's innings' ever played in a Test Match.

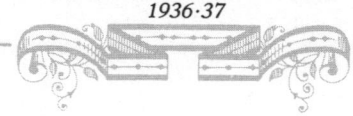

# THE SCORES.

## AUSTRALIA.—First Innings.

| | | |
|---|---|---:|
| J. H. Fingleton, c Sims, b Robins .. | | 38 |
| W. A. Brown, c Ames, b Voce ...... | | 1 |
| D. G. Bradman, c Robins, v Verity .. | | 13 |
| K. Rigg, c Verity, b Allen .......... | | 16 |
| S. J. McCabe, c Worthington, b Voce . | | 63 |
| L. S. Darling, c Allen, b Verity .... | | 20 |
| M. W. Sievers, st Ames, b Robins .... | | 1 |
| W. A. Oldfield, not out ............ | | 27 |
| W. J. O'Reilly, c Sims, b Hammond | | 4 |
| F. A. Ward, st Ames, b Hammond .. | | 7 |
| Byes 2, leg-byes 6, no-balls 2 .... | | 10 |

Nine wickets for ............. 200
Innings declared closed.
Fall of wickets: 7, 33, 69, 79, 122, 130, 183, 190, 200.

### BOWLING.

| | O. | M. | R. | W. |
|---|---:|---:|---:|---:|
| Voce ........... | 18 | 3 | 49 | 2 |
| Allen ........... | 12 | 2 | 35 | 1 |
| Sims ........... | 9 | 1 | 35 | 0 |
| Verity .......... | 14 | 4 | 24 | 2 |
| Robins .......... | 7 | 0 | 31 | 2 |
| Hammond ....... | 5.3 | 0 | 16 | 2 |

Allen bowled two no-balls.

### Second Innings.

| | |
|---|---:|
| W. J. O'Reilly, c and b Voce ..... | 0 |
| L. Fleetwood-Smith, c Verity, b Voce | 0 |
| F. A. Ward, c Hardstaff, b Verity .. | 18 |
| K. Rigg, lbw, b Sims ............. | 47 |
| W. A. Brown, c Barnett, b Voce .... | 20 |
| J. Fingleton, c Ames, b Sims ..... | 136 |
| D. G. Bradman, c Allen, b Verity .. | 270 |
| S. J. McCabe, lbw, b Allen ......... | 22 |
| L. S. Darling, b Allen ............. | 0 |
| M. Sievers, not out ............... | 25 |
| W. A. Oldfield, lbw, b Verity ...... | 7 |
| Byes 6, leg-byes 2, no-balls 10, wide 1 | 19 |

Total ..................... 564
Fall of wickets: 0, 3, 38, 74, 97, 443, 511, 511, 549, 564.

### BOWLING.

| | O. | M. | R. | W. |
|---|---:|---:|---:|---:|
| Voce ........... | 29 | 2 | 120 | 3 |
| Hammond ....... | 22 | 3 | 89 | 0 |
| Allen ........... | 23 | 2 | 84 | 2 |
| Verity .......... | 37.7 | 9 | 79 | 3 |
| Robins .......... | 11 | 2 | 46 | 0 |
| Sims ........... | 23 | 1 | 109 | 2 |
| Worthington ...... | 4 | 0 | 18 | 0 |

Voce bowled six no-balls, Sims three, and Allen one.

## ENGLAND.—First Innings.

| | |
|---|---:|
| T. S. Worthington, c Bradman, b McCabe ..................... | 0 |
| C. J. Barnett, c Darling, b Sievers ... | 11 |
| W. R. Hammond, c Darling, b Sievers | 32 |
| M. Leyland, c Darling, b O'Reilly .... | 17 |
| J. M. Sims, c Brown, b Sievers ...... | 3 |
| L. E. G. Ames, b Sievers ............ | 3 |
| R. W. V. Robins, c O'Reilly, b Sievers | 0 |
| J. Hardstaff, b O'Reilly ............. | 3 |
| G. O. Allen, not out ................ | 0 |
| H. Verity, c Brown, b O'Reilly ...... | 0 |
| Byes 5, leg-byes 1, no-ball 1 ...... | 7 |

Nine wickets for ................ 76
Innings declared closed.
Fall of wickets: 0, 14, 56, 68, 71, 71, 76, 76, 76.

### BOWLING.

| | O. | M. | R. | W. |
|---|---:|---:|---:|---:|
| McCabe .......... | 2 | 1 | 7 | 1 |
| Sievers ........... | 11.2 | 5 | 21 | 5 |
| O'Reilly .......... | 12 | 5 | 28 | 3 |
| Fleetwood-Smith .. | 3 | 1 | 13 | 0 |

Fleetwood-Smith bowled a no-ball.

## ENGLAND.—Second Innings.

| | |
|---|---:|
| C. J. Barnett, lbw, b O'Reilly ...... | 23 |
| T. S. Worthington, c Sievers, b Ward | 16 |
| W. R. Hammond, b Sievers .......... | 51 |
| M. Leyland, not out ................ | 111 |
| L. E. G. Ames, b Fleetwood-Smith .. | 19 |
| J. Hardstaff, c Ward, b Fleetwood-Smith ...................... | 17 |
| G. O. Allen, c Sievers, b Fleetwood-Smith ...................... | 11 |
| R. W. V. Robins, b O'Reilly ....... | 61 |
| H. Verity, c McCabe, b O'Reilly ...... | 11 |
| J. M. Sims, lbw, b Fleetwood-Smith | 0 |
| W. Voce, c Bradman, b Fleetwood-Smith ...................... | 0 |
| Leg-byes ...................... | 3 |

Total ........................ 323
Fall of wickets: 29, 65, 117, 155, 179, 195, 306, 322, 323, 323.

### BOWLING.

| | O. | M. | R. | W. |
|---|---:|---:|---:|---:|
| Sievers ........... | 2 | 2 | 39 | 1 |
| McCabe .......... | 8 | 0 | 32 | 0 |
| O'Reilly .......... | 21 | 6 | 65 | 3 |
| Fleetwood-Smith .. | 25.6 | 2 | 124 | 5 |
| Ward ............ | 12 | 1 | 60 | 1 |

Australia won by 365 runs.

How Bradman was dismissed for 13, in the third Test in Melbourne. He turned a ball from Verity neatly to short leg, and right into Robins' safe hands.

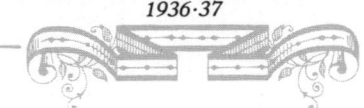

# AUSTRALIANS MAKE POOR START.

## SIX WICKETS DOWN FOR 181.

## Rain May Make Pitch Sticky.

### McCABE, 63 NOT OUT, TOP SCORE.

### Hammond Bruises Ligament in Knee.

(From Our Special Representative.)

MELBOURNE, Friday.

Australia, in the vital Third Test match against England at the Melbourne Cricket Ground to-day, lost six wickets for 181 runs. It was a disappointing performance, even though the pitch did not play truly.

Steady rain, which caused suspension of play, may bring about a "sticky" wicket to-morrow, giving Australia the chance to reap the benefit of the toss.

The weather in the city to-night cleared shortly before 8 p.m., and remained fine. The English captain, Allen, expressed the opinion that the wicket to-morrow would roll out splendidly if fine weather continued.

A special weather forecast for to-morrow reads: "A tendency to some slight showers early in the morning. Otherwise fine. Southerly winds."

Hopes of a big score were dashed early with the failure of Bradman. The wicket before lunch caused the batsmen concern, and later some of the spin bowlers were able to turn the ball, but there were some unsatisfactory features of the batting.

Fingleton defended stubbornly for two hours for 38 runs. McCabe (63), and Oldfield (21), engaged in the best partnership of the day, and they had put on 51 runs in smart time, when an appeal against the light was upheld at 5.56 p.m.

Hammond, England's greatest batsman, slipped and fell when about to deliver a ball, and he did not field after tea. He bruised a ligament in his right knee, but Hammond does not think that it will seriously affect his batting.

# WHEN WICKETS TOPPLED.

## Day of Thrills.

## MEMORABLE TEST.

## Pitch Played a Villain's Part.

(BY DENZIL BATCHELOR.)

MELBOURNE, Sunday.

The most venerable habitue of the Melbourne Cricket Ground can hardly have seen a more thrilling or a more absorbingly interesting afternoon's cricket than that famous, or rather infamous, wicket provided on Saturday. Long before the first ball was bowled the stern battle of tactics began.

It was obvious that that innocent-seeming strip of wet turf, with the fierce glare of the Melbourne sun beating down on it, concealed as much villainy as ever lurked behind a smiling face. This was to be a wicket in a mood far removed from that skittish naughtiness during the first hour's play for which Melbourne turf is famous. This was a black-hearted wicket without any element of kindliness in it; without so much as a single speck of honest, impartial mud from the grass on top right down to the volcanic fires beneath.

### PARADOX OF PLAY.

At the beginning, the match developed into something as abstract and as intellectually exhausting as a game of chess between the two captains. As soon as play was possible, one wanted to continue the game and the other did not. Doubtless, Allen realised that the gift of the last four Australian wickets without cost would not compensate for exposing the batting strength of his team to such a certain death trap.

From the moment the game began, the paradox of the play was obvious. Except during the early batting of the English team, both sides were determined not to stay in (generally the one reasonable ambition of a cricket team), but, to commit suicide as quickly as possible, to have the earliest opportunity of murdering their opponents. The paradox went deeper still. At the finish of the English innings, the English batsmen, hopelessly far behind Australia's score, were not more eager to get out than the Australian bowlers were to keep them in. For the end, Allen had to declare, to get a few overs at the Australian batsmen; and even then Bradman contrived to thwart him by sending in nothing but bowlers, until Fleetwood-Smith was able to persuade the umpires that not sufficient light remained for him to do himself justice as an opening batsman.

### PROCESSION BEGINS.

As soon as play began, the remaining Australian batsmen hurried out as soon as they had hurried in, and Bradman did not trouble Fleetwood-Smith, the last man in, to make his perfunctory return trip to the crease at all. No doubt he was keeping him fresh to open Australia's second innings.

Oldfield batted firmly, and O'Reilly at least patted and gardened the damaged wicket with as much dignity and zeal as a first-wicket batsman. O'Reilly appears to take his batting far more seriously than anyone else does—except, perhaps, those philanthropic gentlemen who give five-pound notes for sixes. An innings by O'Reilly generally furnishes the only discoverable answer to the old nonsense riddle about the higher the fewer: The higher O'Reilly hits the ball, the fewer runs he is likely to make. On Saturday, however, his first innings ended with a bowler's shot into the slips.

Hammond looked the best of the English bowlers. If only Australia's best batsmen could be trusted to bat as well as England's best batsman can bowl!

### IMPENDING DOOM.

England's innings began in an atmosphere of impending doom. The medium-paced bowlers, from the first, were able to make the ball rear from the pitch as high and as unnaturally as a circus pony, and the only strokes that could be made were dead-bat shots which, according to the liveliness of the delivery, might, or might not, be caught by silly point or silly leg. Worthington played just such a shot before a run was scored, and the ball went to Bradman as gently as if he himself had bounced it on the middle of the bat.

The greatest single roar of excited applause that has ever been heard at a cricket match greeted Worthington's downfall. It was more than a cheer at the defeat of a batsman; it was a cry of recognition of victory on the horizon; it was a shout of welcome to the renaissance of Australian cricket.

From the moment Worthington left, the cricket provided two great individual achievements, apart from the enthralling intricacy of the tactical war waged between the two captains. One was the heroic innings of Hammond, and the other the memorable bowling of Sievers. Saturday's play showed a rather puzzled world of cricket enthusiasts wherein lies the strength of Sievers as a bowler. On a vicious wicket, he was able to make the ball rise more unplayably than any other bowler on either side. He kept an impeccable length, and bowled with fine accuracy; and the wicket and inspired fielding could be trusted to do the rest.

### HAMMOND FIGHTS.

While Hammond and Leyland were together, it was still possible that England would weather the storm. Hammond played an innings that will be remembered by those who saw it as long as his double century in Sydney. He actually contrived to defy destiny by playing an occasional forcing shot. He off-drove Sievers to the boundary so vigorously that, even on that dead outfield, the eye could not follow the flash of the speeding ball.

Leyland, too, batted as if the best bowling and the worst wicket could not prevail against him. It took an unforgettable catch to get rid of him, Darling swooping with eagle-swift instantaneousness on to a leg glide, brilliantly played only a few feet from the fieldsman. With the departure of Hammond, England batted like a doomed side. Had Allen known that once his best batsman was gone five wickets would fall for eight runs, he must have declared with four wickets down and obtained an invaluable extra half-hour's bowling at Australia. As it was,

Sims, unduly promoted, was sent in at half past four, apparently in the pathetically optimistic hope that he would stay for an hour and a half. He batted as immovably as a statue, that is to say, he did not bat at all, but was bowled at for a few balls.

### CROWD'S REACTIONS.

The suspense became intolerable, and towards the end of England's innings, the spectacle of a ball bowled which did not get a wicket was so shockingly startling that the crowd became hysterically vocal. They gave Sievers three cheers every time he took a wicket, with a spontaneity and unison which would have done credit to the coaching of an American cheer leader.

Throughout the day, much had happened to play upon their feelings. There had been the sight of the two captains inspecting the wicket at noon—that was worth a boo. Then the appearance of three policemen, ironically enough wearing sun helmets, going out to guard the waterlogged wicket, won a respectful cheer. The appearance of O'Reilly and Fleetwood-Smith to open Australia's innings evoked a new sort of ovation—they were heartily laughed at all the way to the wicket.

The day's play ended with a typical Melbourne cloudburst. What of it! A rainbow glittered above the new stand, which seemed to prove that there is sunshine in Melbourne —and the wicked wicket almost winked.

Residents of Bowral, Don Bradman's home town, listening to a Test broadcast from his brother's sports store on Saturday.

# THIRD TEST IN AUSTRALIA'S GRIP

## BETTER HALF OF TEAM STILL TO BAT

### Bradman Cuts Loose; Rigg, Fingleton And Ward In Grim Fight

#### By ARTHUR MAILEY

MELBOURNE, Monday.

THE Australian batting today has placed the third Test firmly in our grip. England has no hope of escape, outside of a miracle.

Following on a first innings lead of 124, we have 194 more runs on the board, and by far the better half of the side yet to be disposed of.

That advantage of 318 runs would, in itself, be a hurdle for any team in a fourth innings. But the Australian side, looking more and more like a real Test XI every day, will make it a much stiffer obstacle before the match is over.

# HUGE CROWD'S FRENZY HOLDS UP GAME

## Fingleton A Grand Partner For Bradman

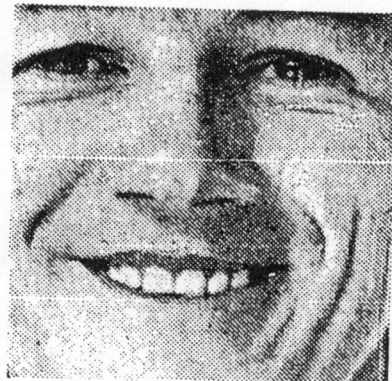

Bradman, the Conqueror.

## Scoring Was Easy On Lifeless Pitch

## GRAVE DUG FOR ENGLAND'S HOPES

MELBOURNE, Tuesday.

WILD acclaim from the packed ground greeted Bradman's century shortly after lunch to-day. Being Bradman he reached three figures by hitting Voce for four and the frenzied cheers of the crowd of 70,000 held up the game for some minutes. Another tremendous roar of relief and delight marked Fingleton's century.

The grave of England's third Test hopes was dug grimly by Bradman and Fingleton, says Neville Cardus. The wicket gave little help to the bowlers. A flying ball was a miracle and the Australians steadily added runs to a total that was becoming a nightmare to England.

THE dynamic batsman of old, Bradman was himself again. That much was obvious from the beauty of his strokemaking, but he took no risks in consolidating Australia's position.

### By Neville Cardus

A lovely morning for the fourth day, soft sunshine and sailing white clouds, like any summer day at Old Trafford. And again a fine crowd to see Bradman; work and all forms of manual labor are rigidly dismissed from the mind by Melbourne whenever Test cricket is shaking the continent.

This morning as I left my hotel I saw a group of little girls setting forth with wickets and bats; they will I suppose, be ready for action at the first signs of failure in Australian manhood, and no doubt they are already qualified to join the women in the crowd and scream for Australia at the top of their voices.

The wicket was as easy as middle age, old slippers, and vintage port. Voce could scarcely make the new ball rise knee-high, and Bradman pulled him with the familiar dynamic movement. The conditions were his ally.

Allen bowled with so great an effort that, after a single ball, his hair became towsled. He actually sent a ball flying past Fingleton's breastbone to the off, but this miracle was, as miracles should be, exceptional.

Voce then forced Bradman back in a superb over of perfect length and rhythm. Bradman was glad to edge a fine outswinger for a single, and the next ball, a masterpiece of accurate swerve, went through the slips also, behind Fingleton's back, while Fingleton was probably wondering in a flash of apprehension whether anybody had held a catch while he wasn't looking.

It was easy to feel the sense of strain in the efforts of England's fast bowlers to take a wicket. Allen troubled Bradman, who was guilty of a dangerous stroke to point. The batting and the turf frustrated the onslaught. Hammond came to the relief of Voce. It is always good captaincy to give Hammond the ball while it is still new. Fingleton again played perpendicularly, not obviously thinking of runs, which came to him by a sort of interest on the time accumulated during his stay at the wicket. Bradman couldn't unleash himself. His batting was tied to the kennel for a long time. None the less, Australia were attending to the right job, grimly digging the deep hole for England's funeral.

## General War Of Attrition

The England attack was admirably steady, and Voce worked like a Trojan on the wicket sent by heaven to Australia's batsmen so soon after Saturday's shambles. The runs continued to come slowly, a by-product of the general war of attrition. Bradman's cricket was, in the term of Karl Marx, congealed labor.

At lunch Bradman and Fingleton were still not out, and apparently beyond serious error.

After lunch (which by the way consisted of oysters, turkey, asparagus, jelly and trifle, all served with charm and hospitality by the club), Verity proceeded with his precise bowling, which before the interval cost England only seven runs in 56 balls; his length dropped with the persistence of water on a rock; I began to look for stalactites hanging down to the earth; the wicket was easily the best, the most cosy and comfortable seen in the Test matches this season.

Bradman cut Voce brilliantly and reached his 100, a State occasion, related to his cricket in England of six years ago as the honest mason's productions are related to architecture. But, as I say, I expect him to begin at any moment and shed his armor. The dazzling returns of Robins produced further hysterics among the women.

## Robins A Joy To See

Bradman drove Sims with a grand running drive and pulled him voraciously to leg; the banked fires of his innings seemed now to have been struck into blaze but Sims had the honor of beating him in the same over.

This was the only sign of mortality the England attack had witnessed for many, many persevering overs, during which the only really encouraging influence to Allen was Robins's quick-silver attempts to run somebody out; he seemed to cover oceans of space, and cover or back up all the other fieldsmen, himself included. He was a joy to see, and you had to be quick to see him, as he flashed and swooped here, there, and everywhere.

Verity put another shovel of damp coal on Bradman's play. He worried the great man, who, even against a long hop from Sims now and again, pulled prodigiously and got only a single. I judge Bradman from the standard he himself established in England during his wonderful year of 1930, when no bowler could keep him quiet. The thrilling velocity of his hits, the old genius shot out once more as soon as Allen came on at 323. A fierce off-drive from the back foot rendered pursuit the merest vanity.

Imperceptibly but surely England's pit was deepened and Fingleton went his ways, a good second grave digger who might have said that he had been on the job at this cemetery man and boy these many years. He does his job diligently with a straight bat, seldom lifted up higher than his knee, and he is always ready for the cause to contribute his share modestly, even anonymously.

He deserved his sojourn on to-day's heavenly wicket, for he played a brave and lonely hand at Brisbane, while at Sydney he was dependable in difficult straits. They also serve who only stand and wait.

When Fingleton reached his 100 he was given roars of applause, the generous like of which I have seldom heard at a cricket match. It was prolonged, and it culminated in three crashing cheers. It was the sort of ovation the foreigners give to Toscanini after he has conducted an opera.

The England team accepted the situation now with commendable philosohy and Robins, having sought in vain to run the batsmen out, came on to bowl, also, apparently, for runouts.

# SCRAMBLE FOR STUMPS AS TEST ENDS

## PLAYERS DID NOT WAIT TO SEE SKIED BALL CAUGHT

**MELBOURNE, Thursday.**

PLAYERS scrambled for the wickets as the third Test ended to-dya.

Even before Bradman had caught the last catch skied by Voce, the stumps were being pulled out and divided.

### (By A. G. Moyes)

Australia's attack lacked Test Match essentials when play was resumed

Bradman took the field. He was feeling better, but had not recovered completely.

McCabe opened the bowling with a new ball, and two singles and a four to Robins made a bright start. Then Robins took another single, and England needed 446 to win.

Sievers took the Richmond end, and Robins cover-hit him for two, making the partnership 50 in 25 minutes, Robins having made 35 of them.

Robins reached 40, and Leyland then drove McCabe straight to the fence, following it with a single.

### Umpire Hit

Turning Sievers for two, Leyland reached 80 and then glanced him nicely for one, Robins following with a delightful cover-hit for three.

In McCabe's fourth over Leyland drove one hard, and Umpire Scott received the full benefit of it on the shin, but the ball cannoned off and two were run.

Off the first ball of Sievers's fifth over, O'Reilly, at slip, missed a low right-hand chance from Robins and three balls later a chance of stumping went astray, but Robins was not perturbed and drove Sievers straight to the fence.

Then he tried to cover-drive the last of the over, and it just eluded Fleetwood-Smith and two were run, making Robins 50 in 47 minutes. It was an over full of incident.

### Sparkling Innings

At 275 O'Reilly relieved McCabe, and Robins cover-drove him magnificently to the fence. Robins was putting up his best effort in the Test against Australia, and it was a sparkling innings, as breezy as his fielding.

O'Reilly's second over brought three, and then Leyland hit Fleetwood-Smith to the fence, making the partnership 100 in 59 minutes, something exceptional for a Test, but an indication of what can be done when

batsmen are natural.

Three hundred came up in 252 minutes, and Leyland hit Fleetwood-Smith past cover to the fence in great style, reaching 103 in 168 minutes, with 10 fours.

At 12.50, O'Reilly spun his leg break, and it hit the top of Robins's off stump. Robins's was a delightful innings, taking 65 minutes and yielding seven fours. The partnership contributed 111 runs.

### Quick Catches

One feature was the manner in which Oldfield had taken Fleetwood-Smith. He was obviously quite at home.

O'Reilly bowled a slow full toss to Verity, who obligingly hit it to McCabe, who was three-parts of the way to the fence at long-on.

Sims was out at once, l.b.w., to Fleetwood-Smith. Voce skied the next ball and as Bradman caught it, Leyland and Fleetwood-Smith took the stumps, at one end, and others divided them at the other.

Fleetwood-Smith gave his stumps to Bradman, who also got the ball, and Leyland presented a stump to Umpire Borthwick.

Australia thus won at 1.10 p.m. by 365 runs.

Leyland's 111 was made in 194 minutes, and included 11 fours. England's innings lasted 278 minutes.

A crowd congregated outside the players' dressing rooms for a time, and some strolled out to look at the wicket.

Don Bradman, with a lusty drive, sends one from J. M. Sims flashing through the covers.

# NINE BATSMEN ARE INCLUDED IN THE TEST TWELVE

## Chipperfield, Gregory & Badcock Are In

### By J. C. DAVIS ("Not Out")

THE selectors have done their best to stiffen the batting of Australia for the fourth Test match in Adelaide next week. They have gone on the right lines, though there must be a risk in it, because the needed type of all-round players has been hard to find in this land teeming with cricketers.

IN selecting the team the committee had to concentrate more than ever on buttressing the batting by choosing more down-the-list men who are capable batsmen.

This successful policy was carried out in the Australian Eleven v England match in Sydney. The selection of that eleven met hostile criticism in many quarters. Many well-meaning enthusiasts became indignant on contemplating what they alleged was mediocrity in the bowling.

The selectors have now omitted Darling, Ward, and Sievers from the team that played in Melbourne and included Chipperfield, Gregory and McCormick, while retaining Badcock in the twelve.

This team may be found as satisfactory as any that be chosen, provided the captain, Don Bradman, does not make too much use of his slow bowlers. Men of this kind were invariably used as changes in the great teams of old. That is how they should be used and not as stock bowlers. The two bowlers of this sort chosen are first-class batsmen. So is Badcock, who may get into the eleven, hence this side ought to be strengthened in batting.

If Darling had shown his true form in Melbourne there would have been no need to omit him. At his best he is an attacking batsman of high quality.

In the Sydney Australian XI match a team chosen in similar lines worked out effectively. It silenced all the critics. That the batting was not inept after the fall of the sixth wicket at 332 was shown by the others carrying the total to 544 for eight wickets—then the closure.

Australia has needed two cricketers of the all-round type of Alan Fairfax. A right-hander, he was a solid batsman and a medium pace bowler, able to keep a length. H. I. Ebeling might have been one of these, if he had been brought in early and practised hard to develop his absolutely best form and condition and then encouraged to seriously think of his batting. If M. Sievers had a little more fire in the field and a good deal more in batting, he would be the man.

A player little mentioned in this connection and who may yet fill the bill, is the Victorian W. E. Pearson. He is the type, a first-class field, a very active athletic man, a good orthodox forcing batsman and a medium pace bowler. One has never seen him playing, but some of the selectors have had that pleasure.

There is more than a grain of humor in the fact that while the slow leg-break bowlers in the early period of the campaign of the M.C.C. men were so deadly, the garnering where they are concerned in the Tests has been done by the batsmen against them.

F. Ward had his very good periods and would have had more but for catching that was missing.

But now that Fleetwood-Smith has won his way into the team there is hardly room for the other, even in face of Ward having shown in Melbourne that he is a better batsman than some of his early efforts indicated.

With the need to strengthen the batting without unduly impairing the attack, A. G. Chipperfield had to be considered again. On the two bad wickets in Brisbane and Sydney Chipperfield shaped second to none with the bat. One hopes to see him on his toes in every phase of fielding whether in the slips or otherwise, keeping his eye on the placing of his field while bowling and retaining the ginger in his batting.

With England leading two matches to one, the fourth Test at Adelaide was crucial. Knowing the nature of my responsibility I fought hard against a deep set field designed to deprive me of the strike. The result was a double century containing 99 singles.

But the hero of the match was Fleetwood-Smith who bowled Hammond on the last morning with one of the finest deliveries ever sent down.

If ever one single ball won a Test match, that was it.

*Don Bradman*

## Tests In Adelaide

THIS will be the thirteenth Test match between Australia and England at Adelaide, and the results so far have favored Australia, who has seven wins to five there. It is rather remarkable that England won the first two and the last two there, and that her fifth win was sandwiched in between Australia's fifth and sixth wins. Australia had won five games in a row when England gained that fifth win in 1911-12 by seven wickets.

Two of the most remarkable games of all have been played there. In the match of 1924-5 with Arthur Gilligan's team, which was marked by an unusual list of casualties, resulting in England at one time having several substitutes in the field, Australia gained the honors by 11 runs. England might have won that game had not rain stopped play when she needed only 27 runs, and had three wickets in hand. Next day the three wickets fell for only 16 runs. The 1928-9 game was a remarkable struggle which Australia might have won had Bradman not been run out when he was hitting the bowling all over the field. England won that game by only 12 runs. Then there was the remarkable game four years ago, with all its unpleasantness, which England won by 389 runs.

## High Scoring Ground

TESTS on this ground have been notable for high scoring—indeed, the scores there have been more consistently high than on any other ground. The record Test aggregate was recorded there in the 1920-1 game, when 1753 runs were made, and Australia won by 119. The four innings in that game produced totals of 354 and 582 to Australia, and 447 and 370 to England, and there were six individual century scores—four for Australia and two for England. On only two other occasions have so many centuries been made. The 1928-9 game also produced four innings totals exceeding 300. Australia has such scores there as 411, 573, 506, 476 and 582, while England has 490, 501 and 447.

In no Test played there has the scoring been really low, and in not one has there not been at least one innings score exceeding 300. If history is to repeat itself we will see more heavy scoring in the coming game. The Adelaide wicket at one time was regarded as the fastest in Australia, but, like those on the chief grounds in the other capital cities, it has lost some of its pace. It was never a good wicket for fast bowlers, but it appears now more than ever to favor those of the spin type.

# Australia v England
## Fourth Test Match

AUSTRALIA v ENGLAND, Fourth Test Match, at Adelaide, 29, 30 January, 1, 2, 3 and 4 February 1937.

| | | | |
|---|---|---|---|
| Australia | - First Innings | 288 | |
| | - Second Innings | 433 | |
| England | - First Innings | 330 | |
| | - Second Innings | 243 | |

Australia won by 148 runs.

| | | |
|---|---|---|
| DON BRADMAN | - b. G.O. Allen | 26 |
| (Captain) | c. and b. W.R. Hammond | 212 |

Australia on the first day again failed to take advantage of DON BRADMAN's fortune in winning the toss. Going in just after lunch at 72 for 2, he reached an aggregate of 3,000 in England-Australia Tests with his first run, and looked to have settled down for a big score when G.O. Allen bowled him; he tried to hook a ball (his fifty-fourth) which kept rather low, and played it on to his wicket, being out at 136 for 4.

In the second innings, Bradman again set himself to win the match for Australia with another huge innings. Going in at 21 for 1 on the third evening, he made a solid 26 not out in exactly an hour before close of play; and again he batted all through the fourth day. He completed 50 in one and three-quarter hours, was 70 at lunch, and at 3 p.m. reached his century, by pulling R.W.V. Robins for 4, after three hours sixteen minutes at the wicket. At 136 not out at the tea interval he did not accelerate as he usually did in the evening, H. Verity keeping him quiet with some accurate if negative leg-theory to a deep-set field. The result was that he scored only 38 in an hour and forty-two minutes after tea, and was 174 not out, after five hours fifty-eight minutes' batting, when stumps were drawn. When he was 53, he completed his season's 1000 runs; in doing so on 2 February, he was 19 days earlier than the previous best by a South Australian batsman, C. Hill. When he was 130, he passed Hill's aggregate of 11,129, previously the biggest total of runs ever scored in Australia; Hill had 233 innings in Australia, while this was Bradman's 135th innings in that country.

For the second consecutive Test Match, and for the third time out of four altogether, Bradman's innings continued into a third day, when he and R.G. Gregory resumed their fifth-wicket partnership, next morning; this they carried to 135 before Gregory was run out, having stayed for two hours fifty-five minutes. Bradman himself, after playing a maiden over of leg-theory from Verity when 199, completed 200 in two minutes over seven hours and nineteen minutes later, at 1.23 p.m., hit a catch very hard back to the bowler. He was out at 422 for 6, having batted for seven hours twenty-one minutes. Bradman hit only fourteen fours.

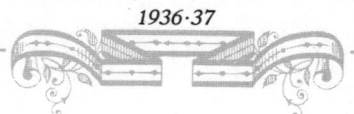

Don Bradman tosses the coin whilst G. O. Allen calls. Allen's optimism in not changing into boots proved unjustified.

# FULL SCORES AND DETAILS OF PLAY.

### AUSTRALIA.—First Innings.

| | |
|---|---|
| J. H. Fingleton, run out | 10 |
| W. A. Brown, c Allen, b Farnes | 42 |
| K. E. Rigg, c Ames, b Farnes | 20 |
| D. G. Bradman, b Allen | 26 |
| S. J. McCabe, c Allen, b Robins | 88 |
| R. Gregory, lbw, b Hammond | 23 |
| A. G. Chipperfield, not out | 57 |
| W. A. Oldfield, run out | 5 |
| W. J. O'Reilly, c Leyland, b Allen | 7 |
| E. L. McCormick, c Ames, b Hammond | 4 |
| L. Fleetwood-Smith, b Farnes | 1 |
| Leg-byes 2, no-balls 3 | 5 |
| **Total** | **288** |

Fall of wickets: 26, 72, 73, 136, 206, 226. 49, 271, 283, 288.

### BOWLING.

| | O. | M. | R. | W. |
|---|---|---|---|---|
| Voce | 12 | 0 | 49 | 0 |
| Allen | 16 | 0 | 60 | 2 |
| Farnes | 20.6 | 1 | 71 | 3 |
| Hammond | 6 | 0 | 30 | 2 |
| Verity | 16 | 4 | 47 | 0 |
| Robins | 7 | 1 | 26 | 1 |

Voce, Allen, and Farnes each bowled a no-ball.

### Second Innings.

| | |
|---|---|
| J. H. Fingleton, lbw, b Hammond | 12 |
| W. A. Brown, c Ames, b Voce | 32 |
| D. G. Bradman, c and b Hammond | 212 |
| S. J. McCabe, c Wyatt, b Robins | 55 |
| K. E. Rigg, c Hammond, b Farnes | 7 |
| R. Gregory, run out | 50 |
| A. G. Chipperfield, c Ames, b Hammond | 31 |
| W. A. Oldfield, c Ames, b Hammond | 1 |
| W. J. O'Reilly, c Hammond, b Farnes | 1 |
| E. L. McCormick, b Hammond | 1 |
| L. Fleetwood-Smith, not out | 4 |
| Byes 10, leg-byes 15, wide 1, no-ball 1 | 27 |
| **Total** | **433** |

Fall of wickets: 21, 88, 197, 237, 372, 422, 426, 427, 429, 433.

### BOWLING..

| | O. | M. | R. | W. |
|---|---|---|---|---|
| Farnes | 24 | 2 | 89 | 2 |
| Hammond | 15.2 | 1 | 57 | 5 |
| Allen | 14 | 1 | 61 | 0 |
| Voce | 20 | 2 | 86 | 1 |
| Verity | 37 | 17 | 54 | 0 |
| Robins | 6 | 0 | 38 | 1 |
| Barnett | 5 | 1 | 15 | 0 |
| Leyland | 2 | 0 | 6 | 0 |

Barnett bowled a wide, and Voce a no-ball.

### ENGLAND.—First Innings.

| | |
|---|---|
| H. Verity, c Bradman, b O'Reilly | 19 |
| C. J. Barnett, lbw, b Fleetwood-Smith | 129 |
| W. R. Hammond, v McCormick, b O'Reilly | 20 |
| M. Leyland, c Chipperfield, b Fleetwood-Smith | 45 |
| R. E. S. Wyatt, c Fingleton, b O'Reilly | 3 |
| L. E. G. Ames, b McCormick | 52 |
| J. Hardstaff, c and b McCormick | 20 |
| G. O. Allen, lbw, b Fleetwood-Smith | 11 |
| R. W. V. Robins, c Oldfield, b O'Reilly | 10 |
| K. Farnes, not out | 0 |
| W. Voce, c Rigg, b Fleetwood-Smith | 9 |
| Sundries | 13 |
| **Total** | **330** |

Fall of wickets: 53, 108, 190, 195, 259, 299, 304, 318, 322, 330.

### BOWLING.

| | O. | M. | R. | W. |
|---|---|---|---|---|
| McCormick | 21 | 2 | 81 | 2 |
| McCabe | 9 | 2 | 18 | 0 |
| Fleetwood-Smith | 41.4 | 10 | 129 | 4 |
| O'Reilly | 30 | 12 | 51 | 4 |
| Chipperfield | 9 | 1 | 24 | 0 |
| Gregory | 3 | 0 | 14 | 0 |

McCormick bowled a wide and three no-balls. O'Reilly bowled a no-ball.

### Second Innings.

| | |
|---|---|
| H. Verity, b Fleetwood-Smith | 17 |
| C. J. Barnett, c Chipperfield, b Fleetwood-Smith | 21 |
| J. Hardstaff, b O'Reilly | 43 |
| W. R. Hammond, b Fleetwood-Smith | 39 |
| M. Leyland, c Chipperfield, b Fleetwood-Smith | 32 |
| R. E. S. Wyatt, c Oldfield, b McCabe | 50 |
| L. E. G. Ames, lbw, b Fleetwood-Smith | 0 |
| G. O. Allen, c Gregory, b McCormick | 9 |
| R. W. V. Robins, b McCormick | 4 |
| W. Voce, b Fleetwood-Smith | 1 |
| K. Farnes, not out | 7 |
| Byes 12, leg-byes 2, no-balls 6 | 20 |
| **Total** | **243** |

### BOWLING.

| | O. | M. | R. | W. |
|---|---|---|---|---|
| McCormick | 13 | 1 | 43 | 2 |
| McCabe | 5 | 0 | 15 | 1 |
| Fleetwood-Smith | 30 | 1 | 110 | 6 |
| O'Reilly | 26 | 8 | 55 | 1 |

McCormick bowled six no-balls.

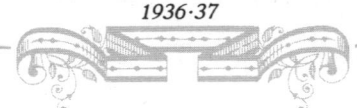

# DRAMATIC CHANGE IN ENGLISH FORTUNES

## TWO WICKETS GO FOR ONE RUN

### (By A. G. Moyes)

ADELAIDE, Friday.

WITH the dismissal of Bradman for 26 by Allen, Australia's position in the vital Test Match to-day became desperate. All the advantage of winning the toss had been lost.

Earlier, Farnes bowled a sensational over, taking two wickets for one run. Rigg and Brown were the victims.

Fingleton was run out with the score at 26.

McCabe made a splendid stand, scoring 88 before being caught by Allen off Robins.

He was followed closely by Gregory and Oldfield.

The Englishmen found it difficult to decide on their team.

Voce opened from the Cathedral end to Fingleton, who took a single off the second ball, and Brown one off the fifth.

Allen had the river end, and three singles resulted.

Off the first ball of Allen's second over, the batsmen picked up a quick single and the bowler in going for the ball seemed to slightly strain his left leg. However, it soon worked off.

A short single came from the sixth ball and Robins took a shot at the wicket, Ames making a grand save with the left hand when four overthrows seemed certain. A single to Brown and two to Fingleton completed the over.

Farnes now relieved Voce, whose two overs cost seven runs. Three came off Farnes, and Brown reached 10.

Voce then took Allen's end, and after two singles Brown got a five. They ran one and decided not to take a second, but Hardstaff threw the ball over Ames's head and it went to the fence. All the same, it was disturbing, and after it was over Fingleton had a word with Brown, who was rather jumpy in his running between the wickets.

### "Shocking Loss"

However, it happened again, and Australia threw away a valuable wicket most foolishly. Brown played Voce back and Fingleton backed up. Brown started to run and then stopped, and Voce, getting the ball, threw down the wicket with Fingleton a foot out.

Rigg followed and started with a single off Farnes, and Brown, who was batting well, turned him for two.

Hitting Farnes past point for two, Brown ran to 21. He hit in a most confident manner. At 34, Hammond was on in place of Voce, and Brown drove him straight for three. Two singles for leg glances followed, and Rigg finished the over with another, making it 40.

### Runs Come Quietly

Runs were coming quietly, and in the first 50 minutes the only boundary came from overthrows. Just before 1 p.m., Rigg missed a chance of getting the first four. He turned a full toss from Hammond a little too fine, and Leyland saved it. The total then was 46, and Rigg added another two with a neat cut.

Verity now took Hammond's place, and Brown, turning him square, would have run had Rigg not been firm. It upset a supporter in the crowd, who advised him to "turn it up." A single off the next ball made him 30, and he faced Allen, who replaced Farnes. He edged the first ball for a single, making the score 50 in 66 minutes. Rigg took two off the seventh ball, and reached 11.

Just before 1.15 p.m., Verity bowled the first maiden of the day, and Rigg then got a funny two. A ball from Allen came rather suddenly at his head and as he ducked out of the way it went off the edge to fine leg.

Verity's third over was another maiden, but the batsmen took four off Allen. It was very peaceful.

The score was now 60. Brown glanced Verity to fine leg for two, then late cut him for another two, and turned him for one.

Rigg brought cheers when he cut the last ball of the over to the fence in fine style.

Robins bowled the last over before the adjournment. Two full-tosses were wasted, and a third hit for two. Another full-toss went straight to

mid-off, but a single came off the last ball.

At lunch, the total was 72—Brown 42, Rigg 20.

After lunch, Farnes bowled to Brown, who turned the second ball to Allen, fielding close at short leg behind the umpire. It was a bad start, and a useful score had been turned by one ball into an indifferent one. Brown had batted 91 minutes.

Bradman took a single off the first ball he received. Two balls later Rigg, who had been batting for 61 minutes, went for a square cut. Ames threw the ball into the air.

Farnes was a last-minute choice, and here in a few balls he had changed the whole aspect of the game. It was as sensational as it was alarming for Australia. When McCabe came in to join Bradman, our stocks had fallen well below par.

His success had inspired Farnes, and he was bowling with more pace than he had shown hitherto in Australia and was getting a bit of lift out of the wicket. At the end of the over, which had yielded two for one, he was given a round of applause.

Each batsman took a single off Voce and McCabe cut Farnes for two, following it with a drive for two. Then came a single off the last ball of the over and McCabe had a strike again.

Voce's second over brought a single and two came off Farnes. The batsmen were taking their time and having a good look at the bowling. Much depended on them and they were content with singles.

Farnes caused mirth when he went through all the action for delivering a ball but let it slip out of his hand towards mid-on.

After a single, Bradman drove Voce straight for three, joining McCabe on 10. Two singles followed and McCabe then made a perfect cover-drive to the fence.

One hundred appeared in 127 minutes when McCabe cut Farnes for a single. Three more came off the over.

At 103, Allen relieved Voce and Bradman drove him for three, a shot which McCabe copied later in the over, reaching 21.

Off the last ball of the over came a loud appeal for a catch at the wicket, and when the umpire (Mr. Borwick) shook his head, the Englishmen stood and looked at him. Bradman was the batsman.

At 109 Verity was back again, and McCabe cut him beautifully to the fence. A single to Bradman and two to McCabe off Allen followed. Robins was frequently being applauded for his fielding.

Verity bowled only one over, Hammond replacing him. Four singles were hit, McCabe reaching 30, and Bradman 20. Verity then took the pavilion end, and McCabe hit him past mid-on for two, making the partnership 51 in 53 minutes.

### Bradman Out

Bradman turned Verity for one, and McCabe drove him for one. Bradman cover-hit the last ball for two. Then came disaster. Bradman tried to hook a short one from Allen. It kept very low, touched the bat, and went into the wicket. Bradman had batted 68 minutes and hit one four.

Australia's position was now desperate. It was a tremendous trial for young Gregory, who received encouraging applause.

He started with a nice onside shot for two and then hooked Verity to the fence. With the total 145, McCabe was 40. There were no sundries —a tribute to fine work by Ames despite his sore back. Two runs later Farnes took over from Allen and McCabe hooked him to the fence, bringing up 150 in 179 minutes.

Using his feet delightfully, McCabe overhit Verity for four and reached a splendid 50 in 88 minutes with three fours.

In the last over before tea, three singles came, and when they adjourned, McCabe was 54, Gregory 11, and the total 163 for four.

### McCabe Brilliant

Robins bowled after tea, and a single came to Gregory, who also took one off Voce. McCabe swung the left-hander to the fine leg fence and drove him for one. In the next over, Robins could not get a proper run up to the wicket, and, after trying a few times and baulking, he registered disgust, to the amusement of the crowd. McCabe hit him past cover for four, and to fine leg for two, finishing the over with a delightful coverdrive for another boundary, making the score 180.

McCabe was now playing brilliantly. He hit Voce to the leg fence, but missed a mighty swing at a no-ball —the first sundry of the innings— and was hit on the knee. The pair had added 50 in 47 minutes. McCabe took two more for a nice cut, and reached 75.

The scoring was too rapid, so Verity was brought back. Gregory glanced the first ball for a single, and McCabe lifted the second to the long-on fence. A single made him 80 and Gregory ran to 16.

### McCabe's Dismissal

Robins transferred to the other end and bowled a good over to Gregory, but five came off Verity, and 200 appeared in 222 minutes.

For McCabe, Robins had his offside men almost on the fence, and McCabe turned him to fine leg for two. Then once again a hook shot was his downfall. He tried one, and gave Allen, wide at mid-on, a gentle catch.

He had batted in grand style for 134 minutes, with nine fours. It is a pity he should have missed his century once again.

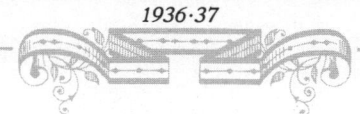

# ONLY 195 RUNS SCORED ON SECOND DAY

## Barnett Makes 92 After Being Missed Early

### By J. C. DAVIS ("Not Out")

ADELAIDE, Saturday

ENGLAND'S tactics as disclosed on Saturday were to make it a Marathon match. In hot weather, ideal for batting, they plugged on from five minutes to one until six o'clock for 174 runs. Their hero was Barnett, 92 not out at the end. Though batting with remarkable solidity, he was missed being caught early, and also missed being run out when O'Reilly failed to pick up an easy ball.

Australia's splendid bowling was a feature, with O'Reilly, Fleetwood-Smith, and McCormick all at their top.

SIMS fielded in place of Voce (back muscles strained). Allen and Farnes —the speed battery—opened spiritedly in biting hot weather with scarcely a zephyr to cool the air. Though batting more soundly than usual O'Reilly, defending for his colleague, pushed a length ball from Allen to Leyland close in at forward short-leg—an easy catch. The eighth wicket put on 21—very useful. Allen now had 2 for 57 and eight were down for 271.

McCormick was batting all right and Chipperfield's judgment was astray when he declined singles to keep the strike. Once when he did this he edged the next ball from Farnes to Wyatt's left hand in the slips, and it was missed. Two runs off it gave him 50. Hammond took the ball and McCormick was snapped up by Ames off a good length ball straightway. Nine were down for 283. There were more declined singles, but at 288 Farnes upset Fleetwood-Smith's sticks with a fast creaser.

### CHIPPERFIELD'S BEST

Chipperfield's 57 not out was the best Test innings he has played in Australia. He made the runs in an hour and a half and next to McCabe, played the finest knock, making strokes with full-blooded power and inclination to attack all the time.

Farnes ended with 3 for 70. He was the best bowler, generally fast, with his speed rarely dropping and length very good. Hammond (2 for 30), was extremely useful. Allen pegged away indomitably. All the bowling was steady. The fielding was clean in close and first-class. Allen placed the field skilfully and his men all bowled to the field.

England gave the crowds a surprise by making Verity the new opening batsman. He started with Barnett against good bowling. Barnett began his knock with a beautiful crack past mid-off off McCormick's shortish ball —a glorious four. McCormick had his pace on. One ball flashed high and Barnett just got his face out of the line of it. The fast bowler then had Verity in sore trouble for the whole eight balls of an over.

But, cool as ice, Verity weathered it. The first half hour produced 14 runs nine off McCormick's bowling, and four off McCabe. Fleetwood-Smith and O'Reilly bowled a very good over each before luncheon. Eighteen without loss were made in 35 minutes.

After luncheon McCormick bowled a peculiar wide. A slowish ball, pitched half-way, bumped so high over Verity's head that umpire Scott called "wide."

### A COSTLY MISS

When Barnett had taken an hour and ten minutes to make 13 out of the first 24 against splendid bowling (mainly by McCormick and Fleetwood-Smith), he gave a dolly return catch to McCormick, slow and breast-high. McCormick closed his fingers on it too soon and the fourth finger of his right hand was injured as well as the chance missed. That turned out to be a misfortune for the bowler and Australia. Barnett remained there for the rest of the day. McCormick left the field for a time to get his finger done up. Barnett, meanwhile, hit a Fleetwood-Smith full-toss clean and hard for six to square leg.

Fleetwood-Smith was bowling the best length one has ever seen from him, but a second full-toss saw Barnett whack it hard to the square-leg fence. Barnett got 28 off the first fifty in an hour and twenty minutes—very slow.

When drinks were brought on at 3.15 p.m. only 74 runs had been made in the day. The batting was of the tense "testitis" type, cool, steady, and Scotch Fleetwood-Smith and O'Reilly bowled spendidly while stewing in the heat.

Verity backed into his sticks and weakly hit it slowly and high to square leg, where Bradman quickly got beneath it and held it. In an hour and 45 minutes Verity made 19 and did his stone-wall job well. O'Reilly's first wicket had cost only three runs. Barnett had made 30 when Hammond was beaten by Fleetwood-Smith and edged the ball low to the left of Chipperfield at first slip and his left hand dropped it.

### STEADY AS A ROCK

Barnett, steady as a rock, got his 50 in two hours 35 minutes, with Fleetwood-Smith and O'Reilly on the spot over after over. Hammond made 21 placidly when he turned round and made a peculiar leg stroke to O'Reilly's length ball on his legs. It went up gently to McCormick at short fine leg, and he held it. Australia sorely needed the stimulus of this wicket. Leyland went in at 108, Barnett having made 61. Seven seagulls now serenaded the field. "Rain is coming," said the crowd. Barnett and Leyland sauntered along picking up singles while the crowd sweltered and some slumbered. Chipperfield, tried at 123, bowled a short one on the leg side to Leyland (14). He turned round to paste it to long leg and, when Oldfield took the ball he appealed sharply for a catch at the wickets. "Not out," said umpire Scott.

Fleetwood-Smith and O'Reilly bowled on as steadily as the Englishmen batted and, at the end of the day, the score was 174 for two wickets. Barnett's 92 was the slowest and steadiest innings he has played. It was splendid from England's angle, but very trying to the crowd's patience, which was exemplary. He should have been run out but O'Reilly again fumbled when he rushed the ball at short-leg.

It might have paid better to have scored 50 more runs in the day as the wicket may not be at its best in England's second innings. O'Reilly (2 for 16) off 15 overs, bowled grandly. Fleetwood-Smith has never bowled such a length, but did not try many bosies His condition was great. McCormick is a unlucky chap. To miss a simple chance was bad enough To injure his bowling hand finger was worse.

Mrs. W. O. Sykes and Mrs. Don Bradman at the Adelaide Oval.

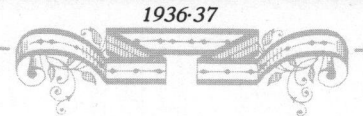

# SUCCESS OF SPIN BOWLERS IS FOREBODING

## ENGLAND WOULD FIND 300 RUNS VERY DIFFICULT TO GET

**By VICTOR RICHARDSON, who led the Australians successfully in South Africa.**

ADELAIDE, Monday.

**T**HE success of the spin bowlers in the fourth Test at the Adelaide Oval today is a foreboding for England.

When England's second innings arrives, 300 runs, if needed, will be very difficult to obtain against Australia's spin bowlers.

The wicket was bone dry when play was resumed, permitting the spin bowlers to extract plenty of pace, and to turn the ball sharply.

**Fleetwood-Smith opened the attack, but could not find a length during his first over. However, from then on began a spell which produced the best bowling of the match.**

Both batsmen found difficulty in meeting him with the full face of the bat, and eventually one spun sharply from the middle stump, across Leyland's bat to find the edge, and fly sharply into Chipperfield's hands.

### South African Ball

We badly needed Leyland's wicket at that stage, and a few minutes later Wyatt fell a victim to O'Reilly's leg trap.

**The ball, a wrong-un on the leg stump, was similar to the one which earned him many wickets in South Africa, where the slower turning wickets made it much more dangerous.**

I could not agree with Bradman's placing of the field when he brought McCormick on with the new ball after 200 had been passed.

He had his slips and leg field as though he expected McCormick to bowl badly.

Agreeing that Barnett has a strong square cut, he has also given evidence of placing his cuts head high around second and fourth slip.

Third man was square at deep point on the fence, third slip was almost close at point, with a huge gap between second and third slip, through which Barnett placed two balls, head high, to the fence.

Had the slip field been regular and watertight, at least two catches may have gone to hand.

McCormick is the fastest bowler in the world, and even allowing for the slow wicket, I think he needs a full slip field for at least his two opening overs.

Allowing an opening upon a man's pet shot when the ball is doing unexpected things is worth a try at the expense of a few runs, for a couple of overs at least.

### McCormick's Miracle

McCormick's dismissal of Hardstaff was ironic. Hardstaff attempted one of his prettily-executed hook shots, but skied it towards the square leg umpire, and McCormick, continuing his run through just reached a wonderful catch.

In comparison with the easy and costly miss of Barnett on Saturday, it was a miracle.

**This was practically the close of England's innings as the tail, although it included Allen and Robins, could not be expected to keep the spin bowlers at bay for long.**

Both groped and swung intermittently until Fleetwood-Smith and O'Reilly claimed one wicket each, to leave the tall fast bowlers to beat holes in the air with an occasional four, until a lofty on-drive was held by Rigg to complete a great recovery by Australia, led by three bowlers, who, with heart and soul in the game, carried the day.

Fingleton and Brown opened cautiously, whilst Hammond was given an opportunity to repeat his first innings success with the new ball. Two rousing appeals for leg before were negatived; but a softer and more pleading appeal succeeded, and Fingleton made way for Bradman.

Bradman absolutely refused to use the hook shot, which was his undoing on Friday, and so safely did he bat, that a continuance of this form will place Australia well on the road to victory.

The game has been one of changing fortunes, and, although Australia appears to hold an advantage, he would be a bold man who dares predict the result.

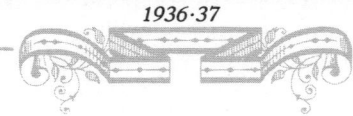

# BRADMAN IN COMMAND.

## Great Innings.

## MASTERY OF BOWLING

### TEST HOPES HIGH.

(By Denzil Batchelor.)

ADELAIDE, Tuesday.

Public holidays and a vital test match attracted smaller crowds than had been expected to the Adelaide Oval, but to-day, the first working day of the week, Don Bradman was batting, and the biggest crowd of the match duly assembled to see him.

Bradman began as if he felt it to be a poor compliment that all Adelaide should turn up so promptly to watch him bat. After all, if you missed him to-day there was always to-morrow, and the next day.

There was from the first a leisurely mastery about his every stroke. Before lunch he hardly drove at all, but stroked the ball through the slips with an insinuating touch, and glided it with feathery lightness to fine leg. He had been batting for two hours before his first boundary came, and then it was from a stroke not generally associated with Bradman—an exquisitely performed late cut that somehow sent the ball to the on boundary behind the wicket.

### BROWN'S DISMISSAL.

When Brown fell to a melodramatic catch on the leg side by Ames the crowd bore it philosophically. Brown was hardly accepted as a personality to-day—he was nothing more than the necessary stop-gap at the other end, whose job it was to run so that Bradman might face the bowling. The arrival of McCabe was a different matter.

McCabe began his innings as if he fully realised the sober fact that a batsman's first duty is not to score runs, but rather to remain in—especially a batsman who is batting with Bradman. He made several insecure forward strokes, and his defence was by no means impeccable at first. But he survived to bat in a way worthy of himself and of the occasion. He thumped the slow bowlers, sliced Farnes for a square cut that curved snakily round third man, and, standing lazily in his crease, timed wristy swings to the on boundary with such fluent ease that Verity had to submit to the indignity of having a fieldsman on the fence at square leg.

Shortly after this Allen set a field for Verity that made cricket history. The left-hander bowled to Bradman with no slip field, and with two men stationed side by side at silly point. The English, or even the Australian, language has as yet no word to describe this formation, and, assuming that the original fieldsman retains his title of silly point, the new position, a few feet nearer in, might perhaps be dignified with the name of lunatic point. The bold policy succeeded fairly well, or at least it was no worse a failure than any other policy adopted against Bradman.

### ROBINS BOWLS McCABE.

After lunch McCabe fell to Robins, whose harlequin exuberance was for once subdued by the solemnity of the occasion. He bowled several earnest overs, which did no more than make the best of batsmen play back thoughtfully, and then, by a wicked stroke of irony, he got the wicket of the day off a full pitch. McCabe volleyed it to leg, and only the fact that the Adelaide ground is not a few yards narrower prevented the shot from being the memorable six it deserved to be. As it was, Wyatt, running as fast as if he had borrowed Robins's seven league boots, held a magnificent catch—or rather three catches, for he juggled the ball, from hand to hand, with the dexterity of a sleight-of-hand artist.

Rigg's innings was a pantomime that might easily have become a tragedy. No able-bodied batsman in history has ever been more adroit at making a perfectly comfortable single into a full-length, five-act drama, fraught with ambition, doubt, eagerness, and a Hamlet-like indecision in quickly recurring order. No one in the English team looked half as likely to bowl or catch Bradman as Rigg looked to run him out. If Rigg ever bats again against England, the Australian captain will not be doing his duty by his side if he does not ask for a runner for him. They were mainly Bradman's strokes for which Rigg ran, or did not run, or, all too often, both. His own innings was quite lacking in strokes and distinction. The mystic poet Blake wrote in an inspired moment of the seer who could find "eternity in an hour." Anyone who watched Rigg bat this afternoon must have grasped what he was driving at. The greatness of Bradman was never more clearly demonstrated than by his refusal to be rattled by the finest English bowling or even by his partner.

### THE TEXT-BOOK BATSMAN.

All through the day's play Bradman endured, and long before the day was over one got the impression that the ambition of England did not soar above getting out the batsman at the other end, and leaving Bradman ultimately thwarted only because he was left unpartnered. So supremely was he master of the situation that he continued to bat as if nothing had happened even in the dark-starred hour of McCabe's downfall. It did not seem to matter who was in with him, or what was bowled to him—he was the text-book batsman, with a pat answer to every problem.

It was not an innings of flaunted aggression. It did not glitter with unforgettable strokes. The sound English bowling was not extinguished or made impotent. Verity's shrewdest bowling was no more than parried, and there was even one second when the robot played a distinctly human cut off Hammond which, if Verity had been a Siamese twin, would have been a palpable chance.

But the salient impression that Bradman's innings gave, during its six infallible hours, was that it was beyond human power to get him out. Perhaps in the fullness of time there will be bowled the ball destined to get rid of him, but it is impossible to expel the suspicion that he will go, not because he must, but because, with an unassailable score on the board, he may.

Small wonder that when Voce managed to hit him on the leg an appeal went up from the English team much louder than a massed choir singing the fortissimo passages of Verdi's "Requiem," and almost as loud as a row of Adelaide ladies greeting the fielding of a bump ball.

### GREGORY'S SUCCESS.

In young Ross Gregory, Bradman found an ideal partner to weather the last difficult hour of the English attack. The Victorian, playing in his first test match, defended resolutely against Farnes inspired to his fastest and most relentless by the fact that he had recently taken a wicket and by the use of the new ball. The ground cheered Gregory's first scoring stroke with a disproportionate enthusiasm that suggested that it feared that the stroke might also be his last. It nursed him as tenderly as a parent through the first dangerous overs, and before the close of play it paid him the pretty compliment of accepting his finest leg glances almost as phlegmatically as it accepted those of Bradman.

A curious feature of the day's play was the number of times that Scott and Borwick, the umpires, were compelled to lift one foot at square-leg to allow the ball to pass to the boundary. McCabe disarranged both the statuesque figures, and Bradman actually succeeded in making each umpire hop.

The end of a glorious innings. D. G. Bradman, when 212, was caught and bowled by W. R. Hammond. The innings is regarded by many cricketers as one of Bradman's greatest efforts.

# HERO-WORSHIP.

## A SEAMAN AND BRADMAN.

### Invasion of Oval with Camera.

(FROM OUR SPECIAL REPRESENTATIVE.)

ADELAIDE, Thursday.
There was an extraordinary scene on the field at Adelaide Oval before play in the fourth test match was resumed after lunch to-day. A man who took a photograph of Bradman was escorted from the ground and subsequently charged and fined.

When the Australian fieldsmen were taking up their positions for the resumption of play and the English captain, Allen, was preparing to take strike at the northern end, a man with a camera, who came from the "hill" near the scoring board, hurried on to the ground. He was carrying a small camera, and the amazed players and spectators soon realised that he was determined to secure a picture of Bradman. Bradman laughingly waved the man away, and Umpires Borwick and Scott hurried towards the man to order him from the field.

There was a delay of a few minutes while the man was being persuaded to depart, and then Allen, in a pretence to throw his bat at the enthusiastic photographer, tossed it along the ground for several yards. The man secured his photograph of Bradman before he ran off the field.

### EXPLANATION IN COURT.

"The only reason I went on was to take Bradman's photo. He is my hero," said James Hobson, seaman, of the Ormonde, then at the Outer Harbour, in the Adelaide Police Court this afternoon. Hobson pleaded guilty to a charge that he had entered the playing arena of the Adelaide Oval during a cricket match contrary to the regulations.

"I looked after him the last time he came to England. I won't pay a fine, as I have not done anything wrong," Hobson informed the magistrate. He said that he was awfully sorry about it. He knew Bradman when the cricketer travelled on the Otranto, and his enthusiasm carried him away. He had only had a few drinks.

A companion stood up in court and said he was the boatswain. "Bradman is a personal friend of Hobson," he said, "but it was really my fault. The ship leaves at 7 p.m. and I need him there. Now you know what Bradman is."

Hobson was fined £2. In default, he was detained in the police cells until about 5 p.m.

# FAMOUS CRICKETER'S WIFE

MRS. DON BRADMAN, who witnessed her husband's magnificent play in the fourth Test match, at Adelaide yesterday, with more joy than any other Australian at the Cricket Ground.

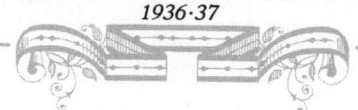

# Fleetwood-Smith Plays Big Part In Test Victory

## Hammond's Dismissal Was End Of England's Hopes

### From ARTHUR MAILEY

#### ADELAIDE, Thursday.

DISMISSING England in the second innings for 243 runs, Australia won the fourth Test at Adelaide Oval today by 148 runs.

The score is now two all, and the fate of the "Ashes" will depend on the final Test, to be played in Melbourne, starting on February 26.

Fleetwood-Smith, the Victorian googly bowler, realised a major ambition today, when, with the sixth ball of his opening over, he clean bowled Walter Hammond with a beautiful ball, which completely baffled the great English batsman.

It was generally thought that if Hammond could be dismissed before lunch victory would be assured for Australia.

In previous games in Australia Hammond had treated Fleetwood-Smith without mercy, being largely responsible for delaying his entry into Test cricket, but in the following season in England Fleetwood-Smith caused Hammond a great deal of discomfort.

In the match just ended the battle was even. Hammond's 39 was scored on a crumbling wicket by superb batsmanship when his side was threatened with annihilation by Fleetwood-Smith, and, although Fleetwood-Smith eventually obtained his wicket, the laurels, I feel, were equally divided.

Hammond had batted magnificently, just as Bradman had under less critical circumstances.

### In Bad Way

When questioned about the ball which bowled him, Hammond said: "It was a humdinger to get so early in the day."

Shortly after Hammond's dismissal, Oldfield missed stumping Wyatt off Fleetwood-Smith. Then the left-handed googly expert claimed Leyland and Ames with consecutive balls.

With six down for 190, and 200 runs still to get, England was in a bad way.

Wyatt was really the only first-class batsman left, and even he was having a rough passage against Fleetwood-Smith's bowling.

Relatively O'Reilly was causing the batsmen very little trouble.

His immaculate length was met with a straight bat, and although the wicket distinctly favored spin bowlers (and has definitely favored spin bowlers since Wednesday morning), O'Reilly, as far as I could see, turned the ball very little.

Still, he had to be watched very carefully, and his good length bowling had a moral effect.

Bradman wisely persevered with the spin bowlers all through the pre-lunch session.

### Stubborn Wyatt

Wyatt batted stubbornly during the morning session, but was never really comfortable, and when the lunch interval arrived it was a question of not how many the Englishmen would get, but how long they would stay at the wickets.

The end came soon after Allen's dismissal, and during the last few moments a little comedy was introduced.

Bradman motioned an outfield deeper, and Voce, who was batting at the time, beckoned the fieldsman closer.

However, Voce made a tremendous swipe at the ball, and none of the fieldsmen were necessary, nor did they take any part in his dismissal.

As far as the Australians were concerned it was certainly Bradman's and the much-criticised Fleetwood-Smith's match.

England put up a great fight in scoring 243, for the wicket was very badly worn on the last day—in fact during the whole of the last innings.

After the match, the curator, Alby Wright, looked sadly at the battered pitch, and said, with almost a sob: "There's not much left of it now."

## ENTHUSIASM AFTER GAME

Scenes of remarkable enthusiasm marked the close of today's game.

When Robins was bowled by McCormick with England's score at 243, the scramble for stumps, bails, and ball resulted in Robins securing one of the wickets and tossing it across to Bradman.

Farnes, the other batsman, and Gregory each grabbed a stump, and O'Reilly got the ball.

Umpires Borwick and Scott each made sure of a bail, and Borwick secured a stump for Fleetwood-Smith.

The players had to run for the gates, as a big section of the crowd of 12,600 was already swarming over the arena.

Thousands gathered in front of the Governor's box, while Bradman and Allen, the rival captains, were presented to Sir Winstan Dugan.

The Governor, after shaking hands with the captains, congratulating one and sympathising with the other, noticed the presence of Lord Somers, president of the M.C.C., and said: "We are going to apply a dictation test to Lord Somers, because wherever he goes he brings bad luck for England. He is a second Mrs. Freer."

The crowd clamored for speeches, and Bradman stepped forward.

He said: "We have had a great match, the result of which was in doubt right up to today. We hope you enjoyed it as much as we have done, and that we will have many more such happy games in the future."

Allen, like Bradman, received an ovation. He said:—

"I want to congratulate Australia, also Don on his wonderful innings. He played a very great innings, to our misfortune. I believe we shall have the luck in Melbourne, and the result there will be different, so don't be too cocky."

At once, thousands set up a cry, "We want Fleetwood-Smith."

An official, at the request of the Governor, went in search of the Victorian bowler, and presently it was announced through the loud-speakers that he could not appear, as he was in the bath.

For 45 minutes crowds waited in front of the grandstand and on the oval for the bowler to appear, and when he did he was surrounded and cheered.

For an hour they also waited for Bradman, and made another demonstration in his favor.

# BRADMAN HAS MORAL EFFECT ON TEAM MATES

## Weaknesses Must Be Eradicated

### INCLUSION OF BARNETT WOULD STRENGTHEN BATTING

#### By ARTHUR MAILEY

**ADELAIDE, Friday.**

AUSTRALIA has won two successive Test matches, but the victories have not been gained by superior teamwork.

The team has certain weaknesses that must be remedied if we are to face the fifth Test, which begins in Melbourne on February 26, with confidence.

It is interesting to look back on the Tests. The Englishmen won the first two Tests mainly because they were favored by the weather conditions.

A rain-damaged wicket, plus a slight tactical error on Allen's part, won the Third Test for Australia.

The winning of the toss was a tremendous advantage to Australia in Adelaide, because England was compelled to face a formidable total on a badly-worn wicket.

Thus it will be seen that, although each team has won two Tests, conditions and luck have had such a strong influence that it is difficult to say at present which is the superior team.

There is still a definite weakness in Australia's batting, or, rather, those batsmen on whom we have depended have not played up to expectations.

### Bradman Pivot

Bradman seems to be the pivot on which the Australian team revolves. If he is out of order, or does not give a characteristic display, it seems to have an influence on the other batsmen.

If, on the other hand, he plays one of his amazing innings, as he did on Wednesday, other players rise to it, and victory is almost assured.

What we want really is a combination of batsmen who are able to pull Australia through without the abnormal assistance of Bradman.

Consequently, our weakness, I feel, lies in collective batting strength. It is difficult to drop players from a winning team, but we cannot be blinded by victory in the face of what happened in the Adelaide Test.

We were behind on the first innings because Bradman failed, although we had first choice of a perfect wicket. Therefore I would suggest that Rigg might stand down for Badcock, Hassett, or Robinson.

### Obvious Choice

Badcock is the obvious choice, because he has been twelfth man for three matches.

Australia's bowling is of sufficient strength to win a Test match, providing, of course, it is supported by the fieldsmen. Therefore I would not add any more bowlers. Another bowler would weaken the batting and, at the same time, make the bowling lopsided, just as England's was when they decided to have three fast bowlers on the Adelaide "cemetery."

The other change that would strengthen the team is the dropping of Oldfield for Barnett.

Oldfield did not keep well in Adelaide, particularly to Fleetwood-Smith, and his batting was indifferent.

Barnett knows Fleetwood-Smith's bowling, and, in addition, is quite a solid left-hand batsman. His inclusion would strengthen the tail, which failed so badly in Adelaide.

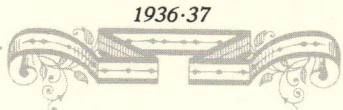

Lord Nuffield, a great cricket lover and benefactor, greets Australia's Captain.

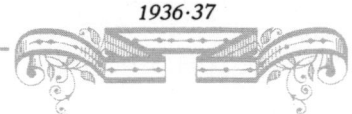

# South Australia v Queensland

SOUTH AUSTRALIA v QUEENSLAND, at Brisbane,
12, 13 and 15 February 1937.

| South Australia | - First Innings | 257 |
| | - Second Innings | 20 for no wicket |
| Queensland | - First Innings | 137 |
| | - Second Innings | 139 |

South Australia won by 10 wickets.

| DON BRADMAN | - st. D. Tallon b. E.R.H. Wyeth | 123 |
| (Captain) | - (did not bat) | - |

DON BRADMAN displaying sound and watchful defence, was again much the most successful batsman. He had sixty-five minutes' batting at the end of the first day, starting at 59 for 3, and was 45 not out when bad light stopped play; next morning he completed 50 in the third over, in seventy-one minutes, being out at 235 for 5 just before lunch, after two and three-quarter hours at the wicket. He hit a six and ten fours.

## FARCICAL FINISH AT BRISBANE

———•———

### SOUTH AUSSIE TO SCORE 13 RUNS ON MONDAY

BRISBANE, Saturday.

QUEENSLAND and South Australia take the dunce's cap, the lop-sided bun, and every other booby prize about the place after to-day's exhibition of leaving the game unfinished at 6 o'clock, with South Australia 10 wickets in hand and needing only 13 runs to win outright.

SOME say, "But it might rain." So it might. Now, the South Aussies have to stay in Brisbane over the week-end to score those 13 runs on Monday.

Bradman could well have been watching the N.S.W.-England game on Monday in his role of Australian selector.

As usual, Bradman was run-getter-in-chief when South Australia scored only 257. 'Twas the much-different, new Bradman. He didn't try to demoralise the bowling. He made many shots which sped to the fence faster than Eddie Tolan, but he showed wise discretion in punishing balls until the last over before lunch, when he dashed out to drive Wyeth, missed, and was stumped by Queensland's Don.

He hit ten fours, one six, and was on view for 165 minutes.

Badcock sparkled on Friday afternoon, but to-day he was quiet as a camel with quinsy. Wyeth, recalled after being dropped against Victoria recently, rubbed it into the selectors by taking four for 54, his victims including Bradman. He spun the ball well from the leg and kept a length that reduced scoring to a minimum.

Dixon's fast bowling was also of high quality and not inferior to that of the same type in South Australia's attack. He may be in Australia's top-class next season.

Oxenham is definitely on the decline. He did not get one wicket.

Bradman's decision to field after winning the toss proved good tactics. Queensland staged one of the worst double innings collapses in history.

Will Bill Brown's double batting failure cost him £30—otherwise exclusion from the fifth Test?

The match proved that Queensland has the same useful players, their chief weakness being inability to play two innings alike. Rogers and Tallon played cricket which could hardly be faulted, though Tallon gave a hard chance when 19. However, neither was able to go on to a big score, as so many young southerners do. Queenslanders who have been hoping for Tallon's promotion to Test cricket may have to wait longer than they think. Walker kept well.

Grimmett had plenty of guile and accuracy in his second innings bowling, but he couldn't repeat the first innings figures.

Queensland's second innings was characterised by extreme poverty of class.

Cotton's fast bowling did not offend Queensland umpires and certainly impressed the critics. Ward came on late to get a harvest of four for three. He bowled very well, despite two presentations.

The attendance was 7,177 and the gate £495/1/3.

After a fascinating and very close rubber, Australia emerged victorious with a big win in the fifth Test.

Australia's first innings total looked to be sufficient, but rain sealed England's doom, as it had sentenced Australia at Brisbane and Sydney. McCabe gave a wonderful display, Badcock's innings was probably the best he ever played for his country, and my own form was more to my satisfaction after the hard grind at Adelaide.

Because of the inclusion of Nash in the Australian team there was much speculation about a bumper war. I would never be a party to any such tactics, neither would Allen, and the match was played in an excellent spirit.

So ended the test career against Australia of a fine opponent in my friend G. O. Allen.

We had restored the good feeling on the cricket field between England and Australia which had been so badly strained by the 1932/33 series.

A message of congratulation from His Majesty the King crowned for me the end of my first trial as Australia's Captain.

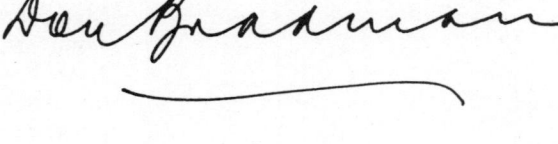

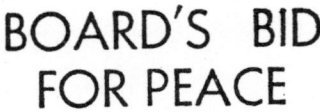

## BOARD'S BID FOR PEACE

### NASH'S BUMPERS UNPOPULAR

(Published in "The Times")

LONDON, Wednesday.

THE general desire to preserve cricket peace is emphasised in a special despatch from the Melbourne correspondent of "The Times."

"Amid around-the-corner rumblings of bodyline, the fifth Test approaches," he says, "but there is little danger of the rumblings becoming a thunderclap and disturbing the pleasant atmosphere of this tour.

"Both captains are firmly opposed to anything approaching intimidatory bowling, and neither wishes to be the first to countenance tactics obliging the umpires to consider the imposition of penalties.

"The Australian Board's desire to convince Allen that no hanky-panky business is intended lies behind the direction to the selectors to reduce the Australian list to 12, although no name has been mentioned. Some members of the Board hope that Nash will be discarded. While Nash was bowling for Victoria, the Englishmen, particularly Barnett and Hammond obviously did not relish having hastily to sway their heads and shoulders out of danger. There was no official demur, but the batsmen made it clear that they considered the bumpers frequent enough to cause a breach of the spirit or the ban on intimidatory bowling. Bradman, who has a mortal's share of distaste for rib-roasters is the last to sanction the firing of the first shot, whether Nash is chosen or not."

# NASH AND McCORMICK WILL PLAY

## "Game Of Bluff, And Bluff Was Called"

# DISLIKE OF BUMPERS

(From A. G. Moyes)

MELBOURNE, Thursday.

NASH and McCormick will both be in the Australian team for the deciding Test Match, which will begin at the Melbourne Cricket Ground to-morrow.

The chairman of the Board of Control (Dr. Robertson) said to-day: "So far as I know the team will not be reduced from 13 until to-morrow morning. My action in seeking a reduction from 13 to 12 was taken to conform with a resolution of the Board, limiting the number to 12."

It was published here to-day that the selectors pleaded to be allowed to retain 13. I don't think there was any "pleading." The selectors' attitude was that 13 had been chosen, approved, and announced, and that their job was to complete the team at a time considered to be best for Australian cricket.

In any case, as E. A. Dwyer, the third selector, was not in Melbourne, the other two, Don Bradman and W Johnson, were not prepared to make any change in his absence.

Thus ended what has been rather a game of bluff, and that bluff has been called.

There have been, and still are, many currents disturbing the cricket pool. Some do not appear on the surface, but are there nevertheless, and I am convinced that the inclusion of Nash was largely the cause of the argument over 13 players.

It is an open secret that Englishmen thought he bowled too many bumpers, but the fact remains that he had only two men on the leg side. Any batsman of skill should be able to handle that situation, though I am definitely against the "bumping" business.

### Why Pre-judge Nash?

As Nash had rarely played first-class cricket, the Englishmen, or some of them, took the view that he had been chosen to "bump" the ball, and they said so, unofficially.

Why they should pre-judge Nash and Bradman is a mystery, and why anyone should listen is a still greater mystery

My view is that this Test will be played in the same spirit as the others. With such captains, how could it be otherwise?

Bradman and Johnson spent some time yesterday with the chairman of the Board of Control (Dr. Robertson), and after the conference Dr Robertson could not be found.

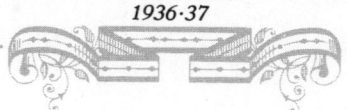

# Australia v England
## Fifth Test Match

AUSTRALIA v ENGLAND, Fifth Test Match, at Melbourne, 26, 27 February, 1, 2 and 3 March 1937.

| Australia | – First Innings | 604 |
|---|---|---|
| | – Second Innings | – |
| England | – First Innings | 239 |
| | – Second Innings | 165 |

Australia won by an innings and 200 runs, won the rubber and retained the Ashes.

DON BRADMAN — b. K. Farnes ... 169
(Captain)

DON BRADMAN again played a big innings.

He went in at 42 for 1, nine minutes before lunch on the first day, and reached 50 in sixty-nine minutes. He had made 90 by tea-time, and at 4.33 p.m. completed his century, after batting for five minutes over two hours. He and S.J. McCabe added 249 for the third wicket in only two hours forty-three minutes. This partnership of 249 with McCabe was the highest for the third wicket by Australia in any Test Match. Next morning, Bradman carried on for another nine minutes and added only 4 runs before being bowled in K. Farnes' second over when trying to force the ball to the on. His faultless innings lasted three hours forty-three minutes, and included fifteen fours; his wicket fell at 346 for 4, and he made his runs off 191 balls.

# Full Scores In Fifth Test
### Played at Melbourne Cricket Ground Feb. 26–March 3.

## AUSTRALIA—First Innings

| | Runs | Mins. | 4's |
|---|---|---|---|
| FINGLETON, c Voce, b Farnes .. | 17 | 89 | 1 |
| RIGG, c Ames, b Farnes ...... | 28 | 78 | 2 |
| BRADMAN, b Farnes ......... | 169 | 223 | 15 |
| McCABE, c Farnes b Verity .... | 112 | 163 | 16 |
| BADCOCK, c Worthington b Voce | 118 | 205 | 15 |
| GREGORY, c Verity, b Farnes ... | 80 | 195 | 5 |
| OLDFIELD, c Ames, b Voce .... | 21 | 76 | 1 |
| NASH, c Ames, b Farnes ...... | 17 | 75 | 0 |
| O'REILLY, b Voce ........... | 1 | 15 | 0 |
| McCORMICK, not out ......... | 17 | 47 | 2 |
| FLEETWOOD-SMITH, b Farnes .. | 13 | 27 | 1 |
| Sundries ............. | 11 | — | — |
| Total .............. | 604 | 606 | 58 |

Fleetwood-Smith also hit a six.
Fall of Wickets: 42, 54, 303, 346, 507, 544, 563, 571, 576, 604.

### BOWLING

| | O. | M. | R. | W. |
|---|---|---|---|---|
| Allen .. .. .. .. .. .. | 17 | 0 | 99 | 0 |
| Voce .. .. .. .. .. .. | 29 | 3 | 123 | 3 |
| Verity .. .. .. .. .. .. | 41 | 5 | 127 | 1 |
| Leyland .. .. .. .. .. .. | 3 | 0 | 36 | 0 |
| Farnes .. .. .. .. .. .. | 28.5 | 5 | 96 | 6 |
| Hammond .. .. .. .. .. .. | 16 | 1 | 62 | 0 |
| Worthington .. .. .. .. .. | 6 | 0 | 60 | 0 |

## ENGLAND—First Innings

| | Runs | Mins. | 4's |
|---|---|---|---|
| BARNETT, c Oldfield, b Nash ... | 18 | 17 | 3 |
| WORTHINGTON, hit wicket, b Fleetwood-Smith | 44 | 98 | 7 |
| HARDSTAFF, c McCormick, b O'Reilly | 83 | 240 | 8 |
| HAMMOND, c Nash, b O'Reilly .. | 14 | 62 | 1 |
| LEYLAND, b O'Reilly ........ | 7 | 13 | 0 |
| WYATT, c Bradman, b O'Reilly .. | 38 | 127 | 1 |
| AMES, b Nash ............ | 19 | 39 | 2 |
| ALLEN, c Oldfield, b Nash ..... | 0 | 9 | 0 |
| VERITY, c Rigg, b Nash ...... | 0 | 17 | 0 |
| VOCE, stp Oldfield, b O'Reilly ... | 3 | 6 | 0 |
| FARNES, not out ........... | 0 | 3 | 0 |
| Sundries ............. | 13 | — | — |
| Total ............... | 239 | 324 | 22 |

Fall of Wickets: 33, 96, 130, 140, 202, 236, 236, 236, 239, 239.

### BOWLING

| | O. | M. | R. | W. |
|---|---|---|---|---|
| McCormick .. .. .. .. .. | 13 | 1 | 54 | 0 |
| Nash .. .. .. .. .. .. .. | 17.5 | 1 | 70 | 4 |
| O'Reilly .. .. .. .. .. .. | 23 | 7 | 51 | 5 |
| Fleetwood-Smith .. .. .. .. | 18 | 3 | 51 | 1 |

McCormick bowled one no-ball.

## ENGLAND.—Second Innings

| | Runs | Mins. | 4's |
|---|---|---|---|
| BARNETT, lbw, b O'Reilly ..... | 41 | 61 | 4 |
| WORTHINGTON, c Bradman, b McCormick | 6 | 18 | 1 |
| HARDSTAFF, b Nash ......... | 1 | 4 | 0 |
| HAMMOND, c Bradman, b O'Reilly | 56 | 95 | 9 |
| LEYLAND, c McCormick, b Fleetwood-Smith | 28 | 95 | 2 |
| WYATT, run out ........... | 9 | 31 | 1 |
| AMES, c McCabe, b McCormick .. | 11 | 41 | 1 |
| ALLEN, c Nash, b O'Reilly ..... | 7 | 18 | 0 |
| VERITY, not out ........... | 2 | 30 | 0 |
| VOCE, c Badcock, b Fleetwood-Smith | 1 | 8 | 0 |
| FARNES, c Nash, b Fleetwood-Smith | 0 | 0 | 0 |
| Sundries ............. | 3 | — | — |
| Total .............. | 165 | 207 | 18 |

Barnett also hit one six.
Fall of Wickets: 9, 10, 70, 121, 142, 142, 153, 163, 165, 165.

### BOWLING

| | O. | M. | R. | W. |
|---|---|---|---|---|
| McCormick .. .. .. .. .. .. | 9 | 0 | 33 | 2 |
| Nash .. .. .. .. .. .. .. | 7 | 1 | 34 | 1 |
| O'Reilly .. .. .. .. .. .. | 19 | 6 | 58 | 3 |
| Fleetwood-Smith .. .. .. .. | 13.2 | 3 | 36 | 3 |
| McCabe .. .. .. .. .. .. .. | 1 | 0 | 1 | 0 |

Australia won by an innings and 200 runs.

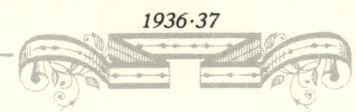

The scene in the outer at Melbourne at the start of the fifth Test.

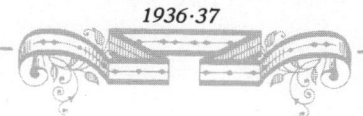

# Bradman & McCabe Tame England's Fast Attack

### By ARTHUR MAILEY

#### MELBOURNE, Friday.

**W**ITH seven wickets in hand, including Bradman's, and 342 runs on the board, Australia has a 3 to 1 on chance of victory in the fifth and deciding Test match, which started on the Melbourne Cricket Ground today.

The weather tonight is fine and clear. The forecast indicates no sign of rain. The wicket is still perfect.

Given a good start tomorrow, Bradman, Badcock, Gregory, Nash, and Oldfield may give England an impossible total to chase.

In the words of Victor Richardson, former Australian captain, only a miracle can now save England from defeat.

*England's fast attack, after the dismissal of Rigg and Fingleton, failed entirely, and Allen found himself sadly in need of a slow spin bowler.*

With Allen and Farnes in the side, Voce, regarded as England's most hostile bowler, was No. 3 in the attack. He could not do himself justice unless he were the opening bowler.

Bradman's 165 not out today was one of the greatest innings I have ever seen him play, and his partnership of 249 with McCabe broke all Test records for a third wicket stand.

## Bowlers Wilted In Melbourne Heat

McCabe capped a brilliant season with a brilliant century, and with his captain laid the foundations of an almost certain win.

Coming together soon after lunch, when Rigg and Fingleton were out for a mere 54, the Australian captain and vice-captain took the score to 303 before they were separated.

During the afternoon they completely collared the English bowling. and only defensive field-placing by Allen prevented a colossal score.

A crowd of 52,342 watched a thrilling day's play. They stood and sang the National Anthem when the Victorian Governor (Lord Huntingfield) arrived.

Saturday's attendance, with Bradman still at the wicket, is likely to approach the 100,000 mark, for which the Melbourne Cricket Ground has been prepared.

I think the writing is on the wall. We saw today the danger of depending on heavy artillery instead of a trench mortar or two.

Two fast bowlers are easy to handle, but it is almost impossible to have three in a team and get best value from each.

One has to be the outcast, so to speak, and use the old ball, but an old ball to a fast bowler is like a broken rod to an angler.

The selection of three fast bowlers was almost forced on England. Robins had an injured shoulder muscle, and Sims was regarded as being unable to trouble Australia's leading batsmen, and again it was probably thought that Verity could do all the spin bowling necessary.

It is quite possible that Australia will score a couple of hundred runs more.

Personally, I believe our batsmen will finish with Gregory, although Nash may score a few runs, and Oldfield seems to be in better batting form.

England's bowlers still have heavy work ahead of them, especially if the heat is as oppressive as it was today.

A couple of the English bowlers said that the heat on the Melbourne ground was worse than they had experienced in the West Indies, and that after two overs yesterday they were done to a frazzle.

Clem Hill told me after the match that England had as much chance of winning as flying over the moon, and I always take notice of what Clem Hill says.

He also said that he had never seen Bradman or McCabe bat better, and I certainly agree.

# HOW ENGLAND RECEIVED HER TEST CRICKET

INDEPENDENT CABLE SERVICE

LONDON, Friday.

London newspapers this evening feature Bradman's score, McCabe's luck, and England's missed catches. The headlines are:—

**The Evening News.**—"Don Not Out 165. Lucky McCabe Goes on to 112. Allen, Victim of Test Nerves, makes disastrous mistake. Faultless Bradman Equals Test Record."

**The Standard.**—"Record Partnership Takes Australia to 3-342. England pays dearly for dropped catches. Allen tries seven bowlers. Facing odds again."

**The Star.**—"New Bradman; Correct Batsman. McCabe, lucky in early stages, gives exhilarating display. Bradman evidently in one of his double-century moods. Cuts, drives, and pulls in usual confident style."

K. Farnes brilliantly stops a hard drive by D. G. Bradman.

# HAPPY END TO NASH TROUBLE

MELBOURNE, Saturday.

**Those who thought there might be trouble in the Test were happy that they were wrong. Allen and Bradman saw to that.**

TALK has been cheap this week. It was known that the Englishmen did not relish the manner in which Nash bowled in the Victorian game against them, and said so.

Many others agreed that he was too persistent with short ones on the body. Something was said to a prominent official, who is also a Board member, and he carried it on until it became almost cricket politics as to whether Nash should play.

It was an amazing position which should never have arisen.

In the first place, any doubt could have been cleared away by a conference between the captains, but the damage was done before Bradman arrived. When he and Allen met the whole matter was discussed and, as was expected, the pair found it easy to agree that the policy of real cricket that has featured other matches should be continued in this.

Why there should have been such hysteria is beyond me. Bradman, as captain of Australia, is quite able to handle his side.

Moreover, selectors are quite able to choose their own side, without help either from the Board of Control or anyone else, and they stood their ground.

## Going To Extremes

There is no doubt that before the match the whole matter was put on a sound basis by Bradman and Allen, and, furthermore, there is no doubt that the friendly spirit which prevailed formerly will continue.

At any rate, England's bowling in the game was scrupulously fair. There were short balls bowled and some hit the batsmen, but that will always happen. England had two days in the field, and Friday was a wretched day. They stuck to it like Trojans and deserve full marks for it.

## Not So Much Fire

There are, however, some who think, and will so reason, that we are likely to go to the other extreme, and curb fast men too much.

It is ridiculous even to think that they will never drop the ball short, and at times one gained the impression in this match that, in order to be absolutely above suspicion, the Englishmen took some of the fire out of their bowling.

On the other hand, it might have been that the wicket was so dead that they did not have pace to get the "lift," for I don't think any of them are as fast as McCormick or Nash.

— A. G. MOYES.

# VETERAN TOUCH BY GREGORY AND BADCOCK

## Australia Has 593 On Board And Wicket In Hand

### By ARTHUR MAILEY

#### MELBOURNE, Sunday.

TWO colts, Badcock and Gregory, with a partnership of 161 runs for the fifth wicket, were mainly responsible for Australia carrying her score from 342 for the loss of three wickets to 593 for the loss of nine wickets in the fifth Test at the Melbourne Cricket Ground yesterday.

Badcock (118) and Gregory (80) began as timorously as youngsters at a party, but soon began batting like old campaigners—except that they were making shots.

The only thing which appeared to affect these young batsmen were broadcasts through loud speakers, which blurted out all the fatal information possible. And the batsmen were not the only people annoyed.

Farnes caught Bradman napping with a ball which seemed to make amazing pace off the wicket, and his early dismissal brought the team's babies, Gregory and Badcock, together.

Bradman's dismissal created a slump in Australian stocks at a time when we expected him to shepherd or nurse Badcock, and probably Gregory.

### Better After Lunch

Badcock was a little more vigorous and more natural than Gregory. He played shots with freedom and with dash, and tried, when the occasion permitted, to score a boundary shot.

Gregory was more subdued, and while he made no serious mistakes, was not so sure of himself.

After lunch the form of Badcock and Gregory assumed a new aspect, and as far as public enthusiasm and team value were concerned, fast approaching the magnificent Bradman-McCabe effort on the day before.

At three o'clock they had put on more than 100 runs, and were batting as though another hundred would be completed before tea.

The English bowlers, refreshed by a cool southerly breeze, which had sprung up after lunch, worked like trojans to break this juvenile partnership, and might have been rewarded earlier had fortune been with them.

Badcock played several uppish shots in the vicinity of point, and Gregory, in one over from Worthington, had two narrow escapes from being caught by Hammond in the slips.

### Enthusiasm Of Youth

These discrepancies, however, were due, probably, to the enthusiasm of youth rather than to any technical shortcoming, but it was noticeable that after these narrow shaves, both batsmen were inclined to close down on adventurous strokes.

The excitement became intense with Badcock within one run of his century, and Gregory on 49.

Verity was bowling, and the field closed in to prevent Badcock getting his coveted century, but, instead of trying to sneak a short run, Badcock jumped yards down the pitch and sent the ball crashing at the fieldsman with terrific force.

This stroke, at such a crucial time, convinced me that Badcock should develop into one of Australia's great batsmen.

Had he been caught off that stroke he would have been marked down as being too impatient. It would have been unfair judgment.

That particular stroke indicated that the maker had imagination, just as that glorious batsman, Archie Jackson, had shown when requiring one run for his first century. He back-cut Larwood brilliantly for four.

This is the stuff that makes cricket lovers happy and stonewallers jealous.

Badcock's magnificent innings came to an end just before tea, when Voce, who had bowled against great odds most of the day, had him caught by the safe hands of Worthington.

There were times when Badcock reminded me of Charles Macartney in his most arrogant and aggressive mood. Being short of stature, probably the smallest man in the team, Badcock was compelled to back cut deliveries that taller men could stand over and hit straight.

Badcock has established himself as a Test batsman, and, despite failures which may come his way, he should be a certainty for the next English tour.

### Relieves Bradman

Bradman has been the sheet-anchor of the Australian Eleven too long—I say this at the risk of annoying many people—but the fact remains that if Bradman did at any time feel the responsibility of captaincy, it was because he was shouldering it from the batting, as well as the administrative, point of view.

However, after Badcock's and Gregory's success, we feel that not only has Australia two batsmen who can score runs, but who can score them with a virility and an aggressiveness that has a great moral advantage, and allows us to estimate the value of bowlers at their true worth.

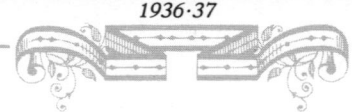

# ALLEN WAS WORRIED

## NASH BUMPERS FEARED

### (From A. G. Moyes)

MELBOURNE, Monday.

WHEN Nash played for Victoria against England many of the latter side considered that he bowled bumpers, and that they constituted an attack on the batsman's body.

When he was chosen in the Australian thirteen it raised a controversy, and the Englishmen considered that if he acted similarly in the Test it might cause retaliation, ending the friendliness that had existed between the teams.

Allen was worried, and pointed out that he had come to Australia to play Tests in the best possible spirit, and did not want trouble arising at the last minute.

He mentioned this to a member of the Board of Control, and that started the cricket politics which were wrapped around the request that the selectors should reduce the selections to 12. Unofficially, Nash's name was mentioned, and the possibilities that his bowling would cause trouble were debated.

The selectors, as is known, declined to allow anyone to interfere with their right to pick the team, and those closely in touch were astounded that anyone should consider the possibility of Bradman allowing his bowlers to infringe the unwritten or written laws of the game.

### Spirit of Game

Bradman, Allen and Robins lunched together on Thursday and discussed matters. All were emphatic that the best of spirits should prevail, and finally, on Friday morning before the game started, there was an unofficial gathering of the captains and the president of the Board of Control. The umpires were naturally left in charge of the game.

The Marylebone Club rule clearly legislates against persistent bowling at a batsman, and lays down certain powers for umpires to handle such a situation.

Obviously it is not possible to consider every bumper as an offence, because many of them are fair. It is only the persistent bowling of bumpers that constitutes an offence.

# BRADMAN WAS HIS PATTERN

## Badcock Ranks With Past Masters

## FOOTWORK

### (By GEORGE THATCHER.)

IN the history of the Anglo-Australian Tests quite a number of colts have staged thrilling innings early in their careers. Jack Badcock, as a result of his 118 at Melbourne on Saturday, has joined the immortals. His knock may not have had the quality of the 135 each by Trumper and Hill at Lord's in 1899. Considering the circumstances, there was more virtue in the late Archie Jackson's 164 at Adelaide in his first innings in a Test.

Still, Badcock followed scintillating knocks by Bradman and McCabe, the most versatile strike-makers in cricket, and his innings did not suffer by comparison.

Early in the series one very famous English commentator referred to Badcock as another Bradman. When the youth failed the same writer conveniently forgot him.

Charles B. Fry, however, has always been a great sticker for Badcock, and I have repeatedly heard the ex-International refer to Badcock as the third best batsman in Australia.

Badcock has modelled his style on that of Bradman. He is not such a vicious hitter as Don, and he has yet to perfect his footwork. Still, he has come on apace in two seasons, and the next Australian season before the team leaves for England should see him at his peak. His inclusion in the Australian XI. for England in 1938 is assured.

### In Three Capitals

Badcock is one of those batsmen who are never worried by environment. In the present season he has scored centuries against England at Perth, Sydney and Melbourne. Last season he made 325 for South Australia against Victoria in Melbourne.

Bradman has very wisely decided that Badcock is not an opening batsman. He is the ideal player to drive home any advantage following a big stand by Don and McCabe.

Badcock and his youthful partner, Gregory, faced anything but an enviable position when Don went early. If another wicket had fallen early our tail, generally ineffective on big occasions, would have had to scratch.

The youths, however, batted with coolness of veterans. Badcock immediately took command, and Gregory gave as much of the strike as possible to the ex-Tasmanian.

In desperation Allen used Worthington and Leyland, much to his sorrow, while Verity, merely a run-saver on our wickets, was treated discourteously.

Badcock's century is merely the forerunner of others. His back foot play is so good that he should be a huge success in England.

Gregory missed his century by a mere 20. Probably, if Badcock had remained he would have achieved his objective.

The Australian tail is very indecisive these days. Old-timers like Howell, Cotter and Carter would have gone for runs in great style in that final hour.

"Chuck" Fleetwood-Smith, who rivals Jack Saunders and Dainty Ironmonger, collected a four and a six. The latter shot was worth a "spin."

### Near Record

Australia is within a few runs of our record total in Tests in Australia—600 in Melbourne against A. E. R. Gilligan's team in 1925.

I feel that we have enough runs to win. In ordinary circumstances Australia should have a first innings lead of 150. Our second innings should be worth at least 250 if the weather holds. Then England would have to make over 400 to win.

With more fast bowlers than usual pounding the wicket rough patches and ridges must appear.

Fleetwood-Smith and O'Reilly may receive some punishment in the first M.C.C. innings. They should have their revenge when England bats the second time, perhaps on Wednesday afternoon and Thursday.

The wicket is sure to disintegrate slowly, and in Melbourne at this time of the year there is always a chance of rain.

Bradman, with an assured first innings lead, won't have to worry about the weather.

Nash, who routed the South Africans, might get his chance before Thursday.

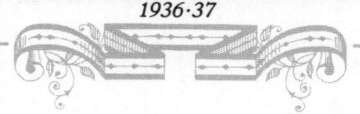

# WICKET AIDS O'REILLY

## BRADMAN'S TRICK WITH FIELD

### (By W. M. Woodfull)

MELBOURNE, Tuesday.

BOTH during the morning and after the luncheon adjournment I thought O'Reilly would be Australia's bowler to get the greatest assistance from the condition of the wicket.

In the afternoon the deliveries of Nash and McCormick were lifting much more sharply than at noon.

When play began to-day the wicket was at the cutting-through stage.

With McCormick and O'Reilly bowling, Bradman had three fieldsmen close on the bat—two forward of the wicket and one at very short square leg.

This is an old Yorkshire trick, for the close proximity of the fieldsmen keeps the batsmen on tenterhooks and has them thinking the wicket is worse than it actually is.

The first 50 minutes brought England 48 more runs. It was excellent going by her batsmen, considering the difficult conditions and the heaviness of the ground.

### Great Innings Ends

Hardstaff certainly tried to make the most for England of the early cut-through stage of the wicket Eventually, however, he picked the wrong ball to hit, and lofted a catch to deep mid-on. He had played a great innings for his side, and was unfortunate to miss recording his first Test century against Australia

After 40 minutes' bowling, Bradman spelled O'Reilly, evidently determined to keep him fresh for the more awkward stage of the wicket's development. When he brought him back at 1.10 p.m., the wicket was just beginning to bite and seemed to cause Wyatt's dismissal.

Ames had been sent back by a ball from Nash, which came well up to him The wicket could not be blamed for anything the ball did on that occasion; but I know that, under these conditions, when a batsman gets so rare a chance as a ball well up to him, he is prone to attempt a stronger forcing stroke than he would play normally, and may hit over the delivery as Ames did.

### Peerless Oldfield

If further proof of Oldfield's peerless ability behind the stumps was needed, he gave it by taking a grand catch off Allen, and then brilliantly stumping Voce to hasten the end of England's first innings.

England had just failed to last out until the adjournment. Had she done so, she would have gained an extra ten minutes after lunch The wicket was likely to be at its worst stage during lunch and for some time afterwards.

O'Reilly was Australia's outstanding bowler, with Nash giving valuable support. He kept the ball well up to the batsmen rather better than McCormick.

England's second innings opened to the fast bowlers Nash and McCormick. While they were on it was difficult to form any accurate opinion of how the wicket was disposed to behave, but I could see that their deliveries were lifting much more sharply than at noon, and this was a fair indication that the wicket immediately after lunch, was at a nasty stage.

### Barnett's Fall

When two for 30 appeared, so did O'Reilly, ball in hand and purpose in his action. But Hammond and Barnett—a possible foundation on which England might build hopes of averting the innings defeat—were combining well to overcome the idiosyncrasies of the wicket. They punched strongly any ball well pitched up to them.

Delightful shots for four and six off O'Reilly preceded Barnett's departure. He was giving a taste of beautiful stroke production; but the burst was his last, O'Reilly trapping him with legs in front.

I think that the excellent showing of Barnett and Hammond in a partnership of 60 was due more to fine batsmanship than to any marked improvement in the pitch.

Hammond and Leyland, England's old guard, were now together, and Hammond was doing more than merely guard. Some of his superb cover-drives were as good as anything seen during the entire match.

### Lefthander's Worry

About 3.30 p.m., with Leyland fresh at the crease, Fleetwood-Smith might well have been given a chance to show what he could do. He is naturally a difficult bowler for lefthanders and might have sent the Yorkshireman back before he had had time to become accustomed to conditions.

Australia had been in the field for three hours to-day before McCabe became her fourth bowler just before tea. The other three, O'Reilly, McCormick and Nash, had bowled continuously and much of the edge had been taken off the fast men.

# TWO BALLS, TWO OUT AND TEST ENDS

## CROWD IN WILD RUSH FOR SOUVENIRS

## Bradman Tells Of Fine Spirit Throughout Games

## TEST TAKINGS £91,912

(From A. G. Moyes)

MELBOURNE, Wednesday.

TWO balls, two wickets—and the final Test was over to-day.

Three minutes sufficed to complete England's defeat by an innings and 200 runs, and to confirm Australia's retention of the Ashes.

The crowd of 10,000—which had been admitted free—rushed the pitch cheering and laughing and, such is the hysteria of cricket these days, many chiselled pieces from the wicket to carry off as a souvenir.

"In appointing me captain and selector," said Bradman later, "the Board of Control gave me a heavy responsibility. I hope that my efforts have shown that all my actions were guided by a desire to maintain all that is best in the history of true cricketing sportsmanship."

"I make no bones about it; I am a disappointed man. But Australia has played wonderful cricket and has fought out of a very difficult position," said Allen.

The attendance at the five Tests totalled 933,294 and the takings £91,912, which is a record.

Bradman, looking back over the season, in an exclusive interview, said:

"It is perfectly natural that I should be very excited and elated over the fact that Australia has won the Ashes."

"I would like now the series is over, to say how much we all enjoyed our games.

"Every match was played in a most friendly spirit, and the happy relationships existing between the teams must be a source of great satisfaction to the cricketing public of both countries."

"Although the weather interfered with four of the Tests, bringing misfortune to each side on two occasions, it was a cruel blow that England should meet with such bad luck in the vital match.

"We were confident of winning the fifth Test, because we believed our team was in better form than at any other time in the season, and that England's team was at its best earlier in the tour.

"The match seemed to bear out this contention. Our batting, bowling and fielding, especially the last-mentioned, were much better in the last game than they had been formerly.

"I want to thank my team-mates for their loyal support, my opponents for their generous sportsmanship, the public for its cordial reception of the efforts of the teams, and the Press for the impartial reviews.

"In appointing me captain and a selector, the Board of Control gave me a heavy responsibility, and I sincerely hope and trust my efforts have shown that all my actions were guided by a desire to maintain all that is best in the history of true cricketing sportsmanship."

Melbourne Cricket Ground, 1985.

Bradman's image in Toby Jugs.

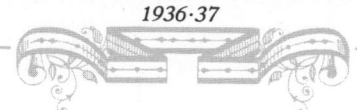

# PLAYERS FLEE FROM CROWDS' WILD ENTHUSIASM

In the players' race to the gate, as the game ended, McCabe, clutching a stump, escaped the crowd's attentions, but the others were overhauled and Fingleton, last in, was subjected to an unmerciful back slapping as he struggled for the dressing-room.

Nash, who held a sky-scraping catch to dismiss the last man, ran off clutching the ball as a souvenir of his first Test Match against England.

As the crowd swarmed over the wicket and massed around the pavilion gates, they were advised through the amplifiers to return to their seats to hear the broadcast speeches from the captains.

Sighting Bradman as he approached the microphone in the official enclosure, the crowd cheered gleefully. Announced as "The man of the moment," Bradman, in his resonant voice, said:—

"I just mentioned to my friend 'Gubby' Allen that this was easily the worst moment in this Test cricket. We don't mind playing before you in the middle, but we become nervous when it is a question of speaking.

"We are delighted to have won. It has been a very hard series, keenly fought; but we have tried very jealously to guard the best traditions of cricket, and I think you will agree that we have succeeded. (Applause.)

"I want to pay a very high tribute to the wonderful sportsmanship displayed by the English team, and especially their captain. (Applause.) When the rain came it dealt them a very cruel blow, seeing that this was the final match for the Ashes, but I have yet to hear one single word of complaint from them. (Applause.)

"I would like to thank the public for their magnificent support, the Press for their generous and impartial reviews, and the umpires for their excellent performance.

"I must also thank my team mates for the magnificent support they have given me right through the series. Without that support we could not possibly have won. It has been a marvellous series, and we are glad it is over, because I doubt if we could have seen the distance had there been another match to play.

"I am sure no one will begrudge us the rest we intend to take from cricket for a little while. It is only another year before an Australian team will go to England. I sincerely hope I will have the privilege to go with it," Bradman added amidst laughter.

# "DISAPPOINTED, AND NO BONES ABOUT IT"—ALLEN

G. O. Allen, who was received with cheers, aroused loud laughter with a reference to Bradman's form with the bat and with "that infernal coin of his."

"You noticed," said Allen to the crowd, "that I was not introduced as the man of the moment. Mr. Bradman, said that this was the moment he liked least. If I stood in his position and had his ability, I think I should be quite happy standing here.

"I make no bones about it. I am a very disappointed man.

"Undoubtedly the best side won on the wickets on which we have had to play here.

"The Australians owe a great deal to their captain. He has shown most magnificent form with the bat and with that infernal coin of his.

"He says that no one has complained of the luck. I am not complaining, but I do not think we shall go down in history as the luckiest team that has ever toured Australia."

"Australia has played wonderful cricket and has fought out of a very difficult position. I can only say that although we have lost, we will live to fight again."

Allen added, that he would like to thank all who had been so kind to his team.

"You had plenty of opportunities at the start to throw bricks, but you refrained from doing so," he said.

"It is probably my last appearance at the Melbourne Ground. It has been a sad one for me, but never mind; thank you all very much."

Although at 9 a.m. there were only 12 in the queues where thousands had stood on other days of the game there were about 10,000 present when play was resumed at noon in bright sunshine.

The rain, having done its damage, had gone.

Voce took strike from Fleetwood-Smith and lifted the first ball to long-on, where Badcock caught him.

Farnes swung at the next and sent it high into the air, but Nash, at mid-on, ran back and never looked like missing it.

Fleetwood-Smith thus finished with three for 36.

Even the announcement that the players would not appear again did not disperse the crowd and half an hour after the game had finished, there were at least 1000 people on the oval and 5000 gathered round the dressing rooms.

More than an hour after the game ended, 20 men and four women were still gazing at the pitch, which had been roped off, and 1000 people clustered around the dressing-rooms to cheer each player as he left.

The attendance at the Test for the four days was 224,388, and the takings £22,267.

As the Captains make their valedictory speeches, an enthusiastic crowd gathers in front of the Members' stand.

HIGH COURT OF AUSTRALIA.

JUDGES' CHAMBERS.

3/3/37

Dear Mr Bradman

Please allow me to congratulate you on three great achievements: first your captaincy during a team and series of unexampled difficulties: it was excellent. Second your performance of the duties of selector in which you showed the courage and imagination required and were not dissuaded either from retaining members of a defeated team or from rejecting members of a victorious team. and finally, your magnificent batting.

I sincerely hope that you will be happily engaged in captaining Australian XI at least for another 10 or 12 years.

Yours very sincerely

H Evatt.

# JARDINE'S STRATEGY TO CHECK BRADMAN

## SET DEEP FIELD AND KEEP HIM FROM STRIKE

*Independent Cable Service*

LONDON, Thursday.

JARDINE, former M.C.C. captain, suggests a plan for coping with Bradman.

"After a doubtful start, Bradman has been reinstated as the bowler's greatest problem," he writes in the Evening Standard.

"In limited matches the problem may well prove insoluble, but in timeless Tests more methodical strategy might reduce the menace.

"**The first essential would be to deprive him of the strike as much as possible, treating his partner, however good, as a rabbit, who should be manoeuvred into getting most of the bowling.**"

Jardine suggests that bowlers should bowl faithfully for two radically different fields.

### GIVEN EARLY SINGLE

Bradman's field should be set deep to enable him to score a single early in the over, thus losing the strike, but preventing him from scoring twos and fours.

The field for his partner should consist of inner and outer rings of fieldsmen, saving ones and threes, but conceding twos and fours.

**The bowlers would not attack Bradman's wicket, but make him "scratch for runs," with big doses of off theory and a packed off-side field.**

"It may be argued that this would not get Bradman out, but it would reduce the scoring rate materially and annoyingly," Jardine contends.

"Even Homer nods—the chances of Bradman getting himself out must often be as good as the bowlers' chances of dismissing him."

### TRIED, FAILED

#### By ARTHUR MAILEY

Douglas Jardine's suggestions to curb Bradman's scoring sound very logical.

Unfortunately they have been tried very thoroughly in five Test matches this year and, judging by Bradman's scores, not too successfully.

**Apparently Jardine has not been kept posted with Allen's tactics.**

From the first Test Allen concentrated primarily on keeping the strike from Bradman. He set "boundary-proof" fields to convert Bradman's best shots into singles and cause him to lose the strike.

This was successful to a certain degree. Bradman's 212 in Adelaide was made up of 99 singles, 18 twos, seven threes, and 14 fours, and he took more than seven hours to make the runs.

**Allen's ideas were sound, but Bradman adapted himself to the conditions, and was content to pick up a great percentage of his runs in singles.**

I am afraid Jardine will have to sit down and think out another one.

# "GRUBBERS" TO KEEP BRADMAN QUIET

## Extraordinary Suggestion By English Writers

### By ARTHUR MAILEY

OF all the extraordinary suggestions made by English writers with the object of "bottling up" Don Bradman, none is more fantastic than that advocating the bowling of "grubbers."

The "grubber," a relic of pre-overarm days, is an underarm ball which never leaves the ground.

It is not a wicket-getter. At best, it might keep a batsman from scoring too freely.

**Bradman must be proud to think that England has at last given up planning his downfall, and is now content to concentrate on keeping him quiet.**

Four years ago Jardine thought of a ball which bounced head-high.

Now we have the ball which never leaves the ground—from headcrackers to corncrackers, as it were.

I would suggest a return to sanity, and recommend to the English selectors to find a good, honest right-hand leg spin bowler, who is a little faster than Robins or Sims, and who can break the ball on any wicket.

This class of bowler seems to be missing from English cricket.

**Until better spin bowlers are found,** Bradman and other Australian batsmen are going to get plenty of runs.

English cricket is suffering, in my opinion, from defective junior or club wickets.

### Wrong Wicket

The wickets one sees around London in club cricket are not in the best interests of good batting or good bowling.

On such wickets a medium paced bowler who bowls on the middle stump and maintains a reasonably good length is sure to get wickets.

**But when the same bowler finds himself on a good wicket there is a different story.**

Junior cricketers in Australia are brought up on matting wickets.

Although they may not be as pleasant as perfect turf wickets, they, at least, compel batsmen to play correct shots and bowlers to develop the art of bowling.

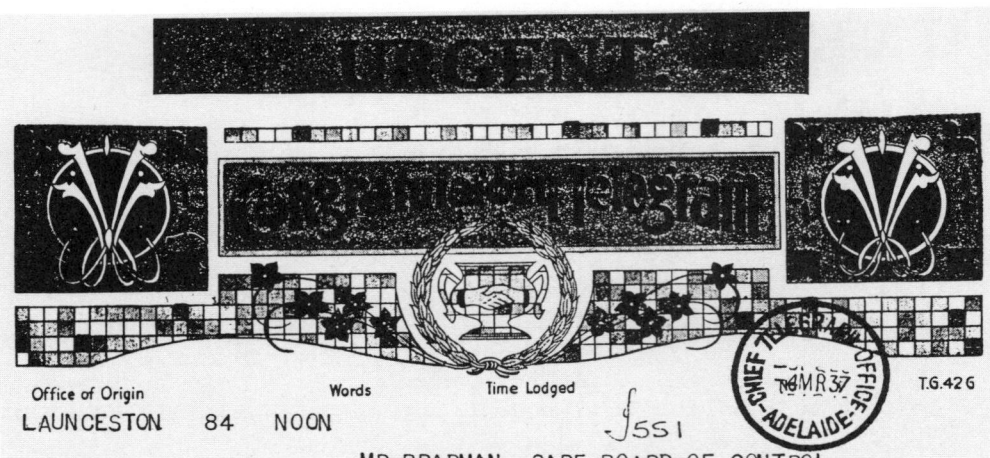

URGENT

Congratulations Telegram

| Office of Origin | Words | Time Lodged | | T.G. 42 G |
|---|---|---|---|---|
| LAUNCESTON | 84 | NOON | 551 | |

MR BRADMAN   CARE BOARD OF CONTROL

MELBOURNE CRICKET CLUB MELBOURNE

I HAVE JUST RECEIVED THE FOLLOWING MESSAGE FROM HIS MAJESTY THE KING

BEGINS PLEASE CONVEY TO MR BRADMAN AND AUSTRALIAN CRICKETERS MY
HEARTY CONGRATULATIONS ON THEIR VICTORY IN THE TEST MATCHES STOP
I HAVE FOLLOWED WITH THE CLOSEST INTEREST THE PROGRESS OF FIVE WELL
CONTESTED MATCHES PLAYED IN THE FRIENDLIEST SPIRIT IN WHICH
MR BRADMAN HAS ONCE MORE GIVEN EVIDENCE OF HIS PREDOMINANT SKILL
AS A BATSMAN GEORGE R I ENDS   ---   GOWRIE GOVERNOR GENERAL

Charge to Governor-General's
    Account.

        VIA IMPERIAL

        PRIVATE SECRETARY TO THE KING

        BUCKINGHAM PALACE

        LONDON

    PLEASE LAY BEFORE THE KING WITH MY HUMBLE DUTY THE FOLLOWING
MESSAGE FROM MR. BRADMAN BEGINS PLEASE CONVEY TO HIS MAJESTY MY
SINCERE THANKS FOR HIS MESSAGE OF CONGRATULATIONS ON THE SUCCESS OF
AUSTRALIA IN TEST MATCHES FULLSTOP MEMBERS OF AUSTRALIAN TEAM FEEL
VERY PROUD TO KNOW THAT HIS MAJESTY TAKES SUCH A GREAT INTEREST IN
OUR NATIONAL GAME FULLSTOP I DEEPLY APPRECIATE THE COMPLIMENT WHICH
HIS MAJESTY HAS PAID TO ME PERSONALLY SIGNED DON BRADMAN ENDS.

Admiralty House, North Sydney.                    GOVERNOR-GENERAL.
    12th March , 1937.

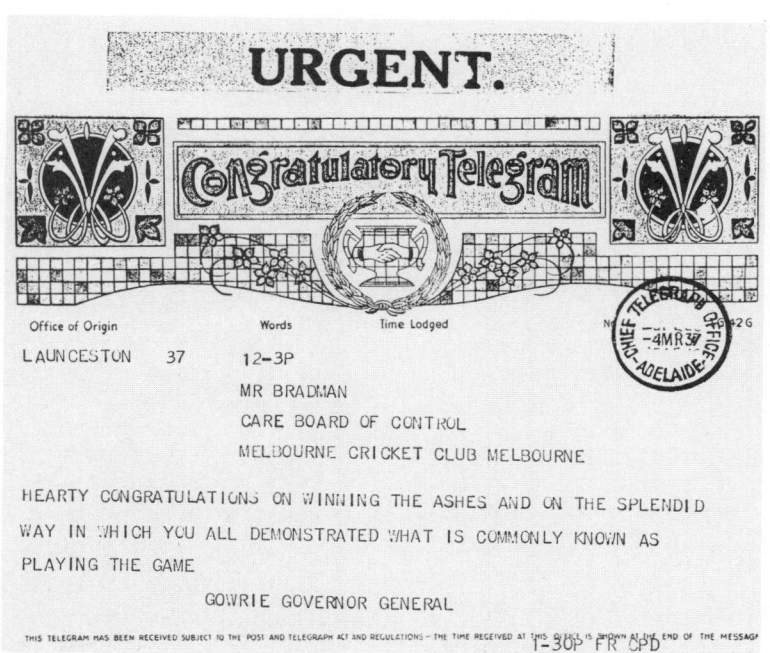

URGENT.

**Congratulatory Telegram**

| Office of Origin | Words | Time Lodged |
|---|---|---|
| LAUNCESTON 37 | 12-3P | |

CHIEF TELEGRAPH OFFICE -4MR37 ADELAIDE

MR BRADMAN
CARE BOARD OF CONTROL
MELBOURNE CRICKET CLUB MELBOURNE

HEARTY CONGRATULATIONS ON WINNING THE ASHES AND ON THE SPLENDID
WAY IN WHICH YOU ALL DEMONSTRATED WHAT IS COMMONLY KNOWN AS
PLAYING THE GAME

GOWRIE GOVERNOR GENERAL

THIS TELEGRAM HAS BEEN RECEIVED SUBJECT TO THE POST AND TELEGRAPH ACT AND REGULATIONS - THE TIME RECEIVED AT THIS OFFICE IS SHOWN AT THE END OF THE MESSAGE

1-30P FR CPD

Don Bradman and his wife home again from the fifth Test in Melbourne.

HUDDART PARKER LINE

M.V. "Wanganella"

March 14.

Dear Don,

Just a line to bid you
a final goodbye and to tell you
once again how much I have
enjoyed my cricket with you on this time.
I am afraid Robbie and I rather upset
you before the last "test" and that
you still think our attitude was
unreasonable. However, I felt
it was much better to discuss
the whole matter before the match
started and I am sorry to thank
you again for sticking to your
side of the bargain so chivalrously.
I have been in bed ever since
the boat passed out of the Sydney
Heads and I am so damned
tired that I don't intend to get
up until we reach Wellington.
Please remember me to Mrs Don
Best of luck.

Yours

Gubby.

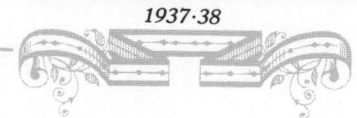

# *1937 - 38* *Season*

The season before a trip to England is always exciting because there is fierce competition amongst the players, who dearly want to be in the most coveted cricket trip of all.

Early in the season, a testimonial match was played on the Adelaide Oval for the benefit of Vic Richardson and Clarrie Grimmett. Naturally a big gate was desirable. However, on the Friday afternoon Grimmett deceived and bowled me with a well flighted ball. He rushed across to his Captain, Vic Richardson, and indicated his pleasure, whereupon, with a few well chosen epithets, Vic made it clear how much money this moment of triumph would cost them both. He was of course referring to the potential increase in the attendance had I been "not out" on Friday night.

I mention the incident partly because there are a few misguided people who argue that cricket matches are sometimes "rigged". I have never known it to happen.

The team ultimately chosen for England did not meet with universal approval and certainly had weak spots, but that is a subject for later comment.

For me, I looked forward to my first overseas trip as Captain, with its opportunities and challenges.

## — SEASON 1937-38 —

| TITLE | GAMES | | | SCORES | |
|---|---|---|---|---|---|
| Second Class | S.A.C.A. | | Nuriootpa | 58 | B. |
| " | " | | Clare | 72 | C. |
| First Grade | Kensington | | Adelaide | 2 | C. |
| " | " | | " | 116 | n.o. |
| " | " | | Sturt | 8 | C. |
| " | " | | " | 53 | r.o. |
| " | " | | Colts | 32 | C. |
| " | " | | Prospect | 88 | C. |
| First Class | South Australia | | New Zealand | 11 | C. |
| " | " | " | Western Australia | 101 | C. |
| " | " | " | " | 102 | S. |
| " | Bradman's XI | | Richardson's XI | 17 | B. |
| " | Australia | | Tasmania | 79 | C. |
| " | " | | " | 144 | B. |
| Sheffield Shield | South Australia | | New South Wales | 91 | C. |
| " | " | " | " | 62 | C. |
| " | " | " | " | 44 | C. |
| " | " | " | " | 104 | n.o. |
| " | " | " | Queensland | 246 | C. |
| " | " | " | " | 39 | n.o. |
| " | " | " | " | 107 | C. |
| " | " | " | " | 113 | C. |
| " | " | " | Victoria | 54 | C. |
| " | " | " | " | 35 | C. |
| " | " | " | " | 3 | B. |
| " | " | " | " | 85 | C. |
| | | | Total runs | 1866 | |

## — SUMMARY —

AVERAGES -

| | Innings | N.O's. | H.S. | Runs | Average |
|---|---|---|---|---|---|
| Sheffield Shield | 12 | 2 | 246 | 983 | 98·3 |
| Other First Class | 6 | 0 | 144 | 454 | 75·6 |
| All First Class | 18 | 2 | 246 | 1437 | 89·8 |
| First Grade | 6 | 1 | 116* | 299 | 59·8 |
| Other Second Class | 2 | 0 | 72 | 130 | 65·0 |
| All Second Class | 8 | 1 | 116* | 429 | 61·2 |
| All Matches | 26 | 3 | 246 | 1866 | 81·1 |

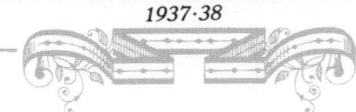

# South Australia v Queensland

SOUTH AUSTRALIA v QUEENSLAND, at Adelaide,
25, 27, 28 and 29 December 1937.

| South Australia | - First Innings | 429 for 8 wickets dec. |
| | - Second Innings | 93 for 2 wickets |
| Queensland | - First Innings | 93 |
| | - Second Innings | 426 |

South Australia won by 8 wickets.

| DON BRADMAN | - c. G. Baker b. P. L. Dixon | 246 |
| (Captain) | - not out | 39 |

DON BRADMAN, going in at 15 for 1, and after three quarters of an hour's batting was 28 not out at the end of the first day.     Next morning, he proceeded to make another huge score off the Queensland bowlers.     He completed 50 in ninety-five minutes, 100 in three hours fourteen minutes, and 200 in five hours twenty-six minutes; and he was eventually out ten minutes from time, caught in the deep after a brilliant burst of hitting, having batted for six hours four minutes.     He hit twenty fours.

This score of 246 was the highest ever made in matches between South Australia and Queensland.

## QUEENSLAND
### First Innings

| | | |
|---|---|---:|
| W. A. BROWN, c. Walker, b. Williams | | 10 |
| G. COOK, b. Williams | | 0 |
| J. COATES, st. Walker, b. Ward | | 21 |
| C. LOXTON, c. Robinson, b. Ward | | 2 |
| R. ROGERS, b. Williams | | 19 |
| D. TALLON, c. Walker, b. Williams | | 3 |
| T. ALLEN, c. Cotton, b. Grimmett | | 6 |
| G. BAKER, c. and b. Williams | | 13 |
| F. R. WYETH, l.b.w., b. Grimmett | | 4 |
| J. GOVAN, not out | | 7 |
| P. L. DIXON, c. Hamence, b. Williams | | 2 |
| Byes 2, wide 1, no-balls 3 | | 6 |
| Total | | 93 |

| 1 | 2 | 3 | 4 | 5 | 6 | 7 | 8 | 9 |
|---|---|---|---|---|---|---|---|---|
| 6 | 19 | 27 | 41 | 55 | 58 | 71 | 76 | 87 |

### Bowling

| | O. | M. | R. | W. |
|---|---|---|---|---|
| H. J. Cotton | 8 | — | 27 | — |
| R. G. Williams | 11.1 | 4 | 21 | 6 |
| M. G. Waite | 3 | — | 12 | — |
| F. A. Ward | 6 | 1 | 16 | 2 |
| C. V. Grimmett | 6 | 1 | 11 | 2 |

Williams bowled three n.-balls and a wide.

### Second Innings

| | | |
|---|---|---:|
| W. A. BROWN, c. Williams, b. Grimmett | | 132 |
| G. Cook, b. Ward | | 11 |
| C. LOXTON, st. Walker, b. Ward | | 0 |
| G. Baker, l.b.w., b. Ward | | 1 |
| D. TALLON, st. Walker, b. Waite | | 24 |
| T. ALLEN, run out | | 26 |
| R. ROGERS, c. Walker, b. Williams | | 181 |
| J. COATS, l.b.w., b. Waite | | 13 |
| F. R. WYETH, c. Badcock, b. Ward | | 7 |
| J. GOVAN, c. Walker, b. Grimmett | | 9 |
| P. L. DIXON, not out | | 5 |
| Byes 5, leg-byes 10, no-balls 2 | | 17 |
| Total | | 426 |

| 1 | 2 | 3 | 4 | 5 | 6 | 7 | 8 | 9 |
|---|---|---|---|---|---|---|---|---|
| 22 | 22 | 24 | 66 | 121 | 273 | 363 | 389 | 415 |

### Bowling

| | O. | M. | R. | W. |
|---|---|---|---|---|
| H. J. Cotton | 20 | 3 | 69 | — |
| R. G. Williams | 16 | 2 | 57 | 1 |
| F. A. Ward | 30 | 2 | 132 | 4 |
| M. G. Waite | 24 | 10 | 51 | 2 |
| C. V. Grimmett | 33.3 | 3 | 107 | 2 |

Williams bowled two no-balls.

## SOUTH AUSTRALIA
### First Innings

| | | |
|---|---|---:|
| C. L. BADCOCK, c. Dixon, b. Cook | | 10 |
| C. W. WALKER, run out | | 11 |
| D. G. BRADMAN, c. Baker, b. Dixon | | 246 |
| F. A. WARD, c. Tallon, b. Loxton | | 0 |
| R. G. WILLIAMS, c. Baker, b. Govan | | 34 |
| R. H. ROBINSON, c. Loxton, b. Dixon | | 49 |
| R. A. HAMENCE, c. Tallon, b. Dixon | | 5 |
| R. S. WHITTINGTON, run out | | 3 |
| M. G. WAITE, not out | | 52 |
| C. V. GRIMMETT, not out | | 5 |
| No-balls 3, byes 3, leg-byes 8 | | 14 |
| Total (for eight wickets) | | 429 |

| 1 | 2 | 3 | 4 | 5 | 6 | 7 | 8 |
|---|---|---|---|---|---|---|---|
| 14 | 50 | 50 | 107 | 217 | 239 | 253 | 414 |

### Bowling

| | O. | M. | R. | W. |
|---|---|---|---|---|
| P. L. Dixon | 24 | — | 130 | 3 |
| G. Cook | 23 | 1 | 87 | 1 |
| C. Loxton | 11 | — | 41 | 1 |
| J. Govan | 12 | — | 72 | 1 |
| E. R. Wyeth | 24 | 3 | 70 | — |
| G. Baker | 3 | 1 | 15 | — |

Dixon bowled two no-balls and Cook one.

### Second Innings

| | | |
|---|---|---:|
| C. L. BADCOCK, st. Tallon, b. Govan | | 45 |
| C. W. WALKER, c. Loxton, b. Dixon | | 0 |
| D. G. BRADMAN, not out | | 39 |
| R. A. HAMENCE, not out | | 9 |
| Total (for two wickets) | | 93 |

| 1 | 2 |
|---|---|
| 1 | 79 |

### Bowling

| | O. | M. | R. | W. |
|---|---|---|---|---|
| P. L. Dixon | 4 | — | 22 | 1 |
| G. Cook | 10 | 1 | 30 | — |
| C. Loxton | 4 | 1 | 11 | — |
| F. R. Wyeth | 3 | — | 12 | — |
| J. Govan | 1.2 | — | 9 | 1 |
| T. Allen | 1 | — | 9 | — |

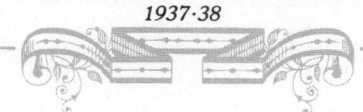

# Bradman's Big Score At Oval Match

## MADE 246 OF 400 RUNS
### WHILE HE WAS AT WICKETS

### Dominates Two Partnerships Of More Than 100—One A State Record

### S.A. 336 RUNS AHEAD WITH TWO WICKETS IN HAND

#### By LONG ON

Batting all day, with the exception of the last 10 minutes of play, Bradman, at the Adelaide Oval yesterday, dwarfed all other features of the Sheffield Shield cricket match between South Australia and Queensland.

He scored 246 of the 400 runs credited to South Australia while he was at the wickets, and was the dominating partner of two partnerships of more than 100—110 for the fifth wicket with Robinson and 161 for the eighth wicket with Waite, the latter being a record for that wicket for the State in Shield cricket.

As a result of his great innings, South Australia, with two wickets in hand, is 336 runs ahead, and faces the almost certain result of an innings victory.

When Bradman reached 208 he passed V. Y. Richardson's aggregate of 6,148 runs for Sheffield Shield matches, and when he was dismissed he was only 87 runs behind C. Hill's record aggregate of 6,274. The figures of the respective players are:—

|  | M. | I. | N.O. | H.S. | Agg. | Avg. |
|---|---|---|---|---|---|---|
| C. Hill | 68 | 126 | 6 | 365x | 6,274 | 52.2 |
| D. G. Bradman | 43 | 67 | 10 | 452x | 6,187 | 108.5 |
| V. Y. Richardson | 78 | 118 | 7 | 203 | 6,148 | 43.6 |

During his long innings—he was at the wickets for six hours and four minutes—Bradman saw six batsmen dismissed, and his partnerships were as follow:—

| Runs. | Wicket. | Partner. |
|---|---|---|
| 36 | Second | Walker |
| 0 | Third | Ward |
| 57 | Fourth | Williams |
| 110 | Fifth | Robinson |
| 22 | Sixth | Hamence |
| 11 | Seventh | Whitington |
| 161 | Eighth | Waite |

Very quiet early in his innings, principally because he did not get much of the strike, and because Brown, the Queensland captain, placed the field deep for him, and concentrated on saving fours. Bradman's times were not remarkably good. He scored off his usual large proportion of the balls he received, but because of Brown's protectively, rather than aggressively, placed field, he was forced to run singles and twos much more frequently. It was an innings which severely tested his stamina and physical condition, and it was not surprising that he showed signs of strain towards its end.

Despite Brown's care in preventing boundary shots, and really fine fielding by the Queenslanders, Bradman reached the fence on 20 occasions, many coming from a brilliant burst of hitting immediately before he was dismissed. His sectional times were:—

| Score. | Time. | Last 50 | Fours |
|---|---|---|---|
| 50 | 95 | 95 | Two |
| 100 | 194 | 99 | Five |
| 150 | 260 | 66 | Seven |
| 200 | 326 | 66 | 13 |
| 246 | 364 | 38 | 20 |

Robinson and he reached 100 in 99 minutes for their fifth wicket partnership, and it was Bradman's third century partnership in three first class matches this season. His fourth followed later in the day.

Bradman went from 98 to 102 without hitting the ball to the boundary or running at all. He played the ball to mid-off, where Baker fielded it and, seeing Robinson out of his ground at the bowler's end, had a shot at the stumps from side on. He missed the wicket and the ball flew to the fence for four overthrow.

The first hundred runs of his partnership with Waite for the seventh wicket were scored in 90 minutes. Waite scoring only 28 of these.

#### Dazzling Strokes

He was more his most brilliant self after he had passed 200 and Richardson's Shield aggregate. He played some dazzling shots towards the end of his innings, astounding the Queenslanders by going right across to turn balls well outside his off-stump to the untenanted field at fine leg. He scored a two for one of these demoralising shots off a ball from Dixon (fast-medium bowler); hit the next over the heads of slips for four; repeated his first amazing stroke, this time for four, off the next, and two balls later loftily off-drove another four. He was caught forward of square-leg off a skier in the same hectic over. His partnership of 161 with Waite lasted only 120 minutes.

Waite was second top-scorer. In the early stages he batted as though he was anxious to make amends for recent low scores, but occasionally he played brilliant shots, and after Bradman's dismissal he assumed his captain's mantle and scored freely. He batted two hours and seven minutes for his half-century, and at that stage had hit four fours.

Williams, who, in his earlier days of district cricket was an all-rounder of ability, but has since ranked almost solely as a bowler, showed batsmanship in his partnership of 57 for the fourth wicket with Bradman. He outscored Bradman during yesterday's play. He made eight of the first 10 runs, playing a good straight bat to the opening fast bowlers and scored with shots behind point. At one stage he was 26 and Bradman 36, the pair having resumed their innings at eight and 28 respectively.

Williams was with Bradman at 12.5 p.m., when, with three wickets down, South Australia passed Queensland's score of 93. He and Bradman reached the 50 partnership for the fourth wicket in 47 minutes. Williams then launched a hard hitting attack on Govan, the slow bowler, who finally had him caught at long-off. Williams had scored 34 runs (two fours) in 51 minutes.

#### Robinson Gets Runs

Robinson began sedately, scoring with late cuts off the slow bowler, Govan, and making only 19 of the first 50 runs scored for the fifth wicket with Bradman in 52 minutes. When 32 he gave a very difficult chance of stumping. The ball flew off his pad just

Cont. over page

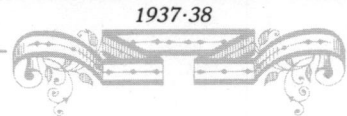

## SOUTH AUSTRALIA

| Score. | Time. | Last 50. |
|---|---|---|
| 50 | 48 | 48 |
| 100 | 100 | 52 |
| 150 | 146 | 46 |
| 200 | 201 | 55 |
| 250 | 248 | 47 |
| 300 | 297 | 49 |
| 350 | 345 | 48 |
| 400 | 374 | 29 |

### ADJOURNMENT SCORES

Resumption—S.A., three for 61 (Bradman 28).

Lunch—S.A., four for 168 (Bradman 81).

Tea—S.A., seven for 288 (Bradman 159).

Stumps—S.A., eight for 429 (Bradman out 246).

out of Tallon's reach with Robinson well out of his ground. He gradually expanded into somethin~ like the stylist he really is, giving one definite glimpse of his artistry with a sizzling shot for four past point off Loxton.

When within one run of his half century, Robinson, facing Dixon with the new ball, was well caught by Loxton at forward short leg, the fieldsman diving headlong to take the catch.

With Bradman, Robinson added 110 runs for the fifth wicket in 107 minutes.

Hamence and Whitington disappointingly failed. The former was a victim of the new ball, being very smartly caught at the wicket, and Whitington was easily run out when, after playing a ball to cover and running, Bradman sent him back.

**Queensland Attack**

Of the Queensland attack, Cook and Wyeth were the most impressive, although Cook took only one wicket and Wyeth none. Cook's medium pace deliveries were never treated with disrespect, and Wyeth bowled left-arm with fine command of length and flight. During the afternoon Wyeth left the ground for a quarter of an hour to have an injured finger on his right hand attended to. He broke a small blood vessel in fielding a hot shot by Bradman.

Dixon (fast medium) took three wickets, but was expensive; and Govan's slows caused little trouble.

Tallon was put out of action with a blow in the lower abdomen from a ball from Loxton when the score was 332 for seven wickets. He was unable to resume his place behind the wickets for several minutes.

# Eight Wicket Win For S.A.

## QUEENSLAND SCORES 426 IN SECOND INNINGS

### Rogers Takes His Score To 181 In Brilliant Display

## WAITE COLLECTS BOWLING HONORS

#### By LONG ON

Queensland forced South Australia to bat for an hour and a half yesterday for an eight wickets win.

Rogers carried his score of 117 to 181 in a brilliantly aggressive innings, in which he dominated the latter half of the Queensland batting list.

South Australia lost the wickets of Walker and Badcock in scoring the 91 runs required for an outright win.

Rogers, who was 117 when play was resumed, continued to hit crisply, especially against Ward, although he was more cautious against Grimmett when that bowler relieved Ward. With Coats he added 90 runs for the seventh wicket in 61 minutes, Coats scoring only 13 of the runs before being out leg-before to Waite. That bowler had then taken two for 20 in more than 20 overs.

The few runs scored by Coats was a tribute to the dominance of Rogers, who reached 150 in 197 minutes (18 fours). He had scored his third 50 in 64 minutes and his last 100 in 97 minutes.

He carefully nursed Wyeth, scoring a single as often as possible off the last ball of an over, and refusing to run singles early in an over. It was inevitable that Wyeth would have to face the bowling for a few balls, and in trying to hit Ward over the infield he was caught at mid-off by Badcock, leaving only Govan and Dixon to partner the century-maker, who seemed bent on reaching 200.

Even when Sides, another Queensland left-hander, scored a brilliant 74 against Grimmett at Adelaide Oval a few years ago, and, more recently, when Levy (another left-hander) scored a dashing century against the Test bowler at Adelaide, the South Australian slow bowlers have never been so completely collared as they were in this match by the burly young Queensland left-hand batsman. He had two international slow bowlers to contend with, and he mastered both of them.

Bradman was forced to avail himself of the new ball privilege after passing

#### QUEENSLAND

| Score. | Time. | Last 50. |
|---|---|---|
| 50 | 81 | 81 |
| 100 | 141 | 60 |
| 150 | 191 | 50 |
| 200 | 245 | 54 |
| 250 | 282 | 37 |
| 300 | 305 | 23 |
| 350 | 341 | 36 |
| 400 | 388 | 47 |

#### SOUTH AUSTRALIA

| Score. | Time. |
|---|---|
| 50 | 57 |
| 93 | 90 |

400, and in Williams's first over Rogers snicked a ball and was well caught by Walker. Rogers had scored his 181 runs in 231 minutes and hit 23 fours. His was one of the best innings from a crisp, but safe-hitting viewpoint, seen at Adelaide Oval for years.

Even after his dismissal the innings dragged on obstinately until 12.40 p.m., when Grimmett took the last wicket with Queensland 90 runs ahead.

##### Walker Fails To Score

Starting at 1.30 p.m. with 91 runs required for outright victory, South Australia lost Walker's wicket as the result of a brilliant catch at forward short leg by Loxton, who threw himself sideways to take it.

When within 12 runs of the required total, Badcock was out to a stumping decision after scoring 45 in 84 minutes (five fours).

Bradman and Hamence were batting when the match ended at 3 p.m., the 93 runs scored being made in 90 minutes.

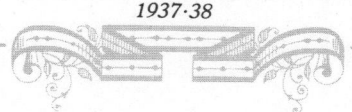

# South Australia
# v
# Queensland

SOUTH AUSTRALIA v QUEENSLAND, at Brisbane,
8, 10, 11 and 12 January 1938.

| | | | |
|---|---|---|---|
| South Australia | - First Innings | 398 | |
| | - Second Innings | 287 for 8 wickets dec. | |
| Queensland | - First Innings | 192 | |
| | - Second Innings | 155 for 8 wickets | |
| | Drawn. | | |
| DON BRADMAN | - c. D. Tallon b. P.L. Dixon | 107 | |
| (Captain) | - c. J. Hackett b. T. Allen | 113 | |

For the second time in a Sheffield Shield Match and for the third time altogether, DON BRADMAN put together two centuries in a match.     In his first innings, starting at 61 for 1 on the first morning, he completed 50 in eighty-five minutes, 100 in two hours thirty-five minutes, and batted altogether for two and three-quarter hours before being caught at the wicket at 264 for 6, just after tea; he hit nine fours and gave no chance.

South Australia batted again with a first-innings lead of 206 and Bradman went in forty minutes from the end of the second day at 2 for 1.     20 not out overnight, he reached 50 next morning after eighty-nine minutes altogether, and then completed his century in a further thirty-three minutes. Altogether, his chanceless 113 lasted two hours twenty-three minutes, and included ten fours, before he was caught in the deep just before lunch, virtually throwing his wicket away, at 177 for 5. Bradman was the first batsman to make a century in each innings of a Sheffield Shield Match on more than one occasion.

# BRADMAN'S
## 9th CENTURY IN QUEENSLAND GAMES
---
## S.A. In Strong Position In Shield Match
---
## 381 FOR 8 WICKETS
---
## Grimmett-Williams Bat Splendidly

BRISBANE, January 9.

South Australia, with eight wickets down for 381, has played itself into a strong position in the Sheffield Shield match begun yesterday against Queensland, and the bowlers tomorrow will have a chance to give the team a winning grip on the game. The attendance was 12,329, and the gate receipts totalled £1,004.

Bradman, who made 107, his ninth century against Queensland, showed that he is still masterful and faultless, but he did not attempt to lift his game to the exhilarating heights which characterised his 300 runs scored on a single day in a Test match in England in 1930. His batting was controlled by singleness of purpose to build for his team. He was determined to take no risks.

### Left-handed Bowlers's Success

Bradman's century was, of course, the highlight of the game, but there were a number of other individual feats which held the crowd's interest. Nothing could have been more captivating than the excellent break and flight bowling of Christ, the young Rockhampton left-hander, who was making his second Sheffield Shield appearance. At one stage in the pre-luncheon session, he had two wickets, those of Whitington and Badcock, for five, off five overs. In this spell he often had Bradman thinking hard. Later he also got Robinson's wicket.

### 94 Runs For Ninth Wicket

When Bradman was dismissed with the total at 264 runs for six wickets just after the tea adjournment, many Queensland optimists thought that the end of South Australia's innings was in sight; but, at 5 o'clock, Grimmett put a different complexion on things by helping Williams to collar the tired Queensland attack. The pair played splendidly through the last hour as if they were opening batsmen. Both made good strokes, Grimmett mixing square cuts with cover drives, while Williams executed a number of powerful sweeping shots, on one occasion lifting a ball from Govan over the square leg fence.

This partnership, which is still unbroken, has added 94 runs for the ninth wicket, the best partnership of the day, being nine runs more than was made in the stand by Bradman and Robinson for the third wicket. There was a remarkable steadiness and balance about the batting of the South Australians, each of the ten batsmen reaching double figures.

### Fine Display By Robinson

Apart from Bradman's effort, the most accomplished and masterful South Australian batting display was given by Robinson, the former New South Wales player. His innings provided a lesson of calm judgment, unerring placing and masterful stroke play, executed with a touch of genius. For skilled aggression he was more entertaining to watch than Bradman. Two of his hard cuts to the boundary off Christ were reminiscent of Alan Kippax. He did more to damage the left-hander's average than any other batsman, four of his six fours being scored off Christ.

Govan had the bad luck to have Badcock, when 33, missed off him by Rogers in the slips. It is many seasons since the Brisbane crowd has seen better fielding from a Queensland Sheffield Shield side.

### Brown Badly Hurt

Turning to make his throw after a fast run in the outfield, W. A. Brown, the Queensland captain and an Australian XI candidate, tore the muscle fibres at the back of his left thigh. He has been medically advised that it may be impossible for him to take further part in the match, and that he might not be fit for the fixture against Victoria opening at Brisbane next Friday.

Brown will be examined again tomorrow morning.

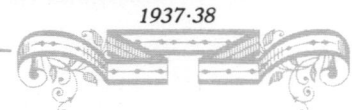

# South Australia v New South Wales

SOUTH AUSTRALIA v NEW SOUTH WALES, at Sydney,
15, 17, 18 and 19 January 1938.

| | | |
|---|---|---|
| South Australia | - First Innings | 187 |
| | - Second Innings | 334 |
| New South Wales | - First Innings | 295 |
| | - Second Innings | 227 for 6 wickets |

South Australia lost by 4 wickets.

| | | |
|---|---|---|
| DON BRADMAN | - c. S.J. McCabe b. L.J. O'Brien | 44 |
| | - not out | 104 |

DON BRADMAN went in at 10 for 1 on the first morning, and early in his innings had a collision with mid-on in going for a quick single, as a result of which he was rather dazed and his lip was cut; but he continued batting, and was out at 93 for 4, just before lunch, caught off an indecisive stroke at second slip after eighty-one minutes at the wicket.

Facing first innings arrears of 108, South Australia had almost cleared them off, with 106 for 1, when Bradman joined C.L. Badcock just after lunch on the third day. Bradman was content to let Badcock be the dominant partner in a stand of 95. He took ninety-five minutes for his 50, completed his 1,000 runs for the season when he was 80, and was 86 when the last man came in; by clever tactics, however, he completed his century, after three hours twenty-six minutes, four minutes before the close of play, when he was 101 not out. It was not one of his best innings, a cut hand interfering with his timing; but W.J. O'Reilly was among the bowlers. The innings soon finished next morning, and Bradman was left with 104ˣ, after three hours thirty-seven minutes; he hit thirteen fours and gave no chance.

In completing his 1,000 runs on 18 January, he was fifteen days earlier than the previous best by a South Australian batsman, he himself having reached this total in 1936-37 on 2 February. He showed his versatility by keeping wicket when C.W. Walker was injured, his record being five byes and a stumping in the first innings, and three byes and three good catches in the second.

# S.A. HAS GOOD FIGHTING
## CHANCE AGAINST N.S.W.

### BADCOCK (132) DASHING, AND
### BRADMAN (101 N.O.) SOLID

SYDNEY, January 18.

Although South Australia was 108 runs behind on the first innings in the match against New South Wales at the Sydney Cricket Ground, the southern team wiped off the deficit today and at stumps had made the position most interesting by holding a lead of 222 with one wicket to fall. Walker, who broke a finger yesterday, will not bat.

The wicket does not appear very worn; but, with the spin bowlers Grimmett and Ward as rivals, New South Wales might find a difficulty in scoring the necessary runs should McCabe and a few others be dismissed early.

Today was Badcock's day. Of the 330 runs scored he made 132, and Bradman 101 not out, but Badcock reigned supreme despite the presence of his more experienced partner. There was a contrast in the two innings, Badcock being dashing and Bradman solid. The former was always in command of the bowling, timing to perfection and hitting anything loose with terrific power. Bradman, on the other hand, timed badly, and did not reveal his customary accuracy in placement, but later this was explained by the fact that he had suffered from a recurrence of a hand injury, the webbing between the thumb and forefinger of the right hand being split.

Badcock was subdued for a few overs when play was resumed, but it was not long before he had command of the situation, and hit the bowling to all parts of the ground. His 132 runs were scored in 199 minutes before McCabe threw his wicket down; but, considering the fact that Whitington was his partner for 136 minutes, scoring only 29, and had quite a lot of the strike, Badcock's scoring rate was fast.

#### All Bowling Alike To Badcock

All bowling was alike to this stock little batsman, for he hooked, glanced, and drove with the greatest of ease. Anything loose was a certain four, and the fieldsmen were not given a chance with many of his square cuts and cover drives. In all he hit 18 fours, a remarkable performance, considering the slowness of the outfield after the heavy rain last night.

When the score was 100 Badcock was 68, and when 150 runs were on the board he was 102. With Bradman, he added 50 in 38 minutes, Bradman scoring only 19 of these. After reaching 132 Badcock cut a ball from Mair fairly slowly to McCabe, at third man, and Bradman appeared to be half-way down the pitch before Badcock realised he had been called. McCabe gathered the ball smartly, and a well-directed throw smashed the stumps at the bowler's end, with Badcock still well out of his crease.

#### 1,000 This Season In First Class Games

Bradman's was a plucky innings, and it was perhaps one of the hardest centuries in his lengthy list. When the last man (Cotton) came in, Bradman was 86, and it was only through determination and brains that he gained his century and added valuable runs to the total. Bradman's 101 took 210 minutes to compile, and included 13 fours. When Bradman had scored 80 it brought his aggregate to 1,000 in first-class matches this season.

The other batsmen did not reveal good form. Whitington was far too slow and Robinson too impetuous, but once again it looked as though Hamence would score well. When 13, however, he succumbed to O'Reilly's "bosey."

O'Reilly was outstanding in the bowling department, taking three for 62 off 25 overs. O'Brien was most innocuous. Bradman and Badcock scoring at will from him. After having none for 65, however, he finished with three of the later batsmen's wickets for 90.

# 'KEEPER BRADMAN CATCHES THREE

---

## Snapped Up McCabe Wide On Leg Side

### By A. G. MOYES

New South Wales to-day beat South Australia by four wickets, in the Sheffield Shield match at the Sydney Cricket Ground. The match finished just before 5 p.m.

It was much closer than the margin indicates, because the two not out batsmen were both missed early in their innings. White was missed when one, and was 36 not out at the finish.

Fingleton played very solidly, and held the side together at a stage when defeat seemed possible. Chipperfield and Barnes also batted in good style.

Waite was the best of the bowlers, while Bradman, despite his sore finger, took three catches behind the wicket.

Play was resumed on time, but only four runs were added to the South Australian innings. Then Chipperfield, who had previously missed Cotton at first slip off O'Reilly, caught that batsman off the same bowler.

N.S.W. thus wanted 227 runs for an outright win.

Despite his injured thumb, which was bound up with adhesive tape, Bradman again kept wickets for South Australia. He had no one who had any experience in this position, and consequently had to do the job himself.

McCabe and Fingleton opened to the bowling of Williams and Waite. Cotton was on the field. He is suffering from an injured foot, and could not bowl.

The first half-hour was very quiet, the only incidents being two unsuccessful appeals for l.b.w. against Fingleton.

When Grimmett came on, McCabe twice hit him for four, but might have been run out during the over. There was a mix-up between the two batsmen, but the ball was returned to the wrong end.

Immediately afterwards, McCabe survived a confident appeal for l.b.w. by Waite. Off the next ball Ridings, who was fielding substitute missed McCabe at first slip.

The 50 came up in 50 minutes, but three runs later McCabe glanced

Waite and Bradman, who was standing back, darted across and took a splendid catch wide on the leg-side. Waite had richly deserved a wicket. He was unlucky that he did not get one earlier.

After McCauley came in, Fingleton twice hit Grimmett to the fence, the first being a powerful drive and the second a nice cover shot. He was 28 not out at lunch, with McCauley 8 and the total one for 77.

### Ward Punished

The second ball after lunch gave Williams his first wicket. McCauley touched it and Bradman caught him.

Barnes came in, and he and Fingleton added 39 in 34 minutes before Waite got Barnes l.b.w.

Ward was bowling into the wind, but lacked the hostility of the first innings. He was irregular, both in length and direction, and Fingleton took two fours off short-pitched ones outside the off stump.

Actually, the spin bowlers, on whom South Australia were relying, had not so far played their part. Easily the outstanding feature had been the medium-paced bowling of Waite, who worried every batsman.

When Chipperfield came in, 111 runs were still needed. Then Fingleton ran to 50 by punching another loose one from Ward through the covers for four. He had been there for 127 minutes and, since lunch, had batted splendidly.

The South Australians were feeling the absence of Cotton, and when Waite had to be relieved, Wil-

liams was the only substitute. This was just the type of bowling that Chipperfield likes, and he drove, hooked, and cut the medium—fast stuff with rare relish.

They ran to 150 in 151 minutes, Fingleton at this stage being 57, and Chipperfield 27.

Ward was now bowling particularly well, and when Waite came back again the batsmen were very quiet. Then Waite clean bowled Chipperfield, and matters became interesting. Jackson, before he scored, edged one from Ward, and Bradman snapped it up very smartly. Half the side was out, with 66 runs still required.

White had made only one when he edged Ward. The ball went from Bradman's gloves just out of reach of Ridings, who had moved across in anticipation. It was a lucky escape, particularly at this stage of the game.

After tea, the two slow bowlers, Ward and Grimmett, took up the attack, and Grimmett got Fingleton. The batsman, in trying to swing him to the square-leg fence, skied the ball to Hamence. Fingleton hit six fours during his 208 minutes of solid batting.

With Oldfield in, White drove Ward for four, and hooked Grimmett to the fence. He was playing much more impressive cricket.

At 204 Robinson, half-way to the square-leg fence, dropped Oldfield, off Ward. He misjudged the ball slightly, got it right near the ground, and injured his finger. He went off the field and Whitington, who had not fielded since tea, came on.

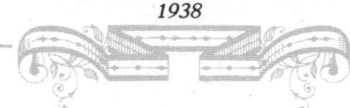

# *1938*
# *Australian Tour of England*

The Australian tour to England of 1938 was my first venture as captain of a team outside Australia and so presented a real challenge.

Those wonderful old stalwarts Oldfield and Grimmett missed selection, thus regrettably ending their Test careers. The team had only one fast bowler, he somewhat physically suspect, but it included O'Reilly, the greatest bowler I ever knew, and with a competent batting line-up I felt reasonably confident.

The young Victorian player, Ross Gregory, was just beaten for a place as an all-rounder by Arthur Chipperfield. I confess Gregory's omission worried me but I was consoled by the thoughts of his youth and the probability that he would get a tour later on. Alas, the only tour he ever had was with the R.A.A.F. in the Second World War in which he gave his life for Australia.

The strength of Australia's batting stood out in the early matches against the Counties and my own consistent good form was encouraging. After batting only seven times I completed (for the second time) 1,000 runs before the end of May. The lowest number of innings to achieve this total was formerly 10, by W. G. Grace in 1895.

The preliminary matches served their purpose for the sterner days ahead.

The more personal aspects of the 1938 tour, as distinct from the cricket side, are chronicled herein.

The diary notes were designed more as a memory reminder than a record of events, hence their brevity. Nevertheless, the passage of time highlights such things as my reference to the ominous nature of naval vessels in Naples harbour. Shades of World War II. In lighter vein is the ribbing I received for taking the salute bareheaded, at Gibraltar. Remarkable how innocent happenings make headline news.

Obviously a cricket tour to England embraces more than sport.

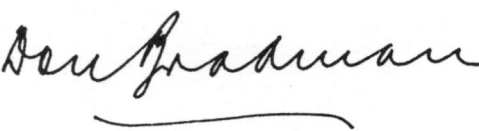

## AUSTRALIA'S 16 YOUNG MEN

*Here are the 16 Australians. Eight are paying their first visit to England for Tests. They are:*

**C. L. Badcock.** Aged 23. They call him Bradman No. 2.

**S. Barnes.** Aged 21. Useful slow bowler; capable wicket-keeper.

**F. Ward.** Aged 29. Good bowler; can be very expensive.

**A. L. Hassett.** Aged 24. Good fieldsman; useful slow bowler; capable wicketkeeper.

**J. H. Fingleton.** Aged 29. If he survives the opening overs he wants a lot of getting out.

**E. S. White.** Aged 24. He is over 6ft. in height. Left-hand bowler.

**E. L. McCormick.** Aged 31. Probably Australia's fastest bowler; not much good with the bat.

**M. G. Waite.** Aged 27. A very good all-rounder; the sort of man any side likes to have.

*Here are the other eight who have been here before:*

**Don Bradman.** Aged 29. Captain. Still holds run-getting record.

**S. J. McCabe.** Aged 28. Vice-captain. His average in 20 Tests is 49.03.

**B. A. Barnett.** Aged 29. Left-handed bat; first choice as wicket-keeper.

**L. O'B. Fleetwood-Smith.** Aged 29. Good left-hand slow bowler when in form. If he isn't, he is very expensive.

**W. A. Brown.** Aged 27. Graceful, straight-bladed, right-handed opening bat.

**A. G. Chipperfield.** Aged 32. Magnificent first slip; a fighting bat; slow leg-break bowler.

**C. W. Walker.** Aged 29. Wicketkeeper; useful defensive bat. Here in 1930.

**W. J. O'Reilly.** Aged 32. One of the best of the Australian bowlers; robs batsmen of all initiative; right-hand spinner.

*But, as "Plum" Warner said recently, we have the men to beat them.*

## "JOE" DARLING GOES FOR SELECTORS: SAYS TWO DON'T KNOW ENGLAND

HOBART (Tasmania), Friday.

STRONG criticism of the Australian cricket selectors and their choice of the Australian team to visit England has been made by the Hon. Joseph Darling, the former Test cricketer, and now member of the Tasmanian Legislative Council.

Darling thinks that R. S. Gregory, the Victorian all-rounder, W. A. Oldfield, the veteran wicket-keeper, C. V. Grimmett, and Ian Lee, the young Victorian left-hander, should have been included.

"Two of the three selectors," he says, "have never played in first-class cricket, have never been to England and are unable to understand English conditions."

Mr. Darling continued.—"The game in Australia has become a fight to make runs. Nobody dared to fail more than once.

"The sooner the public bring their weight to bear, and force the Board to do things in the best interests of cricket, the better for the game it will be."—British United Press.

**G. O. Allen** (captain of England in Australia last year): "It is not quite the Australian side I would have picked, but I suppose that it is a good one. We shall all be sorry not to see Grimmett and Oldfield here again."

**Sir Pelham Warner:** "I have never known an Australian team who were not good. Obviously these are but I hope and believe that they are not invincible. We are looking forward to seeing Bradman here as captain, and to the newcomers

"I notice that their only fast bowler is McCormick, who has been liable to breakdown. No, they are not invincible. We have a chance."

**Sir Stanley Jackson.**—"A very strong side, interesting because of the reliance on the slow and slow medium bowlers—O'Reilly Fleetwood-Smith and Ward—with one fast bowler to supply pace. If he is ineffective for any reason, then the entire burden will be thrown on the others

"We have to find the bowlers somewhere—and our task isn't hopeless by any means."

**R. W. V. Robins** (England vice-captain on the last tour in Australia).—"An excellent side, but I doubt whether good enough. I am surprised that they omitted Ross Gregory.

"I rate our chances as very good. All that is necessary is to pick the usual England team. My honest opinion is that we shall beat them."

**W. R. Hammond.**—"They look a very well-balanced side, though a little bit weak with the new ball I am surprised not to find Gregory in the list.

**W. H. Ponsford** (quoted by Reuter from Melbourne) describes the dropping of Grimmett as "sheer lunacy," and thinks the leaving out of Oldfield is another mistake."

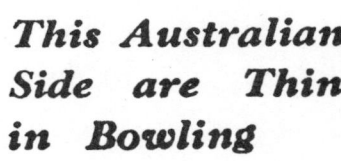

# This Australian Side are Thin in Bowling

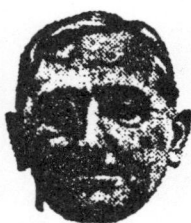

# Double-distilled Tosh to Say We Cannot Beat Them

# ═══ C. B. FRY Says ═══

THE Australian selectors are supposed to have been worried by an *embarras-de-choix* due to an abundance of equality among their younger claimants.

Nothing of the kind. What have worried them are three main points. They know that their bowling is thin; they know that their batting, on a free choice of bowlers and wicket-keepers, would carry a long tail; they have in mind that their tour involves a long list of county fixtures, in addition to the five Tests.

☆   ☆

On the first point, it is informative that they have been unable to rate any of their faster bowlers to back up E. L. McCormick. They have ruled out O'Brien, a new arrival; Cook of Queensland, whom I thought good; and Hynes, the fastish left-hand who I think (if still as good as during G. O. Allen's tour) would have been an asset over here.

They have chosen M. G. Waite, a medium-pace right-hander, up to good county form—something like Jimmy Parks of Sussex and Reginald Sinfield of Gloucestershire, but rather faster. He is useful, but will not win Test matches.

Thus they declare to win on O'Reilly, Fleetwood-Smith, McCormick and Ward, with McCabe and Chipperfield as all-rounders. Probably they will again use McCabe for the depolishing overs at the start. He is so eminent a bat that some of us forget his record as a bowler in big matches.

McCormick, as I saw him, is a good fast bowler for a few overs. But he needs nursing. In any case he has not proved devastating this season in Australia. Fleetwood-Smith, unless the wicket suits him, and he is on his day, can lose a match—a brilliant variable.

This puts the burden of the bowling upon O'Reilly and Ward. O'Reilly we know. Ward is a good slow leg-break bowler with plenty of spin, but he is not a Grimmett; he does not dominate; he has not the resource and tactical knowledge. We have leg-breakers over here as good.

☆   ☆

I do not regard the Australian bowling as strong. I call it thin. And I am pretty sure the Australians think so too. I am pretty sure, too, that what decided them against Grimmett was their fear of too big a batting tail.

The slow left-hand bowler White is an average county bowler.

Then the wicket-keepers. I am sure that tail-fear decided against Oldfield. He is still their best man. But he discussed with me last winter whether he should accept if invited. He did not want to accept and be less than his best self.

I advised him to accept. He may have decided against himself B. A. Barnett is very good, however, and can be a troublesome batsman.

With regard to the batting, Gregory has been left out for a bowler. But had another Queenslander been in their eye, I think Brown would have been left out for Gregory.

☆   ☆

Well, you see an Australian team chosen with a view to reduce its tail.

The idea that our England eleven, if well chosen (as Herbert Sutcliffe says) and well organised (as I say) cannot face this team with fair hopes is simply tosh.
Double distilled tosh.

The Manager of the tour — Mr. W. H. Jeanes.

The Pavilion, Lord's Cricket Ground, 1984.

Canterbury Cricket Ground, 1984. Note the stately tree in the outfield.

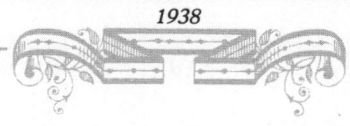

# 1938——
# Australian XI
# Tour in . . .
# Great Britain

## MATCHES IN AUSTRALIA.

| Date | Match Versus | To be Played at |
|---|---|---|
| b. 26, 28, March 1 | Tasmania | Launceston |
| arch 3, 4, 5 | Tasmania | Hobart |
| arch 18, 19, 21 | Western Australia | Perth |

### Playing Hours in Australian Matches.

12 noon to 1.30 p.m.

2.15 p.m. to 4 p.m.

4.15 p.m. to 6 p.m.

## TRAVELLING ITINERARY IN AUSTRALIA.

Journey from Melbourne to Launceston by S.S. "Taroona"; from Hobart to Fremantle by R.M.S. "Maloja."

| | | Miles | | | Hotel Address |
|---|---|---|---|---|---|
| Feb. | 25—Melbourne | | dep. 3.00 p.m. | | Brisbane Hotel |
| " | 26—Launceston | 265 | arr. 8.00 a.m. | | |
| | | | dep. 12 noon | | Hadley's Hote |
| Mar. | 2—Launceston | 133 | arr. 5.25 p.m. | | |
| | Hobart | | dep. 7.00 p.m. | | |
| " | 5—Hobart | 499 | arr. 7.30-8 a.m. | | |
| " | 7—Melbourne | | dep. 4.00 p.m. | | |
| " | 8—Melbourne | 505 | arr. 11.00 p.m. | | |
| " | 9—Adelaide | | dep. 5.00 p.m. | | Palace H |
| " | 10—Adelaide | 1,350 | arr. 7.30-8 a.m. | | |
| " | 14—Fremantle | | | | |
| | | 2,752 | | | |

## COLOMBO MATCH.

A one-day match will be played versus Ceylon March 30th.

## R.M.S. "ORONTES" — JOURNEY TO ENGLAND.

| | | | |
|---|---|---|---|
| FREMANTLE | | | dep. 7.30 p.m. Mar. 21 |
| COLOMBO | 3,126 miles | arr. 6 a.m., Mar. 30 | dep. Midnight Mar. 30 |
| ADEN | 2,094 miles | arr. 8 a.m., Apr. 5 | dep. 12 noon Apr. 5 |
| SUEZ | 1,310 miles | arr. 6 a.m., " 9 | dep. 8 a.m. " 9 |
| PORT SAID | 88 miles | arr. 10 p.m., " 9 | dep. Midnight " 9 |
| NAPLES | 1,112 miles | arr. 7 a.m., " 13 | dep. 5 p.m. " 13 |
| VILLEFRANCHE | 368 miles | arr. 1 p.m., " 14 | dep. 1 a.m. " 15 |
| TOULON | 85 miles | arr. 6 a.m., " 15 | dep. 12 noon " 15 |
| GIBRALTAR | 750 miles | arr. 8 a.m., " 17 | dep. 12 noon " 17 |
| SOUTHAMPTON | 1,142 miles | arr. 2 p.m., " 20 | |
| | 10,075 | | |

## LONDON HOTEL AND MAIL ARRANGEMENTS.

The Team on its visits to London will reside at the—

Victoria Hotel,
Northumberland Avenue,
London, W.C.2

to which address letters should be posted throughout the Tour.

For mail arrangements to connect with the Team on the return journey to Australia, see Page 11.

## R.M.S. "ORONTES" — JOURNEY TO AUSTRALIA.

| | | | |
|---|---|---|---|
| LONDON | | | dep. Noon Sept. 24 |
| GIBRALTAR | 1,332 miles | arr. 8 a.m., Sept. 28 | dep. 12 noon " 28 |
| TOULON | 750 miles | arr. 10 a.m., " 30 | dep. Midnight " 30 |
| NAPLES | 425 miles | arr. 8 a.m., Oct. 2 | dep. 4 p.m. Oct. 2 |
| PORT SAID | 1,112 miles | arr. 8 a.m., " 5 | dep. 12 noon " 5 |
| ADEN | 1,398 miles | arr. 8 a.m., " 9 | dep. Midnight " 9 |
| COLOMBO | 2,094 miles | arr. 6 a.m., " 15 | dep. 12 noon " 15 |
| FREMANTLE | 3,126 miles | arr. 7 a.m., " 25 | dep. 4 p.m. " 25 |
| ADELAIDE | 1,350 miles | arr. 8 a.m., " 29 | dep. 3 p.m. " 29 |
| MELBOURNE | 505 miles | arr. 7 a.m., " 31 | |
| | 12,092 | | |

Steamer arrival and departure hours are approximate only.

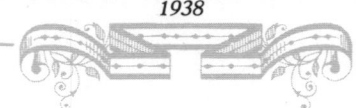

# Australian Test Team Sail from Melbourne

MELBOURNE, Tuesday.

A crowd of 5000 gathered here to see the Australian cricketers, under the captaincy of Don Bradman, leave for Fremantle on their way to England for the coming tour.

EVERY PLAYER was on deck as the Maloja drew away from the Outer Harbor Top—D. G. Bradman and M. G. Waite.

## Bradman Not Playing in Australians' First Match

### ON BOARD S.S. ORONTES, Tuesday.

Don Bradman will stand down from the Australian cricket XI. for their one-day match with Ceylon at Colombo W. J. O'Reilly L. O'B Fleetwood-Smith. E. L. McCormick and B. A. Barnett will also not play, and the team selected is: S. J. McCabe. C. L. Badcock. S. Barnes. A. G. Chipperfield, W. A. Brown, J. H. Fingleton. A. L. Hassett, E. S. White, F. Ward, C. W. Walker, M. G. Waite.—Reuter.

## *Australians in Cairo*

THE AUSTRALIAN cricketers, having emerged from the hot and Red Sea, will land at Suez on Saturday, and dash across to Cairo to play Egypt while their ship is crawling through the canal.

The Egyptian side is made up chiefly from the English fighting services, with a civilian or two and maybe one or two Egyptians. There is a native swing bowler with a fine record against H. M. Martineau's visiting English sides.

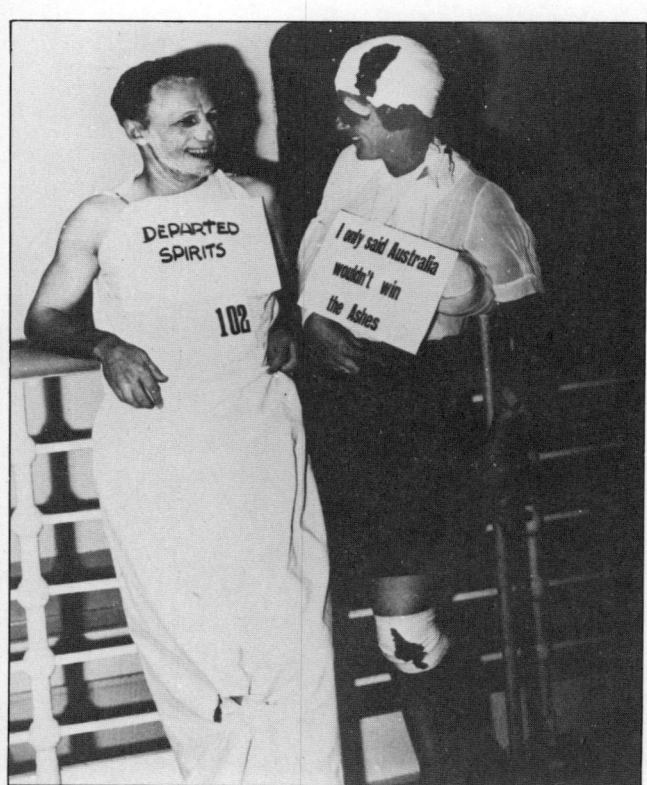

A fancy dress on board.

### *WEDNESDAY, 13 APRIL*

*Arrived at Naples at dawn. Went ashore and walked around. A lot of building has taken place since 1934, but the people looked very poor and quite different to our own. We saw about 36 destroyers, 8 cruisers and 72 submarines in the Harbour. They looked very ominous. Also we saw naval ratings drilling on the wharf. Some boys went to Pompeii. Sailed about 3.*

## *Don's One Mistake*

DON. Bradman is winning golden opinions already as skipper of the Australian cricket team.

His debonair cordiality to all and sundry, including the journalists, is in marked contrast with some earlier Australian cricketers.

He is also developing into a first-class impromptu orator—a sort of cricket Demosthenes of the genial sporting genre.

Even though the Don gets into treble figures in each of his Test innings, he looks like being throughly popular with our cricket crowds and cricketers alike.

When the tourists were at Gibraltar on their voyage to England they attended a church parade.

General "Tim" Harington, who is one of the keenest sportsmen in the British Army, though his chief love is Rugger, invited the Australian captain to stand with him and take the salute as the troops—incidentally, the King's Liverpools, Tim's own regiment—marched past.

A photograph of this interesting occasion reveals the Don standing beside the general, with his hat in one hand and his other hand at the salute.

The Anzacs were better at scrapping than drilling, but even they could have told Bradman that one must never salute bareheaded.

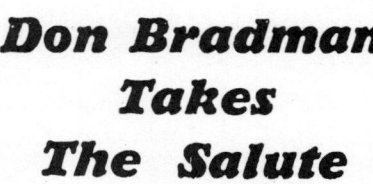

# Don Bradman Takes The Salute

AUSTRALIA'S CRICKET CAPTAIN shared in the salute taken by General Sir Charles Harington when troops marched past after a church parade at Gibraltar.

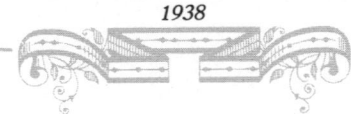

WEDNESDAY, 20 APRIL

*Awoke in a calm sea.*
*Arrived Southampton about 1 p.m. Greeting by Col*
*Hesildene on behalf of M.C.C. and the Mayor and Deputy*
*Mayor of Southampton. Many pictures and movies etc.*
*Got away about 3.10 p.m. on the special train and arrived in*
*London at 5 p.m. where at Waterloo Station we were greeted*
*by a large crowd including Lord Hawke, Sir Plum, Holmes,*
*Allen, Robins, Sir Stanley Jackson, Rait Kerr and others.*
*To the Victoria Hotel. Interviewed pressmen. Got 2 Gunn &*
*Moores and saw hosts of people. At night Dr. Pope and I*
*went to see Sir Douglas Shields. Back by 11. Unpacking.*
*Then bed.*

The Mayor of Southampton, Councillor G. H. Prince, welcomes Don Bradman
to England.

Don Bradman and Lord Hawke.

# BRADMAN'S NEW RESPONSIBILITY

*BY C. G. MACARTNEY*

The Australian cricketers, led by D. G. Bradman, have arrived, and the future success of the team will depend to a large extent on the performances of the new men who constitute half the side. The time has passed for recriminations, and while the omission of Oldfield and Grimmett in the opinion of many has weakened the side in their respective departments, it has yet to be seen whether those appointed will prove the judgment of the selectors to be correct.

D. G. Bradman as the leader and the batsman is a host in himself. For the first time in England he will assume complete responsibility for the side, and his ability to command has given satisfaction in Australia. He possesses the confidence to follow his own policy, and his judgment is good. Instances have occurred in the past where the anxieties of captaincy have interfered seriously with the individual work, but not so in Bradman's case. Judging by his batting against G. O. Allen's team in Australia, the adverse situation in which Australia found herself in the last three Tests merely forced Bradman to bat more cautiously, and with what success is widely known. This caution has been accepted by some as a sign that his erstwhile brilliance has departed and his crashing stroke play of 1930 has for ever disappeared. I should advise English bowlers, however, to be wary, as his aggression is likely to re-appear, and those who hope to keep him on the defensive may be doomed to disappointment. Bradman is still the great driving force of the Australian side, and the captaincy has not yet robbed him of any of his batting or fielding powers.

J. H. Fingleton and Don Bradman walking along the Strand with an admiring escort of London youngsters.

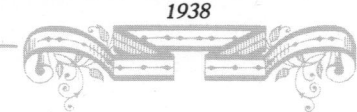
WEDNESDAY, 27 APRIL

*To Selfridges at 10.30 to meet the old man. Hotel. Working
till 12.30 thence to Royal Empire Society lunch. Back to
hotel for meeting of team, then doing mail.*
*To dinner with Geo. Garcia at Hyde Park Hotel with Ann
Bey and thence to see "Bluebeard's Eighth Wife" at the
Plaza.*

Gordon Selfridge knows less about cricket than business but shows his interest in this photograph
taken on the roof of Selfridges.

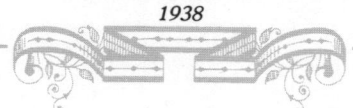

## — SEASON 1938 —

| TITLE | GAMES | | SCORES | | TITLE | GAME | SCORES | |
|---|---|---|---|---|---|---|---|---|
| Test | Australia | England | 51 | C. | – | Lancashire | 12 | C. |
| | " | " | 144 | n.o. | – | " | 101 | n.o. |
| | " | " | 18 | B. | – | Yorkshire | 59 | S. |
| | " | " | 102 | n.o. | – | " | 42 | C. |
| | " | " | 103 | B. | – | Warwickshire | 135 | C. |
| | " | " | 16 | C. | – | Nottingham | 56 | L.B.W. |
| Other First Class | " | Worcester | 258 | C. | – | " | 144 | C. |
| | " | Oxford | 58 | L.B.W. | – | Somerset | 202 | B. |
| | " | Cambridge | 137 | C. | – | Glamorgan | 17 | S. |
| | " | M.C.C. | 278 | C. | – | Kent | 67 | C. |
| | " | Northampton | 2 | C. | | | | |
| | " | Surrey | 143 | C. | | Total runs | 2429 | |
| | " | Hampshire | 145 | n.o. | | | | |
| | " | Middlesex | 5 | C. | | | | |
| | " | " | 30 | n.o. | | | | |
| | " | Gentlemen of England | 104 | C. | | | | |

## THE AUSTRALIANS

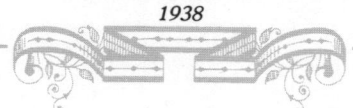

BACK ROW    W. H. Jeanes (Manager), S. G. Barnes (N.S.W.), W. A. Brown (Queensland), E. L. McCormick (Victoria), E. S. White (N.S.W.), W. J. O'Reilly (N.S.W.), L. O'B. Fleetwood-Smith (Victoria), F. A. Ward (South Australia), and W. Ferguson (Official Scorer).

SECOND ROW    J. H. Fingleton (N.S.W.), M. G. Waite (South Australia), S. J. McCabe (N.S.W.), D. G. Bradman (Captain, South Australia), B. A. Barnett (Victoria), A. G. Chipperfield (N.S.W.), C. L. Badcock (South Australia).

SITTING ON GROUND    A. L. Hassett (Victoria), C. W. Walker (South Australia).

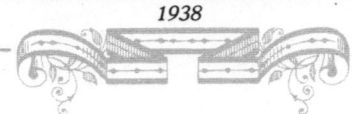

# Australians v Worcestershire

AUSTRALIANS v WORCESTERSHIRE, at Worcester, 30 April, 2 and 3 May 1938.

| | | | |
|---|---|---|---|
| Australians | - | First Innings | 541 |
| | - | Second Innings | - |
| Worcestershire | - | First Innings | 268 |
| | - | Second Innings | 196 |

Australians won by an innings and 77 runs.

DON BRADMAN - c. S.H. Martin b. R. Howorth 258
(Captain)

Worcestershire, winning the toss, surprisingly put the Australians in to bat on a perfect wicket. DON BRADMAN went in at 9 for 1, fifteen minutes after the start of the first day's play, and commenced with great care, taking an hour and three-quarters before lunch to score 37. After the interval, he began to find his form and confidence; completing 50 in two hours seven minutes, he then raced to his century in another thirty-eight minutes. After that, he scored much as he pleased, adding 145 in two hours between lunch and tea; he reached 200 in four hours four minutes, and was at the wicket altogether for four hours fifty-three minutes for his 258. He was then caught in the slips, attempting to cut, with the score 428 for 5; he gave no chance, hit a five and thirty-three fours, and he and C.L. Badcock put on 277 for the fourth wicket in two hours thirty-four minutes. This was the highest fourth wicket partnership made against Worcestershire. The bowlers included R.J. Crisp, R.T.D. Perks and R. Howorth.

In starting a first-class season in England with a double-century in his first innings for the third time, Bradman did something which no other batsman had ever done more than once. 258 was the highest innings ever played by a visiting batsman in his first innings of an English tour. It was also the highest score ever made on the opening day of first-class cricket in any English season and the only double-century.

This was the sixth time that Bradman had made three (or more) centuries in successive innings, thus breaking the record he previously shared with W.G. Grace, J.B. Hobbs and W.H. Ponsford.

## Australians

| | |
|---|---|
| J. H. Fingleton c Crisp b Howorth .. 41 | B. A. Barnett b Crisp ........ 16 |
| W. A. Brown lbw b Crisp .......... 2 | E. S. White b Crisp .......... 26 |
| D. G. Bradman c Martin b Howorth.258 | W. J. O'Reilly b Perks ........ 11 |
| S. J. McCabe b Perks ............ 34 | E. L. McCormick b Crisp ...... 5 |
| C. L. Badcock c Singleton b Perks... 67 | L. O'B. Fleetwood-Smith not out 6 |
| A. L. Hassett c Howorth b Perks..... 43 | B 13, l-b 15, w 2 n-b 2.... 32 |
| | 541 |

## Worcestershire

| | | | |
|---|---|---|---|
| Hon. C. J. Lyttelton b Fleetwood-Smith .. | 50 | — c Badcock b White ........ | 35 |
| C. H. Bull not out .................. | 37 | — c McCormick b Fleetwood-Smith ................. | 69 |
| E. Cooper c Hassett b Fleetwood-Smith . | 61 | — lbw b White .............. | 16 |
| H. H. Gibbons b Fleetwood-Smith ...... | 29 | — c Brown b O'Reilly......... | 9 |
| S. H. Martin b White ................ | 1 | — c Fingleton b O'Reilly .... | 5 |
| Mr. R. H. C. Human c Fingleton b Fleetwood-Smith | 10 | — lbw b Fleetwood Smith ..... | 26 |
| R. Howorth c Hassett b Fleetwood-Smith | 12 | — c McCabe b O'Reilly ..... | 0 |
| Mr. A. P. Singleton st Barnett b Fleetwood-Smith | 5 | — run out .................. | 14 |
| S. Buller lbw b O'Reilly .............. | 5 | — c Fleetwood-Smith b McCormick .................. | 10 |
| R. T. D. Perks c McCabe b Fleetwood-Smith ............................. | 21 | — c McCabe b Fleetwood-Smith | 4 |
| Mr. R. J. Crisp c Hassett b Fleetwood-Smith ............................. | 11 | — not out .................. | 0 |
| B 4, l-b 5, w 1, n-b 16 ............ | 26 | B 5, n-b 3 ............. | 8 |
| | 268 | | 195 |

## Worcestershire Bowling

| | Overs | Mdns. | Runs | Wkts. | Overs | Mdns. | Runs | Wkts. |
|---|---|---|---|---|---|---|---|---|
| Crisp ......... | 37.3 | 5 | 170 | 4 | | | | |
| Perks ......... | 34 | 3 | 147 | 4 | | | | |
| Martin ....... | 29 | 8 | 70 | 0 | | | | |
| Howorth...... | 21 | 1 | 85 | 2 | | | | |
| Singleton ..... | 3 | 0 | 37 | 0 | | | | |

## Australians Bowling

| | Overs | Mdns. | Runs | Wkts. | Overs | Mdns. | Runs | Wkts. |
|---|---|---|---|---|---|---|---|---|
| McCormick .. | 8 | 0 | 44 | 0 | 12 | 2 | 51 | 1 |
| McCabe ....... | 4 | 0 | 16 | 0 | 5 | 1 | 13 | 0 |
| O'Reilly ....... | 14 | 2 | 77 | 1 | 23 | 9 | 56 | 3 |
| Fleetwood-Smith | 29 | 8 | 98 | 8 | 13.1 | 0 | 38 | 3 |
| White ......... | 11 | 7 | 7 | 1 | 10 | 1 | 30 | 2 |

Umpires: J. Smart and H. G. Baldwin

# BRADMAN THE OLD MASTER AGAIN
## Worcester's Bowling Inspected and Then Dismissed

### By Neville Cardus (Cricketer)

WORCESTER, SATURDAY.

For the third time in succession Bradman has opened an Australian cricket season in England with a double century against Worcestershire. He was generally expected to achieve the performance, granted that he himself felt in the mood. The Worcestershire captain, indeed, sensibly resigned himself to it and decided to get it over as quickly and as painlessly as may be, for having won the toss on a thoroughly easy wicket he asked the Australians to bat first, an invitation which was unanimously accepted. The Worcestershire captain's resignation apparently achieved a philosophy so profound that he declined the new ball at 200. Probably he was right; a new ball costs money, and Worcestershire is not a wealthy club and every little counts.

Bradman seldom promised to get out; when he missed a quick-rising out-swinger from Crisp, with his score at twenty-three, and when in the same over a ball struck him on the pads, we were merely rendered surprised, not hopeful. The last innings I saw Bradman play before this one was at Perth, Western Australia, in March; it was done with a bat seemingly all edge. On Saturday the great machine worked as precisely as ever it has worked. Our bowlers must now face the worst—Bradman is to-day, compared with the Bradman of other years, not quite so easy to get out. In other words, he is beginning really to see the ball. This latest innings by him had a plan and an executive skill which were terrifying. He spent two hours and a quarter on his first fifty; then he scored another fifty in half an hour, and another fifty in thirty-five minutes. The awful point is that when he was making a hundred in an hour he concealed the pace, deceived all of us except the alert scorers. He did not barnstorm; not until he passed 200 did his bat swing or hook at all violently. He scored a hundred in an hour with restraint. He played late on the whole, and his touch was so certain that we could almost feel that the blade of his bat was endowed with sight, and also was prehensile. Now and again, true, he reached forward in a way not common for Bradman, who is a back-foot player if ever there was one. The accuracy of his timing, as he forced the ball to leg or square, made one spectator at least catch breath—yes, Bradman can still stir in us astonishment at his powers.

I suppose no man has ever been more of a master of his job than Bradman is a master of his job. He is as good as a batsman as Bach was as a composer. Yet no; he lacks felicity—that effortless touch of nature which makes the difference between a thing that grows and a thing that is constructed. A Bradman innings is designed—it does not fall on him "by grace." There is usually the hint of severe watchfulness, even of suspicion. An innings by a Woolley just happens, like the bloom on the peach on the sun-stained wall. This is not to deny Bradman style and a kind of beauty; people speak nonsense when they say that Bradman does not ever move the æsthetic senses. A constructed thing can be beautiful, if it cannot be spontaneous. The flight of a bird and the flight of an aeroplane mark the difference between an innings by a Woolley and one by a Bradman. And in a war the aeroplane has the grandest eagle beaten.

A large crowd assembled on the pretty Worcester ground to see Bradman and the others. There were some eleven thousand of them, and everybody breathed on everybody else's neck, and pushed and trod and elbowed. The congestion was acute: it spoiled the graciousness of the place. There were scaffoldings for the camera men, and a stand for the battalions of the press. For Worcester cricket the occasion was momentous. At the entrances to the ground the gatemen were on their guard; a policeman with a spike in his hat walked on the field during the interval obviously looking for a case. There was little lunch to be had by the mass of the people, but in spite of a clean, cold day we became soiled as the hours wore on, and sticky. Only the Cathedral kept aloof from the spirit of the age.

Worcestershire bowled well for a long time. Crisp the South African, defeated Brown at once, lbw. Bradman came to the wicket at a quarter to twelve. He subjected the attack to austere scrutiny; for nearly an hour Fingleton was the more interesting batsman. He contrives to lend strength and freedom to strokes which are not announced by the short, cramped lift of his bat. He drove Perks to the off by means of a sudden thrust; he saw a shorter ball swiftly, and he back-cut it strong as an axe. He is clearly a cricketer who senses a ball's flight. Here is another hard nut to crack. Perks, who, according to his fate and custom, bowled ably and unluckily, once found out Fingleton's weakness, which is an involuntary flick at the out-swinger. Fingleton seemed settled for the day until a half-volley provoked him to excitement; he was caught at cover

after an innings of eighty-five minutes—every second bodeful of no good to our bowlers.

McCabe put lightness of touch into the Australian innings; he is never the labourer. His defences have been strengthened more by experience than by application of principles. He is a natural batsman, with strokes which he makes as instinctively as he walks or breathes. The hook is most times a dynamic hit and, as its name denotes, a little awkward. McCabe can hook lissomely; he gives to the stroke a curve, so to say—rounds off the angles. Perks deserved McCabe's wicket, for he took it with a good honest length ball.

Badcock was not at his best. He began vaguely. I could not recognise the fierce little swordsman I had seen in Australia. He groped. He played empirically, and missed many balls, and looked apologetic. But one hit, off the back foot, told the truth; nobody but a fine batsman could have made it. He would not be put down by his mistakes; Australian cricketers seldom respond to the suggestions of circumstances that they should get out. They only get out when they do get out. Badcock did nothing in particular for an hour, and did it badly. Then he proceeded towards his fifty. The innings was a rough study for a finished work to come. He helped Bradman to score 277 for the fourth wicket.

Bradman's innings acquired preposterous immensity. The ruthlessness of it all! First a long critical inspection of the opposition, each bowler weighed in the balance as though by codified law. (Once or twice a quick out-swinger from Crisp disturbed him; possibly the seat of error is here.) Then, as soon as he had put everybody into a class—and worn them out by keeping them in suspense,—he made fools of their pretensions to skill. He would not for hours even batter them—no, a contemptuous flick here, a sardonic cut there, a provoking drive on either side of the wicket. Later in the day the innings became a Juggernaut, and the field a shambles. Perhaps he was trying to get out but just could not. He missed true aim some three or four times in four hours and fifty minutes, and he hit thirty-three fours. I could not decide on what principle he struck these boundaries: I mean I could not work out the periodic law at the bottom of them. Apparently he could have hit a four from every other ball sent to him after lunch.

There were ices for sale on the ground all day, probably made on the premises while you waited. The match is, of course, dead already as a match; the only interest now is how quickly O'Reilly will clear up the mess and leave the Worcestershire field to its proper green peacefulness.

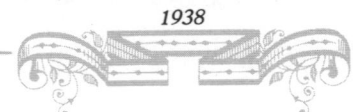

**TUESDAY, 3 MAY**

*Went to Royal Worcester works and got some pottery for Jessie. They expressed their intention of presenting me with a lovely vase in honour of my three 200's.*
*To ground. Continued game and won by an innings. Cold as charity.*
*Train to Oxford. Spent evening writing letters.*

## GIFT TO DON BRADMAN

### Royal Porcelain Works' Memento

When Don Bradman gets back to Australia with the "Ashes" safely in his urn, he will be presented with another urn, made at the Worcester Royal Porcelain Works, and offered as a gift to him by the Directors in recognition of his feat in scoring three consecutive double centuries in opening matches at Worcester.

In 1930 Bradman made 236. Four years later he scored 206, and this summer he surpassed himself with 258.

The urn, which will be on show at the works within the next few days, was designed by Mr. C. B. Simmons, the Company's art director.

It is decorated with the royal blue ground, with a painted panel in front of the Worcestershire cricket ground, showing Bradman batting. The panel is surrounded by a chaste and raised gold design, and the mounts, handles, neck and feet are decorated in royal blue, with burnished and chaste gold.

Mr. H. Davis painted the panel.

The inscription on the back is: "Presented to D. G. Bradman by the Directors of the Worcester Royal Porcelain Company, Worcester, England, in commemoration of his unique record of scoring three consecutive double centuries in the opening matches on the Worcestershire ground. 1930, April 30, 236; 1934, May 2, 206; 1938, April 30, 258."

The urn will be presented by Mr. T. W. Heath, the Company's representative in Sydney, at a function to be arranged when the Australians return home.

See colour plates between pages 544 and 545

S. J. McCabe and D. G. Bradman going out to bat after the lunch interval at Worcester on Saturday.

### SATURDAY, 7 MAY

*After breakfast went to Bank of Australasia and transferred money to Australia and also paid in a cheque to my a/c. at C. Savings Bank, Aust. House.*

*With Chuck to see Guildford at Watermans. Pen and pencil each and promise of cards and sundry other things.*

*Lunch at Charing X Hotel thence to Wembley as guests of League Council. Saw final of game between Salford and Barrow. Salford won 7/4 in last minute.*

*I presented the Cup and medals and met the players on the field at the start.*

*To see "Snow White and the Seven Dwarfs" at New Gallery at night.*

## BRADMAN IN NEW ROLE.

The Australian cricket captain, D. G. Bradman, meeting the members of the Salford team before the British Rugby League Cup Final at Wembley, in which Salford defeated Barrow.

### (NOT) TAKING HIS BOW

I SUPPOSE there is no limit to how far you may bow when shaking hands with a King. But what about when you are shaking hands with a "king" of cricket? Pictures in the morning papers show Don Bradman going the rounds of Saturday's Rugby League finalists, and it is clear what the answer is as far as one member of the Salford team is concerned. This stalwart remains bolt upright as Bradman takes his hand, clearly indicating that the two pastimes, cricket and Rugby League football, meet on an equal footing, and that no subservience is due from the representative of one game to the representative of the other.

# Australians v M.C.C.

Lord's Cricket Ground, 1930s.

AUSTRALIANS v M.C.C., at Lord's, 14 and 16 May 1938.

| Australians | - First Innings | 502 |
| | - Second Innings | - |
| M.C.C. | - First Innings | 214 |
| | - Second Innings | 87 for 1 wicket |

Drawn.

DON BRADMAN - c. R.W.V. Robins b. C.I.J. Smith    278
(Captain)

M.C.C's strong bowling side included K. Farnes, C.I.J. Smith, J.W.A. Stephenson and R.W.V. Robins, but DON BRADMAN played one of his finest innings and put his side into a winning position before rain washed out the last day's play.    He came in at 11 for 1, on the first day, and found that the wicket was helpful to the bowlers.    He soon reached 50 in seventy minutes, and was 68 at lunch; after the interval, he was always the master; and displayed sure defence as well as brilliant strokes. He completed his century in a minute under two and a half hours, and settled down to achieve another double-century which he did after four hours twenty-six minutes at the wicket.    By the close of play, after batting for five hours twenty-six minutes, he had made 257 not out.    He and J.H. Fingleton put on 138 for the second wicket, and he and A.L. Hassett added 162 for the fifth wicket.    Next morning, he carried his score to 278 before being well caught at cover in trying to square-cut a short ball.    His innings lasted five hours forty-nine minutes, included a six and thirty-five fours, and concluded with the score 454 for 6; it was chanceless, and scarcely included a false stroke. This was his eighth successive innings of over 50, a record for an Australian.    This was also the fourteenth successive match in which Bradman made 50 in one innings or the other.    Including his 102 in his last innings in Australia in 1937/8, he had scored 833 runs in five successive innings (102, 258, 58, 137, 278), and including his 132 in his last innings in 1934, he scored 863 in five consecutive innings in England (132, 258, 58, 137, 278), a record for an Overseas player in England.

## Australians
| | |
|---|---|
| J. H. Fingleton b Smith | 44 |
| W. A. Brown b Farnes | 5 |
| D. G. Bradman c Robins b Smith | 278 |
| S. J. McCabe b Smith | 33 |
| C. L. Badcock b Stephenson | 14 |
| A. L. Hassett c Maxwell b Compton | 57 |
| M. G. Waite lbw b Smith | 26 |
| B. A. Barnett lbw b Stephenson | 1 |
| W. J. O'Reilly c Compton b Smith | 17 |
| E. L. McCormick c Maxwell b Smith | 9 |
| L. O'B Fleetwood-Smith not out | 3 |
| B 3, l-b 11, n-b 1 | 15 |
| | 502 |

## M.C.C.
| | | | |
|---|---|---|---|
| Mr. D. R. Wilcox b Waite | 6 | b McCabe | 16 |
| W. J. Edrich c McCabe b Fleetwood-Smith | 31 | not out | 53 |
| D. Compton lbw b O'Reilly | 23 | not out | 12 |
| Mr. R. E. S. Wyatt not out | 84 | | |
| Mr. F. G. H. Chalk lbw b Fleetwood-Smith | 15 | | |
| Mr. J. H. Human b McCormick | 5 | | |
| Mr. C. R. Maxwell b McCormick | 0 | | |
| Mr. R. W. V. Robins c McCabe b O'Reilly | 12 | | |
| Capt. J. W. A. Stephenson c and b Fleetwood-Smith | 1 | | |
| J. Smith c Hassett b Fleetwood-Smith | 17 | | |
| Mr. K. Farnes c Fingleton b O'Reilly | 0 | | |
| B 5, l-b 15 | 20 | B 5, l-b 1 | 6 |
| | 214 | One wkt. | 87 |

### M.C.C. Bowling
| | Overs | Mdns. | Runs | Wkts. | | Overs | Mdns. | Runs | Wkts. |
|---|---|---|---|---|---|---|---|---|---|
| Farnes | 32 | 3 | 88 | 1 | | | | | |
| Smith | 42.5 | 9 | 139 | 6 | | | | | |
| Stephenson | 29 | 5 | 112 | 2 | | | | | |
| Robins | 18 | 2 | 69 | 0 | | | | | |
| Wyatt | 7 | 0 | 27 | 0 | | | | | |
| Compton | 10 | 2 | 37 | 1 | | | | | |
| Edrich | 2 | 0 | 15 | 0 | | | | | |

### Australians Bowling
| | Overs | Mdns. | Runs | Wkts. | | Overs | Mdns. | Runs | Wkts. |
|---|---|---|---|---|---|---|---|---|---|
| McCormick | 13 | 1 | 55 | 2 | | 3 | 1 | 8 | 0 |
| Waite | 11 | 2 | 28 | 1 | | 9 | 3 | 18 | 0 |
| O'Reilly | 16.2 | 6 | 42 | 3 | | 5 | 2 | 8 | 0 |
| Fleetwood-Smith | 20 | 2 | 69 | 4 | | 5 | 0 | 25 | 0 |
| McCabe | | | | | | 7 | 2 | 22 | 1 |

Umpires : J. Hardstaff and J. Newman

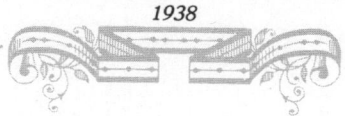

## London needs bigger ground

# Lord's is too small for a Bradman day

### By WILLIAM POLLOCK

LONDON needs a new cricket ground. Lord's wasn't big enough on Saturday for all those who wanted to see the Australians play the M.C.C.

As near as no matter 26,000 people paid their two bobs to enter the ground. It is a fair thing to say that, what with members and whatnot, 30,000 were there. And by three o'clock in the afternoon the gates were closed. Hundreds could not get in; thousands probably did not try to because they had heard the good—bad news.

The Oval holds a few more than Lord's—not many more. London is out of date in its cricket grounds.

Melbourne, with a seventh of London's population, has a ground which has housed a crowd of 87,000—I was there among it; Sydney (a million and a quarter people) can find room for forty thousand spectators.

The objection is, of course, nice work if you can get them—but you can't always. And Melbourne is also a football ground.

\* \* \*

### Don goes lame

AND what did the Lord's thirty thousand see? They saw Don Bradman, saw him almost all the livelong day, make a matter of 257 runs and racing some of them to the pavilion at the finish to escape being affectionately mobbed.

It was Don's Day. He came in with the Australian score 11 runs for one wicket, the up-to-date-unlucky Brown having got a rasper from Ken Farnes which out-swung and removed his off dolly, and he stayed put till the close.

The Don was applauded half way to the wicket—and almost immediately assailed by that super-enthusiastic bowler, Captain Stephenson, of Essex.

"Stevo" first sent him a full toss, which Don missed. The next ball hit him so hard on the outside of the left foot that the ball dribbled back to the bowler, and the batsman hobbled almost to the square-leg umpire in pain. Don was lame for the rest of the day.

\* \* \*

### One bat broken

NOTHING could knock him out. Farnes, big Jim Smith, and the extraordinary Stephenson bowled with spirit, pace—considering the dopey wicket—and some awkward run-away from the bat, but Don was their boss.

It was much the best innings I have seen from him for a long time, either here or in Australia. He was well within himself, with plenty of reserve. He did not "press," only two or three times did he make a false stroke. He batted on an even keel; he was ninety per cent on top of the bowling. He bust one bat to smithereens.

Don Bradman drives a ball off K. Farnes.

The scoreboard showing Don Bradman's enormous score of 278, after being caught by R. W. V. Robins off a ball by J. Smith.

# Australians v Surrey

AUSTRALIANS v SURREY, at the Oval, 21, 23 and 24 May 1938.

| Australians | - First Innings | 528 |
| | - Second Innings | 232 for 2 wickets dec. |
| Surrey | - First Innings | 271 |
| | - Second Innings | 104 for 1 wicket |
| | Drawn. | |

DON BRADMAN went in on the first morning with the score 90 for 1. It took him only sixty-nine minutes to reach 50, and two and a quarter hours to reach 100; but thereafter, rather surprisingly, he slowed down, and his innings lasted altogether for three hours eighteen minutes. He was then well caught at the wicket on the leg side, with the score 349 for 4; he gave no chance, and hit eleven fours. So far this season he had scored 876 runs.

Bradman did not enforce the follow-on, a course which met with some criticism; but by giving some of his later batsmen batting practise, he himself unselfishly missed a great opportunity for raising his aggregate towards his 1,000 runs by the end of May.

| DON BRADMAN | - c. E.W.J. Brooks b. E.A. Watts | 143 |
| (Captain) | - (did not bat) | - |

## Australians

| | | |
|---|---|---|
| J. H. Fingleton b Brown | 47 | |
| W. A. Brown c Brooks b Watts | 96 | |
| D. G. Bradman c Brooks b Watts | 143 | |
| C. L. Badcock c and b Brown | 32 | — c Watts b Gregory ......... 95 |
| A. L. Hassett c Squires b Berry | 98 | |
| A. G. Chipperfield b Gover | 20 | — c Brooks b Gregory ....... 6 |
| M. G. Waite c Brooks b Watts | 35 | |
| B. A. Barnett not out | 33 | — not out ................120 |
| E. S. White b Berry | 7 | — not out .................... 5 |
| F. Ward b Brown | 0 | |
| W. J. O'Reilly c Brooks b Brown | 0 | |
| B 8, l-b 8, n-b 1 | 17 | B 4, l-b 1, n-b 1........ 6 |
| | 528 | Two wkts., dec. 232 |

## Surrey

| | | |
|---|---|---|
| R. J. Gregory c Hassett b O'Reilly | 60 | — retired hurt ............... 5 |
| L. B. Fishlock st Barnett b O'Reilly | 24 | — c White b Chipperfield ..... 93 |
| H. S. Squires b O'Reilly | 7 | — not out .................... 4 |
| T. H. Barling lbw b Ward | 67 | |
| Mr. E. R. T. Holmes c Brown b O'Reilly | 10 | |
| Mr. H. M. Garland-Wells c Brown b O'Reilly | 2 | |
| Mr. F. R. Brown b O'Reilly | 15 | |
| F. Berry st Barnett b Ward | 31 | |
| E. A. Watts b O'Reilly | 22 | |
| E. W. Brooks not out | 16 | |
| A. R. Gover b O'Reilly | 0 | |
| B 8, l-b 9 | 17 | L-b ................ 2 |
| | 271 | One wkt 104 |

## Surrey Bowling

| | Overs | Mdns. | Runs | Wkts. | | Overs | Mdns. | Runs | Wkts. |
|---|---|---|---|---|---|---|---|---|---|
| Gover | 20 | 4 | 100 | 1 | .... | 6 | 0 | 20 | 0 |
| Watts | 23 | 4 | 69 | 3 | .... | 10 | 1 | 47 | 0 |
| Berry | 33 | 6 | 92 | 2 | .... | 6 | 3 | 12 | 0 |
| Brown | 35 | 0 | 147 | 4 | .... | 5 | 0 | 23 | 0 |
| Squires | 20 | 2 | 68 | 0 | .... | 8 | 2 | 29 | 0 |
| Gregory | 9 | 3 | 23 | 0 | .... | 7 | 4 | 10 | 2 |
| Garland-Wells | 3 | 0 | 12 | 0 | .... | 15 | 1 | 62 | 0 |
| Holmes | | | | | .... | 4 | 0 | 23 | 0 |

## Australians Bowling

| | Overs | Mdns. | Runs | Wkts. | | Overs | Mdns. | Runs | Wkts. |
|---|---|---|---|---|---|---|---|---|---|
| Waite | 15 | 3 | 34 | 0 | .... | 7 | 4 | 4 | 0 |
| O'Reilly | 36 | 9 | 104 | 8 | .... | 4 | 2 | 12 | 0 |
| Ward | 30 | 6 | 96 | 2 | .... | 8 | 1 | 50 | 0 |
| White | 17 | 8 | 20 | 0 | .... | 7 | 1 | 16 | 0 |
| Chipperfield | | | | | | 3.1 | 1 | 20 | 1 |

Umpires: E. J. Smith and A. Dolphin

Schoolboys complete with lunch, waiting to see the Australians play Surrey at the Oval to-day.

# DON BRADMAN SCORES YET ANOTHER CENTURY

## SURREY ATTACK WELL MASTERED AT THE OVAL

### *By ELTON EDE*

THE Australians were not very severely tested at the Oval. The wicket was altogether too good for Surrey's fast bowlers, and Gover is not yet bowling with the fire he has shown during the last two seasons. On present from, making due allowance for the wicket and the beautiful light, he must be ranked below Farnes and Jim Smith.

I would have liked to see him on a pitch which held a little life and enabled him to make the length ball lift occasionally. Surrey's change bowlers performed creditably enough; all of them, except Brown, kept a fair length, and they were never collared.

Holmes certainly set his field cleverly, and boundaries had to be placed as well as hit. Brooks was his usual agile and vocal self behind the stumps; but as regards voice-production the honours of the day rested with Dolphin, the umpire. His no-balling of Gover was worthy of Covent Garden—either the opera or the market.

If the afternoon naps of members are to be respected, he should be fitted with a silencer.

### PLENTY OF RUNS

The Australians' batting grows in solidity; Fingleton, Brown, Badcock and Hassett look perfectly capable of making plenty of runs on their own account, without relying on Bradman and McCabe. It will take some exceedingly good bowling, or a lot of help from the wicket, to get them out twice in a four-day match.

Bradman scored his 143 in two hours and a half; he did not hurry himself or take the slightest risk, he just let the runs come. Bradman's mastery and reserve power is comparable with that of a great singer, and his achievement is equally satisfying. He waits for his supreme moments and for the rest makes no effort to strain the context.

If he was a little less dramatic than he sometimes is, his batsmanship is still a marvel of precision and impenetrability. And by impenetrability, as Humpty Dumpty said, I mean that we've had enough of that subject

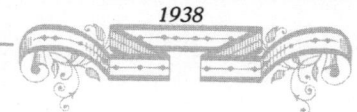

# Don Saves His Bowlers— Angers Crowd

### BY CHARLES BRAY

**M**INOR epidemic of injuries and ailments that has afflicted the Australian team is causing grave anxiety to Don Bradman.

No other possible excuse could be advanced for the remarkable decision of the Australian captain to bat again when Surrey's first innings was quickly brought to an end yesterday at the Oval.

Surrey were 257 runs behind, and the tourists had a nice time in which to win the match, but Don, with an eye on the Test in a fortnight's time, decided to play for a draw, and thus removed all interest from the game.

Don is particularly nervous about O'Reilly. The "Tiger" is the spearhead of his attack against England and, rather than risk giving him too much work to do, Don took the opportunity of giving wicket-keeper Barnett some batting practice, for runs are wanted from the latter in Test matches.

### Unpopular Policy

The decision was most unpopular, and I am afraid that the Australian captain did not do himself or the team any good in the eyes of the public.

He could have rested O'Reilly and also, for that matter, Waite, who is suffering from a sore shoulder, by employing Chipperfield, who has had practically no bowling since the tour began.

Ward and White are slow medium-paced bowlers and they should thrive on plenty of work.

Even as an exhibition—for that is what it had become—the final day had little to commend it. Don achieved his object in giving Barnett batting practice.

The wicket-keeper made a century off Surrey bowling that was deprived of any real incentive. It was his first century in first-class cricket. It was not one, however, he will wish to remember.

The edges of his bat did an astonishing amount of work. Eric Holmes quite rightly used Gover sparingly, and permitted Garland-Wells to turn his arm over far more than he would have done in other circumstances.

Badcock was out when within striking distance of his century, to the undisguised delight of a section of the crowd, who found little merit in anything the Australians did after Don's early decision.

Chipperfield was promoted in the batting order for the same purpose as Barnett, but he failed to take advantage of the opportunity to get some easy batting practice.

### Crowd Knew It

Then Don displeased the crowd still further by letting White bat instead of going in himself. He was No. 4 on the batting list, and the crowd knew it.

I could not understand why, having taken the course he did, the Australian captain did not carry it to its logical conclusion and bat for the rest of the day.

His only justification for not making Surrey follow-on was to rest his bowlers. So why not do it properly? Instead, he declared at 4 p.m., to the further annoyance of the demonstrative section of the crowd.

# Bradman Replies To Hooters

**INDEPENDENT CABLE SERVICE**

SOUTHAMPTON, Wednesday.

**D**ON BRADMAN said today he was sure the spectators who hooted him at The Oval yesterday would have been more tolerant had they known the true position.

"I regret that they disapproved of my action in not forcing Surrey to follow on," said Bradman.

"But my primary duty is to see that the members of the team are fit for the Test matches.

"Three of the players, Fleetwood-Smith (knee), McCormick (ankle), and Waite (shoulder), are suffering from slight injuries.

"McCabe was selected to play against Surrey, but dropped out because of an attack of neuritis in the shoulder.

### "Sorry—Must Look Ahead"

"White had a minor operation to a toe at Northampton, and has not fully recovered, while O'Reilly is suffering from an abscess on a tooth.

"These troubles caused me to think that it would have been detrimental to my bowlers to give them another hard day.

"I was also influenced by the fact that the players had spent a full day in the field and the evening at the Surrey Cricket Club dinner.

"There was the possibility—if Hampshire had batted today—of the bowlers having three consecutive days in the field.

"I am sorry that it was an unpopular move.

"But no reasonable being can refuse to admit that the remainder of the tour must receive serious consideration."

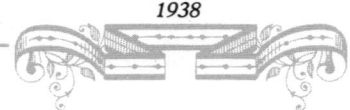

# Australians v Hampshire

AUSTRALIANS v HAMPSHIRE, at Southampton, 26 and 27 May 1938.

| Australians | - First Innings | 320 for 1 wicket dec. |
|---|---|---|
| | - Second Innings | - |
| Hampshire | - First Innings | 157 |
| | - Second Innings | - |
| | Drawn. | |

DON BRADMAN   - not out       145
   (Captain)

Wednesday's play having been washed out, DON BRADMAN put Hampshire in to bat on a drying wicket, which was rather easier when the Australians began their innings.   Bradman went in just before tea, at 78 for 1, and had scored 71 not out in an hour and fifty-seven minutes by the end of the day, having reached 50 in eighty-seven minutes;  he was sometimes worried by the Hampshire spin bowlers, G.S. Boyes and G. Hill, who derived considerable help from the wicket. Next morning, the wicket was again affected by rain and was more difficult.   Bradman and J.H. Fingleton were both uncomfortable at times, but, showing sound defence, they stayed together until lunch-time, adding 242 for the second wicket without being separated.   Bradman reached his century in a minute over two and a half hours, but when he was 109 rain interrupted play for twenty-seven minutes.   He carried his score past 124, and thereby reached his goal of 1,000 runs, this being the second time he had completed 1,000 runs before the end of May;  he batted altogether for three hours twenty-six minutes without giving a chance, and hit twenty-two fours.   He declared at lunch, but rain prevented further play.

## Hampshire
| | |
|---|---|
| N. McCorkell c Chipperfield b O'Reilly | 10 |
| J. Arnold b O'Reilly | 23 |
| Mr. C. G. A. Paris b O'Reilly | 18 |
| W. L. Creese b O'Reilly | 22 |
| Mr. R. H. Moore b Fleetwood-Smith. | 5 |
| A. E. Pothecary c Walker b O'Reilly . | 16 |
| Rev. J. W. J. Steele run out | 24 |
| G. Hill c Fingleton b White | 11 |
| G. S. Boyes c Bradman b O'Reilly | 11 |
| Mr. A. E. G. Baring b White | 0 |
| G. E. M. Heath not out | 4 |
| B 9, l-b 2, n-b 2 | 13 |
| | 157 |

## Australians
| | |
|---|---|
| J. H. Fingleton not out | 123 |
| W. A. Brown c Pothecary b Boyes | 47 |
| D. G. Bradman not out | 145 |
| B 4, l-b 1 | 5 |
| One wkt., dec. | 320 |

A. L. Hassett, A. G. Chipperfield, E. S. White, W. J. O'Reilly, E. L. McCormick, S. J. McCabe, C. W. Walker and L. O'B. Fleetwood-Smith did not bat.

## Australians Bowling
| | Overs | Mdns. | Runs | Wkts. |
|---|---|---|---|---|
| McCormick | 3 | 1 | 16 | 0 |
| McCabe | 3 | 0 | 9 | 0 |
| O'Reilly | 20.5 | 0 | 65 | 6 |
| White | 11 | 3 | 19 | 2 |
| Fleetwood-Smith. | 9 | 0 | 35 | 1 |

## Hampshire Bowling
| | Overs | Mdns. | Runs | Wkts. |
|---|---|---|---|---|
| Baring | 20 | 2 | 97 | 0 |
| Heath | 16 | 1 | 54 | 0 |
| Steele | 15 | 2 | 60 | 0 |
| Boyes | 17 | 5 | 39 | 1 |
| Hill | 19 | 4 | 45 | 0 |
| Creese | 9 | 5 | 20 | 0 |

Umpires: W. Reeves and E. J. Smith

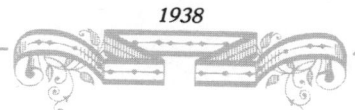

Rain! Lone spectators patiently waiting for play to start.

# Another Bradman Record: Earliest 1,000

---

## Scored in 7 Innings

*By RONALD T. SYMOND*

*'At Southampton (Third Day).—Match drawn, Hampshire, with their second innings to play, needing 167 to avoid an innings defeat.*

**D**ON BRADMAN yesterday added one more to his long list of cricket records. At 1.5 he reached his 1,000 runs for the current season, having enjoyed only seven innings. Never before has any cricketer reached 1,000 runs in England so early as May 27.

The wizard batsman's average now stands at the astounding figure of 170.16.

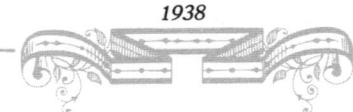

Important as the early matches are, the prime objective of a touring cricket side is to triumph in the Test matches.

We went to Trent Bridge confident and probably favourites. But losing the toss on a perfect wicket was too much for us and we were lucky in the end to avoid defeat.

McCabe made 232 in our first innings. It was the most superb batting I ever saw or ever hope to see. Power, grace and skill were combined to produce a classic innings which taxed the descriptive powers of Neville Cardus to the limit. I called my team mates onto the balcony with the words, "Come and watch this. You'll never see anything like it again." And I'm sure none of them ever did.

A century in 73 minutes against Lancashire was a very satisfying performance because our batting prior to that had been so slow that it incurred the wrath of the Manchester spectators.

In the second Test at Lord's the best we could do was to salvage a shaky but honourable draw after losing the toss.

Then rain saved us against Yorkshire when that county had us at their mercy.

For the third Test it rained incessantly and we didn't even toss the coin. So far as I know this is unprecedented in the whole history of Test cricket.

Smiling Don Bradman surrounded by clamorous autograph hunters when he left the practice nets at Trent Bridge yesterday.

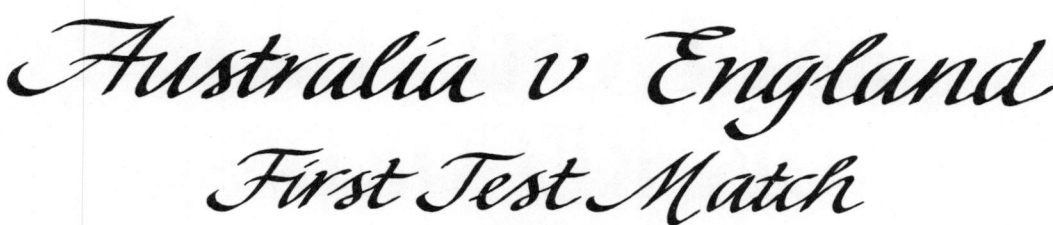

# Australia v England
## First Test Match

AUSTRALIA v ENGLAND, First Test Match, at Nottingham,

10, 11, 13 and 14 June 1938.

| | | | |
|---|---|---|---|
| Australia | - First Innings | 411 | |
| | - Second Innings | 427 for 6 wickets dec. | |
| England | - First Innings | 658 for 8 wickets dec. | |
| | - Second Innings | - | |
| | Drawn. | | |

| | | | |
|---|---|---|---|
| DON BRADMAN | - c. L.E.G. Ames b. R.A. Sinfield | 51 | |
| (Captain) | - not out | 144 | |

England's huge first innings score left Australia nothing to play for except a draw, with about two and a half days' play remaining.

DON BRADMAN went in for his first innings at 34 for 1, on the second afternoon, and was soon in difficulties against D.V.P. Wright, who frequently puzzled and beat him. He was 7 not out at the tea interval, and afterwards gradually settled down, though he was again missed, in the gully off K. Farnes, when he was 47. He reached 50 in eighty-five minutes, but four minutes later was well caught at the wicket, off the inside edge of his bat and then his pads. He hit five fours.

In his second innings, he went in at 89 for 1, twenty minutes before the close of the third day's play, and in that time he made 3 not out; he then batted almost the whole of the last day, in an innings of dour defence and ruthless concentration which saved the game for Australia. Being 44 not out at lunch, he completed his 50 soon afterwards, in two and a half hours. At 118 at the tea interval, he was 144 not out, after six hours five minutes' chanceless batting, when he declared fifteen minutes before the end of the match. He hit five fours.

This was his thirteenth century against England in Test Matches and was his forty-second innings against England. This was the third occasion on which Bradman made over 50 in each innings of a Test Match.

## England

| | | | | |
|---|---|---|---|---|
| L. Hutton lbw b Fleetwood-Smith | ..100 | L. E. G. Ames b Fleetwood-Smith | 46 | |
| C. J. Barnett b McCormick | ........126 | H. Verity b Fleetwood-Smith | .. | 3 |
| W. J. Edrich b O'Reilly | ............ 5 | R. A. Sinfield lbw b O'Reilly | .. | 6 |
| Mr. W. R. Hammond (Capt.) b O'Reilly | 26 | D. V. P. Wright not out | ....... | 1 |
| E. Paynter not out | ........216 | B 1, l-b 22, n-b 4 | ......... | 27 |
| D. Compton c Badcock b Fleetwood- Smith | ........................102 | Eight wkts., dec. | | 658 |

Mr. K. Farnes did not bat.

## Australia

| | | | |
|---|---|---|---|
| J. H. Fingleton b Wright | ............ 9 | — c Hammond b Edrich | ..... 40 |
| W. A. Brown c Ames b Farnes | ........ 48 | — c Paynter b Verity | .........133 |
| D. G. Bradman (Capt.) c Ames b Sinfield | 51 | — not out | ...................144 |
| S. J. McCabe c Compton b Verity | ......232 | — c Hammond b Verity | ...... 39 |
| F. Ward b Farnes | .................. 2 | — not out | ................... 7 |
| A. L. Hassett c Hammond b Wright | ...... 1 | — c Compton b Verity | ........ 2 |
| C. L. Badcock b Wright | ............... 9 | — b Wright | ................. 5 |
| B. A. Barnett c Wright b Farnes | ........ 22 | — lbw b Sinfield | ............. 31 |
| W. J. O'Reilly c Paynter b Farnes | ....... 9 | | |
| E. L. McCormick b Wright | ........ 2 | | |
| L. O'B. Fleetwood-Smith not out | ........ 5 | | |
| B 10, l-b 10, w 1 | ................ 21 | B 5, l-b 16, n-b 5 | ....... 26 |
| | 411 | Six wkts., dec. | 427 |

## Australia Bowling

| | Overs | Mdns. | Runs | Wkts. | Overs | Mdns. | Runs | Wkts. |
|---|---|---|---|---|---|---|---|---|
| McCormick .... | 32 | 4 | 108 | 1 | | | | |
| O'Reilly ....... | 56 | 11 | 164 | 3 | | | | |
| McCabe ....... | 21 | 5 | 64 | 0 | | | | |
| Fleetwood-Smith | 49 | 9 | 153 | 4 | | | | |
| Ward.......... | 30 | 2 | 142 | 0 | | | | |

## England Bowling

| | Overs | Mdns. | Runs | Wkts. | Overs | Mdns. | Runs | Wkts. |
|---|---|---|---|---|---|---|---|---|
| Farnes......... | 37 | 11 | 106 | 4 | 24 | 2 | 78 | 0 |
| Hammond ..... | 19 | 6 | 44 | 0 | 12 | 6 | 15 | 0 |
| Sinfield ....... | 28 | 8 | 51 | 1 | 35 | 8 | 72 | 1 |
| Wright ....... | 39 | 6 | 153 | 4 | 37 | 8 | 85 | 1 |
| Verity ......... | 7.3 | 0 | 36 | 1 | 62 | 27 | 102 | 3 |
| Edrich ...... | | | | | 13 | 2 | 39 | 1 |
| Barnett ...... | | | | | 1 | 0 | 10 | 0 |

## Fall of the Wickets

### England—First Innings

| 1 | 2 | 3 | 4 | 5 | 6 | 7 | 8 |
|---|---|---|---|---|---|---|---|
| 219 | 240 | 244 | 281 | 487 | 577 | 597 | 626 |

### Australia—First Innings

| 1 | 2 | 3 | 4 | 5 | 6 | 7 | 8 | 9 | 10 |
|---|---|---|---|---|---|---|---|---|---|
| 34 | 111 | 134 | 144 | 151 | 194 | 263 | 319 | 334 | 411 |

### Australia—Second Innings

| 1 | 2 | 3 | 4 | 5 | 6 |
|---|---|---|---|---|---|
| 89 | 259 | 331 | 337 | 369 | 417 |

Umpires: F. Chester and E. Robinson

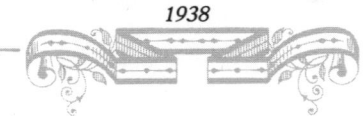

# ENGLAND DAY OF RECORDS

## Paynter 200

### ENGLAND 658 for 8
### Paynter not out 200
### ENGLAND DECLARED

# AUSTRALIA CRASHING !

## We get record 658, dismiss Bradman, Brown and Fingleton for 138—wicket is wearing

Nottingham, Saturday.

NO longer is Trent Bridge a Bridge of Sighs for England.

To-day, after compiling a record-breaking score, we have gone through the first Australian defence like the wind through high corn. We are heading for victory.

Fingleton, Brown, the great Bradman are gone . . . and the remaining Australian batsmen have to face a virile attack on a badly wearing wicket.

In the last twenty minutes to-day young Wright, of Kent, turned the ball more than Fleetwood-Smith ever turned it during the England innings.

We can therefore glory in the doughty deeds of young England, deeds which conjure up visions of a glorious future.

One's head reels as one thinks of England's successes, of young hopefuls doing all that had been asked of them.

And Hammond, the new captain, was masterly in the way he switched his attack. Towards the end he brought Farnes back into the attack. The move succeeded and Brown became our third victim.

But above all this one incident during this marvellous day will remain indelibly in my memory—the silence when Bradman was dismissed.

It was a triangular drama, with Ames as the predominant figure. Quick as a flash he fastened on to a snick off Sinfield. . . . Then, as if to make sure, he whipped off the bails.

Bradman lingered hopefully and doubtfully. In the excitement of the moment nobody knew quite what had happened. The great crowd was hushed until the board showed that the Master had been caught.

Then the storm broke.

After that the crowd cheered almost every ball. Well they might.

Don Bradman hits to leg during his innings of 51.

# —WITH BOGY MAN BRADMAN OUT— CAN ENGLAND DO IT?

A DAY OF TEST THRILLS SUCH AS HAVE RARELY BEEN KNOWN

England declared with 658 for 8—the biggest score ever put up in a Test by England against Australia.

Paynter carried his bat with 216 not out—the highest individual score ever made for England against Australia in England.

### THEN THE SHOCKS.

First Australian wicket—Fingleton's—down at 34.

Bradman, the bogy man, caught for 51; Brown out for 48.

Three wickets down at close of play for a mere 138.

Rarely has the Kangaroo's tail been twisted so thoroughly.

All England faces Monday on tip-toe with excitement.

With two whole days left can we do it after all?

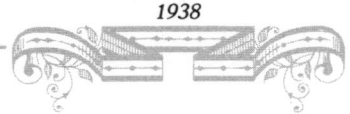

# A MASTERPIECE BY McCABE

## Australia Entrenching for Her Last Desperate Resistance

### RUDE AND SENSELESS BARRACKING

By Neville Cardus (Cricketer)

TRENT BRIDGE, MONDAY.

To-day McCabe honoured the first Test with a great and noble innings. At one time Australia was only 263 for seven, with no survivors to help McCabe except McCormick, O'Reilly, and Fleetwood-Smith. McCabe changed the gravest situation with the ease of a man using a master key; in an hour he smashed the bowling and decimated a field which for long had been a close, keen net. He pulled his side out of a terrible hole and gave Australia a chance to save herself. To-day he scored 213 out of 273 in three and a quarter hours while seven wickets fell. The dear valiance of his play won our hearts. And, believe it or not, when Brown and Fingleton began an uphill job of work a large portion of the crowd actually barracked because Brown and Fingleton played safely and declined to betray McCabe's skill and courage, which they would have done had they attempted indiscreet strokes. Never before have I heard barracking of more stupidity than this. McCabe gave the crowd their money's worth and snatched the match temporarily at least out of England's almost certain grasp. Fingleton and Brown would have been traitors to McCabe had they batted in any but a sound defensive manner; runs now were a secondary condition. Brown and Fingleton possibly carried caution to excess, but the ironical part is that during the period in which they were jeered at they scored only some fifteen runs fewer in two and a quarter hours than England scored in two and a quarter hours after lunch on the first day of the match when Barnett had landed the lunch score at the vantage point of 169 for no wicket.

Fingleton no doubt incensed the crowd by sitting down on the grass, perhaps an unwise gesture. But an appeal against the light was not probably justifiable. But let me get away from paltriness and tell the tale of McCabe's masterpiece. And I will try to describe it in the rhythm of its occurrence, and I hope that my narrative will give the faintest idea of the grand crescendo which crowned all.

Warm sunshine blessed the scene at last that morning and we now had reason to thank Heaven that Bradman got out in Saturday's darkness; this was his own weather and the wicket still contained runs for the picking,

even though marks made by Australia's heavy artillery had slightly roughened the surface. McCabe at once drove Farnes effortlessly through the covers for four; then Farnes bowled Ward. The day began now with Hassett in, small and immaculate as Quaife; he almost played on to Farnes forthwith; the ball gyrated from his bat like a kitten seeking its own tail. Trent Bridge looked handsome; bunting and coloured flags suggest royalty or a fairground with coconut shies at Australia's batsmen two a penny. Wright bowled with Farnes straightway, and Hassett tried to drive a quick leg-break on the half-volley; spin caused him to slice the stroke, and Hammond held the inevitable catch at slip. Wright dropped the ball in the rough stuff high enough up the wicket; it would have been impossible to cause as much spin as this on Friday on any part of the pitch. Australia 151 for five, and, I imagine, much distress in the Athenaeum Club, Melbourne; in the lordly mansions of Toorak, in Castlereagh Street, Sydney, in Wagga Wagga, Bondi, Southport, which is near Brisbane, Adelaide, Perth, and Kalgoorlie; in all these places the time would be evening at nine o'clock and the people would be listening incredulously to the wireless, men and women and boys and girls, even the babies allowed to stay up late for the occasion. And patient ships moving without seeming to move through the blue water of the Pacific on the long way from Colombo to Fremantle would be listening too; cricket girdles the earth nowadays; but I must cease or I shall sound like a cricket dinner at Lord's with Sir Pelham in full song.

McCabe was a great player all the time: he has been out of form, but now, in a severe hour, he held himself calmly, masterfully. But he inspected the pitch once or twice and stabbed late at a ball from Farnes which kept low. This situation became one in which a logical policy of batsmanship was difficult to shape; noon on the third day is too early for defence without runs, yet Australia's position chastened a free swinging stroke. Badcock endured for a while an unnatural life; he reached forward to play back. The English bowling seemed merely steady; I thought to myself now, "Heaven protect this attack the day Bradman and the

others get off with a flying start." Things continued to go awry with Australia: Badcock tried to cut a potential half-volley, and like Fingleton he played on.

The innings was rent in twain now. McCabe was left standing on a solitary rock of sound technique; between him and the rearguard yawned a chasm. He proceeded to play the cricket of heroic loneliness; he hit Farnes for six to square leg with the sweetest sweeping movement. He cut late with the touch of intimate art. Impending disaster did not ruffle him; even a snick through the slips off Farnes was tranquil and graceful. Farnes bowled keenly, accurately, ominously, and fast; Wright at the other end turned his leg-break now and again and avoided too much short stuff. Sinfield's off-breaks had an amiable aspect, but he more than once troubled even McCabe; clearly the turf was now not entirely insensitive to spin. In one other point, too, the English attack at the moment excelled Australia's, a point which had nothing to do with winning the toss; the length was never, or seldom, loose. Barnett defended while McCabe took charge; it is the sure sign of a great batsman that he can at a challenge take charge; what does the term master mean if it does not mean mastery? With his team cornered McCabe played the innings of the match and to make him this compliment is not to forget our Barnett's courage and skill on Friday. But McCabe was so sure an artist, so ripe and, with all his aggression, so stylish and courteous. Australia's Barnett ably put the straight obstructive bat to the ball until after lunch he decided to drive Farnes, in spite of the new ball; ambition was his undoing, but he served Australia well in a last-minute stand of 67.

Now came death and glory, brilliance wearing the dress of culture. McCabe demolished the English attack with aristocratic politeness, good taste, and reserve. Claude Duval never took possession of a stage coach with more charm of manner than this; his boundaries were jewels and trinkets which he accepted as though dangling them in his hands. In half an hour after lunch he scored nearly fifty, unhurried but trenchant. He cut and glanced and drove, upright and lissom; his perfec-

tion of touch moved the aesthetic sense; this was the cricket of felicity, power, and no covetousness, strength and no brutality, opportunism and no meanness, assault and no battery, dazzling strokes and no rhetoric; lovely, brave batsmanship giving joy to the connoisseur, and all done in a losing hour. One of the greatest innings ever seen anywhere in any period of the game's history. Moving cricket which swelled the heart. Not once but many times McCabe has come to Australia's aid in a crucial moment and has played gloriously when others have lost heart: he is in the line of Trumper, and no other batsman to-day but McCabe has inherited Trumper's sword and cloak.

When Cormick was bowled McCabe was 160: he now scored fifty in a little more than a quarter of an hour. He blinded us with four fours in an over from Wright; his innings became incandescent; he reached his two hundred and received worthy acclamation. He passed Paynter's score with a gesture of magnanimity. The English bowling suffered demoralisation; length and accuracy vanished. A majestic on-drive sent Australia's total beyond four hundred. With consummate judgment he kept the bowling; Fleetwood-Smith was almost as much a spectator as I was. This gorgeous sirocco had a calm pivotal spot; McCabe's mind controlled the whirlwind; his shooting stars flashed safely according to an ordered law of gravitation. He scored 72 out of 77 for the last wicket in half an hour; after lunch he scored 127 in eighty minutes. In all, he scored 232 out of 300 runs in 230 minutes, and hit a six and thirty-four fours.

Brown and Fingleton made, or declined to make more than 89 in two and a quarter hours; a wonderful left-handed catch by Hammond then accounted for Fingleton amid universal rejoicing. At the evening's misty fall Bradman was as dour as Brown himself; to-morrow he will move heaven and earth to express his gratitude for McCabe's lifeline; and England will move heaven and earth to overwhelm him and all. Another famous day.

The Worcester Vase.

The back of the Worcester Vase.

## THE WORCESTER VASE

The Directors of the Worcester Royal Porcelain Company Limited in 1938 decided to make a presentation to Don Bradman of a hand painted Royal Worcester vase in recognition of his feat of making three consecutive double centuries in the opening matches at Worcester of the Australian cricket tours of England in 1930, 1934 and 1938.

The urn was designed by Mr. C. B. Simmons, the Company's Art Director. It is decorated with the royal blue ground, with a painted panel in front of the Worcester cricket ground, showing Bradman batting. The panel is surrounded by a chaste and raised gold design and the mounts, handles, neck and feet are decorated in royal blue with burnished and chaste gold. Mr. Harry Davis painted the panel. This spectacular trophy is now on display in the State Library of South Australia, within the Mortlock Library.

This photograph, taken by the *Times*, shows Don Bradman during his innings of 258 at Worcester in 1938. The photograph was used as the basis for the painting on the Worcester Vase. The 1938 crowd of more than 14,000 is reputed to have been the largest attendance ever at the county ground.

# THE WORCESTER VASE

A tribute to the late Harry Davis, who painted the
beautiful panel on the Worcester Vase.

HARRY DAVIS (1885-1970). At factory 1898-1969. Foreman painter 1928-54. His grandfather was Josiah the fine gilder and his father Alfred was a china presser. Harry came to the factory on his 13th birthday in 1898 as a talented young painter taught drawing by Josiah, but his first job was to be set to wash down the Museum steps — "that will teach you to handle a brush", he was told. After twelve months he was formally apprenticed as a painter, and this was to be the last actual indenture of an apprentice on the form dating back to the 18th century. He was fortunate in being apprenticed to Ted Salter, a true and sensitive young artist. They had a common interest in fishing, both in catching and painting fish, and in 1900 Harry won a fishing club prize for a roach caught in the river Teme and a South Kensington national book prize for a water-colour study of that same fish. The shock of Ted Salter's inexplicable suicide remained with Harry until his last days. In an attempt to ease the blow, the Management remitted their share of Harry's earnings, a welcome concession, for the lad was quickly able to hold his own with his more senior colleagues. Landscape painting had always attracted him and he did a great number in the classical style of Claude and the melting colourings of Corot. Every one was an original, for he avoided easy repetition. "Harry", one of the travellers said to him, "if you're ever stuck for an idea, just put your name on a plate — I can sell it." But he was never stuck for an idea and the neat signature, "H. Davis", grew steadily in repute. He made a great speciality of sheep in pastoral or Scottish mountain settings, woodland and garden scenes, rural cottages and town subjects — an extraordinarily wide range.

Harry Davis married in 1910 and joined the army in 1916, keeping his artistic hand in by the drawing of diagrams for instruction purposes and painting a backcloth for regimental show. After the war he took on the demanding task of painting the double service for Ranjitsinhji. In 1928 William Hawkins, the foreman, retired, and Harry was appointed in his place. Much of his time was now claimed by the calls of administration and training. As a means of aiding training he etched a series of subjects, including Cathedrals and Castles, providing a printed outline which, under supervision, could be completed by less experienced hands; some of these are still done to this day. Other etchings which followed were of game birds, fish and coaching scenes and as most of the painters would not sign their own names to the colouring-in of these subjects, so Harry himself used the fictitious name of H. SIVAD (Davis back to front). During the Second World War Harry worked on the painting of a number of the Doughty Birds and other special pieces. After the war he did the colour standard for the study of Princess Elizabeth on Tommy, the Princess sitting for him at Buckingham Palace.

In 1952 his services to the industry were rewarded by the presentation of the B.E.M. and although he relinquished the position of foreman in 1954, he continued to paint in his studio at the factory until a few months before his death in 1970, working especially on the production of a magnificent series of plaques decorated with Corot-type scenes. To celebrate Harry's seventy years of working at the factory, in 1968, the Company arranged a special holiday for him and his wife in Scotland, which would have been his first visit to the Highland scenes that he painted so well, but his wife's illness and death upset this plan. He remained to the end a man of unfailing courtesy, for ever amazed that anyone should be interested in him or his work, an honest and conscientious craftsman of great integrity. Harry Davis is now regarded as the greatest ceramic painter of the twentieth century.

Worcester Cricket Ground, 1984.

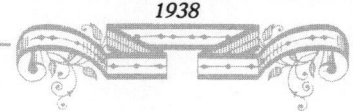

# ANOTHER BRADMAN ON VIEW

## Sacrificed Strokes To Play For Draw In Big Match

"THE SUN" CABLE SERVICE

NOTTINGHAM, Tuesday.

A magnificent example of leadership, with the captain and vice-captain playing contrasting hands, enabled Australia to force a draw in the first Test at Trent Bridge.

Bradman limped wearily from the field to-night after finishing the work begun by McCabe, Brown and Fingleton.

This was another Bradman England had not previously seen. He is more inclined usually to charge at obstacles than to undermine them. However, with a well-founded suspicion of the ability of the middle batsmen to score against clever spin bowling on a worn wicket, he decided that somebody must stay, at whatever sacrifice of natural strokemaking, and except when a loose ball came he could not be tempted.

For Bradman to stay six hours for 144 runs is perhaps remarkable, as a Test record of seven individual centuries was created during the match.

Securing a draw from a seemingly impossible position on Monday morning, was as satisfactory from the Australian viewpoint as a draw could be, but Australia at times was so near defeat that the skill of the salvage work must not be allowed to obscure the fact that the team seriously disappointed.

At moments like these, with a first-class match to face to-morrow, with only 14 fit players, Bradman badly needing rest after the mental and physical strain of Nottingham, and McCabe, earning one if ever a player did, the team feels strongly that the Board ought even now send an additional man.

It is apparent that the regeneration of English cricket in 1938 is going to make the Ashes harder to win than was expected, and the Australians, even when juggernauting over their opponents in early matches, did not delude themselves that the Tests would be a picnic.

The tenseness of the occasion was reflected in Bradman's grimness and pallor. Usually he is capable of laughter, even in a Test, but from the moment he came in at 6.10 on Monday with jutting jaw, his whole attitude was a challenge to England to get him out.

This sternness was intensified when barracking, much milder than yesterday's began.

THE BRADMAN SEVEN'

SEVEN IN THE FIRST HALF HOUR

AT TRENT BRIDGE

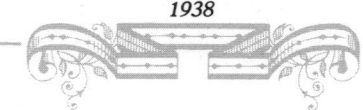

# Australians v Lancashire

AUSTRALIANS v LANCASHIRE, at Manchester, 18, 20 and 21 June 1938.

| | | |
|---|---|---|
| Australians | - First Innings | 303 |
| | - Second Innings | 284 for 2 wickets dec. |
| Lancashire | - First Innings | 289 |
| | - Second Innings | 80 for 3 wickets |
| | Drawn. | |

| | | |
|---|---|---|
| DON BRADMAN | - c. R. Pollard b. W.E. Phillipson | 12 |
| (Captain) | - not out | 101 |

Good bowling on the first morning by W.E. Phillipson on a green pitch accounted for three Australian wickets, including that of DON BRADMAN, falling for 35 in the first innings; Bradman went in at 14 for 1, and was caught at second slip in trying to drive, at 35 for 3. He batted for twenty-nine minutes.

He was in his best form in his second innings; he went in at 153 for 1, on the third afternoon, and reached 50 in forty minutes, and 100 in seventy-three minutes, before declaring four minutes later. Despite the pace at which he scored, he gave no chance, and indeed scarcely appeared to be hurrying; yet he hit fifteen fours.

This was his first century at Old Trafford, in his fourth match there.

## Australians

| | | |
|---|---|---|
| J. H. Fingleton b Nutter | 10 | — c Wilkinson b Phillipson .... 96 |
| W. A. Brown c Farrimond b Phillipson .. | 8 | — b Nutter ............... 70 |
| D. G. Bradman c Pollard b Phillipson .... | 12 | — not out ...................101 |
| C. L. Badcock c Pollard b Phillipson ..... | 96 | — not out ................... 14 |
| A. L. Hassett b Nutter ................118 | | |
| A. G. Chipperfield c Farrimond b Phillipson | 5 | |
| B. A. Barnett c Pollard b Phillipson ...... | 9 | |
| M. G. Waite lbw b Wilkinson ........... | 20 | |
| E. S. White not out ................... | 12 | |
| E. L. McCormick b Pollard ............. | 1 | |
| L. O'B. Fleetwood-Smith absent ill ...... | 0 | |
| B 2, l-b 7, n-b 3 ............... | 12 | B ................... 3 |
| | 303 | Two wkts., dec. 284 |

## Lancashire

| | | |
|---|---|---|
| C. Washbrook b Waite ................. | 7 | — b Chipperfield ............ 11 |
| E. Paynter lbw b Waite ................ | 9 | — b Chipperfield ............ 20 |
| J. Iddon c Badcock b McCormick........ | 44 | — c Waite b White .......... 1 |
| N. Oldfield c Badcock b McCormick .... | 69 | — not out ................... 30 |
| J. L. Hopwood run out ................ | 13 | — not out ................... 17 |
| A. Nutter c and b McCormick.......... | 4 | |
| Mr. W. H. L. Lister c and b Chipperfield . | 7 | |
| W. E. Phillipson b Chipperfield ........ | 52 | |
| W. Farrimond c Bradman b McCormick.. | 49 | |
| R. Pollard not out .................... | 18 | |
| L. L. Wilkinson b White .............. | 1 | |
| B 6, l-b 6, w 1, n-b 3 ............. | 16 | L-b ................ 1 |
| | 289 | Three wkts. 80 |

## Lancashire Bowling

| | Overs | Mdns. | Runs | Wkts. | | Overs | Mdns. | Runs | Wkts. |
|---|---|---|---|---|---|---|---|---|---|
| Phillipson ..... | 35 | 11 | 93 | 5 | .... | 17 | 2 | 71 | 1 |
| Pollard ........ | 30.5 | 5 | 82 | 1 | .... | 13 | 4 | 27 | 0 |
| Nutter ........ | 23 | 7 | 61 | 2 | .... | 20 | 2 | 81 | 1 |
| Wilkinson...... | 16 | 0 | 55 | 1 | .... | 22 | 4 | 63 | 0 |
| Iddon ...... | | | | | | 7 | 0 | 20 | 0 |
| Hopwood ... | | | | | | 4 | 0 | 19 | 0 |

## Australians Bowling

| | Overs | Mdns. | Runs | Wkts. | | Overs | Mdns. | Runs | Wkts. |
|---|---|---|---|---|---|---|---|---|---|
| McCormick .... | 26 | 4 | 84 | 4 | .... | 3 | 0 | 20 | 0 |
| Waite ........ | 21 | 7 | 64 | 2 | .... | 3 | 1 | 7 | 0 |
| White ........ | 21 | 3 | 67 | 1 | .... | 9 | 2 | 30 | 1 |
| Chipperfield ... | 23 | 9 | 58 | 2 | .... | 6 | 2 | 12 | 2 |
| Badcock ..... | | | | | | 2 | 0 | 10 | 0 |

Umpires: A. Dolphin and G. M. Lee

# BRADMAN'S RETURN TO GLORY

**By Neville Cardus (Cricketer)**

A brilliant innings by Bradman came at the right moment yesterday—just in time to restore the crowd's temper and goodwill. For two hours in the morning Brown and Fingleton batted with pointless and dreary caution; they risked playing into the hands of the people who supported the barracking at Nottingham last week. Even a section of the long-suffering Old Trafford crowd barracked; the wonder is that they did not tear the railings down. The Australians were in a safe position; the wicket was good and the bowling merely useful; moreover, stumps were to be drawn at half-past five. Yet in two hours only 90 runs trickled over the field, and even those came less from strokes than from listless pokes and pushes. By these methods Brown and Fingleton tended to gain for their side an unpopular reputation. I have myself always tried to see the Australian point of view; I like the players and I love their country. But yesterday before lunch even my patience was strained almost to disgust. There was no sense in the boring cricket; it was not fair to a crowd which throughout the match had treated the Australians generously. In one period Brown scored two runs in forty minutes; he was 32 not out at lunch—and everybody waiting for Bradman on a day which was purposeless save as an exhibition occasion.

After lunch belated amends were made. Brown and Fingleton themselves exposed the futility and the wilfulness of their methods before lunch. By brilliant strokes 63 were hit in half an hour; then Brown, having cleared his character, was bowled. One of his infrequent fours nearly decapitated Dolphin. Bradman at once attended to his enthusiastic and expectant public. They asked for little—cricket crowds in England are usually not unreasonable. They wish only to feel that a player is doing his best and not denying his true gifts. Dull batting at any period yesterday was unnecessary, and a gratuitous insult to a public that "pays double" to see the Australians. The day was half over before the crowd were allowed to feel that the intentions of the batsmen were excellent. Fingleton did justice to his strokes—and he commands many more fine hits than too often he seems himself to know of. He was out four short of his hundred; he achieved three fours in an innings of three hours' duration.

Bradman reached fifty in forty minutes; he was free from care and he delighted everybody with his swift, masterly hits. This was a return to glory, a revival of the Bradman of 1930, who could not be kept quiet anyhow, Test match or exhibition match. It is, I firmly believe, only his own policy and not any power of our bowlers to-day that has changed Bradman in a Test match from a great batsman who reigned at his own sweet will to a great batsman who obeys a sort of constitutional law. He could demolish the best of our attacks in a Test match to-morrow—if he could get back to his point of view of eight years ago. Moreover, he is a surer player when he is attacking. As a patriotic Englishman I hope he continues to hold a modest opinion of his gifts; as a lover of brilliant cricket I wish he would agree with me that he is a supreme stroke-player yet and most times capable of smashing all bowlers, exactly as he smashed them at Leeds and Lord's in 1930. Yesterday he radiated strokes, made the length he wanted for the performance of each of his great range of hits—drives, cuts, pulls, glances. His cricket burned gaily in the darkening light of the afternoon; the crowd forgot the morning's martyrdom and was happy and grateful. Why do our great cricketers not always value their gifts as jealously as the poet and artist values his? It is not a matter of selfishness; if I were an English bowler I should want Bradman to bat as he did on the Saturday at Nottingham, not as he did yesterday. He annihilated the Lancashire attack; he did not "play" it.

When he was 92 Bradman snicked dangerously off Wilkinson, who earlier on had once troubled him. But these were but the briefest glimpses into his essential mortality; his innings, with all its velocity and dazzling power, was the safest I have seen him play this year. This was the Bradman of my heart's desire, and whenever I write critically of his play it is when he forgets his genius and trusts to talent. If the argument is put to me that the occasion yesterday carried no responsibility for Bradman, my answer is again that this was the Bradman who smashed Tate, Larwood, and the rest in the Test match of Leeds in 1930. He reached his century, his first at Old Trafford, in seventy-three minutes out of 128. This was, I am told, the fastest century of the season so far. It was all done without the turn of a hair—easy as Menuhin on his violin. He certainly removed the blot splashed before lunch on the Australian escutcheon, if they own to a possession so hopelessly class-conscious. It was, as Joxer would say, "a darlin' century."

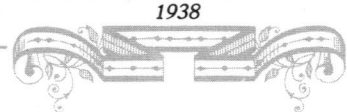

# Australia v England
## Second Test Match

AUSTRALIA v ENGLAND, Second Test Match, at Lord's,
24, 25, 27 and 28 June 1938.

| | | | |
|---|---|---|---|
| Australia | - | First Innings | 422 |
| | - | Second Innings | 204 for 6 wickets |
| England | - | First Innings | 494 |
| | - | Second Innings | 242 for 8 wickets dec. |
| | | Drawn. | |
| DON BRADMAN | - | b. H. Verity | 18 |
| (Captain) | - | not out | 102 |

Going in on the second afternoon at 69 for 1, DON BRADMAN commenced in his best form, but at 101 for 1, after batting for twenty-six minutes, he was deceived by a ball from H. Verity which came in with the arm, and, in attempting a cut, dragged it on to his wicket.

England's declaration, at 3.20 p.m. on the fourth day, set Australia 315 to win, an impossible task in the time available, and the only question was whether Australia could be dismissed by 6.30; Bradman, with another fine innings, soon answered that question. He went in at 8 for 1, forty-two minutes before the tea interval, and had by then scored 38 not out. He completed 50 in sixty-two minutes, and after two hours twenty-two minutes reached his century, five minutes before play ended; he hit fifteen fours.

When Bradman was 18, he passed J.B. Hobbs' aggregate of 3636, the previous record for Tests between England and Australia; this was his forty-fourth innings, whereas Hobbs batted seventy-one times v. Australia.

From the start of the third Test Match, 1936-7, Bradman had scored over 1,000 runs in five consecutive Test Matches, all v. England.

W. R. Hammond and Don Bradman walking out to inspect the pitch.

Don Bradman pats W. R. Hammond on the back upon Hammond completing his century.

Don Bradman shaking hands with King George VI at Lord's, London, during the second Test, when the Australian team members were introduced to His Majesty during the tea interval.

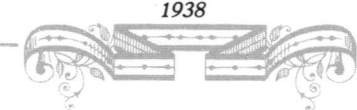
# AUSTRALIA FACE 494 TOTAL

## Bradman Out, Unlucky Accident

# BRADMAN, BOWLED VERITY, 18

## -They Thought This Couldn't Happen, Too!

# WE CAN'T LOSE NOW!

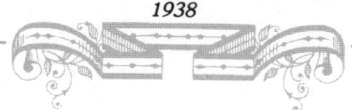

# THE SECOND TEST MATCH

## GREAT STRUGGLE AT LORD'S

FROM OUR CRICKET CORRESPONDENT

The Second Test Match at Lord's on Saturday continued on a note of collapse and recovery as sharply struck as that of the day before. At the end of it all Australia, with five wickets down, were 195 runs behind, and as A. G. Chipperfield, whose hand was severely damaged on Friday, will bat to-day, they should at least save the follow-on. W. Brown, who saved his side from immediate distress, is still there to take as much of the bowling as possible this morning, for, apart from Chipperfield, the remaining Australian batsmen are not distinguished for run-making.

When the game was continued on Saturday morning, with England's total standing at 409 for five wickets, Hammond then being 210 and Ames 50, the crowd seemed if possible to be even more dense than it had been on Friday. Australia began their bowling with McCabe and McCormick, but the wicket played none of those pranks which are expected of it during the first half-hour of play. Ames continued in exactly the same vein as that of the evening before, straight-drove McCabe to the boundary, and for a time seemed intent on monopolizing the scoring. Hammond, not to be outshone, hit McCabe away to the square-leg boundary, and followed this with a stirring blow away past mid-off against the knees of the crowd who were sitting on the grass.

### A GLORIOUS INNINGS

If anything, he seemed to find batting even easier, his mind finally set at rest that his side was safe, until, with the total at 457, he was late and outside a ball from McCormick which broke back and which may have just touched the inside of the bat before it hit the stumps. And so ended an innings superlative in conception and perfect in execution. Mere figures cannot express the virtue of his performance, but he had been in for nearly six hours and had hit 32 4's.

Verity, who came next, was only the shadow of the man who once went in first for England; he was content to do little more than stand erect until O'Reilly, coming on at the Pavilion end, bowled him in his first over. Wellard, who can bat both well and fast, took it into his head to play wildly. He hit one ball away to the square-leg boundary and then hit the next so high that it took an appreciable time to come down again. McCormick waited patiently for its descent, and in

the circumstances must be deemed to have held a very good catch. Wright somehow contrived to prevent Fleetwood-Smith from bowling him until he had lost Ames, who was caught at slip off Fleetwood-Smith. His had been a splendid innings, worth many more runs to his side than those that actually appear against his name in the scoring book. After Farnes had played a stroke worthy of a fast bowler, the innings came to an end just before one o'clock.

England had certainly not made as many runs as was expected of them, and heads wagged when their owners said that the total of 494 was by no means big enough. That it was not greater was due to O'Reilly, who bowled like a lion throughout the innings. He was always ready for work and more work, was continually attacking the batsmen, and an analysis of four wickets for 93 does not begin to do him justice.

### AUSTRALIA'S START

England began their bowling with Farnes, who had three slips, a backward point, and two short legs. Wellard, from the Nursery end, had two slips and a gully. Both Brown and Fingleton, in the manner of Australian batsmen, took the runs which were offered them on the leg side, and together they had scored 26 runs at the luncheon interval.

When they went out again Hammond at once put Wright on at the Nursery end, but he bowled too much on the leg stump, so making little use of what little break he could get out of the wicket. The ball accordingly was placed away to leg. Fingleton pushing rather than striking it. Wellard, when he came on, bowled altogether too short to batsmen who can hook a ball with their eyes shut. Suddenly Fingleton, having cut a short ball from Wright, leant out to the next which was of a better length and was caught at short slip. Enter Bradman, who at once showed us two of his leg strokes, one a delayed leg glide and the other a firm hook to square-leg, both of them off Farnes. Verity was put on to check Bradman's exuberance, but Bradman's answer was two quick steps down the wicket to make the ball a half-volley.

Verity had two slips to Bradman, hoping for a mistake to the leg break, but the 100 was up in 90 minutes and Brown was by then firmly established. Suddenly the unbelievable happened : Bradman dragged a ball well wide of the off stump from Verity on to his stumps and the crowd, having recovered from their first moment of astonishment, roared with delight. Some, may be, were genuinely sorry, for they had travelled far to see Bradman bat.

### VERITY'S GREAT CATCH

There was still McCabe to be dealt with, the McCabe of Trent Bridge, who had massacred England's bowlers, and who started off on Saturday in much the same mood. He had been in less than five minutes when he had hooked Wellard for six ; he treated Verity as if the pride of Yorkshire were an untidy bowler, and in general was well set to become a thorough

nuisance. Brown was nearly out twice; on the first occasion Verity, having beaten him, appealed for leg-before-wicket which must have been very close; and in the next over Brown played a ball from Farnes off the edge of his bat, which fell only just short of first slip.

Wright then came on again to provide McCabe with two fours off successive balls. That he was got rid of so easily was a rare piece of luck for England, for he hit a rather short ball from Farnes fair and square on the middle of his bat; Verity, at backward point, put both hands to the ball which he held close to the ground as he fell. So Bradman and McCabe had gone, Verity being concerned in each case in the matter, and only 152 runs had been scored. There were visions of Australia's downfall, visions which gradually faded away when Brown and Hassett, unconcerned by a few narrow escapes, gradually pulled their side out of imminent danger.

Farnes once made the ball rise so sharply that it flew off Brown's bat over the head of second slip, and Hassett had two very streaky strokes off Verity which slithered through somewhere behind the wicket. Brown, with that stance of his which allows the left shoulder to point straight down the wicket, was for the most part playing the ball securely, never failing to place his runs on the leg side and playing the off-drive with a full follow through of the bat. When he considered the stroke safe he cut hard, with the blade of the bat well over the ball, making deep third man run hard to save a third run and occasionally beating him for pace for a boundary.

Hammond, seeing that Brown was taking upon himself the duty which Bradman and McCabe had left undone, tried all manner of bowling changes. He gave Wright a long spell at the Nursery end hoping that he would find a leg break of the proper length, but Wright persisted in bowling just too short. Hassett, like his partner, was cutting the ball firmly, and, indeed, they both had plenty of opportunities, for the bowling invited it. Edrich was put on, but that achieved little, and an Australian revival was growing more and more threatening, all the more so when Farnes twice beat Brown in one over with the luck still faithful to the batsman. Brown reached his century, but oh ! he was so nearly bowled when he was at 99, a ball from Wellard flirting with the off bail but just not touching it.

Hassett's innings came to an end when he walked in front of his wicket—he had done this several times before—to Wellard, who was now bowling from the Pavilion end, and bowling rather better than before. The score remained at that total, 276, when Badcock was bowled second ball by Wellard, but Barnett stayed in until stumps were drawn, while Brown, apparently deserted by his companions, quite rightly scored runs as quickly as he could. In doing so he sacrificed some of the polish of his batting, but the runs came all the same.

The crisis in this match is likely to occur at lunch time to-day.

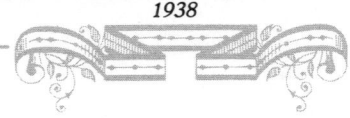

# THE SECOND TEST MATCH

## A RAINY DAY AT LORD'S

## BROWN MAKES HISTORY

FROM OUR CRICKET CORRESPONDENT

There was little more than two and a half hours of play in the Test Match at Lord's yesterday, but during those spells when cricket was possible events were moving to what may be an exciting finish to-day, for England, with two wickets down in their second innings, are 111 runs ahead, and Australia will have to bat last on a wicket which may help the bowlers.

That they will not be faced with an even more formidable task they have to thank W. A. Brown, who, indeed, did for them what Hammond had previously done for England. Although he was never so certain as Hammond had been he had patches in his innings when for the moment his timing deserted him he stuck most manfully to his work and had periods of great brilliance. It was an achievement for him to carry his bat through the innings, all the more so when wickets, and wickets of the illustrious, were tumbling down. The great majority of his runs in an innings which lasted for six hours were scored on the leg side—an estimate of 180 of his total score would not be too high—which, in itself, explains where England's bowling was at fault.

## AN ELEGANT BATSMAN

Australia, when play was begun in the morning, were still 195 runs behind, but it is extremely doubtful, even if those outstanding wickets had fallen quickly, whether Hammond would have enforced the follow-on. As it was Brown could be relied upon if he could find anyone to stay in with him to prevent the possibility of any such indignity.

Farnes, who started the bowling from the Pavilion end, had four slips and a gully, and it must be said that such an array of slip fieldsmen was a luxury to a bowler who pitched the ball consistently on the leg-stump. Only eight runs had been added when Barnett was caught off a skier at cover-point, and Chipperfield was leg-before-wicket when playing no sort of stroke. So far very good for Verity and England, and it was very nearly even better, for O'Reilly was as nearly bowled as ever man could be by the third ball he received from Verity.

Then came a period of acute distress for the English bowlers. O'Reilly was in an attacking mood; he began by hitting Verity away to the leg boundary, drove him straight, and then was missed away on the long-on boundary, the fieldsman coming in too far and then having to go back. Brown was batting quietly and elegantly, taking his runs on the leg-side and playing the ball correctly to the off. O'Reilly hit two 6's running away in the far distance on the leg-side off Verity, who made a mistake in pitching the ball on the wicket instead of just wide of the leg stump. Verity, in fact, was bowling exactly how a hard-hitting left-handed batsman would have chosen him to do.

## GREAT CHANCE LOST

When Wellard came on at the Pavilion end Brown struck him twice to the off for 4, and a change of Wright for Verity had little effect in keeping the rate of run-getting down until, at 393, Farnes bowled O'Reilly.

McCormick was out first ball to Farnes, who was denied a hat trick by Compton's missing an easy catch at second slip off Fleetwood-Smith's bat. And so J. T. Hearne remains the only English bowler who has done the hat-trick against Australia in this country, a feat he performed at Leeds in 1899. The missed catch was not only hard on the bowler; it cost England many runs.

Rain, which had been threatening, fell in earnest soon after half-past 12, and it was not until a quarter-past 4 that the players were out again. It was never a very hard rain, and the ground sucked it in greedily, but it was constant enough to prevent cricket. The players were no sooner out than Brown was missed at

mid-wicket off Wellard, and with Fleetwood-Smith making a thorough nuisance of himself by stopping straight balls the score was taken to 422 before Fleetwood-Smith gave a simple catch to square-leg. Brown had reached his 200, and was still batting in the manner of one who might well have stayed in to all eternity. Australia had certainly scored more runs than they should have been allowed to do; the English bowling had lacked accuracy, and the fielding, more especially the throwing in, was loose.

## A LONG DELAY

England went into bat at 10 minutes past 5, or rather the batsmen arrived at the wickets, and as soon as they were there returned to the Pavilion in a heavy shower of rain before a ball had been bowled. They were out again at 20 minutes to 6. Then McCormick began the bowling with a wide, as a variation from a no-ball. He bowled two more balls, and once more the players fled for shelter. This time they were not away for so long. When they did settle down it was at once obvious that the wicket was vicious and that England would do well if they avoided losing at least three wickets before the end of the day.

McCormick made the ball fly, even when it was of a good length, and O'Reilly at the other end made it stand up almost straight. Barnett scored three leg byes almost off his ear, and with the score at 25 was out to a splendid catch by McCabe in the gully off a firm-enough hit. Hutton was caught at slip off a ball which turned very quickly, and England were in distress.

Hammond, to conserve his resources, had sent Verity in at the fall of the first wicket. Verity also should have been caught in the slips, but he managed to stay there, and Edrich, during the last quarter of an hour, stood his ground well with the ball buzzing all round him.

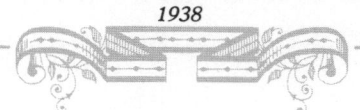

# A GREAT STRUGGLE AT LORD'S DRAWN
## Each Side in Turn Exalted and Mocked by Fortune's Cartwheels
### COMPTON AND BRADMAN KNIGHTS AMONG THEIR SQUIRES

**By Neville Cardus (Cricketer)**

LORD'S, TUESDAY.

Before the second Test match came to an exciting draw England was thrust to the wall this morning, and a young boy of Middlesex forced the way out not by fisticuffs but by elegant gestures of persuasion. The score was 76 for five when he went in to bat and 128 for six when Paynter ran himself out. Moreover, the lame Hammond was back in the pavilion and lunch had not come; Australia could win in the time which remained, and, I think, would have won but for Compton. His cricket foretold a luminous future. Wellard also contributed to the rescue work, and Paynter, as usual, was ready with a hand or a fist or two. But it was mortifying to see the need for salvage at all for England. We have had the Australians twice now in the grip which asks for only one more gentle twist to clinch an issue. When are we going to defeat them, and how, after our advantages at Nottingham and Lord's? Frankly, I think we have missed our chance in the rubber. Bradman has yet to play his real Test-match-winning masterpieces, and they are on the way. And we cannot expect to win the toss every time.

England's batting this morning was deplorable. The Australian attack could, apart from McCormick, do nothing. Yet even McCabe for a long time was regarded with awe. Apparently many of our batsmen can deal with fast bowling in two ways only—the blind hook or the myopic grope towards the slips. Once again we must congratulate the Australians on their own remarkable ability to counter-attack from the last ditch. When yesterday I prophesied some trouble for England to-day I was told I was a pessimist. But I know the Australians—I have known them from my boyhood.

## Comfort for Epicures

On the fourth morning, which promised the best day's cricket of the match, the crowd was merely numerous, not a multitude. Everybody could walk about the ground in comfort; there was no need now to regard the members of the M.C.C. as bloatedly privileged and see them like so many capitalists straight out of a drawing by Will Dyson, with two cigars in the mouth.

An English disaster occurred at once. McCormick's first ball soared over Edrich's head; then Edrich hooked a short one for four. The last ball, another short, rising length, said in unmistakable Australian: "Now hook that, my lad, if you can." And Edrich attempted to hook, head down. McCabe, at forward square-leg, caught him out with ease. Edrich played gallantly on Monday evening, but he should not to-day have allowed his favourite hit to lead him so openly into the Australian trap. McCormick bowled at a rare pace, very rare nowadays, and several times Verity fortunately could not time velocity on the offside. Paynter heartened us with two capital leg-glances for fours off O'Reilly, who could not, thank heaven, make his spin turn viciously. Another wicket to Australia at this point would, we all knew as well as Bradman, mean a struggling English team.

Verity defended admirably, as he did on Monday's flying pitch. It was much easier now; though not always reliable. But when Verity tried to score he journeyed beyond his territory, and a slice through the slips was terribly fortuitous, or, in Paynter's more English English, "off t' edge." Another four by Paynter, a lusty clout from a full toss by O'Reilly, was enough to make the pavilion cat laugh; but the little kangaroo on the Australian balcony watched the stroke with some disdain. At ten minutes past twelve McCormick knocked Verity's off-stump out of the ground, and instead of coming from the field he stayed in the middle of the wicket and consulted with Bradman. Optimists thought Bradman was telling, as most of us have wished to be told when we have had our wickets shattered, that it was all a mistake. But no; they were only arranging for a runner for Hammond, whose strained leg was not yet better. Verity's innings deserved praise; he probably saved other and more technical batsmen, though none could well be more academic than Verity, who holds himself at the wicket as though in degree-day gown and mortar-board.

## Hammond's Handicap

A snick by Paynter off McCormick nearly undid him. The crowd gasped, then silently watched Hammond, who obviously batted under a serious physical handicap. He could not play forward strongly. He pushed once at O'Reilly like a man moving on a cork leg. O'Reilly sent a fine over to Paynter at half-past twelve. He beat the bat with a leg-break, and Paynter put his hand to his mouth to conceal a broad grin, which in the circumstances might have seemed irreverent.

Tragedy overwhelmed us now—McCabe bowled for McCormick, and Hammond, pinned down by his injury, scooped helplessly at a potential full-toss, with one hand, and lobbed a catch to short square-leg. He came back to the pavilion with Verity by his side—like blind Samson. England 76 for five—where now were the reserve of runs thrown away by England during the O'Reilly windstorm of Monday? The wonder was that Hammond attempted a forcing stroke at all. Paynter was missed at first slip almost before Hammond could have got his pads off—and from McCabe of all bowlers. The English innings had become suddenly unnerved, as though suffering from vertigo because of a glimpse of a terrible chasm from a height.

Fleetwood-Smith bowled instead of O'Reilly when England was 84 for five, and Compton cut a short ball brilliantly for four. Compton hit two fours in one over from McCabe, excellent and youthfully eager strokes. The game had arrived at the crucial pivot. Bradman gambled with Fleetwood-Smith—he might easily give runs away and put Australia behind the clock. On the other hand, he might run through the side. Bradman, of course, had no great reserve of bowling to support his spearhead McCormick and the steady infantry of O'Reilly. Compton played perfect cricket in the searching period. He used his feet instinctively; his strokes were sound and pretty. He is, I think, likely to go much farther than Edrich—he has style and temperament. Bradman declined to trust Fleetwood-Smith. O'Reilly was brought back, for the stand of Paynter and Compton was too quickly (for Bradman) putting England in a position from which to dictate terms.

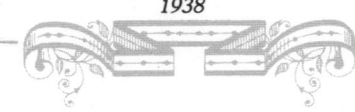

# Australia v England
## Third Test Match

<u>AUSTRALIA v ENGLAND</u>, Third Test Match, at Manchester, 8, 9, 11 and 12 July 1938.

This match was abandoned owing to rain.     The captains did not even toss.

The crowd waiting.

The covered wicket.

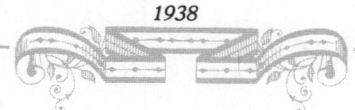

# BRADMAN ON BANNED WIFE SENSATION

## "Very, Very Disappointed"

## MAY TAKE ACTION

*From WILLIAM HALL*

**GRINDLEFORD, Derbyshire, Wednesday.**

"**I** AM very, very disappointed at the Australian Board of Control's decision, but I cannot say at the moment whether I shall do anything further in the matter."

That was the guarded comment Don Bradman made to me here to-night in an exclusive statement on the Board's refusal to allow his wife to join him in London at the end of the Australians' tour.

Don declined to say whether he will issue a statement on the decision, but reading between his smiles, as it were, and significant pauses, I gathered that the world's greatest batsman considers the Board's decision unjustifiable.

### TEAM-MATES' FEARS

It is perfectly obvious from a cricket point of view, a fact that the Australian team are very quick to seize on, that it is regrettable that Bradman should receive such invidious treatment at the hands of the board on the eve of a very important Test match.

**Bradman's team-mates are afraid that it may result in a loss of concentration, and there is a fear that the affair may develop into a first-class cricket sensation.**

" I received news of the decision in a cable yesterday," Bradman told me, " and I am sleeping on it."

Though he would not admit nor deny the possibility, I understand that Bradman may issue a statement to-morrow.

But while he is reticent about the matter his team-mates, rusticating here in the heart of Peakland in readiness for Friday's match at Old Trafford, are of one mind.

**They discussed the matter over dinner here to-night, and it is clear that they deeply resent the ban.**

All the members of the team hope that Bradman will speak out to-morrow. I gathered from the tenor of Bradman's remarks that there is not the slightest suggestion, however, of the affair causing any interference with the original schedule of the tour.

Bradman was obviously looking forward very much indeed to his wife coming to meet him in London. She would have had to leave Australia this month.

### REQUEST TO BOARD

The first week the Australian team arrived in London, a full meeting was called at which it was unanimously decided to send a request to the Board of Control that Bradman's wife should be allowed to come to London at the conclusion of the tour, and that the wives of the other married members should be allowed to come as far as Colombo, Ceylon.

**1 learn that it was expressly stated that no other player desired or expected the privilege which was asked for the captain.**

Such a privilege was extended to the captain of the 1934 Australian team, Mr. Woodfull, and it was expected by the players here that it would be readily extended to Bradman.

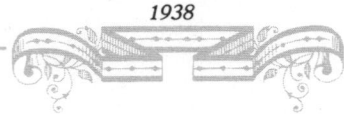

*TUESDAY, 7 JUNE*
*Boys returned from Essex. I had a dust with Bill over Jessie's application and finally we agreed on a cable to be dispatched to the Board. Went to see Van Hardings for shirts, Feldmans for music, then to Bonnys for a suit, Abbotts for slippers and to Royal Typewriters. Then hotel. Charlie Walker's finger is broken. After dinner went to see "Wild Oats" with E. Mc., E.S.W., Ben and Mary Hardwick.*

# "REMOVE BAN ON MRS. BRADMAN"

## Australians' Cable to Board

**O**N the eve of the third Test at Old Trafford, Manchester, the Australian cricket team have taken a hand in the controversy over the refusal of Don Bradman's request that his wife should be allowed to join him in England at the end of the tour.

**Yesterday they held a meeting at their hotel in Manchester — Bradman was not present — and unanimously decided to cable the Australian Board of Control asking them to reconsider their decision not to allow Mrs. Bradman to come to England.**

They told the board they were "heart and soul" in favour of Bradman's request, and declared that if the favour were granted it would not be regarded as "favouritism" to the captain.

**They pointed out that Bradman has carried a very great burden as captain while in England, and said that the team as a whole thought the board should recognise what he has done.**

There could not be any question of "setting embarrassing precedents."

Bradman was told what his team mates had done. He thanked them for their support and decided not to issue a statement on his position, as he hinted he would to a *Daily Mail* representative on Wednesday at Grindleford, in Derbyshire, where the team was then staying.

The latest move is regarded as a supreme gesture of the team's solid regard for their young skipper.

### Spontaneous

The team's action was quite spontaneous. At the start of the tour when Bradman first made his request they gave it their support. When Bradman received the board's refusal they decided that the board had not quite understood the position.

**Yesterday Bradman spent hours considering his next step. The team watched his deep concern for a long time.**

Then one of the senior members of the party called them all together in his room.

Few words were spoken. They decided to cable the board.

The Australian team action has served to temper what had threatened to be a difficult situation. Moreover, it proves that England to-day will face one of the most solidly united Australian teams they have ever met.

Don went to bed early followed by the rest of the team, most of whom had been to a theatre.

## BRADMAN SMILES

**N**EWS from Australia proves that, as the schoolboy wrote, "A human heart can beat beneath a cricket pad." The permission granted to the wives of Australian cricketers to visit this country after the Test series is over shows that their Board of Control are not so unfeeling as their own contract.

Don Bradman, in securing the withdrawal of the ban on his own wife, has obtained a similar privilege for his colleagues. This will surely lead to the removal in future years of a **prohibition which had been applied with unnecessary severity.**

This country will give a hearty greeting to Mrs. Bradman—and all the other wives who wish to make the journey. At the moment, perhaps, the welcome should be qualified. Two more Test matches have to come, and Don Bradman's natural jubilation may give fresh power to his superhuman bat.

Winning the Test at Leeds meant that Australia retained the Ashes. It was one of the most exciting Tests ever played and the result very much more in doubt than the scores indicate.

At one stage I elected to bat on in a light so bad that matches, being lit in the pavilion, shone like beacons. I did this rather than risk batting next day on a rain damaged pitch. Neville Cardus wrote that if we didn't declare he would, because he couldn't see to write his copy.

The final Test at the Oval was a real disaster for Australia.

England batted first on a pitch so perfect that not even the vicious spin of Fleetwood-Smith could make the ball deviate from its course. England's massive score enabled her to win by the biggest margin ever in Tests v. Australia. Fingleton and I were unable to bat through injury and with a broken bone in the ankle I took no further part in the tour.

For me, it was a tragic end, but in retrospect I think Australia performed remarkably well in overcoming severe handicaps, and the players worthily represented their country.

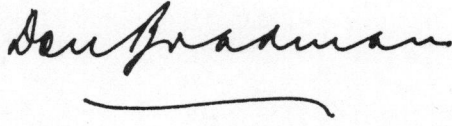

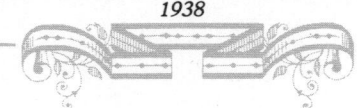

# Australia v England
## Fourth Test Match

AUSTRALIA v ENGLAND, Fourth Test Match, at Leeds, 22, 23 and 25 July 1938.

| Australia | - First Innings | 242 |
| | - Second Innings | 107 for 5 wickets |
| England | - First Innings | 223 |
| | - Second Innings | 123 |

Australia won by 5 wickets, and retained the Ashes.

| DON BRADMAN | - b. W.E. Bowes | 103 |
| (Captain) | - c. H. Verity b. D.V.P. Wright | 16 |

DON BRADMAN's first innings was one of his greatest.    In at 87 for 2, on the second morning, he was 17 not out at lunch.    Thereafter, on a dampish wicket which always gave the bowlers, especially the faster ones some help, and in a light which got steadily worse, he batted easily and commandingly while wickets fell regularly at the other end.    He completed 50 in ninety-two minutes, and when bad light eventually stopped play at 3.57, he was 71;  after a twenty-two-minute interval, he went on to reach 100 in two hours fifty-minutes, and eight minutes later, lost his middle stump to a fine ball from W.E. Bowes.    He gave no chance, hit nine fours. This was his twelfth century of the season, and he thereby broke V.T. Trumper's thirty-six-year-old record for the most centuries scored in a season by an Australian or other Touring batsman in England.

Australia had to work hard on the third afternoon to make 105 to win, again in bad light and with a storm threatening.    Bradman came in at 17 for 1, and was out thirty-five minutes and 31 balls later, caught at second slip in trying to cut a leg-break.

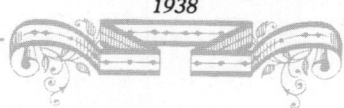
## Dick Moulton says

# DON WON'T GET 300 THIS TIME

*Daily Express Staff Reporter*

LEEDS, Wednesday.

DICK MOULTON, head ground-man at Headingley, who prepared the wickets on which Don Bradman made scores of 334 in 1930 and 304 in 1934, said to me here today–:—

"Don Bradman won't get three hundred this time."

The outfield, soaked by rain, has not quite dried up near the boundaries, and there is still a little "give" about the pitch, though there is no suggestion of a soft wicket.

Heavy clouds hung over the district for a considerable part of today, and the locals say that the south-westerly wind now blowing presages rain.

If there is rain followed by hot sun the bowlers should be right on top.

## England

| | | | |
|---|---|---|---|
| W. J. Edrich b O'Reilly | 12 | — st Barnett b Fleetwood-Smith | 28 |
| C. J. Barnett c Barnett b McCormick | 30 | — c Barnett b McCormick | 29 |
| J. Hardstaff run out | 4 | — b O'Reilly | 11 |
| Mr. W. R. Hammond (Capt.) b O'Reilly | 76 | — c Brown b O'Reilly | 0 |
| E. Paynter st Barnett b Fleetwood-Smith | 28 | — not out | 21 |
| D. Compton b O'Reilly | 14 | — c Barnett b O'Reilly | 15 |
| W. F. Price c McCabe b O'Reilly | 0 | — lbw b Fleetwood-Smith | 6 |
| H. Verity not out | 25 | — b Fleetwood-Smith | 0 |
| D. V. P. Wright c Fingleton b Fleetwood-Smith | 22 | — c Waite b Fleetwood-Smith | 0 |
| Mr. K. Farnes c Fingleton b Fleetwood-Smith | 2 | — b O'Reilly | 7 |
| W. E. Bowes b O'Reilly | 3 | — lbw b O'Reilly | 0 |
| L-b 4, n-b 3 | 7 | L-b 4, w 1, n-b 1 | 6 |
| | 223 | | 123 |

## Australia

| | | | |
|---|---|---|---|
| J. H. Fingleton b Verity | 30 | — lbw b Verity | 9 |
| W. A. Brown b Wright | 22 | — lbw b Farnes | 9 |
| B. A. Barnett c Price b Farnes | 57 | — not out | 15 |
| D. G. Bradman (Capt.) b Bowes | 103 | — c Verity b Wright | 16 |
| S. J. McCabe b Farnes | 1 | — c Barnett b Wright | 15 |
| C. L. Badcock b Bowes | 4 | — not out | 5 |
| A. L. Hassett c Hammond b Wright | 13 | — c Edrich b Wright | 33 |
| M. G. Waite c Price b Farnes | 3 | | |
| W. J. O'Reilly c Hammond b Farnes | 2 | | |
| E. L. McCormick b Bowes | 0 | | |
| L. O'B. Fleetwood-Smith not out | 2 | | |
| B 2, l-b 3 | 5 | B 4, n-b 1 | 5 |
| | 242 | Five wkts. | 107 |

## Australia Bowling

| | Overs | Mdns. | Runs | Wkts. | Overs | Mdns. | Runs | Wkts. |
|---|---|---|---|---|---|---|---|---|
| McCormick | 20 | 6 | 46 | 1 | 11 | 4 | 18 | 1 |
| Waite | 18 | 7 | 31 | 0 | 2 | 0 | 9 | 0 |
| O'Reilly | 34.1 | 17 | 66 | 5 | 21.5 | 8 | 56 | 5 |
| Fleetwood-Smith | 25 | 7 | 73 | 3 | 16 | 4 | 34 | 4 |
| McCabe | 1 | 1 | 0 | 0 | | | | |

## England Bowling

| | Overs | Mdns. | Runs | Wkts. | Overs | Mdns. | Runs | Wkts. |
|---|---|---|---|---|---|---|---|---|
| Farnes | 26 | 3 | 77 | 4 | 11.3 | 4 | 17 | 1 |
| Bowes | 35.4 | 6 | 79 | 3 | 11 | 0 | 35 | 0 |
| Wright | 15 | 4 | 38 | 2 | 5 | 0 | 26 | 3 |
| Verity | 19 | 6 | 30 | 1 | 5 | 2 | 24 | 1 |
| Edrich | 3 | 0 | 13 | 0 | | | | |

## Fall of the Wickets

### England—First Innings

| 1 | 2 | 3 | 4 | 5 | 6 | 7 | 8 | 9 | 10 |
|---|---|---|---|---|---|---|---|---|---|
| 29 | 34 | 88 | 142 | 171 | 171 | 172 | 213 | 215 | 223 |

### Australia—First Innings

| 1 | 2 | 3 | 4 | 5 | 6 | 7 | 8 | 9 | 10 |
|---|---|---|---|---|---|---|---|---|---|
| 28 | 87 | 128 | 136 | 145 | 195 | 232 | 240 | 240 | 242 |

### England—Second Innings

| 1 | 2 | 3 | 4 | 5 | 6 | 7 | 8 | 9 | 10 |
|---|---|---|---|---|---|---|---|---|---|
| 60 | 73 | 73 | 73 | 96 | 116 | 116 | 116 | 123 | 123 |

### Australia—Second Innings

| 1 | 2 | 3 | 4 | 5 |
|---|---|---|---|---|
| 17 | 32 | 50 | 61 | 91 |

Umpires: E. J. Smith and F. Chester

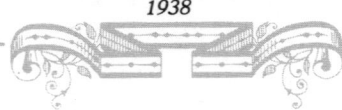

# THE FOURTH TEST MATCH

## ENGLAND'S BAD DAY AT LEEDS

FROM OUR CRICKET CORRESPONDENT

England in the fourth Test Match at Leeds yesterday were spared shame only by the runs scored late in the innings by their bowlers. As it was a total of 223, on a wicket which normal preparation, recent rain, and quiet wind between them had made comfortable and of an easy pace, was meagre, and cannot be attributed to any remarkable quality in the Australian bowling.

W. J. O'Reilly certainly bowled well — he always does — but there was more than a suggestion that the early batsmen, in an attempt to build up a big score which would make their side at least secure during the rest of the match, overlooked the rather important matter of scoring runs. It was an object lesson in how not to do it. Possibly England's bowlers will further retrieve the situation to-day, for last night before the close of play they did have the satisfaction of taking one Australian wicket for only 32 runs.

Australia began their bowling in the morning with McCormick from the Football Ground end and Waite. McCormick had what the covered stands allow to pass by them to help him, and he started off with four slips and two short-legs. The pace of the pitch was not encouraging to a catch behind the wicket, two of the slips accordingly being moved wider, but the men on the leg side remained expectant. Waite, who bowled an excellent length, making the ball go away late, had his two slips and a gully, but the occasional offer which was made of a stroke suggested a deflection or a prod to leg.

### EDRICH CONFIDENT

Barnett was anything but the gay and thrustful opening batsman he can be, but Edrich, playing with more certainty and more time in which to make his stroke, looked the man appropriate to the occasion. It was not long before Waite was put on at McCormick's end and O'Reilly at the other. O'Reilly, be the wicket ever so tame, can wring some life out of it, and he has always that variation of flight and length which worries a batsman of indecision.

So it was with Barnett, who seemed unable to decide whether to go forward to the ball or to wait to see what it would do. He was badly missed at second slip off Waite, and the first hour's play produced only 29 rather indeterminate runs. At the end of that hour Edrich, playing forward, was beaten and bowled by an off-break from O'Reilly, and soon afterwards England suffered an accident which never should have been. Barnett played a ball in the direction of mid-on. Hardstaff backed up unnecessarily vehemently and failed to get back, although he flung himself on to the ground, and was run out. So entered Hammond, and on went McCormick again. It was no fault of Hammond's that two wickets had fallen so cheaply and consequently he was forced to exercise some caution. This he did, no doubt to his own satisfaction and to the pleasure of the crowd while Barnett was gradually shaking off the qualms from which he had been suffering.

Runs were not often noticeable, and there was no manner of doubt that this was a Test Match, for there could have been no other explanation for such sterility. The spectators at the far end of the ground were kept physically and mentally on the move by the sight screen being moved from side to side every few overs, and there was an almost flippant cheer when Hammond hit a full pitch from Fleetwood-Smith straight for 4. Luncheon arrived with the total at 62, a not very liberal score as the result of two hours of cricket.

### BRIGHTER MOMENTS

Hammond must have had a talk to himself during the interval, for the tempo of the game altered entirely afterwards, an attack and a genuine desire to score runs succeeding a policy which had been negative to the point of being suicidal. Hammond led the way by driving McCormick to the off, and then hitting a no-ball into the lofts of the Grand Stand. There were hopes of a revival, for such was needed, when Barnett flicked at a ball outside the off stump and was caught at the wicket.

Hammond and Paynter together was more like an English combination of merit. Fleetwood-Smith bowled particularly well to Hammond, a batsman whom he might well fear more than any other on earth. He pitched the ball perpetually to that length which made Hammond stretch, and he twice beat him with the spin. O'Reilly, when bowling to Paynter, who started much more confidently than he sometimes does, had a very silly mid-off, but the ball was played well down, and never a chance was missed of tickling it away to leg. Hammond, for half an hour or more, was the true majestic Hammond, reaching his 50 with two exquisite drives wide of extra cover-point.

Fleetwood-Smith kept Paynter quiet, although one short ball was cut square for 4, and Waite was given a short spell to rest O'Reilly before Hammond had become too insolent. The first ball Waite bowled to Hammond came back off the bat so violently that there would have been fears for the umpire's life had he not thrown himself on the ground. In any case there was a spare umpire on the ground. Paynter again cut Fleetwood-Smith, and in the first hour after luncheon 63 runs were added, a much more suitable rate of scoring, even if there was a deal of lost time to recover. There was a check, in fact almost a dead halt, when at 142 Hammond's off stump was hit by a ball from O'Reilly which came back sharply. Hammond's had been a good and valuable innings and the end of it must have been joy to the Australians.

### A LUCKY ESCAPE

Compton was no sooner in than he had a lucky escape, a ball from O'Reilly passing from the edge of the bat between the wicketkeeper and first slip. This partnership between Paynter and Compton was regarded as vital to England, for with all due respect to those that were to follow a line could be drawn across the scorecard under Compton's name. Paynter was as comfortable as O'Reilly would allow him to be, and he was content to allow the ball which was breaking away past the off stump to go on its way neglected.

Then, just before tea, came utter disaster to England. Paynter, in attempting to hit the ball ferociously, lost his balance, swung himself off his feet, and was stumped. This was a good wicket for Fleetwood-Smith, who deliberately tossed up this ball to invite indiscretion. Compton was out at the same total, 171, bowled by a beautiful ball which he lost when it left the pitch, and Price, who batted in anything but the manner generally associated with one who has opened the innings for Middlesex, was caught at short slip, or perhaps it would be more accurate to say played the ball into the hands of short slip.

The despised English tail then explained how unkindly it has been spoken of. Wright and Verity, without any ado, hit the bowling hard, frequently, and, for the most part correctly. Certainly the result was correct, and it had the effect of persuading the Australian bowlers, just for a moment, to wilt. There were even a few full pitches, and these Wright banged away to the boundary, and there were long hops, too, which each time were to cost the penalty of 4 runs. Verity, if not so robust as Wright in his methods, played his part, helped from time to time by strokes which sent the ball to unintended places, until, with the 200 up and passed —and at one time it looked as if 200 would be beyond the reach of England's stricken batting—Wright was caught at mid-off. Wright's technique does not prohibit the ball from being hit in the air, and he must be considered unlucky in that there was a fieldsman in the way.

K. Farnes also was caught at mid-off, but this was to a grandly judged running catch, and Bowes, although he was encouraged by a loyal Yorkshire crowd all the way on his amble to the wicket, flourished his bat wildly at a straight ball and was bowled. It was a poor total, but Heaven knows it might have been much worse.

When Australia went in Farnes from the Grand Stand end gave a splendid exhibition of fast bowling. Three times he beat a batsman utterly and completely, but the ball went over the stumps. In his very first over he well might have bowled Fingleton for all that batsman knew of the ball, and in his next over the ball seemed to pierce Brown's bat and body without even the wicket-keeper knowing that it had passed him. Bowes at the other end, without striving for pace, was bowling steadily, while Fingleton and Brown were collecting runs here and there without any marked certainty of execution. With the score at 28, Wright was put on in place of Bowes, a happy thought on the part of Hammond, for Wright, with his first ball hit Brown's leg stump. Barnett was sent in to play out time, which he achieved after he had just, and only just, brought his bat down on to a yorker from Wright.

# DON BRADMAN IN LONE DUEL WITH ENGLAND

## ENGLISH SCHOOLBOYS WELCOME BRADMAN

Don Bradman, hero of young cricketers the world over, was applauded by youngsters as he went in to bat on the second day of the fourth test at Leeds. He made 103.

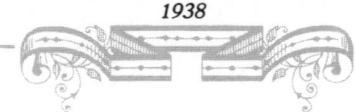

# Impressions by W.L.A.

IT is a long time since I watched so much exciting cricket in a day. The drama reached its height between 4.45, after a break for bad light, and 5.5. At 4.45 the match had assumed the familiar form, Bradman versus England. Australia's captain was playing not merely brilliantly but like a hero. He was three short of his century, and if only he could have the needed support—though this was almost impossible for Australia now to hope for—he looked like making a couple of hundred at least.

Here was the lightning master of batsmanship on a great testing occasion. He swooped on the loose ones like a hawk after a small bird. He showed all the strokes in the text-books. He added one or two special varieties of his own. He maintained all the time most wise and patient care.

But the support he needed had begun to melt away under bowling of sustained excellence and in a troublesome light.

If only the tail could hold on Bradman would do the scoring. Everyone understood how it was. But after Hassett had gone it looked as if Bradman was doomed to carry out his bat. He did his utmost to keep the bowling; he nursed his partners most assiduously.

England's hopes had flickered for hours like a sulky fire that takes a long time to get going. At Hassett's departure hopes brightened. At 4.45 they shot into a flame. Waite was then caught at the wicket. He made way for O'Reilly, with whose arrival the end of the innings was bound to be near.

\* \*

BRADMAN reached his century with a single.

Now you felt he was bound to rush out and wallop every four and six he could while there was a wicket left. He reached 103 out of a total of 240. At 4.52 Bowes sent down what looked to me like a yorker. Bradman, trying to force the pace, missed it. Crash went the middle stump, and he began to run to the pavilion before the bails were on the ground.

How the crowd roared! Bradman fallen—and fallen at the hands of Bowes, bowled middle stump, and the game back in England's hands—oh, but this moment was sweet for Yorkshire!

My opinion is that Bradman, seeing Australia could not stay in much longer, meant to hit as merrily as he could, and then have England in to cope with that tricky light. So he might hope to capture a few of our more valuable wickets before the clock struck 6.30. As it turned out these hopes were fruitless. The remaining Australians were soon polished off, Bowes taking the last wicket, McCormick's, at five minutes past five.

\* \*

AFTER some delay owing to bad light Barnett and Edrich opened the England second innings at 5.35, and, watchful as sentries on a frontier during an ultimatum, carried on with spirited persistence till the end.

Bradman might have appealed against the light before he did. At one time Hassett seemed to be urging him to do it, but I imagine that Don replied, "I'll take care of that, old chap. Just you keep your end up and I'll do the scoring." However bad the light was, and whatever its effect on other people's vision, Bradman could see the ball clearly. But the day got worse.

WHAT I shall remember longest of the match is, I think, the picture presented by Bradman and Bowes as they faced each other. Bradman was all intense concentration, motionless for a full seven seconds as he watched Bowes turn, run up and shoot the ball. Very, very rarely was he puzzled. His footwork was beautiful. He kept the secret of his stroke to the last half-second. There, beyond all question, was a captain of men.

# 25,000 SHOUT FOR DON AFTER TENSE DAY

## Australians' Joy As Hammond Went For A "Duck"

# VITAL BLOW TO HOPES

LEEDS, Monday.

At the close of to-day's dramatic play in the fourth Test, 25,000 people outside the pavilion shouted, "We want Bradman." To-night the Australian captain is wearing a smile that will not come off.

With the Ashes safe in Australia's keeping, as a result of victory by five wickets, there will be a break of three weeks before the fifth Test at the Oval.

Australia won, thanks chiefly to O'Reilly and Bradman. O'Reilly's bowling was beyond praise, and he deserves the major credit.

Bradman took the batting honors with his century, giving the Australians that valuable 19 runs first innings lead, and he is also to be praised for his inspiring leadership.

### *Spectators Give Bradman Ovation*

Although the spectators did not raise a solitary cheer over the result of the match, they gathered in thousands outside the players' balcony and chanted in unison, "We want Bradman."

When he appeared they gave him an ovation.

After the shouting had died down the Australians returned to their hotel and dined together in a private room.

There were brief speeches about victory and some community singing.

The players left for Taunton today to prepare for the match against Somerset, beginning tomorrow.

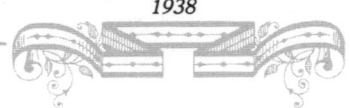

## JACK HOBBS, Reviewing The Test, Says . . . .

# O'Reilly's Brilliant Bowling Plus Bradman's Fighting Century Were Too Much

ENGLAND WERE WELL and truly beaten. We might as well be generous and congratulate Australia on winning the fourth Test and so retaining the Ashes.

They undoubtedly deserved their victory because we won the toss and had the better of a very peculiar wicket. The low scoring suggests it was "funny"; it was never wet.

The wicket was of slower pace than other wickets and the ball didn't go along as it had been doing, to allow the batsmen to make their strokes.

If the game had lasted until the fourth day we should have seen the ball "talk" still more, because the top of the wicket was getting knocked about.

Well as our bowlers worked we hadn't a man who could rise to the heights O'Reilly reached. He was on his mettle and had his tail up all through the match. His flight, change of pace and spin, were too much for our batsmen.

### A FINE INNINGS

O'Reilly's bowling and Bradman's fighting 100 did the trick. This was not one of Bradman's biggest scores, but it was one of his finest innings.

The turning point came yesterday morning when Brown made the snap catch at short leg that dismissed Hammond first ball.

England put up a good performance. I can't say we have been disgraced because another 60 or 70 runs from our batsmen would probably have won the game. Even if we had led by 50 on the first innings, instead of being 19 behind, it might have sufficed.

Goddard would have been useful yesterday—but who could have been left out for him?

Wright got wickets. He mixed bad balls with the good ones in Australia's second innings, so Hammond could only use him in short spells.

### QUERY ABOUT GODDARD

The question is: Would Goddard have done any better in the first innings than the men we had? Farnes was a good bowler all the way through, and I was delighted he was recalled. He was far better than at Lord's.

Bowes did a better job than his figures suggest in Australia's first innings. Hammond was able to bowl him for long spells because his length was so good that he kept the score down.

There were few batting successes apart from those of Bradman and Barnett for Australia and Hammond for England The real point is that their bowlers performed better than our bowlers.

I don't think we can complain about the luck, although Rockley Wilson, the old Yorkshire bowler, remarked to me : "The only things that didn't come off for Australia were the bails."

He was referring to two occasions when they hit the stumps and the bails stayed on.

### THE CAPTAINS PRAISED

I should like to praise the captains Some skippers make a deal of fuss when changing their bowlers and field, but Hammond and Bradman lose nothing of their effectiveness by doing everything unobtrusively.

I am also pleased to notice that in the three Tests to date the captaincy has not affected the abilities of Hammond and Bradman. Both have been successful with the bat.

It has been a most interesting match to watch and report. Batsmen were dismissed for such small scores that all of us were guessing about the result. Also, the fielding was good throughout on both sides.

My only regret is that the honours didn't rest with England. At the same time, I feel they went to the more deserving side. That must be the general opinion of all unbiassed spectators

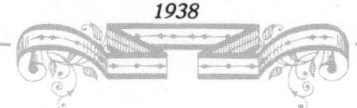

# Australians v Somerset

AUSTRALIANS v SOMERSET, at Taunton, 27, 28 and 29 July 1938.

| Australians | - First Innings | 464 for 6 wickets dec. |
| | - Second Innings | - |
| Somerset | - First Innings | 110 |
| | - Second Innings | 136 |

Australians won by an innings and 218 runs.

On a damp but easy wicket, DON BRADMAN went in at 108 for 1, very early on the second morning, and it was soon apparent that none of the Somerset bowlers was likely to prevent him from getting another century.     He reached 50 in seventy minutes, and 100 in two hours thirty-four minutes;  then forced the pace to reach 200 in three hours forty-three minutes, after which he gave his wicket away two minutes later in the same over.     He gave no chance, and hit thirty-two fours.

This was his thirteenth century of the season, and twelfth double-century made in England.

DON BRADMAN - b. W.H.R. Andrews      202
   (Captain)

## Somerset

| | | | | |
|---|---|---|---|---|
| Mr. M. D. Lyon c Ward b Fleetwood-Smith | 26 | — c Walker b White | 2 |
| F. S. Lee c Chipperfield b McCabe | 0 | — c Chipperfield b White | 4 |
| H. T. F. Buse run out | 0 | — lbw b O'Reilly | 33 |
| Mr. R. J. O. Meyer c Barnes b Fleetwood-Smith | 7 | — c Badcock b O'Reilly | 17 |
| Mr. E. F. Longrigg b White | 7 | — c Chipperfield b Fleetwood-Smith | 23 |
| H. Gimblett c Badcock b Fleetwood-Smith | 7 | — c Hassett b Ward | 6 |
| W. H. R. Andrews c and b Ward | 19 | — c Walker b Fleetwood-Smith | 20 |
| Mr. C. J. P. Barnwell b O'Reilly | 11 | — b Fleetwood-Smith | 18 |
| A. W. Wellard b White | 20 | — lbw b Fleetwood-Smith | 6 |
| W. T. Luckes not out | 5 | — b Fleetwood-Smith | 1 |
| H. L. Hazell c Hassett b White | 3 | — not out | 1 |
| B 1, l-b 1, n-b 3 | 5 | B 4, n-b 1 | 5 |
| | **110** | | **136** |

## Australians

| | | | |
|---|---|---|---|
| C. W. Walker b Andrews | 37 | A. G. Chipperfield b Wellard | 10 |
| C. L. Badcock run out | 110 | S. J. McCabe not out | 56 |
| D. G. Bradman b Andrews | 202 | E. S. White not out | 2 |
| S. Barnes lbw b Wellard | 9 | B 4, l-b 1, w 1, n-b 1 | 7 |
| A. L. Hassett c Gimblett b Buse | 31 | Six wkts., dec. | 464 |

F. Ward, W. J. O'Reilly and L. O'B. Fleetwood-Smith did not bat.

## Australians Bowling

| | Overs | Mdns. | Runs | Wkts. | | Overs | Mdns. | Runs | Wkts. |
|---|---|---|---|---|---|---|---|---|---|
| McCabe | 2 | 2 | 0 | 1 | | | | | |
| Hassett | 6 | 3 | 14 | 0 | .... | 4 | 0 | 8 | 0 |
| O'Reilly | 15 | 5 | 22 | 1 | .... | 6 | 1 | 17 | 2 |
| Fleetwood-Smith | 13 | 3 | 40 | 3 | .... | 11.1 | 1 | 30 | 5 |
| White | 8.3 | 4 | 8 | 3 | .... | 12 | 6 | 13 | 2 |
| Ward | 2 | 0 | 21 | 1 | .... | 15 | 2 | 63 | 1 |

## Somerset Bowling

| | Overs | Mdns. | Runs | Wkts. |
|---|---|---|---|---|
| Wellard | 39 | 8 | 146 | 2 |
| Andrews | 24 | 2 | 108 | 2 |
| Meyer | 17 | 3 | 54 | 0 |
| Buse | 12 | 1 | 82 | 1 |
| Hazell | 11 | 1 | 57 | 0 |
| Lyon | 2 | 1 | 10 | 0 |

Umpires: C. N. Woolley and E. Cooke

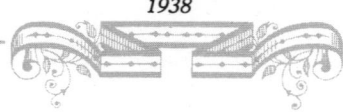

## BRADMAN AT HIS GREATEST

### FINE DOUBLE CENTURY AT TAUNTON

### SOMERSET WANTED A SPIN-BOWLER

#### From WENDELL BILL

TAUNTON, Thursday.

ANOTHER glorious innings by Bradman, who, completing a double century, registered his 13th three-figure score of the tour, was the feature of the cricket here to-day.

Bradman gave the crowd an exhibition of strokes which was faultless in its technique and wide in its repertoire. His second hundred runs were scored in whirlwind fashion.

Australia were able to declare at tea and at the end their bowlers had brought the match very near its conclusion, although some better batting was seen from the county. Buse was particularly impressive with his powerful onside play, and Andrews, who has made some mighty hits, remains to continue to-morrow. This morning the Australians continued their innings brightly, although the county received a spark of encouragement in the fall of Walker's wicket from the third ball of the day.

Badcock and Bradman countered the caprices of the softish turf with fine skill, although it would have been interesting to see how a good spinner could have used the conditions.

#### ATTACK NOT GOOD ENOUGH

At all events, the county did not possess the attack to worry either of the Australians, who produced a variety of firm and polished shots. Badcock did not rise to the heights of yesterday's display, but nevertheless was still sound, gaining valuable experience on a turning pitch.

After reaching his century in just under two hours he was run out, failing to answer Bradman's call quickly enough to beat a smart return.

Bradman carried on in full command, taking severe toll of anything loose or overpitched, and his defence remained impregnable, the despair of all the bowlers. Shortly after lunch yet another century was added to his long list.

Even a widely spread field could not check his brilliant flow of shots, and with a speed and certainty that held the crowd spellbound he raced to the second century, whereupon he threw his wicket away. His last 100 runs took only 70 minutes and included no fewer than 19 boundaries. In all 32 boundaries were marked up to him.

---

## —IS IT BRADMAN'S— LAST TOUR?

### By JACK INGHAM, The Sports Editor

*THEY SAY THAT WE IN ENGLAND WILL NOT SEE BRADMAN AGAIN IN TEST CRICKET ONCE THIS TOUR HAS ENDED.*

*They say that the fearful strain of being a Bradman all the time is too much for anyone. Especially for a man not of notable physique.*

*They say that Bradman will leave cricket while he is on the very peak. That, surely, is now.*

*I do not know if it is true that Bradman is going. I do know that he is not strong; I know that four years must elapse before he could come here again. I know it is the dream of every sport star to go out when the cheering is loudest.*

*I have made no attempt to get the truth about Bradman. I know it is no use trying to get it. Apart from the seal of silence on the players, I question if I would be told the truth.*

*But I sat and thought of it all—cricket without Bradman—as the Australians were beating Kent so easily.*

★

*EVERYBODY TALKS about Bradman. People who don't know one thing from the next in cricket all talk about him. Round this time on Saturday, you will be talking, or thinking, of the little broad-shouldered, slow-speaking Australian.*

*It is strange, but I think true, that all the time, day and night, somewhere in the world somebody is talking about Bradman.*

*In Australia three things count above all else. On the surface anyway. Their harbour, their bridge, and their Bradman.*

*All are the best of their kind in the world.*

*Bradman, of course, is dinkie-die; a true-born Australian. A Bowral kid who learnt much of his cricket by throwing a tennis ball against a wall and then hitting it on the rebound with a cricket stump.*

*Hard application if you like. The other Bradman qualities—judgment of pace, quick feet, a sense of timing and amazingly keen eye-sight, were born in Bradman. Nobody else has them to quite the same extent.*

★

*YOU MAY SAY that Bradman is a walking mass of cricket records. True, of course. But I won't mention a single figure.*

*The queer potency of a Bradman innings can never be shown in figures. They're cold, chilly things. Quite unrelated to what I feel we all feel about Bradman.*

*Let me merely say that Bradman has done everything that can be done with a bat. And I must not forget that fielding; delightful.*

*Bradman lived in Sydney when I met him. He has a house in quiet Adelaide now. The city of churches by the sleepy Torrens under the high curves of Mount Lofty.*

*The town with one of the most beautiful cricket grounds in the world.*

★

*IF BRADMAN needs rest from the noisy adulation that follows him everywhere he will find it in Adelaide.*

*He hates limelight. When an Australian team walks on the field, Bradman, the skipper, seems to hide among his colleagues. I often hear people say: Which is Bradman? He's difficult to find.*

*Bradman is not a showman, though every move he makes on the field screamingly advertises his presence. There is so much he does that no-one else can do.*

*As I say, I made no attempt to get proof that we are looking our last on Bradman in a Test this week-end.*

*One reason why I did not try, a strong reason with me, is that I might have heard officially that it is true.*

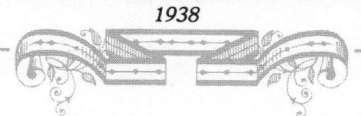

# Australia v England
## Fifth Test Match

AUSTRALIA v ENGLAND, Fifth Test Match, at the Oval, 20, 22, 23 and 24 August 1938.

| | | | |
|---|---|---|---|
| Australia | - | First Innings | 201. |
| | - | Second Innings | 123 |
| England | - | First Innings | 903 for 7 wickets dec. |
| | - | Second Innings | - |

Australia lost by an innings and 579 runs, the rubber being drawn.

DON BRADMAN (Captain) - absent hurt - absent hurt

DON BRADMAN had the misfortune to lose the toss for the fourth consecutive time in Test Matches, and England took advantage of a perfect wicket and a timeless Test to bat until tea-time on the third day.

Finally, with the score 887 for 7, at 4.25 p.m. Bradman slipped while bowling, and fractured a bone in his ankle; he had to be carried off the field, and could not bat. In his absence and that of J.H. Fingleton, and against such a score, Australia did not take things too seriously, and were soon dismissed; but for over two and a half days Bradman fielded magnificently and set his side a splendid example.

Bradman was unable to take any further part in the tour owing to his injury, and in his absence the Australians suffered another defeat, by Mr. H.D.G. Leveson-Gower's XI at Scarborough.

## England

| | |
|---|---|
| L. Hutton c Hassett b O'Reilly | 364 |
| W. J. Edrich c Hassett b O'Reilly | 12 |
| M. Leyland run out | 187 |
| Mr. W. R. Hammond (Capt.) lbw b Fleetwood-Smith | 59 |
| E. Paynter lbw b O'Reilly | 0 |
| D. Compton b Waite | 1 |
| J. Hardstaff not out | 169 |
| A. Wood c and b Barnes | 53 |
| H. Verity not out | 8 |
| B 22, l-b 19, w 1, n-b 8 | 50 |

Mr. K. Farnes and W. E. Bowes did not bat.

Seven wkts., dec. 903

## Australia

| | First Innings | | Second Innings | |
|---|---|---|---|---|
| C. L. Badcock c Hardstaff b Bowes | 0 | — b Bowes | 9 |
| W. A. Brown c Hammond b Leyland | 69 | — c Edrich b Farnes | 15 |
| S. J. McCabe c Edrich b Farnes | 14 | — c Wood b Farnes | 2 |
| A. L. Hassett c Compton b Edrich | 42 | — lbw b Bowes | 10 |
| S. Barnes b Bowes | 41 | — lbw b Verity | 33 |
| B. A. Barnett c Wood b Bowes | 2 | — b Farnes | 46 |
| M. G. Waite b Bowes | 8 | — c Edrich b Verity | 0 |
| W. J. O'Reilly c Wood b Bowes | 0 | — not out | 7 |
| L. O'B. Fleetwood-Smith not out | 16 | — c Leyland b Farnes | 0 |
| D. G. Bradman (Capt.) absent hurt | 0 | — absent hurt | 0 |
| J. H. Fingleton absent hurt | 0 | — absent hurt | 0 |
| B 4, l-b 2, n-b 3 | 9 | B | 1 |
| | 201 | | 123 |

## Australia Bowling

| | Overs | Mdns. | Runs | Wkts. | Overs | Mdns. | Runs | Wkts. |
|---|---|---|---|---|---|---|---|---|
| Waite | 72 | 16 | 150 | 1 | | | | |
| McCabe | 38 | 8 | 85 | 0 | | | | |
| O'Reilly | 85 | 26 | 178 | 3 | | | | |
| Fleetwood-Smith | 87 | 11 | 298 | 1 | | | | |
| Barnes | 38 | 3 | 84 | 1 | | | | |
| Hassett | 13 | 2 | 52 | 0 | | | | |
| Bradman | 3 | 2 | 6 | 0 | | | | |

## England Bowling

| | Overs | Mdns. | Runs | Wkts. | Overs | Mdns. | Runs | Wkts. |
|---|---|---|---|---|---|---|---|---|
| Farnes | 13 | 2 | 54 | 1 | 12.1 | 1 | 63 | 4 |
| Bowes | 19 | 3 | 49 | 5 | 10 | 3 | 25 | 2 |
| Edrich | 10 | 2 | 55 | 1 | | | | |
| Verity | 5 | 1 | 15 | 0 | 7 | 3 | 15 | 2 |
| Leyland | 3.1 | 0 | 11 | 1 | 5 | 0 | 19 | 0 |
| Hammond | 2 | 0 | 8 | 0 | | | | |

## Fall of the Wickets

### England—First Innings

| 1 | 2 | 3 | 4 | 5 | 6 | 7 |
|---|---|---|---|---|---|---|
| 29 | 411 | 546 | 547 | 555 | 770 | 876 |

### Australia—First Innings

| 1 | 2 | 3 | 4 | 5 | 6 | 7 | 8 |
|---|---|---|---|---|---|---|---|
| 0 | 19 | 70 | 145 | 147 | 160 | 160 | 201 |

### Australia—Second Innings

| 1 | 2 | 3 | 4 | 5 | 6 | 7 | 8 |
|---|---|---|---|---|---|---|---|
| 15 | 18 | 35 | 41 | 115 | 115 | 117 | 123 |

Umpires: F. Chester and F. Walden

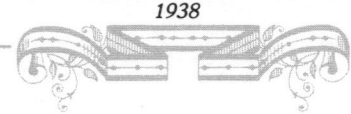

# THE LAST TEST MATCH

## A RECORD STAND

FROM OUR CRICKET CORRESPONDENT

England, by scoring 347 runs for the loss of only one wicket, made a great start at the Oval on Saturday to the Test Match which is to decide whether Australia is to win the rubber or whether honours are to remain easy.

The type of cricket which is known as time-limitless is rare in this country, and any excuse that there may be for its existence, or any suggestion that the practice should become more common, was exposed for all to see. The affair being reduced to a run-making competition, bowlers were to be regarded essentially as a luxury, and it is questionable whether the combined bowling strength of the two teams in a match between England and Australia has ever been so weak. Australia, to be sure, were handicapped by the fact that E. L. McCormick was suffering from neuritis, but it is more than doubtful whether he would have played in any case. As it was, Hutton and Leyland accepted the opportunity offered to them, smashed to smithereens the record stand for England's second-wicket partnership of 188 which had been established by Sutcliffe and Hammond at Sydney during the tour of 1932-33, and are already in a position to attack the Australia record of 451 set up by W. H. Ponsford and D. Bradman at the Oval in 1934.

## NO NEED TO HURRY

There being no need to hurry, with no threat that the quality of the bowling or the condition of the wicket would alter as the day advanced, both Hutton and Leyland took their runs as they came to them, and in so doing allowed us to see as many strokes as they considered to be profitable and safe. Leyland was a little uncertain at the beginning of his innings, and his running between the wickets was never reliable; Hutton might have been stumped when he had made 39; but for the rest the Australians can have seen very little hope of breaking up the partnership. The bowling, or what there was of it, never became loose—there were remarkably few balls short of a length bowled during the day—and the bowlers were splendidly supported by their fieldsmen, the manner in which Bradman gathered the ball on a bumpy ground being one of the very best things of the whole long day.

Hammond, having again won the toss, sent in Hutton and Edrich, put his own pads on, and kept them on, except during the luncheon interval, for the rest of the day. M. G. Waite and S. McCabe, who began the bowling, both had two slips and a gulley, but the scoring strokes during the first quarter of an hour were made to the on-side until Hutton cut a ball from McCabe to the boundary. Edrich, who assuredly has been given plenty of chances to show his worth, was once beaten by

McCabe, and he looked to be none too comfortable when W. J. O'Reilly came on to bowl to two short-legs, one of whom was crouching only just wide of the pitch. O'Reilly took Edrich's wicket, and his 100th in Test Match cricket, when the score was 29 with a googly to which the batsman played back and was leg-before.

There was a mild surprise when Leyland came in at the fall of the first wicket, but Leyland is a suitable person at any position in the batting order. He had not been in long before he was beaten by a leg-break from L. O'B. Fleetwood-Smith, who had come on at the Pavilion end in an attempt to make the ball do something after it had pitched on a wicket which throughout the day was just too slow even for O'Reilly. Leyland, quick on his feet, was watching O'Reilly, who twice forced Hutton back to play hurried defensive strokes, very carefully. Hutton once forced a ball from O'Reilly past extra cover, and Leyland twice in one over drove Fleetwood-Smith away to the long-off boundary, beautifully contained and strong strokes. O'Reilly was used in short spells only, and he had a habit of starting off with a no-ball. Fleetwood-Smith, bowling a good length, twice in one over got the ball past the bat, and with O'Reilly a little troublesome with his variation of pace England's passage before the luncheon interval, when the score stood at 89, was by no means so smooth as it might appear to have been.

## A CHANCE MISSED

It was in the second over after luncheon that Australia might have had their second wicket, but the ball rose awkwardly for the wicket-keeper when Hutton was well out of his ground to Fleetwood-Smith, and such an opportunity was not to come again. Hutton, with that clipped defensive stroke which he plays with a roll of the wrist, had the measure of Fleetwood-Smith and McCabe, and Waite's attempt to make himself appear to be two separate entities by bowling first round and then over the wicket did no more than emphasize the opinion that he is an ordinary bowler. Leyland and Hutton, who in a friendly way kept their scores as level as possible during the afternoon, each treated themselves to an off-drive off Fleetwood-Smith, who had relapsed to a purely defensive setting of his field, which almost formed a complete circle at a respectful distance from the wicket. Leyland once hit him straight to the boundary with a gloriously cross-batted stroke, but in the same over he edged a ball only just wide of first slip, and a little later he must have been very near to chopping a ball from Waite on to his stumps. These were minor events only during a period in which Hutton and Leyland, having established a foundation to their partnership, were adding solidly to it with a nice piece of mortar between each brick. S. Barnes may be a good bowler, but when he came on it did seem that the poverty of the Australian attack was fully demonstrated, and he did little to suggest any alteration in the method of

either Hutton or Leyland.

Fleetwood-Smith kept on bowling away, and Hutton with a grand off-drive and a full-blooded blow to leg off his bowling was the first to reach his 100, the result of about 3½ hours' batting. Waite and McCabe were given the new ball, which made very little difference to their bowling or to the rate of scoring, Leyland greeting it with a lovely off-drive and his century. New ball or no new ball, O'Reilly had to come on again as soon as possible, and Fleetwood-Smith was once more trying to make the ball spin from the other end. The Australian bowling was in fact then expended, and not even a heavy shower which fell at the tea interval could persuade the ball to be unfriendly to the batsmen. Only twice in the day did a ball rise in the least awkwardly: once a ball from Waite nearly knocked Leyland's cap off, and once Hutton had a rap on the knuckles from O'Reilly; for the rest Barnett patted his gloved hands together and watched it hit the bat.

As the afternoon turned into evening Fleetwood-Smith still toiled on, and it is to his credit that while still attempting the effects of a spin bowler against two thoroughly well set batsmen only for two overs did his bowling become in the least untidy. Leyland considered that the situation was best covered by use of the drive, which generally counted four runs (once all run), or the purely defensive stroke with an occasional deflection to long-leg. Hutton was more catholic in his taste, several times employing the on-drive proper, which beat mid-on either by altitude or breadth and then ran along to the boundary. Bradman, without following the stroke, placed his fieldsmen where he thought the situation most demanded them, but he soon found himself in the same difficulty which he had so often set other captains—he had not got enough fieldsmen.

Leyland when he had made 139 would have been run out had the bowler in his anxiety to see the last of him not broken the wicket before he had gathered the ball. That was the nearest that he was to being out, although Barnes, when he was put on again, did once get the ball past his off stump. Hutton had once cut a ball so late that some said that it went through the wicket-keeper's gloves, which is another way of describing a stroke which earned four runs and was actually a beautifully timed stroke. O'Reilly well might have been tired, but his last two overs of the evening were as good as any he had sent down all day. A wicket at 25 minutes past 6 is as valuable as one at any other time of the day, but Leyland stayed there, and if the present state of affairs goes on much longer the pitch, everlasting as it is said to be, will show signs of wear before the Australians are allowed their first use of it.

The Oval, Surrey, 1985, looking towards the members' pavilion.

# CRICKET
## 1938 - Australian Team in England

◆ Not First Class Fixtures. Figures in these Matches are not included in the Averages.

### BATTING

| | INNS. | N.O. | H.S. | RUNS | AVGE. |
|---|---|---|---|---|---|
| BRADMAN D.G. | 26 | 5 | 278 | 2429 | 115·66 |
| BROWN W.A. | 37 | 5 | 265* | 1854 | 57·93 |
| HASSETT A.L. | 32 | 3 | 220 | 1589 | 54·79 |
| BADCOCK C.L. | 39 | 4 | 198 | 1604 | 45·82 |
| BARNES S.G. | 19 | 2 | 94 | 720 | 42·35 |
| FINGLETON J.A. | 32 | 2 | 124 | 1141 | 38·03 |
| McCABE S.J. | 33 | 2 | 232 | 1124 | 36·25 |
| WALKER C.W. | 9 | 4 | 42 | 175 | 35·00 |
| BARNETT B.A. | 29 | 4 | 126* | 737 | 29·48 |
| CHIPPERFIELD A. | 18 | 3 | 104* | 424 | 28·26 |
| WAITE M.G. | 30 | 3 | 77 | 684 | 25·33 |
| WAITE E.C. | 19 | 7 | 52 | 290 | 24·16 |
| O'REILLY W.J. | 17 | 3 | 42 | 224 | 16·00 |
| WARD F.A. | 17 | 5 | 31 | 162 | 13·50 |
| FLEETW-SMITH L. | 20 | 9 | 16* | 99 | 9·00 |
| McCORMICK E.L. | 15 | 4 | 12 | 49 | 4·45 |

### BOWLING

| | O. | M. | R. | W. | AVGE. |
|---|---|---|---|---|---|
| O'REILLY W.J. | 709·4 | 214 | 1732 | 104 | 16·65 |
| WARD F.A. | 523 | 99 | 1773 | 92 | 19·27 |
| FLEETW-SMITH L. | 550 | 98 | 1719 | 88 | 19·53 |
| WAITE E.C. | 375 | 148 | 708 | 30 | 23·60 |
| CHIPPERFIELD A. | 54·1 | 18 | 155 | 6 | 25·83 |
| WAITE M.G. | 641·1 | 185 | 1448 | 56 | 25·85 |
| McCORMICK E.L. | 338 | 52 | 1136 | 34 | 33·41 |
| McCABE S.J. | 212 | 53 | 523 | 14 | 37·35 |
| BARNES S.G. | 44 | 4 | 116 | 2 | 58·00 |
| HASSETT A.L. | 30 | 9 | 78 | 1 | 78·00 |
| BRADMAN D.G. | 3 | 2 | 6 | 0 | — |
| BROWN W.A. | 3 | 0 | 10 | 0 | — |
| BADCOCK C.L. | 2 | 0 | 10 | 0 | — |

FINGLETON 2-17 & WALKER 0-0 ALSO BOWLED - AGAINST SCOTLAND (2ND CLASS MATCH ONLY)

Compiled & Drawn by E.A. Keeble.

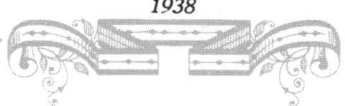

## *A Very Useful Lamp-post*

There was only room for three, but they got a good view of the Test match over the wall surrounding the Oval today.

An attempt to run out Hutton off a smart return from Don Bradman.

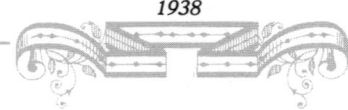

# THE FINAL TEST MATCH

## FIVE WICKETS IN TWO DAYS

### HUTTON 300 NOT OUT

Hours of Play, 11.30 to 6.30

FROM OUR CRICKET CORRESPONDENT

The Test Match at the Oval between England and Australia is perceptibly advancing. England's first innings has not yet by any means been completed, but when bad light stopped play yesterday evening at a quarter past 6 they had lost five wickets and they had already amassed 634 runs. No Test Match that is worth the name can be allowed to pass without its quota of broken records. Yesterday two new records were established. Hutton and Leyland, by scoring 382 runs while they were in together, were associated in the highest partnership ever made for any wicket by a pair of English batsmen, the previous highest being the 323 for the first wicket made by Hobbs and Rhodes at Melbourne in 1912; Hutton himself made the highest individual score to the credit of any English batsman in these matches by passing the 287 of the late R. E. Foster, a record which had hitherto stood intact for 35 years.

The Australian bowlers, in spite of the encouragement they received when three wickets fell unexpectedly quickly in the afternoon, had a tiring and unprofitable day, but once again they stuck manfully to their work. The amount of loose balls bowled was remarkably low, and more alert fielding could not be imagined. Hutton's innings was the perfect continuation of the task he had set himself when he went in on Saturday morning. In so long an innings mistakes are expected to creep in here and there; yet Hutton seems to have found a method of eliminating to the greatest possible extent such errors. His range of stroke play is sufficient for any reasonable purpose—none of the Australian bowlers in this match could curb it—and he has the quiet confidence which would remain undisturbed in any circumstances.

### A SHORT DELAY

A shower of rain in the morning prevented play from being begun until five minutes to 12, when the scoring board bore the imposing score of 347 for one wicket, Hutton's share then being 160 and Leyland's 156. Bradman, discarding any preliminaries, at once began with O'Reilly and Fleetwood-Smith. O'Reilly did make one ball fly over the wicket-keeper's head, but in the main the pitch was in the same mood as it had been when stumps were drawn on Saturday evening. O'Reilly had his two short-legs perhaps a little closer to the batsmen than usual, a form of intimidation to which neither batsman paid much attention. For some time they showed an inclination to employ the cut to any ball of a normal length which was outside the off-stump until Leyland set the example of solid off-driving. Fleetwood-Smith, when bowling to Leyland, had a wide mid-off, another mid-off finer and deeper, and a deep extra cover-point, and each of them in turn had some hard blows to stop.

Waite provided no difficulties whatsoever when he came on, but Leyland when he had made 174 was well and truly beaten by a ball from Fleetwood-Smith which whipped across the wicket. Even so the talk was still of how many records these two Yorkshiremen would break before some phenomenal chance should separate them. That chance was soon to come, and it was promptly, and thankfully, accepted. Leyland had made yet one more off-drive and a perfect stroke which sent the ball whizzing past cover-point before, in attempting a second run to a stroke which mid-off had misfielded, he was run out at the bowler's end, Bradman having dashed up from the region of mid-on to whip off the bails. So came the end of a truly magnificent innings, and never was the adage which declares that there is no run for a misfield more clearly demonstrated. He had batted in all for six and a half hours, during which time he had established a mastery over the bowlers as complete both in defence and attack as could be asked for.

### HUTTON IMPERTURBABLE

This wicket fell soon after 1 o'clock, which allowed Hammond a short spell of batting before luncheon. He took the opportunity to score 12 runs in one over off Fleetwood-Smith and when the interval did arrive the score had been taken to 434, of which Hutton had made 191. Afterwards Waite and McCabe started off full of good intentions with a new ball, and they certainly received some slight encouragement when Hammond twice in one over played out to the ball and missed it. Hutton, who had varied neither in his rate of scoring nor in his method from the very beginning of his innings, reached his 200 out of 447 runs on the board, and when O'Reilly came on again he first glided him to the leg boundary and followed this with a drive to the off which beat even Bradman for pace. Hammond was quiet to the point of being static, but the crowd, now accustomed to the atmosphere of time-limitless cricket, were prepared for anything but the fall of a wicket.

Both O'Reilly and Waite were allowed to bowl a series of maiden overs, and with O'Reilly concentrating on attacking Hammond's leg stump an hour of neutral cricket produced only 43 runs. Once Hammond drove a ball away to long-on, but for the rest he was content to play it back to the bowler, occasionally picking up an odd run here and there with the help of some excellent running between the wickets. Hutton was more inclined to force the ball through a line of off-side fieldsmen, but with Bradman doing the work of two, the bowlers, McCabe, in particular, could afford to bowl outside the off-stump without any fear of the scoring getting out of control. The 500 went up as it was bound to do sooner or later, and when Fleetwood-Smith came on again he did seem at first to be spinning the ball more sharply than he had done before. Hammond, to whom O'Reilly had no slip, reached his 50 with a drive past cover-point, the first of his real strokes that he had shown us. It is no disrespect to the bowlers who were toiling away, to the fieldsmen who were leaping about with continual enthusiasm, nor even to the batsmen, who were placidly doing their part, but as a game of cricket it was frankly passing through a dull phase.

### QUICK WICKETS

Suddenly nodding heads sprang with a jerk when Hammond, attempting to place to leg a ball from Fleetwood-Smith which came straight through, was leg-before-wicket. When in the very next over Paynter also was leg-before-wicket without having scored the game had indeed returned to life, and the whole state of affairs was altered, all this elaborate and careful building of a big score was almost wrecked, when Compton played well over a ball and was bowled. Leg-before-wicket or run out, yes one could understand that, but for someone to be cleaned bowled was bordering on the miraculous, so too was the bare fact that three wickets had tumbled down while only nine runs had been added.

Hardstaff, when his turn came to bat—and he is a handy and polished batsman to come in at the fall of the fifth wicket—made some of Fleetwood-Smith's bowling appear to be a little ragged and he had the opportunity to flog one ball away to the leg boundary and make two delicious off drives. Hutton as he was approaching R. E. Foster's score edged one ball off O'Reilly past first slip, a false stroke which obviously vexed so accurate a batsman, but he continued on his way afterwards with never the suggestion of a mistake.

More than 31,000 watched the cricket, and they must have left the ground convinced that whether it rains or whether it keeps fine England are in a position which even the might of Bradman will find hard to assail.

During the afternoon Fingleton had to leave the field with a strained leg-muscle, and he may not be able to field again in the match. White, the twelfth man, acted as substitute.

THE RECORD BREAKER. — L. Hutton, the young Yorkshire batsman, being congratulated by Bradman and Hardstaff after beating the record held by Bradman for the highest individual score in a match between England and Australia. There were rousing scenes at the Oval when he accomplished the feat.

The scoreboard at the close of England's innings.

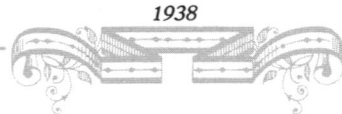

The end of the tour for Don Bradman.
Fracturing an ankle bone whilst bowling he had to be carried from the field.

# PHENOMENAL

ENGLAND, 903 for seven, declared. Hutton, 364. So England yesterday, in a Test match which rattled all the old records, carried first-class cricket figures to new peaks.

In Australia, no less than in this country, there will be unstinted admiration for England's tremendous batting and for the iron endurance which carried Hutton through more than 13 hours at the wicket.

And equally in both countries there will be deep disappointment and regret that Bradman, Australia's great mainstay, and Fingleton will be prevented by injury from helping to reply to this vast total. Our victory—which now seems inevitable—will be robbed of much zest.

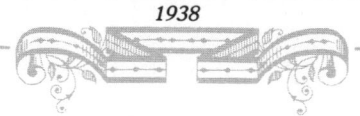

# "TIMELESS TESTS" NOT WANTED.

## ENGLISH REACTION TO OVAL MATCH.

### "Doping" of Wickets Condemned.

The fifth test match at The Oval, in which England defeated Australia by an innings and 579 runs, and so recorded the biggest win in test history, has aroused keen discussion on the question of whether test matches in England should be played to a finish and whether wickets should undergo such extensive "doping" as has been apparent at certain grounds.

There appears to be a preponderance of responsible opinion in favour of a time limit being restored for all tests in England. J. B. Hobbs says that the match at The Oval has completely altered his views on the matter.

R. E. S. Wyatt says it is imperative that the authorities should move to deal with the question of the over-preparation of wickets.

English critics express optimism regarding the future of English cricket, and they declare that England, all-round, was the superior team.

## HOBBS CHANGES HIS OPINION.

LONDON, Aug. 25.

Strong views on the question of what have come to be termed "timeless tests" are expressed by officials, former international players, and Press correspondents.

J. B. Hobbs writes in the "Star": "If Bradman and Fingleton had been able to bat and Australia had scored 400 or 500 in the first innings, England would have had to go in again, which would have been purgatory to any cricket lover. This match has completely altered my views on limitless tests. I do not want to see another in England. It was nice to see Hutton beat a record which I thought would stand perpetually, but one hour of the Leeds test was worth three and a half days at the Oval. We do not know whether Australia, assisted by Bradman and Fingleton, could have put up a fight; but I am convinced that if they had won the toss they would have scored much faster, as they play a natural game in timeless tests."

Sir Pelham Warner, who is a member of the M.C.C. and chairman of England's selection committee, and who has been a strong advocate of an extension of the time limit to five days, says: "It is certain that the English public will not stand for timeless tests, which are unsuited to our temperament. They are different in Australia. I may be influenced by the fact that England would have won at Nottingham and Lord's if there had been a fifth day's play, but I consider that five days is the right length. The wickets generally—and certainly those at The Oval—are too good and gave a tremendous advantage to the winner of the toss. The Oval wicket was easier than anything I have seen in Australia, and it was like playing on a feather bed."

Howard Marshall, writing in the "Daily Telegraph," says: "One thing is certain; there will never be another timeless test in this country. The match was a trial of endurance. Real cricket was knocked out with a wicket so unhelpful to the bowlers. The batting was largely a matter of patience and stamina. The second lesson is that the authorities will be forced to take drastic action against over-prepared wickets. The conditions were totally unfitted for a fair test of cricketing ability. But for the weather uncertainty, Australia might well have conceded England the match when Bradman called incorrectly."

R. E. S. Wyatt, writing in the "Daily Mail," says: "Each successive day added emphasis to the absurdity of timeless tests on the easy-paced, doped wickets provided for tests in England. It is imperative that the authorities move to prevent treatment of wickets that makes them useless to the bowlers."

Wilfred Rhodes, writing in the "Yorkshire Post," says that the luck has gone cruelly against England's opponents. He argues that five days is ample time to finish a test match, and says that a time limit eliminates the danger of batsmen sacrificing enterprise for the sake of monotonous safety-first methods.

# SPECULATION on Don Bradman's future can cease forthwith. ... He has rejected the last of many offers of employment in England, and leaves London to-day preparatory to returning to Australia and his regular job of stockbroking in Adelaide.

Which means, of course, that he will continue playing cricket for Australia. At the moment he could not play if he were offered £1 a run. He is still a cripple from that leg injury in the Oval Test.

Some of the firms who have been after him have painted rosy pictures of Don B. as a big business man. He could have had £50 a week to start—and more, if he had stuck out for it. In fact, his loyalty to Australian cricket has been put to a fairly severe test this last week or two.

He was bound by contract, in common with his team-mates, to return home at the end of the tour, but there would have been nothing to prevent his early return here.

Bradman, however, has plumped for home and glory, happy in the knowledge that the Ashes are going with him.

## Will He Return?

THE Australians are off to-day to Scarborough, where they are to meet Leveson-Gower's XI. After that they go to Dublin and Belfast, and then it will be homeward-bound.

Those who give Bradman a farewell handshake are sure to take it for granted he will be back again in 1942—but will he? For all we know, we may have seen the last of the great little man on English wickets.

Such a wonderful player may, of course, prove the exception to the general order, which is that Australian cricketers rarely pay more than three visits to England. You see, there is a four-years gap between each tour.

For proof, study the team which came in 1926 . . . Collins, Bardsley, MacCartney, Woodfull, Andrews, Gregory, Taylor, Richardson, Ryder, Oldfield, Mailey, Grimmett, Ponsford. Some returned on the next two tours, but by the fourth (1938) they were all written off the list by Father Time, loss of form, and other causes.

Happily, Bradman will be only 34 in 1942, but don't forget he has been playing Test cricket in England since 1930 and was doing so in Australia before that. The mere suggestion of not seeing those flashing Bradman strokes again is unpleasant—but one has got to take notice of cricket's history book.

Mrs. McCabe and Mrs. Bradman chat to Mrs. West whilst at Colombo.

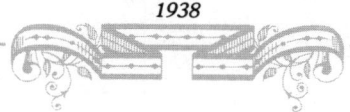

# Bradman hides in the country

*Daily Express Staff Reporter*

DON BRADMAN, his right foot in a red leather slipper, is hiding himself from fans in a two-storey, gabled, red-brick house in Buckinghamshire. He has been ordered complete rest and quiet.

On Monday he drove to London to see his doctor, who said that the ankle injured during the last Test match at the Oval is progressing well.

But Bradman may play no active games over here. Cricket must be ruled right out, even billiards—and the Lambeth Walk, which he used to perform with gusto before his accident.

## PLAYS BRIDGE

So his days at present are quiet. He breakfasts on the verandah at nine o'clock, then settles down to answering letters of sympathy from all over the world. He taps these out on his portable typewriter—at sixty words a minute—gets through sixty letters at a sitting.

After luncheon teetotaler, non-smoker Bradman has a snooze; then daily massage for the ankle.

The rest of the time he amuses himself playing bridge, the piano, or reading.

His host said to me that he knew nothing of any rumour that Bradman will stay in this country, accepting a business contract which he has been offered. He will return to Australia. And by the time he gets there, promised the doctor on Monday, he will be able to play cricket again.

# CRICKET WIVES
## AT MARSEILLES

### DON WAITS NEAR LONDON FOR MRS. BRADMAN

### ARRIVAL TO-MORROW

THE P. and O. liner Strathmore, with Mrs. Don Bradman, Mrs. McCabe and Mrs. W. H. Jeanes, wife of the manager of the Australian team, on board, reached Marseilles to-day. By travelling across France the cricket wives may arrive at Victoria at 3.30 to-morrow afternoon.

The Strathmore is due at Plymouth on the 15th and in the Port of London the following day.

Don Bradman is remaining near London to-day in readiness to meet his wife.

He has been staying for the past few days with friends in Buckinghamshire.

#### Last Games

Mr. Jeanes and the members of the Australian team left London before noon to-day for Scarborough where they begin their last match in England to-morrow against Mr. H. D. G. Leveson-Gower's XI.

They then wind up the tour at Dublin with a match against the Gentlemen of Ireland on the 15th.

Mrs. Bradman came over to England in 1934 to find her husband convalescing after an operation.

#### Recovering From Injury

Now he is recovering from the injury to his ankle caused when he was bowling in the Test at the Oval.

"Don is able to walk without a stick," Mr. Jeanes told an *Evening News* representative to-day, "and will be all right soon. He cannot yet run, and he is not accompanying the team north.

"There is no question of him accepting any business offer to stay in England. He has turned them all down, as we all knew he would.

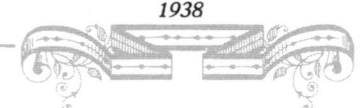

MRS BRAD-MAN has joined her famous cricket husband at Burnham (Buckinghamshire).

They are spending a few days there as the guests of a former English cricket captain, R. W. V. Robins, and Mrs Robins.

The Bradmans are on the left in the picture taken in the garden.

The Bradmans and the Robinses in the latter's garden at Slough.

Relaxing at the home of Mr. and Mrs. Robins.

## HERE'S A 'DOING FINE' BRADMAN BULLETIN

HAND raised to emphasise the point, Australia captain Don Bradman—he injured a foot in the last Test—has the last word (or hopes to) in a playful argument with his wife. Mrs. R. W. V. Robins (right), wife of the Middlesex cricketer, looks on. The Bradmans are her guests near Maidenhead. Mrs. Don arrived in England last week ; is spending a fortnight's holiday before returning with her husband to Australia.

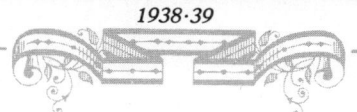

# *1938 ~ 39, 1939 ~ 40 Seasons*

Returning from the hard 1938 English tour, my ten years Test experience probably enabled me to combine mental and physical assets to the maximum. As evidence thereof, my seven first class innings in 1938–39 produced five centuries and one double century.

Nevertheless, I became conscious for the first time of a definite slowing up in muscle reaction and privately was contemplating retirement from cricket.

These thoughts were magnified in 1939–40 when it became increasingly difficult to combine an exacting sporting career with growing business responsibilities. But, as the later years reveal, other factors suddenly intruded and changed the course of history.

*Don Bradman*

## — SEASON 1938-39 —

| TITLE | GAMES | | SCORES | |
|---|---|---|---|---|
| Second Class | S.A.C.A. | Strathalbyn | 131 | C. |
| | " | Broken Hill | 37 | C. |
| | " | " " | 74 | C. |
| First Grade | Kensington | East Torrens | 49 | r.o. |
| | " | University | 146 | C. |
| | " | " | 110 | B. |
| | " | Glenelg | 11 | C. |
| | " | Port Adelaide | 37 | r.o. |
| | " | Colts | 34 | C. |
| | " | " | 22 | St. |
| First Class | Bradman's XI | Rigg's | 118 | B. |
| Sheffield Shield | South Australia | N.S.W. | 143 | B. |
| | " " | " | 135 | n.o. |
| | " " | Queensland | 225 | C. |
| | " " | " | 186 | C. |
| | " " | Victoria | 107 | C. |
| | " " | " | 5 | C. |
| | | Total runs | 1570 | |

## - SUMMARY -

AVERAGES -

| | Innings | N.O's | H.S. | Runs | Average |
|---|---|---|---|---|---|
| Sheffield Shield | 6 | 1 | 225 | 801 | 160·2 |
| Other First Class | 1 | 0 | 118 | 118 | 118·0 |
| All First Class | 7 | 1 | 225 | 919 | 153·1 |
| First Grade | 7 | 0 | 146 | 409 | 58·4 |
| Other Second Class | 3 | 0 | 131 | 242 | 80·6 |
| All Second Class | 10 | 0 | 146 | 651 | 65·1 |
| All Matches | 17 | 1 | 225 | 1570 | 98·1 |

# South Australia v New South Wales

SOUTH AUSTRALIA v NEW SOUTH WALES, at Adelaide, 16, 17, 19 and 20 December 1938.

South Australia — First Innings — 600 for 8 wickets dec.
— Second Innings — -

New South Wales — First Innings — 389
— Second Innings — 155

South Australia won by an innings and 54 runs.

DON BRADMAN — b. J. Murphy — 143
(Captain)

A wicket falling to the first ball of the match, DON BRADMAN was soon in, and he made a very quiet start, scoring only 39 before lunch. He took an hour and fifty-five minutes to reach 50, and three hours five minutes for his 100, his 143 lasting altogether three hours fifty minutes; it included eleven fours and as many as ninety-one singles. He gave no chance, and when he was out, soon after tea, at 242 for 3, playing a rather weary drive, he had helped C.L. Badcock add 175 for the third wicket. The match was played in great heat.

## South Australia

| | |
|---|---|
| K. Ridings b O'Reilly | 31 |
| R. S. Whitington c James b Murphy | 0 |
| D. G. Bradman b Murphy | 143 |
| C. L. Badcock not out | 271 |
| R. A. Hamence c Barnes b Fitzpatrick | 90 |
| C. W. Walker lbw b O'Reilly | 0 |
| M. G. Waite run out | 21 |
| F. A. Ward b Barnes | 0 |
| C. V. Grimmett run out | 35 |
| B 3, l-b 4, n-b 2 | 9 |

H. Cotton and J. Scott did not bat.

Eight wkts, dec 600

## New South Wales

| | | | |
|---|---|---|---|
| J. H. Fitzpatrick b Grimmett | 23 | — b Cotton | 5 |
| A. G. Cheetham st Walker b Grimmett | 27 | — c Cotton b Scott | 9 |
| C. M. Solomon c Walker b Grimmett | 1 | — c and b Grimmett | 13 |
| S. G. Barnes b Cotton | 117 | — c Whitington b Ward | 28 |
| J. H. Fingleton c Walker b Scott | 0 | — c Ward b Grimmett | 3 |
| A. G. Chipperfield c Walker b Cotton | 154 | — lbw b Ward | 13 |
| R. James lbw b Grimmett | 9 | — lbw b Grimmett | 42 |
| F. A. Easton c Walker b Grimmett | 17 | — not out | 7 |
| E. S. White lbw b Grimmett | 14 | — c and b Ward | 21 |
| W. J. O'Reilly lbw b Grimmett | 20 | — c Bradman b Ward | 7 |
| J. Murphy not out | 3 | — c Badcock b Grimmett | 4 |
| B 1, n-b 3 | 4 | B 1, l-b 2 | 3 |
| | **389** | | **155** |

## New South Wales Bowling

| | Overs | Mdns. | Runs | Wkts. | Overs | Mdns. | Runs | Wkts. |
|---|---|---|---|---|---|---|---|---|
| Murphy | 32 | 1 | 126 | 2 | | | | |
| Cheetham | 20 | 1 | 85 | 0 | | | | |
| O'Reilly | 36 | 9 | 99 | 2 | | | | |
| White | 28 | 1 | 103 | 0 | | | | |
| Chipperfield | 8 | 0 | 60 | 0 | | | | |
| Barnes | 15 | 2 | 62 | 1 | | | | |
| James | 1 | 0 | 13 | 0 | | | | |
| Fitzpatrick | 11 | 0 | 40 | 1 | | | | |
| Fingleton | 5 | 0 | 3 | 0 | | | | |

## South Australia Bowling

| | Overs | Mdns. | Runs | Wkts. | Overs | Mdns. | Runs | Wkts. |
|---|---|---|---|---|---|---|---|---|
| Cotton | 23 | 1 | 76 | 2 | 6 | 0 | 24 | 1 |
| Waite | 15 | 3 | 37 | 0 | 5 | 0 | 17 | 0 |
| Ward | 20 | 2 | 81 | 0 | 14 | 3 | 40 | 4 |
| Scott | 29 | 10 | 75 | 1 | 5 | 1 | 12 | 1 |
| Grimmett | 36.6 | 11 | 116 | 7 | 14.7 | 1 | 59 | 4 |

Umpires: J. D. Scott and A. G. Jenkins

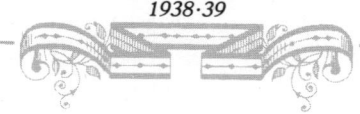

# Shield Cricket In Two States

## DETERMINED FIGHT BY
### NEW SOUTH WALES

### Barnes And Chipperfield Score Centuries

### GRIMMETT CAUSES EARLY COLLAPSE

#### By LONG ON

New South Wales, losing four wickets for 67 runs, in reply to South Australia's score of 600, in the Sheffield Shield cricket match at the Adelaide Oval, fought back in determined fashion yesterday.

From 67 the score was taken to 252 in a fine fifth-wicket partnership by Barnes (117), Chipperfield (149 not out), and then followed another useful unfinished stand of 58 for the seventh wicket by Chipperfield and Easton.

Grimmett's bowling was the feature of South Australia's out cricket yesterday. He took the first three wickets, and finished the day with four of the six which fell.

With four wickets in hand, New South Wales still requires 254 runs today—the last day—to stave off a first innings defeat.

There would have been some excuse for New South Wales, in view of the serious position into which it was forced by Grimmett's fine bowling before lunch, if it had adopted purely defensive tactics, but it did not.

Barnes and Chipperfield did not allow the position of the side to warp their judgment of the right ball to hit, and their partnership of 185 in 184 minutes compared favorably with the batting times of the Badcock-Hamence stand of Saturday.

Barnes is a more polished batsman than before he went abroad, but, probably because of his restraint in view of the position of the game, his front-of-the-wicket strokes lacked timing and power. He scored many runs square with the wicket on the off-side, cutting so late sometimes that his bat seemd to be within inches of the stumps. His was a most attractive innings, and his century was reached in only 19 minutes longer time than Badcock's on Saturday.

Chipperfield apparently needs a crisis to bring out his best cricket. Adelaide cricket-lovers have never seen him bat in better style. He was always master of the situation, despite the fact that he had one or two narrow squeaks, and his solidity was most discouraging to the South Australian attack, which saw its apparently impregnable position gradually weakened.

At lunch time New South Wales semed likely to follow on, but by tea, with the addition of 115 runs without loss there entered into the minds of South Australians some doubt as to whether even a first innings win was certain. By stumps, with the capture of two wickets for an additional 106 runs, the doubt was still there.

New South Wales, with Chipperfield and Easton at the wickets, and White, O'Reilly, and Murphy to bat, today, needs 105 to avoid the follow on, and 254 to avert defeat on the first innings.

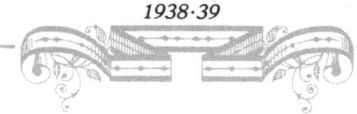

# South Australia
# v
# Queensland

SOUTH AUSTRALIA v QUEENSLAND, at Adelaide, 24, 26, 27 and 28 December 1938.

| | | |
|---|---|---|
| South Australia | - First Innings | 462 |
| | - Second Innings | - |
| Queensland | - First Innings | 131 |
| | - Second Innings | 311 |

South Australia won by an innings and 20 runs.

DON BRADMAN - c. G. Baker b. C. Christ          225
(Captain)

In at 17 for 1, DON BRADMAN had two hours and ten minutes' batting at the end of the first day's play, and had scored 83 not out at the close; he reached 50 in seventy-eight minutes. He took another twenty-five minutes to complete his century next morning, but good defensive bowling by C. Christ, a slow-medium left-hander, thereafter prevented him from quickening his scoring-rate as usual, and it took him five hours four minutes to score 200, and five hours twenty-nine minutes to reach 225; he was then caught at forward short-leg. He gave only one chance and hit fourteen fours.

This was his third century in succession, the seventh time that he had made three (or more) hundreds in consecutive innings.

## SOUTH AUSTRALIA
### First Innings

R. S. WHITINGTON, st. D. Tallon, b. Cook .. .. .. .. .. .. .. .. .. 11
K. RIDINGS, c. D. Tallon, b. Ellis .. 7
D. G. BRADMAN, c. Baker, b. Christ 225
C. L. BADCOCK, c. W. Tallon, b. Ellis 100
R. A. HAMENCE, c. and b. W. Tallon .. 17
M. G. WAITE, c. Guttormsen, b. Cook 52
C. W. WALKER, b. Baker .. .. .. .. 32
F. A. WARD, run out .. .. .. .. .. 9
C. V. GRIMMETT, not out .. .. .. .. 0
H. J. COTTON, b. Baker .. .. .. .. 0
J. SCOTT, b. Baker .. .. .. .. .. 0
Byes 6, leg-byes 2, wide 1 .. .. .. 9

Total .. .. .. .. .. .. 462

| 1 | 2 | 3 | 4 | 5 | 6 | 7 | 8 | 9 |
|---|---|---|---|---|---|---|---|---|
| 17 | 23 | 225 | 271 | 105 | 426 | 456 | 462 | 462 |

### Bowling

| | O. | M. | R. | W. |
|---|---|---|---|---|
| J. Ellis | 26 | — | 87 | 2 |
| G. C. Cook | 25 | 2 | 85 | 2 |
| C. Christ | 33 | 3 | 102 | 1 |
| G. Baker | 8.5 | — | 36 | 3 |
| W. Tallon | 18 | 1 | 90 | 1 |
| R. E. Rogers | 8 | 1 | 12 | 1 |
| T. Allen | 2 | — | 11 | — |

Baker bowled a wide.
Innings—131 minutes.

## QUEENSLAND
### First Innings

W. A. BROWN, c. Walker, b. Scott .. 12
R. ROGERS, c. Walker, b. Waite .. 0
T. ALLEN, b. Grimmett .. .. .. .. 21
D. TALLON, b. Grimmett .. .. .. .. 6
G. C. COOK, not out .. .. .. .. .. 34
G. BAKER, l.b.w., b. Grimmett .. .. 22
D. HANSEN, run out .. .. .. .. .. 12
M. GUTTORMSEN, c. K. Ridings, b. Ward .. .. .. .. .. .. .. .. .. 8
W. TALLON, b. Grimmett .. .. .. .. 6
J. ELLIS, l.b.w., b. Grimmett .. .. 1
C. CHRIST, st. Walker, b. Grimmett .. 0
Bye 1, leg-byes 3, no-balls 6 .. .. 10

Total .. .. .. .. .. .. 131

| 1 | 2 | 3 | 4 | 5 | 6 | 7 | 8 | 9 |
|---|---|---|---|---|---|---|---|---|
| 4 | 28 | 41 | 46 | 82 | 105 | 118 | 131 | 131 |

### Bowling

| | O. | M. | R. | W. |
|---|---|---|---|---|
| H. J. Cotton | 10 | 1 | 51 | — |
| M. G. Waite | 4 | — | 9 | 1 |
| J. Scott | 7 | 3 | 11 | 1 |
| C. V. Grimmett | 11.7 | 2 | 33 | 6 |
| F. A. Ward | 6 | — | 17 | 1 |

Cotton bowled six no-balls.
Innings—160 minutes.

### Second Innings

W. A. BROWN, not out .. .. .. .. .. 174
R. E. ROGERS, c. Bradman, b. Cotton 2
T. ALLEN, l.b.w., b. Ward .. .. .. 16
D. HANSEN, run out .. .. .. .. .. 11
D. TALLON, b. Cotton .. .. .. .. .. 11
G. C. COOK, b. Grimmett .. .. .. .. 35
G. BAKER, st. Walker, b. Ward .. .. 43
M. GUTTORMSEN, run out .. .. .. .. 7
W. TALLON, l.b.w., b. Grimmett .. .. 0
J. ELLIS, b. Grimmett .. .. .. .. 0
C. CHRIST, st. Walker, b. Ward .. .. 0
Byes 10, leg-bye 1, wide 1 .. .. .. 12

Total .. .. .. .. .. .. 311

| 1 | 2 | 3 | 4 | 5 | 6 | 7 | 8 | 9 |
|---|---|---|---|---|---|---|---|---|
| 3 | 53 | 73 | 98 | 206 | 301 | 310 | 310 | 310 |

### Bowling

| | O. | M. | R. | W. |
|---|---|---|---|---|
| H. J. Cotton | 18 | 2 | 62 | 2 |
| M. G. Waite | 9 | 1 | 20 | — |
| F. A. Ward | 38.4 | 8 | 106 | 3 |
| C. V. Grimmett | 31 | 3 | 96 | 3 |
| J. Scott | 9 | 7 | 15 | — |

Cotton bowled a wide.
Innings—351 minutes.

# S.A. And Victoria Well Ahead In Shield Cricket

## BRADMAN DOMINATES
### S.A. INNINGS AGAINST QUEENSLAND

### Visiting Team Needs 331 To Avoid Innings Defeat

#### By LONG ON

The dependence of South Australia for its runs upon Bradman and Badcock was strikingly exemplified yesterday, the second day of the Sheffield Shield match against Queensland at the Adelaide Oval. The Test pair between them scored 325 of the team's total of 462 runs, giving Queensland the task of making 331 to avoid an innings defeat with two days left for play.

Bradman, who scored 225 in less than five and a half hours play, added 202 for the third wicket in 151 minutes with Badcock, who was dismissed immediately he reached three figures.

Although Bradman did not at any time score at the breakneck speed with which he used to startle cricket crowds a few years ago, his innings was almost a perfect example of batsmanship. It was flawless until after he had passed his first century, and he was dismissed only because he relaxed his determination to play accurate left-arm bowling in the proper manner, and attempted a spectacular hit off Christ, whose ability to pin the batsmen to their creases was a feature of the day's play.

# OUTRIGHT WIN FOR S.A.
## IN SHIELD MATCH

## Queensland Beaten By An Innings And 20 Runs

### BROWN (174) CARRIES BAT

#### By LONG ON

South Australia, with nearly three hours to spare, defeated Queensland in the Sheffield Shield cricket match at Adelaide Oval yesterday by an innings and 20 runs.

The Queensland tail-enders collapsed before the slow bowling of Grimmett and Ward, the score at 2 p.m.—an hour before the finish, being five for 269.

Brown (Queensland captain) carried his bat throughout the innings for 174 not out—undoubtedly the best innings of the match.

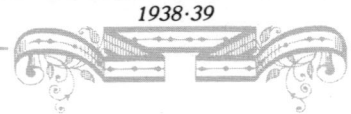

# South Australia
# v
# Victoria

SOUTH AUSTRALIA v VICTORIA, at Melbourne, 30, 31 December 1938, 2 and 3 January 1939.

| South Australia | - First Innings | 488 |
| | - Second Innings | 50 for no wicket |
| Victoria | - First Innings | 499 |
| | - Second Innings | 283 for 7 wickets dec. |

Drawn.

| DON BRADMAN | - c. A.L. Hassett b. M.W. Sievers | 107 |
| (Captain) | - (did not bat) | |

DON BRADMAN went in at 70 for 1 on the second afternoon, and had made only 6 when he was missed at square-leg off M.W. Sievers; thereafter, despite a sore throat, he batted very brightly, against bowlers who also included E.L. McCormick, D.T. Ring and L.O'B. Fleetwood-Smith. He reached 50 in sixty-two minutes, and 100 in an hour and forty-one minutes, before being caught at cover. He hit nine fours, and batted for only an hour and forty-six minutes. This December, as in December 1937, he made 593 runs, his highest in one month in Australia, a record for a South Australian batsman. This was his fourth century in successive innings, the second time he had done this in Australia.

He brought his aggregate for the year 1938 to 3838 (in forty innings), the second highest total by an Australian batsman for a year's cricket; his own 4368 (fifty-two innings) in 1930 is the highest. His forty innings (six not-outs) this year included twenty-two centuries and seven other innings of over 50 - an extraordinary example of his consistency.

## Victoria

| | | | |
|---|---|---|---|
| K. E. Rigg b Waite | 7 | — b Waite | 51 |
| L. S. Lee c Walker b Scott | 6 | — b Waite | 51 |
| R. G. Gregory st Walker b Ward | 71 | — c Sub b Ward | 9 |
| A. L. Hassett not out | 211 | — st Walker b Ward | 54 |
| J. A. Ledward c Scott b Waite | 2 | — c and b Ward | 0 |
| F. W. Sides run out | 44 | — c Scott b P. Ridings | 61 |
| B. A. Barnett lbw b Ward | 50 | — b Ward | 54 |
| M. W. Sievers b Ward | 1 | — not out | 20 |
| D. Ring c Hamence b Waite | 51 | — st Walker b Ward | 19 |
| R. L. McCormick b P. Ridings | 0 | — not out | 1 |
| L. O'B. Fleetwood-Smith b Ward | 43 | | |
| L-b 6, n-b 7 | 13 | B 6, l-b 2, w 1, n-b 5 | 14 |
| | **499** | Seven wkts., dec. | **283** |

## South Australia

| | | | |
|---|---|---|---|
| R. S. Whitington lbw b Sievers | 100 | — not out | 27 |
| K. L. Ridings c Lee b Sievers | 27 | — not out | 18 |
| D. G. Bradman c Hassett b Sievers | 107 | | |
| C. L. Badcock c and b McCormick | 1 | | |
| C. W. Walker b Sievers | 14 | | |
| F. A. Ward c Barnett b Sievers | 62 | | |
| R. A. Hamence b Sievers | 84 | | |
| M. G. Waite lbw b Ring | 0 | | |
| P. Ridings c and b Ring | 33 | | |
| C. V. Grimmett st Barnett b Ring | 34 | | |
| J. Scott not out | 4 | | |
| B 5, l-b 15, n-b 2 | 22 | B 5 | 5 |
| | **488** | No wkt. | **50** |

## South Australia Bowling

| | Overs | Mdns. | Runs | Wkts. | Overs | Mdns. | Runs | Wkts. |
|---|---|---|---|---|---|---|---|---|
| P. Ridings | 19.2 | 3 | 73 | 1 | 9 | 0 | 37 | 1 |
| Waite | 32 | 5 | 123 | 3 | 24 | 6 | 63 | 1 |
| Scott | 17 | 2 | 67 | 1 | 13 | 1 | 43 | 0 |
| Grimmett | 25 | 0 | 98 | 0 | | | | |
| Ward | 25 | 1 | 125 | 4 | 27 | 4 | 126 | 5 |

## Victoria Bowling

| | Overs | Mdns. | Runs | Wkts. | Overs | Mdns. | Runs | Wkts. |
|---|---|---|---|---|---|---|---|---|
| McCormick | 22 | 4 | 78 | 1 | 3 | 1 | 13 | 0 |
| Sievers | 43 | 11 | 95 | 6 | 3 | 0 | 9 | 0 |
| Ring | 31.1 | 2 | 116 | 3 | 6 | 1 | 8 | 0 |
| Fleetwood-Smith | 35 | 4 | 152 | 0 | 3 | 1 | 2 | 0 |
| Gregory | 4 | 0 | 25 | 0 | 4 | 3 | 3 | 0 |
| Hassett | | | | | 2 | 0 | 10 | |

Umpires: A. N. Barlow and G. A. Browne

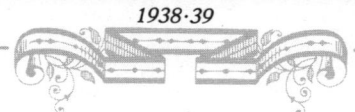

# VICTORIA 363
## FOR 7 WICKETS

### Good Recovery After Poor Start

## HASSETT, 151 n.o., SAVES COLLAPSE

### Cotton Unable To Play

MELBOURNE, December 30.

Recovering well after a poor start, in which two wickets were lost for 23 runs, Victoria batted consistently to score 363 for the loss of seven wickets in the Sheffield Shield cricket match against South Australia, which began on the Melbourne Cricket Ground today. Victoria's total was mainly due to a splendid score of 151 not out from Hassett, who defied the South Australian bowlers for four hours and a half, and good hands from Gregory, Barnett, and Sides.

When Victoria's fourth wicket fell at 134 a collapse appeared imminent, but Hassett and Sides stopped the rot, and Barnett helped Hassett to strengthen the advantage by making a splendid 50.

Ward, who took three for 78 off 18 overs, was South Australia's most successful bowler. Cotton, who is suffering from an attack of influenza, was not available for selection, and Moyle was 12th man for the visitors. The Victorian 12th man was Bromley.

The attendance of 16,706 was the best for the season, and the gate receipts were £736 1/2.

# S.A. FACES
## DEFEAT

### Heavy Scoring On Saturday

## BRILLIANT 211 N.O. TO HASSETT

### Centuries To Whitington And Bradman

MELBOURNE, January 1.

A brilliant recovery by Victoria, which included a double century by Lindsay Hassett, and centuries from Bradman and Whitington for South Australia, made the second day of play on Saturday in the Sheffield Shield cricket match between Victoria and South Australia one of the most interesting of the season.

When play was continued in the morning Victoria had lost seven for 363, and, before the last wicket fell, its total had been carried on to 499. Hassett's splendid 211 not out and surprise scores of 51 from Ring and 43 from Fleetwood-Smith were the main factors in the recovery.

South Australia appeared to be set for a big score when Bradman and Whitington became associated, and the pair scored 157 for the second wicket, but both were dismissed within a few overs of each other and at stumps South Australia had lost four for 240.

Bradman, in making 107 in 106 minutes, displayed his very best form after a shaky start, and gave a glorious exhibition. Whitington, who made 100, was more sedate, but did great work for his side.

The attendance was the largest for the season, numbering 28,637, and the takings were £1,280. The total attendances and takings are now 45,890 and £2,030.

# VICTORIA LEADS
## IN SHIELD MATCHES

### First Innings Win Against S.A.

## LITTLE INTEREST IN LAST DAY'S PLAY

### Three Members Of Teams Absent

MELBOURNE, January 3.

Little interest was left in the match when the last day of play in the Sheffield Shield game between Victoria and South Australia began on the Melbourne Cricket Ground today, and it eventually ended in a first innings win for the home team.

With a first innings lead of 11 runs, Victoria resumed its second innings today and carried its overnight score of none for 16 to seven for 283 before it closed soon after tea. South Australia was then content to play quietly until stumps.

Only for a short time today, when Victoria had lost four wickets for the addition of only 42 runs and it appeared that South Australia might make another fighting recovery, did the game become really interesting, but a partnership between Hassett and Sides, followed by another between Sides and Sievers, made the game safe for Victoria.

South Australia was again without the services of Bradman, its captain, who rested following an attack of laryngitis, and Grimmett, who strained a leg while batting yesterday. Rigg, the Victorian captain, who is also suffering from a strained groin, did not bat or field.

The total takings and attendance figures for the match were 68,131 and £2,897 4/ respectively.

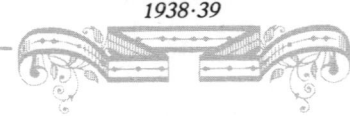

# South Australia v Queensland

SOUTH AUSTRALIA v QUEENSLAND, at Brisbane,
7, 9, 10 and 11 January 1939.

| South Australia | - First Innings | 557 |
| | - Second Innings | 14 for no wicket |
| Queensland | - First Innings | 336 |
| | - Second Innings | 233 |

South Australia won by 10 wickets.

DON BRADMAN — c. C. Christ b. W. Tallon     186
(Captain)    - (did not bat)     -

When DON BRADMAN went in seventy-two minutes from the end of the second day's play, R.S. Whitington and K.L. Ridings had added 197 for the first wicket, and there was little in the bowling to prevent Bradman scoring another century. 42 not out overnight, he reached 50 next morning after eighty-eight minutes' batting, and progressed slowly to his hundred; he was 92 not out at lunch, having taken the whole morning session of one and three-quarter hours to add 50 to his overnight score. However, he reached 100 soon after the interval, after three hours twelve minutes, and his 186 took altogether four hours forty-seven minutes; it was a catch at square-leg which dismissed him, at 530 for 6. He gave no chance, and hit nineteen fours.

This was his fifth successive century, a record for Australia.

## Queensland

| | | | | | |
|---|---|---|---|---|---|
| W. A. Brown c K. Ridings b Waite | 1 | — lbw b K. Ridings | 81 |
| G. G. Cook b Cotton | 22 | — b K. Ridings | 2 |
| T. Allen c Ward b Cotton | 5 | — b Cotton | 5 |
| R. Rogers run out | 11 | — c K. Ridings b Ward | 45 |
| D. Tallon b Cotton | 115 | — absent hurt | 0 |
| C. Stibe c Walker b K. Ridings | 58 | — lbw b Scott | 23 |
| G. Baker b K. Ridings | 78 | — b K. Ridings | 17 |
| W. Tallon c Walker b Ward | 23 | — not out | 40 |
| P. L. Dixon b Cotton | 2 | — b K. Ridings | 4 |
| J. Ellis b Cotton | 1 | — c K. Ridings b Cotton | 5 |
| C. Christ not out | 2 | — run out | 1 |
| B 6, l-b 9, n-b 3 | 18 | B 4, l-b 2, w 1, n-b 3 | 10 |
| | **336** | | **233** |

## South Australia

| | | | |
|---|---|---|---|
| K. L. Ridings b Ellis | 122 | — not out | 10 |
| R. S. Whitington c D. Tallon b W. Tallon | 125 | | |
| D. G. Bradman c Christ b W. Tallon | 186 | | |
| C. L. Badcock c Rogers b Christ | 1 | — not out | 4 |
| R. A. Hamence c Stibe b Christ | 13 | | |
| E. J. R. Moyle c Brown b Cook | 46 | | |
| C. W. Walker c and b W. Tallon | 20 | | |
| F. A. Ward b Ellis | 18 | | |
| H. J. Cotton st Brown b W. Tallon | 2 | | |
| J. Scott not out | 5 | | |
| M. W. Waite absent ill | 0 | | |
| B 3, l-b 9, w 5, n-b 2 | 19 | | |
| | **557** | No wkt. | **14** |

## South Australia Bowling

| | Overs | Mdns. | Runs | Wkts. | Overs | Mdns. | Runs | Wkts. |
|---|---|---|---|---|---|---|---|---|
| Cotton | 25 | 5 | 49 | 5 | 16.6 | 4 | 49 | 2 |
| Waite | 21 | 2 | 86 | 1 | | | | |
| Scott | 23 | 6 | 48 | 0 | 15 | 1 | 55 | 1 |
| Ward | 24 | 1 | 108 | 1 | 25 | 6 | 93 | 1 |
| K. Ridings | 5 | 1 | 27 | 2 | 6 | 1 | 26 | 4 |

## Queensland Bowling

| | Overs | Mdns. | Runs | Wkts. | Overs | Mdns. | Runs | Wkts. |
|---|---|---|---|---|---|---|---|---|
| Ellis | 32.7 | 1 | 126 | 2 | | | | |
| Cook | 25 | 0 | 101 | 1 | | | | |
| Dixon | 19 | 2 | 93 | 0 | | | | |
| Christ | 43 | 9 | 110 | 2 | | | | |
| W. Tallon | 20 | 2 | 80 | 4 | | | | |
| Allen | 1 | 0 | 4 | 0 | | | | |
| Baker | 3 | 0 | 24 | 0 | 1 | 1 | 0 | 0 |
| Stibe | | | | | 1 | 0 | 9 | 0 |
| Rogers | | | | | 0.7 | 0 | 5 | 0 |

Umpires: K. Fagg and F. J. Bartlett

Reproduction of a painting of Don Bradman by J. C. Goodhart, an Adelaide artist, *c.* 1940.

A portrait of Sir Donald Bradman, by Ivor Hele, *c.* 1946.

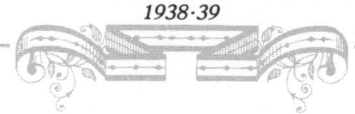

# BRADMAN'S
## FIFTH CENTURY
## IN SUCCESSION

---

## S.A. Consolidates
## Strong Position

---

## FIRST INNINGS
## LEAD OF 221

---

BRISBANE, January 10.
By making 186 in the Shield match today Bradman scored his fifth consecutive century in Australian first-class cricket and created another record, eclipsing the previous one of four successive centuries held by himself and C. G. Macartney. It was Bradman's 86th century in all first-class cricket. His score so consolidated South Australia's position that Queensland's only chance tomorrow is to save an outright defeat.

South Australia's total of 557 left Queensland 221 in arrears. The home team, in the second innings, lost one for 73. Both sides were handicapped to-day. A thumb injury caused D. Tallon to retire and Brown substituted as wicketkeeper. Waite, who is still in hospital, did not bat for South Australia.

A posed photograph showing Bradman making a straight drive.

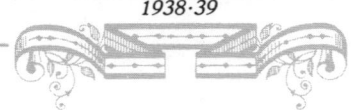

# South Australia
# v
# New South Wales

SOUTH AUSTRALIA v NEW SOUTH WALES, at Sydney, 14 and 18 January 1939.

| South Australia | - First Innings | 349 for 4 wickets dec. |
| | - Second Innings | - |
| New South Wales | - First Innings | 246 |
| | - Second Innings | 156 for 5 wickets |
| | Drawn. | |

| DON BRADMAN | - not out | 135 |
| (Captain) | | |

In 1901, seven years before DON BRADMAN was born, C. B. Fry made six centuries in successive innings, a feat which had hitherto stood unapproached, until in this match Bradman equalled it; no one else had ever made more than four in succession.

On the first day - when incidentally he kept wicket throughout the New South Wales innings in stifling heat - he went in at 76 for 1, and scored 22 not out in thirty-five minutes' batting before the close of play; rain then prevented any play at all on 16 and 17 January. When the game was resumed, he continued to bat soundly if rather cautiously; he completed 50 in one and a quarter hours, and finally reached his century in two hours fifty minutes. Just before that, when 87, he mishit a ball which luckily did not go to hand. He batted for three hours twenty minutes, and hit seven fours.

This was Bradman's fifth century in succession for South Australia and in Sheffield Shield Matches, only C. Hill and Bradman having previously made as many as three in succession for South Australia. This was also his eighth successive hundred on Australian wickets.

### SOUTH AUSTRALIA
#### First Innings

| | | |
|---|---|---|
| R. S. WHITINGTON, l.b.w., b. Barnes | .. | 59 |
| K. RIDINGS, l.b.w., b. Cheetham .. | .. | 28 |
| D. G. BRADMAN, not out .. | .. | 135 |
| F. A. WARD, c. O'Brien, b. Hynes .. | .. | 18 |
| C. L. BADCOCK, c. and b. Hynes .. | .. | 98 |
| Sundries—Bye 1, Leg-byes 2, no-balls 8 | | 11 |
| | | |
| Total (for four wickets) .. .. .. | .. | 349 |
| Innings declared closed. | | |

#### Bowling

| | O. | M. | R. | W. |
|---|---|---|---|---|
| O'Brien .. .. .. .. .. | 15 | — | 76 | — |
| Hynes .. .. .. .. .. | 16.3 | — | 80 | 2 |
| Cheetham .. .. .. .. | 28 | 1 | 104 | 1 |
| Pepper .. .. .. .. .. | 7 | — | 47 | — |
| Barnes .. .. .. .. .. | 8 | 2 | 28 | 1 |

### NEW SOUTH WALES
#### First Innings

| | | |
|---|---|---|
| A. CHEETHAM, c. Bradman, b. Grimmett .. .. .. .. .. .. | .. | 10 |
| B. McCAULEY, l.b.w., b. Grimmett .. | .. | 25 |
| S. BARNES, b. P. Ridings .. | .. | 12 |
| A. G. CHIPPERFIELD, c. Cotton, b. Waite .. .. .. .. .. | .. | 15 |
| C. SOLOMON, c. P. Ridings, b. Ward | .. | 34 |
| C. PEPPER, c. Waite, b. Grimmett .. | .. | 17 |
| V. McCAFFREY, c. P. Ridings, b. Grimmett .. .. .. .. .. | .. | 6 |
| R. JAMES, b. Cotton .. .. .. | .. | 45 |
| L. C. HYNES, not out .. .. .. | .. | 63 |
| S. SISMEY, c. P. Ridings, b. Cotton .. | .. | 6 |
| L. O'BRIEN, b. Cotton .. .. .. | .. | 0 |
| Sundries .. .. .. .. .. .. | .. | 13 |
| | | |
| Total .. .. .. .. .. | .. | 246 |

Fall of wickets—32, 46, 50, 90, 102, 118, 148, 226, 246.

#### Bowling

| | O. | M. | R. | W. |
|---|---|---|---|---|
| Cotton .. .. .. .. | 10.6 | 1 | 44 | 3 |
| Waite .. .. .. .. .. | 11 | 1 | 49 | 1 |
| Grimmett .. .. .. .. | 15 | 3 | 53 | 4 |
| P. Ridings .. .. .. .. | 7 | 1 | 37 | 1 |
| Ward .. .. .. .. .. | 7 | — | 41 | 1 |
| K. Ridings .. .. .. .. | 2 | — | 9 | — |

Waite bowled a wide, and P. Ridings and Cotton each two no-balls.

#### Second Innings

| | | |
|---|---|---|
| B. V. McAULEY, run out .. .. .. | .. | 76 |
| A. G. CHEETHAM, c. Moyle, b. P. Ridings | .. | 25 |
| S. G. BARNES, c. Cotton, b. Grimmett .. | .. | 33 |
| A. G. CHIPPERFIELD, st. Moyle, b. Waite | .. | 12 |
| C. SOLOMON, c. P. Ridings, b. Grimmett | .. | 0 |
| R. JAMES, not out .. .. .. .. | .. | 4 |
| C. PEPPER, not out .. .. .. .. | .. | 0 |
| Sundries—Byes 3, leg-byes 3 .. .. | .. | 6 |
| | | |
| Total (for five wickets) .. .. .. | .. | 156 |

#### Bowling

| | O. | M. | R. | W. |
|---|---|---|---|---|
| Cotton .. .. .. .. .. | 3 | — | 14 | — |
| Waite .. .. .. .. .. | 8 | 1 | 18 | 1 |
| P. Ridings .. .. .. .. | 8 | — | 19 | 1 |
| Grimmett .. .. .. .. | 15 | 1 | 51 | 2 |
| Ward .. .. .. .. .. | 9 | — | 51 | — |

# Bradman Equals World's Record

## SCORES SIXTH CENTURY IN SUCCESSION

## South Aust. Wins Easily On First Innings

### By ARTHUR MAILEY.

WITHOUT giving a chance, Don Bradman yesterday equalled C. B. Fry's world record by scoring his sixth successive century in first-class cricket.

He was playing for South Australia in the Sheffield Shield game against New South Wales. South Australia won on the first innings.

When Bradman reached his 100 with a straight drive players ran in from the outfield to congratulate him.

The stroke that gave him the necessary runs brought an excited shout from the spectators, and loud cheers greeted his feat.

Bradman's century had taken 173 minutes, and included only three fours, but the heavy outfield slowed up the scoring rate.

When his partner, Badcock, was caught and bowled by Hynes for 98, Bradman, who was then 135, closed his side's innings.

South Australia had then lost four for 349, and was 103 in front of New South Wales on the first innings.

### Five Wickets Lost

New South Wales, who began the second innings at 3.30 p.m., lost five wickets for 156 before an appeal against the light was upheld at 5.48 p.m.

The Badcock-Bradman partnership, which yielded 186 runs in 126 minutes, was the highlight of the day.

Badcock scored a little faster than Bradman, but he had more of the strike.

He had a couple of lives—the first when he was only two—but he punched the ball powerfully.

He reached 50 in 75 minutes. His 98, in 126 minutes, included eight fours.

Bradman was never troubled, but he seemed bent on equalling Fry's record, and did not reveal any daring until he had accomplished the feat.

### Opens Shoulders

Then he jumped down the wicket and drove all bowlers with great force.

His last 35 runs, which included four fours, took only 28 minutes. His sole chance was at 133, when Hynes missed him in the covers off Cheetham.

McCauley again did well as an opening batsman for New South Wales, but had the misfortune to be run out for 76.

It was his call for a shot into the covers, but James sent him back.

Moyle, who kept wickets for South Australia, caught one and stumped another.

The attendance was 4464, and the takings were £211/7/6.

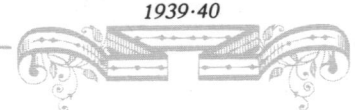

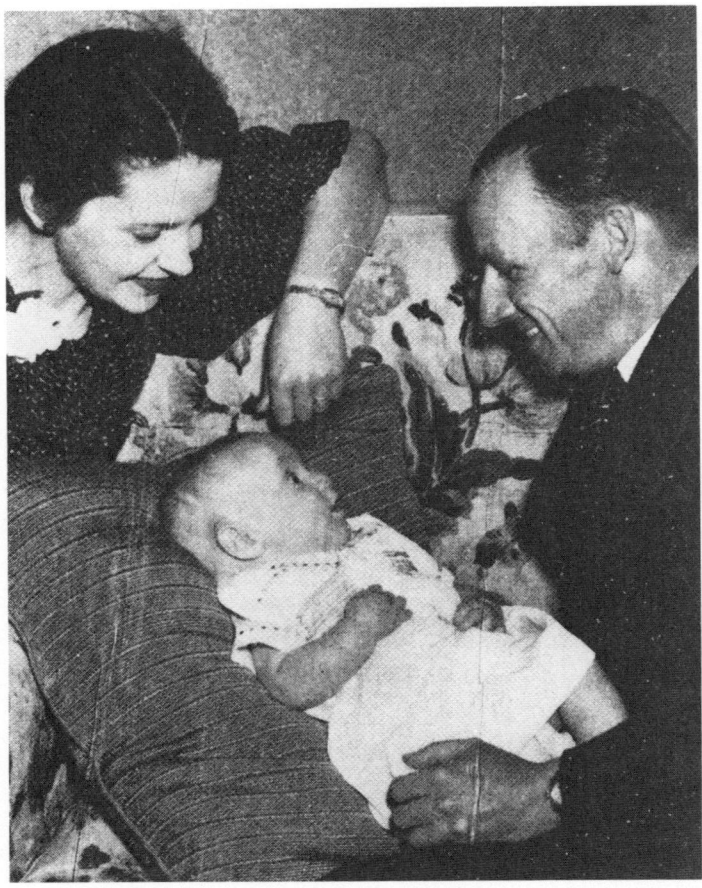

A special study by a staff photographer of Mr. and Mrs. Don Bradman and their son, John Russell, born on July 10. This photograph, taken at their home, Kensington Gardens, last night, is the first family group.

## — SEASON 1939-40 —

| TITLE | GAMES | | SCORES | |
|---|---|---|---|---|
| Second Class | S.A.C.A. | Kadina | 62 | C. |
| | " | Port Lincoln | 1 | B. |
| | " | " | 32 | C. |
| First Grade | Kensington | Sturt | 3 | C. |
| | " | " | 27 | B. |
| | " | Port Adelaide | 188 | B. |
| | " | West Torrens | 49 | C. |
| | " | Glenelg | 303 | C. |
| | " | East Torrens | 11 | B. |
| | " | " | 32 | n.o. |
| | " | West Torrens | 125 | C. |
| First Class | The Rest | N.S.W. | 25 | C. |
| | " | " | 2 | C. |
| | South Australia | Western Australia | 42 | C. |
| | " " | " " | 209 | n.o. |
| | " " | " " | 135 | C. |
| | " " | Victoria | 76 | r.o. |
| | " " | " | 64 | L.B.W. |
| | " " | N.S.W. | 251 | n.o. |
| | " " | " | 90 | n.o. |
| | " " | " | 39 | L.B.W. |
| | " " | " | 40 | C. |
| | " " | Queensland | 138 | C. |
| | " " | " | 0 | C. |
| | " " | " | 97 | C. |
| | " " | Victoria | 267 | C. |
| | | Total runs | 2308 | |

## — SUMMARY —

AVERAGES -

| | Innings | N.O.'s | H.S. | Runs | Average |
|---|---|---|---|---|---|
| Sheffield Shield | 10 | 2 | 267 | 1062 | 132·7 |
| Other First Class | 5 | 1 | 209* | 413 | 103·2 |
| All First Class | 15 | 3 | 267 | 1475 | 122·7 |
| First Grade | 8 | 1 | 303 | 738 | 105·4 |
| Other Second Class | 3 | 0 | 62 | 95 | 31·6 |
| All Second Class | 11 | 1 | 303 | 833 | 83·3 |
| All Matches | 26 | 4 | 303 | 2308 | 104·9 |

Don Bradman's home in Adelaide.

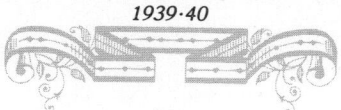

# South Australia
# v
# New South Wales

SOUTH AUSTRALIA v NEW SOUTH WALES, at Adelaide, 15, 16 and 18 December 1939.

| | | |
|---|---|---|
| South Australia | - First Innings | 430 |
| | - Second Innings | 156 for 3 wickets |
| New South Wales | - First Innings | 336 |
| | - Second Innings | 248 |

South Australia won by 7 wickets.

| | | |
|---|---|---|
| DON BRADMAN | - not out | 251 |
| (Captain) | - not out | 90 |

DON BRADMAN was in his most masterful form in this game, and played two superb innings. He started his first innings forty minutes from the end of the first day's play, at 17 for 1, and in that time made 27 not out; next morning, his 50 was achieved in an hour and twenty-three minutes, and his century, just before lunch, in two hours nineteen minutes. Batting one short, South Australia were 19 runs behind on the first innings, when the seventh wicket fell, Bradman's score was 164; thereafter he took complete control of the game. Bradman's 200 took four hours eight minutes, and he then added a further 51 in twenty-three minutes, batting for four hours thirty-one minutes altogether for his 251 not out, which was sixty-two per cent of his side's total. He hit two sixes and thirty-eight fours. In scoring 164 in boundaries, Bradman broke his own Sheffield Shield record for South Australia, 160 (forty fours) in his 357 v. Victoria in 1935-6. Bradman again dominated the scene when South Australia required 155 to win on the third afternoon. In at 9 for 1, he reached 50 in sixty-four minutes, and batted for an hour and forty minutes for his 90 not out, the game being over just before the tea interval; he hit fourteen fours.

## PLAY IN FIGURES
### Scoreboard

**SOUTH AUSTRALIA**
**First Innings**

| | |
|---|---|
| R. S. WHITINGTON, c. Sismey, b. Roper | 6 |
| K. RIDINGS, c. Sismey, b. Walsh | 29 |
| D. G. BRADMAN, not out | 251 |
| A. HAMENCE, l.b.w., b. Pepper | 41 |
| M. G. WAITE, b. Cheetham | 46 |
| T. KLOSE, c. and b. O'Reilly | 4 |
| J. TREGONING, b. O'Reilly | 0 |
| W. WALKER, b. O'Reilly | 1 |
| A. WARD, b. O'Reilly | 4 |
| C. V. GRIMMETT, b. O'Reilly | 17 |
| H. J. COTTON, absent (injured) | 0 |
| Byes, 21; leg-byes 4; no-balls, 6 | 31 |
| **Total** | **430** |

| 1 | 2 | 3 | 4 | 5 | 6 | 7 | 8 |
|---|---|---|---|---|---|---|---|
| 17 | 69 | 161 | 308 | 313 | 313 | 317 | 349 |

**Bowling**

| | O. | M. | R. | W. |
|---|---|---|---|---|
| A. Roper | 14 | — | 83 | 1 |
| A. G. Cheetham | 15 | 1 | 80 | 1 |
| W. J. O'Reilly | 22.1 | 4 | 108 | 5 |
| C. Pepper | 9 | — | 56 | 1 |
| J. Walsh | 12 | — | 72 | 1 |

Roper bowled three no-balls; Cheetham two and O'Reilly one.
Innings—293 minutes.

**Second Innings**

| | |
|---|---|
| K. RIDINGS, b. Cheetham | 20 |
| T. KLOSE, b. Roper | 2 |
| D. G. BRADMAN, not out | 90 |
| R. A. HAMENCE, l.b.w., b. Pepper | 12 |
| M. G. WAITE, not out | 28 |
| Bye 1, leg-byes 3 | 4 |
| **Total (for three wickets)** | **156** |

| 1 | 2 | 3 |
|---|---|---|
| 9 | 57 | 87 |

**Bowling**

| | O. | M. | R. | W. |
|---|---|---|---|---|
| A. Roper | 3 | — | 26 | 1 |
| A. G. Cheetham | 7 | — | 33 | 1 |
| W. J. O'Reilly | 10 | — | 29 | — |
| C. Pepper | 8 | — | 31 | 1 |
| J. Walsh | 2.2 | — | 33 | — |

Innings—112 minutes.

**NEW SOUTH WALES**
**First Innings**

| | |
|---|---|
| S. J. McCABE, l.b.w., b. Grimmett | 40 |
| J. H. FINGLETON, c. Bradman, b. Grimmett | 29 |
| S. G. BARNES, b. Waite | 2 |
| C. SOLOMON, c. Tregonning, b. Klose | 131 |
| A. G. CHIPPERFIELD, b. Cotton | 32 |
| A. G. CHEETHAM, c. Bradman, b. Tregonning | 32 |
| C. PEPPER, l.b.w., b. Klose | 22 |
| A. ROPER, c. K. Ridings, b. Grimmett | 15 |
| W. J. O'REILLY, c. Walker, b. Klose | 16 |
| S. SISMEY, not out | 5 |
| J. WALSH, b. Klose | 1 |
| Byes 2, leg-byes 8, wide 1 | 11 |
| **Total** | **336** |

| 1 | 2 | 3 | 4 | 5 | 6 | 7 | 8 | 9 |
|---|---|---|---|---|---|---|---|---|
| 63 | 70 | 74 | 130 | 225 | 283 | 298 | 322 | 330 |

**Bowling**

| | O. | M. | R. | W. |
|---|---|---|---|---|
| H. J. Cotton | 12 | — | 51 | 1 |
| M. G. Waite | 10 | 1 | 98 | 1 |
| C. V. Grimmett | 20 | — | 102 | 3 |
| F. A. Ward | 5 | — | 42 | — |
| J. Tregonning | 3 | — | 9 | 1 |
| T. Klose | 5.4 | 1 | 23 | 4 |

Tregonning bowled a wide.
Innings—253 minutes.

**Second Innings**

| | |
|---|---|
| S. J. McCABE, l.b.w., b. Grimmett | 47 |
| J. H. FINGLETON, b. Klose | 2 |
| C. SOLOMON, c. Tregonning, b. Grimmett | 46 |
| A. G. CHIPPERFIELD, l.b.w., b. Grimmett | 57 |
| A. ROPER, c and b. Ward | 0 |
| S. G. BARNES, c. Walker, b. Ward | 33 |
| A. G. CHEETHAM, b. Grimmett | 5 |
| C. PEPPER, c. Grimmett, b. Klose | 47 |
| W. J. O'REILLY, c. Tregonning, b. Grimmett | 5 |
| S. SISMEY, c. Tregoning, b. Grimmett | 3 |
| J. WALSH, not out | 0 |
| Bye 1, leg-byes 5 | 6 |
| **Total** | **248** |

| 1 | 2 | 3 | 4 | 5 | 6 | 7 | 8 | 9 |
|---|---|---|---|---|---|---|---|---|
| 16 | 60 | 122 | 139 | 171 | 179 | 238 | 244 | 248 |

**Bowling**

| | O. | M. | R. | W. |
|---|---|---|---|---|
| M. G. Waite | 12 | 1 | 22 | — |
| T. Klose | 7 | 1 | 37 | 2 |
| C. V. Grimmett | 20.5 | 1 | 122 | 6 |
| F. A. Ward | 15 | 4 | 61 | 2 |

Innings—183 minutes.

## Outright Shield Cricket Win For S.A.

### N.S.W. BEATEN BY SEVEN WICKETS

### Bradman Again Dominates Batting

### GRIMMETT TAKES SIX WICKETS

**By LONG-ON**

South Australia won the Sheffield Shield cricket match against New South Wales by seven wickets at the Adelaide Oval yesterday. It was Bradman's match. Having scored 251 not out in the first innings, he held South Australia together in the second, scoring 90 not out of the side's score of 156 for three wickets, thus making 341 of the 586 runs scored by South Australia during the match without once being dismissed.

Bradman has dominated many games during his brilliant career, but probably never before has he been such an outstanding figure as he was in this match. In the two first-class matches already played he has scored 481 runs at an average of 240.5, an astonishing figure, even for the high standard he has set.

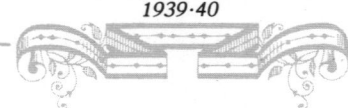

# South Australia v Queensland

SOUTH AUSTRALIA v QUEENSLAND, at Adelaide,
22, 23, 25 and 26 December 1939.

| | | |
|---|---|---|
| South Australia | - First Innings | 821 for 7 wickets dec. |
| | - Second Innings | - |
| Queensland | - First Innings | 222 |
| | - Second Innings | 377 |

South Australia won by an innings and 222 runs.

DON BRADMAN    - c. D. Hansen b. J. Ellis           138
    (Captain)

DON BRADMAN, in brilliant form, started South Australia on the path to their highest score, though he himself was not the largest contributor to it.    In at 36 for 1 on the first morning, he hit up 50 in thirty-seven minutes' batting.    He completed his century only ten minutes after lunch, and altogether made 138 in an hour and fifty-five minutes, before being caught off a skier behind square-leg when mistiming a hook; his strokes included twenty-two fours.

The 80 not out he made before lunch on this occasion was the nearest he ever got to a century before lunch on the first morning of a match in Australia and it was the most ever made before lunch on the first day of a Shield Match for South Australia.    This was his fifth century in successive innings against Queensland; no one else had ever made five centuries in succession off another State's bowling in Australia.

## PLAY IN FIGURES

### SOUTH AUSTRALIA
#### First Innings

| | |
|---|---|
| K. RIDINGS, l.b.w., b. Baker | 151 |
| T. KLOSE, c. Ellis, b. Cook | 13 |
| D. G. BRADMAN, c. Hansen, b. Ellis | 138 |
| R. A. HAMENCE, l.b.w., b. Cook | 6 |
| C. L. BADCOCK, b. Dixon | 236 |
| M. G. WAITE, c. and b. Dixon | 137 |
| R. S. WHITTINGTON, c. Rogers, b. Christ | 67 |
| P. RIDINGS, not out | 44 |
| Byes 10, leg-byes 17, no-balls 2 | 29 |
| **Total (for seven wickets)** | **821** |

| 1 | 2 | 3 | 4 | 5 | 6 | 7 |
|---|---|---|---|---|---|---|
| 36 | 232 | 268 | 101 | 685 | 713 | 821 |

#### Bowling

| | O. | M. | R. | W. |
|---|---|---|---|---|
| J. Ellis | 14 | — | 95 | 1 |
| G. Cook | 22 | 1 | 129 | 2 |
| P. Dixon | 24 | — | 142 | 2 |
| C. Christ | 27.1 | 3 | 144 | 1 |
| G. Baker | 22 | — | 127 | 1 |
| D. Watt | 14 | 1 | 135 | — |
| R. Rogers | 4 | — | 20 | — |

Dixon bowled two wides.
Innings—505 min.

### QUEENSLAND
#### First Innings

| | |
|---|---|
| W. A. BROWN, b. Grimmett | 20 |
| G. COOK, st. Walker, b. Ward | 27 |
| T. ALLEN, c. Klose, b. Ward | 35 |
| R. ROGERS, c. Waite, b. Grimmett | 49 |
| G. BAKER, c. Walker, b. Klose | 0 |
| D. TALLON, c. Badcock, b. Ward | 70 |
| D. Hansen, b. Grimmett | 2 |
| D. WATT, c. Waite, b. Grimmett | 6 |
| C. CHRIST, c. Walker, b. Ward | 1 |
| F. L. DIXON, not out | 3 |
| J. ELLIS, c. Badcock, b. Ward | 5 |
| Leg-byes 3, no-ball 1 | 4 |
| **Total** | **222** |

| 1 | 2 | 3 | 4 | 5 | 6 | 7 | 8 | 9 |
|---|---|---|---|---|---|---|---|---|
| 41 | 76 | 91 | 93 | 199 | 207 | 213 | 214 | 216 |

#### Bowling

| | O. | M. | R. | W. |
|---|---|---|---|---|
| P. Ridings | 5 | — | 29 | — |
| M. G. Waite | 9 | 2 | 40 | — |
| C. V. Grimmett | 19 | 2 | 71 | 4 |
| F. A. Ward | 16.7 | 2 | 62 | 5 |
| T. Klose | 4 | 1 | 16 | 1 |

Ridings bowled a no-ball.
Innings—190 min.

#### Second Innings

| | |
|---|---|
| W. A. BROWN, st. Walker, b. Ward | 156 |
| G. COOK, c. Waite, b. Grimmett | 15 |
| T. ALLEN, c. Waite, b. Ward | 22 |
| R. ROGERS, c. Klose, b. Grimmett | 50 |
| G. BAKER, l.b.w., b. Grimmett | 52 |
| D. TALLON, c. Waite, b. Ward | 14 |
| D. HANSEN, c. Walker, b. Grimmett | 15 |
| C. CHRIST, b. Ward | 12 |
| D. WATT, l.b.w., b. Grimmett | 8 |
| F. L. DIXON, c. Walker, b. Grimmett | 17 |
| J. ELLIS, not out | 1 |
| Byes 8, leg-byes 3, wide 1, no-balls 3 | 15 |
| **Total** | **377** |

| 1 | 2 | 3 | 4 | 5 | 6 | 7 | 8 | 9 |
|---|---|---|---|---|---|---|---|---|
| 27 | 84 | 205 | 291 | 311 | 329 | 348 | 350 | 464 |

#### Bowling

| | O. | M. | R. | W. |
|---|---|---|---|---|
| P. Ridings | 11 | 1 | 48 | — |
| M. G. Waite | 13 | 2 | 21 | — |
| C. V. Grimmett | 33.4 | 5 | 124 | 6 |
| F. A. Ward | 30 | 3 | 165 | 4 |
| T. Klose | 3 | — | 4 | — |

Ridings bowled a no-ball and a wide and Waite two no-balls.
Innings—303 minutes.

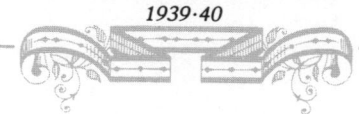

# Record-Breaking Innings By S.A.

## REACHES HIGHEST TOTAL
### IN FIRST-CLASS CRICKET

### Four Centurymakers In Big Score Of Seven (Dec.) For 821

### QUEENSLAND FOUR FOR 177

#### By LONG ON

IN a welter of rungetting such as has never previously been seen at Adelaide Oval, South Australia scored 821 runs for the loss of seven wickets in the Sheffield Shield cricket match against Queensland. The innings was declared closed at 3.15 p.m. on Saturday. Queensland lost four wickets for 92, and the almost hopeless position of the visiting team was only slightly improved by the dashing batting of D. Tallon in association with Rogers, with whom he has added 85 in an unfinished fifth wicket partnership.

Badcock, despite the handicap of sciatica which prevented him from running many singles and which forced him to run with a pronounced limp, and Waite joined Bradman and K. Ridings as century-makers. Badcock was top scorer for the innings with 236 in 249 minutes, hitting four sixes, and Waite's century was his first in first-class cricket.

# QUEENSLAND FOLLOWS
## ON, BUT BATS WELL

## Marathon Effort By South Australian Slow Bowlers

### BROWN SCORES ATTRACTIVE CENTURY

#### By LONG ON

HAVING collapsed before the wiles of the South Australian slow bowlers, Queensland followed on yesterday in the Sheffield Shield cricket match at Adelaide Oval.

Queensland was 599 runs behind on the first innings, but in its second it batted with much greater confidence. Held together by Brown, who batted with delightful grace to score 156, it reached 346 for the loss of six wickets by stumps. At that stage it still required 253 runs to avoid an innings defeat.

Apart from Brown's batting, the outstanding features of the day's play were the marathon bowling efforts of Grimmett and Ward and the brilliant fielding of Waite, who took five catches during the day.

# S.A. WINS BY
## INNINGS

## Slow Bowlers Take All Wickets

#### By LONG ON

Twenty-eight minutes' play, before practically deserted stands at the Adelaide Oval yesterday, sufficed to bring to an end the Sheffield Shield cricket match between South Australia and Queensland. The remaining few wickets fell for the addition of 31 runs, and South Australia had won by an innings and 222 runs.

The slow bowlers, Grimmett and Ward, bowled unchanged from the resumption to the finish, Grimmett taking three wickets and Ward one.

Of the 20 Queensland wickets which fell in the match, the slow bowling pair took all but one (Klose dismissed Baker in the first innings). Grimmett's figures were 10, at an average of 19.5, and Wards, nine at 25.2.

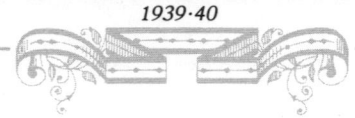

# South Australia
# v
# Victoria

SOUTH AUSTRALIA v VICTORIA, at Melbourne, 29, 30 December 1939, 1 and 2 January 1940.

| South Australia | - First Innings | 610 |
| | - Second Innings | 60 for 1 wicket |
| Victoria | - First Innings | 475 |
| | - Second Innings | 313 |
| | Drawn. | |

DON BRADMAN - c. I.W. Johnson b. L.O'B. Fleetwood-Smith 267
(Captain) - (did not bat)

DON BRADMAN went in late on the second day, at 108 for 1, and, completing 50 in eighty minutes just before 6 p.m., was 52 not out at the close. Next morning, he played a bad stroke through the slips off the fast bowling of R.B. Scott, when 61, and he made another mishit soon after passing 150, though neither of these was a chance; otherwise he batted without the semblance of a mistake until just before 5 p.m. He reached 100 in two hours thirteen minutes, proceeding from 88 by hitting three fours off 4 balls from D.T. Ring; 142 not out at lunch, he reached 200 after batting for four hours eighteen minutes, and continued to bat soundly, his 267 taking five hours forty minutes altogether. He was out, caught in the slips, at 556 for 7, having hit twenty-seven fours and seen South Australia into the lead. This was his thirty-fourth double-century, passing W.R. Hammond's then total of thirty-three. His last five innings thus produced 810 runs which was a South Australian record.

## SOUTH AUSTRALIA
### First Innings

| | |
|---|---|
| K. RIDINGS, c. Johnson, b. Ring | 56 |
| KLOSE, b. Scott | 51 |
| BRADMAN, c. Johnson, b. F.-Smith | 267 |
| BADCOCK, l.b.w., b. Ring | 58 |
| HAMENCE, l.b.w., b. F.-Smith | 20 |
| WHITTINGTON, c. Ring, b. Scott | 41 |
| WALKER, l.b.w., b. Scott | 1 |
| WAITE, c. Hassett, b. Ring | 61 |
| WARD, c. and b. Ring | 26 |
| GRIMMETT, c. Sievers, b. Ring | 6 |
| BURTON, not out | 1 |
| Sundries (six byes, nine leg-byes, one wide) | 16 |
| **Total** | **610** |

Fall of wickets—

| 1 | 2 | 3 | 4 | 5 | 6 | 7 | 8 | 9 |
|---|---|---|---|---|---|---|---|---|
| 108 | 122 | 259 | 330 | 420 | 430 | 556 | 596 | 609 |

### Bowling

| | O. | M. | R. | W. |
|---|---|---|---|---|
| Scott | 25 | — | 135 | 3 |
| Sievers | 29 | 1 | 120 | — |
| Ring | 25.4 | 1 | 123 | 5 |
| Fleetwood-Smith | 27 | — | 156 | 2 |
| Johnson | 13 | — | 60 | — |

Scott bowled one wide.

### Second Innings

| | |
|---|---|
| K. RIDINGS, not out | 29 |
| KLOSE, l.b.w., b. Ring | 15 |
| HAMENCE, not out | 11 |
| Sundries (three byes, one leg-bye, one no ball) | 5 |
| **Total (for one wicket)** | **60** |

Wicket fell at 36.

### Bowling

| | O. | M. | R. | W. |
|---|---|---|---|---|
| Scott | 3 | — | 9 | — |
| Sievers | 3 | — | 12 | — |
| Johnson | 5 | 2 | 11 | — |
| Ring | 4 | 1 | 13 | 1 |
| Hassett | 1 | — | 7 | — |

Ring bowled one no ball.

## VICTORIA
### First Innings

| | |
|---|---|
| LEE, b. Klose | 36 |
| HASSETT, st. Walker, b. Grimmett | 92 |
| MILLER, c. Bradman, b. Burton | 108 |
| JOHNSON, l.b.w., b. Waite | 14 |
| BEAMES, c. and b. Burton | 104 |
| BARNETT, b. Burton | 7 |
| SIEVERS, l.b.w., b. Burton | 16 |
| TAMBLYN, c. Walker, b. Ward | 38 |
| RING, st. Walker, b. Grimmett | 32 |
| SCOTT, c. Waite, b. Burton | 7 |
| FLEETWOOD-SMITH, not out | 11 |
| Sundries (byes 5, leg-byes 5) | 10 |
| **Total** | **475** |

| 1 | 2 | 3 | 4 | 5 | 6 | 7 | 8 | 9 |
|---|---|---|---|---|---|---|---|---|
| 60 | 225 | 275 | 277 | 289 | 313 | 353 | 440 | 460 |

### Bowling

| | O. | M. | R. | W. |
|---|---|---|---|---|
| Burton | 20.2 | — | 99 | 5 |
| Waite | 20 | 3 | 90 | 1 |
| Grimmett | 33 | 2 | 136 | 2 |
| Klose | 21 | 3 | 42 | 1 |
| Ward | 19 | — | 98 | 1 |

### Second Innings

| | |
|---|---|
| BARNETT, l.b.w., b. Klose | 46 |
| SIEVERS, c. Badcock, b. Grimmett | 36 |
| HASSETT, c. and b. Ward | 66 |
| MILLER, c. Bradman, b. Klose | 1 |
| JOHNSON, l.b.w., b. Klose | 23 |
| BEAMES, b. Burton | 32 |
| LEE, c. Grimmett, b. Ward | 39 |
| RING, not out | 41 |
| SCOTT, b. Grimmett | 17 |
| FLEETWOOD-SMITH, st. Walker, b. Ward | 4 |
| TAMBLYN (absent injured) | 0 |
| Sundries (five byes, three leg-byes) | 8 |
| **Total** | **313** |

### Fall Of Wickets

| 1 | 2 | 3 | 4 | 5 | 6 | 7 | 8 | 9 |
|---|---|---|---|---|---|---|---|---|
| 74 | 96 | 102 | 178 | 178 | 239 | 261 | 298 | 313 |

### Bowling

| | O. | M. | R. | W. |
|---|---|---|---|---|
| Burton | 11 | 1 | 11 | 1 |
| Waite | 10 | 1 | 38 | — |
| Grimmett | 21 | 2 | 78 | 2 |
| Klose | 17 | 4 | 43 | 3 |
| Ward | 14.1 | 2 | 102 | 3 |

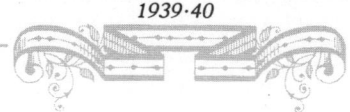

# S.A.'s FINE START WITH TWO FOR 213

## Victoria Carry Score To 475

## GOOD INNINGS BY K. RIDINGS

MELBOURNE, December 31.

With South Australia having lost two wickets for 213 in response to Victoria's 475 on the second day of the Sheffield Shield match on the Melbourne ground, the game is in an interesting position. The crowd of 29,660 (takings £1,337) saw some spectacular play.

For Victoria, Beames carried on from seven not out to make a splendid century. His enterprise made him a favorite with the crowd. In the morning Victoria added 148 runs. Then two young South Australians, K. Ridings and Klose, made 108 for the opening partnership, and Bradman and Badcock carried on quietly, although punishing anything loose.

Beames, who was seven not out on Friday, went on to make 104 in the smart time of 143 minutes. With the exception of an almost impossible chance to silly mid-on when 11, it was chanceless. He was after the runs all the time, used his feet fearlessly and showed good judgment in his handling of the various bowlers. His off and cover driving were bullet-like in force, and the off field was reinforced and deep when he was batting. Although one or two cuts were involuntary, most of them were hit perfectly, and his leg hitting was sound.

He had an exciting passage toward his century when Scott joined him. He needed nine runs. Scott defended stoutly and ran well between the wickets to give Beames the strike, when an almost impossible run was negotiated with ease to give him his first Shield century. The large crowd gave the popular Melbourne footballer a great reception.

### Tamblyn Resumes Innings

Sievers, who had not scored when the appeal against the light was granted on Friday, made 16 quietly before he was out l.b.w. He lifted Grimmett nicely for his only four. Tamblyn, who retired hurt on the first day, followed Sievers and seemed to be suffering no ill effects. He had added only 17 to his 21 when he tried to turn Ward to leg, just touched it and Walker took a smart catch. He was batting splendidly to that stage.

Ring again showed that he is more than a bowler, and it was his solid support that enabled Beames to reach his century. He defended stoutly, used his feet cleverly for powerful off drives, glanced the pace and slow bowlers neatly for fours, and was never in trouble until Grimmett deceived him by the flight and had him stumped.

Fleetwood-Smith cut and drove like a real batsman, and, after helping Beames reach 100, took a hand himself by driving Klose nicely for four.

Although Burton took three wickets fairly cheaply, making his total five for 99, those figures flattered him. Ward took only one wicket, but seemed to worry the batsmen more than did the other bowlers. He had plenty of life, whipping off the wicket quickly. Grimmett also bowled well.

The fielding was not as brilliant as on the first day, but nevertheless was first-class, with Bradman and Hamence the shining stars. Bradman in particular was a brick wall in the covers. Walker kept wickets excellently, and Waite took a sharp catch in the slips with an air of nonchalance.

### First Wicket Partnership

K. Ridings and Klose gave South Australia a great start by putting on 108 before Ridings, mistiming a drive off Ring, was caught at deep mid-off by Johnson. Beames also ran for the catch and could have taken it. For a moment it looked as if they would clash, but Beames saw the danger and dropped back.

Ridings, who is regarded in Adelaide as a coming Test opening batsman, almost bore out that high reputation. He is solid rather than brilliant, but has all the shots, supported by a sound defence. He seemed rather too anxious to connect with off theory bowled by Sievers, and was fortunate in missing it. Early in his innings he was struck on the elbow by a fast ball from Scott, but he cut the next delightfully for four. At 33 Fleetwood-Smith beat him. Ridings was out of his crease, but the ball jumped and hit Barnett on the chest, and the batsman escaped. He was in trouble against Fleetwood-Smith, who was bowling extremely well, and whom he snicked unsafely through slips. He reached a valuable 50 in 80 minutes, and in the next over brought up 100 in 83 minutes. Then he was caught.

Klose also created a fine impression. He scored all round the wicket, glancing Sievers for fours. Swinging Ring to the boundary, and cutting and driving neatly, if with no great force, unhurried and unflurried, he looked the ideal opening batsman. Fleetwood-Smith morally bowled him at 46, and the batsman almost unbalanced in a desperate attempt to keep in the crease. He celebrated his escape by swinging the next ball, a short one, for four. He was bowled for an excellent 54 when Scott came back in place of Ring.

### Bradman And Badcock Quiet

Badcock and Bradman took matters quietly, waiting for a fresh start on Monday. Bradman began with six singles and then hit a full toss from Fleetwood-Smith for four, to bring up 150 in 126 minutes. A delightful shot behind point off Scott gave him another four.

Badcock was not entirely at home and snicked Scott and Sievers dangerously. They brought up 200 in 165 minutes. Then Bradman hit Johnson gloriously through the covers for four and reached 50 in 80 minutes.

# BRADMAN'S 34th DOUBLE CENTURY

## Brilliant 267 Puts S.A. Ahead

## FIRST INNINGS LEAD OF 135

## Waite's Hard Hitting

MELBOURNE, January 1.

Bradman completed his 34th double century and his 90th three-figure score on the Melbourne ground today when through his great efforts and solid batting support from the rest of the side South Australia is well ahead of Victoria's 475, having made 610 runs. It was a magnificent reply to the formidable Victorian total.

South Australia is assured of at least a first innings win, but there is the possibility of an outright victory, as, with Tamblyn unable to play because of his knee injury and Lee indisposed, the Victorian batting has been weakened. A few cheap wickets before lunch tomorrow would place the home team in an extremely difficult position.

Bradman played all the shots with his customary certainty and power, but he was worried much more than usual by the bowlers. He was missed in the slips at 61 and was beaten several times by the bowlers. Nevertheless, it was a remarkable achievement, and he made the other batsmen look almost second-rate against bowling that rarely flagged.

This was Bradman's 12th century and his third double century on the Melbourne ground. He had previously made 357 here in his first season with South Australia in 1935-36, and 270 in the third Test match against the last English team. By making 34 scores of 200 or more he has passed the record of W. R. Hammond with 33. In six innings in Shield games this season he has made 886 runs—76 and 64 in Adelaide against Victoria; 251 not out and 90 not out against New South Wales; 138 against Queensland; and now 267 against Victoria. His average is the phenomenal one of 221.5.

Lee, one of Victoria's best fieldsmen, did not attend. He is suffering from gastritis, and Fothergill took his place. Then, early in the day, Tamblyn fell against the fence in trying to save a four. He had three stitches inserted in a wound in his knee, and will take no further part in the game. Moyle (S.A.) fielded for him in the morning, and Ross Gregory took his place in the afternoon.

The takings were £1,388, and the attendance 30,567, making the totals £3,245 and 73,087 in the three days of the match. Last year the takings were £2,897.

# South Australia v Western Australia

SOUTH AUSTRALIA v WESTERN AUSTRALIA, at Perth,
10, 12 and 13 February 1940.

| South Australia | - First Innings | 248 |
| | - Second Innings | 306 for 3 wickets dec. |
| Western Australia | - First Innings | 275 |
| | - Second Innings | 121 for 3 wickets |

Drawn.

| DON BRADMAN | - c. O.I. Lovelock b. C. MacGill | 42 |
| (Captain) | - not out | 209 |

DON BRADMAN went in on the first morning, and seemed to have played himself in comfortably, when he reached for a wide out-swinger and was caught at the wicket. He batted for sixty-five minutes, and helped to take the score from 28 for 2 to 97 for 3.

His second innings was a dazzling exhibition; going in on the third morning at 25 for 1, he completed his fifty in forty-five minutes, and his century in ninety-nine minutes, while his 200 took him a further fifty-six minutes, or only two hours thirty-five minutes altogether. When he declared at the tea interval, he had made 209 not out in two hours forty-one minutes, and had hit one six and thirty fours. He gave very difficult chances when 161, 183 and 207, but otherwise his display was chanceless; he and L. Michael added 171 unfinished for the fourth wicket in a hundred minutes, and of the 281 added while he was in, his share was seventy-four per cent, the highest proportion he had achieved in a double-century innings. His time for reaching 200, two hours thirty-five minutes, was the fastest of his career until then, and the fastest by any Australian in Australia.

## SOUTH AUSTRALIA
### First Innings

| | | |
|---|---|---|
| RIDINGS, c. Bandy, b. Halcombe | | 46 |
| KLOSE, b. MacGill | | 6 |
| HAMENCE, c. Lovelock, b. Eyres | | 3 |
| BRADMAN, c. Lovelock, b. MacGill | | 42 |
| MICHAEL, c. Eyres, b. MacGill | | 5 |
| WAITE, l.b.w., b. MacGill | | 37 |
| GIBSON, c. A Jeffreys, b. Zimbulis | | 35 |
| KIERSE, c. A. Jeffreys, b. Watt | | 23 |
| WARD, c. K. Jeffreys, b. Halcombe | | 15 |
| GRIMMETT, c. Inverarity, b. Zimbulis | | 14 |
| WALKER, not out | | 2 |
| Sundries | | 20 |
| **Total** | | **2 4 8** |

| 1 | 2 | 3 | 4 | 5 | 6 | 7 | 8 | 9 |
|---|---|---|---|---|---|---|---|---|
| 21 | 28 | 97 | 103 | 115 | 155 | 200 | 227 | 227 |

### Bowling

| | O. | M. | R. | W. |
|---|---|---|---|---|
| Eyres | 22 | 2 | 81 | 1 |
| MacGill | 18 | 1 | 49 | 4 |
| Halcombe | 13 | 1 | 52 | 2 |
| Zimbulis | 9.1 | — | 36 | 2 |
| Watt | 3 | 1 | 5 | 1 |
| Barras | 2 | 1 | 5 | — |

### Second Innings

| | | |
|---|---|---|
| WARD, b. Eyres | | 12 |
| WALKER, c. Inverarity, b. Zimbulis | | 34 |
| BRADMAN, not out | | 209 |
| HAMENCE, c. and b. Eyres | | 14 |
| MICHAEL, not out | | 27 |
| Sundries | | 10 |
| **Total (for three wickets, closed)** | | **306** |

### Bowling

| | O. | M. | R. | W. |
|---|---|---|---|---|
| MacGill | 15 | 3 | 66 | — |
| Zimbulis | 5 | — | 50 | 1 |
| Halcombe | 9 | — | 59 | — |
| Barras | 4 | — | 28 | — |
| K. Jeffreys | 2 | — | 28 | — |
| Eyres | 16 | 2 | 65 | 2 |

## WESTERN AUSTRALIA
### First Innings

| | | |
|---|---|---|
| MACGILL, c. Ward, b. Grimmett | | 78 |
| A. JEFFREYS, c. Klose, b. Ward | | 36 |
| WATT, st. Walker, b. Ward | | 18 |
| BARRAS, l.b.w. b. Klose | | 11 |
| BANDY, c. Klose, b. Ward | | 1 |
| K. JEFFREYS, st. Walker, b. Ward | | 7 |
| INVERARITY, st. Walker, b. Ward | | 57 |
| LOVELOCK, b. Grimmett | | 13 |
| ZIMBULIS, not out | | 42 |
| EYRES, c. Ward, b. Grimmett | | 9 |
| HALCOMBE, b. Ward | | 2 |
| Sundry | | 1 |
| **Total** | | **276** |

### Bowling

| | O. | M. | R. | W. |
|---|---|---|---|---|
| Waite | 8 | 1 | 26 | — |
| Kierse | 3 | 1 | 6 | — |
| Grimmett | 33 | 8 | 91 | 3 |
| Gibson | 12 | 3 | 25 | — |
| Klose | 10 | 2 | 18 | 1 |
| Ward | 26.3 | 1 | 105 | 6 |

### Second Innings

| | | |
|---|---|---|
| MacGILL, run out | | 11 |
| A. JEFFREYS, c Bradman, b. Kierse | | 8 |
| WATT, b. Ridings | | 52 |
| BANDY, not out | | 20 |
| K. JEFFREYS, not out | | 27 |
| Sundries | | 3 |
| **Total (for three wickets)** | | **121** |

### Bowling

| | O. | M. | R. | W. |
|---|---|---|---|---|
| Kierse | 7 | 2 | 19 | 1 |
| Gibson | 7 | 1 | 21 | — |
| Grimmett | 4 | — | 26 | — |
| Ward | 7 | 1 | 32 | — |
| Ridings | 4 | — | 12 | 1 |
| Klose | 6 | 4 | 8 | — |

## BRADMAN GIVES PERTH A TREAT

### Scores 209 Not Out In 161 Minutes

PERTH, February 13.

For ten years cricket lovers in Western Australia have waited for D. G. Bradman to reproduce his form in Perth. Today he more than compensated for his previous "failures" by scoring a brilliant 209 not out in the final day's play of the interstate match between South Australia and Western Australia. Bradman scored 70 before lunch and continued until tea, when he declared South Australia's second innings at three for 306.

When Bradman went in the score was 25, so that while he was there he scored 209 of the 281 obtained. In its second innings Western Australia made 121 for the loss of three wickets.

Ward and Walker continued the South Australian innings and carried the score to 25 before Ward was bowled by Eyres. Walker was troubled by a leg injury and could not run sharp singles. Bradman soon showed he was in a run-getting mood and scored freely all round the wicket. He made his first 50 in 45 minutes. Walker was caught in attempting a big hit and two were down for 83.

Hamence shaped promisingly before lunch, but was dismissed soon afterwards. Bradman was subdued for a while after lunch, but he brought up his century in 99 minutes. Michael supported Bradman ably and was content to let his partner have the centre of the stage. Bradman relished the slow bowlers and fours flowed from his bat. His 150 was reached in 125 minutes and 30 minutes later he passed the 200 mark.

At tea, when the innings was closed, his score was 209, made in 161 minutes. He hit one six and reached the boundary 30 times. He gave a c. and b. chance at 161, and catching chances at 183 and 207.

In Western Australia's second innings Watt batted brilliantly for 52. He square cut beautifully and showed a liking for anything loose on the leg side.

The attendance was about 3 000, and the gate receipts were £177.

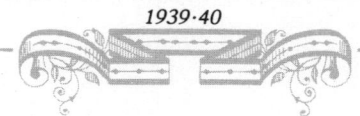

# South Australia v Western Australia

SOUTH AUSTRALIA v WESTERN AUSTRALIA, at Perth, 16, 17 and 19 February 1940.

| South Australia | - First Innings | 429 |
| | - Second Innings | - |
| Western Australia | - First Innings | 275 |
| | - Second Innings | 206 |

Drawn.

DON BRADMAN    - c. A.G. Zimbulis b. G. Eyres   135
(Captain)

Going in just after lunch on the second day, at 79 for 1, DON BRADMAN batted easily, if rather sedately, for two hours twenty-eight minutes before being caught on the leg-boundary for 135. He completed 50 in seventy-nine minutes, and 100 in two hours twelve minutes; he hit fourteen fours, gave no chance, and helped to raise the score to 303 for 4, his stand for the third wicket with R.A. Hamence realizing 150 in ninety-eight minutes.

## WESTERN AUSTRALIA
### First Innings

| | | |
|---|---|---:|
| READ, c. Teisseire, b. Grimmett | | 55 |
| MACGILL, b. Klose | | 17 |
| WATT, c. Walker, b. Grimmett | | 1 |
| BARRAS, run out | | 6 |
| INVERARITY, b. Gibson | | 52 |
| K. JEFFREYS, l.b.w. b. Grimmett | | 26 |
| BANDY, c. Klose, b. Ward | | 30 |
| LOVELOCK, c. Walker, b. Grimmett | | 45 |
| ZIMBULIS, c. Michael, b. Klose | | 13 |
| PUCKETT, c. Waker, b. Grimmett | | 4 |
| EYRES, not out | | 1 |
| Sundries | | 5 |
| **Total** | | **275** |

Fall of wickets—21, 24, 31, 133, 141, 189, 195, 270, 272, 275.

### Bowling

| | O. | M. | R. | W. |
|---|---:|---:|---:|---:|
| Waite | 17 | 4 | 43 | 0 |
| Gibson | 15 | 5 | 39 | 1 |
| Klose | 21 | 12 | 24 | 2 |
| Grimmett | 33.6 | 6 | 67 | 5 |
| Ward | 21 | 2 | 97 | 1 |

### Second Innings

| | | |
|---|---|---:|
| MACGILL, c. Klose, b. Gibson | | 17 |
| READ, b. Grimmett | | 45 |
| ZIMBULIS, c. and b. Ward | | 1 |
| BARRAS, c. Teisseire, b. Grimmett | | 23 |
| INVERARITY, b. Ward | | 3 |
| BANDY, st. Walker, b. Grimmett | | 4 |
| LOVELOCK, c. Klose, b. Ward | | 29 |
| WATT, b. Grimmett | | 10 |
| K. JEFFREYS, not out | | 21 |
| EYRES, b. Grimmett | | 30 |
| PUCKETT, l.b.w. b. Grimmett | | 2 |
| Sundries | | 11 |
| **Total** | | **206** |

42 43 73 82 93 94 120 147 200

### Bowling

| | O. | M. | R. | W. |
|---|---:|---:|---:|---:|
| Gibson | 9 | 5 | 20 | 1 |
| Waite | 6 | — | 26 | — |
| Ward | 21 | 3 | 81 | 3 |
| Grimmett | 10.2 | 6 | 57 | 6 |
| Ridings | 4 | 1 | 11 | — |
| Klose | 3 | 3 | — | — |

## SOUTH AUSTRALIA
### First Innings

| | | |
|---|---|---:|
| RIDINGS, b. Barras, b. Zimbulis | | 34 |
| KLOSE, c. Zimbulis, b. Eyres | | 60 |
| BRADMAN, c. Zimbulis, b. Eyres | | 135 |
| HAMENCE, run out | | 63 |
| MICHAEL, c. and b. Zimbulis | | 10 |
| TEISSEIRE, b. Macgill | | 56 |
| WAITE, c. Eyres, b. Zimbulis | | 24 |
| GIBSON, c. and b. Puckett | | 21 |
| WALKER, b. Puckett | | 3 |
| WARD, run out | | 8 |
| GRIMMETT, not out | | 5 |
| Sundries | | 10 |
| **Total** | | **429** |

1   2   3   4   5   6   7   8   9

79 113 263 303 319 365 400 410 424

### Bowling

| | O. | M. | R. | W. |
|---|---:|---:|---:|---:|
| Eyres | 23 | 3 | 79 | 2 |
| Macgill | 22 | 3 | 108 | 1 |
| Puckett | 21.3 | 4 | 89 | 2 |
| Zimbulis | 22 | — | 131 | 3 |
| Bandy | 1 | — | 12 | — |

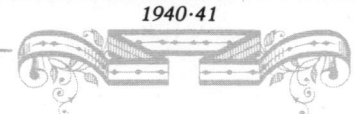

# *1940 – 41, 1945 – 46 Seasons*

**W**ith the world literally in flames I, like so many tens of thousands of others, enlisted and offered to serve my country in any required capacity.

Regrettably, my patriotic motives were cut short by a severe and crippling illness and my eventual return to the cricket field was against my own personal desires and purely in response to appeals for assistance in trying to resuscitate the game.

Where possible I engaged in charitable activity and in my own mind did not contemplate any more than token participation in a side of national life which had perforce been put aside.

*Don Bradman*

## — SEASON 1940-41 —

| TITLE | GAMES | | SCORES | |
|---|---|---|---|---|
| Second Class | Army School | Frankston School | 83 | C. |
| | " | R.A.A.F. | 35 | r. o. |
| | " | Fire Brigade | 112 | B. |
| First Grade | Kensington | West Torrens | 212 | C. |
| First Class | South Australia | Victoria | 0 | C. |
| | " " | " | 6 | B. |
| | Bradman's Team | McCabe's Team | 0 | C. |
| | " " | " " | 13 | B. |
| | | Total runs | 461 | |

## — SUMMARY —

AVERAGES -

| | Innings | N.O's. | H.S. | Runs | Average |
|---|---|---|---|---|---|
| All First Class | 4 | 0 | 13 | 19 | 4·7 |
| First Grade | 1 | 0 | 212 | 212 | 212·0 |
| Other Second Class | 3 | 0 | 112 | 230 | 76·6 |
| All Second Class | 4 | 0 | 212 | 442 | 110·5 |
| All Matches | 8 | 0 | 212 | 461 | 57·6 |

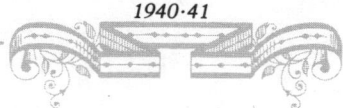

KENSINGTON v WEST TORRENS, at Thebarton Oval, on 19 and 26 October, 1940.

Kensington - First Innings     370
         - Second Innings     -

West Torrens · - First Innings .     305 for 7 wickets dec.
         - Second Innings     -

DON BRADMAN - c Woolcock b Bell 212

# Bradman Dominates District Cricket

## SCORES DOUBLE CENTURY
### IN FIRST INNINGS OF SEASON

#### By LONG ON

PLAYING his first innings for the season, Bradman immediately struck typical batting form in district cricket on Saturday. Going in when the first wicket fell for one run, the Australian captain mercilessly punished the West Torrens bowling to score 212 of the 313 runs made while he was at the wickets. He was out shortly after Kensington had passed the score set by West Torrens.

Niehuus (Glenelg) and Bennett (University) also scored centuries.

Port Adelaide, with the last man at the wickets, scored the winning run against East Torrens, and Glenelg, with two wickets in hand, beat Prospect with three runs hit off the second to last ball of the match.

### HOW TEAMS STAND

| | | |
|---|---|---|
| Sturt | .. .. .. .. | 12 |
| Glenelg | .. .. .. .. | 12 |
| West Torrens | .. .. .. .. | 6 |
| University | .. .. .. .. | 6 |
| Kensington | .. .. .. .. | 6 |
| Port Adelaide | .. .. .. .. | 6 |
| East Torrens | .. .. .. .. | — |
| Prospect | .. .. .. .. | — |
| Adelaide | .. .. .. .. | — |

### BEAT THE CLOCK
#### (26 or more runs)

D. G. Bradman (Kensington), 212 in 195 minutes.

A. W. G. Dawkins (East Torrens), 54 in 41 minutes.

A sparkling 212 in 195 minutes by Don Bradman, Australian Test captain, won the match for Kensington against West Torrens at Thebarton Oval.

Kearney, one of Kensington's opening batsmen, was bowled for none with the second ball of the afternoon. Bradman then went to the wickets, and dominated the batting.

The largest crowd seen at Thebarton for a district cricket match was not disappointed. Batting steadily for 45 in the first hour, Bradman opened a bright patch by clipping King's first three deliveries to the pickets, another four followed, and the over yielded 18. If Bradman had gone for the strike he would have scored much faster, but he unselfishly ran singles to give his younger partners a chance of scoring. Woodcock established a strong partnership of 136 with Bradman, of which the latter made 93. Woodcock's 43 in 104 minutes yielded two to the boundary.

Bradman's century came in 118 minutes, and then he hit 17 off one over from Dooland, including one six, and in the next over from Scott he registered another six and 17 from the over. He made 150 in 149 minutes, 200 in 186 minutes, and 212 in 195 minutes. He skied a ball off Bell close in, and Woolcock and the wicketkeeper Heairfield rushed for it and both got their hands on the ball, but Woolcock held it. Bradman's score included 28 fours and two sixes. Burgess batted soundly for 33, to make a fourth wicket partnership of 123 with Bradman. Grimmett was back at his old Test form to make 35 not out, including several nice boundary shots.

West Torrens appeared to lack change bowlers for batsmen of the Bradman calibre, but E. Bell, a slow lefthander from B grade last year, was the most troublesome.

#### University Bats Better

Sturt, striving for an outright victory against University on Saturday declared immediately at four for 96. The students, however, aided by a fine innings by F. C. Bennett, who reached 101, scored 231. Bennett and Page were associated in a splendid second wicket partnership which added 75 runs in 66 minutes before the latter was run out. Bennett proceeded sedately without being unduly troubled by any of the bowling and reached his century in 184 minutes; his score included five boundaries. The University side showed much sounder form than in the first innings. Hutton returned the best figures, but the bowling was generally unimpressive with the wicket lending little assistance. Sturt had only 19 minutes to bat in the second innings.

#### Stern Fight

After a stern fight for runs, Port Adelaide scored a first innings win over East Torrens at Norwood Oval. Rilstone, Workman, and Roberts were the outstanding batsmen for Port which required five runs to win when the last man, Beck, came in. The two batsmen passed the home team's score after the side had been batting for 212 minutes. Roberts (57) was at the crease for 90 minutes, and his score included five fours.

Workman's 52 was a particularly good effort. Although he took 118 minutes to get his score, he batted steadily. Cocks and Schultz shared the bowling honors for East Torrens.

Dawkins had a merry time in East Torrens' second innings hitting 54 in 41 minutes. His score included 10 fours.

#### Excitement At Prospect

In an exciting finish at Prospect Oval Glenelg just beat the home team by three runs at stumps.

Glenelg wanted 15 with eight minutes to play, and when Cotton opened his last over seven were required. Cooper's wicket fell, but the Glenelg batsmen made 10. Lecher, the opening batsman bungled a call and was run out for 22. Niehuus, winner of last season's cup for the fastest century, proved the rock for Glenelg. He was at the wickets 209 minutes to score 118, and his partnership with Waite (50) yielded 94.

With bowlers and fieldsmen on the alert in the last half-hour it was evident that Glenelg batsmen would have to hit out to secure a win. Some sacrificed their wickets in hitting at everything and taking almost impossible runs. On the second to last ball of the day Mortimer ran from the pavilion to the wickets, and hit a three over Cotton's head

### WEST TORRENS V. KENSINGTON
#### (Thebarton Oval)
#### WEST TORRENS
##### First Innings

| | |
|---|---|
| K. Ridings, c. Bradman, B. White | 2 |
| A. Sampson, c. Smith, b. Grimmett | 54 |
| R. A. Hamence, c. Moyle, b. Grimmett | 24 |
| G. Tuck, c. Grimmett, b. Walkley | 96 |
| B. Dooland, st. G. Inglis, b. Walkley | 26 |
| P. Ridings, not out | 66 |
| N. King, c. Moyle, b. Burton | 15 |
| A. N. Woolcock, c. Moyle, b. Grimmett | 2 |
| H. V. Heairfield, not out | 9 |
| Byes 5, leg-byes 4, wide 1, no-ball 1 | 11 |

Total (for seven wickets dec.)    305

| 1 | 2 | 3 | 4 | 5 | 6 | 7 |
|---|---|---|---|---|---|---|
| 20 | 67 | 96 | 174 | 229 | 253 | 256 |

##### Bowling

| | O. | M. | R. | W. |
|---|---|---|---|---|
| G. Burton | 13 | 1 | 47 | 1 |
| G. White | 6 | — | 28 | 1 |
| C. V. Grimmett | 22 | 1 | 104 | 3 |
| L. Walkley | 12 | 1 | 62 | 2 |
| R. T. Smith | 10 | — | 53 | — |

Burton, one wide; Smith, one no-ball.
Innings—235 minutes.

#### KENSINGTON
##### First Innings

| | |
|---|---|
| L. Woodcock c. Dooland, b King | 43 |
| W Kearney b P Ridings | 0 |
| D G Bradman, c. Woolcock, b. Bell | 212 |
| E. J. R. Moyle, c Dooland, b Bell | 10 |
| T. Burgess, c. P. Ridings, b. King | 33 |
| C. V Grimmett, not out | 35 |
| G Inglis, st. Heairfield, b. King | 9 |
| G Burton, c. Tuck, b. Bell | 6 |
| L Walkley, b. Bell | 4 |
| R. T. Smith c. Heairfield, b. Dooland | 10 |
| G. White, st. Heairfield, b. Dooland | 0 |
| Byes 1, leg-byes 4, wide 1, no- balls 2 | 8 |

Total    370

| 1 | 2 | 3 | 4 | 5 | 6 | 7 | 8 | 9 |
|---|---|---|---|---|---|---|---|---|
| 1 | 137 | 161 | 284 | 314 | 329 | 306 | 341 | 358 |

##### Bowling

| | O. | M. | R. | W. |
|---|---|---|---|---|
| P Ridings | 14 | 1 | 76 | 1 |
| J. Scott | 15 | 2 | 67 | — |
| N. King | 16 | — | 108 | 3 |
| E. Bell | 13 | — | 81 | 4 |
| B. Dooland | 3.1 | — | 30 | 2 |

Ridings, two no-balls; Bell, one wide.
Innings—237 minutes.

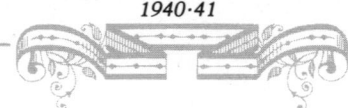

# DON BRADMAN ENLISTS IN AIR FORCE

DON Bradman today joined the Royal Australian Air Force.

With flying colors the Australian Test captain passed his medical examination at the North terrace recruiting depot and subsequently was sworn in for service in an R.A.A.F. air crew. He was placed on reserve and will be called up later for training.

**Don Bradman**

In the meantime, Bradman with other members of the air crew reserve, will attend special study classes organised for reservists.

The Lord Mayor (Mr. Barrett), who is chairman of the Air Force Recruiting Committee, said: "It should be an inspiration to every sportsman in Australia to see a cricketer of such international fame in the R.A.A.F. Let us hope now that Bradman will get centuries as readily in the air as he has on the ground."

## The Bradmans . . .

AUSTRALIA taking its hat off to Don Bradman and son. Don just enlisted with the Air Force, and son John Russell celebrates his first birthday this Wednesday. "No party, he is too little," says his mother.

Animals are John's first love, but lately he's been intrigued with a miniature bat. He doesn't hesitate to swing it, and loves to tap it on the crazy pavement in the garden.

Mrs. Bradman is not yet making any special plans for herself and John when Don is called up, but she will probably keep their Adelaide home going.

She's an expert knitter, and is a member of the Kensington Park Red Cross circle.

5 Taylors Road,
Townsville,
28th June '40

Dear Don,

It was with pride and admiration that I read of your joining up.

Following our talk at the "Belle Vue," I fully realise the sacrifices you and your good wife are making.

I am sure that your action will be an inspiration to all South Australian and Australian cricketers to fall into line.

Congratulations Don, and all the best of luck.

Yours Sincerely,
Hugh Bridgman

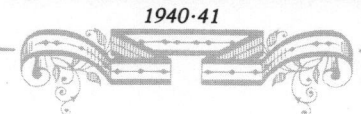

THE TRAINEES *do this and other exercises for hours. Bradman is fourth from the left.*

# Famous athletes train to be A.I.F. gym. instructors

Don Bradman, Australia's number one sporting hero, is in the Army now. He is Lieutenant Don Bradman, and he has gone back to school.

With 74 other athletic lads he is doing an intensive three weeks' course at the Army School of Physical and Recreational Training, Frankston, Vic., which turns out instructors for the A.I.F. and Militia all over Australia.

On completing his course, Lieutenant Bradman will return to Adelaide to become supervisor of Physical and Recreational Training to the A.I.F. in South Australia.

BRADMAN joined the R.A.A.F. intending to become an air observer, but was released to transfer to the Army for physical training duties. Later, he may go overseas.

The training school is a pleasant place. It was the Church of England Boys' Camp before the war.

Work—physical jerks that limber up every part of the body, long jumps, high jumps, wrestling, boxing,. medicine ball, shot putt, all branches of athletics—begins at 9 a.m. and goes on till 4.30 p.m. with brief spells for rest and lunch.

This is a school where Energy is spelt with a capital E, but where students must acquire a good working knowledge of anatomy, physiology, and hygiene as well.

They must also learn how to arrange and conduct every kind of sporting event, from a wrestling match to a sports meeting.

Bradman is one of the smallest, most lightly built men in the school, but he puts just as much pep into the exercises as the young giants twice his size. A considerable amount of skin is peeling off his sunburnt brow, nose and shoulders, but he still wears the famous cheery grin.

"They tell us we will be fitter than we have ever been before when we leave here," said Bradman, walking across the drill ground as the squads broke up for a spell.

"As a matter of fact, you have to be in pretty good nick before you come here. If you weren't, you would probably crack up by the third day."

## Takes orders now

ASKED if the work is harder than a long day at the wicket, he smiled. "Perhaps I had better not say anything about that. You know I take orders here. But we didn't begin a day at the wicket till after eleven. Here, we start work at nine.

"Yes, we had a cricket match the other day, and were well beaten. We played the R.A.A.F. School at Somers. No, they didn't have one interstate player, but they had a good all round team."

The school has many notables. The Chief Instructor, Major W. J. Dickens, is a splendid athlete. He was at Aldershot for a time after the last war, and since then has handled physical training instruction for the Army in many parts of Australia.

"This school is modelled on Aldershot lines," he said. "But we have speeded up the training. These students get through what in peace time would be a three-months' course in three weeks.

"They have to work hard to do that. We have been at work since April, and by Christmas we will have turned out 1000 instructors for the A.I.F. and Militia.

"The men come from all over Australia, from Darwin to Tasmania and W.A. They are specially selected from their units and commands, and most of them will return to their units as instructors."

The staff bristles with famous names. The Senior Instructor is tall, dark, good-looking Sergeant-Major Bruce Cupitt, a product of Aldershot.

Then there are Sergeant-Major E. Jones, Sergeant-Major L. O'B. Fleetwood-Smith, the Test bowler; Sergeant-Majors Bonnie Muir and King Elliott, of wrestling fame; and Sergeant-Major Max Carpenter, the International Rugby player.

Max was in England with the Rugby team when war broke out.

"We went over to play Rugby," he said. "But we ended up filling sandbags in Torquay. The only match we played was in ___bay. I've always been in traini_; for one sport or another, but this is the finest training I've ever had in my life."

Bonnie Muir and King Elliott have promised to give a wrestling match at Allard Park, East Brunswick, on November 30, to help the Red Cross.

Don will referee.

Lieutenant Bradman.

P.T. squad at Frankston, December 1940.

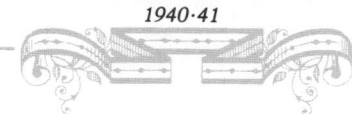
# TEST CRICKETERS IN A.I.F.

Lieutenant Don Bradman with Warrant-Officer Fleetwood-Smith.

Max Carpenter, Don Bradman and Mr. and Mrs. Harry Hopman. Frankston, April 1941.

## Daughter to Mrs. Don Bradman

A daughter was born yesterday to Mrs. Don Bradman, wife of the Australian Test cricketer. They have a son aged 21 months. It was reported this morning that both Mrs. Bradman and the baby are well.

Don Bradman has been engaged on military duties since last year.

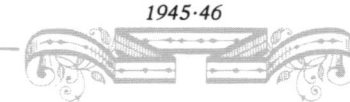

The two Bradman children, Shirley and John.

## — SEASON 1945-46 —

| TITLE | GAMES | | SCORES | |
|---|---|---|---|---|
| First Class | South Australia | Queensland | 68 | C. |
| " " | " " | " | 52 | n. o. |
| " " | " " | Services Team | 112 | C. |
| | | Total runs | 232 | |

## — SUMMARY —

AVERAGES -

| | Innings | N.O's. | H.S. | Runs | Average |
|---|---|---|---|---|---|
| First Class | 3 | 1 | 112 | 232 | 77·3 |
| All Matches | 3 | 1 | 112 | 232 | 77·3 |

# South Australia v Australian Services

SOUTH AUSTRALIA v AUSTRALIAN SERVICES, at Adelaide,
29, 31 December 1945, 1 January 1946.

| | | |
|---|---|---|
| South Australia | - First Innings | 319 |
| | - Second Innings | 130 for 1 wicket |
| Austn. Services | - First Innings | 314 |
| | - Second Innings | 255 |
| | Drawn. | |
| DON BRADMAN | - c. D.K. Carmody b. R.G. Williams | 112 |
| (Captain) | - (did not bat) | - |

Going in on the second morning at 68 for 2, DON BRADMAN showed good form against bowlers who included A.G. Cheetham, R.G. Williams, C.G. Pepper, R.S. Ellis and D.R. Cristofani. He took only three-quarters of an hour to reach 50, and ninety-five minutes to complete his century, before throwing away his wicket, caught at long-on, after batting for an hour and fifty-two minutes. Out at 241 for 3, he and R.J. Craig added 173 for the third wicket; Bradman hit eleven fours, and gave no chance.

## SOUTH AUSTRALIA
### First Innings

| | |
|---|---|
| R. J. Craig, c. Williams, b. Ellis | 141 |
| C. Webb, c. and b. Ellis | 25 |
| R. A. Hamence, b. Pepper | 5 |
| D. G. Bradman, c. Carmody, b. Williams | 112 |
| F. C. Bennett, c. Sismey, b. Pepper | 4 |
| L. Michael, c. Sismey, b. Ellis | 1 |
| T. Klose, b. Pepper | 1 |
| M. G. Waite, l.b.w., b. Pepper | 0 |
| B. Dooland, l.b.w., b. Ellis | 0 |
| J. Noblet, st. Sismey, b. Ellis | 11 |
| J. L. Mann, not out | 5 |
| Byes 8, leg-byes 1, wides 3, no-balls 2 | 14 |
| Total | 319 |

Fall of wickets:—63, 68, 241, 282, 293, 296, 296, 297, 312.

### Bowling

| | O. | M. | R. | W. |
|---|---|---|---|---|
| A. G. Cheetham | 6 | — | 41 | — |
| R. G. Williams | 7 | 1 | 31 | 1 |
| C. G. Pepper | 20 | — | 100 | 4 |
| R. S. Ellis | 22.3 | 2 | 88 | 5 |
| D. R. Cristofani | 6 | — | 30 | — |
| R. S. Whittington | 2 | — | 15 | — |

Cheetham bowled two no-balls; Williams two wides and Pepper one.

### Second Innings

| | |
|---|---|
| L. Michael c. and b. Cristofani | 54 |
| F. C. Bennett, not out | 56 |
| T. Klose, not out | 15 |
| Byes 4, wide 1 | 5 |
| Total (for 1 wicket) | 130 |

Fall of wicket—83

### Bowling

| | O. | M. | R. | W. |
|---|---|---|---|---|
| R. G. Williams | 4 | — | 23 | — |
| A. G. Cheetham | 6 | 1 | 9 | — |
| R. S. Ellis | 5 | — | 18 | — |
| C. G. Pepper | 7 | — | 22 | — |
| D. R. Cristofani | 7 | — | 26 | 1 |
| R. M. Stanford | 2 | — | 13 | — |
| A. L. Hassett | 2 | — | 9 | — |
| D. K. Carmody | 2 | — | 5 | — |

Williams bowled a wide.

## SERVICES
### First Innings

| | |
|---|---|
| R. S. Whittington, b. Bennett | 77 |
| D. K. Carmody, c. Craig, b. Mann | 8 |
| J. A. Workman, b. Mann | 8 |
| A. L. Hassett, c. Michael, b. Dooland | 1 |
| C. G. Pepper, c. Webb, b. Dooland | 63 |
| A. G. Cheetham, c. Craig, b. Dooland | 6 |
| R. Cristofani, c. Klose, b. Dooland | 25 |
| R. Stanford, not out | 59 |
| R. G. Williams, b. Noblet | 21 |
| S. G. Sismey, b. Dooland | 35 |
| R. Ellis, l.b.w., b. Hamence | 9 |
| Wide 1, no-ball 1 | 2 |
| Total | 314 |

Fall of wickets—15, 39, 59, 157, 159, 189, 190, 220, 304.

### Bowling

| | O. | M. | R. | W. |
|---|---|---|---|---|
| J. Noblet | 16 | 3 | 39 | 1 |
| M. G. Waite | 14 | 7 | 21 | — |
| J. L. Mann | 19 | 5 | 59 | 2 |
| T. Klose | 14 | 4 | 42 | — |
| B. Dooland | 22 | — | 104 | 5 |
| F. C. Bennett | 8 | — | 40 | 1 |
| R. A. Hamence | 2 | — | 7 | 1 |

Mann bowled one wide; Bennett one no-ball.

### Second Innings

| | |
|---|---|
| D. K. Carmody, b. Noblet | 4 |
| R. S. Whittington, b. Noblet | 4 |
| J. A. Workman run out | 0 |
| A. L. Hassett, c. Klose, b. Waite | 92 |
| C. G. Pepper, l.b.w., b. Mann | 2 |
| A. G. Cheetham, b. Noblet | 1 |
| D. R. Cristofani, c. Bradman, b Klose | 58 |
| R. M. Stanford, b. Dooland | 57 |
| R. G. Williams, run out | 4 |
| S. G. Sismey, c. Craig, b. Mann | 18 |
| R. S. Ellis, not out | 5 |
| Leg-byes | 10 |
| Total | 255 |

Fall of wickets:—7, 8, 9, 13, 16, 108, 192, 199, 243.

### Bowling

| | O. | M. | R. | W. |
|---|---|---|---|---|
| J. Noblet | 22 | 6 | 44 | 3 |
| M. G. Waite | 14.4 | 1 | 34 | 1 |
| J. L. Mann | 18 | 6 | 52 | 2 |
| B. Dooland | 20 | 3 | 92 | 1 |
| T. Klose | 8 | 1 | 23 | 1 |

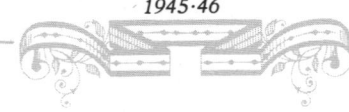

# BRADMAN AND CRAIG SCORE CENTURIES

## Second Innings Collapse By Services Cricketers

### By HARRY KNEEBONE

Don Bradman is fit, in cricket form and in physical condition, to resume big cricket. Yesterday, at Adelaide Oval, he scored a brilliant century for South Australia against the Services team. He did not make a mistake, played all bowlers with sublime confidence, made his runs in time which would bear comparison with any in his hey-day, and sprinted up the grandstand steps at the end of his innings.

Obviously undistressed, all that he would say in the dressing room was that he felt well. He had previously publicly announced that he would in no circumstances be available for the eastern tour by the SA team and that a decision as to his cricket future must wait until next season.

# RECOVERY BY SERVICES

## Draw Forced With S.A.

### By HARRY KNEEBONE

A fighting recovery by the Services side gave South Australia little chance of forcing an outright win in the cricket match which finished at Adelaide Oval yesterday.

Requiring 251 runs in 115 minutes when it began its second innings, South Australia made no attempt to get the runs, and the game finished tamely, with the South Australians taking the opportunity for batting practice.

The Services recovered from five for 16 to reach 255. Hassett was the sheet anchor of this rally, but a dashing innings by Cristofani when the outlook was black for his side, was the outstanding feature.

Stanford also gave Hassett capable support, and outscored his captain while at the wickets. Hassett was overshadowed by both his partners in the two big stands—92 for the sixth wicket (with Cristofani), and 84 for the seventh wicket (with Stanford). Of Hassett's 92 runs, 46 were singles.

Flattered to some extent by the generally unenterprising batting, the South Australian bowling figures nevertheless bore a more satisfactory appearance than before in this season. Noblet, who took his three wickets very cheaply the previous day, did not add to them, but continued to bowl remarkably well.

Mann further strengthened his position in the side by giving another good display of left-arm accuracy.

The improved batting of Michael in the South Australian second innings was timely, in view of the impending selection of the State team to tour the eastern States.

### Cristofani Bats Well

Cristofani and Hassett scored steadily against the bowling of Noblet and Dooland, reaching their 50 partnership in 38 minutes. Cristofani's half century was scored in only three minutes longer than even time. His enterprise and stroke play were the chief factors in the total being taken from 50 to 100 in 25 minutes.

The pair had added 92 runs for the sixth wicket when Cristofani, attempting to cover-drive Klose, did not get over the ball, and gave Bradman an easy catch at mid-off.

Chief responsibility for saving the Services from outright defeat then rested on Hassett, for with six wickets down, the team was only 103 ahead.

The scoring rate slackened after Cristofani's departure. Stanford began unimpressively, having several uncertain moments against the slow bowling of Dooland, but he weathered the settling down period, and began to produce attractive strokes, notably a cut behind point and vigorous off-drives.

When Mann and Waite came on, the Sturt left-arm bowler sent down three successive maidens. Only eight runs were scored from Waite's first four overs. An off-driven four by Stanford off Waite broke a long spell of dreary cricket.

In contrast to the speed with which the team's second 50 was scored, the Services third 50 took an hour and three minutes. Hassett and Stanford (who scored 35 of them) added 50 for the seventh wicket in 71 minutes. Hassett at lunch had been batting two and a half hours for his 49 runs.

### Brighter Batting

Stanford, improving as his innings progressed, threatened to overhaul his captain. He hit Dooland for two successive fours. He was only four runs behind Hassett at 57 to 61, when Dooland got him with the last ball of his fifth over after lunch. Stanford had scored 57 of the seventh-wicket partnership of 84 in 101 minutes. He snicked the ball which was on the leg side on to his pads, whence it went on to hit the stumps.

Smart fielding by Dooland gave Waite (the bowler) the chance to steady himself for a successful shot at the stumps to run out Williams and give South Australia a ray of hope. Services were then 194 ahead with two wickets to fall and more than three hours to play.

The ray became a dull glimmer and finally vanished completely as Sismey, with a reputation for dour defence, played right up to it. He took no chances and every minute he held up the South Australian attack was as good as a run scored—from the point of view of the Services.

Sismey held the fort for two minutes short of an hour. He was then snapped up on the leg side by Craig at the wicket.

Hassett, with the last man at the wicket, and faced with the prospect of being robbed of his century after all, hit out wildly, and was finally caught at mid-on off a skied pull to give Waite his first wicket for the match.

### S.A. In Again

Bradman sent Michael and Bennett to open the second innings, South Australia needing 251 runs in 115 minutes to win outright. The fast attack did not last long. Ellis relieving Williams after two overs, and Pepper completing the double change at the other end.

South Australia's prospects had deteriorated at the end of the first half-hour's play, 219 being then required in 85 minutes. Michael showed the greater initiative of the pair jumping out to drive Ellis. He scored 32 of the first 50 in 40 minutes, Bennett getting only 15 of them.

Although Michael continued to hit the loose ball hard, reaching his 50 in an hour, it was apparent, with an hour to play, that South Australia had no hope of forcing an outright win.

Bennett scored 18 singles in succession at one stage of his innings, and, with Klose playing without confidence, the batting was not inspiring in the closing stages.

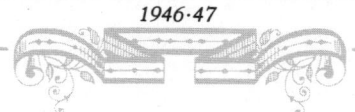
# 1946 - 47 *Season*

The 1946–47 season became one of destiny.

Apart from the illness which had terminated my activities in the services, I had to submit to surgery for an internal complaint which was painful and debilitating.

There was no way in the world I could be 100 per cent fit to play Test cricket.

A newspaper offered me the staggering fee of £10,000 to write the Test series. On all sides there was tremendous pressure for me to play. What should I do? If I played, the risk of failure was very great and the possible adverse effects on my business had to be considered. The financial reward for not playing was tempting.

I considered the diverse aspects of the situation from all angles and finally decided to play. The over-riding consideration which I could not dismiss from my conscience was that it was my duty to do whatever lay in my power to assist my country in the restoration of a sport which meant so much to Australians.

In retrospect, that decision was the most satisfying of my cricket career.

Fate handsomely repaid me by decreeing that my gamble did not fail.

## — SEASON 1946-47 —

| TITLE | GAMES | | SCORES | |
|---|---|---|---|---|
| Second Class | S.A. Team | South Perth | 30 | C. |
| " | " | " | 133 | C. |
| First Grade | Kensington | Glenelg | 117 | B. |
| " | | Prospect | 63 | C. |
| " | | West Torrens | 1 | B. |
| " | | " | 207 | B. |
| " | | Sturt | 86 | B. |
| First Class | South Australia | England | 76 | C. |
| " | " | " | 3 | C. |
| | An Australian XI | " | 106 | C. |
| | South Australia | " | 5 | C. |
| Sheffield Shield | " " | Victoria | 43 | St. |
| " | " " | " | 119 | St. |
| Test Matches | Australia | England | 187 | B. |
| " | " | " | 234 | L.B.W. |
| " | " | " | 79 | B. |
| " | " | " | 49 | C. |
| " | " | " | 0 | B. |
| " | " | " | 56 | n.o. |
| " | " | " | 12 | B. |
| " | " | " | 63 | C. |
| | | Total runs | 1669 | |

## — SUMMARY —

AVERAGES -

| | Innings | N.O's. | H.S. | Runs | Average |
|---|---|---|---|---|---|
| Test Matches | 8 | 1 | 234 | 680 | 97·1 |
| Sheffield Shield | 2 | 0 | 119 | 162 | 81·0 |
| Other First Class | 4 | 0 | 106 | 190 | 47·5 |
| All First Class | 14 | 1 | 234 | 1032 | 79·4 |
| First Grade | 5 | 0 | 207 | 474 | 94·8 |
| Other Second class | 2 | 0 | 133 | 163 | 81·5 |
| All Second class | 7 | 0 | 207 | 637 | 91·0 |
| All matches | 21 | 1 | 234 | 1669 | 83·4 |

## Hasn't Touched Bat This Season

# BRADMAN STILL NOT CERTAIN ABOUT FUTURE

### By A. G. MOYES

**Don Bradman's future in first-class cricket is still completely uncertain.**

**He wants to play against England—he has always wanted to —but it can be stated authoritatively that he is not fit to take part in a four-day game, nor is he in any batting form.**

He is not yet had a bat in his hand this season.

The Englishmen play South Australia tomorrow week.

**Bradman must make up his mind at the weekend, but a decision to play for his State against England would not be proof that he would be available for Test matches.**

Before Bradman came to Sydney last month for the meeting of the Board of Control, he had had gastric trouble and looked jaded and weary.

On his return to Adelaide, a minor operation was necessary and then, when he thought he would be able to attend net practice, a recurrence of gastric trouble sent him to bed for about 10 days.

Obviously, he is neither in proper condition nor proper form for a first-class match and particularly one against England.

Another round of club matches will start in Adelaide on Saturday and no doubt he will play. Today is his last chance to have a knock at the nets.

**The South Australian team will be announced at the weekend, and Bradman must play for his club on Saturday if he is to lead the State against England.**

There is a general desire for Bradman to captain Australia but the early games must be regarded merely as trials, and not as an indication that he will be available for Tests.

If Bradman does play against England next week, he will be short of condition and of form, but he has done everything possible, including sacrificing a fantastic financial offer to cover the tour for an English newspaper, to make himself available.

Everything depends on his health.

# M.C.C.
## TOUR IN AUSTRALIA & NEW ZEALAND
### 1946-47

*W. R. Hammond*
CAPTAIN

*R. H. Gibb*     *L. B. Fishlock*     *W. Bedser*

*(Nor) Yardley*     *W. Edrich*

*D. V. P. Wright*     *Joe Hardstaff*

*Cyril Washbrook*     *W. Voce*

*Denis Compton*

*L. Hutton*     *T. G. Evans*     *T. P. B. Smith*

*R. Pollard*

*J. Ikin*     *James Langridge*

*R. Howard*
MANAGER

# Adelaide's Warm Welcome

**The MCC cricket team was kept busy with official engagements during its first day in Adelaide yesterday, and had only a short net practice in the afternoon in preparation for the four-day match against South Australia, starting at noon today.**

About 1,300 people attended the civic reception given by the Lord Mayor (Mr. McLeay) in the Adelaide Town Hall at noon. The Englishmen were tendered a Ministerial luncheon at Parliament House, and His Excellency the Governor (Sir Willoughby Norrie) gave a late afternoon party to the team and to English press representatives

At the Town Hall, there was prolonged clapping as the Englishmen took their places on the dais. The official party included the Premier (Mr. Playford), members of the State Ministry, members of the Adelaide City Council, officials of the South Australian Cricket Association, and the State captain (Don Bradman). The South Australian cricket team was in the body of the hall.

Welcoming the guests, the Lord Mayor referred to the English captain (W. R. Hammond, who is making his fourth Australian tour, as "one of the greatest sportsmen of all time."

"We hope that Don Bradman will be fit enough to play, and thereby equalise things for us," he added.

## Hammond "Stacked"

Mr. McLeay recalled that Hammond must remember Adelaide rather well, because Bradman had once "stacked" him here with a full toss, with the last ball of a day's play and with the worst ball of the match.

"We want you to remind people at home how proud we are to be members of the great British Empire," added the Lord Mayor.

The Premier spoke on behalf of the State Government and the people of South Australia, and Mr. R. F. Middleton for the SACA and Australian Board of Cricket Control.

Before Hammond responded, he introduced each member of his team, and designated each man's county.

He said that enthusiasm in England for cricket was greater than he could remember. The news that Don Bradman would play against them had pleased all the visitors.

"In all sports, good health is essential," he said. "You can do nothing without it. There is not one of us who does not wish Bradman good health. The very fact that his name is among those playing will be a great service to the game."

The manager of the MCC side (Maj. Rupert Howard) said that the English team was impressed by the improvement in Western Australian cricket.

"It might be worth while to see if it is possible to let them see a little more of your good players from the other States," he said.

## Net Practice

Australian food parcels had made all the difference to the "dull, monotonous and strengthless diet" which the people of England had had to endure, said Maj. Howard.

After the reception, members of the team were introduced to Mr. and Mrs. E. Walker, parents of the late C. W. Walker, South Australian and Australian wicketkeeper.

About 150 people watched the Englishmen at a short net practice at the Adelaide Oval in the afternoon. The only absentees were Hammond, Gibb and Wright.

Hutton and Compton confirmed reports of their batting prowess.

All the men hit freely, but Edrich stole the show with some lusty if chancey slogging, and bowled with astonishing energy. With Voce and Pollard content to bowl at reduced pace, he was the most entertaining bowler, although Bedser had a good work-out with the ball.

# BRADMAN JUNIOR MAKES A FRIEND

John Bradman, seven-year-old son of Don Bradman, met Alec Bedser, of the
English cricket team, on his first day in Adelaide, and since then John has
constantly sought out his new friend. He went to the English dressing room on
Saturday and asked for "Mr. Bedser, please." Bedser came out and was soon
engaged in a rapid fire cricket conversation led by young Bradman, in which
some of the youngster's mates joined. In this picture Bradman junior is seen
watching the game with Bedser.

# South Australia
## v
## M.C.C. Team

SOUTH AUSTRALIA v M.C.C. TEAM, at Adelaide, 25, 26, 27 and 29 October 1946.

| South Australia | - First Innings | 266 |
| | - Second Innings | 276 for 8 wickets |
| M.C.C. Team | - First Innings | 506 for 5 wickets dec. |
| | - Second Innings | - |
| | Drawn. | |

| DON BRADMAN | - c. and b. T.P.B. Smith | 76 |
| (Captain) | - c. W.J. Edrich b. R. Pollard | 3 |

DON BRADMAN played in this game although obviously very far from well. England batted first and he had to field for two days against the big M.C.C. score. In the circumstances, it was a considerable achievement on his part to score 76 in the first innings; he went in at 26 for 2 before lunch on the third day, and was soon in difficulties against R. Pollard, who had him missed at the wicket when 15. However, he gradually settled down, and managed to attain better co-ordination and timing; he completed 50 in ninety-seven minutes, and was out to his first ball after the tea interval, having played an innings lasting two hours thirty-three minutes. He hit six fours.

In at 69 for 2 after lunch on the fourth day, he soon hit out wildly, to be caught at mid-off at 72 for 3; he stayed for only six minutes.

### M.C.C. Team

| | |
|---|---|
| L. Hutton c and b Dooland.......... 136 | N. W. D. Yardley not out............. 54 |
| C. Washbrook c Englefield b O'Neill............................. 113 | J. T. Ikin not out .......................... 35 |
| W. J. Edrich st Englefield b Dooland.................................. 71 | B 6, l-b 4, w 2, n-b 5............ 17 |
| D. Compton c O'Neill b Mann ..... 71 | |
| W. R. Hammond st Englefield b Dooland.................................. 9 | Five wkts., dec. 506 |

T. P. B. Smith, J. Langridge, T. G. Evans and R. Pollard did not bat.

### South Australia

| | | | |
|---|---|---|---|
| R. J. Craig c Evans b Pollard ............... | 14 | — b Pollard ............................. | 111 |
| P. L. Ridings b Langridge...................... | 57 | — c Hammond b Compton..... | 20 |
| R. A. Hamence b Smith ....................... | 0 | — st Evans b Compton........... | 7 |
| D. G. Bradman c and b Smith............... | 76 | — c Edrich b Pollard ............. | 3 |
| R. James b Langridge ........................... | 58 | — run out................................ | 15 |
| K. Gogler b Smith ............................... | 19 | — c Compton b Langridge....... | 1 |
| B. Dooland b Smith............................. | 12 | — c Hammond b Langridge ... | 16 |
| K. O'Neill c Evans b Edrich .................. | 8 | — b Edrich ............................. | 3 |
| J. Mann b Langridge ............................ | 3 | — not out................................ | 62 |
| G. Noblet b Edrich .............................. | 8 | — not out................................ | 25 |
| W. Englefield not out.......................... | 6 | | |
| L-b 3, n-b 2 ................................ | 5 | B 11, l-b 1, n-b 1.............. | 13 |
| | 266 | Eight wkts. | 276 |

### South Australia Bowling

| | O. | M. | R. | W. | O. | M. | R. | W. |
|---|---|---|---|---|---|---|---|---|
| O'Neill.............. | 25 | 1 | 104 | 1 | | | | |
| Noblet .............. | 29 | 5 | 54 | 0 | | | | |
| Ridings............. | 19 | 3 | 57 | 0 | | | | |
| Mann................ | 40 | 18 | 65 | 1 | | | | |
| Dooland ........... | 40 | 2 | 142 | 3 | | | | |
| James............... | 5 | 1 | 20 | 0 | | | | |
| Gogler .............. | 6 | 0 | 27 | 0 | | | | |
| Craig................. | 7 | 0 | 20 | 0 | | | | |

### M.C.C. Bowling

| | O. | M. | R. | W. | | O. | M. | R. | W. |
|---|---|---|---|---|---|---|---|---|---|
| Pollard.............. | 26 | 8 | 66 | 1 | .... | 11 | 3 | 23 | 2 |
| Edrich.............. | 9.3 | 1 | 38 | 1 | .... | 10 | 1 | 37 | 1 |
| Smith................ | 27 | 4 | 93 | 5 | .... | 19 | 1 | 70 | 0 |
| Langridge ......... | 20 | 2 | 60 | 3 | .... | 26 | 7 | 73 | 2 |
| Ikin .................. | 1 | 0 | | | | 4 | 0 | | |
| Compton | | | | | .... | 17 | 5 | 46 | 2 |
| Hutton | | | | | .... | 1 | 0 | 6 | 0 |
| Hammond | | | | | .... | 3 | 0 | 8 | 0 |

# BRADMAN FAR FROM BEST

## Makes 76, Lacks Old-Time Dash

*From ARTHUR MAILEY*

**ADELAIDE, Monday.—Although Don Bradman scored 76 runs for South Australia against England today, it is obvious he is not completely fit.**

He lacked his old-time resilience, vitality, and aggressive suppleness.

When play ended for the day, South Australia were 9-262 in reply to England's 5-506 (declared closed).

The match will end tomorrow, and England's captain, Wally Hammond, is expected to make South Australia bat again, in the hope of dismissing them cheaply.

Today, in the first over after tea, Smith caught and bowled Bradman.

Thus ended the innings of a man whose physical condition could not quite keep pace with his tremendous mental energy and powers of concentration.

**The post-war Bradman did all the things the pre-war Bradman did—but with physical reservations.**

His traditional viciousness had mellowed.

Instead of a lightning flash of the bat sending the ball skimming to the leg-side boundary, we saw a stroke played by a bat that might have been made, not of willow, but of kauri.

### Steady, Subdued

Bradman showed flashes of pre-war brilliance, but was for the most part steady and subdued.

He took nearly two hours to score 63 runs, and his running between the wickets lacked customary speed and alertness.

If Bradman did appear uncomfortable at times, it was against Pollard who, after lunch, seemed to make the ball swing more than when it was new.

Pollard had been very consistent without being particularly dangerous.

**Occasionally he sent down a ball that might have obtained a wicket, and that particular ball seemed to appear more often as the day wore on.**

Pollard often threw his arms up and registered disgust, particularly when Bradman, at 56, seemed to be missed behind the wickets.

On a slowish, easy wicket, not receptive to medium-paced bowling, Pollard battled along gamely despite his bad luck.

His determination and tenacity alone deserved reward.

### James' Two Sides

James, the New South Wales player, began aggressively by punching a couple of fours, faded away, then suddenly came to life and hit Langridge for six in front of the members' stand.

These periods of immobility and aggression apparently had nothing to do with the quality of the bowling.

They were merely inspired by James' varying mental moods.

Bradman and James, by somewhat unorthodox methods, carried the score to nearly 200 runs at tea, and the partnership had then added 75 valuable runs.

James' spasmodic innings ended at 58, shortly after Bradman had left.

It included two sixes and six fours.

**It was an entertaining mixture of excellent stroke-making and shots that were inspired by imagination rather than by reason.**

After Bradman and James had left, the batting was in the hands of an unconvincing array of young men, who found Smith's sophistication embarrassing.

They played him gingerly, and it was not until Ikin came on with an imperfect length that they felt at ease.

But four more wickets fell quickly, three to Smith, who finished the day with 5-93.

The more I see of England's opening attack, whether in the hands of Pollard Voce, Bedser, or Edrich, the more doubtful I am of its success against first-class Australian batsmen.

This morning Pollard and Edrich opened the bowling against Craig and Ridings, two batsmen who can hardly be regarded as potential Test openers.

**Three-quarters of an hour later Craig was caught behind off Pollard, but that was the only ball that passed his bat.**

He seemed at ease and unconcerned throughout his stay.

Shortly after, when slow bowler Smith came on, the batsmen began to show more concern.

Hamence lost his wicket quickly, and Ridings should have been caught shortly after.

Ridings was always in trouble against Smith.

## DEFENDS BRADMAN

*From ARTHUR MAILEY*

ADELAIDE, Monday. — Don Bradman has often gone out of his way to be frank and helpful to pressmen.

But he has never done that to win pressmen and players' popularity.

The South Australian branch of the Australian Journalists' Association have asked Bradman to substantiate or withdraw a statement he made about being mis-reported by pressmen.

He made the statement at a recent meeting of the Federal Institute of Accountants at Adelaide.

It was reported to last Friday's A.J.A. meeting.

**Apparently there are journalists who are always ready to criticise Bradman, but I am certain this does not apply to all of them.**

Recently in Perth, a Sydney cricket writer criticised England's captain, Wally Hammond, for his alleged discourtesy to newspapermen.

### Never Discourteous

I have had as much to do with Bradman and Hammond as any pressman, and I have never found either discourteous.

On the contrary, both have been friendly and helpful.

I think the A.J.A. will try to clear up the present dispute and be as fair as possible to Bradman.

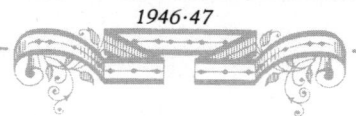

"THE SUN" (DAILY)
"SUNDAY SUN & GUARDIAN"
"POCKET BOOK WEEKLY"
"THE WORLD'S NEWS"
"WOMAN"
"RADIO & HOBBIES"
"PIX"

**The Sun**

ASSOCIATED NEWSPAPERS LIMITED
(Successors to Sun Newspapers Limited)

TELEPHONES:
GENERAL B 0333
ADVERTISING DEPT. B 6821

CABLE ADDRESS:
EDITORIAL "JAGANATHA"
BUSINESS "SUNBUSI"
TELEGRAMS "SUN" SYDNEY
CODE: "BENTLEY'S"

60-70 ELIZABETH STREET
SYDNEY, N.S.W.

ADDRESS ALL COMMUNICATIONS TO BOX 2728 C. G.P.O.

Tuesday

Dear Don,

You may be batting at this moment in Adelaide and you may make a duck or a hundred. To me it does not matter overmuch. What does matter is that you have never in all your career done anything as notable as now. You have pledged your health and your reputation to help Australian cricket and that counts for more than all the records ever made and broken. There has always been a very soft spot in my heart for you as you well know but never have I thought so much of you as now. Only a real man could do it. It isnt that I am surprised. I always expect to find you doing the right thing at the right time. It is just that in these days it is a thrill to find one who puts honor above everything else. Good luck to you and may it bring you blessings and not affect your health.

Yours

*John*

The above letter was from A. G. Moyes, sporting editor of the Sydney *Sun* and Bradman's former boss.

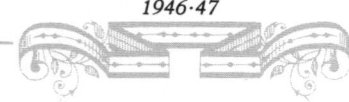

# An Australian XI
# v
# M.C.C. Team

AN AUSTRALIAN XI v M.C.C. TEAM, at Melbourne, 9, 11 and 13 November 1946.

| An Austn. XI | - First Innings | 327 for 5 wickets |
|---|---|---|
| | - Second Innings | - |
| M.C.C. Team | - First Innings | 314 |
| | - Second Innings | - |
| | Drawn. | |

DON BRADMAN - c. R. Pollard b. D.C.S. Compton 106
(Captain)

In rather better health by this time, DON BRADMAN took the opportunity for further batting practice in a game much interfered with by rain. He had fifty-six minutes' batting before the close of the second day, starting at 39 for 1, and remained 28 not out overnight; on the last morning he completed 50 in ninety-two minutes, but soon afterwards strained his leg. However, after twenty-five minutes in the nineties, he reached 100 in three hours thirty-five minutes, and four minutes later threw his wicket away with a catch in the deep. He gave a stumping chance off D.C.S. Compton when 78, but otherwise batted in much better form; he hit five fours.

**AUSTRALIA**
**First Innings**

| | | |
|---|---|---|
| M. HARVEY, c. Ikin, b. Smith | | 22 |
| A. MORRIS, c. Evans, b. Yardley | | 115 |
| D. G. BRADMAN, c. Pollard, b. Compton | | 106 |
| A. L. HASSETT, c. Sutton, b. Smith | | 28 |
| K. R. MILLER, c. Evans, b. Smith | | 5 |
| J. PETTIFORD, not out | | 27 |
| C. L. McCOOL, not out | | 22 |
| Sundries (byes 1, leg-byes 1) | | 2 |
| Total (for five wickets) | | 327 |

Fall of wickets—39, 235, 255, 270, 289.

| | O. | M. | R. | W. |
|---|---|---|---|---|
| R. Pollard | 21 | 5 | 69 | — |
| W. Voce | 27 | 2 | 98 | — |
| T. P. B. Smith | 32 | 2 | 111 | 3 |
| J. T. Ikin | 3 | — | 13 | — |
| D. Compton | 14 | 3 | 26 | — |
| N. W. D. Yardley | 4 | — | 8 | 1 |

**M.C.C.**
**First Innings**

| | |
|---|---|
| L. HUTTON, c. Freer, b. McCool | 71 |
| C. WASHBROOK, b. McCool | 57 |
| W. J. EDRICH, l.b.w., b. McCool | 4 |
| D. COMPTON, stpd. Saggers, b. McCool | 24 |
| W. R. HAMMOND, c. Miller, b. McCool | 51 |
| N. W. D. YARDLEY, b. McCool | 11 |
| J. T. IKIN, b. Puckett | 15 |
| T. G. EVANS, c. Ellis, b. Freer | 18 |
| T. P. B. SMITH, b. Ellis | 28 |
| W. VOCE, c. Freer, b. McCool | 15 |
| R. POLLARD, not out | 11 |
| Sundries (leg-byes 8, wide 1) | 9 |
| Total | 314 |

Fall of wickets—122, 136, 139, 172, 198, 231, 249, 267, 287.

**Bowling**

| | O. | M. | R. | W. |
|---|---|---|---|---|
| J. Ellis | 18.5 | 2 | 47 | 1 |
| C. Puckett | 15 | 4 | 58 | 1 |
| F. W. Freer | 26 | 5 | 60 | 1 |
| J. Pettiford | 5 | — | 26 | — |
| C. L. McCool | 38 | 6 | 106 | 7 |
| K. R. Miller | 4 | — | 8 | — |

## M.C.C. OUT FOR 314

# McCool, 7/106, Now Looks Test Certainty

### MELBOURNE, November 11.

Colin McCool, stockily built Queenslander, practically bowled himself into the first Test by taking seven for 106 in England's 314 on the Melbourne Cricket Ground today.

Bradman, after a brief period of uncertainty, settled down splendidly. Perhaps he did not time the ball as well as before, but it was a very satisfying re-entry to the Melbourne ground, where he last played in 1941.

McCool, who bowled 38 overs in the match, took four for 68 off 23 overs today, showing remarkable stamina from midday until the innings closed just before 4 p.m.

Rarely has McCool shown greater control. He was seen in Melbourne last year, when he was most unsuccessful. Today, however, he interspersed his leg breaks with an occasional top spinner and wrong 'uns.

Fine fielding and a well-placed field helped him. Naturally, the other bowlers took second place to McCool.

It was unfortunate for Pettiford, the leg spinner, that he bowled only four overs on the first day and one today.

Hammond, the outstanding batsman of the day, was most restrained—for which the Australians have to thank McCool. Unlike most of his team mates, Hammond was not afraid to use his feet. He was often yards down the wicket smacking the ball hard, but usually unable to get through the field. Once or twice he scored lofty fours, and it was in attempting another shot of that nature that he was neatly caught by Miller.

Mervyn Harvey, who opened the Australian innings with Morris, and who is a candidate for the position of opening batsman in the first Test, will now find it hard to gain that place. He played some nice shots, but his impetuosity was his downfall.

Morris, the NSW left-hander, who is also a candidate for a place in the Test side, gave nothing away. He concentrated on defence, and he is yet to be seen as a strokemaker.

The attendance was 23,841 and the takings were £2,259.

## BRADMAN "WILL BE HEADACHE"

### Morris Seen As New Bardsley

LONDON, November 13.—AAP.

Bradman confirmed in Melbourne today the impression formed in Adelaide that he has lost none of his skill, and that he will again be England's biggest headache, says Norman Preston, Reuter commentator travelling with the MCC team.

Making his 94th century, Bradman proved that he is still a master of batting technique. Except for a chance of stumping off Compton when 78, Bradman never looked to be in difficulty.

The merit of his innings was heightened because of a slight strain of a calf muscle. This did not interfere with his stroke play.

There is still no difference from the Bradman known in his three English tours as far as his genius to co-ordinate brain and footwork is concerned. His sight remains acute and his brain and feet respond readily to deal with any type of delivery, whether he decides to play forward or off the back foot.

Preston says that he feels more confident than ever that Australia has found another Bardsley in Morris. This 24-year-old auburn-haired batsman displayed remarkable coolness considering his limited experience in first-class cricket. He is assured of a place in the first Test.

For five hours he displayed a solid defence without offering a chance. At present his driving lacks power. Development in this regard may be expected, and will be necessary if he is to reach the Bardsley and Leyland class.

# South Australia v Victoria

SOUTH AUSTRALIA v VICTORIA, at Adelaide, 15, 16, 18 and 19 November 1946.

| South Australia | - | First Innings | 270 |
| | - | Second Innings | 356 |
| Victoria | - | First Innings | 548 |
| | - | Second Innings | 79 for 1 wicket |

South Australia lost by 9 wickets.

| DON BRADMAN | - | st. E.A. Baker b. I.W. Johnson | 43 |
| (Captain) | - | st. E.A. Baker b. G.E. Tribe | 119 |

In his only Sheffield Shield match of the season, DON BRADMAN again showed improved form and fitness. In at 75 for 3 after lunch on the first day, he batted for one and a quarter hours before jumping out to drive, missing the ball, and being unable to get back in time. His strained leg prevented him from fielding during Victoria's big first innings, and it again bothered him when he went in to bat early on the fourth day. He joined R.A. Hamence at 62 for 2, and the pair added 195 for the third wicket in a great effort to save the game for South Australia, who were 278 behind on the first innings. He survived a stumping chance off I.W. Johnson when 26, reached 50 in two minutes over one and a half hours, and his century in two hours forty-eight minutes, despite having a pronounced limp. He batted altogether for three hours three minutes, and hit eight fours; when he was out, stumped well down the pitch, at 284 for 4, at 3.30 p.m., the innings defeat had just been saved, but thereafter there was a collapse, the last six wickets falling for 72. Victoria had thirty-five minutes to make 79 to win, and succeeded with two minutes to spare.

## South Australia

| | | | |
|---|---|---|---|
| R. J. Craig b Tribe | 36 | — c Hassett b Johnson | 3 |
| V. R. Gibson b Miller | 5 | — b Tribe | 1 |
| P. L. Ridings lbw b Tribe | 27 | — b Tribe | 9 |
| R. A. Hamence lbw b Tribe | 2 | — c and b Freer | 116 |
| D. G. Bradman st Baker b Johnson | 43 | — st Baker b Tribe | 119 |
| R. James b Miller | 73 | — c Meuleman b Ring | 34 |
| K. Gogler lbw b Tribe | 36 | — b Tribe | 33 |
| J. L. Mann c and b Tribe | 20 | — lbw b Tribe | 5 |
| B. Dooland c and b Tribe | 2 | — not out | 16 |
| G. Noblet b Tribe | 9 | — lbw b Tribe | 1 |
| W. Englefield not out | 4 | — b Ring | 4 |
| B 4, l-b 8, w 1 | 13 | B 11, l-b 3, n-b 1 | 15 |
| | **270** | | **356** |

## Victoria

| | | | |
|---|---|---|---|
| G. E. Tamblyn c and b Dooland | 75 | | |
| K. Meuleman c Englefield b Dooland | 87 | | |
| M. Harvey c Englefield b Gibson | 9 | — not out | 3 |
| K. R. Miller run out | 188 | — c Englefield b Mann | 33 |
| A. L. Hassett b Ridings | 114 | — not out | 36 |
| I. Johnson c Dooland b Gibson | 17 | | |
| F. Freer run out | 15 | | |
| D. Ring b Ridings | 5 | | |
| E. A Baker st Englefield b Dooland | 1 | | |
| G. Tribe b Dooland | 7 | | |
| W. Johnston not out | 5 | | |
| B 12, l-b 8, w 2, n-b 3 | 25 | B 7 | 7 |
| | **548** | One wkt. | **79** |

### Victoria Bowling

| | O. | M. | R. | W. | O. | M. | R. | W. |
|---|---|---|---|---|---|---|---|---|
| Johnston | 8 | 0 | 30 | 0 | 13 | 1 | 35 | 0 |
| Freer | 7 | 1 | 19 | 0 | 21 | 8 | 84 | 1 |
| Miller | 11 | 1 | 32 | 2 | 2 | 0 | 10 | 0 |
| Johnson | 20 | 4 | 55 | 1 | 14 | 3 | 43 | 1 |
| Tribe | 30.5 | 4 | 85 | 7 | 23 | 2 | 68 | 6 |
| Ring | 10 | 0 | 36 | 0 | 25 | 1 | 99 | 2 |
| Hassett | | | | | 1 | 0 | 2 | 0 |

### South Australia Bowling

| | O. | M. | R. | W. | O. | M. | R. | W. |
|---|---|---|---|---|---|---|---|---|
| Noblet | 24 | 7 | 57 | 0 | 2 | 0 | 21 | 0 |
| Gibson | 36 | 11 | 96 | 2 | 2 | 0 | 25 | 0 |
| Ridings | 27 | 5 | 79 | 2 | 2 | 0 | 14 | 0 |
| Dooland | 54.3 | 2 | 229 | 4 | | | | |
| Mann | 28 | 10 | 50 | 0 | 1.7 | 0 | 12 | 1 |
| Gogler | 4 | 0 | 12 | 0 | | | | |

Umpires: J. D. Scott and L. A. Smith.

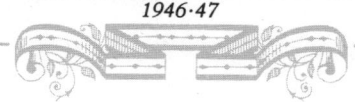

# BRADMAN, HAMENCE SCORE BRIGHT CENTURIES

### By Lawrie Jervis, Jun.

RON Hamence broke a long drought and Don Bradman garnered his usual harvest of runs in scoring centuries for South Australia against Victoria at Adelaide Oval today. Their partnership was worth 195 runs.

HAMENCE, who is second only to Bradman in length of service with State teams returned to form in first class cricket after a spell of low scores.

Hamence first appeared for the State in the 1935-6 season, and in the next year played against Gubby Allen's M.C.C. team. Last year he was a member of the Australian team which toured New Zealand and was reckoned among the batsmen worthy of serious consideration for the Tests.

**He had dropped out of discussion lately after his run of outs, but today's innings will place his name in the notebooks of Australian selectors again under the heading of "Watch closely."**

In the game against the M.C.C. last month he showed hesitation, being often caught between a desire to get out to the ball—his natural game—and to stay back defensively. He showed no such indecision today and went for the bowling.

The whole morning's play was practically Bradman's and Hamence's, as Gogler fell to the same ball with which Tribe got four wickets in the first innings. Gogler tried to sweep it to leg and the ball curled far round his leg to take the stumps.

It seemed obvious that Hassett was not risking Tribe getting a pounding from either of the South Australian pair.

Tribe's four overs today cost 17 runs, but with Hamence in form and partial to slow bowlers, and Bradman likely to splatter Tribe round the field at any moment, Hassett put Tribe back into the field.

With Freer on in place of Tribe at the cathedral end, Bradman survived a confident and full-throated appeal for a catch behind, when he played forward and missed.

The 101 was up in 102 minutes, this morning's 53 taking 43 minutes.

Hamence cover-drove Freer to the fence near the main gate to reach 53 in 97 minutes, making the partnership worth 50 in 42 minutes.

Bradman was keeping a wary eye on Ian Johnson, who got him on Friday.

One ball which he failed to connect on the leg side was a possible stumping chance, although a hard one. Bradman was out of his ground, but Baker failed to take the ball.

Hamence gathered another boundary when he cover drove Freer,

but the next ball yorkered him, although it was off the wicket. Twice Bradman got right on to Freer, and each time Tamblyn, sprinting fast, cut off the shot for a two.

Hamence then put his shoulders into an off-drive off Ian Johnson, which gave Keith Miller a race to the boundary and beat him by a foot. Miller, loping back to his position, cut off the same shot off the next ball, for a single.

## Smartly Run Single

Bradman reached 50 with a smartly run single off Johnston after he had cover-driven that bowler to the fence. Then Bradman had to stretch out in earnest on the second run of two which took Hamence to 78.

Hamence was still "seeing them," and scored the easiest four of his innings past mid-off from a no-ball by Ring. When the 200 was reached in 192 minutes, Miller was brought on to bowl with the new ball.

**Hamence reached his century in Miller's second over, hooking a short pitcher to the fine-leg fence.**

A few balls later he waved the bat round his head like a tennis racket to send a flier to fine leg, but Hassett cut it off for a single, Hamence's century had taken 180 minutes, with 11 fours.

## Powerful Hitting

Bradman and Hamence were both hitting powerfully, and Hamence brought off one of the prettiest shots of the day to take Johnston off his toes, the ball giving no fieldsman a chance as it sped to the square-leg fence.

With Freer at the cathedral end, Hamence was lured forward by a well-flighted ball and patted it back to the bowler for an easy catch. Hamence took 214 minutes for his 116 (12 fours) total. His partnership with Bradman had been worth 195.

Bradman went along confidently to his century (in 168 minutes). The crowd were beginning to ask Hassett pertinent questions about Tribe, and when he was called on to bowl from the Cathedral end there were ironical cheers.

**Bradman jumped out to Tribe but instead of immediately swinging round to ground his bat he hesitated. Amazingly so did Baker, who must have fumbled with the ball slightly, but the keeper was still able to take off the bails with Bradman out of his crease.**

# AUSTRALIA'S TEST SIDE CHOSEN

## 12 Players Announced By Selectors

### By HARRY KNEEBONE

*Twelve players have been chosen by the Australian selectors (Messrs. D. G. Bradman, E. A. Dwyer and J. Ryder) to represent Australia in the First Test match against England, to be played in Brisbane, beginning on Friday week.*

The players, announced in Sydney last night by the chairman of the Australian Board of Control (Mr. R. A. Oxlade) are (in alphabetical order):—

- **S. G. BARNES** (NSW)
- **D. G. BRADMAN** (SA)
- **A. L. HASSETT** (V)
- **I. JOHNSON** (V)
- **R. LINDWALL** (NSW)
- **C. McCOOL** (QLD)
- **K. MEULEMAN** (V)
- **K. R. MILLER** (V)
- **A MORRIS** (NSW)
- **D. TALLON** (Q)
- **E. TOSHACK** (NSW)
- **G. TRIBE** (V)

The captain will be announced by the Board of Control today, and the vice-captain on Thursday. The twelfth man has not yet been named.

J. D. Scott (SA) and G. Borwick (V) have been appointed as umpires for the First Test.

The selectors' choice will be generally applauded as the best side available. Brown's hand injury prevented him from submitting his name for selection.

Any doubts as to Miller's form were removed by the fine cricket he has played in the Sheffield Shield match in Adelaide. Tribe's inclusion, if in doubt after his apparent failure against the Englishmen, was assured after he took 13 South Australian wickets for fewer than 11 runs each.

It seems likely that Meuleman will be named as twelfth man. The reserve is sure to come from among the batsmen in the side and the young Victorian has less in the way of current form to recommend him than Morris, his rival for the opening batsman's position

# Australia v England
## First Test Match

AUSTRALIA v ENGLAND, First Test Match, at Brisbane, 29, 30 November, 2, 3, 4 and 5 December 1946.

| Australia | - First Innings | 645 |
| | - Second Innings | - |
| England | - First Innings | 141 |
| | - Second Innings | 172 |

Australia won by an innings and 332 runs.

| DON BRADMAN | - b. W.J. Edrich | 187 |
| (Captain) | | |

DON BRADMAN for the first time in a Test Match, beat W.R. Hammond in the toss, and in doing so virtually won the match for his side.    Bradman himself went in at 9 for 1, at 12.15 p.m. on the first morning, and made one of the shakiest starts of his career; his first 7 runs took him forty minutes, and in one and a quarter hours before lunch he managed to make 28, but at no time had he looked secure; just before the interval, when 28, he survived a very confident appeal for a catch at second slip off W. Voce.    Thereafter, in great heat, he and A.L. Hassett gradually mastered the bowling; Bradman's 50 came in an hour and fifty-five minutes, and by the tea interval, when he was 82, he was batting with much more of his old authority.    He completed his first century against England at Brisbane after three hours fourteen minutes, and after that began to increase his rate of scoring, so that at the close, after four hours forty-four minutes, he was 162 not out; he had by then quite recovered his old confidence.    When he had made 160, he reached 4,000 runs in Tests between England and Australia, the first batsman to do so.
He continued for a further thirty-four minutes next morning, adding 25 before W.J. Edrich bowled him off his pads with a good ball, at 322 for 3.    He batted altogether for five hours eighteen minutes and 305 balls, hit nineteen fours, and gave no actual chance; he and Hassett added 276 for the third wicket in 278 minutes.    Torrential rain after the end of Australia's innings made the wicket impossible, and England had no chance.
His partnership of 276 with Hassett was the highest for the third wicket by Australia against any Touring team in Australia.    His 187 was the highest score in a Test Match between England and Australia on the Brisbane Cricket Ground.

# AUSTRALIA v. ENGLAND
## First Test Match, Brisbane

BACK ROW   K. Miller, E. Toshack, D. Tallon.
CENTRE ROW   I. Johnson, A. R. Morris, R. Lindwall, C. McCool.
FRONT ROW   K. Meuleman, A. L. Hassett, D. G. Bradman, S. G. Barnes, G. Tribe.

## Australia

| | |
|---|---|
| S. G. Barnes c Bedser b Wright... 31 | D. Tallon lbw b Edrich ......... 14 |
| A. Morris c Hammond b Bedser.. 2 | R. Lindwall c Voce b Wright..... 31 |
| D. G. Bradman b Edrich.........187 | G. Tribe c Gibb b Edrich........ 1 |
| A. L. Hassett c Yardley b Bedser..128 | E. Toshack not out ........... 1 |
| K. R. Miller lbw b Wright....... 79 | B 5, l-b 11, w 2, n-b 11 ...... 29 |
| C. McCool lbw b Wright........ 95 | — |
| I. W. Johnson lbw b Wright...... 47 | 645 |

## England

| | |
|---|---|
| L. Hutton b Miller ................. 7 | — c Barnes b Miller ......... 0 |
| C. Washbrook c Barnes b Miller ....... 6 | — c Barnes b Miller ......... 13 |
| W. J. Edrich c McCool b Miller ....... 16 | — lbw b Toshack ........... 7 |
| D. Compton lbw b Miller ........... 17 | — c Barnes b Toshack ....... 15 |
| W. R. Hammond lbw b Toshack ...... 32 | — b Toshack ............... 23 |
| J. T. Ikin c Tallon b Miller ........... 0 | — b Tribe ................. 32 |
| N. W. D. Yardley c Tallon b Toshack .. 29 | — c Hassett b Toshack ...... 0 |
| P. A. Gibb b Miller ............... 13 | — lbw b Toshack .......... 11 |
| W. Voce not out .................. 1 | — c Hassett b Tribe ....... 18 |
| A. V. Bedser lbw b Miller ......... 0 | — c and b Toshack ......... 18 |
| D. V. P. Wright c Tallon b Toshack .... 4 | — not out ................. 10 |
| B 8, l-b 3, w 2, n-b 3 ........... 16 | B 15, l-b 7, w 1, n-b 2 . 25 |
| | — |
| 141 | 172 |

## England Bowling

| | O. | M. | R. | W. | O. | M. | R. | W. |
|---|---|---|---|---|---|---|---|---|
| Voce ......... | 28 | 9 | 92 | 0 | | | | |
| Bedser ....... | 41 | 4 | 159 | 2 | | | | |
| Wright ........ | 43 6 | 4 | 167 | 5 | | | | |
| Edrich ....... | 25 | 2 | 107 | 3 | | | | |
| Yardley ....... | 13 | 1 | 47 | 0 | | | | |
| Ikin........... | 2 | 0 | 24 | 0 | | | | |
| Compton ..... | 6 | 0 | 20 | 0 | | | | |

## Australia Bowling

| | O. | M. | R. | W. | O. | M. | R. | W. |
|---|---|---|---|---|---|---|---|---|
| Lindwall ....... | 12 | 4 | 23 | 0 | | | | |
| Miller ........ | 22 | 4 | 60 | 7 | 11 | 3 | 17 | 2 |
| Toshack ...... | 16.5 | 11 | 17 | 3 | 20.7 | 2 | 82 | 6 |
| McCool ....... | 1 | 0 | 5 | 0 | | | | |
| Tribe ......... | 9 | 2 | 19 | 0 | 12 | 2 | 48 | 2 |
| Barnes ..... .. | 1 | 0 | 1 | 0 | | | | |

### FALL OF WICKETS

AUSTRALIA:

| 1 | 2 | 3 | 4 | 5 | 6 | 7 | 8 | 9 | 10 |
|---|---|---|---|---|---|---|---|---|---|
| 9 | 46 | 322 | 428 | 465 | 596 | 599 | 629 | 643 | 645 |

ENGLAND—First Innings:

| 1 | 2 | 3 | 4 | 5 | 6 | 7 | 8 | 9 | 10 |
|---|---|---|---|---|---|---|---|---|---|
| 10 | 25 | 49 | 56 | 56 | 121 | 134 | 136 | 136 | 141 |

ENGLAND—Second Innings:

| 1 | 2 | 3 | 4 | 5 | 6 | 7 | 8 | 9 | 10 |
|---|---|---|---|---|---|---|---|---|---|
| 0 | 13 | 33 | 62 | 65 | 65 | 112 | 114 | 143 | 172 |

Umpires: J. D. Scott and G. Borwick.

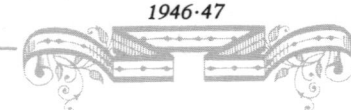

# BRADMAN'S FIGHTING CENTURY

BRISBANE, Friday. — Don Bradman scored a century in the first Test at Brisbane today, and with his vice-captain, Hassett, retrieved the situation for Australia after a disastrous opening.

On 97, Bradman hit the ball to the boundary, and the entire crowd rose to its feet and cheered the ball along. There was a mighty roar as it reached the fence.

*Left-hander Morris (2) snicked a ball within reach of Hammond's clutching hands and Barnes (31) was out to a sensational catch by the 6ft. 3in. Bedser. A shorter man would have had no possible chance of making the catch. Barnes had batted brilliantly.*

**A record crowd for the opening day of a Test at Brisbane applauded every scoring shot as Bradman and Hassett fought to retrieve Australia's position.**

Bradman opened scratchily and struggled for runs before lunch. But this afternoon he suddenly found touch, and at tea he and Hassett had put on 139 for the third wicket.

Bradman slips after failing to connect with a no-ball from Bedser. It was one of 21 no-balls bowled—Bedser 12, Wright 5, Voce 3, Edrich 1.

# Australia's Position "Almost Unbeatable"

### From C. V. GRIMMETT

*BRISBANE, November 29.*

*The end of the first day's play in the First Test has placed Australia in an almost unbeatable position —three hundred runs on the board and only two wickets down. What a happy ending after the first day. This has been brought about by the captain himself, ably assisted by his first lieutenant Hassett.*

The England bowlers gave their best performance to date. Bedser in particular being outstanding. England was really unlucky to lose Bedser's services through indisposition for a long part of the day. Without him, England could make no progress. Australia's winning of the toss promised the big advantage which usually accompanies first use of the wicket. When Morris lost his wicket after scoring two, one of Australia's most likely-looking openers was back in the pavilion.

This was followed shortly afterwards by a sensational catch by Bedser to dismiss Barnes.

Bedser started off with plenty of hostility and bowled better than I have previously seen him. He made the ball move both ways and obtained plenty of nip off the pitch.

## Bradman "Scratchy"

With Morris out, Bradman joined Barnes and had a very worried time. He was very scratchy at first and might have been out several times. On one occasion he attempted to hit a ball through the covers from Voce. The ball flew straight to Ikin at second slip. Bradman made no attempt to move and an appeal was made but it was disallowed by Umpire Borwick.

Several other times edged strokes through the slips made the Englishmen feel optimistic, but Bradman weathered the storm.

From a critical position, Bradman gradually got on top of the bowling. Although restrained in comparison with the old Bradman, he soon showed that he was far from being a back number.

Barnes had settled down and was playing good cricket. He took no risks, but punished anything loose. Wright bowled several shortish balls which Barnes hooked to the fence. However, one particularly short one he hit hard to Bedser, fielding near the umpire and just behind square leg. Bedser reached up and stopped the ball, which he caught at the second attempt. It was a great catch.

The bowling at this stage was very hostile, with the exception of a few shortish balls from Wright. Voce also had been doing a good job, although he was not as dangerous as Bedser. I thought Bedser was kept on too long in his first spell—70 minutes without a break

## Heat Trying

The heat was very trying and it was only to be expected that the bowlers would wilt under the conditions. This made it more important to keep them as fresh as possible by short bursts.

I realise how difficult it is for a captain to relieve a bowler who is doing well. All the bowlers to-day stuck to the job gamely—a heart-breaking task against two such great batsmen.

Wright did not worry them a great deal, although occasionally he beat them with good balls.

After seeing today's play I am more convinced than ever that no team should take the field without a slow spin bowler. Even though a bowler of this type is not high class, the spinning ball always has a chance of being mis-hit.

The pitch today was a good batting one and many more runs should be possible on it. No fault could be found with Hammond's field placing today.

What can one say about that breaker of bowlers' hearts—Bradman? He is unlike anyone else and a law unto himself. Although not the dashing player we saw in pre-war days, Bradman is still a great player. He seems to be able to do just what he wants. Nothing is beyond him.

## Masterly Hassett

Bradman played a captain's part and saw to it that Hassett took no risks. With Hassett's end blocked up the moral effect was great, and it was noticeable how surely and relentlessly Bradman had things worked out. He lost no opportunities to score and took full toll of anything loose.

Hassett never took the slightest risk. He was as safe as it was possible to be and played a masterly innings.

One grand feature was the splendid sustained effort in the field. Each and everyone pulled his weight, and great dash was shown to the end.

## Don Draws A Crowd

DON BRADMAN, the cricketer, was responsible for this crowd gathered outside the Grenfell street office of Mr. Bradman, the stockbroker, yesterday afternoon. The picture was taken when Bradman was making his brilliant score of 162 not out.

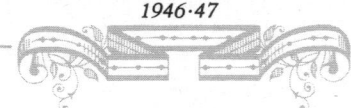

# BRADMAN-HASSETT BREAK RECORDS IN TEST

FROM ROY COLMER

**B**RISBANE.—Don Bradman added 25 to his overnight score before he was bowled by Edrich for 187 in the first Test against England here today, and three records had then been established.

Bradman's partnership with Hassett had set a record for the third wicket by an Australian pair against England and soon afterwards had beaten the record (held by Hammond and Jardine) for third wicket in Anglo-Australian Tests. The captain's score was the highest in a Brisbane Test between the two countries.

After Bradman's dismissal Hassett went on to score his first Test century against England and his new partner, Miller, hit out freely at the English bowlers to bring up 400 with three wickets down.

## 20,000 at Resumption

**N**EARLY 20,000 people, most of them sitting in hot sunshine, saw Hammond lead the Englishmen on to the field. The row was deafening as Bradman and Hassett followed.

Bedser opened the bowling, Bradman scoring two singles, and Hassett one. After Voce had bowled one ball, Hammond sent Yardley from third slip to strengthen the cover field. Bradman promptly scored a single with an on-drive.

The 250-run partnership had broken the Australian Test record for a third wicket stand—established by Bradman and McCabe at Melbourne in 1936-7.

Bradman and Hassett had been together for 248 minutes.

The next over from Bedser saw the tally reach 300 in 309 minutes. Both batsmen were batting confidently, although Bedser found the edge of Bradman's bat once in his second over.

The English pace attack with the old ball and a day's hard work behind them, was nowhere near as hostile as at the opening of the game.

Hassett was again playing the rock, and Bradman added 10 while the Victorian was putting on two.

A record for a third-wicket partnership in Anglo-Australian Tests was established in the next over from Bedser. Bradman square cut him for four to beat the record of 262 standing to the credit of Hammond and Jardine in Adelaide in 1928-9.

Bradman was in full cry now and going at full speed for his double century. He on drove a no-ball from Voce to the boundary and repeated the shot off the next ball. He had raced on 22 in 20 minutes.

**Hassett was very slow, making no attempt to force the pace but allowing Bradman to do the scoring. He scored three in the first half-hour while Bradman was adding 25.**

Edrich opened his first bowling spell with a wide. Off his fourth ball Bradman played defensively, but the ball whipped fast from the pitch and appeared to swing late to take the off stump

Bradman had taken 316 minutes for his 187, which included 19 fours. His partnership with Hassett had put on 276 in even time.

Bradman had added 25 to his overnight score. His 187 is the highest individual tally ever scored in a Test between England and Australia in Brisbane.

Miller opened dashingly against Edrich, swinging him twice to square leg for two. Hassett did not attempt to take over the attacking role with the dismissal of Bradman. He was content to keep his end going. A crisp late cut by Miller gave him a single off Edrich.

Then Hassett scored two for a shot to square leg. This shot gave him five runs in 40 minutes. He scored a single from the next ball with an on drive.

Two grand late cuts by Miller were stopped on the fence by Hutton at deep third man, the first for a single, the second placed finer for two.

# BALL THAT BOWLED BRADMAN

THIS PICTURE graphically illustrates how Don Bradman was clean-bowled by English all-rounder Bill Edrich, after Bradman had scored 187—highest Test score ever made at Brisbane. Edrich's ball made pace off the wicket and beat Bradman all the way. The innings gave Bradman an England-Australia Test aggregate scoring record of more than 4000 runs.

# McCOOL TOO HOT FOR ENGLISHMEN

### (By EX-INTERNATIONAL H. L. ("STORK") HENDRY)

BRISBANE, Saturday.—The glory of today's cricket belongs to local lad Colin McCool whose brilliant batting from the first ball bowled to him, lifted the game out of the doldrums into which it had drifted in the period between lunch and tea.

McCool gave a perfect demonstration of how tired bowling should be dealt with, and by his magnificent partnership with Ian Johnson has completely sealed the position for Australia.

**These two young players did what everyone on the ground knew our earlier batsmen should have attempted.**

McCool has had a sensational introduction into big cricket this year.

**He was picked purely as a slow bowler and now in his first Test has stolen the show with brilliant batting.**

## Time Will Tell

McCool has established himself as Australia's greatest all-rounder of the moment for his slip fielding ability is fully acknowledged.

The result of the Test is now only a matter of time as two days in the field will have taken heavy toll of the visitors, and as a result their batting is certain to suffer.

I speak from experience, knowing the dreadful feeling a bowler has when he is compelled to "come up" next morning after a hard day in the field.

We went through all this in the hidings Wally Hammond and Co. gave us in 1928-29.

That is why my sympathies were all with the Englishmen yesterday morning.

It was like starting the match over again, but with a tired set of bowlers Still, they were lucky they did not get their leather-hunting right at the start instead of at the end of the day.

Colin McCool.

Why Bradman adopted defence and not attack tactics is known only to himself. Unquestionably it was very bad captaincy and unworthy of such a player.

Personally, I consider Bradman should have sent Tallon in as soon as Miller got out, with instructions to get runs or get out. As these two Queenslanders are such great friends and have co-operated so well as a bowling-keeping combination it was reasonable to assume that McCool would have inspired Tallon as a batting partner in a hurricane knock.

Lindwall, too, would have been a faster scorer than Johnson, although no fault could be found with the manner in which this other all-rounder carried on in the right spirit to the best of his ability.

When Bradman started off in his top form this morning hopes were entertained that he would proceed to deal with the bowling as it deserved late on the first day. But the wicket was a little faster and in trying to force a straight ball to the on he was beaten by the pace off the wicket.

**Don had played a remarkable innings. From a very poor first half hour during which he looked like a batsman out of place in a Test, he had, by sheer determination and concentration, re-established himself in Test cricket.**

Bradman's dismissal was like a cold shower to the Englishmen, but its effect was only as lasting for Miller began with a brilliance that promised to cause them more trouble than even Don at his best.

Meanwhile, Hassett had ceased to be a batsman at all, but with his partner scoring well Hassett's immobility was not so noticeable. When

Lindsay Hassett.

on resuming Miller proceeded to square cut, late cut, and cover drive it really looked as though the tempo would be appreciably increased, especially when he walked into a half volley from Wright and hit it for six.

Hassett had played the rock so long he seemed incapable of making a stroke and after being missed twice—once by Hammond off Wright and then by Bedser off Compton—he hit a feeble catch to Yardley.

I have always been a great admirer of Hassett, but today I was ashamed of him.

## Bowlers Battled

Admittedly his knock had been invaluable to the team, as when he came in the position was delicate, and his impregnable defence was welcome. However, there are few batsmen more capable of thrashing a cornered attack than Hassett and the stage was all set for him to play his natural game. But he became more helpless.

When the new ball was taken after the 400 was reached, new life was introduced into the attack, and it was grand to see Voce and Bedser coming back with such energy and vigor.

They were both very unlucky and should have collected a couple of wickets; not only were catches dropped, but snicks were flying just out of reach of slips.

Edrich did a grand job with his fastish bowling, and Wright, except in the closing stages, bowled consistently well to have all the batsmen on the defensive.

Anything the Englishmen could not stop with their hands was done so with their feet, and many runs were saved thereby

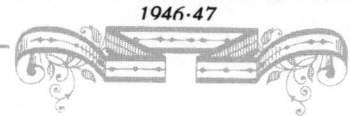

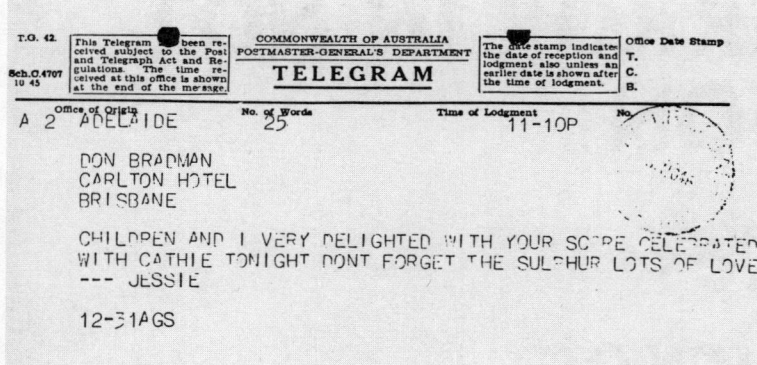

Telegram to DON BRADMAN, CARLTON HOTEL, BRISBANE, from ADELAIDE:

CHILDREN AND I VERY DELIGHTED WITH YOUR SCORE CELEBRATED WITH CATHIE TONIGHT DONT FORGET THE SULPHUR LOTS OF LOVE --- JESSIE

Telegram to DON BRADMAN, CRICKET GROUND BRISBANE, from BOWRAL:

CONGRATULATIONS ON YOUR MARVELLOUS RECOVERY FROM ALL DISTRICT CRICKETERS AND MYSELF BEST REGADS

ALF STEPHENS

Telegram to DON BRADMAN, CARLTON HOTEL BRIBANE, from ADELAIDE:

CONGRATULATIONS PLEASE DO IT AGAIN AND AGAIN ALL AT NO SIXTY THINKING OF YOU REGARDS

FORBES

# As Cardus Sees The Test

## By NEVILLE CARDUS.

BRISBANE, Monday.—The third day of play in the first Test match began to-day in a steam of heat with no sun.

Australia's first innings proceeded on a wicket still easy, and the remaining Australian batsmen came in probably intent on a sort of pillage in the already plundered citadel of England's attack.

But the Australian rearguard was not at all impressive, either in offence or defence, until Lindwall laid about Wright, who began the morning by removing Johnson and McCool as unceremoniously as a waiter clears away empty bottles the morning after.

These wickets fell to his proper length, curving not too quickly to a point just short of the half-volley. Much too frequently Wright bowls along a trajectory straight down to the blockhole.

And when Lindwall drove him for six, Wright seemed at once to rearrange his field for sixes, leaving Hammond with the wicketkeeper as his only conversational refuge.

None of the Australians except Lindwall this morning threw his wicket away. Mainly they struggled as though sternly saving the match.

## But For Bradman—

After witnessing and sitting through this vast total of Australia, I am satisfied that the position in the Test matches remains more or less as in 1938. But for Bradman England could at least entertain furtive hopes of winning the rubber in spite of their less than great attack.

In circumstances as trying to Englishmen as any likely to be experienced again on the tour, only Miller and Bradman (in the second part of his innings) suggested a class and ability beyond the means of tolerably good bowling to get rid of on reasonably profitable terms.

A match more or less becalmed was quickened dramatically into motion as soon as Lindwall bowled.

He compelled Hutton into involuntary twitchy jerks and at least one ducking or genuflection.

Lindwall runs a long way to bowl, he gallops with the true fast bowler's gathering of momentum, and his arm comes over with a vehement body swing. He is not a McDonald or a Gregory, but probably he commands a velocity that is becoming almost fabulous in English cricket.

Miller, too, provoked most hurried thrusts and stabs from both Hutton and Washbrook.

The sky darkened and immediately after lunch thunder rumbled, even as Hutton succumbed to nothing but a pace unusual in his experience nowadays.

## Edrich, Gladiator

The fall of Hutton's wicket, the exultant roar of the crowd, and the sense of gathering storm stimulated the imagination.

A strong—almost reckless—on-drive by Edrich as soon as, gladiatorially, he entered the arena was like an act propitiatory to the gods, who were now threatening England with sinful fortune.

Then, as an added touch of irony, a shower of rain drove the combatants into the pavilion. It was as though the curtain had fallen by accident at the wrong moment while the players were all working up truly histrionic attitudes.

This first pause was brief: In less than no time Lindwall made Edrich rear on his right foot and found him seeking the handle of his bat.

Miller, not as quick as Lindwall in general, sent one ball every now and again that enlivened the slips to expectation.

Another irritating shower occurred just before 3 o'clock.

If the gods wish England to lose the match on a sticky wicket, let them mercifully show their hands here and now—and no half measures. Or, as Lady Bracknell says, no shilly-shallying.

To have to bat against an aggregate of more than 600 after two days of hard labour is an ordeal enough in itself. The spectre of a bowler's pitch lurking overhead in the vacillating clouds comes as an unjust influence to an issue in which resolution and technique on both sides would prefer to fend for themselves.

# BRADMAN'S ERROR IN NOT USING JOHNSON

## England Struggles On Hostile Wicket

### From ARTHUR MAILEY

**BRISBANE, Tuesday. —** Australia's captain, Don Bradman, erred in the First Test today by not using slow bowler Ian Johnson when England were fighting desperately on a hostile wicket.

**England had lost 5-117 when bad light ended play for the day at 4.22 p.m.**

Johnson's good-length spinners would probably have caused a complete collapse of the English team.

This was Bradman's only mistake.

The manner in which he handled the other bowlers was commendable.

**Miller's bowling was the highlight, and Toshack's medium-paced left-hand deliveries the poorest feature of the day's play.**

Miller, who took all five wickets, worried all the batsmen.

After his first few overs he slackened pace and bowled off-spinners.

Only 10 runs were scored from Toshack's 11 overs, but this economy was the result of his lack of direction rather than his hostility.

In one of Toshack's overs Edrich ignored nearly every ball.

At times Toshack made poor use of the pitch which the elements had made to order for him.

Bradman repeatedly walked up and spoke to Toshack, who was allowing a splendid opportunity—and apparently the ball—to slip through his fingers.

From an Australian point of view, the pre-lunch period was disappointing.

### Cordon Of Fieldsmen

At least six wickets were expected, but this hope was destroyed by the failure of Toshack to take advantage of the conditions.

The fact that Bradman replaced him after he had sent down only eight overs for eight runs was proof of this.

If Toshack had given the assistance required of him, Australia would have broken the back of England's batting.

Six-foot Miller and tiny Edrich, both former Air Force pilots, became engaged in a friendly "dog-fight."

Although Miller slackened his pace to bowl off-spinners, he struck Edrich time after time.

Edrich breathed a sigh of relief when he managed to scramble to the other end to face the less aggressive Toshack.

England lost only one wicket, Washbrook, during the first hour of the battle.

This was either a great reflection on the efficiency of Australia's attack, or a well-deserved recommendation of England's tenacity and stubbornness.

After Compton had made 17 runs by courageous batting, he was given out leg-before-wicket from a sinister-looking shooter which did not lift from the pitch.

Miller at this stage had taken 3-20.

Toshack, whose seven somewhat negative overs had cost only eight runs, was then replaced by Lindwall.

I was told in England that Edrich could take anything, and he proved this today.

He was hit everywhere and finally had to leave the field to have a split finger dressed.

Miller dismissed Edrich and Ikin with successive balls in his first over after lunch.

In each case the batsmen played a quite unnecessary stroke.

Edrich appeared to lose his concentration, which was so intense during the pre-lunch period.

He made only 16 runs in an hour and a half, but the time he spent at the wickets was of much greater value to his team than the number of runs he scored.

**Bradman's decision to replace Miller with Tribe was a matter of speculation.**

I would have preferred to have seen Johnson get a chance.

### Another Chance

He is a bowler of greater experience and more consistent length, and he might have caused a complete rout.

His first over was a good one, but the pitch proved to be better suited to other types of bowlers.

Toshack, who should have been the ideal bowler, was given another chance.

He was again economical but unconvincing.

After rain had caused an adjournment a greasy ball inconvenienced the spin bowlers and enabled Hammond and Yardley to collect 20 or 30 valuable runs.

Bradman tried Toshack, McCool, and Miller in turn, but none of them worried the batsmen.

It became an even greater mystery then why Johnson was not given a chance.

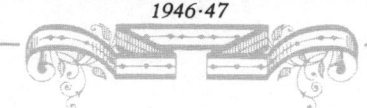

# AUSTRALIA'S INNINGS VICTORY IN FIRST TEST

# England Out For 141, 172

*(From Our Special Representative)*

**B**RISBANE, Wednesday.—In a sensational day's cricket, Australia has beaten England by an innings in the first Test.

*England's best batsmen, fighting desperately for runs and time, were bundled out in rapid order on a bad wicket by Miller, Toshack and Tribe.*

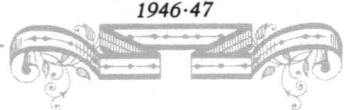

# Australia v England
## Second Test Match

The second Test at Sydney virtually decided the 1946–47 series. England won the toss, had every opportunity to profit by the tactical advantage this gave her, even derived some benefit from the inclement weather, but the resourceful all round strength of the Australian side was too much.

*Don Bradman*

AUSTRALIA v ENGLAND, Second Test Match, at Sydney, 13, 14, 16, 17, 18 and 19 December 1946.

| | | |
|---|---|---|
| Australia | - First Innings 659 for 8 wickets dec. | |
| | - Second Innings | |
| England | - First Innings | 255 |
| | - Second Innings | 371 |

Australia won by an innings and 33 runs.

DON BRADMAN (Captain) - lbw. b. N.W.D. Yardley 234

Suffering both from a leg injury and gastric trouble, DON BRADMAN did not field on the second day, and batted sixth, joining S.G. Barnes at 159 for 4 at 3.50 p.m. on the third day. Five not out at the interval, he took sixty-three minutes to make 14, but thereafter batted well to be 52 not out overnight; he completed 50, four minutes before the close, in an hour and fifty-one minutes. Next day, he and Barnes continued their fifth-wicket stand, and were not separated until seventeen minutes from the close of play, by which time they had added 405. Bradman, adding 34 in eighty-eight minutes, was 86 at the lunch interval, and at 2.35 p.m. completed his century in two minutes under three and three-quarter hours; he had made 151 by tea, reached 200 at 5.21 p.m., after six hours eleven minutes at the wicket, and then hit out, adding a further 34 in twenty-two minutes, before being lbw. swinging wildly at N.W.D. Yardley. He batted altogether for three minutes longer than six and a half hours, hit twenty fours, and gave no chance.

This was Bradman's eight century in successive Test Matches in which he batted, all against England, but his first against England at Sydney. He was the only batsman to make centuries in England v. Australia Test Matches in all four Australian cities, and the only one to make double-centuries in Test Matches at Sydney, Melbourne, Adelaide and both grounds at Brisbane. It was also Bradman's twenty-third century in all Test cricket. His partnership of 405 for the fifth wicket with Barnes broke numerous records, and was a world record for that wicket. It was the highest for any wicket against any Touring team in Australia. With this partnership, Bradman completed an extraordinary sequence, being concerned in the record partnerships in Test Matches for the second, third, fourth, fifth and sixth wickets, all v. England. This was the eighth time that he had scored three (or more) centuries in successive innings in first-class cricket; it was the fifth time he had done so wholly in Australia, equal to Ponsford's record. This was his fourth century in successive innings in Test Matches in Australia all against England.

Bradman was the oldest (as well as the youngest) player to make a double-century in Tests between England and Australia; he was thirty-eight years 112 days old.

## England

| | | | | |
|---|---|---|---|---|
| L. Hutton c Tallon b Johnson | 39 | — hit wkt b Miller | 37 |
| C. Washbrook b Freer | 1 | — c McCool b Johnson | 41 |
| W. J. Edrich lbw b McCool | 71 | — b McCool | 119 |
| D. Compton c Tallon b McCool | 5 | — c Bradman b Freer | 54 |
| W. R. Hammond c Tallon b McCool | 1 | — c Toshack b McCool | 37 |
| J. T. Ikin c Hassett b Johnson | 60 | — b Freer | 17 |
| N. W. D. Yardley c Tallon b Johnson | 25 | — b McCool | 35 |
| T. P. B. Smith lbw b Johnson | 4 | — c Hassett b Johnson | 2 |
| T. G. Evans b Johnson | 5 | — st Tallon b McCool | 9 |
| A. V. Bedser b Johnson | 14 | — not out | 3 |
| D. V. P. Wright not out | 15 | — c Tallon b McCool | 0 |
| B 4, l-b 11 | 15 | B 8, l-b 6, w 1, n-b 2 | 17 |
| | **255** | | **371** |

## Australia

| | | | | |
|---|---|---|---|---|
| S. G. Barnes c Ikin b Bedser | 234 | C. McCool c Hammond b Smith | 12 |
| A. Morris b Edrich | 5 | D. Tallon c and b Wright | 30 |
| I. W. Johnson c Washbrook b Edrich | 7 | F. Freer not out | 28 |
| A. L. Hassett c Compton b Edrich | 34 | G. Tribe not out | 25 |
| K. R. Miller c Evans b Smith | 40 | L-b 7, w 1, n-b 2 | 10 |
| D. G. Bradman lbw b Yardley | 234 | Eight wkts., dec. | 659 |

E. Toshack did not bat.

## Australia Bowling

| | O. | M. | R. | W. | | O. | M. | R. | W. |
|---|---|---|---|---|---|---|---|---|---|
| Miller | 9 | 2 | 24 | 0 | | 11 | 3 | 37 | 1 |
| Freer | 7 | 1 | 25 | 1 | | 13 | 2 | 49 | 2 |
| Toshack | 7 | 2 | 6 | 0 | | 6 | 1 | 16 | 0 |
| Tribe | 20 | 3 | 70 | 0 | | 12 | 0 | 40 | 0 |
| Johnson | 30.1 | 12 | 42 | 6 | | 29 | 7 | 92 | 2 |
| McCool | 23 | 2 | 73 | 3 | | 32.4 | 4 | 109 | 5 |
| Barnes | | | | | | 3 | 0 | 11 | 0 |

## England Bowling

| | O. | M. | R. | W. |
|---|---|---|---|---|
| Bedser | 46 | 7 | 153 | 1 |
| Edrich | 26 | 2 | 79 | 3 |
| Wright | 46 | 8 | 169 | 1 |
| Smith | 37 | 1 | 172 | 2 |
| Ikin | 3 | 0 | 15 | 0 |
| Compton | 6 | 0 | 38 | 0 |
| Yardley | 9 | 0 | 23 | 1 |

### FALL OF THE WICKETS

ENGLAND—First Innings:

| 1 | 2 | 3 | 4 | 5 | 6 | 7 | 8 | 9 | 10 |
|---|---|---|---|---|---|---|---|---|---|
| 10 | 88 | 97 | 99 | 148 | 187 | 197 | 205 | 234 | 255 |

ENGLAND—Second Innings:

| 1 | 2 | 3 | 4 | 5 | 6 | 7 | 8 | 9 | 10 |
|---|---|---|---|---|---|---|---|---|---|
| 49 | 118 | 220 | 280 | 309 | 327 | 346 | 366 | 369 | 371 |

AUSTRALIA:

| 1 | 2 | 3 | 4 | 5 | 6 | 7 | 8 |
|---|---|---|---|---|---|---|---|
| 24 | 37 | 96 | 169 | 564 | 564 | 595 | 617 |

Umpires: J. D. Scott and G. Borwick.

Bradman, going out to practise,
is besieged by youthful autograph hunters.

# "AUSSIE BOWLERS MAGNIFICENT"

### By W. E. BOWES, former English Test player, Special to the Globe

I am not going to waste time making excuses for the failure of the English batsmen. Here and now I am a bowler, praising to the fullest fellow bowlers. Seldom does the bowler receive credit for his performance.

Critics write that the batsmen are in error—they played forward when they should have played back.

The wicket was wet, green, sticky or crumbling—always they find the alibi for the batsman.

Never indeed do you find that the bowler, by his ability to flight the ball, spin it, or by clever positioning of the fieldsmen, has dominated the day's play. Well, in this second Test match you have it.

The Australian bowlers were magnificent, and, if you can show me a better bowling performance than that of offspinner Johnson, who on a first day Test wicket bowled 30 overs for 42 runs — never mind the six wickets—and attacked the batsmen all the time, well, I would like to hear of it.

### JOHNSON SECURE

There was none of the negative safety-first tactics of Toshack about his bowling. He tossed it high, quicker, slower.

He varied his attack perceptibly and cleverly, and I give him main honors.

If he does not get another wicket this tour, I am convinced that, in 1948, when you visit England, Johnson should be a first choice.

He will get 100 wickets easily on our wetter, slower wickets, especially if he learns to bowl round the wickets, too.

As for Colin McCool, I have heard, so many times from experienced colleagues, that he is not to be compared with your bowlers of old. In view of their experience I will not presume to argue.

May I suggest, however, that no player of the past has had a more convincing debut than this lad. He has done his stuff with the ball on every occasion, and his innings of 95 at Brisbane was not the innings of a mug, either.

Let me be perfectly honest, the Australian bowling side is far better balanced and much more varied than that of the Englishmen.

What is more, they took advantage of the slight help to be derived from a Sydney wicket, responsive to spin.

I said in a previous article that the Test match might well be a bowlers' Test, and I still hold that view — it has still to be proved that England's spin bowlers cannot use it so well as yours.

If they do, then it has also to to be proved that your batsmen are better than ours.

And now here comes the rain. The match is far from over. We have got 255 runs on the book, and you have got to get them.

# Only 63 runs scored in 93 minutes batting

## By GEORGE THATCHER

**Sixty-three runs were scored in the 93 minutes' play on the second day of the Second Test at the Cricket Ground yesterday.**

**England lost the wickets of Ikin and Bedser for an addition of 36 runs to the overnight score of 8 for 219.**

Australia have lost the wicket of Morris for 27.

A heavy thunderstorm at one o'clock and bad light interrupted play.

England's tail-enders added 36 to the overnight score of eight for 219.

Bradman, who has a pulled leg muscle, did not field. Hassett taking over the captaincy.

The 12th man, Meuleman, fielded in Bradman's place.

McCool and Johnson resumed the Australian attack.

Ikin survived two early chances.

Tallon dropped a snick from Johnson when Ikin was 58.

In the following over by McCool, Tallon missed a difficult stumping.

McCool then dropped Bedser off Johnson.

Two balls later Hassett caught Ikin at mid-off from Johnson.

Ikin, 60 (three fours), batted 174 minutes.

Wright and Bedser displayed greater confidence than the earlier Englishmen.

Bedser cover-drove Johnson to the boundary, and Wright swept a full-toss from McCool to the fence.

Tribe relieved McCool at 247.

He opened with three long hops.

The 250 came up in 330 minutes.

Then Wright straight-drove Tribe to the southern sightboard.

## Bedser Out

Two balls later Johnson bowled Bedser with a ball that made pace.

Bedser batted 51 minutes.

Wright, 15 (two fours), scored his runs in even time.

The Englishmen batted 332 minutes.

Morris and Barnes opened for Australia at 12.45.

The light was dull, and occasional lightning flashes illuminated the ground.

The umpires refused a light appeal by Barnes before Bedser opened the English attack.

Bedser used three slips, a short and silly leg.

Barnes scored three twos from Bedser's over and made two more unsuccessful light appeals.

Edrich bowled from the northern end, Morris glancing his second ball to fine leg for a single.

Barnes' fourth light appeal succeeded after Edrich had bowled three balls.

Play was suspended at 12.55.

Rain began to fall at 1.5.

Hill patrons rushed for shelter as a wild southerly swept the ground at 1.10.

Torrential rain then fell, and thousands of Hill patrons were drenched.

At the luncheon adjournment there were pools of water on the wicket.

Rain had stopped at 2.15, the usual time of resumption after lunch, but the ground was still wet, and it was not until 2.55 that Bradman and Hammond made an inspection.

The covers had been removed five minutes earlier.

The adjoining wicket was very wet and an absorbent roller was used to pick up the water.

The captains decided to make a further inspection at 3.30.

Bradman limped during the inspection.

An army of groundsmen used bags of sawdust to dry up soft patches near the wicket.

Several patrons from the Hill strolled on the ground and inspected the pitch.

A groundsman escorted them from the arena.

Freshly-cut grass had been rolled into the damp patches near the wicket before Bradman and Hammond made a second inspection of the wicket at 3.30 p.m.

The crowd hooted when the notice, "Inspection at 4 o'clock," was semaphored.

A minute later the notice was changed to, "Play at four."

The bowling approaches and the portion of the wicket where the batsmen stand, which had been covered, were not affected by the heavy shower.

The wicket appeared damp.

The crowd had dwindled to 25,000 when Edrich took up the attack to Barnes.

Edrich cut up the wicket with his foot when delivering the first ball, and placed sawdust in the hole.

Edrich cut straight through, the last ball making pace.

Bedser resumed at the Randwick end.

Morris snicked the third ball through the slips, and the players were off the field for a minute owing to a light shower.

## Hammond's Appeal

Barnes drove Bedser for a single, and Hammond appealed against the rain.

The rain had stopped before the players reached the stand.

In the excitement, umpire Borwick forgot to replace the bails.

Bedser now employed four slips to Morris, who was knocked on the hand from the last ball.

After Barnes had scored two down the gully off Edrich, Hammond brought in a fourth slip.

Barnes went to 10 with a leg glance off Edrich, and straight drove Bedser for two. He took a single from a tap to mid-on.

Barnes went to 15 with a lucky hook for two from Edrich.

Morris got Bedser through the covers for a single and Barnes forced Bedser wide of mid-on for three.

At 4.30 the score was 21, Barnes being 18, Morris 3.

Morris broke a quiet spell by hooking Bedser for a single.

Morris went at 24.

He turned his back to a short one from Edrich that turned late and the ball trickled from his legs on to his stumps.

The ball was the last of Edrich's fifth over.

Morris batted 45 minutes.

## Crowd Demonstrates

The next batsman, Ian Johnson, survived an l.b.w. appeal from the second ball of Bedser's fifth over.

His light appeal before the next delivery was refused. Then came a similar request by Barnes.

A third light appeal in two overs brought hoots from the crowd.

Another light request at 4.55 was successful.

Australia's 27 was made in 61 minutes.

Apart from the bowlers' footprints the turf was unmarked.

None of the bowlers' deliveries cut into the wicket, which probably has benefited by the rain.

Five policemen and a groundsman chased a fan who souvenired one of the stumps.

He was caught before he regained the grandstand enclosure.

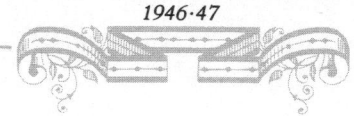

# TALKS ON TEST INCIDENTS LIKELY

**Two controversial incidents during play in the Second Test at Sydney Cricket Ground on Saturday were certain to be discussed at the New South Wales Cricket Association meeting tonight, Mr. Reg Herford, an official, said yesterday.**

The incidents were:

● Australian Sid Barnes' frequent appeals against the light;

● Englishman Bill Edrich's action in depositing sawdust on the pitch to obtain a firm foothold when bowling.

Barnes' appeals were hooted by spectators on the Hill and in the members' reserve.

Barnes appealed before Australia's innings started.

**After several more appeals, the umpires stopped play at 12.53 p.m.**

When play resumed at 4 p.m., after rain, Barnes immediately appealed again.

The umpires ruled against him, but he continued to appeal frequently, and eventually play was stopped.

Mr. Herford said that the association, in the interests of cricket, were duty bound to discuss the incidents.

He added: "I felt very sorry for the spectators. I was once a 'Hillite' myself.

"Other officials were indignant when they had an impromptu discussion on Saturday afternoon.

"It was bad enough for the spectators to see only 93 minutes' play, without having to put up with Barnes' monotonous appeals against the light

**"From my observations, it was not so much the light as the dark clouds and lightning behind the southern end that worried the batsmen.**

"In the circumstances, I don't think a light meter, if one had been available, could have been of any assistance to the umpires.

"There was no rule to prevent Barnes appealing so frequently, but there was no excuse for him doing so

"The umpires couldn't change their decision in such a short space of time, and the monotony of it all only tended to annoy the spectators.

"Edrich's action in depositing sawdust on the pitch to provide a firm foothold when bowling should have been subject to a decision under the Fair and Unfair Play Rule.

"I didn't think the use of sawdust was fair

## Appeals In Order

"We don't want a repetition of these incidents, or it will do the game harm.

"The association must do something about it."

Gordon Club secretary, Mr. P. C. Harrison, said that Barnes' appeals were in order, although they annoyed the public.

He added: "When the umpires eventually stopped play, they proved that Barnes could not have been far out in his judgment.

"Barnes was severely criticised.

"If he had taken no action, and Australia had lost three or four wickets, he would have been criticised for not having appealed."

# *Umpires to inspect test wicket today*

*By GEORGE THATCHER*

**Umpires George Borwick and Jack Scott will inspect the Test wicket at the Sydney Cricket Ground today.**

They have asked Curator Wal Gorman to be in attendance.

The umpires' powers are limited.

They will probably request Gorman to:

● Remove the sawdust from the wicket placed there by Bedser and Edrich for footholds.

● Remove the covers temporarily from the bowling approaches.

● Sweep the cut grass from the wickets near the Test strip.

The cut grass was used to dry up the moisture after yesterday's rain.

It slowed hard drives by Sid Barnes.

Curator Gorman believes yesterday's rain will assist the wicket.

He said: "If there is no more rain after 10 o'clock tomorrow morning, the wicket will be better than at any time during the match.

"There was not one ball-mark on the wicket when play ceased.

Bradman ordered the lightest of rollings when England were dismissed.

The use of a heavy roller in the absence of moisture might have cracked the surface.

The wicket will be rolled before play starts tomorrow.

The light rolling should remove the ridges caused by Edrich's footwork on the pitch.

If the wicket dries slowly, England's spin bowlers may find the strip slower and easier than when McCool and Johnson operated so successfully.

The wicket is expected to take plenty of spin late on Tuesday.

English pressmen expected Edrich to "lift" after yesterday's rain.

A former English player said: "If we have half an hour's fierce sun England's 255 might be good enough to win the game."

The sun lacked fierceness, and the drying process, particularly worrying on Australian wickets, did not eventuate.

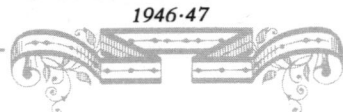

# EDRICH GETS HASSETT FOR 34

### By RAY ROBINSON

## Australia suffered a severe blow shortly after lunch in the Second Test today when vice-captain Lindsay Hassett went for 34.

On a wicket which appeared to make English bowlers, Bedser, Edrich and Wright hostile, batsmen struggled for runs.

The wicket had rolled out well and, refreshed by rain early in the weekend, looked in as good condition for batting as when Australia's spin bowlers were turning the ball off its dry surface on Friday afternoon and Saturday morning.

The prospect of its lasting out the match (timed to end at 6 pm on Thursday) had probably been improved by the rain, and by the fact that instead of five hours' wear and tear on Saturday there had been only 1½ hours' play.

Greatest risk of the surface being damaged and the wicket's life lessened had been during play after the rain on Saturday.

But only 87 balls had been bowled on the pitch while its surface was wet.

**Scars left by Edrich and Bedser's boots are 2ft. outside the leg stumps.**

When Australian captain Don Bradman and vice-captain Lindsay Hassett inspected the wicket about 11 am, they scarcely looked at these scars, but Bradman pointed to one apparently doubtful spot short of where a length ball would pitch at the southern end.

## Gasp From Crowd

A quarter of an hour before resumption, Bradman had the light roller run over the wicket for seven minutes.

Bradman had had since Friday evening to rest the pulled muscle in the back of his left leg. But he still limped slightly.

Before play, the umpires took R. L. Jones, of the Sydney Cricket Ground Trust, to the wicket to indicate that the sight-screen at the members' stand end was inadequate.

Players had told the umpires that it was not high enough to provide a white background for a tall bowler such as Bedser (6ft. 3½in.).

A bookmaker's umbrella which a group on the rails at the foot of the hill had been using as a parasol was furled before Bedser resumed bowling from the southern end into a north-east wind, which helped him to vary his late in-swingers with an occasional out-swinger.

The early crowd of 35,000 (which grew to 40,000 by lunch) gave a great gasp 15 minutes after resumption when England's fast bowler, Edrich, utterly tricked Johnson (7) by ringing in a slower ball.

Playing too soon, the Victorian all-rounder spooned up a catch to Washbrook (doubling as both cover and point).

Australia's second wicket had gone for 37, and 219 were needed to pass England's first innings when vice-captain Lindsay Has-sett came in because Bradman had lowered himself to number six in the batting order.

As in the first Test, Hassett appeared at a moment when the innings needed bracing.

Edrich, who had taken two for 15 in eight overs, flung himself so wholeheartedly into his bowling that batsmen are grateful that he has not greater height than 5ft. 6in. to enable him to make the ball fly.

**As it was, he made one or two get up rib-high to Barnes and Hassett.**

When Wright came on at 46 with the breeze over his left shoulder, his long-stepping run tickled the crowd, and many on the hill called "Oh, oh, oh," in time with his stride.

The Kent leg-spin bowler has changed his routine, at least temporarily, by discarding his former opening steps and the wing-like spread of his arms halfway through his approach.

The batsmen did not share the crowd's amusement at Wright's bowling.

## Whirled In Alarm

One quick-turning leg-break found the outer half of the bat when Hassett pushed forward cautiously and Barnes twice narrowly escaped playing on-balls, which Wright straightened up.

The second time Barnes whirled around in alarm and was relieved to find that the ball had not hit the stumps.

After 54 balls today for 12 runs, Bedser was replaced by dapper Peter Smith, aged 38, who bowled for the first time in a test against Australia.

To that stage, Bedser, Edrich and Wright had pinned Australia down to 28 runs in an hour.

Smith walks up disarmingly with six short steps, as if it were merely practice instead of an international match.

Though a short one gave Barnes the chance for his favorite square-cut to the fence, the Essex slow bowler tossed up several good leg-breaks which commanded respect from both batsmen.

The crowd enjoyed the joke when a throw-in by Edrich caught Barnes bending as he pushed his bat over the crease.

They enjoyed even more a powerful leg hit by Hassett which sent a no-ball from Wright bounding over the fence.

**Two balls later when an off-drive by Hassett beat the sprinting Hutton to the fence good spirits reigned all around the ground after the sobriety of the first hour.**

Though Smith was turning his leg breaks well enough, the balls did not come from the pitch with the snap obtained by the quicker Wright.

Once Barnes skipped back from his wicket to cut a shortish one off the middle stump for two.

Wright knelt by the pitch to relace his left boot and, firmly shod, appealed for lbw against Hassett (27).

**Then he made the vice-captain stretch to an awkward leg break which skidded wide of slip.**

Hammond, who had been setting attacking fields all the time, immediately put Ikin close up in the gully.

Next time Barnes faced Wright he was encircled by silly mid-on, silly point, close gully, and slip.

Despite this, Hassett and Barnes scored 33 in the last half-hour before lunch, when the score was 88 for two wickets (Barnes 44, Hassett 30).

Civil war broke out on the Hill when people stood up, blocking the view of hundreds sitting close wedged on the grass.

# BARNES, BRADMAN DOUBLE CENTURIES
# Test Records Go In Mammoth Partnership

By R. S. WHITINGTON

Sid Barnes and Don Bradman both passed the double century in the Test Match at the SCG today. Several Test records went during the day.

They set a new fifth wicket partnership record for Tests between Australia and England. Barnes, when he ran to 203 after tea, became the highest Australian scorer in Sydney Cricket Ground Tests.

Bradman's double century was his 11th in Anglo-Australian Tests. Official attendance was 29,673.

Don Bradman and Barnes leave the wicket for tea.

# HUTTON, WASHBROOK GO CHASING RUNS

## By RAY ROBINSON

Len Hutton opened sensationally when England began its second innings at the SCG today, 404 runs behind Australia, scoring 37 in 25 minutes.

However, trying to hook Miller's last ball before lunch he hit his wicket. At tea, after Johnson got Washbrook, two were out for 153.

*In the first 50 minutes' play today, Tallon, McCool, Freer and Tribe had added 88 runs, to create a new Test innings record in Australia, before Bradman closed the innings at 8-659.*

## Fireworks by Hutton

Bowling fast down the slope into a diagonal south-easterly breeze, Miller made the Yorkshireman duck under a rearing bumper, but Hutton forced the ball off his toes to the leg fence for his third boundary in 10 minutes.

As Hutton dodged under another bumper his left arm swung above his head, bat in hand.

The ball touched some part of the arm, and when Tallon took it, several Australians on the field appealed and about 2000 outside the fence.

Umpire Scott disallowed the appeal, apparently on the ground that the ball hit Hutton no lower on the arm than the wrist.

Drives between bowler and wicket and bowler and mid-off in Freer's third over sped to the fence, and an on-drive in fast bowler Miller's third over brought Hutton his sixth boundary in 20 minutes.

He placed the ball with a precision that could not have been bettered if his bat had been fitted with radar to detect the positions of fieldsmen.

This unexpected onslaught caused Bradman to spread the field wider. The captain was fielding at second slip—an unaccustomed position for him—to spare his leg.

When Miller hit Hutton in the back, the crowd mumbled, but whether the disapproval was at the batsman or the bowler could not be told, but the word "Larwood" could be distinguished.

Stepping back to force the last ball before lunch to the on side Hutton touched his wicket with the back of his bat.

**As he played the shot he sensed that he had played back too far and he anxiously looked behind to see the bails off.**

The crowd gasped then burst into applause, so warm that Hutton broke into a run for the last few yards to the gate. The defiance and artistry of his batting had stirred the crowd and they were sorry to see him go.

Hutton scored 37 (6 fours) of England's 49 in 25 minutes before lunch. He had so much of the strike and dominated the scene so completely that his partner Washbrook (1) seemed as idle a a gas-worker.

Two of England's shortest batsmen, Washbrook and Edrich, faced a spin attack after lunch—McCool from the south end and Johnson from the north. These were the ends they had used in the first innings, when the wind was from the north-east.

Today's south-easter was more helpful to Johnson, aiding the flight and turn of his off-spinners, but its only value to McCool was to quicken the turn of his leg-breaks.

Vigorous hooks by the capless Edrich twice made Johnson's close leg sentries. Barnes and McCool, blink and turn their heads away, but McCool had his eyes open when a ball in the Victorian's 10th over glanced off Washbrook's bat.

Diving flat on his stomach, McCool clutched the catch just above the grass four yards from the edge of the pitch.

The downfall of Washbrook (41) at 118, after an hour and a half, left England 286 in arrears with eight wickets and 7½ hours to go.

Before Compton scored, Bradman, fielding like a slip on the leg side, dived vainly for a snick off Johnson.

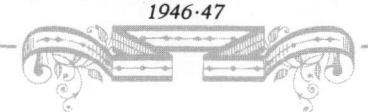

# Australia Wins Test By Innings And 33 Runs

### By RAY ROBINSON

*Dismissing England for 371 in the second innings at the SCG today, Australia won the second Test by an innings and 33 runs. Seven wickets had fallen today for 124 runs, and Australia was two up in the Test series.*

With square-cuts off Miller, Hammond took England past 250 in 235 minutes, then became involved in a stern struggle with McCool.

In his first two overs, which held England's captain scoreless, the Queensland slow bowler tossed up more testing balls than he and Tribe had bowled in 25 overs yesterday, when, in seeking the right spots, they had looked for them in the wrong place—too far down the wicket.

**Edrich had batted 23 minutes today before he scored by clumping McCool past cover to the fence.**

Forty minutes after resumption, England suffered a disastrous blow, when McCool won his contest with Hammond (37) in his seventh over.

A majestic straight drive off the first ball had got through to the fence past Toshack, who seemed slow in starting for it.

**Three balls later Hammand lifted another straight drive, and this time Toshack** ran across smartly for the catch, 20 yards behind the bowler.

At last Edrich reached his 100 with an on-shot off Johnson. The crowd was small but they made a brave noise in recogition of the stocky Middlesex batsman's indomitable effort, and the Australian fieldsmen joined in the applause.

Hammond shook his head ruefully as he walked away. Perhaps the fate of the match had depended on the length of his innings.

In his partnership of 60 in 64 minutes with Edrich he hit a six and two fours, but did not reach full certainty of touch.

Slackening his pace and apparently using off-spin instead of swing Freer bowled to an onside field of six and skittled Ikin (17), at 309.

He tricked the left-hander by suddenly ringing-in a quicker one which swung in as Ikin made a convulsive jab with the bat.

## McCool's Deadly Spell

With half the side out and the last dependable batsman, Yardley, at the wicket, the Englishmen went to lunch with the sombre outlook that 88 runs were still needed to avert an innings defeat and three and a half hours remained for play.

Edrich had been in since the first wicket fell at 49 and had overcome the difficulties of bowling and pitch while 260 were scored.

In the air war he won the DFC. There is no decoration to honor his devotion to duty in this match, though his unwavering courage "in the face of the enemy" gains him "mention in despatches" to all parts of the Empire.

In his long fight, Edrich had put a rein on his natural quick-footedness, but at 115 he made one of his skips forward to a ball which Johnson flighted cleverly into the south-easter.

**It dropped and left him stranded up the pitch, but lodged in the kneeflaps of Tallon's pads.**

While the 'keeper, hampered by his injured finger, groped for it there, Edrich scrambled back. It was his first chance.

Deceiving Edrich into playing back to a low-trajectory ball which came well up and nipped through McCool bowled him for 119. Edrich, who hit seven fours in his five and a quarter huors at the wicket, had held the innings together.

Yardley hit 12 off Johnson's 26th over, including a cover-drive through the off spaces and a hook.

At 346, Smith (2) lifted Johnson over the inner ring into Hassett's hands at wide long on. Twenty runs later Yardley (36) (four fours) misjudged McCool's flight and was bowled.

No match for McCool. Evans (9) became the leg-break bowler's fourth victim, stumped Tallon, and Australia won by an innings and 33 runs, when the wicket-keeper darted around for a catch cocked up by Wright.

When Tallon whirled around to grab a stump as a souvenir he found they had been swiped while his back was turned, making the catch. He won a scramble for a bail.

**At the other end Bedser grabbed all three stumps, apparently nobody felt up to battling with the giant for possession of them.**

Tallon gave the ball to McCool as a fitting trophy of his match-winning feat of five wickets for 55 in 16½ overs today, making his figures for the innings five for 109 of 32 overs.

Excitedly the crowd swarmed over the fence to see the wicket. Policemen kept them from walking on it. It was fitting that the pitch should take the match's curtain, because it had been prepared in a way that never denied the bowlers a chance from the very first day.

A draw in the third Test meant the Ashes stayed in Australia. It was the first drawn test in this country for sixty-five years. The playing conditions imposed a time limit whereas for so long matches had been played to a finish.

Other countries could be excused their bewilderment that a match, failing to produce a win for either side, could result in the highest gross gate takings up to that time of any cricket match in history. Highlights of the game were the great batting of Arthur Morris and the thrilling partnership between Lindwall and Tallon.

*Don Bradman*

# Melbourne ground has played many tricks

*By GEORGE THATCHER*

**Melbourne Cricket Ground, on which the Third Test will begin on Wednesday, is the Jekyll and Hyde pitch of Test cricket.**

**The two highest scores in first-class cricket have been made there and Test bowlers have staged eight of the best 24 performances in the series.**

Sutcliffe, Hobbs, and Bradman regard Melbourne as their favorite-ground.

But Trumper, Macartney, Andrews, and Bardsley were allergic to it.

Bradman and Hobbs made five Test centuries there, and Sutcliffe four.

Hammond's only Melbourne success was his 200 in 1928.

That was the game in which six centuries were made—Kippax 100, Ryder 112, Woodfull 107, and Bradman 112 for Australia, and Hammond 200 and Sutcliffe 135 for England.

Test records created at Melbourne are:

● 323 by Rhodes (179) and Hobbs (178) for the first wicket (Test record), in 1911-12.

● 283 by Hobbs (154) and Sutcliffe (176) for the first wicket in 1924-25, in which they batted throughout a whole day.

● 249 by Bradman (169) and McCabe (112) for the third wicket, in 1936-7.

● 346 by Bradman (270) and Fingleton (136) for the sixth wicket in 1936-7.

● 120 by R. A. Duff (104) and Armstrong (45 n.o.) for last wicket in 1901-2. Both players were making their Test debut.

● Hat tricks by Spofforth and Trumble (twice) for Austral'a, and by W. Bates (England).

● Scores of 604 (1936-7) and 600 (1924-5), by Australia.

● Dismissal of England twice for 61, and for 75.

● Wicket (A. C. MacLaren) by A. Conningham with the first ball of the 1894-5 match.

● Double "ducks" by the late Victor Trumper in 1904.

● Don Bradman bowled first ball by Bill Bowes in 1932.

## Mailey's Record

Bradman's 270 in 1936 is the highest by an Australian in Australia.

Arthur Mailey took nine wickets for 121 in 1921. No other Test bowler has duplicated that feat.

But Rhodes and Braund (England) each took eight wickets in one innings in 1903-4, and Noble, Mailey, and Spofforth, for Australia, and Bates and Barnes (England) have taken 13 wickets in one Melbourne Test.

Rhodes created a world's record when he took 15 for 124 in 1903.

Thirty-one years later another left-hander, Hedley Verity, eclipsed the feat by dismissing 15 Australians for 104 at Lord's.

Melbourne Tests have provided two records that will be difficult to surpass.

● The bowlers in the 1928-29 Test sent down 4244 deliveries.

● The January, 1937, Test attracted 350,534 people, who paid £30,124.

The crowd on January 4 of that match was 87,798 (a world's record), and the gate £7405.

The first of the two Tests played in Melbourne in the 1936-7 series brought condemnation of English captain "Gubby" Allen.

Australia had lost the Brisbane and Sydney Tests. They had had to bat twice on wet wickets, and had failed miserably.

## "Worst" Wicket

The Australian team had not combined, and before the Melbourne Test, which began on January 1, 1937, the Board of Control carpeted a number of the team, and demanded greater support for Bradman.

Australia won the toss, and, on a perfect wicket, had lost six for 181 at the end of the first day.

Heavy rain fell during the night. Australia closed with nine for 200.

The late Hugh Trumble said the wicket was the worst he had ever seen.

Hammond stayed 80 minutes for 32. Allen delayed the closure on the Saturday afternoon. George Duckworth pleaded with him to close immediately after Hammond had been dismissed.

A half-volley removed Ames' cap.

Australian bowler M. Sievers, usually commonplace, was unplayable.

He took five for 21, but was dropped for the rest of the Tests.

England made 76, and at stumps that day Australia had lost O'Reilly's wicket for three. Ward and Rigg stayed for an hour next day, and at stumps Australia were five for 194.

Bradman and Fingleton subsequently added 346 for the sixth wicket, Don going on to 270—the best by an Australian at home.

He had influenza, and was languid on the third day of his innings.

England were beaten by 365.

A month later Australia won the deciding Test by an innings and 200 runs.

Australia made 600 (Bradman 169,

Bradman . . . likes Melbourne.

McCabe 112, Badcock 118, and the late Ross Gregory 80).

The 1907-8 Test should have provided the dream finish—a tie.

Australia scored 266 and 397. England made 382 in the first innings, and needed 282 in the second for a win.

Thirty-nine were required when S. F. Barnes joined Fielder. Both were regarded as batting "rabbits."

Amazingly they stayed until the scores were level. Then Barnes played a ball to Hazlitt in the covers.

Hazlitt, a magnificent fieldsman, became rattled, and threw wildly to the 'keeper.

The ball went for overthrows, and England won by one wicket.

The Melbourne Cricket Ground has magnificent stands and accommodation for 95,000.

Since new stands have been erected the players complain of an absence of breeze on the field.

The rain-threat is always the biggest Melbourne hazard.

The Melbourne wicket can be very, very good. But with rain in the offing, batsmen lose hours of sleep.

# Australia v England
## Third Test Match

AUSTRALIA v ENGLAND, Third Test Match, at Melbourne, 1, 2, 3, 4, 6 and 7 January 1947.

| Australia | - First Innings | 365 |
|---|---|---|
| | - Second Innings | 536 |
| England | - First Innings | 351 |
| | - Second Innings | 310 for 7 wickets |

Drawn.

| DON BRADMAN | - b. N.W.D. Yardley | 79 |
|---|---|---|
| (Captain) | - c. and b. N.W.D. Yardley | 49 |

This was DON BRADMAN's sixth Test Match against England at Melbourne, and for the first time he failed to make a century there; in both innings he was dismissed by N.W.D. Yardley when well set and batting at his best. His first innings began at 32 for 1, thirty-eight minutes before lunch on the first day; he started well, making 30 by the interval, but thereafter he went more sedately. He reached 50 in seventy-nine minutes, and was 73 by the tea interval, but soon afterwards played too late at an off-break and dragged it on to his wicket. Fourth out at 188, he batted for two hours forty-nine minutes, and hit only two fours in a sound innings.

The score was 68 for 1 when he went in for his second innings on the fourth morning, and he again started very hesitantly, making 3 in half an hour, and surviving some edgy strokes, as well as an appeal for lbw. by D.V.P. Wright when he was 3. He was 19 at the lunch interval, and thereafter settled down in more confident style; he was missed at the wicket off A.V. Bedser when 44, but the mistake was not expensive for soon afterwards he gave Yardley an easy return catch. He was second out at 159, having played an innings lasting an hour and thirty-nine minutes and 88 balls.

This was the first drawn Test Match in Australia for sixty-five years.

## Australia

| | | | |
|---|---|---|---|
| S. G. Barnes lbw b Bedser | 45 | — c Evans b Yardley | 32 |
| A. Morris lbw b Bedser | 21 | — b Bedser | 155 |
| D. G. Bradman b Yardley | 79 | — c and b Yardley | 49 |
| A. L. Hassett c Hammond b Wright | 12 | — b Wright | 9 |
| K. R. Miller c Evans b Wright | 33 | — c Hammond b Yardley | 34 |
| I. W. Johnson lbw b Yardley | 0 | — run out | 0 |
| C. McCool not out | 104 | — c Evans b Bedser | 43 |
| D. Tallon c Evans b Edrich | 35 | — c and b Wright | 92 |
| R. Lindwall b Bedser | 9 | — c Washbrook b Bedser | 100 |
| B. Dooland c Hammond b Edrich | 19 | — c Compton b Wright | 1 |
| E. Toshack c Hutton b Edrich | 6 | — not out | 2 |
| N-b 2 | 2 | B 14, l-b 2, n-b 3 | 19 |
| | **365** | | **536** |

## England

| | | | |
|---|---|---|---|
| L. Hutton c McCool b Lindwall | 2 | — c Bradman b Toshack | 40 |
| C. Washbrook c Tallon b Dooland | 62 | — b Dooland | 112 |
| W. J. Edrich lbw b Lindwall | 89 | — lbw b McCool | 13 |
| D. Compton lbw b Toshack | 11 | — run out | 14 |
| W. R. Hammond c and b Dooland | 9 | — b Lindwall | 26 |
| J. T. Ikin c Miller b Dooland | 48 | — c Hassett b Miller | 5 |
| N. W. D. Yardley b McCool | 61 | — not out | 53 |
| T. G. Evans b McCool | 17 | — not out | 0 |
| W. Voce lbw b Dooland | 0 | | |
| A. V. Bedser not out | 27 | — lbw b Miller | 25 |
| D. V. P. Wright b Johnson | 10 | | |
| B 1, l-b 12, n-b 2 | 15 | B 15, l-b 6, w 1 | 22 |
| | **351** | Seven wkts. | **310** |

## England Bowling

| | O. | M. | R. | W. | O. | M. | R. | W. |
|---|---|---|---|---|---|---|---|---|
| Voce | 10 | 2 | 40 | 0 | 6 | 1 | 29 | 0 |
| Bedser | 31 | 4 | 99 | 3 | 34.3 | 4 | 176 | 3 |
| Wright | 26 | 2 | 124 | 2 | 32 | 3 | 131 | 3 |
| Yardley | 20 | 4 | 50 | 2 | 20 | 0 | 67 | 3 |
| Edrich | 10.3 | 2 | 50 | 3 | 18 | 1 | 86 | 0 |
| Hutton | | | | | 3 | 0 | 28 | 0 |

## Australia Bowling

| | O. | M. | R. | W. | O. | M. | R. | W. |
|---|---|---|---|---|---|---|---|---|
| Lindwall | 20 | 1 | 64 | 2 | 16 | 2 | 59 | 1 |
| Miller | 10 | 0 | 34 | 0 | 11 | 0 | 41 | 2 |
| Toshack | 26 | 5 | 88 | 1 | 16 | 5 | 39 | 1 |
| McCool | 19 | 3 | 53 | 2 | 24 | 9 | 41 | 1 |
| Dooland | 27 | 5 | 69 | 4 | 21 | 1 | 84 | 1 |
| Johnson | 6.5 | 1 | 28 | 1 | 12 | 4 | 24 | 0 |

## FALL OF WICKETS

AUSTRALIA—First Innings:

| 1 | 2 | 3 | 4 | 5 | 6 | 7 | 8 | 9 | 10 |
|---|---|---|---|---|---|---|---|---|---|
| 32 | 108 | 143 | 188 | 192 | 192 | 255 | 272 | 355 | 365 |

AUSTRALIA—Second Innings:

| 1 | 2 | 3 | 4 | 5 | 6 | 7 | 8 | 9 | 10 |
|---|---|---|---|---|---|---|---|---|---|
| 68 | 159 | 177 | 212 | 333 | 335 | 341 | 495 | 511 | 536 |

ENGLAND—First Innings:

| 1 | 2 | 3 | 4 | 5 | 6 | 7 | 8 | 9 | 10 |
|---|---|---|---|---|---|---|---|---|---|
| 8 | 155 | 167 | 176 | 179 | 292 | 298 | 298 | 351 | 351 |

ENGLAND—Second Innings:

| 1 | 2 | 3 | 4 | 5 | 6 | 7 |
|---|---|---|---|---|---|---|
| 138 | 163 | 186 | 197 | 221 | 249 | 294 |

Umpires: J. D. Scott and G. Borwick.

# Bowling Puts England Ahead

*From E. M. WELLINGS*

**MELBOURNE, Wednesday.—For the first time in this Test series, England are well placed at the end of the first day's play in the Third Test match today.**

Needing to win this vital Test to hold interest in the Ashes, they pulled something right out of the bag.

It could have been a tragic day with Edrich and Voce, half the main bowling strength, early out of action with leg injuries.

That put a tremendous burden on Wright and Bedser, but they shouldered it magnificently.

They bowled with great heart and much skill, and got unexpectedly good support from Yardley.

Yardley, a medium-pace bowler, is not often used by his county, Yorkshire.

Hammond, who made a fine job of handling his reduced bowling strength, used Yardley as a relief for Wright and Bedser in turn.

Yardley did the job very well, starting off economically with runs, and then appearing in the successive roles of wicket-taker, Bradman-slayer, and new-ball bowler.

He began an eventful quarter of an hour, in which three wickets fell for four runs, by dismissing Bradman and Johnson with successive balls.

So far as could be seen, the pitch did not favor the bowlers after the usual lively morning period of about an hour.

Wright, however, appeared to be turning the ball slightly.

The bowling was really good, and not even Bradman could master it.

He was not at his best, although he played some fine shots.

The day's honors went to the bowling trio, supported by very keen fielding and Hammond's sure captaincy.

McCool and Tallon checked the Australian landslide with plucky and attractive batting.

They put up a very good performance.

Hopes are that Edrich will play tomorrow, but Voce is unlikely to be fit enough to bowl.

Don Bradman returning to the pavilion after his dismissal.

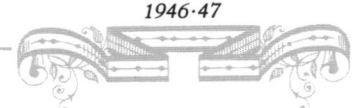

# ENGLAND FIGHTS HARD FOR LEAD

## McCool Hero Of Great Recovery

### From TOM GOODMAN

MELBOURNE, Thursday.—After a second gripping day's play of varying fortunes, the third Test match at the Melbourne Cricket Ground is in the balance.

England has one wicket down for 147 runs, in reply to Australia's total of 365. Four days remain for the match, and the pitch is playing very well.

England's batting to-morrow will need to have greater stability than in the second Test in Sydney, for she needs to obtain a first innings lead of 150 runs to have a chance of forcing a win, if not to stave off defeat.

The pendulum swung England's way right at the start to-day, when the irrepressible Edrich had Tallon caught behind the wicket off his opening ball.

But Colin McCool played a magnificent fighting innings for 104 not out, in 183 minutes, during 78 minutes of which he was assisted by plucky Bruce Dooland, who was batting for the first time in a Test.

They carried Australia's score to 110 more than the overnight 255 for six wickets.

### McCool Inspiring

McCool and Edrich dominated the hour and 50 minutes of the Australian innings to-day.

McCool inspired Australia to hit back, after England's bowling successes early in the day, and Edrich not only took the first wicket, but claimed the last two also.

The crowd hung on McCool's century, remembering that he had been dismissed at 95 in his first Test innings in Brisbane.

When 98 he failed to make the most of a no-ball, but he gained his century, and an ovation which recalled the one accorded Bradman here ten years ago.

McCool gave a hard "caught and bowled" chance to Wright when 44. He made a few uncertain shots early, but he pulled himself together and first grimly, and then aggressively, met the English bowlers.

He played his favourite pull stroke freely, but he introduced greater variety than in some previous innings. Undoubtedly he is a batsman of high technical skill, as well as one of courage and intelligence.

Dooland showed promise by the manner of his defence, and his general behaviour at a critical stage of the innings.

Another feature was the continued superb wicketkeeping of 25-year-old Godfrey Evans, who not only saved many runs by his agility on the leg side, but did not concede a bye.

Evans has kept wickets in two Tests, and has not allowed a bye in 1,024 runs.

This performance has never been excelled, and it is the more amazing coming from a young player in his first Test series.

The Australians were in high glee when Len Hutton, in the second fast over by Ray Lindwall, "felt" for the last ball and snicked it fast and low to the left side of McCool at first slip.

Hutton's scores in the Test series have been 7 and 0 in the first Test in Brisbane, 39 and 37 in the second Test in Sydney, and now two in the first innings here.

### Edrich Again

Once again the responsibility not only of assisting to overcome the new ball period, but also to fight off keen attackers and build up a score fell upon England's "mighty atom," Bill Edrich. Once again he was equal to the occasion.

He top-scored in each innings in Sydney, with 71 and 119; he is 85 not out in Melbourne.

Edrich when 47, with the total 87, was dropped by Sid Barnes a few yards from the bat at silly leg, off tall left-hander Toshack. He hit that ball hard.

He and Washbrook had some uncertain moments in Toshack's early overs, and Edrich, with one wild swing, mishit the ball over slips.

But he won out in the duel with Toshack, and five of his ten fours have come from that bowler.

Edrich, more than any other English batsman, has shown an inclination to chance his arm against the spin bowlers, and has looked like getting away with it.

He used discretion to-day. Twice he lifted Toshack straight to the fence, and later he stepped out to off-spinner Ian Johnson, and clouted him over the outfieldsmen, straight to the boundary.

### Highest Stand

Edrich and Washbrook already have figured in an unfinished partnership of 139 runs—England's highest stand of this series.

The previous best English partnership in this series was 102 for the third wicket by Edrich and Compton in Sydney.

Cyril Washbrook was worried a good deal by Toshack's steadiness and ability to move the ball, but he plugged along doggedly, content to play second fiddle to Edrich.

This is his first 50 in a Test against Australia.

Washbrook has batted for 170 minutes, and has hit one four—a hook shot off Toshack. Edrich has been with him for 153 minutes.

# England Misses Chance In Vital Test Match

### From WARWICK ARMSTRONG, *Former Australian Captain.*

**MELBOURNE, Friday.**—England, by bad batting in the Third Test today, threw away an excellent chance of gaining a first innings lead which would have given it bright prospects of victory.

England, who resumed batting with 1-147 in reply to Australia's 365, was dismissed for 351.

It now appears to have no chance of winning if the weather remains fine.

The best England can hope for is a draw.

England missed a great chance on a wicket which did not assist any of the bowlers.

England was unlucky this morning when it lost Edrich leg-before-wicket to Lindwall, after he had added only four runs to his overnight score of 85.

This was a bad decision, as Edrich played a straight ball hard on to his pads.

Compton also was dismissed soon afterwards leg-before-wicket to Toshack for nine.

He showed plainly that he was not satisfied.

**But from my position directly behind the stumps I was certain that the batsman missed a straight ball, and the umpire's decision was correct.**

I was disappointed at the way Compton carried on over the decision.

## Washbrook Stubborn

The early loss of Edrich and Compton completely changed the aspect of the game.

Washbrook, who opened the innings, continued to bat stubbornly until the sixth wicket.

He scored 62 and was dismissed when trying to cover drive Dooland.

He hit inside the ball and snicked it to be caught at the wicket by Tallon.

Of the batsmen who followed, only Ikin and Yardley, appeared at ease. They were associated in a century partnership.

However, Ikin was missed at silly-point before he had scored. He went on to make 48.

This was his best innings of the tour

Yardley (61) batted well, but played two or three lucky strokes just out of the reach of first slip.

The Australians fielded well, and the field-placing was good, but I thought Bradman handled his bowlers badly.

He had his two fast bowlers operating together, and his two slow bowlers were on for most of the remaining time.

He should have varied the bowling.

# UMPIRES' DECISIONS DISPUTED

## Dismissals "Doubtful"

MELBOURNE, Friday. — English players and cricket writers today disputed leg-before-wicket decisions against Edrich and Compton in the Third Test.

Many people in line with the stumps believed that Compton was out but that Edrich was not.

Compton's behavior in openly disputing umpire Scott's decision was freely condemned in the Members' Stand.

## Compton Angry

Compton stood for a few seconds glaring first at Scott and then at his pads before walking away.

When umpire Borwick gave Edrich out, the Englishman hesitated, then held up his bat to indicate that he had hit the ball.

Both umpires rejected half a dozen confident appeals for l.b.w. against English batsmen.

Former Australian Test captain Warwick Armstrong, who is covering the Tests for the Daily Telegraph, says the decision against Edrich was wrong, but that against Compton was correct.

Some former Australian internationals in the Press box, who thought Edrich had hit the ball, called "not out" as soon as Lindwall appealed.

EDRICH holding his bat in the air after umpire Borwick had given him out l.b.w. in the Third Test at Melbourne yesterday. Edrich had scored 89.

E. M. Wellings, writing in the London Evening Standard a criticism which has been cabled back to Australia, declares flatly that Edrich played the ball on to his pads.

He adds: "It was a hasty decision, as all decisions are here where deliberation by an umpire is regarded as a sign of weakness and indecision.

"This unfortunate decision against Edrich may decide the Ashes.

"Soon after Edrich's dismissal, there was another l.b.w. decision, which was obviously disagreeable to Compton.

"The English players were clearly upset by both decisions."

Bruce Harris, writing in the London Evening Standard, says Edrich appeared to hit the ball on to his pads, but adds that it was impossible to tell from the Press box whether Compton was out.

Harris adds: "Right or wrong, these decisions ruined our chances and opened the door to two more disasters of a less debatable sort—the dismissals of Hammond and Washbrook."

## "Not Squealing"

A British United Press writer says: "Once again the trend of a Test match has been altered by a doubtful decision.

"English players, rather than be accused of squealing in the face of defeat, have maintained silence throughout the tour.

"There is no suggestion of anything more than human fallibility, but it savors of incompetent umpiring."

The London Star's L. N. Bailey claims England has been the chief sufferer in umpiring decisions which "only serve to show the Australian umpiring standard is below that of England."

English pressmen claim that Bradman was given not out wrongly in both the first and second Tests.

In the First Test, in Brisbane, they say Ikin caught Bradman in the slips when he was 28. Bradman made 187.

In the Second Test, in Sydney, they consider Bedser caught Bradman at square leg when he was 170. Bradman went on to make 234.

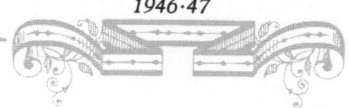

# ENGLISH CRICKET TEAM ANNOYED

# MISREPRESENTED AS BAD SPORTSMEN

**MELBOURNE, Saturday.—The English cricketers are annoyed at being misrepresented as a "team of squealers" by some English Press critics travelling with the team.**

These critics have cabled a "heap of stuff and nonsense" about two l.b.w. decisions by Umpire Jack Scott in the third Test as though the adverse criticism came from the players.

The players have not complained nor have they authorised the publication of any alleged complaints.

A similar howl was made by the same critics during the first Test in Brisbane. They suggested in their newspapers that the English captain Walter Hammond had decided to object to the appointment of umpire Jack Scott for the second Test in Sydney.

**Hammond treated the suggestion with scorn. He has yet to prove that he is not a thoroughly good sportsman who can take an adverse decision on the chin.**

The campaign against Australian umpires by a small but powerful section of the English Press is sinister. It deserves no other term. It deserves to be sneered at. It is publicity of a low degree designed to throw dust in the eyes of the British public by explaining the failures of the English team in Australia.

The truth is that the English team is not good enough.

### "Stupid Suggestion"

It will be recalled that when they arrived in Australia they were then misrepresented on all sides by the Press, not only of England, but of Australia, that they were a team of mighty batsmen.

This section of the Press even suggested that all Tests would be drawn.

The public knows how stupid this suggestion has been.

**This alleged greatness was exploded in the first few weeks of the tour in Truth and the Daily Mirror which stated that the English batsmen would fall before Australia's spin onslaught.**

This view has been confirmed.

But the English Press apparently found the pill too hard to swallow.

Now they are talking about "umpires who cheat" or "umpires who are fair, but who are incompetent."

One writer moaned that the two decisions which dismissed Edrich and Compton had "rendered the game morally null and void," and that the scores are "fictitious."

He said the "morale of the whole side is shaken and they do not know whom to fear most—the bowler or the umpire."

It is time a halt was called to the patronising platitudes of this English critic towards the English cricketers It doesn't please the cricketers and it offends Australians.

**How can a Press critic, sitting in a pavilion, side on to the wicket, 200 yards away, tell whether a batsman has put his leg in front of a ball, or whether he has snicked it on to his pads?**

Answer that question and you will agree that some English pressmen can't take it.

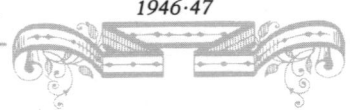

# AUSTRALIA IN STRONG POSITION
## Morris back to form with fine century

*From ARTHUR MAILEY*

**MELBOURNE, Sat.—With a lead of 307 runs and with six wickets still in hand Australia is in a very strong position in the Third Test.**

For the first time in Tests this year the Englishmen achieved their objective of getting Bradman out comparatively cheaply but it doesn't seem to have helped them much.

Other Australian batsmen, particularly McCool today, showed commendable efficiency.

While Australia's position is undoubtedly excellent, there are still opportunities in this match for Hutton, Hammond, and Compton to show their real skill.

If these batsmen get a start on Monday afternoon, Dooland, McCool, and Johnson might find the same trouble that other slow bowlers have found on this easy Melbourne pitch. I happen to know.

The Third Test had another of its grim, dour periods yesterday when Bradman and Morris gave the crowd a lesson in patience.

After batting an hour and a half, Bradman was still in his thirties, and Morris, equally as tenacious, scored at about the same rate.

We saw a flash of Bradman's real form in a vicious half-arm jolt at a shortish ball on the leg stump, and then, seemingly satisfied that he had convinced the public that he is still a genius, he took things easy and waited for runs to come.

I think Bradman had planned a day of leisure in his bath on Saturday morning.

He took a leisurely breakfast, then sat in the lounge reading letters until it was time to meander down to the ground, and, after padding up, Barnes gave him sufficient time to yawn, stretch himself, and stroll out on the field.

Bradman had a little time to play with, and there was no need to get hot and bothered about this business of winning Test matches.

Even the shot which cost him his wicket was a casual one, which appeared to be made without his usual concentration.

I had never seen Bradman look more comfortable and less likely to lose his wicket, and I think Yardley was as surprised as everybody else when Bradman gently patted the ball back into his hands.

Yardley, the ugly duckling of the English team, had taken the two wickets which had fallen for 25 runs.

I have a feeling that Bradman was deceived by the slower pace of the ball and played forward too soon.

Although there were 159 runs on the board at the time, the Englishmen were pleased that the Sydney Test record breakers, Bradman and Barnes, had been dismissed for 81.

This success was like a tonic to the Englishmen, who then attacked Morris and the newcomer, Hassett, as though their lives depended on the complete annihilation of Australia.

## Runs Were Hard

With three wickets down for 177, and Wright and Yardley bowling particularly well, England, if not in a favorable position, was in one that made the Australians realise their own danger.

The Englishmen have always felt throughout these Tests that Bradman was the main obstacle, and if they could dismiss him for a reasonable score the game was as good as won.

Whether this will work out according to expectations remains to be seen, but Australians have a habit, too, of fighting back.

The bowling was mainly in the hands of Yardley and Wright, who appeared to rise to great heights.

Runs were very difficult to get against this pair, and the fact that the Englishmen worked like trojans in the field made this business of run collecting more hazardous.

Miller is by no means a dodderer, yet he took nearly half an hour to score five runs.

He made several very fine strokes, but brilliant fielding made them as valueless as a Portuguese coin in Fiji or somewhere.

Whatever doubts there may have been regarding Morris' ability as opening batsman before this match it is now obvious that he will be Australia's first batsman for years to come.

His defence today was beyond criticism, and one of the most pleasing features of his innings was his desire to play the ball with his bat and not his pads.

Morris was just as attractive and entertaining as his captain, and there were times when he appeared to be much more at ease.

Yesterday Morris did what Bradman has a habit of doing—breaking England's heart.

# LINDWALL, 100, AND TALLON, 92, RUN RIOT: 62 FROM 5 OVERS!

## From RAY ROBINSON

**MELBOURNE, Monday.—In a riot of rungetting in the third Test today Don Tallon and Ray Lindwall put on 154 for the eighth wicket in 88 minutes, thrilling a crowd of 50,000.**

Amid spots of rain and heaps of sawdust, Morris and McCool carried on their fifth wicket partnership from 51, but the sun broke through and the sky began to clear from the west.

The wind was veering about the west and when it came from the north-west, it blew down the slope for the first time in the match.

Refusal of two appeals against McCool (29) and Morris (145), doubtless gave a fresh opportunity for mischief-making comments about the umpiring.

**However, bowler Bedser did not appear to support the wicketkeeper's plea for a leg-side catch and Voce's appeal for lbw also was a solo effort.**

Hardly recognisable as the man who batted five and a half hours on Friday and Saturday for 132, left-hander Morris served his side in a different role by chasing runs.

His lofty hook bounded over the leaping Yardley's hand for four.

He drove Bedser past mid-off for his 8th boundary, then tried to glance another and lost his leg stump.

**The fair-haired left-hander, who will turn 25 in a fortnight, was in 364 minutes for his 155 and is the fifth Australian to bat on three days in one innings.**

The others were Alec Bannerman, in the early days of Tests, C. E. Kellaway, in 1921, Bradman, in 1930, and Barnes, in the second Test.

Morris-McCool partnership of 91 had taken the score to 333.

Two runs later, Johnson anxious to avoid a second blob, tried to steal a single for an off-push

**Unluckily the nearest fieldsman was the pouncing Washbrook who swiftly threw the wicket down as Johnson desperately flung himself at the crease.**

## Another For Evans

This is the 26th time in 146 Tests that a batsman has collected a "pair" of spectacles—eight times by Englishmen and 18 times by an Australian, including such front-line batsmen as Trumper, Noble, Richardson, Fingleton and Badcock.

When McCool (43) snicked an off ball from Bedser to the wicketkeeper. Australia was 355 ahead, but Bradman did not repeat his second Test tactics by declaring the innings closed before lunch to compel England's opening batsmen to make two starts.

For dragging over the line, Bedser was no-balled twice in succession and Tallon, whose high grip helps to make him one of the best drivers in the game, slammed both to the fence.

**Though six days old and parched by a hot Sunday, the wicket was still behaving so well that England's captain, Hammond, did not call on Wright's leg spin until the last quarter of an hour before lunch.**

At the interval, Tallon was 36, Lindwall 12, and the total 385 for seven wickets.

This put Australia 399 in front and many expected Bradman to close the innings.

Commanding stroke play by Tallon and batsmanlike driving by Lindwall, rattled on 100 for the eighth wicket.

## Compton's Miss

Misjudging a high hook off Voce against the upper deck of the grandstand Compton moved a pace the wrong way—enough to make him finish a yard short of a chance to catch Lindwall (16).

Use of the new ball adds life to the bowling, but this time its arrival after 400 enlivened the batting even more.

**One over by Bedser yielded 14, and the pair lashed up 100 in 58 minutes, the second 50 in 20 minutes.**

With footwork, driving, hooking and cutting, worthy of a number three batsman, Tallon hit six fours and 21 scoring strokes after lunch, and Lindwall got five boundaries in 16 scoring shots

**With a wriggle of the shoulders Lindwall lifted a ball from Hutton for the first six of the match.**

It seemed as if the only people in the crowd not roaring deliriously were the dozens who scattered as the ball landed 25 yards over the fence.

Tallon was within eight of a glorious 100 when he tried to turn a leg break from Wright and it cocked up off the side of his bat.

As is recalling the earlier misses, Wright waited fearfully under the catch and looked relieved when he held it safely.

Tallon was cheered out of sight for his sparkling 92 (10 fours) in only 105 minutes.

His partnership with Lindwall carved 154 off the bowling in 88 minutes and Australia was 495 for eight wickets.

An acrobat's catch by Compton at deep square leg dismissed Dooland (1), to give Wright his third victim.

On the run Compton clutched the ball about knee high and fell over backwards with his ankles waving together in the air.

Lidwall needed 19 for 100 when the last man, Toshack, came in.

**The crowd rocked with laughter at the signs that Toshack gave of his determination to stay in to give his fellow bowler a chance for century.**

He held his bat so straight, so firm, that often it was in position as the ball had left the bowler's fingers, as if he were playing by appointment.

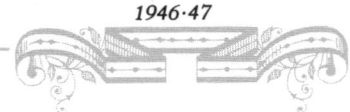

# AUSTRALIA HOLDS ASHES THOUGH ENGLAND FOUGHT OUT TEST DRAW

### From TOM GOODMAN

**MELBOURNE, Tuesday.—The third Test match was drawn to-day, and Australia will retain the "Ashes", held since Woodfull's team regained them in England in 1934.**

The match ended after a tense last hour and a half, with England having three wickets intact and 310 runs on the board.

The Englishmen, in their fight against time to force a draw to-day, were aided by light showers, which caused four interruptions. The total lost time was 47 minutes.

Nevertheless it was an excellent performance on the part of vice-captain Norman Yardley and of bowler Alec Bedser.

They held the fort for an hour after Hammond had gone in the second over after tea.

Yardley had wicketkeeper Godfrey Evans with him during the final 14 minutes, but Evans received only three balls, so well did Yardley keep the strike.

Yardley and Bedser shared the major batting honours of the day with dour Cyril Washbrook, who scored his first Test century against Australia, and carried his overnight score of 60 to 112.

The wicket continued to behave extremely well for the sixth day, and this fact largely discounted the advantage which Australia normally would have gained by winning the toss.

I consider the match proved a good advertisement for a time limit—especially such a more than reasonable time limit as six days.

It will be said that Australia undoubtedly would have won had the match been played to a finish; that Bradman might have considered the doubtful weather outlook, and closed round about three o'clock yesterday to allow for some lost time.

### "Fighting" Test

But the match had an atmosphere of "fight" about it, and to-day was a more interesting day than if England had been merely delaying the defeat which a played-out match would have ensured.

It must be noted, too, that Australia would not have forced the pace so furiously after lunch yesterday had it not been that to-day was to provide the concluding five hours of play.

When Hammond had his wicket skittled by Lindwall's fast yorker in the second over after tea, and there were only Bedser, Evans, Voce, and Wright to support Yardley, most of the onlookers thought that England's position, previously precarious, had become absolutely hopeless.

But Hammond made a successful move when he promoted the huge, smiling Bedser two places in the batting order—above both Evans and Voce.

He performed extremely well in a difficult situation, and Yardley, impressed by his confidence and soundness, did not worry about taking the strike from his partner.

There were three interruptions of approximately ten minutes each, caused by rain, after tea.

There might have been more lost time, as there were periods when the light was bad enough to justify the batsmen appealing.

The crowd stayed on with an eye on the clock, rather than on the scoreboard. Runs did not matter.

But Yardley and Bedser scored freely enough to make it a worthwhile batting exhibition, as well as a test of defence and stubbornness against keen bowling.

The spectators seemed sorry to see Bedser go lbw to Miller at 5.44 p.m.

They encouraged Evans, and wildly applauded Yardley as, with free strokes in the last couple of overs,

he gained his half-century.

It was a great match for Yardley. He had a fine batting double, and he had surprising bowling successes; indeed, he has performed a bowling miracle by dismissing Bradman in his last three Test innings.

Len Hutton, although he batted in all for three hours, never seemed to be quite himself in this innings.

His 40 is his highest score in the series, and his partnership of 138 with Washbrook is easily their best, so perhaps with the strain of the fight for the Ashes gone, Hutton will improve.

Washbrook played a sound, patient and defiant role. He occupied the creases for just over four hours—a remarkable performance in itself, when his team's main object was to play out the hours.

### Hammond Missed

Hammond, although he played rather well in his 77 minutes, was missed behind the wicket off Lindwall with the new ball when 20.

A feature was several successful bowling changes by Bradman.

Altogether this was a remarkable match, with several grand individual performances, including three new centurions for Australia—McCool, Morris, and Lindwall.

This is one fact that serves to emphasise how much better off Australia is at present in the production of worthwhile material.

# Australia v England
## Fourth Test Match

**A**lthough it had already been decided that the Ashes must remain in Australia, much interesting cricket was still played in the last two Tests.

The Adelaide match was distinguished by Compton and Morris both getting a century in each innings. It also saw Evans bat for 95 minutes without scoring and my stumps scattered by Bedser for 0 with the best ball ever bowled to me.

The final Test at Sydney goes down in my memory as one of the greatest. It produced all the best and most exciting features of cricket.

And so ended a series which did much to restore life to normal after the grim years of war. I believe the public were grateful to have their hearts and minds diverted towards happier days.

*Don Bradman*

AUSTRALIA v ENGLAND, Fourth Test Match, at Adelaide,
31 January, 1, 3, 4, 5 and 6 February 1947.

| Australia | - First Innings | 487 |
| | - Second Innings | 215 for 1 wicket |
| England | - First Innings | 460 |
| | - Second Innings | 340 for 8 wickets dec. |

Drawn; Australia won the rubber.

| DON BRADMAN | - b. A.V. Bedser | 0 |
| (Captain) | - not out | 56 |

DON BRADMAN went in at 18 for 1, eighteen minutes from the close of the second day, and played 7 balls from A.V. Bedser, in ten minutes, before being completely beaten and bowled by the eighth, with the score still 18.

England's declaration left Australia three and a quarter hours to make 314 to win on the last day, and Australia did not accept the challenge.    Bradman went in at 116 for 1 soon after tea, and nearly played his second ball, from N.W.D. Yardley, on to his wicket, going close to obtaining a "pair of spectacles".    He reached 50 in sixty-eight minutes, and finished the game in very dull fashion with only 6 more in the last twenty-three minutes.    He hit four fours, and batted for ninety-one minutes and 99 balls.

The match was played in very hot, humid weather.

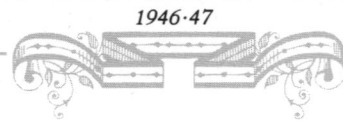

## England

| | | | | | |
|---|---|---|---|---|---|
| L. Hutton lbw b McCool | 94 | — | b Johnson | | 76 |
| C. Washbrook c Tallon b Dooland | 65 | — | c Tallon b Lindwall | | 39 |
| W. J. Edrich c and b Dooland | 17 | — | c Bradman b Toshack | | 46 |
| W. R. Hammond b Toshack | 18 | — | c Lindwall b Toshack | | 22 |
| D. Compton c and b Lindwall | 147 | — | not out | | 103 |
| J. Hardstaff b Miller | 67 | — | b Toshack | | 9 |
| J. T. Ikin c Toshack b Dooland | 21 | — | lbw b Toshack | | 1 |
| N. W. D. Yardley not out | 18 | — | c Tallon b Lindwall | | 18 |
| A. V. Bedser b Lindwall | 2 | — | c Tallon b Miller | | 3 |
| T. G. Evans b Lindwall | 0 | — | not out | | 10 |
| D. V. P. Wright b Lindwall | 0 | | | | |
| B 4, l-b 5, w 2 | 11 | | B 5, l-b 3, w 2, n-b 3 | | 13 |
| | **460** | | Eight wkts., dec. | | **340** |

## Australia

| | |
|---|---|
| M. Harvey b Bedser | 12 |
| A. Morris c Evans b Bedser | 122 |
| D. G. Bradman b Bedser | 0 |
| A. R. Hassett c Hammond b Wright | 78 |
| K. R. Miller not out | 141 |
| I. W. Johnson lbw b Wright | 52 |
| C. McCool c Bedser b Yardley | 2 |
| D. Tallon b Wright | 3 |
| R. Lindwall c Evans b Yardley | 20 |
| B. Dooland c Bedser b Yardley | 29 |
| E. Toshack run out | 0 |
| B 16, l-b 6, w 2, n-b 4 | 28 |
| | **487** |

| | |
|---|---|
| b Yardley | 31 |
| not out | 124 |
| not out | 56 |
| B 2, n-b 2 | 4 |
| One wkt. | **215** |

## Australia Bowling

| | O. | M. | R. | W. | | O. | M. | R. | W. |
|---|---|---|---|---|---|---|---|---|---|
| Lindwall | 23 | 5 | 52 | 4 | .... | 17.1 | 4 | 60 | 2 |
| Miller | 16 | 0 | 45 | 1 | .... | 11 | 0 | 34 | 1 |
| Toshack | 30 | 12 | 59 | 1 | .... | 36 | 6 | 76 | 4 |
| McCool | 29 | 1 | 91 | 1 | .... | 19 | 3 | 41 | 0 |
| Johnson | 22 | 3 | 69 | 0 | .... | 25 | 8 | 51 | 1 |
| Dooland | 33 | 1 | 133 | 3 | .... | 17 | 2 | 65 | 0 |

## England Bowling

| | O. | M. | R. | W. | | O. | M. | R. | W. |
|---|---|---|---|---|---|---|---|---|---|
| Bedser | 30 | 6 | 97 | 3 | .... | 15 | 1 | 68 | 0 |
| Edrich | 20 | 3 | 88 | 0 | .... | 7 | 2 | 25 | 0 |
| Wright | 32.4 | 1 | 152 | 3 | .... | 9 | 0 | 49 | 0 |
| Yardley | 31 | 7 | 101 | 3 | .... | 13 | 0 | 69 | 1 |
| Ikin | 2 | 0 | 9 | 0 | | | | | |
| Compton | 3 | 0 | 12 | 0 | | | | | |

### FALL OF WICKETS

ENGLAND—First Innings:

| 1 | 2 | 3 | 4 | 5 | 6 | 7 | 8 | 9 | 10 |
|---|---|---|---|---|---|---|---|---|---|
| 137 | 173 | 196 | 202 | 320 | 381 | 455 | 460 | 460 | 460 |

ENGLAND—Second Innings:

| 1 | 2 | 3 | 4 | 5 | 6 | 7 | 8 |
|---|---|---|---|---|---|---|---|
| 100 | 137 | 178 | 188 | 207 | 215 | 250 | 255 |

AUSTRALIA—First Innings:

| 1 | 2 | 3 | 4 | 5 | 6 | 7 | 8 | 9 | 10 |
|---|---|---|---|---|---|---|---|---|---|
| 18 | 18 | 207 | 222 | 372 | 389 | 396 | 423 | 486 | 487 |

AUSTRALIA—Second Innings:

| 1 |
|---|
| 116 |

Umpires: J. D. Scott and G. Borwick.

# England Threw Away Early Advantages

## From W. J. O'REILLY

**ADELAIDE, Friday.—The encouraging effect of a fine opening partnership and the tremendous moral advantage of winning the toss were thrown to the winds by England in one unhappy hour after the tea adjournment.**

For dismissing Cyril Washbrook, Bill Edrich, Len Hutton, and Walter Hammond while only 65 runs were added, the Australian bowlers deserve the highest praise for an excellent effort.

The only condition in their favour was the cool day. The wicket favoured the batsmen.

Denis Compton and Joe Hardstaff were quietly playing themselves in when play ended.

Each had scored a century in Tests against Australia. The present position of their team demands nothing but their best efforts to-morrow.

After Bill Edrich's departure Don Bradman brought Bruce Dooland up to examine the pitch at the end to which he was bowling.

I had a look after play and was surprised to find a depression near the southern end in line with the middle stump and at about a good length for a medium-paced bowler.

Ern Toshack and, later, England's Douglas Wright, may cause some trouble on this spot.

It was very early in the game for a Test wicket to show signs of wear. If it should be affected now the consequences should definitely favour England.

The Australian fielding was not quite as good as it was in former games, but Keith Miller, Colin McCool, and Lindsay Hassett did some brilliant work.

## Stolen Singles

Washbrook and Hutton stole many singles to Don Bradman in the covers but were lucky on two occasions to have made the ground before the wicket had been thrown over. Washbrook was the fortunate one on each occasion.

Hutton batted just outside the crease when facing Ray Lindwall. This practice tends to lessen the value of the rising ball.

Bill Edrich started well. He hit the loose ball with plenty of power and looked likely to force home the advantage gained by the patient opening partnership.

Dooland bowled exceptionally well. He tossed the ball higher in the air than usual and accordingly forced the batsmen to use their feet carefully.

It was clever bowling that accoun-

ted for Edrich—Dooland "held the ball back" a trifle, and Edrich went through with his shot, hitting the pitch in doing so before the ball reached his bat.

This young bowler has outstanding ability and will improve considerably with the experience which will come to him on a trip to England.

Colin McCool deserved Hutton's wicket. Hutton did not play McCool very confidently. One ball completely beat him and narrowly missed his wicket.

His downfall came from a half-hearted flat-footed defensive shot which a batsman of Hutton's ability does not generally play when within six runs of a century.

## Toshack's Best

Hammond was bowled by a "world-beating" ball from left-hander, Ern Toshack.

Any bowler who can hit Hammond's wicket when that batsman is in form—as he is, and defending grimly—may be excused for congratulating himself.

Toshack's negative leg-side attack may have lulled Hammond into a false sense of security.

Toshack put up his best bowling performance of the series. He maintained an extraordinarily good length and kept an end going for a very long period. It was exteremely difficult to score from him.

These legside tactics of his are not nearly so innocuous as some critics think.

With a well-placed field—and Bradman arranged that for him—he is a constant menace to those who attempt to force him to the onside.

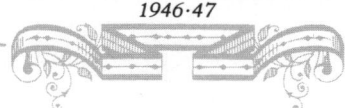

# England Aims At Test Draw

*From H. L. ("Stork") Hendry, Ex-Australian International.*

**ADELAIDE, Saturday. — The methods adopted by the English batsmen throughout their innings in the fourth Test indicated that they are playing for a draw and not to win.**

SCORING rate was again slow, and chances were missed of getting more runs.

Compton and Hardstaff were not happy when play was resumed today until the new ball was taken, with the total 245, and slow bowler McCool taken off.

They looked different batsmen against the fast attack of Lindwall and Miller.

In the hope of sneaking a quick wicket, Bradman opened with McCool, and gave him two overs, making Lindwall bowl his first over with the old ball.

The tactics were good, for these English batsmen fairly dread the slow bowlers coming on.

However, the new ball had to be taken, and immediately the batting became less apprehensive.

Hardstaff, looking a different player, made splendid leg glances.

Only continued brilliant fielding by Hassett reduced their value to singles.

Neither Lindwall or Miller caused the batsmen the slightest anxiety. Miller was relieved by Johnson after only two overs.

With the advent of Toshack the scoring rate fell, and only one run was made in 15 minutes whereas 26 had been scored in the first half hour.

When Dooland took over the whole of the Australian bowling strength had been used in the first hour's play, yet the batsmen were content merely to keep poking the ball away, when it could just as easily have been hit to the open spaces with no risks.

Hardstaff early gave promise of playing an innings full of fine strokes, but he closed up again.

Compton often spoilt good footwork in getting to the ball by merely tapping it to a fieldsman.

The ground fielding had been good and all the bowlers had been fairly accurate.

### Fluke Wicket

Slow batting continued after lunch and the crowd started to barrack — justifiably, too.

Then the partnership was broken unexpectedly. Miller bowled a very short bumper. Hardstaff tried to hook it without getting into proper position for the stroke, mistimed, and dragged the ball into his wicket.

It was a fluke wicket for it was a shocking ball.

Hardstaff had played his knock in patches. He showed himself capable of troubling all pace bowling, but was afraid to use his feet to the slows.

England had not half enough runs yet to have a chance.

# Lindwall's Four Balls, 3 Wickets: Bradman Out 0

## By ROY COLMER

**Ray Lindwall, Australian fast bowler, was the star of a day of sensational cricket in the fourth Test match at Adelaide Oval today. He took three wickets in four balls to finish off the English innings. In his last spell he took four for two in two overs.**

**Another sensation came late in the day with the dismissal of Don Bradman, Australian captain, for a "duck." With two Australian wickets down for 24 at stumps in reply to England's 460, the Englishmen were in a good position.**

**Denis Compton provided the highlight of the English innings, scoring 147. This was the highest score for England, and only the third century by an Englishman in this Test series.**

## Third Ball Shaved Stumps

LINDWALL'S performance electrified the crowd of 30,761, who paid £4,365 for admission to the ground.

The feat came like a lone hailstone out of a clear blue sky. It seemed that Australia would have a hard fight to break the Compton-Yardley partnership when Bradman threw Lindwall the ball to warm up before taking the new ball.

Catching Compton with the first delivery of his last over with the old ball, Lindwall took the new ball for his first delivery to Bedser.

He did everything but bowl Bedser for the remainder of the over.

In his next over he bowled Bedser with the fifth ball, Evans with the sixth, shaved Wright's stumps with the seventh, and bowled him with the last.

This was the first time the feat of taking three wickets in four balls had been performed in Tests between England and Australia, in Australia.

It had been done only twice before in the history of the Tests. F. S. Jackson did it for England at Nottingham in 1905 and W. J. O'Reilly at Manchester in 1934.

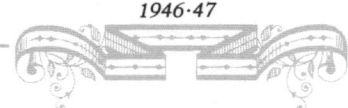

# Australia May Regret Slow Batting In Test

*From ARTHUR MAILEY*

**ADELAIDE, Monday.—If rain falls overnight, which is very likely, Australia will regret that its batsmen were not more enterprising in the Fourth Test today when England's bowling fell below standard.**

Australia added 269 runs and carried its first innings score from 2-24 to 4-293 in reply to England's 460.

This number of runs was not sufficient for a day's cricket under conditions particularly suitable for batsmen.

Morris (122) and Hassett (78) were associated in a long, dreary third-wicket partnership.

They added 189 runs, a valuable contribution to Australia's score, but they could have made them quicker.

Hassett was particularly dreary.

He is at his best when attacking the bowling, as he showed when playing for Victoria against New South Wales in Sydney last week.

It was a pity that he topped his 1000 runs for the season today during one of his poorest periods.

**This princely purveyor of jewels again, as in the First Test at Brisbane, became a common street pedlar.**

Johnson and Miller gave a better assessment of the English attack later in the day, and as a consequence many more runs are expected tomorrow.

The pitch is worn a little, but should not trouble the batsmen unless rain comes overnight.

## Plan Fails

When play resumed today, Hammond persisted with the plan of attack which caused Bradman's downfall on Saturday.

He opened the bowling with Bedser and Wright and placed a cordon of fieldsmen close to the batsmen, Morris and Hassett.

**Bedser and Wright bowled a defective length and the cordon of fieldsmen was wasted.**

Hassett was most sedate and made little or no attempt to punish these loose deliveries.

Morris never missed an opportunity of bashing the bowlers, particularly Wright, to the boundary on the least provocation.

Wright's first four overs were very poor and it was not surprising to see him throw the ball to Edrich, take a large white hat from the umpire, and drift into the outfield.

Edrich and Yardley continued the attack, which became completely negative and purposeless.

Wright again gave his hat to the umpire and bowled—I was nearly going to say attacked—from the other end.

But he again bowled short of good length and without guile.

The bowlers' lack of industry and action seemed to spread to the batsmen, and Hassett's first two hours at the wickets produced only 23 runs.

Even the sound of distant thunder and big black clouds rolling up did not shake the batsmen out of their reverie.

It was thought that at 2.45 p.m. the batsmen might have tried to get runs a little quicker in case of rain coming and damaging the pitch.

But the threat of rain was ignored, and after batting three hours, Australia's total was 2-110—Morris 60 and Hassett 32.

The only time either batsman showed some life was when a no-ball came along.

They drove the no-balls lustily. Morris drove one into the members' reserve for six.

**Morris, when in the sixties, seemed to become bored with his own immobility.**

He started to score attractively and reached his century after three and a half hours' batting.

During this bright period he played beautiful shots through the covers, well-timed leg-glances, and hit another ball for a beautiful six.

Hassett, on the other hand, was content to plod along at a pace well below his usual standard.

When Australia's score was approaching 200, Wright began to worry Hassett.

Wright, who began early with a defective length, seemed to gain much more control and Hassett made several lunges at his deliveries and missed badly.

Instead of using his feet, Hassett continued to push his bat out to good length balls and eventually was caught in the slips by Hammond off one of Wright's deliveries which broke abruptly.

Hammond had refrained from using the new ball. He preferred to keep the old one, because it suited Wright in the battle against Hassett.

Hassett's innings was disappointing.

For some unknown reason he decided to play a defensive innings against probably the weakest three hours' spell of bowling I have seen from the Englishmen.

## New Ball Success

After Hassett's dismissal, Hammond called for the new ball and gave it to Bedser.

The move was successful almost immediately, and Bedser had Morris caught at the wicket by Evans for 122.

**The Morris-Hassett partnership added 189 runs, but it had little or no moral effect on the bowling.**

Morris played a sound innings.

His defence was as perfect as his self-control, but he seldom missed an opportunity of scoring a boundary off a loose ball or a six off a no-ball.

Some of his shots were beautifully timed and safely executed, but for the most part he preferred to let the bowler make the mistakes.

Hassett and Morris, who throughout their innings were determined not to lose their wickets by taking risks, lost them by playing defensive cricket.

It was left to Miller and Johnson to provide the best cricket of the day.

The dream of all young Australian cricketers. This was the blazer worn by Don Bradman when, for the last time, he captained Australia in Australia.

LEFT    Sykes bat used by Don Bradman in making his 100th century in first class cricket in 1947 in Sydney.
RIGHT    The first Don Bradman bat ever used in Australia. With it Don Bradman made a new record score,
187, for his club, St. George, 1929–30.

# ENGLAND MAKES BID FOR TEST VICTORY AND SETS BRADMAN PROBLEM

## From TOM GOODMAN

**ADELAIDE, Tuesday.—Opening batsmen Hutton and Washbrook, putting on 96 runs in the closing 82 minutes of play to-day, showed that England is making a bid for victory in the fourth Test.**

Hammond will be hoping that the wicket during the fourth innings of the match will help his bowlers, Wright in particular, to drive home the advantage gained to-day.

Altogether, the day belonged to England, despite Keith Miller's spectacular first hour and his subsequent defiance.

He reached his first Test century, and went on to a score of 141 not out, when the last man, Toshack, was thrown out by Edrich as he galloped down the wicket to give Miller the strike.

Australia was all out for 487.

It was up to Edrich to do something about it, for it was he who had missed Miller, then 116, in the deep field off Wright with the score at 433 for eight wickets. It was an easy chance.

Hutton and Washbrook, however, not only quickly wiped off the first innings arrears but proceeded to slam loose deliveries to the fence.

### Threat Of Rain

No doubt they were influenced by two desires: to give England a reasonable chance to force a win, and to get as many runs as possible on the board in case the weather should play a vital part in the Test drama.

A light thundershower did interrupt play after the Englishmen had batted for eight minutes, and they were off the field for 25 minutes.

But the sky soon cleared, and the sweltering conditions in which England's bowlers had toiled against Miller returned.

Hutton and Washbrook, with Hutton the faster—he scored England's first 20 runs—rattled up their first 50 in 38 minutes.

Hutton gained his own half century in 57 minutes.

They slowed down over the last 20 minutes because of steadier bowling by Toshack and Dooland, the latter having Washbrook in trouble on two occasions.

### Used Hook

The hook stroke played a prominent part. Washbrook gained his square leg six off Lindwall and one four each off Lindwall and Toshack. by savage hooking.

A more noteworthy feature was that Hutton, who previously had neglected this profitable scoring medium, hooked shortish balls from Miller and Lindwall for four.

In a most impressive innings during which he was sound, yet often scintillating, Hutton already has hit seven fours.

It will be a grand achievement by the pair if they complete their second century partnership for the match.

**English captain, Wally Hammond,** with the gallant support of Douglas Wright and Norman Yardley, had his most creditable day in the field in the series.

It was a fine performance, under gruelling weather conditions, on a slow wicket, and with Alec Bedser indisposed, to gather in Australia's remaining six wickets by 3.56 p.m., and especially to have restricted the scoring powers of such an aggressive and accomplished stroke-maker as Keith Miller.

It looked like a bad day for England when Miller, resuming with a score of 33, and the total 293 for four wickets, sent Wright's opening no-ball soaring over the members' stand for six.

Miller then proceeded to drive, cut, and glance in the manner which first won him cricket stardom as a member of the Services team in England.

But Hammond, with Yardley as his chief conspirator, not only prevented Miller from taking complete control. but managed to subdue him to a rate that was surprisingly low.

The clock told the intriguing story

Miller contributed 71 of the 103 runs added by Australia in 90 minutes before lunch, but 50 of the 71 came in the first 40 minutes.

Miller added only 17 runs in an hour after lunch, and only 37 in 100 minutes.

There were five fours among his first 50 runs and only four fours in his next 91 runs.

It was not that Miller lost the art of his glorious stroke play; just that he was given fewer chances to exploit it.

Wright, with enough help from the pitch to turn the ball now and again required to be watched when he bowled a good length.

Yardley, pegging away at the leg stump with a packed on-side field, kept the play "tight."

Miller, who lost both Johnson and McCool before lunch, Tallon soon after the interval, and Lindwall half an hour later, could not fight his way out of the English net, try as he might

Miller batted in all for 270 minutes. His fifth wicket partnership with Ian Johnson, who scored 52, produced 150 runs in 118 minutes.

Wright was unlucky not to claim Miller as a victim, for after being dropped by Edrich, Miller, when 140, survived a stumping chance to Evans.

### Yardley's Effort

Most striking bowling effort, however, was Yardley's. The pleasant young Yorkshire amateur, marked down as a stock bowler because of his surprising stop-gap work in the Melbourne Test, showed a high degree of cricket intelligence as well as the right temperament.

Not only did he pin down Miller, but he claimed the wickets of McCool and Dooland, both caught by Bedser close in on the leg side and behind the wicket.

Miller, when 104, gave an almost impossible chance off Yardley to Fishlock, substitute for Bedser, at forward short-leg. Fishlock did well to stop the ball with his right hand.

Yardley bowled seven overs straight before lunch, and six more at his next turn.

He maintained remarkable control of length and direction. He finished with three wickets for 103 runs, but his figures for to-day were 14 overs, three maidens, 44 runs, three wickets.

Bedser, who was ill during the luncheon interval, resumed his place in the field before the innings ended.

The attendance was 19,717, and gross takings were £2,711.

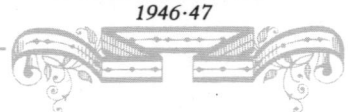

# EXCELLENT CHANCE FOR AUSTRALIA; ENGLISH BATTING SLUMP

### From TOM GOODMAN

**ADELAIDE, Wednesday.—Australia has an excellent chance to force a win in the fourth Test at Adelaide Oval to-morrow.**

**Some of the English batsmen "fell down on the job" very badly.**

**Bradman set a defensive field for Compton in the closing stages to-day, but he must go all out for the win to-morrow.**

Bradman will have to resume a battle of tactics with Compton, who remains the lion in Australia's path after a dogged innings to-day for 52 not out in 195 minutes.

During the last hour Compton sought to control the strike and to play for time rather than force runs.

Evans has been with him for 44 minutes and has yet to score.

The wicket, after five days of play, is remarkably good. Only an occasional ball turned to-day.

Although Bradman played medium-paced left-handed Toshack and slow-medium right-hand spinner Ian Johnson as his aces, there were not the terrors in the pitch that some of the English batsmen appeared to imagine.

## Toshack At His Best

Toshack bowled remarkably well. He took four wickets cheaply in an inspired spell after lunch.

England had fought back on Tuesday to gain a satisfactory position with a first innings deficit of or'y 27 runs and with 96 runs on the board without loss in the second innings.

The loss of both Washbrook and Hutton before lunch to-day was a jar to English hopes.

The departure of Edrich soon after lunch, following his brief burst of aggressive play, brought realisation that the next hour would be vital to England's prospects of continuing a bid for victory.

When, at 2.40 p.m., Hammond went, England was thrown on to grim defence.

## Fight Against Time

It was a fight against time as well as against the Australian bowlers.

Compton, hero of the first innings, carried the burden of the struggle for a draw.

Compton readily accepted the role of defender. It meant curbing of his naturally aggressive style, but he likes a fight.

He continued grimly picking up runs here and there, but making no effort to build up a substantial score.

He had Yardley, last of the recognised first-class batsmen, as his partner for 54 minutes.

Then he lost both Yardley and Bedser in quick succession. When Evans, the tenth man, joined him three-quarters of an hour before stumps it seemed that Australia would be batting again to-day.

Compton took control of the situation. He worked the strike and robbed Evans of some easy singles when that young player must have yearned to take at least one, for he had been bowled first ball in the first innings.

Evans has yet to score, but he defended bravely.

His job again to-morrow will be to hang on at all costs and play for Compton.

How long this pair can stay together may be all important, for there is only Wright to follow them.

On a sweltering day the feat of Toshack and Johnson in bowling unchanged from lunch until afternoon tea was extraordinarily fine.

Edrich hit 11 runs from Johnson's first over after lunch. Actually four of his six boundaries were hit from that spin bowler.

But the last 13 of Johnson's 15 overs between lunch and tea included five maidens and yielded only 10 runs.

Toshack bowled with such good control and to such good effect that several English critics who had described him as a "false alarm" was prepared to eat his words.

Toshack went far towards breaking England's back. Only Compton remained as the toughest fibre he could not sever.

When he dismissed Ikin lbw he had taken four wickets for 25 runs in 13 overs since lunch.

Toshack's full figures for the session of 105 minutes were 15 overs, one maiden, 34 runs, four wickets.

He came back immediately after the tea interval and sent down six overs, including three maidens, for six runs.

On a slow pitch he yet bowled with some life, and his accuracy was almost mechanical.

With Johnson at the other end giving nothing away, those of the English batsmen who fret under enforced restraint were most unhappy—and they showed it, particularly Hardstaff.

Fast bowler Lindwall began the good work for Australia in his eventful first over.

Hutton and Washbrook took four runs from the first three balls to complete their third consecutive century opening partnership in Tests.

They thus equalled the record of Hobbs and Sutcliffe, who, in their initial pairing for England, scored 157 and 110 in the first Test in Sydney and 283 in their next innings in Melbourne in 1924-25.

It was a fast century, taking only 85 minutes.

Hutton stayed for another hour but added only 18 runs.

Johnson bowled him with a ball that unexpectedly made pace.

By lunch time England, with two out for 164, was 137 to the good.

When play was resumed it seemed that Edrich had been given the job of forcing the pace.

In Toshack's second over he mistimed a lofted drive and was out to Bradman's well-judged catch beyond deep mid-on.

## Hammond Fails

It was up to Hammond then to set about retrieving an awkward situation.

In Toshack's next over Hammond seemed to overlook the presence of Lindwall at fine-leg and swept the ball straight to l ..

Hardstaff struggled painfully for nearly 40 minutes, making streaky shots before Toshack bowled him. The left-hander also got Ikin l.b.w when he had made one.

Compton and Yardley were together at tea with six out for 225, but when a last Bradman decided to bring on his pace bowlers the move succeeded.

The score was 250, but Lindwall was using the old ball when he had Yardley caught behind off his first delivery.

He immediately took the new ball for Bedser, but it was Miller who dismissed Bedser.

That player, who seems to have left his best batting form in Tasmania, reached for an off-side ball and gave the safe Tallon his third catch.

Evans joined the indomitable Compton and remained with him.

England's 274 runs have occupied 378 minutes.

# MORRIS, COMPTON SET RECORD
# 100 Each In Both Innings; Test Draw

## *Scramble For Souvenirs As Fourth Test Match Ends*

The usual scramble for souvenirs took place at the end of the fourth Test yesterday. The upper picture shows Hardstaff (carrying a stump) and Edrich moving off the ground as a host of boys and girls swarm on to it. Umpire Borwick also won a stump. In the lower picture, Bradman and Evans appear to be dividing the honors.

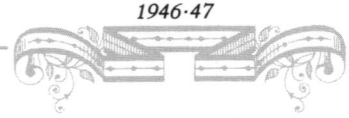

# Australia v England
## Fifth Test Match

AUSTRALIA v ENGLAND, Fifth Test Match, at Sydney, 28 February, 3, 4 and 5 March 1947.

| Australia | - First Innings | 253 |
| | - Second Innings | 214 for 5 wickets |
| England | - First Innings | 280 |
| | - Second Innings | 186 |

Australia won by 5 wickets.

| DON BRADMAN | - b. D.V.P. Wright | 12 |
| (Captain) | - c. D.C.S. Compton b. A.V. Bedser | 63 |

Having had no match practice for almost a month, DON BRADMAN was not at his best in his first innings; he went in after tea on the second day at 126 for 1, and batted for twenty-seven minutes before going down the wicket to D.V.P. Wright. Hitting across and missing a full-pitch, he would have been stumped if he had not been bowled, being third out at 146.

His second innings was a much better one, and virtually won the match for his side. He went in after lunch on the fourth day, at 45 for 1, and found that the wicket was worn, and that Wright and A.V. Bedser were bowling splendidly with its assistance. Cutting at Wright when 2, he gave a sharp chance to slip, but thereafter he batted well, despite the difficult conditions. Reaching 32 by the tea interval, he completed 50 in ninety-seven minutes, and had been in for an hour and fifty-seven minutes when he gave mid-off an easy catch in trying to drive. The score was then 149 for 3, and he had hit seven fours; he and A.L. Hassett added 98 for the third wicket; and when he was 31, he reached 1,000 runs for the season.

Thereafter, Australia always had the match in hand; but England might well have won had it not been for Bradman's innings - and the missed catch.

## England

| | | | |
|---|---|---|---|
| L. Hutton retired ill | 122 | — absent ill | 0 |
| C. Washbrook b Lindwall | 0 | — b McCool | 24 |
| W. J. Edrich c Tallon b Lindwall | 60 | — st Tallon b McCool | 24 |
| L. B. Fishlock b McCool | 14 | — lbw b Lindwall | 0 |
| D. Compton hit wkt b Lindwall | 17 | — c Miller b Toshack | 76 |
| N. W. D. Yardley c Miller b Lindwall | 2 | — b McCool | 11 |
| J. T. Ikin b Lindwall | 0 | — st Tallon b McCool | 0 |
| T. G. Evans b Lindwall | 29 | — b Miller | 20 |
| T. P. B. Smith b Lindwall | 2 | — c Tallon b Lindwall | 24 |
| A. V. Bedser not out | 10 | — st Tallon b McCool | 4 |
| D. V. P. Wright c Tallon b Miller | 7 | — not out | 1 |
| B 7, l-b 8, w 1, n-b 1 | 17 | B 1, l-b 1 | 2 |
| | 280 | | 186 |

## Australia

| | | | |
|---|---|---|---|
| S. G. Barnes c Evans b Bedser | 71 | — c Evans b Bedser | 30 |
| A. Morris lbw b Bedser | 57 | — run out | 17 |
| D. G. Bradman b Wright | 12 | — c Compton b Bedser | 63 |
| A. L. Hassett c Ikin b Wright | 24 | — c Ikin b Wright | 47 |
| K. R. Miller c Ikin b Wright | 23 | — not out | 34 |
| R. A. Hamence not out | 30 | — c Edrich b Wright | 1 |
| C. McCool c Yardley b Wright | 3 | — not out | 13 |
| D. Tallon c Compton b Wright | 0 | | |
| R. Lindwall c Smith b Wright | 0 | | |
| G. Tribe c Fishlock b Wright | 9 | | |
| E. Toshack run out | 5 | | |
| B 7, l-b 6, n-b 6 | 19 | B 4, l-b 1, n-b 4 | 9 |
| | 253 | Five wkts. | 214 |

### Australia Bowling

| | O. | M. | R. | W. | O. | M. | R. | W. |
|---|---|---|---|---|---|---|---|---|
| Lindwall | 22 | 3 | 63 | 7 | 12 | 1 | 46 | 2 |
| Miller | 15.3 | 2 | 31 | 1 | 6 | 1 | 11 | 1 |
| Tribe | 28 | 2 | 95 | 0 | 14 | 0 | 58 | 0 |
| Toshack | 16 | 4 | 40 | 0 | 4 | 1 | 14 | 1 |
| McCool | 13 | 0 | 34 | 1 | 21.4 | 5 | 14 | 5 |
| Barnes | | | | | 3 | 0 | 11 | 0 |

### England Bowling

| | O. | M. | R. | W. | O. | M. | R. | W. |
|---|---|---|---|---|---|---|---|---|
| Bedser | 27 | 7 | 49 | 2 | 22 | 4 | 75 | 2 |
| Edrich | 7 | 0 | 34 | 0 | 2 | 0 | 14 | 0 |
| Smith | 8 | 0 | 38 | 0 | 2 | 0 | 8 | 0 |
| Wright | 29 | 4 | 105 | 7 | 22 | 1 | 93 | 2 |
| Yardley | 5 | 2 | 8 | 0 | 3 | 1 | 7 | 0 |
| Compton | | | | | 1.2 | 0 | 8 | 0 |

### FALL OF WICKETS

ENGLAND—First Innings:

| 1 | 2 | 3 | 4 | 5 | 6 | 7 | 8 | 9 | 10 |
|---|---|---|---|---|---|---|---|---|---|
| 1 | 151 | 188 | 215 | 225 | 225 | 244 | 269 | 280 | 280 |

ENGLAND—Second Innings:

| 1 | 2 | 3 | 4 | 5 | 6 | 7 | 8 | 9 | 10 |
|---|---|---|---|---|---|---|---|---|---|
| 0 | 42 | 65 | 65 | 85 | 120 | 157 | 184 | 186 | 186 |

AUSTRALIA—First Innings:

| 1 | 2 | 3 | 4 | 5 | 6 | 7 | 8 | 9 | 10 |
|---|---|---|---|---|---|---|---|---|---|
| 126 | 146 | 146 | 187 | 218 | 230 | 230 | 233 | 245 | 253 |

AUSTRALIA—Second Innings:

| 1 | 2 | 3 | 4 | 5 |
|---|---|---|---|---|
| 45 | 51 | 149 | 173 | 180 |

Umpires: J. D. Scott and G. Borwick.

# ENGLAND AGAIN ON DEFENSIVE
## Collapse Follows 150 Partnership By Hutton, Edrich

*By ARTHUR MAILEY*

**The dismissal of Yardley and Ikin during the closing stages of yesterday's play in the Fifth Test at Sydney Cricket Ground has again placed England in a defensive position.**

**Batting on a pitch which was a little "sporty" before lunch, but perfect for the rest of the day, England lost 6-237.**

Hutton is 122 not out.

A second-wicket partnership of 150 runs, by Hutton and Edrich, deserved better support.

Should the weather remain fine Australia should score much more heavily than England.

**England's chances depend greatly on whether Hutton can remain at the wickets this morning.**

The early play yesterday was a very grim prelude to a match which was expected to be the brightest of the season.

England lost its first wicket for one run when Washbrook was bowled by Lindwall.

Then Hutton and Edrich became associated.

Hutton scored his first 50 runs in a little over two hours. Edrich took an hour and a half over his first 38.

There was a time when batsmen scored a century before lunch.

The combined effort of the English batsmen and sundries yesterday produced the first 100 at three o'clock.

This gloomy curtain-raiser was not altogether the fault of the batsmen.

The opening bowlers, Miller and Lindwall, bowled fairly fast and with a reasonable amount of accuracy.

### Edrich Opens Out

The tantalising Toshack sent down his first six overs, off which a paltry nine runs were scored.

Toshack bowled a perfect length to a strong leg-side field.

This brand of cricket was served up until three o'clock, when Edrich seemed to realise that the bowling was not as devastating as it seemed.

**He looked at his score on the board, looked at the clock, took a** firm grip of his bat, and promptly **knocked two fours of Toshack's seventh over.**

Then he treated McCool similarly.

Toshack's average jumped from 0-9 to 0-32 in a couple of overs, and he and McCool soon left the bowling crease.

This glorious half-hour's cricket produced about 50 runs.

The partnership, which ended with Edrich trying to back cut a high-flying ball from Lindwall, produced 150 runs—England's best second-wicket partnership of the tour.

The faster scoring towards the end of the partnership was partly due to an improvement in the pitch, which seemed to be hardened by the sun.

Fishlock, who followed Edrich, had the stage set for his type of batting, but he was indecisive and scratchy.

Hutton played a grand innings, which was a combination of Yorkshire and Kent or Sussex styles.

Hutton, perhaps a little shaky against Tribe, and somewhat concerned when facing Miller and Lindwall, was nevertheless mainly responsible for England's favorable position at tea.

### Hostile Bowling

Australia's bowling had been rather hostile throughout the day, and Hutton could hardly be expected to score runs at a faster rate.

After lunch Miller and Lindwall bowled particularly fast, and both bumped the ball disconcertingly.

They maintained their pace till the end of the day and there was no period for Hutton, at any rate, when it was a case of taking advantage of a tired attack.

# Wicket Is Saturated

### (By JIM MATHERS)

RAIN prevented any play today in the fifth Test at the S.C.G. With heavy rain falling, the captains agreed at 2.30 p.m. that play would be impossible.

*Drizzling rain began about 8.40 a.m., continued for nearly two hours, started again less than half an hour later, and grew steadily worse.*

UNTIL the drizzle started the wicket was in good condition, despite 10 points of rain during the night, and it looked capable of being rolled into a good easy wicket, although the first half-hour or so might have been worrying to batsmen.

There was a dampness in the wicket, but it was only "skin deep" and could have been offset by using the heavy roller on it, which the curator (Mr. Wal Gorman) thought would be preferable to the light one.

Provided no rain fell, said Mr. Gorman, the game would be resumed on time at noon. Within half an hour, however, the rain started.

The heavy roller would have brought the moisture to the surface, and so prevented a thin crust being formed on top of the wicket.

At noon, the scheduled time for resumption of play, the gates had not been opened, but about 200 enthusiasts were queued up outside.

The Prime Minister (Mr. Chifley) flew from Canberra this morning for the Test and had lunch with the players.

First announcement about playing prospects was that the captains, Don Bradman and Norman Yardley, would make a decision at 1.30 p.m., the usual time for play to be adjourned for lunch.

## No Match Extension

At that time, however, heavy rain was falling and the players and the captains went to lunch without making an announcement.

Mr. George Borwick, one of the umpires, said at 2 p.m. that he was under the impression that the wicket was to be inspected at 2.15 p.m., not 1.30 p.m.

Bradman, however, visited the Englishmen's dressing-room at 1.30 to ask about an inspection, and Yardley said he would consider the matter at 2.15 p.m.

Rain was falling very heavily at the time, and it seemed obvious that there was no possibility of play to-day.

With rain still falling at 2.30 p.m. it was officially stated there would be no play today.

The match will conclude as scheduled on Thursday.

Test matches are limited to six days in Australia provided that the fifth Test can have no bearing on the rubber, in which case the fifth Test would be played to a finish

As Australia has already won two matches to nil and two have been drawn, the rubber has been decided.

The match is in the same position as at the drawing of stumps last night, when England was 6-237.

## Waited In Vain To See Test

TEST HOPEFULS. Despite heavy rain, this crowd, wearing raincoats and carrying umbrellas, waited outside Sydney Cricket Ground.

# ENGLAND (WITHOUT HUTTON) TOTALS 280

## Lindwall Bags Seven; Morris, Barnes Batting

By R. S. WHITINGTON

**England with Hutton unable to bat lost its three remaining wickets for 43 in the fifth Test at the S.C.G. today and totalled 280.**

Lindwall, bowling seven overs today, took two more wickets for 17 and finished with seven for 63 off 22 overs.

Morris and Barnes who opened confidently for Australia had put on 16 at lunch.

Yardley gave instructions that the wicket be neither rolled nor cut.

The wicket, which had not been cut since Friday morning, had quite a bit of grass growing on its surface at the Paddington end.

The ground had been closely cut.

Lindwall, quite fit again, opened the bowling from the Paddington end to Evans. Smith was the other batsman.

Lindwall started at fast medium pace and gradually clapped on speed during his over, the last ball of which was attractively cover-driven for three by Evans, taking England to six for 240.

Tribe bowled from the Randwick end and his first over was a maiden to Evans.

Lindwall then bowled a maiden to Smith who chopped one ball down very close to his leg stump.

There was a crowd of about 15,000 when play started and it was rapidly growing, giving promise of exceeding Friday's disappointing attendance.

Evans took two to mid-wicket off Tribe's second over and then Smith smashed Lindwall straight back along the ground for two more.

Two balls later Lindwall bowled his first bumper of the day, apparently now thinking Smith was worthy of it.

Two balls later Smith again tried to straight drive Lindwall, but played over and outside it, and lost his leg stump.

Lindwall now had six for 51 and England was seven for 244.

Tribe who had bowled without luck on Friday suffered further misfortune in his third over today.

The second ball was driven sharply to Barnes at forward short leg about five yards from the batsman, hit Barnes in the lower ribs on his left side and fell to the ground.

Evans by cover hitting a shortish ball from Tribe for four made England 252 in 330 minutes. Two balls later he cover drove Tribe to the boundary again to take his own score to 20.

## Tail-enders Show Aggression

Evans, who bats first wicket for Frank Woolley's old county, Kent, and has played several plucky innings for England, went to 26 by back-cutting Tribe for three, turning the first ball of Lindwall's next over past the umpire for two and late-cutting the next for one.

After Bedser had cover driven Lindwall for three, Evans then hit him back over his head for three more.

Lindwall, however, put an end to this belated aggression by bowling Evans for 29 and taking his average to seven for 61. It was the last ball of his over.

Evans had batted 49 minutes and hit two fours. Wright batted through Tribes next over despite the presence of Bradman at silly point and Barnes at silly leg.

Bradman, after Lindwall had bowled seven overs (three maidens) for 17 runs and two wickets today, bowled Miller in his place, and Miller's first ball accounted for Wright, who was caught behind.

England's total was 280, made in 358 minutes.

Bradman lost no time in getting the three-ton roller on the wicket but was not allowed under Test rules to have it cut.

Next cutting is permitted before play tomorrow if the batting captain desires.

Barnes and Morris opened for Australia and Barnes took two for a nicely executed leg glance off Bedser's third ball.

The fifth ball of Bedser's first over was cover driven shoulder-high for two by Morris.

After Morris had corrected a fault in his equipment, umpire Jack Scott lost count of the number of balls and had to ask the scorer.

Morris went to nine with a fine cover drive off Edrich, this time along the ground.

# BRADMAN, MORRIS FAIL
# Lose Wickets By Poor Batting

*By WARWICK ARMSTRONG*

**Bradman and Morris lost their wickets in the third day's play of the Fifth Test yesterday at Sydney Cricket Ground because of bad batting.**

**Thousands of people were at the ground specially to see Bradman bat.**

They were unlucky to see him on one of his worst days, and as soon as he was dismissed for 12 runs most of them left the ground.

● Wright bowled Bradman with practically a full-toss. Bradman hit right across the ball in trying to force it to the on-side.

● Morris walked in front of his wicket to a straight ball from Bedser, and was out leg-before-wicket.

**Morris walks in front of his wicket to almost every ball.**

Because of this, his feet are in a position to make only strokes to the on-side.

This is a bad habit, which Morris must remedy if he wants to remain one of the leading batsmen.

Morris played a fine innings in the Fourth Test at Adelaide, when he hit the ball hard and played a good variety of strokes.

I looked forward for a similar innings from him today, but instead he played like a schoolboy.

Barnes started well, and at times batted brilliantly.

But after he had made about 40 he, too, adopted a negative style, and from then on batted no better than Morris.

Miller played one or two good strokes, but was not comfortable at any stage of his innings.

He seemed to be out of form, and was out, caught in the slips.

The ball, bowled by Wright, lifted sharply from the pitch, turned from the leg, and snicked off Miller's bat to Ikin.

## Bowlers Good

The batting of the English tailender, Evans, early in the day, should have been a lesson to the stars.

Because Hutton was ill and could not resume his innings, Evans took responsibility for the English batting.

He played some beautiful strokes and carried his score from six to 29 before he was out, bowled by Lindwall.

England scored 280 runs, but if Hutton had been able to continue his innings he would probably have scored another 50.

Lindwall, who finished with 7-63, was by far Australia's best bowler.

But, in my opinion, he did not bowl as well as his figures indicate.

A leg injury prevented him from bowling at top pace.

The English bowlers were splendid during Australia's innings, particularly Bedser and Wright.

BRADMAN bowled by Wright for 12. The ball passes over wicketkeeper Evans.

BRADMAN laughs and runs back to the pavilion.

# DRAMATIC PLAY IN TEST —12 BATSMEN FAIL ON WEARING PITCH

### By TOM GOODMAN

After a dramatic day's play, during which bowlers, especially Wright and Bedser, of England, and McCool, of Australia, triumphed, the fifth Test match, at the drawing of stumps yesterday, gave promise of a fighting finish.

England, with six wickets down for 144 runs, and a first innings lead of 27, is 171 runs to the good. Yesterday 12 wickets fell for 208 runs.

## FIGHTING CHANCE FOR ENGLAND

England's man for the crisis, Denis Compton, is still there, with Peter Smith his partner, and Bedser and Wright to follow; but England is not likely to have the services to-day of Len Hutton, who is still in hospital.

When it is noted that Australia failed against Wright on the spinners' pitch in the first innings, when the score changed from no wicket for 126 to all out for 253, England cannot be denied a fighting chance.

But the effect of the rain forecast for to-day remains to be seen—not only how much play is interrupted, but whether the rain is to help bind the wearing pitch, or whether it will cause a soaking to be followed by warm sunshine and the possibility of a "sticky."

Australia's remaining six wickets yesterday added only 64 runs to the overnight score of 189. Then England lost six more (virtually seven with Hutton absent).

### Wright Inspired

Mild-mannered Douglas Wright bowled with tigerish hostility to take his five for 42 in 11 overs, and so earn seven for 105 for the innings.

It was an inspired performance, and easily the best for England in the series.

Wright's nip from the pitch enabled him to exact most help from the conditions. He turned his leg-break considerably at times.

The best feature of his attack was his excellent control of length—especially noteworthy by a bowler who has had bad patches of short-pitched deliveries.

Wright, indeed, at times yesterday reminded me of Bill O'Reilly at his fiery best.

His seven wickets was a grand reward for a hard-worked bowler who has not been lucky.

It gave Wright a tally for this series of 21 wickets, the nearest to him at the end of that innings being Ray Lindwall, with 16.

Alec Bedser, although he did not take wickets yesterday, also played a major part, for he bowled unchanged with Wright, and his 11 overs for 15 runs showed how economically he operated.

He was a grand foil for Wright, because he bowled with sufficient sting to trouble the batsmen, and at times caused the ball to work away off the pitch.

Wright had Hamence, then seven, missed by Ikin at second slip in his fifth over of the day; but two overs later Ikin made amends by brilliantly anticipating and dismissing Lindsay Hassett with a diving left-handed catch.

It was a vital happening. Hassett had batted doggedly for 115 mins., and Hamence, who in his first Test innings, hung on for 106 mins. in all, was the only other batsman to cause the bowlers much worry yesterday.

Wright, after that first miss by Ikin, was brilliantly supported by fieldsmen. He used three slips to McCool, and Yardley, the extra man, cleverly caught that batsman. Fishlock and Smith also held fine catches.

Wright at one stage dismissed McCool, Tallon, and Lindwall in nine balls at a cost of three runs.

Laurie Fishlock, substitute for Hutton as Washbrook's opening partner when England's second innings began at 2.40 p.m., had a depressing finish to his disappointing season's batting when he went lbw to Lindwall's first ball.

Then McCool, who became Bradman's trump card in the spin attack when Tribe again failed to penetrate, troubled all the batsmen with the exception of Compton.

When his sharp leg-breaks had accounted for Washbrook, Edrich, and Ikin, he had taken three wickets for 11 runs in six overs, and he bowled Yardley also before tea, to make it four for 14.

### Compton In Command

McCool finished with four for 32, having bowled 19 overs—remarkably economical figures for a slow spinner even on this pitch.

But the way Denis Compton handled McCool suggested that the Queenslander, splendidly though he bowled, had been flattered by his early figures.

McCool spun prodigiously at times, but without Wright's nip off the pitch, and Compton was able to watch the break all the way.

There was a repetition in miniature of the Adelaide Compton-Evans partnership, as Evans stayed on gallantly for 41 minutes, during which he made 20 of the 35 runs for the sixth wicket.

Miller struck a telling blow for his team by getting rid of Evans; but Smith stayed the last half-hour with Compton.

Compton was superbly sound on the wearing pitch. He has carried a great deal of responsibility in many big matches. If there was a fault to find yesterday it was that he made no strong effort to push the score along late in the day.

He quietly picked up runs, and he concentrated on remaining there. Perhaps he had an idea that Len Hutton might be fit to join him to-day.

The attendance was 20,114 and the gate takings were £2,621.

To-day and to-morrow remain for play.

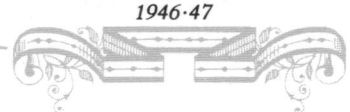

# BRADMAN, HASSETT TO RESCUE OF AUSTRALIA

# Test Win In Sight

*(By JIM MATHERS)*

**M**ISSED in slips when he was only two, Don Bradman went on to score 63 in the fifth Test today, and in a partnership of 98 with Hassett put Australia in sight of victory. Earlier a tense crowd had watched a dramatic battle for runs.

NEEDING 214 runs to win, Australia lost Morris for 17 and Barnes for 30, but when Bradman left Australia needed only 65.

Hassett and Hamence went quickly, but Australia then needed only 34.

England, with a first innings lead of 27, had been dismissed for 186 in the second innings, the last three wickets today having added 42.

Skilfully playing for the strike and attacking the bowling in the closing stages, Compton took his overnight score of 51 to 76.

Len Hutton, who is in St. Vincent's Hospital suffering from severe tonsilitis, today asked for permission to bat for England, but his doctor forbade him to do so.

The hospital reported that he was still very sick, and that it was even problematical whether he would be well enough to leave with the English team for New Zealand on Saturday.

Tribe's first over today left no room for doubt that the wicket had deteriorated under the grinding process of the three-ton roller which the English captain, N. Yardley, ordered to be used before the game began.

The slow bowler's spin off the wicket was much greater than it was yesterday.

However, five runs came off the over, which contained two full tosses, and Smith smacked another full toss in Tribe's second over to the leg boundary.

Lindwall bowled with the breeze from the Randwick end.

The 150 was posted in 193 minutes.

The sixth ball of Lindwall's first over kicked up sharply and nearly caused Compton's dismissal. Compton put his bat to the ball defensively, and spooned it up gently in the direction of Tribe at third slip. The ball, however, fell safely.

In Lindwall's second over, a sharp rising ball, pitched short of good length, hit Smith on the hip. The wicket was "doing" things.

Smith drew away from another bouncer, but fell a victim to Lindwall, snicking a ball that came at even height into the hands of wicket keeper Tallon, who was standing 12 yards behind. Tallon dropped the ball, but grabbed it at the second attempt when it was about 18 inches from the ground. Seven wickets had now fallen for 157 runs.

In Tribe's third over a ball pitched a foot outside Compton's off stump came back very sharply to the leg stump and the batsman chopped down on it just in time.

Compton evidently made up his mind to go for runs with the arrival of Bedser. He brilliantly pulled a short ball from Lindwall to the fence, chopped the next ball hard behind point for two, and brilliantly square-cut another which Tribe just as magnificently fielded, preventing a score.

Compton then powerfully square-drove the last ball of the over for two.

Ten runs came off the over.

Facing McCool, who replaced Tribe with the score at 170, Compton also pulled him hard to the fence.

His onslaught on Lindwall caused Bradman to take the fast bowler off with the score at 178, and Toshack came on. Compton leg-glanced the first ball for two. This stroke made him 73. Two balls later Toshack appealed loudly for leg before against Compton, without success.

Compton's grand innings ended when he was 76 in remarkable fashion. He hit a ball pitched on the leg side by Toshack on to wicketkeeper Tallon's pads, and the ball rebounded to Miller at fine leg who took the catch.

Compton did not appear to quite grasp the situation when umpire George Borwick gave him out after hesitating slightly.

Compton batted 173 minutes and hit five fours. It was a magnificent effort under difficult conditions.

At 12.45 England's innings closed for 186 runs, made in 230 minutes, when Bedser was stumped by Tallon off McCool.

Australia required 214 runs to win.

Barnes and Morris opened for Australia at exactly one o'clock. The scene was set for a thrilling finish.

Bedser and Edrich began the attack. Morris was first to score with a single behind point off Edrich. Barnes opened his scoring with a nice glance for two. He dangerously flicked at a bouncer from Edrich but the ball flew yards wide of Ikin at second slip for two.

It was obvious that Yardley was using Edrich only to take the shine off the ball, for after only one over he was replaced by Wright, who proved so devastating in the first innings. The score was then only six.

Two runs came from Wright's first over and Australia was eight after 16 minutes' batting.

Morris played every ball from Bedser with the full blade of his bat.

Morris cut a single off Bedser and 10 runs came up in 19 minutes.

The crowd was silent during the tense opening struggle between bat and ball.

The first cheer came after 22 minutes when Barnes hit a glorious shot behind point to the fence off Wright.

Yardley at once went to cover, leaving only two men in slips. Another roar came from the crowd when Barnes repeated the stroke two balls later—a beautiful shot between Yardley and Washbrook at deep point. This took the score to 19.

Next ball Barnes hit to Washbrook at point and raced head down to score a single. Morris just managed to beat Washbrook's return to wicketkeeper Evans.

When Barnes was 15, a ball from Bedser lifted sharply and rapped him on the gloves. He walked down the wicket to inspect the offending spot.

At lunch Barnes and Morris had knocked up a handy total of 22 runs leaving 192 runs for victory.

# BRADMAN'S GREAT INNINGS WINS AUSTRALIA TEST

*By E. M. WELLINGS*

**Australia's captain, Don Bradman, won a great victory for Australia yesterday in the Fifth Test.**

His superb batting against Wright tamed England's main and only bowling hope on a pitch helping spin.

His great effort laid the way open for the Australian success.

Yet England could have had him out for two.

In his first over he gave a slip chance off Wright, which Edrich missed.

That proved the turning point in a thrilling match, which, from the English point of view, was far from unsatisfactory, even though Hutton, one of the two main batting hopes, was out of the game after the first day.

Australia's team work and Bradman's batting genius won the match.

England relied overmuch on a few players.

Of the main batsmen, only Hutton, Edrich, and Compton, who batted soundly in the second innings, pulled their weight; and Wright and Bedser were the only bowlers.

Bedser did a fine job as a foil to Wright, who, however, badly needed spin bowling support which Smith could not supply when under pressure.

Wright worked splendidly throughout.

He was not as consistently aggressive and dangerous yesterday as he was the previous day, but this was due largely to Bradman's fine batting against him.

Wright had to carry too heavy a burden, but he did extremely well in this match, and went closer than the score suggests to giving England success.

# TEST UMPIRE HITS BACK AT CRITICS

## *"Had Cricket," Says Scott*

## 'NASTIEST SEASON I'VE EXPERIENCED'

### *(By JIM MATHERS)*

**C**RICKET umpire Jack Scott made a stinging reply today to English Press criticism of some of his decisions in the Tests between England and Australia.

*Explaining his decision to retire, Scott said: "I'm getting out of the game. I will never officiate again as an umpire in Tests. I've 'had' it."*

SCOTT said: "The critics have said that they and the English players would heave sighs of relief when the tour was over.

"But their sighs could not be nearly as deep as the one I heaved yesterday on the Sydney Cricket Ground when McCool made the winning hit.

"**That winning hit closed the nastiest and most acrimonious season I've ever experienced in 39 years of cricket, including 15 years as an umpire.**

"I really don't know what the game has degenerated into when certain Press critics can sit in the pavilion, and literally tear to pieces an umpire, who alone is in the position to judge whether a batsman is out or not.

"But I was pilloried and lampooned by certain critics simply because I did my duty fearlessly. Whether a decision meant the dismissal of an English or Australian player mattered not one jot to me.

"I gave no decision that I regret. Nor did I feel afterwards that I would have liked to have withdrawn any decision. I was scrupulously fair. Any doubt I had, I gave the benefit to the batsman. And I had those doubts," he added.

### Disputed Decisions

Scott was invited to comment on his much-discussed l.b.w. decisions against Compton and Edrich in the third Test match in Melbourne.

The feeling was so bad that some English critics suggested that Scott would be sacked by the Board of Control. But the board appointed him for the remainder of the Test season.

Scott's version of Compton's dismissal was: "Toshack bowled a couple of balls going away to the leg side and Compton held his bat out and let them pass. When Toshack saw what Compton was doing he sent through a straight ball which caught Compton unawares.

"Compton bent his knees and the ball hit his pads. I gave him out leg before wicket. After the decision had been given, Compton straightened his legs, but when the ball hit his pads he was right in front of the middle stump.

"Compton didn't appear to like the decision. Washbrook, who was the batsman at my end of the wicket, turned to me and said: 'What's the matter? That ball would have hit his middle stump.'"

Yet certain English critics howled for days afterwards and said that Compton was cheated out.

Here is Scott's version of the "Edrich incident" (the critics claimed that Edrich had hit the ball on which he was given out l.b.w.):

"Edrich got a ball from Lindwall, pitched outside the leg stump. The ball dipped from the off, and Edrich was plumb in front of his wicket.

"**I saw daylight between bat and ball. Edrich did not hit that ball.**"

Yet some of the critics reckoned they saw the mark of the ball on the bat!

Scott says he will answer the critics more fully in a book dealing with disputed decisions and other incidents in the tour.

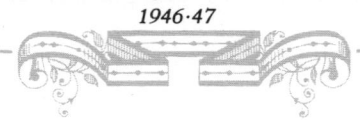

206 Page Street
Middle Park, S.C.6

8 · 3 · 47

Dear Don,

I'd like to thank you for the letter you sent me. I can't say just how much I appreciated it, but it was almost worth a broken finger.

I naturally enjoyed the season immensely but most of all I enjoyed playing under your captaincy. It was an education, as well as an inspiration, to the whole team and the success was, without question, due largely to your leadership.

For myself I have never enjoyed playing under a captain as much; particularly was this so when bowling - you were a tremendous help and taught me a lot in your methods of handling your bowlers.

My one regret is that I didn't bat with you in any match. I would have liked that!

In conclusion Don let me congratulate you on your really wonderful season & the way in which you made the critics eat their words in every way.

Thanks again Don for my most wonderful cricket experience,

Yours Very Sincerely

Ian Johnson

---

| T.G.42E. | This Telegram has been received subject to the Post and Telegraph Act and Regulations. The time received at this office is shown at the end of the message. | COMMONWEALTH OF AUSTRALIA. POSTMASTER-GENERAL'S DEPARTMENT. **TELEGRAM** | The date stamp indicates the date of reception lodgment also, unless earlier date is shown after the time of lodgment. | Office Date Stamp. |
|---|---|---|---|---|

Office of Origin.　　No. of Words.　　Time of Lodgment.

URGT W 212 CANBERRA SUB 36 8 P

DON BRADMAN
CAPT AUSTRALIAN ELEVEN USHERS SYDNEY

PLEASE ACCEPT MY SINCERE CONGRATULATIONS ON EXCELLENT PERFORMANCE
OF YOURSELF AND YOUR TEAM STOP YOUR OWN PERSONAL ACHIEVEMENT
ADDS ANOTHER SERIES TO AN IMPERISHABLE RECORD
... EVATT DEPUTY PRIME MINISTER

THE PARLIAMENT OF THE COMMONWEALTH.

LEADER OF THE OPPOSITION,
CANBERRA, A.C.T.

20th March, 1947.

My dear Don,

I would not like the 1946/47 Test Season to pass into Limbo without dropping you a line to say how much I admired your unique contribution to victory.

As a highly interested onlooker I was constantly fascinated by the skill with which you controlled the game at all stages. There are very many of us who think that we have never seen a better or more subtle exhibition of Captaincy.

You no doubt have your critics and I suppose, like all the rest of us, you occasionally deserve them! But you can certainly look back over these Test victories with unadulterated pride.

With very kind regards,

I am,

Yours truly,

(R.G. MENZIES.)

D.G. Bradman, Esq.
————————

# BRADMAN MAY PLAY AGAINST INDIAN TEAM

SYDNEY.—Don Bradman may lead Australia against the Indian cricket team when it tours Australia next season.

He said last night he hoped it would be possible for him to play in some of the games, at least.

He would not commit himself as to whether he would be available for the 1948 tour of England

## Current Tour Figures

From Roy Colmer

SYDNEY.—The Test cricket series between Australia and England has been a financial success.

Total attendance for the five games was 846,263. Gross gate takings were £115,856.

Figures for the fifth Test were 93,011, and takings £12,617.

The smallest crowds were in Brisbane (77,344 attendance), but takings were £14,515.

This made the fifth Test takings the lowest.

"Sir Vithaldas Chambers",
16, Apollo Street, Fort,
Bombay, 24th April 1947.

Don Bradman, Esq.,
C/O Don Bradman & Co.,
Cowra Chambers,
23, Grenfell Street,
ADELAIDE. (SOUTH AUSTRALIA).

Dear Don,

I thank you for your kind letter of the 16th instant and am grateful to you for the very kind sentiments expressed - therein.

I am very much looking forward to the Indian Team's visit to Australia and the great experience such a tour will - give to me and my colleagues.

Australian's hospitality is proverbial and I have - not the slightest doubt that we shall all enjoy ourselves.

It is indeed very nice of you to offer your assistance and help in making our visit and stay enjoyable. I shall certainly avail myself of it whenever necessary.

With kindest regards to you and Mrs. Bradman and - with best wishes,

Yours sincerely,

Vijay Merchant.

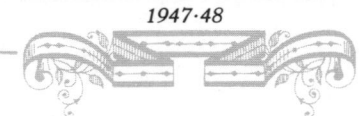

# *1947 - 48  Season*

The visit of the Indians in 1947–48 resulted in some very interesting cricket.
Early in the season I made my hundredth century in first class cricket, and was delighted to do this on my favourite ground, Sydney. It put me in form for the Tests, in which Australia proved too strong for India.

I announced that this would be my last season in Australia but deferred a decision concerning the 1948 Tour of England until later.

*Don Bradman*

### — SEASON 1947-48 —

| TITLE | GAMES | | SCORES | |
|---|---|---|---|---|
| Second Class | Bradman's Team | Ridings' Team | 0 | B. |
| | Australia | Colombo | 20 | C. |
| | " | Tasmania | 45 | C. |
| First Grade | Kensington | University | 11 | n.o. |
| | " | Woodville | 94 | n.o. |
| | " | Port Adelaide | 36 | C. |
| | " | " | 21 | n.o. |
| First Class | South Australia | India | 156 | C. |
| | " | " | 12 | St. |
| | An Australian XI | " | 172 | C. |
| | " | " | 26 | C. |
| | Australia | Western Australia | 115 | C. |
| Sheffield Shield | South Australia | Victoria | 100 | L.B.W. |
| Test Matches | Australia | India | 185 | H.W. |
| | " | " | 13 | B. |
| | " | " | 132 | L.B.W. |
| | " | " | 127 | n.o. |
| | " | " | 201 | B. |
| | " | " | 57 | R.H. |
| | | Total runs | 1523 | |

### — SUMMARY —

AVERAGES -

| | Innings | N.O's. | H.S. | Runs | Average |
|---|---|---|---|---|---|
| Test Matches | 6 | 2 | 201 | 715 | 178·8 |
| Sheffield Shield | 1 | 0 | 100 | 100 | 100·0 |
| Other First Class | 5 | 0 | 172 | 481 | 96·2 |
| All First Class | 12 | 2 | 201 | 1296 | 129·6 |
| First Grade | 4 | 3 | 94* | 162 | 162·0 |
| Other Second Class | 3 | 0 | 45 | 65 | 21·7 |
| All Second Class | 7 | 3 | 94* | 227 | 56·8 |
| All Matches | 19 | 5 | 201 | 1523 | 108·7 |

## INDIAN TEAM IN AUSTRALIA
### 1947-48

BACK ROW    W. Ferguson (Scorer), G. Kishenchand, C. R. Rangachari, J. K. Irani, K. M. Rangnekar, K. Rai Singh, P. Sen,
K. S. Ranvirsinhji, D. G. Phadkar, H. R. Adhikari and P. Gupta (Manager).

FRONT ROW    C. T. Sarwate, Gul Mahomed, S. W. Sohoni, V. S. Hazare (Vice-Captain), L. Amarnath (Captain), V. Mankad,
C. S. Nayudu and Amir Elahi.

# INDIANS WANT BRADMAN TO GET 100th CENTURY AGAINST THEM

**DARWIN, Saturday.—Any member of the visiting Indian cricket team who gets Don Bradman out too cheaply courts censure from his team-mates.**

The Indians regard Bradman as a cricketing colossus, and, as their manager (Mr I. Gupta) says, "they would prefer to lose every match and see Bradman play than win every match and not see him."

Another Indian said: "Bradman has 97 first-class centuries, and we hope he will get his century of centuries against us. We don't mind how many the Australians make, or how many we make. It's a game and we are going to enjoy it."

The Indians impress immediately as men passionately fond of the game for its own sake.

They are young men and some are obviously nervous at the pros-

pect of meeting "giants" of the game. Although every man will be doing his best to make a double century, it won't matter much whether it is win, lose or draw.

The Indians feel that Australian wickets will probably take some getting used to and that their first performances may not be outstanding.

Indian cricket is all played on matting, because, as one member said sorrowfully, "we can't afford the water from the more important business of growing food."

They are keenly interested in water and several asked about Darwin's water supply.

Prince Duleepsinhji, famous

English Test team batsman, who has made many centuries against the Australians, is accompanying the team as a correspondent for Reuter's.

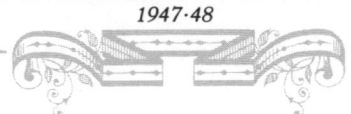

# South Australia
# v
# Indians

SOUTH AUSTRALIANS v INDIANS, at Adelaide, 24, 25, 27 and 28 October 1947.

| South Australia | - First Innings | 518 for 8 wickets dec. |
| | - Second Innings | 219 for 8 wickets dec. |
| Indians | - First Innings | 451 |
| | - Second Innings | 235 for 5 wickets |

Drawn.

| DON BRADMAN | - c. C.T. Sarwate b. V. Mankad | 156 |
| (Captain) | - st. P. Sen b. V. Mankad | 12 |

The Indian bowlers had been punished in an opening stand of 226 before DON BRADMAN came to the wicket five minutes after tea on the first day. He gave a chance at deep square-leg off C.T. Sarwate, when 23, but was otherwise in his most brilliant form, taking only forty-seven minutes to reach 50, and he completed his century, in ninety-eight minutes, in the last over of the day. Starting next morning at 102 not out, he hit out recklessly, carrying his score to 156 in another fifty-four minutes, before being caught off a skier at mid-on; he batted for two hours thirty-two minutes, and hit twenty-two fours. He had also scored a century in his first match v. English (1928-9) and South African (1931-2) Touring teams, and now added the Indians to the list; no other Australian had done this against Touring teams from three countries.

His second innings took place late on the third day, when he went in at 58 for 1, and lasted seventeen minutes; he was then stumped, reaching forward to V. Mankad, with the score 76 for 2.

## South Australia

| | | |
|---|---|---|
| R. D. Niehuus c Nayudu b Mankad | 137 | — lbw b Phadkar ............ 49 |
| R. J. Craig b Sarwate | 100 | — st Sen b Mankad ......... 24 |
| D. G. Bradman c Sarwate b Mankad | 156 | — st Sen b Mankad ......... 12 |
| R. A. Hamence c and b Mankad | 31 | — b Phadkar ............... 10 |
| R. James c Mankad b Amarnath | 3 | — c and b Phadkar ......... 0 |
| P. L. Ridings b Mankad | 26 | — b Sarwate ............... 17 |
| R. Vaughton not out | 17 | — b Mankad ................ 0 |
| B. Dooland b Sarwate | 14 | — b Phadkar ............... 21 |
| J. Noblet b Sarwate | 1 | — not out ................. 50 |
| K. O'Neill not out | 12 | — not out ................. 23 |
| B 16, l-b 5 | 21 | B 9, l-b 4 ............ 13 |
| | **Eight wkts., dec. 518** | **Eight wkts., dec. 219** |

N. Oswald did not bat.

## India

| | | |
|---|---|---|
| V. Mankad b O'Neill | 57 | — not out ................. 116 |
| H. R. Adhikari lbw b O'Neill | 0 | — lbw b O'Neill ........... 0 |
| G. Kishenchand lbw b Noblet | 1 | — b Dooland ............... 9 |
| V. S. Hazare c Ridings b Noblet | 95 | — b Noblet ................ 7 |
| Gul Mahomed c Vaughton b Oswald | 18 | — b Noblet ................ 2 |
| P. Sen b Noblet | 4 | |
| L. Amarnath st Vaughton b Dooland | 144 | — not out ................. 94 |
| C. T. Sarwate c O'Neill b Ridings | 47 | |
| D. G. Phadkar lbw b Ridings | 8 | |
| S. W. Sohoni not out | 27 | — lbw b O'Neill ........... 2 |
| C. S. Nayudu c Dooland b Oswald | 19 | |
| B 19, l-b 6, w 3, n-b 3 | 31 | B 3, l-b 1, w 1 ....... 5 |
| | **451** | **Five wkts. 235** |

## India Bowling

| | O. | M. | R. | W. | | O. | M. | R. | W. |
|---|---|---|---|---|---|---|---|---|---|
| Phadkar | 16 | 1 | 72 | 0 | .... | 15 | 0 | 59 | 4 |
| Amarnath | 12 | 1 | 48 | 1 | .... | 2 | 0 | 7 | 0 |
| Mankad | 36 | 1 | 127 | 4 | .... | 22 | 4 | 51 | 3 |
| Nayudu | 9 | 0 | 62 | 0 | .... | 3 | 1 | 8 | 0 |
| Sarwate | 16 | 1 | 83 | 3 | .... | 10 | 0 | 39 | 1 |
| Hazare | 18 | 1 | 95 | 0 | .... | 7 | 0 | 26 | 0 |
| Sohoni | 3 | 0 | 10 | 0 | .... | 6 | 1 | 16 | 0 |

## South Australia Bowling

| | O. | M. | R. | W. | | O. | M. | R. | W. |
|---|---|---|---|---|---|---|---|---|---|
| O'Neill | 21 | 0 | 110 | 2 | .... | 9 | 0 | 40 | 2 |
| Noblet | 25 | 4 | 65 | 3 | .... | 10 | 0 | 48 | 2 |
| James | 7 | 2 | 23 | 0 | | | | | |
| Dooland | 22 | 2 | 123 | 1 | .... | 12 | 0 | 59 | 1 |
| Oswald | 20.6 | 0 | 70 | 2 | .... | 10 | 0 | 53 | 0 |
| Ridings | 9 | 3 | 29 | 2 | .... | 4 | 0 | 17 | 0 |
| Craig | | | | | | 1 | 0 | 13 | 0 |

*From the Hill* by Wesley Walters. Don Bradman scores the single that gives him 100 first class centuries, Sydney Cricket Ground, 15 November 1947.

Commemorative plate produced by Coalport, England, to recognise Don Bradman's 100 centuries in first class cricket.
Issued in 1979 and limited to 500 pieces.

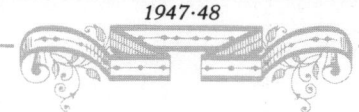

# BRADMAN STILL THE CHAMPION

## Needs Two For 100 Centuries

*By P. J. MILLARD*

**Bowlers still can't stop Don Bradman, as the Indians can ruefully testify! Of his 98 first-class centuries, his first and last (to date) have been scored on the Adelaide Oval.**

It now seems certain that he will achieve his ambition of 100 centuries — a goal that only 10 players, all English have reached — before this season is far advanced. And Don's cricket creed is never to stop at 100.

His present century against the Indians is his 16th at Adelaide, and he has also scored the same number at Melbourne.

**But Sydney — scene of his world record score of 452 not out against Queensland, in 1929-30 — remains his happy hunting ground. There he has reeled off 21 first-class centuries.**

Bradman has hit 10 three-figure scores at Brisbane; five on other Australian grounds; and 30 in England.

Don began his uncanny century habit in his very first innings in big cricket, with 118 for New South Wales against South Australia, at Adelaide, in 1927-28 season. He was then 19.

In his dazzling career, now spanning 20 years (including the wartime break), he has stood out as the greatest batsman and run-getter of all time.

## ANSWERED CRITICS

Nearly two years ago the pessimists practically wiped him off as a Test batsman. He was "a spent force," they said.

Don promptly answered them with a brilliant 112 in 112 minutes, with 11 fours, for South Australia against the returning Australian Services' team, at Adelaide, on December 31, 1945.

That was his 93rd first-class century, and his first since 1939-40. Last season he added four, besides heading the Test averages for either side, totalling 680 runs, av. 97.1, with his highest score, 234, in the second Test against England at Sydney.

Before this he had, last season, made 106 for An Australian XI against England at MCG; 187 in the first Test at Brisbane; and 119 for SA against Victoria at Adelaide.

Record number of first-class centuries in world cricket is 197, by Jack Hobbs (Surrey and England); but his career extended over 29 years (1905-34), and he played 1315 first-class innings (106 not out) for 61,221 runs (another world record), av. 50.63. Hobbs's best score was 316 not out.

Don Bradman's record, compressed into far less big cricket, is much more spectacular.

Before his present hand, Don had played 291 first-class innings (37 not out) for 24,127 runs, at the phenomenal average of 94.9.

And his present blaze of runs lifts his average even higher!

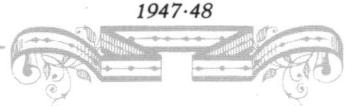

# BRADMAN AND HAZARE PROVIDE THRILLS

## By ROY COLMER

**Bradman and Hazare were the stars in the second day's play of the cricket match between South Australia and India at Adelaide Oval today. Both men gave batting displays that were a sheer delight.**

BRADMAN raced the clock, finishing with 156 in 152 minutes, while Hazare made 95 in a fighting stand for the third wicket after the first two Indian wickets had fallen for two runs.

Estimated at 12,000, the crowd were treated to a day's cricket without a dull moment.

Bradman started the day with 102 runs on the board. He wasted no time in launching a full-blooded attack on the bowling, and soon had the scoring board indicators spinning.

**Even allowing for the easy wicket and that the Indian bowlers were obviously feeling the lack of practice, Bradman's display was a gem.**

He pulled every shot out of the bag in a display of rungetting that worked up quickly to a hurricane rate. He reached his 150 in even time.

### Long Handle

When he took the long handle to Mankad, he gave the Indian left-hander a torrid time. It was clear that Bradman was preparing to call it a day, but he carried my memory back to a Sheffield Shield match before the war when he gave Bill O'Reilly a savage mauling at Adelaide Oval.

Bradman threw his hand away today as on another occasion, when I saw him make a present of his wicket—against Tasmania here—he had to make two attempts to give a catch.

After Bradman left, the remaining South Australians did not worry about wickets falling. They hit out merrily.

India's early batsmen strengthened my belief that they are a side badly handicapped by lack of practice. It must be remembered too, that this was the first day for the tour on which they had experienced clear sunshine.

Merit was added to a grand display by Hazare, by the fact that he went to the wickets with two batsmen out for two runs. It was a position that could well have hobbled any batsman.

But Hazare, after getting a look at the bowling, and accustoming himself to the wicket, gave a display of stroke play that will make him remembered for a long time.

It would be impossible to compare his knock with Bradman's. Where Bradman ripped and tore at the bowling, Hazare was as smooth as oil on the tongue.

It was only to be expected that the start of the Mankad—Hazare partnership should be slow. They had 15 singles in their first 20 runs, but Hazare had hit a three and a two in that time.

When he punched Dooland through the covers for his first four, spectators cheered wildly. However, I thought his best shots came later in his innings.

Square cuts off James, a gem of a pull shot off O'Neill, and then a straight drive, also off the fast bowler, would have done credit to any batsman in the world.

**His 150 partnership with Mankad took only 137 minutes. That rate of scoring was typical of the Indian batting to the end of the day.**

Mankad must be given full credit for his knock for 57. It was a valuable innings, not without its bright moments, but compared to Hazare's, it was notable only for its fighting qualities.

### Lack Practice

Gul Mahomed demonstrated the Indians' lack of practice. He went through all the actions of a forcing batsman, but his timing was so astray that he rarely connected. At the end of the day Amarnath was maintaining the non-stop flow of runs. He put his 38 on the board in 39 minutes.

Gul Mahomed was out of touch with his batting. He made vigorous attempts to force the scoring, but mistimed many of his shots.

Soon after Sarwate joined Amarnath for the seventh wicket the score went to 200 after 195 minutes.

**The scoring rate has been a feature of the game The batsmen have scored 742 runs in two days, and there have been some brilliant bursts.**

In this regard the Indians must be given full credit, because they scored their 224 runs today in 210 minutes, when most teams would have been inclined to take no risks.

With the easy wicket against them, it was to be expected that the bowlers should play a minor role. Dooland, South Australia's Test man, did not take a wicket in 12 overs, which cost 62 runs.

On the other hand Noblet, off the same number of overs took three for 29. Still, I should think the spin bowler's turn will come later when the wicket is giving some assistance

Peter Gupta looks at a photograph of Don Bradman's children.

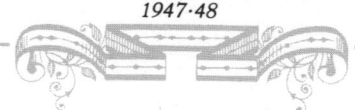

# South Australia v Victoria

SOUTH AUSTRALIA v VICTORIA, at Adelaide,
7, 8, 10 and 11 November 1947.

| South Australia | - First Innings | 536 |
| | - Second Innings | 87 for 1 wicket |
| Victoria | - First Innings | 440 |
| | - Second Innings | 182 |

South Australia won by 9 wickets.

| DON BRADMAN | - lbw. b. I.W. Johnson | 100 |
| (Captain) | - (did not bat) | - |

DON BRADMAN went in at 17 for 1, soon after lunch on the second day, and played a sound and chanceless innings, against bowlers who included W.A. Johnston, .F. Freer, S.J.E. Loxton, I.W. Johnson and D.T. Ring.    He completed 50 in one and a quarter hours, and 100 in two hours forty-two minutes, being lbw. 2 balls later, playing across a straight ball;  second out at 190, he added 173 with R.J. Craig for the second wicket, and reached the boundary eight times.    This was his ninety-ninth century in first-class cricket, and his only Sheffield Shield appearance for South Australia this season.

## SOUTH AUSTRALIA v. VICTORIA.

### Played at Adelaide, November 7, 8, 10, 11, 1947.

### Won by South Australia by 9 wickets

#### VICTORIA

| | | | | |
|---|---|---|---|---|
| K. Meuleman, c Ridings, b O'Neill | 30 | c Noblet, b Oswald | 29 |
| M. Harvey, b O'Neill | 89 | b Noblet | 3 |
| A. L. Hassett (Capt.), c Bradman, b Oswald | 118 | c Noblet, b Craig | 0 |
| S. Loxton, c Vaughton, b Oswald | 13 | b Craig | 21 |
| R. N. Harvey, c Oswald, b Ridings | 10 | c Oswald, b Craig | 13 |
| D. Fothergill, c Dooland, b Ridings | 102 | c Noblet, b Oswald | 31 |
| I. W. Johnson, b Hamence, b Dooland | 34 | b Noblet | 14 |
| F. Freer, c Bradman, b Ridings | 4 | b Noblet | 23 |
| E. A. Baker, b Dooland | 5 | b O'Neill | 5 |
| D. T. Ring, c Craig, b Ridings | 15 | not out | 23 |
| W. A. Johnston, not out | 0 | lbw, b Noblet | 1 |
| B. 13, L.B. 2, N.B. 4, W. 1 | 20 | B. 6, L.B. 8, W. 5 | 19 |
| Total | 440 | Total | 182 |

Fall: 83, 174, 193, 226, 322, 402, 417, 422, 432.

Fall: 10, 47, 77, 77, 83, 116, 145, 162, 167.

#### SOUTH AUSTRALIA

| | | | | |
|---|---|---|---|---|
| R. D. Niehuus, c Freer, b Johnston | 4 | | |
| R. J. Craig, lbw, b Ring | 97 | | |
| D. G. Bradman (Capt.), lbw, b Johnson | 100 | | |
| R. A. Hamence, lbw, b Ring | 14 | run out | 27 |
| R. James, b Freer | 27 | not out | 42 |
| P. Ridings, b Freer | 151 | not out | 17 |
| R. Vaughton, c Loxton, b Johnson | 14 | | |
| B. Dooland, c and b Ring | 62 | | |
| G. Noblet, c Meuleman, b Hassett | 32 | | |
| K. O'Neill, c Meuleman, b Ring | 4 | | |
| N. Oswald, not out | 5 | | |
| B. 18, L.B. 6, N.B. 4, W. 1 | 26 | B. 1 | 1 |
| Total | 536 | One wicket for | 87 |

Fall: 17, 190, 214, 233, 266, 319, 438, 522, 528.

Fall: 46.

#### SOUTH AUSTRALIA—BOWLING

| | O. | M. | R. | W. | O. | M. | R. | W. |
|---|---|---|---|---|---|---|---|---|
| O'Neill | 23 | 1 | 76 | 2 | 11 | 1 | 42 | 1 |
| Noblet | 22 | 5 | 71 | — | 8.7 | 2 | 19 | 4 |
| Ridings | 16.6 | 1 | 66 | 4 | | | | |
| Dooland | 20 | 1 | 99 | 2 | 18 | 4 | 49 | — |
| Oswald | 17 | 1 | 91 | 2 | 15 | 6 | 16 | 2 |
| Craig | 3 | — | 17 | | 13 | 2 | 37 | 3 |

O'Neill, 2 no-balls
Ridings, 2 no-balls
Oswald, 1 wide

Noblet, 1 wide
Craig, 4 wides

#### VICTORIA—BOWLING

| | O. | M. | R. | W. | O. | M. | R. | W. |
|---|---|---|---|---|---|---|---|---|
| Johnston | 33 | 5 | 94 | 1 | 7 | — | 32 | — |
| Freer | 24 | 4 | 87 | 2 | 8 | — | 37 | — |
| Loxton | 10 | 2 | 30 | — | | | | |
| Johnson | 34 | 7 | 89 | 2 | | | | |
| Ring | 46.3 | 3 | 176 | 4 | 1.6 | — | 17 | — |
| Fothergill | 2 | — | 11 | — | | | | |
| Hassett | 3 | — | 23 | 1 | | | | |

Johnston, 1 wide
Freer, 1 no-ball

Umpires: J. D. Scott and G. S. Cooper.

# BRADMAN'S 99th CENTURY: CRAIG, 80 n.o.

## By ROY COLMER

DON Bradman scored his ninety-ninth century in first-class cricket today in the Sheffield Shield match against Victoria at Adelaide Oval. With Craig, he put on 173 for the second wicket.

South Australia were in a satisfactory position at stumps with 202 runs on the board for two wickets. Victoria were dismissed for 440, five wickets falling today for 80 runs.

Bradman's century was almost unique. He was never able to make a full-blooded attack on the bowling, and yet he was never in trouble.

Judged by his own standards, it was a slow knock, but there were contributing factors outside his control.

**Craig's dominance of the strike, coupled with Hassett's field placings, kept a check rein on Bradman. I doubt whether** Bradman has ever seen a partner take so much of the batting.

The scoring showed the staccato rate at which Bradman progressed to his century. There were 47 singles in his 100 runs, which took 162 minutes. The second 50 took 85 minutes. At one stage of his innings, Bradman scored 15 singles in a row.

It was only rarely that the South Australian captain was able to open out. One pull landed the ball on the pickets and an off drive went through so fast that there would have needed to be an extra man or two about to cut it off.

In the main, however, Hassett had his field so well placed that shot after shot was cut off to restrict the score to singles.

**It was obvious Bradman realised he would have been wasting energy to hit the ball hard. Still he kept his score moving whenever he got the opportunity.**

Craig's innings was valuable, but he could not handle the bowling to give him an even flow of runs. The Victorian tactics called for something foreign to his game and, wisely, he did not attempt to break away from style.

He was dropped at 69, but few begrudged him his slice of luck.

Altogether, South Australia had reason to be satisfied with the day's play. Their effort in dismissing the remaining five Victorian batsmen for 80 in the morning session was good.

Ridings played the main role with the ball. He took three for 17 this morning in 2.6 overs.

Fothergill scored the 31 runs to complete his century—his first in a shield game—but after he and Johnson were dismissed the end of the innings was in sight.

**It was not an exciting day's cricket, but still it was interesting. The battle between the bat and the ball was too keen for fireworks.**

On an easy-paced wicket the bowlers maintained length and accuracy to make the batsmen earn every run.

# An Australian XI v Indians

AN AUSTRALIAN XI v INDIANS, at Sydney,
14, 15, 17 and 18 November 1947.

| An Australian XI | - First Innings | 380 |
| | - Second Innings | 203 |
| Indians | - First Innings | 326 |
| | - Second Innings | 304 for 9 wickets dec. |

An Australian XI lost by 47 runs.

| DON BRADMAN | - c. L. Amarnath b. V.S. Hazare | 172 |
| (Captain) | - c. C.T. Sarwate b. V. Mankad | 26 |

With his hundredth century in prospect, DON BRADMAN took this innings very seriously when he went in at 11 for 1 on the second morning, playing himself in with great care and taking no risks. He reached 50 in seventy-eight minutes, and thereafter hit out more freely, but as his century approached he again exercised great caution.     He was 99 when the last over before tea was due, and L. Armanath, the Indian Captain gave the ball to G. Kishenchand, who was no bowler, and had not so far bowled a ball on the tour; Bradman pushed his second ball to leg for a single, to complete his century after batting for two hours twelve minutes.     After tea, freed from the nervous tension, he added a further 72 runs in forty-five minutes of glorious stroke-play before giving a catch to deep mid-off.     He batted altogether for two hours fifty-seven minutes, gave no chance, and hit a six and eighteen fours.     He and K.R. Miller put on 252 for the third wicket, in two hours thirty-four minutes, their partnership being the highest for the third wicket against any Indian Touring team anywhere.

This was his 295th innings in first-class cricket.     Bradman was the only batsman to make 100 centuries scored at the first attempt, i.e. immediately after his ninety-ninth, and the only Australian ever to make 100 centuries.

Set to make 251 to win in two and a half hours on the last day, the Australians accepted the challenge.     Bradman went in at 60 for 1, and hit up 26 in thirty-two minutes before being caught at forward short-leg off a half-cock shot; the score had slumped to 120 for 5 by the time he was out.

## AN AUSTRALIAN XI v INDIANS
### Sydney, November 1947

BACK ROW    R. Saggers, S. Loxton, B. Dooland, W. Johnston, R. Rogers, M. Herbert.
FRONT ROW    K. Miller, R. Hamence, W. A. Brown, D. G. Bradman (Captain), N. Harvey,
J. Pettiford.

# MILLER HELPS CAPTAIN

**SYDNEY, Saturday. — Keith Miller played a great supporting hand in the second wicket stand with Bradman, allowing the champion to race along and reach his century before the tea adjournment.**

Brown and Rogers went cheaply and two wickets were down for 24, before Bradman and Miller became associated in the third wicket stand.

BRADMAN began to sparkle soon after Miller joined him. They posted the first 100 in 83 minutes, Bradman being 46 and Miller 31.

Bradman reached his 50 in 78 minutes (two fours) by tapping Mankad to mid-wicket for a single. He went to 60 with a cover-drive off Mankad, and had scored 31 while Miller, 36, was adding 7. A similar stroke off Mankad brought up the 100 partnership in 73 minutes, Bradman being 66 and Miller 40.

Bradman received a tremendous ovation from the pre-lunch crowd of 25,000, but was only seven when he lost Rogers. Bradman played a ball into the covers, and Rogers, backing up, had to turn when Bradman sent him back. A brilliant return by Nayudu hit the stumps with Rogers just out of his ground. He had made 16 and was batting soundly.

Miller joined Bradman, and at lunch they had taken the score from 31 to 44 after 30 minutes against good bowling by Sohoni and Amarnath.

After lunch, Bradman and Miller had to bat carefully against accurate bowling by Mankad and Amarnath. Their 50 partnership was posted in 43 minutes, Miller being 38.

Amarnath, who had opened the bowling, made Bradman fight hard, and once he rapped the champion's pads with a ball that beat him. With Bradman as the magnet, the crowd had risen above 50,000 after lunch. Bradman was content to move along quietly, and in 70 minutes had not hit a boundary.

Mankad and Sarwate also pinned down Bradman and Miller, until Bradman pulled a short ball from Sarwate to the square leg fence. Mankad at this stage had bowled five overs for eight runs.

Bradman went to 80 as the 150 came up in 113 minutes, the third 50 having taken 30 minutes. At 83, Bradman survived a confident lbw appeal from Mankad, and then swept the next ball to fine leg for four.

Just after Miller had square cut Sarwate to reach 50 (three 4's) in 98 minutes, Bradman moved on to 90. After three singles Bradman turned Mankad to leg for two, and an on drive enabled him and Miller to run an audacious two, making Don 97.

The crowd was tense as he played out the rest of Mankad's over. Miller then gave Bradman the strike against Sarwate. Off the last ball of that over Bradman and Miller sneaked another single, Amarnath's return hitting the stumps.

Another sharp single to square leg made Bradman 99.

**For the next over Amarnath called on Kishenchand for his first over of the tour and an on-drive from the second ball gave Bradman his hundredth century in first-class cricket.**

Bradman had batted 132 minutes in a chanceless knock and had hit only six fours. It was his 21st century on the Sydney Cricket Ground. He was congratulated by Amarnath, Kishenchand and Miller.

At tea, when Bradman was 101, the New South Wales Cricket Association president (Mr Syd Smith) walked on to the ground to congratulate Bradman. There was a very brief handshake and Bradman and Miller continued walking, leaving Mr Smith astern.

**Shortly after tea the 200 came up in 140 minutes.**

As play went on Miller reclaimed some of the brilliance which had characterised the beginnings of his innings, and Bradman and he treated the crowd to a great display of stroke-making.

It was a great relief after the tenseness and suspense of the mid-afternoon session.

In 28 minutes after tea, Bradman made 34 runs, two overs from Amarnath each producing 13 runs. The next over from Hazare saw Bradman at his best, scoring with shots to the fence on all sides to reach 150 in 161 minutes.

His third 50 took 29 minutes and included nine fours. The score rocketed from 200 to 250 in 18 minutes as Bradman took 20 from this over by Hazare.

Two runs later, Miller was beaten and bowled by Mankad with a ball that nipped through sharply. He had made 86 in 154 minutes.

Four runs later, Bradman went for a big hit off Hazare, and was caught by Amarnath, deep at mid-off. He had batted 177 minutes for 172 runs, hitting 18 fours and a six. The crowd immediately began to leave.

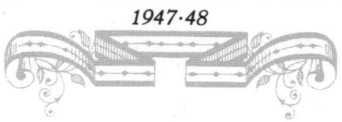

Don Bradman races for his 100th run in his 100th century in first class cricket.

## India

| Batsman | Runs | | Runs |
|---|---|---|---|
| V. Mankad c Miller b Johnston | 3 | — c Saggers b Dooland | 34 |
| C. T. Sarwate c Saggers b Miller | 32 | — c Bradman b Johnston | 58 |
| Gul Mahomed c Saggers b Loxton | 85 | — b Dooland | 20 |
| V. S. Hazare run out | 38 | — c Saggers b Miller | 15 |
| L. Amarnath b Loxton | 10 | — b Johnston | 7 |
| H. R. Adhikari c Saggers b Johnston | 4 | — c Loxton b Johnston | 46 |
| K. M. Rangnekar b Loxton | 6 | — c Harvey b Johnston | 13 |
| G. Kishenchand not out | 75 | — not out | 63 |
| W. S. Sohoni run out | 14 | — b Loxton | 31 |
| C. S. Nayudu c Hamence b Dooland | 3 | — not out | 3 |
| J. K. Irani lbw b Dooland | 43 | — run out | 0 |
| B 6, l-b 7 | 13 | B 2, l-b 12 | 14 |
| | **326** | **Nine wkts., dec.** | **304** |

## An Australian XI

| Batsman | Runs | | Runs |
|---|---|---|---|
| R. Rogers run out | 16 | — b Mankad | 31 |
| W. A. Brown c Hazare b Sohoni | 8 | — run out | 30 |
| D. G. Bradman c Amarnath b Hazare | 172 | — c Sarwate b Mankad | 26 |
| K. R. Miller b Mankad | 86 | — st Irani b Mankad | 13 |
| R. A. Hamence c Hazare b Sohoni | 27 | — c Amarnath b Mankad | 2 |
| R. N. Harvey c Mankad b Hazare | 32 | — not out | 56 |
| S. J. Loxton c Irani b Sohoni | 0 | — lbw b Mankad | 6 |
| R. A. Saggers c Irani b Sohoni | 1 | — b Mankad | 0 |
| B. Dooland lbw b Mankad | 5 | — c Kishenchand b Mankad | 31 |
| M. Herbert not out | 26 | — c Gul Mahomed b Amarnath | 1 |
| W. A. Johnston c Irani b Amarnath | 2 | — c Sohoni b Mankad | 2 |
| B 3, l-b 2 | 5 | B 5 | 5 |
| | **380** | | **203** |

## An Australian XI Bowling

| | O. | M. | R. | W. | | O. | M. | R. | W. |
|---|---|---|---|---|---|---|---|---|---|
| Loxton | 22 | 3 | 70 | 3 | .... | 25 | 9 | 43 | 1 |
| Johnston | 24 | 5 | 70 | 2 | .... | 31 | 9 | 71 | 4 |
| Dooland | 15.1 | 0 | 58 | 2 | .... | 26 | 4 | 76 | 2 |
| Miller | 13 | 0 | 36 | 1 | .... | 9 | 1 | 24 | 2 |
| Herbert | 17 | 0 | 73 | 0 | .... | 15 | 1 | 76 | 0 |
| Hamence | 2 | 0 | 6 | 0 | | | | | |

## India Bowling

| | O. | M. | R. | W. | | O. | M. | R. | W. |
|---|---|---|---|---|---|---|---|---|---|
| Sohoni | 17 | 2 | 89 | 4 | .... | 4 | 0 | 31 | 0 |
| Amarnath | 15.1 | 2 | 53 | 1 | .... | 11 | 0 | 54 | 1 |
| Mankad | 24 | 2 | 93 | 2 | .... | 12 | 0 | 84 | 8 |
| Sarwate | 16 | 0 | 51 | 0 | .... | 2 | 0 | 24 | 0 |
| Nayudu | 4 | 0 | 19 | 0 | | | | | |
| Kishenchand | 1 | 0 | 3 | 0 | | | | | |
| Hazare | 14 | 1 | 67 | 2 | | | | | |
| | | | | | Mahomed | 1 | 0 | 5 | 0 |

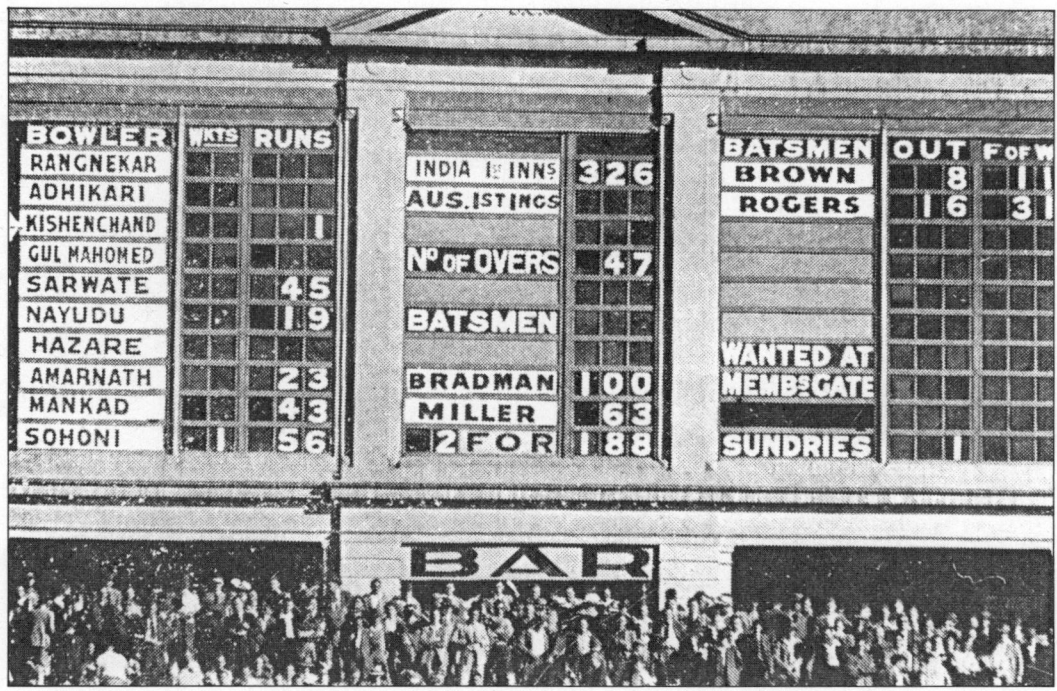

An historic photograph. The Sydney scoreboard at the moment of Don Bradman's 100th century, a feat not achieved by any other Australian.

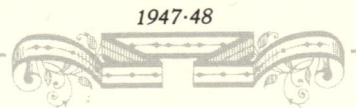

Schoolmates of John Bradman (near radio, fourth from right) cheered with him when his father passed the century.

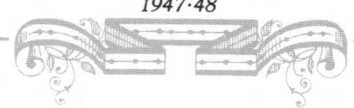

# BRADMAN'S 100 CENTURIES
## Made at Average of One In Every 3 Hands

### By E. H. M. BAILLIE

IN making his 100 centuries Don Bradman averaged a score of 100 runs, or more, once in every three hands.  No player in the world has such a record.  When one adds that only one other Australian, Warren Bardsley, has scored even fifty centuries in first class cricket, Bradman's feat — achievement of opportunity —is phenomenal.

TEN Englishmen, J. B. Hobbs (197), E. Hendren (170), W. R. Hammond (167), C. P. Mead (153), H. Sutcliffe (149), F. E. Woolley (145), W. G. Grace (126), A. Sandham (107), T. Hayward (104) and E. Tyldesley (102) have made more.

They, of course, playing almost every day for season after season, have had a great many more opportunities of making big scores.

### EXCEPTIONAL RATE

Not one of them can approach his consistently remarkable rate of scoring in making the runs.  In only six of the 100 centuries has he scored at a rate of less than 30 an hour, and in most of these cases he was fighting to get his side out of difficulties, or to avoid defeat.

In 22 instances he averaged more than 60 runs an hour, in six of them more than 70 an hour, in six 80 or more, and in one instance 94 an hour. Such rates would have been remarkable for such noted hitters as Jack Lyons, Hugh Massie or Gilbert Jessop, but in the case of a batsman like Bradman they are amazing..

The 94 rate was recorded when he made 149 not out against Lancashire in 95 minutes in 1934.  Immediately afterwards he made 132 in 90 minutes against Leverson-Gower's eleven, a rate of 88 an hour.  In the same season in England he made 160 in 120 minutes against Middlesex—80 an hour—and 140 against Yorkshire in 120 minutes—76 an hour.  In 1935-36 he made 369 for South Australia against Tasmania at 87 an hour, and 233 against Queensland at 73 an hour.

When the 1938 Australian team played against Tasmania before leaving for England he made 144 at 88 an hour, and in England he made 101 not out against Lancashire at 83 an hour.

### 80 AN HOUR

For NSW against Victoria in 1933-34 his 128 were made at a rate of 80 an hour after he had stonewalled in the early part of his innings to enable W. A. Brown to reach a century before the new ball came on.  His last 80 were scored at the rate of 120 an hour.

In test cricket his highest rate against England was 53 an hour when he made 334 at Leeds in 1930, while in five other three figure scores he averaged more than 40 an hour. Against South Africa he averaged more than 40 an hour in each of his four centuries, the fastest being 55; while against the West Indies (two centuries) he averaged 45 and 59.

His six scores exceeding 300 (340 not out, 452 not out (world's record), 334, 304, 357 and 369), and his 36 scores of 200 or more are world records for any batsman.  His 17 against England and 23 for all Tests are also records.  His 13 in England is a record for an Australian batsman in a season there, and his seven centuries three times in an Australian season is unequalled.  Only W. R. Hammond (once) has made so many in an Australian season.  His six centuries in 1938-39 were made in successive hands thus equalling the record of C. B. Fry in England in 1901.

Bradman has made two centuries in a match three times—131 and 133 not out for NSW v. Queensland in 1928-29, 124 and 235 in a Test Trial at Sydney in 1929-30, and 107 and 113 for SA v. Queensland in 1937-38.

His 100 century scores have accounted for 17,812 of 124,467 runs he has made in first-class cricket, at a scoring rate of 46 an hour.

# Australia v India
## First Test Match

AUSTRALIA v INDIA, First Test Match, at Brisbane, 28, 29 November, 1, 2 and 4 December 1947.

| | | |
|---|---|---|
| Australia | - First Innings | 382 for 8 wickets dec. |
| | - Second Innings | - |
| India | - First Innings | 58 |
| | - Second Innings | 98 |

Australia won by an innings and 226 runs.

DON BRADMAN (Captain) - hit wicket b. L. Amarnath    185

DON BRADMAN's success in the toss at Brisbane in the first Test Match ever played between Australia and India virtually won his side the match, for after Australia had taken advantage of a perfect wicket, torrential rain made the conditions impossible for India.    Bradman went in thirty-five minutes before lunch on the first day, at 38 for 1, and made 21 before the interval; he completed 50 in eighty-three minutes, as the sky gradually got darker, and had reached 86 by the tea interval, when a slight drizzle held up play for twenty minutes.    When the game resumed, he ran to his century in two hours fifty-one minutes, and thereafter hit out in devastating fashion, in light scarcely fit for cricket, adding a further 60 in forty-five minutes before play ceased at 5.40 p.m.    He was 160 not out, after three hours thirty-six minutes' batting.    Next day no play was possible until 5 p.m., and Bradman carried his score to 179 in fifty-nine minutes, the conditions being damp and unpleasant.    On the third day, on a wicket which was rapidly becoming sticky, he stayed for a further thirteen minutes before sacrificing his wicket in search of quick runs prior to declaring; he tried to cut a ball which kept low, and hit his stumps with the bat.    He batted for four hours forty-eight minutes and hit twenty fours.

This was the thirteenth successive Test Match (in which he batted) in which he played an innings of over 50 in one innings or the other.    Bradman is the only Australian to make a century in his first Test v. India, and the only Australian to make a century in his first Test against two different countries (he also did so v. South Africa).    This was the fourth Test Match innings in which Bradman batted on three different days.

Brisbane Cricket Ground.

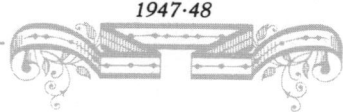

## Australia

| | |
|---|---|
| W. A. Brown c Irani b Amarnath.. | 11 |
| A. R. Morris hit wkt b Sarwate... | 47 |
| D. G. Bradman hit wkt b Amarnath | 185 |
| A. L. Hassett c Gul Mahomed b Mankad .................... | 48 |
| K. R. Miller c Mankad b Amarnath | 58 |
| C. L. McCool c Sohoni b Amarnath | 10 |
| R. R. Lindwall st Irani b Mankad . | 7 |
| W. A. Johnston did not bat. | |
| D. Tallon not out ............. | 3 |
| I. W. Johnson c Rangnekar b Mankad ................. | 6 |
| E. R. H. Toshack not out ....... | 0 |
| B 5, l-b 1, w 1 ............. | 7 |
| Eight wkts., dec. | 382 |

## India

| | | | |
|---|---|---|---|
| V. Mankad c Tallon b Lindwall ........ | 0 | — b Lindwall ............... | 7 |
| C. T. Sarwate c Johnston b Miller ...... | 12 | — b Johnston ............... | 26 |
| Gul Mahomed b Lindwall ........... | 0 | — b Toshack ............ | 13 |
| H. R. Adhikari c McCool b Johnston ... | 8 | — lbw b Toshack ......... | 13 |
| G. Kishenchand c Tallon b Johnston ... | 1 | — c Bradman b Toshack ...... | 0 |
| V. S. Hazare c Brown b Toshack ....... | 10 | — c Morris b Toshack ....... | 18 |
| K. M. Rangnekar c Miller b Toshack ... | 1 | — c Hassett b Toshack ...... | 0 |
| S. W. Sohoni c Miller b Toshack ....... | 2 | — c Brown b Miller ....... | 4 |
| L. Amarnath c Bradman b Toshack ... | 22 | — b Toshack .............. | 5 |
| C. S. Nayudu not out ............. | 0 | — c Hassett b Lindwall ...... | 6 |
| J. K. Irani c Hassett b Toshack ....... | 0 | — not out ................. | 2 |
| B 1, l-b 1 .................... | 2 | B 3, n-b 1 ............ | 4 |
| | 58 | | 98 |

### India Bowling

| | O. | M. | R. | W. | O. | M. | R. | W. |
|---|---|---|---|---|---|---|---|---|
| Sohoni ........ | 23 | 4 | 81 | 0 | | | | |
| Amarnath ..... | 39 | 10 | 84 | 4 | | | | |
| Mankad ...... | 34 | 3 | 113 | 3 | | | | |
| Sarwate ...... | 5 | 1 | 16 | 1 | | | | |
| Hazare ...... | 11 | 1 | 63 | 0 | | | | |
| Nayudu ....... | 3 | 0 | 18 | 0 | | | | |

### Australia Bowling

| | O. | M. | R. | W. | O. | M. | R. | W. |
|---|---|---|---|---|---|---|---|---|
| Lindwall ...... | 5 | 2 | 11 | 2 | 10.7 | 2 | 19 | 2 |
| W. Johnston ... | 8 | 4 | 17 | 2 | 9 | 6 | 11 | 1 |
| Miller ........ | 6 | 1 | 26 | 1 | 10 | 2 | 30 | 1 |
| Toshack ...... | 2.3 | 1 | 2 | 5 | 17 | 6 | 29 | 6 |
| I. Johnson .... | | | | | 3 | 1 | 5 | 0 |

### FALL OF WICKETS

AUSTRALIA—First Innings:

| 1 | 2 | 3 | 4 | 5 | 6 | 7 | 8 |
|---|---|---|---|---|---|---|---|
| 38 | 97 | 198 | 318 | 344 | 373 | 373 | 380 |

INDIA—First Innings:

| 1 | 2 | 3 | 4 | 5 | 6 | 7 | 8 | 9 |
|---|---|---|---|---|---|---|---|---|
| 0 | 0 | 19 | 23 | 23 | 53 | 56 | 58 | 58 |

INDIA—Second Innings:

| 1 | 2 | 3 | 4 | 5 | 6 | 7 | 8 | 9 |
|---|---|---|---|---|---|---|---|---|
| 14 | 27 | 41 | 41 | 72 | 80 | 80 | 89 | 94 |

# RAIN MAY BEAT INDIA

## Australia In Good Position

*From GEORGE THATCHER*

**BRISBANE, Friday.—Heavy rain tonight has spoilt any chance India may have had of winning the First Test, which began today at Brisbane Cricket Ground.**

**Australia lost three wickets for 273 runs (Bradman 160 not out), which will be sufficient for a first innings lead if the wicket becomes "sticky."**

Should the wet ball handicap the Indian bowlers, as it did today, Australia should make about 500 runs in the first innings.

The weather forecast for tomorrow is: Unsettled; some rain and local thunder.

The Indians will not win Tests until their approach is toughened Test cricket is grim and should be played within the rules.

For instance, Mankad today could have run Morris out for backing up before the ball had left the bowler's hand

Mankad pointed out the error to Morris

The Indians carried on late in the afternoon with a ball so greasy it had to be wiped with a towel after each delivery.

This meant Indian captain Amarnath presented Bradman with easy runs. A light appeal by the fielding captain was justified

### Best In Brisbane

Bradman's 160 not out (19 fours) in 216 minutes was his best innings in Brisbane.

He had decided early on aggressive tactics because he realised rain was in the offing and that quick runs were necessary to make the game safe

Bradman's sectional times were: 50 in 83 minutes; 100 in 171 min., 150 in 204 min. and 160 in 216 min.

Bradman gave Mankad who might have been a "terror," no chance He and Hassett added 50 in 55 minutes and 108 in 88 minutes

Bradman and Miller added 50 in 41 min.

The Indians, as usual, missed chances. They were:

**Morris at 8 by Nayudu off Sohoni; Hassett at 7 by Kishenchand at silly mid-on off Amarnath; Hassett at 19 by Irani off Sohoni; Miller at one by Irani, and by Sarwate off Mankad.**

Yet Irani's leg-side catch of Brown off Amarnath was outstanding.

Brown batted 53 minutes for his 11. He may have to give way to Barnes as opener in the Second Test.

Morris took 118 minutes for 47. That was too long.

His on-side timing was astray.

Hassett 48 (three fours) in 89 minutes helped Bradman to swing the game in Australia's favor.

He has shaken off the lethargy that has affected his recent displays

### Bad Light

Miller was 25 minutes before he scored He went to the wicket in a shocking light, and had narow escapes.

He effaced himself to give Bradman as much of the strike as possible

**Australia's scoring rate was: 100 in 125min., 150 in 171min., 200 in 212min., 250 in 251min., 273 in 270min.**

Australian batsmen tomorrow morning probably will be under instructions to speed up the scoring

Apart from dropped catches, India's outcricket was very good.

Mahomed at cover was superb. Several times he hit the wicket with rapid returns.

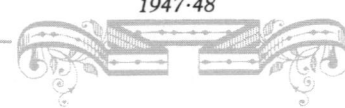

# Crowd hoots Bradman, angry scene

From Ray Robinson

BRISBANE, Saturday.

IN a demonstration at Brisbane Cricket Ground this afternoon angry spectators demanded their money back when a wet wicket delayed the Test Match for nearly four hours.

● The umpires were hooted and counted out before they decided that the wicket was fit, and Australian captain Don Bradman was booed when he came in to bat.

About 100 men who surged to the main street gates shouting for refund of their admittance money were quietened by a detachment of police.

Additional police were called to the ground.

A ground official said: "If play had not begun the crowd would have torn the place to pieces."

The demonstration occurred after a third inspection of the wicket at 3 pm when the captains postponed a decision.

The attendants at the turnstiles told the crowd they had no authority to refund the money.

White-helmeted police broke up the demonstration.

### Long delays

Rain in the night had soaked the wicket and the gates, due to open at 9 am, were not opened to the public until the captains, Don Bradman, and Lala Amarnath, decided at an inspection at 11 am to look at it again at 2 pm.

Those who paid 5/11 to the grandstand and 3/3 to the outer enclosure were given slips entitling them to admittance on Monday if there was no play.

At the 2 pm inspection about 10,000 people watched Bradman and Amarnath gingerly test the pitch for seven minutes, with shoe-soles and thumbs.

Hostility in the outer had increased by the time of the captains' third inspection.

Some of the crowd counted the captains out.

Disagreement by the captains put the decision in the hands of umpires G. Borwick (NSW) and A. Barlow (Victoria), who was umpiring his first Test Match.

The umpires' first inspection, soon after 3 pm, was made in comparative silence.

Hooting broke out in most parts of the ground when they decided on another inspection at 4 pm, and when they examined it at 4.35 pm before deciding that it was fit for play.

The crowd cheered the Indians as they took the field.

But there was widespread hooting as Bradman and Miller entered as if a number of the crowd held the Australian captain responsible for the delay.

Officials would not reveal which captain had been against play when the skippers disagreed at 3 pm.

Scores of barrackers shouted encouraging cries to the Indian bowlers.

Some called "out" as Bradman pushed at a ball from Mankad.

Counter-cheers came from a greater number when Bradman scored his first single.

### Bad light

Later, Bradman was applauded when he hit three fours. A six by Miller put those who remained to the finish in a good mood.

As if to try to compensate the crowd for its earlier disappointment Bradman batted on in poor visibility until 5.50 pm before he appealed against the light.

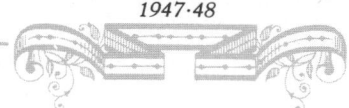

# INDIANS ROUTED; ALL OUT FOR 58 ON BAD WICKET

## 5 Toshack victims for only 2 runs

By R. S. WHITINGTON

**BRISBANE, Monday.**—India failed sensationally on a rain-affected wicket in the first Test today, and were all out for 58 runs after Australia had closed at 8 for 382.

Lindwall, the NSW fast bowler began the rout by dismissing 2-0 in the opening over, and Toshack completed it by taking 5-2.

Lindwall's victims were Mankad and Gul Mohamed, both of whom failed to score.

After this sensational opening over, India's score read—2 for 0.

Sarwate and Amarnath defied the bowlers for a time on the tricky pitch, the Indian captain hitting out lustily.

When Toshack came on, however, Amarnath soon fell, Bradman taking an easy catch. Toshack finished off the others in quick time.

Keith Miller this morning gave an exhibition of hurricane hitting, including four sixes.

**Off five successive balls he hit 6, 6, 4, 2, 2.**

The wicket was sprouting mushrooms early this morning as the result of a weekend drenching by rainstorms.

So soft was the wicket that one could press one's thumb in up to the hilt.

However, under a drying sun, play was possible at 12.30 pm.

### Bradman hit

The ball rose alarmingly at times and Bradman was hit on the right shoulder and groin.

Stepping back to the legside to force Amarnath past point, he hit his wicket and was out for 185 (adding six to his weekend score).

He failed by 15 runs to score his 37th double century. He and Walter Hammond at present share the honor of 36 double centuries.

Miller was missed twice off lofty shots. Then he rattled up 35 in half an hour.

Lowest Test scores are 30 and 45, by South Africa (both in same match) against Australia at Melbourne, 1931-32.

Australia's lowest is 36, at Egbaston against England, in 1902.

India's previous lowest was 93, against England at Lord's, in 1936.

Coincidentally, Australia was dismissed for 58 at Brisbane against England in 1936.

Early this morning attractive, courteous Mrs. McLean (head of the 'Gabba catering staff) also inspected the wicket (and the mushrooms).

"These will do for my staff's breakfast, or the members' lunch," she said, gathering in the mushrooms.

Don Bradman, hit wicket, bowled Amarnath for 185.

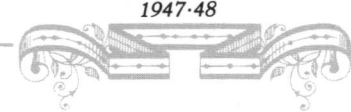

# Rain Expected To Wash Out Test, Save Indian Defeat

BRISBANE, Tuesday.—Rain is expected to wash out the First Test between India and Australia and save India from defeat.

Immediately after stumps were drawn today at 4.37 p.m., rain began to fall.

Heavy rain fell tonight, and it is unlikely play will resume at the scheduled starting time —noon—tomorrow.

Rain is expected tomorrow and on Thursday, when the match is due to end.

India, which overnight was 4-41 in its second innings, today scored 29 runs in 62 minutes without loss.

**India still requires 254 runs to save an innings defeat.**

Australia in its first innings scored eight (closed) for 382.

India was all out for 58 in its first innings.

Today Sarwate and Hazare batted on a rain-affected pitch as though they were playing on a shirt-front wicket.

### Learnt Lesson

It was obvious they had learnt a lesson regarding batting on a rain-damaged wicket.

Yesterday the Indians, with the exception of their captain, Amarnath, showed little or no knowledge about batting on a sticky wicket.

Today Sarwate and Hazare held a dead bat to a good length ball on the wicket.

**They attempted a scoring shot only when the ball was a simple long hop or a full toss.**

If these batsmen can convince most of their team mates that the moral effect of sticky pitches is more dangerous than the physical side, India may be a different side if it bats to-morrow.

### 3.35 p.m. Start

Play today did not start until 3.35 p.m., because of the overnight rain.

**The wicket was wetter than it was yesterday.**

The ball skidded through and did not "hang" as it did yesterday.

The bowling was accurate.

Toshack bowled at one end while Johnston, Miller, Johnson, and Lindwall used the other.

Toshack bowled a good length and kept the batsmen quiet without looking dangerous.

Selection of the Australian team for the Second Test, starting in Sydney on December 12, has been postponed from tonight until tomorrow night.

# Indignant At Umpires

**From GEORGE THATCHER**

BRISBANE, Tuesday.—The Indian cricketers were indignant tonight that Hazare had to appeal five times today in a poor light before the umpires stopped play.

They pointed out that Bradman appealed once on Saturday and the game was stopped immediately.

Hazare, who batted today with Sarwate, in the First India-Australia Test appealed five times in three overs.

Indian manager Mr. Gupta will fly the Indian team to Sydney for the Second Test, starting on December 12 in Sydney.

He will ask the S.C.G. Trust to provide a centre wicket at S.C.G. No. 2 for a full day's practice before the Test.

Poor attendances in the current Test are worrying the Board of Control.

Today's attendance was 1020, and the takings were £117, just enough to pay the staff wages, players, officials, and the Press luncheon.

India will receive about £1600 as its share of the total gate.

Mr. Gupta admitted today he had expected £5000.

# PLAY IMPOSSIBLE ON BRISBANE MUD PATCH

## From GEORGE THATCHER

BRISBANE, Wednesday.—Because the wicket was a mud patch, play was impossible today in the First India-Australia Test at Brisbane Cricket Ground.

The match will end to-morrow.

Australia, in its first innings, scored eight (closed) for 382.

India has scored 58 and four for 70.

**The captains, Bradman and Amarnath, inspected the wicket today at 11 a.m.**

They made another inspection at 2 p.m. and then called off play for the day.

The captains knew when they first looked at the wicket that play was impossible.

The public was not admitted to the ground today.

It is practically certain that if rain falls after midnight to-night play tomorrow will be impossible, and the match will be drawn.

The approaches to the wicket today were slippery and dangerous.

The Brisbane Cricket Ground staff today made no effort to dry the wicket to enable play to be resumed.

The Indians are caught on a sticky wicket at Brisbane.

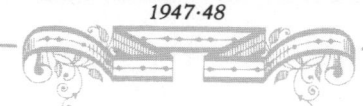

# Australia v India
## Second Test Match

AUSTRALIA v INDIA, Second Test Match, at Sydney, 12, 13, 17 December 1947.

| | | |
|---|---|---|
| Australia | - First Innings | 107 |
| | - Second Innings | - |
| India | - First Innings | 188 |
| | - Second Innings | 61 for 7 wickets |
| | Drawn. | |
| DON BRADMAN (Captain) | - b. V.S. Hazare | 13 |

Rain ruined this match, less than ten hours' cricket being played altogether.   DON BRADMAN went in, at 25 for 1, in the last over of the second day, and did not have to face the bowling that evening; after two blank days owing to rain, the wicket was very difficult when he resumed his innings on the third morning, but he stayed for forty minutes, batting well under the tricky conditions, before playing a hesitant defensive stroke and being bowled at 48 for 4.

## AUSTRALIA v INDIA
### Sydney, December 1947

BACK ROW    N. Harvey, D. Tallon, W. A. Johnston, K. Miller, R. Lindwall, I. Johnson, W. H. Jeanes.
FRONT ROW    R. Hamence, A. Morris, W. Brown, D. G. Bradman (Captain), L. Hassett, C. McCool.

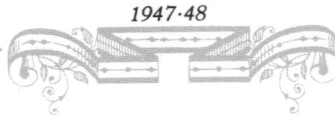

## India

| | | | | |
|---|---|---|---|---|
| V. Mankad b Lindwall | 5 | — b Lindwall | 5 |
| C. T. Sarwate b Johnston | 0 | — c Johnson b Johnston | 3 |
| Gul Mahomed c Brown b Miller | 29 | — c Bradman b Johnson | 5 |
| V. S. Hazare b Miller | 16 | — not out | 13 |
| L. Amarnath b Johnson | 25 | — c Morris b Johnson | 14 |
| G. Kishenchand b Johnson | 44 | — c McCool b Johnston | 0 |
| H. R. Adhikari lbw b Johnston | 0 | — not out | 0 |
| D. G. Phadkar c Miller b McCool | 51 | — c Tallon b Miller | 2 |
| C. S. Nayudu c and b McCool | 6 | | |
| Amir Elahi c Miller b McCool | 4 | — c Miller b Johnston | 13 |
| J. K. Irani not out | 1 | | |
| B 5, lb 2 | 7 | B 3, l-b 3 | 6 |
| | **188** | Seven wkts. | **61** |

## Australia

| | | | | |
|---|---|---|---|---|
| W. A. Brown run out | 18 | C. L. McCool b Phadkar | 9 |
| A. R. Morris lbw b Amarnath | 10 | R. R. Lindwall b Hazare | 0 |
| D. G. Bradman b Hazare | 13 | D. Tallon c Irani b Hazare | 6 |
| A. L. Hassett c Adhikari c Hazare | 6 | W. A. Johnston not out | 0 |
| K. R. Miller lbw b Phadkar | 17 | B 1, l-b 1 | 2 |
| R. A. Hamence c Adhikari b Mankad | 25 | | |
| I. W. Johnson lbw b Phadkar | 1 | | **107** |

### Australia Bowling

| | O. | M. | R. | W. | O. | M. | R. | W. |
|---|---|---|---|---|---|---|---|---|
| Lindwall | 12 | 3 | 30 | 1 | 5 | 1 | 13 | 1 |
| W. Johnston | 17 | 4 | 33 | 2 | 13 | 5 | 15 | 3 |
| Miller | 9 | 3 | 25 | 2 | 6 | 2 | 5 | 1 |
| McCool | 18 | 2 | 71 | 3 | | | | |
| I. Johnson | 14 | 3 | 22 | 2 | 13 | | 22 | 2 |

### India Bowling

| | O. | M. | R. | W. |
|---|---|---|---|---|
| Phadkar | 10 | 2 | 14 | 3 |
| Amarnath | 14 | 4 | 31 | 1 |
| Mankad | 9 | 0 | 31 | 1 |
| Hazare | 13.2 | 3 | 29 | 4 |

### FALL OF WICKETS

INDIA—First Innings:

| 1 | 2 | 3 | 4 | 5 | 6 | 7 | 8 | 9 |
|---|---|---|---|---|---|---|---|---|
| 2 | 16 | 52 | 57 | 94 | 95 | 165 | 174 | 182 |

INDIA—Second Innings:

| 1 | 2 | 3 | 4 | 5 | 6 | 7 |
|---|---|---|---|---|---|---|
| 17 | 19 | 26 | 29 | 34 | 53 | 55 |

AUSTRALIA—First Innings:

| 1 | 2 | 3 | 4 | 5 | 6 | 7 | 8 | 9 |
|---|---|---|---|---|---|---|---|---|
| 28 | 30 | 43 | 48 | 86 | 92 | 92 | 97 | 105 |

For his last Test at Sydney Don Bradman goes through the familiar Members' gate and appears to have no regrets.

# True Wicket: Bad Batting Cause Lapses

### By H. A. de LACY, at Sydney for the Test

SYDNEY, Saturday. — India made conditions more difficult than they were when they resumed batting in the Second Test today.

While there seemed little prospect of play early, the wicket actually played true, while the improvement in the ground was amazing.

From 2/38 overnight they lost another two wickets for 22 by lunch and then allowed 4/94 quickly to degenerate to 6/95. At tea the score was 6/136.

There was nothing wrong with the pitch, and the Australian bowling, while accurate, was never dangerous. It was bad batting that caused the trouble. The innings closed for 188.

After an initial inspection of the ground at 11.30, captains Bradman and Amarnath decided to make another at 12.30. Early this morning the curator despaired of play.

The disused pitches on either side of the Test wicket were pools of water. With the aid of a drying north-easterly wind and of fresh-cut grass rolled into the turf, the ground was a different prospect by noon.

The sun struggled to break through the clouds, promising a sticky wicket later in the afternoon.

The Indians required quick runs to enable them to get Australia in on that "sticky." A week-end without rain would dry the wicket into a "slow and easy" from which Bradman and Co. could take a bag of runs.

The crowd was not admitted to the ground until 11.45.

## BATTLE OF TACTICS

The 12.30 inspection by Amarnath and Bradman was clearly a battle of tactics. Amarnath walked briskly to the pitch, inspected both ends and the nearby turf and obviously wanted to get on with the game.

Bradman pondered, hand to chin, walked slowly along the length of the pitch and seemed very undecided.

The wicket was wet and the ball was expected to cut through. In the circumstances, quick runs were possible. Later, the sun might make the wicket difficult for batting. Then if he had sufficient runs, Amarnath could declare and hope to break Australia's batting backbone.

So Amarnath wanted to play. To further his purpose, he ordered the light roller. The wicket was wet half-way across its width over the full length, but the wicket and ground had made such an amazing recovery that, as players took the field, it was anybody's guess how it would play.

Punctually at 1 o'clock India, 2/38 (Gul Mohamed 24, and Hazare 5) resumed.

Hazare opened with two for a shot towards mid-on and another two for a glorious cover drive. Then he drove Bill Johnston straight for three. Gul Mahomed hooked one from Johnston off his off stump and swung recklessly.

The 50 came up in 106 minutes.

The pitch was without vice, and quite unexpectedly Hazare was bowled by Miller. The ball came in with the arm and amazed Hazare, who stood nonplussed.

The loss of Hazare was a severe blow to India. Hazare was batting well and looked set for a big score. Worse was to follow. After Amarnath had played two clever leg glances Gul Mahomed propped defensively at a rising ball from Miller and spooned it to Bill Brown at silly leg.

He had played a dashing if reckless 29 and hit two fours. It was an innings of extreme caution and rank audacity. Finally Mahomed fell to an ultra-cautious stroke immediately after he had shattered orthodoxy by pulling a good length ball from his off stump to fine leg.

Four wickets were down for 57. The half-hour's play before lunch had been costly for India. two good wickets falling for 22 on an easy wicket.

## OFF HIS PADS

While I was away from the Test watching Clarrie Hayes run a poor 100 yards Kishenchand and Amarnath developed their pre-lunch partnership most promisingly. However, when it had reached 37, with Amarnath batting brilliantly. the captain stepped across the off stump to a ball from Ian Johnson. It turned back, hitting the pads, and bowled him.

Adhikari came in and Bradman gave the new ball to Bill Johnston. The ball kept low and Adhikari was out lbw for a duck. 4/94 quickly became 6/95.

Amarnath had hit Bradman solidly on the leg with a drive prior to his dismissal and the captain limped for some time afterward.

The next incident came when Kishenchand objected to a mirror in the outer and Umpire Barlow walked to the fence and spoke about the flashing.

Miller took the ball from Lindwall without result, and the 100 came up in 185 minutes when Kichenchand cut a full toss from Johnston through the slips.

# Brown, Morris started well

### By GEORGE THATCHER

Australian batsmen Billy Brown and Arthur Morris appeared set for a big opening stand against India before Brown was run out.

Brown was out for 18 and Morris, not out 10, to make Australia 1-28 in reply to India's first innings of 188 at stumps.

Bradman, who went in at 5.59 p.m., watched Morris play out time.

Play began at 1 p.m. on a wicket that was dry on top, and without viciousness.

India lost Hazare and Gul Mahomed for 22 in the half an hour's play before luncheon.

Hazare did not make a shot at the ball from Miller, which knocked out his off stump.

Miller bowled from wide out on the return crease. The ball turned about six inches.

Then Gul Mahomed held out his bat to a ball from Miller that popped from a wet patch.

Amarnath accepted a challenge from McCool, who went on at 60, and went down the crease to half-volley his bowling.

He appeared to have gained the mastery when he tried to defend an off-spinner by Ian Johnson with his body, and was out l.b.w.

Adhikari fell l.b.w. to Johnston, whom, for variety, swung one from the off.

Kishenchand and Phadkir then added 70 for the seventh wicket in 68 minutes.

Phadkar introduced a touch of adventure that had been missing from the early players' batting.

He hit Lindwall for three fours in his opening over with the second new ball.

Kishenchand, 44, batted 137 minutes and hit four fours. He glided Ian Johnson on to his wicket.

Phadkir reached the half-century, the first of the Indians to achieve the feat in Tests.

He scored a run every two minutes.

Phadkir sacrificed when joined by Irani.

Only 12 fours (Mahomed 2, Amarnath 2, Kishenchand 4, and Phadkir 4), were scored in the Indians' innings.

Lindwall bowled a bumper or two and once again had to leave the field for boot attention.

India's scoring rate: Fifty in 86 minutes; lunch 4-60 (Kishenchand 2, Amarnath 3), 100 in 181. Tea, 6-136 (Kishenchand 35, Phadkir 19), 150 in 218. 188 in 268 minutes.

Attendance was 20.027, and the takings £1986.

# BRADMAN OBJECTS TO 'UNFAIR' STORY

**Australian XI captain Don Bradman has complained to the Board of Control because of reports that Ray Lindwall and Keith Miller have bowled unfairly in recent matches.**

A Sydney evening paper's cricket writer wrote the reports of which Bradman has complained.

The Board of Control and the South Australian Cricket Association have written to the cricket writer

Bradman, a member of the board, captains the South Australian Sheffield Shield team

The board is believed to have told the writer that his reports were unfair

Bradman has refused to discuss his action in complaining

On Friday, the first day of the Second Test, Lindwall made the ball bump and fly

Two of his deliveries hit Indian batsman Hazare on the shoulder and hands

Miller also made the ball bump around the batsmen's heads.

A small section of the crowd criticised the bowlers' methods

Prince Duleepsinhji, a former English Test player, said yesterday that fast bowlers without a packed field had every right to bowl an occasion:! short ball.

He was referring to accusations that Lindwall and Miller had bowled unfairly.

## Only "Variation"

Duleepsinhji said: "The short ball is a fast bowler's variation, as flight is a slow bowler's

"If India had a fast bowler we never would have heard Lindwall and Miller accused of unfair bowling at a batsman

"The Indian fast bowler also would have bowled an occasional short bumper

"During my cricket career every fast bowler bowled an occasional bumper, but nobody thought of calling it bowling at the batsman.

"Uncle Ranji's comment on this incident would have been 'Didn't the batsman have a bat?'"

## *Bradman Bowled Hazare-13*

# HAMENCE HAS LIVES AFTER UNEASY START

**Australia with four good wickets down was struggling hard for runs after lunch, as the wicket had deteriorated in the hot sun. No fewer than eight Indians, including the wicketkeeper were huddled around the batsmen waiting to claim their victims.**

*Bradman, who was not happy when opposed to left-hand spinner Mankad, was beaten by a good one from Hazare and was out for 13.*

CONTRARY to anticipation, the wicket was fairly easy when play was resumed at 12.30.

The ball had just a tendency to cut through occasionally. This was due to the fact that the wicket had patches of dampness at both ends.

At the Paddington end the damp patch was on the leg side, and at the Randwick end it was on the off-side of the wicket.

The Indians were very keen to begin at once. In fact, they indulged in fielding practice on the No. 1 ground at 11.30.

Amarnath, the Indian captain, showed his keenness to begin play by restlessly walking into the Australian dressing room at 11.55 for Bradman to accompany him on an inspection of the wicket at noon.

Both Morris and Bradman, the not-out batsmen, began very soberly today to the bowling of Amarnath and Phadkar. They watched every ball closely and frequently patted the wicket down after playing the ball.

## After Bradman

It was obvious the Indians were keen to get Bradman's wicket early, for when he was only one, one of the most absurd appeals for leg before wicket ever made on S.C.G. occurred when he moved to a ball from Amarnath at least a foot outside the leg stump.

On the last ball of this over Bradman stepped right across the wicket to Amarnath and the ball struck the back of his leg, which was outside the off stump. No appeal was made.

Fifteen minutes after play began Morris lost his wicket. He stepped in front of a ball that kept a little lower than usual, and he was out leg before wicket for 10 made in 55 minutes.

Bradman, who was batting quietly, pulled Amarnath to the fence to bring his score to nine.

Hassett remained 11 minutes, and when he made a forward push stroke off Hazare he was nicely caught by Adhikari at silly mid-off for only six.

Three wickets had fallen for 43 runs.

Miller came next. Mankad merely changed ends. He replaced Amarnath, who had bowled four overs this morning for eight runs. Mankad got tremendous turn from the wicket.

## Mankad Accurate

He quickly had Bradman on the defensive.

Bradman, in fact, was in difficulties for the first few balls, but he was applauded when he swung hard at a short ball from Mankad to score a single which made him 10 and the total three for 44.

A sensation came with the score at 48. Bradman was beaten neck and crop by a good length ball from Hazare and was clean bowled.

The wicket had nothing to do with Bradman's dismissal. The ball came through at even height, he moved forward half-heartedly to play a defensive shot, but the ball beat the bat and knocked the stumps over.

Bradman made 13 runs and batted 40 minutes (one four).

Miller pleased the crowd with a full-blooded drive to the fence off Mankad, bringing the total to 52 in 81 minutes.

Hamence was batting very gingerly, but he swung at a ball which he sent hard to the fence, to make his score five and the total four for 59.

When Hamence was six he edged a ball from Hazare into the hands of Nayudu at second slip, but was badly missed and a single was taken.

Hamence gave another chance off Amarnath when he was seven.

He scooped a ball to square leg where Amir Elihi moved slowly for the catch and took it on the half volley.

Hamence was nearly run out before he had added to his score.

Miller glanced a ball from Amarnath. There was an easy run in it, but Miller slipped before he began his run and Hamence had to return to his crease and just scampered home in time.

The wicket developed some bite after lunch due to the hot sun, and was not playing as well now as it was earlier in the day.

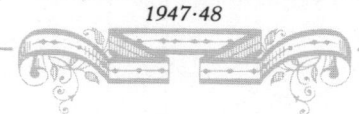

# INDIAN BATS FAIL TO CLINCH THEIR GRIP IN TEST MATCH

### By W. J. O'REILLY

Dispirited batting in its second innings has placed India in a tight corner against Australia at the S.C.G.

With seven down for 61 runs after a first-innings lead of 81, India is 142 in front in the second Test, which ends to-day.

In Australia's innings of 107, Hazare (4-29) and Phadkar (3-14) had bowled the Indians into a position in which Australia would need to fight hard to avoid defeat.

## TEST MATCH DRAW

### By OUR CRICKET REPORTER

**Almost continuous drizzling rain yesterday washed out play in the second Test, which was drawn.**

India scored 188 and 7-61. Australia scored 107 and was 142 runs behind when rain caused the abandonment of play.

For the first time in the history of Tests in Australia, three complete days were lost because of rain.

Actual play occupied nine hours and 38 minutes, out of the 30 hours set down for the match.

During a lull in the weather at 12.45 p.m. yesterday, the umpires ruled that play could begin as soon as the pitch was prepared.

However, rain began again as the groundsmen were marking the creases, and the umpires ordered the covers to be replaced on the ends of the pitch.

Rain continued after lunch. The umpires did not inspect again until 3.15 p.m., when they postponed a decision to 3.45 p.m., but the rain had returned, and at 4.25 p.m. play was abandoned.

Some members of the Indian team assured themselves of souvenirs when they accompanied the umpires on their last inspection.

After making sure they each had a stump themselves, the umpires gave the signal, and Ranvirsinhji, Adhikari, Rangachari, and Rangnekar took the remaining stumps.

Kishenchand secured one set of bails, and Amir Elahi was given the ball by umpire Borwick, who had had it in his charge during the day.

Special transport services to the Cricket Ground were cancelled at midday, when it was realised that the rain would discourage any large attendance.

Miller left by plane soon after play was abandoned to join the New South Wales Sheffield Shield team in Adelaide.

The other New South Wales Test men, Lindwall and Morris, will leave to-day. The Shield match against South Australia starts to-morrow.

# Australia v India
## Third Test Match

AUSTRALIA v INDIA, Third Test Match, at Melbourne, 1, 2, 3 and 5 January 1948.

| Australia | - First Innings | 394 |
|---|---|---|
| | - Second Innings | 255 for 4 wickets dec. |
| India | - First Innings | 291 for 9 wickets dec. |
| | - Second Innings | 125 |

Australia won by 233 runs.

| DON BRADMAN | - lbw. b. D.G. Phadkar | 132 |
|---|---|---|
| (Captain) | - not out | 127 |

DON BRADMAN scored a century in each innings of this Test Match, and again dominated the unfortunate Indian bowlers. His first innings commenced on the first morning, at 29 for 1; 37 by lunch, he reached 50 in eighty-four minutes, and had made 99 by the tea interval. He completed his century just afterwards, after two hours thirty-nine minutes' batting, and carried his score to 132 before being attacked by cramp; he went on with his innings, before properly recovering, swung wildly at the next ball, and was lbw. His chanceless innings lasted three hours seventeen minutes and included eight fours; he and A.L. Hassett put on 169 in a minute under two hours for the third wicket. This was the highest third wicket partnership in all Test Matches against India. Bradman's twenty-ninth run was his 6,000th in all Test Matches.

When India declared on the third day after rain had made the wicket tricky, Bradman countered by putting in his tail-enders first; however, he had to go in himself when four batsmen were out for 32 soon after lunch, when he joined A.R. Morris in a long and unbroken stand. The wicket had by then lost much of its venom, although Bradman had to exercise some caution early on, taking an hour over his first 23.

Forty not out at the tea interval, he reached 50 in eighty-six minutes, and his century forty-two minutes later, in two hours eight minutes. The pair added 223 for the fifth wicket, and Bradman batted for two minutes under three hours and hit thirteen fours. More rain overnight made the wicket sticky again and Bradman declared at once next morning. This was the fourth time he had made a century in each innings, the only Australian to do so more than twice.

The partnership of 223 between Bradman and Morris was a record for the fifth wicket for all Test Matches v. India.

## Australia

| | | | |
|---|---|---|---|
| S. G. Barnes b Mankad | 12 | — c Sen b Amarnath | 15 |
| A. R. Morris b Amarnath | 45 | — not out | 100 |
| D. G. Bradman lbw b Phadkar | 132 | — not out | 127 |
| A. L. Hassett lbw b Mankad | 80 | | |
| K. R. Miller lbw b Mankad | 29 | | |
| R. A. Hamence st Sen b Amarnath | 25 | | |
| R. R. Lindwall b Amarnath | 26 | | |
| D. Tallon c Mankad b Amarnath | 2 | | |
| B. Dooland not out | 21 | — lbw b Phadkar | 6 |
| I. W. Johnson lbw b Mankad | 16 | — c Hazare b Amarnath | 0 |
| W. A. Johnston run out | 5 | — lbw b Amarnath | 3 |
| Extras | 1 | B 3, n-b 1 | 4 |
| | **394** | Four wkts., dec. | **255** |

## India

| | | | |
|---|---|---|---|
| V. Mankad c Tallon b Johnston | 116 | — b Johnston | 13 |
| C. T. Sarwate c Tallon b Johnston | 36 | — b Johnston | 1 |
| Gul Mahomed c and b Dooland | 12 | — c Morris b Johnson | 28 |
| V. S. Hazare c Tallon b Barnes | 17 | — c Barnes b Miller | 10 |
| L. Amarnath lbw b Barnes | 0 | — b Lindwall | 8 |
| D. G. Phadkar not out | 55 | — c Barnes b Johnston | 13 |
| H. R. Adhikari st Tallon b Johnson | 26 | — c Lindwall b Johnson | 1 |
| Rai Singh c Barnes b Johnson | 2 | — c Tallon b Johnston | 24 |
| K. M. Rangnekar c and b Johnson | 6 | — c Hamence b Johnson | 18 |
| P. Sen b Johnson | 4 | — c Hassett b Johnson | 2 |
| C. S. Nayudu not out | 4 | — not out | 0 |
| B 9, l-b 3, n-b 1 | 13 | B 6, l-b 1 | 7 |
| Nine wkts., dec. | **291** | | **125** |

## India Bowling

| | O. | M. | R. | W. | O. | M. | R. | W. |
|---|---|---|---|---|---|---|---|---|
| Phadkar | 15 | 1 | 80 | 1 | 10 | 1 | 28 | 1 |
| Amarnath | 21 | 5 | 78 | 4 | 20 | 3 | 52 | 3 |
| Hazare | 16.1 | 0 | 62 | 0 | 11 | 1 | 55 | 0 |
| Mankad | 37 | 4 | 135 | 4 | 18 | 4 | 74 | 0 |
| Sarwate | 3 | 0 | 16 | 0 | 5 | 0 | 41 | 0 |
| Nayudu | 2 | 0 | 22 | 0 | | | | |
| Gul Mahomed | | | | | 1 | 0 | 1 | 0 |

## Australia Bowling

| | O. | M. | R. | W. | O. | M. | R. | W. |
|---|---|---|---|---|---|---|---|---|
| Lindwall | 12 | 0 | 47 | 0 | 3 | 0 | 10 | 1 |
| Miller | 13 | 2 | 46 | 0 | 7 | 0 | 29 | 1 |
| W. Johnston | 12 | 0 | 33 | 2 | 10 | 1 | 44 | 4 |
| I. Johnson | 14 | 1 | 59 | 4 | 6 | 0 | 35 | 4 |
| Dooland | 12 | 0 | 68 | 1 | | | | |
| Barnes | 6 | 1 | 25 | 2 | | | | |

AUSTRALIA—Second Innings:

| 1 | 2 | 3 | 4 |
|---|---|---|---|
| 1 | 11 | 13 | 32 |

INDIA—First Innings:

| 1 | 2 | 3 | 4 | 5 | 6 | 7 | 8 | 9 |
|---|---|---|---|---|---|---|---|---|
| 124 | 145 | 188 | 188 | 198 | 260 | 264 | 280 | 284 |

INDIA—Second Innings:

| 1 | 2 | 3 | 4 | 5 | 6 | 7 | 8 | 9 |
|---|---|---|---|---|---|---|---|---|
| 10 | 27 | 44 | 60 | 60 | 69 | 100 | 107 | 125 |

# BRADMAN SCORES ANOTHER 100; BARNES CHEAPLY

### From R. S. WHITINGTON

**MELBOURNE, Thursday.—After Barnes had gone for 12 and Morris for 45, Bradman scored yet another century in the thrid Test against India at Melbourne Cricket Ground today.**

**At tea, when Australia was 2-204, Bradman was 99, and he and Hassett had put on 105 for the third wicket.**

Bradman won the toss and Morris and Barnes opened for Australia.

The Australians and the umpires wore black armbands in memory of Col McCool's mother.

**Barnes off-drove Phadkar's second ball through Amarnath's legs for three and took five to Morris' one from the first over.**

Amarnath, who spent yesterday trying to lessen stiffness in his legs caused by 'keeping at Canberra, opened from the members' end with a maiden to Morris.

Phadkar appealed for lbw against Barnes, but Barnes hopped quickly to the leg side while the umpire was making up his mind.

Phadkar, swinging the ball considerably each way, was more accurate in his second over, from which only two were scored.

When Barnes powerfully late cut Hazare wide of third man, he started for a second run just as Rangnekar was releasing his throw.

**Barnes, Sen and ball arrived at the same spot at** the same time, and the two players collided. The lighter Sen was slightly winded and received attention from Barnes.

Morris got three when Rangnekar misfielded a cover-drive off Mankad. Two balls later, Barnes was beaten as he tried to off-drive a good length ball from Mankad.

The ball appeared to come in with the bowler's arm and Barnes played outside it. One for 29 in 35 minutes.

**Mankad's wicket was his 44th in first-class matches for the tour, equalling Verity's best year in Australia, 1932-33.**

Bradman received a great cheer, and started very cautiously.

Mankad, obviously freshened by week's rest from cricket, was bowling almost perfect length, flighting the ball cleverly and making both batsmen grope forward.

The first 34 came in 45 minutes, of which Morris, now playing well, had scored 19. Bradman's first good stroke a delightful late cut off Hazare.

## Morris dismissed

Morris, who was a little sluggish early, began to move more freely to the ball.

Bradman, too, loosened up, with perfectly-executed late cuts, cover drives and effortless leg glides.

Australia's first 50 appeared in 65 minutes of real Test cricket.

**As Bradman began to drop into his demoralising stride, Amarnath spread-eagled even Mankad's field, giving away singles to save the fours.**

This tacit admission of defeat came a little prematurely, and handicapped the bowler, whose task was to concentrate on getting Bradman and Morris early, and not to save runs.

The 90-minute pre-lunch spell saw 91 runs on board.

Bradman reached 41 by pulling Mankad hard for four immediately after lunch.

**Amarnath, replacing Sarwate, bowled Morris for a well-made 45 in 102 minutes (three fours). The ball appeared to swing late from the leg side and come off the batsman's pad.**

With Barnes and Morris out for 99, India was doing well, but Hazare then missed a low, left-handed chance, at first slip, from Hassett.

Dismissal of Morris cheered the Indians and Mankad bowled an excellent maiden to Bradman.

Amarnath, bowling magnificently, just missed the top of Hassett's stump with a late out-swinger. As the ball was 30 overs old, the swing India's captain was getting was remarkable.

# INDIA'S TEST FIGHT

## Needs 300 More Runs

*From ARTHUR MAILEY*

**MELBOURNE, Friday.**—The Indians need at least 300 more runs to give them a winning chance in the Third Test.

The failure of India's captain, Amarnath, at a crucial moment was a big blow to the Indians but Mankad's glorious century somewhat made up for the failure of India's best batsmen.

### Barnes Wrecks Hopes

India has lost six for 262 in reply to Australia's 394.

The weather tomorrow is expected to be chiefly fine, with occasional showers.

Rain is not expected to be heavy enough to interrupt play.

If India loses this Test, most of the blame may be attributed to the problem child of cricket, Sid Barnes, who, being a batsman-bowler, a first-class wicketkeeper, and a grand fieldsman in any position, may be described as the world's most complete all-rounder.

Barnes, whose hatred for bowling and humbugging is identical, completely wrecked India's hopes with consecutive deliveries which masqueraded under the heading of leg-breaks.

**In other words, what were expected by Hazare and Amarnath to be leg-breaks, skidded through and diverted the destiny of the Third Test match in Australia's favor.**

Barnes hates bowling, and does not take it seriously.

### In Bad Way

He doesn't mind sending down an over or two, but he recoils at the thought of being a stock bowler.

When he appeared at the bowling crease yesterday Australia was in a bad way.

Hazare and the resolute Mankad were batting beautifully, and Bradman had employed all his regular bowlers. The score was 180 odd for two wickets.

Bradman, driven to desperation, scratched his head, and saw Barnes browsing in midfield, and threw the ball to him with a somewhat apologetic air.

A few minutes later, Barnes broke the annoying Mankad-Hazare partnership by getting Hazare's wicket.

The next ball completely deceived the great Amarnath, and two of India's best three batsmen were out, and the score was four for 188.

At that particular period, the stage was set for Amarnath. The Australian attack had almost come to the end of its resources, and here at least was one batsman who was expected to take advantage of the position.

### Mankad Hero

Mankad, of course, was the hero of the day.

The fact that he scored his century in 20 minutes less time than Bradman had scored his was sufficient testimony of his enterprise and industry.

Later, a leg strain handicapped him, and he was compelled to have a runner.

This severely handicapped his stroke-making and, being unable to run, prevented him from stealing the strike to save his batting companions.

**Sarwate and Mankad, in scoring 124 for the first wicket, gave the Indians their best start to date.**

A fine partnership by Adhikari and Phadkar during the closing stages somewhat redeemed the ground lost when India's most efficient batsmen, Hazare, Amarnath, and Mankad were dismissed.

OPENING BATSMEN, Mankad (left) and Sarwate, who gave India her best start in a Test against Australia, in Melbourne yesterday. They scored 124 for the first wicket.

# CENTURIES ARE STILL A HABIT
# Bradman Slashes Indian Bowlers In 3rd Test

Bradman.   Morris.

**MELBOURNE, Saturday. — Don Bradman scored a century in both innings in a Test for the first time today when he knocked up 127 not out for Australia against India in Melbourne. Bardsley and Morris are the only other Australians to have achieved this honor.**

**Bradman has scored six centuries this season, including his century today. He has also scored 103 centuries altogether in first-class cricket.**

Here are the scores of this amazing rungetting machine this season—156, 12, 100, 172, 26, 185, 13, 132, and today's score to fill in.

Bradman pulled the game out of the fire after he had committed the blunder of sending his tailenders into bat before lunch.

When the tailenders began the innings for Australia, 35 minutes remained before lunch. The Indians at once sprang to their toes but they gave such a shocking exhibition of fielding that they failed to drive home their advantage.

No fewer than four lollypop chances were missed, three by Nayudu, and one by Phadkar that any school boy would have held

### Three Chances

Bill Johnston gave three chances and Dooland one

Bradman completely demoralised his side changing his batting order.

He saw how the wicket had played when the Indians resumed in the morning and at least he should have appreciated that it was not difficult.

Had he opened the innings with Barnes and Morris they should easily have overcome any tricks the wicket might have played

Instead Bradman threw his tail-enders to the lions.

The fact is that the wicket did not play tricks. Every ball came through at even height

Miller did not even fly head high, as he has done this season in Brisbane and Sydney

Not by any stretch of imagin-

ation could the wicket have been described as dangerous But it was the old story of batsmen developing a "wet-wicket complex" and playing to the tune of this obsession to the advantage of bowling that was elevated from commonplace to class

### Batsmen Tricked

The tailenders made the bowling look hostile. Amarnath assumed the role of a tiger hungry to claim his victims.

He bamboozled the batsmen by placing seven fieldsmen in a huddle around the wicket a few yards from the bat.

**The result was that the batsmen became terrorised and they batted like a lot of old hens on the brood.**

Accordingly when Bradman came in to bat four wickets had fallen for the paltry score of 32 runs and the Indians had their tails up.

Admittedly Bradman retrieved the situation for Australia with a magnificent innings after a very streaky start, but it must be agreed that his blunder placed a much heavier responsibility on his shoulders than it otherwise would have been.

If the wicket was so bad before lunch, however, then surely Amarnath blundered too by not closing his innings earlier than he did

**But he was prepared to waste precious time by allowing his batsmen to remain at the wickets during 40 precious minutes while a paltry 29**

runs were being scored. Those 40 minutes could have won the match if the wicket had been bad. But it wasn't.

Bradman and Morris soon overcame the "wet wicket" bogey and settled down to a match-winning partnership.

V. Mankad   Amarnath

and the longer they batted the more they played the Indian bowling, which earlier had presented such unjustifiable terrors.

**Bradman took longer than usual to get going. He took 88 minutes to reach 50. He scored at the rate of only one run every two minutes.**

But he scintillated the longer he batted, and passed his century—a glorious knock—in 130 minutes (11 fours)

He drove, pulled, and hooked with the abandon of youth at picnic cricket, and gave the crowd one long thrill after he was thoroughly set.

Morris was always the sheet-anchor and steadying

influence during the danger period, and his innings could not be faulted. Morris passed his 50 in 132 minutes.

By 5.30 Bradman and Morris had pulverised the Indian bowling to pulp, and the fieldsmen who earlier paraded like young tigers eager for their first kill, looked more like something the cat had dragged in through the back door.

**Bradman and Morris had 200 runs on the board. They had completely retrieved a dangerous position when four wickets were down for 32 runs.**

The 200 came up in 211 minutes, which was smart time considering the fact that the first 100 occupied 139 minutes

Great excitement prevailed in the last five minutes, when Bradman did everything under the sun to enable Morris to get his century Bradman nearly ran himself out

### Passed Century

Morris passed the century two minutes before stumps by pulling Mankad towards the boundary Sprinting like a pair of greyhounds, they ran four

Morris passed his 100 in 195 minutes (seven fours) The unfinished partnership **was 223** runs in 175 minutes.

At stumps Australia was four for 255 and was in an impregnable position.

**The position is that with the lead of 103 runs in the first innings Australia is now ahead with 358 runs and four wickets down.**

# TEST ENDS SUDDENLY: INDIA CRASHES IN WET

### From R. S. WHITINGTON

**MELBOURNE, Monday. — Don Bradman made another dramatic Test move today when he closed Australia's innings at Saturday's score of 4-255 following rain.**

**India, set 359 to win, quickly struck trouble on a wet pitch and the side was out for 125, 30 minutes after lunch.**

Warm morning sunshine and drying wind made a start on time possible.

When the captains inspected at 11.30 am, the wicket was very soft, but the bowling approaches and batting foothold were playable.

**Bradman, after inspecting the wicket, smiled broadly, and announced the immediate closure of Australian innings at 4-255— 358 ahead of India.**

It is reported that when the captains were inspecting the wicket Bradman said to Amarnath: "Do you want to play?"

Amarnath: "Yes."

Bradman: "Well, you bat."

As Bradman placed his field for Miller, a loud voice from the outer ground called, "You're tough, Bradman."

In Miller's second over Mankad snicked a ball through slips for four to take the total to 10 in even time.

**India's first wicket fell for 10, when Sarwate (1) played over a yorker from Bill Johnston. He could not blame the wicket.**

When Gul Mohamad batted barrackers yelled "hit them over the fence."

Mankad (13), then was bowled by a well pitched up ball from Johnston who had 2-7 out of 2-27.

**Gul Mohamad reached 20 in 33 minutes by snicking Bill Johnston for his second four.**

The crowd had grown to 25,000 by the time Barnes very close in at silly mid-on, took an excellent catch to dismiss Hazare (10) off Miller, to make the score 3-44.

## Crowd sympathetic

Amarnath came in to loud and sympathetic applause from all round the ground

Miller was loudly derided when he jumped into the air and appealed for lbw off the first ball.

**A great hook by Gul Mohamad off Bill Johnston flashed to the fine leg rails, but the wicket was not improving.**

After 52 had appeared in 58 minutes Lindwall replaced Miller, 1-29.

Ian Johnson replaced Bill Johnson (2-32).

Gul Mohamad, however, was caught by Morris at second slip off Ian Johnson, and the score was 4-60. Mohamad had made 28 in 54 minutes.

Lindwall yorked Amarnath (8) when the score was still 60 The wicket was becoming nasty. Lindwall kicking awkwardly from good length.

**Adhikari hooked Ian Johnson, but was well-caught by Lindwall behind square leg to make it 6-69.**

Johnson had 2-8.

At lunch, with the wicket becoming sticky, India was 6 for 84—still 274 behind

Phadkar limping badly, should have been given a runner.

India scored 16 runs off the first two overs after lunch and raised 100 in 97 minutes.

**The wicket was worse than before lunch, but Rai Singh drove Ian Johnson for six.**

Rai Singh then was caught by Tallon for 24 in 19 minutes, when trying for a hook off Bill Johnston.

Phadkar's courageous stay of 38 minutes for 13 runs, ended when he mis-hit an attempted hook off Bill Johnston, softly to Barnes.

Sen came in smiling at 8-107.

**Three beautifully-executed boundaries, off Bill Johnston, took Rangnekar to 18 in 13 minutes, before Hamence took a well-judged catch off Ian Johnson to dismiss him.**

Nine were out for 125.

When Sen was caught by Hassett off Ian Johnson, who had 4-35, Australia had won by 233 runs at 2.45 pm, and was two up with two to play in the rubber.

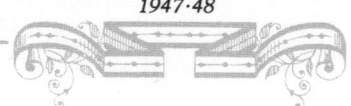

# Australia v India
## Fourth Test Match

AUSTRALIA v INDIA, Fourth Test Match, at Adelaide, 23, 24, 26, 27 and 28 January 1948.

| | | |
|---|---|---|
| Australia | - First Innings | 674 |
| | - Second Innings | - |
| India | - First Innings | 381 |
| | - Second Innings | 277 |

Australia won by an innings and 16 runs, and won the rubber.

| | | |
|---|---|---|
| DON BRADMAN (Captain) | - b. V.S. Hazare | 201 |

The Indian bowlers came in for further heavy punishment when DON BRADMAN won the toss on a perfect wicket and made the thirty-seventh double-century of his career. He went in at 20 for 1 on the first morning, and took an hour before lunch to score only 20; having completed 50 in an hour and forty-one minutes, he was 94 not out at the tea interval, completing his century (his third in successive innings, all in Test Matches) soon afterwards in three hours eleven minutes. Thereafter he forced the pace brilliantly taking only seventy-nine minutes over his second century; he threw his wicket away two minutes later with a wild swing, having batted for four hours and thirty-two minutes, and hit a six and twenty-one fours. His innings was faultless, and he reached his 1,000 runs for the season, for the twelfth time, when he was 77.

This was the sixth time that he had made 200 runs or more in a day's play in a Test Match, three times in Australia and three times in England. For the ninth time, he scored three (or more) successive centuries in first-class cricket. At the age of thirty-nine years 149 days, Bradman was the oldest batsman ever to score 200 for Australia in a Test Match. He was also the youngest. His 201 was the highest score in Australia v. India Test Matches, and his second-wicket stand of 236 with S.G. Barnes was the highest for that wicket in any Test Match against India. He was the only batsman to make double-centuries against four different countries in Test Matches (v. England, South Africa, West Indies and India) - a unique achievement.

## Australia

| | | |
|---|---|---|
| S. G. Barnes lbw b Mankad | ..... | 112 |
| A. R. Morris b Phadkar | ......... | 7 |
| D. G. Bradman b Hazare | ........ | 201 |
| A. L. Hassett not out | ......... | 198 |
| K. R. Miller b Rangachari | ....... | 67 |
| R. N. Harvey lbw b Rangachari | .. | 13 |
| C. L. McCool b Phadkar | ........ | 27 |
| I. W. Johnson b Rangachari | ..... | 22 |
| R. R. Lindwall b Rangachari | .... | 2 |
| D. Tallon lbw b Mankad | ........ | 1 |
| E. R. H. Toshack lbw b Hazare | .. | 8 |
| B 8, l-b 6, n-b 2 | ............. | 16 |
| | | 674 |

## India

| | | | | |
|---|---|---|---|---|
| V. Mankad b McCool | ................ | 49 | — c Tallon b Lindwall | 0 |
| C. T. Sarwate b Miller | ............... | 1 | — b Toshack | 11 |
| P. Sen b Miller | ................... | 0 | — not out | 0 |
| L. Amarnath c Bradman b Johnson | .... | 46 | — b Lindwall | 0 |
| V. S. Hazare lbw b Johnson | .......... | 116 | — b Lindwall | 145 |
| Gul Mahomed st Tallon b Johnson | ..... | 4 | — b Barnes | 34 |
| D. G. Phadkar lbw b Toshack | ........ | 123 | — lbw b Lindwall | 14 |
| G. Kishenchand b Lindwall | .......... | 10 | — b Lindwall | 0 |
| H. R. Adhikari run out | ............. | 2 | — lbw b Miller | 51 |
| K. M. Rangnekar st Tallon b Johnson | .. | 8 | — b Lindwall | 0 |
| C. R. Rangachari not out | ............ | 0 | — c McCool b Lindwall | 0 |
| B 18, l-b 3, n-b 1 | ............ | 22 | Extras | 22 |
| | | 381 | | 277 |

## India Bowling

| | O. | M. | R. | W. | | O. | M. | R. | W. |
|---|---|---|---|---|---|---|---|---|---|
| Phadkar | 15 | 0 | 74 | 2 | | | | | |
| Amarnath | 9 | 0 | 42 | 0 | | | | | |
| Rangachari | 41 | 5 | 141 | 4 | | | | | |
| Mankad | 43 | 8 | 170 | 2 | | | | | |
| Sarwate | 22 | 1 | 121 | 0 | | | | | |
| Hazare | 21.3 | 1 | 110 | 2 | | | | | |

## Australia Bowling

| | O. | M. | R. | W. | | O. | M. | R. | W. |
|---|---|---|---|---|---|---|---|---|---|
| Lindwall | 21 | 5 | 61 | 1 | .... | 16.5 | 4 | 38 | 7 |
| Miller | 9 | 1 | 39 | 2 | .... | 9 | 3 | 13 | 1 |
| McCool | 28 | 2 | 102 | 1 | .... | 4 | 0 | 26 | 0 |
| Johnson | 23.1 | 5 | 64 | 4 | .... | 20 | 4 | 54 | 0 |
| Toshack | 18 | 2 | 66 | 1 | .... | 25 | 8 | 73 | 1 |
| Barnes | 9 | 0 | 23 | 0 | .... | 18 | 4 | 51 | 1 |
| Bradman | 1 | 0 | 4 | 0 | | | | | |

### FALL OF THE WICKETS

AUSTRALIA—First Innings:

| 1 | 2 | 3 | 4 | 5 | 6 | 7 | 8 | 9 |
|---|---|---|---|---|---|---|---|---|
| 20 | 256 | 361 | 503 | 523 | 576 | 634 | 640 | 641 |

INDIA—First Innings:

| 1 | 2 | 3 | 4 | 5 | 6 | 7 | 8 | 9 |
|---|---|---|---|---|---|---|---|---|
| 1 | 6 | 69 | 124 | 133 | 321 | 353 | 359 | 375 |

INDIA—Second Innings:

| 1 | 2 | 3 | 4 | 5 | 6 | 7 | 8 | 9 |
|---|---|---|---|---|---|---|---|---|
| 0 | 0 | 33 | 99 | 139 | 139 | 271 | 273 | 273 |

# TEST BOWLERS FLAYED

## Bradman Gets 201 Despite Leg Cramp

*From ARTHUR MAILEY*

**ADELAIDE, Friday.—Don Bradman, who scored his 37th double century in first-class cricket when he was out for 201 in the Fourth Test against India today, limped during his innings because of leg cramp.**

**Australia, batting on a wicket which did not help the Indian bowlers, has lost three wickets—Morris, Bradman, and Barnes—for 370.**

Bradman's 37 double centuries exceeds Englishman Walter Hammond's by one.

Bradman's leg cramp prevented free footwork, but he stood his ground and played Phadkar and Rangachari off his back foot.

These strokes would have put to shame many batsmen who had two perfectly sound legs.

There were times when Sid Barnes appeared to be a greater batsman than Bradman.

**Early in his innings, Bradman was fidgety and suspici-** ous of the pitch because one or two balls kept low.

Bradman nudged the ball away, while Barnes, oozing confidence, threw his whole weight behind each stroke.

The difference was that Bradman usually scored, while his aggressive partner hit the ball straight to the fieldsman.

The Barnes-Bradman partnership of 236 placed Australia in a good position after a bad start.

The bad start in this case was more by accident than design.

### Captain's Scheme

Morris played an ordinary looking ball, which rolled back and disturbed the stumps.

Phadkar, who got the wicket, never looked dangerous throughout the day, and I was surprised to see him open the bowling in preference to Rangachari, who is much faster.

Indian captain Amarnath's deep-laid scheme of directing his two fast bowlers against Bradman missed fire.

The popular opinion amongst cricketers that Bradman does not relish fast bowling may have influenced Amarnath's action.

But because Phadkar is only little faster than medium, and Rangachari is fast medium on the Adelaide pitch, the theory could not be tested.

From 3 o'clock both batsmen scored without trouble.

Amarnath, who was suffering a knee injury, did not bowl with his usual consistency.

As far as I know, the batsmen gave only one chance.

When 61, Barnes was missed by Amarnath in the slips off Rangachari.

The Indians probably gave their best fielding display up to date.

There was little or no wild throwing, and the ground fielding was first-class.

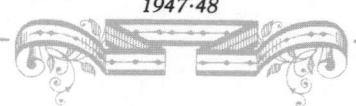

# INDIAN SKIPPER FIGHTS BACK; CAUGHT AT 46

### From R. S. WHITINGTON

**ADELAIDE, Monday.** — India's captain, Lala Amarnath batted brilliantly when his side resumed against Australia in the fourth Test today.

Facing a hat-trick by Miller, Amarnath glanced the first ball for four, and was out shortly before lunch for 46. India, at lunch, was three for 85.

The temperature was over 100 degrees when Amarnath, having recovered from his lumbago, took the field with Mankad.

Amarnath, facing a hat-trick, stylishly leg-glanced Miller's first ball of the day to the boundary, but the third kept low and he just got down on it.

The Indians started very confidently. Mankad straight-driving Miller for three.

**Lindwall still appeared to be dragging over a few inches, but, despite a photograph taken on Saturday and published in an Adelaide newspaper, umpire Wright did not no-ball him.**

Miller, at umpire Borwick's end, kept his back foot for the most part two feet behind the line.

McCool replaced Lindwall and, batting gloriously, Amarnath took 14 (two cover boundaries, three on-drives for twos) from his first over.

**Amarnath reached 22 in 20 minutes with an attractive shot past gully. The crowd of 7000 thrilled to** the cricket, despite the blistering heat. **Thirty-three runs came in 20 minutes.**

Bradman's fibrositis seemed improved by the heat. He was fielding excellently.

Though McCool's length improved in his second over, Amarnath's brilliant footwork always took him to the pitch of the ball, unless it was very short.

Bradman replaced Miller (2-17 off four overs) with Lindwall at the cathedral end, favored by slight breeze.

When Mankad was 12, and the total 43, he glanced Lindwall about a foot high wide to the right of Ian Johnson at close leg gully. Johnson dived, but the ball bounced from his hands and his elbows hit the ground.

When Amarnath was 27 he pounced on a McCool full toss and hit it fiercely towards Bradman's foot on the full, but it was an almost impossible chance.

**The next ball was straight driven to the sightboard to make Amarnath 34 in 30 minutes.**

## Lindwall's bumper

When Lindwall bowled a bumper past Mankad's ears, somebody yelled, "Play the game." Some barrackers seem to resent fast bowlers using a very legitimate part of their armament these days.

Lindwall was definitely not gaining distance over the crease, as in Sydney.

When Morris, at long on, was a second slow in picking up an on-drive by Amarnath, the alert batsman quickly snatched two runs, an example some Australian batsmen could profitably follow.

Lindwall pegged away in the heat at Mankad, but the Indian's bat was straight as a die, and well behind the ball.

After McCool's four overs for 25. Ian Johnson was called on, the batsmen taking four for an over of good length.

When Toshack replaced Lindwall, it seemed that the fast bowlers had had their day.

**Amarnath reached 42 by cover-driving Toshack for three. His placements had been delightful all the morning.**

Amarnath straight-drove the first ball of Johnson's next over for four, and then caught a high full-toss on the edge of his bat, and Bradman, running to the right from deepish mid-on, held a good catch.

Amarnath's brilliant 46 had been made in six minutes less than the hour. Hazare entered at 3-69.

Judging from the difficulties in which Hazare found himself, Ian Johnson must have been spinning and flighting the ball well in his early overs.

When Borwick no-balled Toshack, Mankad hit him high over mid-off to the sightboard.

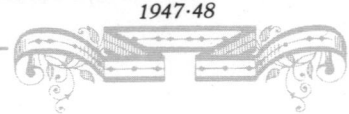

# PHADKAR REACHES TEST 100, BUT HAZARE OUT

### From R. S. WHITINGTON

**ADELAIDE, Tuesday** — Phadkar reached his century in the fourth Test today and was top-scorer with 117 not out in India's 8-369 at lunch.

India at that stage still needed 106 to save a follow-on. Hazare had gone, lbw to Johns on—for 116 with the total 6-321.

Adelaide temperature was not quite as hot as yesterday, when Bradman, wearing khaki topee, led the Australians on to the field.

Official attendance aggregate for the first three days was just under 45,000 and net takings £5500.

Heat again kept thousands away from the ground t\lay.

Lindwall's first over was a maiden, Hazare wisely playing his eye in.

**McCool bowled from the river end to Phadkar, who raised 300 with a lofty pull out to Morris at long on.**

McCool beat Hazare with a leg break and Tallon flashed off the bails, but Hazare's foot had not lifted.

First boundary of the day was a quickly-turned stroke to square leg off Lindwell by Phadkar, who went into the 80's.

More pieces hopped out of the pitch at the river end during Lindwall's third over, which was the second maiden of the day.

Phadkar carefully replaced the divots.

Only 10 runs came in the first half-hour.

McCool then spun a huge leg-break sharply across both Phadkar and Tallon to increase byes to nine.

With five overs left before the new ball, Ian Johnson replaced Lindwall and bowled around the wicket.

**After Hazare had pulled Johnson hard to the mid-wicket fence and had leg-glanced a two, Johnson trapped him lbw at 116.**

It broke a valuable partnership of 188 and made the score six for 321.

The partnership was easily a sixth-wicket record for India.

Johnson had three for 54.

Phadkar went into the 90's by pulling McCool for four. It was Phadkar's 11th four.

Both McCool and Johnson appeared to be gaining occasional sharp spin.

Kischenchand opened confidently, but lost several runs for Phadkar by refusing easy calls when Phadkar was approaching his century.

Phadkar reached a fine century (12 fours) by going way down the wicket and lifting Johnson high and cleanly over the infield to the sightboard.

When Phadkar went for a smashing drive off Johnson, Barnes three yards away wisely turned his back and was hit a hard blow on the shoulder.

Barnes made light of the incident, but Bradman sent him to the outfield at the end of the over.

**At 351 Bradman gave Lindwall the new ball. There was a delay when Phadkar was hit on a finger.**

Lindwall clean bowled Kishenchand (10) with the third ball of his 20th over. It was his first wicket for 49 runs.

Adhikari entered at 7-353.

Hassett accounted for Adhikari with a brilliant underhand throw from extra cover which hit the only stump visible to him at the bowler's wicket.

Umpire Borwick, who had been watching Lindwall closely from square leg yesterday, did not no-ball him today.

## REFLECTIONS ON CURRENT TEST MATCH SERIES.

(By S. P. FOENANDER, sports editor, Ceylon Associated Newspapers Ltd., travelling with the Indian team.)

Now that Australia has won the rubber most decisively against India, following on the defeat of the English team led by Walter Hammond in last season's rubber, it has become more apparent than ever that Bradman and his team mates are undisputed champions of the world in cricket. The last occasion on which England lost the rubber and the ashes was in 1932-33 when Jardine led the English team. I was privileged to see that series of tests, made most memorable by the unfortunate introduction of "body line" bowling. Since then Australian stock in cricket has risen to its wonted heights of the past when Monty Noble and Warwick Armstrong led the Cornstalks to victory in the tests. I remember having seen Australia lose the rubber and the ashes at the Kennington oval in 1926, when A. P. F. Chapman captained England and Herby Collins led the Australians.

Last week at Adelaide I met Clarrie Grimmett, who had been one of the stars of Australian cricket for many years, and had toured England in 1926. While giving all due credit to Bradman and his team for having beaten the Indians so decisively in this season's rubber, Grimmett remarked to me that the bowling strength of Australia has deteriorated in the past quarter-century. I agree with this expert's opinion, and say that Australia, even though the strongest cricket nation, to-day is short of really great bowlers of the type of O'Reilly, Grimmett, Jack Gregory, and Charlie Macartney.

The recent tests have emphasised the greatness of Don Bradman as a batsman and captain. Don is still a wizard with the bat, and a phenomenal run-getter. He set up more than one record this season against a touring team. He obtained centuries against the Indians, for South Australia, an Australian Eleven, and for Australia in three tests. His feat of scoring two centuries in one match was another amazing achievement.

Without Bradman the Australian team in this year's tests would have been appreciably weakened. He always scored runs when they were most needed. But Australia cannot go on depending on Don for ever. I believe he will retire from test cricket after the tour in England. It will be then only that Australia will fully realise the real greatness of Bradman, who since 1928 has been the mightiest match winner in the world.

# BRADMAN TO RETIRE

## No Cricket After English Tour

### MELBOURNE, February 5.

*Don Bradman, the world's greatest cricketer, will play his last first-class game in Australia in the Fifth Test against India to begin tomorrow.*

*He will, however, go with the Australian team to England, after which he will retire completely from the game.*

A characteristic Bradman stance.

Announcing his decision at his hotel tonight, Bradman said :—

"I have today advised my co-selectors I am available for the Australian tour of England. At the same time, I wish to say that this will be my last first-class match in Australia, as I shall retire from cricket at the conclusion of the English tour.

"I recognise that to undertake another tour at my age (Bradman is in his 40th year) would be a heavy responsibility and one which I feel reluctant to accept.

"But if I am required to do so, then I feel this will be the final opportunity of service to he game which has played such a big part in my life."

Bradman explained that while he said the Fifth Test against India would be his last first-class game in Australia, it would still be possible that he could play in an A grade match before the departure of the Australian team for England.

He said emphatically, however, that he would retire from all classes of cricket in Australia when he returned from England.

### In 40th Year

Bradman was born on August 27, 1908. He has shattered almost every world cricket record in his career, and is generally considered to have no peer as a captain. No other player has ever been such a draw in countries where cricket is played.

Although not in the best of health after defence duties during the war and suffering severely from fibrositis, which threatened to end his sporting career, he made a shattering comeback against England last season.

In much better health this year, he opened the season with a century for South Australia against India. A few weeks later he added his 100th century to his amazing string of records, and two weeks ago in Adelaide broke his own world record (held with Hammond) by scoring his 37th double century in first-class cricket.

# Australia v India
## Fifth Test Match

AUSTRALIA v INDIA, Fifth Test Match, at Melbourne, 6, 7, 9 and 10 February 1948.

| Australia | - First Innings | 575 for 8 wickets dec. |
|---|---|---|
| | - Second Innings | - |
| India | - First Innings | 331 |
| | - Second Innings | 67 |

Australia won by an innings and 177 runs.

| DON BRADMAN | - retired hurt | 57 |
|---|---|---|
| (Captain) | | |

DON BRADMAN went in at 48 for 1, three-quarters of an hour before lunch on the first day, and made 35 by the interval; he settled down in his best form afterwards, completed 50 in seventy-three minutes, and was 57, after an hour and twenty-five minutes, when he tore a muscle in his left side and was compelled to retire; he had been batting so well that it seemed likely that he would complete his fifth century of the series. He gave no chance and hit four fours.

He was unable to resume his innings, but had recovered sufficiently after the weekend to field on the last two days, mainly in the slips.

## Australia

| | | | | |
|---|---|---|---|---|
| S. G. Barnes run out | 33 | D. Tallon c Sen b Sarwate | 37 | |
| W. A. Brown run out | 99 | L. Johnson not out | 25 | |
| D. G. Bradman retired hurt | 57 | D. Ring c Kishenchand b Hazare | 11 | |
| K. R. Miller c Sen b Phadkar | 14 | W. A. Johnston not out | 23 | |
| R. N. Harvey c Sen b Mankad | 153 | B 4, l-b 4 | 8 | |
| S. J. Loxton c Sen b Amarnath | 80 | | | |
| R. R. Lindwall c Phadkar b Mankad | 35 | Eight wkts., dec. | 575 | |

## India

| | | | |
|---|---|---|---|
| V. Mankad c Tallon b Loxton | 111 | — c Tallon b Lindwall | 0 |
| C. T. Sarwate b Lindwall | 0 | — lbw b W. Johnston | 10 |
| H. R. Adhikari c Tallon b Loxton | 38 | — c Bradman b Loxton | 17 |
| V. S. Hazare lbw b Lindwall | 74 | — c and b L. Johnson | 10 |
| L. Amarnath c Barnes b Ring | 12 | — c L. Johnson b Ring | 8 |
| D. G. Phadkar not out | 56 | — lbw b W. Johnston | 0 |
| Gul Mahomed c Lindwall b L. Johnson | 1 | — c Barnes b Ring | 4 |
| G. Kishenchand b Ring | 14 | — c Barnes b L. Johnson | 0 |
| C. S. Nayudu c Bradman b Ring | 2 | — c Brown b Ring | 0 |
| P. Sen b L. Johnson | 13 | — b L. Johnson | 10 |
| C. R. Rangachari b L. Johnson | 0 | — not out | 0 |
| B 6, l-b 2 n-b 2 | 10 | B 6, l-b 1, n-b 1 | 8 |
| | **331** | | **67** |

## India Bowling

| | O. | M. | R. | W. | O. | M. | R. | W. |
|---|---|---|---|---|---|---|---|---|
| Phadkar | 9 | 0 | 58 | 1 | | | | |
| Amarnath | 23 | 1 | 79 | 1 | | | | |
| Rangachari | 17 | 1 | 97 | 0 | | | | |
| Hazare | 14 | 1 | 63 | 1 | | | | |
| Mankad | 33 | 2 | 107 | 2 | | | | |
| Sarwate | 18 | 1 | 82 | 1 | | | | |
| Nayudu | 13 | 0 | 77 | 0 | | | | |
| Adhikari | 1 | 0 | 4 | 0 | | | | |

## Australia Bowling

| | O. | M. | R. | W. | O. | M. | R. | W. |
|---|---|---|---|---|---|---|---|---|
| Lindwall | 25 | 4 | 66 | 2 | 3 | 0 | 9 | 1 |
| L. Johnson | 30 | 8 | 66 | 3 | 5.2 | 2 | 8 | 3 |
| Loxton | 19 | 1 | 61 | 2 | 4 | 1 | 10 | 1 |
| W. Johnston | 8 | 4 | 14 | 0 | 7 | 0 | 15 | 2 |
| Ring | 36 | 8 | 103 | 3 | 5 | 1 | 17 | 3 |
| Miller | 3· | 0 | 10 | 0 | | | | |
| Barnes | ·2 | 1 | 1 | 0 | | | | |

## FALL OF WICKETS

AUSTRALIA—First Innings:

| 1 | 2 | 3 | 4 | 5 | 6 | 7 | 8 |
|---|---|---|---|---|---|---|---|
| 48 | 182 | 219 | 378 | 457 | 497 | 527 | 544 |

INDIA—First Innings:

| 1 | 2 | 3 | 4 | 5 | 6 | 7 | 8 | 9 |
|---|---|---|---|---|---|---|---|---|
| 3 | 127 | 206 | 231 | 257 | 260 | 284 | 286 | 331 |

INDIA—Second Innings:

| 1 | 2 | 3 | 4 | 5 | 6 | 7 | 8 | 9 |
|---|---|---|---|---|---|---|---|---|
| 0 | 22 | 28 | 35 | 51 | 51 | 56 | 56 | 66 |

## *Bradman Retires Hurt When 57 In Fifth Test Match*

Bradman leaving the wicket during the fifth Test match in Melbourne yesterday. He had made 57 when he retired.

# BRADMAN HURT, RETIRES AT 57

MELBOURNE, Friday. — A torn back muscle compelled Don Bradman to retire in the fifth Test against India today when he was 57 not out

Sympathetic applause from all parts of the ground greeted Bradman as he limped to the pavilion.

Dr. Keon-Cohen diagnosed Bradman's injury as a torn muscle under the rib.

**India's captain, Amarnath, sportingly agreed to allow Bradman to continue his innings later, though this will depend on Bradman's fitness.**

After passing 50, Bradman began to hold his left side, and appeared in pain after every stroke.

He refused a couple of short, risky runs.

Amarnath spoke to him (evidently suggesting that he could retire), but Don went on batting.

When 57, Bradman walked slowly off the field, holding his side.

He had been batting for 85 minutes, and hit four fours.

Australia was then one for 140.

Bradman, after having his back bound with an elastic strap, changed into civilian clothes and watched play from the dressing-room. He will not bat again today.

# BRADMAN TO FIELD TOMORROW—IF POSSIBLE

Australian Test captain Don Bradman, who did not play yesterday in the Fifth Test against India at Melbourne, said he would field tomorrow if possible.

On Friday Bradman tore a rib muscle during Australia's first innings and retired when he had made 57.

Yesterday he denied a report in a Sydney evening paper that he was suffering from an attack of fibrositis, which might prevent him from touring England.

Brisbane hotelkeeper Jim Burton and his nephew, Bob Burton, who had offered Bradman 10/ for each run he scored in the Fifth Test, said last night they would give him £100 because they thought he would have scored 200 runs if he had completed his innings.

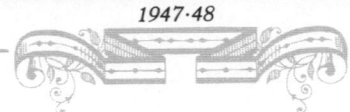

# MANKAD'S TEST 100; BRADMAN TAKES FIELD

### From R. S. WHITINGTON

**MELBOURNE, Monday.—Mankad, continuing his fine fighting innings for India, reached 100 just before tea in the fifth Test today.**

**Don Bradman made a surprise re-appearance, leading the Australians out to field.**

Bradman fielded at first slip. Bradman's motive in playing today doubtless was to watch closely the bowling of Ring, Loxton and Len Johnson.

**Lindwall bowled with plenty of pace, and Mankad, who scored the first 10 today, got most of them from snicks along the ground, past second slip.**

Johnson seemed to waste chances by often bowling too short, and Ring by tossing up too many leg breaks, inches outside the off stump.

The second new ball became available at probably the record low of 89 runs, but Bradman left Miller, Bill Johnston and Lindwall in the field and persevered with Ring and Len Johnson.

**The Indians were showing definite signs of settling down when Loxton replaced Johnson.**

### Near run out

Only excitement in a dull period before lunch came when Mankad was nearly run out. Australian fieldsmen appeared to obscure umpire Barlow's view of the spread-eagled wicket.

At lunch, Mankad was 69, Adhikari 26, and the score 1-99.

**Ring's opening over after lunch was greeted by barrackers with calls of "put them on the wicket."**

Then the match was restored to its proper status by Lindwall coming on at 1-105.

Loxton was Lindwall's new-ball partner this time, and Mankad snicked him along the ground between Bradman and Miller to the fence. Bradman came up holding his left side.

Later in the over, Adhikari snicked Loxton low past Tallon for four.

Having added 124, Mankad and Adhikari were beginning to present a problem, when Loxton took his first Test wicket for 32, having Adhikari caught by Tallon.

Lindwall bowled his first bumper of the day to Hazare, who is believed not to appreciate bumpers.

With Hazare and Mankad together, the Indians for the first time appeared to be on top of the bowling.

Bill Johnston then had his second spell for the innings and the crowd, now about 25,000, applauded his third maiden out of four overs for the innings.

# INNINGS LOSS FOR INDIANS

### From OUR CRICKET REPORTER

**MELBOURNE, Tuesday. — Forced to follow on, 244 behind in the final Test to-day, India offered no resistance to the Australian attack in its second innings, and was dismissed in less than two hours for 67, losing the match by an innings and 177 runs.**

India's first innings totalled 331.

Five Indian batsmen failed to score in the second innings, and at one stage four wickets fell for five runs within 12 minutes.

India suffered from a number of bad decisions to-day, which helped to take heart from the side's batting. Generally, the match was marked by bad umpiring.

In the first innings Hazare was given out by umpire Barlow lbw to Lindwall in a very doubtful decision, and in the second innings, Hazare also hesitated before walking out.

He had played down on a ball from Len Johnson, which curled up from the bat and the bowler caught it. When the bowler appealed, umpire Cooper raised his hand.

India's second innings began sensationally, when Mankad was given out by umpire Cooper, caught behind by Tallon off Lindwall's second ball.

Mankad was using a new bat for the first time, and when he returned to the pavillion, no mark of any kind could be found on its surface or on the edges.

It seemed that Mankad had been unfortunate.

Indian players recalled that when Australia's opening batsman, Brown, snicked a ball before he had scored, umpire Barlow gave him not out.

Brown, who had started to walk out, went on to make 99, and make certain his place in the team for England.

In the hour before tea to-day, India lost four wickets for 36 runs, including that of Phadkar, who batted defensively for 11 minutes, then lost his wicket without scoring, four minutes before the interval.

Amarnath again threw away his hand, making a foolish attempt to hit Ring out of the ground. Of the later batsmen, only Sen offered any resistance.

Len Johnson, bowling with accuracy and life, took three wickets for eight runs and helped Ring break the back of the Indian innings.

Attendance to-day was 9,281, with net gate of £828, making total attendance for the match 97,365, and net takings £9,366.

India's share of the gate will be £4,340, which should enable the team to cover all expenses for the tour, with a small profit.

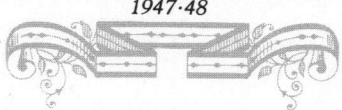

Following a successful season against India, I finally decided to risk one more tour of England, despite personal misgivings that my health and fitness would justify the wisdom of my doing so.

It would have been nice to finish on a high note at Melbourne but, unfortunately, I had to retire hurt when 57. At that time I fully expected to be able to bat again next day but the injury turned out to be a torn cartilage between the ribs and the extreme pain made it impossible for me to continue my innings.

Despite this disappointment I had the satisfaction of having contributed everything I could to the rehabilitation of cricket in Australia following the war.

A humorous sidelight of 1947–48 was the press report that I proposed entering politics. No such thought crossed my mind but I suppose journalists require good imagination.

*Don Bradman*

# BRADMAN AS MEMBER OF PARLT. ?

MELBOURNE.—Will Don Bradman ever seek a place in the field of politics?

Several Victorian members put the suggestion to him last night when he was a guest at dinner at State Parliament House.

Similar suggestions have been made to him by Liberal members of the Federal and South Australian Parliaments. He has been urged to stand for a metropolitan seat in South Australia.

Although Bradman was non-committal last night on the subject of his political ambitions, he showed a keen interest in Parliamentary procedure and listened for a while to the debate on the Gas Commission Bill.

Then he went back to his hotel to have an early night before today's big match.

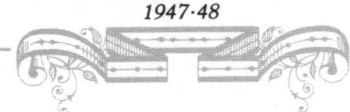

# "WALL" OF BATSMEN KEY TO SIDE'S STRENGTH

### From R. S. WHITINGTON

**MELBOURNE, Thursday. — Judged on modern Test standards, Australia's cricket team for England is a strong one—especially in batting, captaincy, wicket-keeping and fielding. There is no apparent reason why Australia should lose the "Ashes."**

The team includes that arbiter of Test destiny, Don Bradman, Sid Barnes, A. Morris, K. Miller (a 30 per cent. finer batsman in England), Bill Brown (a 50 per cent. better bat over there), L. Hassett and N. Harvey to get the runs.

**Has England the bowlers to get them out twice for match losing totals on the batting paradises of Nottingham, Lord's, Leeds and The Oval?**

Best of the English bowlers appear to be Bedser (very much under a cloud), Douglas Wright, H. J. Butler (another fastish county colleague of Larwood and Voce), Cranston, Gladwin, Edrich and Howarth.

None of them are "worldbeaters" (except Bedser and Wright on their occasional days), and they will need abnormal assistance from weather and wicket to break down this wall of batting resistance.

Our actual winning of the rubber, however, may be delayed until late in the series.

England, smarting under her failure last summer, and now playing as a team under Yardley, will also be hard to dismiss twice in the required time.

We have no leg spin bowler who even approaches the class of O'Reilly, Grimmett or Mailey.

**The selectors have thought fit to leave home the googly bowler whom leading English, Australian and Indian batsmen unanimously regard as our best —Bruce Dooland.**

To the credit of the selectors, I believe they spent the greater part of their five hours' deliberation deciding between Ring and Dooland.

Nevertheless, if Hutton, Compton and Edrich really strike form together in England, it could easily be a case of "God save our Ring."

## Doubts on Toshack

Apart from the googlies, our bowling combination looks well on paper, but it has many "ifs" about it.

Melbourne photographers told me that Lindwall's dragging foot was again nearer to the batting than the bowling crease during the fifth Test.

I hate to have to keep harping on this, but someone has to do the unpleasant job.

**English umpires simply will not tolerate Lindwall's dragging under the existing new rule, which does not help Lindwall at all. It seems more designed to help Edrich and Bedser.**

Toshack, fit and well, would be our main bowling hope,

but he should have had his leg operated upon months ago.

**After watching him nurse his leg in the last few games it was no wonder the selectors demanded a searching medical examination.**

Keith Miller, because of a back injury and his batting, hates being used as a bowler, except for a few shock overs.

Bill Johnston still has to gain the extreme accuracy required to dismiss back-playing English professionals on slower English wickets.

Ian Johnson will have to quicken up his pace and rely more on spin than in his Australian trump card—flight.

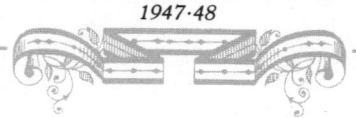

# Australians v Western Australia

AUSTRALIANS v WESTERN AUSTRALIA, at Perth,
13, 15 and 16 March 1948.

| Australians | - First Innings | 442 for 7 wickets dec. |
| | - Second Innings | - |
| Western Aust. | - First Innings | 348 |
| | - Second Innings | 62 for 3 wickets |
| | Drawn. | |

| DON BRADMAN | - c. T. Outridge b. T. O'Dwyer | 115 |
| (Captain) | | |

DON BRADMAN went in at 48 for 1, on the second afternoon, and was soon scoring freely; he reached 50 in forty-seven minutes, and though he spent forty minutes in the nineties, against the new ball, he reached 100 in a minute more than two hours.    Just before the close, after two hours twenty-one minutes at the wicket, he was caught in the covers; second out at 249, he and A.R. Morris added 201 for the second wicket.    Bradman hit sixteen fours in a chanceless innings; this was his eighth century of the season, another record for Australian cricket.

## Bradman Signs Autograph Books At Hospital

Australia's Test captain, Don Bradman, signing autograph books for patients at the Perth Children's Hospital on Thursday.

Visiting the patients at the Children's Hospital today, Test captain Don Bradman was put to work signing their autograph books. Shown with him is 10-year-old Maurice who was deputised to present them.

# *1948*
# *Australian Tour of England*

**M**y decision to once again tour England as a player was made with some reservations. I was not sure that physically I would be able to stand the strain.

A badly torn rib cartilage in the final Test at Melbourne against India had not completely healed when the first match of the English tour commenced. I suffered some pain and inconvenience during that opening match at Worcester and deliberately got out rather than risk further injury.

For me, in 1948, the risk of failure could not be dismissed. But I was imbued with an intense desire to give my all in a final attempt to serve cricket, and through this noble game, my country.

Fate was kind to me as the following pages chronicle.

It was a strange experience as I played match after match realising I would never again appear in those centres. One game of great nostalgia was at Lords against the Gentlemen during which I made 150 and celebrated my 40th birthday. A former Australian Governor General, Lord Gowrie, cut the cake at lunch.

The pictures of our happy afternoon at Balmoral with the Royal family provide eloquent testimony to cricket's place in history.

There was the moving function at which I received a replica of the Warwick Vase as a token of esteem from the people of England. The latter occasion gave me special pleasure because all the money subscribed beyond that needed to acquire the trophy was, at my request, used to install concrete cricket pitches for young players in the public parks and playing fields of England.

There is an undeniable satisfaction in having served one's country to the best of one's ability. Having achieved that I was relieved to face the prospect of returning to a life wherein the pressures of a public existence were substantially reduced.

*Don Bradman*

# WHARFIES CHEER BRADMAN ON HIS WAY

Wharfies line up and farewell Don Bradman, just before he boards the Strathaird for England.

# NO EXTRA FOOD RATION FOR TEST CRICKETERS IN ENGLAND

**PERTH, Saturday.—The Australian cricket team sailed yesterday for England with £650 worth of food parcels—but not for themselves.**

THE team's manager (Keith Johnson) said that definitely no arrangements had been made for the team to have extra rations.

"I want to make it clear," he said, "that our boys will be eating the ordinary rations of the British people.

"Of course, some may get private parcels from home. I know I will.

"**We'll do a lot of visiting, and it will be most welcome in today's Britain to bring a few extra table tid-bits.**"

A seagull farewelled Test captain Don Bradman in its own peculiar manner as the Strathaird left Fremantle with the team.

Grinning, Bradman exclaimed: "It's a new hat too —the first time I've worn it."

Most players were farewelled by West Australian friends. Others have close friends making the voyage.

As soon as the ship left port the players met to form a committee to decide on voyage activities.

Some previous teams have banned deck sports, but manager Johnson said this was unlikely on this trip.

"My personal view is that the boys should be left to look after their own physical fitness," he said.

Only unfit member at present is vice-captain Lindsay Hassett, who has 'flu. He went straight to bed after going aboard.

Departure of the liner was delayed for 90 minutes, tugs being engaged on a salvage job in the harbor, but an army of cricket officials and fans who choked the decks and wharf waited to cheer as the ship pulled out.

"Don't leave the Ashes there," shouted a lumper as the Strathaird headed out to sea.

Several team members replied with the thumbs up sign.

Don Bradman with Captain Allen en route to England.

Betty Beblovsky, Bill Hipkiss, Elonore Martin, Dr. Woods, Toody Askew, and Don
Bradman on R.M.S. *Strathaird*.

♦ **AUSTRALIAN TEST CAPTAIN** Don Bradman rips off his hat and enthusiastically returns the wild welcome of Tilbury c r o w d s as the Strathaird docks from Australia. With him on the boatdeck are Australian Deputy High Commissioner Norman Mitchell and MCC secretary Colonel Rait-Kerr.—RADIOPHOTO.

## — SEASON 1948 —

| TITLE | GAMES | | SCORES | |
|---|---|---|---|---|
| Second Class | Australia | Scotland | 27 | B. |
| | " | | 123 | n.o. |
| First Class | " | Worcestershire | 107 | B. |
| | " | Leicestershire | 81 | C. |
| | " | Surrey | 146 | B. |
| | " | Essex | 187 | B. |
| | " | M.C.C. | 98 | C. |
| | " | Lancashire | 11 | B. |
| | " | | 43 | St. |
| | " | Nottinghamshire | 86 | B. |
| | " | Sussex | 109 | B. |
| | " | Yorkshire | 54 | C. |
| | " | | 86 | C. |
| | " | Surrey | 128 | C. |
| | " | Middlesex | 6 | C. |
| | " | Derbyshire | 62 | B. |
| | " | Warwickshire | 31 | B. |
| | " | | 13 | n.o. |
| | " | Lancashire | 28 | C. |
| | " | | 133 | n.o. |
| | " | Kent | 65 | C. |
| | " | Gentlemen of England | 150 | C. |
| | " | South of England | 143 | C. |
| | " | Leveson-Gower's XI | 153 | C. |
| Test Matches | " | England | 138 | C. |
| | " | " | 0 | C. |
| | " | " | 38 | C. |
| | " | " | 89 | C. |
| | " | " | 7 | L.B.W. |
| | " | " | 30 | n.o. |
| | " | " | 33 | B. |
| | " | " | 173 | n.o. |
| | " | " | 0 | B. |
| | | Total runs | 2578 | |

## — SUMMARY —

AVERAGES -

| | Innings | N.O's. | H.S. | Runs | Average |
|---|---|---|---|---|---|
| Test Matches | 9 | 2 | 173* | 508 | 72·6 |
| Other First Class | 22 | 2 | 187 | 1920 | 96·0 |
| All First Class | 31 | 4 | 187 | 2428 | 89·9 |
| All Second Class | 2 | 1 | 123* | 150 | 150·0 |
| All Matches | 33 | 5 | 187 | 2578 | 92·1 |

# WELCOME, THE AUSTRALIANS

## By R. C. ROBERTSON-GLASGOW

IT will be seventy years on May 27 since the first Australian cricketers, " practically unrecognised by a handful of spectators," drove into Lord's in a horse-brake, and, within one day, beat the flower of English cricket as represented by the Marylebone Cricket Club. In all the years since, no greater bowler has come from Australia, perhaps not from England, than "The Demon" F. R. Spofforth. In M.C.C.'s first innings he took 6 wickets for 4 runs in 5.3 overs. That evening, the crowds gathered outside the Tavistock Hotel in Covent Garden to wonder at the visiting heroes.

### HAPPY FEVER

Well, here they are again; and the crowds will gather in wonder and tens of thousands; and every run and every move in the five Tests will reach the uttermost parts of the earth nearly as quick as a cat can wink her eye. Murders will slide into obscure paragraphs, and what Mr. Molotov said will not be evidence. There is no fever like Anglo-Australian Test cricket. And so, we must be careful; careful to see that the fierce, almost frantic, urge for victory does not kill the enjoyment and overturn the values for which cricket was invented. Cricket was meant to be a sociable game. Therefore, its highest manifestation, the Tests, should be, like Caesar's wife, above suspicion.

Bradman is here again, captain of Australia for the third time. His old admirers will be glad. After ten years' absence, he will also have a new public—those who, in 1938, were still at school, or, even, perambulator cases. We want him to do well, but not too well. We feel we have a share in him. He is more than Australian. He is a world batsman.

Besides Bradman, Hassett, the vice-captain, Brown, and Barnes are the only three who played at the Oval in August, 1938, when our own Len Hutton made what is still the record Test score of 364. Hassett entertained us here during War years with the best type of captaincy and batting. During Hammond's tour of Australia, he adopted, doubtless under orders, a tranquillity foreign to his nature. Now, we are hoping for the return of Hassett I, an artist of footwork and attack. Brown, we remember for a double-century made in the classic manner in the Lord's Test ten years ago. He has recovered from a troublesome injury to his hand.

### THE MERRY MILLER

Barnes is a batsman who excels in the short-arm strokes, with a hook reminiscent of Pat Hendren's. He also delights to field murderously close to the bat on the leg side. Keith Miller, like Hassett, we saw and admired during the war, when he was serving with the Royal Australian Air Force. He is all freedom, power, and daring; a natural hero for boy and man. There are dents in the masonry of the Lord's pavilion to remind us of Miller's batting.

Of the Australian bowlers, expectation most eagerly attends Lindwall. Here we have almost forgotten the sight of a fast bowler, since the prime of Larwood, Allen, and Farnes. Lindwall is connected with a tendency to the no-ball; and our umpires will risk stiff necks in deciding this problem of space and time.

### MATTERS OF AGE

The Australians come as winners of the last Rubber, and, perhaps, with a reputation beyond their deserts. I can hear the older critics rudely murmur "Amongst the blind the one-eyed man is king." They find us, as to cricket, in a somewhat Gummidge-like state, thinking of the old 'uns and wondering where the new 'uns will come from. This won't do; not at all, it won't. We must at least pretend to optimism. We must find ourselves unready to believe that the Australians are as good as all that. After all, they verge on senility! They are the first Australian team to visit us with only one player under the age of 26. O'Reilly and Grimmett are bygone terrors, though the former will be here as critic making the adjectives instead of the ball spin merrily. McCool and Ring have yet to prove themselves in England. Besides, we hear rumours of secret weapons being forged in our winter schools of cricket.

So, welcome Australia, old friends and enemies. You are the best news for many a month.

Keen rivals for the Test tour, Norman Yardley (right), probable England captain, and Australian captain, Don Bradman, greeting each other at a reception in London today. Mr. J. A. Beasley, Australian High Commissioner is also in the picture.

# *Bradman To Play In First Match*

### *From PHIL TRESIDDER*

**LONDON, Friday.—Australian Test captain, Don Bradman, will play in the first match of the Australians' tour, at Worcester, on April 28.**

Bradman, who announced this at a Press conference after the team's arrival today at Tilbury, said he would make as many appearances on the tour as he could.

Bradman has scored a double-century at each of his three previous appearances against Worcestershire.

Asked to compare his team with past Australian sides, he said that, on paper, it compared very favorably.

**Whether it would be a success was a matter for conjecture.**

Asked whether Lindwall had overcome the no-ball problem, Bradman replied, "I didn't know there was any problem.

"I'll remind you it's the umpires who decide what are no-balls, not the newsreel cameras."

Bradman said the Australian team would probably loosen up tomorrow at Lord's.

Hundreds of people waited on the docks to give the team a warm reception when the Strathaird berthed at 5 a.m.

Looking bronzed and fit, the 17 players and manager Keith Johnson stood patiently for an hour before a battery of cameras and newsreels.

Most of the team wore overcoats, because the weather was dull, and a cold, fresh wind blew across the water.

**The only casualty on the voyage was Ray Lindwall, who suffered mild gastritis.**

Lindwall, who had been in bed for several days, joined the team as it was photographed.

Bradman, in high spirits, shook hands with English selector R. W. V. Robins, and cracked: "I hear you're a selector now.

"In that case, I reckon we are a cinch to win the series."

## HONOURED FRIENDS AND ADVERSARIES

### THIS YEAR'S AUSTRALIAN TEST TEAM

BACK ROW   R. Lindwall, K. R. Miller and W. A. Brown.

MIDDLE ROW   W. Ferguson (Scorer), R. N. Harvey, D. Ring, E. R. H. Toshack, W. A. Johnston,
R. A. Saggers, S. G. Barnes and K. O. Johnson (Manager).

FRONT ROW   S. Loxton, R. A. Hamence, A. L. Hassett, D. G. Bradman (Captain), C. L. McCool,
A. R. Morris and I. Johnson. Wicket-keeper D. Tallon is absent from the group.

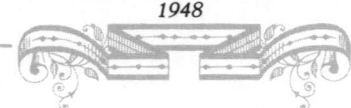

Lord McGowan, Don Bradman, J. Beasley (Aust. High Commissioner), Mrs. Beasley, Lady McGowan, The Mayor of Westminster and C. B. Fry at the Coliseum Theatre to see a performance of *Annie Get Your Gun*.

# BRADMAN UNDER FIRE FROM CRITICS

## *Australian Writer's Book Quoted*

*(Daily Mirror World Cables)*

LONDON, Monday.—Within 48 hours of his arrival in England, Bradman has become the victim of an unfair attack by a section of the English Press, who do not like to remember the pitiful display by the M.C.C. team in Australia last year.

THE latest English journalist to join the anti-Bradman school is Peter Wilson, of the Sunday Pictorial.

Yesterday the paper devoted three-quarters of a column to telling Bradman not to repeat the errors which marked the last Test series.

Wilson has never been to Australia, but apparently, from the tone of his article, went to great pains to drag every anti-Bradman card out of the pack.

"This series must be played in the spirit which has generally prevailed when matches are played in England, but which has not always been the case when they were played in Australia," said Wilson.

*Don Bradman*

"During the last series it was said that England went out primarily on a goodwill mission to Australia, while Australia, under Bradman's captaincy, went out to win, and did so," he said.

Wilson also quoted from Clif Cary's book, Cricket Controversy, which vigorously criticises Bradman and which has been freely quoted by every anti-Bradman cricket writer in London.

### "Not Read Book"

Bradman told a Daily Mirror reporter yesterday that he had not read Cary's book and did not intend to do so.

English humorist Sir Alan Herbert, writing in the Sunday Graphic, said that England for the time being should forget about the unaccountable things the Molotovs do.

"Let us think of happier names such as Bradman, Hassett, Miller and the rest of their illustrious crew," Sir Alan said.

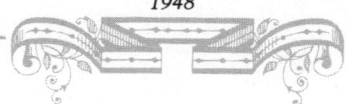

# NEW APPEAL BY BRADMAN

**Staff Correspondent And A.A.P.**

LONDON, April 23.—Don Bradman again has appealed to English journalists not to spoil the Australian team's tour by subordinating cricket to sensations.

"We do not think the game should be used as a vehicle for distortion or exaggeration of events," he declared in a speech at the Cricket Writers' dinner.

"I think there are other legitimate events for stirring up a sensation, even though capital punishment has been abolished."

Discussing the responsibilities of cricket journalists, Bradman said that every cricketer of note was a subject for legitimate criticism.

The Australians expected acute analysis of their batting, bowling, fielding, and captaincy.

Bradman promised that the Australians would do everything to make this a happy and successful tour.

"By the end of the tour, we hope we shall have done much to restore to its proper pedestal the greatest game in the British Empire," he declared.

## Last Tour

Bradman reminded his audience that this was his last tour of England, and that he would not play cricket again in Australia.

Referring to the Duke of Edinburgh's presence at the dinner, he said:—

"I detected in the films of the Duke that he has a perfect action for a right-hand off-spin bowler.

"We have been accused of being ungenerous at times, so I submit that to the English selectors for serious consideration. (Laughter.)

"If they are not prepared to take the hint seriously, we are prepared to give the Duke a knock or a bowl with us at Lord's."

Bradman, whose speech was broadcast, gave a message from Australia to British children.

"We know they have been having a very tough time," he said.

"Australia is behind them in spirit, and will continue to do all she possibly can to make their lot a little easier in future."

The "Daily Telegraph's" columnist, Peterborough, says that after hearing Bradman's speech he can testify that Bradman approaches the microphone not much less skilfully than he approaches the wicket.

Bradman spoke, he says, with a short smile, a coolness, and ease which the most polished after-dinner speaker might have envied.

## On-side Practice

Determined to polish up his on-side play, which has been weak during the last few practices, Bradman had Toshack and Ian Johnson concentrate on the leg side at Lord's this morning.

He showed, when he had settled down, that he has returned to his old flashing form, making a series of brilliant on-drives and sweeps to leg.

All the batsmen had a morning of hard-hitting practice, with Miller outstanding.

Lindwall, bowling a few balls at nearly top speed to Ring, knocked the leg stump out of the ground with an inswinger.

Two balls later, he knocked it out again.

Ring picked up the stump to replace it for a second time, then turned ruefully to the amused crowd and threw it into a corner of the net.

He left Lindwall only the off and middle stumps to aim for in the remainder of his knock.

## Bradman Hands Over Food Gift

Don Bradman, captain of the Australian Test team, and Mr Keith Johnson, team manager, presented Mr Strachey, at the Food Ministry, today, with a specimen case of tinned meats, one of 200 that the team brought with them from Australia on behalf of the Australian Cricket Board of Control.

The food, about three and a quarter tons, will be distributed through local authorities in various parts of Britain.

Mr Strachey, thanking them said, "I think the crowds, when they watch Bradman and his chaps playing, will really like to remember you brought this gift, and they will feel the better for it if they see the game going the wrong way from their point of view—which may happen."

Mr. Johnson, Manager of the Australian team speaking at the presentation of food at the Ministry of Food Headquarters.

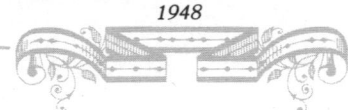

# Australians v Worcestershire

AUSTRALIANS · v WORCESTERSHIRE, at Worcester, 28, 29 and 30 April 1948.

| Australians | - First Innings | 462 for 8 wickets dec. |
|---|---|---|
| | - Second Innings | - |
| Worcestershire | - First Innings | 233 |
| | - Second Innings | 212 |

Australians won by an innings and 17 runs.

DON BRADMAN - b. P.F. Jackson        107
   (Captain)

Although he did not on this occasion start the tour with a double-century, DON BRADMAN for the fourth time made over 100 at Worcester in his first match, and could probably have doubled his score had he wished.    In cold and unpleasant weather, he went in on the second morning at 79 for 1, and in company with A.R. Morris raised the score by 186, to 265 for 2, before he threw his wicket away just after tea.    He reached 50 in seventy-one minutes, and 100 in two hours eighteen minutes, just before the interval;  he batted altogether for two hours thirty-two minutes, gave no chance, and hit fifteen fours.

This was Bradman's second century in April, the first being his 258 in 1938;  no other visiting batsman had done this more than once.

## Worcestershire

| | | | |
|---|---|---|---|
| E. Cooper c Hassett b Toshack | 51 | — lbw b Toshack | 22 |
| D. Kenyon lbw b Lindwall | 0 | — st Tallon b McCool | 17 |
| C. H. Palmer c Johnson b Toshack | 85 | — st Tallon b McCool | 34 |
| R. E. S. Wyatt st Tallon b McCool | 18 | — absent hurt | 0 |
| L. Outschoorn b Lindwall | 1 | — c Tallon b Barnes | 54 |
| A. F. T. White c Tallon b Miller | 1 | — c Barnes b McCool | 11 |
| R. Jenkins b Johnson | 7 | — lbw b Johnson | 21 |
| R. Howorth not out | 37 | — lbw b McCool | 0 |
| R. T. D. Perks c Toshack b McCool | 0 | — c Barnes b Johnson | 27 |
| H. Yarnold c Barnes b Johnson | 15 | — c Lindwall b Johnson | 11 |
| P. F. Jackson c Barnes b Johnson | 1 | — not out | 9 |
| B 7, l-b 10 | 17 | B 4, l-b 1, w 1 | 6 |
| | **233** | | **212** |

## Australians

| | | | | |
|---|---|---|---|---|
| S. G. Barnes lbw b Howorth | 44 | W. A. Brown st Yarnold b Howorth | 25 |
| A. R. Morris c Jenkins b Jackson | 138 | K. R. Miller not out | 50 |
| D. G. Bradman b Jackson | 107 | I. W. Johnson not out | 12 |
| R. R. Lindwall lbw b Jackson | 32 | B 6; l-b 5, w 4 | 15 |
| C. L. McCool b Jackson | 0 | | |
| D. Tallon b Jackson | 4 | | |
| A. L. Hassett c Wyatt b Jackson | 35 | Eight wkts., dec. | 462 |

E. R. H. Toshack did not bat.

## Australian Bowling

| | O. | M. | R. | W. | O. | M. | R. | W. |
|---|---|---|---|---|---|---|---|---|
| Lindwall | 15 | 2 | 41 | 2 | 3 | 0 | 19 | 0 |
| Miller | 12 | 1 | 36 | 1 | 8 | 3 | 18 | 0 |
| McCool | 19 | 9 | 38 | 2 | 17 | 5 | 29 | 4 |
| Toshack | 14 | 3 | 39 | 2 | 18 | 8 | 40 | 1 |
| Johnson | 23 | 8 | 52 | 3 | 13.3 | 1 | 75 | 3 |
| Barnes | 9 | 6 | 10 | 0 | 8 | 2 | 25 | 1 |

## Worcestershire Bowling

| | O. | M. | R. | W. |
|---|---|---|---|---|
| Perks | 26 | 3 | 95 | 0 |
| Palmer | 16 | 5 | 56 | 0 |
| Wyatt | 1 | 0 | 4 | 0 |
| Jenkins | 7 | 0 | 47 | 0 |
| Jackson | 39 | 4 | 135 | 6 |
| Howorth | 38 | 6 | 109 | 2 |
| Outschoorn | 1 | 0 | 1 | 0 |

Umpires: F. Root and D. Davies.

Cheery Don Bradman, who began smiling when he docked at Tilbury and has been in humorous mood ever since, looked in a happy frame of mind when he stepped off the train at Worcester to be greeted by the Mayor, Coun. Basil Edwards, last night. Brig. M. A. Green, the county secretary, and the club captain, A. F. T. White, were also there. Among the enthusiastic crowd who gave the Australians a cheer as they came out of the station was a girl who hustled a floral cricket into Bradman's car.

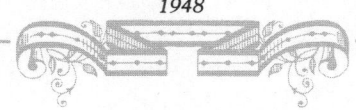

# They queue for Bradman

Brilliant sunshine streamed on a hard and fast wicket at Worcester to-day for the opening match of the Australian tour.

The Australians are fielding what appears to be their strongest team.

Don Bradman in 1930, 1934 and 1938 scored double centuries at Worcester in the first matches of his tours.

Groundsman George Platt said to-day: "There is nothing wrong with the wicket so he should have the best possible chance of doing it again."

Flags are flying everywhere in Worcester. Some shops are closing this afternoon and many schoolchildren have been given a half-holiday.

The ground has room for about 15,000 people and three extra stands have been built but all seats in the stands were sold weeks ago.

To-day a queue formed outside the ground several hours before the gates were opened.

# BRADMAN OPENS LAST TOUR WITH A CENTURY

WORCESTER, April 29 (A.A.P.). —Don Bradman opened his last English tour with a sparkling century against Worcestershire to-day, making 107 before being bowled by Jackson.

He and Arthur Morris added 186 for the second wicket, Morris going on to make an impressive 138. Three more wickets then fell for 38 runs in a sudden batting slump.

## GOOD DEBUT BY MORRIS

Opening batsman Arthur Morris impressed in his first innings on English wickets.

He was held in check before lunch, however, by left-arm bowler R. Howorth, who used a packed off field.

Barnes and Morris opened quietly on an easy-paced wicket.

Barnes broke through the well-placed cordon of fieldsmen four times for three sweeps to the leg boundary and an immaculate square-cut.

Howorth, bowling round the wicket to a tightly guarded off-field, was accurate but did not look dangerous.

Barnes produced another two boundaries—one a rather streaky shot, just out of reach of the slips—and a series of singles before he played forward to Howorth's first ball of his eighth over, and was out leg-before.

Morris, meanwhile, was missed by Howorth when he drove a ball hard and low back to that bowler's left hand.

The left-hander opened up after Barnes's dismissal and three fours took him to 50 in 115 minutes.

At lunch Bradman was 17, Morris 59, and Australia had one down for 121.

Bradman jumped out to Howorth and drove one straight back hard past the bowler for his first boundary. It made him 30.

The pitch was showing signs of developing patches and a few balls kicked up dust.

Howorth made some deliveries turn sharply and others whipped through low and quickly.

Perks and Palmer returned to the attack with the new ball.

Bradman steered Palmer past third man for four and drove him through the covers for another, to bring up his half-century in 70 minutes.

He was in sparkling form since lunch and had put on 41 to seven by Morris.

A sharp hailstorm stopped play for 25 minutes.

There was a great cheer when Bradman sauntered a single to make his thirty-first century in England, a couple of minutes after Morris had reached his first.

Bradman's century took 125 minutes, and Morris's 225, each with 14 fours.

A spectacular race to the century began when Morris produced five and Bradman four boundaries.

Bradman hit Jackson for four, two, and a single to reach 90.

Two fours took Bradman to 99, but Morris beat him to it with a two to fine leg.

Bradman threw away his wicket after tea when he jumped out twice to Jackson.

He missed a sixer by a few feet on the first attempt, and missed the ball entirely on the second mighty lunge.

The painstaking Jackson had Morris caught by Jenkins soon after.

When he bowled McCool and Tallon in quick succession, he had taken four quick wickets.

Lindwall hit six fours in a bright 32.

## Scoreboard

**WORCESTERSHIRE.**
First Innings, 233.

**AUSTRALIA.**
First Innings.

| | |
|---|---|
| A. MORRIS, c Jenkins, b Jackson | 138 |
| S. G. BARNES, lbw, b Howorth | 44 |
| D. G. BRADMAN, b Jackson | 107 |
| R. LINDWALL, lbw, b Jackson | 32 |
| C. McCOOL, b Jackson | 0 |
| D. TALLON, b Jackson | 4 |
| A. L. HASSETT, not out | 7 |
| W. A. BROWN, not out | 1 |
| Sundries | 5 |
| Six wickets for | 340 |

Fall of wickets: 79, 265, 297, 314, 320, 335.

To bat: K. R. Miller, I. Johnson, E. Toshack.

# AUSTRALIA WINS

## McCool Takes Four Wickets

LONDON, April 30: The Australian cricket team won its first match of the English tour when it defeated Worcestershire today by an innings and 15 runs. Australia declared at 462 for eight wickets and then dismissed the county for 214. McCool took four for 29 off 17 overs.

Bradman, who seemed in pain in his last few minutes of his magnificent innings yesterday, was quite fit today. He said that the back muscle which he strained in the fifth test against India became a little sore, but it was nothing to worry about.

The Hassett (33)-Brown (12) partnership, which seemed steady enough last night, did not continue long this morning. Hassett went first. He stepped out to drive Jackson but the ball spun in sharply and he skied it to Wyatt behind point. Brown went a few minutes later when he also went out for a hit and the wicketkeeper, Yarnold, removed the bails. Jackson, Worcestershire's bowler of the day yesterday, was getting a lot of assistance from the pitch.

Miller, who came in just as the total reached 400, quickly set about the bowling in cavalier fashion. He hit three mighty sixes in three successive overs—one off Howorth, whom he straight drove almost out of the ground at the pavilion end, two off Jackson, whom he hooked out of the ground into an adjoining backyard, and then straight drove the ball over the river end sightboard.

Johnson played a passive part at the other end while Miller carried on in hurricane style to reach his half-century in 40 minutes. Bradman almost immediately declared with the score at 8 for 462, leaving Worcester 230 to get to avoid an innings defeat.

Bradman gave Lindwall and Miller only three overs each to take the shine off the ball before bringing on Toshack and McCool. Worcestershire's opener, Cooper, again began confidently, though he once snicked Lindwall dangerously through the slips for four. Toshack sent down a couple of maidens and was unlucky not to have had Cooper's wicket. The batsman popped one up to Miller at cover, but he dropped it. McCool began very erratically, but smart fielding kept runs down.

Perks added life to the end of Worcestershire's innings with a dashing display, in which he hit Johnson once over the boundary and was unlucky not to get another six when the ball hit a sight board inside the boundary.

Wyatt was unable to bat because of an injured thumb.

## A hay-making swipe was Bradman's first gesture of his goodwill tour. It followed—

# DON'S 100 HABIT

CENTURY-MAKER Don Bradman (107) forces the ball through the covers in masterly style as Worcestershire wicket-keeper Yarnold shapes hopefully for a catch. It was one of many flashing shots that reached the boundary.

DON has scored 739 (average 184.75) in his last six innings—132 and 127 not out v India at Melbourne, 201 v India at Adelaide, 57 not out (retired hurt) v India at Melbourne, and 115 for the touring side against Western Australia.

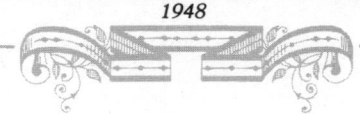

# DINNER

IN HONOUR OF THE

## AUSTRALIAN CRICKET TEAM

IN THE HARCOURT ROOM OF

## THE HOUSE OF COMMONS

MONDAY, 10th MAY, 1948

Chairman - - SIR J. STANLEY HOLMES, M.P.

## *Test Cricketers At House Of Commons Dinner*

Australian Test cricketers with the British Prime Minister, Mr. Attlee, and other M.P.s at the recent dinner tendered to the Australians at the House of Commons. Photograph shows, from left, D. G. Bradman, Mr. Oliver Lyttleton (at rear), Mr. Attlee, W. A. Brown, and Sir Stanley Holmes on the terrace before the dinner.

# Australians v Surrey

AUSTRALIANS v SURREY, at the Oval, 8, 10 and 11 May 1948.

| Australians | - First Innings | 632 |
| | - Second Innings | - |
| Surrey | - First Innings | 141 |
| | - Second Innings | 195 |

Australians won by an innings and 296 runs.

| DON BRADMAN | - b. A.V. Bedser | 146 |
| (Captain) | | |

After the Surrey bowlers had been worn down on the first day in an opening stand of 136, which ended just before lunch, DON BRADMAN joined S.G. Barnes in a second-wicket partnership of 207 in two hours eighteen minutes.    Bradman made a most confident start, and batted at his best; he reached 50 in seventy-seven minutes, and completed his century in two hours sixteen minutes.    When he was 137, he made his first mistake, putting up a catch to mid-wicket off J.C. Laker, and soon afterwards, at 403 for 3, he was bowled, playing a defensive stroke, by a fine ball from A.V. Bedser.    He hit fifteen fours in an innings lasting two hours fifty-four minutes.

## Australians
| | | |
|---|---|---|
| S. G. Barnes lbw b Squires | ......176 | |
| A. R. Morris lbw b McMahon | .... 65 | |
| D. G. Bradman b Bedser | ........146 | |
| A. L. Hassett b Bedser | ..........110 | |
| R. N. Harvey b McMahon | ...... 7 | |
| I. W. Johnson c Fishlock b Bedser | 46 | |
| R. R. Lindwall b Bedser | ......... 4 | |
| D. Tallon not out | .............. | 50 |
| D. Ring b McMahon | | 2 |
| W. A. Johnston lbw b Laker | ..... | 6 |
| E. R. H. Toshack c and b McMahon | | 8 |
| B 6, l-b 5, n-b 1 | .......... | 12 |
| | | 632 |

## Surrey
| | | | |
|---|---|---|---|
| L. B. Fishlock not out | ................ 81 | — c Tallon b Johnston | ...... 5 |
| D. G. W. Fletcher b Lindwall | ......... 1 | — b Johnston | ............. 2 |
| H. S. Squires lbw b Lindwall | .......... 3 | — c Harvey b Johnson | ....... 54 |
| T. H. Barling c Ring b Johnson | ...... 10 | — retired hurt | ............... 10 |
| M. R. Barton c Barnes b Johnson | ...... 4 | — c Johnston b Lindwall | ... 15 |
| A. J. McIntyre c and b Ring | ........... 6 | — c Tallon b Toshack | ........ 23 |
| E. R. T. Holmes b Johnson | .......... 0 | — b Johnson | ................ 3 |
| J. C. Laker b Ring | ................ 9 | — c Johnson b Johnston | ...... 20 |
| A. V. Bedser c Morris b Ring | ......... 2 | — c Johnson b Johnston | ..... 20 |
| W. S. Surridge c Harvey b Johnson | ..... 15 | — c Harvey b Johnson | ....... 20 |
| J. W. McMahon lbw b Johnson | ....... 0 | — not out | .................. 0 |
| B 9, l-b 1 | .................... 10 | B 15, l-b 6, w 1, n-b 1 | 23 |
| | 141 | | 195 |

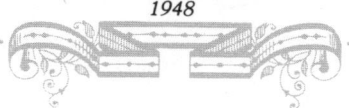

# Bedser missed Don—
# then bowled him

## *479 runs but no big hitting*

### By JACK HOBBS

BATTING all day on an Oval wicket which was as good as always, the Australians scored 479 against Surrey for the loss of four batsmen, including a Barnes-Bradman stand of 207 in two and a quarter hours.

Judged by any standards, the score must be summarised as a good one—well above the ordinary, in fact—but it was rather a quaint day's cricket.

At no time did the rate of scoring seem fast. There were no displays of enthusiasm by the 30,000 spectators such as big hitting arouses.

There wasn't any big hitting.

The answer to it all, I should say, was that the Surrey bowling, generally speaking, was such that the runs just came without any necessity for really forceful measures.

### *Many full tosses*

There were a lot of full tosses from the slow bowlers, and other deliveries of indifferent lengths which asked for, and duly received, punishment.

It will take something with more sting, more venom, from the England bowlers to dispose of the best Australian batsmen.

Morris, Barnes, Bradman, and Hassett gave us further glimpses of their masterly power.

Just a thought occurs to me about Don—a consoling thought for the bowlers we shall have to find.

His powers of concentration may not stand up to the task of adding to his record of huge scores.

Yesterday he got a typical hundred. After he had been missed by Bedser at 137 he opened out, and was bowled when 146 by the player who had missed him in playing a trifle loosely.

He may summon up the habitual concentration of Test matches, or he may not.

But, given good weather, he may get sufficient single hundreds this season to take a record from Denis Compton.

The whole day's cricket saw only one lofty hit—by Hassett.

The Australians did not take command, did not dictate, as completely as I thought they might have done. Probably, the ball was not coming to them quite quickly enough off the wicket, and, as they could take the runs anyway, why worry?

### *Laker not deadly*

Just once Alec Bedser discovered that solid left-hander Morris has an edge to the bat, and McMahon might have had his wicket earlier than he did if wicketkeeper McIntyre had not been so eager to stump him when he might have taken a catch.

Jim Laker, who is on a rather long list of possible bowlers for the first Test at Trent Bridge, did quite well without being deadly. He nearly bowled Barnes before lunch.

Laker is of the Tom Goddard type: off-breaks bowled over the wicket, but a little slower than the Gloucestershire man, giving the ball a bit more air.

On this pitch he did not make many turn, and those which did gave the batsmen time to watch them.

For those who like figures, Barnes got his first 100 in 158 minutes. Bradman took 136 minutes to run to the almost inevitable three figures, and before Squires found Barnes with his leg in front he had registered 18 boundaries, most of them on the leg side, where all the Australians are so strong.

I do hope that the many boys who were watching, and who hope to be real cricketers one day, were taking the lessons in running between the wickets which were handed out when Bradman was there.

The short ones were taken in the effort to upset a field well placed by skipper Holmes. The first run also taken at top speed, just in case. The Australians may not force runs, but they certainly don't waste them.

I must add a word for the Surrey men. They stuck it well.

Don Bradman bowled Bedser for 146.

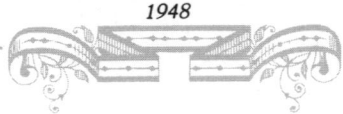

# AUST. INNINGS WIN LIKELY

*From E. M. WELLINGS and A.A.P.*

**KENNINGTON OVAL, Monday.—**
**The Australian attack routed Surrey on a crumbling wicket today, and made an innings win almost certain.**

Surrey collapsed for 141 in reply to Australia's 632 and was 2-25 in the follow-on at stumps.

Bill Johnston took Surrey's first two wickets in the second innings within half an hour.

A short bumper from Johnston knocked out Barling, who swung at the ball, and missed. He retired hurt.

In the first innings Lindwall (2-10), bowling his fastest so far on tour, started the rout.

Johnson (5-53), bowled particularly well, flighting the ball awkwardly and spinning it considerably.

Ring took 3-34.

Australia, which resumed at 4-479 this morning, was out for 632 after six wickets had fallen for 153 before lunch.

Hassett, who scored 110 (five boundaries) in 156 minutes, was associated with Ian Johnson in a century partnership, the third of the innings.

Hassett, who is suffering a cold, later left the field, and Hamence (12th man) replaced him.

## Four Wickets

Bedser took three of today's wickets, and McMahon two, to give them each four wickets for the innings

Lindwall and Bill Johnston opened to Fishlock and Fletcher after lunch.

**Lindwall warmed up in the second over and clean-bowled Fletcher with a beautiful in-swinger.**

Lindwall's speed beat Squires, who went l.b.w. when covering up to a good-length ball.

Johnson was successful in his first over when Barling gave Ring an easy catch at mid-off.

Barnes, at silly leg, made no mistake when Barton popped up another catch later off Johnson.

McIntyre went out to an easy catch by Ring.

Holmes joined the Surrey retreat when Ian Johnson bowled him second ball for a duck, and Laker was bowled soon afterwards by Ring.

Surridge lofted one from Ian Johnson to Harvey, who took a good catch at long-on.

McMahon, stepping in front of a straight ball, gave Ian Johnson his fifth wicket, and Surrey followed on.

Surrey began its second innings disastrously when Bill Johnston clean-bowled Fletcher with the score at four.

# VICTORY BY INNINGS

## Bradman's Bowling Changes

LONDON, May 11: Plucky batting by Squires and McIntyre threatened to deprive the Australian cricketers of victory over Surrey at Kennington Oval today but W. Johnston and Ian Johnson dismissed the county for 195 in its second innings with 23 minutes to spare. Australia won by an innings and 296 runs. A brilliant running catch by N. Harvey ended the Surrey innings. Bradman had been compelled to change his bowlers quickly.

The Australians will meet Cambridge University tomorrow. Bradman, Barnes, Loxton, Tallon and I. Johnson will stand down and W. Johnston will be 12th.

Only a few hundred people watched the Australians go out two hours after play was due to begin to seal what looked like certain victory over Surrey. A heavy shower earlier had left the wicket slow and the light was poor when Barton and Squires resumed Surrey's second innings with two wickets down for 25—466 behind Australia's total.

Morris missed Barton at second slip in W. Johnston's second over. Lindwall, despite the slow wicket, made a few balls lift and Tallon, reaching for one, bruised his right hand.

With both batsmen staying firmly in their creases Surrey's score mounted slowly, mainly by lucky snicks. Squires, cutting a ball from Lindwall shoulder high, gave a very difficult chance to Harvey in the gully but the fast bowler dismissed Barton in his next over when the batsman cocked a bumper up to W. Johnston at second slip.

### LINDWALL NO-BALLED

H. Haldwin, the umpire who had penalised McCormick so severely in 1938, called a no-ball against Lindwall—the first against him in England. Toshack did not trouble the batsmen in his first six overs when he profitlessly pegged away at the leg stump.

Squires, if rather lucky, was giving Surrey a slim hope of forcing a draw. Ninety minutes' play yielded 73 runs for the loss of one wicket today and the century soon came up of which 15 were byes. Tallon was not in his usual form.

Bradman made quick bowling changes to try to break the stubborn stand and was rewarded when Squires (54) stepped out and skied a ball from Ian Johnson to Harvey, who took a brilliant catch at deep mid-on. Squires had batted pluckily for nearly two and a half hours and hit seven fours.

McIntyre soon followed Squires, Tallon catching a snick against Toshack with one hand. Holmes uneasily played four balls lift from Ian Johnson before the off-spinner bowled him.

Bedser and Laker defied the bowlers until W. Johnston, using a new ball, had the former caught. I. Johnson took another catch in slips to dismiss Laker and then secured Surridge's wicket when Harvey took a good catch at long-off.

# Australians v Essex

AUSTRALIANS v ESSEX, at Southend, 15 and 17 May 1948.

| Australians | - First Innings | 721 |
|---|---|---|
| | - Second Innings | - |
| Essex | - First Innings | 83 |
| | - Second Innings | 187 |

Australians won by an innings and 451 runs.

DON BRADMAN - b. T.P.B. Smith          187
(Captain)

DON BRADMAN went in to bat at 145 for 1, twenty-two minutes before lunch on the first day, and by the interval he had made 42 not out; he used his last over, from F. H. Vigar, to score 20 (five fours). From that extraordinary start, he completed 50 after lunch in thirty-four minutes, 100 in seventy-four minutes, and was at the wicket for only two hours four minutes altogether when he was bowled for 187, swinging across a straight ball; his last 87 came in fifty minutes.     He hit a five and thirty-two fours (133 runs in boundaries, or seventy-one per cent) and had played the fastest innings of his career, averaging 90 runs an hour.

This was the second time that the Australians had played at Southend, and his 187 was the highest score made on the ground for them.     Essex was the twelfth English county against which he had made a century, thus passing W. Bardsley's record of centuries v. eleven different counties.

## Australians Score 721 In A Day

THE Australian cricketers, scoring at the phenomenal rate of 120 runs an hour, amassed 721 runs against Essex at Southend yesterday. This is believed to be a record for one day's batting of six hours in a first-class match.   Last season Middlesex made 663 in one day against Leicestershire.

D. G. Bradman (187), W. A. Brown (153), S. Loxton (120), and R. A. Saggers (104 not out) all scored centuries, but it was Bradman, playing for the first time against Essex, who made the pace.   He scored 42 in 20 minutes before lunch, 102 in 70 minutes, 152 in 115 minutes, and 187 in 125 minutes.   He twice hit 20 in an over, and his innings included a five and 32 fours.   His stand with Brown yielded 219 runs in 90 minutes.   Loxton and Saggers followed this with a stand of 166 in little more than an hour.

### Ran Out of Numbers

So rapid was the scoring that near the close one board ran out of numbers, and the scorers themselves found difficulty in keeping pace with the runs.

Though Bradman's rate of scoring was extremely fast, it is not a record for this country.   In 1907 G. L. Jessop scored 191 runs out of 234 in 90 minutes.   He reached 50 in 24 minutes, 100 in 42, and 150 in 63. P. G. H. Fender, playing for Surrey at Northampton in 1920, made 100 in 35 minutes, and C. I. J. Smith, batting for Middlesex against Gloucestershire in 1938 at Bristol, scored 50 in the record time of 11 minutes.

## Australians

| | |
|---|---|
| S. G. Barnes hit wkt b R. Smith... | 79 |
| W. A. Brown c Horsfall b Bailey .153 | |
| D. G. Bradman b P. Smith ......187 | |
| K. R. Miller b Bailey .......... | 0 |
| R. A. Hamence c P. Smith b R. Smith ...................... | 46 |
| S. J. Loxton c Rist b Vigar ......120 | |
| R. A. Saggers not out...........104 | |
| I. W. Johnson st Rist b P. Smith .. | 9 |
| D. Ring c Vigar b P. Smith ...... | 1 |
| W. A. Johnston b Vigar ......... | 9 |
| E. R. H. Toshack c Vigar b P. Smith | 4 |
| B 7, n-b 2 ............... | 9 |
| | **721** |

## Essex

| | | | |
|---|---|---|---|
| T. C. Dodds c Ring b Miller ......... | 0 | — b Toshack ............... | 16 |
| S. J. Cray b Miller ................. | 5 | — b Johnson............... | 15 |
| A. V. Avery b Johnston ........... | 10 | — c Brown b Johnson....... | 3 |
| F. H. Vigar c Saggers b Miller ........ | 0 | — c Johnson b Toshack ...... | 0 |
| R. Horsfall b Toshack .............. | 11 | — b Johnson............... | 8 |
| T. N. Pearce c Miller b Toshack ...... | 8 | — c and b Johnson ......... | 71 |
| R. Smith c Barnes b Toshack ......... | 25 | — c Ring b Johnson ......... | 0 |
| T. P. B. Smith b Toshack ........... | 3 | — lbw b Barnes ............ | 54 |
| F. Rist c Barnes b Toshack .......... | 8 | — b Johnson............... | 1 |
| E. Price not out .................. | 4 | — not out ................. | 4 |
| T. E. Bailey absent hurt ............. | 0 | — absent hurt ............. | 0 |
| B 2, l-b 6, n-b 1 ............... | 9 | B 6, l-b 3, n-b 6....... | 15 |
| | **83** | | **187** |

### Essex Bowling

| | O. | M. | R. | W. | O. | M. | R. | W. |
|---|---|---|---|---|---|---|---|---|
| Bailey ........ | 21 | 1 | 128 | 2 | | | | |
| R. Smith ...... | 37 | 2 | 169 | 2 | | | | |
| P. Smith...... | 38 | 0 | 193 | 4 | | | | |
| Price ......... | 20 | 0 | 156 | 0 | | | | |
| Vigar ......... | 13 | 1 | 66 | 2 | | | | |

### Australian Bowling

| | O. | M. | R. | W. | | O. | M. | R. | W. |
|---|---|---|---|---|---|---|---|---|---|
| Miller ........ | 8 | 3 | 14 | 3 | .... | 2 | 1 | 4 | 0 |
| Johnston ...... | 7 | 1 | 10 | 1 | .... | 10 | 4 | 26 | 0 |
| Toshack ...... | 10.5 | 0 | 31 | 5 | .... | 17 | 2 | 50 | 2 |
| Ring ......... | 11 | 4 | 19 | 0 | .... | 7 | 3 | 16 | 0 |
| Loxton ...... | | | | | | 12 | 3 | 28 | 0 |
| Johnson ...... | | | | | | 21 | 6 | 37 | 6 |
| Barnes ....... | | | | | | 9.4 | 5 | 11 | 1 |

Umpires: W. H. Ashdown and D. Hendren.

# ESSEX BATSMEN CRUMPLE IN TWO INNINGS

**SOUTHEND, May 17 (A.A.P.).**—Ern Toshack and Keith Miller today bundled out the Essex batsmen for 83 in the first innings. Essex was all out 187 in the second, with Ian Johnson the chief destroyer.

Australia won the match by an innings and 451 runs.

## BARNES, MILLER INJURED

Miller and Barnes both went off the field with injuries in Essex's second innings. Barnes returned later.

Miller was hurt in the County's first innings when he was struck on the back by a return from Bradman.

Barnes had been struck on the foot when fielding this morning.

Facing Australia's record score of 721, the Essex batsmen offered feeble resistance on a pitch that was fast and true.

Miller broke the backbone of the Essex batting in his first five overs of the day.

Bowling very fast with the wind from the northern end, he had the opener, Dodds, caught by Ring at second slip in his second over, before a run was on the board.

He clean-bowled Cray and had Vigar caught by Saggers with successive balls in his fifth over.

His average then was three wickets for nine, and three wickets were down for 13.

### Johnston's Wicket

Bill Johnston bowled Avery.

Toshack quickly struck a length and quickly dismissed Pearce and Horsfall.

Ray and Peter Smith, who added 16 runs in 15 minutes, were the only remaining batsmen to make any showing.

Trevor Bailey did not bat. He injured a hand fielding on Saturday, and is having it X-rayed this morning.

Essex had five minutes of its second innings before lunch.

Loxton and Bill Johnston carried on with the new ball after Miller had bowled one over and left the field.

Ian Johnson replaced Loxton and bowled Cray with his first ball.

Barnes relieved Bill Johnston at the other end and bowled a maiden to Dodds.

Barnes then limped off the field, and Bradman had to call on Essex for a substitute. Rist came on to field.

Barnes was fielding close to the wicket this morning when a ball hit him sharply on the foot. His leg later became painful.

Harvey, who was at the ground, later took Rist's place in the field.

Ian Johnson had Avery caught by Brown at silly mid-on, and then Toshack had Vigar caught and clean-bowled Dodds.

Horsfall and Ray Smith fell to successive balls from Ian Johnson, and Essex had lost six for 46.

The score was six for 90 at tea, with Pearce 31 and Peter Smith 11.

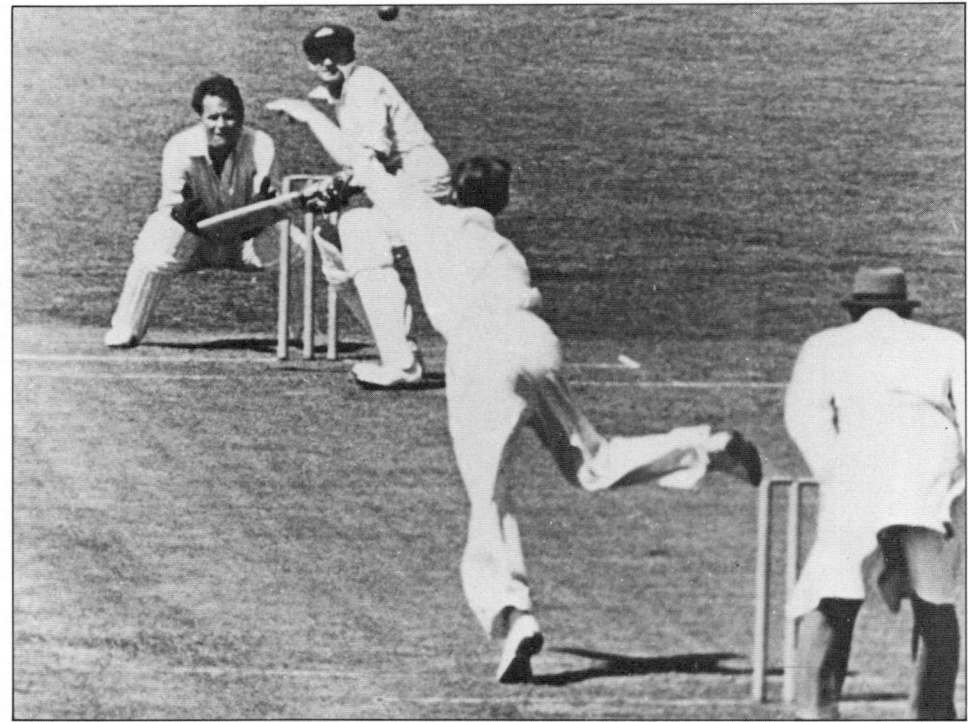

Peter Smith bowling to Bradman.

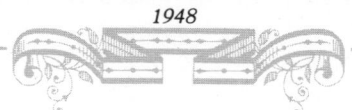

# There's something about the Aussies . . .

WHY ARE THE Australian cricketers different? Why is a Test Match against Australia different from a Test Match against any other country? And why do we *feel* that it is different?

Now, I am sure it is not only, or even basically, because the Australians are our senior Test opponents. If it were, then South African, West Indian and Indian cricket followers would not have this same feeling about the Australians to a greater degree than about the English teams—as they have.

No, it is the quality of "Australianism" which makes the difference. Historically, "Australianism" dates from that momentous day at the Oval in 1882 when England twice seemed to have the solitary Test Match of that season won, only for Massie, by his batting, and then Spofforth, by his bowling, to snatch it away in the face of all cricket probability and eleven great English cricketers. It has gone on through the forty-four Test Tours.

I remember, as a boy, hearing with steadily growing awe of the two Australian fast bowlers in Warwick Armstrong's 1921 team, Gregory and Macdonald, and of how they passed through English cricket like a scourge. More than human those two men seemed to me—almost devilish in their relentless destruction of English batting.

This feeling does not come from regular Australian victory; they have won sixty Tests to our fifty-five—and we have won twenty-one to their sixteen in England.

Australia has had her great players, certainly, but against their Bradman, Ponsford, Woodfull, Miller we can place Hammond, Hobbs, Sutcliffe and Compton. Grimmett and Mailey and O'Reilly took many wickets—but not one of them ever took so many in a single series as Maurice Tate's thirty-eight in 1925-26 in Australia.

## Hardly the Same Game!

The difference does not lie in comparative excellence in any department of the game but in the whole Australian *attitude* to cricket. Australian cricket is not the same game as English cricket.

Why should it be? The Australians come from a country at the opposite end of the world, their setting is different, their very atmosphere is different. Australia has her own character and that character is in her cricket because it is part of the life of her people.

This difference, this "Australianism," is not always admitted by those who follow cricket here. Some try to pretend that there is no difference between the cricket of the two countries. Others, over-conscious of the difference, have tried to capitalize it with stories of "crises" and "controversies" which ignore the essential *humanity* of the difference.

Let me try to capture that difference for you in one game.

On the Saturday of Whit weekend this year the Australians made 721 runs in a day against Essex. On Whit Monday Essex came out to bat: the Australian bowlers were at them like tigers.

Miller bowled faster and more grimly than he had done all the tour; the fielding was as tight as in a Test Match. There was going to be no nonsense about "giving Essex a chance."

## Barnes Glared and Waited

Things were grim indeed when Ray Smith came in. Five Essex wickets were down, one batsman, Bailey, unable to bat because of injury, and fifty not yet on the board. Toshack was bowling from the railway end. Sidney Barnes at silly mid-on was so close to the batsman that if Smith had held his bat out at full arm's stretch and Barnes had reached out his hand the two would have touched.

Ray Smith has in him a blend of courage and gaiety that cannot be quelled even by a deficit of almost six hundred runs and a Test attack against him. Almost at once he drove a ball from Toshack past Barnes's ear like a bullet for four. Barnes looked at him undisturbed. "You cain't drive me away," he said. Square, self-reliant and grim, he put his hands on his knees and glared at the batsman.

In Toshack's next over Ray Smith hit a half-volley straight on to Barnes's foot — from which it rebounded to the boundary! Barnes did not say a word.

Smith had scored twenty-five when he received another half-volley from Toshack. Ray hit that ball from Toshack like a ton of bricks, and it headed straight for Barnes. Barnes put up his hands to the ball. It forced them apart and struck against his chest. As it bounced off he darted out his right hand and caught it. Ray Smith, caught Barnes, bowled Toshack—twenty-five.

As Ray looked at him unbelievingly, Sidney Barnes said: "I told you you cain't drive me away," and he casually tossed the ball to Toshack.

The Australians bowled and fielded seriously, almost grimly, to the last Essex wicket, and they won by an innings and 451 runs. They never gave away a run, never relaxed; the field was always placed as tightly as it would stretch round the batsman.

The Australians play their hardest and they expect their opponents to do the same. Unless we are prepared to play as hard as the Australians, then we ought not to play Test cricket against them.

There has long been a custom in English cricket for the batsman to "give the bowler a chance" after he has scored a hundred. An Australian batsman merely takes guard afresh after the first hundred; of Bradman's 108 scores of over one hundred, thirty-seven have also been over two hundred.

The Australians set out to win Tests. There is a single-mindedness about their cricket — Lindwall, Loxton and Miller gave up football in the last Australian season so as to be certain of being fit for this tour of England.

Recall, too, that there is no full-time professionalism at cricket in Australia and that many of the men making this tour are doing so at a financial loss. There are strict rules against players being accompanied by their wives and against their broadcasting or writing.

They are here to play cricket and they will not be diverted from that purpose.

## Believe in the Impossible

We are faced with Australian batting, bowling, fielding, captaincy—and "Australianism."

And "Australianism" means single-minded determination to win—to win within the laws but, if necessary, to the last limit within them. It means that where the "impossible" is within the realms of what the human body can do, there are Australians who *believe* that they can do it. It means that they have never lost a match—particularly a Test Match—until the last run is scored or their last wicket has fallen.

Dear Daddy

2 HOLDEN STREET.
KENSINGTON PARK.
SOUTH AUSTRALIA.

Page 1

I are killing off my chooks and are stating all over again with sussex and blacks sussex are very good table birds. I have a new rooster he is a show bird but the.

Page 2

only thing that is rong with him is that he crows too early in the morning. we have eaten the two red ones for the same reason and as well we wanted some more food.

Page 3

I brought two new silver wine dots. they are only very young yet but when they grow up they are very good layers. Marulin Aunty jene and romer have come Marulin is ~~terribly~~ scared of ~~puppy~~ the

Page 4

pupps but is not a bit scared of sally I will fatten up a rooster and have it the day you come back. I hope you do very well in the Test Matches

~~Page~~ Page 5
Mummy is
going to let me listen in
on Friday night.
please daddy will you
bring me a watch
please can I have a
waterproof one with a
little leather case
that has a little click to
do it up. thankyou
I am trying very hard
Page 6
to be good and help
mummy with Shirley.
daddy please can I have
a two wheeler next
Xmas. be cause I can
ride a size 28 quite
easily. I am very ~~glad~~
~~you~~ made a ~~watch~~

century in the Test
match~~es~~. daddy I ~~know~~ I
want everything
but please can I have
for my birth day
a pellet gun, they arent
very dangerous
because they cant
~~~~ even kill a chook

Page 7

I hope you are well

daddy lots of love from
~~John daddy~~ X X XX X X XXX
X X X X X X X X X + + X X
X X X X X X X X X X X X X X
X X X X + X X X X X X X X X X X56

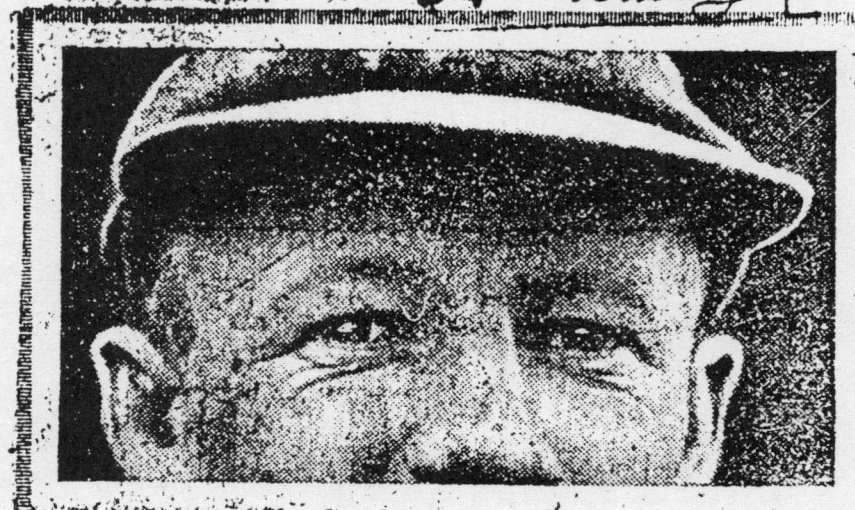

To Mr.

SOMEWHERE    playing
IN
ENGLAND

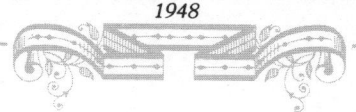

After an interval of ten years and the experience of a devastating war, the people of England welcomed the chance to see once again Test matches against Australia.

In the first of the series they blooded some youngsters who performed creditably and in due course became legendary figures in English cricket history.

Australia proved too strong but tremendous interest was kindled.

The following match against Yorkshire, played on a typical testing North of England pitch, tested Australia and attracted an enormous crowd.

The revival of peace time pleasures in a war torn country undoubtedly helped the morale of our kith and kin in the motherland.

*Don Bradman*

# Australia Names 13 For Test

Daily Telegraph Service

NOTTINGHAM, Wednesday. — Australia's team for the First Test, to begin at Trent Bridge tomorrow, will be chosen from these 13 players:

Bradman
Brown
Morris
Barnes
Miller
Hassett
Harvey
Tallon
Lindwall
Ring
Toshack
Johnson
Johnston

The final selection will be made just before the captains toss tomorrow.

The English Test selectors tonight dramatically added George Pope (Derbyshire) to the players from whom their Test side will be selected.

The panel now reads: Yardley (capt.), Edrich, Barnett, Hardstaff, Hutton, Washbrook, Compton, Wright, Evans, Bedser, Young, Laker, and Pope. Simpson will be 12th man.

The wicket is expected to be wet.

The forecast is for rain, with thunder.

Groundsmen will cover the wicket if rain falls today or tomorrow morning.

After the game begins the pitch cannot be covered.

Play each day will start at 11.30 a.m. (8.30 p.m., Sydney time) and end at 6.30 p.m (3.30 a.m., Sydney time)

## Barnes In Pain

Australian batsman Sid Barnes complained of stomach pains during practice this morning

Barnes is 9lb. underweight after a week's illness with food-poisoning.

He spent three days in bed while the Australians were in Sussex.

Barnes said stomach pains were worrying him at lunch-time, and he is resting in his room this afternoon

He looks very off-color

Inclusion in the English team of Douglas Wright, its main bowling hope, is in doubt.

Wright is suffering from lumbago, and his try-out at Lord's yesterday was a failure

## More Treatment

He managed a slow run up to the wicket, only with a painful effort, and could then bowl only at half-pace.

He had more treatment this morning, and later visited Lord's again

After this second practice he said he felt much better.

He will continue treatment today before he leaves for Nottingham, where he will have a final try-out tomorrow

If Wright cannot play, off-spin bowler J. Laker will probably replace him

# TEST BROADCASTS DIRECT FROM U.K.

"There will be nothing synthetic about Test broadcasts from England this time. Cricket commentaries and summaries will come from England, not from Australia," said ABC State sporting superintendent Ron Halcombe today.

During the tests, listeners would be able to listen to a ball-to-ball description of the play until 1.30 a.m. he said.

Programme arrangements made difficult the broadcasting of county matches, but short summaries of the play would probably be given at night.

At 6.25 each Test night there would be a five-minute summary before the start of play at 6.30.

A ball-to-ball description of play would follow until 6.45 p.m., when the broadcasts would close down until 7.15 p.m.

From 7.15 p.m. until 1.30 a.m. the description would be continuous except for lunch and afternoon tea breaks.

Country listeners to ABC regionals 6WA and 6GF would have the benefit of the same broadcasts.

At 9.15 p.m. tonight there would be a 15-minute summary of the first match played in England, against Worcester.

Bulk of the description would be given by prominent Australian cricketer and commentator Alan McGilvray and ABC Federal

Sporting Superintendent Dudley Leggett, who are both in England at present.

## Commercials

Because of programme and sponsor difficulties, commercial stations 6PR-6TZ and 6KY will not broadcast Test cricket.

Spokesmen for the stations said that, as it would be impossible to give as complete a coverage as the ABC, it was not worthwhile.

Two other commercials 6AM-6PM and 6IX-WD-MD reported that nothing had been finalised yet in the matter of Test broadcasts.

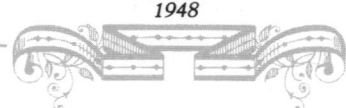

# Australia v England
## First Test Match

AUSTRALIA v ENGLAND, First Test Match, at Nottingham, 10, 11, 12, 14 and 15 June 1948.

| Australia | - First Innings | 509 |
| | - Second Innings | 98 for 2 wickets |
| England | - First Innings | 165 |
| | - Second Innings | 441 |

Australia won by 8 wickets.

| DON BRADMAN | - c. L. Hutton b. A.V. Bedser | 138 |
| (Captain) | - c. L. Hutton b. A.V. Bedser | 0 |

DON BRADMAN's first innings began at 73 for 1, at 12.50 p.m. on the second day, and he had scored 19 by the lunch interval.    He was at first uncomfortable against both A.V. Bedser and J.C. Laker, but later he played very soundly, though always exercising great care.    He reached 50 in an hour and forty minutes, and was 78 at the tea interval, having failed to add to his score in the last twenty-five minutes; his last 32 runs to his century took him eighty-six minutes, and the 100 took him three hours thirty-one minutes, a slow rate of scoring which was induced mainly by the defensive tactics and field-placing of the England bowlers.    By the close of play, after four hours forty minutes of watchful batting, he was 130 not out.    He lasted only another eight minutes next morning; when 132, he completed his 1,000 runs for the season.    In the third over he played an in-swinger into the hands of backward short-leg, with the score 305 for 5.    He hit ten fours, gave no chance, and, with A.L. Hassett, added 120 for the fifth wicket in two hours forty-three minutes.    His partnership of 120 with Hassett for the fifth wicket is a Test Match record for Australia against England in England.    This was the third English season in which he had been the first batsman, English or Australian, to reach 1,000 runs.    His 138 was his fifth successive Test Match innings of over 50, a record for Australia.

Despite a fighting recovery by England, Australia had ample time to make 98 to win on the last afternoon, but Bradman, who came in at 38 for 1, was out thirteen minutes later to his tenth ball, at 48 for 2, in the same way as in the first innings, caught at backward short-leg, for his first 'duck' in a Test Match in England.

## England

| L. Hutton b Miller | 3 | — b Miller | 74 |
| C. Washbrook c Brown b Lindwall | 6 | — c Tallon b Miller | 1 |
| W. J. Edrich b Johnston | 18 | — c Tallon b Johnson | 13 |
| D. C. S. Compton b Miller | 19 | — hit wkt b Miller | 184 |
| J. Hardstaff c Miller b Johnston | 0 | — c Hassett b Toshack | 43 |
| C. J. Barnett b Johnston | 8 | — c Miller b Johnston | 6 |
| N. W. D. Yardley lbw b Toshack | 3 | — c and b Johnston | 22 |
| T. G. Evans c Morris b Johnston | 12 | — c Tallon b Johnston | 50 |
| J. C. Laker c Tallon b Miller | 63 | — b Miller | 4 |
| A. V. Bedser c Brown b Johnston | 22 | — not out | 3 |
| J. A. Young not out | 1 | — b Johnston | 9 |
| B 5, l-b 5 | 10 | B 12, l-b 17, n-b 3 | 32 |
| | 165 | | 441 |

## Australia

| S. G. Barnes c Evans b Laker | 62 | — not out | 64 |
| A. R. Morris b Laker | 31 | — b Bedser | 9 |
| D. G. Bradman c Hutton b Bedser | 138 | — c Hutton b Bedser | 0 |
| K. R. Miller c Edrich b Laker | 0 | | |
| W. A. Brown lbw b Yardley | 17 | | |
| A. L. Hassett b Bedser | 137 | — not out | 21 |
| I. W. Johnson b Laker | 21 | | |
| D. Tallon c and b Young | 10 | | |
| R. R. Lindwall c Evans b Yardley | 42 | | |
| W. A. Johnston not out | 17 | | |
| E. R. H. Toshack lbw b Bedser | 19 | | |
| B 9, l-b 4, w 1, n-b 1 | 15 | L-b 2, w 1, n-b 1 | 4 |
| | 509 | Two wkts. | 98 |

## Australia Bowling

| | O. | M. | R. | W. | O. | M. | R. | W. |
|---|---|---|---|---|---|---|---|---|
| Lindwall | 13 | 5 | 30 | 1 | | | | |
| Miller | 19 | 8 | 38 | 3 | 44 | 10 | 125 | 4 |
| Johnston | 25 | 11 | 36 | 5 | 59 | 12 | 147 | 4 |
| Toshack | 14 | 8 | 28 | 1 | 33 | 14 | 60 | 1 |
| Johnson | 5 | 1 | 19 | 0 | 42 | 15 | 66 | 1 |
| Morris | 3 | 1 | 4 | 0 | | | | |
| Barnes | | | | | 5 | 2 | 11 | 0 |

## England Bowling

| | O. | M. | R. | W. | O. | M. | R. | W |
|---|---|---|---|---|---|---|---|---|
| Edrich | 18 | 1 | 72 | 0 | 4 | 0 | 20 | 0 |
| Bedser | 44.2 | 12 | 113 | 3 | 14.3 | 4 | 46 | 2 |
| Barnett | 17 | 5 | 36 | 0 | | | | |
| Young | 60 | 28 | 79 | 1 | 10 | 3 | 28 | 0 |
| Laker | 55 | 14 | 138 | 4 | | | | |
| Compton | 5 | 0 | 24 | 0 | | | | |
| Yardley | 17 | 6 | 32 | 2 | | | | |

### FALL OF WICKETS

ENGLAND—First Innings:

| 1 | 2 | 3 | 4 | 5 | 6 | 7 | 8 | 9 |
|---|---|---|---|---|---|---|---|---|
| 9 | 15 | 46 | 46 | 48 | 60 | 74 | 74 | 163 |

ENGLAND—Second Innings:

| 1 | 2 | 3 | 4 | 5 | 6 | 7 | 8 | 9 |
|---|---|---|---|---|---|---|---|---|
| 5 | 39 | 150 | 243 | 264 | 321 | 405 | 413 | 423 |

AUSTRALIA—First Innings:

| 1 | 2 | 3 | 4 | 5 | 6 | 7 | 8 | 9 |
|---|---|---|---|---|---|---|---|---|
| 73 | 121 | 121 | 185 | 305 | 338 | 365 | 472 | 476 |

AUSTRALIA—Second Innings:

| 1 | 2 |
|---|---|
| 38 | 48 |

Umpires: F. Chester and E. Cooke.

*Bradman Family
Listen In*

# LAKER-BEDSER GIVE SOME HOPE TO ENGLAND

### *From Arthur Mailey*

**Nottingham, Thursday.—Thanks to a plucky ninth-wicket partnership by Jim Laker and Alec Bedser yielding 89 runs, England is in a position to fight back against Australia in the First Test.**

*TEST CAPTAIN'S WIFE, Mrs. Don Bradman, with their children, Shirley and John, listening to a broadcast of Test play at their Kensington Park home last night.*

The partnership began in poverty against a very hostile opposition, lifted the score from 74 to 163, and brought England back into the game.

The moral effect of the Bedser-Laker innings is important as far as the second innings is concerned.

**If English batsmen ever thought Australian bowling was too hostile, this partnership should do much to dissipate that complex.**

## Annoying Hold-Up

Australia's inability to break the annoying partnership was another instance of history repeating itself.

On many occasions this tour the Australian attack has been held up by relative batting nonentities.

**Some might say Bradman did not want to bat in the fading light and deliberately kept the batsmen in.**

This was not the case today. The placing of the field and the choice of tactics of bowlers showed positively that the Australians tried hard to dismiss the tailenders.

Further proof is that Bedser and Laker scored valuable runs too quickly, and these runs may be difficult for Australia to get if overnight rain should present Australian batsmen with a sticky wicket.

**In desperation, Bradman even tried Morris as a bowler—and he seldom bowls in any class of cricket.**

Miller and Johnston, the two bowlers who had earlier embarrassed the cream of England's batting, never looked more punishable than when this somewhat rabbitish pair was in action.

## Johnston's Effort

Johnston, earlier, had bowled magnificently, compelling the recognised batsmen to play every ball, which swerved viciously.

Hutton was confident when he opened for England, in spite of bad visibility.

When bowled by Miller he seemed to lose sight of the ball against the murky pavilion background of darkish red tiles; similar in color to the ball.

I don't know what happened in the dressing rooms when rain interrupted play, but for a considerable time when rain was not falling the players did not appear.

This, of course, was an advantage to the Australians.

**I felt Yardley could have sought an earlier resumption. His generosity was more apparent than his strategy.**

Yardley, whose selection had hinged partly on his capacity to fight back, faced an unenviable situation.

He batted stolidly and doggedly, but made little headway.

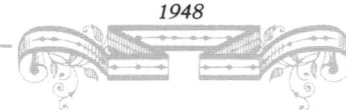

# BRADMAN'S CENTURY IN 1st TEST

# Australia 293 For 4

*From ARTHUR MAILEY*

**TRENT BRIDGE, Friday.—Bradman, 130 not out, today put Australia well in front in the First Test.**

**With Hassett (46 not out) he took the score from 184 for four to 293 for four at stumps.**

Off-spin bowler Laker, last-minute English selection, took three wickets for 77—Barnes (62), Morris (32), and Miller (0).

Yardley took the other wicket, getting Brown leg-before for 17.

Australian batsmen, although facing an English total of only 165, were subdued by accurate English bowling.

The wicket dried out perfectly overnight, and was unmarked from yesterday's play.

Barnes and Morris started confidently enough, although Morris early showed some concern facing Bedser.

Barnes was always neat and sure.

## Barnett "Fishing"

When Barnett was bowling to him, the situation resembled fishing with a set-line, with the fisherman relying on his bait rather than his skill to land his fish.

Four men in a circle on the legside waited patiently for Barnes to, mis-hit one of the balls aimed at his legs.

Young made his Test debut against Australia by presenting Morris with a four off his first ball.

This was a great relief to Morris, who had been batting against Bedser and Barnett for an hour for 17 runs.

At the other end, Laker, who came into the team when Douglas Wright withdrew because of lumbago, also made his Test debut against Australia.

He sent down an offering of gentle-looking, but somewhat sinister off-breaks.

Although runs came a little more quickly than when Bedser and Barnett were bowling, there was something more imaginative and more thoughtful about this spin attack.

The batsmen were compelled to use their feet to counteract spin and flight.

Morris was the first to discover that Laker was not as innocent as he looked.

He mistimed a ball which rolled against the stumps and dislodged a bail.

Morris had batted patiently for about 95 minutes.

Bradman's appearance caused a change of strategy.

Bedser replaced Young, and three men who had been waiting at midfield for an indiscreet stroke from Barnes came up on the leg side to within whispering distance of the suspicious Bradman.

These tactics disturbed him.

He was obviously ill at ease, and scored once in 20 minutes.

**He nearly chopped balls from Bedser and Laker into his wicket.**

This was one of the grimmest batting periods I have ever seen, Bradman go through.

He was greatly relieved when Yardley unaccountably removed the suicide squad.

The English attack was definitely on top.

Shortly before lunch, with Edrich and Compton bowling, a less relentless spirit came into the attack.

Yardley loosened his field, and runs came a little more frequently.

When, shortly after lunch, Laker had Barnes caught behind, and then dismissed Miller, English supporters were happier than they had been for seasons.

Bradman and Brown settled in doggedly.

They painstakingly took the total to 184.

Then Yardley put himself on.

His fourth ball shot through low, and Brown who had played a defensive shot, was leg before.

Bradman and Hassett played as cautiously as if the team needed 600.

After tea both batsmen scored much more freely.

Bradman, who had seemed tired at tea, hit the ball harder and reached his century with his seventh four.

The bowlers were obviously tired, but towards the end of the day Bradman and Hassett obviously concentrated on keeping their wickets up.

In the last half-hour they scored slowly.

Bradman had played perhaps his most determined innings

# WILD OUTBURST OF PROTEST AT MILLER'S BOWLING

### From Tom Goodman

NOTTINGHAM, June 13.—Australian fast bowler Keith Miller was loudly hooted during his last two overs at Trent Bridge yesterday after he had struck England's opener Len Hutton on the left shoulder with one of two short-pitched bumpers.

As stumps were drawn, a large section of the crowd ran on to the field and staged a demonstration against Miller as he walked up the pavilion steps. Many of the members in the pavilion area joined in the hooting. Police hurried to head off the demonstrators.

With two days left for play in the first Test, England has lost two wickets in its second innings for 121 runs, and is still 223 runs short of Australia's first innings score of 509.

## EFFORT TO UNSETTLE HUTTON

When the disturbance took place, Miller, with a reduced run, was bowling at fast-medium pace with two short-leg fieldsmen.

It was plain that Bradman had kept Miller on in the concluding stages in an attempt to unsettle Hutton.

His wicket would probably have sealed England's fate.

There had been some mild barracking just previously when Miller dropped a couple of balls short.

On one occasion when Hutton ducked away from the ball, Miller motioned to the crowd as if making a hook shot, thus indicating what the batsman might have done with a short ball.

The crowd roared with delight when Hutton, in Miller's next over, hit three beautiful fours.

The early barracking had come mostly from a number of young men, but people of all ages joined the "booing" when Hutton was hit in Miller's last over.

### Game Held Up

When the hooting continued as he began his run up for the next delivery, Miller stopped half-way to the bowling crease and waited for the noise to subside.

Hooting broke out again as he resumed his run, but he completed bowling.

Miller's short balls at his reduced pace and with the field placing as it was were quite legitimate.

Obviously he bowled in an attempt to unsettle Hutton, who had succumbed to him on several occasions during the tour of Australia in 1946-7.

Miller displays great nervous energy and undoubtedly the crowd disturbed him yesterday.

The demonstration was featured on front pages of English Sunday newspapers and referred to in B.B.C. broadcasts.

Some of the comments were:

**Arthur Gilligan,** former English Test captain, in a B.B.C. broadcast condemned the booing and was particularly critical of those in the members' stand who had joined the demonstration.

He added: "It is ridiculous to start this nonsense. It makes me furious."

**Jack Hobbs,** in the "Sunday Express," writes: "It was a pity the day ended on an unpleasant note.

"It had been a keen struggle with Hutton and Compton fighting with backs to the wall."

**George Duckworth** says in the "Empire News": "To me it seemed a bit of a tall order that Lindwall did not field after his sprightly batting."

That Hutton quickly recovered from the blow on the shoulder was shown when he picked the last ball of the over off his toes and turned it to the fine-leg boundary—one of the most brilliant shots of the match.

It remains to be seen whether the crowd on Monday will display any reactions to Saturday's incidents.

Since the bodyline sensation, in which Notts bowlers Larwood and Voce were central figures, the Nottingham ground has provided some turbulent scenes for Australian players.

In 1934, when Australia was playing Notts, Voce operated with a bodyline field in the first innings, and the Australian captain, Woodfull, protested.

Voce was withdrawn from the Notts team for the second innings.

It was announced that Voce had injured a shin and the crowd vigorously hooted the Australians when they took the field.

In 1938 J. H. Fingleton, who was barracked for slow batting in the Test match, sat on the pitch until the disorder subsided.

On Friday there had been some mild barracking of Bradman and Hassett for their slow batting, and Bradman was irritated by this.

His demeanour showed that he considered England's defensive bowling at that stage was responsible.

With two out for 121 after two hours' batting, Hutton, 63 (11 fours), and Dennis Compton, 36, will resume to-morrow on a pitch which late yesterday showed slight signs of wear.

With off-spinner Ian Johnson. in particular, threatening trouble and two days left for play, England is in a desperate situation.

The Australians took the field yesterday without fast-bowler Ray Lindwall who, with his injured right leg strapped, had batted for nearly two hours and had scored 42.

He was replaced in the field by the twelfth man, Neil Harvey, who is a brilliant fieldsman.

This caused some comment.

### Johnson Turns Ball
(Australian Associated Press.)

Unlike England's spinners, Laker and Young, Ian Johnson was able to make the ball turn on an easy pitch when England began its second innings.

In two and a half hours at the wicket before stumps, England lost two for 121 and still needs 223 to avoid an innings defeat.

Australia was all out in its first innings for 509 in reply to England's 165.

Bradman batted for only eight minutes yesterday before he was out for 138. He batted 289 minutes and hit 10 fours.

He became the first batsman to score 1,000 runs in England this season.

He beat Jack Robertson, of Middlesex, by 13 minutes.

The Australian tail wagged freely after lunch when Hassett completed his century.

He was out for 137, made in 351 minutes. He hit 20 fours and a six.

### Early Blood

Miller, as in England's first innings, had an early success when Washbrook was caught by Tallon after only five minutes.

Johnson dealt another sharp blow by dismissing Edrich with the score at 39.

Hutton meanwhile uneasily faced Bill Johnston and Ian Johnson.

Each gained assurance when Johnson was relieved after 14 overs, five of which had been maidens, for 15 runs.

Hutton luckily snicked a ball from Bill Johnston past Miller in slips to bring up England's 50.

Compton immediately survived a confident lbw appeal by Johnson.

When Miller returned to bowl medium-pace off-spinners, Hutton immediately ran into the fifties with three beautiful boundaries.

Miller in his last two overs of the day made the ball lift sharply from a good length.

As though by signal, the crowd began a demonstration as Compton blocked one high up.

He bowled his last over to a continuous chorus.

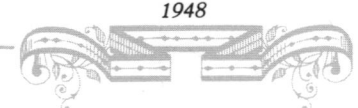

# Compton's Dismissal From Bumper And Duck By Bradman: Thrills Of Test

### From TOM GOODMAN

NOTTINGHAM, June 15.—Denis Compton's great innings came to a sensational, and rather tragic, ending when at 1.18 p.m. to-day he fell over his wicket in trying to avoid a violent bumper from Miller.

A later sensation at Trent Bridge to-day, the fifth and last day of the first Test of this series, was when Don Bradman was caught out before he had scored.

Australia won by eight wickets, two wickets having fallen before the 98 runs needed for outright victory were obtained. England's second innings had yielded 441 runs.

A few shouts were directed at Miller when Compton lost his wicket, but the English captain, Norman Yardley, did not support the implied criticism.

Yardley said:—

"Compton's innings was one of the greatest fighting knocks I have ever seen.

"I have no complaints about the manner of his dismissal. It was just 'one of those things.'"

Umpire Chester said he had given Compton out from square-leg because it was not possible for Umpire Cook to say whether Compton had completed his stroke.

The light was comparatively good when Compton was dismissed. He had scored 184.

The ball which Miller bowled was only his second bumper of this innings, and certainly more pronounced than the one he had sent down to Compton yesterday.

It reared sharply, and Compton, trying to hook the high-flier, failed to connect, and over-balanced.

Compton stumbled backwards, opened his legs wide in a desperate attempt to avoid the stumps, but fell back across them, and finished full length behind the shattered wicket.

There was an immediate appeal to Umpire Chester at square-leg, and Chester raised his finger.

Compton was out "hit wicket."

He hurried from the field a picture of disappointment and annoyance.

There were some shouts directed against Miller from the uncovered portions of the ground and further booing when he resumed bowling, but the demonstration soon subsided.

In three successive Test innings, Bradman was out to the Bedser–Hutton leg-trap. Here is Don's dismissal in Australia's second innings at Trent Bridge — for 0!

# Australia v England
## Second Test Match

A splendid all round team effort won the second Test for Australia at Lord's by the big margin of 409 runs. Even that did not reflect the complete story because Australia lost only 7 wickets in her second innings.

To me it was a most gratifying finish because I would never again play a Test there.

A handsome victory over Surrey preceded the third Test at Manchester where, as had been the case for decades, the weather was the victor.

We were deeply concerned over the terrible injury suffered by Barnes fielding at short leg. Fortunately he made a complete recovery but the incident highlighted the dangers to close-in fieldsmen. The miracle is that more serious injuries don't occur.

The draw at Manchester sealed the fate of the Ashes once more. And so to Leeds.

*Don Bradman*

---

AUSTRALIA v ENGLAND, Second Test Match, at Lord's, 24, 25, 26, 28 and 29 June 1948.

| Australia | - First Innings | 350 |
| | - Second Innings | 460 for 7 wickets dec. |
| England | - First Innings | 215 |
| | - Second Innings | 186 |

Australia won by 409 runs.

| DON BRADMAN | - c. L. Hutton b. A.V. Bedser | 38 |
| (Captain) | - c. W.J. Edrich b. A.V. Bedser | 89 |

DON BRADMAN's first innings began at 3 for 1, soon after the start of play, on a rather damp and green wicket and in a heavy atmosphere, and for the first hour he was most uncertain. After making 35 in an hour and forty-eight minutes before lunch, he appeared to have settled down; but soon afterwards he gave yet another catch to L. Hutton at backward short-leg off A.V. Bedser's in-swinger - the third time in successive innings in Test Matches that he had failed to time his leg-glance properly against Bedser's bowling. He made 38 in an hour and fifty-five minutes and helped to raise the score to 87 for 2.

His second innings was much better; he went in at 2.52 p.m. on the third afternoon, at 122 for 1, and though he was not comfortable at first against J.C. Laker or Bedser, he soon settled down to a long partnership with S.G. Barnes. He resisted the temptation to glance Bedser's in-swingers, playing them mainly with his pads, and this checked his rate of scoring; however, he was 50 at the tea interval, having reached 50 in the last over after ninety-eight minutes' batting, and looked certain to reach his century when Bedser took his wicket for the sixth time in successive innings, and for the fifth time in successive Test Match innings. This time he was caught in the slips.

This was the fourteenth successive Test Match v. England (in which he batted), in which he made at least 50 in one innings or the other - an achievement of extraordinary consistency.

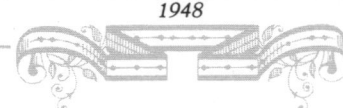

## Australia

| | 1st | 2nd | |
|---|---|---|---|
| S. G. Barnes c Hutton b Coxon | 0 | c Washbrook b Yardley | 141 |
| A. R. Morris c Hutton b Coxon | 105 | b Wright | 62 |
| D. G. Bradman c Hutton b Bedser | 38 | c Edrich b Bedser | 89 |
| A. L. Hassett b Yardley | 47 | b Yardley | 0 |
| K. R. Miller lbw b Bedser | 4 | c Bedser b Laker | 74 |
| W. A. Brown lbw b Yardley | 24 | c Evans b Coxon | 32 |
| I. W. Johnson c Evans b Edrich | 4 | not out | 9 |
| D. Tallon c Yardley b Bedser | 53 | | |
| R. R. Lindwall b Bedser | 15 | st Evans b Laker | 25 |
| W. A. Johnston st Evans b Wright | 29 | | |
| E. R. H. Toshack not out | 20 | | |
| B 3, l-b 7, n-b 1 | 11 | B 22, l-b 5, n-b 1 | 28 |
| | 350 | Seven wkts., dec. | 460 |

## England

| | 1st | 2nd | |
|---|---|---|---|
| L. Hutton b Johnson | 20 | c Johnson b Lindwall | 13 |
| C. Washbrook c Tallon b Lindwall | 8 | c Tallon b Toshack | 37 |
| W. J. Edrich b Lindwall | 5 | c Johnson b Toshack | 2 |
| D. C. S. Compton c Miller b Johnston | 53 | c Miller b Johnston | 29 |
| H. E. Dollery b Lindwall | 0 | b Lindwall | 37 |
| N. W. D. Yardley b Lindwall | 44 | b Toshack | 11 |
| A. Coxon c and b Johnson | 19 | lbw b Toshack | 0 |
| T. G. Evans c Miller b Johnston | 9 | not out | 24 |
| J. C. Laker c Tallon b Johnson | 28 | b Lindwall | 0 |
| A. V. Bedser b Lindwall | 9 | c Hassett b Johnston | 9 |
| D. V. P. Wright not out | 13 | c Lindwall b Toshack | 4 |
| L-b 3, n-b 4 | 7 | B 16, l-b 4 | 20 |
| | 215 | | 186 |

### England Bowling

| | O. | M. | R. | W. | O. | M. | R. | W. |
|---|---|---|---|---|---|---|---|---|
| Bedser | 43 | 14 | 100 | 4 | 34 | 6 | 112 | 1 |
| Coxon | 35 | 10 | 90 | 2 | 28 | 3 | 82 | 1 |
| Edrich | 8 | 0 | 43 | 1 | 2 | 0 | 11 | 0 |
| Wright | 21.3 | 8 | 54 | 1 | 19 | 4 | 69 | 1 |
| Laker | 7 | 3 | 17 | 0 | 31.2 | 6 | 111 | 2 |
| Yardley | 15 | 4 | 35 | 2 | 13 | 4 | 36 | 2 |
| Compton | | | | | 3 | 0 | 11 | 0 |

### Australia Bowling

| | O. | M. | R. | W. | O. | M. | R. | W. |
|---|---|---|---|---|---|---|---|---|
| Lindwall | 27.4 | 7 | 70 | 5 | 23 | 9 | 61 | 3 |
| Johnston | 22 | 4 | 43 | 2 | 33 | 15 | 62 | 2 |
| Johnson | 35 | 13 | 72 | 3 | 2 | 1 | 3 | 0 |
| Toshack | 18 | 11 | 23 | 0 | 20.1 | 6 | 40 | 5 |

### FALL OF WICKETS

AUSTRALIA—First Innings:

| 1 | 2 | 3 | 4 | 5 | 6 | 7 | 8 | 9 |
|---|---|---|---|---|---|---|---|---|
| 3 | 87 | 166 | 173 | 216 | 225 | 246 | 275 | 320 |

AUSTRALIA—Second Innings:

| 1 | 2 | 3 | 4 | 5 | 6 | 7 |
|---|---|---|---|---|---|---|
| 122 | 296 | 296 | 329 | 416 | 445 | 460 |

ENGLAND—First Innings:

| 1 | 2 | 3 | 4 | 5 | 6 | 7 | 8 | 9 |
|---|---|---|---|---|---|---|---|---|
| 17 | 32 | 46 | 46 | 133 | 134 | 145 | 186 | 197 |

ENGLAND—Second Innings:

| 1 | 2 | 3 | 4 | 5 | 6 | 7 | 8 | 9 |
|---|---|---|---|---|---|---|---|---|
| 42 | 52 | 65 | 106 | 133 | 133 | 141 | 141 | 158 |

Umpires: C. N. Woolley and D. Davies.

DAY AND NIGHT TEST QUEUE

ADMISSION INCLUDING TAX 40

**DAY—Bill Davies.**
*First man in.*

**NIGHT: Part of the queue at midnight.**

To-day's Test Match queue outside Lord's started forming yesterday—at 10.30 a.m. and by midnight more than 100 enthusiasts had arrived. Some bedded down and others prepared to sit the night out on camp stools and blankets.

First man in was 60-year-old Bill Davies, of Camberwell. Bill was not taking any chances. In the last Test match played at Lord's he was just about to buy his ticket when the "ground full" notice was hoisted and he had to go disappointed away.

So Bill started early: bought a supply of cigarettes and was promised a hot meal in the night to be delivered by his family. "I don't care if it rains," he said, "I'm here to stay."

# AUSTRALIANS 7-258

# Bradman Out To Bedser Trap

LONDON, June 24.—England's bowlers took the honours in the first day's play of the second Test at Lord's, and at stumps Australia had lost seven for 258.

Bradman again fell to the Bedser-Hutton leg-trap and was out for 38. A brilliant 105 by Morris saved Australia after Barnes had gone for a "duck."

It was the third time Hutton had caught Bradman off Bedser's bowling in Bradman's three Test innings.

Jack Young was omitted from England's team and Emmett made 12th man. Australia's team was unchanged from that which won the first Test at Nottingham.

## LUCK OF TOSS CHANGES
### From DENZIL BATCHELOR

To-day it was the Don's turn to be lucky.

After enough cameramen to cover a Royal wedding had photographed the half-crown tails uppermost, Bradman waved to the Australian balcony and patted his shin.

Morris and Barnes dived for the dressing room and reappeared in pads in time which would have done credit to quick change artists.

Ghoulish oracles began to quote the highest scores ever made in a Lord's Test.

Bedser's opening gave these cheerful pessimists fresh heart.

He was bowling hectoringly —the only stroke that could be shaped at him was a respectful push along the carpet towards the hip-bath hands of Tom Dollery at mid-off.

### COXON'S TRIUMPH

To Coxon fell the first success of the day—a triumph glorious as the capture of a standard in battle.

Barnes caressed towards fine leg an in-swinger that snapped like elastic from the pitch, and Hutton swooped on the catch like a hawk on a feeble sparrow.

Bradman came in to escape being bowled by the width off the seam on the ball.

Then he survived an optimistic appeal for lbw from the tall rangy Coxon, whose lean face was impassive. but purposeful as a chasing greyhound's.

Bradman continued to alarm and thrill.

Twice in one over from Bedser came the fatal flick to leg which has succeeded the hook in popularity as a method of suicide among Australian batsmen.

When Edrich replaced Coxon, Bradman played the most speculative stroke of his career since he swished at a golf ball with a stick in his back garden at Bowral.

The hook was aimed to pick off the five film cameras on the roof of the tavern behind mid-wicket, but the ball floated over the slips to where a deep third man could not have failed to catch it—if there had been a deep third man.

The English fielding was terrier-keen, but the throwing-in does not compare with the Australian, where the ball travels from outfield to wicket-keeper with the precision of a zip fastener being snapped home.

Arthur Morris defended with unruffled skill. The middle of his white blade was decorated with brown circles, honourable scars of war earned by stemming the English attack at its boldest and best.

Once in a while Morris emitted a hearty drive, but it was left to Bradman to carry the battle to the enemy.

The little Australian danced down the pitch—two skips and a slash—to rocket Laker far beyond long-off.

It had been a stern two hours up to lunch, with Australia's lost ground bravely retrieved.

## LEG GLIDE AGAIN FATAL

Once again it was a neat glide to fine leg that encompassed the downfall of Bradman.

It is a stroke alluring as hashish, and as destructive.

The howl of acclamation was in the air almost before Hutton's hands had engulfed the cosy catch.

It was a wicket Bedser had earned with bitter toil.

He had kept at his enemy's throat all through the early overs.

Only a charmed life had preserved Bradman then through a crisis in which the most genial diagnostician with the blandest bedside manner, laying his hand on his heart, must have warned the relatives to prepare for the worst.

Now he had cut him off in flourishing middle life.

The contest was evenly poised again, and seemed to be swinging England's way.

### MORRIS OPENS UP

By mid-afternoon Morris's lifetime of prudence was beginning to pay rich dividends.

He dealt with Yardley on his merits, which were not considerable.

He sent a roaring pull—one of his typical full-blooded shots—skipping the ropes at mid-wicket. To prove that his bat was as subtle as an Oriental scimitar as well as doughty as a broadsword, he cleft a late-cut so fine that he might have been dividing a hair in two.

Beside him Hassett was an automaton.

His runs came—at longish intervals—from restrained leg glances and dabs through slips from Coxon and Bedser as they strove to impart some special diabolism to the new ball.

Morris went to 90 with a leg-glide from Bedser which all Australian batsmen should be set to copy a hundred times before breakfast as an imposition.

It was no mere slip or flick, but went to boundary with the centre of the bat, urging onward the flow of the out-swinger.

Morris's hundred came from an effortless cover-drive. one of three elegant boundaries embellishing a perfectly good over from Coxon.

The left-hander was neatly pocketed in the gully by Hutton with the flavour of his century still sweet in the mouth.

A fourth wicket by tea was needed to swing the game England's way.

It came in a strange manner.

Hassett had cut a ball from Coxon into and out of Bedser's hands at third man, and there was a feeling in the air that the neglected chance had spelt doom for England, but Bedser was to atone in his own way.

### UNHAPPY MILLER

The unfortunate Miller, never shaping like a batsman, had been frequently peppered about the thighs.

Now he hobbled across the wicket with bat in the air, was hit on the back of the leg, and, on turning round, found himself adjudged lbw.

By tea the pull was still on and no one could say how the tug-of-war would go.

Morris and Bedser had, of course, been the anchormen of two authentic Grecian teams.

# No Excuses For England

## DRAW, OR DEFEAT?

### From Arthur Mailey

*Lord's, Friday.—No excuses can be found for England's failure in the second Test at Lord's today.*

The pitch was easy and less lively than when the Australians batted.

**Reason for England's failure was simply inability to play fastish swing bowling.**

With all due credit to Bill Johnston, who bowled really well, it's just as well for England that Keith Miller was unable to bowl because of a strained side.

With his speed to supplement that of Lindwall, the Australian fast attack might have brought complete disaster.

### Needed 450

As it is. England now has little chance of winning. However, by avoiding the follow-on England may be able to make a drawn game of it.

England needed to make 450 in their first innings to insure themselves against the disadvantage of batting on a much-worn pitch.

**Although I felt that Lindwall bowled no faster than usual, he was much too fast for most of the batsmen.**

Had Lindwall used intimidatory tactics or bowled bumpers, there might have been some excuse for England, but almost every ball was of good length or a half-volley, and gave the impression, as on previous occasions when Miller bowled, that England's leading batsmen have lost the art of dealing effectively with fast bowling.

This, too, might apply to the Australians if they were facing Lindwall and Miller.

### Beautiful Ball

While Lindwall was resting the Englishmen batted confidently.

**When he bowled after tea with the new ball he dismissed Yardley with a beautiful ball that must have swung a foot.**

A useful partnership between Laker and Coxon saved the follow-on for England. This stand may mean the difference between England losing, or making a drawn game of the Test

Had those runs not been scored, Bradman would have had the option of sending England in again, and would have exercised that option had overnight rain turned the reasonably easy pitch into a sticky one.

Australia has benefited from fielding that has been much superior to England's.

The Australians h a v e dropped no catches and their ground work has been splendid

Bedser was England's outstanding bowler, but was not supported fully by the fieldsmen or other bowlers.

An efficient slow leg spin bowler might have dissipated Australia's tail-end more quickly. but since Yardley doesn't seem to possess one. batsmen in the second flight were allowed to score runs against medium pacers with considerable comfort.

# BEDSER ONCE AGAIN GETS BRADMAN

### (FROM TRUTH'S SPECIAL REPRESENTATIVE)

**LORD'S, Saturday.—At stumps today Australia, with four for 343 in its second innings, had an iron grip on the second Test. Barnes compiled a brilliant 141 after an early life, and Bedser, for the fourth time in the series, dismissed Bradman (89). England was all out for 215, a first innings deficit of 135.**

Gates were closed at 10.50 with the crowd packing every vantage point inside t h e ground

After 25 minutes in which the last wicket had added eight runs today, Lindwall bowled Bedser.

England was all out for 215 —135 runs behind on the first innings.

Lindwall had been the destroyer and finished with the fine figures of five for 70 from 27.4 overs, including seven maidens.

Morris and Barnes opened Australia's second innings to England's fast-medium attack, Bedser and Coxon.

Both shaped confidently and Barnes cracked Bedser for four through the cover field.

The bright opening posted 15 runs in 12 minutes, then Coxon appealed confidently for l.b.w. against Barnes.

A complete change was made at 28, Edrich and Wright taking over the attack

Six runs came from Wright's first over including four byes. Morris reached 24 with a neat late cut off a rising ball from Edrich. Barnes, with less of the strike and batting at a slower tempo than his partner, was 14.

Runs came at an alarmingly fast rate for England and 50 was posted in 49 minutes.

Yardley, worried by the confident batting, elected to rapidly switch his bowlers, and Laker came on.

**The move should have been crowned with success, for Barnes was beaten neck and crop when he stepped out to drive Laker, but 'keeper Evans fumbled. Barnes regained his crease, and a golden stumping chance was lost.**

### Fast Scoring

Wright's bowling was anything but accurate. A full toss was driven out near the fence by Morris and the next delivery, a no-ball, was hit for six, also by Morris.

Those scoring shots took Morris to 40, Barnes 25, and Australia none for 73.

The first maiden of the innings was bowled by Wright to Morris after 70 minutes play. In itself that fact was an indication of the batting freedom of the Australian openers.

Morris gave a hot chance to Yardley when he powerfully drove Laker, but Yardley barely stopped the ball and then wrung his hand in pain. Morris hit his sixth four off the last ball of the over.

At lunch Australia was 88, Barnes 33 and Morris 47.

Morris reached 51 (seven fours, six) with a slashing

boundary off Coxon's first over after lunch. He had been batting 90 minutes.

Barnes brought up the 100 (97 minutes) with a single.

England's position could be termed nothing else but desperate, and Yardley appeared at his wits' end to break the partnership.

Laker with his off-spinners was brought on in place of Coxon.

The wicket was definitely beginning to take spin, and Laker's first ball to Barnes turned back sharply.

Wright's bowling since lunch was accurate and he sent down a series of maidens.

Barnes reached 51 (four fours) with a boundary off Laker.

The strong opening partnership was broken by Wright who tricked Morris with his wrong 'un and clean bowled him for 62.

### Crowd's Buzz

Australia was one for 122 and Bradman followed.

**Yardley immediately set his leg trap for Bradman, placing three men close in on the leg for Wright's first ball.**

Bradman replied by forcing the ball wide of the leg trap for a single.

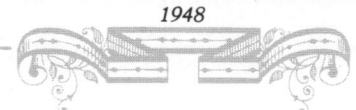
The leg trap complex for Bradman was completed by Yardley switching Bedser to the bowling crease in place of Laker and placing Hutton at short fine leg.

Three times the Bedser-Hutton trap had dismissed Bradman, and Yardley's pointed move brought a buzz of expectation from the capacity crowd and a dour tug at the cap by Bradman.

**Bradman's next three scoring shots were boundaries, a back cut and then two powerful pulls crashing through the cordon of leg fieldsmen to the fence.**

Bradman continued in punishing mood and again flashed a four through the leg trap off Bedser. He reached 19 with four fours, a two and a single, and Yardley took Bedser off and bowled himself.

Laker took the new ball and bowled to Bradman, who scattered the leg-side field with a pull which was brilliantly fielded by Compton on the fence. The shot brought up Australia's 151, Bradman 22, Barnes 57, and the innings had been in progress 155 minutes.

### Barnes Retreats

Barnes, set and seeing the ball every inch of the pitch, inexplicably adopted negative tactics and would not be tempted into anything approaching an offensive shot.

He was mildly barracked as he patted ball after ball back along the wicket.

Yardley brought Bedser back with the new ball, bowling to Bradman. The first ball beat him badly, but went through to Evans. The next ball, another in-swinger, again beat Bradman, but the third was snicked safely to the fence.

Bradman's sixth four was a carpet drive off Coxon past long-on.

Barnes broke his passive spell with a four off Coxon. The shot brought ironical applause, which Barnes playfully acknowledged by doffing his cap.

Barnes went to 78 with a powerful boundary pull off Wright. More fours by Barnes followed and it was Bradman in his 30's who was marking time.

Bradman brought up 200 in 210 minutes. Australia's position was impregnable.

Bradman spurted, and a succession of aggressive scoring shots took him to 50 (nine fours) in 95 minutes.

At tea Barnes was 93, Bradman 50, and Australia one for 217.

Barnes reached his carefully compiled century with a four from a full toss served up by Laker. His 102 included nine fours and it was his second Test century against England.

**Barnes opened his shoulders to Laker and hit him hard and high out of the ground for successive sixes.**

Compton bowled with the

score at one for 276. It was a desperation move by Yardley.

The partnership was eventually broken by Yardley, who tempted Barnes into a big hit and he was caught inches inside the boundary by Washbrook. Barnes' score was 141 (14 fours, two sixes) and his second wicket stand with Bradman added 175.

### MILLER HAS SORE SIDE

LORD'S, Saturday.—Australian team manager Keith Johnson denied that Test all-rounder Keith Miller was to be examined by a specialist before play in the second Test today. "Miller is not suffering from a strain, but there is a certain soreness in his side," Johnson said.

Washbrook split his finger taking the catch.

Hassett followed, shaped up to Yardley, was beaten neck and crop, and his off stump sent flying by the first ball. Australia three for 296.

The successes brought a roar of appreciation from the crowd.

Miller hit Wright for three to bring up 302.

Miller hit Yardley into the stand at square leg for six and the next ball for four.

Bedser for the fourth time in this series dismissed Bradman, but this time to a woeful stroke. Bradman, 89 (13 fours), disinterestedly hung out his bat to a ball outside the off stump and spooned a simple catch to Edrich.

Brown followed and scored three from the remainder of Bedser's over.

At stumps Miller was not out 22, Brown not out seven, Australia four for 343.

Bradman cuts a ball to third man, eluding the outstretched hand of Bill Edrich.

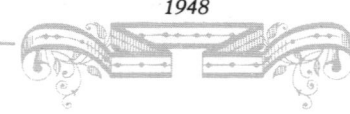

# HUTTON, EDRICH OUT EARLY

## Australia Declares At 7-460

LONDON, June 28.—England, needing 596 runs in nine hours to win the second Test at Lord's, lost the wickets of Hutton (13), Edrich (2), and Washbrook (37). At stumps, the score was 3-106, with Compton not out 29 and Dollery not out 21.

**Australia's second innings was closed at 7-460 soon after 3 p.m.**

**Heavy rain interrupted play for 67 minutes before lunch and again for 53 minutes soon after England had gone in to bat.**

## SUN AND RAIN ALTERNATE
### From DENZIL BATCHELOR

A short-lived sun came out with the cricketers at 11.30.

Until then a great crowd, ranging from ex-England captains to girls in pigtails, had filled in the drenching hours writing down the names of the English team and crossing out all except Compton, Hutton, Bedser, and Evans.

So far this game was easy.

The problem then arose of how to fill the seven vacant places for Manchester, and there was sympathy with the view that it would perhaps be better not to attempt to do so, but take the field seven short.

To such depths has the English morale done a swallow dive.

After seven minutes of cricket the major rainstorm of the morning further water-logged the outfield and the spirits of the spectators.

Bradman gazed through the plate-glass window of the Australian dressing-room with an expression on his face of Montgomery when the weather report compelled him to postpone D-Day.

Whoever else was due for sacking from England's side J. Pluvius was earning his place for his home ground of Manchester by a brave effort to force a drawn game.

### STORM OVER

The storm swept over in half an hour and the sun shone uncertainly.

The announcement that unless further rain fell the captains would inspect the wicket at 12.30 was fraught with drama.

Was England to be saved by further downpours, reducing the ground to a genuine snipe marsh, or would the sun turn Quisling and present Bradman with a lethal wicket for England's second innings, thus hastening the execution already tentatively arranged?

When play was resumed three-quarters of an hour before lunch, the melodrama was temporarily suspended.

The sun was not hot enough to bedevil the wicket, which was drying out in a west wind.

Coxon spurred a little pace from the pitch, and beat Miller once.

Brown, however, dealt with Coxon with a defensive back stroke as if batsmanship was as slow and methodical a hobby as collecting stamps.

Miller hit thunderous leg and straight drives from Bedser, interspersed with a dynamic square cut: each stroke a certain boundary on dry turf, but now moving sluggishly as if across a ploughed field.

This batsman had chosen to play an innings flamboyantly beautiful with its sparkling straight drives in conditions almost as unfriendly to his technique as the bottom of a swimming bath.

The new ball did not daunt him.

### CHANCE MISSED

At 58 Miller enjoyed an escape deserved by so venturesome a batsman.

A hook from Bedser sent the ball as high as the cross on St. Paul's.

Dollery made ground to reach the catch, which he then spilled on the floor.

## ENGLAND'S HOPELESS TASK

By lunch, Australia led by 544, a margin which no English opium addict could expect to bridge.

Though the sun shone, a pall of black cloud loomed low on the horizon.

While a minor rainstorm drenched Lord's at the lunch interval, two loud reports of thunder were heard across the ground.

A cynic put forward the theory that Dollery, despairing at his continued bad luck, had shot himself, and, being Dollery, had missed with the first barrel.

But there was Dollery fielding the first ball after the interval.

### PITCH UNAFFECTED

The sun had still not got its teeth into the wicket.

The bowlers toiled, strewing sawdust in heaps down the pitch, the outfield held up the ball like a policeman on traffic duty, and Miller blazed his Wagnerian way towards the Pantheon.

And then Miller perished magnificently.

He swung a hook, gaudy rather than neat, at Laker's off-break, and the ball went with the buzz of a small-calibre shell into the big hands of Bedser, raised to save his face, at short leg.

Meanwhile, Lindwall had been batting with all the confidence of an opening batsman.

The crowd was only moderately appreciative—it had seen too many such performances in this innings.

Enthusiasm was aroused by the glimpse of Ian Johnson as a hitter of sixes and by the neatness and despatch with which Evans stumped Lindwall when he attempted to poach this role.

But the sight of Bradman waving his team back to the pavilion was the first really rescuscitating sight the Lord's crowd had enjoyed since Thursday evening.

There remained only to get 596 to win—and, of course, to pray for rain.

The few overs of England's innings that were possible before more rain stopped play at 3.45 revealed a Washbrook who had foresworn hooking.

Dourly he played off the back foot to keep a ravening Lindwall at bay.

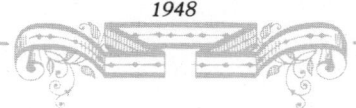

# CRUSHING TEST DEFEAT FOR ENGLAND

## Australia Wins By 409 Runs

From Tom Goodman And A.A.P.

LONDON, June 29.—Australia won the second Test at Lord's soon after lunch to-day. England made only 186 runs in its second innings and was crushingly beaten by 409 runs.

The last seven English wickets fell in less than two hours play for 80 runs though both Dollery and Evans fought stubbornly against the accurate and hostile Australian attack.

## TOSHACK HEADS ATTACK

Ern Toshack, who took three for 12 from nine overs to-day, finished with five wickets for 40 runs.

He was ably supported by Ray Lindwall, who took two wickets for 14 runs this morning, and Bill Johnston.

There have been several heavier defeats in Tests. The record was at the Oval in 1938, when England won by an innings and 579 runs.

Australia's biggest win was by an innings and 332 at Brisbane in 1946-47.

Only once has the team that lost the first two Tests won the remaining three. That was Australia, in 1936-7.

England's last authentic chance of saving the game seemed to have gone with Compton's dismissal in the first over of the day, and that of Yardley 20 minutes later.

### Amazing Catch

Compton went to an amazing catch by Miller, at second slip.

The batsman cut the ball hard and low, but Miller dived forward to his right and picked it up when rolling over.

Compton stood indecisively, wondering whether he was out, and the umpire gave no sign, until Miller shouted "Yes." Compton walked away immediately.

Toshack, bowling to a strong attacking field, pinned Yardley down for several overs, and finally bowled him with a faster ball.

All-rounder Coxon finished a not-too-successful Test debut with a "duck."

He played two balls from Toshack's same over and was instantly given out lbw. when Toshack appealed.

Dollery, undisturbed by the calamities around him, had then made 34, and the score was 133 for six wickets when Evans joined him.

Black, threatening clouds were rolling over from the south-west when Bradman took the new ball immediately it was due, in an effort to shift the imperturable Dollery.

Toshack had bowled eight overs, five of which were maidens, for seven runs and two wickets in his morning spell.

Evans consulted Dollery and immediately appealed unsuccessfully against the light.

Lindwall opened below top speed and bowled to four slips.

A heavy shower stopped play after 60 minutes, in which England added 35 to the overnight score.

It was all over bar the final tallying of statistics when Lindwall bowled Dollery and Laker in the first over after the resumption.

Dollery ducked and did not make a stroke at a shortish ball he thought would bump. It did not, but went straight through to send the bails flying.

### Cautious Evans

Evans survived two maidens from Lindwall, by dint of placing his bat firmly in front of straight balls and leaving everything else severely alone.

He then lost Bedser, who attempted to off-drive a slower ball from Bill Johnston and gave Hassett at mid-off a sitter.

Evans, lapsing from his policy of caution, cocked up an easy catch off Lindwall, but the fieldsmen, in their rush to get souvenir stumps, omitted to catch the ball.

Evans raised shouts of mirth from the crowd when, running like a hare, he lapped Wright as they took three byes.

At lunch the total was 179 for nine wickets.

Australia had won by 409 runs when Wright stepped out and slogged at a short ball in Toshack's second over after lunch.

The catch went high to Lindwall, who pocketed the ball and ran off the field.

The match ended at 2.23 p.m. Twenty minutes later the heaviest rain of the week swept across the ground, and continued for a quarter of an hour.

To-day's attendance of 18,000 brought the total for the match to 133,000, and the gross gate takings to £24,035/8/.

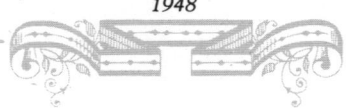

# Australians v Surrey

AUSTRALIANS v SURREY, at the Oval, 30 June, 1 and 2 July 1948.

| Australians | - First Innings | 389 |
| | - Second Innings | 122 for no wicket |
| Surrey | - First Innings | 221 |
| | - Second Innings | 289 |

Australians won by 10 wickets.

| DON BRADMAN | - c. M.R. Barton b. H.S. Squires | 128 |
| (Captain) | - (did not bat) | |

There was little in Surrey's weakened attack to prevent DON BRADMAN from scoring his sixth century of the season. He went in at 6 for 1 on the first evening, and had ninety-one minutes' batting before the close, hitting up 84 not out; his fifty took fifty-six minutes. Next morning he completed his century in a further twenty minutes, and threw his wicket away half an hour later, caught at mid-on off a wild heave; he was in altogether for two hours twenty-one minutes, gave no chance, and hit fifteen fours, being second out at 237.

Bradman had previously won the toss and put Surrey in to bat.

## Surrey

| | | | |
|---|---|---|---|
| L. B. Fishlock c McCool b Hamence | 31 | st Saggers b McCool | 61 |
| D. G. W. Fletcher c Hassett b Toshack | 26 | st Saggers b McCool | 18 |
| H. S. Squires c Bradman b Loxton | 0 | c Toshack b McCool | 13 |
| M. R. Barton c Ring b Loxton | 4 | c Miller b Loxton | 18 |
| J. F. Parker lbw b Ring | 76 | c McCool b Ring | 81 |
| A. J. McIntyre lbw b Ring | 6 | b Toshack | 11 |
| E. A. Bedser c Saggers b Hamence | 0 | st Saggers b Toshack | 3 |
| E. R. T. Holmes c Harvey b Toshack | 23 | st Saggers b McCool | 54 |
| B. Constable run out | 2 | b McCool | 4 |
| E. A. Watts b Ring | 30 | not out | 1 |
| W. S. Surridge not out | 4 | c sub b McCool | 12 |
| B 9, l-b 7, n-b 3 | 19 | B 9, l-b 3, n-b 1 | 13 |
| | 221 | | 289 |

## Australians

| | | | |
|---|---|---|---|
| A. L. Hassett c Holmes b Watts | 139 | | |
| R. A. Hamence c Parker b Watts | 0 | | |
| D. G. Bradman c Barton b Squires | 128 | | |
| K. R. Miller c McIntyre b Surridge | 9 | | |
| R. N. Harvey run out | 43 | not out | 73 |
| S. J. Loxton c Surridge b Parker | 8 | not out | 47 |
| C. L. McCool b Surridge | 26 | | |
| R. A. Saggers b Squires | 12 | | |
| D. Ring not out | 15 | | |
| E. R. H. Toshack lbw b Constable | 1 | | |
| W. A. Brown absent hurt | 0 | | |
| B 5, l-b 1, n-b 2 | 8 | L-b 1, n-b 1 | 2 |
| | 389 | No wkt. | 122 |

## Australian Bowling

| | O. | M. | R. | W. | | O. | M. | R. | W. |
|---|---|---|---|---|---|---|---|---|---|
| Loxton | 25 | 7 | 47 | 2 | | 18 | 3 | 53 | 1 |
| Hamence | 13 | 4 | 24 | 2 | | 8 | 0 | 30 | 0 |
| Toshack | 20 | 2 | 76 | 2 | | 12 | 6 | 29 | 2 |
| Ring | 21.2 | 5 | 51 | 3 | | 24 | 6 | 51 | 1 |
| McCool | 3 | 1 | 4 | 0 | | 45.5 | 10 | 113 | 6 |
| Miller | 1 | 1 | 0 | 0 | | | | | |

## Surrey Bowling

| | O. | M. | R. | W. | | O. | M. | R. | W. |
|---|---|---|---|---|---|---|---|---|---|
| Surridge | 22 | 0 | 123 | 2 | | 7 | 1 | 43 | 0 |
| Watts | 10 | 0 | 64 | 2 | | | | | |
| Parker | 25 | 5 | 62 | 1 | | 5 | 0 | 22 | 0 |
| E. A. Bedser | 20 | 1 | 85 | 0 | | 5 | 0 | 23 | 0 |
| Constable | 7.1 | 1 | 23 | 1 | | 3.1 | 0 | 32 | 0 |
| Squires | 10 | 2 | 24 | 2 | | | | | |

Umpires: G. M. Lee and F. S. Lee.

# AUSTRALIANS HIT OUT AT OVAL

## Bradman's 6th 100

### By L. N. BAILEY

SURREY'S weakened attack came in for punishment against the Australians at the Oval where Bradman and Hassett both completed centuries in a stand of 231.

A quick third run for an off-drive off Parker gave Bradman his sixth hundred of the tour scored in the quick time of 110 minutes, but Hassett took 35 minutes longer to get his fourth century of the season.

Bradman tried to leave by hitting the ball in the air with some lusty drives and neat flicks through the slips, but the ball never went to hand until he mistimed Squires and was caught at mid-on off a skier.

He batted 140 minutes for his 128 which makes his aggregate for the season 1,401 in 16 innings.

## Bowral Boy's Triumph

*Daily Mirror World Cables*
LONDON, Saturday.—Don Bradman (the "boy from Bowral") received a telegram yesterday morning at the Oval from a "cricket fan" advising him to back Bowral Boy at Newmarket (England) yesterday.

*Don Bradman*

Bradman, a non-punter, passed the news on to the rest of the Australian team, but no one took the telegram seriously.

Bowral Boy won at 25/1 and paid £6 2s 6d on the tote.

# AUSTRALIA'S QUICK FINISH

### (By Maurice Tate, English ex-International)

LONDON, Saturday. — By scoring 122 runs without loss in 57 minutes, the Australians finished off the Surrey match yesterday in time to enable them to see the Wimbledon tennis final.

HARVEY was in brilliant form for 73, hitting both pace bowlers, Surridge and Constable, for sixes. It would not surprise to see him make the team for the third Test starting on July 8.

It must have been refreshing to Bradman to see McCool finish with six wickets, although he bowled better on Thursday than he did on yesterday's easy wicket.

For the second time in the match, Parker reached 50.

Before the war he was one of England's best all-rounders and although he has not a wide range of strokes, he plods along on orthodox lines.

Holmes, also middle-aged, who just failed to make the grade as a regular Test player, figured in an entertaining partnership with Parker.

Holmes rushed down the wicket, tried to hit McCool out of the ground, missed and was easily stumped by Saggers, who finished with four stumpings, three off McCool's bowling and one off Toshack's.

The Australian team to play Gloucester today is: Hassett, Morris, Barnes, Harvey, Miller, Loxton, Lindwall, Johnson, Ring, McCool, Saggers, Hamence (12th).

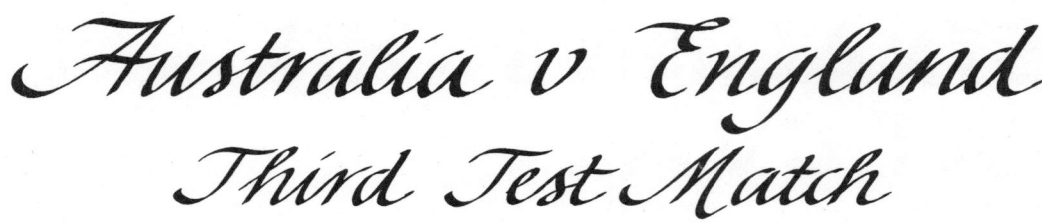

# *Australia v England*
## *Third Test Match*

AUSTRALIA v ENGLAND, Third Test Match, at Manchester, 8, 9, 10 and 13 July 1948.

| Australia | - First Innings | 221 |
| | - Second Innings | 92 for 1 wicket |
| England | - First Innings | 363 |
| | - Second Innings | 174 for 3 wickets dec. |

Drawn; Australia retained the Ashes.

| DON BRADMAN | - lbw. b. R. Pollard | 7 |
| (Captain) | - not out | 30 |

Going in at 3 for 1 on the second afternoon, DON BRADMAN had his first innings ended after nine minutes and 7 balls by an in-swinger at 13 for 2.     By the end of the third day, England had played themselves into an encouraging position, but rain prevented any further play until 2.15 p.m. on the last day, and though N.W.D. Yardley declared at once, Australia had little difficulty in forcing a draw.     On a very soft wicket, which was too slow and lifeless to give much help to the bowlers, Bradman and A.R. Morris defended grimly; the former, coming in at 2.49 p.m. with the score 10 for 1, took 35 balls and twenty-eight minutes before opening his score. Further rain interrupted the game for four minutes during the afternoon, and again at 4.10 p.m., when Bradman was 24; this shower prevented further play until 5.45 p.m., after which there were only forty-five minutes left.     Bradman scored only 6 more runs in these forty-five minutes;  indeed, he scored only 2 in the last forty-two minutes, but time was what mattered, not runs.     At the close, Bradman had been in for two minutes over two hours; this was his fiftieth Test Match.

## England

| | | | |
|---|---|---|---|
| C. Washbrook b Johnston | 11 | — not out | 85 |
| G. M. Emmett c Barnes b Lindwall | 10 | — c Tallon b Lindwall | 0 |
| W. J. Edrich c Tallon b Lindwall | 32 | — run out | 53 |
| D. C. S. Compton not out | 145 | — c Miller b Toshack | 0 |
| J. F. Crapp lbw b Lindwall | 37 | — not out | 19 |
| H. E. Dollery b Johnston | 1 | — | |
| N. W. D. Yardley c Johnson b Toshack | 22 | | |
| T. G. Evans c Johnston b Lindwall | 34 | | |
| A. V. Bedser run out | 37 | | |
| R. Pollard b Toshack | 3 | | |
| J. A. Young c Bradman b Johnston | 4 | | |
| B 7, l-b 17, n-b 3 | 27 | B 9, l-b 7, w 1 | 17 |
| | 363 | Three wkts., dec. | 174 |

## Australia

| | | | |
|---|---|---|---|
| A. R. Morris c Compton b Bedser | 51 | — not out | 54 |
| I. W. Johnson c Evans b Bedser | 1 | — c Crapp b Young | 6 |
| D. G. Bradman lbw b Pollard | 7 | — not out | 30 |
| A. L. Hassett c Washbrook b Young | 38 | | |
| K. R. Miller lbw b Pollard | 31 | | |
| S. G. Barnes retired hurt | 1 | | |
| S. J. Loxton b Pollard | 36 | | |
| D. Tallon c Evans b Edrich | 18 | | |
| R. R. Lindwall c Washbrook b Bedser | 23 | | |
| W. A. Johnston c Crapp b Bedser | 3 | | |
| E. R. H. Toshack not out | 0 | | |
| B 5, l-b 4, n-b 3 | 12 | N-b 2 | 2 |
| | 221 | One wkt. | 92 |

## Australia Bowling

| | O. | M. | R. | W. | O. | M. | R. | W. |
|---|---|---|---|---|---|---|---|---|
| Lindwall | 40 | 8 | 99 | 4 | 14 | 4 | 37 | 1 |
| Johnston | 45.5 | 13 | 67 | 3 | 14 | 3 | 34 | 0 |
| Loxton | 7 | 0 | 18 | 0 | 8 | 1 | 29 | 0 |
| Toshack | 41 | 20 | 75 | 2 | 12 | 5 | 26 | 1 |
| Johnson | 38 | 16 | 77 | 0 | 7 | 3 | 16 | 0 |
| Miller | | | | | 14 | 7 | 15 | 0 |

## England Bowling

| | O. | M. | R. | W. | O. | M. | R. | W. |
|---|---|---|---|---|---|---|---|---|
| Bedser | 36 | 12 | 81 | 4 | 19 | 12 | 27 | 0 |
| Pollard | 32 | 9 | 53 | 3 | 10 | 8 | 6 | 0 |
| Edrich | 7 | 3 | 27 | 1 | 2 | 0 | 8 | 0 |
| Yardley | 4 | 0 | 12 | 0 | | | | |
| Young | 14 | 5 | 36 | 1 | 21 | 12 | 31 | 1 |
| Compton | | | | | 9 | 3 | 18 | 0 |

### FALL OF WICKETS

ENGLAND—First Innings:

| 1 | 2 | 3 | 4 | 5 | 6 | 7 | 8 | 9 |
|---|---|---|---|---|---|---|---|---|
| 22 | 28 | 96 | 97 | 119 | 141 | 216 | 337 | 352 |

ENGLAND—Second Innings:

| 1 | 2 | 3 |
|---|---|---|
| 1 | 125 | 129 |

AUSTRALIA—First Innings:

| 1 | 2 | 3 | 4 | 5 | 6 | 7 | 8 | 9 |
|---|---|---|---|---|---|---|---|---|
| 3 | 13 | 82 | 135 | 139 | 172 | 208 | 219 | 221 |

AUSTRALIA—Second Innings:

| 1 |
|---|
| 10 |

Umpires: D. Davies and F. Chester.

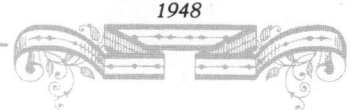

## THIRD TEST MATCH
# England Openers Fail Again

**Australian Associated Press And Our Special Representative**

**MANCHESTER, July 8.**

England's new opening pair, Washbrook and Emmett, did little better at the outset of the third Test match at Old Trafford today than had Hutton and Washbrook at Nottingham and Lord's, both being out in the first three-quarters of an hour.

Ten minutes before Yardley won the toss, the following teams were announced:—

| ENGLAND | AUSTRALIA |
|---|---|
| Yardley (c.) | Bradman (c.) |
| Edrich | Hassett |
| Compton | Barnes |
| Bedser | Morris |
| Evans | Miller |
| Washbrook | Tallon |
| Dollery | Lindwall |
| Emmett | Johnson |
| Crapp | Johnston |
| Young | Toshack |
| Pollard | Loxton |
| Wardle (12th) | Harvey (12th) |

Laker, who played in the first two Tests, was discarded from England's original 13. Loxton was given preference over Harvey because of a lingering doubt as to Miller's fitness.

Although it is reported that Miller has suffered no discomfort from his strained side for several days, Johnston opened the bowling with Lindwall when the match began, and Loxton, not Miller, sent down the third over of the innings to enable Lindwall to change ends.

From the first ball of the match, Emmett was nearly run out when he did not respond quickly enough to Washbrook's call for a second run; but, apart from that brief moment of excitement, the first half-hour's play, which produced 20, was uneventful.

### Washbrook Out

Neither Lindwall nor Johnston was able to obtain much lift from the grassy pitch, and the ball which skittled Washbrook with the total at 22 did not even hit the ground.

A full toss from Johnston swung late, and Washbrook's jab was too late to prevent the ball wrecking his wicket.

A quarter of an hour later, Emmett attempted a one-handed swing at a short rising ball outside the off stump from Lindwall and skied it to Barnes at short leg. Two wickets were down for 28.

After Compton had helped Edrich to add seven, he tried to hook a short no-ball from Lindwall, but snicked it on to his forehead, which was badly cut. After a pause, he was helped off the field by Edrich, Bradman and Barnes.

Seventy minutes' play produced 40 runs, at which stage Bradman took off both fast bowlers, replacing them with Toshack and Johnson, who each opened with a maiden.

Edrich made only two scoring strokes—a four and a two—in his first 50 minutes.

The first run scored from Toshack's bowling came in his sixth over. Two balls later Crapp broke the monotony with a four to long leg.

A leg-bye brought up 50 in 1¾ hours. Seven minutes before lunch Edrich hit Johnson for a beautiful four past mid-off off his back foot and, reached double figures after having batted for 73 minutes.

Only 16 runs were scored from the last 20 overs before the luncheon interval. Fourteen maidens were sent down in this period.

England's total was 57 for two at the adjournment.

### Crapp Hits Six

Five minutes after lunch, Crapp jumped into a no-ball from Johnson and straight-drove it over the sightboard for six.

Crapp, a few overs later, hit a four and a three in successive overs from Johnson. Edrich at the other end was almost immobile.

In Toshack's next over, Barnes missed Crapp off a fairly easy one-handed chance at silly mid-on. Crapp took another four when he slammed Johnson over Barnes's head.

Thirty runs were added in three-quarters of an hour after lunch, Edrich's share being five.

Lindwall returned with the new ball with the score at 87 and sent down a maiden to Edrich.

### Edrich's Luck

An edged shot through the slips gave Edrich a lucky boundary off Lindwall—his first scoring stroke for half an hour—and his luck held when, two balls later, he snicked an extra fast ball head-high between second and third slips for another four.

In the next over, Lindwall completely deceived Crapp with an in-swinger at which he attempted no stroke and which hit him on the foot. He was given out l.b.w., and, with one added, Johnston knocked back Dollery's off stump.

A beautiful sweeping shot by Edrich to the long leg boundary off Lindwall brought up 103 in 200 minutes.

Edrich fell on his wrist in trying to hook Lindwall, and the game was held up for a few moments while Barnes massaged the affected part.

Yardley had an unhappy over from Johnston and then snicked Lindwall through the slips for four. He followed this stroke by hooking the next ball to the square leg boundary. Ten came from the over.

At 119, Edrich's long and plucky three-hour vigil ended when he edged a kicker to the wicket-keeper.

**Wearing plaster above his eye, Compton followed to resume his innings.**

Compton did not seem unduly inconvenienced and played quite confidently.

### Missed Chance

The crowd groaned when Yardley snicked one from Johnston apparently into Miller's hands at second slip and then applauded Miller who shook his head to signify that the ball had hit the ground just before he caught it.

Toshack and Loxton relieved the fast bowlers a quarter of an hour before tea. Barnes missed another chance, a very hot one, from Yardley off Toshack.

After a scoreless 12 minutes following the tea interval, Yardley tried to force Toshack over the infieldsmen and lifted the ball to Johnson at mid-wicket. Six wickets were down for 141.

Compton welcomed Evans with a four past square leg and four leg-byes brought up 150 in 4¼ hours.

Compton hit two flowing boundaries off successive balls from Toshack, and 28 were added in a quarter of an hour after Yardley's dismissal.

Tallon and Lindwall appealed loudly for stumping when Compton played forward to Johnson and missed.

Compton went into the forties with a beautiful square cut to the boundary off Johnson, and he turned Toshack off his toes for another four. A four to Evans made the stand worth 50 in 38 minutes.

Compton soon afterwards reached 50 in 105 minutes, and the 200 came up in 315 minutes.

The partnership realised 75 in 70 minutes—the first time today in which a scoring rate of a run a minute had been bettered, and then Evans made a wild swing at Lindwall and was caught by Johnston at mid-on.

Determined to be first in the queue at Old Trafford to-day, 17-year-old Terry Burke had his tent pitched outside the gates long before darkness fell last night.

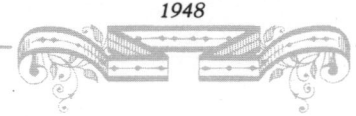

# AUSTRALIA'S TURN TO FIGHT

## Deficit Of 237 With Three Men Out

LONDON, July 9: An excellent eighth-wicket stand by Compton, who scored 145 not out, and Bedser enabled England to compile 363 in the first innings of the third Test match against Australia at Manchester today. Suddenly the game swung decidedly in England's favour as, with Barnes injured, Australia lost Johnson and Bradman with the score only 13. At stumps three were out for 126.

England had good reason to feel satisfied with its batting recovery from 141 for six wickets to a total of 363. It could be excused its jubilation when Bedser had Johnson caught for one—the all-rounder had been promoted in the batting order because of Barnes's injury received in the field—and Pollard dismissed Bradman l.b.w. for seven. It was Australia's turn to fight and for the first time in the current Test series England had more than vague hopes of success.

The first turning point in the game came when Bedser managed to make a plucky stand with Compton. They deservedly had luck with them—Tallon missed difficult chances offered by Compton—and they added 121 for the eighth wicket. This was the best partnership for that wicket ever recorded in Tests in England between the two countries and only three short of the record for England established by Hendren and Larwood at Brisbane in the 1928-29 series. A suicidal attempt at a single ended the partnership.

Compton, serenely confident in a difficult situation, completed his fifth Test century catch. Bedser bore a charmed life. He snicked a ball from Lindwall just out of Johnson's reach in slips and another just clear of Tallon. Both balls went to the boundary. Compton ran into the eighties with two powerful cover shots.

Compton's ninth four—a perfectly-timed on-drive made his score 101 in 234 minutes. A similar shot brought up England's 300.

Bedser's luck continued. Toshack might have bowled him with any one of half a dozen balls that completely baffled him but missed the stumps by a hair's breadth.

### EXTRA SPEED.

Lindwall came back to the Stretford end a quarter of an hour before lunch and Bedser cut a ball for one to make the partnership worth 100 and England's score 316.

Lindwall's second last over before lunch was very fast. Compton ducked to avoid a "bumper." Then a good-length ball rose sharply and hit him painfully on a hand. Compton for the first time in the innings looked really uncomfortable.

In the next over, which was probably the fastest Lindwall has bowled in England, Compton stepped away and flicked at the first ball but blocked the rest of the over with a dead bat.

An injudicious call for a single by Compton led to Bedser's dismissal when the pair had added 121. Pollard, joining Compton, swung hard at a ball from Johnson and hit it fiercely to leg. Barnes, close in, was hit a severe blow and was carried off the field.

England's ninth wicket fell at 352 when Pollard played half-heartedly forward over a good-length ball from Toshack and was bowled. Compton went on soundly to 145 before the last man, Young, gave Bradman an easy catch off Johnston's bowling with England's total 363.

### A BAD START.

Ian Johnson, promoted to opening batsman in Barnes's absence, stayed less than ten minutes before he touched a rising out-swinger from Bedser into Evans's hands. Bradman, who thus was virtually an opening batsman, scored a single from the first ball he received.

Bradman had added only a single, four for a beautifully timed late cut and a single before Pollard dismissed him

l.b.w. A ball of perfect length, swinging late, beat him and hit his pads. The crowd shouted wildly and tossed caps and hats into the air when the umpire (Dai Davies) raised his finger.

Australia, with two down for 13, had now experienced what has been common to England —quick losses against an opening attack. Pollard had covered himself with glory by dismissing the Australian captain —a valued scalp for a bowler in his first Test against Australia.

Morris, who reached double figures with a powerful cover-drive to the boundary, played Bedser's bowling confidently but treated Pollard's swinging deliveries with great respect. Pollard's first seven overs cost ten runs and Bedser's, 21.

### POLLARD ACCURATE.

Edrich relieved Bedser shortly before tea but Yardley persisted with Pollard, whose figures at tea were 10-2-13-1.

Twice in two overs after tea Pollard beat Hassett with excellent deliveries swinging away from the bat and only five runs were added in 25 minutes. Both batsmen were content to defend and wear down the aggressive English attack.

Two leg-byes made Australia's score 50. Then Morris and Hassett entered their twenties with beautifully placed boundary strokes. Yardley relieved Bedser after an accurate spell of seven overs but Pollard bowled unchanged for 17 overs before Young went on at 76.

Six runs later Hassett amazed the crowd by suddenly lapsing from his sound tactics and attempting a big hit against Young with a disastrous result. He skied the ball to Washbrook in the covers and was out for 38.

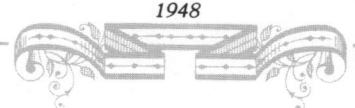

# AUSTRALIA OUT, 142 BEHIND
# Washbrook, Edrich make stand after Emmett goes

SUNDAY TELEGRAPH SERVICE AND A.A.P.

**OLD TRAFFORD, Sat.—England, leading Australia by 142 on the first innings, lost Emmett early, but was saved by a sound partnership between Washbrook and Edrich.**

**Emmett, who opened with Washbrook, was caught behind for a "duck" on Lindwall's third ball.**

Near tea, England was 363 and 1-82 in reply to Australia's 221.

The wicket was good at the start, and the weather was warm and sunny.

Miller (23) and Morris (48) resumed for Australia at 3-126.

Bedser and Pollard opened the bowling.

The ground was packed two hours before play began. A crowd of 35,000 was present.

Morris and Miller opened slowly, scoring only seven runs in the first half-hour.

At 135, Miller played forward to an in-swinger from Pollard, which beat him, and he was out l.b.w.

Pollard had just taken the new ball.

Barnes, who was injured while fielding yesterday but had recovered sufficiently to bat today, then joined Morris.

He was given a great ovation.

Barnes tried himself out at the Old Trafford nets half an hour before play was due to begin.

He batted for only 10 minutes at the nets before the pain in his side forced him to give up.

Barnes had scored only one when Morris, at 51, followed Miller to the pavilion.

Morris was caught by Compton on the boundary off Bedser two minutes after he had got his 50 in 305 minutes.

Loxton then joined Barnes, but Barnes retired soon afterwards because of the pain in his side, and Tallon came in.

## Barnes Unfit

Barnes was later examined by a doctor, who announced that Barnes would not play again in this match.

Yardley had kept Pollard and Bedser on unchanged.

Tallon's first scoring shot was an off-drive off Bedser for two, while Loxton appeared to have settled down with shots around the wicket.

Young relieved Pollard, and Loxton swept him to the fine leg boundary.

Young bowled his second over, and Tallon drove him through the covers and past mid-off for two successive fours.

Edrich relieved Bedser and had Tallon caught at the wicket off his first ball. Lindwall went in.

Tallon and Loxton were together for a brief but lively 33.

The ball which got Tallon was a chest-high bumper at which Tallon swung, and snicked to Evans, standing well back.

Australia, at 6-172, still needed 41 if Yardley was not to have the choice of enforcing the follow-on.

Edrich, heartened by his success, flung himself into the attack.

He unleashed three head-high bumpers.

Lindwall swung wildly at the first two, and failed to connect each time.

The third bumper caught Lindwall a painful blow on the right hand.

He had to kick the ball away to prevent it hitting the wicket.

Loxton, deciding that his natural aggressive game was the best defence, scored comparatively freely off the later overs of Pollard and Bedser.

Powerful strokes in front of the wicket brought his 14 up in even time.

He was confident, if less productive, against the slow left-hander Young.

Lindwall took Australia to 6-182 with a beautiful cut between point and gully to the boundary off Edrich.

He repeated the shot uppishly in Edrich's next over.

From this over, Loxton also hit two powerful boundaries.

Off Young, Loxton made Australia 6-202 at lunch.

At lunch, Bedser had taken 2-66, Pollard 2-50, Edrich 1-27, and Young 1-36.

After the resumption, only five runs had been added when Pollard bowled Loxton, who had hit six fours in his 36.

## Saved "Follow-On"

Lindwall saved a follow-on when he edged Bedser over slips for four.

Lindwall went to 23 when he on-drove Bedser for two.

Trying to repeat the shot two balls later, Lindwall hit an easy catch to Washbrook at deep mid-on.

Bill Johnston cover-drove Bedser for two, but two balls later reached out and snicked a ball outside the off stump to Crapp at second slip.

Australia was all out for 221, with Toshack, the not out batsman, nil.

Washbrook and Emmett opened for England.

Washbrook took a single to fine leg off Lindwall's first ball.

Emmett, groping forward to the third ball, edged it behind the wicket and Tallon, diving full-length, took a brilliant catch.

Edrich then joined Washbrook.

Miller, showing no sign of his back injury, opened at the other end.

Washbrook hit Lindwall uppishly to Hassett at fine leg, who dropped a hard chance.

Johnston relieved Miller, and bowled medium pace round the wicket.

Washbrook pushed him away to square leg for a single, and Edrich hooked him for two.

Loxton made it a double change when he took over from Lindwall.

Washbrook went to 30 with a beautiful shot to mid-wicket off Johnston.

The first ball of Johnston's next over was a full-toss, which Washbrook slammed behind square leg for four, to bring up England's 50.

### ... Then Came Bradman ... England's Hopes Faded ... Vanished

# DON'S PERFECT ANSWER TO EVERY BALL

## By ARCHIE LEDBROOKE

RAIN, combined with some indifferent bowling and some wonderfully correct batting by Bradman and Morris, settled the 1948 rubber.

Australia drew the third Test match at Old Trafford and, having won the games at Nottingham and Lord's, retain the Ashes, which we last won in the 1932-33 (body-line) series.

No play was possible yesterday until after lunch and then only because artificial drying of the wicket had been undertaken in the most vigorous fashion.

A hint of sunshine suggested that the pitch, obviously sodden, might eventually become difficult and the huge crowd were prepared for a real scrap when Ian Johnson, once more the stop-gap opener, was caught low down at slip after 35 minutes of patient defence.

When Bradman came in it was a moment for the connoisseur.

His reputation for throwing his wicket away on bad pitches, the memory of Verity at Lord's in 1934, his recent display against Hilton on the same stretch of turf, his reckless (but how brilliant!) stroke-play on the wet Oval pitch in 1930—all these things came back to the mind of one who has seen much of Bradman in four tours.

Here was the occasion for a great innings . . . or one to leave for ever a blot on his reputation.

Here was the situation: A turning wicket (not yet sticky, it is true), Australia sent in on a prompt declaration, Barnes absent, and most of three and a half hours to play.

To see Bradman fight out this crisis would be a cricket treat indeed.

A treat suggests cakes, sweets, trifles. Shall we say we passed the sandwich stage and were about to enjoy the tastier morsels when further rain broke into the match?

For eighty minutes we saw Bradman "middle" every ball at which he played except one from Bedser, and even then I am not sure that the Australian captain did not check his shot in the last split second.

His footwork to Young and Compton was perfect for every situation: when the ball was dropped short he hooked the two slow left-handers with a vigour, an intensity, and a boyish enthusiasm we have hardly seen from him all summer.

With Morris firmly entrenched at the Manchester end, and judging the pace nicely, Bradman decided to stay at the Stretford crease.

So they hit fours, ran safe twos, and remained at their respective ends for 70 minutes while 27 overs were bowled.

## NOT A MURMUR

At the start of his innings, Bradman played 35 consecutive balls from Young, Compton and Pollard without scoring, then getting off the mark with a sweeping leg hit off Compton.

Twenty-one runs was the total at the end of the first hour, and so keen was the cricket, so skilled the batsmanship, that no one in the vast crowd murmured a word of criticism.

By this time everything on the scoreboard, except the number of wickets down, had ceased to matter.

Yardley had runs enough and to spare . . . but he could not get down the wicket of either of these master batsmen.

The bowler all pitched on the short side unable or unwilling to make the batsmen grope forward towards a false hit, so at last Edrich was called up for duty.

Apparently this was to bring into the attack the air of hostility which is nowadays the favourite description of mediocre fast-medium bowlers.

The hostility was all on one side, for Bradman hooked Edrich through the leg trap for four, and then drove his slow ball past mid-off, again to the boundary; and that was the end of Edrich for that spell.

A shower freshened the pitch and enabled Bedser at last to make two deliveries leave the pitch in haste and run away from the bat; and then another downfall sent the players in to early tea and settled the result of the match.

## FORMALITY

The play late in the afternoon, when further cricket was possible for 45 minutes, was merely a formality so far as the players were concerned, and an opportunity for humour from the remnants of the crowd.

Well, the Lancashire crowd commanded success, but the English players hardly deserved it when things came to a crisis.

Would better bowling have won the match in the limited time available? Could the Australians have held out had there been a full day's play yesterday? Would another bowler (an off-spinner for preference) have turned the balance?

Those are questions which will frequently be asked and never answered to the satisfaction of all.

The following pages deal primarily with the fourth Test at Leeds where Australia achieved a victory unparalleled in the annals of cricket.

On the fifth and final day the English captain left Australia 344 minutes in which to make 404 runs. The feat was achieved with 15 minutes to spare. No Test team had previously made over 400 to win on the last day. Arthur Morris and I put on 301 in 217 minutes.

I was then within a month of my 40th birthday and my first Test century was made 19½ years earlier, a longer span than anyone else had achieved.

So I had cause to thank nature for having endowed me with the strength to see out the journey.

*Don Bradman*

## Leeds—Baby Of England Test Grounds

### By SIDNEY DOWNER

THE Headingley ground at Leeds, where the fourth Test match will begin today, is the youngest of all English Test match grounds. Its history is not as vivid as the panorama unfolded by Lord's, nor has it been punctuated by the climatic disturbances of Old Trafford. Yet since the first Test match was played there in 1905, distinction has crowded the pages of its brief saga.

No cricket field could be altogether neutral and anonymous whose turf had been nursed by Roy Kilner, or whose "texture" had been felt by Wilfred Rhodes. The old order has changed somewhat; Kilner is dead, Rhodes long out of the game, and Bowes and Leyland, too, have passed from the Yorkshire scene, now filled with almost unknown aspirants for high honor.

Until 1946, Australia had never won at Brisbane; it remains for England in this match to lay her own ghosts at Leeds.

*   *   *   *

LEEDS seemed to do things to Macartney and Bradman. They both made a hundred before lunch in a Test match there; Bradman scored 334 in the 1930 match and 304 in 1934 as well as 103 in 1938, and Macartney not only made two centuries on the ground but, in his salad days, took seven wickets for 30 in an England innings.

Macartney was all out of character in that match—18 runs occupied him two hours, and then, far exceeding his prerogatives as a change bowler, he skittled England for 87. The story is told how Hobbs, dismissed second with the total 60, had his reflections in his bath suddenly disturbed by pandemonium without. Through the steam Hobbs called out to all whom it might concern: "What's happened? Has another wicket fallen?" "Another wicket be blowed!" came the response. "The whole dashed side's out!"

England has often met with disaster at Leeds. The last occasion was at the outset of the third day in 1938 when, in face of a deficit of 19, she had scored 60 without loss. Those first 20 minutes which Barnett and Edrich endured that day were delusory. They were struck down together, at the same total. The third wicket added little, and then came Hammond. There was impatience among the Australians as he took guard. At last the great man prepared to receive the first ball. O'Reilly sent it down on a teasing length. Unseeing, Hammond groped, tried to recover when he found he had made his stroke too soon, and jabbed the ball towards the ground in the direction of short leg. Brown dived for the prize, and Hammond walked away amid the silence of the tomb.

What happened afterwards is almost unprintable. In a couple of hours, England was out for 75 runs—the result of fine bowling, supported by opportunist fielding—and the direst panic.

*   *   *   *

FOUR years before, Bradman had accompanied Ponsford to the wicket at the start of the second day's play in the unusually low station of No. 5. That was the beginning of their two legendary partnerships. They batted all that day until, 20 minutes from time, Ponsford hit Verity to the long-on boundary and trod on his wicket in doing so.

The wonder of Ponsford was that Bradman's virtuosity never blotted him out of the firmament. At no stage did he go into eclipse as any other living batsman must have done.

# Australia v England
## Fourth Test Match

AUSTRALIA v ENGLAND, Fourth Test Match, at Leeds, 22, 23, 24, 26 and 27 July 1948.

| Australia | - First Innings | 458 |
|---|---|---|
| | - Second Innings | 404 for 3 wickets |
| England | - First Innings | 496 |
| | - Second Innings | 365 for 8 wickets dec. |

Australia won by 7 wickets, and won the rubber.

| DON BRADMAN | - b. R. Pollard | 33 |
|---|---|---|
| (Captain) | - not out | 173 |

DON BRADMAN went in for his first innings at 13 for 1, fifty-one minutes from the end of the second day, and thanks to some explosive hooking, reached 31 overnight. Next morning, a shower had livened the pitch, and Bradman, after being hit on the thigh by a lifting ball from A.V. Bedser, was out in the second over after another eight minutes; he was late in playing back to R. Pollard and lost his off-stump, with the score 68 for 3.

On the fifth day, N.W.D. Yardley's declaration set Australia 404 to win in five hours forty-four minutes (70 runs an hour) on a worn wicket which took spin, but Bradman and A.R. Morris put together a huge partnership which won the match against all the odds. Bradman came in at 1 p.m. with the score 57 for 1, and had some unhappy moments against D.C.S. Compton's bowling; he was 35 at lunch-time after half an hour, and afterwards reached 50 in an hour, before giving a hard chance when 59 off K. Cranston. He completed his century at 4.10 p.m. in two hours twenty-five minutes, and just before tea, when 108, he might have been stumped off J.C. Laker. By the tea interval, when he was still 108, Australia needed 116 in one and three-quarter hours, and they eventually won with fifteen minutes to spare; Bradman and Morris added 301 for the second wicket in three hours thirty-seven minutes. Bradman's 173 not out took him four and a quarter hours and included twenty-nine fours.

## England

| | | | | |
|---|---|---|---|---|
| L. Hutton b Lindwall | 81 | — c Bradman b Johnson | 57 |
| C. Washbrook c Lindwall b Johnston | 143 | — c Harvey b Johnston | 65 |
| W. J. Edrich c Morris b Johnson | 111 | — lbw b Lindwall | 54 |
| A. V. Bedser c and b Johnson | 79 | — c Hassett b Miller | 17 |
| D. C. S. Compton c Saggers b Lindwall | 23 | — c Miller b Johnston | 66 |
| J. F. Crapp b Toshack | 5 | — b Lindwall | 18 |
| N. W. D. Yardley b Miller | 25 | — c Harvey b Johnston | 7 |
| K. Cranston b Loxton | 10 | — c Saggers b Johnston | 0 |
| T. G. Evans c Hassett b Loxton | 3 | — not out | 47 |
| J. C. Laker c Saggers b Loxton | 4 | — not out | 15 |
| R. Pollard not out | 0 | | |
| B 2, l-b 8, w 1, n-b 1 | 12 | B 4, l-b 12, n-b 3 | 19 |
| | **496** | Eight wkts., dec. | **365** |

## Australia

| | | | | |
|---|---|---|---|---|
| A. R. Morris c Cranston b Bedser | 6 | — c Pollard b Yardley | 182 |
| A. L. Hassett c Crapp b Pollard | 13 | — c and b Compton | 17 |
| D. G. Bradman b Pollard | 33 | — not out | 173 |
| K. R. Miller c Edrich b Yardley | 58 | — lbw b Cranston | 12 |
| R. N. Harvey b Laker | 112 | — not out | 4 |
| S. J. Loxton b Yardley | 93 | | |
| I. W. Johnson c Cranston b Laker | 10 | | |
| R. R. Lindwall c Crapp b Bedser | 77 | | |
| R. A. Saggers st Evans b Laker | 5 | | |
| W. A. Johnston c Edrich b Bedser | 13 | | |
| E. R. H. Toshack not out | 12 | | |
| B 9, l-b 14, n-b 3 | 26 | B 6, l-b 9, n-b 1 | 16 |
| | **458** | Three wkts. | **404** |

### Australia Bowling

| | O. | M. | R. | W. | | O. | M. | R. | W |
|---|---|---|---|---|---|---|---|---|---|
| Lindwall | 38 | 10 | 79 | 2 | .... | 26 | 6 | 84 | 2 |
| Miller | 17.1 | 2 | 43 | 1 | .... | 21 | 5 | 53 | 1 |
| Johnston | 38 | 13 | 86 | 1 | .... | 29 | 5 | 95 | 4 |
| Toshack | 35 | 6 | 112 | 1 | | | | | |
| Loxton | 26 | 4 | 55 | 3 | .... | 10 | 2 | 29 | 0 |
| Johnson | 33 | 9 | 89 | 2 | .... | 21 | 2 | 85 | 1 |
| Morris | 5 | 0 | 20 | 0 | | | | | |

### England Bowling

| | O. | M. | R. | W. | | O. | M. | R. | W |
|---|---|---|---|---|---|---|---|---|---|
| Bedser | 31.2 | 4 | 92 | 3 | .... | 21 | 2 | 56 | 0 |
| Pollard | 38 | 6 | 100 | 2 | .... | 22 | 6 | 55 | 0 |
| Cranston | 14 | 1 | 51 | 0 | .... | 7.1 | 0 | 28 | 1 |
| Edrich | 3 | 0 | 19 | 0 | | | | | |
| Laker | 30 | 8 | 113 | 3 | .... | 32 | 11 | 93 | 0 |
| Yardley | 17 | 6 | 38 | 2 | .... | 13 | 1 | 44 | 1 |
| Compton | 3 | 0 | 15 | 0 | .... | 15 | 3 | 82 | 1 |
| | | | | | Hutton | 4 | 1 | 30 | 0 |

### FALL OF WICKETS

**ENGLAND—First Innings:**

| 1 | 2 | 3 | 4 | 5 | 6 | 7 | 8 | 9 |
|---|---|---|---|---|---|---|---|---|
| 168 | 268 | 423 | 426 | 447 | 473 | 486 | 490 | 496 |

**ENGLAND—Second Innings:**

| 1 | 2 | 3 | 4 | 5 | 6 | 7 | 8 |
|---|---|---|---|---|---|---|---|
| 129 | 129 | 232 | 260 | 277 | 278 | 293 | 330 |

**AUSTRALIA—First Innings:**

| 1 | 2 | 3 | 4 | 5 | 6 | 7 | 8 | 9 |
|---|---|---|---|---|---|---|---|---|
| 13 | 65 | 68 | 189 | 294 | 329 | 344 | 355 | 403 |

**AUSTRALIA—Second Innings:**

| 1 | 2 | 3 |
|---|---|---|
| 57 | 358 | 396 |

Umpires: F. Chester and H. G. Baldwin.

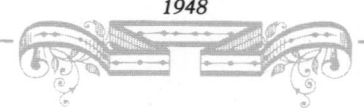

# EARLY AUST. SETBACK

## Morris Out For 6; England Gets 496

*Daily Telegraph Service and A.A.P.*

**HEADINGLEY, Friday.—Australia was 1-63 at stumps today in the first innings of the Fourth Test against England.**

England's innings ended shortly after tea at 496 after having been 3-423.

Australia lost Morris (6) with the total 13.

England's last eight batsmen added only 73 runs.

The collapse followed the end of the third-wicket partnership at 155 by Edrich (111) and Bedser (79).

**This was the third century partnership of the innings.**

Openers Hutton and Washbrook made 168, and Washbrook and Edrich 100.

England today was 2-360 at lunch and 7-488 at tea.

Bedser's wicket was the first to fall today, and Edrich's followed a few minutes later.

Bedser, sent in as a stop-gap during the last over yesterday, hit 14 off one over from Toshack, and had him taken off.

He also hit two sixes.

Edrich hit one six.

At one stage of the Edrich-Bedser partnership, Bradman had to call on Morris to bowl. The move did not succeed.

There was no rain last night, and this morning, when Edrich (41) and Bedser (0) resumed England's innings, the weather was cool with the sky half clouded.

The forecast was for fine weather throughout the day.

**Only four runs were scored in the first half hour's play.**

Lindwall and Johnston, who opened the attack today, bowled better than they did yesterday.

Lindwall swung the ball, and Johnston reduced pace and added spin.

Johnston beat Bedser four times in his second over and twice in his third.

In Lindwall's third over,

Edrich nearly played one ball on to his wicket.

Bradman claimed the new ball at 275, and again Edrich had a lucky escape when he played forward to Lindwall and the ball missed his off stump narrowly.

**Bedser at eight snicked one from Johnston close to Hassett at short leg, and then snicked another between Lindwall and Miller, in slips, for the day's first boundary.**

A cover drive for three by Edrich was the only forceful shot in the first hour, in which the pair put on 22.

Edrich took 62 minutes to get the nine he needed for his 50.

The half-century took him 193 minutes, and included six fours.

Bedser, when 10, again was nearly out when he turned a short, fast ball from Lindwall just short of Hassett at square leg.

In four overs each with the new ball Lindwall and Johnston failed to break the partnership.

Bradman then made a double change.

The new bowlers, Loxton and Toshack, were less dangerous.

### Lucky Hits

Edrich went into the 60's, and Bedser became 30 when he unscientifically but effectively, hit three fours and a two from Toshack's fourth over.

Bradman immediately called on Johnson to replace Toshack.

Bedser played one over from Johnson as a "sighter" and then in the next over punished him just as effectively, but more scientifically, with two fours and a six over long-on.

Fifty had been added in 30 minutes when England's total reached 350.

**Bedser soon pushed Miller for a single for his own half-century, made in 117 minutes.**

At lunch, England was 2-360 (Edrich 76, Bedser 52).

The determined attack by the batsmen after lunch suggested that it was time for England to force the pace.

Neither Lindwall nor Johnston, who resumed the bowling, produced his earlier "fire."

Morris was soon given his chance in place of Johnston.

Johnson relieved Lindwall.

**Edrich stepped out and drove a short one from Johnson high into the grandstand.**

The shot made him 96

### Reaches Century

A single and a four to leg off Morris made him 101 in 293 minutes.

He had then hit 11 fours and one six.

Bedser hit his second six, a hook off Morris, but was out soon afterwards for 79 (eight fours, two sixes).

Johnson caught and bowled him.

The partnership of 155 runs lasted 173 minutes.

England's total was 3-423.

Edrich was then 111.

**Compton added three, and then Edrich, who had not increased his score, mistimed a hook off Johnson, and Morris at mid-wicket took an easy catch.**

England was then 4-426.

Edrich had batted 318 minutes and hit 13 fours and one six.

With the addition of only 21 to the total, Crapp (5) tried to

play a forcing shot off Toshack and was bowled.

**Compton and Yardley had added 47 when Compton (23) was caught by 'keeper Saggers off Lindwall.**

England was then 6-473 (Yardley n o. 19)

Loxton jumped gleefully when he sent down a good ball which broke in and tumbled Cranston's leg stump five minutes before tea. That made England 7-486.

Two more runs were added before the interval.

England's last three wickets fell for eight runs in 22 minutes after tea.

The wicket seemed to be showing signs of wear when Morris and Hassett opened Australia's innings at 5.20, but it couldn't be blamed for Morris' dismissal.

**He made a bad shot at a near half-volley from Bedser and gave Cranston an easy catch at mid-wicket.**

Hassett, unperturbed by Morris' dismissal, blocked steadily for 45 minutes, in which he scored only six.

But Bradman was more enterprising. He hit the first ball for three, and soon after got his first boundary with a square-cut.

At stumps, Bradman was 31 and Hassett 13.

# Harvey's brilliant century against England in 4th Test

*From ARTHUR MAILEY*

**LEEDS, Sat.**——Nineteen-year-old Neil Harvey today scored a brilliant fighting 112 in his first Test innings against England.

Going in when Hassett and Bradman had failed, he added 121 runs with Miller and in a partnership of 105 with Loxton.

Only other Australian 19-year-old to make a century against England was the late Archie Jackson.

He scored 164 at Adelaide in 1928-29.

Harvey last season scored a century in a Test against India.

He is only playing in to-day's match because Barnes is injured.

Shortly before tea Australia was six for 329, Loxton being 78 not out and Lindwall 0 not out.

Johnson was out for 10.

Australia, three down for 68 when Hassett and Bradman went, were in a bad position.

England had made 496.

## Bradman Bowled

Bradman and Hassett went in Pollard's first over, Hassett caught at slip, and Bradman bowled.

The wicket might then have been doing a little because of early rain.

Harvey started dashingly, and with Miller hit the English bowling for boundary after boundary.

He lost Miller at 58, with the score four for 189.

Fellow Victorian Loxton joined Harvey, who protected him from the bowling for 20 minutes before lunch.

After lunch, England took the new ball, and Harvey faced it with the confidence of an experienced opener.

He gradually wore down the attack, which had dismissed Bradman and Hassett, set sail after runs again, paused for a while, nearing his century.

He was obviously not over-awed, and the crowd took him to its heart for his debonair, cavalier run-chasing.

After he reached 100, he hit three fours, and was out bowled trying to pull Laker for another.

Loxton opened out under the influence of Harvey's brilliance, and hit seven fours and a six in his first 50.

Headingley Cricket Ground, Leeds, 1985.

Reproduction by Coalport of English County Cricket Club emblems in 1973, with the emblem of the 1973 County champions, Hampshire County Cricket Club, in the centre.

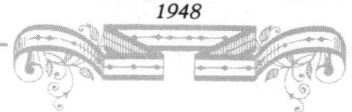

# GRINS AT 'SIR DONALD' TALE

From Arthur Mailey

*London, Saturday.—Don Bradman grinned when I asked him if there were any truth in rumors that he is to be knighted.*

"IT was something in the papers, but apart from that, I know nothing officially or otherwise," Bradman said.

I asked him if, in the event of a knighthood being offered, would he accept it.

"I cannot answer a question which, as far as I know, has no foundation," he said.

"It's just like a full toss coming along. You don't know what you'll do until it comes along."

Then I said, "Yes, but you usually know what to do with a full toss beforehand."

Bradman grinned.

"This is different," he said, grinned and disappeared into the night.

[There have been many reports that Bradman is to receive a knighthood on his retirement from cricket this year.]

# ENGLAND MAKES ALL-OUT BID FOR TEST VICTORY

From ARTHUR MAILEY

**LEEDS, Monday.—Forcing the pace, in a gallant bid for victory, England today established a lead of 400 over Australia in the Fourth Test.**

Beginning the second innings today with a lead of 38, England had scored 362 for the loss of eight wickets at stumps.

England today played to a bold plan.

It was obvious that it was better for England to go for runs and lose if the gamble failed, rather than repeat the dreariness of the Manchester Test, and allow the game to develop into a dull draw.

Hutton and Washbrook laid the foundations.

**They took the edge off the Australian attack until it was hammered and impotent.**

Both went at 129, forcing the pace.

Washbrook (65) was the victim of one of the greatest catches of the tour.

Harvey, Australia's baby-faced hero, took a running catch, inches from the ground, as Washbrook hooked Johnston to long-leg.

The English batsmen handled Australia's fast attack with amazing and—to Bradman—disturbing ease.

Without Toshack, Bradman brought Ian Johnson in to rest the fast men, but Compton and Edrich drove him out of the attack.

After tea Compton and Edrich cut loose, and when Edrich went l.b.w., Crapp carried on the plan of campaign.

## Wickets Fall

Wickets fell, but the English batsmen still chased runs.

Crapp, Yardley, and Cranston came and went, but the picture changed somewhat when Denis Compton departed.

England then had a lead of 331.

**Evans and Bedser, the heroes of England's first innings, however maintained the run-getting policy.**

Evans, playing with more enterprise than art, scored 47, and was not out at stumps.

Runs came freely from the edge of his bat.

The wicket today showed signs of wear from bowlers' footmarks.

Lindwall once switched to round the wicket, to avoid the holes, but the umpire ordered him to continue bowling over the wicket because Lindwall's spikes were damaging the pitch.

## Gates Shut

The fluctuating fortunes of the game drew a huge crowd.

**At 11.15, a quarter of an hour before play began, officials closed the gates.**

They estimated the crowd inside the ground at 40,000 and the crowd outside at 25,000.

Spectators crowded on to the playing area, seven or eight deep, inside the fence.

The two umpires and police tried for 10 minutes to persuade the crowd to leave the arena.

**They drew back to the boundary, but no farther—they had nowhere to go.**

As excitement mounted during the afternoon, and especially in the torrid after-tea session, the crowd pushed forward on to the field.

Twice umpire Chester walked to the edge of the crowd to check whether the ball had crossed the boundary.

Australia's first innings ended a few minutes after play started this morning.

Lindwall tried to force Bedser's second ball, and Crapp took a good one-handed catch at second slip.

Australia was out for 458.

TEST QUEUE COMEDY is shown in this Y.E. News picture at Headingley to-day, as two Wigan lads, James Russell (right) and John Woodcock, are kindly but firmly advised by the policeman that, Test or no Test, they can't pitch their tent on the pavement.

# Australia Set Big Test Task

Australian Associated Press

## LEEDS, July 27.

As a result of Yardley's delay in declaring until two overs had been bowled today, Australia was left with about 340 minutes to make 404 runs and win the fourth Test match, a scoring rate of nearly 72 runs an hour.

In the two overs at their disposal, Evans and Laker added three runs—one to Laker and a couple of leg-byes.

Morris and Hassett opened for Australia and showed no disposition to go after the target set by England.

Apart from 13 hit off Laker's first over, the first 40 minutes, which produced 31 runs, were uneventful. Laker made amends by sending down his next four overs for a single.

Only an occasional kicking ball from Bedser gave evidence of the wear and tear of five days' intensive play.

Morris broke the tranquillity by sweeping Laker to the long-eg boundary. Another boundary to Morris off Yardley, who had replaced Bedser, raised 50 in 58 minutes.

At 54, Evans should have stumped Morris off Compton when the Australian essayed a straight drive but missed the ball.

### Hassett Out

In his third over Compton beat Hassett badly and appealed unsuccessfully for l.b.w. Hassett played forward to the next ball and returned it gently to the bowler, the first Australian wicket falling for 57.

Morris greeted Bradman, once again received tumultuously by the crowd, by back-cutting Laker to the boundary.

Bradman made a powerful hook for four in Compton's next over, from which he took seven.

**In an effort to extract all the spin he could from the wicket and his bowlers, Yardley brought Hutton on instead of Compton. Unhappily, Hutton could not hit the pitch and Morris belted two full tosses for four. A third four from another full tosss gave Morris 51 in 85 minutes out of 82. He had hit nine fours.**

Hutton began his second over with two more full tosses—both hit for four by Bradman. Hutton's two overs cost 21 runs.

Hutton succeeded in hitting the pitch more often in his third over which was a maiden to Bradman, who was lucky in Compton's next over when he swung a ball just out of reach of Cranston for his fifth four. Then Bradman was missed at slip by Crapp.

The 100 was reached in 95 minutes, 10 minutes before lunch. Morris hit two more fours off Hutton's next over, and Bradman took the score to 120 by sweeping Compton to the long leg boundary.

At lunch, 121 had been made in an hour and three-quarters, the last 64 in half an hour.

Morris hit seven fours from the first nine balls he received from Compton after the interval, scoring 30 out of 34 in 14 minutes. Compton's first two after-lunch overs cost 31.

Morris brought up the 100 partnership in 47 minutes by on-driving Laker for four and reached 98 with the stroke.

Another four in Bedser's next over gave Morris his 100 in 127 minutes, his last 39 in 25 minutes, while Bradman was making eight.

Bedser checked the riot of runs with a maiden to Morris. A glorious late cut off Bedser took Bradman to 50 in 62 minutes with nine fours.

Cranston and Laker slowed down Australia's progress until a half-volley to Bradman cost Laker four, and Morris hit a boundary in the same over.

When Bradman mishit an off drive off Cranston, Yardley dropped a very difficult chance at point.

Two full-pitches from Laker to Morris both went for four to raise 201 in 160 minutes, and a lovely on-drive for four off Cranston made Bradman 66.

The stroke appeared to hurt him, and he walked back to the crease holding his left side as if suffering from cramp. Three balls later, Bradman hit another four—this time from a hook.

**With three hours left for play, Australia needed 195 runs.**

Bradman was clearly in considerable pain, hobbling between the wickets when he cut Bedser for a single after which Bedser took the new ball.

### Bradman Boundaries

Bradman skied a Bedser no-ball over the heads of the slips for four to reach 80 in 100 minutes, and he square-cut another boundary in Bedser's next over.

Amid deafening applause, Bradman hooked a short ball from Laker to the square-leg boundary to reach 103, and he repeated the stroke an over later, before being badly beaten and almost bowled by the next ball.

Bradman might have been stumped and Morris caught in successive overs from Laker and Compton respectively. Morris's chance went off Laker's hand at short leg for four.

Just before tea, Morris hit two fours off Laker to reach 150 in 235 minutes. The score at the interval was 288 for one wicket.

Bradman square-cut the first ball after tea from Laker for four, and hooked another boundary two balls later.

Yardley bowled for the first time in the innings and Morris hit another four to raise 300 in four hours.

Eighteen runs were scored in 10 minutes, leaving Australia only 98 behind with 95 minutes left.

Bradman added 23 in 17 minutes after tea and put Australia well ahead of the clock. Even Yardley, bowling to a tight leg field, could not check the scoring rate.

Two fours off Pollard took Morris to 169 and the total to 339. Morris had just passed his 1,000 in Tests and Bradman wanted three for his 5,000 when Morris skied Yardley and was caught by Pollard for 182 at mid-on after having batted for five hours.

Partnered by Miller, Bradman reached 152 in 230 minutes. He had hit 25 fours. Each batsman hit a four to leave Australia with only 20 required, with more than half an hour left.

A hooked four by Bradman off Cranston took Australia to 391, and he square-cut another boundary two balls later. Pollard then bowled a maiden to Miller.

Cranston took his first wicket in a Test match when, with eight needed, he had Miller l.b.w. for 12.

A four to Bradman off Pollard brought up 400 16 minutes before time. Harvey made the winning hit by flicking Cranston wristily to the long-on boundary.

# Bradman Goes For Those 404 Runs

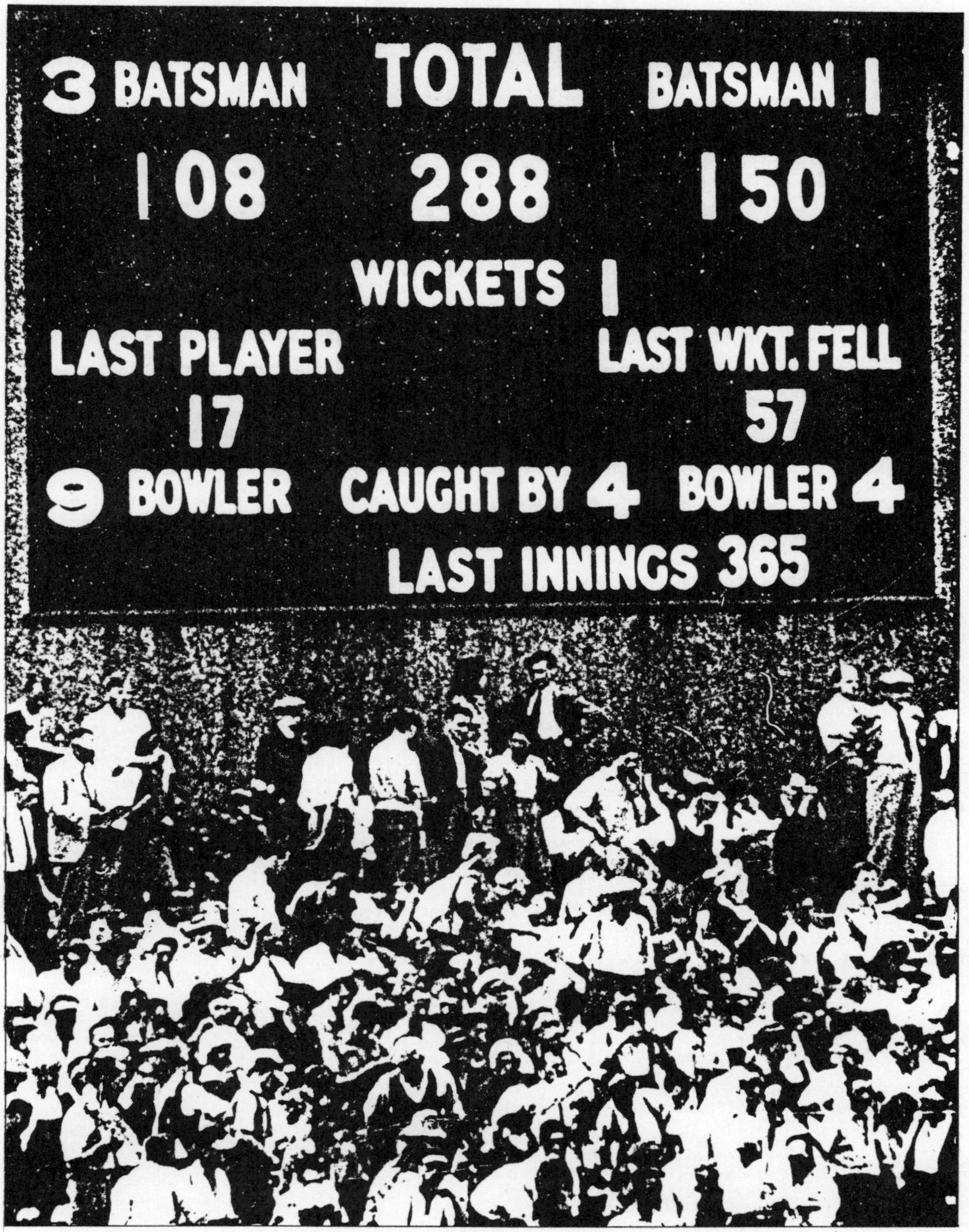

| 3 BATSMAN | TOTAL | BATSMAN 1 |
|---|---|---|
| 108 | 288 | 150 |

WICKETS 1

| LAST PLAYER | | LAST WKT. FELL |
|---|---|---|
| 17 | | 57 |

9 BOWLER  CAUGHT BY 4  BOWLER 4

LAST INNINGS 365

The scoreboard during the Bradman–Morris partnership.

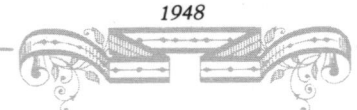

# AUSTRALIA WINS TEST
## Morris, Bradman Make Fast-Scoring Centuries

*Daily Telegraph Service and A.A.P.*

**HEADINGLEY, Tuesday.—Australia won the Fourth Test today by seven wickets and with 15 minutes to spare.**

**England had set Australia 404 in 345 minutes for victory. Morris (182) and Bradman (173 n.o.) made the win possible with fast scoring.**

England's captain, Yardley, had closed England's second innings at 8-365 after five minutes' batting this morning.

Morris reached his century in 127 minutes, and hit 20 fours.

Bradman's took 147 minutes and included 15 fours.

Before play began, Yardley announced that he would continue the second innings. and ordered the heavy roller

The wicket had stood up well to four days play. but Yardley saw a couple of doubtful patches which he hoped the roller would enlarge.

The weather was hot and sultry when Evans (47) and Laker (14) resumed England's second innings.

Evans took strike to Lindwall, whose third ball hit Evans pad and went to fine, leg for a single.

Miller bowled at the other end, and his second ball also went for a leg-bye.

Laker took a single with a push to the off from Miller's last ball, and Yardley then closed at 8-365—a lead of 403.

Hassett and Morris opened Australia's second innings to the bowling of Bedser and Pollard

Hassett took strike. and Bedser's first over produced four byes.

Morris scored a single in Pollard's first over and a three in Bedser's second.

Pollard's second over was a maiden

In Bedser's third over Hassett started his score with a two.

Pollard's third over was a maiden.

Then Laker replaced Bedser, and 13 were scored off his first over.

The Australian openers continued steadily, with Morris batting the brighter.

After Pollard had bowled six overs for six runs, Bedser was brought back to replace him.

At the other end Laker bowled four successive maidens.

After four more overs from Bedser. Yardley called on Compton, a slow left-hand spinner, to relieve him.

With a four in Compton's first over, Morris brought up Australia's 50 in 65 minutes.

In Compton's next over, Evans missed a chance of stumping Morris, who was 32.

With the fourth ball of his third over, Compton appealed confidently but unsuccessfully for l.b.w. against Hassett.

However, with the last ball of the over he got Hassett caught and bowled.

Hassett, who had been uncomfortable against Compton, played forward to a wrong 'un and spooned the ball back to the bowler.

Hassett was 17 and Australia 1-57.

## Five Fours In Row Off Hutton

When Laker had bowled 12 overs for 25 runs. Hutton, right-hand leg-break bowler. replaced him.

Morris hit the last three balls of the over for fours. to reach his half-century

He had batted 85 minutes and hit nine fours.

Bradman hit the first two balls of Hutton's second over to the fence. to take his score to 21.

Five successive fours had been taken from Hutton.

In his seventh over, Compton should have dismissed Bradman with the third and fifth balls.

The first chance was a snick from a forward defensive stroke to leg.

The ball went towards Crapp. in the slips, but he was not quick enough.

Edrich came up to second slip next ball, but Bradman turned it to leg for four to reach 30.

Next ball, another sharply turning-leg-break, went from the top of his bat to Crapp, who dropped one of the simplest catches of the match.

The last ball again beat Bradman completely

Morris and Bradman continued to hit out, and for the last over before lunch Hutton, whose four overs had cost 30 (seven fours and one two). was relieved by Laker.

At lunch Australia was 1-121. Morris was 63 and Bradman 35.

Bradman had batted 30 minutes and hit seven fours

Morris gave the total a spectacular boost in the quarter hour after lunch. when he took seven fours and two singles off two overs by Compton, to reach 93

Laker came back to curb the scoring rate, but Morris on-drove his first ball for four

A streaky four snicked off Bedser gave Morris his century in 126 minutes. He had then hit 20 fours.

Bradman was 43 and Australia 1-168.

Cranston. with his accurate but not hostile offbreaks, was put on to reduce the scoring rate.

He allowed only seven in his first four overs.

Bradman had another "life" at 59

He cut Cranston high to backward-point, but Yardley dropped the "hot" chance.

Australia had half the runs needed in 165 minutes. but Yardley took the new ball at 212 and again quietened the batsmen.

Bradman was in the 70's when he got a sudden twinge in the left side.

A perfectly-timed square cut to the boundary off Bedser and a four to fine leg off the handle of the bat, took Bradman to 89 and Australia to 243. 90 minutes after lunch.

Another flawless late-cut to the boundary off Bedser made Bradman 97 and the partnership worth 200 in two and a quarter hours.

A few minutes later Bradman reached his century with his 15th four.

Morris hit Laker to the square-leg boundary and brought up Australia's 200.

Later, a similar stroke off the same bowler brought the 250 up

Morris hit Compton's last ball before tea through the covers for four, and made his score 150.

Bradman chopped Bedser through slips to make the partnership worth 200.

Bradman, at 108, was feet out of his ground when Evans again fumbled a stumping chance off Laker.

Then Laker dropped an easy catch at square leg when Morris was 136.

After tea both batsmen continued to hit powerfully.

Morris off-drove Pollard for four, and took the partnership to 300.

Then, when 182, he was caught by Pollard off Yardley's bowling.

Bradman was then 143, and Australia 2-358—only 46 short of victory.

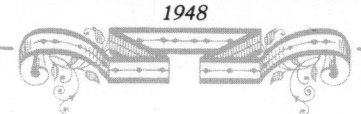

# Australians v Lancashire
## (C. Washbrook's Benefit)

AUSTRALIANS v LANCASHIRE (C. Washbrook's Benefit),
at Manchester, 7, 9 and 10 August 1948.

| Australians | - First Innings | 321 |
| | - Second Innings | 265 for 3 wickets dec. |
| Lancashire | - First Innings | 130 |
| | - Second Innings | 199 for 7 wickets |
| | Drawn. | |

| DON BRADMAN | - c. A.E. Wilson b. W.B. Roberts | 28 |
| (Captain) | - not out | 133 |

DON BRADMAN's first innings, on a green wicket, was one of his least impressive; he went in on the first afternoon, at 123 for 1, and took forty minutes for his first 4 runs, before giving a stumping chance off W.B. Roberts. He then tried to force the pace, but after giving another stumping chance off Roberts when 27, was soon afterwards caught at the wicket off that bowler, at 175 for 3; he was in for an hour and thirteen minutes.

He had sixty-six minutes' batting at the end of the second day, when he went in at 21 for 1, and reached 25 not out by the close, steady bowling keeping him on the defensive; next morning, he batted much more confidently, and, after twenty-three minutes in the forties, ran to 50 in an hour and fifty-six minutes. He completed his century in three hours six minutes, and by the lunch interval, when he declared, he had made 133 in three hours thirty-six minutes, having added 108 in two and a half hours before lunch. He hit seventeen fours and gave no chance. His declaration left Lancashire only two and three-quarter hours' batting.

This was the eighth occasion altogether, and the fourth in England, on which he added over 100 runs before lunch.

## Australians

| | | | | |
|---|---|---|---|---|
| S. G. Barnes c Ikin b Roberts | 67 | — | c Wilson b Pollard | 90 |
| A. R. Morris c Wilson b Roberts | 49 | — | c Place b Pollard | 16 |
| D. G. Bradman c Wilson b Roberts | 28 | — | not out | 133 |
| K. R. Miller lbw b Ikin | 24 | — | c Howard b Pollard | 11 |
| R. A. Hamence c and b Roberts | 14 | — | not out | 10 |
| S. J. Loxton c G. Edrich b Roberts | 2 | | | |
| R. R. Lindwall c Wilson b Roberts | 17 | | | |
| I. W. Johnson c and b | 48 | | | |
| D. Tallon c Pollard b Greenwood | 33 | | | |
| D. Ring not out | 17 | | | |
| E. R. H. Toshack c Howard b Pollard | 2 | | | |
| B 16, l-b 3, w 1 | 20 | | B 4, l-b 1 | 5 |
| | 321 | | Three wkts., dec. | 265 |

## Lancashire

| | | | | |
|---|---|---|---|---|
| C. Washbrook c Miller b Lindwall | 38 | | | |
| W. Place c Ring b Lindwall | 5 | — | b Lindwall | 11 |
| G. A. Edrich c Tallon b Lindwall | 0 | — | lbw b Ring | 25 |
| J. T. Ikin c Bradman b Loxton | 9 | — | b Lindwall | 99 |
| A. Wharton c Bradman b Miller | 5 | — | c Tallon b Johnson | 1 |
| N. D. Howard not out | 28 | — | b Lindwall | 8 |
| K. Cranston st Tallon b Ring | 18 | — | c Johnson b Ring | 16 |
| P. Greenwood st Tallon b Johnson | 3 | — | not out | 16 |
| R. Pollard c Lindwall b Ring | 1 | — | b Lindwall | 0 |
| W. B. Roberts c Loxton b Johnson | 1 | — | not out | 0 |
| A. E. Wilson c and b Johnson | 4 | | | |
| B 13, l-b 4, w 1 | 18 | | B 10, l-b 12, w 1 | 23 |
| | 130 | | Seven wkts. | 199 |

## Lancashire Bowling

| | O. | M. | R. | W. | O. | M. | R. | W. |
|---|---|---|---|---|---|---|---|---|
| Pollard | 27 | 6 | 58 | 2 | 27 | 8 | 58 | 3 |
| Greenwood | 19 | 4 | 62 | 1 | 13 | 2 | 53 | 0 |
| Cranston | 3 | 0 | 24 | 0 | 8 | 2 | 34 | 0 |
| Wharton | 1 | 0 | 4 | 0 | | | | |
| Ikin | 39 | 12 | 80 | 1 | 15 | 3 | 51 | 0 |
| Roberts | 42 | 14 | 73 | 6 | 22 | 4 | 64 | 0 |

## Australian Bowling

| | O. | M. | R. | W. | O. | M. | R. | W. |
|---|---|---|---|---|---|---|---|---|
| Lindwall | 16 | 3 | 32 | 3 | 11 | 2 | 27 | 4 |
| Miller | 11 | 3 | 22 | 1 | 5 | 1 | 10 | 0 |
| Loxton | 9 | 4 | 11 | 1 | 7 | 2 | 21 | 0 |
| Toshack | 7 | 4 | 17 | 0 | | | | |
| Ring | 11 | 4 | 25 | 2 | 22 | 3 | 88 | 2 |
| Johnson | 5 | 2 | 5 | 3 | 12 | 6 | 30 | 1 |

Umpires: T. J. Bartley and J. Smart.

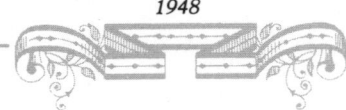

# AUST. IN DRAW
## Failed To Force Win

*Daily Telegraph Service and A.A.P.*

**OLD TRAFFORD, Tuesday.—Australia failed by two wickets to force a win against Lancashire today.**

**The match was drawn after Bradman had closed Australia's second innings, leaving his bowlers 165 minutes to get Lancashire out and force a win.**

At stumps Lancashire was 130 and 7-119 in reply to Australia's 321 and 3-265 (closed).

Lancashire went in 456 behind after lunch, one man short with Washbrook not playing because of an injured right thumb.

Lindwall took two wickets with successive balls 10 minutes before stumps, but Roberts saved the hat-trick by edging the ball.

One of his wickets was that of Ikin, whom he yorked for 99.

Earlier, Lindwall, bowling his fastest of the tour, had taken Lancashire's first two wickets in the first half an hour.

Bradman got his eighth century of the tour with 133 not out.

Bradman (25) and Barnes (39) resumed for Australia at 1-81.

The wicket was good and the weather fine.

Barnes batted for 122 minutes before he reached 50 with a single off Roberts.

### Misses Century

Barnes, at 90, snicked an out-swinger from Pollard to wicket-keeper Wilson.

Barnes had batted 178 minutes, and hit 10 fours, and, with Bradman, set up a partnership of 167.

Miller was caught by Howard off Pollard for 11.

Bradman's century came up from a neat glance to the boundary off Cranston.

He had then batted 186 minutes and hit 13 fours.

In Lancashire's innings, only Ikin appeared comfortable against the Australian bowling. Ring got two wickets and Ian Johnson one.

The Australian team to play Durham at Sunderland, starting tomorrow, is: A. L. Hassett (captain), W. A. Brown, R. A. Hamence, K. R. Miller, N. Harvey, S. Loxton, D. Tallon, R. Saggers, I. Johnson, C. V. McCool, D. Ring, W. Johnston (12th.).

## MATCH ENDS IN DRAW

### Bradman's Century In 186 Minutes

LONDON, Aug. 10: Batting with unusual caution Bradman scored a century at Old Trafford today when the match against Lancashire was continued. At the luncheon interval Bradman declared Australia's second innings closed with three wickets down for 265 and at stumps the county had lost seven wickets for 199. Thus the game was drawn.

Bradman has now made 1,917 runs for the tour and scored his eighth century. He brought up his 100 in 186 minutes.

After making 90 in 178 minutes Barnes snicked an outswinger and was caught by the wicket-keeper, Wilson. He and Bradman added 167 runs. Miller was caught for 11 in attempting a big hit.

**BRADMAN HONOURED.**
The Lancashire Club has elected Don Bradman a life member in appreciation of his services to English-Australian cricket.

The following material brings to a close my cricket on foreign soil; in particular, my final test at the Oval.

For me personally, a duck, out second ball, was of course a sad exit from the Test arena. But for Australia the match was an incredible victory. England won the toss and her captain elected to bat so the wicket could scarcely have been villainous, yet the whole side was out for 52, the lowest score ever recorded by England against Australia in the home country.

What a contrast from the 907 for 7 wickets, scored by England in the last Test of the previous tour.

The Australian team continued to the end undefeated, a feat not achieved by any of its predecessors. The whole performance reflected a side splendidly equipped for all occasions with players dedicated to the service of their country and with a spirit to match their talent. It was truly a marvellous team.

Finishing the tour with three first class centuries was some consolation for my Test match failure and it was a real thrill to close my overseas cricket with a century at Aberdeen. A perfect Scottish summer day and an appreciative audience produced for me an inner feeling of great satisfaction that on the cricket field I had faithfully served my fellow men.

*Don Bradman*

# Australia v England
## Fifth Test Match

AUSTRALIA v ENGLAND, Fifth Test Match, at the Oval, 14, 16, 17 and 18 August 1948.

| Australia | - First Innings | 389 |
| | - Second Innings | - |
| England | - First Innings | 52 |
| | - Second Innings | 188 |

Australia won by an innings and 149 runs.

DON BRADMAN    - b. W.E. Hollies        0
(Captain)

After England's lamentable first innings on a wet but easy pitch, S.G. Barnes and A.R. Morris added 117 for Australia's first wicket, and set the stage for a big score by DON BRADMAN in his last Test Match; he went in at 5.50 p.m. on the first evening, and the England team, led by N.W.D. Yardley, greeted him by giving him three cheers. Possibly affected by this reception, Bradman played his first ball, a leg-break, hesitantly to silly mid-off, and tried to play the same stroke, equally hesitantly to his second; this time it was a googly, which turned back just enough to beat his bat and dislodge his off-bail. His Test Match career thus ended on a note of anticlimax and disappointment, so far as his personal performance was concerned; but Australia's easy victory was some consolation. Had he scored 4 runs, he would have completed an aggregate of 7,000 runs in all Test Matches, and would have had a career Test average of 100.

### England

| | 1st | | 2nd |
|---|---|---|---|
| L. Hutton c Tallon b Lindwall | 30 | c Tallon b Miller | 64 |
| J. G. Dewes b Miller | 1 | b Lindwall | 10 |
| W. J. Edrich c Hassett b Johnston | 3 | b Lindwall | 28 |
| D. C. S. Compton c Morris b Lindwall | 4 | c Lindwall b Johnston | 39 |
| J. F. Crapp c Tallon b Miller | 0 | b Miller | 9 |
| N. W. D. Yardley b Lindwall | 7 | c Miller b Johnston | 9 |
| A. Watkins lbw b Johnston | 0 | c Hassett b Ring | 2 |
| T. G. Evans b Lindwall | 1 | b Lindwall | 8 |
| A. V. Bedser b Lindwall | 0 | b Johnston | 0 |
| J. A. Young b Lindwall | 0 | not out | 3 |
| W. E. Hollies not out | 0 | c Morris b Johnston | 0 |
| B 6 | 6 | B 9, l-b 4, n-b 3 | 16 |
| | 52 | | 188 |

### Australia

| | | | | |
|---|---|---|---|---|
| S. G. Barnes c Evans b Hollies | 61 | R. R. Lindwall c Edrich b Young | 9 |
| A. R. Morris run out | 196 | D. Tallon c Crapp b Hollies | 31 |
| D. G. Bradman b Hollies | 0 | D. Ring c Crapp b Bedser | 9 |
| A. L. Hassett lbw b Young | 37 | W. A. Johnston not out | 0 |
| K. R. Miller st Evans b Hollies | 5 | B 4, l-b 2, n-b 3 | 9 |
| R. N. Harvey c Young b Hollies | 17 | | |
| S. J. Loxton c Evans b Edrich | 15 | | 389 |

### Australia Bowling

| | O. | M. | R. | W. | O. | M. | R. | W. |
|---|---|---|---|---|---|---|---|---|
| Lindwall | 16.1 | 5 | 20 | 6 | 25 | 3 | 50 | 3 |
| Miller | 8 | 5 | 5 | 2 | 15 | 6 | 22 | 2 |
| Johnston | 16 | 4 | 20 | 2 | 27.3 | 12 | 40 | 4 |
| Loxton | 2 | 1 | 1 | 0 | 10 | 2 | 16 | 0 |
| Ring | | | | | 28 | 13 | 44 | 1 |

### England Bowling

| | O. | M. | R. | W. |
|---|---|---|---|---|
| Bedser | 31.2 | 9 | 61 | 1 |
| Watkins | 4 | 1 | 19 | 0 |
| Young | 51 | 16 | 118 | 2 |
| Hollies | 56 | 14 | 131 | 5 |
| Compton | 2 | 0 | 6 | 0 |
| Edrich | 9 | 0 | 38 | 1 |
| Yardley | 5 | 1 | 7 | 0 |

### FALL OF WICKETS

ENGLAND—First Innings:

| 1 | 2 | 3 | 4 | 5 | 6 | 7 | 8 | 9 |
|---|---|---|---|---|---|---|---|---|
| 2 | 10 | 17 | 23 | 35 | 42 | 45 | 45 | 47 |

ENGLAND—Second Innings:

| 1 | 2 | 3 | 4 | 5 | 6 | 7 | 8 | 9 |
|---|---|---|---|---|---|---|---|---|
| 20 | 64 | 125 | 153 | 164 | 167 | 178 | 181 | 188 |

AUSTRALIA—First Innings:

| 1 | 2 | 3 | 4 | 5 | 6 | 7 | 8 | 9 |
|---|---|---|---|---|---|---|---|---|
| 117 | 117 | 226 | 243 | 265 | 304 | 332 | 359 | 389 |

Umpires: D. Davies and H. G. Baldwin.

A great leader emerges with his men for the last time: Don Bradman, now concluding his fourth tour of England and his second as captain, leading his men on to the field for the last Test at the Oval. In all the Tests he has played against England, Bradman has scored an average of 89.77, made eleven single centuries, six doubles, and two innings over 300. He now retires definitely from the arena.

Don Bradman b. Hollies 0.

# England All Out 52—Don A "Duck"

(TRUTH'S SPECIAL SERVICE.)

**THE OVAL, Saturday.**—After Yardley had won the toss, England collapsed dramatically in the Fifth Test today and were all out after two and a half hours for 52—the lowest Test score ever recorded by them in England.

The first wicket fell five minutes after play began and from then on there was a continuous procession of batsmen making their way dejectedly back to the pavilion.

Hutton played a valiant lone-hand innings, scoring 30 of England's total. He was the last man dismissed, and was unfortunate not to join R. Abel, who remains the only Englishman to carry his bat through a Test innings.

The innings was a personal triumph for Australian fast bowler Ray Lindwall who took 6 wickets (four bowled) for 20 runs. Miller took 2 for 5.

Today's collapse was a particularly bitter pill for the English as in the corresponding game on the last tour of England in 1938 England compiled the record Test score of 903 for 7 wickets and beat Australia by the record margin of an innings and 579 runs.

Of the three players who represented England in that game who played for England today, two recognised batsmen failed utterly on both occasions—Edrich 12 in '38 and 3 today, Compton 1 in 1938 and 4 today—while the third, Hutton, scored the world's individual record Test score of 364 in 1938 and today proved the only prop in the English side.

England's lowest score in all Anglo-Australian Tests is 45, recorded at Sydney in 1886.

Their previous lowest in England stood at 53, made at Leeds in 1888.

Lowest Test score ever recorded was Australia's 36 at Birmingham in 1902.

The Australian openers, Morris and Barnes passed the English total before tea in 57 minutes.

Morris and Barnes doubled the English total before Barnes was caught behind off Hollies, the Warwickshire spinner, who had taken eight for 107 against the tourists early this month—including Bradman and Harvey.

Bradman, playing in his final Test, received a magnificent ovation as he walked out to bat, the entire oval standing as a man and cheering him all the way. Yardley met him near the crease, and, after shaking his hand, called for three cheers from the English team.

The day of sensations, however, had not ended. After blocking the first ball he received from Hollies, Don went forward to the next and was completely beaten and bowled.

Bradman returned to the pavilion with as big a grin as he had when he left it.

Stumps score was two for 152—Morris 77, Hassett 10.

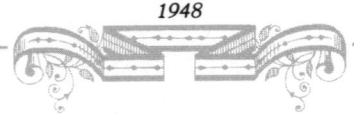

# AUSTRALIA'S LEAD NOW 283

## Morris Misses Double Century

LONDON, Aug. 16: Although the consistent Morris scored 196, Australia was out for 389 in its first innings of the fifth Test match at Kennington Oval today. England, whose main bowler was Hollies, began its second innings 337 in arrears and at stumps had lost Dewes's wicket for 54.

Morris overshadowed the other Australian batsmen and was most unlucky to be run out when only four runs short of his double century and when Australia's total was 359. His was a chanceless display and the more meritorious because his partners in succession today were all ill-at-ease. He batted for 406 minutes and hit 16 fours.

Until he and Tallon went for that cheeky single Morris looked likely to become one of the few players who have batted right through a Test innings and remained not out. At least he deserved the satisfaction of scoring 200 in a Test against England—a feat performed by D. G. Bradman (eight times), W. H. Ponsford, S. J. McCabe, W. L. Murdoch, W. A. Brown, S. E. Gregory, J. Ryder and S. Barnes. His score of 196 was the highest made in the current series, beating Compton's 184 and his own 182. Morris has now made 1,199 runs against England and his average is 79.9.

The 36-year-old E. Hollies, who earned Test selection very late in his career, bowled with admirable accuracy, flighting the ball cleverly. He took five for 131 off 56 overs and gave the best performance by a slow bowler against Australia this season.

After Dewes had again failed at the start of England's second innings, Hutton and Edrich determinedly played out time. Ring, bowling for the first time against England, delivered a succession of maiden overs. The half-century was posted in 70 minutes.

### NEW BALL USED.

Yardley claimed a new ball in the second over but Bedser and Edrich could not penetrate the calm defence of Morris and Hassett in the early overs.

Four through covers against Edrich and three wide of Dewes at point against Hollies gave Morris his century. He continued with unrelaxed vigilance and showed no desire to improve the scoring rate which had slackened temporarily while Hassett carefully played Hollies's leg-breaks.

Australia's 200 came up in 235 minutes. Both batsmen studied Hollies's slows with great deliberation. He bowled six overs which cost only four runs before Morris drove an over-pitched ball powerfully past Simpson at extra cover to the boundary.

At the pavilion end Young did not seem dangerous. He bowled six overs for 11 runs before Yardley put himself on. Hassett, who had scored only 13 in the first hour today, earned ironic cheers when he jumped out and straight-drove a ball from Hollies for three.

England had its first success for the day when Young and Hollies changed ends. Young, with his third ball from the Vauxhall end, had Hassett l.b.w. with a slightly faster ball. Hassett had taken 133 minutes to make 37 (two fours).

Miller had made only five when he stretched out to drive a ball from Hollies in the last over before lunch and was beaten by the spin. He was out of his ground when Evans smartly brought off a stumping.

Harvey played a sparkling but short-lived innings, scoring 17 in 23 minutes. He began with fours, straight-driven and hooked, against Young and treated Hollies, who was still England's most dangerous bowler, with scant respect. Aggression led to his downfall. He jumped out to drive a shorter ball from Hollies, mistimed the stroke, and gave Young a waist-high catch at mid-off.

### UNHURRIED.

Precise and unhurried, Morris continued to score effortlessly with shots placed skilfully through gaps in the field. A single for a gentle pat towards mid-off took his score to 150.

Yardley delayed use of the third new ball until Young seemed likely to prove too expensive. Bedser took it at 299 and Loxton's shot to mid-wicket for two made the total 301 in 315 minutes. In Edrich's next over he swung at a short, rising ball which went off the edge of the bat to Evans, the keeper.

Lindwall, the seventh man out, had contributed nine to the relatively modest total of 332 when he skied a catch to Edrich behind point. Young had then taken two for 91 off 42 overs and was now making the ball turn appreciably.

Morris seemed certain to score his first Test double century when he called for a very risky single for a square-cut by Tallon. Simpson picked up the ball smartly and his accurate throw found Morris just out of his ground.

Tallon, with perfect drives to the on and the off, carried the score on to 380 but nine runs later the side was out.

England had 80 minutes in which to bat before stumps when Dewes and Hutton opened its second innings. Dewes took strike to Lindwall and swung hopefully at the last ball of the first over which bumped and which he snicked for four.

It was not long, however, before Lindwall captured Dewes's wicket, as at ten the young left-hander did not even put his bat near a late-swinger and was bowled off his pads.

# DON TAKES HIS CURTAIN

## Longest hat-trick ever may be completed —two years from now

"This is the last time I shall play in a test." Don Bradman says farewell to Test cricket as he speaks to the crowd at the end of yesterday's final Test at the Oval.

On the Oval balcony Norman Yardley (dark jacket) calls for cheers for "the greatest cricketer of all time." Bradman is second from left.

## By VICTOR LEWIS

AUSTRALIAN Test bowler W. A. Johnston will have to wait two years for the chance to complete a Test hat-trick.

It took 20 minutes yesterday to finish off the game. Johnston took the three remaining England wickets: two of them with the last two balls of the match.

So the first English batsman to face him in Australia two years from now will be trying to stave off the longest hat-trick ever.

After the match which England lost by an innings and 149 runs. Australian captain Don Bradman, confirming the announcement that he had played in his last Test, paid this rather ambiguous compliment to Norman Yardley:

"In Norman Yardley," he said, "I have found a very lovable opposition skipper. He has been very kind to us in every sense, and it has been a great pleasure to find him captaining the England team."

Bradman went on to say that Yardley had been in an unfortunate position because "I think he has been up against one of the strongest Australian sides ever to visit this country."

Yardley, for his part said, "We are saying good-bye to the greatest cricketer of all time: a great cricketer and a very great sportsman."

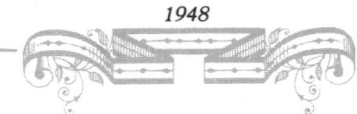

## SALUTE TO BRADMAN

"We are saying good-bye," said the English captain at the close of Bradman's last Test match, "to a man who, without doubt, is the greatest cricketer of all time." Yardley's valedictory tribute, like much else in Don Bradman's career, may be a theme of controversy. "Greatest" is always a term of challenge. Partisans of the giants of other days will be slow to concede that Bradman's surpassing powers as a run-getter place him first among the heroes of cricket.

Such disputations may be left to the historians and statisticians of the game. The mass of his countrymen now will prefer to recall, with gratitude and admiration, how much Australian cricket owes to Bradman. He gave it new life and interest. He conferred international predominance upon it, between the wars and since. Records cluster thick about his name. Centuries flowed miraculously from his bat. In his heyday a Bradman failure was news, so thoroughly had he accustomed his admirers —even his idolaters among generations of schoolboys—to expect glittering and phenomenal success.

And to the last his capacity to amass vast scores on occasion remained undimmed. Or almost to the last. The ironies and uncertainties of cricket decreed that, after his triumph at Headingley, he should finish his Test career at The Oval with a "duck." This final lapse of genius matters only as being contrary to the natural fitness of things. Bradman should have gone out in a blaze of glory— and indeed he has, for under his masterly leadership a great Australian team has been the first to win four Tests in a series in England. "Don" has still much to offer Australian cricket on the administrative side. In the field we shall not soon, we may not ever, look upon his like again.

Don Bradman cuts the special cake to commemorate his last appearance in English Test matches.

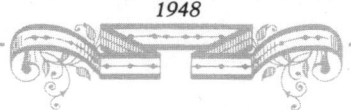

# HERBERT J. LONG,

### Journalist, Football, Cricket and Sports Correspondent,

ooo ESTABLISHED 1899. ooo

*Leading Provincial, Midland and Southern Newspapers Catered for.*
*Special Criticism for Morning Papers by Train.*
*Reports Telephoned to London Office of Provincial Newspapers.*

*Telephone work a speciality.*

*Reliable Reports and Comments by Trunk Telephone.*

*Experienced Telephone Operators.*

*Reports & Comments promptly by Press Telegram.*

*Special Cyclist Messengers.*

*Cup-tie matter a speciality.*

TEMPORARY OFFICE:-
RD.
PLUMSTEAD, LONDON, S.E.18.

D. Bradman Esq.,                                    16th August, 1948.
Captain,
Australia Cricket Team (in England) 1948.
Kennington Oval, S. E. 11.

My dear Don,

I am now nearly 70 years of age, and, have been Reporting Test Cricket matches in England 43 years. Next to Mr. Hubert Preston, Editor of "Wisden" my great friend, and, at one time my Colleague on the staff of the Cricket Reporting Agency, I believe I was the second oldest Pressman in the Press Box at the Oval on Saturday last, 14th August:

I feel I must write to you to say I thank God I have been spared to witness the unforgettable scene at the Oval on Saturday when you emerged from the pavilion to take your place at the crease. First, the Surrey Members and, their Guests, in the pavilion seats, stood up and set the cheering going. The whole community on the ground were upstanding like a flash, Men, Women, of all ages, Youths, young Girls, and Children, Boys and Girls, who, through their Parents, had been privileged to be present on this historic occasion, shouted and clapped their hands with an enthusiasm that I, in my long lifetime, have never seen on a Cricket Field before. And, I have seen all the old masters receptions in their last Test match, Mc. Laren, Hobbs, Ranji, Hendren, Woolley and the rest of them. Then the climax to your wonderful reception came. The sight of the England team, spread out, but facing the pavilion to greet you and clap you in right up to the crease. Then came Norman Yardley, England's Captain, HATLESS, to go forward to you and, as I saw through the powerful glasses, to give you a real PAL'S right hearty grip of the hand of congratulation. Then suddenly, Yardley raises his Cap and calls for THREE CHEERS for Don Bradman, and, the whole assembly give it as I have never seen it on a First Class Cricket Ground before.

To me, an old man, it was an amazing sight. I was thrilled to the bone, and, suddenly, I felt a tear trickling down my cheek, and, I am not ashamed of it. The Oval crowd have always been a great cricket public. The British crowd, as well as the multitude of Australians, who were at the Oval on Saturday, were keyed right up, and, how sincere was their shouts and hand-clapping for Don Bradman. It was a wonderful day for them and, a wonderful day for me. In this wonderful atmosphere Don, none of us, who witnessed it, can exactly vision what your emotion could have been. We can just assume. My greatest thrill on a cricket field was many years ago, when I bowled out W. G. Grace, and, sent his middle stump spinning out of the ground. My thrill at the Oval on Saturday was as great. It will remain with me for the rest of my day's short though they may be.

Don, you are shortly going back to Australia. And, in your mind will be the fact that, the Bristish public have not only admired your cricket. BUT, also your sportsmanship. You, too, have the consolation of knowing that the lads you have with you on the 1948 tour have set a standard for future Australian Cricketers that will be difficult to emulate. What a great joy it must have been to you to lead such a great lot of lads, efficient in their job as cricketers, and faultless in their behaviour both on, and off the field You can go back to your retirement with the knowledge that

"YOU HAVE ALWAYS PLAYED THE GAME"

To win. Yes, of course, we cricketers always want to win. It is cricket. BRADMAN'S POLICY has always been to WIN. BUT with the right sporting instinct behind it all the time..

DON. BRAVO: Well done, and, this applies to all the members of your splendid team. I am an Englishman. BUT you have, with the assistance of the rest of your team, TROUNCED our chaps true and proper by superior cricket in all departments.

FIELDIND, BATTING and BOWLING

I congratulate you all.

Don, just one final word. May you live many years to enjoy your retirement, enjoy first class health, without the troubles athletes usually have in advancing years. That is the sincere wish of an old campaigner, a man, whole heart and soul has been in cricket since I was at school.

To you all I say a safe journey when you sail back.

Yours very sincerely,

*Herbert J. Long.*

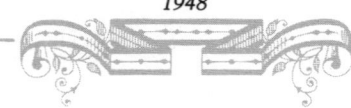

# Australians v Gentlemen of England

AUSTRALIANS v GENTLEMEN OF ENGLAND, at Lord's,
25, 26 and 27 August 1948.

| Australians | - First Innings | 610 for 5 wickets dec. |
| | - Second Innings | - |
| Gents. of Eng. | - First Innings | 245 |
| | - Second Innings | 284 |

Australians won by an innings and 81 runs.

DON BRADMAN - c. M.P. Donnelly b. F.R. Brown      150
(Captain)

DON BRADMAN's last innings at Lord's was one of his best and most assured; starting at 40 for 1 on the first morning, he soon made the 18 he required to complete an aggregate of 2,000 runs for the tour, this being the fourth occasion he had done so.    He reached 50 just after lunch in eighty-two minutes, and 100 in two and a half hours; but after batting for three hours thirty-two minutes, he threw away his wicket, being caught off a skier at wide mid-on.    He hit nineteen fours in a chanceless innings.

On the last day of the match he celebrated his fortieth birthday, and thus became the oldest (as he had been the youngest) Touring batsman to make 2,000 runs in an English season.

## Australians

| | | | |
|---|---|---|---|
| S. G. Barnes c Wooller b Bailey... | 19 | S. J. Loxton c Griffith b Bailey ... | 17 |
| W. A. Brown c Bailey b Wooller | .120 | R. A. Hamence not out ......... | 24 |
| D. G. Bradman c Donnelly b Brown | 150 | B 6, l-b 4, w 1 ............. | 11 |
| A. L. Hassett not out ..........| 200 | | |
| K. R. Miller c Simpson b Wooller | 69 | Five wkts., dec. | 610 |

I. W. Johnson, R. R. Lindwall, R. A. Saggers and D. Ring did not bat.

## Gentlemen

| | | | | |
|---|---|---|---|---|
| R. T. Simpson c Brown b Johnson ..... | 60 | — c Bradman b Ring ........ | 27 |
| W. J. Edrich b Ring ................. | 27 | — c Saggers b Ring ........ | 128 |
| C. H. Palmer c and b Johnson ........ | 3 | — b Miller ............... | 29 |
| M. P. Donnelly lbw b Johnson ....... | 15 | — c Barnes b Miller ........ | 8 |
| N. W. D. Yardley b Miller ........... | 25 | — b Ring................. | 18 |
| F. G. Mann lbw b Lindwall ......... | 7 | — c and b Ring ............ | 0 |
| R. W. V. Robins b Johnson........... | 30 | — b Johnson.............. | 19 |
| W. Wooller c Johnson b Hamence ... | 11 | — c Loxton b Ring ......... | 5 |
| T. E. Bailey c Hamence b Ring ....... | 20 | — not out ............... | 14 |
| F. R. Brown c Hamence b Ring ....... | 18 | — c Brown b Johnson....... | 17 |
| S. C. Griffith not out................. | 13 | — b Johnson.............. | 0 |
| B 8, l-b 8 ................. | 16 | B 11, l-b 7, w 1 ...... | 19 |
| | 245 | | 284 |

## Gentlemen Bowling

| | O. | M. | R. | W. |
|---|---|---|---|---|
| Bailey ........ | 27 | 4 | 112 | 2 |
| Wooller....... | 24 | 1 | 131 | 2 |
| Palmer....... | 21 | 3 | 58 | 0 |
| Edrich ........ | 16 | 3 | 49 | 0 |
| Yardley ....... | 24 | 5 | 88 | 0 |
| Brown ........ | 27 | 0 | 121 | 1 |
| Robins ....... | 4 | 0 | 22 | 0 |
| Donnelly...... | 6 | 0 | 18 | 0 |

## LAST BRADMAN 100 AT LORD'S

### STROKES SHOW NO SIGN OF AGE

#### From E. W. SWANTON
LORD'S, Wednesday.

Bradman made his farewell to Lord's and to London this afternoon with an innings of 150 and when he came in the pavilion rose and to a man doffed its hat, in case there may be no second chance.

The Australians always seemed assured of a long score for the pitch was wonderfully easy and the Gentlemen's bowling not above average contemporary quality, so that Bradman's runs were not especially hardly come by.

His was mostly a serene, equable piece of batsmanship, the runs always accruing quickly without anything violent except when someone bowled a long hop; then the ball was invariably murdered. As when he was young, he scarcely ever hooks for less than four.

Bradman to-day is inevitably slower to judge the length of the ball than in his youth. Thus he was sometimes caught leaning forward, especially to F. R. Brown, where in 1930 he would have been playing back very firmly. But much of his execution shows no sign of age, and he played exquisite off-drives and late cuts which could have been taken from his 254 against England here, perhaps the most technically perfect innings ever played.

It was Barnes who began the day in a particularly punitive mood, but it was Brown, strangely enough, who contributed the fastest innings of all, for Barnes fell to an admirable low catch at third slip. Brown played beautifully, always perfectly balanced, the stroke so easy and yet so powerful. The Canterbury spectators must have cheered him if they had seen him to-day, and it was a startling thought that we were watching someone apparently not quite good enough for the Australian Test side.

#### LIMITED BOWLING

Hassett played second to Bradman until the great man, after 3½ hours' batting, got underneath an on-drive and hit it high to mid-on. Then Hassett broadened out with the strokes he can always show at will, while Miller, though beaten now and then, batted powerfully at the other end.

The Gentlemen, after an unfortunate beginning in which they stayed out in persistent rain and so had a wet ball to bowl with, made the best they could of an unfavourable situation. A good deal of the fielding was excellent, and Robins stretched his limited bowling as far as it would go, even to the extent of Donnelly, who had a very creditable bowl, slow left-arm into the strong wind.

Don Bradman's 40th birthday cake presented to him by all at Lord's.

## Bradman Gets Birthday Cake

LONDON, Thursday.—Don Bradman celebrated his 40th birthday at Lord's today

The M.C.C presented him with a cake, made in the shape of a large open book.

Four confectionery kangaroos held the book, on which rested a confectionery spray of rose, wattle, and maiden hair.

The president of the M.C.C. (Lord Gowrie) presented the cake to Bradman, who cut it and was toasted in champagne.

# INNINGS WIN TO AUSTRALIANS

LONDON, Aug. 27 (A.A.P.).—Despite a brilliant century before lunch by W. J. Edrich, the Gentlemen were dismissed for 284 in their second innings to-day, the Australians winning by an innings and 81 runs.

On a pitch responsive to spin, Ring and Ian Johnson called the tune after lunch.

The Gentlemen had followed on this morning still 365 runs short of Australia's score of 610.

The Australian attack was without fast bowler Ray Lindwall, in bed suffering from a chill.

Simpson, highest scorer in the first innings, helped Edrich to put on 60 for the first wicket before he skied a ball from Ring to Bradman at mid-on.

Then in a brilliant burst Edrich ran to the nineties with seven fours from consecutive scoring strokes.

Another two fours to Edrich.

## Serenade To Bradman

LONDON, Aug. 27 (A.A.P.).—Elderly gentlemen basking in the sun in front of Lord's pavilion looked on benignly when the Australians gathered round Bradman on the field this morning and sang "Happy Birthday."

Bradman grinned hugely at the unprecedented serenade in the solemn precincts of Lord's. He is 40 to-day.

off Miller, who was bowling offbreaks, took the Englishman to 100 in 130 minutes. He had then hit 18 fours.

Miller dismissed both Palmer and Donnelly soon after lunch.

A well pitched-up leg-break, snicked to Saggers, gave Ring Edrich's wicket at 217.

Edrich batted 195 minutes and hit 22 fours.

In the same over he neatly caught and bowled Mann, and 13 balls later Yardley played a wrong-un on to his wicket.

Ring had taken five for 57 when Loxton took a chest-high catch at long leg from Wooller.

Ian Johnson soon routed the tail, Australia winning with 35 minutes to spare.

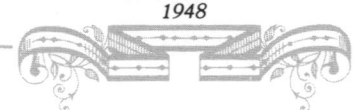

# Australians
# v
# South of England

AUSTRALIANS v SOUTH OF ENGLAND, at Hastings, 1, 2 and 3 September 1948.

Australians    - First Innings    522 for 7 wickets dec.
   - Second Innings    -

S. of England    - First Innings    298
   - Second Innings    -

   Drawn.

DON BRADMAN    - c. F.G. Mann b. T.E. Bailey    143
   (Captain)

With a wicket falling to the first ball of the match, DON BRADMAN went in at 0 for 1, and was again at his best, reaching 50 in exactly an hour, and 100 in two hours thirteen minutes, before being caught at mid-on after three hours five minutes at the wicket; he gave no chance, and hit a six and seventeen fours. The score when he was out was 237 for 3.

## Australians

| | |
|---|---|
| S. G. Barnes c Griffith b Bailey ... | 0 |
| W. A. Brown c Edrich b Mallett .. | 13 |
| D. G. Bradman c Mann b Bailey.. | 143 |
| A. L. Hassett c Mallett b Perks ... | 151 |
| R. N. Harvey c Griffith b Perks... | 110 |
| R. A. Hamence lbw b Mallett .... | 7 |
| S. J. Loxton not out ............ | 67 |
| C. L. McCool b Perks ........... | 5 |
| R. R. Lindwall not out .......... | 17 |
| B 2, l-b 6, n-b 1 .......... | 9 |
| Seven wkts., dec. | 522 |

D. Tallon and W. A. Johnston did not bat.

## South of England

| | |
|---|---|
| C. J. Barnett c Hassett b Loxton . | 35 |
| W. J. Edrich c Harvey b Johnston. | 52 |
| G. H. G. Doggart c Tallon b Lindwall ........................ | 8 |
| D.C.S.Compton c Brown b McCool | 82 |
| T. E. Bailey c Lindwall b Harvey . | 25 |
| F. G. Mann c Loxton b Brown ... | 31 |
| B. H. Valentine c Tallon b Brown. | 25 |
| S. C. Griffith b McCool.......... | 11 |
| A. W. H. Mallett c Harvey b Brown | 1 |
| R. T. D. Perks c Tallon b Brown . | 10 |
| C. Cook not out ................ | 0 |
| B 13, l-b 2, w 3 .......... | 18 |
| | 298 |

# BRADMAN GETS CENTURY

Daily Telegraph Service & A.A.P.

**HASTINGS, Wednesday.**—Australian captain Don Bradman scored his 10th century of the tour against South of England today.

The match is Bradman's second last first-class match.

He scored his century in 133 minutes, and went on to 143, when he was caught by Mann off Bailey.

Bradman and Hassett added 188.

Bradman won the toss and decided to bat on a good wicket in warm, cloudy weather.

Australia began badly, with two wickets falling in the first half-hour.

Barnes was caught off fast bowler Bailey for a "duck" off the first ball.

Bradman joined Brown, and the pair forced the pace.

## Fast Scoring

Bradman began with a cut for four off Bailey's second ball and, in Bailey's next over, hit him for two boundaries.

In the first half-hour, he had made 34 of the 46 on the board.

Brown, at 13, snicked a swinger from Mallett on to the wicket-keeper Griffith's boot, from where it bounced to Edrich at short fine-leg, who took the catch.

Bradman reached 45 in even time.

By lunch, Bradman had taken his score to 64, with Hassett 19, and Australia 2-99.

After lunch, Bradman went on to his century. Hassett, scoring equally as well, passed his 50 in 100 minutes.

Bradman went at 143. His score, made in 185 minutes, included 17 fours and one six.

Harvey, following him, reached his 1000 runs for the tour when he was four.

A miniature cricket bat crafted out of Queensland cabinet timber, and a souvenir cricket ball. The cricket ball was presented to Don Bradman to commemorate his last innings for Australia, 123 not out v. Scotland, at Aberdeen, 18 September 1948.

# CRICKET
## — 1948 - Australian Team in England —

◆ Not First Class Fixtures. Figures in these Matches are not included in the Averages.

## BATTING

| | I. | N.O. | H.S. | AGG. | AV. |
|---|---|---|---|---|---|
| BRADMAN D.G. | 31 | 4 | 187 | 2428 | 89·92 |
| HASSETT A.L. | 27 | 6 | 200* | 1563 | 74·42 |
| MORRIS A.R. | 29 | 2 | 290 | 1922 | 71·18 |
| BROWN W.A. | 26 | 1 | 200 | 1448 | 57·92 |
| LOXTON S. | 22 | 5 | 159* | 973 | 57·23 |
| BARNES S.G. | 27 | 3 | 176 | 1354 | 56·41 |
| HARVEY N.R. | 27 | 6 | 126 | 1129 | 53·76 |
| MILLER K.R. | 26 | 3 | 202* | 1088 | 47·30 |
| HAMENCE R.A. | 22 | 4 | 99 | 582 | 32·33 |
| JOHNSON I.W. | 22 | 4 | 113* | 543 | 30·16 |
| TALLON D. | 13 | 2 | 53 | 283 | 25·72 |
| LINDWALL R.R. | 20 | 3 | 77 | 411 | 24·17 |
| SAGGERS R. | 12 | 3 | 104* | 209 | 23·22 |
| McCOOL C.L. | 18 | 3 | 76 | 306 | 20·40 |
| JOHNSTON W.A. | 18 | 8 | 29 | 188 | 18·80 |
| RING D. | 14 | 5 | 53 | 150 | 16·66 |
| TOSHACK E.R. | 12 | 3 | 20* | 78 | 8·66 |
| Sundries | | | | | |

## BOWLING

| | O. | M. | R. | W. | AV. |
|---|---|---|---|---|---|
| LINDWALL R.R. | 573 | 139 | 1358 | 86 | 15·79 |
| JOHNSTON W.A. | 850 | 279 | 1699 | 102 | 16·65 |
| MILLER K.R. | 429 | 117 | 992 | 56 | 17·71 |
| McCOOL C.L. | 399 | 98 | 1018 | 57 | 17·85 |
| JOHNSON I.W. | 668 | 228 | 1562 | 85 | 18·37 |
| TOSHACK E.R. | 502 | 171 | 1069 | 50 | 21·38 |
| HAMENCE R.A. | 56 | 13 | 151 | 7 | 21·57 |
| LOXTON S. | 361 | 91 | 709 | 32 | 22·15 |
| RING D. | 542 | 155 | 1328 | 60 | 22·13 |

ALSO BOWLED (First Class Matches)

| | O | M | R | W | AV |
|---|---|---|---|---|---|
| BROWN | 4 | 4 | 16 | 4 | 4·00 |
| HARVEY | 10 | 2 | 29 | 1 | 29·00 |
| MORRIS | 35 | 9 | 45 | 1 | 45·50 |
| BARNES | 65 | 26 | 121 | 2 | 60·50 |
| HASSETT | 12 | 0 | 48 | 0 | — |
| BRADMAN | 1 | 0 | 0 | 0 | — |

Compiled & Drawn by C.A.Kable.

COPYRIGHT APPLIED FOR

# Australians
## v
# Mr. H.D.G. Leveson-Gower's XI

AUSTRALIANS v MR. H.D.G. LEVESON-GOWER'S XI, at Scarborough, 8, 9 and 10 September 1948.

| | | |
|---|---|---|
| Australians | - First Innings | 489 for 8 wickets dec. |
| | - Second Innings | - |
| Leveson-Gower's | - First Innings | 177 |
| | - Second Innings | 75 for 2 wickets |
| | Drawn. | |

DON BRADMAN - c. L. Hutton b. A.V. Bedser    153
(Captain)

DON BRADMAN ended his cricket career in England with another triumph, hitting his eleventh century of the season and his third in successive innings, and also ensuring that his team retained their unbeaten record - the only Australian team to do so. In a match interfered with by rain, he went in late on the second evening, at 102 for 1, and made 30 not out in thirty-six minutes before the close, on a wicket which took a certain amount of spin. Next morning, on an easier wicket, he started slowly, and completed 50 in ninety-one minutes, and 100 in two hours twenty minutes shortly before lunch; after the interval, when he was 109, he hit out and added 44 in thirty-eight minutes before giving his wicket away to A.V. Bedser, being caught off a skier in the covers from a wild swing. He batted faultlessly for three hours fourteen minutes altogether, and hit two sixes and nineteen fours. For the tenth and last time, and for the second time in England, Bradman made three (or more) centuries in successive innings.
The tour finished with Bradman bowling the last over of the match.

## Leveson Gower's XI

| | | | | |
|---|---|---|---|---|
| L. Hutton b Lindwall | 0 | — lbw b Johnson | 27 | |
| L. B. Fishlock c Harvey b Johnson | 38 | — c Morris b Johnson | 26 | |
| W. J. Edrich b Johnston | 15 | — not out | 20 | |
| M. P. Donnelly c Miller b Johnson | 36 | — not out | 2 | |
| N. W. D. Yardley b Johnson | 34 | | | |
| R. W. V. Robins b Lindwall | 7 | | | |
| F. R. Brown c Johnson b Lindwall | 0 | | | |
| T. G. Evans b Lindwall | 0 | | | |
| A. V. Bedser b Lindwall | 23 | | | |
| J. C. Laker c Johnson b Lindwall | 7 | | | |
| T. L. Pritchard not out | 4 | | | |
| B 7, l-b 6 | 13 | | | |
| | **177** | Two wkts. | **75** | |

## Australians

| | | | |
|---|---|---|---|
| S. G. Barnes c Yardley b Laker | 151 | I. W. Johnson c Hutton b Brown | 38 |
| A. R. Morris b Yardley | 62 | D. Tallon c Edrich b Bedser | 2 |
| D. G. Bradman c Hutton b Bedser | 153 | A. L. Hassett not out | 7 |
| S. J. Loxton retired hurt | 12 | W. A. Johnston not out | 26 |
| R. N. Harvey b Brown | 23 | L-b 7, w 1, n-b 1 | 9 |
| R. R. Lindwall c Evans b Brown | 5 | | |
| K. R. Miller c Evans b Bedser | 1 | Eight wkts., dec. | 489 |

### Australian Bowling

| | O. | M. | R. | W. | O. | M. | R. | W. |
|---|---|---|---|---|---|---|---|---|
| Lindwall | 25.3 | 10 | 59 | 6 | 2 | 0 | 11 | 0 |
| Johnston | 13 | 3 | 20 | 1 | 2 | 0 | 9 | 0 |
| Miller | 8 | 0 | 28 | 0 | | | | |
| Loxton | 5 | 2 | 12 | 0 | | | | |
| Johnson | 15 | 5 | 45 | 3 | 7 | 4 | 12 | 2 |
| Harvey | | | | | 4 | 1 | 14 | 0 |
| Hassett | | | | | 4 | 0 | 12 | 0 |
| Morris | | | | | 6 | 1 | 15 | 0 |
| Bradman | | | | | 1 | 0 | 2 | 0 |

### H. D. G. Leveson Gower's XI Bowling

| | O. | M. | R. | W. |
|---|---|---|---|---|
| Pritchard | 19 | 4 | 60 | 0 |
| Bedser | 27 | 7 | 72 | 3 |
| Laker | 20 | 4 | 95 | 1 |
| Brown | 40 | 4 | 171 | 3 |
| Robins | 3 | 1 | 9 | 0 |
| Yardley | 13 | 2 | 56 | 1 |
| Edrich | 3 | 0 | 17 | 0 |

Umpires: H. G. Baldwin and A. R. Coleman.

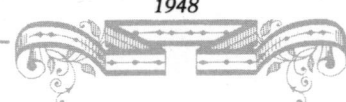

# Bradman Had Magic Touch

*By P. J. MILLARD*

Don Bradman has ended his great career as he began it — with a brilliant century. He has retained the Midas touch to the end, reeling off three centuries in his last three hands — 150 against Gentlemen, 143 against South of England, and now 153 in a grand finale.

As "the boy from Bowral," Bradman—then a callow youth of 19—joined the cricket elite by hitting a quick 118 in his first hand in big cricket.

It was for New South Wales against South Australia at Adelaide in 1927. Even in the blistering December heat, the crowd sat up and took notice. Here was a batsman—they sensed it, saw it.

Now, amid ringing applause from the whole cricketing world, the greatest batsman and most dynamic personality in the history of the game, and regarded as one of the two best-known men in the Empire (Churchill being the other), finally puts away his magic bat, two weeks after his 40th birthday.

A mighty "Well played, Sir!" echoes around the globe, with emphasis on the "Sir."

[For there is a confident belief in England that Bradman will be knighted in December or when the King and Queen visit Australia next year.]

Bradman, the batting prodigy, was never coached. As a small country boy he got his eye in early by constant practice—not with a bat, but by hitting a golf ball against a wall with a cricket stump! One of the secrets of his success was his ultra-quick eye.

Whenever the first wicket fell in Don's side, the air became electric, and the crowd buzzed with expectation.

For the great Bradman was next to bat, in his traditional role of No. 3.

He always had the crowd on edge as he eagerly—almost impatiently—tried to break his "duck" with a sharp single. But he knew what he was doing. In his 334 first-class hands he collected only 16 "ducks."

For the last 15 years his "career" average has not been below 90.

Don's phenomenal career has not been an uninterrupted succession of triumphs. He had his setbacks . . . and overcame them. There were some grim phases:

When Larwood and Voce tried to knock him off his throne with "bodyline" in Australia in 1932-33.

When he was seriously ill in England at the end of the 1934 tour, and some newspapers got his "obituary" ready.

When, a sick man, he managed only 18 runs in his brief, disastrous 1940-41 season in Australia.

It is amusing to recall that, since an English cricket writer accompanying Hammond's team described Don as "a frail little man, full of good spirits, struggling with ill-health," after watching him at practice in October, 1946, the "F.L.M." has proved the prime factor in Australia winning three Test rubbers! Not bad work for an "invalid"!

Unlike many a champion in sport, Donald George Bradman goes out of the game WHILE STILL ON TOP OF IT.

Fortunately, he will still serve Australia as a member of the Board of Control, and also, probably, Test selector.

He will not play again, after the present tour, even in club cricket, except perhaps to appear in his testimonial match, proposed for December 3-7 at Melbourne Cricket Ground.

Here are Bradman's summarised first-class batting figures, year by year:

| | Inns. | N.O. | H.S. | Runs | Av. for Season | Av. for Career |
|---|---|---|---|---|---|---|
| 1927-28 | 10 | 1 | 134* | 416 | 46.2 | 46.2 |
| 1928-29 | 24 | 6 | 340* | 1690 | 93.8 | 78 |
| 1929-30 | 16 | 2 | 452* | 1586 | 113.2 | 90 |
| '30, Eng. | 36 | 6 | 334 | 2960 | 98.6 | 93.6 |
| 1930-31 | 18 | — | 258 | 1422 | 79 | 90.7 |
| 1931-32 | 13 | 1 | 229* | 1403 | 116.9 | 93.8 |
| 1932-33 | 21 | 2 | 238 | 1171 | 61.6 | 88.7 |
| 1933-34 | 11 | 2 | 253 | 1192 | 132.4 | 91.7 |
| '34, Eng. | 27 | 3 | 304 | 2020 | 84.1 | 90.5 |
| 1935-36 | 9 | — | 369 | 1173 | 130.3 | 92.7 |
| 1936-37 | 19 | 1 | 270 | 1552 | 86.3 | 92.1 |
| 1937-38 | 18 | 2 | 246 | 1437 | 89.6 | 91.9 |
| '38, Eng. | 26 | 5 | 278 | 2429 | 115.6 | 94.2 |
| 1938-39 | 7 | 1 | 225 | 919 | 153.1 | 95.8 |
| 1939-40 | 15 | 3 | 267 | 1475 | 122.9 | 97.2 |
| 1940-41 | 4 | — | 12 | 18 | 4.5 | 95.6 |
| 1945-46 | 3 | 1 | 112 | 232 | 116 | 95.8 |
| 1946-47 | 14 | 1 | 234 | 1032 | 79.3 | 94.9 |
| 1947-48 | 12 | 2 | 201 | 1296 | 129.6 | 96.2 |
| '48, Eng. | 31 | 4 | 187 | 2428 | 89.9 | 95.7 |
| Totals | 334 | 43 | — | 27,851 | | 95.7 |

* Not out. (Did not play in Australia in 1934-35 season; began with SA in 1935-36 season.)

Australia's two concluding games against Scotland (at Edinburgh on September 13-14, and Aberdeen on September 17-18) are second-class.

"Bon-Accord's" camera-men sum-up the great occasion.—Top, left—Led by Don Bradman, the Australians take the field.

## Bradman of Yorks

Don Bradman was made an honorary life member of Yorkshire County Cricket Club yesterday in recognition of "the joy he has given to Yorks crowds by his wonderful display in Test matches at Headingley, Leeds."

## Scotland

| | 1st | | 2nd |
|---|---|---|---|
| G. L. Willatt b Johnston | 16 | — b Ring | 52 |
| T. Crosskey c Ring b Morris | 49 | — b Ring | 14 |
| J. C. Wykes b Morris | 11 | — c Ring b Johnston | 10 |
| I. J. M. Lumsden c Johnson b Morris | 1 | — b Brown | 16 |
| W. Nicol lbw b McCool | 37 | — c McCool b Tallon | 1 |
| J. Aitchison c Lindwall b McCool | 32 | — c Brown b Tallon | 9 |
| B. G. W. Atkinson lbw b Johnson | 1 | — b Harvey | 11 |
| W. A. Edwards b McCool | 5 | — lbw b Ring | 0 |
| W. K. Laidlaw lbw b Johnson | 5 | — st Johnson b Ring | 6 |
| F. Colledge b Johnson | 1 | — b Harvey | 8 |
| G. W. Youngson not out | 5 | — not out | 2 |
| B 14, n-b 1 | 15 | B 12, n-b 1 | 13 |
| | **178** | | **142** |

## Australians

| | |
|---|---|
| C. L. McCool c Lumsden b Edwards | 108 |
| R. A. Hamence lbw b Colledge | 15 |
| R. N. Harvey c Aitchison b Youngson | 4 |
| R. R. Lindwall b Laidlaw | 15 |
| I. W. Johnson c Crosskey b Youngson | 95 |
| D. G. Bradman not out | 123 |
| A. R. Morris c Aitchison b Youngson | 10 |
| W. A. Brown not out | 24 |
| B 10, l-b 2, n-b 1 | 13 |
| Six wkts., dec. | **407** |

W. A. Johnston, D. Ring and D. Tallon did not bat.

## Australian Bowling

| | O. | M. | R. | W. | O. | M. | R. | W. |
|---|---|---|---|---|---|---|---|---|
| Lindwall | 10 | 5 | 12 | 0 | 4 | 0 | 16 | 0 |
| Johnston | 13 | 4 | 35 | 1 | 4 | 0 | 13 | 1 |
| Ring | 14 | 4 | 42 | 0 | 10 | 1 | 30 | 4 |
| Johnson | 20.2 | 11 | 26 | 3 | 3 | 0 | 6 | 0 |
| Morris | 9 | 1 | 17 | 3 | 4 | 1 | 8 | 0 |
| McCool | 16 | 2 | 31 | 3 | 7 | 1 | 19 | 0 |
| Brown | | | | | 5 | 0 | 9 | 1 |
| Tallon | | | | | 9 | 3 | 15 | 2 |
| Harvey | | | | | 5 | 0 | 13 | 2 |

## Scotland Bowling

| | O. | M. | R. | W. |
|---|---|---|---|---|
| Youngson | 35 | 3 | 114 | 3 |
| Colledge | 27 | 4 | 93 | 1 |
| Laidlaw | 10 | 0 | 62 | 1 |
| Nicol | 15 | 5 | 56 | 0 |
| Edwards | 18 | 5 | 69 | 1 |

Umpires: L. E. Tyson and W. Nelson.

Don Bradman and his men at Aberdeen.

## Bradman Thrills Aberdeen Crowd

LONDON, Sept. 19.—AAP.

The Australian cricketers, in the last match of their tour, defeated Scotland yesterday by an innings and 87 runs with 40 minutes to spare, Bradman giving a record Aberdeen crowd a fitting farewell with 123 not out in 87 minutes. Scores:—

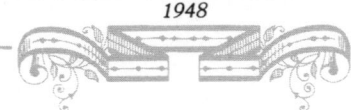

# SPARKLING DISPLAY ENDS 'BRADMAN ERA'

*From Ray Robinson*

**LONDON, Mon:** An era in cricket history closed when Don Bradman walked from a cricket field in Britain for the last time on Saturday.

Bradman will turn his last leaf when he makes a farewell appearance in a big cricketing testimonial match in Australia.

The Australian captain's step was slow as he left the field at Aberdeen after his last innings. But he was smiling happily.

He was bidding farewell to British cricket after a firecracker 123 not out and he had achieved his great ambition of captaining the first Australian team to go through a tour unbeaten.

Bradman and Victorian all rounder Ian Johnson were the only two of the 17 to play in 25 of team's 34 matches. Don scored most runs (2428 in first class, 2578 in all games), most centuries (11, first class and another against Scotland) and headed first class averages (89) and was third in Tests (72).

## 50 Centuries

He and his men made 50 centuries, 47 in first class matches. Pen point studies of the players achievements are:

**Hassett:** Popular deputy to a busy captain. Deserves much credit for keeping team a companionable band. Second in first class averages. Seven centuries.

**Lindwall:** Almost demoralised England's Test batsmen. Thoroughly earned finest figures by Australian fast bowler in Britain since McDonald and Gregory of 1921.

**Miller:** Only Australian to exceed 1000 runs 50 wickets, but figures fail to reflect value of world's best all rounder as matchwinner at critical times.

**W. Johnston:** Intelligence in adapting pace and style of bowling to all kinds of wickets won him the distinction of only bowler to take 100 wickets.

**Morris:** On one of the most successful first trips ever had. Best Test aggregate 696 and average 87 of both sides. Highest individual score of tour 290 is record for an Australian left-hander in England.

**Tallon:** World's finest wicketkeeper was a telling influence in Australia's battery.

**Barnes:** Most confident player of new-ball bowling. Second in Test Averages (82). Greatest close fielder in Test cricket.

## Dashing

**Brown:** Scorer of eight centuries in first class matches. Fourth in first class averages.

**Harvey:** Delighted English crowds with dashing strokeplay and fielding. Seventh of team to score 1000.

**Loxton:** Forceful batsman. Second to Miller as hitter of sixes. Brilliant fieldsman and useful bowler.

**Ian Johnson:** Second largest harvest of wickets for all matches.

**Ring:** Opportunities limited but took 60 wickets in 19 first class matches. 69 in 22 games in all.

**McCool:** Opportunities even more restricted. Tore callous on chief spinning finger three times yet 57 wickets in 17 first class matches. 63 in 20 games in all.

**Saggers:** Accomplished deputy to Tallon who kept wickets excellently in his only Test (fourth).

**Toshack:** Proved his value on English wickets. Took 50 wickets in 15 matches.

**Hamence:** Primarily a forward player he seldom approached his normal confidence on English wickets.

# TOUR ENDS WITH INNINGS WIN

**LONDON, Sept. 19:** The Australian captain (D. G. Bradman) closed his cricket career in Great Britain yesterday with a chanceless century and the team concluded its tour with a win over Scotland by an innings and 87 runs.

Declaring with the total at six for 407 and his own score 123 not out after 87 minutes of free, forceful hitting, Bradman set the bowlers the task of dismissing Scotland for the second time in just over three hours. They did so with 40 minutes to spare.

Don Bradman and Bill Brown leaving the field at Aberdeen. This was Bradman's last innings on the 1948 English tour and therefore the end of his overseas career. Bradman scored 123 not out in this innings.

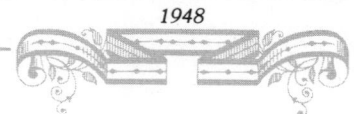
# Party For Test Men At Balmoral Castle

AAP And Our Special Representative

LONDON, Sept. 19.

Their Majesties the King and Queen will entertain the Australian Test team at tea at Balmoral Castle today.

It will be one of the biggest parties held at Balmoral, with over 50 guests, when the Queen presides at tea in the drawing room.

Their Royal Highnesses Princess Elizabeth, Princess Margaret, the Duke of Edinburgh, the Duchess of Kent and the son of the Duke of Kent will help to entertain the Australians.

The party will be informal.

The King has given the Australians permission to take photographs and has promised to show them round the castle grounds.

A last-minute change in the itinerary of the Australians' tour was made when Their Majesties' Private Secretary (Sir Alan Lascelles) let the manager of the team (Mr. Keith Johnson) know that Their Majesties particularly wanted to say good-bye to the team and to talk about their Australian visit in 1949.

The team, which was due to leave Aberdeen yesterday, will leave this evening and the Australians will now have only two days to get their baggage packed for the trip home.

Princess Elizabeth expects her baby about the middle of November. It will be born at Buckingham Palace because the Princess and the Duke of Edinburgh still have not their own home.

They are renting Windlesham Moor at Sunningdale, and also have a suite at Buckingham Palace. Their official home, Clarence House, will not be ready before next year.

# King jokes with Bradman

London, Sunday.—Banter was exchanged between the King and Don Bradman as the Australian cricketers sat for press photographs at Balmoral Castle this afternoon.

Genial informality marked the visit of the Australian and Scotland teams to the castle

**The King, the Queen, Princesses Elizabeth and Margaret, the Duke of Edinburgh, and the Duchess of Kent shook hands with the whole party, and chatted with each player, quickly putting them at ease.**

Most of the Australians and Scots had cameras, and Their Majesties encouraged them to capture mementoes of the occasion.

The young Duke of Kent, who is very keen on cricket, made the most of the opportunity to take photographs, as did the majority of the Royal House party.

**The Queen presided at one of the biggest afternoon parties at the castle for a long time. There were about 60 guests.**

The visit closed with members of the Royal Family seeing visitors off from the front hall of castle in a hum of lively chat and laughing exchanges

Both the King and Queen talked enthusiastically about their coming visit to Australia.

They specially mentioned they were looking forward to witnessing an Australian rules football match in Melbourne.

Princess Elizabeth said she regretted she was not going, and hoped to go later

The Australian manager (Mr Keith Johnson) said:— "The Royal Family are marvellous. They made a deep impression on all of us. We enjoyed Scotland immensely, and are sorry to rush away."— A.A.P.

The King and Queen with Australian players and cricket officials.

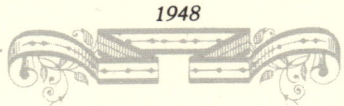

Don Bradman chatting in the grounds of Balmoral with the Queen and Princess Margaret.

AUSTRALIA
1948

*A Luncheon
and Presentation
to
Don Bradman*

*Savoy Hotel, London
September 20th
1948*

*This Luncheon and Presentation is given
by "The People," Britain's National
Sunday Newspaper, as a tribute to a great
sportsman.*

## Menu

*Le Suprême de Turbotin Riviera*

\*

*Le Caneton Pôele aux Petits Pois
Les Haricots Verts
Les Pommes Cocotte*

\*

*Le Parfait Glacé Frutti
Les Gaufrettes*

\*

*Le Café*

HIS MAJESTY THE KING
*Proposed by* ARTHUR G. COUSINS, ESQ., C.B.E.
*Chairman, Odhams Press Ltd.*

*Speakers*
ARTHUR G. COUSINS, ESQ., C.B.E.
BRIG. GEN. THE RT. HON. EARL OF GOWRIE, V.C., P.C.
N. W. D. YARDLEY, ESQ.

## Presentation

PRESENTATION OF ANTIQUE SILVER REPLICA
OF THE WARWICK VASE TO DON BRADMAN
*by*
BRIG. GEN. THE RT. HON. EARL OF GOWRIE, V.C., P.C.

*Response by* DON BRADMAN, ESQ.

## "THE PEOPLE"
### FAREWELL LUNCHEON AND PRESENTATION
### to DON BRADMAN at the
### SAVOY HOTEL · LONDON · W·C₂
### Monday, September 20th. 1948

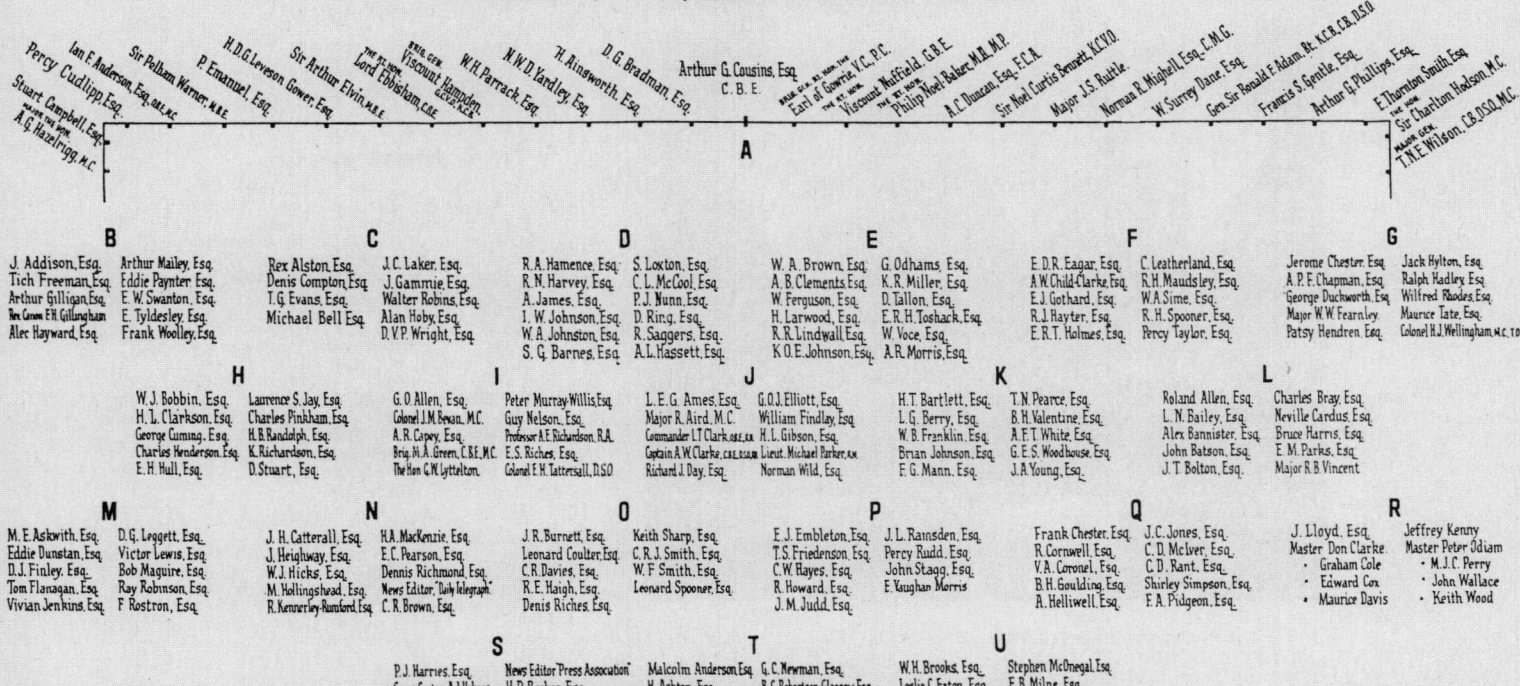

Table A (head): Stuart Campbell, Esq. · A. G. Hazlerigg, M.C. · Percy Cudlipp, Esq. · Ian F. Anderson, Esq., O.B.E., M.C. · Sir Pelham Warner, M.B.E. · P. Emanuel, Esq. · H. D. G. Leveson Gower, Esq. · Sir Arthur Elvin, M.B.E. · Lord Ebbisham, C.B.E. · Brig. Gen. Viscount Hampden, G.C.V.O., K.C.B. · W. H. Parrack, Esq. · N. W. D. Yardley, Esq. · H. Ainsworth, Esq. · D. G. Bradman, Esq. · Arthur G. Cousins, Esq. C.B.E. · Brig. Gen. Rt. Hon. The Earl of Gowrie, V.C., P.C. · The Rt. Hon. Viscount Nuffield, G.B.E. · Philip Noel-Baker, M.A., M.P. · A. C. Duncan, Esq., F.C.A. · Sir Noel Curtis Bennett, K.C.V.O. · Major J. S. Kettle · Norman R. Mighell, Esq., C.M.G. · W. Surrey Dane, Esq. · Gen. Sir Ronald F. Adam, Bt., K.C.B., C.B., D.S.O. · Francis S. Gentle, Esq. · Arthur G. Phillips, Esq. · E. Thornton Smith, Esq. · The Hon. Sir Charlton Hodson, M.C. · Major Gen. T. N. F. Wilson, C.B., D.S.O., M.C.

**B**
J. Addison, Esq. · Arthur Mailey, Esq.
Tich Freeman, Esq. · Eddie Paynter, Esq.
Arthur Gilligan, Esq. · E. W. Swanton, Esq.
Rev. Canon F. H. Gillingham · E. Tyldesley, Esq.
Alec Hayward, Esq. · Frank Woolley, Esq.

**C**
Rex Alston, Esq. · J. C. Laker, Esq.
Denis Compton, Esq. · J. Gammie, Esq.
T. G. Evans, Esq. · Walter Robins, Esq.
Michael Bell, Esq. · Alan Hoby, Esq.
D. V. P. Wright, Esq.

**D**
R. A. Hamence, Esq. · S. Loxton, Esq.
R. N. Harvey, Esq. · C. L. McCool, Esq.
A. James, Esq. · P. J. Nunn, Esq.
I. W. Johnson, Esq. · D. Ring, Esq.
W. A. Johnston, Esq. · R. Saggers, Esq.
S. G. Barnes, Esq. · A. L. Hassett, Esq.

**E**
W. A. Brown, Esq. · G. Odhams, Esq.
A. B. Clements, Esq. · K. R. Miller, Esq.
W. Ferguson, Esq. · D. Tallon, Esq.
H. Larwood, Esq. · E. R. H. Toshack, Esq.
R. R. Lindwall, Esq. · W. Voce, Esq.
K. O. E. Johnson, Esq. · A. R. Morris, Esq.

**F**
E. D. R. Eagar, Esq. · C. Leatherland, Esq.
A. W. Child-Clarke, Esq. · R. H. Maudsley, Esq.
E. J. Gothard, Esq. · W. A. Sime, Esq.
R. J. Hayter, Esq. · R. H. Spooner, Esq.
E. R. T. Holmes, Esq. · Percy Taylor, Esq.

**G**
Jerome Chester, Esq. · Jack Hylton, Esq.
A. P. F. Chapman, Esq. · Ralph Hadley, Esq.
George Duckworth, Esq. · Wilfred Rhodes, Esq.
Major W. W. Fearnley · Maurice Tate, Esq.
Patsy Hendren, Esq. · Colonel H. J. Wellingham, M.C., T.D.

**H**
W. J. Bobbin, Esq. · Laurence S. Jay, Esq.
H. L. Clarkson, Esq. · Charles Pinkham, Esq.
George Cuming, Esq. · H. B. Randolph, Esq.
Charles Henderson, Esq. · K. Richardson, Esq.
E. H. Hull, Esq. · D. Stuart, Esq.

**I**
G. O. Allen, Esq. · Peter Murray-Willis, Esq.
Colonel J. M. Bevan, M.C. · Guy Nelson, Esq.
A. R. Capey, Esq. · Professor A. E. Richardson, R.A.
Brig. M. A. Green, C.B.E., M.C. · E. S. Riches, Esq.
The Hon. G. W. Lyttelton · Colonel E. H. Tattersall, D.S.O.

**J**
L. E. G. Ames, Esq. · G. O. J. Elliott, Esq.
Major R. Aird, M.C. · William Findlay, Esq.
Commander L. T. Clark, O.B.E., R.N. · H. L. Gibson, Esq.
Captain A. W. Clarke, O.B.E., R.N.(R.) · Lieut. Michael Parker, R.N.
Richard J. Day, Esq. · Norman Wild, Esq.

**K**
H. T. Bartlett, Esq. · T. N. Pearce, Esq.
L. G. Berry, Esq. · B. H. Valentine, Esq.
W. B. Franklin, Esq. · A. F. T. White, Esq.
Brian Johnson, Esq. · G. E. S. Woodhouse, Esq.
F. G. Mann, Esq. · J. A. Young, Esq.

**L**
Roland Allen, Esq. · Charles Bray, Esq.
L. N. Bailey, Esq. · Neville Cardus, Esq.
Alex Bannister, Esq. · Bruce Harris, Esq.
John Batson, Esq. · E. M. Parks, Esq.
J. T. Bolton, Esq. · Major R. B. Vincent

**M**
M. E. Askwith, Esq. · D. G. Leggett, Esq.
Eddie Dunstan, Esq. · Victor Lewis, Esq.
D. J. Finley, Esq. · Bob Maguire, Esq.
Tom Flanagan, Esq. · Ray Robinson, Esq.
Vivian Jenkins, Esq. · F. Rostron, Esq.

**N**
J. H. Catterall, Esq. · H. A. MacKenzie, Esq.
J. Heighway, Esq. · E. C. Pearson, Esq.
W. J. Hicks, Esq. · Dennis Richmond, Esq.
M. Hollingshead, Esq. · News Editor, "Daily Telegraph"
R. Kennerley-Rumford, Esq. · C. R. Brown, Esq.

**O**
J. R. Burnett, Esq. · Keith Sharp, Esq.
Leonard Coulter, Esq. · C. R. J. Smith, Esq.
C. R. Davies, Esq. · W. F. Smith, Esq.
R. E. Haigh, Esq. · Leonard Spooner, Esq.
Denis Riches, Esq.

**P**
E. J. Embleton, Esq. · J. L. Rainsden, Esq.
T. S. Friedenson, Esq. · Percy Rudd, Esq.
C. W. Hayes, Esq. · John Stagg, Esq.
R. Howard, Esq. · E. Vaughan Morris
J. M. Judd, Esq.

**Q**
Frank Chester, Esq. · J. C. Jones, Esq.
R. Cornwell, Esq. · C. D. McIver, Esq.
V. A. Coronel, Esq. · C. D. Rant, Esq.
B. H. Goulding, Esq. · Shirley Simpson, Esq.
A. Helliwell, Esq. · F. A. Pidgeon, Esq.

**R**
J. Lloyd, Esq. · Jeffrey Kenny
Master Don Clarke · Master Peter Odiam
· Graham Cole · M. J. C. Perry
· Edward Cox · John Wallace
· Maurice Davis · Keith Wood

**S**
P. J. Harries, Esq. · News Editor Press Association
Group Captain A. J. Holmes · H. D. Rochez, Esq.
H. Kingsley Long, Esq. · News Editor "Star"
D. R. Lloyd, Esq. · E. W. Thomas, Esq.
F. J. Kellaway, Esq. · Peter Wilson, Esq.

**T**
Malcolm Anderson, Esq. · G. C. Newman, Esq.
H. Ashton, Esq. · R. C. Robertson-Glasgow, Esq.
George Geary, Esq. · C. H. Taylor, Esq.
Cricket Correspondent, "Evening Telegraph" · E. Tempest, Esq.
N. Harwood, Esq.

**U**
W. H. Brooks, Esq. · Stephen McDnegal, Esq.
Leslie C. Eaton, Esq. · E. B. Milne, Esq.
E. J. Gilling, Esq. · Morley Richards, Esq.
Philip Grune, Esq. · News Editor "Daily Mail"
A. J. Hollobone, Esq. · News Editor, "The Times"

Lord Gowrie shakes hands with Don Bradman at *The People* farewell dinner.

*Don Bradman and Harold Larwood, England's fastest-ever bowler, met to-day at a Savoy luncheon in honour of Australia's captain. The last time they met was in 1933 in Sydney.*

## They Meet Again

THE last time Harold Larwood, England's fastest-ever bowler, saw Don Bradman was in Sydney in 1933 when the body-line bowling controversy was at its height. They met again to-day—at a West End luncheon in the Don's honour.

It is the first time Larwood has been to London since 1938; and with him are three other famous North Country players—Eddie Paynter, Ernest Tyldesley and George Duckworth. Harold keeps a tobacconist shop in Blackpool—but doesn't smoke.

A silver replica of the Warwick Vase.

# THE WARWICK VASE

The vase was found in 1770 during excavations carried on in the bed of a small lake called Pantanello, overlooking the Vale of Temple, near Tivoli, 16 miles from Rome. How it came there is not known. Hadrian's Villa was occupied by the Ostro-Gothic King, Totila, 540 A.D., when he laid siege to Rome, and the vase may have been cast into the lake to save it from the invaders.

The villa was finished about 138 A.D., but this work is of an earlier date, and is attributed to Lysippus, of Sicyon, a Greek artist of the close of the 4th century B.C., when the beautiful or elegant style began to replace the noble severity of Phidias and his school. The vase is of white marble and is circular in form. It is 5ft 6in high and 5ft 8in in diameter at the lip, and is placed on a square pedestal of modern construction. The handles are formed in pairs of vine stems, the smaller branches of which twine around the upper lip and, with drooping bunches of grapes, form a symmetrical frieze.

The lower rim is covered by two tiger or panther skins, of which the heads and the forepaws adorn the sides of the vase, while the hind legs interlace and hang down between the handles. Arranged along the tiger skins are several heads, all except one being those of Silene, or male attendants of Bacchus, the single exception being that of a female head, probably that of a Bacchante or Faun. Between the heads are thyrsi or bacchi staves twined round with ivy and vine shoots and litui, or laugural wands, used in taking omens.

The uses of the vase, which holds 163 gallons, have been the theme of speculation. Many suppose it to have been a vessel designed to contain wine, mixed with water, and intended for the centre of a chamber devoted to festive uses, but it was more probably constructed solely for decorative purposes, and may have formed the ornament of a temple of Bacchus.

Many good stories can be told about the vase, and one, at least, must not go unrecorded. Adorning the vase you will see a row of heads, all representing satyrs. All, that is, with one exception. And here you will find no satyr's face, but the features of one of the most striking beauties of the 18th century. The face is that of Lady Hamilton, famous the world over as the mistress of the one and only Nelson. But Nelson had nothing to do with milady's face being immortalised in this 2,300 year old vase. It was, in fact, her husband, Sir William Hamilton, who was responsible for that.

It was he who, in the year 1770, at a time when he was English ambassador at the court of Naples, found the vase. Being something of an archaeologist, he employed his spare time draining a lake and digging in the ruins of the villa at Tiber, about 12 miles from Rome, which was held in high delight by the Roman Emperor Hadrian. Sir William had no difficulty in finding the villa, or at least part of it, for in its original state, Hadrian had a cosy little place about seven miles long, with innumerable halls, courts and libraries. And he found many rich treasures there, including the vase, complete except for one missing head. Sir William immediately set about restoring the vase and had the bright idea of substituting his wife's head for the original satyr's.

He engaged an Italian sculptor (name unknown) and persuaded Lady Hamilton to sit for him. But the artist was temperamental, Lady Hamilton more so. Sitting after sitting ended in fierce quarrels.

Then the day came when the great work was done. Sir William found himself gazing at a striking resemblance of his wife — but for one thing. The vengeful sculptor had concentrated on milady's ears. They were wonderful ears. They were the long delicate ears of a Greek faun. Naturally Lady Hamilton did not like her new ears. And it may have been to preserve the domestic peace of his household that Sir William parted with this precious relic. He presented it to his maternal nephew, George, Earl of Warwick. It now stands, a dream of white marble, in the special conservatory built for it at Warwick Castle.

It stands on a marble pedestal, bearing the Latin inscription: "This monument of ancient Roman art and magnificence was dug out of the ruins at Tiber, which was held in high delight by the Emperor Hadrian. The knight, William Hamilton, envoy from George III, the great British King to the Sicilian King, Ferdinand IV, caused it to be restored, and, despatching it to his country, dedicated it to the father genius of fine arts in the year of Our Lord 1774."

Close-up of the Warwick Vase showing Lady Hamilton's face.

# THE WARWICK VASE

Towards the end of the Australian cricket tour of England in 1948, *The People* newspaper of London conceived the idea of British public paying a tribute to Bradman.

To start the ball rolling, the appeal in the press began with these words:— "*THE PEOPLE* believes that cricket lovers of Britain would like to do more than send Bradman home for the last time with its thanks and good wishes. We have therefore decided to open a "BRADMAN SHILLING FUND" to enable everyone who admires his genius to pay tribute to him in tangible form."

The paper raised a substantial sum by way of donations, but Bradman refused to accept the money. He did, however, agree to accept a memento, and the newspaper decided it should take the form of a replica of the Warwick Vase. Bradman requested that the balance of the fund should be used to lay concrete pitches in the parks of England for the use and benefit of young cricketers. The replica was presented to Don Bradman at a special luncheon held at the Savoy Hotel, London, on 20th September 1948.

Arthur Cousens, Chairman of Odhams Press Ltd, proprietors of *The People* presided over a notable gathering of over 200 people who came to pay tribute to Bradman. In addition to England's captain Norman Yardley, there were seven former captains of England, nine county captains, and ten boys selected to represent the thousands of subscribers.

A former Governor General of Australia, the Earl of Gowrie, then President of M.C.C., made the formal presentation on behalf of the donors. This was a nice gesture. Lord Gowrie remembered with gratitude that Bradman had acted as Honorary Secretary and Organiser in South Australia for the Gowrie Scholarship Trust Fund which raised about $280,000, from which amount scholarships are awarded every year to members of the services or their children.

The replica of the Warwick Vase is a magnificent silver edifice containing 378 ounces of silver. It sits on a solid silver plinth on which is engraved the following:

Presented to
**DON BRADMAN**
by cricket lovers of Britain.
This trophy, a tribute to a great Australian
sportsman, was subscribed for by people
through "The People" newspaper, London,
1948.

In order that this splendid trophy should remain as a permanent memorial Bradman donated it to the State Library of South Australia where it will be held on display in perpetuity within the Mortlock Library.

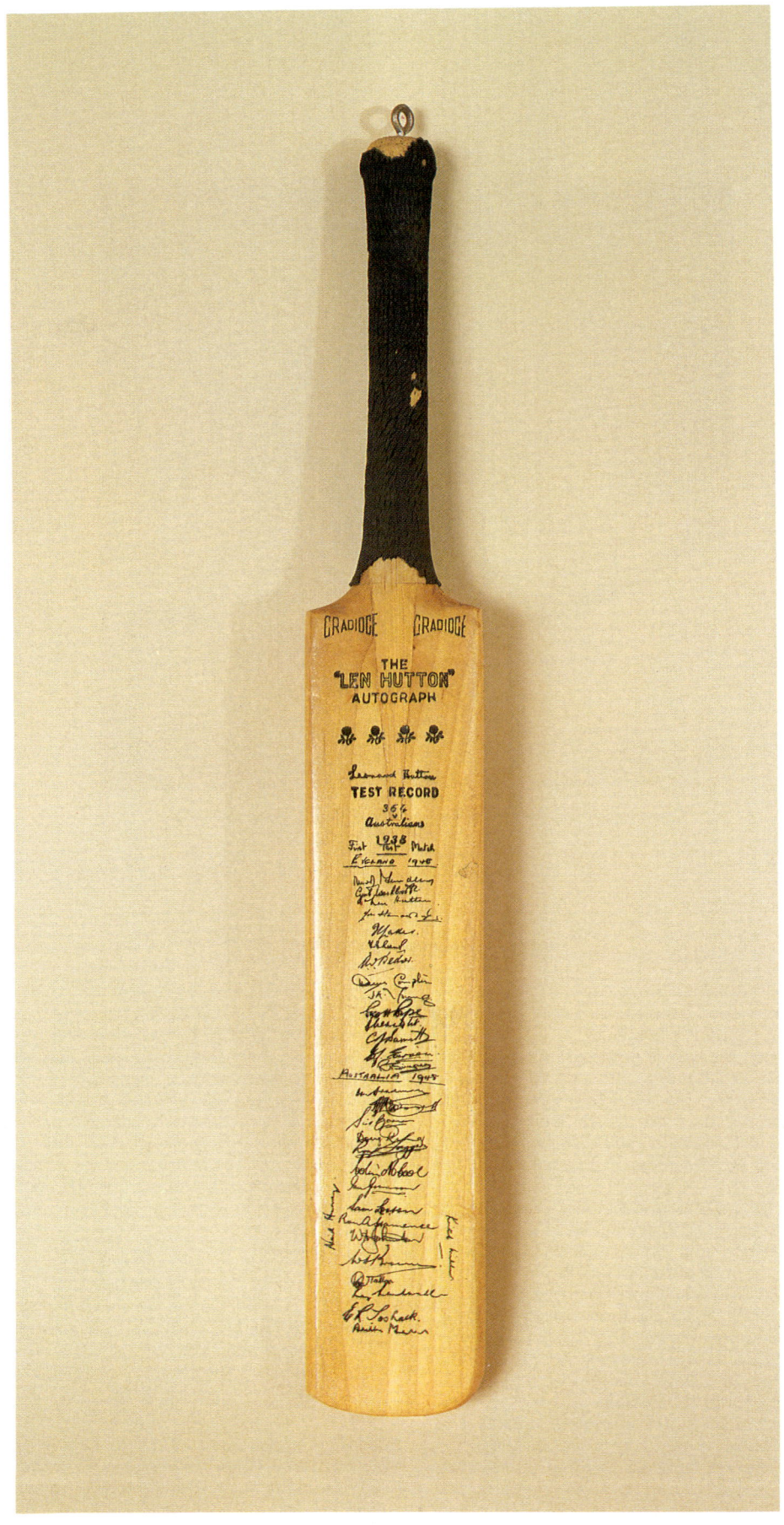

Miniature cricket bat with the signatures of the 1948 English and Australian teams.

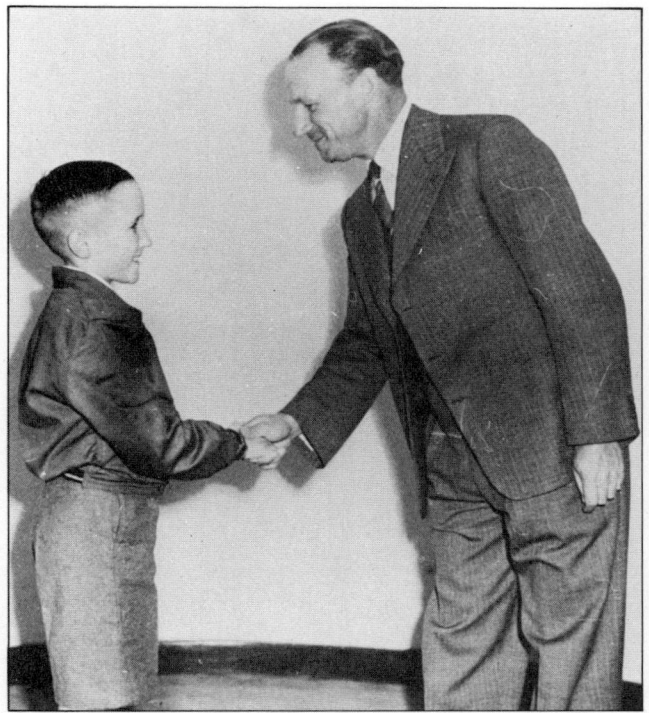

Don Bradman met eleven-year-old Don Clark, named after the cricketer, at a farewell party held at the Savoy Hotel for the Australian captain. Don was presented with an antique silver replica of the Warwick vase.

Australian Test captain Don Bradman was presented with a silver trophy by Lord Gowrie, president of Marylebone Cricket Club and a former Governor of South Australia, at a farewell luncheon at the Savoy Hotel, London. The trophy was bought from proceeds of a newspaper shilling fund.

Auld Lang Syne.

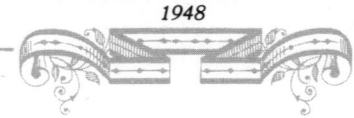

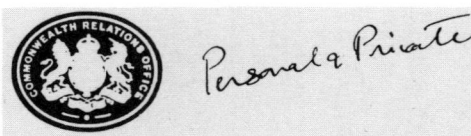

COMMONWEALTH RELATIONS OFFICE,
DOWNING STREET, S.W.1.
25th September,1948

*Personal & Private*

My dear Bradman,

I enclose an "official" letter to you and your team about your tour here. I want, if I may, to take the liberty of adding a personal note.

I know something of international sporting contests and of taking teams abroad. In my belief, no-one in the history of sport has ever done it with such masterly success as you. I know that it must have meant infinite work and infinite trouble, and that over these months it must often have been a great strain. That you should have been able to carry the burden, and to keep your cricket up to your own standard, is almost a miracle. I feel that we in the United Kingdom owe you a personal debt of gratitude for what you have done; and I know we shall all look back on your magnificent career not only with gratitude, but with pride. In these days, it is not easy to know what is of real and lasting value in what we call our civilisation. The more I deal in politics, the more convinced I am that our modern games are among the best things in our national life! I agree with every word you said yesterday in your splendid speech at the Savoy. Cricket is indeed a great affair, and its greatness will grow in every country where it is played. As that happens, so we shall the more remember what you, the greatest master of the game, have done for it and for us all. *With all good wishes, & again my warmest congratulations,*

*Yours ever sincerely,*

*Philip Noel-Baker*

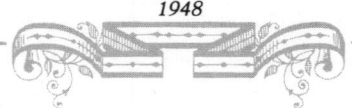

FOND WELCOME HOME

DON BRADMAN, Australian Test captain, was met by his children when the Orontes berthed at Outer Harbor today. He is holding his daughter Shirley in his arms while Mrs. Bradman and their son John watch the reunion. Mrs. Bradman joined the ship at Fremantle.

# BRADMAN'S MEN WELCOMED BY 3,000 AT OUTER HARBOR

**More than 3,000 people lined the wharf at Outer Harbor today to welcome the Australian cricketers returning in the Orontes from their Test tour of England.**

COMMENT by South Australian members of the team was:—

**Don Bradman**—I will play in my testimonial game at Melbourne in December. Otherwise my appearances this season are indefinite.

**Ron Hamence**—I have had two offers to transfer to Lancashire League. One is a very good offer and I will discuss it with my wife.

Members of the team were besieged by child autograph hunters and curious fans who poured into the ship in hun-dreds. Other people waited for two hours at the bottom of the gangway until Bradman left the ship.

Among them were 25 boys and girls of Eden Hills Aboriginal School. They had passes to go aboard the Orontes, but preferred to wait on the wharf so they might see Bradman leaving

**Bradman said his team, unbeaten on the tour, was the best he had ever accompanied abroad.**

He could see no reason why English cricket should not re-gain strength. Experience had shown strength and weakness went in cycles.

**Hamence said he would get straight into club cricket. He would play for West Torrens in their next match.**

Bill Johnston would not comment further on his offer to play with Nedlands (WA), apart from admitting it was a "good offer and worth considering."

Ray Lindwall said his £700-a-year offer from the West would receive earnest consideration.

Ern Toshack has made a complete recovery from the knee operation which he underwent a month before leaving England. He said it was possible he would play immediately on his return to Sydney.

At his home at Seaview road. Grange, tonight, Hamence entertained at a big family gathering. Dozens of presents completely covered a table, and in another room was a stream-lined tricycle, a present he had brought home for his four-year-old daughter, Lynette.

Bradman spent a quiet homecoming with his wife and two children at his home at Holden street, Kensington Park.

# *1948 - 49 Season*

Upon returning from my final tour of England I had no intention of ever playing another first class match. However, the Australian cricket authorities generously arranged a testimonial game in my honour on the Melbourne Cricket Ground. Miraculously, the game ended in a tie, and 94,035 spectators attended.

Having participated in this game I regarded it as a duty (as well as a pleasure) to play in the Kippax-Oldfield Testimonial in Melbourne and finally the Arthur Richardson Testimonial in Adelaide.

In the latter, my final act was to sprain my ankle (due to a sunken water tap) and limp from the field where I had played my initial first class innings.

So ended the last chapter. If life could be re-lived I would gladly do it all again.

*Don Bradman*

## — SEASON 1948-49 —

| TITLE | GAMES | | SCORES | |
|-------|-------|---|--------|---|
| Second Class | Vollugi's XI | St. Peters' College | 47 | L.B.W. |
| " | " | " | 117 | C. |
| First Class | Bradman's XI | Hassett's XI | 123 | C. |
| " | " | " | 10 | C. |
| " | Morriss's XI | " | 53 | C. |
| Sheffield Shield | South Australia | Victoria | 30 | B. |
| | | Total runs | 380 | |

## — SUMMARY —

AVERAGES -

| | Innings | N.O's. | H.S. | Runs | Average |
|---|---------|--------|------|------|---------|
| Sheffield Shield | 1 | 0 | 30 | 30 | 30·0 |
| Other First Class | 3 | 0 | 123 | 186 | 62·0 |
| All First Class | 4 | 0 | 123 | 216 | 54·0 |
| All Second Class | 2 | 0 | 117 | 164 | 82·0 |
| All Matches | 6 | 0 | 123 | 380 | 62·3 |

DON BRADMAN, here today for the testimonial game at the Melbourne Cricket Ground, pins a gardenia on the lapel of his wife's coat at Spencer Street Station. In the centre is the secretary of the Board of Control (Mr W. H. Jeanes).

## Glad it's end to limelight

From Roy Colmer

*Mrs. Bradman*

MELBOURNE. — Mrs. Don Bradman said today she was glad that, with her husband's retirement from cricket, the "limelight days" had passed.

"I was never keen on having the international news spotlight focused on my home and family," she said.

She could not bear to think, however, Don would entirely shed his cricket connections. She was pleased he would retain his interest in cricket as an Australian selector.

Mrs. Bradman said she would find it strange for Don not to be in the thick of international cricket, but she was happy at the prospect of having uninterrupted family life.

In their 16 years of married life Don had made four trips to England—she had been with him on the latter stages of two of them—and he had been away on many trips with Sheffield Shield games.

"Don's long absences left me with the responsibility of home and children, and it was something of a strain," said Mrs. Bradman. "The children—John (9) and Shirley (7)—were too young to miss him on his earlier tours, and as long as I was there they were happy."

Asked about her feelings when Don went in to bat, Mrs. Bradman said, "I have never been more than a little apprehensive. His calmness always inspired me with confidence."

# D.G.Bradman's XI
# v
# A.L.Hassett's XI
# (D.G.Bradman Testimonial)

D.G. BRADMAN'S XI v A.L. HASSETT'S XI (D.G. Bradman Testimonial), at Melbourne, 3, 4, 6 and 7 December 1948.

| D.G. Bradman's XI | - First Innings | 434 |
| | - Second Innings | 402 for 9 wickets |
| A.L. Hassett's XI | - First Innings | 406 |
| | - Second Innings | 430 |

A Tie

| DON BRADMAN | - c. R.N. Harvey  b. B. Dooland | 123 |
| (Captain) | - c. R.A. Saggers  b. W.A. Johnston | 10 |

DON BRADMAN's Testimonial Match proved to be a brilliant success, and produced some splendid cricket; while in the first innings, Bradman himself went in at 3 p.m. on the second day (Saturday), and made his 117th century in first-class cricket.    Starting at 138 for 2 with a single off his first ball, he played himself in carefully, but nevertheless reached his 50 in an hour just before tea, and after the interval carried on majestically towards his hundred.    However, when he was 97, he tried to force W.A. Johnston to leg, and sent up a skier off the edge of his bat to wide mid-on, where C.L. McCool dropped the catch and enabled him to run 3 and complete his century.    He had then been in for two hours seventeen minutes.    Bradman played R.R. Lindwall, who was at his fastest, particularly well, though he was sometimes troubled by that bowler when he took the new ball just after the tea interval.    After completing his century, he lashed out, and finally threw his wicket away, caught at deep square-leg off a full-pitch, ten minutes from the close of play.    He was in for two hours thirty-four minutes and hit thirteen fours.

His last three innings in England having been centuries, this was his fourth century in succession; this was the third time that he had made four or more centuries in successive innings.    Bradman took the last two wickets in Hassett's XI's second innings for 12 runs, thus taking a wicket with the last ball he ever bowled.    The final stages were remarkable for a magnificent innings by D. Tallon, who, after 9 wickets had fallen for 302, helped to add 100, of which his own share was 91, in the last hour and, scoring 12 off the last over, levelled the scores off the last ball.

## Ovation for Cricket Hero

**DON BRADMAN,** going on to the Melbourne Cricket Ground in his last match, received a tremendous ovation from the large crowd. Prominent among his admirers were the younger generation of cricket enthusiasts.

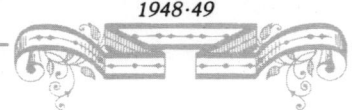

# Bradman Hits 123 In Own Testimonial

### From HARRY KNEEBONE

##### MELBOURNE, December 5.

*With that uncanny certainty which has characterised his career, and which unkind critics have tried to ascribe to luck, Don Bradman kept another assignation with fate at the Melbourne Cricket Ground on Saturday. What was needed on top of warm sunshine and a record crowd for a match other than a Test, to make the day supremely successful, was a Bradman century. So he produced one.*

It was a typical Bradman 100. Not perhaps as slashingly murderous as those of 15 to 20 years ago, but truly one which the thousands of youngsters in the crowd could store away in their memory.

Bradman not only withstood Lindwall, bumpers and all, demonstrated how a fast bowler's strength and speed could be harnessed to do the will of the batsman.

It was a thrilling day. The crowd thrilled itself by its own size—52,960—and then came the long-awaited duel between Lindwall and Bradman.

#### Catch Dropped

Then there was the hysteria of a skied on-drive off Bill Johnston when Bradman was 97.

**McCool, at short mid-on, ran round in a circle under the dropping ball, finished up with his back to the pitch, muffed the catch, then "accidentally" kicked the ball as it dropped from his hands, and had to chase it.**

It was very convincingly done. While all that was happening, Bradman ran the three he required for his century.

Then followed an amazing period, during which Bradman tried hard, but unsuccessfully, to throw his wicket away. He put his head in the air and lashed at everything. Two stumping chances were missed, and Loxton dropped a skier at first slip.

All the time the runs came at a great rate. Finally, baseballer Neil Harvey, at deep square-leg, took a beautifully-judged catch, to put an end to Bradman's innings—his 117th first-class century.

**Bradman's runs were worth £1 each to him, for Melbourne sportsman, John Wren, had contracted to pay him at that rate, with a minimum of £100 for each of his two innings.**

Altogether from his testimonial—State subscription lists and the match proceeds—Bradman is likely to get £10,000.

The net gate takings on Saturday were £4,488, bringing the aggregate to £5,674, and members' gate contributions are about £200 so far.

Bill Johnston and Bruce Dooland gave the day a light-hearted start by adding 23 runs in a quarter of an hour for the last wicket for Hassett's side.

Morris's cavalier treatment of McCool's short-pitched first over—the left-hander repeatedly swept him behind square leg—was avenged when the Queensland slow bowler dived to take a fine catch off his own bowling in his fourth over.

**The crowd, already 40,000, roared salvoes of cheers as the next batsman walked through the gate. It was Ron Hamence, and he accepted the role of Bradman by waving his bat and lifting his cap as he strode to the wicket.**

Lindwall, at first slip, aided the deception by walking up to Hamence and giving him a warm handshake.

The crowd still was not convinced that it was wrong when Hamence's name went on the scoreboard, for when the new batsman neatly placed McCool's first delivery to mid-on for a single a burst of applause came from the stands.

Lindwall, working up great pace and accuracy after lunch, bowled a blistering over in which Hamence was twice beaten by pace and struck on a leg, and Meuleman was missed low down by Saggers.

#### Six To Hamence

Hamence celebrated by loftily driving McCool for six, tried to do the same next over, was stumped, and made way for the master.

**It was a most stirring tribute the crowd gave Bradman. He was cheered all the way to the wicket, and when he arrived there Hassett's team gathered round him and cheered him again. When he took guard there were more cheers, and still more when he scored a single off the first ball he received.**

Playing the bowling with confidence, yet attempting nothing rash, Bradman's score mounted steadily. He overshadowed Meuleman, who was much more dogged than daring.

# BRADMAN FUND

## £10,200 In Hand

MELBOURNE, Tuesday. — Don Bradman's Testimonial fund to-day passed the £10,000 mark when 14,178 people paid £1,035 to see the final day's play of his benefit match.

To-night more than £10,200 had been received from gate takings, donations, and other functions.

Total attendance at the match on the Melbourne Cricket Ground was 94,035 for an aggregate gate of £7,484.

In addition, members of the Melbourne Cricket Club donated £629/7/6 through collection boxes placed at the gates.

#### GAVE £300

This morning Mr. John Wren, who had promised to subsidise Bradman's run-getting at the rate of £1 per run, or a minimum of £100 per innings, wrote out a cheque for £300 after seeing Bradman score his last 10 runs.

He gave the cheque to Australian selector Mr. Jack Ryder, who later introduced Mr. Wren to Bradman.

Entertained at lunch to-day by the M.C.C. members, Bradman said he felt very keenly the great honour which had been paid to him during his testimonial match.

"I feel very deeply because, as a product of N.S.W. and a resident of South Australia, this match is being played in another State," he said.

"So far as I know that has not been done on any other occasion, and it is something for which I am very grateful indeed."

#### PLAYERS' SUPPORT

Bradman said that he was very appreciative of the manner in which the players had helped, although there never was any need to question their support.

"In the 1948 team that visited England we had the grandest lot of players that it has been my good fortune to travel with," Bradman said.

"You who have witnessed this match have seen for yourselves the benefit they have derived from that tour."

The feared or expected sensations did not occur when Lindwall took the new ball. Except for failure to connect with half-arm hooks on the leg side, Bradman did not seem seriously troubled by Lindwall. He gloriously back cut a four off him and forced him through the covers with confidence and certainty.

Meuleman, having attained his 100 after more than three and a half hours of concentrated determination, mistimed a drive to give Queensland fast-medium bowler L. Johnson an easy catch.

Still batting delightfully, Bradman's score mounted with its characteristically deceptive speed and Lindwall tested him with a vicious bumper which caused Bradman to duck hastily, making the crowd roar.

Bradman's century was scored in 137 minutes and included nine fours. His full innings occupied 154 minutes and included 13 fours. He and Meuleman added 112 in 86 minutes for the third wicket.

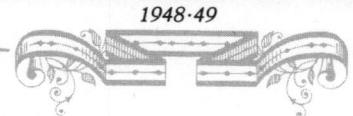

### Four Days' Cricket Yields 1,672 Runs

# BRADMAN MATCH ENDS IN DRAMATIC TIE

### By ARTHUR MAILEY

DON BRADMAN'S testimonial cricket match ended in a dramatic tie at the MCG yesterday with each team scoring a total of 836 runs.

With 10 minutes to go, Bradman's team needed 20 runs to win.

Tallon batted brilliantly, and before the last ball was bowled the difference was only two. Tallon scored the necessary runs, and the match ended with the teams all square.

Morris gave Bradman's team an excellent start, but it was a one-man effort owing to the loss of Meuleman, Bradman, and Miller for 72 runs.

Then Hamence and Morris became associated and carried the score to 170-odd before Morris was caught and bowled by Johnston.

### BRADMAN GOES EARLY

Bradman's pre-lunch dismissal probably cost him hundreds of pounds. If he had batted lower down the list and after lunch, the crowd probably would have doubled.

A fine catch by Saggers ended the champion's innings shortly before the lunch interval.

Hamence continued, and gave a measure of opposition to the attack, but the wickets of Raymer and Loxton fell fairly rapidly and the position looked rather hopeless.

At the tea interval Bradman's team, with seven out for 242, was 160 behind, with only Tallon and a couple of mediocre wickets in hand.

Noblet arrived on the scene at 5 o'clock to assist Tallon in what seemed a hopeless position. Noblet stonewalled, and Tallon went for the runs.

Hassett, the opposing captain, tried all his bowlers and placed the field so that Tallon might lose the strike. He did everything possible to clinch a victory which he felt was beginning to slip through his fingers.

Tallon was batting beautifully. He passed his 100 in 99 minutes, and had clouted twelve 4's.

The crowd, which had begun to drift away, paused and returned to see a sensational finish.

Morris' and Tallon's centuries were most entertaining.

Morris seems to have improved in every way since his trip to England, and now must be regarded as one of Australia's best lefthand batsmen of all time.

His drives were both powerful and beautifully timed. In one over he hit 23 off McCool,

AT HIS TESTIMONIAL MATCH at Melbourne Don Bradman for once agreed to sign autograph books publicly for young admirers. Previously he had made it a firm rule to sign only books sent to the dressing room.

and while not so aggressive against the medium and pace bowlers, he was equally confident.

The attack, as in the preceding days, was not particularly hostile. Lindwall obtained three cheap wickets, but he lacked the fire he showed in England, and appeared to be a little jaded.

Bill Johnston, who depended mainly on medium-slow bowling, was not particularly dangerous.

The following pages refer to the Knighthood which the King graciously bestowed on me. Included are press reports, letters, telegrams etc. and the bestowal of the accolade by the Governor-General of Australia.

When I started my Test career I had no thoughts of anything but the love of the game, the joy of playing it and the honour of representing my country.

I stood in awe when informed of the King's wish, and sincerely believe I would have declined the honour had there been nothing to consider but my personal feelings. However, I recognised it was intended as a compliment to the game of cricket and Australian cricket in particular. To refuse would have been ungracious. So I accepted, even though I knew that life would never be quite the same again.

I did not feel any different, but when my very close friends started to address me as "Sir Donald", I felt as though an invisible barrier had been erected between us. Convention seemed to demand respect rather than comradeship.

I hope that over the years I was able to successfully harmonise these qualities.

The flood of congratulatory messages which poured in were proof beyond doubt that there was widespread appreciation of my being the vehicle of this honour to cricket.

I must confess that I felt a sense of pride that my wife could thus share in a positive way some reflected glory and she always bore her new found status with a grace and dignity worthy of any title.

But for me personally, as a private man and citizen, I always preferred to think of myself just as plain Don Bradman, the boy from Bowral.

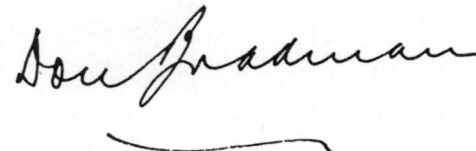

Melbourne *Herald* poster announcing the knighthood conferred on Don Bradman in 1949.

Sir Donald Bradman, painted by R. Hannaford, 1972. The original of this painting is hung in the Long Room at Lord's.

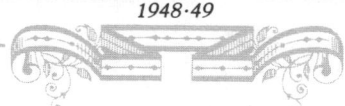

# Sir Donald Bradman

## NEW YEAR HONOURS

NEWS CHRONICLE REPORTER

A KNIGHTHOOD for Don Bradman, a barony for Sir John Boyd Orr, and knighthoods for Mr. Will Lawther and Mr. James Turner (president of the National Farmers' Union) are included in the New Year Honours list.

In the 25th honours list of the reign the King has created three barons, three Privy Councillors and 30 knights (in the home list); and has appointed two new Companions of Honour.

The new Privy Councillors are Dr. Edith Summerskill, Parliamentary Secretary, Ministry of Food (fourth woman so honoured); Mr. H. A. Marquand, Pensions Minister; and Lord Hailey, chairman, Colonial Research Committee.

Art, literature, drama and music claim 13 honours. Awards go to leaders in industry, the Civil Service and the man and woman in the street with striking records in social associations and trade unions.

The Archbishop of Canterbury, Dr. Geoffrey Fisher, receives from the King the Royal Victorian Chain.

Don Bradman, the new cricket knight, spent New Year's Eve watching a Sheffield Shield match at Melbourne

Sir Donald and Lady Bradman with their children, John and Shirley.

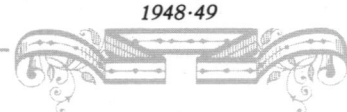

# "ARISE, SIR DON," SAYS LONDON
## *Papers Acclaim Knighthood*

## CLIMAX OF FINE CAREER

*(Daily Mirror World Cables)*

LONDON, Saturday.—"Arise, Sir Don." This was the front page banner line of the Morning Advertiser today, announcing the knighthood conferred on Bradman, the world's leading cricketer.

### *All morning newspapers splashed the announcement.*

THE Daily Express, in an editorial, says: "Hail, Sir Don. His knighthood brings the climax of an outstanding career that has captivated and exhilarated boys of all ages.

"But why not Sir Jack Hobbs? He was, of course, a professional. Will we ever see Sir Denis Compton carrying his bat for England?"

[The Melbourne Cricket Club and the Victorian Cricket Association are giving a luncheon at the Melbourne Cricket Ground in honor of Bradman's elevation as Australia's first cricketing knight. About 200 cricket fans huddled in shelters outside the Cricket Ground today to await Bradman's arrival, but he had not reached the ground by noon.]

Bradman, Claude Plowman, Professor Bernard Heinze, Brigadier E. G. B. Knox, Norman Angus Martin, Mr. Justice Walter Dwyer, and John Clifford Valentine Behan all receive knighthoods in the Dominions New Year Honors list.

*Sir Don*

Among those honored in the British list are Sir Winston Dugan, Governor of Victoria, granted a barony, and Australian-born singer Miss Astra Desmond, C.B.E.

A knighthood is conferred on Bradman in recognition of his services for many years as a cricketer, Australian Test captain, and for public services.

Don Bradman, born at Cootamundra on August 27, 1908, and now living in South Australia, has been the leader of Australian cricket for many years and hailed the world over as the greatest batsman of his time.

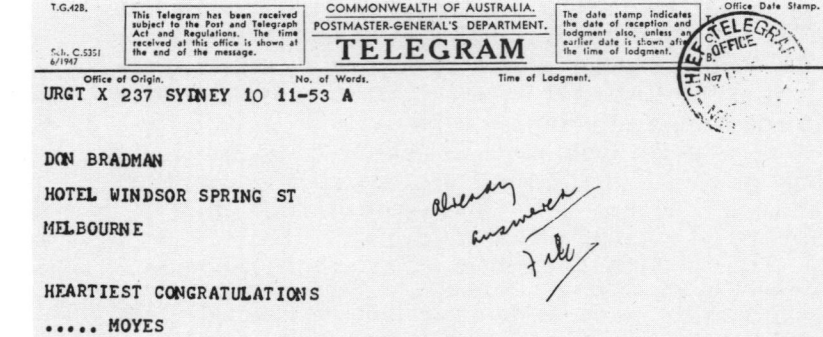

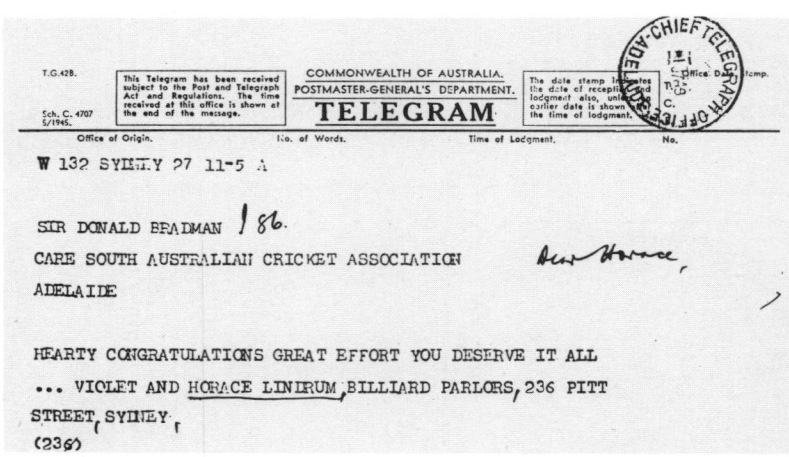

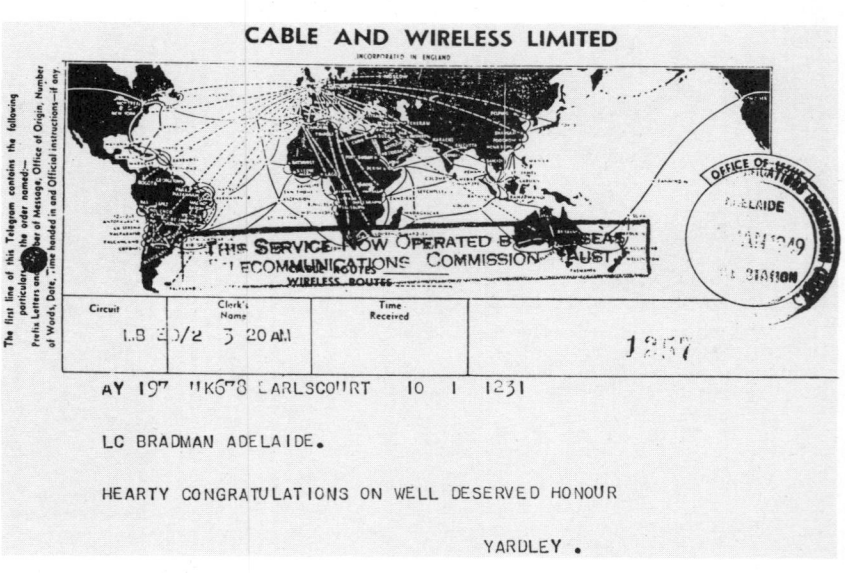

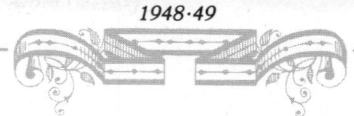

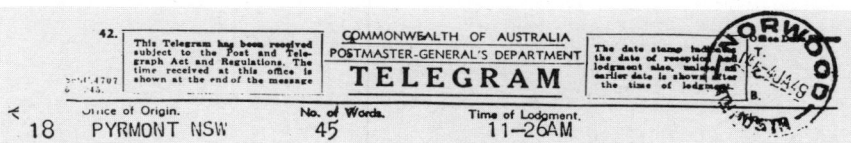

**COMMONWEALTH OF AUSTRALIA**
**POSTMASTER-GENERAL'S DEPARTMENT**
**TELEGRAM**

42.
This Telegram has been received subject to the Post and Telegraph Act and Regulations. The time received at this office is shown at the end of the message

The date stamp indicates the date of reception and lodgment also, unless an earlier date is shown after the time of lodgment.

| Office of Origin. | No. of Words. | Time of Lodgment. |
|---|---|---|
| 18  PYRMONT NSW | 45 | 11—26AM |

SIR DONALD BRADMAN
KENSINGTON ADELAIDE SA

HEARTY CONGRATULATIONS UPON HONOUR CONFERRED AND RICHLY DESERVED
STOP ALL AT ELLIMATTA DELIGHTED AND SHARE WITH YOU THE HONOUR
AND PRICE THAT JESSIE MERITS HER LOVELY TITLE ALSO AND OUR
CONGRATULATIONS ARE EXTENDED TO HER

FRANK CUSH AND FAMILY

1—50P L

---

T.G.42B.
This Telegram has been received subject to the Post and Telegraph Act and Regulations. The time received at this office is shown at the end of the message.

Sch. C. 4707
5/1945.

**COMMONWEALTH OF AUSTRALIA.**
**POSTMASTER-GENERAL'S DEPARTMENT.**
**TELEGRAM**

The date stamp indicates the date of reception and lodgment also, unless an earlier date is shown after the time of lodgment.

Office Date Stamp.

| Office of Origin. | No. of Words. | Time of Lodgment. |
|---|---|---|
| X 119  SYDNEY 16 11 A | | |

SIR DONALD BRADMAN
SOUTH AUSTRALIAN CRECKET ASSN ADELAIDE

HEARTY CONGRATULATIONS AN HONOUR WELL DESERVED

.... ALAN KIPPAX *Esq, Martin Place, Sydney.*

---

T.G.42B.
This Telegram has been received subject to the Post and Telegraph Act and Regulations. The time received at this office is shown at the end of the message.

Sch. C. 4707
5/1945.

**COMMONWEALTH OF AUSTRALIA.**
**POSTMASTER-GENERAL'S DEPARTMENT.**
**TELEGRAM**

The date stamp indicates the date of reception and lodgment also, unless an earlier date is shown after the time of lodgment.

Office Date Stamp.

| Office of Origin. | No. of Words. | Time of Lodgment. |
|---|---|---|
| W 19  ORCADES SYDNEYRADIO 11 3_A | | |

*2 Holden St Kensington Park*

SLT LADY BRADMAN ~~ADELAIDE~~

*aus*

CONGRATULATIONS AND HAPPY WISHES BOTH

NEVILLE CARDUS

---

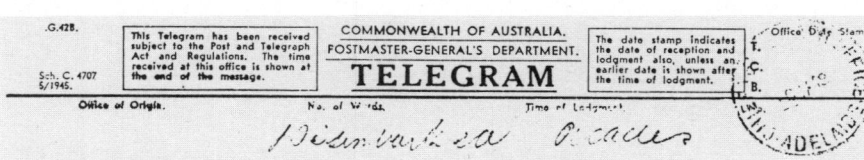

.G.42B.
This Telegram has been received subject to the Post and Telegraph Act and Regulations. The time received at this office is shown at the end of the message.

Sch. C. 4707
5/1945.

**COMMONWEALTH OF AUSTRALIA.**
**POSTMASTER-GENERAL'S DEPARTMENT.**
**TELEGRAM**

The date stamp indicates the date of reception and lodgment also, unless an earlier date is shown after the time of lodgment.

Office Date Stamp.

*Disembarked Orcades*

| Office of Origin. | No. of Words. | Time of Lodgment. |
|---|---|---|
| W341  PERTH SUB 15 2.23P | | |

SIR DONALD BRADMAN

GRENFELL ST ADELAIDE

I AM DELIGHTED AT YOUR HONOUR

R G MENZIES

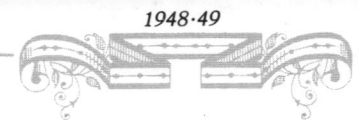

Government House,
CANBERRA.

14th. February, 1949.

Dear Sir,

His Excellency the Governor-General will hold
an Investiture, on behalf of His Majesty The King, at
10.30 a.m. on the 15th. March, 1949 in Queen's Hall,
Parliament House, Melbourne, and I am directed to invite
you to be present to receive the accolade of a Knight
Bachelor.

This invitation is extended as His Excellency
is not expected to visit South Australia in the near future
and it is thought that you may prefer to take advantage of
this occasion rather than wait an indefinite period to
receive the accolade.

If you so desire you may be accompanied at the
Investiture by two relatives or friends and arrangements
will be made for them to witness the ceremony.   The simple
procedure to be followed will be explained to you upon
arrival.

In order that arrangements may be completed, the
favour of your early reply is requested.

For the purpose of record, and this ceremony,
would you please indicate in your reply by which of your
Christian names you wish to be known.

Yours, faithfully,

(M.L. Tyrrell)
Official Secretary and Comptroller
to the Governor-General.

Sir Donald George Bradman,
2 Holden Street,
KENSINGTON PARK.
South Australia.

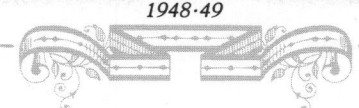

# A. R. Morris's XI
# v
# A. L. Hassett's XI
# (A. F. Kippax & W. A. Oldfield Testimonial)

<u>A.R. MORRIS'S XI v A.L. HASSETT'S XI</u> (A.F. Kippax and W.A. Oldfield Testimonial), at Sydney, 25, 26, 28 February, and 1 March 1949.

| | | |
|---|---|---|
| A.R. Morris's XI | - First Innings | 581 |
| | - Second Innings | 62 for 2 wickets |
| A.L. Hassett's XI | - First Innings | 204 |
| | - Second Innings | 437 |

A.R. Morris's XI won by 8 wickets.

| | | |
|---|---|---|
| <u>DON BRADMAN</u> | - c. K. Meulemann b. K.R. Miller | 53 |
| | - (did not bat) | |

DON BRADMAN played under A.R. Morris's captaincy in this game, the first time for over fourteen years that he did not captain his side. He went in at 111 for 1, at 2.48 p.m. on the second day (Saturday), on a slow, easy wicket, and, despite being completely out of practice, at once settled down confidently. He had to face a strong bowling side, including three fast bowlers in K.R. Miller, A.K. Walker and W.A. Johnston, and he played them as though he were years younger; the way he hooked bumpers from Miller was thrilling to watch, and without appearing to hit hard or to force the pace, he reached 50 in sixty-three minutes, mainly by skilful placing. Just afterwards, he mistimed Miller's slower ball, spooning it to mid-on, where K. Meulemann took a brilliant catch, one-handed, when running at full speed. Bradman hit only three fours, batted for sixty-five minutes and was out for 194 for 2.

BACK ROW    J. Moroney (M.), J. Burke (H.), K. Archer (M.), G. A. Langley (M.), W. Donaldson (12th man), P. Ridings (H.)

CENTRE ROW    H. Elphinston (Umpire), K. Meuleman (H.), F. Johnston (H.), K. R. Miller (H.), D. Ring (M.), W. Johnston (M.), R. A. Saggers (H.), L. Johnson (M.), I. Johnson (M.), G. Borwick (Umpire)

FRONT ROW    V. N. Raymer (H.), A. Walker (H.), R. A. Hamence (M.), R. N. Harvey (H.), A. L. Hassett, A. R. Morris, D. G. Bradman (M.), R. R. Lindwall (M.), S. Loxton (H.)

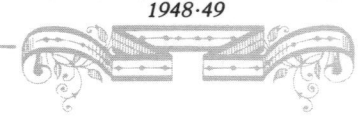

# BOYS SEIZE CHANCE TO GET AUTOGRAPH

## Scoreboard

**HASSETT'S ELEVEN.**
First Innings.

| | |
|---|---|
| K. MEULEMAN, lbw, b Lindwall | 36 |
| J. BURKE, c Morris, b I. Johnson | 11 |
| A. L. HASSETT, c I. Johnson, b Ring | 73 |
| K. R. MILLER, c W. Johnston, b Ring | 15 |
| N. HARVEY, b Ring | 8 |
| S. LOXTON, b Archer | 5 |
| P. RIDINGS, b Ring | 7 |
| V. N. RAYMER, b Ring | 0 |
| R. SAGGERS, c I. Johnson, b Lindwall | 21 |
| F. JOHNSTON, c Langley, b Lindwall | 8 |
| A. WALKER, not out | 8 |
| Sundries | 12 |
| **Total** | **204** |

Fall: 30, 99, 126, 134, 157, 159, 159, 168, 189, 204.

BOWLING.

| | O. | M. | R. | W. |
|---|---|---|---|---|
| Lindwall | 11.4 | 0 | 27 | 3 |
| W. Johnston | 14 | 3 | 43 | 0 |
| L. Johnson | 11 | 0 | 28 | 0 |
| I. Johnson | 12 | 1 | 45 | 1 |
| Ring | 18 | 0 | 49 | 5 |
| Archer | 1 | 1 | 0 | 1 |

Byes 8, leg-byes 4.

Second Innings.

| | |
|---|---|
| Meuleman, c and b I. Johnson | 13 |
| Burke, b Ring | 19 |
| Hasset, c Morris, b I. Johnson | 159 |
| Miller, b I. Johnson | 6 |
| Harvey, st Langley, b Ring | 87 |
| Loxton, c Lindwall, b W. Johnston | 93 |
| Ridings, run out | 12 |
| Raymer, st Langley, b I. Johnson | 2 |
| Saggers, b Morris | 8 |
| F. Johnston, not out | 7 |
| Walker, st Langley, b Ring | 9 |
| Sundries | 22 |
| **Total** | **437** |

Fall: 28, 42, 49, 253, 327, 351, 356, 387, 425, 437.

BOWLING.

| | O. | M. | R. | W. |
|---|---|---|---|---|
| Lindwall | 7 | 0 | 29 | 0 |
| W. Johnston | 12 | 2 | 47 | 1 |
| L. Johnson | 15 | 1 | 35 | 0 |
| I. Johnson | 25 | 3 | 86 | 4 |
| Ring | 30.3 | 3 | 152 | 3 |
| Archer | 8 | 2 | 34 | 0 |
| Hamence | 1 | 0 | 3 | 0 |
| Morris | 3 | 0 | 29 | 1 |

**MORRIS' XI.—First Innings**

| | |
|---|---|
| A. R. MORRIS, c Miller, b Ridings | 96 |
| J. MORONEY, c Walker, b Miller | 217 |
| D. G. BRADMAN, c Meuleman, b Miller | 53 |
| R. HAMENCE, st Saggers, b Raymer | 23 |
| K. ARCHER, st Saggers, b Harvey | 12 |
| I. JOHNSON, b Ridings | 41 |
| G. LANGLEY, c Hassett, b W. Johnston | 11 |
| R. LINDWALL, c Harvey, b Meuleman | 78 |
| D. RING, b F. Johnston | 31 |
| L. JOHNSON, c Burke, b Meuleman | 29 |
| W. JOHNSTON, not out | 9 |
| Sundries | 16 |
| **Total** | **581** |

Fall: 111, 194, 235, 269, 395, 430, 435, 497, 562, 581.

BOWLING.

| | O. | M. | R. | W. |
|---|---|---|---|---|
| Walker | 20 | 1 | 70 | 0 |
| Miller | 15 | 1 | 63 | 2 |
| F. Johnston | 23 | 0 | 181 | 2 |
| Loxton | 5 | 0 | 11 | 0 |
| Raymer | 15 | 1 | 103 | 1 |
| Ridings | 8 | 0 | 69 | 2 |
| Burke | 5 | 0 | 20 | 0 |
| Harvey | 3 | 0 | 13 | 1 |
| Hassett | 1 | 0 | 8 | 0 |
| Meuleman | 2.5 | 0 | 27 | 2 |

Second Innings.

| | |
|---|---|
| Morris, c F. Johnston, b Walker | 12 |
| Moroney, c Ridings, b Hassett | 25 |
| Archer, not out | 17 |
| Hamence, not out | 5 |
| **Total for two wickets** | **62** |

Fall: 14, 47.

BOWLING.

| | O. | M. | R. | W. |
|---|---|---|---|---|
| Walker | 6 | 0 | 20 | 1 |
| Loxton | 1 | 0 | 9 | 0 |
| Ridings | 2 | 0 | 4 | 0 |
| F. Johnston | 4 | 0 | 20 | 0 |
| Hassett | 2 | 0 | 9 | 1 |

Morris's Eleven won by eight wickets.

Small boys get Sir Donald Bradman's autograph as he goes out to the practice nets at Sydney Cricket Ground yesterday. Sir Donald, who is playing in the Kippax-Oldfield Testimonial match, is making his farewell appearance at S.C.G.

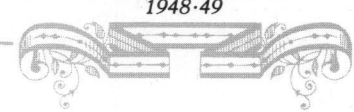

# Sir Donald's Farewell Appearance

### By OUR SPECIAL REPORTER

A gale of wild cheering stormed from all sections of the crammed Sydney Cricket Ground when Sir Donald Bradman walked through the players' gate at exactly 2.44 p.m. yesterday.

Sir Donald was going out to bat in his farewell match, the Oldfield-Kippax Testimonial.

Before it was his turn to bat, I watched him looking at the play from behind the glassed enclosure in the pavilion.

Now and then his eyes would turn from the field of younger men to the packed Hill and the stands as if he was remembering something.

He was not smiling at all yet—his lips were a straight line—only his deep, thoughtful eyes spoke of the things in his head.

Then he was standing up, pulling on a glove, reaching for his bat. Morris, the man just out, touched his cap as he walked into the pavilion.

### STORM BROKE

Sir Donald stepped into view, and that's when the storm broke.

Sir Donald smiled.

He walked slowly down through the clapping and back-slaps of the stand into the brilliant sunshine, and now everybody could see him clearly and the storm grew louder as the shouting lifted up from the Hill.

There were cries of "Good luck, Bradman—Leave it to Don" —"Garn, he ain't too old"— "Have a go, Bradman," as he moved over the bright, green oval to the crease and waited for Moroney to score a single.

Everything went still as Bradman took block—everything seemed to stop and hold breath as he leaned on his bat, looked twice around the field, and Ridings turned to bowl.

Bradman turned the first ball sweetly away to fine leg, and, like

**SIR DONALD and the boy who wanted his autograph.**

mass relief, the storm broke out again as the batsmen ran two.

As the players came back to the pavilion for the tea adjournment, a small boy burst from the crowd and raced towards Bradman, with an autograph book.

The master laid his arm over the lad's shoulders and led him through the players' entrance.

The lad couldn't talk when Sir Donald signed his book.

Bradman's appearance at the crease yesterday, helped pack the ground for the Oldfield-Kippax testimonial.

Both Oldfield and Kippax had played in Bradman's first interstate match—Adelaide, 1927— and in his first Test at Brisbane in 1928.

## The Courier-Mail

## The Don again

BACK briefly from the shadows of retirement, Don Bradman on Saturday demonstrated that he is still incomparably the greatest batsman in the world's greatest cricketing nation.

For a fleeting hour he charmed the crowded Sydney Cricket Ground with strokes compounded of skill and youthful zest. And yet he is 40, and lost now to cricket lovers.

In the cold language of the record books the last word has already been written to the Bradman story. But in the minds of reminiscent cricket lovers the Bradman legend is just beginning to take on heroic shape and colour. On Saturday Bradman provided more of the stuff of future legend.

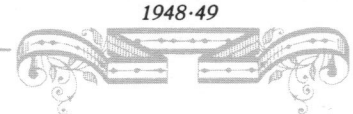

# BRADMAN'S FIGHTING 53 WILL RANK WITH HIS FINEST DEEDS

## The hook—as it is played

By R. S. WHITINGTON

**B**EFORE 41,575 worshippers, Sir Donald Bradman yet again rose grandly to the big occasion and scored one of his finest fifties at the Sydney Cricket Ground yesterday.

**Having had no match and little net practice since early December, Bradman made his batting farewell at his favorite cricket ground more than memorable.**

At the Kippax-Oldfield Testimonial match, his 53 in 65 minutes was technically a far finer innings than the century he scored in his own Testimonial three months ago at Melbourne.

At stumps, Morris' team had scored four for 294 in 240 minutes, in reply to Hassett's team's 204.

**Highlight of the whole Bradman knock was a perfectly executed hook stroke off Miller.**

Stepping across the flight of the ball as it rose toward his head. Bradman crashed it along the ground to the midwicket boundary.

Most modern batsmen hook the ball into the air, and behind square-leg.

So well did Bradman play that Walker, bowling well but unluckily against other batsmen, could neither make much impression on Bradman's defence. nor curb Bradman's scoring-rate.

All things considered, this innings by the 40-year-old.

unpractised champion, can fittingly take its place in his gallery of great cricketing deeds.

Apart from the hook I've mentioned, Bradman's best strokes, to my mind, were his pivoting cover-drive off Johnston and his well-placed, perfectly-executed leg glances off Walker's in-swingers.

Bradman richly deserved the warmest reception I've ever heard at SCG.

A solid, unfinished, opening 128 by faithful, dependable Jack Moroney, has made things awkward for his rivals for selection for the South African tour.

Though Moroney took exactly four hours for his runs he played many powerful strokes.

He hit a ball on to the gravel in front of the men's member stand after passing the century.

**Moroney has scored almost 900 runs this summer and he heads the first-class batting averages.**

## Fine cover drives

His best strokes were the drive and the pull, but he also played one or two attractive square-cuts and cover drives.

Morris, who hooked the first ball of his team's innings to the boundary, played another swashbuckling knock.

He used his feet so well to pull, drive and force the ball to the offside that the bowlers were at a loss to know where next to pitch it.

Morris' 66 in 94 minutes included seven fine boundaries, and Moroney's 128 not out 11 fours and a six.

At this stage it is only fair to say that the bowling of Hassett's team, taken as a whole, was far inferior to that of Morris' team.

Moroney, Hamence and the otherwise unlucky Archer had much less to worry them in the bowling line than did Burke, Meuleman and their successors.

Hassett, who tried nine bowlers, including himself, also had a far more difficult time as captain than did Morris. with Lindwall, Bill Johnston, Len Johnson, Ian Johnson and Ring under his wing.

As Hassett found today, no captain can place a field for bowling that lacks both length and direction.

Best of the Hassett team bowlers, I thought, was Alan Walker, who failed to take a wicket, but could easily have had those of Morris and Moroney (twice) in his first two overs.

**He also got two balls past Bradman, one of them not so far outside the off stump.**

Miller mixed some good balls with some very ordinary ones.

Saggers' leg-side stumping of the stylish Archer was worthy of Bert Oldfield at his best.

**Early in the day Hobart-born 30-year-old Doug Ring effaced some of the memory of an indifferent season by a good performance, which gave him the figures 18-0-49-5.**

**Takings were £3348/14/9.**

Sir Donald Bradman, A. C. Taken at his home in Adelaide, 1985.

Sir Donald Bradman A.C. and Lady Bradman at home. Adelaide, 1987.

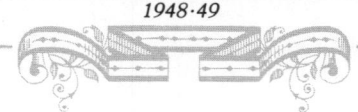

**PUNISHER.** Bradman made no mistake with this shot when he pulled a short ball from Fred Johnston to the square leg fence.

# SYDNEY HAS FAREWELL GLIMPSE OF THE MASTER

DON BRADMAN, playing his farewell match on the Sydney Cricket Ground yesterday, gave the crowd of more than 40,000 a glimpse of his old mastery. LEFT: He pushes a ball from Ridings into the covers, as he settles down. CENTRE: On the defensive as Walker attacks with speed and swing. RIGHT: For a flashing moment the Bradman of other days is recalled as he hooks a bumping ball from Walker hard to the on fence.

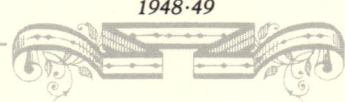
Don Bradman walking off the Sydney Cricket Ground after his last innings there in February 1949.

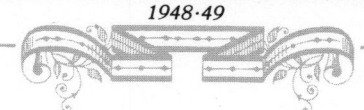

# South Australia
# v
# Victoria
# (A. J. Richardson Testimonial)

## BRADMAN'S LAST MATCH

SOUTH AUSTRALIA v VICTORIA (A.J. Richardson Testimonial),
at Adelaide, 4, 5, 7 and 8 March 1949.

| South Australia | - First Innings | 154 |
| | - Second Innings | 132 |
| Victoria | - First Innings | 229 |
| | - Second Innings | 328 |

South Australia lost by 271 runs.

DON BRADMAN - b. W.A. Johnston 30
- absent hurt

DON BRADMAN played under the captaincy of P.L. Ridings on his last appearance in a first-class match.    He went in at 26 for 2, thirty-seven minutes from the close of the first day's play, and defended rather anxiously to make 18 not out;  S.J.E. Loxton had him missed at backward short-leg. Next morning, he stayed for another three-quarters of an hour, but was well below his best form, and never really timed the ball properly, until he chopped on to his stumps a ball which kept low; he was out at 84 for 4, having batted for eighty-two minutes, and his 30 was top score for his side. Later that day he trod on a ball while fielding, turned his right ankle over, and had to be helped off the field;  with his ankle very swollen and painful, he was unable to bat in the second innings, and his last appearance was thus something of an anticlimax.

Scores:—

### VICTORIA.

| | |
|---|---|
| C. McDonald, b Noblet | 1 |
| R. Howard, b Noblet | 35 |
| K. Stackpole, c Bradman, b Gogler | 33 |
| N. Harvey, b McLean | 41 |
| S. J. Loxton, lbw b O'Neill | 25 |
| H. Turner, b O'Neill | 22 |
| I. W. Johnson, c Langley, b O'Neill | 1 |
| D. Ring, b O'Neill | 1 |
| I. McDonald, b O'Neill | 2 |
| J. Baird, not out | 13 |
| W. A. Johnston, c Bradman, b McLean | 38 |
| Extras | 17 |
| | 229 |

### SOUTH AUSTRALIA BOWLING.

| | O | M | R | W |
|---|---|---|---|---|
| O'Neill | 13 | 2 | 45 | 5 |
| Noblet | 14 | 3 | 39 | 2 |
| Bowley | 6 | 1 | 30 | 0 |
| McLean | 15.4 | 1 | 66 | 2 |
| Gogler | 4 | 0 | 19 | 1 |
| Ridings | 4 | 2 | 13 | 0 |

### VICTORIA.
#### Second Innings.

| | |
|---|---|
| C. McDonald, c Langley, b O'Neill | 9 |
| R. Howard, c Noblet, b McLean | 26 |
| K. Stackpole, c Langley, b Noblet | 15 |
| N. Harvey, c and b McLean | 9 |
| S. J. Loxton, lbw b Noblet | 135 |
| H. Turner, lbw b O'Neill | 29 |
| I. W. Johnson, lbw b McLean | 22 |
| D. Ring, lbw b Noblet | 32 |
| I. McDonald, not out | 32 |
| J. Baird, run out | 1 |
| W. A. Johnston, c Gogler, b Noblet | 7 |
| Extras | 11 |
| | 328 |

### SOUTH AUSTRALIA BOWLING.

| | O | M | R | W |
|---|---|---|---|---|
| O'Neill | 12 | 1 | 40 | 2 |
| Noblet | 26.6 | 7 | 54 | 4 |
| Bowley | 5 | 1 | 20 | 0 |
| McLean | 21 | 2 | 139 | 3 |
| Gogler | 8 | 0 | 53 | 0 |
| Ridings | 5 | 1 | 11 | 0 |

### SOUTH AUSTRALIA.

| | |
|---|---|
| K. Lewis, c Howard, b Loxton | 16 |
| K. Gogler, c McDonald, b Baird | 6 |
| R. A. Hamence, b Baird | 11 |
| Sir D. G. Bradman, b Johnston | 30 |
| P. Ridings, c Howard, b Baird | 17 |
| B. Bowley, c Howard, b Johnson | 12 |
| G. R. Langley, c and b Johnson | 15 |
| P. Bednall, st McDonald, b Ring | 7 |
| K. O'Neill, b Baird | 10 |
| A. R. McLean, c and b Ring | 10 |
| G. Noblet, not out | 8 |
| Extras | 12 |
| | 154 |

### VICTORIA BOWLING.

| | O | M | R | W |
|---|---|---|---|---|
| Baird | 15 | 1 | 69 | 4 |
| Johnston | 14 | 4 | 28 | 1 |
| Loxton | 8 | 1 | 19 | 1 |
| Ring | 6.3 | 2 | 15 | 2 |
| Johnson | 6 | 3 | 11 | 2 |

### SOUTH AUSTRALIA.
#### Second Innings.

| | |
|---|---|
| K. Lewis, run out | 20 |
| K. Gogler, c Johnson, b Loxton | 20 |
| R. A. Hamence, c Stackpole, b Ring | 10 |
| Sir D. G. Bradman, absent hurt | 0 |
| P. Ridings, c Stackpole, b Johnston | 4 |
| B. Bowley, st McDonald, b Johnson | 8 |
| G. R. Langley, run out | 36 |
| P. Bednall, b Ring | 3 |
| K. O'Neill, c McDonald, b Baird | 3 |
| A. R. McLean, run out | 19 |
| G. Noblet, not out | 0 |
| Extras | 9 |
| | 132 |

### VICTORIA BOWLING.

| | O | M | R | W |
|---|---|---|---|---|
| Baird | 7 | 2 | 28 | 1 |
| Johnston | 23.2 | 10 | 51 | 1 |
| Loxton | 4 | 0 | 10 | 1 |
| Ring | 9 | 1 | 30 | 2 |
| Johnson | 8 | 6 | 4 | 1 |

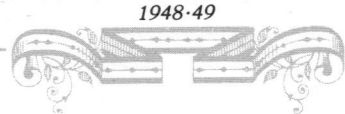

# BRADMAN'S 30 IN LAST SHIELD GAME

**ADELAIDE, Saturday.—Sir Donald Bradman was out for 30 in the final 1948-49 Shield game between SA and Victoria today.**

With Victoria all out for 229, Bradman went in when SA had lost 3-44 yesterday.

Batting quietly, he was 18 not out at stumps.

Today, he again had a good look at the ball, and took 35 minutes to score seven.

**He lashed unsuccessfully at two balls wide on the leg from Baird.**

Test all-rounder Sam Loxton bowled with pace and good length, and kept Bradman anchored.

However, B r a d m a n pounced on a loose one, and swung it beautifully for four.

Soon after, he survived a confident appeal for a catch behind.

A few balls later, Bradman cut a Johnston swinger into his stumps, and had a swing at the ball in disgust.

**His 30 took 82 minutes and included two fours.**

SA was then 5-84.

The batsmen strugled along but Bowley, when shaping nicely, lofted Johnson to give Howard his second good catch.

Bednall did not last long and at lunch SA was 8-123.

Baird was next to go, and nine were down for 132.

McLean and Noblet were still together when the score passed 150.

**South Australia all out for 154 in 205 minutes.**

Victoria again started badly in its second knock, losing the first two wickets for 31.

McDonald leg-glanced to Langley, who took a great catch wide on the leg side for the first-wicket fall at 12.

Harvey was again bright, but, in trying to drive Mc-Lean, hit the ball straight back to the bowler.

SIR DONALD BRADMAN chats at the Adelaide Oval with veteran international A. J. Richardson, during the match between South Australia and Victoria which has been made a Testimonial game for Richardson. It also is the last first-class cricket match in which Bradman will play.

# Sir Donald Bradman Receives

# Accolade

MELBOURNE, Mar. 15.

Mr. Don Bradman became Sir Donald Bradman, Kt., officially at Melbourne today.

With 201 recipients of honors and decorations, he went to the Queen's Hall, at Parliament House, for investiture by the Governor-General (Mr. McKell).

Only two others were present to receive the accolade as Knight Bachelor—Sir John Behan, former warden of Trinity College, Melbourne University, and Sir Charles Lowe, University Chancellor.

Sir Donald Bradman looked unusually short as he sat between the two university men —one 6 ft. 2 in. and the other 6 ft.

The 500 spectators had been asked to remain quiet throughout the ceremony, but a murmur arose when an aide called "Donald George Bradman, Esquire."

Sir Donald stepped forward with his head down and a half-smile on his face. He bowed and kneeled on the red plush cushion before Mr. McKell, who with a shining infantry sword touched him on each of his shoulders.

Then, almost inaudibly, Mr. McKell said. "Arise, Sir Donald."

He smiled warmly as he shook hands and quietly said, "Congratulations!"

Sir Donald was smiling, too, as he walked, still with head down, back to his seat.

Lady Bradman, who had watched rather anxiously from a seat among the crowd, gave a sigh of relief and smiled with them.

Capt. Vivian Bullwinkel, sole survivor of the Banka Island massacre. was among the Army nursing sisters honored She received the award of the Associate of the Order of the Royal Red Cross.

Capt. Bullwinkel had a miraculous escape wnen the Japanese murdered 29 nurses at Banka Island. She is now a sister at the blood bank at the Heidelberg Repatriation Hospital. Melbourne.

# They Called: 'Donald Bradman, Esq.'

"Arise, Sir Donald," said the Governor General (Mr McKell) in the sedate, plum-carpeted Queen's Hall at Parliament House today.

And the crowd of 500 who were looking on (earlier asked by officials to keep silent) could not restrain a little flutter of excitement.

Sir Donald received the accolade of Knight Bachelor between two elderly University men—Sir John Behan, Warden of Trinity College for 28 years, and the Chancellor, Sir Charles Lowe.

Mr McKell stood in morning dress before a raised dais with a huge Union Jack at his back.

Behind him on the dais sat the Lieutenant - Governor (Sir Edmund Herring), the three service chiefs, the Minister for Labor (Mr Holloway), representing the Federal Government, and the Victorian Premier (Mr Hollway).

Before him the carpeted aisle stretched forward to the towering marble statue of Queen Victoria.

## Shining Sword

When an aide called, "Donald George Bradman, Esq.," Sir Donald walked forward a few yards from his chair with his head down and a half smile on his face.

He kneeled on the red plush cushion before Mr McKell as an aide stepped forward with a shining infantry sword.

Mr McKell touched the sword lightly on Sir Donald's left and right shoulders and almost inaudibly told him to rise.

Both men broke into wide smiles as Mr McKell shook hands and said almost in a whisper, "Congratulations."

Still with his head down, Bradman walked back to his chair, where the two tall University knights stood up, according to the practice, on his arrival.

Lady Bradman came from South Australia with her husband for the investiture. They will return home tonight.

A Naval Royal guard of 100 men was drawn up in Spring Street at the foot of Parliament House steps when Mr McKell arrived. He inspected the guard before walking into Queen's Hall.

## Not Talking

Rumors of Sir Donald Bradman's imminent entry into the commercial world—this time as an importer of Scottish wools—continue, but Sir Donald remains noncommittal.

"I have nothing to say on that subject whatsoever," he said emphatically today, when approached in Parliament Buildings before the investiture.

## Then:

# 'ARISE DONALD'

The Governor-General, Mr. McKell, chatting with Sir Donald and Lady Bradman after he had bestowed the accolade of knighthood upon Sir Donald at yesterday's investiture in Melbourne. Photograph shows, from left, Capt. V. Bullwinkle of Fullarton, who was made an Associate of the Royal Red Cross, Mr. McKell, Sir John Behan (background), Sir Donald Bradman and Lady Bradman.

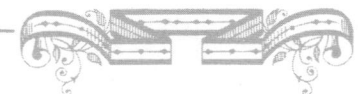

... It is idle, if alluring, to compare the champions of different epochs: we may wonder indefinitely how H. L. Doherty would have fared with Budge, or Harry Vardon with Henry Cotton: whether Alex James in his prime would have bewildered the brothers Walters in theirs, whether Ronnie Poulton's swerve would have been checkmated by the closer defensive tactics of a modern international. Would "W.G." have been really bothered by the googly and the leg-side field, and how would Hammond have fared on the old fiery wickets of Lord's in the seventies? Such questions cannot be answered, but we may with a feeling of absolute security assert that in no age and at no game has any man more dominated his contemporaries than has Don Bradman in the dozen years—and they are no more—of his first-class career. How many runs on a good wicket would England barter for the surety of seeing Bradman's back twice disappearing into the pavilion? What odds would any man lay, when he reaches a century, against that hundred going into two? How much of Test Match history in those dozen years can be assigned to him and him alone? Figures can lie, but in cricket, taken in the large, they tell the truth, and in his case defy all argument. In that period twenty-three matches have been finished, England winning 13 and Australia 10: and in nine out of those ten Bradman has made over 100, in six of the ten over 200. It has been the same in all his cricket from Test Match to second grade in Australia: no one in the game has approached him for consistency over anything like the same period. He has already far outstripped in aggregate all other Australian batsmen: Trumper, Macartney, Clem Hill and Joe Darling, Sidney Gregory and Warren Bardsley are all as "The Field" to Eclipse.

To total 1,000 runs in a domestic season in the Dominion is a tremendous achievement: only Ponsford and Kippax have done it more than once—in each case twice. Bradman has done it every season except one since he first appeared.

What then, is the secret of this astonishing phenomenon? Let us consider first the physical equipment. Bradman is a small man and were a stranger to meet him standing still in ordinary clothes he would notice nothing remarkable about him except a pair of exceptionally high shoulders, an unusually resolute jaw and a keen pair of eyes. But see the same figure in flannels and in action and the first secret is not far to seek. For here is obviously a perfectly co-ordinated body, balanced on feet as neat, and at the same time as strong, as any professional dancer's, which ensure maximum speed and accuracy of movement: add to this that flexibility of hip which is a hall-mark of nearly all great games-players, great power of forearm, wrist and (often forgotten) hand, and you have some idea of the machine that turns out the runs. Machines need looking after and Bradman has always known how to keep his not merely, it would seem, in good running, but in racing trim. But greatest of all his natural assets is a speed of reaction which, I believe, scientific tests have proved to be quite abnormal; perhaps only with Ranji was there so small a time-lag between conception and execution, and this is the secret of his stroke play whether in defence or attack. He sees the ball sooner, watches it longer, and can play the stroke later than anyone else. Remember, too, that in his case each stroke decision is regulated by a singularly acute cricket brain and a, by now, immense batting experience.

It would be illogical to expect in a man of his build the effortless ease of stroke play which one associated with Frank Woolley or the power of Walter Hammond's driving, though in all conscience there is power enough; nor can he rival one of the greatest of English batsmen—George Gunn—in giving the impression that he has "all day to play his shot in": the tempo of his batting is staccato. But the power and versatility of his stroke play are astonishing; unlike the vast majority of his contemporaries he can fight a war on two fronts, for he seems equally at home with an off-side or leg-side attack: he can hit the ball through the covers with equal facility off the front or back leg, and he is a brilliant cutter, both square and late; but it is on the other side of the wicket that his mastery is most impressive. He is the finest hooker in the world and can direct this stroke at will anywhere from wide mid-on to fine leg with the vital, and very rare, security of hardly ever lifting the ball, whilst to bowl even a fairly accurate length on the line of his leg-stumps or legs is to ask for punishment; here, perhaps, his peculiar genius is most pronounced, in his ability to force the ball through any inviting gap, generally off the back foot, meeting it very near his body, and with a combined thrust of the forearms and flick of the wrists played with a perfection of timing that makes a utilitarian stroke into a work of art. Allied with this great variety of stroke play there goes an extraordinary facility for placing the ball, and only very accurate bowling and the most skilfully adjusted placing of the field has any chance of keeping him even moderately quiet on a good wicket. In his earlier years, and even now when the whim takes him, he could and can go the pace of a pure hitter, and for a time in the early part of the 1934 tour he seemed practically to have selected that rôle for himself: then I believe an almost stern remonstrance from Woodfull sobered him, with the monumental result that we all remember, and since then, though his stroke play could never be anything but remarkable, runs rather than strokes appear to have become his main objective.

For the extraordinary consistency with which he pursues that aim we must look beyond the mere technique of a superlative defence coupled with outstanding physical fitness and a stamina that sustains him through the longest day. If I may borrow terms

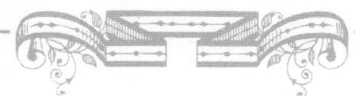

from another sphere, Bradman is not a romantic but a realist: he finds his satisfaction in achievement rather than in method; he is not tempted, as Jack Hobbs often was, to try dangerous strokes simply because the mere making of runs by ordinarily secure means had begun to pall, or to regard a mere century as the signal for "chancing his arm", either as a concession to his physical nature or from the feeling that made Michaelangelo want to give up painting in favour of sculpture, "because it was too easy". He will always play to the clock and the state of the game and very rarely fails to take drastic toll of a tiring attack during the last ninety minutes of a day's play; but, other things being equal, he is content to go on his way from his first century to his second and from his second to his third with the same deliberate speed, unwearied, unexcited and, above all, undiverted.

It is sometimes said that "Bradman cannot play on a sticky wicket": that is nonsense. With his natural gifts he could not help being good under those conditions, when the ability to move the feet quickly and play a delayed stroke accurately mean so much: in the Leeds Test Match of 1938 the ball was consistently on top of the bat, but he made his century as usual and that century settled the match, whilst in that absorbing game, in which all Yorkshire to this day believes they were robbed of victory by rain, he played Verity, on his own admission, as well as he ever remembers being played.

Another statement that I have sometimes heard made, in a sort of vague disparagement, against Bradman is that he is "inhuman". If this means that he is uniquely immune from the ordinary frailties of the cricketing flesh, he certainly stands condemned, for he does not tire, he does not relax, and even on the days when he is, for him, palpably out of form, a long score remains more probable than a short one. But if it implies that he lacks personality or the capacity to enjoy the game himself and make others enjoy it, it is ludicrously false. His immense vitality, for one thing, gives it the lie: one cannot be bored with a man who is so tremendously alive every moment he is on the field. But it was finally and utterly disproved by his captaincy of the Australians in 1938. No one can have been surprised at his tactical shrewdness on that tour, but I doubt whether anyone was quite prepared for the personal ascendancy which he established over his team. I do not think I have ever admired anything on the cricket field so much as his leadership through those heartbreaking days at the Oval in August: his own fielding was an inspiration in itself, and as hour succeeded hour with nothing going right and the prospect of the rubber receding over a hopeless horizon, it was, one felt, his courage and gaiety that alone sustained his side. And when the tragic accident came, the game was over, the balloon was pricked and his team was a team no more.

I have written much more than I meant: much more, indeed,

than my friend the Editor asked me: more perhaps than he will see fit to publish, and I have caught myself wondering whether a sense of proportion in time as well as space has not been left out in a schoolmaster's "arrested development". But if Falstaff in a tavern in Eastcheap "babbled o' green fields", may we not find comfort in remembering our own Arcadies? I am the happier now for having seen "W.G." bat and Kortright bowl, for having fielded to "Ranji" and Archie MacLaren, and for having been comprehensively bowled by Colin Blythe. But, as I have written in another place, "In the many pictures that I have stored in my mind from the 'burnt-out Junes' of forty years, there is none more dramatic or compelling than that of Bradman's small, serenely-moving figure in its big-peaked green cap coming out of the pavilion shadows into the sunshine, with the concentration, ardour and apprehension of surrounding thousands centred upon him, and the destiny of a Test Match in his hands."

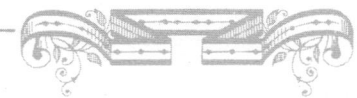

# ACKNOWLEDGEMENTS

The material in these volumes has been selected from the fifty-two volumes entitled *Don Bradman Scrapbooks* which are held in the Mortlock Library, State Library of South Australia. The Publisher gratefully acknowledges the ready help and cooperation extended by the Mortlock Library throughout the preparation of this publication, and, in particular, would like to thank the Librarian, Margy Burn.

Much of the collected material carries no source, accreditation or date. Every attempt has been made to identify and seek permission of the copyright holders, but in many cases this has proved impossible. The Publisher would be pleased to hear from anyone who feels they should have been acknowledged here.

Thanks are extended to the publishers and copyright holders for granting permission to include the material listed below:

The *Advertiser*, Adelaide (photograph, p. 362); Allans Music (Australia) Pty Ltd (song sheet, p. 290); Australian Cricket Board (cables, pp. 346–9; letter, p. 75; instructions, p. 76); Rosalind Carrodus, née Evatt (letters, pp. 251, 254, 506); The *Courier-Mail* (editorial, p. 783); David Higham Associates Ltd, London (articles by Denzil Batchelor, pp. 461, 475, 488, 729, 732); Margaret Hughes (articles by Neville Cardus, pp. 343, 456, 457, 477–8, 529, 544, 547, 553); Hurstville Municipal Council (letter, p. 22); Ian Johnson (letter p. 660); *Mail* Newspapers plc (articles, pp. 120, 365, 366, 405, 422); Marylebone Cricket Club (cables, pp. 346–9); Dame Pattie Menzies (letter, p. 661); N.S.W. Cricket Association (letters, pp. 16, 359; team photographs, p. 18, and other unaccredited N.S.W. team photographs); W. J. O'Reilly (articles, pp. 646, 683); *Punch*, London (cartoons, pp. 373, 388); St. George District Cricket Club (article, p. 21); *Southern Highland News*, Bowral (articles, pp. 13, 21, 25, 27); South Australian Cricket Association (letters, pp. 433, 444); The *Wagga Daily Advertiser* (article, p. 246).

Grateful acknowledgement is made to Sir Donald Bradman, A.C., for making available items from his private collection for plates facing pages 16, 145, 288, 289, 401, 569, 665, 745 and 761.

Colour plates are also by courtesy of: British Columbia Mainland Cricket League (facing p. 273); Anthony Buckley and Constantine Ltd (facing p. 784); Patrick Eagar (facing pp. 520, 521, 545, 568, 744); Donald Gee (facing p. 441); Sir Ivor Hele and South Australian Cricket Association (facing p. 585), photographer Donald Gee; Hutchinson, London: *Don Bradman's Book* by D. G. Bradman, 1930 (facing p. 208); John Knight (facing p. 456); Marylebone Cricket Club (facing p. 777); G. W. & J. Sparkes Pty Ltd (facing p. 504).

All other items photographed for the colour plates were kindly provided by the Mortlock Library in Adelaide.

Photographs of items in the Mortlock Library and from the private collection of Sir Donald Bradman were taken by Ray Joyce and Donald Gee.

The commentaries and innings scores which appear at the beginning of each game, the season summaries and the Appendices have been taken from B. J. Wakley, *Bradman the Great*, Nicholas Kaye, London, 1959. The Tribute to Don Bradman on page 790 has been taken from Hubert Doggart (ed.), *The Heart of Cricket. A Memoir of H. S. Altham*, Century Hutchinson, London, 1967.

Thanks are also extended to the following for their invaluable help: Australian Cricket Board; Melbourne Cricket Club; N.S.W. Cricket Association; Queensland Cricket Association; South Australian Cricket Association; West Australian Cricket Association; *Australian Cricket Magazine*; Kent County Cricket Club; Marylebone Cricket Club, Lord's Ground, London; Worcestershire County Cricket Club; W. J. O'Reilly; F. Ivory, Commercial Travellers Association; Bruce Collins; Dr Cedric Lamb; Keith Lamb.

## Appendix I
### Career Summary, 1927–49

| | Matches | Innings | NO | HS | Runs | Average | Centuries |
|---|---|---|---|---|---|---|---|
| All First-Class Matches | 234 | 338 | 43 | 452* | 28067 | 95·14 | 117 |
| All Matches in Australia | 142 | 218 | 25 | 452* | 18230 | 94·45 | 76 |
| All Matches in England | 92 | 120 | 18 | 334 | 9837 | 96·44 | 41 |
| All Test Matches | 52 | 80 | 10 | 334 | 6996 | 99·94 | 29 |
| Test Matches *v.* England | 37 | 63 | 7 | 334 | 5028 | 89·78 | 19 |
| *v.* England in England | 19 | 30 | 4 | 334 | 2674 | 102·84 | 11 |
| *v.* England in Australia | 18 | 33 | 3 | 270 | 2354 | 78·46 | 8 |
| All Tests in Australia | 33 | 50 | 6 | 299* | 4322 | 98·22 | 18 |
| All Sheffield Shield Matches | 62 | 96 | 15 | 452* | 8926 | 110·19 | 36 |
| Shield Matches for New South Wales | 31 | 52 | 9 | 452* | 4633 | 107·74 | 17 |
| Shield Matches for South Australia | 31 | 44 | 6 | 357 | 4293 | 112·97 | 19 |
| All Matches for New South Wales | 41 | 69 | 10 | 452* | 5813 | 98·52 | 21 |
| All Matches for South Australia | 44 | 63 | 8 | 369 | 5753 | 104·60 | 25 |
| All Matches *v.* Touring Teams | 54 | 84 | 8 | 299* | 6259 | 82·35 | 25 |
| Matches *v.* M.C.C. Teams | 32 | 55 | 5 | 270 | 3352 | 67·04 | 11 |

## Appendix III
### Season-by-Season Record in Test Matches

| | Opponents | Matches | Innings | NO | HS | Runs | Average | Centuries |
|---|---|---|---|---|---|---|---|---|
| 1928–9 | England | 4 | 8 | 1 | 123 | 468 | 66·85 | 2 |
| 1930 | England | 5 | 7 | 0 | 334 | 974 | 139·14 | 4 |
| 1930–1 | West Indies | 5 | 6 | 0 | 223 | 447 | 74·50 | 2 |
| 1931–2 | South Africa | 5 | 5 | 1 | 299* | 806 | 201·50 | 4 |
| 1932–3 | England | 4 | 8 | 1 | 103* | 396 | 56·57 | 1 |
| 1934 | England | 5 | 8 | 0 | 304 | 758 | 94·75 | 2 |
| 1936–7 | England | 5 | 9 | 0 | 270 | 810 | 90·00 | 3 |
| 1938 | England | 4 | 6 | 2 | 144* | 434 | 108·50 | 3 |
| 1946–7 | England | 5 | 8 | 1 | 234 | 680 | 97·14 | 2 |
| 1947–8 | India | 5 | 6 | 2 | 201 | 715 | 178·75 | 4 |
| 1948 | England | 5 | 9 | 2 | 173* | 508 | 72·57 | 2 |
| *Totals:* | | | | | | | | |
| *v.* England in Australia | | 18 | 33 | 3 | 270 | 2354 | 78·46 | 8 |
| *v.* England in England | | 19 | 30 | 4 | 334 | 2674 | 102·84 | 11 |
| Total *v.* England | | 37 | 63 | 7 | 334 | 5028 | 89·78 | 19 |
| All Tests in Australia | | 33 | 50 | 6 | 299* | 4322 | 98·22 | 18 |
| TOTAL | | 52 | 80 | 10 | 334 | 6996 | 99·94 | 29 |

## Appendix II
### Season-by-Season Record in all First Class Matches

| | Matches | Innings | NO | HS | Runs | Average | Centuries |
|---|---|---|---|---|---|---|---|
| 1927–8 | 5 | 10 | 1 | 134* | 416 | 46·22 | 2 |
| 1928–9 | 13 | 24 | 6 | 340* | 1690 | 93·88 | 7 |
| 1929–30 | 11 | 16 | 2 | 452* | 1586 | 113·28 | 5 |
| 1930 | 27 | 36 | 6 | 334 | 2960 | 98·66 | 10 |
| 1930–1 | 12 | 18 | 0 | 258 | 1422 | 79·00 | 5 |
| 1931–2 | 10 | 13 | 1 | 299* | 1403 | 116·91 | 7 |
| 1932–3 | 11 | 21 | 2 | 238 | 1171 | 61·63 | 3 |
| 1933–4 | 7 | 11 | 2 | 253 | 1192 | 132·44 | 5 |
| 1934 | 22 | 27 | 3 | 304 | 2020 | 84·16 | 7 |
| 1934–5 | — | — | — | — | — | — | — |
| 1935–6 | 8 | 9 | 0 | 369 | 1173 | 130·33 | 4 |
| 1936–7 | 12 | 19 | 1 | 270 | 1552 | 86·22 | 6 |
| 1937–8 | 12 | 18 | 2 | 246 | 1437 | 89·81 | 7 |
| 1938 | 20 | 26 | 5 | 278 | 2429 | 115·66 | 13 |
| 1938–9 | 7 | 7 | 1 | 225 | 919 | 153·16 | 6 |
| 1939–40 | 9 | 15 | 3 | 267 | 1475 | 122·91 | 5 |
| 1940–1 | 2 | 4 | 0 | 12 | 18 | 4·50 | 0 |
| 1945–6 | 2 | 3 | 1 | 112 | 232 | 116·00 | 1 |
| 1946–7 | 9 | 14 | 1 | 234 | 1032 | 79·38 | 4 |
| 1947–8 | 9 | 12 | 2 | 201 | 1296 | 129·60 | 8 |
| 1948 | 23 | 31 | 4 | 187 | 2428 | 89·92 | 11 |
| 1948–9 | 3 | 4 | 0 | 123 | 216 | 54·00 | 1 |
| In Australia | 142 | 218 | 25 | 452* | 18230 | 94·45 | 76 |
| In England | 92 | 120 | 18 | 334 | 9837 | 96·44 | 41 |
| TOTAL | 234 | 338 | 43 | 452* | 28067 | 95·14 | 117 |

## Appendix IV
### Season-by-Season Record in Sheffield Shield Matches

| | Matches | Innings | NO | HS | Runs | Average | Centuries |
|---|---|---|---|---|---|---|---|
| *For New South Wales* | | | | | | | |
| 1927–8 | 5 | 10 | 1 | 134* | 416 | 46·22 | 2 |
| 1928–9 | 5 | 9 | 3 | 340* | 893 | 148·83 | 4 |
| 1929–30 | 6 | 10 | 2 | 452* | 894 | 111·75 | 1 |
| 1930–1 | 4 | 6 | 0 | 258 | 695 | 115·83 | 3 |
| 1931–2 | 3 | 5 | 0 | 167 | 213 | 42·60 | 1 |
| 1932–3 | 3 | 5 | 1 | 238 | 600 | 150·00 | 2 |
| 1933–4 | 5 | 7 | 2 | 253 | 922 | 184·40 | 4 |
| *For South Australia* | | | | | | | |
| 1935–6 | 6 | 6 | 0 | 357 | 739 | 123·16 | 3 |
| 1936–7 | 4 | 6 | 1 | 192 | 416 | 83·20 | 2 |
| 1937–8 | 6 | 12 | 2 | 246 | 983 | 98·30 | 4 |
| 1938–9 | 6 | 6 | 1 | 225 | 801 | 160·20 | 5 |
| 1939–40 | 6 | 10 | 2 | 267 | 1062 | 132·75 | 3 |
| 1946–7 | 1 | 2 | 0 | 119 | 162 | 81·00 | 1 |
| 1947–8 | 1 | 1 | 0 | 100 | 100 | — | 1 |
| 1948–9 | 1 | 1 | 0 | 30 | 30 | — | 0 |
| For New South Wales | 31 | 52 | 9 | 452* | 4633 | 107·74 | 17 |
| For South Australia | 31 | 44 | 6 | 357 | 4293 | 112·97 | 19 |
| TOTAL | 62 | 96 | 15 | 452* | 8926 | 110·19 | 36 |

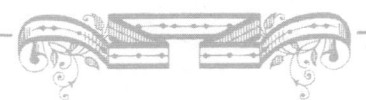

# INDEX

Sir Donald Bradman is featured on practically every page of this book. To avoid a proliferation of entries under his name these entries have been confined, in principle, to topics which cannot be entered as headings in their own right. Matches in which Sir Donald Bradman played are entered twice: under the name of the team for which he played and also under the name of the team against which he played.

In general, apart from Bradman himself, only players who are entered in Christopher Martin-Jenkins's *Who's Who of Test Cricketers* (Rigby, 1980) have been indexed. Games in which they played are entered as sub-entries under their respective names, the team for which they played being cited first, whether or not it was the home team.

Writers of material in the albums have been indexed if they have works cited in *A Bibliography of Cricket*, edited by E. W. Padmore (Library Association, 1977).

Pages 1–424 are in Volume 1, 432–791 are in Volume 2. Numbers in italic refer to illustrations. Entries are arranged alphabetically word-by-word. An asterisk * beside a score indicates not out.

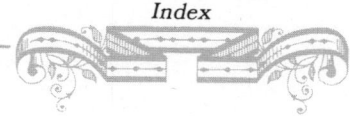

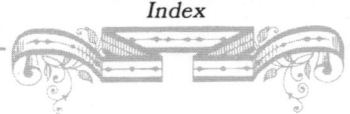

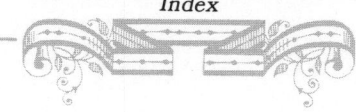

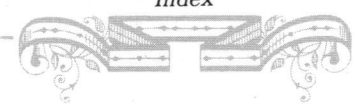